D0326938

WORDSWORTH
POETICAL WORKS

WILLIAM WORDSWORTH
Born at Cockermouth, Cumberland, 7 April 1770
Died at Rydal Mount, Westmorland, 23 April 1850

WORDSWORTH

POETICAL WORKS

With Introductions and Notes

Edited by
THOMAS HUTCHINSON

A new Edition, revised by
ERNEST DE SELINCOURT

Oxford New York
OXFORD UNIVERSITY PRESS

Oxford University Press, Walton Street, Oxford OX2 6DP

Oxford New York Toronto
Delhi Bombay Calcutta Madras Karachi
Petaling Jaya Singapore Hong Kong Tokyo
Nairobi Dar es Salaam Cape Town
Melbourne Auckland

and associated companies in
Berlin Ibadan

Oxford is a trade mark of Oxford University Press

First published in this edition 1904
New edition first published in the
Oxford Standard Authors series
by Oxford University Press 1936
Reprinted seventeen times
First issued as an Oxford University Press paperback 1969
Reprinted 1973, 1975, 1978, 1981, 1985, 1986, 1987, 1988

ISBN 0–19–281052–9

PR
5850
. F69

74590768

Printed in Great Britain
at the University Printing House, Oxford
by David Stanford
Printer to the University

If thou indeed derive thy light from Heaven,
Then, to the measure of that heaven-born light,
Shine, Poet! in thy place, and be content:—
The stars pre-eminent in magnitude,
And they that from the zenith dart their beams,
(Visible though they be to half the earth,
Though half a sphere be conscious of their brightness)
Are yet of no diviner origin,
No purer essence, than the one that burns,
Like an untended watch-fire, on the ridge
Of some dark mountain; or than those which seem
Humbly to hang, like twinkling winter lamps,
Among the branches of the leafless trees;
All are the undying offspring of one Sire:
Then, to the measure of the light vouchsafed,
Shine, Poet! in thy place, and be content.

PREFACE

In this Edition of the Poems of William Wordsworth there will be found—now for the first time within the compass of a single volume of convenient size and modest price—every piece of original verse which we know to have been published by the poet himself, or of which he can be shown to have authorised the posthumous publication.

The OXFORD WORDSWORTH comprises (1) the Minor or Miscellaneous Poems, reprinted from the standard edition of 1849–50—the last issued during the lifetime and under the direct authority of the poet; (2) a reprint of the original text of the two Poems of 1793, viz. An Evening Walk, and Descriptive Sketches; (3) a Supplement, giving, so far as it has been possible to ascertain, every piece published by Wordsworth on any other occasion whatsoever, but omitted by him from the final edition of 1849–50; (4) The Prelude,[1] or Growth of a Poet's Mind; an Autobiographical Poem; (5) The Excursion (text of ed. 1849–50); (6) all the Author's Notes of ed. 1849–50, together with many notes found in various early editions, but subsequently omitted; (7) sundry Prefaces, Postscripts, &c., given at the end of Vol. V, ed. 1849–50; (8) a Chronological Table of the Life of Wordsworth; and (9) some few miscellaneous Notes by the Editor, who is also accountable for (10) the Chronological Data prefixed to the individual poems.

Great pains have been taken to ensure a high degree of accuracy in the text of this Edition. The poet's use of capital letters—a sure index to his intentions of stress—has been carefully and, it is hoped, in every instance reproduced; but it seemed idle to preserve with scrupulous exactness certain oddities and inconsistencies of spelling—a matter to which Wordsworth, unlike his brother-poet, Walter Savage Landor, appears never to have given serious attention. The editor has throughout compared the punctuation of the standard text of 1849–50 with that of the Aldine Wordsworth, issued in 1892.[2] In most instances of divergence between them he has followed the recent authority; but in a few cases a regard—it may be, a superstitious regard—for the metrical design of the poet has compelled him to revert (not without misgiving) to the pointing of the standard text. Be this as it may, we must always bear in mind the fact that Wordsworth's system of punctuation was no mere logical or intellectual organ, but rather—in the words of the Aldine Editor—'an elaborate and ingenious instrument, intended at once to guide the reader to the meaning and to serve a metrical purpose'.

In three places, where a misprint in the text of 1849–50, while not absolutely demonstrable, was yet in the highest degree probable, the Editor has substituted a reading of one or more of the earlier editions, taking care to add in a footnote the precise authority attaching to the adopted reading. On behalf of the change thus introduced into line 3 of Misc. Son., II. xxiv: 'a lamp sullenly (vice suddenly) glaring,' it will probably suffice to refer the reader to the three passages cited in the footnote on page 211; bidding him add thereto, from Eccles. Sonnets, II. xv, line 13: 'Ambition . . . is no sullen fire;' and also, from Inscriptions, X., lines 27, 28: 'by sullen weeds forbidden To resume its native light.'[3] In defence of 'choral (vice coral) fountains' (p. 173) it may be observed, first: that Wordsworth was not a writer of nonsense-verses; secondly: that he had a rooted aversion to slip-shod grammar, and, in particular, to the very solecism exemplified in the phrase (of text 1849–50), 'coral fountains,' i.e. to the adjectival misuse of a substantive pur et simple. We may feel confident that the poet-critic who found fault with W. Rowan Hamilton's phrase: weariness of that gold sphere, and remonstrated with R. P. Gillies for having written: where the lake gleams beneath the autumn

---

[1] Published, shortly after the poet's death, in 1850.
[2] Edited by Edward Dowden, LL.D., &c., &c., Professor of Oratory and English Literature in the University of Dublin.
[3] [Mr. T. E. Casson (1926) points out another parallel in 'Guilt and Sorrow' (p. 21), l. 183.]

PREFACE

sun; who vehemently advocated the employment of *vernal* and *autumnal* as being both 'unexceptionable words,' and declared it to be a matter of regret that Miss Seward's bantling, *hybernal*, was not in more familiar use;—we may, surely, feel quite satisfied that this severe precisian would never have condescended to the vile phrase, *coral fountains*; all the more because, in the words, *fountains coralline*, he had a phrase ready to his hand which (had it but been possible on the score of sense) was undeniably 'unexceptionable,' as well from the metrist's as from the grammarian's point of view. It should be added that the *Aldine* Editor led the way in adopting both readings—*sullenly* and *choral*—into his text.[1] The third instance above referred to (see page 390) calls for no particular comment in this place.

In the extract from Chaucer's *Troilus and Cresida*, contributed by Wordsworth to the volume projected by Thomas Powell in 1840, line 118, as it appears in the original issue of that volume (1841), runs precisely as it runs in Chaucer's original, and as it now runs in the *OXFORD WORDSWORTH*:—

'With a soft voice, he of his Lady dear'—

When, however, in the following year, this extract, along with the poet's other adaptations from Chaucer, was being reprinted for publication amongst his Collected Poems, the compositor perpetrated the ludicrous and (one would have thought) quite palpable blunder of foisting in the word 'night' (evidently caught from the expression 'night by night,' which occurs four lines below), between the words 'soft' and 'voice.' From that day to this, the line has run, in every edition of the Poems:—

'With a soft night voice, he of his Lady dear'—

an arrangement which obviously yields neither good metre nor common sense. It seems strange that neither Wordsworth himself, nor his clerk and proof-reader, Mr. John Carter, should, while revising the several editions of the Poems that appeared between 1842 and 1850, have detected so manifest an error of the press. But we may perhaps suppose that their attention on these occasions was wholly given to Wordsworth's original compositions, and that the text of the adaptations from Chaucer, having been settled once for all, was simply left to take care of itself. Professor Dowden, in a paper read to the Wordsworth Society in May, 1882, was the first to suggest the possibly intrusive character of 'night'; he has, however, retained that word in the text of the *Aldine* Edition (1892). The Editor of the *OXFORD WORDSWORTH*, finding himself unable to conceive the possibility of any difference of opinion as to the true character and origin of 'night' in the line under notice, has summarily removed it from the text, without note, comment or apology of any kind whatsoever.

In a very few instances—possibly not more than half-a-dozen in all—where a passage either of striking beauty or otherwise interesting had been rejected from the text of ed. 1849–50, the Editor has ventured to restore the cancelled lines to their original position, placing them within brackets, to indicate that they form no part of the standard text, and adding in a footnote the precise amount of authority which they derive from the numerous earlier editions. The second stanza of *Louisa* has been replaced after this fashion; so, too, have the opening stanza of *Dion*, and a stanza (originally the sixth) of the *Ode to Duty*. Thus restored, the passages in question are sure to catch the eye of the reader; whereas, had they been relegated to the 'Notes and Illustrations' at the end of the volume, they would necessarily have escaped the notice of that numerous class who read poetry readily enough, but turn with instant aversion from anything in the shape of a Note.

The Minor Poems are here presented in the order in which they stand in ed. 1849–50. The notion of that order or arrangement was, as is well known, first

[1] [But see 'The Triad' (p. 175), l. 11.—T. E. Casson, 1926.]

PREFACE

conceived by Wordsworth in 1812, and, after three years of sedulous elaboration, was finally perfected and embodied by him in the Collective Edition of 1815. To it, despite much ridicule and hostile criticism, the poet adhered with unwavering faith throughout the rest of his life. On this question of arrangement, the Editor is fain to confess, his affections are most humble; he has no ambition to see a goodlier scheme than Wordsworth's. Accordingly, those who purchase the OXFORD WORDSWORTH must needs content themselves with the works of the poet arranged according to an antiquated scheme of his own devising. As to the advantages alleged by some to accompany a chronological arrangement of the poems, it will be time enough to discuss them when the materials for the construction of such an arrangement are in our hands. At present, our knowledge of the chronology[1] of the poems is very far from complete; and, accordingly, every attempt to set the poems in their true chronological order must of necessity be largely tentative and conjectural.

In compiling the Chronological Life-Table, the Editor has, of course, freely availed himself of the two great Sources for the Biography of Wordsworth, viz. the *Memoirs* of the poet, published in 1851 by his nephew Christopher, late Bishop of Lincoln, and the *Life* in three volumes by Professor Knight of St. Andrews, published in 1889. Though not very inviting to look at, this Life-Table will, the Editor trusts, be found useful by sundry persons in divers ways. To the old Wordsworthian it will prove convenient for occasional reference; the young reader may pick out thence the leading dates and events of the poet's life; while the more advanced student may, it is hoped, learn by its aid something at least concerning the affinities—moral, poetical and intellectual—which connect Wordsworth with the preceding generation, and with the men of his own troubled and disjointed times.

It may be well to point out that in the OXFORD WORDSWORTH no attempt has been made to annotate the poems systematically; nor has the Editor thought it fair to cumber the pages with such information as the student can, without any difficulty, obtain for himself from Biographies, &c., now-a-days within the reach of all. Here and there, in order to facilitate the continuous reading of the poet, the Editor has thrown in a brief footnote, for the most part giving a name or a date referred to in the text; and to these footnotes he has added a very few notes (printed along with the Author's Notes at the end of the volume), to convey some novel suggestion, or else to supply some necessary or interesting fact regarding the text. Beyond this he has not attempted to go. The main object of the Series to which this Edition belongs is to provide the public, not with notes or commentary, but with a thoroughly sound, complete and legible text; and in the volume now before the reader this object, the Editor ventures to believe, has been realised to the fullest extent possible.

In view of the vague and unsettled character of the chronology of much of Wordsworth's poetry, the Editor has deemed it inexpedient to print a formal Chronological Table or List of the Author's Works, such as that given in Vol. VII of the *Aldine* Edition. He has, however, used all diligence in testing the accuracy of the dates here prefixed to the individual poems. In the interest of the student and for purposes of reference, the lines have been numbered throughout the entire volume.

In conclusion, the Editor's best thanks are due to Professor William Knight, LL.D., of St. Andrews, for permission, granted in the readiest and most cordial fashion, to make use of certain particulars regarding the chronology of the

---

[1] In this matter of chronology, be it observed, the poet himself is little better than a blind guide. Whenever he attempts to assign dates to his several compositions, he frequently errs, and not seldom contradicts himself. Nevertheless, in many instances, Wordsworth's testimony is all we at present have to go upon; and, wherever the date he gives is not discredited by evidence from another source, it has been thought best to adopt it in this Edition, as at least provisionally correct.

PREFACE

Sonnets of 1802–3, which he himself had, at considerable pains, hunted up for use in his forthcoming Edition of the Poems. To Professor Dowden the Editor stands indebted for good counsel, assistance, and encouragement during the continuance of his task, as at many other times. Here, too, what has he to offer in return but grateful thanks?—

'Evermore thanks, the exchequer of the poor.'

Lastly, his warmest acknowledgments are due to the Rev. Thomas Hutchinson of Kimbolton, Leominster, the poet's nephew by marriage, who, at considerable inconvenience to himself, in the kindest manner undertook to read a proof of the Chronological Life-Table, marked several errors therein for correction, and suggested certain improvements, which, so far as was found practicable, have been carried into effect.

T. H.

NOTE

I have taken four verbal and six punctual corrections from Mr. Nowell Smith's three-volume edition (London, 1908).

March, 1910.   T. H.

CONTENTS

CONTENTS

CONTENTS

CONTENTS

CONTENTS

CONTENTS

CONTENTS

CONTENTS

CONTENTS

CONTENTS

CONTENTS

xxi

CHRONOLOGICAL TABLE

OF THE

LIFE OF WILLIAM WORDSWORTH

THE following Table is intended to show (1) the chief events of the poet's life, (2) the dates of the publication of his principal works, and (3) his chronological relations to certain of his predecessors and contemporaries.

W. = William Wordsworth, the Poet.
John, &c. W. = John, &c. Wordsworth.
H. = Hutchinson.
S. T. C. = Samuel Taylor Coleridge.

A.D.	ÆT.	
1725	—	About this year Richard Wordsworth migrates from Yorkshire to Westmoreland, is made Superintendent of the Lowther estates, marries, and purchases the property of Sockbridge, in the parish of Barton, near Penrith.
1745	—	Richard W. Receiver-General of the County of Westmoreland.
1754	—	[George Crabbe born.]
1762	—	[Wm. Lisle Bowles born. Joanna Baillie born.]
1763	—	[Samuel Rogers born.]
1764	—	[*The Traveller* (O. Goldsmith).]
1765	—	[Bp. Percy's *Reliques of Ancient English Poetry*.]
1766	—	John Wordsworth, attorney, of Cockermouth, chief law-agent to Sir Jas. Lowther, and Steward of the Manor and Forest of Ennerdale (born 1741, second son of Richard W.), marries Anne, daughter of Wm. Cookson, mercer, of Penrith, by Dorothy Crackanthorp, his wife (of the Newbiggin Hall family). To him are born:
1768	—	(1) Richard W. (May 19th; died May 19th, 1816).
1769	—	[*The Beggar's Petition* (Rev. Thos. Moss).]
1770	—	(2) WILLIAM WORDSWORTH, BORN APRIL 7th. [Mary Hutchinson born Aug. 16th (died Jan. 17th, 1859). James Hogg born. Chatterton died. *The Deserted Village* (Goldsmith).]
1771	1	(3) Dorothy W. (Dec. 25th; died Jan. 25th, 1855). [Gray died. Scott born. *The Minstrel* (Beattie).]
1772	2	(4) John W. (Dec. 4th; drowned Feb. 5th, 1805. [S. T. Coleridge born.]
1774	4	(5) Christopher W. (June 9th; died Feb. 2nd, 1846). [Goldsmith died. Southey born. *The Country Justice* (Langhorne, 1774–5).]
1775	5	[Chas. Lamb born. W. Savage Landor born.]
1777	7	During 1776–7 W. W. and Mary H. attend Anne Birkett's infant school at Penrith. [H. Hallam born. Thos. Campbell born.]
1778	8	Mother dies. W. lodges at Anne Tyson's cottage and attends Hawkshead Grammar-school. [Wm. Hazlitt born.]
1779	9	[Thos. Moore born.]
1781	11	[Ebenezer Elliott born. *The Library* (Crabbe). *Triumphs of Temper* (Hayley).]
1782	12	[*Poems* (Wm. Cowper). *Edwin and Elfrida* (Helen M. Williams).]
1783	13	John W. (father) dies, leaving his five children in the guardianship of their uncles, Richard Wordsworth and Christ. Crackanthorp. [*Poetical Sketches* (Blake). *The Village* (Crabbe).]

xxiii

A.D.	ÆT.	
1784	14	[Dr. Johnson died. Leigh Hunt born. *Elegiac Sonnets* (Charlotte Smith).]
1785	15	'And has the sun his flaming chariot driven,' &c. written (W.'s earliest extant verses). [De Quincey born. Thos. Love Peacock born. *The Newspaper* (Crabbe). *The Task* (Cowper).]
1786	16	'Dear native Regions,' &c.; 'Calm is all Nature,' &c. written. [*Poems* (Robt. Burns: Kilmarnock Ed.).]
1787	17	Enters at S. John's College, Cambridge. Studies Italian under Agostino Isola. *Evening Walk* begun. [B. W. Procter born.]
1788	18	Long Vacation¹ at Hawkshead. First visit to London (autumn). [Byron born. *Lewesdon Hill* (Wm. Crowe).]
1789	19	Long Vac. with Dorothy W. and Mary H. at Penrith. *Evening Walk* finished. [*The Loves of the Plants* (Darwin). *Sonnets* (W. L. Bowles). *Songs of Innocence* (Blake).]
1790	20	Walking tour in Long Vac. with Robt. Jones through France and Switzerland. [*Julia: a Novel* (with *Sonnet to Hope:* Helen M. Williams).]
1791	21	B.A. Camb. (Jan.). Forncett Rectory, Norfolk; London; Plas-yn-llan, N. Wales (with Robt. Jones); Paris (Nov.); Orleans. *Descriptive Sketches* begun. *Guilt and Sorrow* begun.
1792	22	Orleans; Blois (friendship with Michel Beaupuy: in love with Marie Anne Vallon (Annette). Nature now yields the first place to Man in W.'s affections and imagination); Paris (Oct.): W., on the point of offering himself as a leader of the Girondins; his daughter Caroline born (Dec. 15); he is recalled to England; London; *Descriptive Sketches* finished. [Shelley born. Keble born. *Pleasures of Memory* (Rogers). *The Economy of Vegetation* (Darwin).]
1793	23	*Evening Walk* publ. (Feb.); *Descriptive Sketches* publ.; London; Isle of Wight, with Wm. Calvert (July); walking tour by Salisbury—Stonehenge—Bath—Bristol—Tintern Abbey—Goodrich Castle—to Plas-yn-llan. Visit to France (Oct.)?; wanderings through N. Wales (autumn). Shocked by England's declaration of war against France (Feb.). Indites a '*Letter to the Bishop of Llandaff, &c. By a Republican*'. [Felicia Hemans born. *Tam o' Shanter*, &c. (Burns).]
1794	24	At Armathwaite near Keswick; joins Dorothy W. at Halifax (Feb.) and with her to Windybrow, the Calverts' cottage, under Skiddaw; Whitehaven; wanderings through Lancashire and the Lake Country. Proposes to start 'The Philanthropist, a monthly Miscellany'; searches in vain for congenial employment; anxious and perplexed. Rampside (Aug.); nursing Raisley Calvert (Oct.–Dec.); *Guilt and Sorrow* finished. [*Fall of Robespierre* (S. T. C.). *Songs of Experience* (Blake). Robespierre executed (July 28th): see *Prelude* X. 570–603.]
1795	25	At Penrith with Raisley Calvert, who dies (Jan.) leaving W. £900: London; settles with Dorothy W. at Racedown, Dorset (Oct.). Meets S. T. C. at the house of Mr. Pinney, Bristol (prob. late in Sept.). *The Borderers* begun: writes some Juvenalian satire. *Margaret; or, The Ruined Cottage* begun. [Keats born. Carlyle born.]
1796	26	Racedown. *The Borderers* finished. [Burns died. Hartley Coleridge born. *Poems*, 1st issue (S. T. C.). *Joan of Arc* (Southey).]
1797	27	Racedown. Intimacy with S. T. C. leads to an outburst of poetic activity. W. and sister visit S. T. C. at Nether Stowey cottage (July 2–16), whence they move to Alfoxden, some three miles distant. Charles Lamb visits S. T. C. (July 9–16). *Lyrical Ballads* planned with S. T. C.

¹ It was during either this vacation or that of 1794, that W. spent four weeks with his cousin Mrs. Barker in Rampside, a village of Low Furness, Lancashire, right opposite Peel Castle, which lies between Walney Isle and the mainland. Cf. the *Elegiac Stanzas suggested by a Picture of Peele Castle*.

A.D.	ÆT.	
		Margaret finished (aft. merged in *Excursion*, Bk. I). W. in London (Dec.). [*Poems* (S. T. C.; Lamb and Lloyd). *Poems* (Southey).]
1798	28	Alfoxden (Jan.–June). 1300 lines of blank verse 'on Man, Nature, & Society' written, also several *Lyrical Ballads* and *Peter Bell*. [Hazlitt visits S. T. C. and W.] Bristol (July); two short visits to Wales; London (Aug. 27th). *Lyrical Ballads* publ. (Sept.). Viâ Yarmouth to Hamburg with Dorothy W. and S. T. C. (Sept. 16th); arrives at Goslar (Oct. 6th).[1] [*Epistle to a Friend* (Rogers). *Plays on the Passions*, Vol. I (Joanna Baillie: Vol. II, 1802; Vol. III, 1812). *Gebir* (W. S. Landor).]
1799	29	Goslar; Göttingen; whence (April 21st) viâ Hamburg to Yarmouth; with Thos. and Mary Hutchinson at Sockburn-on-Tees (May 1st?). Much of *Prelude*, Bks. I, II, *Lucy Gray*, and the chief 'Lucy' poems written in Germany. Walking tour through Lake Country with S. T. C. and John W. (Oct.). Settles, with Dorothy W., in Dove Cottage, Townend, Grasmere (Friday, Dec. 20th). Bks. I and II of the *Prelude* were probably finished before the close of the year. [T. Hood born. *Pleasures of Hope* (Campbell).]
1800	30	Dove Cottage. John W. sojourns (Jan.–Sept. 29th). S. T. C. visits Grasmere (Apr., May), and, with wife and Hartley, sojourns at Dove Cottage (June 29th–July 24th). Mary H. visits Dove Cottage twice in 1800. S. T. C. settles at Greta Hall, Keswick (Aug.). Frequent intercourse between W. and S. T. C. Poetic activity fully maintained in 1800; *The Recluse*, Bk. I (publ. 1888); *The Brothers, Michael, Poems on naming of Places*, and famous *Preface* written. [Cowper died. Macaulay born.]
1801	31	Dove Cottage. Visits Scotland to be present at Basil Montagu's second marriage (summer). *Lyrical Ballads*, 2nd ed., two vols. publ. (Jan.). Unproductive interval, Jan.–Dec. 1801. [*Thalaba* (Southey). *John Woodvil* (Lamb). *Poems* ('Thos. Little').]
1802	32	Dove Cottage. Second period of productive energy (Dec. 1801–Dec. 1803: declining somewhat in 1803). Thirty-nine of the poems publ. in 1807 now written; also much of Bks. I and II of *The Excursion*. The Sonnet now (May 21st onwards) regularly and frequently cultivated. Four weeks' visit to Annette and Caroline at Calais (Aug.). London (Sept.). W. marries Mary H. at Brompton near Scarborough (Oct. 4th); returns to Grasmere (Oct. 6th). *Lyrical Ballads*, 3rd. ed. [Darwin died.]
1803	33	Dove Cottage. Birth of W.'s son John (June 18th). W. and Dorothy start with S. T. C. on a tour in Scotland (Aug. 16th). They visit Scott at Lasswade, and return to Grasmere (Oct. 14th). Sir Geo. Beaumont buys and presents to W. the little estate of Applethwaite, three miles from Greta Hall. S. T. C. ill at Grasmere (Dec.). *Yarrow Unvisited* written (Nov.). [*Temple of Nature* (Darwin).]
1804	34	Dove Cottage. *The Prelude* continued, Bks. III–VII (Feb.–Apr.); Bks. VIII–XI (Oct.–Dec.). Dora W. born (Aug. 16th). S. T. C. starts for Malta, Apr. 2nd. [*Triumphs of Music* (Hayley).]
1805	35	Dove Cottage. *The Prelude* finished, Bks. XII–XIV (Apr., May). Feb. 1804–May 1805 may be regarded as W.'s third period of productive activity. John W. (brother) drowned in the wreck of the *Earl of*

---

[1] During this six months' sojourn abroad, W.'s republican ardour evanesced, and with it his resentment towards England as the foe of France. 'We are right glad to find ourselves in England,' he writes on his return to Cottle, '*for we have learned to know its value*.' Cf. the lines beginning: 'I travelled among unknown men.'

A.D.	ÆT.	
		Abergavenny (Feb. 5th). W. ascends Helvellyn along with Walter Scott and Humphry Davy. *The Waggoner* written. *Lyrical Ballads*, 4th ed. [*Madoc* (Southey). *Lay of the Last Minstrel* (Scott).]
1806	36	Dove Cottage. Visit to London (April–May). Thomas W. born (June 16th). S. T. C. returns to England (Aug.). W. moves into the farm-house at Coleorton (lent by Sir G. Beaumont) in October. Meets S. T. C. at Kendal (Oct. 26th). S. T. C. at Coleorton (Dec. 1806–Feb. 1807). Fourth period of poetic productiveness (Nov. 1806–Feb. 1808). [*Simonidea* (Landor). *Odes and Epistles* (T. Moore).]
1807	37	Coleorton farm-house. *Poems in Two Volumes* publ. (prob. early in May). W. visits London (April), returning to Coleorton with W. Scott. Home to Grasmere viâ Halifax and Yorkshire dales (Aug.). De Quincey calls at Dove Cottage (Nov. 4th). *Poems in Two Volumes* savagely attacked in *Edinburgh Review*. W. visits John H. (wife's brother) at Stockton-on-Tees, where part of *The White Doe of Rylstone* is written (Dec.). [*Parish Register* (Crabbe). *Hours of Idleness* (Byron).]
1808	38	Dove Cottage. *The White Doe* (first draft) finished (Feb.). Visit to London (March). Moves from Dove Cottage into Allan Bank (June). Catharine W. born (Sept. 6th). S. T. C. and De Quincey domesticated at Allan Bank (Sept.). [*Marmion* (Scott). Lord Houghton born.]
1809	39	Allan Bank. *The Excursion* continued and completed during this and the four following years. Tract on the *Convention of Cintra* (written Nov., Dec., 1808) publ. (end of May). *The Friend* publ. by S. T. C. (No. 1 on June 1st) at Penrith. De Quincey settles at Dove Cottage (Nov.). *Reply to the Letter of Mathetes* (in *The Friend*) publ. (Dec.). [*English Bards and Scotch Reviewers* (Byron). *Gertrude of Wyoming* (Campbell). A. Tennyson, Elizabeth Barrett, W. E. Gladstone, Chas. Darwin born.]
1810	40	Allan Bank. *Essay on Epitaphs* (in *The Friend*) publ. (Feb.). *Description of the Scenery of the English Lakes*, publ. as Introd. to Wilkinson's *Select Views* (Apr.). William W. born (May 12th). S. T. C. quits Allan Bank for Keswick (May); passes a night there on his way to London with Basil Montagu (Oct.); estrangement between W. and S. T. C. (Oct.). About this time W.'s poetic ill-repute is at its height (De Quincey). [*The Borough* (Crabbe). *Lady of the Lake* (Scott). *Curse of Kehama* (Southey).]
1811	41	Allan Bank. W. moves into the Rectory (May). Sojourns at Bootle (Aug.: see *Poetical Epistles to Sir Geo. Beaumont*). [Thackeray born. Bp. Percy died. *Don Roderick* (Scott).]
1812	42	The Rectory. W. seeks through Lord Lonsdale for some office of emolument (Feb.). Visits London and is reconciled to S. T. C. (May). Catharine (June 4th) and Thomas (Dec. 1st) W. died. [Chas. Dickens born. Robert Browning born. *Tales in Verse* (Crabbe). *Count Julian* (Landor). *Childe Harold*, Cantos I, II (Byron). *The Isle of Palms* (Wilson).]
1813	43	The Rectory. Appointed Stamp-Distributor for Westmorland (March). Moves into Rydal Mount (May 1st). [*Rokeby; The Bridal of Triermain* (Scott). *Remorse* (S. T. C.), performed at Drury Lane (Jan.).]
1814	44	Rydal Mount. Tour in Scotland with wife and Sara H. (July): *Yarrow Visited*. *The Excursion* publ. (Aug.). [*Roderick* (Southey). *The Feast of the Poets* (Leigh Hunt).]
1815	45	Rydal Mount. *The first collective ed. of the poems* publ. (March). Visit to London (Apr.). *The White Doe of Rylstone* publ. (May). [*The Lord of the Isles* (Scott).]

CHRONOLOGICAL TABLE

A.D.	ÆT.	
1816	46	Rydal Mount. *A Letter to a Friend of Robert Burns* publ. *Thanksgiving Ode*, Jan. 18, 1816, &c., publ. W.'s daughter Caroline married to Jean Baptiste Baudouin (Feb.); W.'s granddaughter Louise Marie Caroline Baudouin born (Dec. 27). [*Alastor* (Shelley). *Christabel*, &c. (S. T. C.). *The Story of Rimini* (Leigh Hunt).]
1817	47	Rydal Mount. W. visits Dr. Christopher W. (brother) at Lambeth Rectory (Dec.). W. and Keats meet at Haydon's 'immortal dinner' (Dec.). W.'s poetry cordially praised in *Blackwood*. [*Sibylline Leaves; Biographia Literaria* (S. T. C.). *Poems*, 1st issue (Keats). *Lalla Rookh* (Moore). *Harold the Dauntless* (Scott). The *Whistlecraft* Poem (J. H. Frere).]
1818	48	Rydal Mount. Correspondence with Lord Lonsdale on public affairs. *Two Addresses to the Freeholders of Westmorland*, publ. at Kendal. [*Childe Harold*, Cantos III, IV (Byron). *Revolt of Islam* (Shelley). *Poems* (Chas. Lamb, in his collected *Works*). *Foliage* (Leigh Hunt). *Endymion* (Keats). *Rhododaphne* (T. L. Peacock).]
1819	49	Rydal Mount. J.P. for Westmorland. *Peter Bell* publ. (Apr.). *The Waggoner* publ. (May). [*Don Juan*, Canto I, &c. (Byron). *Tales of the Hall* (Crabbe). *Dramatic Scenes* (Procter). *Rosalind and Helen—The Cenci* (Shelley). Arthur H. Clough born. Chas. Kingsley born.)
1820	50	Rydal Mount. Oxford (May 30th); Lambeth Rectory (June–July). Tour with wife and sister through Switzerland to Italian Lakes and home through Paris (July 11th–Nov. 9th). Fortnight in London; do. at the Lodge, Trinity Coll., Cambr. (where Dr. Christ. W. is now Master); do. at Coleorton Hall. Home at Rydal (Dec. 24th). *The River Duddon: a Series of Sonnets*, &c., publ. (May). Also, *The Miscellaneous Poems of W. W.* in four vols. (July), and *The Excursion*, 2nd ed. [*Lamia, Isabella, Hyperion*, &c. (Keats). *Idyllia Heroica Decem* (Landor). *Prometheus Unbound* (Shelley). *Marcian Colonna* (Procter).]
1821	51	Rydal Mount. W. busy with the *Ecclesiastical Sketches*. [Keats died. *Adonais; Epipsychidion* (Shelley). *Cain*, &c. (Byron). *Mirandola; A Sicilian Story* (Procter).]
1822	52	Rydal Mount. *Memorials of a Tour on the Continent*, 1820, and *Ecclesiastical Sketches* publ. (Feb. or March). Also, *Description of the Scenery of the Lakes*, now first publ. separately (publ. as appendix to *Duddon* vol. in 1820; see also under 1810). [Shelley drowned. *Hellas* (Shelley).]
1823	53	Rydal Mount. Coleorton Hall (Feb.); London (Mar., Apr.); Lee Priory near Canterbury (May). Tour through the Netherlands (May 16th–June 30th). 'Every year shows more and more how strongly W.'s poetry has leavened the rising generation' (Southey). 'Up to 1820 the name of W. was trampled under foot; from 1820 to 1830 it was militant; from 1830 to 1835 it has been triumphant' (De Quincey, 1835). [*The Loves of the Angels* (T. Moore).]
1824	54	Rydal Mount. London; Cambridge; Coleorton Hall (Apr., May). Tour in N. Wales, and visits to Robt. Jones, now Curate of Glyn Mavyr, and to Thos. H. at Hindwell, Radnorshire (Aug., Sept., Oct.). [Byron died.]
1825	55	Rydal Mount. Coleorton Hall (July). Lowther Castle (Aug.). Alaric Watts tries in vain to get a London publisher for an ed. of W.'s collected poems.
1826	56	Rydal Mount. *The Excursion*, and the shorter poems, carefully revised and corrected, and the *Miscellaneous Sonnets* re-arranged in groups on the principle of mutual illustration, for the projected five-vol. ed.

A.D.	ÆT.	
1827	57	Rydal Mount. Sir Geo. Beaumont died (Feb.). *An ed. in five vols. (the third collective ed.) of the poems* publ., including (for the first time) *The Excursion. [Poems* (T. Hood). *The Christian Year* (Keble).]
1828	58	Rydal Mount. W., Dora W., and S. T. C. go on a fortnight's tour up the Rhine (June). John W. takes holy orders, and after a year as Curate at Whitwick near Coleorton obtains from Lord Lonsdale the living of Moresby, Cumberland.
1829	59	Rydal Mount. Carriage tour through Ireland with J. Marshall, M.P. for Leeds (Aug., Sept.). Dorothy W. taken seriously ill at Whitwick (Apr.).
1830	60	Rydal Mount. Felicia Hemans (July) and W. Rowan Hamilton (Aug.) visit W. Rev. John W. marries dau. of H. Curwen, Workington Hall, Cumberland (Oct.). W. rides from Lancaster to Cambridge (Nov.); London (Dec.). [Hazlitt died. *Poems, chiefly Lyrical* (A. Tennyson).]
1831	61	Buxted Rectory, Sussex (the home of Dr. Christ. W.); home at Rydal (June). W., Dora W., and Charles W. (nephew), aft. Bishop of S. Andrews, visit Sir Walter Scott at Abbotsford (Sept. 21st), and travel through the Highlands. *Yarrow Revisited. [Corn Law Rhymes* (Eb. Elliott).]
1832	62	Rydal Mount. Moresby Rectory (June), where W. is visited by W. Savage Landor. Correspondence on Reform with Lord Lonsdale, Henry Taylor, and H. Crabb Robinson (Sept., Oct.). *Edition in four vols. (the fourth collective ed.) of the poems* publ. [Sir W. Scott died (Sept. 21st). Rev. Geo. Crabbe died. Dr. Arnold purchases Fox How. *English Songs* (B. W. Procter).]
1833	63	Rydal Mount. Moresby Rectory (Apr.), where several of the *Evening Voluntaries* were written. Tour in the Isle of Man and in Scotland with John W. and H. Crabb Robinson (Sept., Oct.). [*Pauline* (R. Browning). *Poems* (Hartley Coleridge).]
1834	64	Rydal Mount. [S. T. C. died (July 25th). Chas. Lamb died (Dec. 27th). *Italy* completed (first draft publ. 1822): Rogers]
1835	65	Rydal Mount. London (Feb., Mar.), Cambridge (Apr.). Sara Hutchinson (sister-in-law) died (June 23rd). Dorothy W.'s mind gives way. W. visits Thos. H. at Brinsop Court, Herefordshire (Aug.–Nov.). *Yarrow Revisited and other Poems* publ. (prob. Jan.), containing the *Itinerary Sonnets* of 1831, and those of 1833; *Evening Voluntaries; The Egyptian Maid,* &c. [Mrs. Hemans died. Jas. Hogg died. Rev. Robt. Jones died. *Prometheus Bound,* &c. (Eliz. Barrett).]
1836	66	Rydal Mount. London (May), where W. attends first night of *Ion* (Talfourd). Back at Rydal in June; and from June–Dec. engaged in revising poems for the projected stereotyped ed. [*Pericles and Aspasia* (Landor).]
1837	67	Rydal Mount. *New ed. in six vols. (the fifth collective ed.) of the poems* (Vols. I, II, 1836; Vols. III–VI, 1837). Poems reprinted in the United States, ed. Henry Reed. Tour with H. Crabb Robinson through France and Italy to Rome (March–Aug.). Brinsop Court (Sept.). [*Strafford* (R. Browning). W. S. Landor, in requital of W.'s fancied depreciation of Southey, parodies *We are Seven,* and prints the *Satire on Satirists, and Admonition to Detractors.*]
1838	68	Rydal Mount. D.C.L. Univ. Durham (summer.) *The Sonnets of W. W. collected in one vol.,* publ. (June). Lengthy correspondence with Talfourd, H. C. Robinson, W. E. Gladstone and others on the copyright question. Julius Hare dedicates the 2nd edition of *Guesses at Truth* to W. [*The Seraphim,* &c. (Eliz. Barrett).]
1839	69	Rydal Mount. W. petitions the House of Commons in support of Talfourd's Copyright Bill (May). D.C.L. Oxford (July). Presented by Keble, and greeted with acclamation. [*Romaunt of the Page* (Eliz. Barrett).]

CHRONOLOGICAL TABLE

A.D.	ÆT.	
1840	70	Rydal Mount. Pickersgill paints a portrait of W. for the Drayton Manor Gallery (summer). Miss Fenwick settles at Rydal Mount (Oct.). [Francis Hare died. *Sordello* (R. Browning). *Fugitive Verses* (Joanna Baillie).]
1841	71	Rydal Mount. W. and his family visit Taunton and Brinsop (Apr.). Dora W. married to Edw. Quillinan (May 11th) at Bath. W. revisits old haunts—Alfoxden, Tintern, Goodrich Castle, &c.; then to London (Aug.), and home to Rydal (Sept.). [*Bells and Pomegranates* (R. Browning), Nos. i–viii. (1841–1846).]
1842	72	Rydal Mount. London (May, June). *Poems, Chiefly of Early and Late Years*, publ. (Apr.). Resigns the Stamp-Distributorship (July). Pension of £300 per annum from Civil List conferred on W. by Sir Robt. Peel (Oct.). [*Poems in two Volumes* (A. Tennyson).]
1843	73	Rydal Mount. At home (spring and summer). The Quillinans at Windermere. Accepts the Laureateship (Apr.). [Robt. Southey died (March 21st). *Song of the Shirt* (T. Hood). *Lays of Ancient Rome* (Macaulay).]
1844	74	Rydal Mount. Keble dedicates his *Prælectiones Academicæ* to W. (March). Tour through the Duddon Valley with the Quillinans and Lady Richardson (Sept.). [Thos. Campbell died. *Poems*, 2 vols. (Eliz. Barrett). *The Bridge of Sighs* (T. Hood).]
1845	75	Rydal Mount. The Quillinans go to Oporto (spring). W. attends Levée and State Ball in London (May). At Brinsop Court (Sept., Oct.). *New ed. of the poems in one vol.*, royal 8vo. *Kendal and Windermere Railway: Two Letters Reprinted from the Morning Post*, publ. at Kendal (Jan.; or, possibly, Dec., 1844). [Thos. Hood died.]
1846	76	Rydal Mount. Elected hon. mem. Royal Irish Academy (March). Nominated for Lord Rectorship of Glasgow Univ., and obtained a majority of twenty-one votes over Lord John Russell, who however was seated by means of the Sub-Rector's vote. The Quillinans return and settle at Loughrigg Holm (July). [*Hellenics* (W. S. Landor).]
1847	77	Rydal Mount. William W. marries Miss Fanny E. Graham of Brighton (Jan.). Dora Quillinan died (July 9th). The *Installation Ode* performed in the Senate-House, Cambr. (July). [*The Princess* (A. Tennyson).]
1848	78	Rydal Mount. H. Crabb Robinson comes down to Rydal, as in 1835 and 1838, for the Christmas season. [*The Saint's Tragedy* (C. Kingsley). *The Bothie of Tober-na-vuolich* (A. H. Clough). *Casa Guidi Windows* (Eliz. Barrett Browning).]
1849	79	Rydal Mount. Hartley Coleridge died, Jan. 6th. W. and wife visit Thos. Hutchinson at West Malvern (June). *An ed. of the poems, in six vols.*, giving the results of W.'s final revision of the text, publ. 1849–50. [*The Strayed Reveller*, &c. (M. Arnold). *Ambarvalia* (A. H. Clough).]
1850	80	WILLIAM WORDSWORTH DIED, April 23rd. Buried in Grasmere Churchyard (April 27th). *The Prelude; or, Growth of a Poet's Mind* publ. [Rev. W. L. Bowles died.]

The stereotyped edition of the poems in six volumes, published in 1836–7, was re-issued, with a revised and slightly altered text, in 1840; and this edition of 1840 again was also reprinted in 1841, 1842, 1843, 1846, and 1849. To the six-vol. ed. of 1842 the volume, originally published under the title of *Poems, Chiefly of Early and Late Years*, was added in the course of that same year, with the title: *The Poetical Works of William Wordsworth. Volume VII.* London: Edward Moxon. 1842.

The one-vol. edition of 1845 has also been frequently reprinted. After 1850 the contents were enlarged by the addition of *The Prelude*, and of the nine poems first published in 1849–50. Moxon's familiar one-vol. edition—that which has a prefatory notice from the pen of Mr. W. M. Rossetti—is in fact but a re-issue of this ed. of 1845, with *The Prelude*, but without the poems of 1849–50.

In 1857 a six-volume edition of the poems appeared, in which the notes dictated in 1843 by the poet to Miss Fenwick were first published, being prefixed to the individual pieces to which they severally refer.

CHRONOLOGICAL TABLE

The *Letter to the Bishop of Llandaff*, mentioned under 1793 in the foregoing Table, remained unpublished until 1876, when it was included in the collective edition of *Wordsworth's Prose Works* put forth by Dr. A. B. Grosart.

Besides the prose writings already noticed, Wordsworth wrote (1) the famous *Preface* to the second edition (1800) of the *Lyrical Ballads*; (2) the *Appendix on Poetic Diction* to the third edition (1802); (3) the *Preface* to *The Excursion;* (4) the *Preface* and the *Essay Supplementary to the Preface* of the edition of 1815; and (5) the *Postscript* to the *Yarrow Revisited* volume.[1] Many notes also from Wordsworth's pen appeared in the several successive issues of his poems between 1793 and 1845; of which notes the poet subsequently saw fit to cancel not a few. One or two of these, which seemed well worth restoring, will be found in this volume amongst the notes of ed. 1849–50, from which they are distinguished by the addition of their proper date after the signature (W.).   T. H.

[1] All of these will be found in the present edition.

POEMS WRITTEN IN YOUTH

Of the Poems in this class, 'THE EVENING WALK' and 'DESCRIPTIVE SKETCHES' were first published in 1793. They are reprinted with some alterations that were chiefly made very soon after their publication.

. . . .

This notice, which was written some time ago, scarcely applies to the Poem, 'Descriptive Sketches,' as it now stands. The corrections, though numerous, are not, however, such as to prevent its retaining with propriety a place in the class of Juvenile Pieces[1].
1836.

I

EXTRACT

FROM THE CONCLUSION OF A POEM, COMPOSED IN ANTICIPATION OF LEAVING SCHOOL

[Composed 1786.—Published 1815.]

DEAR native regions, I foretell,
From what I feel at this farewell,
That, wheresoe'er my steps may tend,
And whensoe'er my course shall end,
If in that hour a single tie   5
Survive of local sympathy,
My soul will cast the backward view,
The longing look alone on you.

Thus, while the Sun sinks down to rest
Far in the regions of the west,   10
Though to the vale no parting beam
Be given, not one memorial gleam,
A lingering light he fondly throws
On the dear hills where first he rose.

II

WRITTEN IN VERY EARLY YOUTH

[Composed 1786 (?).—Published *Morning Post* February 13, 1802; ed. 1807.]

CALM is all nature as a resting wheel.
The kine are couched upon the dewy grass;
The horse alone, seen dimly as I pass,
Is cropping audibly his later meal:
Dark is the ground; a slumber seems to steal   5
O'er vale, and mountain, and the starless sky.
Now, in this blank of things, a harmony,
Home-felt, and home-created, comes to heal
That grief for which the senses still supply
Fresh food; for only then, when memory   10
Is hushed, am I at rest. My Friends! restrain
Those busy cares that would allay my pain;
Oh! leave me to myself, nor let me feel
The officious touch that makes me droop again.

[1] See *Appendix: Poems of* 1793, pp. 462–482.

III

AN EVENING WALK[2]

ADDRESSED TO A YOUNG LADY

[Composed 1787–89.—Published 1793.]

General Sketch of the Lakes—Author's regret of his Youth which was passed amongst them—Short description of Noon—Cascade—Noontide Retreat—Precipice and sloping Lights—Face of Nature as the Sun declines—Mountain-farm, and the Cock—Slate-quarry—Sunset—Superstition of the Country connected with that moment—Swans—Female Beggar—Twilight-sounds—Western Lights—Spirits—Night—Moonlight—Hope—Night-sounds—Conclusion.

FAR from my dearest Friend, 'tis mine to rove
Through bare grey dell, high wood, and pastoral cove;
Where Derwent rests, and listens to the roar
That stuns the tremulous cliffs of high Lodore;
Where peace to Grasmere's lonely island leads,   5
To willowy hedge-rows, and to emerald meads;
Leads to her bridge, rude church, and cottaged grounds,
Her rocky sheepwalks, and her woodland bounds;
Where, undisturbed by winds, Winander[3] sleeps;
'Mid clustering isles, and holly-sprinkled steeps;   10
Where twilight glens endear my Esthwaite's shore,
And memory of departed pleasures, more.

Fair scenes, erewhile, I taught, a happy child,
The echoes of your rocks my carols wild:

[2] So many and so important changes have been made in this Poem since its first appearance, that it has been thought well to reprint the original text of 1793. See Appendix, page 462.—ED.
[3] These lines are only applicable to the middle part of that lake.

1   B

The spirit sought not then, in cherished
sadness,   15
A cloudy substitute for failing gladness.
In youth's keen eye the livelong day was
bright,
The sun at morning, and the stars at
night,
Alike, when first the bittern's hollow bill
Was heard, or woodcocks¹ roamed the
moonlight hill.   20

In thoughtless gaiety I coursed the
plain,
And hope itself was all I knew of pain;
For then the inexperienced heart would
beat
At times, while young Content forsook
her seat,
And wild Impatience, pointing upward,
showed,   25
Through passes yet unreached, a brighter
road.
Alas! the idle tale of man is found
Depicted in the dial's moral round;
Hope with reflection blends her social
rays
To gild the total tablet of his days;   30
Yet still, the sport of some malignant
power,
He knows but from its shade the present
hour.

But why, ungrateful, dwell on idle
pain?
To show what pleasures yet to me remain,
Say, will my Friend, with unreluctant
ear,   35
The history of a poet's evening hear?

When, in the south, the wan noon,
brooding still,
Breathed a pale steam around the glaring
hill,
And shades of deep-embattled clouds
were seen,
Spotting the northern cliffs with lights
between;   40
When crowding cattle, checked by rails
that make
A fence far stretched into the shallow
lake,
Lashed the cool water with their restless
tails,
Or from high points of rock looked out
for fanning gales;
When school-boys stretched their length
upon the green;   45
And round the broad-spread oak, a glimmering scene,

¹ In the beginning of winter these mountains are
frequented by woodcocks, which in dark nights retire
into the woods.

In the rough fern-clad park, the herded
deer
Shook the still-twinkling tail and glancing
ear;
When horses in the sunburnt intake²
stood,
And vainly eyed below the tempting
flood,   50
Or tracked the passenger, in mute distress,
With forward neck the closing gate to
press—
Then, while I wandered where the hud-
dling rill
Brightens with water-breaks the hollow
ghyll³
As by enchantment, an obscure retreat
Opened at once, and stayed my devious
feet.   56
While thick above the rill the branches
close,
In rocky basin its wild waves repose,
Inverted shrubs, and moss of gloomy
green,
Cling from the rocks, with pale wood-
weeds between;   60
And its own twilight softens the whole
scene,
Save where aloft the subtle sunbeams
shine
On withered briars that o'er the crags
recline;
Save where, with sparkling foam, a small
cascade
Illumines, from within, the leafy shade;
Beyond, along the vista of the brook,   66
Where antique roots its bustling course
o'erlook,
The eye reposes on a secret bridge,⁴
Half grey, half shagged with ivy to its
ridge;
There, bending o'er the stream, the listless
swain   70
Lingers behind his disappearing wain.
—Did Sabine grace adorn my living line,
Bandusia's praise, wild stream, should
yield to thine!
Never shall ruthless minister of death
'Mid thy soft glooms the glittering steel
unsheath;   75
No goblets shall, for thee, be crowned
with flowers,
No kid with piteous outcry thrill thy
bowers;
The mystic shapes that by thy margin
rove
A more benignant sacrifice approve—

² The word *intake* is local, and signifies a mountain-inclosure.
³ Ghyll is also, I believe, a term confined to this
country: ghyll and dingle have the same meaning.
⁴ The reader, who has made the tour of this country, will recognise, in this description, the features
which characterise the lower waterfall in the grounds
of Rydal.

2

A mind that, in a calm angelic mood 80
Of happy wisdom, meditating good,
Beholds, of all from her high powers
    required,
Much done, and much designed, and
    more desired,—
Harmonious thoughts, a soul by truth
    refined,
Entire affection for all human kind. 85

Dear Brook, farewell! To-morrow's
    noon again
Shall hide me, wooing long thy wildwood
    strain;
But now the sun has gained his western
    road,
And eve's mild hour invites my steps
    abroad.

While, near the midway cliff, the sil-
    vered kite   90
In many a whistling circle wheels her flight;
Slant watery lights, from parting clouds,
    apace
Travel along the precipice's base;
Cheering its naked waste of scattered
    stone,
By lichens grey, and scanty moss, o'er-
    grown;   95
Where scarce the foxglove peeps, or
    thistle's beard;
And restless stone-chat, all day long, is
    heard.

How pleasant, as the sun declines, to
    view
The spacious landscape change in form
    and hue!
Here, vanish, as in mist, before a flood 100
Of bright obscurity, hill, lawn, and wood;
There, objects, by the searching beams
    betrayed,
Come forth, and here retire in purple
    shade;
Even the white stems of birch, the cottage
    white,
Soften their glare before the mellow
    light;   105
The skiffs, at anchor where with umbrage
    wide
Yon chestnuts half the latticed boat-
    house hide,
Shed from their sides, that face the sun's
    slant beam,
Strong flakes of radiance on the tremu-
    lous stream:
Raised by yon travelling flock, a dusty
    cloud   110
Mounts from the road, and spreads its
    moving shroud;
The shepherd, all involved in wreaths of
    fire,
Now shows a shadowy speck, and now is
    lost entire.

Into a gradual calm the breezes sink,
A blue rim borders all the lake's still
    brink;   115
There doth the twinkling aspen's foliage
    sleep,
And insects clothe, like dust, the glassy
    deep:
And now, on every side, the surface
    breaks
Into blue spots, and slowly lengthening
    streaks;
Here, plots of sparkling water tremble
    bright   120
With thousand thousand twinkling points
    of light;
There, waves that, hardly weltering, die
    away,
Tip their smooth ridges with a softer
    ray;
And now the whole wide lake in deep
    repose
Is hushed, and like a burnished mirror
    glows,   125
Save where, along the shady western
    marge,
Coasts, with industrious oar, the charcoal
    barge.

Their panniered train a group of pot-
    ters goad,
Winding from side to side up the steep
    road;
The peasant, from yon cliff of fearful edge
Shot, down the headlong path darts with
    his sledge;   131
Bright beams the lonely mountain-horse
    illume
Feeding 'mid purple heath, 'green rings',[1]
    and broom;
While the sharp slope the slackened team
    confounds,
Downward the ponderous timber-wain
    resounds;   135
In foamy breaks the rill, with merry song,
Dashed o'er the rough rock, lightly leaps
    along;
From lonesome chapel at the mountain's
    feet
Three humble bells their rustic chime re-
    peat;
Sounds from the water-side the ham-
    mered boat;   140
And *blasted* quarry thunders, heard re-
    mote!

Even here, amid the sweep of endless
    woods,
Blue pomp of lakes, high cliffs and falling
    floods,
Not undelightful are the simplest charms,
Found by the grassy door of mountain-
    farms.   145

[1] 'Vivid rings of green.'—GREENWOOD'S *Poem on
Shooting.*

3

Sweetly ferocious,[1] round his native
walks,
Pride of his sister-wives, the monarch
stalks;
Spur-clad his nervous feet, and firm his
tread;
A crest of purple tops the warrior's head.
Bright sparks his black and rolling eyeball
hurls   150
Afar, his tail he closes and unfurls;
On tiptoe reared, he strains his clarion
throat,
Threatened by faintly-answering farms
remote:
Again with his shrill voice the mountain
rings,
While, flapped with conscious pride, re-
sound his wings!   155

Where, mixed with graceful birch, the
sombrous pine
And yew-tree o'er the silver rocks recline,
I love to mark the quarry's moving trains,
Dwarf panniered steeds, and men, and
numerous wains: 159
How busy all the enormous hive within,
While Echo dallies with its various din!
Some (hear you not their chisels' clinking
sound?)
Toil, small as pygmies in the gulf pro-
found;
Some, dim between the lofty cliffs de-
scried,
O'erwalk the slender plank from side to
side;   165
These, by the pale-blue rocks that cease-
less ring,
In airy baskets hanging, work and sing.

Just where a cloud above the mountain
rears
An edge all flame, the broadening sun
appears;
A long blue bar its aegis orb divides,   170
And breaks the spreading of its golden
tides;
And now that orb has touched the purple
steep,
Whose softened image penetrates the
deep.
'Cross the calm lake's blue shades the
cliffs aspire,
With towers and woods, a 'prospect all
on fire;'   175
While coves and secret hollows, through
a ray
Of fainter gold, a purple gleam betray.
Each slip of lawn the broken rocks
between
Shines in the light with more than earthly
green:

Deep yellow beams the scattered stems
illume,   180
Far in the level forest's central gloom:
Waving his hat, the shepherd, from the
vale,
Directs his winding dog the cliffs to
scale,—
The dog, loud barking, 'mid the glittering
rocks,
Hunts, where his master points, the intercepted flocks.   185
Where oaks o'erhang the road the radi-
ance shoots
On tawny earth, wild weeds, and twisted
roots;
The druid-stones a brightened ring unfold;
And all the babbling brooks are liquid
gold;
Sunk to a curve, the day-star lessens
still,   190
Gives one bright glance, and drops be-
hind the hill.[2]

In these secluded vales, if village fame,
Confirmed by hoary hairs, belief may
claim;
When up the hills, as now, retired the
light,
Strange apparitions mocked the shep-
herd's sight.   195

The form appears of one that spurs his
steed
Midway along the hill with desperate
speed;
Unhurt pursues his lengthened flight,
while all   198
Attend, at every stretch, his headlong fall.
Anon, appears a brave, a gorgeous show
Of horsemen-shadows moving to and fro;
At intervals imperial banners stream,
And now the van reflects the solar beam;
The rear through iron brown betrays a
sullen gleam.
While silent stands the admiring crowd
below,   205
Silent the visionary warriors go,
Winding in ordered pomp their upward
way,[3]
Till the last banner of their long array
Has disappeared, and every trace is fled
Of splendour—save the beacon's spiry
head   210
Tipt with eve's latest gleam of burning
red.

Now, while the solemn evening shadows sail,
On slowly-waving pinions, down the vale;

---

[1] 'Dolcemente feroce.'—TASSO.—In this description of the cock, I remembered a spirited one of the
same animal in L'Agriculture, ou Les Géorgiques
Françoises, of M. Rossuet.

[2] From Thomson.

[3] See a description of an appearance of this kind
in Clark's Survey of the Lakes, accompanied by
vouchers of its veracity, that may amuse the reader.

And, fronting the bright west, yon oak entwines
Its darkening boughs and leaves in stronger lines;   215
'Tis pleasant near the tranquil lake to stray
Where, winding on along some secret bay,
The swan uplifts his chest, and backward flings
His neck, a varying arch, between his towering wings:
The eye that marks the gliding creature sees   220
How graceful, pride can be, and how majestic, ease.
While tender cares and mild domestic loves
With furtive watch pursue her as she moves,
The female with a meeker charm succeeds,
And her brown little-ones around her leads,   225
Nibbling the water lilies as they pass,
Or playing wanton with the floating grass.
She, in a mother's care, her beauty's pride
Forgetting, calls the wearied to her side;
Alternately they mount her back, and rest   230
Close by her mantling wings' embraces prest.

Long may they float upon this flood serene;
Theirs be these holms untrodden, still, and green,
Where leafy shades fence off the blustering gale,
And breathes in peace the lily of the vale!   235
Yon isle, which feels not even the milkmaid's feet,
Yet hears her song, 'by distance made more sweet,'
Yon isle conceals their home, their hutlike bower;
Green water-rushes overspread the floor;
Long grass and willows form the woven wall,   240
And swings above the roof the poplar tall.
Thence issuing often with unwieldy stalk,
They crush with broad black feet their flowery walk;
Or, from the neighbouring water, hear at morn
The hound, the horse's tread, and mellow horn;   245
Involve their serpent-necks in changeful rings,
Rolled wantonly between their slippery wings,
Or, starting up with noise and rude delight,
Force half upon the wave their cumbrous flight.

AN EVENING WALK

Fair Swan! by all a mother's joys caressed,   250
Haply some wretch has eyed, and called thee blessed;
When with her infants, from some shady seat
By the lake's edge, she rose—to face the noontide heat;
Or taught their limbs along the dusty road
A few short steps to totter with their load.   255

I see her now, denied to lay her head,
On cold blue nights, in hut or straw-built shed,
Turn to a silent smile their sleepy cry,
By pointing to the gliding moon on high.
—When low-hung clouds each star of summer hide,   260
And fireless are the valleys far and wide,
Where the brook brawls along the public road
Dark with bat-haunted ashes stretching broad,
Oft has she taught them on her lap to lay
The shining glow-worm; or, in heedless play,   265
Toss it from hand to hand, disquieted;
While others, not unseen, are free to shed
Green unmolested light upon their mossy bed.

Oh! when the sleety showers her path assail,
And like a torrent roars the headstrong gale;   270
No more her breath can thaw their fingers cold;
Their frozen arms her neck no more can fold,
Weak roof a cowering form two babes to shield,
And faint the fire a dying heart can yield!
Press the sad kiss, fond mother! vainly fears   275
Thy flooded cheek to wet them with its tears;
No tears can chill them, and no bosom warms,
Thy breast their death-bed, coffined in thine arms!

Sweet are the sounds that mingle from afar,
Heard by calm lakes, as peeps the folding star,   280
Where the duck dabbles 'mid the rustling sedge,
And feeding pike starts from the water's edge,
Or the swan stirs the reeds, his neck and bill
Wetting, that drip upon the water still;

And heron, as resounds the trodden
    shore,   285
Shoots upward, darting his long neck
    before.

Now, with religious awe, the farewell
    light
Blends with the solemn colouring of
    night;
'Mid groves of clouds that crest the
    mountain's brow,
And round the west's proud lodge their
    shadows throw,   290
Like Una shining on her gloomy way,
The half-seen form of Twilight roams
    astray;
Shedding, through paly loop-holes mild
    and small,
Gleams that upon the lake's still bosom
    fall;
Soft o'er the surface creep those lustres
    pale   295
Tracking the motions of the fitful gale.
With restless interchange at once the
    bright
Wins on the shade, the shade upon the
    light.
No favoured eye was e'er allowed to gaze
On lovelier spectacle in faery days;   300
When gentle Spirits urged a sportive
    chase,
Brushing with lucid wands the water's
    face:
While music, stealing round the glimmer-
    ing deeps,
Charmed the tall circle of the enchanted
    steeps.
—The lights are vanished from the watery
    plains: 305
No wreck of all the pageantry remains.
Unheeded night has overcome the vales:
On the dark earth the wearied vision
    fails;
The latest lingerer of the forest train,
The lone black fir, forsakes the faded
    plain;   310
Last evening sight, the cottage smoke, no
    more,
Lost in the thickened darkness, glimmers
    hoar;
And, towering from the sullen dark-
    brown mere,
Like a black wall, the mountain-steeps
    appear.
—Now o'er the soothed accordant heart
    we feel   315
A sympathetic twilight slowly steal,
And ever, as we fondly muse, we find
The soft gloom deepening on the tranquil
    mind.
Stay! pensive, sadly-pleasing visions,
    stay!
Ah no! as fades the vale, they fade
    away: 320

Yet still the tender, vacant gloom re-
    mains;
Still the cold cheek its shuddering tear
    retains.

The bird, who ceased, with fading light,
    to thread
Silent the hedge or steamy rivulet's bed,
From his grey re-appearing tower shall
    soon   325
Salute with gladsome note the rising moon,
While with a hoary light she frosts the
    ground,
And pours a deeper blue to Æther's
    bound;
Pleased, as she moves, her pomp of clouds
    to fold
In robes of azure, fleecy-white, and gold.

Above yon eastern hill, where darkness
    broods   331
O'er all its vanished dells, and lawns, and
    woods;
Where but a mass of shade the sight can
    trace,
Even now she shows, half-veiled, her
    lovely face:
Across the gloomy valley flings her
    light,   335
Far to the western slopes with hamlets
    white;
And gives, where woods the chequered
    upland strew,
To the green corn of summer, autumn's
    hue.

Thus Hope, first pouring from her
    blessed horn
Her dawn, far lovelier than the moon's
    own morn,   340
Till higher mounted, strives in vain to
    cheer
The weary hills, impervious, blackening
    near;
Yet does she still, undaunted, throw the
    while
On darling spots remote her tempting
    smile.

Even now she decks for me a distant
    scene,   345
(For dark and broad the gulf of time be-
    tween)
Gilding that cottage with her fondest ray,
(Sole bourn, sole wish, sole object of my
    way;
How fair its lawns and sheltering woods
    appear!
How sweet its streamlet murmurs in
    mine ear!)   350
Where we, my Friend, to happy days
    shall rise,
Till our small share of hardly-paining
    sighs

(For sighs will ever trouble human breath)
Creep hushed into the tranquil breast of
  death.

But now the clear bright Moon her
  zenith gains,   355
And, rimy without speck, extend the
  plains:
The deepest cleft the mountain's front
  displays
Scarce hides a shadow from her searching
  rays;
From the dark-blue faint silvery threads
  divide
The hills, while gleams below the azure
  tide;   360
Time softly treads; throughout the landscape breathes
A peace enlivened, not disturbed, by
  wreaths
Of charcoal-smoke, that, o'er the fallen
  wood,
Steal down the hill, and spread along the
  flood.

The song of mountain-streams, unheard
  by day,   365
Now hardly heard, beguiles my home-
  ward way.
Air listens, like the sleeping water, still,
To catch the spiritual music of the hill,
Broke only by the slow clock tolling deep,
Or shout that wakes the ferry-man from
  sleep,   370
The echoed hoof nearing the distant
  shore,
The boat's first motion—made with dash-
  ing oar;
Sound of closed gate, across the water
  borne,
Hurrying the timid hare through rustling
  corn;   374
The sportive outcry of the mocking owl;
And at long intervals the mill-dog's howl;
The distant forge's swinging thump pro-
  found;
Or yell, in the deep woods, of lonely
  hound.

IV

LINES

WRITTEN WHILE SAILING IN A BOAT
AT EVENING

[Composed 1789.—Published 1798.]

How richly glows the water's breast
Before us, tinged with evening hues,
While, facing thus the crimson west,
The boat her silent course pursues!
And see how dark the backward stream!
A little moment past so smiling!   6
And still, perhaps, with faithless gleam,
Some other loiterers beguiling.

DESCRIPTIVE SKETCHES, ETC.

Such views the youthful Bard allure;
But, heedless of the following gloom,   10
He deems their colours shall endure
Till peace go with him to the tomb.
—And let him nurse his fond deceit,
And what if he must die in sorrow!
Who would not cherish dreams so sweet,
Though grief and pain may come to-
  morrow?   16

V

REMEMBRANCE OF COLLINS

COMPOSED UPON THE THAMES NEAR
RICHMOND

[Composed 1789.—Published 1798.]

GLIDE gently, thus for ever glide,
O Thames! that other bards may see
As lovely visions by thy side
As now, fair river! come to me.
O glide, fair stream! for ever so,   5
Thy quiet soul on all bestowing,
Till all our minds for ever flow
As thy deep waters now are flowing.

Vain thought!—Yet be as now thou art,
That in thy waters may be seen   10
The image of a poet's heart,
How bright, how solemn, how serene!
Such as did once the Poet bless,
Who, murmuring here a later¹ ditty,
Could find no refuge from distress   15
But in the milder grief of pity.

Now let us, as we float along,
For *him* suspend the dashing oar;
And pray that never child of song
May know that Poet's sorrows more.   20
How calm! how still! the only sound,
The dripping of the oar suspended!
—The evening darkness gathers round
By virtue's holiest Powers attended.

VI

DESCRIPTIVE SKETCHES²

TAKEN DURING A PEDESTRIAN TOUR AMONG
THE ALPS

[Composed 1791-92.—Published 1793.]

TO

THE REV. ROBERT JONES,

FELLOW OF ST. JOHN'S COLLEGE,
CAMBRIDGE.

DEAR SIR,
    However desirous I might have been of giving
you proofs of the high place you hold in my

¹ Collins' Ode on the death of Thomson, the last
written, I believe, of the poems which were published
during his life-time. This Ode is also alluded to in
the next stanza.
² The original (1793) text of this Poem will be
found in the Appendix, pp. 469-482. It differs in
many important particulars from the finally revised
text here given.—ED.

POEMS WRITTEN IN YOUTH

esteem, I should have been cautious of wounding your delicacy by thus publicly addressing you, had not the circumstance of our having been companions among the Alps seemed to give this dedication a propriety sufficient to do away any scruples which your modesty might otherwise have suggested.

In inscribing this little work to you I consult my heart. You know well how great is the difference between two companions lolling in a post-chaise and two travellers plodding slowly along the road, side by side, each with his little knapsack of necessaries upon his shoulders. How much more of heart between the two latter!

I am happy in being conscious that I shall have one reader who will approach the conclusion of these few pages with regret. You they must certainly interest, in reminding you of moments to which you can hardly look back without a pleasure not the less dear from a shade of melancholy. You will meet with few images without recollecting the spot where we observed them together; consequently, whatever is feeble in my design, or spiritless in my colouring, will be amply supplied by your own memory.

With still greater propriety I might have inscribed to you a description of some of the features of your native mountains, through which we have wandered together, in the same manner, with so much pleasure. But the sea-sunsets, which give such splendour to the vale of Clwyd, Snowdon, the chair of Idris, the quiet village of Bethgelert, Menai and her Druids, the Alpine steeps of the Conway, and the still more interesting windings of the wizard stream of the Dee, remain yet untouched. Apprehensive that my pencil may never be exercised on these subjects, I cannot let slip this opportunity of thus publicly assuring you with how much affection and esteem,

I am, dear Sir,
Most sincerely yours,
London, 1793.   W. WORDSWORTH.

Happiness (if she had been to be found on earth) among the charms of Nature—Pleasures of the pedestrian Traveller—Author crosses France to the Alps—Present state of the Grande Chartreuse—Lake of Como—Time, Sunset—Same Scene, Twilight—Same Scene, Morning; its voluptuous Character; Old man and forest-cottage music—River Tusa—Via Mala and Grison Gipsy—Sckellenen-thal—Lake of Uri—Stormy sunset—Chapel of William Tell—Force of local emotion—Chamois-chaser—View of the higher Alps—Manner of life of a Swiss mountaineer, interspersed with views of the higher Alps—Golden age of the Alps—Life and views continued—Ranz des Vaches, famous Swiss Air—Abbey of Einsiedlen and its pilgrims—Valley of Chamouny—Mont Blanc—Slavery of Savoy—Influence of liberty on cottage-happiness—France—Wish for the Extirpation of slavery—Conclusion.

WERE there, below, a spot of holy ground
Where from distress a refuge might be found,
And solitude prepare the soul for heaven;
Sure, nature's God that spot to man had given
Where falls the purple morning far and
wide   5
In flakes of light upon the mountain-side;

Where with loud voice the power of water shakes
The leafy wood, or sleeps in quiet lakes.

Yet not unrecompensed the man shall roam,
Who at the call of summer quits his home,   10
And plods through some wide realm o'er vale and height,
Though seeking only holiday delight;
At least, not owning to himself an aim
To which the sage would give a prouder name.
No gains too cheaply earned his fancy cloy,   15
Though every passing zephyr whispers joy;
Brisk toil, alternating with ready ease,
Feeds the clear current of his sympathies.
For him sod-seats the cottage-door adorn;
And peeps the far-off spire, his evening bourn!   20
Dear is the forest frowning o'er his head,
And dear the velvet green-sward to his tread:
Moves there a cloud o'er mid-day's flaming eye?
Upward he looks—'and calls it luxury':
Kind Nature's charities his steps attend;   25
In every babbling brook he finds a friend;
While chastening thoughts of sweetest use, bestowed
By wisdom, moralise his pensive road.
Host of his welcome inn, the noon-tide bower,
To his spare meal he calls the passing poor;   30
He views the sun uplift his golden fire,
Or sink, with heart alive like Memnon's lyre;[1]
Blesses the moon that comes with kindly ray,
To light him shaken by his rugged way.
Back from his sight no bashful children steal;   35
He sits a brother at the cottage-meal;
His humble looks no shy restraint impart;
Around him plays at will the virgin heart.
While unsuspended wheels the village dance,
The maidens eye him with enquiring glance,   40
Much wondering by what fit of crazing care,
Or desperate love, bewildered, he came there.

A hope, that prudence could not then approve,
That clung to Nature with a truant's love,

---

[1] The lyre of Memnon is reported to have emitted melancholy or cheerful tones, as it was touched by the sun's evening or morning rays.

O'er Gallia's wastes of corn my footsteps
led; 45
Her files of road-elms, high above my
head
In long-drawn vista, rustling in the
breeze;
Or where her pathways straggle as they
please
By lonely farms and secret villages.
But lo! the Alps, ascending white in air, 50
Toy with the sun and glitter from afar.

And now, emerging from the forest's
gloom,
I greet thee, Chartreuse, while I mourn
thy doom.
Whither is fled that Power whose frown
severe
Awed sober Reason till she crouched in
fear? 55
That Silence, once in deathlike fetters
bound,
Chains that were loosened only by the
sound
Of holy rites chanted in measured round?
—The voice of blasphemy the fane
alarms,
The cloister startles at the gleam of
arms. 60
The thundering tube the aged angler
hears,
Bent o'er the groaning flood that sweeps
away his tears.
Cloud-piercing pine-trees nod their
troubled heads,
Spires, rocks, and lawns a browner night
o'erspreads;
Strong terror checks the female peasant's
sighs, 65
And start the astonished shades at female
eyes.
From Bruno's forest screams the af-
frighted jay,
And slow the insulted eagle wheels away.
A viewless flight of laughing Demons
mock
The Cross, by angels planted[1] on the
aerial rock. 70
The 'parting Genius' sighs with hollow
breath
Along the mystic streams of Life and
Death.[2]
Swelling the outcry dull, that long re-
sounds
Portentous through her old woods' track-
less bounds,
Vallombre,[3] 'mid her falling fanes, de-
plores, 75
For ever broke, the sabbath of her
bowers.

[1] Alluding to crosses seen on the tops of the spiry
rocks of Chartreuse, which have every appearance
of being inaccessible.
[2] Names of rivers at the Chartreuse.
[3] Name of one of the valleys of the Chartreuse.

More pleased, my foot the hidden margin roves
Of Como, bosomed deep in chestnut
groves.
No meadows thrown between, the giddy
steeps
Tower, bare or sylvan, from the narrow
deeps. 80
—To towns, whose shades of no rude
noise complain,
From ringing team apart and grating
wain—
To flat-roofed towns, that touch the
water's bound,
Or lurk in woody sunless glens pro-
found,
Or, from the bending rocks, obtrusive
cling, 85
And o'er the whitened wave their shadows
fling—
The pathway leads, as round the steeps
it twines;
And Silence loves its purple roof of vines.
The loitering traveller hence, at evening,
sees
From rock-hewn steps the sail between
the trees; 90
Or marks, 'mid opening cliffs, fair dark-
eyed maids
Tend the small harvest of their garden
glades;
Or stops the solemn mountain-shades to
view
Stretch o'er the pictured mirror broad
and blue,
And track the yellow lights from steep
to steep, 95
As up the opposing hills they slowly
creep.
Aloft, here, half a village shines, arrayed
In golden light; half hides itself in shade:
While, from amid the darkened roofs,
the spire,
Restlessly flashing, seems to mount like
fire: 100
There, all unshaded, blazing forests throw
Rich golden verdure on the lake below.
Slow glides the sail along the illumined
shore,
And steals into the shade the lazy oar;
Soft bosoms breathe around contagious
sighs, 105
And amorous music on the water dies.

How blest, delicious scene! the eye that
greets
Thy open beauties, or thy lone retreats;
Beholds the unwearied sweep of wood
that scales
Thy cliffs; the endless waters of thy
vales; 110
Thy lowly cots that sprinkle all the shore,
Each with its household boat beside the
door;

Thy torrents shooting from the clear-blue
    sky;
Thy towns that cleave, like swallows'
    nests, on high;
That glimmer hoar in eve's last light,
    descried   115
Dim from the twilight water's shaggy
    side,
Whence lutes and voices down the en-
    chanted woods
Steal, and compose the oar-forgotten
    floods;
—Thy lake that, streaked or dappled,
    blue or grey,
'Mid smoking woods gleams hid from
    morning's ray   120
Slow-travelling down the western hills,
    to enfold
Its green-tinged margin in a blaze of
    gold;
Thy glittering steeples, whence the matin
    bell
Calls forth the woodman from his desert
    cell,
And quickens the blithe sound of oars
    that pass   125
Along the steaming lake, to early mass.
But now farewell to each and all—adieu
To every charm, and last and chief to you,
Ye lovely maidens that in noontide shade
Rest near your little plots of wheaten
    glade;   130
To all that binds the soul in powerless
    trance,
Lip-dewing song, and ringlet-tossing
    dance;
Where sparkling eyes and breaking smiles
    illume
The sylvan cabin's lute-enlivened gloom.
—Alas! the very murmur of the streams
Breathes o'er the failing soul voluptuous
    dreams,   136
While Slavery, forcing the sunk mind to
    dwell
On joys that might disgrace the captive's
    cell,
Her shameless timbrel shakes on Como's
    marge,
And lures from bay to bay the vocal
    barge.   140

Yet are thy softer arts with power in-
    dued
To soothe and cheer the poor man's soli-
    tude.
By silent cottage-doors, the peasant's
    home
Left vacant for the day, I loved to roam.
But once I pierced the mazes of a wood
In which a cabin undeserted stood;   146
There an old man an olden measure
    scanned
On a rude viol touched with withered
    hand.

As lambs or fawns in April clustering lie
Under a hoary oak's thin canopy,   150
Stretched at his feet, with steadfast up-
    ward eye,
His children's children listened to the
    sound;
—A Hermit with his family around!

But let us hence; for fair Locarno
    smiles
Embowered in walnut slopes and citron
    isles: 155
Or seek at eve the banks of Tusa's stream,
Where, 'mid dim towers and woods, her[1]
    waters gleam.
From the bright wave, in solemn gloom,
    retire
The dull-red steeps, and, darkening still,
    aspire
To where afar rich orange lustres glow
Round undistinguished clouds, and rocks,
    and snow: 161
Or, led where Via Mala's chasms con-
    fine
The indignant waters of the infant Rhine,
Hang o'er the abyss, whose else imper-
    vious gloom
His burning eyes with fearful light il-
    lume.   165

The mind condemned, without re-
    prieve, to go
O'er life's long deserts with its charge of
    woe,
With sad congratulation joins the train
Where beasts and men together o'er the
    plain
Move on—a mighty caravan of pain: 170
Hope, strength, and courage, social suf-
    fering brings,
Freshening the wilderness with shades
    and springs.
—There be whose lot far otherwise is
    cast:
Sole human tenant of the piny waste,
By choice or doom a gipsy wanders
    here,   175
A nursling babe her only comforter;
Lo, where she sits beneath yon shaggy
    rock,
A cowering shape half hid in curling
    smoke!

When lightning among clouds and
    mountain-snows
Predominates, and darkness comes and
    goes,   180
And the fierce torrent at the flashes
    broad
Starts, like a horse, beside the glaring
    road—

[1] The river along whose banks you descend in
crossing the Alps by the Simplon Pass.

10

She seeks a covert from the battering
   shower
In the roofed bridge;[1] the bridge, in that
   dread hour,
Itself all trembling at the torrent's power.

Nor is she more at ease on some *still*
   night,   186
When not a star supplies the comfort of
   its light;
Only the waning moon hangs dull and red
Above a melancholy mountain's head,
Then sets. In total gloom the Vagrant
   sighs,   190
Stoops her sick head, and shuts her weary
   eyes;
Or on her fingers counts the distant clock,
Or to the drowsy crow of midnight cock
Listens, or quakes while from the forest's
   gulf
Howls near and nearer yet the famished
   wolf.   195

From the green vale of Urseren smooth
   and wide
Descend we now, the maddened Reuss
   our guide;
By rocks that, shutting out the blessed
   day,
Cling tremblingly to rocks as loose as
   they;
By cells[2] upon whose image, while he
   prays,   200
The kneeling peasant scarcely dares to
   gaze;
By many a votive death-cross[3] planted
   near,
And watered duly with the pious tear,
That faded silent from the upward eye
Unmoved with each rude form of peril
   nigh;   205
Fixed on the anchor left by Him who
   saves
Alike in whelming snows and roaring
   waves.

But soon a peopled region on the sight
Opens—a little world of calm delight;
Where mists, suspended on the expiring
   gale,   210
Spread rooflike o'er the deep secluded
   vale,
And beams of evening, slipping in be-
   tween,
Gently illuminate a sober scene:—

Here, on the brown wood-cottages[4] they
   sleep,   214
There, over rock or sloping pasture creep.
On as we journey, in clear view displayed,
The still vale lengthens underneath its shade
Of low-hung vapour: on the freshened
   mead
The green light sparkles;—the dim bowers
   recede.
While pastoral pipes and streams the
   landscape lull,   220
And bells'of passing mules that tinkle dull,
In solemn shapes before the admiring eye
Dilated hang the misty pines on high,
Huge convent domes with pinnacles and
   towers,
And antique castles seen through gleamy
   showers.   225

From such romantic dreams, my soul,
   awake
To sterner pleasure, where, by Uri's lake,
In Nature's pristine majesty outspread,
Winds neither road nor path for foot to
   tread:
The rocks rise naked as a wall, or stretch
Far o'er the water, hung with groves of
   beech;   231
Aerial pines from loftier steeps ascend,
Nor stop but where creation seems to end.
Yet here and there, if 'mid the savage
   scene   234
Appears a scanty plot of smiling green,
Up from the lake a zigzag path will creep
To reach a small wood-hut hung boldly
   on the steep.
—Before those thresholds (never can they
   know
The face of traveller passing to and fro,
No peasant leans upon his pole, to tell 240
For whom at morning tolled the funeral
   bell;
Their watch-dog ne'er his angry bark for-
   goes,
Touched by the beggar's moan of human
   woes;
The shady porch ne'er offered a cool seat
To pilgrims overcome by summer's heat.
Yet thither the world's business finds its
   way   246
At times, and tales unsought beguile the day,
And *there* are those fond thoughts which
   Solitude,
However stern, is powerless to exclude.
There doth the maiden watch her lover's
   sail   250
Approaching, and upbraid the tardy gale;
At midnight listens till his parting oar,
And its last echo, can be heard no more.

And what if ospreys, cormorants,
   herons cry,   254
Amid tempestuous vapours driving by,

---

[1] Most of the bridges among the Alps are of wood,
and covered: these bridges have a heavy appearance,
and rather injure the effect of the scenery in some
places.
[2] The Catholic religion prevails here: these cells
are, as is well known, very common in the Catholic
countries, planted, like the Roman tombs, along the
road side.
[3] Crosses, commemorative of the deaths of travellers, by the fall of snow and other accidents, are very
common along this dreadful road.

[4] The houses in the more retired Swiss valleys are
all built of wood.

Or hovering over wastes too bleak to rear
That common growth of earth, the food-
 ful ear;
Where the green apple shrivels on the
 spray,
And pines the unripened pear in sum-
 mer's kindliest ray;
Contentment shares the desolate domain
With Independence, child of high Dis-
 dain.   261
Exulting 'mid the winter of the skies,
Shy as the jealous chamois, Freedom flies,
And grasps by fits her sword, and often
 eyes;
And sometimes, as from rock to rock she
 bounds,   265
The Patriot nymph starts at imagined
 sounds,
And, wildly pausing, oft she hangs aghast,
Whether some old Swiss air hath checked
 her haste,
Or thrill of Spartan fife is caught between
 the blast.

 Swoln with incessant rains from hour
  to hour,   270
All day the floods a deepening murmur
 pour:
The sky is veiled, and every cheerful
 sight:
Dark is the region as with coming night;
But what a sudden burst of overpowering
 light!
Triumphant on the bosom of the storm,
Glances the wheeling eagle's glorious
 form!   276
Eastward, in long perspective glittering,
 shine
The wood-crowned cliffs that o'er the lake
 recline;
Those lofty cliffs a hundred streams un-
 fold,
At once to pillars turned that flame with
 gold: 280
Behind his sail the peasant shrinks, to
 shun
The *west*, that burns like one dilated sun,
A crucible of mighty compass, felt
By mountains, glowing till they seem to
 melt.

 But, lo! the boatman, overawed, before
The pictured fane of Tell suspends his
 oar;   286
Confused the Marathonian tale appears,
While his eyes sparkle with heroic tears.
And who, that walks where men of an-
 cient days
Have wrought with godlike arm the deeds
 of praise,   290
Feels not the spirit of the place control,
Or rouse and agitate his labouring soul?
Say, who, by thinking on Canadian hills,
Or wild Aosta lulled by Alpine rills,

On Zutphen's plain, or on that highland
 dell,   295
Through which rough Garry cleaves his
 way, can tell
What high resolves exalt the tenderest
 thought
Of him whom passion rivets to the spot,
Where breathed the gale that caught
 Wolfe's happiest sigh,
And the last sunbeam fell on Bayard's
 eye;   300
Where bleeding Sidney from the cup re-
 tired,
And glad Dundee in 'faint huzzas' ex-
 pired?

 But now with other mind I stand alone
Upon the summit of this naked cone,
And watch the fearless chamois-hunter
 chase   305
His prey, through tracts abrupt of deso-
 late space,
[1]Through vacant worlds where Nature
 never gave
A brook to murmur or a bough to wave,
Which unsubstantial Phantoms sacred
 keep;
Thro' worlds where Life, and Voice, and
 Motion sleep;   310
Where silent Hours their death-like sway
 extend,
Save when the avalanche breaks loose, to
 rend
Its way with uproar, till the ruin, drowned
In some dense wood or gulf of snow pro-
 found,
Mocks the dull ear of Time with deaf
 abortive sound.   315
—'Tis his, while wandering on from
 height to height,
To see a planet's pomp and steady light
In the least star of scarce-appearing night;
While the pale moon moves near him, on
 the bound,   319
Of ether, shining with diminished round,
And far and wide the icy summits blaze,
Rejoicing in the glory of her rays:
To him the day-star glitters small and
 bright,
Shorn of its beams, insufferably white,
And he can look beyond the sun, and
 view   325
Those fast-receding depths of sable blue
Flying till vision can no more pursue!
—At once bewildering mists around him
 close,
And cold and hunger are his least of
 woes;   329
The Demon of the snow, with angry roar
Descending, shuts for aye his prison door.

[1] For most of the images in the next sixteen verses,
I am indebted to M. Raymond's interesting observa-
tions, annexed to his translation of Coxe's Tour in
Switzerland.

Soon with despair's whole weight his
  spirits sink;
Bread has he none, the snow must be his
  drink;
And, ere his eyes can close upon the day,
The eagle of the Alps o'ershades her prey.

Now couch thyself where, heard with
  fear afar,   336
Thunders through echoing pines the head-
  long Aar;
Or rather stay to taste the mild delights
Of pensive Underwalden's[1] pastoral
  heights.
—Is there who 'mid these awful wilds
  has seen   340
The native Genii walk the mountain
  green?
Or heard, while other worlds their charms
  reveal,
Soft music o'er the aerial summit steal?
While o'er the desert, answering every
  close,
Rich steam of sweetest perfume comes and
  goes.   345
—And sure there is a secret Power that
  reigns
Here, where no trace of man the spot
  profanes,
Nought but the *chalets*,[2] flat and bare, on
  high
Suspended 'mid the quiet of the sky;
Or distant herds that pasturing upward
  creep,   350
And, not untended, climb the dangerous
  steep.
How still! no irreligious sound or sight
Rouses the soul from her severe delight.
An idle voice the sabbath region fills
Of Deep that calls to Deep across the
  hills,   355
And with that voice accords the soothing
  sound
Of drowsy bells, for ever tinkling round;
Faint wail of eagle melting into blue
Beneath the cliffs, and pine-wood's steady
  sugh;[3]
The solitary heifer's deepened low;   360
Or rumbling, heard remote, of falling
  snow.
All motions, sounds, and voices, far and
  nigh,
Blend in a music of tranquillity;
Save when, a stranger seen below, the boy
Shouts from the echoing hills with savage
  joy.   365

[1] The people of this Canton are supposed to be of
a more melancholy disposition than the other inhabitants of the Alps; this, if true, may proceed from
their living more secluded.
[2] This picture is from the middle region of the
Alps. *Chalets* are summer huts for the Swiss herdsmen.
[3] *Sugh*, a Scotch word expressive of the sound of
the wind through the trees.

When, from the sunny breast of open
  seas,
And bays with myrtle fringed, the
  southern breeze
Comes on to gladden April with the sight
Of green isles widening on each snow-
  clad height;
When shouts and lowing herds the valley
  fill,   370
And louder torrents stun the noon-tide
  hill,
The pastoral Swiss begin the cliffs to
  scale,
Leaving to silence the deserted vale;
And, like the Patriarchs in their simple
  age,
Move, as the verdure leads, from stage
  to stage;   375
High and more high in summer's heat
  they go,
And hear the rattling thunder far below;
Or steal beneath the mountains, half-
  deterred,
Where huge rocks tremble to the bellow-
  ing herd.

One I behold who, 'cross the foaming
  flood,   380
Leaps with a bound of graceful hardi-
  hood;
Another high on that green ledge;—he
  gained
The tempting spot with every sinew
  strained;
And downward thence a knot of grass
  he throws,
Food for his beasts in time of winter
  snows.   385
—Far different life from what Tradition
  hoar
Transmits of happier lot in times of
  yore!
Then Summer lingered long; and honey
  flowed
From out the rocks, the wild bees' safe
  abode:
Continual waters welling cheered the
  waste,   390
And plants were wholesome, now of
  deadly taste:
Nor Winter yet his frozen stores had
  piled,
Usurping where the fairest herbage
  smiled:
Nor Hunger driven the herds from pastures bare,
To climb the treacherous cliffs for scanty
  fare.   395
Then the milk-thistle flourished through
  the land,
And forced the full-swoln udder to demand,
Thrice every day, the pail and welcome
  hand.

Thus does the father to his children tell
Of banished bliss, by fancy loved too
    well.   400
Alas! that human guilt provoked the rod
Of angry Nature to avenge her God.
Still, Nature, ever just, to him imparts
Joys only given to uncorrupted hearts.

'Tis morn: with gold the verdant moun-
    tain glows;   405
More high, the snowy peaks with hues
    of rose.
Far stretched beneath the many-tinted
    hills,
A mighty waste of mist the valley fills,
A solemn sea! whose billows wide around
Stand motionless, to awful silence
    bound: 410
Pines, on the coast, through mist their
    tops uprear,
That like to leaning masts of stranded
    ships appear.
A single chasm, a gulf of gloomy blue,
Gapes in the centre of the sea—and,
    through
That dark mysterious gulf ascending,
    sound   415
Innumerable streams with roar pro-
    found.
Mount through the nearer vapours notes
    of birds,
And merry flageolet; the low of herds,
The bark of dogs, the heifer's tinkling
    bell,
Talk, laughter, and perchance a church-
    tower knell: 420
Think not the peasant from aloft has
    gazed
And heard with heart unmoved, with soul
    unraised:
Nor is his spirit less enrapt, nor less
Alive to independent happiness,
Then, when he lies, out-stretched, at
    even-tide   425
Upon the fragrant mountain's purple
    side:
For as the pleasures of his simple day
Beyond his native valley seldom stray,
Nought round its darling precincts can
    he find
But brings some past enjoyment to his
    mind;   430
While Hope, reclining upon Pleasure's
    urn,
Binds her wild wreaths, and whispers his
    return.

Once, Man entirely free, alone and
    wild,
Was blest as free—for he was Nature's
    child.
He, all superior but his God disdained,
Walked none restraining, and by none
    restrained: 436

Confessed no law but what his reason
    taught,
Did all he wished, and wished but what
    he ought.
As man in his primeval dower arrayed
The image of his glorious Sire dis-
    played,   440
Even so, by faithful Nature guarded,
    here
The traces of primeval Man appear;
The simple dignity no forms debase;
The eye sublime, and surly lion-grace:
The slave of none, of beasts alone the
    lord,   445
His book he prizes, nor neglects his
    sword;
—Well taught by that to feel his rights,
    prepared
With this 'the blessings he enjoys to
    guard.'

And as his native hills encircle ground
For many a marvellous victory re-
    nowned,   450
The work of Freedom daring to oppose,
With few in arms,[1] innumerable foes,
When to those famous fields his steps are
    led,
An unknown power connects him with
    the dead:
For images of other worlds are there; 455
Awful the light, and holy is the air.
Fitfully, and in flashes, through his soul,
Like sun-lit tempests, troubled transports
    roll;
His bosom heaves, his Spirit towers
    amain,
Beyond the senses and their little
    reign.   460

And oft, when that dread vision hath
    past by,
He holds with God himself communion
    high,
There where the peal of swelling torrents
    fills
The sky-roofed temple of the eternal hills;
Or, when upon the mountain's silent
    brow   465
Reclined, he sees, above him and below,
Bright stars of ice and azure fields of
    snow;
While needle peaks of granite shooting
    bare
Tremble in ever-varying tints of air.

[1] Alluding to several battles which the Swiss in very
small numbers have gained over their oppressors, the
House of Austria; and, in particular, to one fought at
Næffels near Glarus, where three hundred and thirty
men are said to have defeated an army of between
fifteen and twenty thousand Austrians. Scattered
over the valley are to be found eleven stones, with
this inscription, 1388, the year the battle was fought,
marking out, as I was told upon the spot, the several
places where the Austrians, attempting to make a
stand, were repulsed anew.

And when a gathering weight of shadows
brown   470
Falls on the valleys as the sun goes down;
And Pikes, of darkness named and fear
and storms,[1]
Uplift in quiet their illumined forms,
In sea-like reach of prospect round him
spread,
Tinged like an angel's smile all rosy
red—   475
Awe in his breast with holiest love unites,
And the near heavens impart their own
delights.

When downward to his winter hut he
goes,
Dear and more dear the lessening circle
grows;
That hut which on the hills so oft em-
ploys   480
His thoughts, the central point of all his
joys.
And as a swallow, at the hour of rest,
Peeps often ere she darts into her nest,
So to the homestead, where the grandsire
tends
A little prattling child, he oft descends,
To glance a look upon the well-matched
pair;   486
Till storm and driving ice blockade him
there.
There, safely guarded by the woods be-
hind,
He hears the chiding of the baffled wind,
Hears Winter calling all his terrors
round,   490
And, blest within himself, he shrinks not
from the sound.

Through Nature's vale his homely plea-
sures glide,
Unstained by envy, discontent, and
pride;
The bound of all his vanity, to deck,
With one bright bell a favourite heifer's
neck;   495
Well pleased upon some simple annual
feast,
Remembered half the year and hoped the
rest,
If dairy-produce, from his inner hoard,
Of thrice ten summers dignify the board.
—Alas! in every clime a flying ray   500
Is all we have to cheer our wintry way;
And here the unwilling mind may more
than trace
The general sorrows of the human race:
The churlish gales of penury, that blow
Cold as the north-wind o'er a waste of
snow,   505
To them the gentle groups of bliss deny
That on the noon-day bank of leisure lie.

Yet more;—compelled by Powers which
only deign
That *solitary* man disturb their reign,
Powers that support an unremitting strife
With all the tender charities of life, 511
Full oft the father, when his sons have
grown
To manhood, seems their title to disown;
And from his nest amid the storms of
heaven
Drives, eagle-like, those sons as he was
driven;   515
With stern composure watches to the
plain—
And never, eagle-like, beholds again!

When long familiar joys are all re-
signed,
Why does their sad remembrance haunt
the mind?
Lo! where through flat Batavia's willowy
groves,   520
Or by the lazy Seine, the exile roves;
O'er the curled waters Alpine measures
swell,
And search the affections to their inmost
cell;
Sweet poison spreads along the listener's
veins,
Turning past pleasures into mortal pains;
Poison, which not a frame of steel can
brave,   526
Bows his young head with sorrow to the
grave.[2]

Gay lark of hope, thy silent song re-
sume!
Ye flattering eastern lights, once more
the hills illume!
Fresh gales and dews of life's delicious
morn,   530
And thou, lost fragrance of the heart,
return!
Alas! the little joy to man allowed
Fades like the lustre of an evening cloud;
Or like the beauty in a flower installed,
Whose season was, and cannot be re-
called.   535
Yet, when opprest by sickness, grief, or
care,
And taught that pain is pleasure's natural
heir,
We still confide in more than we can
know;
Death would be else the favourite friend
of woe.

'Mid savage rocks, and seas of snow
that shine,   540
Between interminable tracts of pine,
Within a temple stands an awful shrine,

----

[1] As Schreck-Horn, the pike of terror; Wetter-
Horn, the pike of storms, &c., &c.

[2] The well-known effect of the famous air, called
in French Ranz des Vaches, upon the Swiss troops.

By an uncertain light revealed, that falls
On the mute Image and the troubled
walls.
Oh! give not me that eye of hard dis-
dain 545
That views, undimmed, Einsiedlen's[1]
wretched fane.
While ghastly faces through the gloom
appear,
Abortive joy, and hope that works in
fear;
While prayer contends with silenced
agony,
Surely in other thoughts contempt may
die. 550
If the sad grave of human ignorance bear
One flower of hope—oh, pass and leave it
there!

The tall sun, pausing on an Alpine
spire,
Flings o'er the wilderness a stream of fire:
Now meet we other pilgrims ere the
day 555
Close on the remnant of their weary way;
While they are drawing toward the sacred
floor
Where, so they fondly think, the worm
shall gnaw no more.
How gaily murmur and how sweetly taste
The fountains[2] reared for them amid the
waste! 560
Their thirst they slake:—they wash their
toil-worn feet,
And some with tears of joy each other
greet.
Yes, I must see you when ye first behold
Those holy turrets tipped with evening
gold,
In that glad moment will for you a sigh 565
Be heaved of charitable sympathy;
In that glad moment when your hands
are prest
In mute devotion on the thankful breast!

Last, let us turn to Chamouny that
shields
With rocks and gloomy woods her fertile
fields: 570
Five streams of ice amid her cots descend,
And with wild flowers and blooming
orchards blend;—
A scene more fair than what the Grecian
feigns
Of purple lights and ever-vernal plains;
Here all the seasons revel hand in
hand: 575
'Mid lawns and shades by breezy rivulets
fanned,

[1] This shrine is resorted to, from a hope of relief,
by multitudes, from every corner of the Catholic
world, labouring under mental or bodily afflictions.
[2] Rude fountains built and covered with sheds for
the accommodation of the Pilgrims, in their ascent
of the mountain.

They sport beneath that mountain's
matchless height
That holds no commerce with the sum-
mer night.
From age to age, throughout his lonely
bounds
The crash of ruin fitfully resounds; 580
Appalling havoc! but serene his brow,
Where daylight lingers on perpetual
snow;
Glitter the stars above, and all is black
below.

What marvel then if many a Wanderer
sigh,
While roars the sullen Arve in anger
by, 585
That not for thy reward, unrivail'd Vale!
Waves the ripe harvest in the autumnal
gale;
That thou, the slave of slaves, art doomed
to pine
And droop, while no Italian arts are
thine,
To soothe or cheer, to soften or refine. 590

Hail Freedom! whether it was mine to
stray,
With shrill winds whistling round my
lonely way,
On the bleak sides of Cumbria's heath-
clad moors,
Or where dank sea-weed lashes Scotland's
shores;
To scent the sweets of Piedmont's breath-
ing rose, 595
And orange gale that o'er Lugano blows;
Still have I found, where Tyranny pre-
vails,
That virtue languishes and pleasure fails,
While the remotest hamlets blessings
share
In thy loved presence known, and only 600
there;
Heart-blessings—outward treasures too
which the eye
Of the sun peeping through the clouds
can spy,
And every passing breeze will testify.
There, to the porch, belike with jasmine
bound
Or woodbine wreaths, a smoother path is
wound; 605
The housewife there a brighter garden
sees,
Where hum on busier wing her happy
bees;
On infant cheeks there fresher roses blow;
And grey-haired men look up with livelier
brow,—
To greet the traveller needing food and
rest; 610
Housed for the night, or but a half-hour's
guest.

And oh, fair France! though now the traveller sees
Thy three-striped banner fluctuate on the breeze;
Though martial songs have banished songs of love,
And nightingales desert the village grove,
Scared by the fife and rumbling drum's alarms,   616
And the short thunder, and the flash of arms;
That cease not till night falls, when far and nigh,
Sole sound, the Sourd[1] prolongs his mournful cry;
—Yet hast thou found that Freedom spreads her power   620
Beyond the cottage hearth, the cottage-door:
All nature smiles, and owns beneath her eyes
Her fields peculiar, and peculiar skies.
Yes, as I roamed where Loiret's waters glide
Through rustling aspens heard from side to side,   625
When from October clouds a milder light
Fell where the blue flood rippled into white;
Methought from every cot the watchful bird
Crowed with ear-piercing power till then unheard;
Each clacking mill, that broke the murmuring streams,   630
Rocked the charmed thought in more delightful dreams;
Chasing those pleasant dreams, the falling leaf
Awoke a fainter sense of moral grief;
The measured echo of the distant flail
Wound in more welcome cadence down the vale;   635
With more majestic course[2] the water rolled,
And ripening foliage shone with richer gold.
—But foes are gathering—Liberty must raise
Red on the hills her beacon's far-seen blaze;
Must bid the tocsin ring from tower to tower!—   640
Nearer and nearer comes the trying hour!
Rejoice, brave Land, though pride's perverted ire
Rouse hell's own aid, and wrap thy fields in fire:

[1] An insect so called, which emits a short, melancholy cry, heard at the close of the summer evenings, on the banks of the Loire.
[2] The duties upon many parts of the French rivers were so exorbitant, that the poorer people, deprived of the benefit of water carriage, were obliged to transport their goods by land.

Lo, from the flames a great and glorious birth;
As if a new-made heaven were hailing a new earth!   645
—All cannot be: the promise is too fair
For creatures doomed to breathe terrestrial air:
Yet not for this will sober reason frown
Upon that promise, nor the hope disown;
She knows that only from high aims ensue   650
Rich guerdons, and to them alone are due.

Great God! by whom the strifes of men are weighed
In an impartial balance, give thine aid
To the just cause; and, oh! do thou preside
Over the mighty stream now spreading wide: 655
So shall its waters, from the heavens supplied
In copious showers, from earth by wholesome springs,
Brood o'er the long-parched lands with Nile-like wings!
And grant that every sceptred child of clay
Who cries presumptuous, 'Here the flood shall stay,'   660
May in its progress see thy guiding hand,
And cease the acknowledged purpose to withstand;
Or, swept in anger from the insulted shore,
Sink with his servile bands, to rise no more!

To-night, my Friend, within this humble cot   665
Be scorn and fear and hope alike forgot
In timely sleep; and when, at break of day,
On the tall peaks the glistening sunbeams play,
With a light heart our course we may renew,
The first whose footsteps print the mountain dew.   670

VII

LINES

Left upon a Seat in a Yew-tree, which stands near the lake of Esthwaite, on a desolate part of the shore, commanding a beautiful prospect.

[Begun 1787.—Completed 1795.—Published 1798.]

NAY, Traveller! rest. This lonely Yew-tree stands
Far from all human dwelling: what if here
No sparkling rivulet spread the verdant herb?

POEMS WRITTEN IN YOUTH

What if the bee love not these barren
    boughs?
Yet, if the wind breathe soft, the curling
    waves,   5
That break against the shore, shall lull
    thy mind
By one soft impulse saved from vacancy.
————————Who he was
That piled these stones and with the
    mossy sod
First covered, and here taught this aged
    Tree   10
With its dark arms to form a circling
    bower,
I well remember.—He was one who
    owned
No common soul. In youth by science
    nursed,
And led by nature into a wild scene
Of lofty hopes, he to the world went
    forth   15
A favoured Being, knowing no desire
Which genius did not hallow; 'gainst the
    taint
Of dissolute tongues, and jealousy, and
    hate,
And scorn,—against all enemies pre-
    pared,
All but neglect. The world, for so it
    thought,   20
Owed him no service; wherefore he at
    once
With indignation turned himself away,
And with the food of pride sustained his
    soul
In solitude.—Stranger! these gloomy
    boughs
Had charms for him; and here he loved
    to sit,   25
His only visitants a straggling sheep,
The stone-chat, or the glancing sand-
    piper:
And on these barren rocks, with fern and
    heath,
And juniper and thistle, sprinkled o'er,
Fixing his downcast eye, he many an
    hour   30
A morbid pleasure nourished, tracing
    here
An emblem of his own unfruitful life:
And, lifting up his head, he then would
    gaze
On the more distant scene,—how lovely
    'tis
Thou seest,—and he would gaze till it
    became   35
Far lovelier, and his heart could not
    sustain
The beauty, still more beauteous! Nor,
    that time,
When nature had subdued him to herself,
Would he forget those Beings to whose
    minds
Warm from the labours of benevolence 40

The world, and human life, appeared a
    scene
Of kindred loveliness: then he would sigh,
Inly disturbed, to think that others felt
What he must never feel: and so, lost
    Man!
On visionary views would fancy feed,   45
Till his eye streamed with tears. In this
    deep vale
He died,—this seat his only monument.

If Thou be one whose heart the holy
    forms
Of young imagination have kept pure,
Stranger! henceforth be warned; and
    know that pride,   50
Howe'er disguised in its own majesty,
Is littleness; that he who feels contempt
For any living thing, hath faculties
Which he has never used; that thought
    with him
Is in its infancy. The man whose eye 55
Is ever on himself doth look on one,
The least of Nature's works, one who
    might move
The wise man to that scorn which wisdom
    holds
Unlawful, ever. O be wiser, Thou!
Instructed that true knowledge leads to
    love;   60
True dignity abides with him alone
Who, in the silent hour of inward thought,
Can still suspect, and still revere himself,
In lowliness of heart.

VIII

GUILT AND SORROW

OR

INCIDENTS UPON SALISBURY PLAIN

[Begun 1791–92.—Completed 1793–94.—Published 1842.]

ADVERTISEMENT,

PREFIXED TO THE FIRST EDITION OF THIS POEM,
PUBLISHED IN 1842.

NOT less than one-third of the following poem,
though it has from time to time been altered in
the expression, was published so far back as the
year 1798, under the title of 'The Female Vagrant.'
The extract is of such length that an apology seems
to be required for reprinting it here: but it was
necessary to restore it to its original position, or
the rest would have been unintelligible. The whole
was written before the close of the year 1794, and
I will detail, rather as matter of literary biography
than for any other reason, the circumstances under
which it was produced.
    During the latter part of the summer of 1793,
having passed a month in the Isle of Wight, in
view of the fleet which was then preparing for sea
off Portsmouth at the commencement of the war,
I left the place with melancholy forebodings. The
American war was still fresh in memory. The
struggle which was beginning, and which many

18

thought would be brought to a speedy close by
the irresistible arms of Great Britain being added
to those of the Allies, I was assured in my own
mind would be of long continuance, and productive of distress and misery beyond all possible
calculation. This conviction was pressed upon me
by having been a witness, during a long residence
in revolutionary France, of the spirit which prevailed in that country. After leaving the Isle of
Wight, I spent two days in wandering on foot over
Salisbury Plain, which, though cultivation was
then widely spread through parts of it, had upon
the whole a still more impressive appearance than
it now retains.

The monuments and traces of antiquity, scattered in abundance over that region, led me
unavoidably to compare what we know or guess
of those remote times with certain aspects of
modern society, and with calamities, principally
those consequent upon war, to which, more than
other classes of men, the poor are subject. In
those reflections, joined with particular facts that
had come to my knowledge, the following stanzas
originated.

In conclusion, to obviate some distraction in
the minds of those who are well acquainted with
Salisbury Plain, it may be proper to say that, of
the features described as belonging to it, one or
two are taken from other desolate parts of England.

I

A Traveller on the skirt of Sarum's
    Plain
Pursued his vagrant way, with feet half
    bare;
Stooping his gait, but not as if to gain
Help from the staff he bore; for mien
    and air
Were hardy, though his cheek seemed
    worn with care   5
Both of the time to come, and time long
    fled:
Down fell in straggling locks his thin grey
    hair;
A coat he wore of military red
But faded, and stuck o'er with many a
    patch and shred.

II

While thus he journeyed, step by step
    led on,   10
He saw and passed a stately inn, full
    sure
That welcome in such house for him was
    none.
No board inscribed the needy to allure
Hung there, no bush proclaimed to old
    and poor
And desolate, 'Here you will find a
    friend!'   15
The pendent grapes glittered above the
    door;—
On he must pace, perchance till night
    descend,
Where'er the dreary roads their bare
    white lines extend.

III

The gathering clouds grew red with
    stormy fire,
In streaks diverging wide and mounting
    high;   20
That inn he long had passed; the distant
    spire,
Which oft as he looked back had fixed his
    eye,
Was lost, though still he looked, in the
    blank sky.
Perplexed and comfortless he gazed
    around,
And scarce could any trace of man descry,
Save cornfields stretched and stretching
    without bound;   26
But where the sower dwelt was nowhere
    to be found.

IV

No tree was there, no meadow's pleasant
    green,
No brook to wet his lip or soothe his ear;
Long files of corn-stacks here and there
    were seen,   30
But not one dwelling-place his heart to
    cheer.
Some labourer, thought he, may per-
    chance be near;
And so he sent a feeble shout—in vain;
No voice made answer, he could only hear
Winds rustling over plots of unripe grain,
Or whistling thro' thin grass along the
    unfurrowed plain.   36

V

Long had he fancied each successive slope
Concealed some cottage, whither he
    might turn
And rest; but now along heaven's dark-
    ening cope
The crows rushed by in eddies, homeward
    borne.   40
Thus warned he sought some shepherd's
    spreading thorn
Or hovel from the storm to shield his
    head,
But sought in vain; for now, all wild,
    forlorn,
And vacant, a huge waste around him
    spread;
The wet cold ground, he feared, must be
    his only bed.   45

VI

And be it so—for to the chill night shower
And the sharp wind his head he oft hath
    bared;
A Sailor he, who many a wretched hour
Hath told; for, landing after labour hard,
Full long endured in hope of just reward,
He to an armèd fleet was forced away   51
By seamen, who perhaps themselves had
    shared

Like fate; was hurried off, a helpless prey,
'Gainst all that in *his* heart, or theirs
    perhaps, said nay.

VII

For years the work of carnage did not
    cease,   55
And death's dire aspect daily he surveyed,
Death's minister; then came his glad re-
    lease,
And hope returned, and pleasure fondly
    made
Her dwelling in his dreams. By Fancy's
    aid
The happy husband flies, his arms to
    throw   60
Round his wife's neck; the prize of vic-
    tory laid
In her full lap, he sees such sweet tears
    flow
As if thenceforth nor pain nor trouble she
    could know.

VIII

Vain hope! for fraud took all that he had
    earned.
The lion roars and gluts his tawny brood
Even in the desert's heart; but he, re-
    turned,   66
Bears not to those he loves their needful
    food.
His home approaching, but in such a
    mood
That from his sight his children might
    have run,
He met a traveller, robbed him, shed his
    blood;   70
And when the miserable work was done
He fled, a vagrant since, the murderer's
    fate to shun.

IX

From that day forth no place to him
    could be
So lonely, but that thence might come a
    pang   74
Brought from without to inward misery.
Now, as he plodded on, with sullen clang
A sound of chains along the desert rang;
He looked, and saw upon a gibbet high
A human body that in irons swang,
Uplifted by the tempest whirling by;   80
And, hovering, round it often did a raven
    fly.

X

It was a spectacle which none might view,
In spot so savage, but with shuddering
    pain;
Nor only did for him at once renew
All he had feared from man, but roused
    a train   85
Of the mind's phantoms, horrible as vain.
The stones, as if to cover him from day,
Rolled at his back along the living plain;

He fell, and without sense or motion lay;
But, when the trance was gone, feebly
    pursued his way.   90

XI

As one whose brain habitual frenzy fires
Owes to the fit in which his soul hath
    tossed
Profounder quiet, when the fit retires,
Even so the dire phantasma which had
    crossed
His sense, in sudden vacancy quite lost,
Left his mind still as a deep evening
    stream.   96
Nor, if accosted now, in thought en-
    grossed,
Moody, or inly troubled, would he seem
To traveller who might talk of any casual
    theme.

XII

Hurtle the clouds in deeper darkness
    piled,   100
Gone is the raven timely rest to seek;
He seemed the only creature in the wild
On whom the elements their rage might
    wreak;
Save that the bustard, of those regions
    bleak
Shy tenant, seeing by the uncertain light
A man there wandering, gave a mournful
    shriek,   106
And half upon the ground, with strange
    affright,
Forced hard against the wind a thick
    unwieldy flight.

XIII

All, all was cheerless to the horizon's
    bound;
The weary eye—which, wheresoe'er it
    strays,   110
Marks nothing but the red sun's setting
    round,
Or on the earth strange lines, in former
    days
Left by gigantic arms—at length surveys
What seems an antique castle spreading
    wide;
Hoary and naked are its walls, and raise
Their brow sublime: in shelter there to
    bide   116
He turned, while rain poured down
    smoking on every side.

XIV

Pile of Stone-henge! so proud to hint yet
    keep
Thy secrets, thou that lov'st to stand and
    hear
The Plain resounding to the whirlwind's
    sweep,   120
Inmate of lonesome Nature's endless
    year;

Even if thou saw'st the giant wicker rear
For sacrifice its throngs of living men,
Before thy face did ever wretch appear,
Who in his heart had groaned with dead-
    lier pain   125
Than he who, tempest-driven, thy shelter
    now would gain?

xv

Within that fabric of mysterious form
Winds met in conflict, each by turns
    supreme;
And, from the perilous ground dislodged,
    through storm
And rain he wildered on, no moon to
    stream   130
From gulf of parting clouds one friendly
    beam,
Nor any friendly sound his footsteps led;
Once did the lightning's faint disastrous
    gleam
Disclose a naked guide-post's double head,
Sight which, tho' lost at once, a gleam of
    pleasure shed.   135

xvi

No swinging sign-board creaked from
    cottage elm
To stay his steps with faintness overcome;
'Twas dark and void as ocean's watery
    realm
Roaring with storms beneath night's
    starless gloom;
No gipsy cower'd o'er fire of furze or
    broom;   140
No labourer watched his red kiln glaring
    bright,
Nor taper glimmered dim from sick
    man's room;
Along the waste no line of mournful light
From lamp of lonely toll-gate streamed
    athwart the night.

xvii

At length, though hid in clouds, the moon
    arose;   145
The downs were visible—and now revealed
A structure stands, which two bare slopes
    enclose.
It was a spot where, ancient vows fulfilled,
Kind pious hands did to the Virgin build
A lonely Spital, the belated swain   150
From the night terrors of that waste to
    shield:
But there no human being could remain,
And now the walls are named the 'Dead
    House' of the plain.

xviii

Though he had little cause to love the abode
Of man, or covet sight of mortal face, 155
Yet when faint beams of light that ruin
    showed,
How glad he was at length to find some
    trace

Of human shelter in that dreary place.
Till to his flock the early shepherd goes,
Here shall much-needed sleep his frame
    embrace.   160
In a dry nook where fern the floor be-
    strows
He lays his stiffened limbs,—his eyes be-
    gin to close;

xix

When hearing a deep sigh, that seemed
    to come
From one who mourned in sleep, he
    raised his head,
And saw a woman in the naked room 165
Outstretched, and turning on a restless
    bed:
The moon a wan dead light around her
    shed.
He waked her—spake in tone that would
    not fail,
He hoped, to calm her mind; but ill he
    sped,
For of that ruin she had heard a tale 170
Which now with freezing thoughts did all
    her powers assail;

xx

Had heard of one who, forced from
    storms to shroud,
Felt the loose walls of this decayed
    Retreat
Rock to incessant neighings shrill and
    loud,
While his horse pawed the floor with
    furious heat;   175
Till on a stone, that sparkled to his feet,
Struck, and still struck again, the troubled
    horse:
The man half raised the stone with pain
    and sweat,
Half raised, for well his arm might lose
    its force
Disclosing the grim head of a late mur-
    dered corse.   180

xxi

Such tale of this lone mansion she had
    learned,
And when that shape, with eyes in sleep
    half drowned,
By the moon's sullen lamp she first dis-
    cerned,
Cold stony horror all her senses bound.
Her he addressed in words of cheering
    sound;   185
Recovering heart, like answer did she
    make;
And well it was that of the corse there
    found
In converse that ensued she nothing
    spake;
She knew not what dire pangs in him
    such tale could wake.

XXII

But soon his voice and words of kind
   intent   190
Banished that dismal thought; and now
   the wind
In fainter howlings told its *rage* was spent:
Meanwhile discourse ensued of various
   kind,
Which by degrees a confidence of mind
And mutual interest failed not to create.
And, to a natural sympathy resigned, 196
In that forsaken building where they sate
The Woman thus retraced her own un-
   toward fate.

XXIII

'By Derwent's side my father dwelt—a man
Of virtuous life, by pious parents bred;
And I believe that, soon as I began   201
To lisp, he made me kneel beside my bed,
And in his hearing there my prayers I
   said:
And afterwards, by my good father
   taught,
I read, and loved the books in which I
   read;   205
For books in every neighbouring house
   I sought,
And nothing to my mind a sweeter plea-
   sure brought.

XXIV

'A little croft we owned—a plot of corn,
A garden stored with peas, and mint, and
   thyme,
And flowers for posies, oft on Sunday
   morn   210
Plucked while the church bells rang their
   earliest chime.
Can I forget our freaks at shearing time!
My hen's rich nest through long grass
   scarce espied;
The cowslip-gathering in June's dewy
   prime;
The swans that with white chests up-
   reared in pride   215
Rushing and racing came to meet me at
   the waterside!

XXV

'The staff I well remember which upbore
The bending body of my active sire;
His seat beneath the honied sycamore
Where the bees hummed, and chair by
   winter fire;   220
When market-morning came, the neat
   attire
With which, though bent on haste, myself
   I decked;
Our watchful house-dog, that would tease
   and tire
The stranger till its barking-fit I checked;
The red-breast, known for years, which
   at my casement pecked.   225

XXVI

'The suns of twenty summers danced
   along,—
Too little marked how fast they rolled
   away:
But, through severe mischance and cruel
   wrong,
My father's substance fell into decay:
We toiled and struggled, hoping for a day
When Fortune might put on a kinder
   look;   231
But vain were wishes, efforts vain as they;
He from his old hereditary nook
Must part; the summons came;—our
   final leave we took.

XXVII

'It was indeed a miserable hour   235
When, from the last hill-top, my sire sur-
   veyed,
Peering above the trees, the steeple tower
That on his marriage day sweet music
   made!
Till then he hoped his bones might there
   be laid
Close by my mother in their native
   bowers: 240
Bidding me trust in God, he stood and
   prayed;—
I could not pray:—through tears that fell
   in showers
Glimmered our dear-loved home, alas!
   no longer ours!

XXVIII

'There was a Youth whom I had loved
   so long,
That when I loved him not I cannot say:
'Mid the green mountains many a
   thoughtless song   246
We two had sung, like gladsome birds in
   May;
When we began to tire of childish play,
We seemed still more and more to prize
   each other;
We talked of marriage and our marriage
   day;   250
And I in truth did love him like a brother,
For never could I hope to meet with such
   another.

XXIX

'Two years were passed since to a distant
   town
He had repaired to ply a gainful trade:
What tears of bitter grief, till then un-
   known,   255
What tender vows our last sad kiss de-
   layed!
To him we turned:—we had no other aid:
Like one revived, upon his neck I wept;
And her whom he had loved in joy, he
   said,

He well could love in grief; his faith he
      kept;   260
And in a quiet home once more my father
      slept.

XXX

'We lived in peace and comfort; and
      were blest
With daily bread, by constant toil sup-
      plied.
Three lovely babes had lain upon my
      breast;
And often, viewing their sweet smiles, I
      sighed,   265
And knew not why. My happy father
      died,
When threatened war reduced the chil-
      dren's meal:
Thrice happy! that for him the grave
      could hide
The empty loom, cold hearth, and silent
      wheel,
And tears which flowed for ills which
      patience might not heal.   270

XXXI

''Twas a hard change; an evil time was
      come;
We had no hope, and no relief could
      gain:
But soon, with proud parade, the noisy
      drum
Beat round to clear the streets of want
      and pain.
My husband's arms now only served to
      strain   275
Me and his children hungering in his
      view;
In such dismay my prayers and tears
      were vain:
To join those miserable men he flew,
And now to the sea-coast, with numbers
      more, we drew.

XXXII

'There were we long neglected, and we
      bore   280
Much sorrow ere the fleet its anchor
      weighed;
Green fields before us, and our native
      shore,
We breathed a pestilential air, that made
Ravage for which no knell was heard.
      We prayed
For our departure; wished and wished—
      nor knew,   285
'Mid that long sickness and those hopes
      delayed,
That happier days we never more must
      view.
The parting signal streamed—at last the
      land withdrew.

XXXIII

'But the calm summer season now was
      past.
On as we drove, the equinoctial deep 290
Ran mountains high before the howling
      blast,
And many perished in the whirlwind's
      sweep.
We gazed with terror on their gloomy
      sleep,
Untaught that soon such anguish must
      ensue,
Our hopes such harvest of affliction reap,
That we the mercy of the waves should
      rue: 296
We reached the western world, a poor
      devoted crew.

XXXIV

'The pains and plagues that on our heads
      came down,
Disease and famine, agony and fear, 299
In wood or wilderness, in camp or town,
It would unman the firmest heart to hear.
All perished—all in one remorseless year,
Husband and children! one by one, by
      sword
And ravenous plague, all perished: every
      tear
Dried up, despairing, desolate, on board
A British ship I waked, as from a trance
      restored.'   306

XXXV

Here paused she, of all present thought
      forlorn,
Nor voice, nor sound, that moment's pain
      expressed,
Yet Nature, with excess of grief o'er-
      borne,
From her full eyes their watery load re-
      leased.   310
He too was mute: and, ere her weeping
      ceased,
He rose, and to the ruin's portal went,
And saw the dawn opening the silvery
      east
With rays of promise, north and south-
      ward sent;
And soon with crimson fire kindled the
      firmament.   315

XXXVI

'O come,' he cried, 'come, after weary
      night
Of such rough storm, this happy change
      to view.'
So forth she came, and eastward looked;
      the sight
Over her brow like dawn of gladness
      threw;
Upon her cheek, to which its youthful
      hue   320

23

Seemed to return, dried the last lingering
   tear,
And from her grateful heart a fresh one
   drew:
The whilst her comrade to her pensive
   cheer
Tempered fit words of hope; and the lark
warbled near.

XXXVII

They looked and saw a lengthening road,
   and wain   325
That rang down a bare slope not far re-
   mote:
The barrows glistered bright with drops
   of rain,
Whistled the waggoner with merry note,
The cock far off sounded his clarion
   throat;
But town, or farm, or hamlet, none they
   viewed,   330
Only were told there stood a lonely cot
A long mile thence. While thither they
   pursued
Their way, the Woman thus her mournful
talo renewed.

XXXVIII

'Peaceful as this immeasurable plain
Is now, by beams of dawning light im-
   prest,   335
In the calm sunshine slept the glittering
   main;
The very ocean hath its hour of rest.
I too forgot the heavings of my breast.
How quiet 'round me ship and ocean
   were!
As quiet all within me. I was blest,   340
And looked, and fed upon the silent air
Until it seemed to bring a joy to my
   despair.

XXXIX

'Ah! how unlike those late terrific sleeps,
And groans that rage of racking famine
   spoke;
The unburied dead that lay in festering
   heaps,   345
The breathing pestilence that rose like
   smoke,
The shriek that from the distant battle
   broke,
The mine's dire earthquake, and the
   pallid host
Driven by the bomb's incessant thunder-
   stroke
To loathsome vaults, where heart-sick
   anguish tossed,   350
Hope died, and fear itself in agony was lost!

XL

'Some mighty gulf of separation passed,
I seemed transported to another world;
A thought resigned with pain, when from
   the mast

The impatient mariner the sail unfurled,
And, whistling, called the wind that
   hardly curled   356
The silent sea. From the sweet thoughts
   of home
And from all hope I was for ever hurled.
For me—farthest from earthly port to
   roam
Was best, could I but shun the spot where
   man might come.   360

XLI

'And oft I thought (my fancy was so
   strong)
That I, at last, a resting-place had found;
"Here will I dwell," said I, "my whole
   life long,
Roaming the illimitable waters round;
Here will I live, of all but heaven dis-
   owned,   365
And end my days upon the peaceful
   flood."—
To break my dream the vessel reached its
   bound;
And homeless near a thousand homes I
   stood,
And near a thousand tables pined and
   wanted food.

XLII

'No help I sought; in sorrow turned
   adrift,   370
Was hopeless, as if cast on some bare
   rock;
Nor morsel to my mouth that day did lift,
Nor raised my hand at any door to knock.
I lay where, with his drowsy mates, the
   cock
From the cross-timber of an outhouse
   hung: 375
Dismally tolled, that night, the city clock!
At morn my sick heart hunger scarcely
   stung,
Nor to the beggar's language could I fit
   my tongue.

XLIII

'So passed a second day; and, when the
   third
Was come, I tried in vain the crowd's
   resort.   380
—In deep despair, by frightful wishes
   stirred,
Near the sea-side I reached a ruined fort;
There, pains which nature could no more
   support,
With blindness linked, did on my vitals
   fall;
And, after many interruptions short   385
Of hideous sense, I sank, nor step could
   crawl:
Unsought for was the help that did my
   life recall.

24

XLIV

'Borne to a hospital, I lay with brain
Drowsy and weak, and shattered memory;
I heard my neighbours in their beds com-
 plain   390
Of many things which never troubled
 me—
Of feet still bustling round with busy
 glee,
Of looks where common kindness had no
 part,
Of service done with cold formality,
Fretting the fever round the languid
 heart,   395
And groans which, as they said, might
 make a dead man start.

XLV

'These things just served to stir the slum-
 bering sense,
Nor pain nor pity in my bosom raised.
With strength did memory return; and,
 thence
Dismissed, again on open day I gazed,
At houses, men, and common light, a-
 mazed.   401
The lanes I sought, and, as the sun retired,
Came where beneath the trees a faggot
 blazed;
The travellers saw me weep, my fate in-
 quired,
And gave me food—and rest, more wel-
 come, more desired.   405

XLVI

'Rough potters seemed they, trading so-
 berly
With panniered asses driven from door to
 door;
But life of happier sort set forth to me,
And other joys my fancy to allure—
The bag-pipe dinning on the midnight
 moor   410
In barn uplighted; and companions boon,
Well met from far with revelry secure
Among the forest glades, while jocund
 June
Rolled fast along the sky his warm and
 genial moon.

XLVII

'But ill they suited me—those journeys
 dark   415
O'er moor and mountain, midnight theft
 to hatch!
To charm the surly house-dog's faithful
 bark,
Or hang on tip-toe at the lifted latch.
The gloomy lantern, and the dim blue
 match,
The black disguise, the warning whistle
 shrill,   420
And ear still busy on its nightly watch,

Were not for me, brought up in nothing
 ill:
Besides, on griefs so fresh my thoughts
 were brooding still.

XLVIII

'What could I do, unaided and unblest?
My father! gone was every friend of
 thine: 425
And kindred of dead husband are at best
Small help; and, after marriage such as
 mine,
With little kindness would to me incline.
Nor was I then for toil or service fit;
My deep-drawn sighs no effort could con-
 fine;   430
In open air forgetful would I sit
Whole hours, with idle arms in moping
 sorrow knit.

XLIX

'The roads I paced, I loitered through
 the fields;
Contentedly, yet sometimes self-accused,
Trusted my life to what chance bounty
 yields,   435
Now coldly given, now utterly refused.
The ground I for my bed have often used:
But what afflicts my peace with keenest
 ruth,
Is that I have my inner self abused,
Forgone the home delight of constant
 truth,   440
And clear and open soul, so prized in
 fearless youth.

L

'Through tears the rising sun I oft have
 viewed,
Through tears have seen him towards that
 world descend
Where my poor heart lost all its fortitude:
Three years a wanderer now my course I
 bend—   445
Oh! tell me whither—for no earthly friend
Have I.'—She ceased, and weeping turned
 away;
As if because her tale was at an end,
She wept; because she had no more to say
Of that perpetual weight which on her
 spirit lay.   450

LI

True sympathy the Sailor's looks ex-
 pressed,
His looks—for pondering he was mute
 the while.
Of social Order's care for wretchedness,
Of Time's sure help to calm and reconcile,
Joy's second spring and Hope's long-
 treasured smile,   455
'Twas not for *him* to speak—a man so
 tried.
Yet, to relieve her heart, in friendly style

25

Proverbial words of comfort he applied,
And not in vain, while they went pacing
   side by side.

LII

Ere long, from heaps of turf, before their
   sight,   460
Together smoking in the sun's slant beam,
Rise various wreaths that into one unite
Which high and higher mounts with
   silver gleam:
Fair spectacle,—but instantly a scream
Thence bursting shrill did all remark pre-
   vent;   465
They paused, and heard a hoarser voice
   blaspheme,
And female cries. Their course they
   thither bent,
And met a man who foamed with anger
   vehement.

LIII

A woman stood with quivering lips and
   pale,
And, pointing to a little child that lay 470
Stretched on the ground, began a piteous
   tale;
How in a simple freak of thoughtless play
He had provoked his father, who straight-
   way,
As if each blow were deadlier than the
   last,
Struck the poor innocent. Pallid with
   dismay   475
The Soldier's Widow heard and stood
   aghast;
And stern looks on the man her grey-
   haired Comrade cast.

LIV

His voice with indignation rising high
Such further deed in manhood's name
   forbade;
The peasant, wild in passion, made reply
With bitter insult and revilings sad; 481
Asked him in scorn what business there
   he had;
What kind of plunder he was hunting
   now;
The gallows would one day of him be
   glad;—
Though inward anguish damped the
   Sailor's brow,   485
Yet calm he seemed as thoughts so
   poignant would allow.

LV

Softly he stroked the child, who lay outstretched
With face to earth; and, as the boy turned round
His battered head, a groan the Sailor
   fetched

As if he saw—there and upon that
   ground—   490
Strange repetition of the deadly wound
He had himself inflicted. Through his
   brain
At once the griding iron passage found;
Deluge of tender thoughts then rushed
   amain,
Nor could his sunken eyes the starting
   tear restrain.   495

LVI

Within himself he said—What hearts
   have we!
The blessing this a father gives his child!
Yet happy thou, poor boy! compared
   with me,
Suffering not doing ill—fate far more
   mild.
The stranger's looks and tears of wrath
   beguiled   500
The father, and relenting thoughts awoke;
He kissed his son—so all was reconciled.
Then, with a voice which inward trouble
   broke
Ere to his lips it came, the Sailor them
   bespoke.

LVII

'Bad is the world, and hard is the world's
   law   505
Even for the man who wears the warmest
   fleece;
Much need have ye that time more closely
   draw
The bond of nature, all unkindness cease,
And that among so few there still be
   peace:
Else how can ye hope but with such numerous
   foes   510
Your pains shall ever with your years
   increase?'—
While from his heart the appropriate
   lesson flows,
A correspondent calm stole gently o'er his
   woes.

LVIII

Forthwith the pair passed on; and down
   they look
Into a narrow valley's pleasant scene 515
Where wreaths of vapour tracked a wind-
   ing brook,
That babbled on through groves and
   meadows green;
A low-roofed house peeped out the trees
   between;
The dripping groves resound with cheer-
   ful lays,
And melancholy lowings intervene 520
Of scattered herds, that in the meadow
   graze,
Some amid lingering shade, some touched
   by the sun's rays.

LIX

They saw and heard, and, winding with
  the road
Down a thick wood, they dropt into the
  vale;
Comfort by prouder mansions unbe-
  stowed   525
Their wearied frames, she hoped, would
  soon regale.
Ere long they reached that cottage in the
  dale:
It was a rustic inn;—the board was spread,
The milk-maid followed with her brim-
  ming pail,
And lustily the master carved the bread,
Kindly the housewife pressed, and they in
  comfort fed.   531

LX

Their breakfast done, the pair, though
  loth, must part;
Wanderers whose course no longer now
  agrees.
She rose and bade farewell! and, while
  her heart
Struggled with tears nor could its sorrow
  ease,   535
She left him there; for, clustering round
  his knees,
With his oak-staff the cottage children
  played;
And soon she reached a spot o'erhung
  with trees
And banks of ragged earth; beneath the
  shade
Across the pebbly road a little runnel
  strayed.   540

LXI

A cart and horse beside the rivulet stood;
Chequering the canvas roof the sunbeams
  shone.
She saw the carman bend to scoop the
  flood
As the wain fronted her,—wherein lay
  one,   544
A pale-faced Woman, in disease far gone.
The carman wet her lips as well behoved;
Bed under her lean body there was none,
Though even to die near one she most had
  loved
She could not of herself those wasted
  limbs have moved.

LXII

The Soldier's Widow learned with honest
  pain   550
And homefelt force of sympathy sincere,
Why thus that worn-out wretch must
  there sustain
The jolting road and morning air severe.
The wain pursued its way; and following
  near
In pure compassion she her steps re-
  traced   555
Far as the cottage. 'A sad sight is here,'
She cried aloud; and forth ran out in
  haste
The friends whom she had left but a few
  minutes past.

LXIII

While to the door with eager speed they
  ran,
From her bare straw the Woman half
  upraised   560
Her bony visage—gaunt and deadly wan;
No pity asking, on the group she gazed
With a dim eye, distracted and amazed;
Then sank upon her straw with feeble
  moan.
Fervently cried the housewife—'God be
  praised,   565
I have a house that I can call my own;
Nor shall she perish there, untended and
  alone!'

LXIV

So in they bear her to the chimney seat,
And busily, though yet with fear, untie
Her garments, and, to warm her icy feet
And chafe her temples, careful hands
  apply.   571
Nature reviving, with a deep-drawn sigh
She strove, and not in vain, her head to
  rear;
Then said—'I thank you all; if I must die,
The God in heaven my prayers for you
  will hear;   575
Till now I did not think my end had been
  so near.

LXV

'Barred every comfort labour could pro-
  cure,
Suffering what no endurance could as-
  suage,   578
I was compelled to seek my father's door,
Though loth to be a burthen on his age.
But sickness stopped me in an early stage
Of my sad journey; and within the wain
They placed me—there to end life's pil-
  grimage,
Unless beneath your roof I may remain:
For I shall never see my father's door
  again.   585

LXVI

'My life, Heaven knows, hath long been
  burthensome;
But, if I have not meekly suffered, meek
May my end be! Soon will this voice be
  dumb:
Should child of mine e'er wander hither,
  speak
Of me, say that the worm is on my
  cheek.—   590

Torn from our hut, that stood beside the
sea
Near Portland lighthouse in a lonesome
creek,
My husband served in sad captivity
On shipboard, bound till peace or death
should set him free.

LXVII

'A sailor's wife I knew a widow's cares,
Yet two sweet little ones partook my
bed;   596
Hope cheered my dreams, and to my
daily prayers
Our heavenly Father granted each day's
bread;
Till one was found by stroke of violence
dead,
Whose body near our cottage chanced to
lie;   600
A dire suspicion drove us from our shed;
In vain to find a friendly face we try,
Nor could we live together those poor
boys and I;

LXVIII

'For evil tongues made oath how on that
day
My husband lurked about the neighbourhood;   605
Now he had fled, and whither none could
say,
And he had done the deed in the dark
wood—
Near his own home!—but he was mild
and good;
Never on earth was gentler creature
seen;
He'd not have robbed the raven of its
food.   610
My husband's loving kindness stood between
Me and all worldly harms and wrongs
however keen.'

LXIX

Alas! the thing she told with labouring
breath
The Sailor knew too well. That wickedness
His hand had wrought; and when, in the
hour of death,   615
He saw his Wife's lips move his name to
bless
With her last words, unable to suppress
His anguish, with his heart he ceased to
strive;
And, weeping loud in this extreme distress,
He cried—'Do pity me! That thou
shouldst live   620
I neither ask nor wish—forgive me, but
forgive!'

LXX

To tell the change that Voice within her
wrought
Nature by sign or sound made no essay;
A sudden joy surprised expiring thought,
And every mortal pang dissolved away.
Borne gently to a bed, in death she lay;
Yet still, while over her the husband bent,
A look was in her face which seemed to
say,
'Be blest: by sight of thee from heaven
was sent
Peace to my parting soul, the fulness of
content.'   630

LXXI

She slept in peace,—his pulses throbbed
and stopped,
Breathless he gazed upon her face,—then
took
Her hand in his, and raised it, but both
dropped,
When on his own he cast a rueful look.
His ears were never silent; sleep forsook
His burning eyelids stretched and stiff as
lead;   636
All night from time to time under him
shook
The floor as he lay shuddering on his bed;
And oft he groaned aloud, 'O God, that
I were dead!'

LXXII

The Soldier's Widow lingered in the cot;
And, when he rose, he thanked her pious
care   641
Through which his Wife, to that kind
shelter brought,
Died in his arms; and with those thanks
a prayer
He breathed for her, and for that mer-
ciful pair.
The corse interred, not one hour he re-
mained   645
Beneath their roof, but to the open air
A burthen, now with fortitude sustained,
He bore within a breast where dreadful
quiet reigned.

LXXIII

Confirmed of purpose, fearlessly prepared
For act and suffering, to the city straight
He journeyed, and forthwith his crime
declared: 651
'And from your doom,' he added, 'now
I wait,
Nor let it linger long, the murderer's fate.'
Not ineffectual was that piteous claim:
'O welcome sentence which will end
though late,   655
He said, 'the pangs that to my conscience
came
Out of that deed. My trust, Saviour! is
in thy name!'

LXXIV

His fate was pitied. Him in iron
case
(Reader, forgive the intolerable thought)
They hung not:—no one on *his* form or
face   660
Could gaze, as on a show by idlers sought;

No kindred sufferer, to his death-place
brought
By lawless curiosity or chance,
When into storm the evening sky is
wrought,
Upon his swinging corse an eye can
glance,   665
And drop, as he once dropped, in misera-
ble trance.

THE BORDERERS

A TRAGEDY

[Composed 1795–96.—Published 1842.]

DRAMATIS PERSONÆ

MARMADUKE. ⎫
OSWALD.   ⎪
WALLACE.   ⎬ *Of the Band of*
LACY.   ⎪   *Borderers.*
LENNOX.   ⎭
HERBERT.
WILFRED, *Servant to* MARMADUKE.
Host.

Forester.
ELDRED, *a Peasant.*
Peasant, Pilgrims, &c.

IDONEA.
Female Beggar.
ELEANOR, *Wife of* ELDRED.

SCENE, *Borders of England and Scotland.*

TIME, *The Reign of Henry III.*

READERS already acquainted with my Poems will recognise, in the following composition, some eight or ten lines, which I have not scrupled to retain in the places where they originally stood. It is proper however to add that they would not have been used elsewhere, if I had foreseen the time when I might be induced to publish this Tragedy.
February 28, 1842.

ACT I

SCENE, *Road in a Wood*

WALLACE and LACY.

Lacy. The Troop will be impatient;
let us hie
Back to our post, and strip the Scottish
Foray
Of their rich Spoil, ere they recross the
Border.
—Pity that our young Chief will have no
part
In this good service.
Wal.   Rather let us grieve 5
That, in the undertaking which has caused
His absence, he hath sought, whate'er his
aim,
Companionship with One of crooked
ways,
From whose perverted soul can come no
good
To our confiding, open-hearted, Leader.
Lacy. True; and, remembering how
the Band have proved   11
That Oswald finds small favour in our
sight,

Well may we wonder he has gained such
power
Over our much-loved Captain.
Wal.   I have heard
Of some dark deed to which in early life
His passion drove him—then a Voyager
Upon the midland Sea. You knew his
bearing   17
In Palestine?
Lacy.   Where he despised alike
Mohammedan and Christian. But enough,
Let us begone—the Band may else be
foiled.   [*Exeunt.*

Enter MARMADUKE *and* WILFRED.

Wil. Be cautious, my dear Master!
Mar.   I perceive
That fear is like a cloak which old men
huddle
About their love, as if to keep it warm.
Wil. Nay, but I grieve that we should
part. This Stranger,   24
For such he is—
Mar.   Your busy fancies, Wilfred,
Might tempt me to a smile; but what of
him?
Wil. You know that you have saved
his life.

Mar.   I know it.
Wil. And that he hates you!—Pardon
  me, perhaps
That word was hasty.
Mar.   Fy! no more of it.
Wil. Dear Master! gratitude's a heavy
  burden   30
To a proud Soul.—Nobody loves this
  Oswald—
Yourself, you do not love him.
Mar.   I do more,
I honour him. Strong feelings to his heart
Are natural; and from no one can be learnt
More of man's thoughts and ways than
  his experience   35
Has given him power to teach: and then
  for courage
And enterprise—what perils hath he
  shunned?
What obstacles hath he failed to over-
  come?
Answer these questions, from our common
  knowledge,   39
And be at rest.
Wil.   Oh, Sir!
Mar.   Peace, my good Wilfred;
Repair to Liddesdale, and tell the Band
I shall be with them in two days at
  farthest.
Wil. May He whose eye is over all
  protect you!   [*Exit.*

Enter OSWALD [*a bunch of plants in
  his hand*].

Osw. This wood is rich in plants and
  curious simples.   44
Mar. [*looking at them*]. The wild rose,
  and the poppy, and the nightshade:
Which is your favourite, Oswald?
Osw.   That which, while it is
Strong to destroy, is also strong to heal—
                    [*Looking forward.*
Not yet in sight!—We'll saunter here
  awhile;
They cannot mount the hill, by us unseen.
Mar. [*a letter in his hand*]. It is no com-
  mon thing when one like you   50
Performs these delicate services, and
  therefore
I feel myself much bounden to you,
  Oswald;
'Tis a strange letter this!—You saw her
  write it?
Osw. And saw the tears with which she
  blotted it.
Mar. And nothing less would satisfy
  him?
Osw.   No less;   55
For that another in his Child's affection
Should hold a place, as if 'twere robbery,
He seemed to quarrel with the very
  thought.
Besides, I know not what strange prejudice

Is rooted in his mind; this Band of ours,
Which you've collected for the noblest
  ends,   61
Along the confines of the Esk and Tweed
To guard the Innocent—he calls us
  'Outlaws;'
And, for yourself, in plain terms he asserts
This garb was taken up that indolence 65
Might want no cover, and rapacity
Be better fed.
Mar. Ne'er may I own the heart
That cannot feel for one, helpless as he is.
Osw. Thou know'st me for a Man not
  easily moved,
Yet was I grievously provoked to think 70
Of what I witnessed.
Mar.   This day will suffice
To end her wrongs.
Osw.   But if the blind Man's tale
Should *yet* be true?
Mar.   Would it were possible!
Did not the Soldier tell thee that himself,
And others who survived the wreck,
  beheld   75
The Baron Herbert perish in the waves
Upon the coast of Cyprus?
Osw.   Yes, even so,
And I had heard the like before: in sooth
The tale of this his quondam Barony
Is cunningly devised; and, on the back 80
Of his forlorn appearance, could not fail
To make the proud and vain his tribu-
  taries,
And stir the pulse of lazy charity.
The seignories of Herbert are in Devon;
We, neighbours of the Esk and Tweed:
  'tis much   85
The Arch-impostor——
Mar.   Treat him gently, Oswald;
Though I have never seen his face,
  methinks,
There cannot come a day when I shall
  cease
To love him. I remember, when a Boy
Of scarcely seven years' growth, beneath
  the Elm   90
That casts its shade over our village school,
'Twas my delight to sit and hear Idonea
Repeat her Father's terrible adventures,
Till all the band of playmates wept to-
  gether;
And that was the beginning of my love. 95
And, through all converse of our later
  years,
An image of this old Man still was present,
When I had been most happy. Pardon me
If this be idly spoken.
Osw.   See, they come, 99
Two Travellers!
Mar. [*points*]. The woman is Idonea.
Osw. And leading Herbert.
Mar.   We must let them pass—
This thicket will conceal us.
                    [*They step aside.*

Enter IDONEA, *leading* HERBERT *blind.*

Idon. Dear Father, you sigh deeply;
    ever since
We left the willow shade by the brookside
Your natural breathing has been troubled.
Her.   Nay, 105
You are too fearful; yet must I confess,
Our march of yesterday had better suited
A firmer step than mine.
Idon.   That dismal Moor—
In spite of all the larks that cheered our
    path,
I never can forgive it: but how steadily
You paced along, when the bewildering
    moonlight   111
Mocked me with many a strange fantastic
    shape!—
I thought the Convent never would
    appear;
It seemed to move away from us; and yet
That you are thus the fault is mine; for
    the air   115
Was soft and warm, no dew lay on the
    grass,
And midway on the waste ere night had
    fallen
I spied a Covert walled and roofed with
    sods—
A miniature; belike some Shepherd-boy,
Who might have found a nothing-doing
    hour   120
Heavier than work, raised it: within that
    hut
We might have made a kindly bed of
    heath,
And thankfully there rested side by side
Wrapped in our cloaks, and, with re-
    cruited strength,
Have hailed the morning sun. But 125
    cheerily, Father,—
That staff of yours, I could almost have
    heart
To fling 't away from you: you make no
    use
Of me, or of my strength;—come, let me
    feel
That you do press upon me. There—
    indeed
You are quite exhausted. Let us rest
    awhile   130
On this green bank. [*He sits down.*
Her. [*after some time*]. Idonea, you are
    silent,
And I divine the cause.
Idon.   Do not reproach me:
I pondered patiently your wish and will
When I gave way to your request; and
    now,
When I behold the ruins of that face, 135
Those eyeballs dark—dark beyond hope
    of light,
And think that they were blasted for my
    sake,

The name of Marmaduke is blown away:
Father, I would not change that sacred
    feeling
For all this world can give.
Her.   Nay, be composed: 140
Few minutes gone a faintness overspread
My frame, and I bethought me of two
    things
I ne'er had heart to separate—my grave,
And thee, my Child!
Idon.   Believe me, honoured Sire!
'Tis weariness that breeds these gloomy
    fancies,   145
And you mistake the cause: you hear the
    woods
Resound with music, could you see the
    sun,
And look upon the pleasant face of
    Nature——
Her. I comprehend thee—I should be
    as cheerful
As if we two were twins; two songsters
    bred   150
In the same nest, my spring-time one
    with thine.
My fancies, fancies if they be, are such
As come, dear Child! from a far deeper
    source
Than bodily weariness. While here we
    sit
I feel my strength returning. The be-
    quest   155
Of thy kind Patroness, which to receive
We have thus far adventured, will suffice
To save thee from the extreme of penury;
But when thy Father must lie down and
    die,
How wilt thou stand alone?
Idon.   Is he not strong? 160
Is he not valiant?
Her.   Am I then so soon
Forgotten? have my warnings passed so
    quickly
Out of thy mind? My dear, my only,
    Child;
Thou wouldst be leaning on a broken
    reed—
This Marmaduke—
Idon. O could you hear his voice: 165
Alas! you do not know him. He is one
(I wot not what ill tongue had wronged
    him with you)
All gentleness and love. His face be-
    speaks
A deep and simple meekness: and that
    Soul,
Which with the motion of a virtuous act
Flashes a look of terror upon guilt, 171
Is, after conflict, quiet as the ocean,
By a miraculous finger stilled at once.
Her. Unhappy Woman!
Idon.   Nay, it was my duty
Thus much to speak; but think not I
    forget—   175

31

Dear Father! how *could* I forget and
live?—
You and the story of that doleful night
When, Antioch blazing to her topmost
     towers,
You rushed into the murderous flames,
     returned
Blind as the grave, but, as you oft have
     told me,   180
Clasping your infant Daughter to your
     heart.
  Her. Thy Mother too!—scarce had I
     gained the door,
I caught her voice; she threw herself
     upon me,
I felt thy infant brother in her arms;
She saw my blasted face—a tide of
     soldiers   185
That instant rushed between us, and I
     heard
Her last death-shriek, distinct among a
     thousand.
  Idon. Nay, Father, stop not; let me
     hear it all,
  Her. Dear Daughter! precious relic of
     that time—
For my old age, it doth remain with thee
To make it what thou wilt. Thou hast
     been told,   191
That when, on our return from Palestine,
I found how my domains had been usurped,
I took thee in my arms, and we began
Our wanderings together. Providence 195
At length conducted us to Rossland,—
     there,
Our melancholy story moved a Stranger
To take thee to her home—and for myself,
Soon after, the good Abbot of St. Cuth-
     bert's
Supplied my helplessness with food and
     raiment,   200
And, as thou know'st, gave me that
     humble Cot
Where now we dwell.—For many years I
     bore
Thy absence, till old age and fresh infir-
     mities
Exacted thy return, and our reunion.
I did not think that, during that long
     absence,   205
My Child, forgetful of the name of
     Herbert,
Had given her love to a wild Freebooter,
Who here, upon the borders of the Tweed,
Doth prey alike on two distracted Coun-
     tries,   209
Traitor to both.
  Idon.   Oh, could you hear his voice!
I will not call on Heaven to vouch for me,
But let this kiss speak what is in my heart.

          Enter a Peasant.

  Pea. Good morrow, Strangers! If you
     want a Guide,

Let me have leave to serve you!
  Idon.   My Companion
Hath need of rest; the sight of Hut or
     Hostel   215
Would be most welcome.
  Pea.   Yon white hawthorn gained,
You will look down into a dell, and there
Will see an ash from which a sign-board
     hangs;
The house is hidden by the shade. Old
     Man,
You seem worn out with travel—shall I
     support you?   220
  Her. I thank you; but, a resting-place
     so near,
'Twere wrong to trouble you.
  Pea.   God speed you both.
                             [*Exit* Peasant.
  Her. Idonea, we must part. Be not
     alarmed—
'Tis but for a few days—a thought has
     struck me.
  Idon. That I should leave you at this
     house, and thence   225
Proceed alone. It shall be so; for strength
Would fail you ere our journey's end be
     reached.
[*Exit* HERBERT *supported by* IDONEA.

  Re-enter MARMADUKE *and* OSWALD.

  Mar. This instant will we stop him—
  Osw.   Be not hasty,
For sometimes, in despite of my con-
     viction,
He tempted me to think the Story true;
'Tis plain he loves the Maid, and what he
     said   231
That savoured of aversion to thy name
Appeared the genuine colour of his soul—
Anxiety lest mischief should befall her
After his death.
  Mar.   I have been much deceived.
  Osw. But sure he loves the Maiden, and
     never love   236
Could find delight to nurse itself so
     strangely,
Thus to torment her with *inventions!*—
     death—
There must be truth in this.
  Mar.   Truth in his story!
He must have felt it then, known what it
     was,   240
And in such wise to rack her gentle heart
Had been a tenfold cruelty.
  Osw.   Strange pleasures
Do we poor mortals cater for ourselves!
To see him thus provoke her tender-
     ness
With tales of weakness and infirmity! 245
I'd wager on his life for twenty years.
  Mar. We will not waste an hour in
     such a cause.
  Osw. Why, this is noble! shake her off
     at once.

Mar. Her virtues are his instruments.
   —A Man
Who has so practised on the world's cold
   sense,   250
May well deceive his Child—What! leave
   her thus,
A prey to a deceiver?—no—no—no—
'Tis but a word and then——
   Osw.   Something is here
More than we see, or whence this strong
   aversion?
Marmaduke! I suspect unworthy tales
Have reached his ear—you have had
   enemies.   256
   Mar. Enemies!—of his own coinage.
   Osw.   That may be,
But wherefore slight protection such as
   you
Have power to yield? perhaps he looks
   elsewhere.—
I am perplexed.
   Mar. What hast thou heard or seen?
   Osw. No—no—the thing stands clear
   of mystery;   261
(As you have said) he coins himself the
   slander
With which he taints her ear;—for a
   plain reason;
He dreads the presence of a virtuous man
Like you; he knows your eye would
   search his heart,   265
Your justice stamp upon his evil deeds
The punishment they merit. All is plain:
It cannot be——
   Mar.   What cannot be?
   Osw.   Yet that a Father
Should in his love admit no rivalship,
And torture thus the heart of his own
   Child——   270
   Mar. Nay, you abuse my friendship!
   Osw.   Heaven forbid!—
There was a circumstance, trifling in-
   deed—
It struck me at the time—yet I believe
I never should have thought of it again
But for the scene which we by chance
   have witnessed.   275
   Mar. What is your meaning?
   Osw.   Two days gone I saw,
Though at a distance and he was dis-
   guised,
Hovering round Herbert's door, a man
   whose figure
Resembled much that cold voluptuary,
The villain, Clifford. He hates you, and
   he knows   280
Where he can stab you deepest.
   Mar.   Clifford never
Would stoop to skulk about a Cottage
   door—
It could not be.
   Osw.   And yet I now remember
That, when your praise was warm upon
   my tongue,

And the blind Man was told how you had
   rescued   285
A maiden from the ruffian violence
Of this same Clifford, he became im-
   patient
And would not hear me.
   Mar.   No—it cannot be—
I dare not trust myself with such a
   thought—
Yet whence this strange aversion? You
   are a man   290
Not used to rash conjectures——
   Osw.   If you deem it
A thing worth further notice, we must act
With caution, sift the matter artfully.
   [*Exeunt* MARMADUKE *and* OSWALD.

SCENE, *The door of the Hostel*

HERBERT, IDONEA, *and* Host

   Her. [*seated*]. As I am dear to you, re-
   member, Child!
This last request.
   Idon. You know me, Sire; farewell!
   Her. And are you going then? Come,
   come, Idonea,   296
We must not part,—I have measured
   many a league
When these old limbs had need of rest,—
   and now
I will not play the sluggard.
   Idon.   Nay, sit down.
   [*Turning to* Host.
Good Host, such tendance as you would
   expect   300
From your own Children, if yourself were
   sick,
Let this old Man find at your hands;
   poor Leader,   [*Looking at the dog.*
We soon shall meet again. If thou neglect
This charge of thine, then ill befall thee!
   —Look,
The little fool is loth to stay behind. 305
Sir Host! by all the love you bear to
   courtesy,
Take care of him, and feed the truant
   well.
   Host. Fear not, I will obey you;—but
   One so young,
And One so fair, it goes against my heart
That you should travel unattended, Lady!—
I have a palfrey and a groom: the lad 311
Shall squire you, (would it not be better,
   Sir?)
And for less fee than I would let him run
For any lady I have seen this twelve-
   month.
   Idon. You know, Sir, I have been too
   long your guard   315
Not to have learnt to laugh at little fears.
Why, if a wolf should leap from out a
   thicket,
A look of mine would send him scouring
   back,

Unless I differ from the thing I am   319
When you are by my side.
Her.   Idonea, wolves
Are not the enemies that move my fears.
Idon. No more, I pray, of this. Three
     days at farthest
Will bring me back—protect him, Saints
     —farewell!   [*Exit* IDONEA.
Host. 'Tis never drought with us—
St. Cuthbert and his Pilgrims,
Thanks to them, are to us a stream of
     comfort: 325
Pity the Maiden did not wait a while;
She could not, Sir, have failed of company.
Her. Now she is gone, I fain would
     call her back.
Host [*calling*]. Holla!
Her. No, no, the business must be
     done.—
What means this riotous noise?
Host.   The villagers
Are flocking in—a wedding festival—   331
That's all—God save you, Sir.

Enter OSWALD

Osw.   Ha! as I live,
The Baron Herbert.
Host.   Mercy, the Baron Herbert!
Osw. So far into your journey! on my
     life,
You are a lusty Traveller. But how fare
     you?   335
Her. Well as the wreck I am permits.
     And you, Sir?
Osw. I do not see Idonea.
Her.   Dutiful Girl,
She is gone before, to spare my weariness.
But what has brought you hither?
Osw.   A slight affair,
That will be soon despatched.
Her.   Did Marmaduke   340
Receive that letter?
Osw.   Be at peace.—The tie
Is broken, you will hear no more of *him.*
Her. This is true comfort, thanks a
     thousand times!—
That noise!—would I had gone with her
     as far
As the Lord Clifford's Castle: I have
     heard   345
That, in his milder moods, he has ex-
     pressed
Compassion for me. His influence is great
With Henry, our good King;—the Baron
     might
Have heard my suit, and urged my plea
     at Court.
No matter—he's a dangerous Man.—That
     noise!—   350
'Tis too disorderly for sleep or rest.
Idonea would have fears for me,—the
     Convent
Will give me quiet lodging. You have
     a boy, good Host,

And he must lead me back.
Osw.   You are most lucky;
I have been waiting in the wood hard by
For a companion—here he comes; our
     journey   356

Enter MARMADUKE

Lies on your way; accept us as your
     Guides.
Her. Alas! I creep so slowly.
Osw.   Never fear;
We'll not complain of that.
Her.   My limbs are stiff
And need repose. Could you but wait
     an hour?   360
Osw. Most willingly!—Come, let me
     lead you in,
And, while you take your rest, think not
     of us;
We'll stroll into the wood; lean on my
     arm.
     [*Conducts* HERBERT *into the house.*
                    Exit MARMADUKE.

Enter Villagers

Osw. [*to himself coming out of the
     Hostel*]. I have prepared a most apt
     Instrument—
The Vagrant must, no doubt, be loitering
     somewhere   365
About this ground; she hath a tongue
     well skilled,
By mingling natural matter of her own
With all the daring fictions I have taught
     her,
To win belief, such as my plot requires.
                    [*Exit* OSWALD.

Enter more Villagers, *a* Musician *among
     them*

Host [*to them*]. Into the court, my
     Friend, and perch yourself   370
Aloft upon the elm-tree. Pretty Maids,
Garlands and flowers, and cakes and
     merry thoughts,
Are here, to send the sun into the west
More speedily than you belike would
     wish.

SCENE *changes to the Wood adjoining the
     Hostel*—MARMADUKE *and* OSWALD
     entering

Mar. I would fain hope that we de-
     ceive ourselves: 375
When first I saw him sitting there, alone,
It struck upon my heart I know not how.
Osw. To-day will clear up all.—You
     marked a Cottage,
That ragged Dwelling, close beneath a
     rock
By the brook-side: it is the abode of One,
A Maiden innocent till ensnared by
     Clifford,   381
Who soon grew weary of her; but, alas!

What she had seen and suffered turned
   her brain.
Cast off by her Betrayer, she dwells alone,
Nor moves her hands to any needful
   work: 385
She eats her food which every day the
   peasants
Bring to her hut; and so the Wretch has
   lived
Ten years; and no one ever heard her
   voice;
But every night at the first stroke of twelve
She quits her house and, in the neigh-
   bouring Churchyard   390
Upon the self-same spot, in rain or storm,
She paces out the hour 'twixt twelve and
   one—
She paces round and round an Infant's
   grave,
And in the Churchyard sod her feet have
   worn
A hollow ring; they say it is knee-
   deep——   395
Ah! what is here?
   [*A female* Beggar *rises up, rubbing her
   eyes as if in sleep—a Child in her
   arms.*
   Beg. Oh! Gentlemen, I thank you;
I've had the saddest dream that ever
   troubled
The heart of living creature.—My poor
   Babe
Was crying, as I thought, crying for bread
When I had none to give him; whereupon
I put a slip of foxglove in his hand,   401
Which pleased him so, that he was hushed
   at once:
When into one of those same spotted bells
A bee came darting, which the Child with
   joy   404
Imprisoned there, and held it to his ear,
And suddenly grew black, as he would die.
   Mar. We have no time for this, my
   babbling Gossip;
Here's what will comfort you.
              [*Gives her money.*
   Beg.   The Saints reward you
For this good deed!—Well, Sirs, this
   passed away;   409
And afterwards I fancied, a strange dog,
Trotting alone along the beaten road,
Came to my child as by my side he slept,
And, fondling, licked his face, then on a
   sudden
Snapped fierce to make a morsel of his
   head:
But here he is, [*kissing the Child*] it must
   have been a dream.   415
   Osw. When next inclined to sleep, take
   my advice
And put your head, good Woman, under
   cover.
   Beg. Oh, Sir, you would not talk thus,
   if you knew

What life is this of ours, how sleep will
   master
The weary-worn.—You gentlefolk have
   got   420
Warm chambers to your wish. I'd rather
   be
A stone than what I am.—But two nights
   gone,
The darkness overtook me—wind and rain
Beat hard upon my head—and yet I saw
A glow-worm, through the covert of the
   furze,   425
Shine calmly as if nothing ailed the sky:
At which I half accused the God in
   Heaven.—
You must forgive me.
   Osw.   Ay, and if you think
The Fairies are to blame, and you should
   chide
Your favourite saint—no matter—this
   good day   430
Has made amends.
   Beg.   Thanks to you both; but,
   Oh Sir!
How would you like to travel on whole
   hours
As I have done, my eyes upon the ground,
Expecting still, I knew not how, to find
A piece of money glittering through the
   dust?   435
   Mar. This woman is a prater. Pray,
   good Lady!
Do you tell fortunes?
   Beg.   Oh Sir, you are like the rest.
This Little-one—it cuts me to the heart—
Well! they might turn a beggar from
   their doors,
But there are Mothers who can see the
   Babe   440
Here at my breast, and ask me where I
   bought it:
This they can do, and look upon my face—
But you, Sir, should be kinder.
   Mar.   Come hither, Fathers,
And learn what nature is from this poor
   Wretch!
   Beg. Ay, Sir, there's nobody that feels
   for us.   445
Why now—but yesterday I overtook
A blind old Greybeard and accosted him,
I' th' name of all the Saints, and by the
   Mass
He should have used me better!—Charity!
If you can melt a rock, it is your man;
But I'll be even with him—here again 451
Have I been waiting for him.
   Osw.   Well, but softly,
Who is it that hath wronged you?
   Beg.   Mark you me;
I'll point him out;—a Maiden is his guide,
Lovely as Spring's first rose; a little dog,
Tied by a woollen cord, moves on before
With look as sad as he were dumb; the
   cur,   457

I owe him no ill will, but in good sooth
He does his Master credit.
Mar.   As I live,
'Tis Herbert and no other!
Beg.   'Tis a feast to see him,
Lank as a ghost and tall, his shoulders
    bent,   461
And long beard white with age—yet ever-
    more,
As if he were the only Saint on earth,
He turns his face to Heaven.
Osw.   But why so violent
Against this venerable Man?
Beg.   I'll tell you: 465
He has the very hardest heart on earth;
I had as lief turn to the Friar's school
And knock for entrance, in mid holiday.
Mar. But to your story.
Beg.   I was saying, Sir—
Well!—he has often spurned me like a
    toad,   470
But yesterday was worse than all; at last
I overtook him, Sirs, my Babe and I,
And begged a little aid for charity:
But he was snappish as a cottage cur.
Well then, says I—I'll out with it; at
    which   475
I cast a look upon the Girl, and felt
As if my heart would burst; and so I left
    him.
Osw. I think, good Woman, you are the
    very person
Whom, but some few days past, I saw in
    Eskdale,   479
At Herbert's door.
Beg.   Ay; and if truth were known
I have good business there.
Osw.   I met you at the threshold,
And he seemed angry.
Beg.   Angry! well he might;
And long as I can stir I'll dog him.—
    Yesterday,
To serve me so, and knowing that he owes
The best of all he has to me and mine. 485
But 'tis all over now. That good old Lady
Has left a power of riches; and I say it,
If there's a lawyer in the land, the knave
Shall give me half.
Osw.   What's this?—I fear, good
    Woman,
You have been insolent.
Beg.   And there's the Baron,
I spied him skulking in his peasant's
    dress.   491
Osw. How say you? in disguise?—
Mar.   But what's your business
With Herbert or his Daughter?
Beg.   Daughter! truly—
But how's the day?—I fear, my little
    Boy,
We've overslept ourselves.—Sirs, have
    you seen him?   [*Offers to go.*
Mar. I must have more of this;—you
    shall not stir   496

An inch, till I am answered. Know you
    aught
That doth concern this Herbert?
Beg.   You are provoked,
And will misuse me, Sir!
Mar.   No trifling, Woman!—
Osw. You are as safe as in a sanctuary;
Speak.   501
Mar. Speak!
Beg.   He is a most hard-hearted Man.
Mar. Your life is at my mercy.
Beg.   Do not harm me,
And I will tell you all!—You know not,
    Sir,
What strong temptations press upon the
    Poor.
Osw. Speak out.
Beg.   Oh, Sir, I've been a wicked
    Woman.   505
Osw. Nay, but speak out!
Beg.   He flattered me, and said
What harvest it would bring us both;
    and so
I parted with the Child.
Mar.   Parted with whom?
Beg. Idonea, as he calls her; but the Girl
Is mine.
Mar. Yours, Woman! are you Her-
    bert's wife?   510
Beg. Wife, Sir! his wife—not I; my
    husband, Sir,
Was of Kirkoswald—many a snowy
    winter
We've weathered out together. My poor
    Gilfred!
He has been two years in his grave.
Mar.   Enough.
Osw. We've solved the riddle—Mis-
    creant!
Mar. Do you,   515
Good Dame, repair to Liddesdale and
    wait
For my return; be sure you shall have
    justice.
Osw. A lucky woman!—go, you have
    done good service.   [*Aside.*
Mar. [*to himself*]. Eternal praises on
    the power that saved her!—   519
Osw. [*gives her money*]. Here's for your
    little boy, and when you christen him
I'll be his Godfather.
Beg. Oh Sir, you are merry with me.
In grange or farm this Hundred scarcely
    owns
A dog that does not know me.—These
    good Folks,—
For love of God I must not pass their
    doors;
But I'll be back with my best speed: for
    you—   525
God bless and thank you both, my gentle
    Masters.   [*Exit Beggar.*
Mar. [*to himself*]. The cruel Viper!—
    Poor devoted Maid,

Now I *do* love thee.
Osw.   I am thunderstruck.
Mar. Where is she—holla!
[*Calling to the* Beggar, *who returns;*
he looks at her stedfastly.
          You are Idonea's Mother?—
Nay, be not terrified—it does me good   530
To look upon you.
   Osw. [*interrupting*]. In a peasant's dress
You saw, who was it?
   Beg.   Nay, I dare not speak;
He is a man, if it should come to his ears
I never shall be heard of more.
   Osw.   Lord Clifford?
Beg. What can I do? believe me, gentle
   Sirs,   535
I love her, though I dare not call her
   daughter.
   Osw. Lord Clifford—did you see him
   talk with Herbert?
   Beg. Yes, to my sorrow—under the
   great oak
At Herbert's door—and when he stood
   beside
The blind Man—at the silent Girl he
   looked   540
With such a look—it makes me tremble,
   Sir,
To think of it.
   Osw.   Enough! you may depart.
Mar. [*to himself*]. Father!—to God
   himself we cannot give   543
A holier name; and, under such a mask,
To lead a Spirit, spotless as the blessed,
To that abhorrèd den of brutish vice!—
Oswald, the firm foundation of my life
Is going from under me; these strange
   discoveries—
Looked at from every point of fear or
   hope,
Duty, or love—involve, I feel, my ruin. 550

ACT II

SCENE, *A Chamber in the Hostel*—OSWALD
alone, rising from a Table on which he
had been writing

   Osw. They chose *him* for their Chief!—
   what covert part
He in the preference, modest Youth,
   might take,
I neither know nor care. The insult bred
More of contempt than hatred; both are
   flown;
That either e'er existed is my shame: 555
'Twas a dull spark—a most unnatural fire
That died the moment the air breathed
   upon it.
—These fools of feeling are mere birds of
   winter
That haunt some barren island of the
   north,
Where, if a famishing man stretch forth
   his hand,   560

They think it is to feed them. I have left
   him
To solitary meditation;—now
For a few swelling phrases, and a flash
Of truth, enough to dazzle and to blind,
And he is mine for ever—here he comes.

Enter MARMADUKE

Mar. These ten years she has moved
   her lips all day   566
And never speaks!
   Osw.   Who is it?
   Mar.   I have seen her.
Osw. Oh! the poor tenant of that
   ragged homestead,
Her whom the Monster, Clifford, drove to
   madness.
Mar. I met a peasant near the spot; he
   told me,   570
These ten years she had sate all day alone
Within those empty walls.
   Osw.   I too have seen her;
Chancing to pass this way some six
   months gone,
At midnight, I betook me to the Church-
   yard:
The moon shone clear, the air was still,
   so still   575
The trees were silent as the graves beneath
   them.
Long did I watch, and saw her pacing
   round
Upon the self-same spot, still round and
   round,
Her lips for ever moving.
   Mar.   At her door
Rooted I stood; for, looking at the
   woman,   580
I thought I saw the skeleton of Idonea.
   Osw. But the pretended Father——
   Mar.   Earthly law
Measures not crimes like his.
   Osw.   *We* rank not, happily,
With those who take the spirit of their
   rule
From that soft class of devotees who feel
Reverence for life so deeply, that they
   spare   586
The verminous brood, and cherish what
   they spare
While feeding on their bodies. Would
   that Idonea
Were present, to the end that we might
   hear
What she can urge in his defence; she
   loves him.   590
Mar. Yes, loves him; 'tis a truth that
   multiplies
His guilt a thousand-fold.
   Osw.   'Tis most perplexing:
What must be done?
   Mar.   We will conduct her hither;
These walls shall witness it—from first to
   last

He shall reveal himself.

Osw.   Happy are we, 595
Who live in these disputed tracts, that own
No law but what each man makes for
    himself;
Here justice has indeed a field of triumph.

Mar. Let us begone and bring her
    hither;—here
The truth shall be laid open, his guilt
    proved   600
Before her face. The rest be left to me.

Osw. You will be firm: but though we
    well may trust
The issue to the justice of the cause,
Caution must not be flung aside; re-
    member,
Yours is no common life. Self-stationed
    here,   605
Upon these savage confines, we have seen
    you
Stand like an isthmus 'twixt two stormy
    seas
That oft have checked their fury at your
    bidding.
'Mid the deep holds of Solway's mossy
    waste,
Your single virtue has transformed a
    Band   610
Of fierce barbarians into Ministers
Of peace and order. Aged men with tears
Have blessed their steps, the fatherless
    retire   613
For shelter to their banners. But it is,
As you must needs have deeply felt, it is
In darkness and in tempest that we seek
The majesty of Him who rules the world.
Benevolence, that has not heart to use
The wholesome ministry of pain and evil,
Becomes at last weak and contemptible.
Your generous qualities have won due
    praise,   621
But vigorous Spirits look for something
    more
Than Youth's spontaneous products; and
    to-day
You will not disappoint them; and here-
    after——

Mar. You are wasting words; hear me
    then once for all: 625
You are a Man—and therefore, if com-
    passion,
Which to our kind is natural as life,
Be known unto you, you will love this
    Woman,
Even as I do; but I should loathe the
    light,
If I could think one weak or partial
    feeling——   630

Osw. You will forgive me——
Mar.   If I ever knew
My heart, could penetrate its inmost core,
'Tis at this moment.—Oswald, I have loved
To be the friend and father of the op-
    pressed,

A comforter of sorrow;—there is some-
    thing   635
Which looks like a transition in my soul,
And yet it is not.—Let us lead him
    hither.

Osw. Stoop for a moment; 'tis an act
    of justice;
And where's the triumph if the delegate
Must fall in the execution of his office? 640
The deed is done—if you will have it so—
Here where we stand—that tribe of vulgar
    wretches
(You saw them gathering for the festival)
Rush in—the villains seize us——

Mar.   Seize!
Osw.   Yes, they—
Men who are little given to sift and
    weigh—   645
Would wreak on us the passion of the
    moment.

Mar. The cloud will soon disperse—
    farewell—but stay,
Thou wilt relate the story.

Osw.   Am I neither
To bear a part in this Man's punishment,
Nor be its witness?

Mar.   I had many hopes 650
That were most dear to me, and some
    will bear
To be transferred to thee.

Osw.   When I'm dishonoured!
Mar. I would preserve thee. How may
    this be done?

Osw. By showing that you look beyond
    the instant.
A few leagues hence we shall have open
    ground,   655
And nowhere upon earth is place so fit
To look upon the deed. Before we enter
The barren Moor, hangs from a beetling
    rock
The shattered Castle in which Clifford oft
Has held infernal orgies—with the gloom,
And very superstition of the place,   661
Seasoning his wickedness. The Debauchee
Would there perhaps have gathered the
    first fruits
Of this mock Father's guilt.

Enter Host *conducting* HERBERT

Host.   The Baron Herbert
Attends your pleasure.

Osw. [to Host*].*   We are ready—
                  [*to* HERBERT] Sir! 665
I hope you are refreshed.—I have just
    written
A notice for your Daughter, that she may
    know
What is become of you.—You'll sit down
    and sign it;
'Twill glad her heart to see her father's
    signature.
            [*Gives the letter he had written.*
Her. Thanks for your care.

[*Sits down and writes. Exit* Host.
Osw. [*aside to* MARMADUKE]. Perhaps
it would be useful   670
That you too should subscribe your name.
[MARMADUKE *overlooks* HERBERT—*then
writes—examines the letter eagerly*.
Mar. I cannot leave this paper.
                    [*He puts it up, agitated*.
Osw. [*aside*].   Dastard! Come.
[MARMADUKE *goes towards* HERBERT
and supports him—MARMADUKE
tremblingly beckons OSWALD *to take
his place*.
Mar. [*as he quits* HERBERT]. There is a
palsy in his limbs—he shakes.
[*Exeunt* OSWALD *and* HERBERT—MAR-
MADUKE *following*.

SCENE *changes to a Wood*—*a Group of*
Pilgrims *and* IDONEA *with them*
First Pil. A grove of darker and more
lofty shade
I never saw.
Sec. Pil. The music of the birds   675
Drops deadened from a roof so thick with
leaves.
Old Pil. This news! it made my heart
leap up with joy.
Idon. I scarcely can believe it.
Old Pil.   Myself, I heard
The Sheriff read, in open Court, a letter
Which purported it was the royal pleasure
The Baron Herbert, who, as was supposed,
Had taken refuge in this neighbourhood,
Should be forthwith restored. The hear-
ing, Lady,
Filled my dim eyes with tears.—When
I returned
From Palestine, and brought with me a
heart,   685
Though rich in heavenly, poor in earthly,
comfort,
I met your Father, then a wandering
Outcast:
He had a Guide, a Shepherd's boy; but
grieved
He was that One so young should pass
his youth
In such sad service; and he parted with
him.   690
We joined our tales of wretchedness
together,
And begged our daily bread from door
to door.
I talk familiarly to you, sweet Lady!
For once you loved me.
Idon.   You shall back with me
And see your Friend again. The good old
Man   695
Will be rejoiced to greet you.
Old Pil.   It seems but yesterday
That a fierce storm o'ertook us, worn with
travel,
In a deep wood remote from any town.

A cave that opened to the road presented
A friendly shelter, and we entered in. 700
Idon. And I was with you?
Old Pil.   If indeed 'twas you—
But you were then a tottering Little-one—
We sate us down. The sky grew dark and
darker:
I struck my flint, and built up a small fire
With rotten boughs and leaves, such as
the winds   705
Of many autumns in the cave had piled.
Meanwhile the storm fell heavy on the
woods;
Our little fire sent forth a cheering
warmth
And we were comforted, and talked of
comfort;
But 'twas an angry night, and o'er our
heads   710
The thunder rolled in peals that would
have made
A sleeping man uneasy in his bed.
O Lady, you have need to love your
Father.
His voice—methinks I hear it now, his
voice
When, after a broad flash that filled the
cave,   715
He said to me, that he had seen his Child,
A face (no cherub's face more beautiful)
Revealed by lustre brought with it from
heaven;
And it was you, dear Lady!
Idon.   God be praised,
That I have been his comforter till now!
And will be so through every change of
fortune   721
And every sacrifice his peace requires.—
Let us begone with speed, that he may hear
These joyful tidings from no lips but
mine.   724
                    [*Exeunt* IDONEA *and* Pilgrims.

SCENE, *The Area of a half-ruined Castle*—
on one side the entrance to a dungeon—
OSWALD *and* MARMADUKE *pacing back-
wards and forwards*
Mar. 'Tis a wild night.
Osw.   I'd give my cloak and bonnet
For sight of a warm fire.
Mar.   The wind blows keen;
My hands are numb.
Osw.   Ha! ha! 'tis nipping cold.
                    [*Blowing his fingers*.
I long for news of our brave Comrades;
Lacy
Would drive those Scottish Rovers to
their dens
If once they blew a horn this side the
Tweed.   730
Mar. I think I see a second range of
Towers;
This castle has another Area—come,
Let us examine it.

Osw.   'Tis a bitter night;
I hope Idonea is well housed. That horseman,
Who at full speed swept by us where the wood   735
Roared in the tempest, was within an ace
Of sending to his grave our precious Charge:
That would have been a vile mischance.
Mar.   It would.
Osw. Justice had been most cruelly defrauded.
Mar. Most cruelly.
Osw.   As up the steep we clomb,
I saw a distant fire in the north-east; 741
I took it for the blaze of Cheviot Beacon:
With proper speed our quarters may be gained
To-morrow evening.
[*Looks restlessly towards the mouth of the dungeon.*
Mar.   When, upon the plank,
I had led him 'cross the torrent, his voice blessed me: 745
You could not hear, for the foam beat the rocks
With deafening noise,—the benediction fell
Back on himself; but changed into a curse.
Osw. As well indeed it might.
Mar.   And this you deem
The fittest place?
Osw. [*aside*]. He is growing pitiful. 750
Mar. [*listening*]. What an odd moaning that is!—
Osw.   Mighty odd
The wind should pipe a little, while we stand
Cooling our heels in this way!—I'll begin
And count the stars.
Mar. [*still listening*]. That dog of his, you are sure,
Could not come after us—he *must* have perished;   755
The torrent would have dashed an oak to splinters.
You said you did not like his looks— that he
Would trouble us; if he were here again,
I swear the sight of him would quail me more
Than twenty armies.
Osw.   How?
Mar.   The old blind Man,
When you had told him the mischance, was troubled   761
Even to the shedding of some natural tears
Into the torrent over which he hung,
Listening in vain.
Osw.   He has a tender heart!
[*Oswald offers to go down into the dungeon.*
Mar. How now, what mean you?
Osw.   Truly, I was going
To waken our stray Baron. Were there not

A farm or dwelling-house within five leagues,   767
We should deserve to wear a cap and bells,
Three good round years, for playing the fool here
In such a night as this.
Mar.   Stop, stop.
Osw.   Perhaps, 770
You'd better like we should descend together,
And lie down by his side—what say you to it?
Three of us—we should keep each other warm:
I'll answer for it that our four-legged friend
Shall not disturb us; further I'll not engage;   775
Come, come, for manhood's sake!
Mar.   These drowsy shiverings,
This mortal stupor which is creeping over me,
What do they mean? were this my single body
Opposed to armies, not a nerve would tremble:
Why do I tremble now?—Is not the depth   780
Of this Man's crimes beyond the reach of thought?
And yet, in plumbing the abyss for judgment,
Something I strike upon which turns my mind
Back on herself, I think, again—my breast   784
Concentres all the terrors of the Universe:
I look at him and tremble like a child.
Osw. Is it possible?
Mar.   One thing you noticed not:
Just as we left the glen a clap of thunder
Burst on the mountains with hell-rousing force.
This is a time, said he, when guilt may shudder;   790
But there's a Providence for them who walk
In helplessness, when innocence is with them.
At this audacious blasphemy, I thought
The spirit of vengeance seemed to ride the air.
Osw. Why are you not the man you were that moment?   795
[*He draws* MARMADUKE *to the dungeon.*
Mar. You say he was asleep,—look at this arm,
And tell me if 'tis fit for such a work.
Oswald, Oswald! [*Leans upon* OSWALD.
Osw.   This is some sudden seizure!
Mar. A most strange faintness,—will you hunt me out
A draught of water?
Osw.   Nay, to see you thus 800

40

Moves me beyond my bearing.—I will try
To gain the torrent's brink. [*Exit* OSWALD.
Mar. [*after a pause*].   It seems an age
Since that Man left me.—No, I am not
    lost.
Her. [*at the mouth of the dungeon*].   Give
    me your hand; where are you,
    Friends? and tell me
How goes the night.
    Mar.   'Tis hard to measure time
In such a weary night, and such a place.
Her. I do not hear the voice of my friend
    Oswald.   807
Mar. A minute past, he went to fetch
    a draught
Of water from the torrent. 'Tis, you'll say,
A cheerless beverage.
    Her.   How good it was in you
To stay behind!—Hearing at first no
    answer,   811
I was alarmed.
    Mar.   No wonder; this is a place
That well may put some fears into *your*
    heart.
    Her. Why so? a roofless rock had been
    a comfort,
Storm-beaten and bewildered as we were;
And in a night like this to lend your
    cloaks   816
To make a bed for me!—My Girl will weep
When she is told of it.
    Mar.   This Daughter of yours
Is very dear to you.
    Her.   Oh! but you are young;
Over your head twice twenty years must
    roll,   820
With all their natural weight of sorrow
    and pain,
Ere can be known to you how much a
    Father
May love his Child.
    Mar.   Thank you, old Man, for this!
                                  [*Aside.*
Her. Fallen am I, and worn out, a use-
    less Man;   824
Kindly have you protected me to-night,
And no return have I to make but prayers;
May you in age be blest with such a
    daughter!—
When from the Holy Land I had returned
Sightless, and from my heritage was
    driven,
A wretched Outcast—but this strain of
    thought   830
Would lead me to talk fondly.
    Mar.   Do not fear;
Your words are precious to my ears; go on.
    Her. You will forgive me, but my heart
    runs over.
When my old Leader slipped into the
    flood
And perished, what a piercing outcry you
Sent after him. I have loved you ever
    since.   836

You start—where are we?
    Mar.   Oh, there is no danger;
The cold blast struck me.
    Her.   'Twas a foolish question.
Mar. But when you were an Outcast?—
    Heaven is just;
Your piety would not miss its due re-
    ward;   840
The little Orphan then would be your
    succour,
And do good service, though she knew it
    not.
Her. I turned me from the dwellings
    of my Fathers,
Where none but those who trampled on
    my rights
Seemed to remember me. To the wide
    world   845
I bore her in my arms; her looks won
    pity;
She was my Raven in the wilderness,
And brought me food. Have I not cause
    to love her?
Mar. Yes.
    Her.   More than ever Parent
    loved a Child?   849
Mar. Yes, yes.
    Her. I will not murmur, merciful God!
I will not murmur, blasted as I have been,
Thou hast left me ears to hear my Daugh-
    ter's voice,
And arms to fold her to my heart. Sub-
    missively   853
Thee I adore, and find my rest in faith.

            Enter OSWALD

Osw. Herbert!—confusion! [*aside*].
    Here it is, my Friend, [*Presents the
    Horn.*
A charming beverage for you to carouse
This bitter night.
    Her. Ha! Oswald! ten bright crosses
I would have given, not many minutes
    gone,
To have heard your voice.
    Osw. Your couch, I fear, good Baron,
Has been but comfortless; and yet that
    place,   860
When the tempestuous wind first drove
    us hither,
Felt warm as a wren's nest. You'd better
    turn
And under covert rest till break of day,
Or till the storm abate.
    [*To* MARMADUKE *aside.*] He has restored
    you,
No doubt you have been nobly enter-
    tained?   865
But soft!—how came he forth? The Night-
    mare Conscience
Has driven him out of harbour?
    Mar.   I believe
You have guessed right.
    Her. The trees renew their murmur:

                   41

Come, let us house together.
[OSWALD *conducts him to the dungeon.*
Osw. [*returns*]. Had I not
Esteemed you worthy to conduct the affair 870
To its most fit conclusion, do you think
I would so long have struggled with my Nature,
And smothered all that's man in me?—away!—
[*Looking towards the dungeon.*
This man's the property of him who best
Can feel his crimes. I have resigned a privilege; 875
It now becomes my duty to resume it.
Mar. Touch not a finger——
Osw. What then must be done?
Mar. Which way soe'er I turn, I am perplexed.
Osw. Now, on my life, I grieve for you. The misery
Of doubt is insupportable. Pity, the facts
Did not admit of stronger evidence; 881
Twelve honest men, plain men, would set us right;
Their verdict would abolish these weak scruples.
Mar. Weak! I am weak—there does my torment lie,
Feeding itself.
Osw. Verily, when he said 885
How his old heart would leap to hear her steps,
You thought his voice the echo of Idonea's.
Mar. And never heard a sound so terrible.
Osw. Perchance you think so now?
Mar. I cannot do it:
Twice did I spring to grasp his withered throat, 890
When such a sudden weakness fell upon me,
I could have dropped asleep upon his breast.
Osw. Justice—is there not thunder in the word?
Shall it be law to stab the petty robber
Who aims but at our purse; and shall this Parricide— 895
Worse is he far, far worse (if foul dishonour
Be worse than death) to that confiding Creature
Whom he to more than filial love and duty
Hath falsely trained—shall he fulfil his purpose?
But you are fallen.
Mar. Fallen should I be indeed—900
Murder—perhaps asleep, blind, old, alone,
Betrayed, in darkness! Here to strike the blow—
Away! away!——[*Flings away his sword.*
Osw. Nay, I have done with you:
We'll lead him to the Convent. He shall live,

And she shall love him. With unquestioned title 905
He shall be seated in his Barony,
And we too chant the praise of his good deeds.
I now perceive we do mistake our masters,
And most despise the men who best can teach us:
Henceforth it shall be said that bad men only 910
Are brave: Clifford is brave; and that old Man
Is brave.
[*Taking* MARMADUKE'S *sword and giving it to him.*
To Clifford's arms he would have led
His Victim—haply to this desolate house.
Mar. [*advancing to the dungeon*]. It must be ended!—
Osw. Softly; do not rouse him; 915
He will deny it to the last. He lies
Within the Vault, a spear's length to the left.
[MARMADUKE *descends to the dungeon.*
[*Alone*]. The Villains rose in mutiny to destroy me;
I could have quelled the Cowards, but this Stripling
Must needs step in, and save my life. The look
With which he gave the boon—I see it now! 920
The same that tempted me to loathe the gift.—
For this old venerable Grey-beard—faith
'Tis his own fault if he hath got a face
Which doth play tricks with them that look on it:
'Twas this that put it in my thoughts— that countenance— 925
His staff—his figure—Murder!—what, of whom?
We kill a worn-out horse, and who but women
Sigh at the deed? Hew down a withered tree,
And none look grave but dotards. He may live
To thank me for this service. Rainbow arches, 930
Highways of dreaming passion, have too long,
Young as he is, diverted wish and hope
From the unpretending ground we mortals tread;—
Then shatter the delusion, break it up
And set him free. What follows? I have learned 935
That things will work to ends the slaves o' the world
Do never dream of. I *have* been what he—
This Boy—when he comes forth with bloody hands—
Might envy, and am now,—but he shall know

42

What I am now—
   [*Goes and listens at the dungeon.*
      Praying or parleying?—tut! 940
Is he not eyeless? He has been half-dead
These fifteen years——

Enter female Beggar *with two or three of
      her Companions*
[*Turning abruptly*]. Ha! speak—what
   Thing art thou?
[*Recognises her*]. Heavens! my good
   Friend!   [*To her.*
Beg.   Forgive me, gracious Sir!—
Osw. [*to her companions*]. Begone, ye
   Slaves, or I will raise a whirlwind
And send ye dancing to the clouds, like
   leaves.   [*They retire affrighted.*
Beg. Indeed we meant no harm; we
   lodge sometimes   946
In this deserted Castle—*I repent me.*
   [OSWALD *goes to the dungeon—listens
   —returns to the* Beggar.
Osw. Woman, thou hast a helpless In-
   fant—keep
Thy secret for its sake, or verily
That wretched life of thine shall be the
   forfeit.   950
Beg. I *do* repent me, Sir; I fear the curse
Of that blind Man. 'Twas not your mo-
   ney, Sir,——
Osw. Begone!
Beg. [*going*]. There is some wicked
   deed in hand: [*Aside.*
Would I could find the old Man and his
   Daughter.   [*Exit Beggar.*

MARMADUKE *re-enters from the dungeon*
Osw. It is all over then;—your foolish
   fears   955
Are hushed to sleep, by your own act and
   deed,
Made quiet as he is.
Mar.   Why came you down?
And when I felt your hand upon my
   arm
And spake to you, why did you give no
   answer?
Feared you to waken him? he must have
   been   960
In a deep sleep. I whispered to him thrice.
There are the strangest echoes in that
   place!
Osw. Tut! let them gabble till the day
   of doom.
Mar. Scarcely, by groping, had I reach-
   ed the Spot,
When round my wrist I felt a cord drawn
   tight,   965
As if the blind Man's dog were pulling
   at it.
Osw. But after that?
Mar.   The features of Idonea
Lurked in his face——

Osw.   Pshaw! Never to these eyes
Will retribution show itself again 969
With aspect so inviting. Why forbid me
To share your triumph?
Mar.   Yes, her very look,
Smiling in sleep——
Osw.   A pretty feat of Fancy!
Mar. Though but a glimpse, it sent me
   to my prayers.
Osw. Is he alive?
Mar.   What mean you? who alive?
Osw. Herbert! since you will have it, 975
   Baron Herbert;
He who will gain his Seignory when
   Idonea
Hath become Clifford's harlot—is *he* liv-
   ing?
Mar. The old Man in that dungeon *is*
   alive.
Osw. Henceforth, then, will I never in
   camp or field
Obey you more. Your weakness, to the
   Band,   980
Shall be proclaimed: brave Men, they all
   shall hear it.
You a protector of humanity!
Avenger you of outraged innocence!
Mar. 'Twas dark—dark as the grave;
   yet did I see,
Saw him—his face turned toward me; and
   I tell thee   985
Idonea's filial countenance was there
To baffle me—it put me to my prayers.
Upwards I cast my eyes, and, through a
   crevice,
Beheld a star twinkling above my head,
And, by the living God, I could not do it.
   [*Sinks exhausted.*
Osw. [*to himself*]. Now may I perish if
   this turn do more   991
Than make me change my course.
   [*To* MARMADUKE].   Dear Marmaduke,
My words were rashly spoken; I recall
   them:
I feel my error; shedding human blood
Is a most serious thing.
Mar.   Not I alone, 995
Thou too art deep in guilt.
Osw.   We have indeed
Been most presumptuous. There *is* guilt
   in this,
Else could so strong a mind have ever
   known
These trepidations? Plain it is that Hea-
   ven
Has marked out this foul Wretch as one
   whose crimes   1000
Must never come before a mortal judg-
   ment-seat,
Or be chastised by mortal instruments.
Mar. A thought that's worth a thou-
   sand worlds!
   [*Goes towards the dungeon.*
Osw.   I grieve

43

That, in my zeal, I have caused you so much pain.
Mar. Think not of that! 'tis over—we are safe. 1005
Osw. [*as if to himself, yet speaking aloud*].
The truth is hideous, but how stifle it?
[*Turning to* MARMADUKE.
Give me your sword—nay, here are stones and fragments,
The least of which would beat out a man's brains;
Or you might drive your head against that wall. 1009
No! this is not the place to hear the tale:
It should be told you pinioned in your bed,
Or on some vast and solitary plain
Blown to you from a trumpet.
Mar. Why talk thus?
Whate'er the monster brooding in your breast
I care not: fear I have none, and cannot fear—— 1015
[*The sound of a horn is heard.*
That horn again—'Tis some one of our Troop;
What do they here? Listen!
Osw. What; dogged like thieves!

Enter WALLACE *and* LACY, &c.

Lacy. You are found at last, thanks to the vagrant Troop
For not misleading us.
Osw. [*looking at* WALLACE]. That subtle Grey-beard— 1019
I'd rather see my father's ghost.
Lacy [*to* MARMADUKE]. My Captain,
We come by order of the Band. Belike
You have not heard that Henry has at last
Dissolved the Barons' League, and sent abroad
His Sheriffs with fit force to reinstate
The genuine owners of such Lands and Baronies 1025
As, in these long commotions, have been seized.
His Power is this way tending. It befits us
To stand upon our guard, and with our swords
Defend the innocent.
Mar. Lacy! we look 1029
But at the surfaces of things; we hear
Of towns in flames, fields ravaged, young and old
Driven out in troops to want and nakedness;
Then grasp our swords and rush upon a cure
That flatters us, because it asks not thought:
The deeper malady is better hid; 1035
The world is poisoned at the heart.
Lacy. What mean you?

Wal. [*whose eye has been fixed suspiciously upon* OSWALD]. Ay, what is it you mean?
Mar. Harkee, my Friends;—
[*Appearing gay.*
Were there a Man who, being weak and helpless
And most forlorn, should bribe a Mother, pressed 1039
By penury, to yield him up her Daughter,
A little Infant, and instruct the Babe,
Prattling upon his knee, to call him Father——
Lacy. Why, if his heart be tender, that offence
I could forgive him.
Mar. [*going on*]. And should he make the Child
An instrument of falsehood, should he teach her 1045
To stretch her arms, and dim the gladsome light
Of infant playfulness with piteous looks
Of misery that was not——
Lacy. Troth, 'tis hard—
But in a world like ours——
Mar. [*changing his tone*]. This selfsame Man—
Even while he printed kisses on the cheek
Of this poor Babe, and taught its innocent tongue 1051
To lisp the name of Father—could he look
To the unnatural harvest of that time
When he should give her up, a Woman grown, 1054
To him who bid the highest in the market
Of foul pollution——
Lacy. The whole visible world
Contains not such a Monster!
Mar. For this purpose
Should he resolve to taint her Soul by means
Which bathe the limbs in sweat to think of them;
Should he, by tales which would draw tears from iron, 1060
Work on her nature, and so turn compassion
And gratitude to ministers of vice,
And make the spotless spirit of filial love
Prime mover in a plot to damn his Victim
Both soul and body——
Wal. 'Tis too horrible; 1065
Oswald, what say you to it?
Lacy. Hew him down,
And fling him to the ravens.
Mar. But his aspect
It is so meek, his countenance so venerable.
Wal. [*with an appearance of mistrust*].
But how, what say you, Oswald?
Lacy [*at the same moment*]. Stab him, were it
Before the Altar.

Mar.   What, if he were sick,   1070
Tottering upon the very verge of life,
And old, and blind——
    Lacy.   Blind, say you?
    Osw. [coming forward]. Are we Men,
Or own we baby Spirits? Genuine courage
Is not an accidental quality,
A thing dependent for its casual birth
On opposition and impediment.   1076
Wisdom, if Justice speak the word, beats
    down
The giant's strength; and, at the voice of
    Justice,
Spares not the worm. The giant and the
    worm—
She weighs them in one scale. The wiles
    of woman,   1080
And craft of age, seducing reason, first
Made weakness a protection, and obscured
The moral shapes of things. His tender
    cries
And helpless innocence—do they protect
The infant lamb? and shall the infirmi-
    ties,   1085
Which have enabled this enormous Culprit
To perpetrate his crimes, serve as a Sanc-
    tuary
To cover him from punishment? Shame!—
    Justice,
Admitting no resistance, bends alike
The feeble and the strong. She needs not
    here   1090
Her bonds and chains, which make the
    mighty feeble.
—We recognise in this old Man a victim
Prepared already for the sacrifice.
    Lacy. By heaven, his words are reason!
    Osw.   Yes, my Friends,
His countenance is meek and vener-
    able;   1095
And, by the Mass, to see him at his
    prayers!—
I am of flesh and blood, and may I perish
When my heart does not ache to think
    of it!—
Poor Victim! not a virtue under heaven
But what was made an engine to ensnare
    thee;   1100
But yet I trust, Idonea, thou art safe.
    Lacy. Idonea!
    Wal.   How! what? your Idonea?
                        [*To* MARMADUKE.
    Mar.   Mine;
But now no longer mine. You know
    Lord Clifford;
He is the Man to whom the Maiden—pure
As beautiful, and gentle and benign, 1105
And in her ample heart loving even me—
Was to be yielded up.
    Lacy.   Now, by the head
Of my own child, this Man must die; my
    hand,   ·
A worthier wanting, shall itself entwine
In his grey hairs!—

    Mar. [to LACY. I love the Father in
    thee.   1110
You know me, Friends; I have a heart
    to feel,
And I have felt, more than perhaps be-
    comes me
Or duty sanctions.
    Lacy. We will have ample justice.
Who are we, Friends? Do we not live on
    ground
Where Souls are self-defended, free to
    grow   1115
Like mountain oaks rocked by the stormy
    wind.
Mark the Almighty Wisdom, which de-
    creed
This monstrous crime to be laid open—
    here,
Where Reason has an eye that she can
    use,
And Men alone are Umpires. To the
    Camp   1120
He shall be led, and there, the Country
    round
All gathered to the spot, in open day
Shall Nature be avenged.
    Osw.   'Tis nobly thought;
His death will be a monument for ages.
    Mar. [to LACY]. I thank you for that
    hint. He shall be brought   1125
Before the Camp, and would that best
    and wisest
Of every country might be present. There
His crime shall be proclaimed; and for
    the rest
It shall be done as Wisdom shall decide:
Meanwhile, do you two hasten back and
    see   1130
That all is well prepared.
    Wal.   We will obey you.
[*Aside*]. But softly! we must look a little
    nearer.
    Mar. Tell where you found us. At
    some future time
I will explain the cause.   [*Exeunt.*

                ACT III

SCENE, *The door of the Hostel, a group of*
    Pilgrims *as before;* IDONEA *and the*
    Host *among them*

Host. Lady, you'll find your Father at
    the Convent   1135
As I have told you: He left us yesterday
With two Companions; one of them, as
    seemed,
His most familiar Friend. [*Going.*] There
    was a letter
Of which I heard them speak, but that I
    fancy
Has been forgotten.
    Idon. [to Host]. Farewell!
    Host.   Gentle pilgrims,

                        45

St. Cuthbert speed you on your holy
   errand.   1141
     [*Exeunt* IDONEA *and* Pilgrims.

     SCENE, *A desolate Moor*
       OSWALD [*alone*]

Osw. Carry him to the Camp! Yes, to
   the Camp.
Oh, Wisdom! a most wise resolve! and
   then,
That half a word should blow it to the
   winds!
This last device must end my work.—
   Methinks   1145
It were a pleasant pastime to construct
A scale and table of belief—as thus—
Two columns, one for passion, one for
   proof;
Each rises as the other falls: and first,
Passion a unit and *against* us—proof—
Nay, we must travel in another path, 1151
Or we're stuck fast for ever;—passion,
   then,
Shall be a unit *for* us; proof—no, passion!
We'll not insult thy majesty by time, .
Person, and place—the where, the when,
   the how,   1155
And all particulars that dull brains re-
   quire
To constitute the spiritless shape of Fact,
They bow to, calling the idol, Demonstra-
   tion.
A whipping to the Moralists who preach
That misery is a sacred thing: for me,
I know no cheaper engine to degrade a
   man,   1161
Nor any half so sure. This Stripling's
   mind
Is shaken till the dregs float on the sur-
   face;
And, in the storm and anguish of the
   heart,
He talks of a transition in his Soul, 1165
And dreams that he is happy. We dis-
   sect
The senseless body, and why not the
   mind?—
These are strange sights—the mind of
   man, upturned,
Is in all natures a strange spectacle;
In some a hideous one—hem! shall I
   stop?   1170
No.—Thoughts and feelings will sink
   deep, but then
They have no substance. Pass but a few
   minutes,
And something shall be done which
   Memory
May touch, whene'er her Vassals are at
   work.

   Enter MARMADUKE, *from behind*

Osw. [*turning to meet him*]. But listen,
   for my peace——

Mar.   Why, I *believe* you.
Osw. But hear the proofs——
Mar.   Ay, prove that when two peas
Lie snugly in a pod, the pod must
   then   1177
Be larger than the peas—prove this—
   'twere matter
Worthy the hearing. Fool was I to
   dream
It ever could be otherwise!
Osw.   Last night,   1180
When I returned with water from the
   brook,
I overheard the Villains—every word
Like red-hot iron burnt into my heart.
Said one, 'It is agreed on. The blind
   Man
Shall feign a sudden illness, and the
   Girl,   1185
Who on her journey must proceed alone,
Under pretence of violence, be seized.
She is,' continued the detested Slave,
'She is right willing—strange if she were
   not!—
They say Lord Clifford is a savage
   man;   1190
But, faith, to see him in his silken tunic,
Fitting his low voice to the minstrel's
   harp,
There's witchery in't. I never knew a
   maid
That could withstand it. True,' con-
   tinued he,
'When we arranged the affair, she wept
   a little   1195
(Not the less welcome to my Lord for
   that)
And said, "My Father he will have it
   so."'
Mar. I am your hearer.
Osw.   This I caught, and more
That may not be retold to any ear.
The obstinate bolt of a small iron door
Detained them near the gateway of the
   Castle.   1201
By a dim lantern's light I saw that
   wreaths
Of flowers were in their hands, as if de-
   signed
For festive decoration; and they said,
With brutal laughter and most foul allu-
   sion,   1205
That they should share the banquet with
   their Lord
And his new Favorite.
Mar.   Misery!—
Osw.   I knew
How you would be disturbed by this dire
   news,
And therefore chose this solitary Moor,
Here to impart the tale, of which, last
   night,   1210
I strove to ease my mind, when our two
   Comrades,

Commissioned by the Band, burst in
    upon us.
Mar. Last night, when moved to lift
    the avenging steel,
I did believe all things were shadows—yea,
Living or dead all things were bodi-
    less,   1215
All but the mutual mockeries of body,
Till that same star summoned me back
    again.
Now I could laugh till my ribs ached.
    Oh, Fool!
To let a creed, built in the heart of
    things,
Dissolve before a twinkling atom!—Os-
    wald,   1220
I could fetch lessons out of wiser schools
Than you have entered, were it worth the
    pains.
Young as I am, I might go forth a
    teacher,
And you should see how deeply I could
    reason
Of love in all its shapes, beginnings,
    ends;   1225
Of moral qualities in their diverse as-
    pects;
Of actions, and their laws and tendencies.
Osw. You take it as it merits——
Mar.   One a King,
General or Cham, Sultan or Emperor,
Strews twenty acres of good meadow-
    ground   1230
With carcasses, in lineament and shape
And substance, nothing differing from his
    own,
But that they cannot stand up of them-
    selves;
Another sits i' th' sun, and by the hour
Floats kingcups in the brook—a Hero one
We call, and scorn the other as Time's
    spendthrift;   1236
But have they not a world of common
    ground
To occupy—both fools, or wise alike,
Each in his way?
Osw.   Troth, I begin to think so.
Mar. Now for the corner-stone of my
    philosophy: 1240
I would not give a denier for the man
Who, on such provocation as this earth
Yields, could not chuck his babe beneath
    the chin,
And send it with a fillip to its grave.
Osw. Nay, you leave me behind.
Mar.   That such a One,
So pious in demeanour! in his look   1246
So saintly and so pure!——Harkee, my
    Friend,
I'll plant myself before Lord Clifford's
    Castle,
A surly mastiff kennels at the gate,
And he shall howl and I will laugh, a
    medley   1250

Most tunable.
Osw.   In faith, a pleasant scheme;
But take your sword along with you, for
    that
Might in such neighbourhood find seemly
    use.—
But first, how wash our hands of this old
    Man?
Mar. Oh yes, that mole, that viper in
    the path;   1255
Plague on my memory, him I had for-
    gotten.
Osw. You know we left him sitting—
    see him yonder.
Mar. Ha! ha!—
Osw.   As 'twill be but a moment's
    work,
I will stroll on; you follow when 'tis done.
                                    [*Exeunt.*

SCENE *changes to another part of the Moor
    at a short distance*—HERBERT *is dis-
    covered seated on a stone*

Her. A sound of laughter, too!—'tis
    well—I feared   1260
The Stranger had some pitiable sorrow
Pressing upon his solitary heart.
Hush!—'tis the feeble and earth-loving
    wind
That creeps along the bells of the crisp
    heather.
Alas! 'tis cold—I shiver in the sun-
    shine—   1265
What can this mean? There is a psalm
    that speaks
Of God's parental mercies—with Idonea
I used to sing it.—Listen!—what foot is
    there?

Enter MARMADUKE

Mar. [*aside—looking at* HERBERT]. And
    I have loved this Man! and *she* hath
    loved him!
And I loved her, and she loves the Lord
    Clifford!   1270
And there it ends;—if this be not enough
To make mankind merry for evermore,
Then plain it is as day that eyes were made
For a wise purpose—verily to weep with!
                                [*Looking round.*
A pretty prospect this, a masterpiece 1275
Of Nature, finished with most curious
    skill!
[*To* HERBERT]. Good Baron, have you
    ever practised tillage?
Pray tell me what this land is worth by
    the acre.
Her. How glad I am to hear your voice!
    I know not   1279
Wherein I have offended you;—last night
I found in you the kindest of Protectors;
This morning, when I spoke of weariness,
You from my shoulder took my scrip and
    threw it

47

About your own; but for these two hours
past
Once only have you spoken, when the
lark   1285
Whirred from among the fern beneath our
feet,
And I, no coward in my better days,
Was almost terrified.
Mar.   That's excellent!—
So you bethought you of the many ways
In which a man may come to his end,
whose crimes   1290
Have roused all Nature up against him—
pshaw!—
Her. For mercy's sake, is nobody in
sight?
No traveller, peasant, herdsman?
Mar.   Not a soul:
Here is a tree, ragged, and bent, and
bare,
That turns its goat's-beard flakes of pea-
green moss   1295
From the stern breathing of the rough
sea-wind;
This have we, but no other company:
Commend me to the place. If a man
should die
And leave his body here, it were all one
As he were twenty fathoms underground.
Her. Where is our common Friend?
Mar.   A ghost, methinks—
The Spirit of a murdered man, for in-
stance—
Might have fine room to ramble about
here,
A grand domain to squeak and gibber in.
Her. Lost Man! if thou have any close-
pent guilt   1305
Pressing upon thy heart, and this the
hour
Of visitation——
Mar.   A bold word from *you!*
Her. Restore him, Heaven!
Mar.   The desperate
Wretch!—A Flower,
Fairest of all flowers, was she once, but
now
They have snapped her from the stem—
Poh! let her lie   1310
Besoiled with mire, and let the houseless
snail
Feed on her leaves. You knew her well—
ay, there,
Old Man! you were a very Lynx, you
knew
The worm was in her——
Her.   Mercy! Sir, what mean you?
Mar. You have a Daughter!
Her.   Oh that she were here!—
She hath an eye that sinks into all
hearts,   1316
And if I have in aught offended you,
Soon would her gentle voice make peace
between us.

Mar. [*aside*]. I do believe he weeps—
I could weep too—
There is a vein of her voice that runs
through his: 1320
Even such a Man my fancy bodied forth
From the first moment that I loved the
Maid;
And for his sake I loved her more: these
tears—
I did not think that aught was left in me
Of what I have been—yes, I thank thee,
Heaven!   1325
One happy thought has passed across my
mind.
—It may not be—I am cut off from man;
No more shall I be man—no more shall I
Have human feelings!—[*To* HERBERT]—
Now, for a little more
About your Daughter!
Her.   Troops of armed men,
Met in the roads, would bless us; little
children,   1331
Rushing along in the full tide of play,
Stood silent as we passed them! I have
heard
The boisterous carman, in the miry road,
Check his loud whip and hail us with
mild voice,   1335
And speak with milder voice to his poor
beasts.
Mar. And whither were you going?
Her.   Learn, young Man,—
To fear the virtuous, and reverence misery,
Whether too much for patience, or, like
mine,
Softened till it becomes a gift of mercy.
Mar. Now, this is as it should be!
Her.   I am weak!—   1341
My Daughter does not know how weak
I am;
And, as thou see'st, under the arch of
heaven
Here do I stand, alone, to helplessness,
By the good God, our common Father,
doomed!—   1345
But I had once a spirit and an arm——
Mar. Now, for a word about your
Barony:
I fancy when you left the Holy Land,
And came to—what's your title—eh?
your claims
Were undisputed!
Her.   Like a mendicant, 1350
Whom no one comes to meet, I stood
alone;—
I murmured—but, remembering Him who
feeds
The pelican and ostrich of the desert,
From my own threshold I looked up to
Heaven
And did not want glimmerings of quiet
hope.   1355
So from the court I passed, and down the
brook,

Led by its murmur, to the ancient oak
I came; and when I felt its cooling shade,
I sate me down, and cannot but believe—
While in my lap I held my little Babe
And clasped her to my heart, my heart
　　that ached　　　　　　　　　　　1361
More with delight than grief—I heard a
　　voice
Such as by Cherith on Elijah called;
It said, 'I will be with thee.' A little boy,
A shepherd-lad, ere yet my trance was
　　gone,　　　　　　　　　　　　　1365
Hailed us as if he had been sent from
　　heaven,
And said, with tears, that he would be
　　our guide:
I had a better guide—that innocent
　　Babe—
Her, who hath saved me, to this hour,
　　from harm,
From cold, from hunger, penury, and
　　death;　　　　　　　　　　　　1370
To whom I owe the best of all the good
I have, or wish for, upon earth—and more
And higher far than lies within earth's
　　bounds:
Therefore I bless her: when I think of
　　Man,
I bless her with sad spirit,—when of
　　God,　　　　　　　　　　　　　1375
I bless her in the fulness of my joy!
　　Mar. The name of daughter in his
　　mouth, he prays!
With nerves so steady, that the very flies
Sit unmolested on his staff.—Innocent!
If he were innocent—then he would
　　tremble　　　　　　　　　　　　1380
And be disturbed, as I am. [*Turning
aside*]. I have read
In Story, what men now alive have wit-
　　nessed,
How, when the People's mind was racked
　　with doubt,
Appeal was made to the great Judge: the
　　Accused
With naked feet walked over burning
　　ploughshares.　　　　　　　　　1385
Here is a Man by Nature's hand prepared
For a like trial, but more merciful.
Why else have I been led to this bleak
　　Waste?
Bare is it, without house or track, and
　　destitute
Of obvious shelter, as a shipless sea.　1390
Here will I leave him—here—All-seeing
　　God!
Such as *he* is, and sore perplexed as I am,
I will commit him to this final *Ordeal!*—
He heard a voice—a shepherd-lad came to
　　him
And was his guide; if once, why not
　　again,　　　　　　　　　　　　1395
And in this desert? If never—then the
　　whole

Of what he says, and looks, and does,
　　and is,
Makes up one damning falsehood. Leave
　　him here
To cold and hunger!—Pain is of the
　　heart,
And what are a few throes of bodily
　　suffering　　　　　　　　　　　1400
If they can waken one pang of remorse?
　　　　　　　　[*Goes up to* HERBERT.
Old Man! my wrath is as a flame burnt
　　out,
It cannot be rekindled. Thou art here
Led by my hand to save thee from per-
　　dition;
Thou wilt have time to breathe and
　　think——
　　Her.　　　　　　　　Oh, Mercy!
　　Mar. I know the need that all men
　　have of mercy,　　　　　　　　1406
And therefore leave thee to a righteous
　　judgment.
　　Her. My Child, my blessèd Child!
　　Mar.　　　　No more of that;
Thou wilt have many guides if thou art
　　innocent;
Yea, from the utmost corners of the
　　earth,　　　　　　　　　　　　1410
That Woman will come o'er this Waste
　　to save thee.
[*He pauses and looks at* HERBERT'S *staff.*
Ha! what is here? and carved by her
　　own hand! 　[*Reads upon the staff.*
'I am eyes to the blind, saith the Lord.
He that puts his trust in me shall not
　　fail!'
Yes, be it so;—repent and be forgiven—
God and that staff are now thy only
　　guides.　　　　　　　　　　　1416
　　　　　　　[*He leaves* HERBERT *on the Moor.*

SCENE, *An eminence, a Beacon on the
summit*
LACY, WALLACE, LENNOX, &c. &c.
Several of the Band [*confusedly*]. But
patience!
One of the Band. Curses on that
Traitor, Oswald!
Our Captain made a prey to foul device!—
　　Len. [*to* WALLACE]. His tool, the
wandering Beggar, made last night
A plain confession, such as leaves no
　　doubt,　　　　　　　　　　　　1420
Knowing what otherwise we know too
　　well,
That she revealed the truth. Stand by
　　me now;
For rather would I have a nest of vipers
Between my breast-plate and my skin
　　than make
Oswald my special enemy, if you　　1425
Deny me your support.
　　Lacy.　　　　We have been fooled—

But for the motive?
Wal.   Natures such as his
Spin motives out of their own bowels,
    Lacy!
I learn'd this when I was a Confessor.
I know him well; there needs no other
    motive   1430
Than that most strange incontinence in
    crime
Which haunts this Oswald. Power is life
    to him
And breath and being; where he cannot
    govern,
He will destroy.
Lacy.   To have been trapped like
    moles!—
Yes, you are right, we need not hunt for
    motives: 1435
There is no crime from which this man
    would shrink;
He recks not human law; and I have
    noticed
That often, when the name of God is
    uttered,
A sudden blankness overspreads his face.
Len. Yet, reasoner as he is, his pride
    has built   1440
Some uncouth superstition of its own.
Wal. I have seen traces of it.
Len.   Once he headed
A band of Pirates in the Norway seas;
And when the King of Denmark sum-
    moned him
To the oath of fealty, I well remember,
'Twas a strange answer that he made; he
    said,   1446
'I hold of Spirits, and the Sun in heaven.'
Lacy. He is no madman.
Wal.   A most subtle doctor
Were that man, who could draw the line
    that parts
Pride and her daughter, Cruelty, from
    Madness,   1450
That should be scourged, not pitied.
    Restless Minds,
Such Minds as feed amid their fellow-men
No heart that loves them, none that they
    can love,
Will turn perforce and seek for sympathy
In dim relation to imagined Beings. 1455
One of the Band. What if he mean to
    offer up our Captain
An expiation and a sacrifice
To those infernal fiends!
Wal.   Now, if the event
Should be as Lennox has foretold, then
    swear,
My Friends, his heart shall have as many
    wounds   1460
As there are daggers here.
Lacy.   What need of swearing!
One of the Band. Let us away!
Another.   Away!
A third.   Hark! how the horns

Of those Scotch Rovers echo through the
    vale.
Lacy. Stay you behind; and, when
    the sun is down,
Light up this beacon.
One of the Band. You shall be obeyed.
                        [*They go out together.*

SCENE, *The Wood on the edge of the Moor*
            MARMADUKE [*alone*]

Mar. Deep, deep and vast, vast be-
    yond human thought,
Yet calm.—I could believe that there
    was here
The only quiet heart on earth. In terror,
Remembered terror, there is peace and
    rest.   1469

            Enter OSWALD

Osw. Ha! my dear Captain.
Mar.   A later meeting, Oswald,
Would have been better timed.
Osw.   Alone, I see;
You have done your duty. I had hopes,
    which now
I feel that you will justify.
Mar.   I had fears,
From which I have freed myself—but 'tis
    my wish
To be alone, and therefore we must part.
Osw. Nay, then—I am mistaken.
    There's a weakness   1476
About you still; you talk of solitude—
I am your friend.
Mar.   What need of this assurance
At any time? and why given now?
Osw.   Because
You are now in truth my Master; you
    have taught me   1480
What there is not another living man
Had strength to teach;—and therefore
    gratitude
Is bold, and would relieve itself by praise.
Mar. Wherefore press this on me?
Osw.   Because I feel
That you have shown, and by a signal
    instance,   1485
How they who would be just must seek
    the rule
By diving for it into their own bosoms.
To-day you have thrown off a tyranny
That lives but in the torpid acquiescence
Of our emasculated souls, the tyranny
Of the world's masters, with the musty
    rules   1491
By which they uphold their craft from
    age to age:
You have obeyed the only law that sense
Submits to recognise; the immediate law,
From the clear light of circumstances,
    flashed   1495
Upon an independent Intellect.
Henceforth new prospects open on your
    path;

Your faculties should grow with the
    demand;
I still will be your friend, will cleave to
    you
Through good and evil, obloquy and
    scorn,   1500
Oft as they dare to follow on your steps.
Mar. I would be left alone.
Osw. [*exultingly*]. I know your motives!
I am not of the world's presumptuous
    judges,
Who damn where they can neither see
    nor feel,
With a hard-hearted ignorance; your
    struggles   1505
I witness'd, and now hail your victory.
Mar. Spare me awhile that greeting.
Osw.   It may be
That some there are, squeamish half-
    thinking cowards,
Who will turn pale upon you, call you
    murderer,
And you will walk in solitude among
    them.   1510
A mighty evil for a strong-built mind!—
Join twenty tapers of unequal height
And light them joined, and you will see
    the less
How 'twill burn down the taller; and
    they all   1514
Shall prey upon the tallest. Solitude!—
The Eagle lives in Solitude!
Mar.   Even so,
The Sparrow so on the house-top, and I,
The weakest of God's creatures, stand
    resolved
To abide the issue of my act, alone.
Osw. Now would you? and for ever?—
    My young Friend,   1520
As time advances either we become
The prey or masters of our own past
    deeds.
Fellowship we *must* have, willing or no;
And if good Angels fail, slack in their
    duty,
Substitutes, turn our faces where we may,
Are still forthcoming; some which, though
    they bear   1526
Ill names, can render no ill services,
In recompense for what themselves re-
    quired.
So meet extremes in this mysterious
    world,
And opposites thus melt into each other.
Mar. Time, since Man first drew breath,
    has never moved   1531
With such a weight upon his wings as
    now;
But they will soon be lightened.
Osw.   Ay, look up—
Cast round you your mind's eye, and you
    will learn
Fortitude is the child of Enterprise: 1535
Great actions move our admiration, chiefly

Because they carry in themselves an
    earnest
That we can suffer greatly.
Mar.   Very true.
Osw. Action is transitory—a step, a
    blow,
The motion of a muscle—this way or
    that—   1540
'Tis done, and in the after-vacancy
We wonder at ourselves like men be-
    trayed:
Suffering is permanent, obscure and dark,
And shares the nature of infinity.
Mar. Truth—and I feel it.
Osw.   What! if you had bid
Eternal farewell to unmingled joy   1546
And the light dancing of the thoughtless
    heart;
It is the toy of fools, and little fit
For such a world as this. The wise ab-
    jure
All thoughts whose idle composition lives
In the entire forgetfulness of pain.   1551
—I see I have disturbed you.
Mar.   By no means.
Osw. Compassion!—pity!—pride can
    do without them;
And what if you should never know them
    more!—
He is a puny soul who, feeling pain, 1555
Finds ease because another feels it too.
If e'er I open out this heart of mine
It shall be for a nobler end—to teach
And not to purchase puling sympathy.
—Nay, you are pale.
Mar.   It may be so.
Osw.   Remorse—
It cannot live with thought; think on,
    think on,   1561
And it will die. What! in this universe,
Where the least things control the great-
    est, where
The faintest breath that breathes can
    move a world;
What! feel remorse, where, if a cat had
    sneezed,   1565
A leaf had fallen, the thing had never
    been
Whose very shadow gnaws us to the
    vitals.
Mar. Now, whither are you wandering?
    That a man,
So used to suit his language to the time,
Should thus so widely differ from him-
    self—   1570
It is most strange.
Osw. Murder!—what's in the word!—
I have no cases by me ready made
To fit all deeds. Carry him to the Camp!—
A shallow project;—you of late have seen
More deeply, taught us that the insti-
    tutes   1575
Of Nature, by a cunning usurpation
Banished from human intercourse, exist

51

Only in our relations to the brutes
That make the fields their dwelling. If
 a snake
Crawl from beneath our feet we do not ask
A license to destroy him: our good gover-
 nors 1581
Hedge in the life of every pest and plague
That bears the shape of man; and for
 what purpose,
But to protect themselves from extirpa-
 tion?—
This flimsy barrier you have overleaped.
 Mar. My Office is fulfilled—the Man is
 now 1586
Delivered to the Judge of all things.
 Osw. Dead!
 Mar. I have borne my burthen to its
 destined end.
 Osw. This instant we'll return to our
 Companions—
Oh how I long to see their faces again!

Enter IDONEA *with* Pilgrims *who continue
 their journey*

Idon. [*after some time*]. What, Marma-
 duke! now thou art mine for ever.
And Oswald, too! [*To* MARMADUKE.] On
 will we to my Father 1592
With the glad tidings which this day
 hath brought;
We'll go together, and, such proof received
Of his own rights restored, his gratitude
To God above will make him feel for ours.
 Osw. I interrupt you?
 Idon. Think not so.
 Mar. Idonea,
That I should ever live to see this mo-
 ment!
 Idon. Forgive me.—Oswald knows it
 all—he knows,
Each word of that unhappy letter fell 1600
As a blood-drop from my heart.
 Osw. 'Twas even so.
 Mar. I have much to say, but for
 whose ear?—not thine.
 Idon. Ill can I bear that look—Plead
 for me, Oswald!
You are my Father's Friend.
 [*To* MARMADUKE]. Alas, you know not,
And never *can* you know, how much he
 loved me. 1605
Twice had he been to me a father, twice
Had given me breath, and was I not to be
His daughter, once his daughter? could I
 withstand
His pleading face, and feel his clasping
 arms,
And hear his prayer that I would not for-
 sake him 1610
In his old age—— [*Hides her face.*
 Mar. Patience—Heaven grant
 me patience!—
She weeps, she weeps—*my* brain shall
 burn for hours

Ere *I* can shed a tear.
 Idon. I was a woman;
And, balancing the hopes that are the
 dearest
To womankind with duty to my Father,
I yielded up those precious hopes, which
 nought 1616
On earth could else have wrested from
 me;—if erring,
Oh let me be forgiven!
 Mar. I *do* forgive thee.
 Idon. But take me to your arms—this
 breast, alas!
It throbs, and you have a heart that does
 not feel it. 1620
 Mar. [*exultingly*]. She is innocent.
 [*He embraces her.*
 Osw. [*aside*]. Were I a Moralist,
I should make wondrous revolution here;
It were a quaint experiment to show
The beauty of truth— [*Addressing them.*
 I see I interrupt you;
I shall have business with you, Marma-
 duke; 1625
Follow me to the Hostel. [*Exit* OSWALD.
 Idon. Marmaduke,
This is a happy day. My Father soon
Shall sun himself before his native doors;
The lame, the hungry, will be welcome
 there.
No more shall he complain of wasted
 strength, 1630
Of thoughts that fail, and a decaying
 heart;
His good works will be balm and life to
 him.
 Mar. This is most strange!—I know
 not what it was,
But there was something which most
 plainly said 1634
That thou wert innocent.
 Idon. How innocent!—
Oh heavens! you've been deceived.
 Mar. Thou art a Woman
To bring perdition on the universe.
 Idon. Already I've been punished to
 the height
Of my offence. [*Smiling affectionately.*
 I see you love me still,
The labours of my hand are still your joy;
Bethink you of the hour when on your
 shoulder 1641
I hung this belt.
 [*Pointing to the belt on which was
 suspended* HERBERT'S *scrip.*
 Mar. Mercy of Heaven! [*Sinks.*
 Idon. What ails you! [*Distractedly.*
 Mar. The scrip that held his food, and
 I forgot
To give it back again!
 Idon. What mean your words?
 Mar. I know not what I said—all may
 be well. 1645
 Idon. That smile hath life in it!

Mar.   This road is perilous;
I will attend you to a Hut that stands
Near the wood's edge—rest there to-night,
        I pray you:
For me, I have business, as you heard,
        with Oswald,   1649
But will return to you by break of day.
                                    [*Exeunt.*

ACT IV

SCENE, *A desolate prospect—a ridge of
rocks—a Chapel on the summit of one—
Moon behind the rocks—night stormy—
irregular sound of a bell*—HERBERT
enters exhausted

Her. That Chapel-bell in mercy seemed
        to guide me,
But now it mocks my steps; its fitful
        stroke
Can scarcely be the work of human hands.
Hear me, ye Men upon the cliffs, if such
There be who pray nightly before the
        Altar.   1655
Oh that I had but strength to reach the
        place!
My Child—my Child—dark—dark—I
        faint—this wind—
These stifling blasts—God help me!

Enter ELDRED

Eld.   Better this bare rock,
Though it were tottering over a man's
        head,
Than a tight case of dungeon walls for
        shelter   1660
From such rough dealing.
                [*A moaning voice is heard.*
        Ha! what sound is that?
Trees creaking in the wind (but none are
        here)
Send forth such noises—and that weary
        bell!
Surely some evil Spirit abroad to-night
Is ringing it—'twould stop a Saint in
        prayer,   1665
And that—what is it? never was sound
        so like
A human groan. Ha! what is here?
        Poor Man—
Murdered! alas! speak—speak, I am your
        friend:
No answer—hush—lost wretch, he lifts
        his hand
And lays it to his heart—[*Kneels to him*].
        I pray you speak!   1670
What has befallen you?
        Her. [*feebly*]. A stranger has done this,
And in the arms of a stranger I must die.
        Eld. Nay, think not so: come, let me
        raise you up: [*Raises him.*
This is a dismal place—well—that is
        well—   1674
I was too fearful—take me for your guide

And your support—my hut is not far off.
        [*Draws him gently off the stage.*

SCENE, *A room in the Hostel*—
        MARMADUKE *and* OSWALD

Mar. But for Idonea!—I have cause to
        think
That she is innocent.
        Osw.   Leave that thought awhile
As one of those beliefs which in their
        hearts
Lovers lock up as pearls, though oft no
        better   1680
Than feathers clinging to their points of
        passion.
This day's event has laid on me the duty
Of opening out my story; you must hear
        it,
And without further preface.—In my
        youth,
Except for that abatement which is paid
By envy as a tribute to desert,   1686
I was the pleasure of all hearts, the dar-
        ling
Of every tongue—as you are now. You've
        heard
That I embarked for Syria. On our
        voyage
Was hatched among the crew a foul Con-
        spiracy   1690
Against my honour, in the which our
        Captain
Was, I believed, prime Agent. The wind
        fell;
We lay becalmed week after week, until
The water of the vessel was exhausted;
I felt a double fever in my veins,   1695
Yet rage suppressed itself;—to a deep
        stillness
Did my pride tame my pride;—for many
        days,
On a dead sea under a burning sky,
I brooded o'er my injuries, deserted
By man and nature;—if a breeze had
        blown,   1700
It might have found its way into my
        heart,
And I had been—no matter—do you
        mark me?
        Mar. Quick—to the point—if any un-
        told crime
Doth haunt your memory,
        Osw.   Patience, hear me further!—
One day in silence did we drift at
        noon   1705
By a bare rock, narrow, and white, and
        bare;
No food was there, no drink, no grass, no
        shade,
No tree, nor jutting eminence, nor form
Inanimate large as the body of man,
Nor any living thing whose lot of life 1710
Might stretch beyond the measure of one
        moon.

To dig for water on the spot, the Captain
Landed with a small troop, myself being
  one:
There I reproached him with his trea-
  chery.
Imperious at all times, his temper rose;
He struck me; and that instant had I
  killed him,   1716
And put an end to his insolence, but my
  Comrades
Rushed in between us: then did I insist
(All hated him, and I was stung to mad-
  ness)
That we should leave him there, alive!—
  we did so.   1720
  Mar. And he was famished?
  Osw.   Naked was the spot;
Methinks I see it now—how in the sun
Its stony surface glittered like a shield;
And in that miserable place we left him,
Alone but for a swarm of minute crea-
  tures   1725
Not one of which could help him while
  alive,
Or mourn him dead.
  Mar.   A man by men cast off,
Left without burial! nay, not dead nor
  dying,
But standing, walking, stretching forth
  his arms,
In all things like ourselves but in the
  agony   1730
With which he called for mercy; and—
  even so—
He was forsaken?
  Osw.   There is a power in sounds:
The cries he uttered might have stopped
  the boat
That bore us through the water——
  Mar.   You returned
Upon that dismal hearing—did you not?
  Osw. Some scoffed at him with hellish
  mockery,   1736
And laughed so loud it seemed that the
  smooth sea
Did from some distant region echo us.
  Mar. We all are of one blood, our
  veins are filled
At the same poisonous fountain!
  Osw.   'Twas an island
Only by sufferance of the winds and
  waves,   1741
Which with their foam could cover it at
  will.
I know not how he perished; but the
  calm,
The same dead calm, continued many days.
  Mar. But his own crime had brought
  on him this doom,   1745
His wickedness prepared it; these expe-
  dients
Are terrible, yet ours is not the fault.
  Osw. The man was famished, and was
  innocent!

  Mar. Impossible!
  Osw. The man had never wronged me.
  Mar. Banish the thought, crush it, and
  be at peace.   1750
His guilt was marked—these things could
  never be
Were there not eyes that see, and for
  good ends,
Where ours are baffled.
  Osw.   I had been deceived.
  Mar. And from that hour the miser-
  able man   1754
No more was heard of?
  Osw.   I had been betrayed.
  Mar. And he found no deliverance!
  Osw.   The Crew
Gave me a hearty welcome; they had laid
The plot to rid themselves, at any cost,
Of a tyrannic Master whom they loathed.
So we pursued our voyage: when we
  landed,   1760
The tale was spread abroad; my power
  at once
Shrunk from me; plans and schemes, and
  lofty hopes—
All vanished. I gave way—do you attend?
  Mar. The Crew deceived you?
  Osw.   Nay, command yourself.
  Mar. It is a dismal night—how the
  wind howls!   1765
  Osw. I hid my head within a Convent,
  there
Lay passive as a dormouse in mid winter.
That was no life for me—I was o'er-
  thrown,
But not destroyed.
  Mar.   The proofs—you ought
  to have seen
The guilt—have touched it—felt it at
  your heart—   1770
As I have done.
  Osw.   A fresh tide of Crusaders
Drove by the place of my retreat: three
  nights
Did constant meditation dry my blood;
Three sleepless nights I passed in sound-
  ing on,
Through words and things, a dim and
  perilous way;   1775
And, wheresoe'er I turned me, I beheld
A slavery compared to which the dungeon
And clanking chains are perfect liberty.
You understand me—I was comforted;
I saw that every possible shape of ac-
  tion   1780
Might lead to good—I saw it and burst
  forth,
Thirsting for some of those exploits that
  fill
The earth for sure redemption of lost
  peace.
    [*Marking* MARMADUKE'S *countenance.*
Nay, you have had the worst. Ferocity
Subsided in a moment, like a wind   1785

54

That drops down dead out of a sky it
    vexed.
And yet I had within me evermore
A salient spring of energy; I mounted
From action up to action with a mind
That never rested—without meat or
    drink   1790
Have I lived many days—my sleep was
    bound
To purposes of reason—not a dream
But had a continuity and substance
That waking life had never power to give.
    Mar. O wretched Human-kind!—
    Until the mystery   1795
Of all this world is solved, well may we
    envy
The worm, that, underneath a stone
    whose weight
Would crush the lion's paw with mortal
    anguish,
Doth lodge, and feed, and coil, and sleep,
    in safety.
Fell not the wrath of Heaven upon those
    traitors?   1800
    Osw. Give not to them a thought.
    From Palestine
We marched to Syria: oft I left the Camp,
When all that multitude of hearts was
    still,
And followed on, through woods of
    gloomy cedar,
Into deep chasms troubled by roaring
    streams;   1805
Or from the top of Lebanon surveyed
The moonlight desert, and the moonlight
    sea:
In these my lonely wanderings I perceived
What mighty objects do impress their
    forms
To elevate our intellectual being; 1810
And felt, if ought on earth deserved a
    curse,
'Tis that worst principle of ill which dooms
A thing so great to perish self-consumed.
—So much for my remorse!
    Mar.   Unhappy Man!
    Osw. When from these forms I turned
    to contemplate   1815
The World's opinions and her usages,
I seemed a Being who had passed alone
Into a region of futurity,
Whose natural element was freedom——
    Mar.   Stop—
I may not, cannot, follow thee.
    Osw.   You must.   1820
I had been nourished by the sickly food
Of popular applause. I now perceived
That we are praised, only as men in us
Do recognise some image of themselves,
An abject counterpart of what they are,
Or the empty thing that they would wish
    to be.   1826
I felt that merit has no surer test
Than obloquy; that, if we wish to serve

The world in substance, not deceive by
    show,
We must become obnoxious to its hate,
Or fear disguised in simulated scorn. 1831
    Mar. I pity, can forgive, you; but
    those wretches—
That monstrous perfidy!
    Osw.   Keep down your wrath.
False Shame discarded, spurious Fame
    despised,
Twin sisters both of Ignorance, I found
Life stretched before me smooth as some
    broad way   1836
Cleared for a monarch's progress. Priests
    might spin
Their veil, but not for me—'twas in fit
    place
Among its kindred cobwebs. I had been,
And in that dream had left my native
    land,   1840
One of Love's simple bondsmen—the soft
    chain
Was off for ever; and the men, from
    whom
This liberation came, you would destroy:
Join me in thanks for their blind services.
    Mar. 'Tis a strange aching that, when
    we would curse   1845
And cannot.—You have betrayed me—I
    have done—
I am content—I know that he is guilt-
    less—
That both are guiltless, without spot or
    stain,
Mutually consecrated. Poor old Man!
And I had heart for this, because thou
    lovedst   1850
Her who from very infancy had been
Light to thy path, warmth to thy blood!—
Together   [*Turning to* OSWALD.
We propped his steps, he leaned upon us
    both.
    Osw. Ay, we are coupled by a chain of
    adamant;
Let us be fellow-labourers, then, to en-
    large   1855
Man's intellectual empire. We subsist
In slavery; all is slavery; we receive
Laws, but we ask not whence those laws
    have come;
We need an inward sting to goad us on.
    Mar. Have you betrayed me? Speak
    to that.
    Osw.   The mask,   1860
Which for a season I have stooped to
    wear,
Must be cast off.—Know then that I was
    urged,
(For other impulse let it pass) was driven,
To seek for sympathy, because I saw
In you a mirror of my youthful self; 1865
I would have made us equal once again,
But that was a vain hope. You have
    struck home,

With a few drops of blood cut short the
business;
Therein for ever you must yield to me.
But what is done will save you from the
blank   1870
Of living without knowledge that you
live:
Now you are suffering—for the future
day,
'Tis his who will command it.—Think of
my story—
Herbert is *innocent*.
   Mar. [*in a faint voice, and doubtingly*].
              You do but echo
My own wild words?
   Osw.   Young Man, the seed must lie
Hid in the earth, or there can be no
harvest;   1876
'Tis Nature's law. What I have done in
darkness
I will avow before the face of day.
Herbert *is* innocent.
   Mar.   What fiend could prompt
This action? Innocent!—oh breaking
heart!—   1880
Alive or dead, I'll find him.   [*Exit.*
   Osw.   Alive—perdition! [*Exit.*

·SCENE, *The inside of a poor Cottage*
   ELEANOR *and* IDONEA *seated*

   Idon.   The storm beats hard—Mercy
for poor or rich,
Whose heads are shelterless in such a
night!
   A Voice without. Holla! to bed, good
Folks, within!
   Elea.   O save us!   1884
   Idon. What can this mean?
   Elea.   Alas, for my poor husband!—
We'll have a counting of our flocks to-
morrow;
The wolf keeps festival these stormy
nights:
Be calm, sweet Lady, they are wassailers
   [*The voices die away in the distance.*
Returning from their Feast—my heart
beats so—
A noise at midnight does *so* frighten me.
   Idon. Hush!   [*Listening.*
   Elea.   They are gone. On such
a night my husband,   1891
Dragged from his bed, was cast into a
dungeon,
Where, hid from me, he counted many
years,
A criminal in no one's eyes but theirs—
Not even in theirs—whose brutal vio-
lence   1895
So dealt with him.
   Idon.   I have a noble Friend
First among youths of knightly breeding,
One
Who lives but to protect the weak or in-
jured.

There again!   [*Listening.*
   Elea.   'Tis my husband's foot.
   Good Eldred   1899
Has a kind heart; but his imprisonment
Has made him fearful, and he'll never be
The man he was.
   Idon.   I will retire;—good night!
                  [*She goes within.*

   Enter ELDRED [*hides a bundle*].
   Eld. Not yet in bed, Eleanor!—there
are stains in that frock which must be
washed out.   1905
   Elea. What has befallen you?
   Eld. I am belated, and you must know
the cause—[*speaking low*] that is the
blood of an unhappy Man.
   Elea. Oh! we are undone for ever. 1910
   Eld. Heaven forbid that I should lift
my hand against any man. Eleanor, I
have shed tears to-night, and it comforts
me to think of it.
   Elea. Where, where is he?   1915
   Eld. I have done him no harm, but—it
will be forgiven me; it would not have
been so once.
   Elea. You have not *buried* anything?
You are no richer than when you left me?
   Eld. Be at peace; I am innocent. 1921
   Elea. Then God be thanked——
   [*A short pause; she falls upon his neck.*
   Eld. To-night I met with an old Man
lying stretched upon the ground—a sad
spectacle: I raised him up with the hope
that we might shelter and restore him.
   Elea. [*as if ready to run*]. Where is
he? You were not able to bring him *all*
the way with you; let us return, I can help
you.   1930
            [ELDRED *shakes his head.*
   Eld. He did not seem to wish for life:
as I was struggling on, by the light of the
moon I saw the stains of blood upon my
clothes—he waved his hand, as if it were
all useless; and I let him sink again to the
ground.   1936
   Elea. Oh that I had been by your side!
   Eld. I tell you his hands and his body
were cold—how could I disturb his last
moments? he strove to turn from me as
if he wished to settle into sleep.   1941
   Elea. But, for the stains of blood——
   Eld. He must have fallen, I fancy, for
his head was cut; but I think his malady
was cold and hunger.   1945
   Elea. Oh, Eldred, I shall never be able
to look up at this roof in storm or fair but
I shall tremble.
   Eld. Is it not enough that my ill stars
have kept me abroad to-night till this
hour? I come home, and this is my comfort!   1952
   Elea. But did he say nothing which
might have set you at ease?

Eld. I thought he grasped my hand while he was muttering something about his Child—his Daughter—[*starting as if he heard a noise*]. What is that?   1958

Elea. Eldred, you are a father.

Eld. God knows what was in my heart, and will not curse my son for my sake.

Elea. But you prayed by him? you waited the hour of his release?   1964

Eld. The night was wasting fast; I have no friend; I am spited by the world—his wound terrified me—if I had brought him along with me, and he had died in my arms!——I am sure I heard something breathing—and this chair! 1970

Elea. Oh, Eldred, you will die alone. You will have nobody to close your eyes—no hand to grasp your dying hand —I shall be in my grave. A curse will attend us all.   1975

Eld. Have you forgot your own troubles when I was in the dungeon?

Elea. And you left him alive?

Eld. Alive!—the damps of death were upon him—he could not have survived an hour.   1981

Elea. In the cold, cold night.

Eld. [*in a savage tone*]. Ay, and his head was bare; I suppose you would have had me lend my bonnet to cover it.—You will never rest till I am brought to a felon's end.   1987

Elea. Is there nothing to be done? cannot we go to the Convent?

Eld. Ay, and say at once that I murdered him!   1991

Elea. Eldred, I know that ours is the only house upon the Waste; let us take heart; this Man may be rich; and could he be saved by our means, his gratitude may reward us.   1996

Eld. 'Tis all in vain.

Elea. But let us make the attempt. This old Man may have a wife, and he may have children—let us return to the spot; we may restore him, and his eyes may yet open upon those that love him.   2003

Eld. He will never open them more; even when he spoke to me, he kept them firmly sealed, as if he had been blind.

Idon. [*rushing out*]. It is, it is, my Father—

Eld. We are betrayed!
                [*Looking at* IDONEA.

Elea. His Daughter!—God have mercy!
                [*Turning to* IDONEA.

Idon. [*sinking down*]. Oh! lift me up and carry me to the place.   2010 You are safe; the whole world shall not harm you.

Elea. This Lady is his Daughter.

Eld. [*moved*]. I'll lead you to the spot.

Idon. [*springing up*]. Alive! you heard him breathe? quick, quick—
                [*Exeunt.*

ACT V

SCENE, *A Wood on the edge of the Waste*

Enter OSWALD *and a* Forester

For. He leaned upon the bridge that spans the glen,   2015 And down into the bottom cast his eye, That fastened there, as it would check the current.

Osw. He listened too; did you not say he listened?

For. As if there came such moaning from the flood   2019 As is heard often after stormy nights.

Osw. But did he utter nothing?

For.   See him there!

MARMADUKE *appearing*

Mar. Buzz, buzz, ye black and winged freebooters! That is no substance which ye settle on!

For. His senses play him false; and see, his arms Outspread, as if to save himself from falling!—   2025 Some terrible phantom I believe is now Passing before him, such as God will not Permit to visit any but a man Who has been guilty of some horrid crime.
                [MARMADUKE *disappears.*

Osw. The game is up!—

For.   If it be needful, Sir,   2030 I will assist you to lay hands upon him.

Osw. No, no, my Friend, you may pursue your business— 'Tis a poor wretch of an unsettled mind, Who has a trick of straying from his keepers; We must be gentle. Leave him to my care.   [*Exit* Forester. If his own eyes play false with him, these freaks   2036 Of fancy shall be quickly tamed by mine; The goal is reached. My Master shall become A shadow of myself—made by myself.

SCENE, *The edge of the Moor*

MARMADUKE *and* ELDRED *enter from opposite sides*

Mar. [*raising his eyes and perceiving* ELDRED]. In any corner of this savage Waste   2040 Have you, good Peasant, seen a blind old Man?

Eld. I heard——

Mar. You heard him, where? when heard him?

Eld.   As you know,
The first hours of last night were rough
with storm;
I had been out in search of a stray heifer;
Returning late, I heard a moaning sound;
Then, thinking that my fancy had de-
ceived me,   2046
I hurried on, when straight a second moan,
A human voice distinct, struck on my ear.
So guided, distant a few steps, I found
An aged Man, and such as you describe.
Mar. You heard!—he called you to
him? Of all men   2051
The best and kindest!—but where is he?
guide me,
That I may see him.
Eld.   On a ridge of rocks
A lonesome Chapel stands, deserted now:
The bell is left, which no one dares re-
move;   2055
And, when the stormy wind blows o'er
the peak,
It rings, as if a human hand were there
To pull the cord. I guess he must have
heard it;
And it had led him towards the precipice,
To climb up to the spot whence the sound
came;   2060
But he had failed through weakness.
From his hand
His staff had dropped, and close upon the
brink
Of a small pool of water he was laid,
As if he had stooped to drink, and so
remained   2064
Without the strength to rise.
Mar.   Well, well, he lives,
And all is safe: what said he?
Eld.   But few words:
He only spake to me of a dear Daughter,
Who, so he feared, would never see him
more;
And of a Stranger to him, One by whom
He had been sore misused; but he forgave
The wrong and the wrong-doer. You are
troubled—   2071
Perhaps you are his son?
Mar.   The All-seeing knows,
I did not think he had a living Child.—
But whither did you carry him?
Eld.   He was torn,
His head was bruised, and there was
blood about him——   2075
Mar. That was no work of mine.
Eld.   Nor was it mine.
Mar. But had he strength to walk? I
could have borne him
A thousand miles.
Eld.   I am in poverty,
And know how busy are the tongues of
men;
My heart was willing, Sir, but I am one
Whose good deeds will not stand by their
own light;   2081

And, though it smote me more than
words can tell,
I left him.
Mar. I believe that there are phantoms,
That in the shape of man do cross our
path
On evil instigation, to make sport   2085
Of our distress—and thou art one of them!
But things substantial have so pressed on
me——
Eld. My wife and children came into
my mind.
Mar. Oh Monster! Monster! there are
three of us,
And we shall howl together.
                  [*After a pause and in a feeble voice.*
                  I am deserted
At my worst need, my crimes have in a
net   2091
[*Pointing to* ELDRED] Entangled this poor
man? Where was it? where?
                  [*Dragging him along.*
Eld. 'Tis needless; spare your violence.
His Daughter——
Mar. Ay, in the word a thousand scor-
pions lodge:
This old man *had* a Daughter.
Eld.   To the spot   2095
I hurried back with her.—Oh save me, Sir,
From such a journey!——there was a
black tree,
A single tree; she thought it was her
Father.—
Oh Sir, I would not see that hour again
For twenty lives. The daylight dawned,
and now——   2100
Nay; hear my tale, 'tis fit that you should
hear it—
As we approached, a solitary crow
Rose from the spot;—the Daughter clap-
ped her hands,
And then I heard a shriek so terrible
                  [MARMADUKE *shrinks back.*
The startled bird quivered upon the wing.
Mar. Dead, dead!—
Eld. [*after a pause*]. A dismal matter,
Sir, for me,   2106
And seems the like for you; if 'tis your
wish,
I'll lead you to his Daughter; but 'twere
best
That she should be prepared; I'll go be-
fore.
Mar. There will be need of preparation.
                  [ELDRED *goes off.*
Elea. [*enters*].   Master!
Your limbs sink under you, shall I sup-
port you?   2111
Mar. [*taking her arm*]. Woman, I've
lent my body to the service
Which now thou tak'st upon thee. God
forbid
That thou shouldst ever meet a like occa-
sion

58

With such a purpose in thine heart as
        mine was.   2115
Elea. Oh, why have I to do with things
        like these?   [*Exeunt.*
SCENE *changes to the door of* ELDRED'S
cottage—IDONEA *seated—enter* ELDRED
Eld. Your Father, Lady, from a wilful
        hand
Has met unkindness; so indeed he told
        me,
And you remember such was my report:
From what has just befallen me I have
        cause   2120
To fear the very worst.
    Idon.   My Father is dead;
Why dost thou come to me with words
        like these?
    Eld. A wicked Man should answer for
        his crimes.
    Idon. Thou seest me what I am.
    Eld.   It was most heinous,
And doth call out for vengeance.
    Idon.   Do not add,
I prithee, to the harm thou'st done al-
        ready.   2126
    Eld. Hereafter you will thank me for
        this service.
Hard by a Man I met, who, from plain
        proofs
Of interfering Heaven, I have no doubt,
Laid hands upon your Father. Fit it were
You should prepare to meet him.
    Idon.   I have nothing 2131
To do with others; help me to my Father—
    [*She turns and sees* MARMADUKE *leaning
        on* ELEANOR—*throws herself upon his
        neck, and after some time,*
In joy I met thee, but a few hours past;
And thus we meet again; one human stay
Is left me still in thee. Nay, shake not so.
    Mar. In such a wilderness—to see no
        thing,   2136
No, not the pitying moon!
    Idon.   And perish so.
    Mar. Without a dog to moan for him.
    Idon.   Think not of it,
But enter there and see him how he sleeps,
Tranquil as he had died in his own bed.
    Mar. Tranquil—why not?
    Idon.   Oh, peace!
    Mar.   He is at peace; 2141
His body is at rest: there was a plot,
A hideous plot, against the soul of man:
It took effect—and yet I baffled it,
In *some* degree.
    Idon.   Between us stood, I thought,
A cup of consolation, filled from Heaven
For both our needs; must I, and in thy
        presence,   2147
Alone partake of it?—Belovèd Marma-
        duke!
    Mar. Give me a reason why the wisest
        thing

That the earth owns shall never choose to
        die,   2150
But some one must be near to count his
        groans.
The wounded deer retires to solitude,
And dies in solitude: all things but man,
All die in solitude.
        [*Moving towards the cottage door.*
                Mysterious God,
If she had never lived I had not done it!—
    Idon. Alas, the thought of such a cruel
        death   2156
Has overwhelmed him.—I must follow.
    Eld.   Lady!
You will do well; [*she goes*] unjust sus-
        picion may
Cleave to this Stranger: if, upon his
        entering,
The dead Man heave a groan, or from his
        side   2160
Uplift his hand—that would be evidence.
    Elea. Shame! Eldred, shame!
    Mar. [*both returning*]. The dead have
        but one face. [*To himself.*]
And such a Man—so meek and unoffend-
        ing—
Helpless and harmless as a babe: a Man
By obvious signal to the world's protec-
        tion   2165
Solemnly dedicated—to decoy him!—
    Idon. Oh, had you seen him living!—
    Mar.   I (so filled
With horror is this world) am unto thee
The thing most precious that it now con-
        tains:
Therefore through me alone must be re-
        vealed   2170
By whom thy Parent was destroyed,
        Idonea!
I have the proofs!—
    Idon.   O miserable Father!
Thou didst command me to bless all man-
        kind;
Nor to this moment have I ever wished
Evil to any living thing; but hear me,
Hear me, ye Heavens!—[*kneeling*]—may
        vengeance haunt the fiend   2176
For this most cruel murder: let him live
And move in terror of the elements;
The thunder send him on his knees to
        prayer
In the open streets, and let him think he
        sees,   2180
If e'er he entereth the house of God,
The roof, self-moved, unsettling o'er his
        head;
And let him, when he would lie down at
        night,
Point to his wife the blood-drops on his
        pillow!
    Mar. My voice was silent, but my heart
        hath joined thee.   2185
    Idon. [*leaning on* MARMADUKE]. Left
        to the mercy of that savage Man!

How could he call upon his Child!—O
Friend!   [*Turns to* MARMADUKE.
My faithful true and only Comforter.
Mar. Ay, come to me and weep.
                    [*He kisses her.*
[*To* Eldred]. Yes, Varlet, look,
The devils at such sights do clap their
hands.   [ELDRED *retires alarmed.*
Idon. Thy vest is torn, thy cheek is
deadly pale;   2191
Hast thou pursued the monster?
Mar.   I have found him.—
Oh! would that thou hadst perished in
the flames!
Idon. Here art thou, then can I be
desolate?
Mar. There was a time, when this
protecting hand   2195
Availed against the mighty; never more
Shall blessings wait upon a deed of mine.
Idon. Wild words for me to hear, for
me, an orphan,   2198
Committed to thy guardianship by Heaven;
And, if thou hast forgiven me, let me hope,
In this deep sorrow, trust, that I am thine
For closer care;—here, is no malady.
                    [*Taking his arm.*
Mar. There, *is* a malady—
[*Striking his heart and forehead.*] And
here, and here,
A mortal malady. I am accurst:
All nature curses me, and in my heart
Thy curse is fixed; the truth must be laid
bare.   2206
It must be told, and borne. I am the man,
(Abused, betrayed, but how it matters not)
Presumptuous above all that ever breathed,
Who, casting as I thought a guilty Person
Upon Heaven's righteous judgment, did
become   2211
An instrument of Fiends. Through me,
through me,
Thy Father perished.
Idon.   Perished—by what mischance?
Mar. Belovèd! if I dared, so would I
call thee—
Conflict must cease, and, in thy frozen
heart,   2215
The extremes of suffering meet in absolute
peace.   [*He gives her a letter.*
Idon. [*reads*] 'Be not surprised if you
hear that some signal judgment has be-
fallen the man who calls himself your
father; he is now with me, as his signa-
ture will show: abstain from conjecture
till you see me.
                        'HERBERT.
                        'MARMADUKE.'
The writing Oswald's; the signature my
Father's: 2225
[*Looks steadily at the paper*] And here is
yours,—or do my eyes deceive me?
You have then seen my Father?
Mar.   He has leaned

Upon this arm.
Idon. You led him towards the Convent?
Mar. That Convent was Stone-Arthur
Castle. Thither
We were his guides. I on that night re-
solved   2230
That he should wait thy coming till the day
Of resurrection.
Idon.   Miserable Woman,
Too quickly moved, too easily giving way,
I put denial on thy suit, and hence, 2234
With the disastrous issue of last night,
Thy perturbation, and these frantic words.
Be calm, I pray thee!
Mar.   Oswald—
Idon.   Name him not.

Enter female Beggar

Beg. And he is dead!—that Moor—
how shall I cross it?
By night, by day, never shall I be able,
To travel half a mile alone.—Good Lady!
Forgive me!—Saints forgive me. Had I
thought
It would have come to this!—
Idon. What brings you hither? speak!
Beg. [*pointing to* MARMADUKE]. This
innocent Gentleman. Sweet hea-
vens! I told him
Such tales of your dead Father!—God is
my judge,
I thought there was no harm: but that
bad Man,   2245
He bribed me with his gold, and looked
so fierce.
Mercy! I said I know not what—oh pity
me—
I said, sweet Lady, you were not his
Daughter—
Pity me, I am haunted;—thrice this day
My conscience made me wish to be struck
blind;   2250
And then I would have prayed, and had
no voice.
Idon. [*to* MARMADUKE]. Was it my Fa-
ther?—no, no, no, for he
Was meek and patient, old and blind,
Helpless, and loved me dearer than his life.
—But hear me. For *one* question, I have
a heart   2255
That will sustain me. Did you murder
him?
Mar. No, not by stroke of arm. But
learn the process:
Proof after proof was pressed upon me;
guilt
Made evident, as seemed, by blacker guilt,
Whose impious folds enwrapped even
thee; and truth   2260
And innocence, embodied in his looks,
His words and tones and gestures, did
but serve
With me to aggravate his crimes, and
heaped

Ruin upon the cause for which they
pleaded.
Then pity crossed the path of my resolve:
Confounded, I looked up to Heaven, and
cast,   2266
Idonea! thy blind Father on the Ordeal
Of the bleak Waste—left him— and so he
died!
  [IDONEA *sinks senseless;* Beggar,
  ELEANOR, *&c., crowd round, and
  bear her off.*
Why may we speak these things, and do
no more;
Why should a thrust of the arm have
such a power,   2270
And words that tell these things be heard
in vain?
She is not dead. Why!—if I loved this
Woman,
I would take care she never woke again;
But she WILL wake, and she will weep for
me,
And say no blame was mine—and so, poor
fool,   2275
Will waste her curses on another name.
  [*He walks about distractedly.*

   Enter OSWALD

Osw. [*to himself*]. Strong to o'erturn,
strong also to build up.
    [*To* MARMADUKE.
The starts and sallies of our last encounter
Were natural enough; but that, I trust,
Is all gone by. You have cast off the
chains   2280
That fettered your nobility of mind—
Delivered heart and head!
    Let us to Palestine;
This is a paltry field for enterprise.
Mar. Ay, what shall we encounter next?
This issue—
'Twas nothing more than darkness deepen-
ing darkness,   2285
And weakness crowned with the impo-
tence of death!—
Your pupil is, you see, an apt proficient
[*ironically*].
Start not!—Here is another face hard by;
Come, let us take a peep at both together,
And, with a voice at which the dead will
quake,   2290
Resound the praise of your morality—
Of this too much.
  [*Drawing* OSWALD *towards the Cot-
  tage—stops short at the door.*
   Men are there, millions, Oswald,
Who with bare hands would have plucked
out thy heart
And flung it to the dogs: but I am raised
Above, or sunk below, all further sense
Of provocation. Leave me, with the weight
Of that old Man's forgiveness on thy heart,
Pressing as heavily as it doth on mine.

Coward I have been; know, there lies not
now,   2299
Within the compass of a mortal thought,
A deed that I would shrink from;—but
to endure,
That is my destiny. May it be thine:
Thy office, thy ambition, be henceforth
To feed remorse, to welcome every sting
Of penitential anguish, yea with tears.
When seas and continents shall lie be-
tween us—   2306
The wider space the better—we may find
In such a course fit links of sympathy,
An incommunicable rivalship
Maintained, for peaceful ends beyond our
view.   2310
  [*Confused voices—several of the band
  enter—rush upon* OSWALD *and seize
  him.*
  One of them. I would have dogged him
to the jaws of hell—
  Osw. Ha! is it so!—That vagrant
Hag!—this comes
Of having left a thing like her alive!
        [*Aside.*
  Several voices. Despatch him!
  Osw.   If I pass beneath a rock
And shout, and, with the echo of my voice,
Bring down a heap of rubbish, and it
crush me,   2316
I die without dishonour. Famished,
starved,
A Fool and Coward blended to my wish!
  [*Smiles scornfully and exultingly at
  *MARMADUKE.
  Wal. 'Tis done! [*stabs him*].
  Another of the band. The ruthless traitor!
  Mar.   A rash deed!—
With that reproof I do resign a station
Of which I have been proud.
  Wil. [*approaching* MARMADUKE]. O my
poor Master!   2321
  Mar. Discerning Monitor, my faithful
Wilfred,
Why art thou here? [*Turning to* WALLACE.
    Wallace, upon these Borders,
Many there be whose eyes will not want
cause
To weep that I am gone. Brothers in
arms!   2325
Raise on that dreary Waste a monument
That may record my story: nor let words—
Few must they be, and delicate in their
touch
As light itself—be there withheld from
Her
Who, through most wicked arts, was made
an orphan   2330
By One who would have died a thousand
times
To shield her from a moment's harm. To
you,
Wallace and Wilfred, I commend the
Lady,

        61

By lowly nature reared, as if to make her
In all things worthier of that noble birth,
Whose long-suspended rights are now on
   the eve   2336
Of restoration: with your tenderest care
Watch over her, I pray—sustain her——
  Several of the band [eagerly]. Captain!
  Mar. No more of that; in silence hear
  my doom:
A hermitage has furnished fit relief   2340
To some offenders; other penitents,
Less patient in their wretchedness, have
  fallen,
Like the old Roman, on their own sword's
  point.

They had their choice: a wanderer *must*
  I go,
The Spectre of that innocent Man, my
  guide.   2345
No human ear shall ever hear me speak;
No human dwelling ever give me food,
Or sleep, or rest: but over waste and wild,
In search of nothing that this earth can
  give,
But expiation, will I wander on—   2350
A Man by pain and thought compelled to
  live,
Yet loathing life—till anger is appeased
In Heaven, and Mercy gives me leave to
  die.

POEMS REFERRING TO THE PERIOD OF CHILDHOOD

I

[Composed March 26, 1802.—Published 1807.]

MY heart leaps up when I behold
  A rainbow in the sky:
So was it when my life began;
So is it now I am a man;
So be it when I shall grow old,   5
  Or let me die!
The Child is father of the Man;
And I could wish my days to be
Bound each to each by natural piety.

II

TO A BUTTERFLY

[Composed March 14, 1802.—Published 1807.]

STAY near me—do not take thy flight!
A little longer stay in sight!
Much converse do I find in thee,
Historian of my infancy!
Float near me; do not yet depart!   5
Dead times revive in thee:
Thou bring'st, gay creature as thou art!
A solemn image to my heart,
My father's family!

Oh! pleasant, pleasant were the days,   10
The time, when in our childish plays,
My sister Emmeline[1] and I
Together chased the butterfly!
A very hunter did I rush
Upon the prey;—with leaps and springs 15
I followed on from brake to bush;
But she, God love her! feared to brush
The dust from off its wings.

III

THE SPARROW'S NEST

[Composed 1801.—Published 1807.]

BEHOLD, within the leafy shade,
Those bright blue eggs together laid!

On me the chance-discovered sight
Gleamed like a vision of delight.
I started—seeming to espy   5
The home and sheltered bed,
The Sparrow's dwelling, which, hard by
My Father's house, in wet or dry
My sister Emmeline[1] and I
  Together visited.   10

She looked at it and seemed to fear it;
Dreading, tho' wishing, to be near it:
Such heart was in her, being then
A little Prattler among men.
The Blessing of my later years   15
Was with me when a boy:
She gave me eyes, she gave me ears;
And humble cares, and delicate fears;
A heart, the fountain of sweet tears;
  And love, and thought, and joy. 20

IV

FORESIGHT

[Composed April 28, 1802.—Published 1807.]

THAT is work of waste and ruin—
Do as Charles and I are doing!
Strawberry-blossoms, one and all,
We must spare them—here are many:
Look at it—the flower is small,   5
Small and low, though fair as any:
Do not touch it! summers two
I am older, Anne, than you.

Pull the primrose, sister Anne!
Pull as many as you can.   10
—Here are daisies, take your fill;
Pansies, and the cuckoo-flower:
Of the lofty daffodil
Make your bed, or make your bower;
Fill your lap and fill your bosom;   15
Only spare the strawberry-blossom!

[1] See Editor's Note, p. 699.

Primroses, the Spring may love them—
Summer knows but little of them:
Violets, a barren kind,
Withered on the ground must lie;   20
Daisies leave no fruit behind
When the pretty flowerets die;
Pluck them, and another year
As many will be blowing here.

God has given a kindlier power   25
To the favoured strawberry-flower.
Hither soon as spring is fled
You and Charles and I will walk;
Lurking berries, ripe and red,
Then will hang on every stalk,   30
Each within its leafy bower;
And for that promise spare the flower!

V

CHARACTERISTICS OF A CHILD
THREE YEARS OLD

[Composed 1811.—Published 1815.]

LOVING she is, and tractable, though wild;
And Innocence hath privilege in her
To dignify arch looks and laughing eyes
And feats of cunning; and the pretty
      round
Of trespasses, affected to provoke   5
Mock-chastisement and partnership in
      play.
And, as a faggot sparkles on the hearth,
Not less if unattended and alone
Than when both young and old sit ga-
      thered round
And take delight in its activity;   10
Even so this happy Creature of herself
Is all-sufficient; solitude to her
Is blithe society, who fills the air
With gladness and involuntary songs.
Light are her sallies as the tripping
      fawn's   15
Forth-startled from the fern where she
      lay couched;
Unthought-of, unexpected, as the stir
Of the soft breeze ruffling the meadow-
      flowers,
Or from before it chasing wantonly
The many-coloured images imprest   20
Upon the bosom of a placid lake.

VI

ADDRESS TO A CHILD

DURING A BOISTEROUS WINTER EVENING

BY MY SISTER

[Composed 1806.—Published 1815.]

WHAT way does the Wind come? What
      way does he go?
He rides over the water, and over the
      snow,

THE PERIOD OF CHILDHOOD

Through wood, and through vale; and
      o'er rocky height,
Which the goat cannot climb, takes his
      sounding flight;
He tosses about in every bare tree,   5
As, if you look up, you plainly may see;
But how he will come, and whither he
      goes,
There's never a scholar in England knows.

He will suddenly stop in a cunning nook,
And ring a sharp 'larum;—but, if you
      should look,   10
There's nothing to see but a cushion of
      snow,
Round as a pillow, and whiter than milk,
And softer than if it were covered with
      silk.
Sometimes he'll hide in the cave of a
      rock,
Then whistle as shrill as the buzzard cock;
—Yet seek him,—and what shall you find
      in the place?   16
Nothing but silence and empty space;
Save, in a corner, a heap of dry leaves,
That he's left, for a bed, to beggars or
      thieves!

As soon as 'tis daylight to-morrow, with
      me   20
You shall go to the orchard, and then you
      will see
That he has been there, and made a great
      rout,
And cracked the branches, and strewn
      them about;
Heaven grant that he spare but that one
      upright twig
That looked up at the sky so proud and
      big   25
All last summer, as well you know,
Studded with apples, a beautiful show!

Hark! over the roof he makes a pause,
And growls as if he would fix his claws
Right in the slates, and with a huge
      rattle   30
Drive them down, like men in a battle:
—But let him range round; he does us no
      harm,
We build up the fire, we're snug and
      warm;
Untouched by his breath see the candle
      shines bright,
And burns with a clear and steady light;
Books have we to read,—but that half-
      stifled knell,   36
Alas! 'tis the sound of the eight o'clock
      bell.
—Come now we'll to bed! and when we
      are there
He may work his own will, and what
      shall we care?

63

He may knock at the door,—we'll not let
  him in;   40
May drive at the windows,—we'll laugh
  at his din;
Let him seek his own home wherever it be;
Here's a *cozie* warm house for Edward[1]
  and me.

VII

THE MOTHER'S RETURN

BY THE SAME

[Composed April or May, 1807.—Published 1815.]

A MONTH, sweet Little-ones, is past
Since your dear Mother went away,—
And she to-morrow will return;
To-morrow is the happy day.

O blessèd tidings! thought of joy!   5
The eldest heard with steady glee;
Silent he stood; then laughed amain,—
And shouted, 'Mother, come to me!'

Louder and louder did he shout,
With witless hope to bring her near!— 10
'Nay, patience! patience, little boy;
Your tender mother cannot hear.'

I told of hills, and far-off towns,
And long, long vales to travel through;
He listens, puzzled, sore perplexed,   15
But he submits; what can he do?

No strife disturbs his sister's breast;
She wars not with the mystery
Of time and distance, night and day;
The bonds of our humanity.   20

Her joy is like an instinct, joy
Of kitten, bird, or summer fly;
She dances, runs without an aim,
She chatters in her ecstasy.

Her brother now takes up the note,   25
And echoes back his sister's glee;
They hug the infant in my arms,
As if to force his sympathy.

Then, settling into fond discourse,
We rested in the garden bower;   30
While sweetly shone the evening sun
In his departing hour.

We told o'er all that we had done,—
Our rambles by the swift brook's side
Far as the willow-skirted pool,   35
Where two fair swans together glide.

We talked of change, of winter gone,
Of green leaves on the hawthorn spray,
Of birds that build their nests and sing,
And all 'since Mother went away!'   40

  [1] Edward = Johnnie, the household name of
Wordsworth's eldest son. See note on *To a Butterfly*,
p. 699.—ED.

To her these tales they will repeat,
To her our new-born tribes will show,
The goslings green, the ass's colt,
The lambs that in the meadow go.

—But see, the evening star comes forth!
To bed the children must depart;   46
A moment's heaviness they feel,
A sadness at the heart:

'Tis gone—and in a merry fit
They run up stairs in gamesome race; 50
I, too, infected by their mood,
I could have joined the wanton chase.

Five minutes past—and, O the change!
Asleep upon their beds they lie;
Their busy limbs in perfect rest,   55
And closed the sparkling eye.

VIII

ALICE FELL

OR, POVERTY

[Composed March 12, 13, 1802.—Published 1807.]

THE post-boy drove with fierce career,
For threatening clouds the moon had
  drowned;
When, as we hurried on, my ear
Was smitten with a startling sound

As if the wind blew many ways,   5
I heard the sound,—and more and more;
It seemed to follow with the chaise,
And still I heard it as before.

At length I to the boy called out;
He stopped his horses at the word,   10
But neither cry, nor voice, nor shout,
Nor aught else like it, could be heard.

The boy then smacked his whip, and fast
The horses scampered through the rain;
But, hearing soon upon the blast   15
The cry, I bade him halt again.

Forthwith alighting on the ground,
'Whence comes,' said I, 'this piteous
  moan?'
And there a little Girl I found,
Sitting behind the chaise, alone.   20

'My cloak!' no other word she spake,
But loud and bitterly she wept,
As if her innocent heart would break;
And down from off her seat she leapt.

'What ails you, child?'—she sobbed.
  'Look here!'   25
I saw it in the wheel entangled,
A weather-beaten rag as e'er
From any garden scare-crow dangled.

There, twisted between nave and spoke,
It hung, nor could at once be freed;　30
But our joint pains unloosed the cloak,
A miserable rag indeed!

'And whither are you going, child,
To-night along these lonesome ways?'
'To Durham,' answered she, half wild—
'Then come with me into the chaise.'　36

Insensible to all relief
Sat the poor girl, and forth did send
Sob after sob, as if her grief
Could never, never have an end.　40

'My child, in Durham do you dwell?'
She checked herself in her distress,
And said, 'My name is Alice Fell;
I'm fatherless and motherless.

'And I to Durham, Sir, belong.'　45
Again, as if the thought would choke
Her very heart, her grief grew strong;
And all was for her tattered cloak!

The chaise drove on; our journey's end
Was nigh; and, sitting by my side,　50
As if she had lost her only friend
She wept, nor would be pacified.

Up to the tavern-door we post;
Of Alice and her grief I told;
And I gave money to the host,　55
To buy a new cloak for the old.

'And let it be of duffil grey,
As warm a cloak as man can sell!'
Proud creature was she the next day,
The little orphan, Alice Fell!　60

IX
LUCY GRAY
OR, SOLITUDE
[Composed 1799.—Published 1800.]

OFT I had heard of Lucy Gray:
And, when I crossed the wild,
I chanced to see at break of day
The solitary child.

No mate, no comrade Lucy knew;　5
She dwelt on a wide moor,
—The sweetest thing that ever grew
Beside a human door!

You yet may spy the fawn at play,
The hare upon the green;　10
But the sweet face of Lucy Gray
Will never more be seen.

'To-night will be a stormy night—
You to the town must go;
And take a lantern, Child, to light　15
Your mother through the snow.'

'That, Father! will I gladly do:
'Tis scarcely afternoon—
The minster-clock has just struck two,
And yonder is the moon!'　20

At this the Father raised his hook,
And snapped a faggot-band;
He plied his work;—and Lucy took
The lantern in her hand.

Not blither is the mountain roe:　25
With many a wanton stroke
Her feet disperse the powdery snow,
That rises up like smoke.

The storm came on before its time:
She wandered up and down;　30
And many a hill did Lucy climb:
But never reached the town.

The wretched parents all that night
Went shouting far and wide;
But there was neither sound nor sight　35
To serve them for a guide.

At day-break on a hill they stood
That overlooked the moor;
And thence they saw the bridge of wood,
A furlong from their door.　40

They wept—and, turning homeward, cried,
'In heaven we all shall meet;'
—When in the snow the mother spied
The print of Lucy's feet.

Then downwards from the steep hill's
　　edge　45
They tracked the footmarks small;
And through the broken hawthorn hedge,
And by the long stone-wall;

And then an open field they crossed:
The marks were still the same;　50
They tracked them on, nor ever lost;
And to the bridge they came.

They followed from the snowy bank
Those footmarks, one by one,
Into the middle of the plank;　55
And further there were none!

—Yet some maintain that to this day
She is a living child;
That you may see sweet Lucy Gray
Upon the lonesome wild.　60

O'er rough and smooth she trips along,
And never looks behind;
And sings a solitary song
That whistles in the wind.

POEMS REFERRING TO

X

WE ARE SEVEN

[Composed 1798.—Published 1798.]

——A SIMPLE Child,
That lightly draws its breath,
And feels its life in every limb,
What should it know of death?

I met a little cottage Girl: 5
She was eight years old, she said;
Her hair was thick with many a curl
That clustered round her head.

She had a rustic, woodland air,
And she was wildly clad: 10
Her eyes were fair, and very fair;
—Her beauty made me glad.

'Sisters and brothers, little maid,
How many may you be?'
'How many? Seven in all,' she said,   15
And wondering looked at me.

'And where are they? I pray you tell.'
She answered, 'Seven are we;
And two of us at Conway dwell,
And two are gone to sea.   20

'Two of us in the church-yard lie,
My sister and my brother;
And, in the church-yard cottage, I
Dwell near them with my mother.'

'You say that two at Conway dwell,   25
And two are gone to sea,
Yet ye are seven! I pray you tell,
Sweet Maid, how this may be.'

Then did the little Maid reply,
'Seven boys and girls are we;   30
Two of us in the church-yard lie,
Beneath the church-yard tree.'

'You run about, my little Maid,
Your limbs they are alive;
If two are in the church-yard laid,   35
Then ye are only five.'

'Their graves are green, they may be
    seen,'
The little Maid replied,
'Twelve steps or more from my mother's
    door,
And they are side by side.   40

'My stockings there I often knit,
My kerchief there I hem;
And there upon the ground I sit,
And sing a song to them.

'And often after sun-set, Sir,   45
When it is light and fair,
I take my little porringer,
And eat my supper there.

'The first that died was sister Jane;
In bed she moaning lay,   50
Till God released her of her pain;
And then she went away.

'So in the church-yard she was laid;
And, when the grass was dry,
Together round her grave we played,   55
My brother John and I.

'And when the ground was white with
    snow,
And I could run and slide,
My brother John was forced to go,
And he lies by her side.'   60

'How many are you, then,' said I,
'If they two are in heaven?'
Quick was the little Maid's reply,
'O Master! we are seven.'

'But they are dead; those two are dead!
Their spirits are in heaven!'   66
'Twas throwing words away; for still
The little Maid would have her will,
And said, 'Nay, we are seven!'

XI

THE IDLE SHEPHERD-BOYS

OR, DUNGEON-GHYLL FORCE[1]

A PASTORAL

[Composed 1800.—Published 1800.]

THE valley rings with mirth and joy;
Among the hills the echoes play
A never never ending song,
To welcome in the May.
The magpie chatters with delight;   5
The mountain raven's youngling brood
Have left the mother and the nest;
And they go rambling east and west
In search of their own food;
Or through the glittering vapours dart   10
In very wantonness of heart.

Beneath a rock, upon the grass,
Two boys are sitting in the sun;
Their work, if any work they have,
Is out of mind—or done.   15
On pipes of sycamore they play
The fragments of a Christmas hymn;
Or with that plant which in our dale
We call stag-horn, or fox's tail,
Their rusty hats they trim: 20
And thus, as happy as the day,
Those Shepherds wear the time away.

[1] Ghyll, in the dialect of Cumberland and Westmoreland, is a short and, for the most part, a steep
narrow valley, with a stream running through it.
Force is the word universally employed in these
dialects for waterfall.

66

Along the river's stony marge
The sand-lark chants a joyous song;
The thrush is busy in the wood,   25
And carols loud and strong.
A thousand lambs are on the rocks,
All newly born! both earth and sky
Keep jubilee, and, more than all,
Those boys with their green coronal;   30
They never hear the cry,
That plaintive cry! which up the hill
Comes from the depth of Dungeon-Ghyll.

Said Walter, leaping from the ground,
'Down to the stump of yon old yew   35
We'll for our whistles run a race.'
——Away the shepherds flew;
They leapt—they ran—and when they
          came
Right opposite to Dungeon-Ghyll,   .
Seeing that he should lose the prize,   40
'Stop!' to his comrade Walter cries—
James stopped with no good will:
Said Walter then, exulting; 'Here
You'll find a task for half a year.   44

'Cross, if you dare, where I shall cross—
Come on, and tread where I shall tread.'
The other took him at his word,
And followed as he led.
It was a spot which you may see
If ever you to Langdale go;   50
Into a chasm a mighty block
Hath fallen, and made a bridge of rock:
The gulf is deep below;
And, in a basin black and small,
Receives a lofty waterfall.   55

With staff in hand across the cleft
The challenger pursued his march;
And now, all eyes and feet, hath gained
The middle of the arch.
When list! he hears a piteous moan—   60
Again!—his heart within him dies—
His pulse is stopped, his breath is lost,
He totters, pallid as a ghost,
And, looking down, espies
A lamb, that in the pool is pent   65
Within that black and frightful rent.

The lamb had slipped into the stream,
And safe without a bruise or wound
The cataract had borne him down
Into the gulf profound.   70
His dam had seen him when he fell,
She saw him down the torrent borne;
And, while with all a mother's love
She from the lofty rocks above
Sent forth a cry forlorn,   75
The lamb, still swimming round and
          round,
Made answer to that plaintive sound.

THE PERIOD OF CHILDHOOD

When he had learnt what thing it was,
That sent this rueful cry, I ween
The Boy recovered heart, and told   80
The sight which he had seen.
Both gladly now deferred their task;
Nor was there wanting other aid—
A Poet, one who loves the brooks
Far better than the sages' books,   85
By chance had thither strayed;
And there the helpless lamb he found
By those huge rocks encompassed round.

He drew it from the troubled pool,
And brought it forth into the light: 90
The Shepherds met him with his charge,
An unexpected sight!
Into their arms the lamb they took,
Whose life and limbs the flood had spared;
Then up the steep ascent they hied,   95
And placed him at his mother's side;
And gently did the Bard
Those idle Shepherd-boys upbraid,
And bade them better mind their trade.

XII

ANECDOTE FOR FATHERS

'Retine vim istam, falsa enim dicam, si coges.'
                                    EUSEBIUS.

[Composed 1798.—Published 1798.]

I HAVE a boy of five years old;
His face is fair and fresh to see;
His limbs are cast in beauty's mould,
And dearly he loves me.

One morn we strolled on our dry walk, 5
Our quiet home all full in view,
And held such intermitted talk
As we are wont to do.

My thoughts on former pleasures ran;
I thought of Kilve's delightful shore, 10
Our pleasant home when spring began,
A long, long year before.

A day it was when I could bear
Some fond regrets to entertain;
With so much happiness to spare,   15
I could not feel a pain.

The green earth echoed to the feet
Of lambs that bounded through the glade,
From shade to sunshine, and as fleet
From sunshine back to shade.   20

Birds warbled round me—and each
          trace
Of inward sadness had its charm;
Kilve, thought I, was a favoured place,
And so is Liswyn farm.

My boy beside me tripped, so slim   25
And graceful in his rustic dress!   ·
And, as we talked, I questioned him,
In very idleness.

'Now tell me, had you rather be,'
I said, and took him by the arm,⁣ 30
'On Kilve's smooth shore, by the green
⁣ sea,
Or here at Liswyn farm?'

In careless mood he looked at me,
While still I held him by the arm,
And said, 'At Kilve I'd rather be⁣ 35
Than here at Liswyn farm.'

'Now, little Edward, say why so:
My little Edward, tell me why.'—
'I cannot tell, I do not know.'—
'Why, this is strange,' said I;⁣ 40

'For here are woods, hills smooth and
⁣ warm:
There surely must some reason be
Why you would change sweet Liswyn
⁣ farm
For Kilve by the green sea.'

At this my boy hung down his head,⁣ 45
He blushed with shame, nor made
⁣ reply;
And three times to the child I said,
'Why, Edward, tell me why?'

His head he raised—there was in sight,
It caught his eye, he saw it plain—⁣ 50
Upon the house-top, glittering bright,
A broad and gilded vane.

Then did the boy his tongue unlock,
And eased his mind with this reply:
'At Kilve there was no weather-cock;⁣ 55
And that's the reason why.'

O dearest, dearest boy! my heart
For better lore would seldom yearn,
Could I but teach the hundredth part
Of what from thee I learn.⁣ 60

XIII
RURAL ARCHITECTURE

[Composed (probably) 1800.—Published 1800.]

THERE'S George Fisher, Charles Fleming,
⁣ and Reginald Shore,
Three rosy-cheeked school-boys, the high-
⁣ est not more
Than the height of a counsellor's bag;
To the top of GREAT HOW[1] did it please
⁣ them to climb:
And there they built up, without mortar
⁣ or lime,⁣ 5
A Man on the peak of the Crag.

[1] GREAT HOW is a single and conspicuous hill,
which rises towards the foot of Thirlmere, on the
western side of the beautiful dale of Legberthwaite,
along the high road between Keswick and Ambleside.

They built him of stones gathered up as
⁣ they lay:
They built him and christened him all in
⁣ one day,
An urchin both vigorous and hale;
And so without scruple they called him
⁣ Ralph Jones.⁣ 10
Now Ralph is renowned for the length of
⁣ his bones;
The Magog of Legberthwaite dale.

Just half a week after, the wind sallied
⁣ forth,
And, in anger or merriment, out of the
⁣ north,
Coming on with a terrible pother,⁣ 15
From the peak of the crag blew the giant
⁣ away.
And what did these school-boys? The
⁣ very next day
They went and they built up another.

—Some little I've seen of blind bois-
⁣ terous works
By Christian disturbers more savage than
⁣ Turks,⁣ 20
Spirits busy to do and undo:
At remembrance whereof my blood some-
⁣ times will flag;
Then, light-hearted Boys, to the top of
⁣ the crag;
And I'll build up a giant with you.

XIV
THE PET-LAMB

A PASTORAL

[Composed 1800.—Published 1800.]

THE dew was falling fast, the stars began
⁣ to blink;
I heard a voice; it said, 'Drink, pretty
⁣ creature, drink!'
And, looking o'er the hedge, before me
⁣ I espied
A snow-white mountain-lamb with a
⁣ Maiden at its side.

Nor sheep nor kine were near; the lamb
⁣ was all alone,⁣ 5
And by a slender cord was tethered to a
⁣ stone:
With one knee on the grass did the little
⁣ Maiden kneel,
While to that mountain-lamb she gave
⁣ its evening meal.

The lamb, while from her hand he thus
⁣ his supper took,
Seemed to feast with head and ears; and
⁣ his tail with pleasure shook.⁣ 10
'Drink, pretty creature, drink,' she said
⁣ in such a tone
That I almost received her heart into my
⁣ own.

'Twas little Barbara Lewthwaite, a child
  of beauty rare!
I watched them with delight, they were
  a lovely pair.
Now with her empty can the Maiden
  turned away: 15
But ere ten yards were gone her footsteps did she stay.

Right towards the lamb she looked; and
  from a shady place
I unobserved could see the workings of
  her face:
If Nature to her tongue could measured
  numbers bring,
Thus, thought I, to her lamb that little
  Maid might sing: 20

'What ails thee, young One? what? Why
  pull so at thy cord?
Is it not well with thee? well both for bed
  and board?
Thy plot of grass is soft, and green as
  grass can be;
Rest, little young One, rest; what is't
  that aileth thee?

'What is it thou wouldst seek? What is
  wanting to thy heart?   25
Thy limbs, are they not strong? And
  beautiful thou art:
This grass is tender grass; these flowers
  they have no peers;
And that green corn all day is rustling
  in thy ears!

'If the sun be shining hot, do but stretch
  thy woollen chain,
This beech is standing by, its covert thou
  canst gain;   30
For rain and mountain-storms! the like
  thou need'st not fear,
The rain and storm are things that
  scarcely can come here.

'Rest, little young One, rest; thou hast
  forgot the day
When my father found thee first in places
  far away;
Many flocks were on the hills, but thou
  wert owned by none,   35
And thy mother from thy side for evermore was gone.

'He took thee in his arms, and in pity
  brought thee home:
A blessèd day for thee! then whither
  wouldst thou roam?
A faithful nurse thou hast; the dam that
  did thee yean
Upon the mountain-tops no kinder could
  have been.   40

'Thou know'st that twice a day I have
  brought thee in this can
Fresh water from the brook, as clear as
  ever ran;
And twice in the day, when the ground
  is wet with dew,
I bring thee draughts of milk, warm
  milk it is and new.

'Thy limbs will shortly be twice as stout
  as they are now,   45
Then I'll yoke thee to my cart like a pony
  in the plough;
My playmate thou shalt be; and when
  the wind is cold
Our hearth shall be thy bed, our house
  shall be thy fold.

'It will not, will not rest!—Poor creature,
  can it be
That 'tis thy mother's heart which is
  working so in thee?   50
Things that I know not of belike to thee
  are dear,
And dreams of things which thou canst
  neither see nor hear.

'Alas, the mountain-tops that look so
  green and fair!
I've heard of fearful winds and darkness
  that come there;
The little brooks that seem all pastime
  and all play,   55
When they are angry, roar like lions for
  their prey.

'Here thou need'st not dread the raven in
  the sky;
Night and day thou art safe,—our cottage
  is hard by.
Why bleat so after me? Why pull so at
  thy chain?
Sleep—and at break of day I will come
  to thee again!'   60

—As homeward through the lane I went
  with lazy feet,
This song to myself did I oftentimes
  repeat;
And it seemed, as I retraced the ballad
  line by line,
That but half of it was hers, and one half
  of it was *mine*.

Again, and once again, did I repeat the
  song;   65
'Nay,' said I, 'more than half to the
  damsel must belong,
For she looked with such a look, and she
  spake with such a tone,
That I almost received her heart into my
  own.'

POEMS REFERRING TO

XV

TO H. C.

SIX YEARS OLD

[Composed 1802.—Published 1807.]

O THOU! whose fancies from afar are
   brought;
Who of thy words dost make a mock
   apparel,
And fittest to unutterable thought
The breeze-like motion and the self-born
   carol;
Thou faery voyager! that dost float   5
In such clear water, that thy boat
May rather seem
To brood on air than on an earthly
   stream;
Suspended in a stream as clear as sky,
Where earth and heaven do make one
   imagery;   10
O blessèd vision! happy child!
Thou art so exquisitely wild,
I think of thee with many fears
For what may be thy lot in future years.

I thought of times when Pain might
   be thy guest,   15
Lord of thy house and hospitality;
And Grief, uneasy lover! never rest
But when she sate within the touch of thee.
O too industrious folly!
O vain and causeless melancholy!   20
Nature will either end thee quite;
Or, lengthening out thy season of delight,
Preserve for thee, by individual right,
A young lamb's heart among the full-
   grown flocks.
What hast thou to do with sorrow,   25
Or the injuries of to-morrow?
Thou art a dew-drop, which the morn
   brings forth,
Ill fitted to sustain unkindly shocks,
Or to be trailed along the soiling earth;
A gem that glitters while it lives,   30
And no forewarning gives;
But, at the touch of wrong, without a strife
Slips in a moment out of life.

XVI

INFLUENCE OF NATURAL OBJECTS

IN CALLING FORTH AND STRENGTHENING
THE IMAGINATION IN BOYHOOD AND
EARLY YOUTH

[Composed 1798-9.—Published in *The Friend*,
Dec. 28, 1809; ed. 1815.]

FROM AN UNPUBLISHED POEM

[This extract is reprinted from *The Friend*.]

WISDOM and Spirit of the universe!
Thou Soul, that art the Eternity of
   thought!

And giv'st to forms and images a breath
And everlasting motion! not in vain,
By day or star-light, thus from my first
   dawn   5
Of childhood didst thou intertwine for me
The passions that build up our human
   soul;
Not with the mean and vulgar works
   of Man;
But with high objects, with enduring
   things,
With life and nature; purifying thus   10
The elements of feeling and of thought,
And sanctifying by such discipline
Both pain and fear,—until we recognise
A grandeur in the beatings of the heart.

Nor was this fellowship vouchsafed
   to me   15
With stinted kindness. In November
   days,
When vapours rolling down the valleys
   made
A lonely scene more lonesome; among
   woods
At noon; and 'mid the calm of summer
   nights,
When, by the margin of the trembling
   lake,   20
Beneath the gloomy hills, homeward I
   went
In solitude, such intercourse was mine:
Mine was it in the fields both day and
   night,
And by the waters, all the summer long.
And in the frosty season, when the sun   25
Was set, and, visible for many a mile,
The cottage-windows through the twilight
   blazed,
I heeded not the summons: happy time
It was indeed for all of us; for me
It was a time of rapture! Clear and
   loud   30
The village-clock tolled six—I wheeled
   about,
Proud and exulting like an untired horse
That cares not for his home.—All shod
   with steel
We hissed along the polished ice, in
   games
Confederate, imitative of the chase   35
And woodland pleasures,—the resound-
   ing horn,
The pack loud-chiming, and the hunted
   hare.
So through the darkness and the cold we
   flew,
And not a voice was idle: with the din
Smitten, the precipices rang aloud;   40
The leafless trees and every icy crag
Tinkled like iron; while far-distant hills
Into the tumult sent an alien sound
Of melancholy, not unnoticed, while the
   stars,

Eastward, were sparkling clear, and in
  the west   45
The orange sky of evening died away.

Not seldom from the uproar I retired
Into a silent bay, or sportively
Glanced sideway, leaving the tumultuous
  throng,
To cut across the reflex of a star;   50
Image that, flying still before me, gleamed
Upon the glassy plain: and oftentimes,
When we had given our bodies to the
  wind,
And all the shadowy banks on either side
Came sweeping through the darkness,
  spinning still   55
The rapid line of motion, then at once
Have I, reclining back upon my heels,
Stopped short; yet still the solitary cliffs
Wheeled by me—even as if the earth had
  rolled
With visible motion her diurnal round! 60
Behind me did they stretch in solemn
  train,
Feebler and feebler, and I stood and
  watched
Till all was tranquil as a summer sea.

XVII

THE LONGEST DAY

ADDRESSED TO MY DAUGHTER, DORA

[Composed 1817.—Published 1820.]

Let us quit the leafy arbour,
And the torrent murmuring by;
For the sun is in his harbour,
Weary of the open sky.

Evening now unbinds the fetters   5
Fashioned by the glowing light;
All that breathe are thankful debtors
To the harbinger of night.

Yet by some grave thoughts attended
Eve renews her calm career;   10
For the day that now is ended
Is the longest of the year.

Dora! sport, as now thou sportest,
On this platform, light and free;
Take thy bliss, while longest, shortest, 15
Are indifferent to thee!

Who would check the happy feeling
That inspires the linnet's song?
Who would stop the swallow, wheeling
On her pinions swift and strong?   20

Yet, at this impressive season,
Words which tenderness can speak
From the truths of homely reason
Might exalt the loveliest cheek;

THE PERIOD OF CHILDHOOD

And, while shades to shades succeeding 25
Steal the landscape from the sight,
I would urge this moral pleading,
Last forerunner of 'Good night!'

Summer ebbs;—each day that follows
Is a reflux from on high,   30
Tending to the darksome hollows
Where the frosts of winter lie.

He who governs the creation,
In his providence, assigned
Such a gradual declination   35
To the life of human kind.

Yet we mark it not;—fruits redden,
Fresh flowers blow as flowers have blown,
And the heart is loath to deaden
Hopes that she so long hath known. 40

Be thou wiser, youthful Maiden!
And when thy decline shall come,
Let not flowers, or boughs fruit-laden,
Hide the knowledge of thy doom.

Now, even now, ere wrapped in slumber,
Fix thine eyes upon the sea   46
That absorbs time, space, and number;
Look thou to Eternity!

Follow thou the flowing river
On whose breast are thither borne 50
All deceived, and each deceiver,
Through the gates of night and morn;

Through the year's successive portals;
Through the bounds which many a star
Marks, not mindless of frail mortals, 55
When his light returns from far.

Thus when thou with Time hast travelled
Toward the mighty gulf of things,
And the mazy stream unravelled
With thy best imaginings;   60

Think, if thou on beauty leanest,
Think how pitiful that stay,
Did not virtue give the meanest
Charms superior to decay.

Duty, like a strict preceptor,   65
Sometimes frowns, or seems to frown;
Choose her thistle for thy sceptre,
While youth's roses are thy crown.

Grasp it,—if thou shrink and tremble,
Fairest damsel of the green,   70
Thou wilt lack the only symbol
That proclaims a genuine queen;

And ensures those palms of honour
Which selected spirits wear,
Bending low before the Donor, 75
Lord of heaven's unchanging year!

POEMS REFERRING TO

XVIII

THE NORMAN BOY

[Composed (?).—Published 1842.]

HIGH on a broad unfertile tract of forest-
skirted Down,
Nor kept by Nature for herself, nor made
by man his own,
From home and company remote and
every playful joy,
Served, tending a few sheep and goats,
a ragged Norman Boy.

Him never saw I, nor the spot; but from
an English Dame,   5
Stranger to me and yet my friend, a
simple notice came,
With suit that I would speak in verse of
that sequestered child
Whom, one bleak winter's day, she met
upon the dreary Wild.

His flock, along the woodland's edge with
relics sprinkled o'er
Of last night's snow, beneath a sky threatening the fall of more,   10
Where tufts of herbage tempted each,
were busy at their feed,
And the poor Boy was busier still, with
work of anxious heed.

There *was* he, where of branches rent and
withered and decayed,
For covert from the keen north wind, his
hands a hut had made.
A tiny tenement, forsooth, and frail, as
needs must be   15
A thing of such materials framed, by a
builder such as he.

The hut stood finished by his pains, nor
seemingly lacked aught
That skill or means of his could add, but
the architect had wrought
Some limber twigs into a Cross, well-
shaped with fingers nice,
To be engrafted on the top of his small
edifice.   20

That Cross he now was fastening there,
as the surest power and best
For supplying all deficiencies, all wants
of the rude nest
In which, from burning heat, or tempest
driving far and wide,
The innocent Boy, else shelterless, his
lonely head must hide.

That Cross belike he also raised as a
standard for the true   25
And faithful service of his heart in the
worst that might ensue

Of hardship and distressful fear, amid the
houseless waste
Where he, in his poor self so weak, by
Providence was placed.

—Here, Lady! might I cease; but nay,
let *us* before we part
With this dear holy shepherd-boy breathe
a prayer of earnest heart,   30
That unto him, where'er shall lie his life's
appointed way,
The Cross, fixed in his soul, may prove an
all-sufficing stay.

XIX

THE POET'S DREAM

SEQUEL TO 'THE NORMAN BOY'

[Composed (?).—Published 1842.]

JUST as those final words were penned,
the sun broke out in power,
And gladdened all things; but, as chanced,
within that very hour,
Air blackened, thunder growled, fire
flashed from clouds that hid the sky,
And for the Subject of my Verse I heaved
a pensive sigh.

Nor could my heart by second thoughts
from heaviness be cleared,   5
For bodied forth before my eyes the cross-
crowned hut appeared;
And while around it storm as fierce
seemed troubling earth and air,
I saw, within, the Norman Boy kneeling
alone in prayer.

The Child, as if the thunder's voice spake
with articulate call,
Bowed meekly in submissive fear, before
the Lord of All;   10
His lips were moving; and his eyes, upraised to sue for grace,
With soft illumination cheered the dimness of that place.

How beautiful is holiness!—what wonder
if the sight,
Almost as vivid as a dream, produced a
dream at night?
It came with sleep and showed the Boy,
no cherub, not transformed,   15
But the poor ragged Thing whose ways
my human heart had warmed.

Me had the dream equipped with wings,
so I took him in my arms,
And lifted from the grassy floor, stilling
his faint alarms,
And bore him high through yielding air
my debt of love to pay,
By giving him, for both our sakes, an
hour of holiday.   20

72

I whispered, 'Yet a little while, dear
    Child! thou art my own,
To show thee some delightful thing, in
    country or in town.
What shall it be? a mirthful throng? or
    that holy place and calm
St. Denis, filled with royal tombs, or the
    Church of Notre Dame?

'St. Ouen's golden Shrine? Or choose
    what else would please thee most 25
Of any wonder Normandy, or all proud
    France, can boast!'
'My Mother,' said the Boy, 'was born
    near to a blessèd Tree,
The Chapel Oak of Allonville; good
    Angel, show it me!'

On wings from broad and steadfast poise
    let loose by this reply,
For Allonville, o'er down and dale, away
    then did we fly; 30
O'er town and tower we fled, and fields
    in May's fresh verdure drest;
The wings they did not flag; the Child,
    though grave, was not deprest.

But who shall show, to waking sense, the
    gleam of light that broke
Forth from his eyes, when first the Boy
    looked down on that huge oak,
For length of days so much revered, so
    famous where it stands 35
For twofold hallowing—Nature's care,
    and work of human hands?

Strong as an Eagle with my charge I
    glided round and round
The wide-spread boughs, for view of door,
    window, and stair that wound
Gracefully up the gnarled trunk; nor
    left we unsurveyed
The pointed steeple peering forth from
    the centre of the shade.' 40

I lighted—opened with soft touch the
    chapel's iron door,
Past softly, leading in the Boy; and
    while from roof to floor,
From floor to roof, all round his eyes the
    Child with wonder cast,
Pleasure on pleasure crowded in, each
    livelier than the last.

For, deftly framed within the trunk, the
    sanctuary showed, 45
By light of lamp and precious stones,
    that glimmered here, there glowed,
Shrine, Altar, Image, Offerings hung in
    sign of gratitude;
Sight that inspired accordant thoughts;
    and speech I thus renewed:

'Hither the Afflicted come, as thou hast
    heard thy Mother say,
And, kneeling, supplication make to our
    Lady de la Paix; 50
What mournful sighs have here been
    heard, and, when the voice was stopt
By sudden pangs; what bitter tears have
    on this pavement dropt!

'Poor Shepherd of the naked Down, a
    favoured lot is thine,
Far happier lot, dear Boy, than brings
    full many to this shrine;
From body pains and pains of soul thou
    needest no release, 55
Thy hours as they flow on are spent, if
    not in joy in peace.

'Then offer up thy heart to God in
    thankfulness and praise,
Give to Him prayers, and many thoughts,
    in thy most busy days;
And in His sight the fragile Cross, on thy
    small hut, will be
Holy as that which long hath crowned
    the Chapel of this Tree; 60

'Holy as that far seen which crowns the
    sumptuous Church in Rome
Where thousands meet to worship God
    under a mighty Dome;
He sees the bending multitude, He hears
    the choral rites,
Yet, not the less, in children's hymns
    and lonely prayer delights.

'God for His service needeth not proud
    work of human skill; 65
They please Him best who labour most
    to do in peace His will:
So let us strive to live, and to our Spirits
    will be given
Such wings as, when our Saviour calls,
    shall bear us up to heaven.'

The Boy no answer made by words, but,
    so earnest was his look,
Sleep fled, and with it fled the dream—
    recorded in this book, 70
Lest all that passed should melt away in
    silence from my mind,
As visions still more bright have done,
    and left no trace behind.

But oh! that Country-man of thine,
    whose eye, loved Child, can see
A pledge of endless bliss in acts of early
    piety,
In verse, which to thy ear might come,
    would treat this simple theme, 75
Nor leave untold our happy flight in that
    adventurous dream.

Alas the dream, to thee, poor Boy! to
  thee from whom it flowed,
Was nothing, scarcely can be aught, yet
  'twas bounteously bestowed,
If I may dare to cherish hope that gentle
  eyes will read
Not loth, and listening Little-ones, heart-
  touched, their fancies feed.[1]   80

XX

THE WESTMORELAND GIRL

TO MY GRANDCHILDREN

[Composed June 6, 1845.—Published 1845.]

PART I

SEEK who will delight in fable,
I shall tell you truth. A Lamb
Leapt from this steep bank to follow
'Cross the brook its thoughtless dam.

Far and wide on hill and valley   5
Rain had fallen, unceasing rain,
And the bleating mother's Young-one
Struggled with the flood in vain:

But, as chanced, a Cottage-maiden
(Ten years scarcely had she told)   10
Seeing, plunged into the torrent,
Clasped the Lamb and kept her hold.

Whirled adown the rocky channel,
Sinking, rising, on they go,
Peace and rest, as seems, before them 15
Only in the lake below.

Oh! it was a frightful current
Whose fierce wrath the Girl had braved;
Clap your hands with joy my Hearers,
Shout in triumph, both are saved;   20

Saved by courage that with danger
Grew, by strength the gift of love,
And belike a guardian angel
Came with succour from above.

PART II

Now, to a maturer Audience,   25
Let me speak of this brave Child
Left among her native mountains
With wild Nature to run wild.

So, unwatched by love maternal,
Mother's care no more her guide,   30
Fared this little bright-eyed Orphan
Even while at her father's side.

Spare your blame,—remembrance makes
  him
Loth to rule by strict command;
Still upon his cheek are living   35
Touches of her infant hand,

[1] See Note, p. 699.

Dear caresses given in pity,
Sympathy that soothed his grief,
As the dying mother witnessed
To her thankful mind's relief.   40

Time passed on; the Child was happy,
Like a Spirit of air she moved,
Wayward, yet by all who knew her
For her tender heart beloved.

Scarcely less than sacred passions,   45
Bred in house, in grove, and field,
Link her with the inferior creatures,
Urge her powers their rights to shield.

Anglers, bent on reckless pastime,
Learn how she can feel alike   50
Both for tiny harmless minnow
And the fierce sharp-toothed pike.

Merciful protectress, kindling
Into anger or disdain;
Many a captive hath she rescued,   55
Others saved from lingering pain.

Listen yet awhile;—with patience
Hear the homely truths I tell,
She in Grasmere's old church-steeple
Tolled this day the passing bell.   60

Yes, the wild Girl of the mountains
To their echoes gave the sound,
Notice punctual as the minute,
Warning solemn and profound.

She, fulfilling her sire's office,   65
Rang alone the far-heard knell,
Tribute, by her hand, in sorrow,
Paid to One who loved her well.

When his spirit was departed,
On that service she went forth;   70
Nor will fail the like to render
When his corse is laid in earth.

What then wants the Child to temper,
In her breast, unruly fire,
To control the froward impulse   75
And restrain the vague desire?

Easily a pious training
And a steadfast outward power
Would supplant the weeds, and cherish
In their stead each opening flower.   80

Thus the fearless Lamb-deliv'rer,
Woman-grown, meek-hearted, sage,
May become a blest example
For her sex, of every age.

Watchful as a wheeling eagle,   85
Constant as a soaring lark,
Should the country need a heroine,
She might prove our Maid of Arc.

Leave that thought; and here be uttered
Prayer that Grace divine may raise   90
Her humane courageous spirit
Up to heaven, thro' peaceful ways

POEMS FOUNDED ON THE AFFECTIONS

I

THE BROTHERS

[Composed (in or about) February, 1800.—Published 1800.]

'THESE Tourists, heaven preserve us!
  needs must live
A profitable life: some glance along,
Rapid and gay, as if the earth were air,
And they were butterflies to wheel about
Long as the summer lasted: some, as
  wise,   5
Perched on the forehead of a jutting crag,
Pencil in hand and book upon the knee,
Will look and scribble, scribble on and
  look,
Until a man might travel twelve stout
  miles,
Or reap an acre of his neighbour's corn. 10
But, for that moping Son of Idleness,
Why can he tarry *yonder*?—In our
  church-yard
Is neither epitaph nor monument,
Tombstone nor name—only the turf we
  tread
And a few natural graves.'

                              To Jane, his wife,
Thus spake the homely Priest of Enner-
  dale.   16
It was a July evening; and he sate
Upon the long stone-seat beneath the
  eaves
Of his old cottage,—as it chanced, that
  day,
Employed in winter's work. Upon the
  stone   20
His wife sate near him, teasing matted
  wool,
While, from the twin cards toothed with
  glittering wire,
He fed the spindle of his youngest child,
Who, in the open air, with due accord
Of busy hands and back-and-forward
  steps,   25
Her large round wheel was turning. To-
  wards the field
In which the Parish Chapel stood alone,
Girt round with a bare ring of mossy
  wall,
While half an hour went by, the Priest
  had sent
Many a long look of wonder: and at last,
Risen from his seat, beside the snow-
  white ridge   31
Of carded wool which the old man had
  piled

He laid his implements with gentle care,
Each in the other locked; and down the
  path,
That from his cottage to the church-yard
  led,   35
He took his way, impatient to accost
The Stranger, whom he saw still lingering
  there.

'Twas one well known to him in former
  days,
A Shepherd-lad; who ere his sixteenth
  year
Had left that calling, tempted to entrust
His expectations to the fickle winds   41
And perilous waters; with the mariners
A fellow-mariner; and so had fared
Through twenty seasons; but he had been
  reared   44
Among the mountains, and he in his
  heart
Was half a shepherd on the stormy seas.
Oft in the piping shrouds had Leonard
  heard
The tones of waterfalls, and inland sounds
Of caves and trees:—and when the regu-
  lar wind
Between the tropics filled the steady sail,
And blew with the same breath through
  days and weeks,   51
Lengthening invisibly its weary line
Along the cloudless Main, he, in those
  hours
Of tiresome indolence, would often hang
Over the vessel's side, and gaze and gaze;
And, while the broad blue wave and
  sparkling foam   56
Flashed round him images and hues that
  wrought
In union with the employment of his
  heart,
He, thus by feverish passion overcome,
Even with the organs of his bodily eye,
Below him, in the bosom of the deep,   61
Saw mountains; saw the forms of sheep
  that grazed
On verdant hills—with dwellings among
  trees,
And shepherds clad in the same country
  grey
Which he himself had worn.[1]

                         And now, at last,
From perils manifold, with some small
  wealth   66

[1] This description of the Calenture is sketched
from an imperfect recollection of an admirable one
in prose, by Mr. Gilbert, author of the *Hurricane*.

Acquired by traffic 'mid the Indian Isles,
To his paternal home he is returned,
With a determined purpose to resume
The life he had lived there; both for the
    sake   70
Of many darling pleasures, and the love
Which to an only brother he has borne
In all his hardships, since that happy
    time
When, whether it blew foul or fair, they
    two
Were brother-shepherds on their native
    hills.   75
—They were the last of all their race:
    and now,
When Leonard had approached his home,
    his heart
Failed in him; and, not venturing to
    enquire
Tidings of one so long and dearly loved,
He to the solitary church-yard turned; 80
That, as he knew in what particular spot
His family were laid, he thence might
    learn
If still his Brother lived, or to the file
Another grave was added.—He had found
Another grave,—near which a full half-
    hour   85
He had remained; but, as he gazed, there
    grew
Such a confusion in his memory,
That he began to doubt; and even to hope
That he had seen this heap of turf be-
    fore,—
That it was not another grave; but one 90
He had forgotten. He had lost his path,
As up the vale, that afternoon, he walked
Through fields which once had been well
    known to him:
And oh what joy this recollection now
Sent to his heart! he lifted up his eyes, 95
And, looking round, imagined that he saw
Strange alteration wrought on every side
Among the woods and fields, and that the
    rocks,
And everlasting hills themselves were
    changed.

    By this the Priest, who down the field
    had come,   100
Unseen by Leonard, at the church-yard
    gate
Stopped short,—and thence, at leisure,
    limb by limb
Perused him with a gay complacency.
Ay, thought the Vicar, smiling to himself,
'Tis one of those who needs must leave
    the path   105
Of the world's business to go wild alone:
His arms have a perpetual holiday;
The happy man will creep about the
    fields,
Following his fancies by the hour, to
    bring

Tears down his cheek, or solitary smiles
Into his face, until the setting sun   111
Write fool upon his forehead.—Planted
    thus
Beneath a shed that over-arched the gate
Of this rude church-yard, till the stars
    appeared
The good Man might have communed
    with himself,   115
But that the Stranger, who had left the
    grave,
Approached; he recognised the Priest at
    once,
And, after greetings interchanged, and
    given
By Leonard to the Vicar as to one
Unknown to him, this dialogue ensued.
    Leonard. You live, Sir, in these dales,
    a quiet life: 121
Your years make up one peaceful family;
And who would grieve and fret, if, wel-
    come come
And welcome gone, they are so like each
    other,
They cannot be remembered? Scarce a
    funeral   125
Comes to this church-yard once in eighteen
    months;
And yet, some changes must take place
    among you:
And you, who dwell here, even among
    these rocks,
Can trace the finger of mortality,
And see, that with our threescore years
    and ten   130
We are not all that perish.——I re-
    member,
(For many years ago I passed this road)
There was a foot-way all along the
    fields
By the brook-side—'tis gone—and that
    dark cleft!
To me it does not seem to wear the
    face   135
Which then it had!
    Priest. Nay, Sir, for aught I know,
That chasm is much the same—
    Leonard. But, surely, yonder—
    Priest. Ay, there, indeed, your memory
    is a friend
That does not play you false.—On that
    tall pike
(It is the loneliest place of all these
    hills)   140
There were two springs which bubbled
    side by side,
As if they had been made that they might
    be
Companions for each other: the huge
    crag
Was rent with lightning—one hath dis-
    appeared;
The other, left behind, is flowing still. 145
For accidents and changes such as these,

We want not store of them;—a water-
   spout
Will bring down half a mountain; what
   a feast
For folks that wander up and down like
   you,
To see an acre's breadth of that wide
   cliff   150
One roaring cataract! a sharp May-storm
Will come with loads of January snow,
And in one night send twenty score of
   sheep
To feed the ravens; or a shepherd dies
By some untoward death among the
   rocks: 155
The ice breaks up and sweeps away a
   bridge;
A wood is felled:—and then for our own
   homes!
A child is born or christened, a field
   ploughed,
A daughter sent to service, a web spun,
The old house-clock is decked with a new
   face;   160
And hence, so far from wanting facts or
   dates
To chronicle the time, we all have here
A pair of diaries,—one serving, Sir,
For the whole dale, and one for each fire-
   side—
Yours was a stranger's judgment: for
   historians,   165
Commend me to these valleys!
   Leonard.   Yet your Church-yard
Seems, if such freedom may be used with
   you,
To say that you are heedless of the past:
An orphan could not find his mother's
   grave:
Here's neither head nor foot-stone, plate
   of brass,   170
Cross-bones nor skull,—type of our
   earthly state
Nor emblem of our hopes: the dead man's
   home
Is but a fellow to that pasture-field.
   Priest. Why, there, Sir, is a thought
   that's new to me!
The stone-cutters, 'tis true, might beg
   their bread   175
If every English church-yard were like
   ours;
Yet your conclusion wanders from the
   truth:
We have no need of names and epitaphs;
We talk about the dead by our fire-sides.
And then, for our immortal part! *we*
   want   180
No symbols, Sir, to tell us that plain tale:
The thought of death sits easy on the man
Who has been born and dies among the
   mountains.
   Leonard. Your Dalesmen, then, do in
   each other's thoughts

Possess a kind of second life: no doubt 185
You, Sir, could help me to the history
Of half these graves?
   Priest.   For eight-score winters past,
With what I've witnessed, and with what
   I've heard,
Perhaps I might; and, on a winter-
   evening,
If you were seated at my chimney's nook,
By turning o'er these hillocks one by one,
We two could travel, Sir, through a
   strange round;   192
Yet all in the broad highway of the world.
Now there's a grave—your foot is half
   upon it,—
It looks just like the rest; and yet that
   man   195
Died broken-hearted.
   Leonard.   'Tis a common case.
We'll take another: who is he that lies
Beneath yon ridge, the last of those three
   graves?
It touches on that piece of native rock
Left in the church-yard wall.
   Priest.   That's Walter Ewbank. 200
He had as white a head and fresh a cheek
As ever were produced by youth and age
Engendering in the blood of hale four-
   score.
Through five long generations had the
   heart
Of Walter's forefathers o'erflowed the
   bounds   205
Of their inheritance, that single cottage—
You see it yonder! and those few green
   fields.
They toiled and wrought, and still, from
   sire to son,
Each struggled, and each yielded as be-
   fore
A little—yet a little,—and old Walter, 210
They left to him the family heart, and
   land
With other burthens than the crop it
   bore.
Year after year the old man still kept up
A cheerful mind,—and buffeted with bond,
Interest, and mortgages; at last he
   sank,   215
And went into his grave before his time.
Poor Walter! whether it was care that
   spurred him
God only knows, but to the very last
He had the lightest foot in Ennerdale:
His pace was never that of an old
   man: 220
I almost see him tripping down the path
With his two grandsons after him:—but
   you,
Unless our Landlord be your host to-
   night,
Have far to travel,—and on these rough
   paths   224
Even in the longest day of midsummer—

Leonard. But those two Orphans!
Priest. Orphans!—Such they were—
Yet not while Walter lived:—for, though
    their parents
Lay buried side by side as now they lie,
The old man was a father to the boys,
Two fathers in one father: and if tears,
Shed when he talked of them where they
    were not,   231
And hauntings from the infirmity of love,
Are aught of what makes up a mother's
    heart,
This old Man, in the day of his old age,
Was half a mother to them.—If you weep,
    Sir,   235
To hear a stranger talking about strangers,
Heaven bless you when you are among
    your kindred!
Ay—you may turn that way—it is a grave
Which will bear looking at.
    Leonard.   These boys—I hope
They loved this good old Man?—
    Priest.   They did—and truly: 240
But that was what we almost overlooked,
They were such darlings of each other.
    Yes,
Though from the cradle they had lived
    with Walter,
The only kinsman near them, and though he
Inclined to both by reason of his age, 245
With a more fond, familiar, tenderness;
They, notwithstanding, had much love to
    spare,
And it all went into each other's hearts.
Leonard, the elder by just eighteen
    months,
Was two years taller: 'twas a joy to see,
To hear, to meet them!—From their house
    the school   251
Is distant three short miles, and in the
    time
Of storm and thaw, when every water-
    course
And unbridged stream, such as you may
    have noticed
Crossing our roads at every hundred steps,
Was swoln into a noisy rivulet,   256
Would Leonard then, when elder boys
    remained
At home, go staggering through the slip-
    pery fords,
Bearing his brother on his back. I have
    seen him,
On windy days, in one of those stray
    brooks,   260
Ay, more than once I have seen him, mid-
    leg deep,
Their two books lying both on a dry stone,
Upon the hither side: and once I said,
As I remember, looking round these rocks
And hills on which we all of us were
    born,   265
That God who made the great book of
    the world

Would bless such piety—
    Leonard.   It may be then—
    Priest. Never did worthier lads break
    English bread;
The very brightest Sunday Autumn saw,
With all its mealy clusters of ripe nuts,
Could never keep those boys away from
    church,   271
Or tempt them to an hour of sabbath
    breach.
Leonard and James! I warrant, every
    corner
Among these rocks, and every hollow
    place
That venturous foot could reach, to one
    or both   275
Was known as well as to the flowers that
    grow there.
Like roe-bucks they went bounding o'er
    the hills;
They played like two young ravens on the
    crags:
Then they could write, ay, and speak too,
    as well
As many of their betters—and for Leonard!
The very night before he went away, 281
In my own house I put into his hand
A Bible, and I'd wager house and field
That, if he be alive, he has it yet.
    Leonard. It seems, these Brothers have
    not lived to be   285
A comfort to each other—
    Priest.   That they might
Live to such end is what both old and
    young
In this our valley all of us have wished,
And what, for my part, I have often
    prayed:
But Leonard—
    Leonard. Then James still is left among
    you!   290
    Priest. 'Tis of the elder brother I am
    speaking:
They had an uncle;—he was at that time
A thriving man, and trafficked on the seas:
And, but for that same uncle, to this hour
Leonard had never handled rope or
    shroud: .   295
For the boy loved the life which we lead
    here;
And though of unripe years, a stripling
    only,
His soul was knit to this his native soil.
But, as I said, old Walter was too weak
To strive with such a torrent; when he
    died,   300
The estate and house were sold; and all
    their sheep,
A pretty flock, and which, for aught I
    know,
Had clothed the Ewbanks for a thousand
    years:—
Well—all was gone, and they were desti-
    tute,

78

And Leonard, chiefly for his Brother's
  sake,   305
Resolved to try his fortune on the seas.
Twelve years are past since we had tidings
  from him.
If there were one among us who had heard
That Leonard Ewbank was come home
  again,
From the Great Gavel,[1] down by Leeza's
  banks,   310
And down the Enna, far as Egremont,
The day would be a joyous festival;
And those two bells of ours, which there
  you see—
Hanging in the open air—but, O good
  Sir!
This is sad talk—they'll never sound for
  him—   315
Living or dead.—When last we heard of
  him,
He was in slavery among the Moors
Upon the Barbary coast.—'Twas not a
  little
That would bring down his spirit; and no
  doubt,
Before it ended in his death, the Youth 320
Was sadly crossed.—Poor Leonard! when
  we parted,
He took me by the hand, and said to me,
If e'er he should grow rich, he would
  return,
To live in peace upon his father's land,
And lay his bones among us.
    Leonard.   If that day   325
Should come, 'twould needs be a glad day
  for him;
He would himself, no doubt, be happy
  then
As any that should meet him—
    Priest.   Happy! Sir—
    Leonard. You said his kindred all were
  in their graves,
And that he had one Brother—
    Priest.   That is but   330
A fellow-tale of sorrow. From his youth
James, though not sickly, yet was delicate;
And Leonard being always by his side
Had done so many offices about him,
That, though he was not of a timid
  nature,   335
Yet still the spirit of a mountain-boy
In him was somewhat checked; and, when
  his Brother
Was gone to sea, and he was left alone,
The little colour that he had was soon
Stolen from his cheek; he drooped, and

pined, and pined—   340
Leonard. But these are all the graves of
  full-grown men!
Priest. Ay, Sir, that passed away: we
  took him to us;
He was the child of all the dale—he lived
Three months with one, and six months
  with another;
And wanted neither food, nor clothes,
  nor love: 345
And many, many happy days were his.
But, whether blithe or sad, 'tis my belief
His absent Brother still was at his heart.
And, when he dwelt beneath our roof, we
  found
(A practice till this time unknown to
  him)   350
That often, rising from his bed at night,
He in his sleep would walk about, and
  sleeping
He sought his brother Leonard.—You
  are moved!
Forgive me, Sir: before I spoke to you,
I judged you most unkindly.
    Leonard.   But this Youth, 355
How did he die at last?
    Priest.   One sweet May-morning,
(It will be twelve years since when Spring
  returns)
He had gone forth among the new-
  dropped lambs,
With two or three companions, whom
  their course   359
Of occupation led from height to height
Under a cloudless sun—till he, at length,
Through weariness, or, haply, to indulge
The humour of the moment, lagged be-
  hind.
You see yon precipice;—it wears the shape
Of a vast building made of many crags;
And in the midst is one particular
  rock   366
That rises like a column from the vale,
Whence by our shepherds it is called THE
  PILLAR.
Upon its aëry summit crowned with
  heath,
The loiterer, not unnoticed by his com-
  rades,   370
Lay stretched at ease; but, passing by
  the place
On their return, they found that he was
  gone.
No ill was feared; till one of them by
  chance
Entering, when evening was far spent, the
  house
Which at that time was James's home,
  there learned   375
That nobody had seen him all that day:
The morning came, and still he was un-
  heard of:
The neighbours were alarmed, and to the
  brook

---

[1] The Great Gavel, so called, I imagine, from its
resemblance to the gable end of a house, is one of the
highest of the Cumberland mountains. It stands at
the head of the several vales of Ennerdale, Wastdale
and Borrowdale.
   The Leeza is a river which flows into the Lake of
Ennerdale: on issuing from the Lake, it changes its
name, and is called the End, Eyne, or Enna. It falls
into the sea a little below Egremont.

Some hastened; some ran to the lake:
 ere noon
They found him at the foot of that same
 rock   380
Dead, and with mangled limbs. The third
 day after
I buried him, poor Youth, and there he
 lies!
 Leonard. And that then *is* his grave!—
 Before his death
You say that he saw many happy years?
 Priest. Ay, that he did—
 Leonard. And all went well with him?—
 Priest. If he had one, the Youth had
 twenty homes.   386
 Leonard. And you believe, then, that
 his mind was easy?—
 Priest. Yes, long before he died, he
 found that time
Is a true friend to sorrow; and, unless
His thoughts were turned on Leonard's
 luckless fortune,   390
He talked about him with a cheerful love.
 Leonard. He could not come to an un-
 hallowed end!
 Priest. Nay, God forbid!—You recollect
 I mentioned
A habit which disquietude and grief
Had brought upon him; and we all con-
 jectured   395
That, as the day was warm, he had lain
 down
On the soft heath,—and, waiting for his
 comrades,
He there had fallen asleep; that in his
 sleep
He to the margin of the precipice
Had walked, and from the summit had
 fallen headlong: 400
And so no doubt he perished. When the
 Youth
Fell, in his hand he must have grasped,
 we think,
His shepherd's staff; for on that Pillar of
 rock
It had been caught mid-way; and there
 for years
It hung;—and mouldered there.

    The Priest here ended—
The Stranger would have thanked him,
 but he felt   406
A gushing from his heart, that took away
The power of speech. Both left the spot
 in silence;
And Leonard, when they reached the
 church-yard gate,
As the Priest lifted up the latch, turned
 round,—   410
And, looking at the grave, he said, 'My
 Brother!'
The Vicar did not hear the words: and now
He pointed towards his dwelling-place,
 entreating

That Leonard would partake his homely
 fare:
The other thanked him with an earnest
 voice;   415
But added, that, the evening being calm,
He would pursue his journey. So they
 parted.

It was not long ere Leonard reached a
 grove
That overhung the road: he there stopped
 short,
And, sitting down beneath the trees,
 reviewed   420
All that the Priest had said: his early
 years
Were with him:—his long absence, che-
 rished hopes,
And thoughts which had been his an hour
 before,
All pressed on him with such a weight,
 that now,
This vale, where he had been so happy,
 seemed   425
A place in which he could not bear to
 live:
So he relinquished all his purposes.
He travelled back to Egremont: and
 thence,
That night, he wrote a letter to the Priest,
Reminding him of what had passed be-
 tween them;   430
And adding, with a hope to be forgiven,
That it was from the weakness of his
 heart
He had not dared to tell him who he was.
This done, he went on shipboard, and is
 now
A seaman, a grey-headed Mariner. 435

II

ARTEGAL AND ELIDURE

(SEE THE CHRONICLE OF GEOFFREY OF
MONMOUTH, AND MILTON'S HISTORY
OF ENGLAND)

[Composed 1815.—Published 1820.]

WHERE be the temples which in Britain's
 Isle,
For his paternal Gods, the Trojan raised?
Gone like a morning dream, or like a pile
Of clouds that in cerulean ether blazed!
Ere Julius landed on her white-cliffed
 shore,   5
 They sank, delivered o'er
To fatal dissolution; and, I ween,
No vestige then was left that such had
 ever been.

Nathless, a British record (long concealed
In old Armorica, whose secret springs 10
No Gothic conqueror ever drank) revealed
The marvellous current of forgotten things;

80

How Brutus came, by oracles impelled,
  And Albion's giants quelled,
A brood whom no civility could melt,   15
'Who never tasted grace, and goodness
  ne'er had felt.'

By brave Corineus aided, he subdued,
And rooted out the intolerable kind;
And this too-long-polluted land imbued
With goodly arts and usages refined;   20
Whence golden harvests, cities, warlike
    towers,
  And pleasure's sumptuous bowers;
Whence all the fixed delights of house
    and home,
Friendships that will not break, and love
    that cannot roam.

O, happy Britain! region all too fair   25
For self-delighting fancy to endure
That silence only should inhabit there,
Wild beasts, or uncouth savages impure!
But, intermingled with the generous seed,
  Grew many a poisonous weed;   30
Thus fares it still with all that takes its
    birth
From human care, or grows upon the
    breast of earth.

Hence, and how soon! that war of ven-
    geance waged
By Guendolen against her faithless lord;
Till she, in jealous fury unassuaged,   35
Had slain his paramour with ruthless
    sword:
Then into Severn hideously defiled,
  She flung her blameless child,
Sabrina,—vowing that the stream should
    bear
That name through every age, her hatred
  to declare.   40

So speaks the Chronicle, and tells of Lear
By his ungrateful daughters turned adrift.
Ye lightnings, hear his voice!—they can-
    not hear,
Nor can the winds restore his simple gift.
But One there is, a Child of nature meek,
  Who comes her Sire to seek;   46
And he, recovering sense, upon her breast
Leans smilingly, and sinks into a perfect
    rest.

There too we read of Spenser's fairy
    themes,
And those that Milton loved in youthful
    years;   50
The sage enchanter Merlin's subtle
    schemes;
The feats of Arthur and his knightly peers;
Of Arthur,—who, to upper light restored,
  With that terrific sword
Which yet he brandishes for future war,
Shall lift his country's fame above the
  polar star!   56

ARTEGAL AND ELIDURE

What wonder, then, if in such ample field
Of old tradition, one particular flower
Doth seemingly in vain its fragrance yield,
And bloom unnoticed even to this late
    hour?   60
Now, gentle Muses, your assistance grant,
  While I this flower transplant
Into a garden stored with Poesy;
Where flowers and herbs unite, and haply
    some weeds be,
That, wanting not wild grace, are from
    all mischief free!   65

A KING more worthy of respect and love
Than wise Gorbonian ruled not in his day;
And grateful Britain prospered far above
All neighbouring countries through his
    righteous sway;
He poured rewards and honours on the
    good;   70
  The oppressor he withstood;
And while he served the Gods with reve-
    rence due,
Fields smiled, and temples rose, and towns
    and cities grew.

He died, whom Artegal succeeds—his son;
But how unworthy of that sire was he!   75
A hopeful reign, auspiciously begun,
Was darkened soon by foul iniquity.
From crime to crime he mounted, till at
    length
The nobles leagued their strength
With a vexed people, and the tyrant
    chased;   80
And on the vacant throne his worthier
    Brother placed.

From realm to realm the humbled Exile
    went,
Suppliant for aid his kingdom to regain;
In many a court, and many a warrior's
    tent,
He urged his persevering suit in vain.   85
Him, in whose wretched heart ambition
    failed,
  Dire poverty assailed;
And, tired with slights his pride no more
    could brook,
He towards his native country cast a
    longing look.

Fair blew the wished-for wind—the
    voyage sped;   90
He landed; and by many dangers scared,
'Poorly provided, poorly followèd,'
To Calaterium's forest he repaired.
How changed from him who, born to
    highest place,
  Had swayed the royal mace,   95
Flattered and feared, despised yet deified,
In Troynovant, his seat by silver Thames's
  side!

81

From that wild region where the crown-
　　less king
Lay in concealment with his scanty train,
Supporting life by water from the spring,
And such chance food as outlaws can
　　obtain,　　　　　　　　　　101
Unto the few whom he esteems his friends
　　A messenger he sends;
And from their secret loyalty requires
Shelter and daily bread,—the sum of his
　　desires.　　　　　　　　　　105

While he the issue waits, at early morn
Wandering by stealth abroad, he chanced
　　to hear
A startling outcry made by hound and
　　horn,
From which the tusky wild boar flies in
　　fear;
And, scouring toward him o'er the grassy
　　plain,　　　　　　　　　　110
Behold the hunter train!
He bids his little company advance
With seeming unconcern and steady coun-
　　tenance.

The royal Elidure, who leads the chase,
Hath checked his foaming courser:—can
　　it be!　　　　　　　　　　115
Methinks that I should recognise that face,
Though much disguised by long adver-
　　sity!
He gazed rejoicing, and again he gazed,
　　Confounded and amazed—
'It is the king, my brother!' and, by
　　sound　　　　　　　　　　120
Of his own voice confirmed, he leaps upon
　　the ground.

Long, strict, and tender was the embrace
　　he gave,
Feebly returned by daunted Artegal;
Whose natural affection doubts enslave,
And apprehensions dark and criminal. 125
Loth to restrain the moving interview,
　　The attendant lords withdrew;
And, while they stood upon the plain
　　apart,
Thus Elidure, by words, relieved his
　　struggling heart.

'By heavenly Powers conducted, we have
　　met;　　　　　　　　　　130
—O Brother! to my knowledge lost so
　　long,
But neither lost to love, nor to regret,
Nor to my wishes lost;—forgive the
　　wrong,
(Such it may seem) if I thy crown have
　　borne,
　　Thy royal mantle worn:　　135
I was their natural guardian; and 'tis just
That now I should restore what hath been
　　held in trust.'

A while the astonished Artegal stood mute,
Then thus exclaimed: 'To me, of titles
　　shorn,
And stripped of power! me, feeble, desti-
　　tute,　　　　　　　　　　140
To me a kingdom! spare the bitter scorn:
If justice ruled the breast of foreign kings,
　　Then, on the wide-spread wings
Of war, had I returned to claim my right;
This will I here avow, not dreading thy
　　despite.'　　　　　　　　　　145

'I do not blame thee,' Elidure replied;
'But, if my looks did with my words agree,
I should at once be trusted, not defied,
And thou from all disquietude be free.
May the unsullied Goddess of the chase,
　　Who to this blessed place　　151
At this blest moment led me, if I speak
With insincere intent, on me her ven-
　　geance wreak!

'Were this same spear, which in my hand
　　I grasp,
The British sceptre, here would I to thee
The symbol yield; and would undo this
　　clasp,　　　　　　　　　　156
If it confined the robe of sovereignty.
Odious to me the pomp of regal court,
　　And joyless sylvan sport,
While thou art roving, wretched and
　　forlorn,　　　　　　　　　　160
Thy couch the dewy earth, thy roof the
　　forest thorn!'

Then Artegal thus spake: 'I only sought
Within this realm a place of safe retreat;
Beware of rousing an ambitious thought;
Beware of kindling hopes for me un-
　　meet!　　　　　　　　　　165
Thou art reputed wise, but in my mind
　　Art pitiably blind:
Full soon this generous purpose thou
　　may'st rue,
When that which has been done no wishes
　　can undo.

'Who, when a crown is fixed upon his head,
Would balance claim with claim, and
　　right with right?　　　　　　171
But thou—I know not how inspired, how
　　led—
Wouldst change the course of things in
　　all men's sight!
And this for one who cannot imitate
　　Thy virtue, who may hate:　　175
For, if, by such strange sacrifice restored,
He reign, thou still must be his king, and
　　sovereign lord;

'Lifted in magnanimity above
Aught that my feeble nature could per-
　　form,
Or even conceive; surpassing me in love
Far as in power the eagle doth the worm:

I, Brother! only should be king in name,
    And govern to my shame;
A shadow in a hated land, while all
Of glad or willing service to thy share
    would fall.'   185

'Believe it not,' said Elidure; 'respect
Awaits on virtuous life, and ever most
Attends on goodness with dominion
    decked,
Which stands the universal empire's
    boast;
This can thy own experience testify: 190
    Nor shall thy foes deny
That, in the gracious opening of thy reign,
Our father's spirit seemed in thee to
    breathe again.

'And what if o'er that bright unbosoming
Clouds of disgrace and envious fortune
    past!   195
Have we not seen the glories of the spring
By veil of noontide darkness overcast?
The frith that glittered like a warrior's
    shield,
    The sky, the gay green field,
Are vanished; gladness ceases in the
    groves,   200
And trepidation strikes the blackened
    mountain-coves.

'But is that gloom dissolved? how passing
    clear
Seems the wide world, far brighter than
    before!
Even so thy latent worth will re-appear,
Gladdening the people's heart from shore
    to shore;   205
For youthful faults ripe virtues shall
    atone;
    Re-seated on thy throne,
Proof shalt thou furnish that misfortune,
    pain,
And sorrow, have confirmed thy native
    right to reign.

'But, not to overlook what thou may'st
    know,   210
Thy enemies are neither weak nor few;
And circumspect must be our course, and
    slow,
Or from my purpose ruin may ensue.
Dismiss thy followers;—let them calmly
    wait
    Such change in thy estate   215
As I already have in thought devised;
And which, with caution due, may soon
    be realized.'

The Story tells what courses were pur-
    sued,
Until king Elidure, with full consent
Of all his peers, before the multitude, 220
Rose,—and, to consummate this just in-
    tent,

Did place upon his brother's head the
    crown,
    Relinquished by his own;
Then to his people cried, 'Receive your
    lord,
Gorbonian's first-born son, your rightful
    king restored!'   225

The people answered with a loud acclaim:
Yet more;—heart-smitten by the heroic
    deed,
The reinstated Artegal became
Earth's noblest penitent; from bondage
    freed
Of vice—thenceforth unable to subvert
    Or shake his high desert.   231
Long did he reign; and, when he died,
    the tear
Of universal grief bedewed his honoured
    bier.

Thus was a Brother by a Brother saved;
With whom a crown (temptation that
    hath set   235
Discord in hearts of men till they have
    braved
Their nearest kin with deadly purpose
    met)
'Gainst duty weighed, and faithful love,
    did seem
    A thing of no esteem;
And, from this triumph of affection pure,
He bore the lasting name of 'pious Eli-
    dure!'   241

III

TO A BUTTERFLY

[Composed April 20, 1802.—Published 1807.]

I'VE watched you now a full half-hour,
Self-poised upon that yellow flower;
And, little Butterfly! indeed
I know not if you sleep or feed.
How motionless!—not frozen seas   5
More motionless! and then
What joy awaits you, when the breeze
Hath found you out among the trees,
And calls you forth again!

This plot of orchard-ground is ours;   10
My trees they are, my Sister's flowers;
Here rest your wings when they are weary;
Here lodge as in a sanctuary!
Come often to us, fear no wrong;
Sit near us on the bough!   15
We'll talk of sunshine and of song,
And summer days, when we were young;
Sweet childish days, that were as long
As twenty days are now.

POEMS FOUNDED ON THE AFFECTIONS

IV

A FAREWELL

[Finished May 29, 1802.—Published 1815.]

FAREWELL, thou little Nook of mountain-
ground,
Thou rocky corner in the lowest stair
Of that magnificent temple which doth
bound
One side of our whole vale with grandeur
rare;
Sweet garden-orchard, eminently fair,   5
The loveliest spot that man hath ever
found,
Farewell!—we leave thee to Heaven's
peaceful care,
Thee, and the Cottage which thou dost
surround.

Our boat is safely anchored by the shore,
And there will safely ride when we are
gone;   10
The flowering shrubs that deck our hum-
ble door
Will prosper, though untended and alone:
Fields, goods, and far-off chattels we have
none:
These narrow bounds contain our private
store
Of things earth makes, and sun doth
shine upon;   15
Here are they in our sight—we have no
more.

Sunshine and shower be with you, bud
and bell!
For two months now in vain we shall be
sought;
We leave you here in solitude to dwell
With these our latest gifts of tender
thought;   20
Thou, like the morning, in thy saffron
coat,
Bright gowan, and marsh-marigold, fare-
well!
Whom from the borders of the Lake we
brought,
And placed together near our rocky Well.

We go for One to whom ye will be dear;
And she will prize this Bower, this Indian
shed,   26
Our own contrivance, Building without
peer!
—A gentle Maid, whose heart is lowly
bred,
Whose pleasures are in wild fields
gatherèd,
With joyousness, and with a thoughtful
cheer,   30
Will come to you; to you herself will
wed;
And love the blessed life that we lead here.

Dear Spot! which we have watched with
tender heed,
Bringing thee chosen plants and blossoms
blown
Among the distant mountains, flower and
weed,   35
Which thou hast taken to thee as thy
own,
Making all kindness registered and
known;
Thou for our sakes, though Nature's child
indeed,
Fair in thyself and beautiful alone,
Hast taken gifts which thou dost little
need.   40

And O most constant, yet most fickle
Place,
That hast thy wayward moods, as thou
dost show
To them who look not daily on thy
face;
Who, being loved, in love no bounds dost
know,
And say'st, when we forsake thee, 'Let
them go!'   45
Thou easy-hearted Thing, with thy wild
race
Of weeds and flowers, till we return be
slow,
And travel with the year at a soft pace.

Help us to tell Her tales of years gone
by,
And this sweet spring, the best beloved
and best;   50
Joy will be flown in its mortality;
Something must stay to tell us of the
rest.
Here, thronged with primroses, the steep
rock's breast
Glittered at evening like a starry sky;
And in this bush our sparrow built her
nest,   55
Of which I sang one song that will not
die.

O happy Garden! whose seclusion deep
Hath been so friendly to industrious
hours;
And to soft slumbers, that did gently
steep
Our spirits, carrying with them dreams of
flowers,   60
And wild notes warbled among leafy
bowers;
Two burning months let summer over-
leap,
And, coming back with Her who will be
ours,
Into thy bosom we again shall creep.

V

STANZAS

WRITTEN IN MY POCKET-COPY OF
THOMSON'S 'CASTLE OF INDOLENCE'

[Composed May 9–11, 1802.—Published 1815.]

WITHIN our happy Castle there dwelt One
Whom without blame I may not over-
    look:
For never sun on living creature shone
Who more devout enjoyment with us
    took:
Here on his hours he hung as on a book, 5
On his own time here would he float
    away,
As doth a fly upon a summer brook;
But go to-morrow, or belike to-day,
Seek for him,—he is fled; and whither
    none can say.

Thus often would he leave our peaceful
    home,   10
And find elsewhere his business or de-
    light:
Out of our Valley's limits did he roam:
Full many a time, upon a stormy night,
His voice came to us from the neighbour-
    ing height:
Oft could we see him driving full in view
At mid-day when the sun was shining
    bright;   16
What ill was on him, what he had to do,
A mighty wonder bred among our quiet
    crew.

Ah! piteous sight it was to see this Man
When he came back to us, a withered
    flower,—   20
Or like a sinful creature, pale and wan.
Down would he sit; and without strength
    or power
Look at the common grass from hour to
    hour:
And oftentimes, how long I fear to say,
Where apple-trees in blossom made a
    bower,   25
Retired in that sunshiny shade he lay;
And, like a naked Indian, slept himself
    away.

Great wonder to our gentle tribe it was
Whenever from our Valley he withdrew;
For happier soul no living creature has 30
Than he had, being here the long day
    through.
Some thought he was a lover, and did woo:
Some thought far worse of him, and
    judged him wrong;
But verse was what he had been wedded to;
And his own mind did like a tempest
    strong   35
Come to him thus, and drove the weary
Wight along.

With him there often walked in friendly
    guise,
Or lay upon the moss by brook or tree,
A noticeable Man with large grey eyes,
And a pale face that seemed undoubt-
    edly   40
As if a blooming face it ought to be;
Heavy his low-hung lip did oft appear,
Deprest by weight of musing Phantasy;
Profound his forehead was, though not
    severe;
Yet some did think that he had little
    business here: 45

Sweet heaven forefend! his was a lawful
    right;
Noisy he was, and gamesome as a boy;
His limbs would toss about him with
    delight,
Like branches when strong winds the
    trees annoy.   49
Nor lacked his calmer hours device or toy
To banish listlessness and irksome care;
He would have taught you how you might
    employ
Yourself; and many did to him repair,—
And certes not in vain; he had inventions
    rare.

Expedients, too, of simplest sort he tried:
Long blades of grass, plucked round him
    as he lay,   56
Made, to his ear attentively applied,
A pipe on which the wind would deftly
    play;
Glasses he had, that little things display,
The beetle panoplied in gems and gold, 60
A mailèd angel on a battle-day;
The mysteries that cups of flowers enfold,
And all the gorgeous sights which fairies
    do behold.

He would entice that other Man to hear
His music, and to view his imagery: 65
And, sooth, these two were each to the
    other dear:
No livelier love in such a place could be:
There did they dwell—from earthly
    labour free,
As happy spirits as were ever seen;
If but a bird, to keep them company, 70
Or butterfly sate down, they were, I ween,
As pleased as if the same had been a
    Maiden-queen.

VI

LOUISA[1]

AFTER ACCOMPANYING HER ON A MOUN-
TAIN EXCURSION

[Composed (probably) 1801.—Published 1807.]

I MET Louisa in the shade,
And, having seen that lovely Maid,

[1] On the question of the identity of *Louisa*, see
Editor's note on *To a Butterfly*, p. 699.—ED.

Why should I fear to say
That, nymph-like, she is fleet and strong,
And down the rocks can leap along   5
Like rivulets in May?

[And she hath smiles to earth unknown;
Smiles, that with motion of their own
Do spread, and sink, and rise;
That come and go with endless play,
And ever, as they pass away,
Are hidden in her eyes.[1]]

She loves her fire, her cottage-home;
Yet o'er the moorland will she roam
In weather rough and bleak;   9
And, when against the wind she strains,
Oh! might I kiss the mountain rains
That sparkle on her cheek.

Take all that's mine 'beneath the moon,'
If I with her but half a noon
May sit beneath the walls   15
Of some old cave, or mossy nook,
When up she winds along the brook
To hunt the waterfalls.

VII

[Composed 1799.—Published 1800.]

STRANGE fits of passion have I known:
And I will dare to tell,
But in the Lover's ear alone,
What once to me befell.

When she I loved looked every day   5
Fresh as a rose in June,
I to her cottage bent my way,
Beneath an evening-moon.

Upon the moon I fixed my eye,
All over the wide lea;   10
With quickening pace my horse drew nigh
Those paths so dear to me.

And now we reached the orchard-plot;
And, as we climbed the hill,
The sinking moon to Lucy's cot   15
Came near, and nearer still.

In one of those sweet dreams I slept,
Kind Nature's gentlest boon!
And all the while my eyes I kept
On the descending moon.   20

My horse moved on; hoof after hoof
He raised, and never stopped:
When down behind the cottage roof,
At once, the bright moon dropped.

What fond and wayward thoughts will
   slide   25
Into a Lover's head!
'O mercy!' to myself I cried,
'If Lucy should be dead!'

[1] This stanza came second in all edd. from 1807 to 1843. It was most unfortunately omitted—for some reason unknown to us—in edd. 1845 and 1849.—ED.

VIII

[Composed 1799.—Published 1800.]

SHE dwelt among the untrodden ways
Beside the springs of Dove,
A Maid whom there were none to praise
And very few to love:

A violet by a mossy stone   5
Half hidden from the eye!
—Fair as a star, when only one
Is shining in the sky.

She lived unknown, and few could know
When Lucy ceased to be;   10
But she is in her grave, and, oh,
The difference to me!

IX

[Composed 1801.—Published 1807.]

I TRAVELLED among unknown men,
In lands beyond the sea;
Nor, England! did I know till then
What love I bore to thee.

'Tis past, that melancholy dream!   5
Nor will I quit thy shore
A second time; for still I seem
To love thee more and more.

Among thy mountains did I feel
The joy of my desire;   10
And she I cherished turned her wheel
Beside an English fire.

Thy mornings showed, thy nights concealed,
The bowers where Lucy played;
And thine too is the last green field   15
That Lucy's eyes surveyed.

X

[Composed 1826.—Published 1827.]

ERE with cold beads of midnight dew
Had mingled tears of thine,
I grieved, fond Youth! that thou shouldst
   sue
To haughty Geraldine.

Immoveable by generous sighs,   5
She glories in a train
Who drag, beneath our native skies,
An Oriental chain.

Pine not like them with arms across,
Forgetting in thy care   10
How the fast-rooted trees can toss
Their branches in mid air.

The humblest rivulet will take
Its own wild liberties;
And every day the imprisoned lake   15
Is flowing in the breeze.

Then crouch no more on suppliant
   knee,
But scorn with scorn outbrave;
A Briton, even in love, should be
A subject, not a slave!   20

XI

TO ——

[Composed 1824.—Published 1827.]

Look at the fate of summer flowers,
Which blow at daybreak, droop ere even-
   song;
And, grieved for their brief date, confess
   that ours,
Measured by what we are and ought to
   be,
Measured by all that, trembling, we fore-
   see,   5
  Is not so long!

If human Life do pass away,
Perishing yet more swiftly than the flower,
If we are creatures of a *winter's* day;
What space hath Virgin's beauty to dis-
   close   10
Her sweets, and triumph o'er the breath-
   ing rose?
  Not even an hour!

The deepest grove whose foliage hid
The happiest lovers Arcady might boast,
Could not the entrance of this thought
   forbid: 15
O be thou wise as they, soul-gifted Maid!
Nor rate too high what must so quickly
   fade,
  So soon be lost.

Then shall love teach some virtuous
   Youth
'To draw, out of the object of his eyes,' 20
The while on thee they gaze in simple
   truth,
Hues more exalted, 'a refinèd Form,'
That dreads not age, nor suffers from the
   worm,
  And never dies.

XII

THE FORSAKEN

[Dated 1804 (W.).—Probably composed earlier.—
Published 1842.]

The peace which others seek they find;
The heaviest storms not longest last;
Heaven grants even to the guiltiest mind
An amnesty for what is past;
When will my sentence be reversed?   5
I only pray to know the worst;
And wish, as if my heart would burst.

O weary struggle! silent years
Tell seemingly no doubtful tale;
And yet they leave it short, and fears   10
And hopes are strong and will prevail.
My calmest faith escapes not pain;
And, feeling that the hope is vain,
I think that he will come again.

XIII

[Composed 1800.—Published 1800.]

'Tis said that some have died for love:
And here and there a church-yard grave
  is found
In the cold north's unhallowed ground,
Because the wretched man himself had
  slain,
His love was such a grievous pain.   5
And there is one whom I five years have
  known;
He dwells alone
Upon Helvellyn's side:
He loved—the pretty Barbara died;
And thus he makes his moan: 10
Three years had Barbara in her grave
  been laid
When thus his moan he made:

'Oh, move, thou Cottage, from behind
  that oak!
Or let the aged tree uprooted lie,
That in some other way yon smoke   15
May mount into the sky!
The clouds pass on; they from the hea-
  vens depart:
I look—the sky is empty space;
I know not what I trace;
But when I cease to look, my hand is on
  my heart.   20

'O! what a weight is in these shades!
  Ye leaves,
That murmur once so dear, when will it
  cease?
Your sound my heart of rest bereaves,
It robs my heart of peace.
Thou Thrush, that singest loud—and loud
  and free,   25
Into yon row of willows flit,
Upon that alder sit;
Or sing another song, or choose another
  tree.

'Roll back, sweet Rill! back to thy
  mountain-bounds,   29
And there for ever be thy waters chained!
For thou dost haunt the air with sounds
That cannot be sustained;
If still beneath that pine-tree's ragged
  bough
Headlong yon waterfall must come,
Oh let it then be dumb!   35
Be anything, sweet Rill, but that which
  thou art now.

'Thou Eglantine, so bright with sunny
  showers,
Proud as a rainbow spanning half the
  vale,
Thou one fair shrub, oh! shed thy flowers,
And stir not in the gale.   40
For thus to see thee nodding in the air,
To see thy arch thus stretch and bend,
Thus rise and thus descend,—
Disturbs me till the sight is more than I
  can bear.'

The Man who makes this feverish com-
  plaint   45
Is one of giant stature, who could dance
Equipped from head to foot in iron mail.
Ah gentle Love! if ever thought was thine
To store up kindred hours for me, thy
  face
Turn from me, gentle Love! nor let me
  walk   50
Within the sound of Emma's voice, nor
  know
Such happiness as I have known to-day.

XIV

A COMPLAINT

[Composed 1806.—Published 1807.]

THERE is a change—and I am poor;
Your love hath been, nor long ago,
A fountain at my fond heart's door,
Whose only business was to flow;
And flow it did; not taking heed   5
Of its own bounty, or my need.

What happy moments did I count!
Blest was I then all bliss above!
Now, for that consecrated fount
Of murmuring, sparkling, living love,   10
What have I? shall I dare to tell?
A comfortless and hidden well.

A well of love—it may be deep—
I trust it is,—and never dry:
What matter? if the waters sleep   15
In silence and obscurity.
—Such change, and at the very door
Of my fond heart, hath made me poor.

XV

TO ——

[Composed 1824.—Published 1827.]

LET other bards of angels sing,
  Bright suns without a spot;
But thou art no such perfect thing:
  Rejoice that thou art not!

Heed not tho' none should call thee fair;
  So, Mary, let it be   6
If nought in loveliness compare
  With what thou art to me.

True beauty dwells in deep retreats,
  Whose veil is unremoved   10
Till heart with heart in concord beats,
  And the lover is beloved.

XVI

[Composed (?).—Published 1845.]

YES! thou art fair, yet be not moved
  To scorn the declaration,
That sometimes I in thee have loved
  My fancy's own creation.

Imagination needs must stir;   5
  Dear Maid, this truth believe,
Minds that have nothing to confer
  Find little to perceive.

Be pleased that nature made thee fit
  To feed my heart's devotion,   10
By laws to which all Forms submit
  In sky, air, earth, and ocean.

XVII

[Composed 1824.—Published 1827.]

How rich that forehead's calm expanse!
How bright that heaven-directed glance!
—Waft her to glory, wingèd Powers,
Ere sorrow be renewed,
And intercourse with mortal hours   5
Bring back a humbler mood!
So looked Cecilia when she drew
An Angel from his station;
So looked; not ceasing to pursue
Her tuneful adoration!   10

But hand and voice alike are still;
No sound *here* sweeps away the will
That gave it birth: in service meek
One upright arm sustains the cheek,
And one across the bosom lies—   15
That rose, and now forgets to rise,
Subdued by breathless harmonies
Of meditative feeling;
Mute strains from worlds beyond the
  skies,
Through the pure light of female eyes   20
Their sanctity revealing!

XVIII

[Composed (?).—Published 1845.]

WHAT heavenly smiles! O Lady mine,
Through my very heart they shine;
And, if my brow gives back their light,
Do thou look gladly on the sight;
As the clear Moon with modest pride   5
  Beholds her own bright beams
Reflected from the mountain's side
  And from the headlong streams.

XIX

TO ——

[Composed 1824.—Published 1827.]

O DEARER far than light and life are dear,
Full oft our human foresight I deplore;
Trembling, through my unworthiness, with fear
That friends, by death disjoined, may meet no more!

Misgivings, hard to vanquish or control, 5
Mix with the day, and cross the hour of rest;
While all the future, for thy purer soul,
With 'sober certainties' of love is blest.

That sigh of thine, not meant for human ear,
Tells that these words thy humbleness offend; 10
Yet bear me up—else faltering in the rear
Of a steep march: support me to the end.

Peace settles where the intellect is meek,
And Love is dutiful in thought and deed;
Through Thee communion with that Love I seek: 15
The faith Heaven strengthens where *he* moulds the Creed.

XX

LAMENT OF MARY QUEEN OF SCOTS

ON THE EVE OF A NEW YEAR

[Composed 1817.—Published 1820.]

I

SMILE of the Moon!—for so I name
That silent greeting from above;
A gentle flash of light that came
From her whom drooping captives love;
Or art thou of still higher birth? 5
Thou that didst part the clouds of earth
My torpor to reprove!

II

Bright boon of pitying Heaven!—alas,
I may not trust thy placid cheer!
Pondering that Time to-night will pass 10
The threshold of another year;
For years to me are sad and dull;
My very moments are too full
Of hopelessness and fear.

III

And yet the soul-awakening gleam, 15
That struck perchance the farthest cone
Of Scotland's rocky wilds, did seem
To visit me, and me alone;
Me, unapproached by any friend,
Save those who to my sorrows lend 20
Tears due unto their own.

IV

To-night the church-tower bells will ring
Through these wide realms a festive peal;
To the new year a welcoming;
A tuneful offering for the weal 25
Of happy millions lulled in sleep;
While I am forced to watch and weep,
By wounds that may not heal.

V

Born all too high, by wedlock raised
Still higher—to be cast thus low! 30
Would that mine eyes had never gazed
On aught of more ambitious show
Than the sweet flowerets of the fields!
—It is my royal state that yields
This bitterness of woe. 35

VI

Yet how?—for I, if there be truth
In the world's voice, was passing fair;
And beauty, for confiding youth,
Those shocks of passion can prepare
That kill the bloom before its time; 40
And blanch, without the owner's crime,
The most resplendent hair.

VII

Unblest distinction! showered on me
To bind a lingering life in chains:
All that could quit my grasp, or flee, 45
Is gone;—but not the subtle stains
Fixed in the spirit; for even here
Can I be proud that jealous fear
Of what I was remains.

VIII

A Woman rules my prison's key; 50
A sister Queen, against the bent
Of law and holiest sympathy,
Detains me, doubtful of the event;
Great God, who feel'st for my distress,
My thoughts are all that I possess, 55
O keep them innocent!

IX

Farewell desire of human aid,
Which abject mortals vainly court!
By friends deceived, by foes betrayed,
Of fears the prey, of hopes the sport; 60
Nought but the world-redeeming Cross
Is able to supply my loss,
My burthen to support.

X

Hark! the death-note of the year
Sounded by the castle-clock! 65
From her sunk eyes a stagnant tear
Stole forth, unsettled by the shock;
But oft the woods renewed their green,
Ere the tired head of Scotland's Queen
Reposed upon the block! 70

XXI

THE COMPLAINT

OF A FORSAKEN INDIAN WOMAN

[Composed 1798.—Published 1798.]

[When a Northern Indian, from sickness, is unable
to continue his journey with his companions,
he is left behind, covered over with deer-skins,
and is supplied with water, food, and fuel, if
the situation of the place will afford it. He is
informed of the track which his companions
intend to pursue, and if he be unable to follow,
or overtake them, he perishes alone in the
desert, unless he should have the good fortune
to fall in with some other tribes of Indians. The
females are equally, or still more, exposed to
the same fate. See that very interesting work
Hearne's 'Journey from Hudson's Bay to the
Northern Ocean.' In the high northern latitudes,
as the same writer informs us, when the northern
lights vary their position in the air, they make
a rustling and a crackling noise, as alluded to in
the following poem.]

I

BEFORE I see another day,
Oh let my body die away!
In sleep I heard the northern gleams;
The stars, they were among my dreams;
In rustling conflict through the skies,   5
I heard, I saw the flashes drive,
And yet they are upon my eyes,
And yet I am alive;
Before I see another day,
Oh let my body die away!   10

II

My fire is dead: it knew no pain;
Yet is it dead, and I remain:
All stiff with ice the ashes lie;
And they are dead, and I will die.
When I was well, I wished to live,   15
For clothes, for warmth, for food, and
    fire;
But they to me no joy can give,
No pleasure now, and no desire.
Then here contented will I lie!
Alone, I cannot fear to die.   20

III

Alas! ye might have dragged me on
Another day, a single one!
Too soon I yielded to despair;
Why did ye listen to my prayer?
When ye were gone my limbs were
    stronger;   25
And oh, how grievously I rue,
That, afterwards, a little longer,
My friends, I did not follow you!
For strong and without pain I lay,
Dear friends, when ye were gone away.   30

IV

My Child! they gave thee to another,
A woman who was not thy mother.

When from my arms my Babe they took,
On me how strangely did he look!
Through his whole body something ran,
A most strange working did I see;   36
—As if he strove to be a man,
That he might pull the sledge for me:
And then he stretched his arms, how
    wild!
Oh mercy! like a helpless child.   40

V

My little joy! my little pride!
In two days more I must have died.
Then do not weep and grieve for me;
I feel I must have died with thee.
O wind, that o'er my head art flying   45
The way my friends their course did bend,
I should not feel the pain of dying,
Could I with thee a message send;
Too soon, my friends, ye went away;
For I had many things to say.   50

VI

I'll follow you across the snow;
Ye travel heavily and slow;
In spite of all my weary pain
I'll look upon your tents again.
—My fire is dead, and snowy white   55
The water which beside it stood:
The wolf has come to me to-night,
And he has stolen away my food.
For ever left alone am I;
Then wherefore should I fear to die?   60

VII

Young as I am, my course is run,
I shall not see another sun;
I cannot lift my limbs to know
If they have any life or no.
My poor forsaken Child, if I   65
For once could have thee close to me,
With happy heart I then would die,
And my last thought would happy be;
But thou, dear Babe, art far away,
Nor shall I see another day.   70

XXII

THE LAST OF THE FLOCK

[Composed 1798.—Published 1798.]

I

IN distant countries have I been,
And yet I have not often seen
A healthy man, a man full grown,
Weep in the public roads, alone.
But such a one, on English ground,   5
And in the broad highway, I met;
Along the broad highway he came,
His cheeks with tears were wet:
Sturdy he seemed, though he was sad;
And in his arms a Lamb he had.   10

II

He saw me, and he turned aside,
As if he wished himself to hide:
And with his coat did then essay
To wipe those briny tears away.
I followed him, and said, 'My friend,   15
What ails you? wherefore weep you so?'
—'Shame on me, Sir! this lusty Lamb,
He makes my tears to flow.
To-day I fetched him from the rock;
He is the last of all my flock.   20

III

'When I was young, a single man,
And after youthful follies ran,
Though little given to care and thought,
Yet, so it was, an ewe I bought;
And other sheep from her I raised,   25
As healthy sheep as you might see;
And then I married, and was rich
As I could wish to be;
Of sheep I numbered a full score,
And every year increased my store.   30

IV

'Year after year my stock it grew;
And from this one, this single ewe,
Full fifty comely sheep I raised,
As fine a flock as ever grazed!
Upon the Quantock hills they fed;   35
They throve, and we at home did thrive:
—This lusty Lamb of all my store
Is all that is alive;
And now I care not if we die,
And perish all of poverty.   40

V

'Six Children, Sir! had I to feed;
Hard labour in a time of need!
My pride was tamed, and in our grief
I of the Parish asked relief.
They said, I was a wealthy man;   45
My sheep upon the uplands fed,
And it was fit that thence I took
Whereof to buy us bread.
"Do this: how can we give to you,"
They cried, "what to the poor is due?"   50

VI

'I sold a sheep, as they had said,
And bought my little children bread,
And they were healthy with their food;
For me—it never did me good.
A woeful time it was for me,   55
To see the end of all my gains,
The pretty flock which I had reared
With all my care and pains,
To see it melt like snow away—
For me it was a woeful day.   60

VII

'Another still! and still another!
A little lamb, and then its mother!

It was a vein that never stopped—
Like blood-drops from my heart they
    dropped.
Till thirty were not left alive   65
They dwindled, dwindled, one by one;
And I may say, that many a time
I wished they all were gone—
Reckless of what might come at last
Were but the bitter struggle past.   70

VIII

'To wicked deeds I was inclined,
And wicked fancies crossed my mind;
And every man I chanced to see,
I thought he knew some ill of me:
No peace, no comfort could I find,   75
No ease, within doors or without;
And crazily and wearily
I went my work about;
And oft was moved to flee from home,
And hide my head where wild beasts
    roam.   80

IX

'Sir! 'twas a precious flock to me,
As dear as my own children be;
For daily with my growing store
I loved my children more and more.
Alas! it was an evil time;   85
God cursed me in my sore distress;
I prayed, yet every day I thought
I loved my children less;
And every week, and every day,
My flock it seemed to melt away.   90

X

'They dwindled, Sir, sad sight to see!
From ten to five, from five to three,
A lamb, a wether, and a ewe;—
And then at last from three to two;
And, of my fifty, yesterday   95
I had but only one:
And here it lies upon my arm,
Alas! and I have none;—
To-day I fetched it from the rock;
It is the last of all my flock.'   100

XXIII

REPENTANCE

A PASTORAL BALLAD

[Composed 1804.—Published 1820.]

THE fields which with covetous spirit we
    sold,
Those beautiful fields, the delight of the
    day,
Would have brought us more good than a
    burthen of gold,
Could we but have been as contented as
    they.

When the troublesome Tempter beset us,
said I,   5
'Let him come, with his purse proudly
grasped in his hand;
But, Allan, be true to me, Allan,—we'll
die
Before he shall go with an inch of the
land!'

There dwelt we, as happy as birds in their
bowers;
Unfettered as bees that in gardens abide;
We could do what we liked with the land,
it was ours;   11
And for us the brook murmured that ran
by its side.

But now we are strangers, go early or
late;
And often, like one overburthened with
sin,
With my hand on the latch of the half-
opened gate,   15
I look at the fields, but I cannot go in!

When I walk by the hedge on a bright
summer's day,
Or sit in the shade of my grandfather's tree,
A stern face it puts on, as if ready to say,
'What ails you, that you must come
creeping to me!'   20

With our pastures about us, we could not
be sad;
Our comfort was near if we ever were
crost;
But the comfort, the blessings, and wealth
that we had,
We slighted them all,—and our birthright was lost.

Oh, ill-judging sire of an innocent son   25
Who must now be a wanderer! but peace
to that strain!
Think of evening's repose when our
labour was done,
The sabbath's return; and its leisure's
soft chain!

And in sickness, if night had been sparing
of sleep,
How cheerful, at sunrise, the hill where I
stood,   30
Looking down on the kine, and our treasure of sheep
That besprinkled the field; 'twas like
youth in my blood!

Now I cleave to the house, and am dull as
a snail;
And, oftentimes, hear the church-bell
with a sigh,
That follows the thought—We've no land
in the vale,   35
Save six feet of earth where our forefathers lie!

XXIV

THE

AFFLICTION OF MARGARET ——

[Dated 1804 (W.).—Probably composed earlier
(1801?).—Published 1807.]

I

WHERE art thou, my beloved Son,
Where art thou, worse to me than dead?
Oh find me, prosperous or undone!
Or, if the grave be now thy bed,
Why am I ignorant of the same   5
That I may rest; and neither blame
Nor sorrow may attend thy name?

II

Seven years, alas! to have received
No tidings of an only child;
To have despaired, have hoped, believed,
And been for evermore beguiled;   11
Sometimes with thoughts of very bliss!
I catch at them, and then I miss;
Was ever darkness like to this?

III

He was among the prime in worth,   15
An object beauteous to behold;
Well born, well bred; I sent him forth
Ingenuous, innocent, and bold;
If things ensued that wanted grace,
As hath been said, they were not base; 20
And never blush was on my face.

IV

Ah! little doth the young-one dream,
When full of play and childish cares,
What power is in his wildest scream,
Heard by his mother unawares!   25
He knows it not, he cannot guess:
Years to a mother bring distress;
But do not make her love the less.

V

Neglect me! no, I suffered long
From that ill thought; and, being blind,
Said, 'Pride shall help me in my wrong:
Kind mother have I been, as kind   32
As ever breathed:' and that is true;
I've wet my path with tears like dew,
Weeping for him when no one knew.   35

VI

My Son, if thou be humbled, poor,
Hopeless of honour and of gain,
Oh! do not dread thy mother's door;
Think not of me with grief and pain:
I now can see with better eyes;   40
And worldly grandeur I despise,
And fortune with her gifts and lies.

VII

Alas! the fowls of heaven have wings,
And blasts of heaven will aid their flight;
They mount—how short a voyage brings
The wanderers back to their delight!   46

Chains tie us down by land and sea;
And wishes, vain as mine, may be
All that is left to comfort thee.

VIII

Perhaps some dungeon hears thee groan,
Maimed, mangled by inhuman men;   51
Or thou upon a desert thrown
Inheritest the lion's den;
Or hast been summoned to the deep,
Thou, thou and all thy mates, to keep   55
An incommunicable sleep.

IX

I look for ghosts; but none will force
Their way to me: 'tis falsely said
That there was ever intercourse
Between the living and the dead;   60
For, surely, then I should have sight
Of him I wait for day and night,
With love and longings infinite.

X

My apprehensions come in crowds;
I dread the rustling of the grass;   65
The very shadows of the clouds
Have power to shake me as they pass:
I question things and do not find
One that will answer to my mind;
And all the world appears unkind.   70

XI

Beyond participation lie
My troubles, and beyond relief:
If any chance to heave a sigh,
They pity me, and not my grief.
Then come to me, my Son, or send   75
Some tidings that my woes may end;
I have no other earthly friend!

XXV

THE COTTAGER TO HER INFANT

BY MY SISTER

[Composed 1805.—Published 1815.]

THE days are cold, the nights are long,
The north-wind sings a doleful song;
Then hush again upon my breast;
All merry things are now at rest,
Save thee, my pretty Love!   5

The kitten sleeps upon the hearth,
The crickets long have ceased their mirth;
There's nothing stirring in the house
Save one *wee*, hungry, nibbling mouse,
Then why so busy thou?   10

Nay! start not at that sparkling light;
'Tis but the moon that shines so bright
On the window pane bedropped with
rain:
Then little Darling! sleep again,
And wake when it is day.   15

XXVI

MATERNAL GRIEF

[Composed 1810 (?).—Published 1842.]

DEPARTED Child! I could forget thee once
Though at my bosom nursed; this woeful
gain
Thy dissolution brings, that in my soul
Is present and perpetually abides
A shadow, never, never to be displaced   5
By the returning substance, seen or
touched,
Seen by mine eyes, or clasped in my
embrace.
Absence and death how differ they! and
how
Shall I admit that nothing can restore   9
What one short sigh so easily removed?—
Death, life, and sleep, reality and thought,
Assist me, God, their boundaries to
know,
O teach me calm submission to thy Will!

The Child she mourned had over-
stepped the pale
Of Infancy, but still did breathe the air   15
That sanctifies its confines, and partook
Reflected beams of that celestial light
To all the Little-ones on sinful earth
Not unvouchsafed—a light that warmed
and cheered
Those several qualities of heart and mind
Which, in her own blest nature, rooted
deep,   21
Daily before the Mother's watchful eye,
And not hers only, their peculiar charms
Unfolded,—beauty, for its present self,
And for its promises to future years,   25
With not unfrequent rapture fondly
hailed.

Have you espied upon a dewy lawn
A pair of Leverets each provoking each
To a continuance of their fearless sport,
Two separate Creatures in their several
gifts   30
Abounding, but so fashioned that, in all
That Nature prompts them to display,
their looks,
Their starts of motion and their fits of
rest,
An undistinguishable style appears
And character of gladness, as if Spring   35
Lodged in their innocent bosoms, and the
spirit
Of the rejoicing morning were their own?

Such union, in the lovely Girl maintained
And her twin Brother, had the parent
seen,
Ere, pouncing like a ravenous bird of
prey,   40
Death in a moment parted them, and left

93

The Mother, in her turns of anguish, worse
Than desolate; for oft-times from the sound
Of the survivor's sweetest voice (dear child,
He knew it not) and from his happiest looks,   45
Did she extract the food of self-reproach,
As one that lived ungrateful for the stay
By Heaven afforded to uphold her maimed
And tottering spirit. And full oft the Boy,
Now first acquainted with distress and grief,   50
Shrunk from his Mother's presence, shunned with fear
Her sad approach, and stole away to find,
In his known haunts of joy where'er he might,
A more congenial object. But, as time
Softened her pangs, and reconciled the child   55
To what he saw, he gradually returned,
Like a scared Bird encouraged to renew
A broken intercourse; and, while his eyes
Were yet with pensive fear and gentle awe
Turned upon her who bore him, she would stoop   60
To imprint a kiss that lacked not power
to spread
Faint colour over both their pallid cheeks,
And stilled his tremulous lip. Thus they were calmed
And cheered; and now together breathe fresh air
In open fields; and when the glare of day   65
Is gone, and twilight to the Mother's wish
Befriends the observance, readily they join
In walks whose boundary is the lost One's grave,
Which he with flowers hath planted, finding there
Amusement, where the Mother does not miss   70
Dear consolation, kneeling on the turf
In prayer, yet blending with that solemn rite
Of pious faith the vanities of grief;
For such, by pitying Angels and by Spirits
Transferred to regions upon which the clouds   75
Of our weak nature rest not, must be deemed
Those willing tears, and unforbidden sighs,
And all those tokens of a cherished sorrow,
Which, soothed and sweetened by the grace of Heaven   79
As now it is, seems to her own fond heart
Immortal as the love that gave it being.

XXVII

THE SAILOR'S MOTHER

[Composed March 11, 12, 1802.—Published 1807.]

ONE morning (raw it was and wet—
A foggy day in winter time)
A Woman on the road I met,
Not old, though something past her prime:
Majestic in her person, tall and straight;
And like a Roman matron's was her mien
and gait.   6

The ancient spirit is not dead;
Old times, thought I, are breathing there;
Proud was I that my country bred
Such strength, a dignity so fair: 10
She begged an alms, like one in poor estate;
I looked at her again, nor did my pride abate.

When from these lofty thoughts I woke,
'What is it,' said I, 'that you bear,
Beneath the covert of your Cloak,   15
Protected from this cold damp air?'
She answered, soon as she the question heard,
'A simple burthen, Sir, a little Singing-bird.'

And, thus continuing, she said,
'I had a Son, who many a day   20
Sailed on the seas, but he is dead;
In Denmark he was cast away:
And I have travelled weary miles to see
If aught which he had owned might still remain for me.

'The bird and cage they both were his:
'Twas my Son's bird; and neat and trim   26
He kept it: many voyages
The singing-bird had gone with him;
When last he sailed, he left the bird behind;
From bodings, as might be, that hung upon his mind.   30

'He to a fellow-lodger's care
Had left it, to be watched and fed,
And pipe its song in safety;—there
I found it when my Son was dead;
And now, God help me for my little wit!   35
I bear it with me, Sir;—he took so much delight in it.'

XXVIII

THE CHILDLESS FATHER

[Composed 1800.—Published 1800.]

'UP, Timothy, up with your staff and away!
Not a soul in the village this morning will stay;

94

The hare has just started from Hamilton's
    grounds,
And Skiddaw is glad with the cry of the
    hounds.'

—Of coats and of jackets grey, scarlet,
    and green,   5
On the slopes of the pastures all colours
    were seen;
With their comely blue aprons, and caps
    white as snow,
The girls on the hills made a holiday
    show.

Fresh sprigs of green box-wood, not six
    months before,
Filled the funeral basin[1] at Timothy's
    door;   10
A coffin through Timothy's threshold had
    past;
One Child did it bear, and that Child
    was his last.

Now fast up the dell came the noise and
    the fray,
The horse, and the horn, and the hark!
    hark away!
Old Timothy took up his staff, and he
    shut   15
With a leisurely motion the door of his
    hut.

Perhaps to himself at that moment he
    said;
'The key I must take, for my Ellen is
    dead.'
But of this in my ears not a word did he
    speak;
And he went to the chase with a tear on
    his cheek.   20

<h2 style="text-align:center">XXIX</h2>

<h3 style="text-align:center">THE EMIGRANT MOTHER</h3>

[Composed March 16, 17, 1802.—Published 1807.]

ONCE in a lonely hamlet I sojourned
In which a Lady driven from France did
    dwell;
The big and lesser griefs with which
    she mourned
In friendship she to me would often tell.

This Lady, dwelling upon British ground,
Where she was childless, daily would
    repair   6
To a poor neighbouring cottage; as I
    found,
For sake of a young Child whose home
    was there.

[1] In several parts of the North of England, when
a funeral takes place, a basin full of sprigs of box-
wood is placed at the door of the house from which
the coffin is taken up, and each person who attends
the funeral ordinarily takes a sprig of this box-wood,
and throws it into the grave of the deceased.

Once having seen her clasp with fond
    embrace
This Child, I chanted to myself a lay,   10
Endeavouring, in our English tongue, to
    trace
Such things as she unto the Babe might
    say:
And thus, from what I heard and knew,
    or guessed,
My song the workings of her heart ex-
    pressed.

I

'Dear Babe, thou daughter of another, 15
One moment let me be thy mother!
An infant's face and looks are thine
And sure a mother's heart is mine:
Thy own dear mother's far away,
At labour in the harvest field: 20
Thy little sister is at play;—
What warmth, what comfort would it
    yield
To my poor heart, if thou wouldst be
One little hour a child to me!

II

'Across the waters I am come,   25
And I have left a babe at home:
A long, long way of land and sea!
Come to me—I'm no enemy:
I am the same who at thy side
Sate yesterday, and made a nest   50
For thee, sweet Baby!—thou hast tried,
Thou know'st the pillow of my breast;
Good, good art thou:—alas! to me
Far more than I can be to thee.

III

'Here, little Darling, dost thou lie;   35
An infant thou, a mother I!
Mine wilt thou be, thou hast no fears;
Mine art thou—spite of these my tears.
Alas! before I left the spot,
My baby and its dwelling-place,   40
The nurse said to me, "Tears should not
Be shed upon an infant's face,
It was unlucky"—no, no, no;
No truth is in them who say so!

IV

'My own dear Little-one will sigh,   45
Sweet Babe! and they will let him die.
"He pines," they'll say, "it is his doom,
And you may see his hour is come."
Oh! had he but thy cheerful smiles,
Limbs stout as thine, and lips as gay,   50
Thy looks, thy cunning, and thy wiles,
And countenance like a summer's day,
They would have hopes of him; and
    then
I should behold his face again!

V

''Tis gone—like dreams that we forget;
There was a smile or two—yet—yet   56
I can remember them, I see
The smiles, worth all the world to me.
Dear Baby! I must lay thee down;   59
Thou troublest me with strange alarms;
Smiles hast thou, bright ones of thy own;
I cannot keep thee in my arms;
For they confound me;—where—where is
That last, that sweetest smile of his?

VI

'Oh! how I love thee!—we will stay   65
Together here this one half day.
My sister's child, who bears my name,
From France to sheltering England came;
She with her mother crossed the sea;
The babe and mother near me dwell: 70
Yet does my yearning heart to thee
Turn rather, though I love her well:
Rest, little Stranger, rest thee here!
Never was any child more dear!

VII

'—I cannot help it; ill intent   75
I've none, my pretty Innocent!
I weep—I know they do thee wrong,
These tears—and my poor idle tongue.
Oh, what a kiss was that! my cheek
How cold it is! but thou art good;   80
Thine eyes are on me—they would speak,
I think, to help me if they could.
Blessings upon that soft, warm face,
My heart again is in its place!

VIII

'While thou art mine, my little Love,   85
This cannot be a sorrowful grove;
Contentment, hope, and mother's glee,
I seem to find them all in thee:
Here's grass to play with, here are
    flowers;
I'll call thee by my darling's name;   90
Thou hast, I think, a look of ours,
Thy features seem to me the same;
His little sister thou shalt be;
And, when once more my home I see,
I'll tell him many tales of Thee.'   95

XXX

VAUDRACOUR AND JULIA

[Composed probably 1804.—Published 1820.]

The following tale was written as an Episode, in
a work from which its length may perhaps
exclude it. The facts are true; no invention
as to these has been exercised, as none was
needed.

O HAPPY time of youthful lovers (thus
My story may begin) O balmy time,
In which a love-knot on a lady's brow
Is fairer than the fairest star in heaven!

To such inheritance of blessed fancy   5
(Fancy that sports more desperately with
    minds
Than ever fortune hath been known to
    do)
The high-born Vaudracour was brought,
    by years
Whose progress had a little overstepped
His stripling prime. A town of small
    repute,   10
Among the vine-clad mountains of Au-
    vergne,
Was the Youth's birth-place. There he
    wooed a Maid
Who heard the heart-felt music of his suit
With answering vows. Plebeian was the
    stock,
Plebeian, though ingenuous, the stock,   15
From which her graces and her honours
    sprung:
And hence the father of the enamoured
    Youth,
With haughty indignation, spurned the
    thought
Of such alliance.—From their cradles up,
With but a step between their several
    homes,   20
Twins had they been in pleasure; after
    strife
And petty quarrels, had grown fond
    again;
Each other's advocate, each other's stay;
And, in their happiest moments, not
    content,
If more divided than a sportive pair   25
Of sea-fowl, conscious both that they are
    hovering
Within the eddy of a common blast,
Or hidden only by the concave depth
Of neighbouring billows from each other's
    sight.

Thus, not without concurrence of an
    age   30
Unknown to memory, was an earnest
    given
By ready nature for a life of love,
For endless constancy, and placid truth;
But whatsoe'er of such rare treasure lay
Reserved, had fate permitted, for sup-
    port   35
Of their maturer years, his present mind
Was under fascination;—he beheld
A vision, and adored the thing he saw.
Arabian fiction never filled the world
With half the wonders that were wrought
    for him.   40
Earth breathed in one great presence of
    the spring;
Life turned the meanest of her imple-
    ments,
Before his eyes, to price above all gold;
The house she dwelt in was a sainted
    shrine;

96

Her chamber-window did surpass in glory
The portals of the dawn; all Paradise   46
Could, by the simple opening of a door,
Let itself in upon him:—pathways, walks,
Swarmed with enchantment, till his spirit
        sank,
Surcharged, within him, overblest to
        move   50
Beneath a sun that wakes a weary world
To its dull round of ordinary cares;
A man too happy for mortality!

So passed the time, till, whether through
        effect
Of some unguarded moment that dis-
        solved   55
Virtuous restraint—ah, speak it, think it,
        not!
Deem rather that the fervent Youth, who
        saw
So many bars between his present state
And the dear haven where he wished to
        be
In honourable wedlock with his Love, 60
Was in his judgment tempted to decline
To perilous weakness, and entrust his
        cause
To nature for a happy end of all;
Deem that by such fond hope the Youth
        was swayed,
And bear with their transgression, when
        I add   65
That Julia, wanting yet the name of wife,
Carried about her for a secret grief
The promise of a mother.
                        To conceal
The threatened shame, the parents of the
        Maid
Found means to hurry her away by night,
And unforewarned, that in some distant
        spot   71
She might remain shrouded in privacy,
Until the babe was born. When morning
        came,
The Lover, thus bereft, stung with his
        loss,
And all uncertain whither he should turn,
Chafed like a wild beast in the toils; but
        soon   76
Discovering traces of the fugitives,
Their steps he followed to the Maid's
        retreat.
Easily may the sequel be divined—
Walks to and fro—watchings at every
        hour;   80
And the fair Captive, who, whene'er she
        may,
Is busy at her casement as the swallow
Fluttering its pinions, almost within
        reach,
About the pendent nest, did thus espy
Her Lover!—thence a stolen interview, 85
Accomplished under friendly shade of
        night.

I pass the raptures of the pair;—such
        theme
Is, by innumerable poets, touched
In more delightful verse than skill of mine
Could fashion; chiefly by that darling
        bard   90
Who told of Juliet and her Romeo,
And of the lark's note heard before its
        time,
And of the streaks that laced the severing
        clouds
In the unrelenting east.—Through all her
        courts
The vacant city slept; the busy winds, 95
That keep no certain intervals of rest,
Moved not; meanwhile the galaxy dis-
        played
Her fires, that like mysterious pulses beat
Aloft;—momentous but uneasy bliss!
To their full hearts the universe seemed
        hung   100
On that brief meeting's slender filament!

They parted; and the generous Vau-
        dracour
Reached speedily the native threshold,
        bent
On making (so the Lovers had agreed)
A sacrifice of birthright to attain   105
A final portion from his father's hand;
Which granted, Bride and Bridegroom
        then would flee
To some remote and solitary place,
Shady as night, and beautiful as heaven,
Where they may live, with no one to
        behold   110
Their happiness, or to disturb their love.
But *now* of this no whisper; not the less,
If ever an obtrusive word were dropped
Touching the matter of his passion, still,
In his stern father's hearing, Vaudracour
Persisted openly that death alone   116
Should abrogate his human privilege
Divine, of swearing everlasting truth,
Upon the altar, to the Maid he loved.

'You shall be baffled in your mad in-
        tent   120
If there be justice in the court of France,'
Muttered the Father.—From these words
        the Youth
Conceived a terror; and, by night or day
Stirred nowhere without weapons, that
        full soon   124
Found dreadful provocation: for at night,
When to his chamber he retired, attempt
Was made to seize him by three armèd
        men,
Acting, in furtherance of the Father's will,
Under a private signet of the State.
One the rash Youth's ungovernable hand
Slew, and as quickly to a second gave 131
A perilous wound—he shuddered to be-
        hold

97   E

The breathless corse; then peacefully resigned
His person to the law, was lodged in
prison,
And wore the fetters of a criminal.   135

Have you observed a tuft of wingèd seed
That, from the dandelion's naked stalk,
Mounted aloft, is suffered not to use
Its natural gifts for purposes of rest,
Driven by the autumnal whirlwind to and
fro   140
Through the wide element? or have you
marked
The heavier substance of a leaf-clad
bough,
Within the vortex of a foaming flood,
Tormented? by such aid you may con-
ceive
The perturbation that ensued;—ah, no!
Desperate the Maid—the Youth is stained
with blood;   146
Unmatchable on earth is their disquiet!
Yet as the troubled seed and tortured
bough
Is man, subjected to despotic sway.

For him, by private influence with the
Court,   150
Was pardon gained, and liberty procured;
But not without exaction of a pledge,
Which liberty and love dispersed in air.
He flew to her from whom they would
divide him—
He clove to her who could not give him
peace—   155
Yea, his first word of greeting was,—'All
right
Is gone from me; my lately-towering
hopes,
To the least fibre of their lowest root,
Are withered; thou no longer canst be
mine,
I thine—the conscience-stricken must not
woo   160
The unruffled Innocent,—I see thy face,
Behold thee, and my misery is complete!'

'One, are we not?' exclaimed the
Maiden—'One,
For innocence and youth, for weal and
woe?'
Then with the father's name she coupled
words   165
Of vehement indignation; but the Youth
Checked her with filial meekness; for no
thought
Uncharitable crossed his mind, no sense
Of hasty anger, rising in the eclipse
Of true domestic loyalty, did e'er   170
Find place within his bosom.—Once again
The persevering wedge of tyranny
Achieved their separation: and once more
Were they united,—to be yet again

Disparted, pitiable lot! But here   175
A portion of the tale may well be left
In silence, though my memory could add
Much how the Youth, in scanty space of
time,
Was traversed from without; much, too,
of thoughts
That occupied his days in solitude   180
Under privation and restraint; and what,
Through dark and shapeless fear of
things to come,
And what, through strong compunction
for the past,
He suffered—breaking down in heart and
mind!

Doomed to a third and last captivity,
His freedom he recovered on the eve   186
Of Julia's travail. When the babe was
born,
Its presence tempted him to cherish
schemes
Of future happiness. 'You shall return,
Julia,' said he, 'and to your father's
house   190
Go with the child.—You have been
wretched; yet
The silver shower, whose reckless burthen
weighs
Too heavily upon the lily's head,
Oft leaves a saving moisture at its root.
Malice, beholding you, will melt away.195
Go!—'tis a town where both of us were
born;
None will reproach you, for our truth is
known;
And if, amid those once-bright bowers,
our fate
Remain unpitied, pity is not in man.
With ornaments—the prettiest, nature
yields   200
Or art can fashion, shall you deck our boy,
And feed his countenance with your own
sweet looks,
Till no one can resist him.—Now, even
now,
I see him sporting on the sunny lawn;
My father from the window sees him
too;   205
Startled, as if some new-created thing
Enriched the earth, or Faery of the woods
Bounded before him;—but the unweeting
Child
Shall by his beauty win his grandsire's
heart,
So that it shall be softened, and our loves
End happily, as they began!'
                                 These gleams
Appeared but seldom; oftener was he
seen   212
Propping a pale and melancholy face
Upon the Mother's bosom; resting thus
His head upon one breast, while from the
other   215

The Babe was drawing in its quiet food.
—That pillow is no longer to be thine,
Fond Youth! that mournful solace now
   must pass
Into the list of things that cannot be!
Unwedded Julia, terror-smitten, hears
The sentence, by her mother's lip pro-
   nounced,   221
That dooms her to a convent.—Who shall
   tell,
Who dares report, the tidings to the lord
Of her affections? so they blindly asked
Who knew not to what quiet depths a
   weight   225
Of agony had pressed the Sufferer down:
The word, by others dreaded, he can hear
Composed and silent, without visible sign
Of even the least emotion. Noting this,
When the impatient object of his love 230
Upbraided him with slackness, he re-
   turned
No answer, only took the mother's hand
And kissed it; seemingly devoid of pain,
Or care, that what so tenderly he pressed
Was a dependant on the obdurate heart
Of one who came to disunite their lives 236
For ever—sad alternative! preferred,
By the unbending Parents of the Maid,
To secret 'spousals meanly disavowed.
—So be it!
            In the city he remained   240
A season after Julia had withdrawn
To those religious walls. He, too, de-
   parts—
Who with him?—even the senseless Little-
   one.
With that sole charge he passed the city-
   gates,
For the last time, attendant by the side
Of a close chair, a litter, or sedan,   246
In which the Babe was carried. To a hill,
That rose a brief league distant from the
   town,
The dwellers in that house where he had
   lodged
Accompanied his steps, by anxious love
Impelled;—they parted from him there,
   and stood   251
Watching below till he had disappeared
On the hill top. His eyes he scarcely took,
Throughout that journey, from the vehicle
(Slow-moving ark of all his hopes!) that
   veiled   255
The tender infant: and at every inn,
And under every hospitable tree
At which the bearers halted or reposed,
Laid him with timid care upon his knees,
And looked, as mothers ne'er were known
   to look,   260
Upon the nursling which his arms em-
   braced.

   This was the manner in which Vaudracour

Departed with his infant; and thus
   reached
His father's house, where to the innocent
   child
Admittance was denied. The young man
   spake   265
No word of indignation or reproof,
But of his father begged, a last request,
That a retreat might be assigned to him,
Where in forgotten quiet he might dwell,
With such allowance as his wants re-
   quired;   270
For wishes he had none. To a lodge that
   stood
Deep in a forest, with leave given, at the
   age
Of four-and-twenty summers he with-
   drew;
And thither took with him his motherless
   Babe,
And one domestic for their common
   needs,   275
An aged woman. It consoled him here
To attend upon the orphan, and per-
   form
Obsequious service to the precious child,
Which, after a short time, by some mis-
   take
Or indiscretion of the Father, died.— 280
The Tale I follow to its last recess
Of suffering or of peace, I know not
   which:
Theirs be the blame who caused the woe,
   not mine!

   From this time forth he never shared a
   smile
With mortal creature. An Inhabitant 285
Of that same town, in which the pair had
   left
So lively a remembrance of their griefs,
By chance of business coming within
   reach
Of his retirement, to the forest lodge
Repaired, but only found the matron
   there,   290
Who told him that his pains were thrown
   away,
For that her Master never uttered word
To living thing—not even to her.—Be-
   hold!
While they were speaking, Vaudracour
   approached;
But seeing some one near, as on the latch
Of the garden-gate his hand was laid, he
   shrunk—   296
And, like a shadow, glided out of view.
Shocked at his savage aspect, from the
   place
The visitor retired.
               Thus lived the Youth
Cut off from all intelligence with man, 300
And shunning even the light of common
   day;

Nor could the voice of Freedom, which
    through France
Full speedily resounded, public hope,
Or personal memory of his own deep
    wrongs,
Rouse him: but in those solitary shades
His days he wasted, an imbecile mind! 306

XXXI

THE IDIOT BOY

[Composed 1798.—Published 1798.]

'Tis eight o'clock,—a clear March night,
The moon is up,—the sky is blue,
The owlet, in the moonlight air,
Shouts from nobody knows where;
He lengthens out his lonely shout, 5
Halloo! halloo! a long halloo!

—Why bustle thus about your door,
What means this bustle, Betty Foy?
Why are you in this mighty fret?
And why on horseback have you set 10
Him whom you love, your Idiot Boy?

Scarcely a soul is out of bed;
Good Betty, put him down again;
His lips with joy they burr at you;
But, Betty! what has he to do 15
With stirrup, saddle, or with rein?

But Betty's bent on her intent;
For her good neighbour Susan Gale,
Old Susan, she who dwells alone,
Is sick, and makes a piteous moan, 20
As if her very life would fail.

There's not a house within a mile,
No hand to help them in distress;
Old Susan lies a-bed in pain,
And sorely puzzled are the twain, 25
For what she ails they cannot guess.

And Betty's husband's at the wood,
Where by the week he doth abide,
A woodman in the distant vale;
There's none to help poor Susan Gale; 30
What must be done? what will betide?

And Betty from the lane has fetched
Her Pony, that is mild and good;
Whether he be in joy or pain,
Feeding at will along the lane, 35
Or bringing fagots from the wood.

And he is all in travelling trim,—
And, by the moonlight, Betty Foy
Has on the well-girt saddle set
(The like was never heard of yet) 40
Him whom she loves, her Idiot Boy.

And he must post without delay
Across the bridge and through the dale,
And by the church, and o'er the down,
To bring a Doctor from the town, 45
Or she will die, old Susan Gale.

There is no need of boot or spur,
There is no need of whip or wand;
For Johnny has his holly-bough,
And with a *hurly-burly* now 50
He shakes the green bough in his hand.

And Betty o'er and o'er has told
The Boy, who is her best delight,
Both what to follow, what to shun,
What do, and what to leave undone, 55
How turn to left, and how to right.

And Betty's most especial charge,
Was, 'Johnny! Johnny! mind that you
Come home again, nor stop at all,—
Come home again, whate'er befall, 60
My Johnny, do, I pray you, do.'

To this did Johnny answer make,
Both with his head and with his hand,
And proudly shook the bridle too;
And then! his words were not a few, 65
Which Betty well could understand.

And now that Johnny is just going,
Though Betty's in a mighty flurry,
She gently pats the Pony's side,
On which her Idiot Boy must ride, 70
And seems no longer in a hurry.

But when the Pony moved his legs,
Oh! then for the poor Idiot Boy!
For joy he cannot hold the bridle,
For joy his head and heels are idle, 75
He's idle all for very joy.

And, while the Pony moves his legs,
In Johnny's left hand you may see
The green bough motionless and dead:
The Moon that shines above his head 80
Is not more still and mute than he.

His heart it was so full of glee
That, till full fifty yards were gone,
He quite forgot his holly whip,
And all his skill in horsemanship: 85
Oh! happy, happy, happy John.

And while the Mother, at the door,
Stands fixed, her face with joy o'erflows,
Proud of herself, and proud of him,
She sees him in his travelling trim, 90
How quietly her Johnny goes.

The silence of her Idiot Boy,
What hopes it sends to Betty's heart!
He's at the guide-post—he turns right;
She watches till he's out of sight, 95
And Betty will not then depart.

Burr, burr—now Johnny's lips they burr,
As loud as any mill, or near it;
Meek as a lamb the Pony moves,
And Johnny makes the noise he loves,
And Betty listens, glad to hear it. 101

Away she hies to Susan Gale:
Her Messenger's in merry tune;
The owlets hoot, the owlets curr,
And Johnny's lips they burr, burr, burr,
As on he goes beneath the moon.   106

His steed and he right well agree;
For of this Pony there's a rumour
That, should he lose his eyes and ears,
And should he live a thousand years,   110
He never will be out of humour.

But then he is a horse that thinks!
And, when he thinks, his pace is slack;
Now, though he knows poor Johnny well,
Yet, for his life, he cannot tell   115
What he has got upon his back.

So through the moonlight lanes they go,
And far into the moonlight dale,
And by the church, and o'er the down,
To bring a Doctor from the town,   120
To comfort poor old Susan Gale.

And Betty, now at Susan's side,
Is in the middle of her story,
What speedy help her Boy will bring,
With many a most diverting thing,   125
Of Johnny's wit, and Johnny's glory.

And Betty, still at Susan's side,
By this time is not quite so flurried:
Demure with porringer and plate
She sits, as if in Susan's fate   130
Her life and soul were buried.

But Betty, poor good woman! she,
You plainly in her face may read it,
Could lend out of that moment's store
Five years of happiness or more   135
To any that might need it.

But yet I guess that now and then
With Betty all was not so well;
And to the road she turns her ears,
And thence full many a sound she hears,
Which she to Susan will not tell.   141

Poor Susan moans, poor Susan groans;
'As sure as there's a moon in heaven,'
Cries Betty, 'he'll be back again;
They'll both be here—'tis almost ten—   145
Both will be here before eleven.'

Poor Susan moans, poor Susan groans;
The clock gives warning for eleven;
'Tis on the stroke—'He must be near,'
Quoth Betty, 'and will soon be here,   150
As sure as there's a moon in heaven.'

The clock is on the stroke of twelve,
And Johnny is not yet in sight:
—The Moon's in heaven, as Betty sees,
But Betty is not quite at ease;   155
And Susan has a dreadful night.

And Betty, half an hour ago,
On Johnny vile reflections cast:
'A little idle sauntering Thing!'
With other names, an endless string;   160
But now that time is gone and past.

And Betty's drooping at the heart,
That happy time all past and gone,
'How can it be he is so late?
The Doctor, he has made him wait;   165
Susan! they'll both be here anon.'

And Susan's growing worse and worse,
And Betty's in a sad *quandary;*
And then there's nobody to say
If she must go, or she must stay!   170
—She's in a sad *quandary.*

The clock is on the stroke of one;
But neither Doctor nor his Guide
Appears along the moonlight road;
There's neither horse nor man abroad,   175
And Betty's still at Susan's side

And Susan now begins to fear
Of sad mischances not a few,
That Johnny may perhaps be drowned;
Or lost, perhaps, and never found;   180
Which they must both for ever rue.

She prefaced half a hint of this
With, 'God forbid it should be true!'
At the first word that Susan said
Cried Betty, rising from the bed,   185
'Susan, I'd gladly stay with you.

'I must be gone, I must away:
Consider, Johnny's but half-wise;
Susan, we must take care of him,
If he is hurt in life or limb'—   190
'Oh God forbid!' poor Susan cries.

'What can I do?' says Betty, going,
'What can I do to ease your pain?
Good Susan tell me, and I'll stay;
I fear you're in a dreadful way,   195
But I shall soon be back again.'

'Nay, Betty, go! good Betty, go!
There's nothing that can ease my pain.'
Then off she hies; but with a prayer,
That God poor Susan's life would spare,
Till she comes back again.   201

So, through the moonlight lane she goes,
And far into the moonlight dale;
And how she ran, and how she walked,
And all that to herself she talked,   205
Would surely be a tedious tale.

In high and low, above, below,
In great and small, in round and square,
In tree and tower was Johnny seen,
In bush and brake, in black and green;
'Twas Johnny, Johnny, everywhere.   211

And while she crossed the bridge, there
　　came
A thought with which her heart is sore—
Johnny perhaps his horse forsook,
To hunt the moon within the brook,　215
And never will be heard of more.

Now is she high upon the down,
Alone amid a prospect wide;
There's neither Johnny nor his Horse
Among the fern or in the gorse;　220
There's neither Doctor nor his Guide.

'Oh saints! what is become of him?
Perhaps he's climbed into an oak,
Where he will stay till he is dead;
Or sadly he has been misled,　225
And joined the wandering gipsy-folk.

'Or him that wicked Pony's carried
To the dark cave, the goblin's hall;
Or in the castle he's pursuing
Among the ghosts his own undoing;　230
Or playing with the waterfall.'

At poor old Susan then she railed,
While to the town she posts away;
'If Susan had not been so ill,
Alas! I should have had him still,　235
My Johnny, till my dying day.'

Poor Betty, in this sad distemper,
The Doctor's self could hardly spare:
Unworthy things she talked, and wild;
Even he, of cattle the most mild,　240
The Pony had his share.

But now she's fairly in the town,
And to the Doctor's door she hies;
'Tis silence all on every side;
The town so long, the town so wide,　245
Is silent as the skies.

And now she's at the Doctor's door,
She lifts the knocker, rap, rap, rap;
The Doctor at the casement shows
His glimmering eyes that peep and doze!
And one hand rubs his old night-cap.　251

'Oh Doctor! Doctor! where's my Johnny?'
'I'm here, what is't you want with me?'
'Oh Sir! you know I'm Betty Foy,
And I have lost my poor dear Boy,　255
You know him—him you often see;

He's not so wise as some folks be:'
'The devil take his wisdom!' said
The Doctor, looking somewhat grim,
'What, Woman! should I know of him?'
And, grumbling, he went back to bed!　261

'O woe is me! O woe is me!
Here will I die; here will I die;
I thought to find my lost one here,
But he is neither far nor near,　265
Oh! what a wretched Mother I!'

She stops, she stands, she looks about;
Which way to turn she cannot tell.
Poor Betty! it would ease her pain
If she had heart to knock again;　270
—The clock strikes three—a dismal knell!

Then up along the town she hies,
No wonder if her senses fail;
This piteous news so much it shocked her,
She quite forgot to send the Doctor,　275
To comfort poor old Susan Gale.

And now she's high upon the down,
And she can see a mile of road:
'O cruel! I'm almost threescore;
Such night as this was ne'er before,　280
There's not a single soul abroad.'

She listens, but she cannot hear
The foot of horse, the voice of man;
The streams with softest sound are flow-
　　ing,
The grass you almost hear it growing,
You hear it now, if e'er you can.　286

The owlets through the long blue night
Are shouting to each other still:
Fond lovers! yet not quite hob nob,
They lengthen out the tremulous sob,　290
That echoes far from hill to hill.

Poor Betty now has lost all hope,
Her thoughts are bent on deadly sin,
A green-grown pond she just has past,
And from the brink she hurries fast,　295
Lest she should drown herself therein.

And now she sits her down and weeps;
Such tears she never shed before;
'Oh dear, dear Pony! my sweet joy!
Oh carry back my Idiot Boy!　300
And we will ne'er o'erload thee more.'

A thought is come into her head:
The Pony he is mild and good,
And we have always used him well;
Perhaps he's gone along the dell,　305
And carried Johnny to the wood.

Then up she springs as if on wings;
She thinks no more of deadly sin,
If Betty fifty ponds should see,
The last of all her thoughts would be　310
To drown herself therein.

Oh Reader! now that I might tell
What Johnny and his Horse are doing!
What they've been doing all this time,
Oh could I put it into rhyme,　315
A most delightful tale pursuing!

Perhaps, and no unlikely thought!
He with his Pony now doth roam
The cliffs and peaks so high that are,
To lay his hands upon a star,　320
And in his pocket bring it home.

Perhaps he's turned himself about,
His face unto his horse's tail,
And, still and mute, in wonder lost,
All silent as a horseman-ghost,   325
He travels slowly down the vale.

And now, perhaps, is hunting sheep,
A fierce and dreadful hunter he;
Yon valley, now so trim and green,
In five months' time, should he be seen,
A desert wilderness will be!   331

Perhaps, with head and heels on fire,
And like the very soul of evil,
He's galloping away, away,
And so will gallop on for aye,   335
The bane of all that dread the devil!

I to the Muses have been bound
These fourteen years, by strong inden-
     tures:
O gentle Muses! let me tell
But half of what to him befell;   340
He surely met with strange adventures.

O gentle Muses! is this kind?
Why will ye thus my suit repel?
Why of your further aid bereave me?
And can ye thus unfriended leave me; 345
Ye Muses! whom I love so well?

Who's yon, that, near the waterfall,
Which thunders down with headlong force,
Beneath the moon, yet shining fair,
As careless as if nothing were,   350
Sits upright on a feeding horse?

Unto his horse—there feeding free,
He seems, I think, the rein to give;
Of moon or stars he takes no heed;
Of such we in romances read: 355
—'Tis Johnny! Johnny! as I live.

And that's the very Pony, too!
Where is she, where is Betty Foy?
She hardly can sustain her fears;
The roaring waterfall she hears,   360
And cannot find her Idiot Boy.

Your Pony's worth his weight in gold:
Then calm your terrors, Betty Foy!
She's coming from among the trees,
And now all full in view she sees   365
Him whom she loves, her Idiot Boy.

And Betty sees the Pony too:
Why stand you thus, good Betty Foy?
It is no goblin, 'tis no ghost,
'Tis he whom you so long have lost,   370
He whom you love, your Idiot Boy.

She looks again—her arms are up—
She screams—she cannot move for joy;
She darts, as with a torrent's force,
She almost has o'erturned the Horse,   375
And fast she holds her Idiot Boy.

And Johnny burrs, and laughs aloud;
Whether in cunning or in joy
I cannot tell; but, while he laughs,
Betty a drunken pleasure quaffs   380
To hear again her Idiot Boy.

And now she's at the Pony's tail,
And now is at the Pony's head,—
On that side now, and now on this;
And, almost stifled with her bliss,   385
A few sad tears does Betty shed.

She kisses o'er and o'er again
Him whom she loves, her Idiot Boy;
She's happy here, is happy there,
She is uneasy everywhere;   390
Her limbs are all alive with joy.

She pats the Pony, where or when
She knows not, happy Betty Foy!
The little Pony glad may be,
But he is milder far than she,   395
You hardly can perceive his joy.

'Oh! Johnny, never mind the Doctor;
You've done your best, and that is all:'
She took the reins, when this was said,
And gently turned the Pony's head   400
From the loud waterfall.

By this the stars were almost gone,
The moon was setting on the hill,
So pale you scarcely looked at her:
The little birds began to stir,   405
Though yet their tongues were still.

The Pony, Betty, and her Boy,
Wind slowly through the woody dale;
And who is she, betimes abroad,
That hobbles up the steep rough road?
Who is it, but old Susan Gale?   411

Long time lay Susan lost in thought;
And many dreadful fears beset her,
Both for her Messenger and Nurse;
And, as her mind grew worse and worse,
Her body—it grew better.   416

She turned, she tossed herself in bed,
On all sides doubts and terrors met her;
Point after point did she discuss;
And, while her mind was fighting thus,
Her body still grew better.   421

'Alas! what is become of them?
These fears can never be endured;
I'll to the wood.'—The word scarce said,
Did Susan rise up from her bed,   425
As if by magic cured.

Away she goes up hill and down,
And to the wood at length is come;
She spies her Friends, she shouts a greet-
     ing;
Oh me! it is a merry meeting   430
As ever was in Christendom.

The owls have hardly sung their last,
While our four travellers homeward
 wend;
The owls have hooted all night long,
And with the owls began my song,   435
And with the owls must end.

For, while they all were travelling home,
Cried Betty, 'Tell us, Johnny, do,
Where all this long night you have been,
What you have heard, what you have
 seen: 440
And, Johnny, mind you tell us true.'

Now Johnny all night long had heard
The owls in tuneful concert strive;
No doubt too he the moon had seen;
For in the moonlight he had been   445
From eight o'clock till five.

And thus, to Betty's question, he
Made answer, like a traveller bold,
(His very words I give to you,)
'The cocks did crow to-whoo, to-whoo,
And the sun did shine so cold!'   451
—Thus answered Johnny in his glory,
And that was all his travel's story.

XXXII

MICHAEL

A PASTORAL POEM

[Composed October 11–December 9, 1800.—
Published 1800.]

IF from the public way you turn your
 steps
Up the tumultuous brook of Green-head
 Ghyll,
You will suppose that with an upright
 path
Your feet must struggle; in such bold
 ascent
The pastoral mountains front you, face
 to face.   5
But, courage! for around that boisterous
 brook
The mountains have all opened out them-
 selves,
And made a hidden valley of their own.
No habitation can be seen; but they
Who journey thither find themselves
 alone   10
With a few sheep, with rocks and stones,
 and kites
That overhead are sailing in the sky.
It is in truth an utter solitude;
Nor should I have made mention of this
 Dell
But for one object which you might pass
 by,   15
Might see and notice not. Beside the
 brook

Appears a straggling heap of unhewn
 stones!
And to that simple object appertains
A story—unenriched with strange events,
Yet not unfit, I deem, for the fireside, 20
Or for the summer shade. It was the first
Of those domestic tales that spake to me
Of Shepherds, dwellers in the valleys, men
Whom I already loved;—not verily
For their own sakes, but for the fields and
 hills   25
Where was their occupation and abode.
And hence this Tale, while I was yet a
 Boy
Careless of books, yet having felt the
 power
Of Nature, by the gentle agency
Of natural objects, led me on to feel   30
For passions that were not my own, and
 think
(At random and imperfectly indeed)
On man, the heart of man, and human
 life.
Therefore, although it be a history
Homely and rude, I will relate the same 35
For the delight of a few natural hearts;
And, with yet fonder feeling, for the sake
Of youthful Poets, who among these hills
Will be my second self when I am gone.

UPON the forest-side in Grasmere Vale
There dwelt a Shepherd, Michael was his
 name;   41
An old man, stout of heart, and strong of
 limb.
His bodily frame had been from youth to
 age
Of an unusual strength: his mind was
 keen,
Intense, and frugal, apt for all affairs, 45
And in his shepherd's calling he was
 prompt
And watchful more than ordinary men.
Hence had he learned the meaning of all
 winds,
Of blasts of every tone; and oftentimes,
When others heeded not, He heard the
 South   50
Make subterraneous music, like the noise
Of bagpipers on distant Highland hills.
The Shepherd, at such warning, of his
 flock
Bethought him, and he to himself would
 say,
'The winds are now devising work for
 me!'   55
And, truly, at all times, the storm, that
 drives
The traveller to a shelter, summoned him
Up to the mountains: he had been alone
Amid the heart of many thousand mists,
That came to him, and left him, on the
 heights.   60
So lived he till his eightieth year was past.

And grossly that man errs, who should
suppose
That the green valleys, and the streams
and rocks,
Were things indifferent to the Shepherd's
thoughts.
Fields, where with cheerful spirits he had
breathed   65
The common air; hills, which with vigor-
ous step
He had so often climbed; which had
impressed
So many incidents upon his mind
Of hardship, skill or courage, joy or fear;
Which, like a book, preserved the
memory   70
Of the dumb animals, whom he had
saved,
Had fed or sheltered, linking to such acts
The certainty of honourable gain;
Those fields, those hills—what could they
less? had laid
Strong hold on his affections, were to
him   75
A pleasurable feeling of blind love,
The pleasure which there is in life itself.

His days had not been passed in single-
ness.
His Helpmate was a comely matron,
old—
Though younger than himself full twenty
years.   80
She was a woman of a stirring life,
Whose heart was in her house: two
wheels she had
Of antique form; this large, for spinning
wool;
That small, for flax; and, if one wheel had
rest,
It was because the other was at work. 85
The Pair had but one inmate in their
house,
An only Child, who had been born to
them
When Michael, telling o'er his years,
began
To deem that he was old,—in shepherd's
phrase,
With one foot in the grave. This only
Son,   90
With two brave sheep-dogs tried in many
a storm,
The one of an inestimable worth,
Made all their household. I may truly
say,
That they were as a proverb in the vale
For endless industry. When day was
gone,   95
And from their occupations out of doors
The Son and Father were come home,
even then,
Their labour did not cease; unless when
all

Turned to the cleanly supper-board, and
there,
Each with a mess of pottage and skimmed
milk,   100
Sat round the basket piled with oaten
cakes,
And their plain home-made cheese. Yet
when the meal
Was ended, Luke (for so the Son was
named)
And his old Father both betook them-
selves
To such convenient work as might employ
Their hands by the fire-side; perhaps to
card   106
Wool for the Housewife's spindle, or
repair
Some injury done to sickle, flail, or
scythe,
Or other implement of house or field.

Down from the ceiling, by the chim-
ney's edge,   110
That in our ancient uncouth country
style
With huge and black projection over-
browed
Large space beneath, as duly as the light
Of day grew dim the Housewife hung a
lamp;
An aged utensil, which had performed 115
Service beyond all others of its kind.
Early at evening did it burn—and late,
Surviving comrade of uncounted hours,
Which, going by from year to year, had
found,
And left, the couple neither gay perhaps
Nor cheerful, yet with objects and with
hopes,   121
Living a life of eager industry.
And now, when Luke had reached his
eighteenth year,
There by the light of this old lamp they
sate,
Father and Son, while far into the night
The Housewife plied her own peculiar
work,   126
Making the cottage through the silent
hours
Murmur as with the sound of summer
flies.
This light was famous in its neighbour-
hood,
And was a public symbol of the life 130
That thrifty Pair had lived. For, as it
chanced,
Their cottage on a plot of rising ground
Stood single, with large prospect, north
and south,
High into Easedale, up to Dunmail-Raise,
And westward to the village near the
lake;   135
And from this constant light, so regular,
And so far seen, the House itself, by all

Who dwelt within the limits of the vale,
Both old and young, was named THE
  EVENING STAR.

Thus living on through such a length of
  years,   140
The Shepherd, if he loved himself, must
  needs
Have loved his Helpmate; but to Mi-
  chael's heart
This son of his old age was yet more
  dear—
Less from instinctive tenderness, the same
Fond spirit that blindly works in the
  blood of all—   145
Than that a child, more than all other
  gifts
That earth can offer to declining man,
Brings hope with it, and forward-looking
  thoughts,
And stirrings of inquietude, when they
By tendency of nature needs must fail. 150
Exceeding was the love he bare to him,
His heart and his heart's joy! For often-
  times
Old Michael, while he was a babe in arms,
Had done him female service, not alone
For pastime and delight, as is the use 155
Of fathers, but with patient mind enforced
To acts of tenderness; and he had rocked
His cradle, as with a woman's gentle
  hand.

And in a later time, ere yet the Boy
Had put on boy's attire, did Michael
  love,   160
Albeit of a stern unbending mind,
To have the Young-one in his sight,
  when he
Wrought in the field, or on his shepherd's
  stool
Sate with a fettered sheep before him
  stretched
Under the large old oak, that near his
  door   165
Stood single, and, from matchless depth
  of shade,
Chosen for the Shearer's covert from the
  sun,
Thence in our rustic dialect was called
The CLIPPING TREE,[1] a name which yet it
  bears,
There, while they two were sitting in the
  shade,   170
With others round them, earnest all and
  blithe,
Would Michael exercise his heart with
  looks
Of fond correction and reproof bestowed
Upon the Child, if he disturbed the sheep
By catching at their legs, or with his
  shouts   175

[1] Clipping is the word used in the North of England for shearing.

Scared them, while they lay still beneath
  the shears.

And when by Heaven's good grace the
  boy grew up
A healthy Lad, and carried in his cheek
Two steady roses that were five years old;
Then Michael from a winter coppice cut
With his own hand a sapling, which he
  hooped   181
With iron, making it throughout in all
Due requisites a perfect shepherd's staff,
And gave it to the Boy; wherewith equipt
He as a watchman oftentimes was placed
At gate or gap, to stem or turn the flock;
And, to his office prematurely called, 187
There stood the urchin, as you will divine,
Something between a hindrance and a
  help;
And for this cause not always, I believe,
Receiving from his Father hire of praise;
Though nought was left undone which
  staff, or voice,
Or looks, or threatening gestures, could
  perform.

But soon as Luke, full ten years old,
  could stand
Against the mountain blasts; and to the
  heights,   195
Not fearing toil, nor length of weary ways,
He with his Father daily went, and they
Were as companions, why should I relate
That objects which the Shepherd loved
  before
Were dearer now? that from the Boy
  there came   200
Feelings and emanations—things which
  were
Light to the sun and music to the wind;
And that the old Man's heart seemed
  born again?

Thus in his Father's sight the Boy grew
  up:
And now, when he had reached his
  eighteenth year,   205
He was his comfort and his daily hope.

While in this sort the simple household
  lived
From day to day, to Michael's ear there
  came
Distressful tidings. Long before the time
Of which I speak, the Shepherd had been
  bound   210
In surety for his brother's son, a man
Of an industrious life, and ample means;
But unforeseen misfortunes suddenly
Had prest upon him; and old Michael
  now
Was summoned to discharge the for-
  feiture,   215
A grievous penalty, but little less

Than half his substance. This unlooked-
for claim,
At the first hearing, for a moment took
More hope out of his life than he sup-
posed
That any old man ever could have
lost.   220
As soon as he had armed himself with
strength
To look his trouble in the face, it seemed
The Shepherd's sole resource to sell at
once
A portion of his patrimonial fields.
Such was his first resolve; he thought
again,   225
And his heart failed him. 'Isabel,' said
he,
Two evenings after he had heard the
news,
'I have been toiling more than seventy
years,
And in the open sunshine of God's love
Have we all lived; yet, if these fields of
ours   230
Should pass into a stranger's hand, I think
That I could not lie quiet in my grave.
Our lot is a hard lot; the sun himself
Has scarcely been more diligent than I;
And I have lived to be a fool at last   235
To my own family. An evil man
That was, and made an evil choice, if he
Were false to us; and, if he were not false,
There are ten thousand to whom loss
like this
Had been no sorrow. I forgive him;—
but   240
'Twere better to be dumb than to talk
thus.

When I began, my purpose was to
speak
Of remedies and of a cheerful hope.
Our Luke shall leave us, Isabel; the land
Shall not go from us, and it shall be
free;   245
He shall possess it, free as is the wind
That passes over it. We have, thou
know'st,
Another kinsman—he will be our friend
In this distress. He is a prosperous man,
Thriving in trade—and Luke to him shall
go,   250
And with his kinsman's help and his own
thrift
He quickly will repair this loss, and then
He may return to us. If here he stay,
What can be done? Where every one is
poor,
What can be gained?'
      At this the old Man paused, 255
And Isabel sat silent, for her mind
Was busy, looking back into past times.
There's Richard Bateman, thought she to
herself,

He was a parish-boy—at the church-door
They made a gathering for him, shillings,
pence,   260
And halfpennies, wherewith the neigh-
bours bought
A basket, which they filled with pedlar's
wares;
And, with this basket on his arm, the lad
Went up to London, found a master
there,
Who, out of many, chose the trusty boy
To go and overlook his merchandise 266
Beyond the seas; where he grew wondrous
rich,
And left estates and monies to the poor,
And, at his birth-place, built a chapel
floored
With marble, which he sent from foreign
lands.   270
These thoughts, and many others of like
sort,
Passed quickly through the mind of
Isabel,
And her face brightened. The old Man
was glad,
And thus resumed:—'Well, Isabel! this
scheme
These two days has been meat and drink
to me.   275
Far more than we have lost is left us yet.
—We have enough—I wish indeed that I
Were younger;—but this hope is a good
hope.
Make ready Luke's best garments, of the
best
Buy for him more, and let us send him
forth   280
To-morrow, or the next day, or to-night:
If he could go, the Boy should go to-
night.'

Here Michael ceased, and to the fields
went forth
With a light heart. The Housewife for
five days
Was restless morn and night, and all day
long   285
Wrought on with her best fingers to
prepare
Things needful for the journey of her son.
But Isabel was glad when Sunday came
To stop her in her work: for, when she lay
By Michael's side, she through the last
two nights   290
Heard him, how he was troubled in his
sleep:
And when they rose at morning she could
see
That all his hopes were gone. That day
at noon
She said to Luke, while they two by
themselves
Were sitting at the door, 'Thou must
not go: 295

We have no other Child but thee to lose,
None to remember—do not go away,
For if thou leave thy Father he will die.'
The Youth made answer with a jocund
    voice;
And Isabel, when she had told her fears,
Recovered heart. That evening her best
    fare   301
Did she bring forth, and all together sat
Like happy people round a Christmas
    fire.

With daylight Isabel resumed her work;
And all the ensuing week the house
    appeared   305
As cheerful as a grove in Spring: at length
The expected letter from their kinsman
    came,
With kind assurances that he would do
His utmost for the welfare of the Boy;
To which, requests were added, that
    forthwith   310
He might be sent to him. Ten times or
    more
The letter was read over; Isabel
Went forth to show it to the neighbours
    round;
Nor was there at that time on English land
A prouder heart than Luke's. When
    Isabel   315
Had to her house returned, the old Man
    said,
'He shall depart to-morrow.' To this
    word
The Housewife answered, talking much
    of things
Which, if at such short notice he should
    go,
Would surely be forgotten. But at length
She gave consent, and Michael was at
    ease.   321

Near the tumultuous brook of Green-
    head Ghyll,
In that deep valley, Michael had designed
To build a Sheep-fold; and, before he
    heard
The tidings of his melancholy loss,   325
For this same purpose he had gathered up
A heap of stones, which by the stream-
    let's edge
Lay thrown together, ready for the work.
With Luke that evening thitherward he
    walked:
And soon as they had reached the place
    he stopped,   330
And thus the old Man spake to him:—
    'My son,
To-morrow thou wilt leave me: with full
    heart
I look upon thee, for thou art the same
That wert a promise to me ere thy birth,
And all thy life hast been my daily joy.
I will relate to thee some little part   336

Of our two histories; 'twill do thee good
When thou art from me, even if I should
    touch
On things thou canst not know of.——
    After thou
First cam'st into the world—as oft befalls
To new-born infants—thou didst sleep
    away   341
Two days, and blessings from thy Father's
    tongue
Then fell upon thee. Day by day passed
    on,
And still I loved thee with increasing
    love.
Never to living ear came sweeter sounds
Than when I heard thee by our own fire-
    side   346
First uttering, without words, a natural
    tune;
While thou, a feeding babe, didst in thy
    joy
Sing at thy Mother's breast. Month
    followed month,
And in the open fields my life was passed
And on the mountains; else I think that
    thou   351
Hadst been brought up upon thy Father's
    knees.
But we were playmates, Luke: among
    these hills,
As well thou knowest, in us the old and
    young
Have played together, nor with me didst
    thou   355
Lack any pleasure which a boy can know.'
Luke had a manly heart; but at these
    words
He sobbed aloud. The old Man grasped
    his hand,
And said, 'Nay, do not take it so—I see
That these are things of which I need not
    speak.   360
—Even to the utmost I have been to thee
A kind and a good Father: and herein
I but repay a gift which I myself
Received at others' hands; for, though
    now old
Beyond the common life of man, I still 365
Remember them who loved me in my
    youth.
Both of them sleep together: here they
    lived,
As all their Forefathers had done; and,
    when
At length their time was come, they were
    not loth
To give their bodies to the family mould.
I wished that thou shouldst live the life
    they lived,   371
But 'tis a long time to look back, my Son,
And see so little gain from threescore
    years.
These fields were burthened when they
    came to me;

Till I was forty years of age, not more 375
Than half of my inheritance was mine.
I toiled and toiled; God blessed me in
my work,
And till these three weeks past the land
was free.
—It looks as if it never could endure
Another Master. Heaven forgive me,
Luke, 380
If I judge ill for thee, but it seems good
That thou shouldst go.'
At this the old Man paused;
Then, pointing to the stones near which
they stood,
Thus, after a short silence, he resumed:
'This was a work for us; and now, my
Son, 385
It is a work for me. But, lay one stone—
Here, lay it for me, Luke, with thine own
hands.
Nay, Boy, be of good hope;—we both
may live
To see a better day. At eighty-four
I still am strong and hale;—do thou thy
part; 390
I will do mine.—I will begin again
With many tasks that were resigned to
thee:
Up to the heights, and in among the
storms,
Will I without thee go again, and do 394
All works which I was wont to do alone,
Before I knew thy face.—Heaven bless
thee, Boy!
Thy heart these two weeks has been beat-
ing fast
With many hopes; it should be so—yes—
yes—
I knew that thou couldst never have a
wish
To leave me, Luke: thou hast been bound
to me 400
Only by links of love: when thou art
gone,
What will be left to us!—But I forget
My purposes. Lay now the corner-stone,
As I requested; and hereafter, Luke,
When thou art gone away, should evil
men 405
Be thy companions, think of me, my Son,
And of this moment; hither turn thy
thoughts,
And God will strengthen thee: amid all
fear
And all temptation, Luke, I pray that
thou
May'st bear in mind the life thy Fathers
lived, 410
Who, being innocent, did for that cause
Bestir them in good deeds. Now, fare
thee well—
When thou return'st, thou in this place
wilt see
A work which is not here: a covenant 414

'Twill be between us; but, whatever fate
Befall thee, I shall love thee to the last,
And bear thy memory with me to the
grave.'

The Shepherd ended here; and Luke
stooped down,
And, as his Father had requested, laid
The first stone of the Sheep-fold. At the
sight 420
The old Man's grief broke from him; to
his heart
He pressed his Son, he kissèd him and
wept;
And to the house together they returned.
—Hushed was that House in peace, or
seeming peace,
Ere the night fell:—with morrow's dawn
the Boy 425
Began his journey, and, when he had
reached
The public way, he put on a bold face;
And all the neighbours, as he passed their
doors,
Came forth with wishes and with farewell
prayers, 429
That followed him till he was out of sight.

A good report did from their Kinsman
come,
Of Luke and his well-doing: and the Boy
Wrote loving letters, full of wondrous
news,
Which, as the Housewife phrased it, were
throughout 434
'The prettiest letters that were ever seen.'
Both parents read them with rejoicing
hearts.
So, many months passed on: and once
again
The Shepherd went about his daily work
With confident and cheerful thoughts; and now
Sometimes when he could find a leisure
hour 440
He to that valley took his way, and there
Wrought at the Sheep-fold. Meantime
Luke began
To slacken in his duty; and, at length,
He in the dissolute city gave himself
To evil courses: ignominy and shame 445
Fell on him, so that he was driven at last
To seek a hiding-place beyond the seas.

There is a comfort in the strength of
love;
'Twill make a thing endurable, which else
Would overset the brain, or break the
heart: 450
I have conversed with more than one who
well
Remember the old Man, and what he was
Years after he had heard this heavy news.

His bodily frame had been from youth to age
Of an unusual strength. Among the rocks
He went, and still looked up to sun and cloud,   456
And listened to the wind; and, as before,
Performed all kinds of labour for his sheep,
And for the land, his small inheritance.
And to that hollow dell from time to time   460
Did he repair, to build the Fold of which
His flock had need. 'Tis not forgotten yet
The pity which was then in every heart
For the old Man—and 'tis believed by all
That many and many a day he thither went,   465
And never lifted up a single stone.

There, by the Sheep-fold, sometimes was he seen
Sitting alone, or with his faithful Dog,
Then old, beside him, lying at his feet.
The length of full seven years, from time to time,   470
He at the building of this Sheep-fold wrought,
And left the work unfinished when he died.
Three years, or little more, did Isabel
Survive her Husband: at her death the estate
Was sold, and went into a stranger's hand.   475
The Cottage which was named THE EVEN-ING STAR
Is gone—the ploughshare has been through the ground
On which it stood; great changes have been wrought
In all the neighbourhood:—yet the oak is left
That grew beside their door; and the remains   480
Of the unfinished Sheep-fold may be seen
Beside the boisterous brook of Greenhead Ghyll.

XXXIII

THE WIDOW ON WINDERMERE SIDE

[Composed 1837 (?).—Published 1842.]

I

How beautiful when up a lofty height
Honour ascends among the humblest poor,
And feeling sinks as deep! See there the door
Of One, a Widow, left beneath a weight
Of blameless debt. On evil Fortune's spite   5

She wasted no complaint, but strove to make
A just repayment, both for conscience-sake
And that herself and hers should stand upright
In the world's eye. Her work when day-light failed
Paused not, and through the depth of night she kept   10
Such earnest vigils, that belief prevailed
With some, the noble Creature never slept;
But, one by one, the hand of death as-sailed
Her children from her inmost heart be-wept.

II

The Mother mourned, nor ceased her tears to flow,   15
Till a winter's noon-day placed her buried Son
Before her eyes, last child of many gone—
His raiment of angelic white, and lo!
His very feet bright as the dazzling snow
Which they are touching; yea far brighter, even   20
As that which comes, or seems to come, from heaven,
Surpasses aught these elements can show.
Much she rejoiced, trusting that from that hour
Whate'er befell she could not grieve or pine;
But the Transfigured, in and out of season,   25
Appeared, and spiritual presence gained a power
Over material forms that mastered reason.
Oh, gracious Heaven, in pity make her thine!

III

But why that prayer? as if to her could come
No good but by the way that leads to bliss   30
Through Death,—so judging we should judge amiss.
Since reason failed want is her threatened doom,
Yet frequent transports mitigate the gloom:
Nor of those maniacs is she one that kiss
The air or laugh upon a precipice;   35
No, passing through strange sufferings toward the tomb,
She smiles as if a martyr's crown were won:
Oft, when light breaks through clouds or waving trees,
With outspread arms and fallen upon her knees

The Mother hails in her descending Son
An Angel, and in earthly ecstasies   41
Her own angelic glory seems begun.

XXXIV

THE ARMENIAN LADY'S LOVE

[Composed 1830.—Published 1835.]

[The subject of the following poem is from the
Orlandus of the author's friend, Kenelm Henry
Digby: and the liberty is taken of inscribing
it to him as an acknowledgment, however unworthy, of pleasure and instruction derived from
his numerous and valuable writings, illustrative
of the piety and chivalry of the olden time.]

I

You have heard 'a Spanish Lady
   How she wooed an English man;'[1]
Hear now of a fair Armenian,
   Daughter of the proud Soldàn;
How she loved a Christian Slave, and told
   her pain   5
By word, look, deed, with hope that he
   might love again.

II

'Pluck that rose, it moves my liking,'
   Said she, lifting up her veil;
'Pluck it for me, gentle gardener,
   Ere it wither and grow pale.'   10
'Princess fair, I till the ground, but may
   not take
From twig or bed an humbler flower,
   even for your sake!'

III

'Grieved am I, submissive Christian!
   To behold thy captive state;
Women, in your land, may pity   15
   (May they not?) the unfortunate.'
'Yes, kind Lady! otherwise man could
   not bear
Life, which to every one that breathes is
   full of care.'

IV

'Worse than idle is compassion
   If it end in tears and sighs;   20
Thee from bondage would I rescue
   And from vile indignities;
Nurtured, as thy mien bespeaks, in high
   degree,
Look up—and help a hand that longs to
   set thee free.'

V

'Lady! dread the wish, nor venture   25
   In such peril to engage;
Think how it would stir against you
   Your most loving father's rage:

[1] See in Percy's Reliques that fine old ballad, 'The
Spanish Lady's Love;' from which Poem the form
of stanza, as suitable to dialogue, is adopted.

Sad deliverance would it be, and yoked
   with shame,
Should troubles overflow on her from
   whom it came.'   30

VI

'Generous Frank! the just in effort
   Are of inward peace secure:
Hardships for the brave encountered
   Even the feeblest may endure:
If almighty grace through me thy chains
   unbind,   35
My father for slave's work may seek a
   slave in mind.'

VII

'Princess, at this burst of goodness,
   My long-frozen heart grows warm!'
'Yet you make all courage fruitless,
   Me to save from chance of harm: 40
Leading such companion I that gilded
   dome,
Yon minarets, would gladly leave for his
   worst home.'

VIII

'Feeling tunes your voice, fair Princess!
   And your brow is free from scorn,
Else these words would come like
   mockery,   45
   Sharper than the pointed thorn.'
'Whence the undeserved mistrust? Too
   wide apart
Our faith hath been,—O would that eyes
   could see the heart!'

IX

'Tempt me not, I pray; my doom is
   These base implements to wield;   50
Rusty lance, I ne'er shall grasp thee,
   Ne'er assoil my cobwebbed shield!
Never see my native land, nor castle
   towers,
Nor Her who thinking of me there counts
   widowed hours.'

X

'Prisoner! pardon youthful fancies,   55
   Wedded? If you can, say no!
Blessed is and be your consort;
   Hopes I cherished—let them go!
Handmaid's privilege would leave my
   purpose free,
Without another link to my felicity.'   60

XI

'Wedded love with loyal Christians,
   Lady, is a mystery rare;
Body, heart, and soul in union,
   Make one being of a pair.'
'Humble love in me would look for no
   return,   65
Soft as a guiding star that cheers, but
   cannot burn.'

XII

'Gracious Allah! by such title
    Do I dare to thank the God,
Him who thus exalts thy spirit,
    Flower of an unchristian sod!   70
Or hast thou put off wings which thou in
        heaven dost wear?
What have I seen, and heard, or dreamt?
        where am I? where?'

XIII

Here broke off the dangerous converse:
    Less impassioned words might tell
How the pair escaped together,   75
    Tears not wanting, nor a knell
Of sorrow in her heart while through her
        father's door,
And from her narrow world, she passed
        for evermore.

XIV

But affections higher, holier,
    Urged her steps; she shrunk from
        trust   80
In a sensual creed that trampled
    Woman's birthright into dust.
Little be the wonder then, the blame be
        none,
If she, a timid Maid, hath put such bold-
        ness on.

XV

Judge both Fugitives with knowledge:
    In those old romantic days   86
Mighty were the soul's commandments
    To support, restrain, or raise.
Foes might hang upon their path, snakes
        rustle near,
But nothing from their inward selves had
        they to fear.   90

XVI

Thought infirm ne'er came between
        them,
    Whether printing desert sands
With accordant steps, or gathering
    Forest-fruit with social hands;
Or whispering like two reeds that in the
        cold moonbeam   95
Bend with the breeze their heads, beside
        a crystal stream.

XVII

On a friendly deck reposing
    They at length for Venice steer;
There, when they had closed their
        voyage,
    One, who daily on the pier   100
Watched for tidings from the East, beheld
        his Lord,
Fell down and clasped his knees for joy,
        not uttering word.

XVIII

Mutual was the sudden transport;
    Breathless questions followed fast,
Years contracting to a moment,   105
    Each word greedier than the last;
'Hie thee to the Countess, friend! return
        with speed,
And of this Stranger speak by whom her
        lord was freed.

XIX

'Say that I, who might have languished,
    Drooped and pined till life was spent,
Now before the gates of Stolberg   111
    My Deliverer would present
For a crowning recompense, the precious
        grace
Of her who in my heart still holds her
        ancient place.

XX

'Make it known that my Companion
    Is of royal eastern blood,   116
    Thirsting after all perfection,
    Innocent, and meek, and good,
Though with misbelievers bred; but that
        dark night
Will holy Church disperse by beams of
        gospel-light.'   120

XXI

Swiftly went that grey-haired Servant,
    Soon returned a trusty Page
Charged with greetings, benedictions,
    Thanks and praises, each a gage
For a sunny thought to cheer the Stran-
        ger's way,   125
Her virtuous scruples to remove, her fears
        allay.

XXII

And how blest the Reunited,
    While beneath their castle-walls
Runs a deafening noise of welcome!—
    Blest, though every tear that falls 130
Doth in its silence of past sorrow tell,
And makes a meeting seem most like a
        dear farewell.

XXIII

Through a haze of human nature,
    Glorified by heavenly light,
Looked the beautiful Deliverer   135
    On that overpowering sight,
While across her virgin cheek pure blushes
        strayed,
For every tender sacrifice her heart had
        made.

XXIV

On the ground the weeping Countess
    Knelt and kissed the Stranger's hand;
Act of soul-devoted homage,   141
    Pledge of an eternal band:

Nor did aught of future days that kiss
   belie,
Which, with a generous shout, the crowd
   did ratify.

XXV

Constant to the fair Armenian,   145
   Gentle pleasures round her moved,
Like a tutelary spirit
   Reverenced, like a sister loved.
Christian meekness smoothed for all the
   path of life,
Who, loving most, should wiseliest love,
   their only strife.   150

XXVI

Mute memento of that union
   In a Saxon church survives,
Where a cross-legged Knight lies sculp-
   tured
   As between two wedded Wives—
Figures with armorial signs of race and
   birth,   155
And the vain rank the pilgrims bore
   while yet on earth.

XXXV

LOVING AND LIKING

IRREGULAR VERSES

ADDRESSED TO A CHILD

(BY MY SISTER)

[Composed 1832.—Published 1835.]

THERE'S more in words than I can teach:
Yet listen, Child!—I would not preach;
But only give some plain directions
To guide your speech and your affections.
Say not you *love* a roasted fowl   5
But you may love a screaming owl,
And, if you can, the unwieldy toad
That crawls from his secure abode
Within the mossy garden wall
When evening dews begin to fall.   10
Oh! mark the beauty of his eye:
What wonders in that circle lie!
So clear, so bright, our fathers said
He wears a jewel in his head!
And when, upon some showery day,   15
Into a path or public way
A frog leaps out from bordering grass,
Startling the timid as they pass,
Do you observe him, and endeavour
To take the intruder into favour;   20
Learning from him to find a reason
For a light heart in a dull season.
And you may love him in the pool,
That is for him a happy school,
In which he swims as taught by nature, 25
Fit pattern for a human creature,
Glancing amid the water bright,
And sending upward sparkling light.

Nor blush if o'er your heart be stealing
A love for things that have no feeling: 30
The spring's first rose by you espied,
May fill your breast with joyful pride;
And you may love the strawberry-flower,
And love the strawberry in its bower;
But when the fruit, so often praised   35
For beauty, to your lip is raised,
Say not you *love* the delicate treat,
But *like* it, enjoy it, and thankfully eat.

Long may you love your pensioner
   mouse,
Though one of a tribe that torment the
   house: 40
Nor dislike for her cruel sport the cat
Deadly foe both of mouse and rat;
Remember she follows the law of her
   kind,
And Instinct is neither wayward nor blind.
Then think of her beautiful gliding form,
Her tread that would scarcely crush a
   worm,   46
And her soothing song by the winter fire,
Soft as the dying throb of the lyre.

I would not circumscribe your love:
It may soar with the eagle and brood
   with the dove,   50
May pierce the earth with the patient mole,
Or track the hedgehog to his hole.
Loving and liking are the solace of life,
Rock the cradle of joy, smooth the death-
   bed of strife.
You love your father and your mother, 55
Your grown-up and your baby brother;
You love your sister and your friends,
And countless blessings which God sends:
And while these right affections play,
You *live* each moment of your day; 60
They lead you on to full content,
And likings fresh and innocent,
That store the mind, the memory feed,
And prompt to many a gentle deed:
But *likings* come, and pass away; 65
'Tis *love* that remains till our latest day:
Our heavenward guide is holy love,
And will be our bliss with saints above.

XXXVI

FAREWELL LINES

[Composed 1828 (?).—Published 1842.]

'HIGH bliss is only for a higher state,'
But, surely, if severe afflictions borne
With patience merit the reward of peace,
Peace ye deserve; and may the solid good,
Sought by a wise though late exchange,
   and here   5
With bounteous hand beneath a cottage-
   roof
To you accorded, never be withdrawn,
Nor for the world's best promises re-
   nounced.

Most soothing was it for a welcome
   Friend,
Fresh from the crowded city, to behold 10
That lonely union, privacy so deep,
Such calm employments, such entire
   content.
So when the rain is over, the storm laid,
A pair of herons oft-times have I seen,
Upon a rocky islet, side by side,   15
Drying their feathers in the sun, at ease;
And so, when night with grateful gloom
   had fallen,
Two glow-worms in such nearness that
   they shared,
As seemed, their soft self-satisfying light,
Each with the other, on the dewy ground,
Where He that made them blesses their
   repose.—   21
When wandering among lakes and hills
   I note,
Once more, those creatures thus by nature
   paired,
And guarded in their tranquil state of life,
Even, as your happy presence to my mind
Their union brought, will they repay the
   debt,   26
And send a thankful spirit back to you,
With hope that we, dear Friends! shall
   meet again.

XXXVII

THE REDBREAST

(SUGGESTED IN A WESTMORELAND COTTAGE)

[Composed 1834.—Published 1835.]

DRIVEN in by Autumn's sharpening air
From half-stripped woods and pastures
   bare,
Brisk Robin seeks a kindlier home:
Not like a beggar is he come,
But enters as a looked-for guest,   5
Confiding in his ruddy breast,
As if it were a natural shield
Charged with a blazon on the field,
Due to that good and pious deed
Of which we in the Ballad read.   10
But pensive fancies putting by,
And wild-wood sorrows, speedily
He plays the expert ventriloquist;
And, caught by glimpses now—now missed,
Puzzles the listener with a doubt   15
If the soft voice he throws about
Comes from within doors or without!
Was ever such a sweet confusion,
Sustained by delicate illusion?
He's at your elbow—to your feeling   20
The notes are from the floor or ceiling;
And there's a riddle to be guessed,
Till you have marked his heaving chest,
And busy throat whose sink and swell
Betray the Elf that loves to dwell   25
In Robin's bosom, as a chosen cell.

Heart-pleased we smile upon the Bird
If seen, and with like pleasure stirred
Commend him, when he's only heard.
But small and fugitive our gain   30
Compared with *hers* who long hath lain,
With languid limbs and patient head
Reposing on a lone sick-bed;
Where now she daily hears a strain
That cheats her of too busy cares,   35
Eases her pain, and helps her prayers.
And who but this dear Bird beguiled
The fever of that pale-faced Child;
Now cooling, with his passing wing,
Her forehead, like a breeze of Spring;   40
Recalling now, with descant soft
Shed round her pillow from aloft,
Sweet thoughts of angels hovering nigh.
And the invisible sympathy
Of 'Matthew, Mark, and Luke, and
   John,   45
Blessing the bed she lies upon?'[1]
And sometimes, just as listening ends
In slumber, with the cadence blends
A dream of that low-warbled hymn
Which old folk, fondly pleased to trim   50
Lamps of faith, now burning dim,
Say that the Cherubs carved in stone,
When clouds gave way at dead of night
And the ancient church was filled with
   light,
Used to sing in heavenly tone,   55
Above and round the sacred places
They guard, with wingèd baby-faces.

Thrice happy Creature! in all lands
Nurtured by hospitable hands:
Free entrance to this cot has he,   60
Entrance and exit both *yet* free;
And when the keen unruffled weather,
That thus brings man and bird together,
Shall with its pleasantness be past,
And casement closed and door made fast,
To keep at bay the howling blast,   66
He needs not fear the season's rage,
For the whole house is Robin's cage.
Whether the bird flit here or there,
O'er table *lilt*, or perch on chair,   70
Though some may frown and make a
   stir,
To scare him as a trespasser,
And he belike will flinch or start,
Good friends he has to take his part;
One chiefly, who with voice and look   75
Pleads for him from the chimney-nook,
Where sits the Dame, and wears away
Her long and vacant holiday;
With images about her heart,
Reflected from the years gone by,   80
On human nature's second infancy.

[1] The words—
   'Matthew, Mark, and Luke, and John,
      Bless the bed that I lie on,'
are part of a child's prayer, still in general use
through the northern counties.

XXXVIII

HER EYES ARE WILD

[Composed 1798.—Published 1798.]

I

HER eyes are wild, her head is bare,
The sun has burnt her coal-black hair;
Her eyebrows have a rusty stain,
And she came far from over the main.
She has a baby on her arm,   5
Or else she were alone:
And underneath the hay-stack warm,
And on the greenwood stone,
She talked and sung the woods among,
And it was in the English tongue.   10

II

'Sweet babe! they say that I am mad,
But nay, my heart is far too glad,
And I am happy when I sing
Full many a sad and doleful thing:
Then, lovely baby, do not fear!   15
I pray thee have no fear of me;
But safe as in a cradle, here
My lovely baby! thou shalt be:
To thee I know too much I owe;
I cannot work thee any woe.   20

III

'A fire was once within my brain;
And in my head a dull, dull pain;
And fiendish faces, one, two, three,
Hung at my breast, and pulled at me;
But then there came a sight of joy;   25
It came at once to do me good;
I waked, and saw my little boy,
My little boy of flesh and blood;
Oh joy for me that sight to see!
For he was here, and only he.   30

IV

'Suck, little babe, oh suck again!
It cools my blood; it cools my brain;
Thy lips I feel them, baby! they
Draw from my heart the pain away.
Oh! press me with thy little hand;   35
It loosens something at my chest;
About that tight and deadly band
I feel thy little fingers prest.
The breeze I see is in the tree:
It comes to cool my babe and me.   40

V

'Oh! love me, love me, little boy!
Thou art thy mother's only joy;
And do not dread the waves below,
When o'er the sea-rock's edge we go;
The high crag cannot work me harm,   45
Nor leaping torrents when they howl;
The babe I carry on my arm,
He saves for me my precious soul;

Then happy lie; for blest am I;
Without me my sweet babe would die.   50

VI

'Then do not fear, my boy! for thee
Bold as a lion will I be;
And I will always be thy guide,
Through hollow snows and rivers wide.
I'll build an Indian bower; I know   55
The leaves that make the softest bed:
And if from me thou wilt not go,
But still be true till I am dead,
My pretty thing! then thou shalt sing
As merry as the birds in spring.   60

VII

'Thy father cares not for my breast,
'Tis thine, sweet baby, there to rest;
'Tis all thine own!—and if its hue
Be changed, that was so fair to view,
'Tis fair enough for thee, my dove!   65
My beauty, little child, is flown,
But thou wilt live with me in love;
And what if my poor cheek be brown?
'Tis well for me thou canst not see
How pale and wan it else would be.   70

VIII

'Dread not their taunts, my little Life;
I am thy father's wedded wife;
And underneath the spreading tree
We two will live in honesty.
If his sweet boy he could forsake,   75
With me he never would have stayed:
From him no harm my babe can take;
But he, poor man! is wretched made;
And every day we two will pray
For him that's gone and far away.   80

IX

'I'll teach my boy the sweetest things:
I'll teach him how the owlet sings.
My little babe! thy lips are still,
And thou hast almost sucked thy fill.
—Where art thou gone, my own dear
child?   85
What wicked looks are those I see?
Alas! Alas! that look so wild,
It never, never came from me:
If thou art mad, my pretty lad,
Then I must be for ever sad.   90

X

'Oh! smile on me, my little lamb!
For I thy own dear mother am:
My love for thee has well been tried:
I've sought thy father far and wide.
I know the poisons of the shade;   95
I know the earth-nuts fit for food:
Then, pretty dear, be not afraid:
We'll find thy father in the wood.
Now laugh and be gay, to the woods
away!
And there, my babe, we'll live for
aye.'   100

POEMS ON THE NAMING OF PLACES

ADVERTISEMENT

By persons resident in the country, and attached to rural objects, many places will be found unnamed or of unknown names, where little Incidents must have occurred, or feelings been experienced, which will have given to such places a private and peculiar interest. From a wish to give some sort of record to such Incidents, and renew the gratification of such feelings, Names have been given to Places by the Author and some of his Friends, and the following Poems written in consequence.

I

[Composed 1800.—Published 1800.]

It was an April morning: fresh and clear
The Rivulet, delighting in its strength,
Ran with a young man's speed; and yet
    the voice
Of waters which the winter had supplied
Was softened down into a vernal tone. 5
The spirit of enjoyment and desire,
And hopes and wishes, from all living
    things
Went circling, like a multitude of sounds.
The budding groves seemed eager to urge
    on
The steps of June; as if their various hues
Were only hindrances that stood between
Them and their object: but, meanwhile,
    prevailed 12
Such an entire contentment in the air
That every naked ash, and tardy tree
Yet leafless, showed as if the countenance
With which it looked on this delightful
    day 16
Were native to the summer.—Up the
    brook
I roamed in the confusion of my heart,
Alive to all things and forgetting all.
At length I to a sudden turning came 20
In this continuous glen, where down a
    rock
The Stream, so ardent in its course before,
Sent forth such sallies of glad sound, that
    all
Which I till then had heard appeared the
    voice
Of common pleasure: beast and bird, the
    lamb, 25
The shepherd's dog, the linnet and the
    thrush,
Vied with this waterfall, and made a song
Which, while I listened, seemed like the
    wild growth
Or like some natural produce of the air,
That could not cease to be. Green leaves
    were here; 30
But 'twas the foliage of the rocks—the
    birch,
The yew, the holly, and the bright green
    thorn,
With hanging islands of resplendent
    furze:
And on a summit, distant a short space,
By any who should look beyond the dell 35

A single mountain-cottage might be seen.
I gazed and gazed, and to myself I said,
'Our thoughts at least are ours; and this
    wild nook,
My Emma,[1] I will dedicate to thee.'
——Soon did the spot become my other
    home, 40
My dwelling, and my out-of-doors abode.
And of the Shepherds who have seen me
    there,
To whom I sometimes in our idle talk
Have told this fancy, two or three, per-
    haps,
Years after we are gone and in our graves,
When they have cause to speak of this
    wild place, 46
May call it by the name of Emma's Dell.

II

TO JOANNA

[Composed August, 1800.—Published 1800.]

Amid the smoke of cities did you pass
The time of early youth; and there you
    learned,
From years of quiet industry, to love
The living Beings by your own fire-side,
With such a strong devotion, that your
    heart 5
Is slow to meet the sympathies of them
Who look upon the hills with tenderness,
And make dear friendships with the
    streams and groves.
Yet we, who are transgressors in this kind,
Dwelling retired in our simplicity 10
Among the woods and fields, we love you
    well,
Joanna! and I guess, since you have been
So distant from us now for two long years,
That you will gladly listen to discourse
However trivial, if you thence be taught
That they, with whom you once were
    happy, talk 16
Familiarly of you and of old times.

While I was seated, now some ten days
    past,
Beneath those lofty firs, that overtop
Their ancient neighbour, the old steeple-
    tower, 20

[1] *Emma:* the poet's sister Dorothy: *Emmeline* is elsewhere used as a pseudonym for her. See editor's note on *To a Butterfly,* p. 699.—Ed.

116

The Vicar from his gloomy house hard by
Came forth to greet me; and, when he
    had asked,
'How fares Joanna, that wild-hearted
    Maid!
And when will she return to us?' he
    paused;
And, after short exchange of village news,
He with grave looks demanded for what
    cause,   26
Reviving obsolete idolatry,
I, like a Runic Priest, in characters
Of formidable size had chiselled out
Some uncouth name upon the native rock,
Above the Rotha, by the forest-side.   31
—Now, by those dear immunities of
    heart
Engendered between malice and true
    love,
I was not loth to be so catechised,
And this was my reply:—'As it befell,
One summer morning we had walked
    abroad   36
At break of day, Joanna and myself.
—'Twas that delightful season when the
    broom,
Full-flowered, and visible on every steep,
Along the copses runs in veins of gold. 40
Our pathway led us on to Rotha's banks;
And, when we came in front of that tall
    rock
That eastward looks, I there stopped
    short—and stood
Tracing the lofty barrier with my eye
From base to summit; such delight I
    found   45
To note in shrub and tree, in stone and
    flower,
That intermixture of delicious hues,
Along so vast a surface, all at once,
In one impression, by connecting force
Of their own beauty, imaged in the heart.
—When I had gazed perhaps two minutes'
    space,   51
Joanna, looking in my eyes, beheld
That ravishment of mine, and laughed
    aloud.
The Rock, like something starting from a
    sleep,
Took up the Lady's voice, and laughed
    again;   55
That ancient Woman seated on Helm-
    crag
Was ready with her cavern; Hammar-
    scar,
And the tall Steep of Silver-how, sent
    forth
A noise of laughter; southern Loughrigg
    heard,
And Fairfield answered with a mountain
    tone;   60
Helvellyn far into the clear blue sky
Carried the Lady's voice,—old Skiddaw
    blew

His speaking-trumpet;—back out of the
    clouds
Of Glaramara southward came the voice;
And Kirkstone tossed it from his misty
    head.   65
—Now whether (said I to our cordial
    Friend,
Who in the hey-day of astonishment
Smiled in my face) this were in simple
    truth
A work accomplished by the brotherhood
Of ancient mountains, or my ear was
    touched   70
With dreams and visionary impulses
To me alone imparted, sure I am
That there was a loud uproar in the hills.
And, while we both were listening, to my
    side
The fair Joanna drew, as if she wished 75
To shelter from some object of her fear.
—And hence, long afterwards, when
    eighteen moons
Were wasted, as I chanced to walk alone
Beneath this rock, at sunrise, on a calm
And silent morning, I sat down, and there,
In memory of affections old and true, 81
I chiselled out in those rude characters
Joanna's name deep in the living stone:—
And I, and all who dwell by my fireside,
Have called the lovely rock, JOANNA'S
    ROCK.'   85

NOTE.—In Cumberland and Westmoreland are
several Inscriptions, upon the native rock, which,
from the wasting of time, and the rudeness of the
workmanship, have been mistaken for Runic.
They are, without doubt, Roman.

The Rotha, mentioned in this poem, is the River
which, flowing through the lakes of Grasmere and
Rydal, falls into Winandermere. On Helm-crag,
that impressive single mountain at the head of the
Vale of Grasmere, is a rock which from most
points of view bears a striking resemblance to an
old Woman cowering. Close by this rock is one
of those fissures or caverns, which in the language
of the country are called dungeons. Most of the
mountains here mentioned immediately surround
the Vale of Grasmere; of the others, some are at
a considerable distance, but they belong to the
same cluster.

III

[Composed 1800.—Published 1800.]

THERE is an Eminence,—of these our hills
The last that parleys with the setting sun;
We can behold it from our orchard seat;
And, when at evening we pursue our walk
Along the public way, this Peak, so high
Above us, and so distant in its height,   6
Is visible; and often seems to send
Its own deep quiet to restore our hearts.
The meteors make of it a favourite haunt:
The star of Jove, so beautiful and large
In the mid heavens, is never half so fair
As when he shines above it. 'Tis in truth
The loneliest place we have among the
    clouds.

And She who dwells with me, whom I
have loved
With such communion that no place on
earth   15
Can ever be a solitude to me,
Hath to this lonely Summit given my
Name.

IV

[Composed October 10, 1800.—Published 1800.]

A NARROW girdle of rough stones and
crags,
A rude and natural causeway, interposed
Between the water and a winding slope
Of copse and thicket, leaves the eastern
shore
Of Grasmere safe in its own privacy: 5
And there myself and two beloved
Friends,
One calm September morning, ere the mist
Had altogether yielded to the sun,
Sauntered on this retired and difficult
way.
——Ill suits the road with one in haste;
but we   10
Played with our time; and, as we strolled
along,
It was our occupation to observe
Such objects as the waves had tossed
ashore—
Feather, or leaf, or weed, or withered
bough,
Each on the other heaped, along the line
Of the dry wreck. And, in our vacant
mood,   16
Not seldom did we stop to watch some
tuft
Of dandelion seed or thistle's beard,
That skimmed the surface of the dead
calm lake,
Suddenly halting now—a lifeless stand!
And starting off again with freak as
sudden;   21
In all its sportive wanderings, all the while,
Making report of an invisible breeze
That was its wings, its chariot, and its
horse,
Its playmate, rather say, its moving soul.
——And often, trifling with a privilege 26
Alike indulged to all, we paused, one now,
And now the other, to point out, per-
chance
To pluck, some flower or water-weed, too
fair
Either to be divided from the place   30
On which it grew, or to be left alone
To its own beauty. Many such there are,
Fair ferns and flowers, and chiefly that
tall fern,
So stately, of the Queen Osmunda named;
Plant lovelier, in its own retired abode 35
On Grasmere's beach, than Naiad by the
side

Of Grecian brook, or Lady of the Mere,
Sole-sitting by the shores of old romance.
——So fared we that bright morning: from
the fields,
Meanwhile, a noise was heard, the busy
mirth   40
Of reapers, men and women, boys and
girls.
Delighted much to listen to those sounds,
And feeding thus our fancies, we ad-
vanced
Along the indented shore; when suddenly,
Through a thin veil of glittering haze was
seen   45
Before us, on a point of jutting land,
The tall and upright figure of a Man
Attired in peasant's garb, who stood
alone,
Angling beside the margin of the lake.
'Improvident and reckless,' we exclaimed,
'The Man must be, who thus can lose a
day   51
Of the mid harvest, when the labourer's
hire
Is ample, and some little might be stored
Wherewith to cheer him in the winter
time.'
Thus talking of that Peasant, we ap-
proached   55
Close to the spot where with his rod and
line
He stood alone; whereat he turned his
head
To greet us—and we saw a Man worn
down
By sickness, gaunt and lean, with sunken
cheeks
And wasted limbs, his legs so long and
lean   60
That for my single self I looked at them,
Forgetful of the body they sustained.—
Too weak to labour in the harvest field,
The Man was using his best skill to gain
A pittance from the dead unfeeling lake
That knew not of his wants. I will not say
What thoughts immediately were ours,
nor how   67
The happy idleness of that sweet morn,
With all its lovely images, was changed
To serious musing and to self-reproach.70
Nor did we fail to see within ourselves
What need there is to be reserved in
speech,
And temper all our thoughts with charity.
—Therefore, unwilling to forget that day,
My Friend, Myself, and She who then
received   75
The same admonishment, have called the
place
By a memorial name, uncouth indeed
As e'er by mariner was given to bay
Or foreland, on a new-discovered coast;
And POINT RASH-JUDGMENT is the Name
it bears.   80

118

V

TO M. H.

[Composed after December 21, and before December 28, 1799.—Published 1800.]

OUR walk was far among the ancient trees:
There was no road, nor any woodman's path;
But a thick umbrage—checking the wild growth
Of weed and sapling, along soft green turf
Beneath the branches—of itself had made
A track, that brought us to a slip of lawn,
And a small bed of water in the woods. 7
All round this pool both flocks and herds might drink
On its firm margin, even as from a well,
Or some stone-basin which the herds-man's hand 10
Had shaped for their refreshment; nor did sun,
Or wind from any quarter, ever come,
But as a blessing to this calm recess,
This glade of water and this one green field.
The spot was made by Nature for herself;
The travellers know it not, and 'twill remain 16
Unknown to them; but it is beautiful;
And if a man should plant his cottage near,
Should sleep beneath the shelter of its trees,
And blend its waters with his daily meal,
He would so love it, that in his death-hour
Its image would survive among his thoughts: 22
And therefore, my sweet MARY, this still Nook,
With all its beeches, we have named from You!

VI

[Begun August 29, 30, 1800.—Finished 1802.—Published 1815.]

WHEN, to the attractions of the busy world
Preferring studious leisure, I had chosen
A habitation in this peaceful Vale,
Sharp season followed of continual storm
In deepest winter; and, from week to week, 5
Pathway, and lane, and public road, were clogged
With frequent showers of snow. Upon a hill,
At a short distance from my cottage, stands
A stately Fir-grove, whither I was wont
To hasten, for I found, beneath the roof 10
Of that perennial shade, a cloistral place
Of refuge, with an unincumbered floor.

Here, in safe covert, on the shallow snow,
And sometimes on a speck of visible earth,
The redbreast near me hopped; nor was I loth 15
To sympathize with vulgar coppice birds
That, for protection from the nipping blast,
Hither repaired.—A single beech-tree grew
Within this grove of firs! and, on the fork
Of that one beech, appeared a thrush's nest; 20
A last year's nest, conspicuously built
At such small elevation from the ground
As gave sure sign that they, who in that house
Of nature and of love had made their home
Amid the fir-trees, all the summer long 25
Dwelt in a tranquil spot. And oftentimes
A few sheep, stragglers from some moun-tain-flock,
Would watch my motions with suspicious stare,
From the remotest outskirts of the grove,—
Some nook where they had made their final stand, 30
Huddling together from two fears—the fear
Of me and of the storm. Full many an hour
Here did I lose. But in this grove the trees
Had been so thickly planted and had thriven
In such perplexed and intricate array, 35
That vainly did I seek beneath their stems
A length of open space, where to and fro
My feet might move without concern or care;
And, baffled thus, though earth from day to day
Was fettered, and the air by storm dis-turbed, 40
I ceased the shelter to frequent,—and prized,
Less than I wished to prize, that calm recess.

The snows dissolved, and genial Spring returned
To clothe the fields with verdure. Other haunts
Meanwhile were mine; till one bright April day, 45
By chance retiring from the glare of noon
To this forsaken covert, there I found
A hoary pathway traced between the trees,
And winding on with such an easy line
Along a natural opening, that I stood 50
Much wondering how I could have sought in vain

For what was now so obvious. To abide,
For an allotted interval of ease,
Under my cottage-roof, had gladly come
From the wild sea a cherished Visitant;
And with the sight of this same path—
    begun,   56
Begun and ended, in the shady grove,
Pleasant conviction flashed upon my
    mind
That, to this opportune recess allured,
He had surveyed it with a finer eye,   60
A heart more wakeful; and had worn the
    track
By pacing here, unwearied and alone,
In that habitual restlessness of foot
That haunts the Sailor, measuring o'er
    and o'er
His short domain upon the vessel's
    deck,   65
While she pursues her course through the
    dreary sea.

    When thou hadst quitted Esthwaite's
    pleasant shore,
And taken thy first leave of those green
    hills
And rocks that were the play-ground of
    thy youth,
Year followed year, my Brother! and we
    two,   70
Conversing not, knew little in what mould
Each other's mind was fashioned; and at
    length,
When once again we met in Grasmere
    Vale,
Between us there was little other bond
Than common feelings of fraternal love.
But thou, a School-boy, to the sea hadst
    carried   76
Undying recollections; Nature there
Was with thee; she, who loved us both,
    she still
Was with thee; and even so didst thou
    become
A *silent* Poet; from the solitude   80
Of the vast sea didst bring a watchful
    heart
Still couchant, an inevitable ear,
And an eye practised like a blind man's
    touch.[1]
—Back to the joyless Ocean thou art
    gone;
Nor from this vestige of thy musing hours
Could I withhold thy honoured name,—
    and now   86
I love the fir-grove with a perfect love.
Thither do I withdraw when cloudless
    suns

[1] Lines 1–83 were probably written on August 29,
30, 1800; the remainder in 1802, while John W. was
absent on the voyage to China from which he returned in September of that year. Can this be the
Silver How Poem to which (Dorothy W. tells us)
William wrote a conclusion on March 26, 1802? See
Knight's 'Life of W. W.,' vol. I. pp. 302-3.—ED.

Shine hot, or wind blows troublesome
    and strong;
And there I sit at evening, when the steep
Of Silver-how, and Grasmere's peaceful
    lake   91
And one green island, gleam between the
    stems
Of the dark firs, a visionary scene!
And while I gaze upon the spectacle
Of clouded splendour, on this dream-like
    sight   95
Of solemn loveliness, I think on thee,
My Brother, and on all which thou hast
    lost.
Nor seldom, if I rightly guess, while Thou,
Muttering the verses which I muttered
    first
Among the mountains, through the mid-
    night watch   100
Art pacing thoughtfully the vessel's deck
In some far region, here, while o'er my
    head,
At every impulse of the moving breeze,
The fir-grove murmurs with a sea-like
    sound,
Alone I tread this path;—for aught I
    know,   105
Timing my steps to thine; and, with a
    store
Of undistinguishable sympathies,
Mingling most earnest wishes for the day
When we, and others whom we love, shall
    meet   109
A second time, in Grasmere's happy Vale.

NOTE.—This wish was not granted; the lamented
Person not long after perished by shipwreck, in
discharge of his duty as Commander of the
Honourable East India Company's Vessel, the
Earl of Abergavenny.

VII

[Composed 1845.—Published 1845.]

FORTH from a jutting ridge, around whose
    base
Winds our deep Vale, two heath-clad
    Rocks ascend
In fellowship, the loftiest of the pair
Rising to no ambitious height; yet both,
O'er lake and stream, mountain and
    flowery mead,   5
Unfolding prospects fair as human eyes
Ever beheld. Up-led with mutual help,
To one or other brow of those twin Peaks
Were two adventurous Sisters wont to
    climb,
And took no note of the hour while
    thence they gazed,   10
The blooming heath their couch, gazed
    side by side,
In speechless admiration. I, a witness
And frequent sharer of their calm delight
With thankful heart, to either Eminence
Gave the baptismal name each Sister bore.

Now are they parted, far as Death's cold
  hand   16
Hath power to part the Spirits of those
  who love
As they did love. Ye kindred Pinnacles—
That, while the generations of mankind
Follow each other to their hiding-place   20
In time's abyss, are privileged to endure
Beautiful in yourselves, and richly graced

With like command of beauty—grant
  your aid
For MARY'S humble, SARAH'S silent
  claim,[1]
That their pure joy in nature may survive
From age to age in blended memory.   26

[1] MARY, the poet's wife; SARAH, her sister, who died at Rydal Mount on June 23, 1835. See *Miscellaneous Sonnets*, I. XXIX.—ED.

POEMS OF THE FANCY

I

A MORNING EXERCISE

[Composed 1828.—Published 1832.]

FANCY, who leads the pastimes of the glad,
Full oft is pleased a wayward dart to
  throw;
Sending sad shadows after things not sad,
Peopling the harmless fields with signs of
  woe:
Beneath her sway, a simple forest cry   5
Becomes an echo of man's misery.

Blithe ravens croak of death; and when
  the owl
Tries his two voices for a favourite strain—
Tu-whit—Tu-whoo! the unsuspecting fowl
Forebodes mishap or seems but to com-
  plain;   10
Fancy, intent to harass and annoy,
Can thus pervert the evidence of joy.

Through border wilds where naked
  Indians stray,
Myriads of notes attest her subtle skill;
A feathered task-master cries, 'WORK
  AWAY!'   15
And in thy iteration, 'WHIP POOR WILL!'[1]
Is heard the spirit of a toil-worn slave,
Lashed out of life, not quiet in the grave.

What wonder? at her bidding, ancient
  lays
Steeped in dire grief the voice of Philo-
  mel;   20
And that fleet messenger of summer days,
The Swallow, twittered subject to like spell;
But ne'er could Fancy bend the buoyant
  Lark
To melancholy service—hark! O hark!

The daisy sleeps upon the dewy lawn,   25
Not lifting yet the head that evening bowed;
But *He* is risen, a later star of dawn,
Glittering and twinkling near yon rosy
  cloud;
Bright gem instinct with music, vocal
  spark;
The happiest bird that sprang out of the
  Ark!   30

[1] See Waterton's 'Wanderings in South America.'

Hail, blest above all kinds!—Supremely
  skilled
Restless with fixed to balance, high with
  low,
Thou leav'st the halcyon free her hopes to
  build
On such forbearance as the deep may
  show;
Perpetual flight, unchecked by earthly
  ties,   35
Leav'st to the wandering bird of paradise.

Faithful, though swift as lightning, the
  meek dove;
Yet more hath Nature reconciled in thee;
So constant with thy downward eye of
  love,
Yet, in aërial singleness, so free;   40
So humble, yet so ready to rejoice
In power of wing and never-wearied
  voice.

To the last point of vision, and beyond,
Mount, daring warbler!—that love-
  prompted strain,
('Twixt thee and thine a never-failing
  bond),   45
Thrills not the less the bosom of the plain:
Yet might'st thou seem, proud privilege!
  to sing
All independent of the leafy spring.[2]

How would it please old Ocean to par-
  take,   49
With sailors longing for a breeze in vain,
The harmony thy notes most gladly make
Where earth resembles most his own
  domain!
Urania's self might welcome with pleased
  ear
These matins mounting towards her na-
  tive sphere.

Chanter by heaven attracted, whom no
  bars   55
To daylight known deter from that pursuit,

[2] This stanza was transferred in 1845 to its present place from the poem (composed 1825; published 1827) *To a Skylark*, beginning, 'Ethereal minstrel! pilgrim of the sky.'—ED.

'Tis well that some sage instinct, when
  the stars
Come forth at evening, keeps Thee still
  and mute;
For not an eyelid could to sleep incline
Wert thou among them, singing as they
  shine!   60

II

A FLOWER GARDEN

AT COLEORTON HALL, LEICESTERSHIRE

[Composed 1824.—Published 1827.]

TELL me, ye Zephyrs! that unfold,
While fluttering o'er this gay Recess,
Pinions that fanned the teeming mould
Of Eden's blissful wilderness,
Did only softly-stealing hours   5
There close the peaceful lives of flowers?

Say, when the *moving* creatures saw
All kinds commingled without fear,
Prevailed a like indulgent law
For the still growths that prosper here?
Did wanton fawn and kid forbear   11
The half-blown rose, the lily spare?

Or peeped they often from their beds,
And prematurely disappeared,
Devoured like pleasure ere it spreads 15
A bosom to the sun endeared?
If such their harsh untimely doom,
It falls not *here* on bud or bloom.

All summer-long the happy Eve
Of this fair Spot her flowers may bind, 20
Nor e'er, with ruffled fancy, grieve,
From the next glance she casts, to find
That love for little things by Fate
Is rendered vain as love for great.

Yet, where the guardian fence is wound, 25
So subtly are our eyes beguiled,
We see not nor suspect a bound,
No more than in some forest wild;
The sight is free as air—or crost
Only by art in nature lost.   30

And though the jealous turf refuse
By random footsteps to be prest,
And feed on never-sullied dews,
Ye, gentle breezes from the west,
With all the ministers of hope   35
Are tempted to this sunny slope!

And hither throngs of birds resort;
Some, inmates lodged in shady nests,
Some, perched on stems of stately port
That nod to welcome transient guests; 40
While hare and leveret, seen at play,
Appear not more shut out than they.

Apt emblem (for reproof of pride)
This delicate Enclosure shows
Of modest kindness, that would hide 45
The firm protection she bestows;

Of manners, like its viewless fence,
Ensuring peace to innocence.

Thus spake the moral Muse—her wing
Abruptly spreading to depart,   50
She left that farewell offering,
Memento for some docile heart;
That may respect the good old age
When Fancy was Truth's willing Page;
And Truth would skim the flowery glade,
Though entering but as Fancy's Shade. 56

III

[Composed March 18, 1798.—Published 1800.]

A WHIRL-BLAST from behind the hill
Rushed o'er the wood with startling
  sound;
Then—all at once the air was still,
And showers of hailstones pattered
  round.
Where leafless oaks towered high above, 5
I sat within an undergrove
Of tallest hollies, tall and green;
A fairer bower was never seen.
From year to year the spacious floor
With withered leaves is covered o'er, 10
And all the year the bower is green.

But see! where'er the hailstones drop
The withered leaves all skip and hop;
There's not a breeze—no breath of air—
Yet here, and there, and every where 15
Along the floor, beneath the shade
By those embowering hollies made,
The leaves in myriads jump and spring,
As if with pipes and music rare
Some Robin Good-fellow were there, 20
And all those leaves, in festive glee,
Were dancing to the minstrelsy.

IV

THE WATERFALL AND THE EGLANTINE

[Composed 1800.—Published 1800.]

I

'BEGONE, thou fond presumptuous Elf,'
Exclaimed an angry Voice,
'Nor dare to thrust thy foolish self
Between me and my choice!'
A small Cascade fresh swoln with snows 5
Thus threatened a poor Briar-rose,
That, all bespattered with his foam,
And dancing high and dancing low,
Was living, as a child might know,
In an unhappy home.   10

II

'Dost thou presume my course to block?
Off, off! or, puny Thing!
I'll hurl thee headlong with the rock
To which thy fibres cling.'

122

The Flood was tyrannous and strong; 15
The patient Briar suffered long,
Nor did he utter groan or sigh,
Hoping the danger would be past;
But, seeing no relief, at last
He ventured to reply.   20

III

'Ah!' said the Briar, 'blame me not;
Why should we dwell in strife?
We who in this sequestered spot
Once lived a happy life!
You stirred me on my rocky bed—   25
What pleasure through my veins you
        spread
The summer long, from day to day,
My leaves you freshened and bedewed;
Nor was it common gratitude
That did your cares repay.   30

IV

'When spring came on with bud and bell,
Among these rocks did I
Before you hang my wreaths to tell
That gentle days were nigh!
And in the sultry summer hours   35
I sheltered you with leaves and flowers;
And in my leaves—now shed and gone,
The linnet lodged, and for us two
Chanted his pretty songs, when you
Had little voice or none.   40

V

'But now proud thoughts are in your
        breast—
What grief is mine you see,
Ah! would you think, even yet how blest
Together we might be!
Though of both leaf and flower bereft, 45
Some ornaments to me are left—
Rich store of scarlet hips is mine,
With which I, in my humble way,
Would deck you many a winter day,
A happy Eglantine!'   50

VI

What more he said I cannot tell,
The Torrent down the rocky dell
Came thundering loud and fast;
I listened, nor aught else could hear;
The Briar quaked—and much I fear 55
Those accents were his last.

V

THE OAK AND THE BROOM
A PASTORAL
[Composed 1800.—Published 1800.]

I

His simple truths did Andrew glean
Beside the babbling rills;
A careful student he had been
Among the woods and hills.

One winter's night, when through the
        trees   5
The wind was roaring, on his knees
His youngest born did Andrew hold:
And while the rest, a ruddy quire,
Were seated round their blazing fire,
This Tale the Shepherd told.   10

II

'I saw a crag, a lofty stone
As ever tempest beat!
Out of its head an Oak had grown,
A Broom out of its feet.
The time was March, a cheerful noon— 15
The thaw-wind, with the breath of June,
Breathed gently from the warm south-
        west:
When, in a voice sedate with age,
This Oak, a giant and a sage,
His neighbour thus addressed:—   20

III

'"Eight weary weeks, through rock and
        clay,
Along this mountain's edge,
The Frost had wrought both night and
        day,
Wedge driving after wedge.
Look up! and think, above your head 25
What trouble, surely, will be bred;
Last night I heard a crash—'tis true,
The splinters took another road—
I see them yonder—what a load
For such a Thing as you!   30

IV

'"You are preparing as before,
To deck your slender shape;
And yet, just three years back—no
        more—
You had a strange escape:
Down from yon cliff a fragment broke; 35
It thundered down, with fire and smoke,
And hitherward pursued its way;
This ponderous block was caught by me,
And o'er your head, as you may see,
'Tis hanging to this day!   40

V

'"If breeze or bird to this rough steep
Your kind's first seed did bear;
The breeze had better been asleep,
The bird caught in a snare:
For you and your green twigs decoy 45
The little witless shepherd-boy
To come and slumber in your bower;
And trust me, on some sultry noon,
Both you and he, Heaven knows how
        soon!
Will perish in one hour.   50

VI

'"From me this friendly warning take"—
The Broom began to doze,
And thus, to keep herself awake,
Did gently interpose:
"My thanks for your discourse are due;
That more than what you say is true   56
I know, and I have known it long;
Frail is the bond by which we hold
Our being, whether young or old,
Wise, foolish, weak, or strong.   60

VII

'"Disasters, do the best we can,
Will reach both great and small;
And he is oft the wisest man,
Who is not wise at all.
For me, why should I wish to roam?   65
This spot is my paternal home,
It is my pleasant heritage;
My father many a happy year
Spread here his careless blossoms, here
Attained a good old age.   70

VIII

'"Even such as his may be my lot.
What cause have I to haunt
My heart with terrors? Am I not
In truth a favoured plant!
On me such bounty Summer pours,   75
That I am covered o'er with flowers;
And when the Frost is in the sky,
My branches are so fresh and gay
That you might look at me and say,
This Plant can never die.   80

IX

'"The butterfly, all green and gold,
To me hath often flown,
Here in my blossoms to behold
Wings lovely as his own.
When grass is chill with rain or dew,   85
Beneath my shade the mother-ewe
Lies with her infant lamb; I see
The love they to each other make,
And the sweet joy which they partake,
It is a joy to me."   90

X

'Her voice was blithe, her heart was light;
The Broom might have pursued
Her speech, until the stars of night
Their journey had renewed;
But in the branches of the oak   95
Two ravens now began to croak
Their nuptial song, a gladsome air;
And to her own green bower the breeze
That instant brought two stripling bees
To rest, or murmur there.   100

XI

'One night, my Children! from the north
There came a furious blast;
At break of day I ventured forth,
And near the cliff I passed.

The storm had fallen upon the Oak,   105
And struck him with a mighty stroke,
And whirled, and whirled him far away;
And, in one hospitable cleft,
The little careless Broom was left
To live for many a day.'   110

VI

TO A SEXTON
[Composed 1799.—Published 1800.]

LET thy wheel-barrow alone—
Wherefore, Sexton, piling still
In thy bone-house bone on bone?
'Tis already like a hill
In a field of battle made,   5
Where three thousand skulls are laid;
These died in peace each with the other,—
Father, sister, friend, and brother.

Mark the spot to which I point!
From this platform, eight feet square,   10
Take not even a finger-joint:
Andrew's whole fire-side is there.
Here, alone, before thine eyes,
Simon's sickly daughter lies,
From weakness now and pain defended,
Whom the twenty winters tended.   16

Look but at the gardener's pride—
How he glories, when he sees
Roses, lilies, side by side,
Violets in families!   20
By the heart of Man, his tears,
By his hopes and by his fears,
Thou, too heedless, art the Warden
Of a far superior garden.

Thus then, each to other dear,   25
Let them all in quiet lie,
Andrew there, and Susan here,
Neighbours in mortality,
And should I live through sun and rain
Seven widowed years without my Jane,
O Sexton, do not then remove her,   31
Let one grave hold the Loved and Lover!

VII

TO THE DAISY
[Composed 1802.—Published 1807.]

'Her[1] divine skill taught me this,
That from every thing I saw
I could some instruction draw,
And raise pleasure to the height
Through the meanest object's sight.
By the murmur of a spring,
Or the least bough's rustelling;
By a Daisy whose leaves spread
Shut when Titan goes to bed;
Or a shady bush or tree;
She could more infuse in me
Than all Nature's beauties can
In some other wiser man.'

G. WITHER.

IN youth from rock to rock I went,
From hill to hill in discontent
Of pleasure high and turbulent,

[1] His Muse.

124

Most pleased when most uneasy;
But now my own delights I make,—   5
My thirst at every rill can slake,
And gladly Nature's love partake
    Of Thee, sweet Daisy!

Thee Winter in the garland wears
That thinly decks his few grey hairs;   10
Spring parts the clouds with softest airs,
    That she may sun thee;
Whole Summer-fields are thine by right;
And Autumn, melancholy Wight!
Doth in thy crimson head delight   15
    When rains are on thee.

In shoals and bands, a morrice train,
Thou greet'st the traveller in the lane;
Pleased at his greeting thee again;
    Yet nothing daunted,   20
Nor grieved if thou be set at nought:
And oft alone in nooks remote
We meet thee, like a pleasant thought,
    When such are wanted.

Be violets in their secret mews   25
The flowers the wanton Zephyrs choose;
Proud be the rose, with rains and dews
    Her head impearling,
Thou liv'st with less ambitious aim,
Yet hast not gone without thy fame;   30
Thou art indeed by many a claim
    The Poet's darling.

If to a rock from rains he fly,
Or, some bright day of April sky,
Imprisoned by hot sunshine lie   35
    Near the green holly,
And wearily at length should fare;
He needs but look about, and there
Thou art!—a friend at hand, to scare
    His melancholy.   40

A hundred times, by rock or bower,
Ere thus I have lain couched an hour
Have I derived from thy sweet power
    Some apprehension;
Some steady love; some brief delight;   45
Some memory that had taken flight;
Some chime of fancy wrong or right;
    Or stray invention.

If stately passions in me burn,
And one chance look to Thee should turn,
I drink out of an humbler urn   51
    A lowlier pleasure;
The homely sympathy that heeds
The common life our nature breeds;
A wisdom fitted to the needs   55
    Of hearts at leisure.

Fresh-smitten by the morning ray,
When thou art up, alert and gay,
Then, cheerful Flower! my spirits play

With kindred gladness: 60
And when, at dusk, by dews opprest
Thou sink'st, the image of thy rest
Hath often eased my pensive breast
    Of careful sadness.

And all day long I number yet,   65
All seasons through, another debt,
Which I, wherever thou art met,
    To thee am owing;
An instinct call it, a blind sense;
A happy, genial influence,   70
Coming one knows not how, nor whence,
    Nor whither going.

Child of the Year! that round dost run
Thy pleasant course,—when day's begun
As ready to salute the sun   75
    As lark or leveret,
Thy long-lost praise thou shalt regain;
Nor be less dear to future men
Than in old time;—thou not in vain
    Art Nature's favourite.[1]   80

VIII

TO THE SAME FLOWER

[Composed 1802.—Published 1807.]

WITH little here to do or see
Of things that in the great world be,
Daisy! again I talk to thee,
    For thou art worthy,
Thou unassuming Common-place   5
Of Nature, with that homely face,
And yet with something of a grace
    Which love makes for thee!

Oft on the dappled turf at ease
I sit, and play with similes,   10
Loose types of things through all degrees,
    Thoughts of thy raising:
And many a fond and idle name
I give to thee, for praise or blame,
As is the humour of the game,   15
    While I am gazing.

A nun demure of lowly port;
Or sprightly maiden, of Love's court,
In thy simplicity the sport
    Of all temptations;   20
A queen in crown of rubies drest;
A starveling in a scanty vest;
Are all, as seems to suit thee best,
    Thy appellations.

A little Cyclops with one eye   25
Staring to threaten and defy,
That thought comes next—and instantly
    The freak is over,
The shape will vanish—and behold
A silver shield with boss of gold,   30
That spreads itself, some faery bold
    In fight to cover!

[1] See, in Chaucer and the elder Poets, the honours formerly paid to this flower.

I see thee glittering from afar—
And then thou art a pretty star;
Not quite so fair as many are   35
    In heaven above thee!
Yet like a star, with glittering crest,
Self-poised in air thou seem'st to rest;—
May peace come never to his nest,
    Who shall reprove thee!   40

Bright *Flower!* for by that *name* at last,
When all my reveries are past,
I call thee, and to that cleave fast,
    Sweet silent creature!
That breath'st with me in sun and air,   45
Do thou, as thou art wont, repair
My heart with gladness, and a share
    Of thy meek nature!

IX

THE GREEN LINNET

[Composed 1803.—Published 1807.]

BENEATH these fruit-tree boughs that shed
Their snow-white blossoms on my head,
With brightest sunshine round me spread
Of spring's unclouded weather,
In this sequestered nook how sweet   5
To sit upon my orchard-seat!
And birds and flowers once more to greet,
    My last year's friends together.

One have I marked, the happiest guest
In all this covert of the blest: 10
Hail to Thee, far above the rest
    In joy of voice and pinion!
Thou, Linnet! in thy green array,
Presiding Spirit here to-day,
Dost lead the revels of the May;   15
    And this is thy dominion.

While birds, and butterflies, and flowers,
Make all one band of paramours,
Thou, ranging up and down the bowers,
    Art sole in thy employment: 20
A Life, a Presence like the Air,
Scattering thy gladness without care,
Too blest with any one to pair;
    Thyself thy own enjoyment.

Amid yon tuft of hazel trees,   25
That twinkle to the gusty breeze,
Behold him perched in ecstasies,
    Yet seeming still to hover;
There! where the flutter of his wings
Upon his back and body flings   30
Shadows and sunny glimmerings,
    That cover him all over.

My dazzled sight he oft deceives,
A Brother of the dancing leaves;
Then flits, and from the cottage eaves   35
    Pours forth his song in gushes;
As if by that exulting strain
He mocked and treated with disdain
The voiceless Form he chose to feign,
    While fluttering in the bushes.   40

X

TO A SKY-LARK

[Composed 1805.—Published 1807.]

UP with me! up with me into the clouds!
    For thy song, Lark, is strong;
Up with me, up with me into the clouds!
        Singing, singing,
With clouds and sky about thee ringing,   5
    Lift me, guide me, till I find
That spot which seems so to thy mind!

I have walked through wildernesses dreary,
And to-day my heart is weary;
Had I now the wings of a Faery,   10
    Up to thee would I fly.
There is madness about thee, and joy divine
    In that song of thine;
Lift me, guide me, high and high
To thy banqueting place in the sky.   15

        Joyous as morning,
    Thou art laughing and scorning;
Thou hast a nest for thy love and thy rest,
And, though little troubled with sloth,
Drunken Lark! thou wouldst be loth
To be such a traveller as I.   21
    Happy, happy Liver,
With a soul as strong as a mountain river
Pouring out praise to the almighty Giver,
    Joy and jollity be with us both!   25

Alas! my journey, rugged and uneven,
Through prickly moors or dusty ways
        must wind;
But hearing thee, or others of thy kind,
As full of gladness and as free of heaven,
I, with my fate contented, will plod on,   30
And hope for higher raptures, when life's
    day is done.

XI

TO THE SMALL CELANDINE[1]

[Composed April 30, 1802.—Published 1807.]

PANSIES, lilies, kingcups, daisies,
Let them live upon their praises;
Long as there's a sun that sets,
Primroses will have their glory;
Long as there are violets,   5
They will have a place in story:
There's a flower that shall be mine,
'Tis the little Celandine.

Eyes of some men travel far
For the finding of a star;   10
Up and down the heavens they go,
Men that keep a mighty rout!
I'm as great as they, I trow,
Since the day I found thee out,
Little Flower—I'll make a stir,   15
Like a sage astronomer.

[1] Common Pilewort.

Modest, yet withal an Elf
Bold, and lavish of thyself;
Since we needs must first have met
I have seen thee, high and low,   20
Thirty years or more, and yet
'Twas a face I did not know;
Thou hast now, go where I may,
Fifty greetings in a day.

Ere a leaf is on a bush,
In the time before the thrush
Has a thought about her nest,
Thou wilt come with half a call,
Spreading out thy glossy breast
Like a careless Prodigal;   30
Telling tales about the sun,
When we've little warmth, or none.

Poets, vain men in their mood!
Travel with the multitude:
Never heed them; I aver   35
That they all are wanton wooers;
But the thrifty cottager,
Who stirs little out of doors,
Joys to spy thee near her home;
Spring is coming, Thou art come!   40

Comfort have thou of thy merit,
Kindly, unassuming Spirit!
Careless of thy neighbourhood,
Thou dost show thy pleasant face
On the moor, and in the wood,   45
In the lane;—there's not a place,
Howsoever mean it be,
But 'tis good enough for thee.

Ill befall the yellow flowers,
Children of the flaring hours!   50
Buttercups, that will be seen,
Whether we will see or no;
Others, too, of lofty mien;
They have done as worldlings do,
Taken praise that should be thine,   55
Little, humble Celandine.

Prophet of delight and mirth,
Ill-requited upon earth;
Herald of a mighty band,
Of a joyous train ensuing,   60
Serving at my heart's command,
Tasks that are no tasks renewing,
I will sing, as doth behove,
Hymns in praise of what I love!

XII

TO THE SAME FLOWER

[Composed May 1, 1802.—Published 1807.]

PLEASURES newly found are sweet
When they lie about our feet:
February last, my heart
First at sight of thee was glad;
All unheard of as thou art,
Thou must needs, I think, have had,
Celandine! and long ago,
Praise of which I nothing know.

I have not a doubt but he,
Whosoe'er the man might be,   10
Who the first with pointed rays
(Workman worthy to be sainted)
Set the sign-board in a blaze,
When the rising sun he painted,
Took the fancy from a glance   15
At thy glittering countenance.

Soon as gentle breezes bring   25
News of winter's vanishing,
And the children build their bowers,
Sticking 'kerchief-plots of mould   20
All about with full-blown flowers,
Thick as sheep in shepherd's fold!   30
With the proudest thou art there,
Mantling in the tiny square.

Often have I sighed to measure   25
By myself a lonely pleasure,
Sighed to think I read a book
Only read, perhaps, by me;
Yet I long could overlook
Thy bright coronet and Thee,   30
And thy arch and wily ways,
And thy store of other praise.

Blithe of heart, from week to week
Thou dost play at hide-and-seek;
While the patient primrose sits   35
Like a beggar in the cold,
Thou, a flower of wiser wits,
Slip'st into thy sheltering hold;
Liveliest of the vernal train
When ye all are out again.   40

Drawn by what peculiar spell,
By what charm of sight or smell,
Does the dim-eyed curious Bee,
Labouring for her waxen cells,
Fondly settle upon Thee   45
Prized above all buds and bells
Opening daily at thy side,
By the season multiplied?

Thou art not beyond the moon,
But a thing 'beneath our shoon;'   50
Let the bold Discoverer thrid
In his bark the polar sea;
Rear who will a pyramid;
Praise it is enough for me,
If there be but three or four   55
Who will love my little Flower.

XIII

THE SEVEN SISTERS

OR

THE SOLITUDE OF BINNORIE

[Composed before August 17, 1800.—Published 1807.]

I

SEVEN Daughters had Lord Archibald,
All children of one mother:
You could not say in one short day
What love they bore each other.

A garland of seven lilies wrought!   5
Seven Sisters that together dwell;
But he, bold Knight as ever fought,
Their Father, took of them no thought,
He loved the wars so well.
Sing, mournfully, oh! mournfully,   10
The solitude of Binnorie!

II

Fresh blows the wind, a western wind,
And from the shores of Erin,
Across the wave, a Rover brave
To Binnorie is steering: 15
Right onward to the Scottish strand
The gallant ship is borne;
The warriors leap upon the land,
And hark! the Leader of the band
Hath blown his bugle horn.   20
Sing, mournfully, oh! mournfully,
The solitude of Binnorie.

III

Beside a grotto of their own,
With boughs above them closing,
The Seven are laid, and in the shade   25
They lie like fawns reposing.
But now, upstarting with affright
At noise of man and steed,
Away they fly to left, to right—
Of your fair household, Father-knight,   30
Methinks you take small heed!
Sing, mournfully, oh! mournfully,
The solitude of Binnorie.

IV

Away the seven fair Campbells fly,
And over hill and hollow,   35
With menace proud, and insult loud,
The youthful Rovers follow.
Cried they, 'Your Father loves to roam:
Enough for him to find
The empty house when he comes home;
For us your yellow ringlets comb,   41
For us be fair and kind!'
Sing, mournfully, oh! mournfully,
The solitude of Binnorie.

V

Some close behind, some side by side,   45
Like clouds in stormy weather;
They run, and cry, 'Nay, let us die,
And let us die together.'
A lake was near; the shore was steep;
There never foot had been;   50
They ran, and with a desperate leap
Together plunged into the deep,
Nor ever more were seen.
Sing, mournfully, oh! mournfully,
The solitude of Binnorie.   55

VI

The stream that flows out of the lake,
As through the glen it rambles,
Repeats a moan o'er moss and stone,
For those seven lovely Campbells.

Seven little Islands, green and bare,   60
Have risen from out the deep:
The fishers say, those sisters fair
By faeries all are buried there,
And there together sleep.
Sing, mournfully, oh! mournfully,   65
The solitude of Binnorie.

XIV

[Composed 1803.—Published 1807.]

WHO fancied what a pretty sight
This Rock would be if edged around
With living snow-drops? circlet bright!
How glorious to this orchard-ground!
Who loved the little Rock, and set   5
Upon its head this coronet?

Was it the humour of a child?
Or rather of some gentle maid,
Whose brows, the day that she was styled
The shepherd-queen, were thus arrayed?
Of man mature, or matron sage?   11
Or old man toying with his age?

I asked—'twas whispered; The device
To each and all might well belong:
It is the Spirit of Paradise   15
That prompts such work, a Spirit strong,
That gives to all the self-same bent
Where life is wise and innocent.

XV

THE REDBREAST CHASING THE
BUTTERFLY

[Composed April 18, 1802.—Published 1807.]

ART thou the bird whom Man loves best,
The pious bird with the scarlet breast,
    Our little English Robin;
The bird that comes about our doors
When Autumn-winds are sobbing?   5
Art thou the Peter of Norway Boors?
    Their Thomas in Finland,
    And Russia far inland?
The bird that by some name or other
All men who know thee call their brother,
The darling of children and men?   11
Could Father Adam[1] open his eyes
And see this sight beneath the skies,
He'd wish to close them again.
—If the Butterfly knew but his friend,   15
Hither his flight he would bend;
    And find his way to me,
Under the branches of the tree:
In and out, he darts about;
Can this be the bird, to man so good,   20
That, after their bewildering,
Covered with leaves the little children,
    So painfully in the wood?

[1] See 'Paradise Lost', Book XI, where Adam
points out to Eve the ominous sign of the Eagle
chasing 'two Birds of gayest plume', and the gentle
Hart and Hind pursued by their enemy.

What ailed thee, Robin, that thou couldst
    pursue
    A beautiful creature,   25
That is gentle by nature?
Beneath the summer sky
From flower to flower let him fly;
'Tis all that he wishes to do.
The cheerer Thou of our in-door sad-
    ness,   30
He is the friend of our summer gladness:
What hinders, then, that ye should be
Playmates in the sunny weather,
And fly about in the air together!
His beautiful wings in crimson are
    drest,   35
A crimson as bright as thine own:
Wouldst thou be happy in thy nest,
O pious Bird! whom man loves best,
Love him, or leave him alone!

XVI

SONG FOR THE SPINNING WHEEL

FOUNDED UPON A BELIEF PREVALENT
AMONG THE PASTORAL VALES OF
WESTMORELAND

[Composed 1812.—Published 1820.]

SWIFTLY turn the murmuring wheel!
Night has brought the welcome hour,
When the weary fingers feel
Help, as if from faery power;
Dewy night o'ershades the ground;   5
Turn the swift wheel round and round!

Now, beneath the starry sky,
Couch the widely-scattered sheep;—
Ply the pleasant labour, ply!
For the spindle, while they sleep,   10
Runs with speed more smooth and fine,
Gathering up a trustier line.

Short-lived likings may be bred
By a glance from fickle eyes;
But true love is like the thread   15
Which the kindly wool supplies,
When the flocks are all at rest,
Sleeping on the mountain's breast.

XVII

HINT FROM THE MOUNTAINS

FOR CERTAIN POLITICAL PRETENDERS

[Composed 1817.—Published 1820.]

'WHO but hails the sight with pleasure
When the wings of genius rise,
Their ability to measure
    With great enterprise;
But in man was ne'er such daring   5
As yon Hawk exhibits, pairing
His brave spirit with the war in
    The stormy skies!

'Mark him, how his power he uses,
Lays it by, at will resumes!   10
Mark, ere for his haunt he chooses
    Clouds and utter glooms!
There he wheels in downward mazes;
Sunward now his flight he raises,
Catches fire, as seems, and blazes   15
    With uninjured plumes!'

ANSWER

'Stranger, 'tis no act of courage
Which aloft thou dost discern;
No bold *bird* gone forth to forage
    'Mid the tempest stern;   20
But such mockery as the nations
See, when public perturbations
Lift men from their native stations,
    Like yon TUFT OF FERN;

'Such it is; the aspiring creature   25
Soaring on undaunted wing,
(So you fancied) is by nature
    A dull helpless thing,
Dry and withered, light and yellow;—
That to be the tempest's fellow!   30
Wait—and you shall see how hollow
    Its endeavouring!'

XVIII

ON SEEING A NEEDLECASE IN
THE FORM OF A HARP

THE WORK OF E. M. S.

[Composed 1827.—Published 1827.]

FROWNS are on every Muse's face,
    Reproaches from their lips are sent,
That mimicry should thus disgrace
    The noble Instrument.

A very Harp in all but size!   5
    Needles for strings in apt gradation!
Minerva's self would stigmatize
    The unclassic profanation.

Even her *own* needle that subdued
    Arachne's rival spirit,   10
Though wrought in Vulcan's happiest
    mood,
    Such honour could not merit.

And this too from the Laureate's Child,
    A living lord of melody!
How will her Sire be reconciled   15
    To the refined indignity?

I spake, when whispered a low voice,
    'Bard! moderate your ire;
Spirits of all degrees rejoice
    In presence of the lyre.   20

'The Minstrels of Pygmean bands,
    Dwarf Genii, moonlight-loving Fays,
Have shells to fit their tiny hands
    And suit their slender lays.

'Some, still more delicate of ear,   25
  Have lutes (believe my words)
Whose framework is of gossamer,
  While sunbeams are the chords.

'Gay Sylphs this miniature will court,
  Made vocal by their brushing wings, 30
And sullen Gnomes will learn to sport
  Around its polished strings;

'Whence strains to love-sick maiden dear,
  While in her lonely bower she tries
To cheat the thought she cannot cheer,
  By fanciful embroideries.   36

'Trust, angry Bard! a knowing Sprite,
  Nor think the Harp her lot deplores;
Though 'mid the stars the Lyre shine
          bright,
Love *stoops* as fondly as he soars.'   40

XIX

TO A LADY

IN ANSWER TO A REQUEST THAT I WOULD
WRITE HER A POEM UPON SOME DRAW-
INGS THAT SHE HAD MADE OF FLOWERS
IN THE ISLAND OF MADEIRA

[Composed 1845 (?).—Published 1845.]

FAIR Lady! can I sing of flowers
  That in Madeira bloom and fade,
I who ne'er sate within their bowers,
  Nor through their sunny lawns have
          strayed?
How they in sprightly dance are worn 5
  By Shepherd-groom or May-day queen,
Or holy festal pomps adorn,
  These eyes have never seen.

Yet tho' to me the pencil's art
  No like remembrances can give,   10
Your portraits still may reach the heart
  And there for gentle pleasure live;
While Fancy ranging with free scope
  Shall on some lovely Alien set
A name with us endeared to hope,   15
  To peace, or fond regret.

Still as we look with nicer care,
  Some new resemblance we may trace:
A *Heart's-ease* will perhaps be there,
  A *Speedwell* may not want its place. 20
And so may we, with charmèd mind
  Beholding what your skill has wrought,
Another *Star-of-Bethlehem* find,
  A new *Forget-me-not*.

From earth to heaven with motion fleet
  From heaven to earth our thoughts will
          pass,   26
A *Holy-thistle* here we meet
  And there a *Shepherd's weather-glass;*

And haply some familiar name
  Shall grace the fairest, sweetest, plant
Whose presence cheers the drooping
          frame   31
  Of English Emigrant.

Gazing she feels its power beguile
  Sad thoughts, and breathes with easier
          breath;
Alas! that meek, that tender smile   35
  Is but a harbinger of death:
And pointing with a feeble hand
  She says, in faint words by sighs
          broken,
Bear for me to my native land
  This precious Flower, true love's last
          token.   40

XX

[Composed 1845 (?).—Published 1845.]

GLAD sight wherever new with old
  Is joined through some dear homeborn
          tie;
The life of all that we behold
  Depends upon that mystery.
Vain is the glory of the sky,   5
  The beauty vain of field and grove,
Unless, while with admiring eye
  We gaze, we also learn to love.

XXI

THE CONTRAST

THE PARROT AND THE WREN

[Composed 1825.—Published 1827.]

I

WITHIN her gilded cage confined
  I saw a dazzling Belle,
A Parrot of that famous kind
  Whose name is NON-PAREIL.

Like beads of glossy jet her eyes;   5
  And, smoothed by Nature's skill,
With pearl or gleaming agate vies
  Her finely-curvèd bill.

Her plumy mantle's living hues,
  In mass opposed to mass,   10
Outshine the splendour that imbues
  The robes of pictured glass.

And, sooth to say, an apter Mate
  Did never tempt the choice
Of feathered Thing most delicate   15
  In figure and in voice.

But, exiled from Australian bowers,
  And singleness her lot,
She trills her song with tutored powers,
  Or mocks each casual note.   20

No more of pity for regrets
With which she may have striven!
Now but in wantonness she frets,
Or spite, if cause be given;

Arch, volatile, a sportive bird   25
By social glee inspired;
Ambitious to be seen or heard,
And pleased to be admired!

II

THIS moss-lined shed, green, soft, and dry,
Harbours a self-contented Wren,   30
Not shunning man's abode, though shy,
Almost as thought itself, of human ken.

Strange places, coverts unendeared,
She never tried; the very nest
In which this Child of Spring was reared
Is warmed thro' winter by her feathery
          breast.   36

To the bleak winds she sometimes gives
A slender unexpected strain;
Proof that the hermitess still lives,
Though she appear not, and be sought in
          vain.   40

Say, Dora! tell me, by yon placid moon,
If called to choose between the favoured
          pair,
Which would you be,—the bird of the
          saloon,
By lady-fingers tended with nice care,
Caressed, applauded, upon dainties fed,
Or Nature's DARKLING of this mossy
          shed?   46

XXII

THE DANISH BOY

A FRAGMENT

[Composed 1799.—Published 1800.]

I

BETWEEN two sister moorland rills
There is a spot that seems to lie
Sacred to flowerets of the hills,
And sacred to the sky.
And in this smooth and open dell   5
There is a tempest-stricken tree;
A corner-stone by lightning cut,
The last stone of a lonely hut;
And in this dell you see
A thing no storm can e'er destroy,   10
The shadow of a Danish Boy.

II

In clouds above, the lark is heard,
But drops not here to earth for rest;
Within this lonesome nook the bird
Did never build her nest.   15
No beast, no bird, hath here his home;

Bees, wafted on the breezy air,
Pass high above those fragrant bells
To other flowers:—to other dells
Their burdens do they bear;   20
The Danish Boy walks here alone:
The lovely dell is all his own.

III

A Spirit of noon-day is he;
Yet seems a form of flesh and blood;
Nor piping shepherd shall he be,   25
Nor herd-boy of the wood.
A regal vest of fur he wears,
In colour like a raven's wing;
It fears not rain, nor wind, nor dew;
But in the storm 'tis fresh and blue   30
As budding pines in spring;
His helmet has a vernal grace,
Fresh as the bloom upon his face.

IV

A harp is from his shoulder slung;
Resting the harp upon his knee,   35
To words of a forgotten tongue
He suits its melody.
Of flocks upon the neighbouring hill
He is the darling and the joy;
And often, when no cause appears,   40
The mountain-ponies prick their ears,
—They hear the Danish Boy,
While in the dell he sings alone
Beside the tree and corner-stone.

V

There sits he; in his face you spy   45
No trace of a ferocious air,
Nor ever was a cloudless sky
So steady or so fair.
The lovely Danish Boy is blest
And happy in his flowery cove: 50
From bloody deeds his thoughts are far;
And yet he warbles songs of war,
That seem like songs of love,
For calm and gentle is his mien;
Like a dead Boy he is serene.   55

XXIII
SONG

FOR THE WANDERING JEW

[Composed 1800.—Published 1800.]

THOUGH the torrents from their fountains
Roar down many a craggy steep,
Yet they find among the mountains
Resting-places calm and deep.

Clouds that love through air to hasten,
Ere the storm its fury stills,   6
Helmet-like themselves will fasten
On the heads of towering hills.

What if through the frozen centre
Of the Alps the Chamois bound,   10
Yet he has a home to enter
In some nook of chosen ground:

131

And the Sea-horse, though the ocean
Yield him no domestic cave,
Slumbers without sense of motion,   15
Couched upon the rocking wave.

If on windy days the Raven
Gambol like a dancing skiff,
Not the less she loves her haven
In the bosom of the cliff.   20

The fleet Ostrich, till day closes,
Vagrant over desert sands,
Brooding on her eggs reposes
When chill night that care demands.

Day and night my toils redouble,   25
Never nearer to the goal;
Night and day, I feel the trouble
Of the Wanderer in my soul.

XXIV

STRAY PLEASURES

[Composed 1806.—Published 1807.]

'——*Pleasure is spread through the earth
In stray gifts to be claimed by whoever shall find.*'

By their floating mill,
    That lies dead and still,
Behold yon Prisoners three,
The Miller with two Dames, on the breast
    of the Thames!
The platform is small, but gives room for
    them all;   5
And they're dancing merrily.

From the shore come the notes
    To their mill where it floats,
To their house and their mill tethered
    fast:
To the small wooden isle where, their
    work to beguile,   10
They from morning to even take whatever
    is given;—
And many a blithe day they have past.

In sight of the spires,
    All alive with the fires
Of the sun going down to his rest,   15
In the broad open eye of the solitary sky,
They dance,—there are three, as jocund
    as free,
While they dance on the calm river's
    breast.

Man and Maidens wheel,
    They themselves make the reel,
And their music's a prey which they
    seize;   21
It plays not for them,—what matter? 'tis
    theirs;
And if they had care, it has scattered
    their cares
While they dance, crying, 'Long as ye
    please!'

They dance not for me,   25
    Yet mine is their glee!
Thus pleasure is spread through the earth
In stray gifts to be claimed by whoever
    shall find;
Thus a rich loving-kindness, redundantly
    kind,
Moves all nature to gladness and mirth.

The showers of the spring   31
    Rouse the birds, and they sing;
If the wind do but stir for his proper
    delight,
Each leaf, that and this, his neighbour
    will kiss;
Each wave, one and t'other, speeds after
    his brother;   35
They are happy, for that is their right!

XXV

THE PILGRIM'S DREAM

OR, THE STAR AND THE GLOW-WORM

[Composed 1818.—Published 1820.]

A PILGRIM, when the summer day
Had closed upon his weary way,
A lodging begged beneath a castle's roof;
But him the haughty Warder spurned;
And from the gate the Pilgrim turned,   5
To seek such covert as the field
Or heath-besprinkled copse might yield,
Or lofty wood, shower-proof.

He paced along; and pensively,
Halting beneath a shady tree,   10
Whose moss-grown root might serve for
    couch or seat,
Fixed on a Star his upward eye;
Then from the tenant of the sky
He turned, and watched with kindred
    look
A Glow-worm, in a dusky nook,   15
Apparent at his feet.

The murmur of a neighbouring stream
Induced a soft and slumbrous dream,
A pregnant dream, within whose shadowy
    bounds
He recognised the earth-born Star,   20
And *That* which glittered from afar;
And (strange to witness!) from the frame
Of the ethereal Orb there came
Intelligible sounds.

Much did it taunt the humble Light   25
That now, when day was fled, and night
Hushed the dark earth, fast closing weary
    eyes,
A very reptile could presume
To show her taper in the gloom,
As if in rivalship with One   30
Who sat a ruler on his throne
Erected in the skies.

'Exalted Star!' the Worm replied,
'Abate this unbecoming pride,
Or with a less uneasy lustre shine;   25
Thou shrink'st as momently thy rays
Are mastered by the breathing haze;
While neither mist, nor thickest cloud
That shapes in heaven its murky shroud,
Hath power to injure mine.   40

'But not for this do I aspire
To match the spark of local fire,
That at my will burns on the dewy lawn,
With thy acknowledged glories;—No!
Yet, thus upbraided, I may show   45
What favours do attend me here,
Till, like thyself, I disappear
Before the purple dawn.'

When this in modest guise was said,
Across the welkin seemed to spread   50
A boding sound—for aught but sleep
          unfit!
Hills quaked, the rivers backward ran;
That Star, so proud of late, looked wan;
And reeled with visionary stir
In the blue depth, like Lucifer   55
Cast headlong to the pit!

Fire raged: and, when the spangled floor
Of ancient ether was no more,
New heavens succeeded, by the dream
          brought forth:
And all the happy Souls that rode   60
Transfigured through that fresh abode
Had heretofore, in humble trust,
Shone meekly 'mid their native dust,
The Glow-worms of the earth!

This knowledge, from an Angel's voice
Proceeding, made the heart rejoice   66
Of Him who slept upon the open lea:
Waking at morn he murmured not;
And, till life's journey closed, the spot
Was to the Pilgrim's soul endeared,   70
Where by that dream he had been cheered
Beneath the shady tree.

XXVI

THE POET AND THE CAGED TURTLEDOVE

[Composed 1830.—Published 1835.]

As often as I murmur here
My half-formed melodies,
Straight from her osier mansion near
The Turtledove replies:
Though silent as a leaf before,   5
The captive promptly coos;
Is it to teach her own soft lore,
Or second my weak Muse?

I rather think the gentle Dove
Is murmuring a reproof,   10
Displeased that I from lays of love
Have dared to keep aloof;

That I, a Bard of hill and dale,
Have carolled, fancy free,
As if nor dove nor nightingale   15
Had heart or voice for me.

If such thy meaning, O forbear,
Sweet Bird! to do me wrong;
Love, blessed Love, is everywhere
The spirit of my song: 20
'Mid grove, and by the calm fireside,
Love animates my lyre—
That coo again!—'tis not to chide,
I feel, but to inspire.

XXVII

A WREN'S NEST

[Composed 1833.—Published 1835.]

AMONG the dwellings framed by birds
In field or forest with nice care,
Is none that with the little Wren's
In snugness may compare.

No door the tenement requires,   5
And seldom needs a laboured roof;
Yet is it to the fiercest sun
Impervious, and storm-proof.

So warm, so beautiful withal,
In perfect fitness for its aim,   10
That to the Kind by special grace
Their instinct surely came.

And when for their abodes they seek
An opportune recess,
The hermit has no finer eye   15
For shadowy quietness.

These find, 'mid ivied abbey-walls,
A canopy in some still nook;
Others are pent-housed by a brae
That overhangs a brook.   20

There to the brooding bird her mate
Warbles by fits his low clear song;
And by the busy streamlet both
Are sung to all day long.

Or in sequestered lanes they build,   25
Where, till the flitting bird's return,
Her eggs within the nest repose,
Like relics in an urn.

But still, where general choice is good,
There is a better and a best;   30
And, among fairest objects, some
Are fairer than the rest;

This, one of those small builders proved
In a green covert, where, from out
The forehead of a pollard oak,   35
The leafy antlers sprout;

For She who planned the mossy lodge,
Mistrusting her evasive skill,
Had to a Primrose looked for aid
Her wishes to fulfil.   40

133

High on the trunk's projecting brow,
And fixed an infant's span above
The budding flowers, peeped forth the
nest
The prettiest of the grove!

The treasure proudly did I show   45
To some whose minds without disdain
Can turn to little things; but once
Looked up for it in vain:

'Tis gone—a ruthless spoiler's prey,   49
Who heeds not beauty, love, or song,
'Tis gone! (so seemed it) and we grieved
Indignant at the wrong.

Just three days after, passing by
In clearer light the moss-built cell
I saw, espied its shaded mouth;   55
And felt that all was well.

The Primrose for a veil had spread
The largest of her upright leaves;
And thus, for purposes benign,
A simple flower deceives.   60

Concealed from friends who might dis-
turb
Thy quiet with no ill intent,
Secure from evil eyes and hands
On barbarous plunder bent,   64

Rest, Mother-bird! and when thy young
Take flight, and thou art free to roam,
When withered is the guardian Flower,
And empty thy late home,

Think how ye prospered, thou and thine,
Amid the unviolated grove   70
Housed near the growing Primrose-tuft
In foresight, or in love.

XXVIII

LOVE LIES BLEEDING

[Composed 1842 (?).—Published 1842.]

You call it, 'Love lies bleeding,'—so you
may,
Though the red Flower, not prostrate,
only droops,
As we have seen it here from day to day,
From month to month, life passing not
away:
A flower how rich in sadness! Even thus
stoops,   5
(Sentient by Grecian sculpture's marvel-
lous power),
Thus leans, with hanging brow and body
bent
Earthward in uncomplaining languish-
ment,
The dying Gladiator. So, sad Flower!

('Tis Fancy guides me willing to be led,
Though by a slender thread,)   11
So drooped Adonis, bathed in sanguine
dew
Of his death-wound, when he from inno-
cent air
The gentlest breath of resignation drew;
While Venus in a passion of despair   15
Rent, weeping over him, her golden hair
Spangled with drops of that celestial
shower.
She suffered, as Immortals sometimes do;
But pangs more lasting far *that* Lover
knew
Who first, weighed down by scorn, in
some lone bower   20
Did press this semblance of unpitied
smart
Into the service of his constant heart,
His own dejection, downcast Flower!
could share
With thine, and gave the mournful name
which thou wilt ever bear.

XXIX

[Composed 1842 (?).—Published 1842.]

NEVER enlivened with the liveliest ray
That fosters growth or checks or cheers
decay,
Nor by the heaviest rain-drops more
deprest,
This Flower, that first appeared as sum-
mer's guest,
Preserves her beauty 'mid autumnal
leaves,   5
And to her mournful habits fondly
cleaves.
When files of stateliest plants have ceased
to bloom,
One after one submitting to their doom,
When her coevals each and all are fled,
What keeps her thus reclined upon her
lonesome bed?   10

The old mythologists, more impressed
than we
Of this late day by character in tree
Or herb that claimed peculiar sympathy,
Or by the silent lapse of fountain clear,
Or with the language of the viewless air
By bird or beast made vocal, sought a
cause   16
To solve the mystery, not in Nature's laws
But in Man's fortunes. Hence a thousand
tales
Sung to the plaintive lyre in Grecian
vales.
Nor doubt that something of their spirit
swayed   20
The fancy-stricken Youth or heart-sick
Maid,

Who, while each stood companionless
   and eyed
This undeparting Flower in crimson dyed,
Thought of a wound which death is slow
   to cure,   24
A fate that has endured and will endure,
And, patience coveting yet passion feed-
   ing,
Called the dejected Lingerer *Love lies
   Bleeding.*

XXX
RURAL ILLUSIONS

[Composed 1832.—Published 1835.]

SYLPH was it? or a Bird more bright
   Than those of fabulous stock?
A second darted by;—and lo!
   Another of the flock,
Through sunshine flitting from the bough
   To nestle in the rock.   6
Transient deception! a gay freak
   Of April's mimicries!
Those brilliant strangers, hailed with joy
   Among the budding trees,   10
Proved last year's leaves, pushed from the
   spray
   To frolic on the breeze.

Maternal Flora! show thy face,
   And let thy hand be seen,
Thy hand here sprinkling tiny flowers,
   That, as they touch the green, 16
Take root (so seems it) and look up
   In honour of their Queen.
Yet, sooth, those little starry specks,
   That not in vain aspired   20
To be confounded with live growths,
Most dainty, most admired,
Were only blossoms dropped from twigs
   Of their own offspring tired.

Not such the World's illusive shows; 25
   Her wingless flutterings,
Her blossoms which, though shed, out-
   brave
   The floweret as it springs,
For the undeceived, smile as they may,
   Are melancholy things: 30
But gentle Nature plays her part
   With ever-varying wiles,
And transient feignings with plain truth
   So well she reconciles,
That those fond Idlers most are pleased
   Whom oftenest she beguiles.   36

XXXI
THE KITTEN AND FALLING LEAVES

[Composed 1804.—Published 1807.]

THAT way look, my Infant, lo!
What a pretty baby-show!

See the Kitten on the wall,
Sporting with the leaves that fall,
Withered leaves—one—two—and three—
From the lofty elder-tree!   6
Through the calm and frosty air
Of this morning bright and fair,
Eddying round and round they sink
Softly, slowly: one might think, 10
From the motions that are made,
Every little leaf conveyed
Sylph or Faery hither tending,—
To this lower world descending,
Each invisible and mute,   15
In his wavering parachute.
——But the Kitten, how she starts,
Crouches, stretches, paws, and darts!
First at one, and then its fellow,
Just as light and just as yellow; 20
There are many now—now one—
Now they stop and there are none:
What intenseness of desire
In her upward eye of fire!
With a tiger-leap half-way   25
Now she meets the coming prey,
Lets it go as fast, and then
Has it in her power again:
Now she works with three or four,
Like an Indian conjurer;   30
Quick as he in feats of art,
Far beyond in joy of heart.
Were her antics played in the eye
Of a thousand standers-by,
Clapping hands with shout and stare, 35
What would little Tabby care
For the plaudits of the crowd?
Over happy to be proud,
Over wealthy in the treasure
Of her own exceeding pleasure! 40

'Tis a pretty baby-treat;
Nor, I deem, for me unmeet;
Here, for neither Babe nor me,
Other playmate can I see.
Of the countless living things, 45
That with stir of feet and wings
(In the sun or under shade,
Upon bough or grassy blade)
And with busy revellings,
Chirp and song, and murmurings, 50
Made this orchard's narrow space,
And this vale, so blithe a place;
Multitudes are swept away
Never more to breathe the day:
Some are sleeping; some in bands 55
Travelled into distant lands;
Others slunk to moor and wood,
Far from human neighbourhood;
And among the Kinds that keep
With us closer fellowship, 60
With us openly abide,
All have laid their mirth aside.

Where is he that giddy Sprite,
Blue-cap, with his colours bright,

135

Who was blest as bird could be,
Feeding in the apple-tree;
Made such wanton spoil and rout,
Turning blossoms inside out;
Hung—head pointing towards the 65
  ground—
Fluttered, perched, into a round 70
Bound himself, and then unbound;
Lithest, gaudiest Harlequin!
Prettiest Tumbler ever seen!
Light of heart and light of limb;
What is now become of Him? 75
Lambs, that through the mountains went
Frisking, bleating merriment,
When the year was in its prime,
They are sobered by this time.
If you look to vale or hill, 80
If you listen, all is still,
Save a little neighbouring rill,
That from out the rocky ground
Strikes a solitary sound.
Vainly glitter hill and plain, 85
And the air is calm in vain;
Vainly Morning spreads the lure
Of a sky serene and pure;
Creature none can she decoy
Into open sign of joy; 90
Is it that they have a fear
Of the dreary season near?
Or that other pleasures be
Sweeter even than gaiety?

Yet, whate'er enjoyments dwell 95
In the impenetrable cell
Of the silent heart which Nature
Furnishes to every creature;
Whatsoe'er we feel and know
Too sedate for outward show, 100
Such a light of gladness breaks,
Pretty Kitten! from thy freaks,—
Spreads with such a living grace
O'er my little Dora's face;
Yes, the sight so stirs and charms 105
Thee, Baby, laughing in my arms,
That almost I could repine
That your transports are not mine,
That I do not wholly fare
Even as ye do, thoughtless pair! 110
And I will have my careless season
Spite of melancholy reason,
Will walk through life in such a way
That, when time brings on decay,
Now and then I may possess 115
Hours of perfect gladsomeness.
—Pleased by any random toy;
By a kitten's busy joy,
Or an infant's laughing eye
Sharing in the ecstasy; 120
I would fare like that or this,
Find my wisdom in my bliss;
Keep the sprightly soul awake,
And have faculties to take,
Even from things by sorrow wrought,
Matter for a jocund thought, 126

Spite of care, and spite of grief, 65
To gambol with Life's falling Leaf.

XXXII

ADDRESS TO MY INFANT DAUGHTER, DORA

ON BEING REMINDED THAT SHE WAS A
MONTH OLD THAT DAY, SEPTEMBER 16

[Composed September 16, 1804.—Published 1815.]

————HAST thou then survived—
Mild Offspring of infirm humanity,
Meek Infant! among all forlornest things
The most forlorn—one life of that bright
  star,
The second glory of the Heavens?—Thou
  hast; 5
Already hast survived that great decay,
That transformation through the wide
  earth felt,
And by all nations. In that Being's sight
From whom the Race of human kind
  proceed, 9
A thousand years are but as yesterday;
And one day's narrow circuit is to Him
Not less capacious than a thousand years.
But what is time? What outward glory?
  Neither
A measure is of Thee, whose claims extend
Through 'heaven's eternal year.'—Yet
  hail to Thee, 15
Frail, feeble, Monthling!—by that name,
  methinks,
Thy scanty breathing-time is portioned
  out
Not idly.—Hadst thou been of Indian
  birth,
Couched on a casual bed of moss and
  leaves,
And rudely canopied by leafy boughs,
Or to the churlish elements exposed 21
On the blank plains,—the coldness of the
  night,
Or the night's darkness, or its cheerful
  face
Of beauty, by the changing moon adorned,
Would, with imperious admonition, then
Have scored thine age, and punctually
  timed 26
Thine infant history, on the minds of
  those
Who might have wandered with thee.—
  Mother's love,
Nor less than mother's love in other
  breasts,
Will, among us warm-clad and warmly
  housed, 30
Do for thee what the finger of the heavens
Doth all too often harshly execute
For thy unblest coevals, amid wilds
Where fancy hath small liberty to grace
The affections, to exalt them or refine;

And the maternal sympathy itself,⠀⠀36
Though strong, is, in the main, a joyless
⠀⠀tie
Of naked instinct, wound about the heart.
Happier, far happier is thy lot and ours!
Even now—to solemnise thy helpless
⠀⠀state,⠀⠀40
And to enliven in the mind's regard
Thy passive beauty—parallels have risen,
Resemblances, or contrasts, that connect,
Within the region of a father's thoughts,
Thee and thy mate and sister of the sky.
And first;—thy sinless progress, through
⠀⠀a world⠀⠀46
By sorrow darkened and by care dis-
⠀⠀turbed,
Apt likeness bears to hers, through
⠀⠀gathered clouds
Moving untouched in silver purity,
And cheering oft-times their reluctant
⠀⠀gloom.⠀⠀50
Fair are ye both, and both are free from
⠀⠀stain:
But thou, how leisurely thou fill'st thy
⠀⠀horn
With brightness! leaving her to post
⠀⠀along,
And range about, disquieted in change,
And still impatient of the shape she
⠀⠀wears.⠀⠀55
Once up, once down the hill, one journey,
⠀⠀Babe,
That will suffice thee; and it seems that
⠀⠀now
Thou hast foreknowledge that such task
⠀⠀is thine;
Thou travellest so contentedly, and
⠀⠀sleep'st⠀⠀59
In such a heedless peace. Alas! full soon
Hath this conception, grateful to behold,
Changed countenance, like an object
⠀⠀sullied o'er
By breathing mist; and thine appears
⠀⠀to be
A mournful labour, while to her is given
Hope, and a renovation without end.⠀⠀65
—That smile forbids the thought; for on
⠀⠀thy face
Smiles are beginning, like the beams of
⠀⠀dawn,
To shoot and circulate; smiles have there
⠀⠀been seen;
Tranquil assurances that Heaven sup-
⠀⠀ports
The feeble motions of thy life, and cheers
Thy loneliness: or shall those smiles be
⠀⠀called⠀⠀71
Feelers of love, put forth as if to explore
This untried world, and to prepare thy
⠀⠀way
Through a strait passage intricate and
⠀⠀dim?
Such are they; and the same are tokens,
⠀⠀signs,⠀⠀75

Which, when the appointed season hath
⠀⠀arrived,
Joy, as her holiest language, shall adopt;
And Reason's godlike Power be proud to
⠀⠀own.

XXXIII

THE WAGGONER

[Composed 1805.—Published 1819.]

'In Cairo's crowded streets
The Impatient Merchant, wondering, waits in vain,
And Mecca saddens at the long delay.'
⠀⠀⠀⠀⠀⠀⠀⠀⠀⠀⠀⠀⠀⠀⠀THOMSON.

TO CHARLES LAMB, ESQ.

MY DEAR FRIEND,

⠀⠀When I sent you, a few weeks ago, the Tale of
Peter Bell, you asked 'why THE WAGGONER was
not added?'—To say the truth,—from the higher
tone of imagination, and the deeper touches of
passion aimed at in the former, I apprehended
this little Piece could not accompany it without
disadvantage. In the year 1806, if I am not mistaken, THE WAGGONER was read to you in manuscript, and, as you have remembered it for so long
a time, I am the more encouraged to hope that,
since the localities on which the Poem partly depends did not prevent its being interesting to you,
it may prove acceptable to others. Being therefore in some measure the cause of its present
appearance, you must allow me the gratification
of inscribing it to you; in acknowledgment of the
pleasure I have derived from your Writings, and
of the high esteem with which

⠀⠀⠀⠀⠀⠀I am very truly yours,

⠀⠀⠀⠀⠀⠀WILLIAM WORDSWORTH.

RYDAL MOUNT, *May* 20, 1819.

CANTO FIRST

'TIS spent—this burning day of June!
Soft darkness o'er its latest gleams is
⠀⠀stealing;
The buzzing dor-hawk, round and round,
⠀⠀is wheeling,—
That solitary bird
Is all that can be heard⠀⠀5
In silence deeper far than that of deepest
⠀⠀noon!

⠀⠀Confiding Glow-worms, 'tis a night
Propitious to your earth-born light!
But where the scattered stars are seen
In hazy straits the clouds between,⠀⠀10
Each, in his station twinkling not,
Seems changed into a pallid spot.
The mountains against heaven's grave
⠀⠀weight
Rise up, and grow to wondrous height.
The air, as in a lion's den,⠀⠀15
Is close and hot;—and now and then
Comes a tired and sultry breeze
With a haunting and a panting,
Like the stifling of disease;
But the dews allay the heat,⠀⠀20
And the silence makes it sweet.

Hush, there is some one on the stir!
'Tis Benjamin the Waggoner;
Who long hath trod this toilsome way,
Companion of the night and day.   25
That far-off tinkling's drowsy cheer,
Mixed with a faint yet grating sound
In a moment lost and found,
The Wain announces—by whose side
Along the banks of Rydal Mere   30
He paces on, a trusty Guide,—
Listen! you can scarcely hear!
Hither he his course is bending;—
Now he leaves the lower ground,
And up the craggy hill ascending   35
Many a stop and stay he makes,
Many a breathing-fit he takes;
Steep the way and wearisome,
Yet all the while his whip is dumb!

The Horses have worked with right
        good-will,   40
And so have gained the top of the hill;
He was patient, they were strong,
And now they smoothly glide along,
Recovering breath, and pleased to win
The praises of mild Benjamin.   45
Heaven shield him from mishap and snare!
But why so early with this prayer?—
Is it for threatenings in the sky?
Or for some other danger nigh?
No; none is near him yet, though he   50
Be one of much infirmity;
For at the bottom of the brow,
Where once the DOVE and OLIVE-BOUGH
Offered a greeting of good ale
To all who entered Grasmere Vale;   55
And called on him who must depart
To leave it with a jovial heart;
There, where the DOVE and OLIVE-BOUGH
Once hung, a Poet harbours now,
A simple water-drinking Bard;   60
Why need our Hero then (though frail
His best resolves) be on his guard?
He marches by, secure and bold;
Yet, while he thinks on times of old,   64
It seems that all looks wondrous cold;
He shrugs his shoulders, shakes his head,
And, for the honest folk within,
It is a doubt with Benjamin
Whether they be alive or dead!

    Here is no danger,—none at all!   70
Beyond his wish he walks secure;
But pass a mile—and then for trial,—
Then for the pride of self-denial;
If he resist that tempting door,
Which with such friendly voice will call;
If he resist those casement panes,   76
And that bright gleam which thence will fall
Upon his Leaders' bells and manes,
Inviting him with cheerful lure:
For still, though all be dark elsewhere,   80
Some shining notice will be there,
Of open house and ready fare.

The place to Benjamin right well
Is known, and by as strong a spell
As used to be that sign of love   85
And hope—the OLIVE-BOUGH and DOVE;
He knows it to his cost, good Man!
Who does not know the famous SWAN?
Object uncouth! and yet our boast,
For it was painted by the Host;   90
His own conceit the figure planned,
'Twas coloured all by his own hand;
And that frail Child of thirsty clay,
Of whom I sing this rustic lay,
Could tell with self-dissatisfaction   95
Quaint stories of the bird's attraction![1]

    Well! that is past—and in despite
Of open door and shining light.
And now the conqueror essays
The long ascent of Dunmail-raise;   100
And with his team is gentle here
As when he clomb from Rydal Mere;
His whip they do not dread—his voice
They only hear it to rejoice.
To stand or go is at *their* pleasure;   105
Their efforts and their time they measure
By generous pride within the breast;
And while they strain, and while they
        rest,
He thus pursues his thoughts at leisure.

    Now am I fairly safe to-night—   110
And with proud cause my heart is light:
I trespassed lately worse than ever—
But Heaven has blest a good endeavour;
And, to my soul's content, I find
The evil One is left behind.   115
Yes, let my master fume and fret,
Here am I—with my horses yet!
My jolly team, he finds that ye
Will work for nobody but me!   119
Full proof of this the Country gained;
It knows how ye were vexed and strained,
And forced unworthy stripes to bear,
When trusted to another's care.
Here was it—on this rugged slope,
Which now ye climb with heart and hope,
I saw you, between rage and fear,   126
Plunge, and fling back a spiteful ear,
And ever more and more confused,
As ye were more and more abused:
As chance would have it, passing by   130
I saw you in that jeopardy:
A word from me was like a charm;
Ye pulled together with one mind;
And your huge burthen, safe from harm,
Moved like a vessel in the wind!   135
—Yes, without me, up hills so high
'Tis vain to strive for mastery.
Then grieve not, jolly team! though tough
The road we travel, steep, and rough;

[1] This rude piece of self-taught art (such is the progress of refinement) has been supplanted by a professional production.

Though Rydal-heights and Dunmail-
 raise,   140
And all their fellow banks and braes,
Full often make you stretch and strain,
And halt for breath and halt again,
Yet to their sturdiness 'tis owing
That side by side we still are going! 145

While Benjamin in earnest mood
His meditations thus pursued,
A storm, which had been smothered long,
Was growing inwardly more strong;
And, in its struggles to get free, 150
Was busily employed as he.
The thunder had begun to growl—
He heard not, too intent of soul;
The air was now without a breath— 154
He marked not that 'twas still as death.
But soon large rain-drops on his head
Fell with the weight of drops of lead;—
He starts—and takes, at the admonition,
A sage survey of his condition.
The road is black before his eyes, 160
Glimmering faintly where it lies;
Black is the sky—and every hill,
Up to the sky, is blacker still—
Sky, hill, and dale, one dismal room,
Hung round and overhung with gloom;
Save that above a single height 166
Is to be seen a lurid light,
Above Helm-crag[1]—a streak half dead,
A burning of portentous red;
And near that lurid light, full well 170
The ASTROLOGER, sage Sidrophel,
Where at his desk and book he sits,
Puzzling aloft his curious wits;
He whose domain is held in common
With no one but the ANCIENT WOMAN, 175
Cowering beside her rifted cell,
As if intent on magic spell;—
Dread pair that, spite of wind and
 weather,
Still sit upon Helm-crag together!

The ASTROLOGER was not unseen 180
By solitary Benjamin;
But total darkness came anon,
And he and every thing was gone:
And suddenly a ruffling breeze,
(That would have rocked the sounding
 trees,   185
Had aught of sylvan growth been there),
Swept through the Hollow long and bare·
The rain rushed down—the road was
 battered,
As with the force of billows shattered;
The horses are dismayed, nor know 190
Whether they should stand or go;
And Benjamin is groping near them,
Sees nothing, and can scarcely hear them.

[1] A mountain of Grasmere, the broken summit of
which presents two figures, full as distinctly shaped
as that of the famous Cobbler near Arroquhar in
Scotland.

He is astounded,—wonder not,—
With such a charge in such a spot; 195
Astounded in the mountain gap
With thunder-peals, clap after clap,
Close-treading on the silent flashes—
And somewhere, as he thinks, by crashes
Among the rocks; with weight of rain,
And sullen motions long and slow, 201
That to a dreary distance go—
Till, breaking in upon the dying strain,
A rending o'er his head begins the fray
 again.

Meanwhile, uncertain what to do, 205
And oftentimes compelled to halt,
The horses cautiously pursue
Their way, without mishap or fault;
And now have reached that pile of stones,
Heaped over brave King Dunmail's
 bones,   210
He who had once supreme command,
Last king of rocky Cumberland;
His bones, and those of all his Power,
Slain here in a disastrous hour!

When, passing through this narrow
 strait,   215
Stony, and dark, and desolate,
Benjamin can faintly hear
A voice that comes from some one near,
A female voice:—'Whoe'er you be,
Stop,' it exclaimed, 'and pity me!' 220
And less in pity than in wonder,
Amid the darkness and the thunder,
The Waggoner, with prompt command,
Summons his horses to a stand.

While, with increasing agitation, 225
The Woman urged her supplication,
In rueful words, with sobs between—
The voice of tears that fell unseen;
There came a flash—a startling glare,
And all Seat-Sandal was laid bare! 230
'Tis not a time for nice suggestion,
And Benjamin, without a question,
Taking her for some way-worn rover,
Said, 'Mount, and get you under cover!'

Another voice, in tone as hoarse 235
As a swoln brook with rugged course,
Cried out, 'Good brother, why so fast?
I've had a glimpse of you—*avast!*
Or, since it suits you to be civil,
Take her at once—for good and evil!'

'It is my Husband,' softly said 241
The Woman, as if half afraid:
By this time she was snug within,
Through help of honest Benjamin; 244
She and her Babe, which to her breast
With thankfulness the Mother pressed;
And now the same strong voice more near
Said cordially, 'My Friend, what cheer?

Rough doings these! as God's my judge,
The sky owes somebody a grudge!   250
We've had in half an hour or less
A twelvemonth's terror and distress!'

Then Benjamin entreats the Man
Would mount, too, quickly as he can:
The Sailor—Sailor now no more,   255
But such he had been heretofore—
To courteous Benjamin replied,
'Go you your way, and mind not me;
For I must have, whate'er betide,
My Ass and fifty things beside,—   260
Go, and I'll follow speedily!'

The Waggon moves—and with its load
Descends along the sloping road;
And the rough Sailor instantly
Turns to a little tent hard by: 265
For when, at closing-in of day,
The family had come that way,
Green pasture and the soft warm air
Tempted them to settle there.—
Green is the grass for beast to graze,   270
Around the stones of Dunmail-raise!

The Sailor gathers up his bed,
Takes down the canvas overhead;
And after farewell to the place,
A parting word—though not of grace,
Pursues, with Ass and all his store,   276
The way the Waggon went before.

CANTO SECOND

If Wytheburne's modest House of prayer,
As lowly as the lowliest dwelling,
Had, with its belfry's humble stock,
A little pair that hang in air,
Been mistress also of a clock,   5
(And one, too, not in crazy plight),
Twelve strokes that clock would have
   been telling
Under the brow of old Helvellyn—
Its bead-roll of midnight,
Then, when the Hero of my tale   10
Was passing by, and, down the vale
(The vale now silent, hushed, I ween,
As if a storm had never been)
Proceeding with a mind at ease;
While the old Familiar of the seas,   15
Intent to use his utmost haste,
Gained ground upon the Waggon fast,
And gives another lusty cheer;
For, spite of rumbling of the wheels,
A welcome greeting he can hear;—   20
It is a fiddle in its glee
Dinning from the Cherry Tree!

Thence the sound—the light is there—
As Benjamin is now aware,
Who, to his inward thoughts confined,   25
Had almost reached the festive door,
When, startled by the Sailor's roar,

He hears a sound and sees the light,
And in a moment calls to mind
That 'tis the village Merry-night![1]   30

Although before in no dejection,
At this insidious recollection,
His heart with sudden joy is filled,—
His ears are by the music thrilled,
His eyes take pleasure in the road   35
Glittering before him bright and broad;
And Benjamin is wet and cold,
And there are reasons manifold
That make the good, tow'rds which he's
   yearning,
Look fairly like a lawful earning.   40

Nor has thought time to come and go,
To vibrate between yes and no;
For, cries the Sailor, 'Glorious chance
That blew us hither!—let him dance,
Who can or will!—my honest soul,   45
Our treat shall be a friendly bowl!'
He draws him to the door—'Come in,
Come, come,' cries he to Benjamin!
And Benjamin—ah, woe is me!
Gave the word—the horses heard   50
And halted, though reluctantly.

'Blithe souls and lightsome hearts have
   we
Feasting at the Cherry Tree!'
This was the outside proclamation,
This was the inside salutation;   55
What bustling—jostling—high and low!
A universal overflow!
What tankards foaming from the tap!
What store of cakes in every lap!
What thumping—stumping—overhead!
The thunder had not been more busy:
With such a stir you would have said,   62
This little place may well be dizzy!
'Tis who can dance with greatest vigour—
'Tis what can be most prompt and eager;
As if it heard the fiddle's call,   66
The pewter clatters on the wall;
The very bacon shows its feeling,
Swinging from the smoky ceiling!

A steaming bowl, a blazing fire,   70
What greater good can heart desire?
'Twere worth a wise man's while to try
The utmost anger of the sky:
To seek for thoughts of a gloomy cast,
If such the bright amends at last.   75
Now should you say I judge amiss,
The Cherry Tree shows proof of this;
For soon, of all the happy there,
Our Travellers are the happiest pair;
All care with Benjamin is gone—   80
A Cæsar past the Rubicon!

[1] A term well known in the North of England, and applied to rural Festivals where young persons meet in the evening for the purpose of dancing.

He thinks not of his long, long, strife;—
The Sailor, Man by nature gay,
Hath no resolves to throw away;
And he hath now forgot his Wife, 85
Hath quite forgotten her—or may be
Thinks her the luckiest soul on earth,
Within that warm and peaceful berth,
 Under cover,
 Terror over, 90
Sleeping by her sleeping Baby.

With bowl that sped from hand to
 hand,
The gladdest of the gladsome band,
Amid their own delight and fun,
They hear—when every dance is done,
When every whirling bout is o'er— 96
The fiddle's *squeak*[1]—that call to bliss,
Ever followed by a kiss;
They envy not the happy lot,
But enjoy their own the more! 100

While thus our jocund Travellers fare,
Up springs the Sailor from his chair—
Limps (for I might have told before
That he was lame) across the floor—
Is gone—returns—and with a prize; 105
With what?—a Ship of lusty size;
A gallant stately Man-of-war,
Fixed on a smoothly-sliding car.
Surprise to all, but most surprise
To Benjamin, who rubs his eyes, 110
Not knowing that he had befriended
A Man so gloriously attended!

'This,' cries the Sailor, 'a Third-rate
 is—
Stand back, and you shall see her gratis!
This was the Flag-ship at the Nile, 115
The VANGUARD—you may smirk and
 smile,
But, pretty Maid, if you look near,
You'll find you've much in little here!
A nobler ship did never swim,
And you shall see her in full trim: 120
I'll set, my friends, to do you honour,
Set every inch of sail upon her.'
So said, so done; and masts, sails, yards,
He names them all; and interlards 124
His speech with uncouth terms of art,
Accomplished in the showman's part;
And then, as from a sudden check,
Cries out—''Tis there, the quarter-deck
On which brave Admiral Nelson stood—
A sight that would have roused your
 blood! 130
One eye he had, which, bright as ten,
Burned like a fire among his men;
Let this be land, and that be sea,
Here lay the French—and *thus* came we!'

Hushed was by this the fiddle's sound,
The dancers all were gathered round, 136

[1] At the close of each strathspey, or jig, a particular note from the fiddle summons the Rustic to the agreeable duty of saluting his partner.

And such the stillness of the house,
You might have heard a nibbling mouse;
While, borrowing helps where'er he may,
The Sailor through the story runs 140
Of ships to ships and guns to guns;
And does his utmost to display
The dismal conflict, and the might
And terror of that marvellous night!
'A bowl, a bowl of double measure,' 145
Cries Benjamin, 'a draught of length!
To Nelson, England's pride and treasure,
Her bulwark and her tower of strength!'
When Benjamin had seized the bowl,
The mastiff, from beneath the waggon, 151
Where he lay, watchful as a dragon,
Rattled his chain;—'twas all in vain,
For Benjamin, triumphant soul!
He heard the monitory growl;
Heard—and in opposition quaffed 155
A deep, determined, desperate draught!
Nor did the battered Tar forget,
Or flinch from what he deemed his debt:
Then, like a hero crowned with laurel,
Back to her place the ship he led; 160
Wheeled her back in full apparel;
And so, flag flying at mast head,
Re-yoked her to the Ass:—anon
Cries Benjamin, 'We must be gone.'
Thus, after two hours' hearty stay, 165
Again behold them on their way!

CANTO THIRD

RIGHT gladly had the horses stirred,
When they the wished-for greeting heard,
The whip's loud notice from the door,
That they were free to move once more.
You think, those doings must have bred
In them disheartening doubts and dread;
No, not a horse of all the eight, 7
Although it be a moonless night,
Fears either for himself or freight;
For this they know (and let it hide, 10
In part, the offences of their guide)
That Benjamin, with clouded brains,
Is worth the best with all their pains;
And, if they had a prayer to make,
The prayer would be that they may take
With him whatever comes in course, 16
The better fortune or the worse;
That no one else may have business near
 them,
And, drunk or sober, he may steer them.

So forth in dauntless mood they fare,
And with them goes the guardian pair. 21

Now, heroes, for the true commotion,
The triumph of your late devotion!
Can aught on earth impede delight,
Still mounting to a higher height; 25
And higher still—a greedy flight!
Can any low-born care pursue her,
Can any mortal clog come to her?

No notion have they—not a thought,
That is from joyless regions brought! 30
And, while they coast the silent lake,
Their inspiration I partake;
Share their empyreal spirits—yea,
With their enraptured vision see—
O fancy—what a jubilee! 35
What shifting pictures—clad in gleams
Of colour bright as feverish dreams!
Earth, spangled sky, and lake serene,
Involved and restless all—a scene
Pregnant with mutual exaltation, 40
Rich change, and multiplied creation!
This sight to me the Muse imparts;—
And then, what kindness in their hearts!
What tears of rapture, what vow-making,
Profound entreaties, and hand-shaking!
What solemn, vacant, interlacing, 46
As if they'd fall asleep embracing!
Then, in the turbulence of glee,
And in the excess of amity,
Says Benjamin, 'That Ass of thine, 50
He spoils thy sport, and hinders mine:
If he were tethered to the waggon,
He'd drag as well what he is dragging;
And we, as brother should with brother,
Might trudge it alongside each other!' 55

Forthwith, obedient to command,
The horses made a quiet stand;
And to the waggon's skirts was tied
The Creature, by the Mastiff's side,
The Mastiff wondering, and perplext 60
With dread of what will happen next;
And thinking it but sorry cheer
To have such company so near!

This new arrangement made, the Wain
Through the still night proceeds again;
No moon hath risen her light to lend; 66
But indistinctly may be kenned
The VANGUARD, following close behind,
Sails spread, as if to catch the wind!

'Thy wife and child are snug and
warm, 70
Thy ship will travel without harm;
I like,' said Benjamin, 'her shape and
stature:
And this of mine—this bulky creature
Of which I have the steering—this,
Seen fairly, is not much amiss! 75
We want your streamers, friend, you
know;
But, altogether as we go,
We make a kind of handsome show!
Among these hills, from first to last,
We've weathered many a furious blast;
Hard passage forcing on, with head 81
Against the storm, and canvas spread.
I hate a boaster; but to thee
Will say't, who know'st both land and
sea,
The unluckiest hulk that stems the brine
Is hardly worse beset than mine, 86

When cross-winds on her quarter beat;
And, fairly lifted from my feet,
I stagger onward—heaven knows how;
But not so pleasantly as now: 90
Poor pilot I, by snows confounded,
And many a foundrous pit surrounded!
Yet here we are, by night and day
Grinding through rough and smooth our
way; 94
Through foul and fair our task fulfilling;
And long shall be so yet—God willing!'

'Ay,' said the Tar, 'through fair and
foul—
But save us from yon screeching owl!'
That instant was begun a fray
Which called their thoughts another way:
The Mastiff, ill-conditioned carl! 101
What must he do but growl and snarl,
Still more and more dissatisfied
With the meek comrade at his side!
Till, not incensed though put to proof,
The Ass, uplifting a hind hoof, 106
Salutes the Mastiff on the head;
And so were better manners bred,
And all was calmed and quieted.

'Yon screech-owl,' says the Sailor,
turning 110
Back to his former cause of mourning,
'Yon owl!—pray God that all be well!
'Tis worse than any funeral bell;
As sure as I've the gift of sight,
We shall be meeting ghosts to-night!' 115
—Said Benjamin, 'This whip shall lay
A thousand, if they cross our way.
I know that Wanton's noisy station,
I know him and his occupation;
The jolly bird hath learned his cheer 120
Upon the banks of Windermere;
Where a tribe of them make merry,
Mocking the Man that keeps the ferry;
Hallooing from an open throat,
Like travellers shouting for a boat. 125
—The tricks he learned at Windermere
This vagrant owl is playing here—
That is the worst of his employment:
He's at the top of his enjoyment!'

This explanation stilled the alarm, 130
Cured the foreboder like a charm;
This, and the manner, and the voice,
Summoned the Sailor to rejoice;
His heart is up—he fears no evil
From life or death, from man or devil;
He wheels—and, making many stops, 136
Brandished his crutch against the moun-
tain tops;
And, while he talked of blows and scars,
Benjamin, among the stars,
Beheld a dancing—and a glancing; 140
Such retreating and advancing
As, I ween, was never seen
In bloodiest battle since the days of Mars!

CANTO FOURTH

THUS they, with freaks of proud delight,
Beguile the remnant of the night;
And many a snatch of jovial song
Regales them as they wind along;
While to the music, from on high,   5
The echoes make a glad reply.—
But the sage Muse the revel heeds
No farther than her story needs;
Nor will she servilely attend
The loitering journey to its end.   10
—Blithe spirits of her own impel
The Muse, who scents the morning air,
To take of this transported pair
A brief and unreproved farewell;
To quit the slow-paced waggon's side,   15
And wander down yon hawthorn dell,
With murmuring Greta for her guide.
—There doth she ken the awful form
Of Raven-crag—black as a storm—   19
Glimmering through the twilight pale;
And Ghimmer-crag,[1] his tall twin brother,
Each peering forth to meet the other:—
And, while she roves through St. John's
        Vale,
Along the smooth unpathwayed plain,
By sheep-track or through cottage lane,
Where no disturbance comes to intrude
Upon the pensive solitude,   27
Her unsuspecting eye, perchance,
With the rude shepherd's favoured glance,
Beholds the faeries in array,   30
Whose party-coloured garments gay
The silent company betray:
Red, green, and blue; a moment's sight!
For Skiddaw-top with rosy light
Is touched—and all the band take flight.
—Fly also, Muse! and from the dell   36
Mount to the ridge of Nathdale Fell;
Thence look thou forth o'er wood and
        lawn
Hoar with the frost-like dews of dawn;
Across yon meadowy bottom look,   40
Where close fogs hide their parent brook;
And see, beyond that hamlet small
The ruined towers of Threlkeld-hall,
Lurking in a double shade,
By trees and lingering twilight made!   45
There, at Blencathara's rugged feet,
Sir Lancelot gave a safe retreat
To noble Clifford; from annoy
Concealed the persecuted boy,
Well pleased in rustic garb to feed   50
His flock, and pipe on shepherd's reed
Among this multitude of hills,
Crags, woodlands, waterfalls, and rills;
Which soon the morning shall enfold,
From east to west, in ample vest   55
Of massy gloom and radiance bold.

The mists, that o'er the streamlet's bed
Hung low, begin to rise and spread;

[1] The crag of the ewe lamb.

Even while I speak, their skirts of grey
Are smitten by a silver ray;   60
And, lo!—up Castrigg's naked steep
(Where, smoothly urged, the vapours
        sweep
Along—and scatter and divide,
Like fleecy clouds self-multiplied)
The stately waggon is ascending,   65
With faithful Benjamin attending,
Apparent now beside his team—
Now lost amid a glittering steam:
And with him goes his Sailor-friend,
By this time near their journey's end; 70
And, after their high-minded riot,
Sickening into thoughtful quiet,
As if the morning's pleasant hour
Had for their joys a killing power.
And sooth for Benjamin a vein   75
Is opened of still deeper pain,
As if his heart by notes were stung
From out the lowly hedge-rows flung;
As if the warbler lost in light
Reproved his soarings of the night,   80
In strains of rapture pure and holy
Upbraided his distempered folly.

Drooping is he, his step is dull;
But the horses stretch and pull;
With increasing vigour climb,   85
Eager to repair lost time;
Whether, by their own desert,
Knowing what cause there is for shame,
They are labouring to avert
As much as may be of the blame,   90
Which, they foresee, must soon alight
Upon *his* head, whom, in despite
Of all his failings, they love best;
Whether for him they are distrest;
Or, by length of fasting roused,   95
Are impatient to be housed:
Up against the hill they strain
Tugging at the iron chain,
Tugging all with might and main,
Last and foremost, every horse   100
To the utmost of his force!
And the smoke and respiration,
Rising like an exhalation,
Blend with the mist—a moving shroud
To form, an undissolving cloud;   105
Which, with slant ray, the merry sun
Takes delight to play upon.
Never golden-haired Apollo,
Pleased some favourite chief to follow
Through accidents of peace or war,   110
In a perilous moment threw
Around the object of his care
Veil of such celestial hue;
Interposed so bright a screen—
Him and his enemies between!   115

Alas! what boots it?—who can hide,
When the malicious Fates are bent
On working out an ill intent?
Can destiny be turned aside?

No—sad progress of my story!   120
Benjamin, this outward glory
Cannot shield thee from thy Master,
Who from Keswick has pricked forth,
Sour and surly as the north;
And, in fear of some disaster,   125
Comes to give what help he may,
And to hear what thou canst say;
If, as needs he must forbode,
Thou hast been loitering on the road!
His fears, his doubts, may now take flight—
The wished-for object is in sight;   131
Yet, trust the Muse, it rather hath
Stirred him up to livelier wrath;
Which he stifles, moody man!
With all the patience that he can;   135
To the end that, at your meeting,
He may give thee decent greeting.

There he is—resolved to stop,
Till the waggon gains the top;
But stop he cannot—must advance: 140
Him Benjamin, with lucky glance,
Espies—and instantly is ready,
Self-collected, poised, and steady:
And, to be the better seen,
Issues from his radiant shroud,   145
From his close-attending cloud,
With careless air and open mien.
Erect his port, and firm his going;
So struts yon cock that now is crowing;
And the morning light in grace   150
Strikes upon his lifted face,
Hurrying the pallid hue away
That might his trespasses betray.
But what can all avail to clear him,
Or what need of explanation,   155
Parley or interrogation?
For the Master sees, alas!
That unhappy Figure near him,
Limping o'er the dewy grass,
Where the road it fringes, sweet,   160
Soft and cool to way-worn feet;
And, O indignity! an Ass,
By his noble Mastiff's side,
Tethered to the waggon's tail:
And the ship, in all her pride,   165
Following after in full sail!
Not to speak of babe and mother;
Who, contented with each other,
And snug as birds in leafy arbour,
Find, within, a blessed harbour!   170

With eager eyes the Master pries;
Looks in and out, and through and
    through;
Says nothing—till at last he spies
A wound upon the Mastiff's head,   174
A wound where plainly might be read
What feats an Ass's hoof can do!
But drop the rest:—this aggravation,
This complicated provocation,
A hoard of grievances unsealed;
All past forgiveness it repealed;   180

And thus, and through distempered blood
On both sides, Benjamin the good,
The patient, and the tender-hearted,
Was from his team and waggon parted;
When duty of that day was o'er,   185
Laid down his whip—and served no
    more.—
Nor could the waggon long survive,
Which Benjamin had ceased to drive:
It lingered on;—guide after guide
Ambitiously the office tried;   190
But each unmanageable hill
Called for *his* patience and *his* skill;—
And sure it is that through this night,
And what the morning brought to light,
Two losses had we to sustain,   195
We lost both WAGGONER and WAIN!

Accept, O Friend, for praise or blame,
The gift of this adventurous song;
A record which I dared to frame,   199
Though timid scruples checked me long;
They checked me—and I left the theme
Untouched;—in spite of many a gleam
Of fancy which thereon was shed,
Like pleasant sunbeams shifting still
Upon the side of a distant hill: 205
But Nature might not be gainsaid;
For what I have and what I miss
I sing of these;—it makes my bliss!
Nor is it I who play the part,
But a shy spirit in my heart,   210
That comes and goes—will sometimes leap
From hiding-places ten years deep;
Or haunts me with familiar face,
Returning, like a ghost unlaid,
Until the debt I owe be paid.   215
Forgive me then; for I had been
On friendly terms with this Machine:
In him, while he was wont to trace
Our roads, through many a long year's
    space,
A living almanack had we;   220
We had a speaking diary,
That in this uneventful place,
Gave to the days a mark and name
By which we knew them when they came.
—Yes, I, and all about me here,   225
Through all the changes of the year,
Had seen him through the mountains go,
In pomp of mist or pomp of snow,
Majestically huge and slow:
Or with a milder grace adorning   230
The landscape of a summer's morning;
While Grasmere smoothed her liquid
    plain
The moving image to detain;
And mighty Fairfield, with a chime
Of echoes, to his march kept time;   235
When little other business stirred,
And little other sound was heard;

144

In that delicious hour of balm,
Stillness, solitude, and calm,
While yet the valley is arrayed,   240
On this side with a sober shade;
On that is prodigally bright—
Crag, lawn, and wood—with rosy light.
—But most of all, thou lordly Wain!
I wish to have thee here again,   245
When windows flap and chimney roars,
And all is dismal out of doors;
And, sitting by my fire, I see
Eight sorry carts, no less a train!
Unworthy successors of thee,   250
Come straggling through the wind and rain:
And oft, as they pass slowly on,
Beneath my windows, one by one,

See, perched upon the naked height
The summit of a cumbrous freight,   255
A single traveller—and there
Another; then perhaps a pair—
The lame, the sickly, and the old;
Men, women, heartless with the cold;
And babes in wet and starveling plight;
Which once, be weather as it might,   261
Had still a nest within a nest,
Thy shelter—and their mother's breast!
Then most of all, then far the most,
Do I regret what we have lost;   265
Am grieved for that unhappy sin
Which robbed us of good Benjamin;—
And of his stately Charge, which none
Could keep alive when He was gone!

POEMS OF THE IMAGINATION

I

THERE WAS A BOY

[Composed November or December, 1798.
Published 1800.]

THERE was a Boy; ye knew him well, ye cliffs
And islands of Winander!—many a time,
At evening, when the earliest stars began
To move along the edges of the hills,
Rising or setting, would he stand alone,   5
Beneath the trees, or by the glimmering lake;
And there, with fingers interwoven, both hands
Pressed closely palm to palm and to his mouth
Uplifted, he, as through an instrument,
Blew mimic hootings to the silent owls,   10
That they might answer him.—And they would shout
Across the watery vale, and shout again,
Responsive to his call,—with quivering peals,
And long halloos, and screams, and echoes loud
Redoubled and redoubled; concourse wild   15
Of jocund din! And, when there came a pause
Of silence such as baffled his best skill:
Then sometimes, in that silence, while he hung
Listening, a gentle shock of mild surprise
Has carried far into his heart the voice   20
Of mountain-torrents; or the visible scene
Would enter unawares into his mind
With all its solemn imagery, its rocks,
Its woods, and that uncertain heaven received
Into the bosom of the steady lake.   25

This boy was taken from his mates, and died
In childhood, ere he was full twelve years old.
Pre-eminent in beauty is the vale
Where he was born and bred: the church-yard hangs
Upon a slope above the village-school;
And through that churchyard when my way has led   31
On summer-evenings, I believe that there
A long half-hour together I have stood
Mute—looking at the grave in which he lies!

II

TO THE CUCKOO

[Composed March 23–26, 1802.—Published 1807.]

O BLITHE New-comer! I have heard,
I hear thee and rejoice.
O Cuckoo! shall I call thee Bird,
Or but a wandering Voice?

While I am lying on the grass   5
Thy twofold shout I hear;
From hill to hill it seems to pass
At once far off, and near.

Though babbling only to the Vale,
Of sunshine and of flowers,   10
Thou bringest unto me a tale
Of visionary hours.

145

Thrice welcome, darling of the Spring!
Even yet thou art to me
No bird, but an invisible thing,   15
A voice, a mystery;

The same whom in my schoolboy days
I listened to; that Cry
Which made me look a thousand ways
In bush, and tree, and sky.   20

To seek thee did I often rove
Through woods and on the green;
And thou wert still a hope, a love;
Still longed for, never seen.

And I can listen to thee yet;   25
Can lie upon the plain
And listen, till I do beget
That golden time again.

O blessèd Bird! the earth we pace
Again appears to be   30
An unsubstantial, faery place;
That is fit home for Thee!

III

A NIGHT-PIECE

[Composed January 25, 1798.—Published 1815.]

——The sky is overcast
With a continuous cloud of texture close,
Heavy and wan, all whitened by the
     Moon,
Which through that veil is indistinctly
     seen,   4
A dull, contracted circle, yielding light
So feebly spread that not a shadow falls,
Chequering the ground—from rock,
     plant, tree, or tower.
At length a pleasant instantaneous gleam
Startles the pensive traveller while he
     treads
His lonesome path, with unobserving eye
Bent earthwards; he looks up—the clouds
     are split   11
Asunder,—and above his head he sees
The clear Moon, and the glory of the
     heavens.
There in a black-blue vault she sails along,
Followed by multitudes of stars, that,
     small   15
And sharp, and bright, along the dark
     abyss
Drive as she drives: how fast they wheel
     away,
Yet vanish not!—the wind is in the tree,
But they are silent;—still they roll along
Immeasurably distant; and the vault,
Built round by those white clouds, enor-
     mous clouds,   21
Still deepens its unfathomable depth.
At length the Vision closes; and the mind,
Not undisturbed by the delight it feels,
Which slowly settles into peaceful calm,
Is left to muse upon the solemn scene.   26

IV

AIREY-FORCE VALLEY

[Composed (?).—Published 1842]

——Not a breath of air
Ruffles the bosom of this leafy glen.
From the brook's margin, wide around,
     the trees
Are steadfast as the rocks; the brook
     itself,
Old as the hills that feed it from afar,   5
Doth rather deepen than disturb the calm
Where all things else are still and motion-
     less.
And yet, even now, a little breeze, per-
     chance
Escaped from boisterous winds that rage
     without,
Has entered, by the sturdy oaks unfelt,
But to its gentle touch how sensitive   11
Is the light ash! that, pendent from the
     brow
Of yon dim cave, in seeming silence makes
A soft eye-music of slow-waving boughs,
Powerful almost as vocal harmony   15
To stay the wanderer's steps and soothe
     his thoughts.

V

YEW-TREES

[Composed 1803.—Published 1815.]

There is a Yew-tree, pride of Lorton Vale,
Which to this day stands single, in the
     midst
Of its own darkness, as it stood of yore:
Not loth to furnish weapons for the bands
Of Umfraville or Percy ere they marched
To Scotland's heaths; or those that
     crossed the sea   6
And drew their sounding bows at Azin-
     cour,
Perhaps at earlier Crecy, or Poictiers.
Of vast circumference and gloom pro-
     found
This solitary Tree! a living thing   10
Produced too slowly ever to decay;
Of form and aspect too magnificent
To be destroyed. But worthier still of note
Are those fraternal Four of Borrowdale,
Joined in one solemn and capacious grove;
Huge trunks! and each particular trunk
     a growth   16
Of intertwisted fibres serpentine
Up-coiling, and inveterately convolved;
Nor uninformed with Phantasy, and looks
That threaten the profane; a pillared
     shade,   20
Upon whose grassless floor of red-brown
     hue,
By sheddings from the pining umbrage
     tinged

Perennially—beneath whose sable roof
Of boughs, as if for festal purpose decked
With unrejoicing berries—ghostly Shapes
May meet at noontide; Fear and trem-
    bling Hope,   26
Silence and Foresight; Death the Skeleton
And Time the Shadow;—there to cele-
    brate,
As in a natural temple scattered o'er
With altars undisturbed of mossy stone,
United worship; or in mute repose   31
To lie, and listen to the mountain flood
Murmuring from Glaramara's inmost
    caves.

VI

NUTTING

[Composed 1798–9.—Published 1800.]

———————————It seems a day
(I speak of one from many singled out)
One of those heavenly days that cannot
    die;
When, in the eagerness of boyish hope,
I left our cottage-threshold, sallying forth
With a huge wallet o'er my shoulders
    slung,   6
A nutting-crook in hand; and turned my
    steps
Tow'rd some far-distant wood, a Figure
    quaint,
Tricked out in proud disguise of cast-off
    weeds
Which for that service had been hus-
    banded,   10
By exhortation of my frugal Dame—
Motley accoutrement, of power to smile
At thorns, and brakes, and brambles,—
    and in truth
More ragged than need was! O'er path-
    less rocks,
Through beds of matted fern, and tangled
    thickets,   15
Forcing my way, I came to one dear nook
Unvisited, where not a broken bough
Drooped with its withered leaves, un-
    gracious sign
Of devastation; but the hazels rose
Tall and erect, with tempting clusters
    hung,   20
A virgin scene!—A little while I stood,
Breathing with such suppression of the
    heart
As joy delights in; and with wise restraint
Voluptuous, fearless of a rival, eyed
The banquet;—or beneath the trees I sate
Among the flowers, and with the flowers
    I played;   26
A temper known to those who, after long
And weary expectation, have been blest
With sudden happiness beyond all hope.
Perhaps it was a bower beneath whose
    leaves   30

The violets of five seasons re-appear
And fade, unseen by any human eye;
Where fairy water-breaks do murmur on
For ever; and I saw the sparkling foam,
And—with my cheek on one of those
    green stones   35
That, fleeced with moss, under the shady
    trees,
Lay round me, scattered like a flock of
    sheep—
I heard the murmur and the murmuring
    sound,
In that sweet mood when pleasure loves
    to pay
Tribute to ease; and, of its joy secure,   40
The heart luxuriates with indifferent
    things,
Wasting its kindliness on stocks and
    stones,
And on the vacant air. Then up I rose,
And dragged to earth both branch and
    bough, with crash   44
And merciless ravage: and the shady nook
Of hazels, and the green and mossy bower,
Deformed and sullied, patiently gave up
Their quiet being: and unless I now
Confound my present feelings with the
    past,
Ere from the mutilated bower I turned   50
Exulting, rich beyond the wealth of kings,
I felt a sense of pain when I beheld
The silent trees, and saw the intruding
    sky.—
Then, dearest Maiden, move along these
    shades   54
In gentleness of heart; with gentle hand
Touch—for there is a spirit in the woods.

VII

THE SIMPLON PASS

[Composed 1799? (certainly not later than 1803).
Published 1845.]

————————Brook and road
Were fellow-travellers in this gloomy
    Pass,
And with them did we journey several
    hours
At a slow step. The immeasurable height
Of woods decaying, never to be decayed,
The stationary blasts of waterfalls,   6
And in the narrow rent, at every turn,
Winds thwarting winds bewildered and
    forlorn,
The torrents shooting from the clear blue
    sky,
The rocks that muttered close upon our
    ears,   10
Black drizzling crags that spake by the
    wayside
As if a voice were in them, the sick sight
And giddy prospect of the raving stream,

The unfettered clouds and region of the
  heavens,
Tumult and peace, the darkness and the
  light—   15
Were all like workings of one mind, the
  features
Of the same face, blossoms upon one tree,
Characters of the great Apocalypse,
The types and symbols of Eternity,
Of first, and last, and midst, and without
  end.   20

VIII

[Composed 1804.—Published 1807.]

SHE was a Phantom of delight
When first she gleamed upon my sight;
A lovely Apparition, sent
To be a moment's ornament;
Her eyes as stars of Twilight fair;   5
Like Twilight's, too, her dusky hair;
But all things else about her drawn
From May-time and the cheerful Dawn;
A dancing Shape, an Image gay,
To haunt, to startle, and way-lay.   10

I saw her upon nearer view,
A Spirit, yet a Woman too!
Her household motions light and free,
And steps of virgin-liberty;
A countenance in which did meet   15
Sweet records, promises as sweet;
A Creature not too bright or good
For human nature's daily food;
For transient sorrows, simple wiles,
Praise, blame, love, kisses, tears, and
  smiles.   20

And now I see with eye serene
The very pulse of the machine;
A Being breathing thoughtful breath,
A Traveller between life and death;
The reason firm, the temperate will,   25
Endurance, foresight, strength, and skill;
A perfect Woman, nobly planned,
To warn, to comfort, and command;
And yet a Spirit still, and bright
With something of angelic light.   30

IX

[Composed 1806.—Published 1807.]

O NIGHTINGALE! thou surely art
A creature of a 'fiery heart':—
These notes of thine—they pierce and
  pierce;
Tumultuous harmony and fierce!
Thou sing'st as if the God of wine   5
Had helped thee to a Valentine;
A song in mockery and despite
Of shades, and dews, and silent night;
And steady bliss, and all the loves
Now sleeping in these peaceful groves.   10

I heard a Stock-dove sing or say
His homely tale, this very day;
His voice was buried among trees,
Yet to be come-at by the breeze:
He did not cease; but cooed—and cooed;
And somewhat pensively he wooed: 16
He sang of love, with quiet blending,
Slow to begin, and never ending;
Of serious faith, and inward glee;
That was the song—the song for me!   20

X

[Composed 1799.—Published 1800.]

THREE years she grew in sun and shower,
Then Nature said, 'A lovelier flower
On earth was never sown;
This Child I to myself will take;
She shall be mine, and I will make   5
A Lady of my own.

'Myself will to my darling be
Both law and impulse: and with me
The Girl, in rock and plain,
In earth and heaven, in glade and bower,
Shall feel an overseeing power   11
To kindle or restrain.

'She shall be sportive as the fawn
That wild with glee across the lawn
Or up the mountain springs;   15
And hers shall be the breathing balm,
And hers the silence and the calm
Of mute insensate things.

'The floating clouds their state shall lend
To her; for her the willow bend;   20
Nor shall she fail to see
Even in the motions of the Storm
Grace that shall mould the Maiden's
  form
By silent sympathy.

'The stars of midnight shall be dear   25
To her; and she shall lean her ear
In many a secret place
Where rivulets dance their wayward
  round,
And beauty born of murmuring sound
Shall pass into her face.   30

'And vital feelings of delight
Shall rear her form to stately height,
Her virgin bosom swell;
Such thoughts to Lucy I will give
While she and I together live   35
Here in this happy dell.'

Thus Nature spake—The work was
  done—
How soon my Lucy's race was run!
She died, and left to me
This heath, this calm, and quiet scene;   40
The memory of what has been,
And never more will be.

XI

[Composed 1799.—Published 1800.]

A SLUMBER did my spirit seal;
  I had no human fears:
She seemed a thing that could not feel
  The touch of earthly years.

No motion has she now, no force;   5
  She neither hears nor sees;
Rolled round in earth's diurnal course,
  With rocks, and stones, and trees.

XII

[Composed 1804.—Published 1807.]

I WANDERED lonely as a cloud
That floats on high o'er vales and hills,
When all at once I saw a crowd,
A host, of golden daffodils;
Beside the lake, beneath the trees,   5
Fluttering and dancing in the breeze.

Continuous as the stars that shine
And twinkle on the milky way,
They stretched in never-ending line
Along the margin of a bay: 10
Ten thousand saw I at a glance,
Tossing their heads in sprightly dance.

The waves beside them danced; but they
Out-did the sparkling waves in glee:
A poet could not but be gay,   15
In such a jocund company:
I gazed—and gazed—but little thought
What wealth the show to me had brought:

For oft, when on my couch I lie
In vacant or in pensive mood,   20
They flash upon that inward eye
Which is the bliss of solitude;
And then my heart with pleasure fills,
And dances with the daffodils.

XIII

THE REVERIE OF POOR SUSAN

[Composed 1797.—Published 1800.]

AT the corner of Wood Street, when day-
    light appears,
Hangs a Thrush that sings loud, it has
    sung for three years:
Poor Susan has passed by the spot, and
    has heard
In the silence of morning the song of the
    Bird.

'Tis a note of enchantment; what ails her?
    She sees   5
A mountain ascending, a vision of trees;

Bright volumes of vapour through Loth-
    bury glide,
And a river flows on through the vale of
    Cheapside.

Green pastures she views in the midst of
    the dale,
Down which she so often has tripped with
    her pail;   10
And a single small cottage, a nest like a
    dove's,
The one only dwelling on earth that she
    loves.

She looks, and her heart is in heaven:
    but they fade,
The mist and the river, the hill and the
    shade:
The stream will not flow, and the hill will
    not rise,   15
And the colours have all passed away
    from her eyes!

XIV

POWER OF MUSIC

[Composed 1806.—Published 1807.]

AN Orpheus! an Orpheus! yes, Faith
    may grow bold,
And take to herself all the wonders of
    old:—
Near the stately Pantheon you'll meet
    with the same
In the street that from Oxford hath bor-
    rowed its name.

His station is there; and he works on the
    crowd,   5
He sways them with harmony merry and
    loud;
He fills with his power all their hearts to
    the brim—
Was aught ever heard like his fiddle and
    him?

What an eager assembly! what an empire
    is this!
The weary have life, and the hungry have
    bliss;   10
The mourner is cheered, and the anxious
    have rest;
And the guilt-burthened soul is no longer
    opprest.

As the Moon brightens round her the
    clouds of the night,
So He, where he stands, is a centre of
    light;
It gleams on the face, there, of dusky-
    browed Jack,   15
And the pale-visaged Baker's, with basket
    on back.

That errand-bound 'Prentice was passing
  in haste—
What matter! he 's caught—and his time
  runs to waste;
The Newsman is stopped, though he stops
  on the fret;
And the half-breathless Lamplighter—
  he's in the net!   20

The Porter sits down on the weight which
  he bore;
The Lass with her barrow wheels hither
  her store;—
If a thief could be here he might pilfer at
  ease;
She sees the Musician, 'tis all that she
  sees!

He stands, backed by the wall;—he abates
  not his din;   25
His hat gives him vigour, with boons
  dropping in,
From the old and the young, from the
  poorest; and there!
The one-pennied Boy has his penny to
  spare.

O blest are the hearers, and proud be the
  hand
Of the pleasure it spreads through so
  thankful a band;   30
I am glad for him, blind as he is!—all the
  while
If they speak 'tis to praise, and they
  praise with a smile.

That tall Man, a giant in bulk and in
  height,
Not an inch of his body is free from
  delight;
Can he keep himself still, if he would?
  oh, not he!   35
The music stirs in him like wind through
  a tree.

Mark that Cripple who leans on his
  crutch; like a tower
That long has leaned forward, leans hour
  after hour!—
That Mother, whose spirit in fetters is
  bound,
While she dandles the Babe in her arms
  to the sound.   40

Now, coaches and chariots! roar on like a
  stream;
Here are twenty souls happy as souls in
  a dream:
They are deaf to your murmurs—they
  care not for you,
Nor what ye are flying, nor what ye
  pursue!

XV

STAR-GAZERS

[Composed 1806.—Published 1807.]

WHAT crowd is this? what have we here?
  we must not pass it by;
A Telescope upon its frame, and pointed
  to the sky:
Long is it as a barber's pole, or mast of
  little boat,
Some little pleasure-skiff, that doth on
  Thames's waters float.

The Showman chooses well his place, 'tis
  Leicester's busy Square;   5
And is as happy in his night, for the
  heavens are blue and fair;
Calm, though impatient, is the crowd;
  each stands ready with the fee,
And envies him that 's looking;—what an
  insight must it be!

Yet, Showman, where can lie the cause?
  Shall thy Implement have blame,
A boaster that, when he is tried, fails, and
  is put to shame?   10
Or is it good as others are, and be their
  eyes in fault?
Their eyes, or minds? or, finally, is yon
  resplendent vault?

Is nothing of that radiant pomp so good
  as we have here?
Or gives a thing but small delight that
  never can be dear?
The silver moon with all her vales, and
  hills of mightiest fame,   15
Doth she betray us when they're seen? or
  are they but a name?

Or is it rather that Conceit rapacious is
  and strong,
And bounty never yields so much but it
  seems to do her wrong?
Or is it that, when human Souls a journey
  long have had
And are returned into themselves, they
  cannot but be sad?   20

Or must we be constrained to think that
  these Spectators rude,
Poor in estate, of manners base, men of
  the multitude,
Have souls which never yet have risen,
  and therefore prostrate lie?
No, no, this cannot be;—men thirst for
  power and majesty!

Does, then, a deep and earnest thought
  the blissful mind employ   25
Of him who gazes, or has gazed? a grave
  and steady joy,
That doth reject all show of pride, admits
  no outward sign,
Because not of this noisy world, but silent
  and divine!

150

Whatever be the cause, 'tis sure that they
  who pry and pore
Seem to meet with little gain, seem less
  happy than before: 30
One after One they take their turn, nor
  have I one espied
That doth not slackly go away, as if dissatisfied.

XVI

WRITTEN IN MARCH

WHILE RESTING ON THE BRIDGE AT THE
FOOT OF BROTHER'S WATER

[Composed April 16, 1802.—Published 1807.]

THE Cock is crowing,
The stream is flowing,
The small birds twitter,
The lake doth glitter,
The green field sleeps in the sun;   5
The oldest and youngest
Are at work with the strongest;
The cattle are grazing,
Their heads never raising;
There are forty feeding like one!   10

Like an army defeated
The snow hath retreated,
And now doth fare ill
On the top of the bare hill;
The Ploughboy is whooping—anon—
  anon: 15
There's joy in the mountains;
There's life in the fountains;
Small clouds are sailing,
Blue sky prevailing;
The rain is over and gone!   20

XVII

[Composed (?).—Published 1842.]

LYRE! though such power do in thy magic
  live
As might from India's farthest plain
Recall the not unwilling Maid,
    Assist me to detain
    The lovely Fugitive: 5
Check with thy notes the impulse which,
  betrayed
By her sweet farewell looks, I longed to
  aid.
Here let me gaze enrapt upon that eye,
The impregnable and awe-inspiring fort
Of contemplation, the calm port   10
By reason fenced from winds that sigh
Among the restless sails of vanity.
But if no wish be hers that we should
  part,
A humbler bliss would satisfy my heart.
    Where all things are so fair,   15

Enough by her dear side to breathe the
  air
    Of this Elysian weather;
And on or in, or near, the brook, espy
  Shade upon the sunshine lying
    Faint and somewhat pensively;
  And downward Image gaily vying   21
    With its upright living tree
'Mid silver clouds, and openings of blue
  sky
As soft almost and deep as her cerulean
  eye.

Nor less the joy with many a glance   25
Cast up the Stream or down at her be-
  seeching,
To mark its eddying foam-balls prettily
  distrest
By ever-changing shape and want of rest;
  Or watch, with mutual teaching,
  The current as it plays   30
  In flashing leaps and stealthy
    creeps
  Adown a rocky maze;
Or note (translucent summer's happiest
  chance!)
In the slope-channel floored with pebbles
  bright,
Stones of all hues, gem emulous of gem,
So vivid that they take from keenest
  sight   36
The liquid veil that seeks not to hide
  them.

XVIII

BEGGARS

[Composed March 13, 14, 1802.—Published 1807.]

SHE had a tall man's height or more;
Her face from summer's noontide heat
No bonnet shaded, but she wore
A mantle, to her very feet
Descending with a graceful flow,   5
And on her head a cap as white as new-
  fallen snow.

Her skin was of Egyptian brown:
Haughty, as if her eye had seen
Its own light to a distance thrown,
She towered, fit person for a Queen   10
To lead those ancient Amazonian files;
Or ruling Bandit's wife among the Grecian
  isles.

Advancing, forth she stretched her hand
And begged an alms with doleful plea
That ceased not; on our English land   15
Such woes, I knew, could never be;
And yet a boon I gave her, for the creature
Was beautiful to see—a weed of glorious
  feature.

I left her, and pursued my way;
And soon before me did espy   20
A pair of little Boys at play,
Chasing a crimson butterfly;
The taller followed with his hat in hand,
Wreathed round with yellow flowers the
gayest of the land.

The other wore a rimless crown   25
With leaves of laurel stuck about;
And while both followed up and down,
Each whooping with a merry shout,
In their fraternal features I could trace
Unquestionable lines of that wild Sup-
pliant's face.   30

Yet *they*, so blithe of heart, seemed fit
For finest tasks of earth or air:
Wings let them have, and they might flit
Precursors to Aurora's car,
Scattering fresh flowers; though happier
far, I ween,   35
To hunt their fluttering game o'er rock
and level green.

They dart across my path—but lo,
Each ready with a plaintive whine!
Said I, 'not half an hour ago
Your Mother has had alms of mine.'   40
'That cannot be,' one answered—'she is
dead:'—
I looked reproof—they saw—but neither
hung his head.

'She has been dead, Sir, many a day.'—
'Hush, boys! you're telling me a lie;
It was your Mother, as I say!'   45
And, in the twinkling of an eye,
'Come! come!' cried one, and without
more ado
Off to some other play the joyous Vagrants
flew!

XIX

SEQUEL TO THE FOREGOING

COMPOSED MANY YEARS AFTER

[Composed 1817.—Published 1827.]

WHERE are they now, those wanton Boys?
For whose free range the dædal earth
Was filled with animated toys,
And implements of frolic mirth;
With tools for ready wit to guide;   5
And ornaments of seemlier pride,
More fresh, more bright, than princes
wear;
For what one moment flung aside,
Another could repair;
What good or evil have they seen   10
Since I their pastime witnessed here,
Their daring wiles, their sportive cheer?
I ask—but all is dark between!

They met me in a genial hour,
When universal nature breathed   15
As with the breath of one sweet flower.—
A time to overrule the power
Of discontent, and check the birth
Of thoughts with better thoughts at strife,
The most familiar bane of life   20
Since parting Innocence bequeathed
Mortality to Earth!
Soft clouds, the whitest of the year,
Sailed through the sky—the brooks ran
clear;
The lambs from rock to rock were bound-
ing;   25
With songs the budded groves resound-
ing;
And to my heart are still endeared
The thoughts with which it then was
cheered;
The faith which saw that gladsome pair
Walk through the fire with unsinged hair.
Or, if such faith must needs deceive—   31
Then, Spirits of beauty and of grace,
Associates in that eager chase;
Ye, who within the blameless mind
Your favourite seat of empire find—   35
Kind Spirits! may we not believe
That they, so happy and so fair
Through your sweet influence, and the
care
Of pitying Heaven, at least were free
From touch of *deadly* injury?   40
Destined, whate'er their earthly doom,
For mercy and immortal bloom?

XX

GIPSIES

[Composed 1807.—Published 1807.]

YET are they here the same unbroken knot
Of human Beings, in the self-same spot!
Men, women, children, yea the frame
Of the whole spectacle the same!
Only their fire seems bolder, yielding
light,   5
Now deep and red, the colouring of night;
That on their Gipsy-faces falls,
Their bed of straw and blanket-walls.
—Twelve hours, twelve bounteous hours
are gone, while I
Have been a traveller under open sky,   10
Much witnessing of change and cheer,
Yet as I left I find them here!
The weary Sun betook himself to rest;—
Then issued Vesper from the fulgent west,
Outshining like a visible God   15
The glorious path in which he trod.
And now, ascending, after one dark hour
And one night's diminution of her power,
Behold the mighty Moon! this way
She looks as if at them—but they   20

Regard not her:—oh, better wrong and
    strife
(By nature transient) than this torpid life;
    Life which the very stars reprove
    As on their silent tasks they move!
Yet, witness all that stirs in heaven or
    earth!   25
In scorn I speak not;—they are what their
    birth
    And breeding suffer them to be;
    Wild outcasts of society!

XXI

RUTH

[Composed 1799.—Published 1800.]

WHEN Ruth was left half desolate,
Her Father took another Mate;
And Ruth, not seven years old,
A slighted child, at her own will
Went wandering over dale and hill,   5
In thoughtless freedom, bold.

And she had made a pipe of straw,
And music from that pipe could draw
Like sounds of winds and floods;
Had built a bower upon the green,   10
As if she from her birth had been
An infant of the woods.

Beneath her father's roof, alone
She seemed to live; her thoughts her own;
Herself her own delight;   15
Pleased with herself, nor sad, nor gay;
And, passing thus the live-long day,
She grew to woman's height.

There came a Youth from Georgia's
    shore—
A military casque he wore,   20
With splendid feathers drest;
He brought them from the Cherokees;
The feathers nodded in the breeze,
And made a gallant crest.

From Indian blood you deem him sprung:
But no! he spake the English tongue,   26
And bore a soldier's name;
And, when America was free
From battle and from jeopardy,
He 'cross the ocean came.   30

With hues of genius on his cheek
In finest tones the Youth could speak:
—While he was yet a boy,
The moon, the glory of the sun,
And streams that murmur as they run,   35
Had been his dearest joy.

He was a lovely Youth! I guess
The panther in the wilderness
Was not so fair as he;
And, when he chose to sport and play,   40
No dolphin ever was so gay
Upon the tropic sea.

Among the Indians he had fought,
And with him many tales he brought
Of pleasure and of fear;   45
Such tales as told to any maid
By such a Youth, in the green shade,
Were perilous to hear.

He told of girls—a happy rout!
Who quit their fold with dance and shout,
Their pleasant Indian town,   51
To gather strawberries all day long;
Returning with a choral song
When daylight is gone down.

He spake of plants that hourly change   55
Their blossoms, through a boundless range
Of intermingling hues;
With budding, fading, faded flowers
They stand the wonder of the bowers
From morn to evening dews.   60

He told of the magnolia, spread
High as a cloud, high over head!
The cypress and her spire;
—Of flowers that with one scarlet gleam
Cover a hundred leagues, and seem   65
To set the hills on fire.

The Youth of green savannahs spake,
And many an endless, endless lake,
With all its fairy crowds
Of islands, that together lie   70
As quietly as spots of sky
Among the evening clouds.

'How pleasant,' then he said, 'it were
A fisher or a hunter there,
In sunshine or in shade   75
To wander with an easy mind;
And build a household fire, and find
A home in every glade!

'What days and what bright years! Ah
    me!
Our life were life indeed, with thee   80
So passed in quiet bliss,
And all the while,' said he, 'to know
That we were in a world of woe,
On such an earth as this!'

And then he sometimes interwove   85
Fond thoughts about a father's love:
'For there,' said he, 'are spun
Around the heart such tender ties,
That our own children to our eyes
Are dearer than the sun.   90

'Sweet Ruth! and could you go with me
My helpmate in the woods to be,
Our shed at night to rear;
Or run, my own adopted bride,
A sylvan huntress at my side,   95
And drive the flying deer!

'Beloved Ruth!'—No more he said.
The wakeful Ruth at midnight shed
A solitary tear:
She thought again—and did agree   100
With him to sail across the sea,
And drive the flying deer.

'And now, as fitting is and right,
We in the church our faith will plight,
A husband and a wife.'   105
Even so they did; and I may say
That to sweet Ruth that happy day
Was more than human life.

Through dream and vision did she sink,
Delighted all the while to think   110
That on those lonesome floods,
And green savannahs, she should share
His board with lawful joy, and bear
His name in the wild woods.

But, as you have before been told,   115
This Stripling, sportive, gay, and bold,
And, with his dancing crest,
So beautiful, through savage lands
Had roamed about, with vagrant bands
Of Indians in the West.   120

The wind, the tempest roaring high,
The tumult of a tropic sky,
Might well be dangerous food
For him, a Youth to whom was given
So much of earth—so much of heaven,   125
And such impetuous blood.

Whatever in those climes he found
Irregular in sight or sound
Did to his mind impart
A kindred impulse, seemed allied   130
To his own powers, and justified
The workings of his heart.

Nor less, to feed voluptuous thought,
The beauteous forms of nature wrought,
Fair trees and gorgeous flowers;   135
The breezes their own languor lent;
The stars had feelings, which they sent
Into those favoured bowers.

Yet, in his worst pursuits I ween
That sometimes there did intervene   140
Pure hopes of high intent:
For passions linked to forms so fair
And stately needs must have their share
Of noble sentiment.

But ill he lived, much evil saw,   145
With men to whom no better law
Nor better life was known;
Deliberately, and undeceived,
Those wild men's vices he received,
And gave them back his own.   150

His genius and his moral frame
Were thus impaired, and he became
The slave of low desires:
A Man who without self-control
Would seek what the degraded soul   155
Unworthily admires.

And yet he with no feigned delight
Had wooed the Maiden, day and night
Had loved her, night and morn:
What could he less than love a Maid   160
Whose heart with so much nature played?
So kind and so forlorn!

Sometimes, most earnestly, he said,
'O Ruth! I have been worse than dead;
False thoughts, thoughts bold and vain,
Encompassed me on every side   166
When I, in confidence and pride,
Had crossed the Atlantic main.

'Before me shone a glorious world—
Fresh as a banner bright, unfurled   170
To music suddenly:
I looked upon those hills and plains,
And seemed as if let loose from chains,
To live at liberty.

'No more of this; for now, by thee   175
Dear Ruth! more happily set free
With nobler zeal I burn;
My soul from darkness is released,
Like the whole sky when to the east
The morning doth return.'   180

Full soon that better mind was gone:
No hope, no wish remained, not one,—
They stirred him now no more;
New objects did new pleasure give,
And once again he wished to live   185
As lawless as before.

Meanwhile, as thus with him it fared,
They for the voyage were prepared,
And went to the sea-shore,
But, when they thither came, the Youth
Deserted his poor Bride, and Ruth   191
Could never find him more.

God help thee, Ruth!—Such pains she had,
That she in half a year was mad,
And in a prison housed;   195
And there, with many a doleful song
Made of wild words, her cup of wrong
She fearfully caroused.

Yet sometimes milder hours she knew,
Nor wanted sun, nor rain, nor dew,   200
Nor pastimes of the May;
—They all were with her in her cell;
And a clear brook with cheerful knell
Did o'er the pebbles play.

When Ruth three seasons thus had lain,
There came a respite to her pain;   206
She from her prison fled;
But of the Vagrant none took thought;
And where it liked her best she sought
Her shelter and her bread.   210

Among the fields she breathed again:
The master-current of her brain
Ran permanent and free;
And, coming to the Banks of Tone,
There did she rest; and dwell alone   215
Under the greenwood tree.

The engines of her pain, the tools
That shaped her sorrow, rocks and pools,
And airs that gently stir
The vernal leaves—she loved them still;
Nor ever taxed them with the ill   221
Which had been done to her.

A Barn her *winter* bed supplies;
But, till the warmth of summer skies
And summer days is gone,   225
(And all do in this tale agree)
She sleeps beneath the greenwood tree,
And other home hath none.

An innocent life, yet far astray!
And Ruth will, long before her day,   230
Be broken down and old:
Sore aches she needs must have! but less
Of mind than body's wretchedness,
From damp, and rain, and cold.

If she is prest by want of food,   235
She from her dwelling in the wood
Repairs to a road-side;
And there she begs at one steep place
Where up and down with easy pace
The horsemen-travellers ride.   240

That oaten pipe of hers is mute,
Or thrown away; but with a flute
Her loneliness she cheers:
This flute, made of a hemlock stalk,
At evening in his homeward walk   245
The Quantock woodman hears.

I, too, have passed her on the hills
Setting her little water-mills
By spouts and fountains wild—
Such small machinery as she turned   250
Ere she had wept, ere she had mourned,
A young and happy Child!

Farewell! and when thy days are told,
Ill-fated Ruth, in hallowed mould
Thy corpse shall buried be,   255
For thee a funeral bell shall ring,
And all the congregation sing
A Christian psalm for thee.

XXII

RESOLUTION AND
INDEPENDENCE

[Composed May 3–July 4, 1802.—Published 1807.]

I

THERE was a roaring in the wind all night;
The rain came heavily and fell in floods;
But now the sun is rising calm and bright;
The birds are singing in the distant woods;
Over his own sweet voice the Stock-dove
     broods;   5
The Jay makes answer as the Magpie
     chatters;
And all the air is filled with pleasant
     noise of waters.

II

All things that love the sun are out of
     doors;
The sky rejoices in the morning's birth;
The grass is bright with rain-drops;—on
     the moors   10
The hare is running races in her mirth;
And with her feet she from the plashy
     earth
Raises a mist; that, glittering in the sun,
Runs with her all the way, wherever she
     doth run.

III

I was a Traveller then upon the moor;   15
I saw the hare that raced about with joy;
I heard the woods and distant waters roar;
Or heard them not, as happy as a boy:
The pleasant season did my heart employ:
My old remembrances went from me
     wholly;   20
And all the ways of men, so vain and
     melancholy.

IV

But, as it sometimes chanceth, from the
     might
Of joy in minds that can no further go,
As high as we have mounted in delight
In our dejection do we sink as low;   25
To me that morning did it happen so;
And fears and fancies thick upon me came;
Dim sadness—and blind thoughts, I knew
     not, nor could name.   28

V

I heard the sky-lark warbling in the sky;
And I bethought me of the playful hare:
Even such a happy Child of earth am I;
Even as these blissful creatures do I fare;
Far from the world I walk, and from all
     care;
But there may come another day to me—
Solitude, pain of heart, distress, and
     poverty.   35

VI

My whole life I have lived in pleasant
     thought,
As if life's business were a summer mood;
As if all needful things would come un-
     sought
To genial faith, still rich in genial good;
But how can He expect that others should
Build for him, sow for him, and at his
     call   41
Love him, who for himself will take no
     heed at all?

VII

I thought of Chatterton, the marvellous
     Boy,
The sleepless Soul that perished in his
     pride;

POEMS OF THE IMAGINATION

Of Him who walked in glory and in joy
Following his plough, along the mountain-side:
By our own spirits are we deified: 46
We Poets in our youth begin in gladness;
But thereof come in the end despondency
   and madness.

VIII

Now, whether it were by peculiar grace, 50
A leading from above, a something given,
Yet it befell that, in this lonely place,
When I with these untoward thoughts
   had striven,
Beside a pool bare to the eye of heaven
I saw a Man before me unawares·   55
The oldest man he seemed that ever wore
   grey hairs.

IX

As a huge stone is sometimes seen to lie
Couched on the bald top of an eminence;
Wonder to all who do the same espy,
By what means it could thither come, and
   whence;   60
So that it seems a thing endued with
   sense:
Like a sea-beast crawled forth, that on a
   shelf
Of rock or sand reposeth, there to sun
   itself;

X

Such seemed this Man, not all alive nor
   dead,
Nor all asleep—in his extreme old age: 65
His body was bent double, feet and head
Coming together in life's pilgrimage;
As if some dire constraint of pain, or rage
Of sickness felt by him in times long past,
A more than human weight upon his
   frame had cast.   70

XI

Himself he propped, limbs, body, and
   pale face,
Upon a long grey staff of shaven wood:
And, still as I drew near with gentle pace,
Upon the margin of that moorish flood
Motionless as a cloud the old Man stood,
That heareth not the loud winds when
   they call;   76
And moveth all together, if it move at all.

XII

At length, himself unsettling, he the pond
Stirred with his staff, and fixedly did look
Upon the muddy water, which he conned,
As if he had been reading in a book: 81
And now a stranger's privilege I took;
And, drawing to his side, to him did say,
'This morning gives us promise of a
   glorious day.'

XIII

A gentle answer did the old Man make,
In courteous speech which forth he slowly
   drew: 86
And him with further words I thus be-
   spake,
'What occupation do you there pursue?
This is a lonesome place for one like you.'
Ere he replied, a flash of mild surprise   90
Broke from the sable orbs of his yet-vivid
   eyes.

XIV

His words came feebly, from a feeble
   chest,
But each in solemn order followed each,
With something of a lofty. utterance
   drest—
Choice word and measured phrase, above
   the reach   95
Of ordinary men; a stately speech;
Such as grave Livers do in Scotland use,
Religious men, who give to God and man
   their dues.

XV

He told, that to these waters he had come
To gather leeches, being old and poor: 100
Employment hazardous and wearisome!
And he had many hardships to endure:
From pond to pond he roamed, from moor
   to moor;
Housing, with God's good help, by choice
   or chance;
And in this way he gained an honest
   maintenance.   105

XVI

The old Man still stood talking by my
   side;
But now his voice to me was like a stream
Scarce heard; nor word from word could
   I divide;
And the whole body of the Man did seem
Like one whom I had met with in a
   dream;   110
Or like a man from some far region sent,
To give me human strength, by apt ad-
   monishment.

XVII

My former thoughts returned: the fear
   that kills;
And hope that is unwilling to be fed;
Cold, pain, and labour, and all fleshly
   ills;   115
And mighty Poets in their misery dead.
—Perplexed, and longing to be comforted,
My question eagerly did I renew,
'How is it that you live, and what is it
   you do?'

156

XVIII

He with a smile did then his words repeat;
And said that, gathering leeches, far and
    wide   121
He travelled; stirring thus about his feet
The waters of the pools where they abide.
'Once I could meet with them on every
    side;
But they have dwindled long by slow
    decay;   125
Yet still I persevere, and find them where
    I may.'

XIX

While he was talking thus, the lonely
    place,
The old Man's shape, and speech—all
    troubled me:
In my mind's eye I seemed to see him pace
About the weary moors continually,   130
Wandering about alone and silently.
While I these thoughts within myself
    pursued,
He, having made a pause, the same dis-
    course renewed.

XX

And soon with this he other matter
    blended,
Cheerfully uttered, with demeanour kind,
But stately in the main; and, when he
    ended,   136
I could have laughed myself to scorn to
    find
In that decrepit Man so firm a mind.
'God,' said I, 'be my help and stay
    secure;
I'll think of the Leech-gatherer on the
    lonely moor!'   140

XXIII

THE THORN

[Composed 1798.—Published 1798.]

I

'There is a Thorn—it looks so old,
In truth, you'd find it hard to say
How it could ever have been young,
It looks so old and grey.
Not higher than a two years' child   5
It stands erect, this aged Thorn;
No leaves it has, no prickly points;
It is a mass of knotted joints,
A wretched thing forlorn.
It stands erect, and like a stone   10
With lichens is it overgrown.

II

'Like rock or stone, it is o'ergrown,
With lichens to the very top,
And hung with heavy tufts of moss,
A melancholy crop: 15
Up from the earth these mosses creep,
And this poor Thorn they clasp it round
So close, you'd say that they are bent
With plain and manifest intent
To drag it to the ground;   20
And all have joined in one endeavour
To bury this poor Thorn for ever.

III

'High on a mountain's highest ridge,
Where oft the stormy winter gale
Cuts like a scythe, while through the
    clouds   25
It sweeps from vale to vale;
Not five yards from the mountain path,
This Thorn you on your left espy;
And to the left, three yards beyond,
You see a little muddy pond   30
Of water—never dry,
Though but of compass small, and bare
To thirsty suns and parching air.

IV

'And, close beside this aged Thorn,
There is a fresh and lovely sight,   35
A beauteous heap, a hill of moss,
Just half a foot in height.
All lovely colours there you see,
All colours that were ever seen;
And mossy network too is there,   40
As if by hand of lady fair
The work had woven been;
And cups, the darlings of the eye,
So deep is their vermilion dye.

V

'Ah me! what lovely tints are there   45
Of olive green and scarlet bright,
In spikes, in branches, and in stars,
Green, red, and pearly white!
This heap of earth o'ergrown with moss,
Which close beside the Thorn you see,   50
So fresh in all its beauteous dyes,
Is like an infant's grave in size,
As like as like can be:
But never, never any where,
An infant's grave was half so fair.   **55**

VI

'Now would you see this aged Thorn,
This pond, and beauteous hill of moss,
You must take care and choose your
    time
The mountain when to cross.
For oft there sits between the heap,   60
So like an infant's grave in size,
And that same pond of which I spoke,
A Woman in a scarlet cloak,
And to herself she cries,
"Oh misery! oh misery!   65
Oh woe is me! oh misery!"

POEMS OF THE IMAGINATION

VII

'At all times of the day and night
This wretched Woman thither goes;
And she is known to every star,
And every wind that blows;   70
And there, beside the Thorn, she sits
When the blue daylight's in the skies,
And when the whirlwind's on the hill,
Or frosty air is keen and still,
And to herself she cries,   75
"Oh misery! oh misery!
Oh woe is me! oh misery!"'

VIII

'Now wherefore, thus, by day and night,
In rain, in tempest, and in snow,
Thus to the dreary mountain-top   80
Does this poor Woman go?
And why sits she beside the Thorn
When the blue daylight's in the sky
Or when the whirlwind's on the hill,
Or frosty air is keen and still,   85
And wherefore does she cry?—
O wherefore? wherefore? tell me why
Does she repeat that doleful cry?'

IX

'I cannot tell; I wish I could;
For the true reason no one knows: 90
But would you gladly view the spot,
The spot to which she goes;
The hillock like an infant's grave,
The pond—and Thorn, so old and grey;
Pass by her door—'tis seldom shut—   95
And if you see her in her hut—
Then to the spot away!
I never heard of such as dare
Approach the spot when she is there.'

X

'But wherefore to the mountain-top   100
Can this unhappy Woman go,
Whatever star is in the skies,
Whatever wind may blow?'
'Full twenty years are past and gone
Since she (her name is Martha Ray)   105
Gave with a maiden's true good-will
Her company to Stephen Hill;
And she was blithe and gay,
While friends and kindred all approved
Of him whom tenderly she loved.   110

XI

'And they had fixed the wedding day,
The morning that must wed them both;
But Stephen to another Maid
Had sworn another oath;
And, with this other Maid, to church   115
Unthinking Stephen went—
Poor Martha! on that woeful day
A pang of pitiless dismay
Into her soul was sent;
A fire was kindled in her breast,   120
Which might not burn itself to rest.

XII

'They say, full six months after this,
While yet the summer leaves were green,
She to the mountain-top would go,
And there was often seen.   125
What could she seek?—or wish to hide?
Her state to any eye was plain;
She was with child, and she was mad;
Yet often was she sober sad
From her exceeding pain.   130
O guilty Father—would that death
Had saved him from that breach of faith!

XIII

'Sad case for such a brain to hold
Communion with a stirring child!
Sad case, as you may think, for one   135
Who had a brain so wild!
Last Christmas-eve we talked of this,
And grey-haired Wilfred of the glen
Held that the unborn infant wrought
About its mother's heart, and brought   141
Her senses back again:
And, when at last her time drew near,
Her looks were calm, her senses clear.

XIV

'More know I not, I wish I did,
And it should all be told to you;   145
For what became of this poor child
No mortal ever knew;
Nay—if a child to her was born
No earthly tongue could ever tell;
And if 'twas born alive or dead,   150
Far less could this with proof be said;
But some remember well
That Martha Ray about this time
Would up the mountain often climb.

XV

'And all that winter, when at night   155
The wind blew from the mountain-peak,
'Twas worth your while, though in the dark,
The churchyard path to seek:
For many a time and oft were heard
Cries coming from the mountain head:
Some plainly living voices were;   161
And others, I've heard many swear,
Were voices of the dead:
I cannot think, whate'er they say,
They had to do with Martha Ray.   165

XVI

'But that she goes to this old Thorn,
The Thorn which I described to you,
And there sits in a scarlet cloak,
I will be sworn is true.
For one day with my telescope,   170
To view the ocean wide and bright,
When to this country first I came,
Ere I had heard of Martha's name,
I climbed the mountain's height:—
A storm came on, and I could see   175
No object higher than my knee.

XVII

"'Twas mist and rain, and storm and rain:
No screen, no fence could I discover;
And then the wind! in sooth, it was
A wind full ten times over.   180
I looked around, I thought I saw
A jutting crag,—and off I ran,
Head-foremost, through the driving rain,
The shelter of the crag to gain;
And, as I am a man,   185
Instead of jutting crag I found
A Woman seated on the ground.

XVIII

'I did not speak—I saw her face;
Her face!—it was enough for me;
I turned about and heard her cry,   190
"Oh misery! oh misery!"
And there she sits, until the moon
Through half the clear blue sky will go;
And when the little breezes make
The waters of the pond to shake,   195
As all the country know,
She shudders, and you hear her cry,
"Oh misery! oh misery!"'

XIX

'But what's the Thorn? and what the pond?
And what the hill of moss to her?   200
And what the creeping breeze that comes
The little pond to stir?'
'I cannot tell; but some will say
She hanged her baby on the tree;
Some say she drowned it in the pond,   205
Which is a little step beyond:
But all and each agree,
The little Babe was buried there,
Beneath that hill of moss so fair.

XX

'I've heard, the moss is spotted red   210
With drops of that poor infant's blood;
But kill a new-born infant thus,
I do not think she could!
Some say if to the pond you go,
And fix on it a steady view,   215
The shadow of a babe you trace,
A baby and a baby's face,
And that it looks at you;
Whene'er you look on it, 'tis plain
The baby looks at you again.   220

XXI

'And some had sworn an oath that she
Should be to public justice brought;
And for the little infant's bones
With spades they would have sought.
But instantly the hill of moss   225
Before their eyes began to stir!
And, for full fifty yards around,
The grass—it shook upon the ground!
Yet all do still aver
The little Babe lies buried there,   230
Beneath that hill of moss so fair.

XXII

'I cannot tell how this may be,
But plain it is the Thorn is bound
With heavy tufts of moss that strive
To drag it to the ground;   235
And this I know, full many a time,
When she was on the mountain high,
By day, and in the silent night,
When all the stars shone clear and bright,
That I have heard her cry,   240
"Oh misery! oh misery!
Oh woe is me! oh misery!"'

XXIV

HART-LEAP WELL

[Composed January or February, 1800.—Published 1800.]

Hart-Leap Well is a small spring of water, about five miles from Richmond in Yorkshire, and near the side of the road that leads from Richmond to Askrigg. Its name is derived from a remarkable Chase, the memory of which is preserved by the monuments spoken of in the second Part of the following Poem, which monuments do now exist as I have there described them.

THE Knight had ridden down from Wensley Moor
With the slow motion of a summer's cloud,
And now, as he approached a vassal's door,
'Bring forth another horse!' he cried aloud.

'Another horse!'—That shout the vassal heard   5
And saddled his best Steed, a comely grey;
Sir Walter mounted him; he was the third
Which he had mounted on that glorious day.

Joy sparkled in the prancing courser's eyes;
The horse and horseman are a happy pair;   10
But, though Sir Walter like a falcon flies,
There is a doleful silence in the air.

A rout this morning left Sir Walter's Hall,
That as they galloped made the echoes roar;
But horse and man are vanished, one and all;   15
Such race, I think, was never seen before.

Sir Walter, restless as a veering wind,
Calls to the few tired dogs that yet remain:
Blanch, Swift, and Music, noblest of their kind,
Follow, and up the weary mountain strain.   20

159

The Knight hallooed, he cheered and chid
    them on
With suppliant gestures and upbraidings
    stern;
But breath and eyesight fail; and, one by
    one,
The dogs are stretched among the moun-
    tain fern.

Where is the throng, the tumult of the
    race?   25
The bugles that so joyfully were blown?
—This chase it looks not like an earthly
    chase;
Sir Walter and the Hart are left alone.

The poor Hart toils along the mountain-
    side;
I will not stop to tell how far he fled, 30
Nor will I mention by what death he died;
But now the Knight beholds him lying
    dead.

Dismounting, then, he leaned against a
    thorn;
He had no follower, dog, nor man, nor
    boy:
He neither cracked his whip, nor blew his
    horn,   35
But gazed upon the spoil with silent joy.

Close to the thorn on which Sir Walter
    leaned
Stood his dumb partner in this glorious
    feat;
Weak as a lamb the hour that it is yeaned;
And white with foam as if with cleaving
    sleet.   40

Upon his side the Hart was lying stretched:
His nostril touched a spring beneath a
    hill,
And with the last deep groan his breath
    had fetched
The waters of the spring were trembling
    still.

And now, too happy for repose or rest, 45
(Never had living man such joyful lot!)
Sir Walter walked all round, north, south,
    and west,
And gazed and gazed upon that darling
    spot.

And climbing up the hill—(it was at least
Four roods of sheer ascent) Sir Walter
    found   50
Three several hoof-marks which the hunt-
    ed Beast
Had left imprinted on the grassy ground.

Sir Walter wiped his face, and cried,
    'Till now
Such sight was never seen by human eyes:
Three leaps have borne him from this lofty
    brow   55
Down to the very fountain where he lies.

'I'll build a pleasure-house upon this spot,
And a small arbour, made for rural joy;
'Twill be the traveller's shed, the pilgrim's
    cot,
A place of love for damsels that are coy.

'A cunning artist will I have to frame 61
A basin for that fountain in the dell!
And they who do make mention of the
    same,
From this day forth, shall call it HART-
    LEAP WELL.

'And, gallant Stag! to make thy praises
    known,   65
Another monument shall here be raised;
Three several pillars, each a rough-hewn
    stone,
And planted where thy hoofs the turf
    have grazed.

'And in the summer-time, when days are
    long,
I will come hither with my Paramour; 70
And with the dancers and the minstrel's
    song
We will make merry in that pleasant
    bower.

'Till the foundations of the mountains fail
My mansion with its arbour shall en-
    dure;—
The joy of them who till the fields of
    Swale,   75
And them who dwell among the woods
    of Ure!'

Then home he went, and left the Hart
    stone-dead,
With breathless nostrils stretched above
    the spring.
—Soon did the Knight perform what he
    had said;
And far and wide the fame thereof did
    ring.   80

Ere thrice the Moon into her port had
    steered,
A cup of stone received the living well;
Three pillars of rude stone Sir Walter
    reared,
And built a house of pleasure in the dell.

And, near the fountain, flowers of stature
    tall   85
With trailing plants and trees were inter-
    twined,—
Which soon composed a little sylvan hall,
A leafy shelter from the sun and wind.

And thither, when the summer days were
    long,   89
Sir Walter led his wondering Paramour;
And with the dancers and the minstrel's
    song
Made merriment within that pleasant
    bower.

The Knight, Sir Walter, died in course of
   time,
And his bones lie in his paternal vale.—
But there is matter for a second rhyme,   95
And I to this would add another tale.

PART SECOND

The moving accident is not my trade;
To freeze the blood I have no ready arts:
'Tis my delight, alone in summer shade,
To pipe a simple song for thinking hearts.

As I from Hawes to Richmond did repair,
It chanced that I saw standing in a dell
Three aspens at three corners of a square;
And one, not four yards distant, near a
   well.

What this imported I could ill divine: 105
And, pulling now the rein my horse to stop,
I saw three pillars standing in a line,—
The last stone-pillar on a dark hill-top.

The trees were grey, with neither arms
   nor head;
Half wasted the square mound of tawny
   green;   110
So that you just might say, as then I said,
'Here in old time the hand of man hath
   been.'

I looked upon the hill both far and near,
More doleful place did never eye survey;
It seemed as if the spring-time came not
   here,   115
And Nature here were willing to decay.

I stood in various thoughts and fancies
   lost,
When one, who was in shepherd's garb
   attired,
Came up the hollow:—him did I accost,
And what this place might be I then enquired.   120

The Shepherd stopped, and that same
   story told
Which in my former rhyme I have rehearsed.
'A jolly place,' said he, 'in times of old!
But something ails it now: the spot is
   curst.

'You see these lifeless stumps of aspen
   wood—   125
Some say that they are beeches, others
   elms—
These were the bower; and here a mansion stood,
The finest palace of a hundred realms!

'The arbour does its own condition tell;
You see the stones, the fountain, and the
   stream;   130
But as to the great Lodge! you might as
   well
Hunt half a day for a forgotten dream.

'There's neither dog nor heifer, horse nor
   sheep,
Will wet his lips within that cup of stone;
And oftentimes, when all are fast asleep,
This water doth send forth a dolorous
   groan.   136

'Some say that here a murder has been
   done,
And blood cries out for blood: but, for
   my part,
I've guessed, when I've been sitting in the
   sun,
That it was all for that unhappy Hart.

'What thoughts must through the creature's brain have past!   141
Even from the topmost stone, upon the
   steep,
Are but three bounds—and look, Sir, at
   this last—
O Master! it has been a cruel leap.

'For thirteen hours he ran a desperate
   race;   145
And in my simple mind we cannot tell
What cause the Hart might have to love
   this place,
And come and make his death-bed near
   the well.

'Here on the grass perhaps asleep he sank,
Lulled by the fountain in the summer-
   tide;   150
This water was perhaps the first he drank
When he had wandered from his mother's
   side.

'In April here beneath the flowering thorn
He heard the birds their morning carols
   sing;
And he perhaps, for aught we know, was
   born   155
Nor half a furlong from that self-same
   spring.

'Now, here is neither grass nor pleasant
   shade;
The sun on drearier hollow never shone;
So will it be, as I have often said,
Till trees, and stones, and fountain, all
   are gone.'   160

'Grey-headed Shepherd, thou hast spoken
   well;
Small difference lies between thy creed
   and mine:
This Beast not unobserved by Nature fell;
His death was mourned by sympathy
   divine.

'The Being that is in the clouds and air,
That is in the green leaves among the
   groves,   166
Maintains a deep and reverential care
For the unoffending creatures whom he
   loves.

'The pleasure-house is dust:—behind,
before,
This is no common waste, no common
gloom;   170
But Nature, in due course of time, once
more
Shall here put on her beauty and her
bloom.

'She leaves these objects to a slow decay,
That what we are, and have been, may be
known;
But at the coming of the milder day   175
These monuments shall all be overgrown.

'One lesson, Shepherd, let us two divide,
Taught both by what she shows, and what
conceals;
Never to blend our pleasure or our pride
With sorrow of the meanest thing that
feels.'   180

XXV

SONG AT THE FEAST OF BROUGHAM CASTLE

UPON THE RESTORATION OF LORD CLIFFORD,
THE SHEPHERD, TO THE ESTATES AND
HONOURS OF HIS ANCESTORS

[Composed 1807.—Published 1807.]

HIGH in the breathless Hall the Minstrel
sate,
And Emont's murmur mingled with the
Song.—
The words of ancient time I thus translate,
A festal strain that hath been silent long:—

'From town to town, from tower to
tower,   5
The red rose is a gladsome flower.
Her thirty years of winter past,
The red rose is revived at last;
She lifts her head for endless spring,
For everlasting blossoming.   10

Both roses flourish, red and white:
In love and sisterly delight
The two that were at strife are blended,
And all old troubles now are ended.—
Joy! joy to both! but most to her   15
Who is the flower of Lancaster!
Behold her how She smiles to-day
On this great throng, this bright array!
Fair greeting doth she send to all
From every corner of the hall;   20
But chiefly from above the board
Where sits in state our rightful Lord,
A Clifford to his own restored!

'They came with banner, spear, and
shield;
And it was proved in Bosworth-field.   25
Not long the Avenger was withstood—
Earth helped him with the cry of blood:

St. George was for us, and the might
Of blessed Angels crowned the right.
Loud voice the Land has uttered forth,   30
We loudest in the faithful north:
Our fields rejoice, our mountains ring,
Our streams proclaim a welcoming;
Our strong-abodes and castles see
The glory of their loyalty.   5

'How glad is Skipton at this hour—
Though lonely, a deserted Tower;
Knight, squire, and yeoman, page and
groom:
We have them at the feast of Brough'm.
How glad Pendragon—though the sleep
Of years be on her!—She shall reap   41
A taste of this great pleasure, viewing
As in a dream her own renewing.
Rejoiced is Brough, right glad, I deem,
Beside her little humble stream;   45
And she that keepeth watch and ward
Her statelier Eden's course to guard;
They both are happy at this hour,
Though each is but a lonely Tower:—
But here is perfect joy and pride   50
For one fair House by Emont's side,
This day, distinguished without peer,
To see her Master and to cheer—
Him, and his Lady-mother dear!

'Oh! it was a time forlorn   55
When the fatherless was born—
Give her wings that she may fly,
Or she sees her infant die!
Swords that are with slaughter wild
Hunt the Mother and the Child.   60
Who will take them from the light?
—Yonder is a man in sight—
Yonder is a house—but where?
No, they must not enter there.
To the caves, and to the brooks,   65
To the clouds of heaven she looks;
She is speechless, but her eyes
Pray in ghostly agonies.
Blissful Mary, Mother mild,
Maid and Mother undefiled,   70
Save a Mother and her Child!

'Now Who is he that bounds with joy
On Carrock's side, a Shepherd-boy?
No thoughts hath he but thoughts that
pass
Light as the wind along the grass.   75
Can this be He who hither came
In secret, like a smothered flame?
O'er whom such thankful tears were shed
For shelter, and a poor man's bread!   79
God loves the Child; and God hath willed
That those dear words should be fulfilled,
The Lady's words, when forced away
The last she to her Babe did say:
"My own, my own, thy Fellow-guest
I may not be; but rest thee, rest,   85
For lowly shepherd's life is best!"

162

'Alas! when evil men are strong
No life is good, no pleasure long.
The Boy must part from Mosedale's
    groves,   89
And leave Blencathara's rugged coves,
And quit the flowers that summer brings
To Glenderamakin's lofty springs;
Must vanish, and his careless cheer
Be turned to heaviness and fear.
—Give Sir Lancelot Threlkeld praise! 95
Hear it, good man, old in days!
Thou tree of covert and of rest
For this young Bird that is distrest;
Among thy branches safe he lay,
And he was free to sport and play, 100
When falcons were abroad for prey.

'A recreant harp, that sings of fear
And heaviness in Clifford's ear!
I said, when evil men are strong,
No life is good, no pleasure long, 105
A weak and cowardly untruth!
Our Clifford was a happy Youth,
And thankful through a weary time,
That brought him up to manhood's prime.
—Again he wanders forth at will, 110
And tends a flock from hill to hill:
His garb is humble; ne'er was seen
Such garb with such a noble mien;
Among the shepherd-grooms no mate
Hath he, a Child of strength and state!
Yet lacks not friends for simple glee, 116
Nor yet for higher sympathy.
To his side the fallow-deer
Came, and rested without fear;
The eagle, lord of land and sea, 120
Stooped down to pay him fealty;
And both the undying fish that swim
Through Bowscale-tarn did wait on him;
The pair were servants of his eye
In their immortality; 125
And glancing, gleaming, dark or bright,
Moved to and fro, for his delight.
He knew the rocks which Angels haunt
Upon the mountains visitant;
He hath kenned them taking wing: 130
And into caves where Faeries sing
He hath entered; and been told
By Voices how men lived of old.
Among the heavens his eye can see
The face of thing that is to be; 135
And, if that men report him right,
His tongue could whisper words of might.
—Now another day is come,
Fitter hope, and nobler doom;
He hath thrown aside his crook, 140
And hath buried deep his book;
Armour rusting in his halls
On the blood of Clifford calls;—
"Quell the Scot," exclaims the Lance—
Bear me to the heart of France, 145
Is the longing of the Shield—
Tell thy name, thou trembling Field;
Field of death, where'er thou be,

Groan thou with our victory!
Happy day, and mighty hour, 150
When our Shepherd in his power,
Mailed and horsed, with lance and sword,
To his ancestors restored
Like a re-appearing Star,
Like a glory from afar, 155
First shall head the flock of war!'

Alas! the impassioned minstrel did not
    know
How, by Heaven's grace, this Clifford's
    heart was framed:
How he, long forced in humble walks
    to go,
Was softened into feeling, soothed, and
    tamed. 160

Love had he found in huts where poor
    men lie;
His daily teachers had been woods and
    rills,
The silence that is in the starry sky,
The sleep that is among the lonely hills.

In him the savage virtue of the Race, 165
Revenge, and all ferocious thoughts were
    dead:
Nor did he change; but kept in lofty place
The wisdom which adversity had bred.

Glad were the vales, and every cottage-
    hearth;
The Shepherd-lord was honoured more
    and more; 170
And, ages after he was laid in earth,
'The good Lord Clifford' was the name
    he bore.

XXVI

LINES

COMPOSED A FEW MILES ABOVE TINTERN
ABBEY, ON REVISITING THE BANKS OF THE
WYE DURING A TOUR. JULY 13, 1798

[Composed July 13, 1798.—Published 1798.]

FIVE years have past; five summers, with
    the length
Of five long winters! and again I hear
These waters, rolling from their moun-
    tain-springs
With a soft inland murmur.[1]—Once again
Do I behold these steep and lofty cliffs, 5
That on a wild secluded scene impress
Thoughts of more deep seclusion; and
    connect
The landscape with the quiet of the sky.
The day is come when I again repose
Here, under this dark sycamore, and view

---

[1] The river is not affected by the tides a few miles
above Tintern.

These plots of cottage-ground, these orch-
ard-tufts,   11
Which at this season, with their unripe
fruits,
Are clad in one green hue, and lose them-
selves
'Mid groves and copses. Once again I see
These hedge-rows, hardly hedge-rows,
little lines   15
Of sportive wood run wild: these pastoral
farms,
Green to the very door; and wreaths of
smoke
Sent up, in silence, from among the trees!
With some uncertain notice, as might seem
Of vagrant dwellers in the houseless
woods,   20
Or of some Hermit's cave, where by his fire
The Hermit sits alone.

These beauteous forms,
Through a long absence, have not been to
me   23
As is a landscape to a blind man's eye:
But oft, in lonely rooms, and 'mid the din
Of towns and cities, I have owed to them,
In hours of weariness, sensations sweet,
Felt in the blood, and felt along the heart;
And passing even into my purer mind,
With tranquil restoration:—feelings too
Of unremembered pleasure: such, per-
haps,   31
As have no slight or trivial influence
On that best portion of a good man's life,
His little, nameless, unremembered, acts
Of kindness and of love. Nor less, I trust,
To them I may have owed another gift,
Of aspect more sublime; that blessed
mood,   37
In which the burthen of the mystery,
In which the heavy and the weary weight
Of all this unintelligible world,   40
Is lightened:—that serene and blessed
mood,
In which the affections gently lead us on,—
Until, the breath of this corporeal frame
And even the motion of our human blood
Almost suspended, we are laid asleep   45
In body, and become a living soul:
While with an eye made quiet by the
power
Of harmony, and the deep power of joy,
We see into the life of things.
If this
Be but a vain belief, yet, oh! how oft— 50
In darkness and amid the many shapes
Of joyless daylight; when the fretful stir
Unprofitable, and the fever of the world,
Have hung upon the beatings of my
heart—
How oft, in spirit, have I turned to thee,
O sylvan Wye! thou wanderer thro' the
woods,   56
How often has my spirit turned to thee!

And now, with gleams of half-extin-
guished thought,
With many recognitions dim and faint,
And somewhat of a sad perplexity,   60
The picture of the mind revives again:
While here I stand, not only with the sense
Of present pleasure, but with pleasing
thoughts
That in this moment there is life and food
For future years. And so I dare to hope,
Though changed, no doubt, from what I
was when first   66
I came among these hills; when like a roe
I bounded o'er the mountains, by the sides
Of the deep rivers, and the lonely streams,
Wherever nature led: more like a man   70
Flying from something that he dreads
than one
Who sought the thing he loved. For
nature then
(The coarser pleasures of my boyish days,
And their glad animal movements all gone
by)
To me was all in all.—I cannot paint   75
What then I was. The sounding cataract
Haunted me like a passion: the tall rock,
The mountain, and the deep and gloomy
wood,
Their colours and their forms, were then
to me
An appetite; a feeling and a love,   80
That had no need of a remoter charm,
By thought supplied, nor any interest
Unborrowed from the eye.—That time is
past,
And all its aching joys are now no more,
And all its dizzy raptures. Not for this
Faint I, nor mourn nor murmur; other
gifts   86
Have followed; for such loss, I would
believe,
Abundant recompense. For I have learned
To look on nature, not as in the hour
Of thoughtless youth; but hearing often-
times   90
The still, sad music of humanity,
Nor harsh nor grating, though of ample
power
To chasten and subdue. And I have felt
A presence that disturbs me with the joy
Of elevated thoughts; a sense sublime   95
Of something far more deeply interfused,
Whose dwelling is the light of setting suns,
And the round ocean and the living air,
And the blue sky, and in the mind of man:
A motion and a spirit, that impels   100
All thinking things, all objects of all
thought,
And rolls through all things. Therefore
am I still
A lover of the meadows and the woods,
And mountains; and of all that we behold
From this green earth; of all the mighty
world   105

Of eye, and ear,—both what they half
 create,[1]
And what perceive; well pleased to recog-
 nise
In nature and the language of the sense
The anchor of my purest thoughts, the
 nurse,
The guide, the guardian of my heart, and
 soul   110
Of all my moral being.
                    Nor perchance,
If I were not thus taught, should I the
 more
Suffer my genial spirits to decay:
For thou art with me here upon the banks
Of this fair river; thou my dearest Friend,
My dear, dear Friend; and in thy voice I
 catch   116
The language of my former heart, and read
My former pleasures in the shooting lights
Of thy wild eyes. Oh! yet a little while
May I behold in thee what I was once,
My dear, dear Sister! and this prayer I
 make,   121
Knowing that Nature never did betray
The heart that loved her; 'tis her privilege,
Through all the years of this our life, to
 lead   124
From joy to joy: for she can so inform
The mind that is within us, so impress
With quietness and beauty, and so feed
With lofty thoughts, that neither evil
 tongues,
Rash judgments, nor the sneers of selfish
 men,
Nor greetings where no kindness is, nor all
The dreary intercourse of daily life,   131
Shall e'er prevail against us, or disturb
Our cheerful faith, that all which we
 behold
Is full of blessings. Therefore let the
 moon
Shine on thee in thy solitary walk;   135
And let the misty mountain-winds be free
To blow against thee: and, in after years,
When these wild ecstasies shall be ma-
 tured
Into a sober pleasure; when thy mind
Shall be a mansion for all lovely forms,
Thy memory be as a dwelling-place   141
For all sweet sounds and harmonies; oh!
 then,
If solitude, or fear, or pain, or grief,
Should be thy portion, with what healing
 thoughts
Of tender joy wilt thou remember me,   145
And these my exhortations! Nor, per-
 chance—
If I should be where I no more can hear
Thy voice, nor catch from thy wild eyes
 these gleams

[1] This line has a close resemblance to an admirable line of Young's, the exact expression of which
I do not recollect.

Of past existence—wilt thou then forget
That on the banks of this delightful stream
We stood together; and that I, so long
A worshipper of Nature, hither came   152
Unwearied in that service: rather say
With warmer love—oh! with far deeper
 zeal
Of holier love. Nor wilt thou then forget
That after many wanderings, many years
Of absence, these steep woods and lofty
 cliffs,   157
And this green pastoral landscape, were
 to me
More dear, both for themselves and for
 thy sake!

XXVII

[Composed 1803.—Published 1807.]

IT is no Spirit who from heaven hath
 flown,
And is descending on his embassy;
Nor Traveller gone from earth the heavens
 to espy!
'Tis Hesperus—there he stands with glit-
 tering crown,
First admonition that the sun is down!   5
For yet it is broad day-light: clouds pass
 by;
A few are near him still—and now the sky,
He hath it to himself—'tis all his own.
O most ambitious Star! an inquest
 wrought   9
Within me when I recognised thy light;
A moment I was startled at the sight:
And, while I gazed, there came to me a
 thought
That I might step beyond my natural race
As thou seem'st now to do; might one day
 trace
Some ground not mine; and, strong her
 strength above,   15
My Soul, an Apparition in the place,
Tread there with steps that no one shall
 reprove!

XXVIII

FRENCH REVOLUTION

AS IT APPEARED TO ENTHUSIASTS AT ITS
 COMMENCEMENT.[1] REPRINTED FROM
 'THE FRIEND'

Composed 1804.—Published October 26, 1809
 (*The Friend*); ed. 1815.]

OH! pleasant exercise of hope and joy!
For mighty were the auxiliars which then
 stood
Upon our side, we who were strong in
 love!
Bliss was it in that dawn to be alive,

[1] This and the Extract, page 89, and the first Piece
of this Class, are from the unpublished Poem of
which some account is given in the Preface to THE
EXCURSION.

But to be young was very heaven!—Oh!
  times,   5
In which the meagre, stale, forbidding
  ways
Of custom, law, and statute, took at once
The attraction of a country in romance!
When Reason seemed the most to assert
  her rights,
When most intent on making of herself 10
A prime Enchantress—to assist the work
Which then was going forward in her
  name!
Not favoured spots alone, but the whole
  earth,
The beauty wore of promise, that which
  sets
(As at some moment might not be unfelt
Among the bowers of paradise itself) 16
The budding rose above the rose full
  blown.
What temper at the prospect did not wake
To happiness unthought of? The inert
Were roused, and lively natures rapt away!
They who had fed their childhood upon
  dreams,   21
The playfellows of fancy, who had made
All powers of swiftness, subtilty, and
  strength
Their ministers,—who in lordly wise had
  stirred
Among the grandest objects of the sense,
And dealt with whatsoever they found
  there   26
As if they had within some lurking right
To wield it;—they, too, who, of gentle
  mood,
Had watched all gentle motions, and to
  these
Had fitted their own thoughts, schemers
  more mild,   30
And in the region of their peaceful
  selves;—
Now was it that both found, the meek and
  lofty
Did both find, helpers to their heart's
  desire,
And stuff at hand, plastic as they could
  wish;
Were called upon to exercise their skill, 35
Not in Utopia, subterranean fields,
Or some secreted island, Heaven knows
  where!
But in the very world, which is the world
Of all of us,—the place where in the end
We find our happiness, or not at all!

XXIX

[Composed 1806.—Published 1807.]

YES, it was the mountain Echo,
Solitary, clear, profound,
Answering to the shouting Cuckoo,
Giving to her sound for sound!

Unsolicited reply   5
To a babbling wanderer sent;
Like her ordinary cry,
Like—but oh, how different!

Hears not also mortal Life?
Hear not we, unthinking Creatures! 10
Slaves of folly, love, or strife—
Voices of two different natures?

Have not *we* too?—yes, we have
Answers, and we know not whence;
Echoes from beyond the grave, 15
Recognised intelligence!

Such rebounds our inward ear
Catches sometimes from afar—
Listen, ponder, hold them dear;
For of God,—of God they are. 20

XXX

TO A SKYLARK[1]

[Composed 1825.—Published 1827.]

ETHEREAL minstrel! pilgrim of the sky!
Dost thou despise the earth where cares
  abound?
Or, while the wings aspire, are heart and
  eye
Both with thy nest upon the dewy ground?
Thy nest which thou canst drop into at
  will,   5
Those quivering wings composed, that
  music still!

Leave to the nightingale her shady wood;
A privacy of glorious light is thine;
Whence thou dost pour upon the world a
  flood
Of harmony, with instinct more divine; 10
Type of the wise who soar, but never
  roam;
True to the kindred points of Heaven and
  Home!

XXXI

LAODAMIA

[Composed 1814.—Published 1815.]

'WITH sacrifice before the rising morn
Vows have I made by fruitless hope in-
  spired;
And from the infernal Gods, 'mid shades
  forlorn
Of night, my slaughtered Lord have I
  required:
Celestial pity I again implore;—   5
Restore him to my sight—great Jove,
  restore!'

[1] For Stanza ii of this poem, omitted in 1845 and
1849-50, see note 2, page 121.—ED.

So speaking, and by fervent love endowed
With faith, the Suppliant heavenward
    lifts her hands;
While, like the sun emerging from a
    cloud,
Her countenance brightens—and her eye
    expands;   10
Her bosom heaves and spreads, her stature
    grows;
And she expects the issue in repose.

O terror! what hath she perceived?—O
    joy!
What doth she look on?—whom doth she
    behold?   14
Her Hero slain upon the beach of Troy?
His vital presence? his corporeal mould?
It is—if sense deceive her not—'tis He!
And a God leads him, wingèd Mercury!

Mild Hermes spake—and touched her
    with his wand
That calms all fear; 'Such grace hath
    crowned thy prayer,   20
Laodamía! that at Jove's command
Thy Husband walks the paths of upper air:
He comes to tarry with thee three hours'
    space;
Accept the gift, behold him face to face!'

Forth sprang the impassioned Queen her
    Lord to clasp;   25
Again that consummation she essayed;
But unsubstantial Form eludes her grasp
As often as that eager grasp was made.
The Phantom parts—but parts to re-unite,
And re-assume his place before her sight.

'Protesiláus, lo! thy guide is gone!   31
Confirm, I pray, the vision with thy voice:
This is our palace,—yonder is thy throne;
Speak, and the floor thou tread'st on will
    rejoice.
Not to appal me have the gods bestowed
This precious boon; and blest a sad
    abode.'   36

'Great Jove, Laodamía! doth not leave
His gifts imperfect:—Spectre though I be,
I am not sent to scare thee or deceive;
But in reward of thy fidelity.   40
And something also did my worth obtain;
For fearless virtue bringeth boundless
    gain.

'Thou knowest, the Delphic oracle fore-
    told
That the first Greek who touched the
    Trojan strand
Should die; but me the threat could not
    withhold: 45
A generous cause a victim did demand;
And forth I leapt upon the sandy plain;
A self-devoted chief—by Hector slain.'

'Supreme of Heroes—bravest, noblest,
    best!
Thy matchless courage I bewail no more,
Which then, when tens of thousands were
    deprest   51
By doubt, propelled thee to the fatal shore;
Thou found'st—and I forgive thee—here
    thou art—
A nobler counsellor than my poor heart.

'But thou, though capable of sternest
    deed,   55
Wert kind as resolute, and good as brave;
And he, whose power restores thee, hath
    decreed
Thou shouldst elude the malice of the
    grave:
Redundant are thy locks, thy lips as fair
As when their breath enriched Thessalian
    air.   60

'No Spectre greets me,—no vain Shadow
    this;
Come, blooming Hero, place thee by my
    side!
Give, on this well-known couch, one nup-
    tial kiss
To me, this day, a second time thy bride!'
Jove frowned in heaven: the conscious
    Parcæ threw   65
Upon those roseate lips a Stygian hue.

'This visage tells thee that my doom is
    past:
Nor should the change be mourned, even
    if the joys
Of sense were able to return as fast
And surely as they vanish. Earth de-
    stroys   70
Those raptures duly—Erebus disdains:
Calm pleasures there abide—majestic
    pains.

'Be taught, O faithful Consort, to control
Rebellious passion: for the Gods approve
The depth, and not the tumult, of the
    soul;   75
A fervent, not ungovernable, love.
Thy transports moderate; and meekly
    mourn
When I depart, for brief is my sojourn—'

'Ah wherefore?—Did not Hercules by
    force
Wrest from the guardian Monster of the
    tomb   80
Alcestis, a reanimated corse,
Given back to dwell on earth in vernal
    bloom?
Medea's spells dispersed the weight of
    years,
And Æson stood a youth 'mid youthful
    peers.   84

167

'The Gods to us are merciful—and they
Yet further may relent: for mightier far
Than strength of nerve and sinew, or the
      sway
Of magic potent over sun and star,
Is love, though oft to agony distrest,
And though his favourite seat be feeble
      woman's breast.   90

'But if thou goest, I follow—' 'Peace!'
      he said,—
She looked upon him and was calmed and
      cheered;
The ghastly colour from his lips had fled;
In his deportment, shape, and mien,
      appeared
Elysian beauty, melancholy grace,   95
Brought from a pensive though a happy
      place.

He spake of love, such love as Spirits feel
In worlds whose course is equable and
      pure;
No fears to beat away—no strife to heal—
The past unsighed for, and the future
      sure;   100
Spake of heroic arts in graver mood
Revived, with finer harmony pursued;

Of all that is most beauteous—imaged
      there
In happier beauty; more pellucid streams,
An ampler ether, a diviner air,   105
And fields invested with purpureal gleams;
Climes which the sun, who sheds the
      brightest day
Earth knows, is all unworthy to survey.

Yet there the Soul shall enter which hath
      earned   109
That privilege by virtue.—'Ill,' said he,
'The end of man's existence I discerned,
Who from ignoble games and revelry
Could draw, when we had parted, vain
      delight,
While tears were thy best pastime, day
      and night;

'And while my youthful peers before my
      eyes   115
(Each hero following his peculiar bent)
Prepared themselves for glorious enter-
      prise
By martial sports,—or, seated in the tent,
Chieftains and kings in council were de-
      tained;
What time the fleet at Aulis lay enchained.

'The wished-for wind was given:—I then
      revolved   121
The oracle, upon the silent sea;
And, if no worthier led the way, resolved
That, of a thousand vessels, mine should
      be

The foremost prow in pressing to the
      strand,—   125
Mine the first blood that tinged the Trojan
      sand.

'Yet bitter, oft-times bitter, was the pang
When of thy loss I thought, belovèd Wife!
On thee too fondly did my memory hang,
And on the joys we shared in mortal life,—
The paths which we had trod—these foun-
      tains, flowers;   131
My new-planned cities, and unfinished
      towers.

'But should suspense permit the Foe to
      cry,
"Behold they tremble!—haughty their
      array,
Yet of their number no one dares to die?"
In soul I swept the indignity away: 136
Old frailties then recurred:—but lofty
      thought,
In act embodied, my deliverance wrought.

'And Thou, though strong in love, art all
      too weak
In reason, in self-government too slow;
I counsel thee by fortitude to seek   141
Our blest re-union in the shades below.
The invisible world with thee hath sym-
      pathised;
Be thy affections raised and solemnised.

'Learn, by a mortal yearning, to ascend—
Seeking a higher object. Love was given,
Encouraged, sanctioned, chiefly for that
      end;   147
For this the passion to excess was driven—
That self might be annulled: her bondage
      prove
The fetters of a dream opposed to love.'—

Aloud she shrieked! for Hermes re-
      appears!   151
Round the dear Shade she would have
      clung—'tis vain:
The hours are past—too brief had they
      been years;
And him no mortal effort can detain:
Swift, toward the realms that know not
      earthly day,   155
He through the portal takes his silent way,
And on the palace-floor a lifeless corse She
      lay.

Thus, all in vain exhorted and reproved,
She perished; and, as for a wilful crime,
By the just Gods whom no weak pity
      moved,   160
Was doomed to wear out her appointed
      time,
Apart from happy Ghosts, that gather
      flowers
Of blissful quiet 'mid unfading bowers.[1]

[1] For an account of the important changes—
material as well as formal—introduced from time to
time into this stanza, see Editor's note, p. 901.—ED.

—Yet tears to human suffering are due;
And mortal hopes defeated and o'er-
    thrown   165
Are mourned by man, and not by man
    alone,
As fondly he believes.—Upon the side
Of Hellespont (such faith was entertained)
A knot of spiry trees for ages grew
From out the tomb of him for whom she
    died;   170
And ever, when such stature they had
    gained
That Ilium's walls were subject to their
    view,
The trees' tall summits withered at the
    sight;
A constant interchange of growth and
    blight![1]

XXXII

DION

[Composed 1816.—Published 1820.]

(SEE PLUTARCH.)

[1]

[FAIR is the Swan, whose majesty, pre-
    vailing
O'er breezeless water, on Locarno's lake,
Bears him on while proudly sailing
He leaves behind a moon-illumined wake:
Behold! the mantling spirit of reserve 5
Fashions his neck into a goodly curve;
An arch thrown back between luxuriant
    wings
Of whitest garniture, like fir-tree boughs
To which, on some unruffled morning,
    clings
A flaky weight of winter's purest snows!
—Behold!—as with a gushing impulse
    heaves   11
That downy prow, and softly cleaves
The mirror of the crystal flood,
Vanish inverted hill, and shadowy wood,
And pendent rocks, where'er, in gliding
    state,   15
Winds the mute Creature without visible
    Mate
Or Rival, save the Queen of night
Showering down a silver light,
From heaven, upon her chosen Favour-
    ite!]

[II]

[So pure, so bright, so fitted to embrace
Where'er he turned, a natural grace   21
Of haughtiness without pretence,
    &c. &c. &c. (Edd. 1820, 1827, 1832).]

[1] For the account of these long-lived trees, see Pliny's 'Natural History', lib. xvi, cap. 44; and for the features in the character of Protesilaus, see the 'Iphigenia in Aulis' of Euripides. Virgil places the Shade of Laodamia in a mournful region, among unhappy Lovers,
    —— His Laodamia
It comes.——

I

SERENE, and fitted to embrace,
Where'er he turned, a swan-like grace
Of haughtiness without pretence,
And to unfold a still magnificence,
Was princely Dion, in the power   5
And beauty of his happier hour.
And what pure homage *then* did wait
On Dion's virtues, while the lunar beam
Of Plato's genius, from its lofty sphere,
Fell round him in the grove of Academe,
Softening their inbred dignity austere—
    That he, not too elate   12
    With self-sufficing solitude,
But with majestic lowliness endued,
Might in the universal bosom reign, 15
And from affectionate observance gain
Help, under every change of adverse fate.

II

Five thousand warriors—O the rapturous
    day!
Each crowned with flowers, and armed
    with spear and shield,
Or ruder weapon which their course might
    yield,   20
To Syracuse advance in bright array.
Who leads them on?—The anxious people
    see
Long-exiled Dion marching at their head,
He also crowned with flowers of Sicily,
And in a white, far-beaming, corselet clad!
Pure transport undisturbed by doubt or
    fear   26
The gazers feel; and, rushing to the plain,
Salute those strangers as a holy train
Or blest procession (to the Immortals
    dear)
That brought their precious liberty again.
Lo! when the gates are entered, on each
    hand,   31
Down the long street, rich goblets filled
    with wine
    In seemly order stand,
On tables set, as if for rites divine;—
And, as the great Deliverer marches by,
He looks on festal ground with fruits
    bestrown;   36
And flowers are on his person thrown
    In boundless prodigality;
Nor doth the general voice abstain from
    prayer,
Invoking Dion's tutelary care,   40
As if a very Deity he were!

III

Mourn, hills and groves of Attica! and
    mourn
Ilissus, bending o'er thy classic urn!
Mourn, and lament for him whose spirit
    dreads
Your once sweet memory, studious walks
    and shades!   45

For him who to divinity aspired,
Not on the breath of popular applause,
But through dependence on the sacred laws
Framed in the schools where Wisdom dwelt retired,
Intent to trace the ideal path of right 50
(More fair than heaven's broad causeway paved with stars)
Which Dion learned to measure with sublime delight;—
But He hath overleaped the eternal bars;
And, following guides whose craft holds no consent
With aught that breathes the ethereal element, 55
Hath stained the robes of civil power with blood,
Unjustly shed, though for the public good.
Whence doubts that came too late, and wishes vain,
Hollow excuses, and triumphant pain;
And oft his cogitations sink as low 60
As, through the abysses of a joyless heart,
The heaviest plummet of despair can go—
But whence that sudden check? that fearful start!
He hears an uncouth sound—
Anon his lifted eyes 65
Saw, at a long-drawn gallery's dusky bound,
A Shape of more than mortal size
And hideous aspect, stalking round and round!
A woman's garb the Phantom wore,
And fiercely swept the marble floor,—
Like Auster whirling to and fro, 71
His force on Caspian foam to try:
Or Boreas when he scours the snow
That skins the plains of Thessaly,
Or when aloft on Mænalus he stops 75
His flight, 'mid eddying pine-tree tops!

IV

So, but from toil less sign of profit reaping,
The sullen Spectre to her purpose bowed,
Sweeping—vehemently sweeping—
No pause admitted, no design avowed! 80
'Avaunt, inexplicable Guest!—avaunt.'
Exclaimed the Chieftain—'let me rather see
The coronal that coiling vipers make;
The torch that flames with many a lurid flake, 84
And the long train of doleful pageantry
Which they behold, whom vengeful Furies haunt;
Who, while they struggle from the scourge to flee,
Move where the blasted soil is not unworn,
And, in their anguish, bear what other minds have borne!'

V

But Shapes, that come not at an earthly call, 90
Will not depart when mortal voices bid;
Lords of the visionary eye whose lid,
Once raised, remains aghast, and will not fall!
Ye Gods, thought He, that servile Implement
Obeys a mystical intent! 95
Your Minister would brush away
The spots that to my soul adhere;
But should she labour night and day,
They will not, cannot disappear;
Whence angry perturbations,—and that look 100
Which no philosophy can brook!

VI

Ill-fated Chief! there are whose hopes are built
Upon the ruins of thy glorious name;
Who, through the portal of one moment's guilt,
Pursue thee with their deadly aim! 105
O matchless perfidy! portentous lust
Of monstrous crime!—that horror-striking blade,
Drawn in defiance of the Gods, hath laid
The noble Syracusan low in dust!
Shuddered the walls—the marble city wept— 110
And sylvan places heaved a pensive sigh;
But in calm peace the appointed Victim slept,
As he had fallen in magnanimity;
Of spirit too capacious to require
That Destiny her course should change; too just 115
To his own native greatness to desire
That wretched boon, days lengthened by mistrust.
So were the hopeless troubles, that involved
The soul of Dion, instantly dissolved.
Released from life and cares of princely state, 120
He left this moral grafted on his Fate;
'Him only pleasure leads, and peace attends,
Him, only him, the shield of Jove defends,
Whose means are fair and spotless as his ends.'

XXXIII

THE PASS OF KIRKSTONE
[Composed 1817.—Published 1820.]

I

WITHIN the mind strong fancies work,
A deep delight the bosom thrills,
Oft as I pass along the fork
Of these fraternal hills:

Where, save the rugged road, we find 5
No appanage of human kind,
Nor hint of man; if stone or rock
Seem not his handy-work to mock
By something cognizably shaped;
Mockery—or model roughly hewn, 10
And left as if by earthquake strewn,
Or from the Flood escaped:
Altars for Druid service fit;
(But where no fire was ever lit,
Unless the glow-worm to the skies 15
Thence offer nightly sacrifice)
Wrinkled Egyptian monument;
Green moss-grown tower; or hoary tent;
Tents of a camp that never shall be
    razed—
On which four thousand years have
    gazed! 20

II

Ye ploughshares sparkling on the slopes!
Ye snow-white lambs that trip
Imprisoned 'mid the formal props
Of restless ownership!
Ye trees, that may to-morrow fall 25
To feed the insatiate Prodigal!
Lawns, houses, chattels, groves, and
    fields,
All that the fertile valley shields;
Wages of folly—baits of crime,
Of life's uneasy game the stake, 30
Playthings that keep the eyes awake
Of drowsy, dotard Time;—
O care! O guilt!—O vales and plains,
Here, 'mid his own unvexed domains,
A Genius dwells, that can subdue 35
At once all memory of You,—
Most potent when mists veil the sky,
Mists that distort and magnify,
While the coarse rushes, to the sweeping
    breeze,
Sigh forth their ancient melodies! 40

III

List to those shriller notes!—*that* march
Perchance was on the blast,
When, through this Height's inverted
    arch,
Rome's earliest legion passed!
—They saw, adventurously impelled, 45
And older eyes than theirs beheld,
This block—and yon, whose church-like
    frame
Gives to this savage Pass its name.
Aspiring Road! that lov'st to hide
Thy daring in a vapoury bourn, 50
Not seldom may the hour return
When thou shalt be my guide:
And I (as all men may find cause,
When life is at a weary pause,
And they have panted up the hill 55
Of duty with reluctant will)
Be thankful, even though tired and faint,
For the rich bounties of constraint;

Whence oft invigorating transports flow
That choice lacked courage to bestow!

IV

My Soul was grateful for delight 61
That wore a threatening brow;
A veil is lifted—can she slight
The scene that opens now?
Though habitation none appear, 65
The greenness tells, man must be there;
The shelter—that the perspective
Is of the clime in which we live;
Where Toil pursues his daily round;
Where Pity sheds sweet tears—and Love,
In woodbine bower or birchen grove, 71
Inflicts his tender wound.
—Who comes not hither ne'er shall know
How beautiful the world below;
Nor can he guess how lightly leaps 75
The brook adown the rocky steeps.
Farewell, thou desolate Domain!
Hope, pointing to the cultured plain,
Carols like a shepherd-boy;
And who is she?—Can that be Joy! 80
Who, with a sunbeam for her guide,
Smoothly skims the meadows wide;
While Faith, from yonder opening cloud,
To hill and vale proclaims aloud,
'Whate'er the weak may dread, the
    wicked dare, 85
Thy lot, O Man, is good, thy portion
    fair!'

XXXIV

TO ENTERPRISE

[Composed 1820 (?).—Published 1822.]

KEEP for the Young the impassioned
    smile
Shed from thy countenance, as I see thee
    stand
High on that chalky cliff of Britain's Isle,
A slender volume grasping in thy hand—
(Perchance the pages that relate 5
The various turns of Crusoe's fate)—
Ah, spare the exulting smile,
And drop thy pointing finger bright
As the first flash of beacon light;
But neither veil thy head in shadows dim,
Nor turn thy face away 11
From One who, in the evening of his day,
To thee would offer no presumptuous
    hymn!

I

Bold Spirit! who art free to rove
Among the starry courts of Jove, 15
And oft in splendour dost appear
Embodied to poetic eyes,
While traversing this nether sphere,
Where Mortals call thee ENTERPRISE.

Daughter of Hope! her favourite Child,
Whom she to young Ambition bore,　21
When hunter's arrow first defiled
The grove, and stained the turf with gore;
Thee wingèd Fancy took, and nursed
On broad Euphrates' palmy shore,　25
And where the mightier Waters burst
From caves of Indian mountains hoar!
She wrapped thee in a panther's skin;
And Thou, thy favourite food to win,
The flame-eyed eagle oft wouldst scare　30
From her rock-fortress in mid air,
With infant shout; and often sweep,
Paired with the ostrich, o'er the plain;
Or, tired with sport, wouldst sink asleep
Upon the couchant lion's mane!　35
With rolling years thy strength increased;
And, far beyond thy native East,
To thee, by varying titles known
As variously thy power was shown,
Did incense-bearing altars rise,　40
Which caught the blaze of sacrifice,
From suppliants panting for the skies!

II

What though this ancient Earth be trod
No more by step of Demi-god
Mounting from glorious deed to deed　45
As thou from clime to clime didst lead;
Yet still the bosom beating high,
And the hushed farewell of an eye
Where no procrastinating gaze
A last infirmity betrays,　50
Prove that thy heaven-descended sway
Shall ne'er submit to cold decay.
By thy divinity impelled,
The Stripling seeks the tented field;
The aspiring Virgin kneels; and, pale　55
With awe, receives the hallowed veil,
A soft and tender Heroine
Vowed to severer discipline;
Inflamed by thee, the blooming Boy
Makes of the whistling shrouds a toy,　60
And of the ocean's dismal breast
A play-ground,—or a couch of rest;
'Mid the blank world of snow and ice,
Thou to his dangers dost enchain
The Chamois-chaser awed in vain　65
By chasm or dizzy precipice;
And hast Thou not with triumph seen
How soaring Mortals glide between
Or through the clouds, and brave the light
With bolder than Icarian flight?　70
How they, in bells of crystal, dive—
Where winds and waters cease to strive—
For no unholy visitings,
Among the monsters of the Deep;
And all the sad and precious things　75
Which there in ghastly silence sleep?
Or adverse tides and currents headed,
And breathless calms no longer dreaded,
In never-slackening voyage go
Straight as an arrow from the bow;　80

And, slighting sails and scorning oars,
Keep faith with Time on distant shores?
—Within our fearless reach are placed
The secrets of the burning Waste;
Egyptian tombs unlock their dead,　85
Nile trembles at his fountain head;
Thou speak'st—and lo! the polar Seas
Unbosom their last mysteries.
—But oh! what transports, what sublime
reward,
Won from the world of mind, dost thou
prepare　90
For philosophic Sage; or high-souled Bard
Who, for thy service trained in lonely
woods,
Hath fed on pageants floating through
the air,
Or calentured in depth of limpid floods;
Nor grieves—tho' doomed thro' silent
night to bear　95
The domination of his glorious themes,
Or struggle in the net-work of thy dreams!

III

If there be movements in the Patriot's soul,
From source still deeper, and of higher
worth,
'Tis thine the quickening impulse to con-
trol,　100
And in due season send the mandate
forth;
Thy call a prostrate Nation can restore,
When but a single Mind resolves to
crouch no more.

IV

Dread Minister of wrath!
Who to their destined punishment dost
urge　105
The Pharaohs of the earth, the men of
hardened heart!
Not unassisted by the flattering stars,
Thou strew'st temptation o'er the path
When they in pomp depart
With trampling horses and refulgent
cars—　110
Soon to be swallowed by the briny surge;
Or cast, for lingering death, on unknown
strands;
Or caught amid a whirl of desert sands—
An Army now, and now a living hill
That a brief while heaves with convulsive
throes—　115
Then all is still;
Or, to forget their madness and their woes,
Wrapt in a winding-sheet of spotless
snows!

V

Back flows the willing current of my
Song:
If to provoke such doom the Impious
dare,　120
Why should it daunt a blameless prayer?

172

—Bold Goddess! range our Youth among;
Nor let thy genuine impulse fail to beat
In hearts no longer young;
Still may a veteran Few have pride   125
In thoughts whose sternness makes them
     sweet;
In fixed resolves by Reason justified;
That to their object cleave like sleet
Whitening a pine tree's northern side,
When fields are naked far and wide,   130
And withered leaves, from earth's cold
     breast
Up-caught in whirlwinds, nowhere can
     find rest.

VI

But if such homage thou disdain
As doth with mellowing years agree,
One rarely absent from thy train   135
More humble favours may obtain
For thy contented Votary.
She who incites the frolic lambs
In presence of their heedless dams,
And to the solitary fawn   140
Vouchsafes her lessons, bounteous Nymph
That wakes the breeze, the sparkling
     lymph
Doth hurry to the lawn;
She who inspires that strain of joyance
     holy
Which the sweet Bird, misnamed the
     melancholy,   145
Pours forth in shady groves, shall plead
     for me;
And vernal mornings opening bright
With views of undefined delight,
And cheerful songs, and suns that shine
On busy days, with thankful nights, be
     mine.   150

VII

But thou, O Goddess! in thy favourite Isle
(Freedom's impregnable redoubt,
The wide earth's storehouse fenced about
With breakers roaring to the gales   154
That stretch a thousand thousand sails)
Quicken the slothful, and exalt the vile!—
Thy impulse is the life of Fame;
Glad Hope would almost cease to be
If torn from thy society;   159
And Love, when worthiest of his name,
Is proud to walk the earth with Thee!

XXXV

TO ——

ON HER FIRST ASCENT TO THE SUMMIT OF
HELVELLYN

[Composed 1816.—Published 1820.]

INMATE of a mountain-dwelling,
Thou hast clomb aloft, and gazed
From the watch-towers of Helvellyn;
Awed, delighted, and amazed!

Potent was the spell that bound thee   5
Not unwilling to obey;
For blue Ether's arms, flung round thee,
Stilled the pantings of dismay.

Lo! the dwindled woods and meadows;
What a vast abyss is there!   10
Lo! the clouds, the solemn shadows,
And the glistenings—heavenly fair!

And a record of commotion
Which a thousand ridges yield;
Ridge, and gulf, and distant ocean   15
Gleaming like a silver shield!

Maiden! now take flight;—inherit
Alps or Andes—they are thine!
With the morning's roseate Spirit
Sweep their length of snowy line;   20

Or survey their bright dominions
In the gorgeous colours drest
Flung from off the purple pinions,
Evening spreads throughout the west!

Thine are all the choral[1] fountains   25
Warbling in each sparry vault
Of the untrodden lunar mountains;
Listen to their songs!—or halt,

To Niphates' top invited,
Whither spiteful Satan steered;   30
Or descend where the ark alighted,
When the green earth re-appeared;

For the power of hills is on thee,
As was witnessed through thine eye
Then, when old Helvellyn won thee   35
To confess their majesty!

XXXVI

TO A YOUNG LADY

WHO HAD BEEN REPROACHED FOR TAKING
LONG WALKS IN THE COUNTRY

[Composed 1801 (?).—Published *Morning Post*,
     February 11, 1802; ed. 1807.]

DEAR Child of Nature, let them rail!
—There is a nest in a green dale,
A harbour and a hold;
Where thou, a Wife and Friend, shalt see
Thy own heart-stirring days, and be   5
A light to young and old.

There, healthy as a shepherd boy,
And treading among flowers of joy
Which at no season fade,
Thou, while thy babes around thee cling,
Shalt show us how divine a thing   11
A Woman may be made.

Thy thoughts and feelings shall not die,
Nor leave thee, when grey hairs are nigh,
A melancholy slave;   15
But an old age serene and bright,
And lovely as a Lapland night,
Shall lead thee to thy grave.

     [1] 'Choral', edd. 1820, 1827; 'coral', 1832-1849.
                                             —ED.

173

XXXVII
WATER FOWL

[Composed 1812 (?).[1]—Published 1823; ed. 1827.]

'Let me be allowed the aid of verse to describe the evolutions which these visitants sometimes perform, on a fine day towards the close of winter.'
—*Extract from the Author's Book on the Lakes (edition of 1823.*—ED.).

MARK how the feathered tenants of the flood,
With grace of motion that might scarcely seem
Inferior to angelical, prolong
Their curious pastime! shaping in mid air
(And sometimes with ambitious wing that soars   5
High as the level of the mountain-tops)
A circuit ampler than the lake beneath—
Their own domain; but ever, while intent
On tracing and retracing that large round,
Their jubilant activity evolves   10
Hundreds of curves and circlets, to and fro,
Upward and downward, progress intricate
Yet unperplexed, as if one spirit swayed
Their indefatigable flight. 'Tis done—
Ten times, or more, I fancied it had ceased;
But lo! the vanished company again   16
Ascending; they approach—I hear their wings,
Faint, faint at first; and then an eager sound,
Past in a moment—and as faint again!
They tempt the sun to sport amid their plumes;   20
They tempt the water, or the gleaming ice,
To show them a fair image; 'tis themselves,
Their own fair forms, upon the glimmering plain,
Painted more soft and fair as they descend
Almost to touch;—then up again aloft,
Up with a sally and a flash of speed,   26
As if they scorned both resting-place and rest!

XXXVIII
VIEW FROM THE TOP OF BLACK COMB[2]

[Composed 1813.—Published 1815.]

THIS Height a ministering Angel might select:
For from the summit of BLACK COMB (dread name

[1] These lines form portion of *The Recluse, Book I,* much of which was undoubtedly composed in 1800. In 1836 Wordsworth assigned them to the year 1812; but his memory on such matters was treacherous, and it is quite possible that they were written as far back as 1800.—ED.
[2] Black Comb stands at the southern extremity of Cumberland: its base covers a much greater extent of ground than any other mountain in those parts; and, from its situation, the summit commands a more extensive view than any other point in Britain.

Derived from clouds and storms!) the amplest range
Of unobstructed prospect may be seen
That British ground commands:—low dusky tracts,   5
Where Trent is nursed, far southward! Cambrian hills
To the south-west, a multitudinous show;
And, in a line of eye-sight linked with these,
The hoary peaks of Scotland that give birth
To Tiviot's stream, to Annan, Tweed, and Clyde:—   10
Crowding the quarter whence the sun comes forth
Gigantic mountains rough with crags;
beneath,
Right at the imperial station's western base,
Main ocean, breaking audibly, and stretched
Far into silent regions blue and pale;—
And visibly engirding Mona's Isle   16
That, as we left the plain, before our sight
Stood like a lofty mount, uplifting slowly
(Above the convex of the watery globe)
Into clear view the cultured fields that streak   20
Her habitable shores, but now appears
A dwindled object, and submits to lie
At the spectator's feet.—Yon azure ridge,
Is it a perishable cloud? Or there   24
Do we behold the line of Erin's coast?
Land sometimes by the roving shepherd-swain
(Like the bright confines of another world)
Not doubtfully perceived.—Look homeward now!
In depth, in height, in circuit, how serene
The spectacle, how pure!—Of Nature's works,   30
In earth, and air, and earth-embracing sea,
A revelation infinite it seems;
Display august of man's inheritance,
Of Britain's calm felicity and power!

XXXIX
THE HAUNTED TREE

TO ——

[Composed 1819.—Published 1820.]

THOSE silver clouds collected round the sun
His mid-day warmth abate not, seeming less
To overshade than multiply his beams
By soft reflection—grateful to the sky,
To rocks, fields, woods. Nor doth our human sense

Ask, for its pleasure, screen or canopy
More ample than the time-dismantled Oak
Spreads o'er this tuft of heath, which now,
    attired
In the whole fulness of its bloom, affords
Couch beautiful as e'er for earthly use   10
Was fashioned; whether by the hand of
    Art,
That eastern Sultan, amid flowers en-
    wrought
On silken tissue, might diffuse his limbs
In languor; or by Nature, for repose
Of panting Wood-nymph, wearied with
    the chase.   15
O Lady! fairer in thy Poet's sight
Than fairest spiritual creature of the
    groves,
Approach;—and, thus invited, crown with
    rest
The noon-tide hour: though truly some
    there are
Whose footsteps superstitiously avoid   20
This venerable Tree; for, when the wind
Blows keenly, it sends forth a creaking
    sound
(Above the general roar of woods and
    crags)
Distinctly heard from far—a doleful note!
As if (so Grecian shepherds would have
    deemed)   25
The Hamadryad, pent within, bewailed
Some bitter wrong. Nor is it unbelieved,
By ruder fancy, that a troubled ghost
Haunts the old trunk; lamenting deeds
    of which
The flowery ground is conscious. But no
    wind   30
Sweeps now along this elevated ridge;
Not even a zephyr stirs;—the obnoxious
    Tree
Is mute; and, in his silence, would look
    down,
O lovely Wanderer of the trackless hills,
On thy reclining form with more delight
Than his coevals in the sheltered vale   36
Seem to participate, the while they view
Their own far-stretching arms and leafy
    heads
Vividly pictured in some glassy pool,
That, for a brief space, checks the hurrying
    stream!   40

XL
THE TRIAD

[Composed 1828.—Published 1829 (*The Keepsake*); ed. 1832.]

SHOW me the noblest Youth of present
    time,
Whose trembling fancy would to love give
    birth;
Some God or Hero, from the Olympian
    clime
Returned, to seek a Consort upon earth;

Or, in no doubtful prospect, let me see   6
The brightest star of ages yet to be,
And I will mate and match him blissfully.

I will not fetch a Naiad from a flood
Pure as herself—(song lacks not mightier
    power)
Nor leaf-crowned Dryad from a pathless
    wood,   10
Nor Sea-nymph glistening from her coral
    bower;
Mere Mortals, bodied forth in vision still,
Shall with Mount Ida's triple lustre fill
The chaster coverts of a British hill.

'Appear!—obey my lyre's command!
Come, like the Graces, hand in hand!   16
For ye, though not by birth allied,
Are Sisters in the bond of love;
Nor shall the tongue of envious pride   19
Presume those interweavings to reprove
In you, which that fair progeny of Jove
Learned from the tuneful spheres that
    glide
In endless union, earth and sea above.'

—I sing in vain;—the pines have hushed
    their waving:
A peerless Youth expectant at my side,   25
Breathless as they, with unabated craving
Looks to the earth, and to the vacant air;
And, with a wandering eye that seems to
    chide,
Asks of the clouds what occupants they
    hide:—
But why solicit more than sight could
    bear,   30
By casting on a moment all we dare?
Invoke we those bright Beings one by
    one;
And what was boldly promised, truly
    shall be done.

'Fear not a constraining measure!
—Yielding to this gentle spell,   35
Lucida! from domes of pleasure,
Or from cottage-sprinkled dell,
Come to regions solitary,
Where the eagle builds her aery,
Above the hermit's long-forsaken cell!'
—She comes!—behold   41
That Figure, like a ship with snow-white
    sail!
Nearer she draws; a breeze uplifts her
    veil;
Upon her coming wait
As pure a sunshine and as soft a gale   45
As e'er, on herbage covering earthly
    mould,
Tempted the bird of Juno to unfold
His richest splendour—when his veering
    gait
And every motion of his starry train
Seem governed by a strain   50
Of music, audible to him alone.

'O Lady, worthy of earth's proudest throne!
Nor less, by excellence of nature, fit
Beside an unambitious hearth to sit
Domestic queen, where grandeur is unknown;   55
What living man could fear
The worst of Fortune's malice, wert Thou near,
Humbling that lily-stem, thy sceptre meek,
That its fair flowers may from his cheek
Brush the too happy tear?   60
——Queen, and handmaid lowly!
Whose skill can speed the day with lively cares,
And banish melancholy
By all that mind invents or hand prepares;
O Thou, against whose lip, without its smile   65
And in its silence even, no heart is proof;
Whose goodness, sinking deep, would reconcile
The softest Nursling of a gorgeous palace
To the bare life beneath the hawthorn-roof
Of Sherwood's Archer, or in caves of Wallace—   70
Who that hath seen thy beauty could content
His soul with but a *glimpse* of heavenly day?
Who that hath loved thee, but would lay
His strong hand on the wind, if it were bent
To take thee in thy majesty away?   75
—Pass onward (even the glancing deer
Till we depart intrude not here;)
That mossy slope, o'er which the woodbine throws
A canopy, is smoothed for thy repose!'

Glad moment is it when the throng   80
Of warblers in full concert strong
Strive, and not vainly strive, to rout
The lagging shower, and force coy Phœbus out,
Met by the rainbow's form divine,
Issuing from her cloudy shrine;—   85
So may the thrillings of the lyre
Prevail to further our desire,
While to these shades a sister Nymph I call.

'Come, if the notes thine ear may pierce,
Come, youngest of the lovely Three,   90
Submissive to the might of verse
And the dear voice of harmony,
By none more deeply felt than Thee!'
—I sang; and lo! from pastimes virginal
She hastens to the tents   95
Of nature, and the lonely elements.
Air sparkles round her with a dazzling sheen;
But mark her glowing cheek, her vesture green!

And, as if wishful to disarm
Or to repay the potent Charm,   100
She bears the stringèd lute of old romance,
That cheered the trellised arbour's privacy,
And soothed war-wearied knights in raftered hall.
How vivid, yet how delicate, her glee!
So tripped the Muse, inventress of the dance;   105
So, truant in waste woods, the blithe Euphrosyne!

But the ringlets of that head
Why are they ungarlanded?
Why bedeck her temples less
Than the simplest shepherdess?   110
Is it not a brow inviting
Choicest flowers that ever breathed,
Which the myrtle would delight in
With Idalian rose enwreathed?
But her humility is well content   115
With *one* wild floweret (call it not forlorn)
FLOWER OF THE WINDS, beneath her bosom worn—
Yet more for love than ornament.

Open, ye thickets! let her fly,
Swift as a Thracian Nymph o'er field and height!   120
For She, to all but those who love her, shy,
Would gladly vanish from a Stranger's sight;
Though, where she is beloved and loves,
Light as the wheeling butterfly she moves;
Her happy spirit as a bird is free,   125
That rifles blossoms on a tree,
Turning them inside out with arch audacity.
Alas! how little can a moment show
Of an eye where feeling plays
In ten thousand dewy rays;   130
A face o'er which a thousand shadows go!
—She stops—is fastened to that rivulet's side;
And there (while, with sedater mien,
O'er timid waters that have scarcely left
Their birthplace in the rocky cleft   135
She bends) at leisure may be seen
Features to old ideal grace allied,
Amid their smiles and dimples dignified—
Fit countenance for the soul of primal truth;
The bland composure of eternal youth!
What more changeful than the sea?   141
But over his great tides
Fidelity presides;
And this light-hearted Maiden constant is as he.
High is her aim as heaven above,   145
And wide as ether her good-will;
And, like the lowly reed, her love
Can drink its nurture from the scantiest rill:

Insight as keen as frosty star
Is to *her* charity no bar,   150
Nor interrupts her frolic graces
When she is, far from these wild places,
Encircled by familiar faces.

O the charm that manners draw,
Nature, from thy genuine law!   155
If from what her hand would do,
Her voice would utter, aught ensue
Untoward or unfit;
She, in benign affections pure,
In self-forgetfulness secure,   160
Sheds round the transient harm or vague
    mischance
A light unknown to tutored elegance:
Hers is not a cheek shame-stricken,
But her blushes are joy-flushes;
And the fault (if fault it be)   165
Only ministers to quicken
Laughter-loving gaiety,
And kindle sportive wit—
Leaving this Daughter of the mountains
    free,
As if she knew that Oberon king of
    Faery   170
Had crossed her purpose with some quaint
    vagary,
And heard his viewless bands
Over their mirthful triumph clapping
    hands.

'Last of the Three, though eldest born,
Reveal thyself, like pensive Morn   175
Touched by the skylark's earliest note,
Ere humbler gladness be afloat.
But whether in the semblance drest
Of Dawn—or Eve, fair vision of the west,
Come with each anxious hope subdued
By woman's gentle fortitude,   181
Each grief, through meekness, settling
    into rest.
—Or I would hail thee when some high-
    wrought page
Of a closed volume lingering in thy hand
Has raised thy spirit to a peaceful stand
Among the glories of a happier age.'   186

Her brow hath opened on me—see it
    there,
Brightening the umbrage of her hair;
So gleams the crescent moon, that loves
To be descried through shady groves.
Tenderest bloom is on her cheek;   191
Wish not for a richer streak;
Nor dread the depth of meditative eye;
But let thy love, upon that azure field
Of thoughtfulness and beauty, yield   195
Its homage offered up in purity.
What wouldst thou more? In sunny glade,
Or under leaves of thickest shade,
Was such a stillness e'er diffused
Since earth grew calm while angels
    mused?   200

Softly she treads, as if her foot were loth
To crush the mountain dew-drops—soon
    to melt
On the flower's breast; as if she felt
That flowers themselves, whate'er their
    hue,
With all their fragrance, all their glisten-
    ing,   205
Call to the heart for inward listening—
And though for bridal wreaths and tokens
    true
Welcomed wisely; though a growth
Which the careless shepherd sleeps on,
As fitly spring from turf the mourner
    weeps on—   210
And without wrong are cropped the mar-
    ble tomb to strew.
The Charm is over; the mute Phantoms
    gone,
Nor will return—but droop not, favoured
    Youth;
The apparition that before thee shone
Obeyed a summons covetous of truth.
From these wild rocks thy footsteps I will
    guide   216
To bowers in which thy fortune may be
    tried,
And one of the bright Three become thy
    happy Bride.

XLI

THE WISHING-GATE

[Composed 1828.—Published 1829 (*The Keep-sake*); ed. 1832.]

In the vale of Grasmere, by the side of the old highway leading to Ambleside, is a gate, which, time out of mind, has been called the Wishing-gate, from a belief that wishes formed or indulged there have a favourable issue.

HOPE rules a land for ever green:
All powers that serve the bright-eyed
    Queen
    Are confident and gay;
Clouds at her bidding disappear;
Points she to aught?—the bliss draws near,
    And Fancy smooths the way.   6

Not such the land of Wishes—there
Dwell fruitless day-dreams, lawless prayer,
    And thoughts with things at strife;
Yet how forlorn, should *ye* depart,   10
Ye superstitions of the *heart*,
    How poor, were human life!

When magic lore abjured its might,
Ye did not forfeit one dear right,
    One tender claim abate;   15
Witness this symbol of your sway,
Surviving near the public way,
    The rustic Wishing-gate!

Enquire not if the faery race
Shed kindly influence on the place,   20
    Ere northward they retired;
If here a warrior left a spell,
Panting for glory as he fell;
    Or here a saint expired.

Enough that all around is fair,   25
Composed with Nature's finest care,
    And in her fondest love—
Peace to embosom and content—
To overawe the turbulent,
    The selfish to reprove.   30

Yea! even the Stranger from afar,
Reclining on this moss-grown bar,
    Unknowing, and unknown,
The infection of the ground partakes,
Longing for his Beloved—who makes   35
    All happiness her own.

Then why should conscious Spirits fear
The mystic stirrings that are here,
    The ancient faith disclaim?
The local Genius ne'er befriends   40
Desires whose course in folly ends,
    Whose just reward is shame.

Smile if thou wilt, but not in scorn,
If some, by ceaseless pains outworn,
    Here crave an easier lot;   45
If some have thirsted to renew
A broken vow, or bind a true,
    With firmer, holier knot.

And not in vain, when thoughts are cast
Upon the irrevocable past,   50
    Some Penitent sincere
May for a worthier future sigh,
While trickles from his downcast eye
    No unavailing tear.

The Worldling, pining to be freed   55
From turmoil, who would turn or speed
    The current of his fate,
Might stop before this favoured scene,
At Nature's call, nor blush to lean
    Upon the Wishing-gate.   60

The Sage, who feels how blind, how weak
Is man, though loth such help to *seek*,
    Yet, passing, here might pause,
And thirst for insight to allay
Misgiving, while the crimson day   65
    In quietness withdraws;

Or when the church-clock's knell profound
To Time's first step across the bound
    Of midnight makes reply;
Time pressing on with starry crest   70
To filial sleep upon the breast
    Of dread eternity.

XLII

THE WISHING-GATE DESTROYED

[Composed (?)—Published 1842.]

'Tis gone—with old belief and dream
That round it clung, and tempting scheme
    Released from fear and doubt;
And the bright landscape too must lie,
By this blank wall, from every eye,   5
    Relentlessly shut out.

Bear witness ye who seldom passed
That opening—but a look ye cast
    Upon the lake below,
What spirit-stirring power it gained   10
From faith which here was entertained,
    Though reason might say no.

Blest is that ground, where, o'er the springs
Of history, Glory claps her wings,
    Fame sheds the exulting tear;   15
Yet earth is wide, and many a nook
Unheard of is, like this, a book
    For modest meanings dear.

It was in sooth a happy thought
That grafted, on so fair a spot,   20
    So confident a token
Of coming good;—the charm is fled;
Indulgent centuries spun a thread,
    Which one harsh day has broken.

Alas! for him who gave the word;   25
Could he no sympathy afford,
    Derived from earth or heaven,
To hearts so oft by hope betrayed;
Their very wishes wanted aid
    Which here was freely given?   30

Where, for the love-lorn maiden's wound,
Will now so readily be found
    A balm of expectation?
Anxious for far-off children, where
Shall mothers breathe a like sweet air   35
    Of home-felt consolation?

And not unfelt will prove the loss
'Mid trivial care and petty cross
    And each day's shallow grief;
Though the most easily beguiled   40
Were oft among the first that smiled
    At their own fond belief.

If still the reckless change we mourn,
A reconciling thought may turn
    To harm that might lurk here,   45
Ere judgment prompted from within
Fit aims, with courage to begin,
    And strength to persevere.

Not Fortune's slave is Man: our state
Enjoins, while firm resolves await   50
    On wishes just and wise,
That strenuous action follow both,
And life be one perpetual growth
    Of heaven-ward enterprise.

So taught, so trained, we boldly face 55
All accidents of time and place;
    Whatever props may fail,
Trust in that sovereign law can spread
New glory o'er the mountain's head,
    Fresh beauty through the vale. 60

That truth informing mind and heart,
The simplest cottager may part,
    Ungrieved, with charm and spell;
And yet, lost Wishing-gate, to thee
The voice of grateful memory 65
    Shall bid a kind farewell![1]

XLIII

THE PRIMROSE OF THE ROCK

[Composed 1831.—Published 1835.]

A ROCK there is whose homely front
    The passing traveller slights;
Yet there the glow-worms hang their
    lamps,
    Like stars, at various heights;
And one coy Primrose to that Rock 5
    The vernal breeze invites.

What hideous warfare hath been waged,
    What kingdoms overthrown,
Since first I spied that Primrose-tuft
    And marked it for my own; 10
A lasting link in Nature's chain
    From highest heaven let down!

The flowers, still faithful to the stems,
    Their fellowship renew;
The stems are faithful to the root, 15
    That worketh out of view;
And to the rock the root adheres
    In every fibre true.

Close clings to earth the living rock,
    Though threatening still to fall; 20
The earth is constant to her sphere;
    And God upholds them all:
So blooms this lonely Plant, nor dreads
    Her annual funeral.

.   .   .   .   .   .

Here closed the meditative strain; 25
    But air breathed soft that day,
The hoary mountain-heights were cheered,
    The sunny vale looked gay;
And to the Primrose of the Rock
    I gave this after-lay. 30

I sang—Let myriads of bright flowers,
    Like Thee, in field and grove
Revive unenvied;—mightier far,
    Than tremblings that reprove
Our vernal tendencies to hope, 35
    Is God's redeeming love;

That love which changed—for wan disease,
    For sorrow that had bent
O'er hopeless dust, for withered age—

[1] See Note, p. 901.

Their moral element, 40
And turned the thistles of a curse
    To types beneficent.

Sin-blighted though we are, we too,
    The reasoning Sons of Men,
From one oblivious winter called 45
    Shall rise, and breathe again;
And in eternal summer lose
    Our threescore years and ten.

To humbleness of heart descends
    This prescience from on high, 50
The faith that elevates the just,
    Before and when they die;
And makes each soul a separate heaven,
    A court for Deity.

XLIV

PRESENTIMENTS

[Composed 1830.—Published 1835.]

PRESENTIMENTS! they judge not right
Who deem that ye from open light
    Retire in fear of shame;
All *heaven-born* Instincts shun the touch
Of vulgar sense,—and, being such, 5
    Such privilege ye claim.

The tear whose source I could not guess,
The deep sigh that seemed fatherless,
    Were mine in early days;
And now, unforced by time to part 10
With fancy, I obey my heart,
    And venture on your praise.

What though some busy foes to good,
Too potent over nerve and blood,
    Lurk near you—and combine 15
To taint the health which ye infuse;
This hides not from the moral Muse
    Your origin divine.

How oft from you, derided Powers!
Comes Faith that in auspicious hours 20
    Builds castles, not of air:
Bodings unsanctioned by the will
Flow from your visionary skill,
    And teach us to beware.

The bosom-weight, your stubborn gift, 25
That no philosophy can lift,
    Shall vanish, if ye please,
Like morning mist: and, where it lay,
The spirits at your bidding play
    In gaiety and ease. 30

Star-guided contemplations move
Through space, though calm, not raised
    above
    Prognostics that ye rule;
The naked Indian of the wild,
And haply too the cradled Child, 35
    Are pupils of your school.

But who can fathom your intents,
Number their signs or instruments?
    A rainbow, a sunbeam,
A subtle smell that Spring unbinds,   40
Dead pause abrupt of midnight winds,
    An echo, or a dream.

The laughter of the Christmas hearth
With sighs of self-exhausted mirth
    Ye feelingly reprove;   45
And daily, in the conscious breast,
Your visitations are a test
    And exercise of love.

When some great change gives boundless
        scope
To an exulting Nation's hope   50
    Oft, startled and made wise
By your low-breathed interpretings,
The simply-meek foretaste the springs
    Of bitter contraries.

Ye daunt the proud array of war,   55
Pervade the lonely ocean far
    As sail hath been unfurled;
For dancers in the festive hall
What ghastly partners haunt your call
    Fetched from the shadowy world.   60

'Tis said that warnings ye dispense,
Emboldened by a keener sense;
    That men have lived for whom,
With dread precision, ye made clear
The hour that in a distant year   65
    Should knell them to the tomb.

Unwelcome insight! Yet there are
Blest times when mystery is laid bare,
    Truth shows a glorious face,   69
While on that isthmus which commands
The councils of both worlds she stands,
    Sage Spirits! by your grace.

God, who instructs the brutes to scent
All changes of the element,
    Whose wisdom fixed the scale   75
Of natures, for our wants provides
By higher, sometimes humbler, guides,
    When lights of reason fail.

XLV
VERNAL ODE
[Composed 1817.—Published 1820.]
'Rerum Natura tota est nusquam magis quam
in minimis.'—PLIN. *Nat. Hist.*

I

BENEATH the concave of an April sky,
When all the fields with freshest green
        were dight,
Appeared, in presence of the spiritual eye
That aids or supersedes our grosser sight,
The form and rich habiliments of One   5
Whose countenance bore resemblance to
        the sun,

When it reveals, in evening majesty,
Features half lost amid their own pure
        light.
Poised like a weary cloud, in middle air
He hung,—then floated with angelic ease
(Softening that bright effulgence by de-
        grees)   11
Till he had reached a summit sharp and
        bare,
Where oft the venturous heifer drinks the
        noontide breeze.
Upon the apex of that lofty cone
Alighted, there the Stranger stood alone;
Fair as a gorgeous Fabric of the east   16
Suddenly raised by some enchanter's
        power,
Where nothing was; and firm as some old
        Tower
Of Britain's realm, whose leafy crest
Waves high, embellished by a gleaming
        shower!   20

II

Beneath the shadow of his purple wings
Rested a golden harp;—he touched the
        strings;
And, after prelude of unearthly sound
Poured through the echoing hills around,
He sang—
        'No wintry desolations,   25
Scorching blight or noxious dew,
Affect my native habitations;
Buried in glory, far beyond the scope
Of man's enquiring gaze, but to his hope
Imaged, though faintly, in the hue   30
Profound of night's ethereal blue;
And in the aspect of each radiant orb;—
Some fixed, some wandering with no
        timid curb;
But wandering star and fixed, to mortal
        eye,
Blended in absolute serenity,   35
And free from semblance of decline;—
Fresh as if Evening brought their natal
        hour,
Her darkness splendour gave, her silence
        power,
To testify of Love and Grace divine.

III

'What if those bright fires   40
Shine subject to decay,
Sons haply of extinguished sires,
Themselves to lose their light, or pass
        away
Like clouds before the wind,
Be thanks poured out to Him whose hand
        bestows,   45
Nightly, on human kind
That vision of endurance and repose.
—And though to every draught of vital
        breath,
Renewed throughout the bounds of earth
        or ocean,

The melancholy gates of Death   50
Respond with sympathetic motion;
Though all that feeds on nether air
Howe'er magnificent or fair,
Grows but to perish, and entrust
Its ruins to their kindred dust;   55
Yet, by the Almighty's ever-during care,
Her procreant vigils Nature keeps
Amid the unfathomable deeps;
And saves the peopled fields of earth
From dread of emptiness or dearth.   60
Thus, in their stations, lifting tow'rd the sky
The foliaged head in cloud-like majesty,
The shadow-casting race of trees survive:
Thus, in the train of Spring, arrive
Sweet flowers;—what living eye hath
        viewed   65
Their myriads?—endlessly renewed,
Wherever strikes the sun's glad ray;
Where'er the subtle waters stray;
Wherever sportive breezes bend
Their course, or genial showers descend!
Mortals, rejoice! the very Angels quit   71
Their mansions unsusceptible of change,
Amid your pleasant bowers to sit,
And through your sweet vicissitudes to
        range!'

IV

O, nursed at happy distance from the
        cares   75
Of a too-anxious world, mild pastoral
        Muse!
That to the sparkling crown Urania wears,
And to her sister Clio's laurel wreath,
Preferr'st a garland culled from purple
        heath,
Or blooming thicket moist with morning
        dews;   80
Was such bright Spectacle vouchsafed
        to me?
And was it granted to the simple ear
Of thy contented Votary
Such melody to hear!   84
Him rather suits it, side by side with thee,
Wrapped in a fit of pleasing indolence,
While thy tired lute hangs on the haw-
        thorn-tree,
To lie and listen—till o'er-drowsèd sense
Sinks, hardly conscious of the influence—
To the soft murmur of the vagrant Bee.
—A slender sound! yet hoary Time   91
Doth to the *Soul* exalt it with the chime
Of all his years;—a company
Of ages coming, ages gone;
(Nations from before them sweeping,   95
Regions in destruction steeping,)
But every awful note in unison
With that faint utterance, which tells
Of treasure sucked from buds and bells,
For the pure keeping of those waxen
        cells;   100
Where She—a statist prudent to confer
Upon the common weal; a warrior bold,

Radiant all over with unburnished gold,
And armed with living spear for mortal
        fight;
        A cunning forager   105
That spreads no waste; a social builder;
        one
In whom all busy offices unite
With all fine functions that afford delight—
Safe through the winter storm in quiet
        dwells!

V

And is She brought within the power   110
Of vision?—o'er this tempting flower
Hovering until the petals stay
Her flight, and take its voice away!—
Observe each wing!—a tiny van!
The structure of her laden thigh,   115
How fragile! yet of ancestry
Mysteriously remote and high;
High as the imperial front of man;
The roseate bloom on woman's cheek;
The soaring eagle's curvèd beak;   120
The white plumes of the floating swan;
Old as the tiger's paw, the lion's mane
Ere shaken by that mood of stern disdain
At which the desert trembles.—Humming
        Bee!
Thy sting was needless then, perchance
        unknown,   125
The seeds of malice were not sown;
All creatures met in peace, from fierceness
        free,
And no pride blended with their dignity.
—Tears had not broken from their source;
Nor Anguish strayed from her Tartarean
        den;   130
The golden years maintained a course
Not undiversified though smooth and
        even;
We were not mocked with glimpse and
        shadow then,
Bright Seraphs mixed familiarly with men;
And earth and stars composed a universal
        heaven!   135

XLVI

DEVOTIONAL INCITEMENTS

[Composed 1832.—Published 1835.]

'Not to the earth confined,
Ascend to heaven.'

WHERE will they stop, those breathing
        Powers,
The Spirits of the new-born flowers?
They wander with the breeze, they wind
Where'er the streams a passage find;
Up from their native ground they rise   5
In mute aerial harmonies;
From humble violet—modest thyme—
Exhaled, the essential odours climb,
As if no space below the sky
Their subtle flight could satisfy: 10

181

Heaven will not tax our thoughts with
    pride
If like ambition be *their* guide.

Roused by this kindliest of May-
    showers,
The spirit-quickener of the flowers,
That with moist virtue softly cleaves   15
The buds, and freshens the young leaves,
The birds pour forth their souls in notes
Of rapture from a thousand throats—
Here checked by too impetuous haste,
While there the music runs to waste,   20
With bounty more and more enlarged,
Till the whole air is overcharged;
Give ear, O Man! to their appeal,
And thirst for no inferior zeal,
Thou, who canst *think*, as well as feel.   25

Mount from the earth; aspire! aspire!
So pleads the town's cathedral quire,
In strains that from their solemn height
Sink, to attain a loftier flight;
While incense from the altar breathes   30
Rich fragrance in embodied wreaths;
Or, flung from swinging censer, shrouds
The taper-lights, and curls in clouds
Around angelic Forms, the still
Creation of the painter's skill,   35
That on the service wait concealed
One moment, and the next revealed.
—Cast off your bonds, awake, arise,
And for no transient ecstasies!
What else can mean the visual plea   40
Of still or moving imagery—
The iterated summons loud,
Not wasted on the attendant crowd,
Nor wholly lost upon the throng
Hurrying the busy streets along?   45

Alas! the sanctities combined
By art to unsensualise the mind
Decay and languish; or, as creeds
And humours change, are spurned like
    weeds:
The priests are from their altars thrust;
Temples are levelled with the dust;   51
And solemn rites and awful forms
Founder amid fanatic storms.
Yet evermore, through years renewed
In undisturbed vicissitude   55
Of seasons balancing their flight
On the swift wings of day and night,
Kind Nature keeps a heavenly door
Wide open for the scattered Poor.
Where flower-breathed incense to the
    skies   60
Is wafted in mute harmonies;
And ground fresh-cloven by the plough
Is fragrant with a humbler vow;
Where birds and brooks from leafy dells
Chime forth unwearied canticles,   65
And vapours magnify and spread
The glory of the sun's bright head—

Still constant in her worship, still
Conforming to the eternal Will,
Whether men sow or reap the fields,   70
Divine monition Nature yields,
That not by bread alone we live,
Or what a hand of flesh can give;
That every day should leave some part
Free for a sabbath of the heart: 75
So shall the seventh be truly blest,
From morn to eve, with hallowed rest.

XLVII

THE CUCKOO-CLOCK

[Composed (?).—Published 1842.]

WOULDST thou be taught, when sleep has
    taken flight,
By a sure voice that can most sweetly tell,
How far off yet a glimpse of morning
    light,
And if to lure the truant back be well,
Forbear to covet a Repeater's stroke,   5
That, answering to thy touch, will sound
    the hour;
Better provide thee with a Cuckoo-clock,
For service hung behind thy chamber-
    door;
And in due time the soft spontaneous
    shock,
The double note, as if with living power,
Will to composure lead—or make thee
    blithe as bird in bower.   11

List, Cuckoo—Cuckoo!—oft tho' tem-
    pests howl,
Or nipping frost remind thee trees are
    bare,
How cattle pine, and droop the shivering
    fowl,
Thy spirits will seem to feed on balmy air:
I speak with knowledge,—by that Voice
    beguiled,   16
Thou wilt salute old memories as they
    throng
Into thy heart; and fancies, running wild
Through fresh green fields, and budding
    groves among,
Will make thee happy, happy as a child;
Of sunshine wilt thou think, and flowers,
    and song,   21
And breathe as in a world where nothing
    can go wrong.

And know—that, even for him who shuns
    the day
And nightly tosses on a bed of pain;
Whose joys, from all but memory swept
    away,   25
Must come unhoped for, if they come
    again;
Know—that, for him whose waking
    thoughts, severe
As his distress is sharp, would scorn my
    theme,

The mimic notes, striking upon his ear
In sleep, and intermingling with his
    dream,   30
Could from sad regions send him to a dear
Delightful land of verdure, shower and
    gleam,
To mock the *wandering* Voice beside some
    haunted stream.
O bounty without measure! while the
    grace
Of Heaven doth in such wise, from hum-
    blest springs,   35
Pour pleasure forth, and solaces that trace
A mazy course along familiar things,
Well may our hearts have faith that bless-
    ings come,
Streaming from founts above the starry
    sky,
With angels when their own untroubled
    home   40
They leave, and speed on nightly embassy
To visit earthly chambers,—and for
    whom?
Yea, both for souls who God's forbear-
    ance try,
And those that seek his help, and for his
    mercy sigh.

XLVIII

TO THE CLOUDS

[Composed (?).—Published 1842.]

ARMY of Clouds! ye wingèd Host in troops
Ascending from behind the motionless
    brow
Of that tall rock, as from a hidden world,
Oh whither with such eagerness of speed?
What seek ye, or what shun ye? of the gale
Companions, fear ye to be left behind,
Or racing o'er your blue ethereal field   7
Contend ye with each other? of the sea
Children, thus post ye over vale and
    height
To sink upon your mother's lap—and
    rest?   10
Or were ye rightlier hailed, when first
    mine eyes
Beheld in your impetuous march the
    likeness
Of a wide army pressing on to meet
Or overtake some unknown enemy?—
But your smooth motions suit a peaceful
    aim;   15
And Fancy, not less aptly pleased, com-
    pares
Your squadrons to an endless flight of
    birds
Aerial, upon due migration bound
To milder climes; or rather do ye urge
In caravan your hasty pilgrimage   20
To pause at last on more aspiring heights
Than these, and utter your devotion there
With thunderous voice? Or are ye jubilant,

And would ye, tracking your proud lord
    the Sun,
Be present at his setting; or the pomp   25
Of Persian mornings would ye fill, and
    stand
Poising your splendours high above the
    heads
Of worshippers kneeling to their up-risen
    God?
Whence, whence, ye Clouds! this eager-
    ness of speed?
Speak, silent creatures.—They are gone,
    are fled,   30
Buried together in yon gloomy mass
That loads the middle heaven; and clear
    and bright
And vacant doth the region which they
    thronged
Appear; a calm descent of sky conducting
Down to the unapproachable abyss,   35
Down to that hidden gulf from which
    they rose
To vanish—fleet as days and months and
    years,
Fleet as the generations of mankind,
Power, glory, empire, as the world itself,
The lingering world, when time hath
    ceased to be.   40
But the winds roar, shaking the rooted
    trees,
And see! a bright precursor to a train
Perchance as numerous, overpeers the rock
That sullenly refuses to partake
Of the wild impulse. From a fount of
    life   45
Invisible, the long procession moves
Luminous or gloomy, welcome to the vale
Which they are entering, welcome to
    mine eye
That sees them, to my soul that owns in
    them,
And in the bosom of the firmament   50
O'er which they move, wherein they are
    contained,
A type of her capacious self and all
Her restless progeny.
                  A humble walk
Here is my body doomed to tread, this
    path,
A little hoary line and faintly traced,   55
Work, shall we call it, of the shepherd's
    foot
Or of his flock?—joint vestige of them
    both.
I pace it unrepining, for my thoughts
Admit no bondage and my words have
    wings.
Where is the Orphean lyre, or Druid
    harp,   60
To accompany the verse? The mountain
    blast
Shall be our *hand* of music; he shall sweep
The rocks, and quivering trees, and bil-
    lowy lake,

183

And search the fibres of the caves, and they
Shall answer, for our song is of the
 Clouds,   65
And the wind loves them; and the gentle
 gales—
Which by their aid re-clothe the naked lawn
With annual verdure, and revive the
 woods,
And moisten the parched lips of thirsty
 flowers—
Love them; and every idle breeze of air
Bends to the favourite burthen. Moon
 and stars   71
Keep their most solemn vigils when the
 Clouds
Watch also, shifting peaceably their place
Like bands of ministering Spirits, or when
 they lie,
As if some Protean art the change had
 wrought,   75
In listless quiet o'er the ethereal deep
Scattered, a Cyclades of various shapes
And all degrees of beauty. O ye Light-
 nings!
Ye are their perilous offspring; and the
 Sun—
Source inexhaustible of life and joy,   80
And type of man's far-darting reason,
 therefore
In old time worshipped as the god of verse,
A blazing intellectual deity—
Loves his own glory in their looks, and
 showers
Upon that unsubstantial brotherhood
Visions with all but beatific light   86
Enriched—too transient, were they not
 renewed
From age to age, and did not, while we
 gaze
In silent rapture, credulous desire
Nourish the hope that memory lacks not
 power   90
To keep the treasure unimpaired. Vain
 thought!
Yet why repine, created as we are
For joy and rest, albeit to find them only
Lodged in the bosom of eternal things?

XLIX
SUGGESTED BY A PICTURE OF THE BIRD OF PARADISE

[Composed (?).—Published 1842.]

The gentlest Poet, with free thoughts
 endowed,
And a true master of the glowing strain,
Might scan the narrow province with
 disdain
That to the Painter's skill is here allowed.
This, this the Bird of Paradise! disclaim
The daring thought, forget the name;   6
This the Sun's Bird, whom Glendoveers
 might own

As no unworthy Partner in their flight
Through seas of ether, where the ruffling
 sway
Of nether air's rude billows is unknown;
Whom Sylphs, if e'er for casual pastime
 they   11
Through India's spicy regions wing their
 way,
Might bow to as their Lord. What
 character,
O sovereign Nature! I appeal to thee,
Of all thy feathered progeny   15
Is so unearthly, and what shape so fair?
So richly decked in variegated down,
Green, sable, shining yellow, shadowy
 brown,
Tints softly with each other blended,
Hues doubtfully begun and ended;   20
Or intershooting, and to sight
Lost and recovered, as the rays of light
Glance on the conscious plumes touched
 here and there?
Full surely, when with such proud gifts
 of life
Began the pencil's strife,   25
O'erweening Art was caught as in a snare.

A sense of seemingly presumptuous
 wrong
Gave the first impulse to the Poet's song;
But, of his scorn repenting soon, he drew
A juster judgment from a calmer view; 30
And, with a spirit freed from discontent,
Thankfully took an effort that was meant
Not with God's bounty, Nature's love,
 to vie,
Or made with hope to please that inward
 eye   34
Which ever strives in vain itself to satisfy,
But to recall the truth by some faint trace
Of power ethereal and celestial grace,
That in the living Creature find on earth
 a place.

L
A JEWISH FAMILY
(IN A SMALL VALLEY OPPOSITE ST. GOAR, UPON THE RHINE)

[Composed 1828.—Published 1835.]

Genius of Raphael! if thy wings
 Might bear thee to this glen,
With faithful memory left of things
 To pencil dear and pen,
Thou wouldst forego the neighbouring
 Rhine,   5
 And all his majesty—
A studious forehead to incline
 O'er this poor family.

The Mother—her thou must have seen,
 In spirit, ere she came   10
To dwell these rifted rocks between,
 Or found on earth a name;

An image, too, of that sweet Boy,
  Thy inspirations give—
Of playfulness, and love, and joy,   15
  Predestined here to live.

Downcast, or shooting glances far,
  How beautiful his eyes,
That blend the nature of the star
  With that of summer skies!   20
I speak as if of sense beguiled;
  Uncounted months are gone,
Yet am I with the Jewish Child,
  That exquisite Saint John.

I see the dark-brown curls, the brow, 25
  The smooth transparent skin,
Refined, as with intent to show
  The holiness within;
The grace of parting Infancy
  By blushes yet untamed;   30
Age faithful to the mother's knee,
  Nor of her arms ashamed.

Two lovely Sisters, still and sweet
  As flowers, stand side by side;
Their soul-subduing looks might cheat
  The Christian of his pride: 36
Such beauty hath the Eternal poured
  Upon them not forlorn,
Though of a lineage once abhorred,
  Nor yet redeemed from scorn.   40

Mysterious safeguard, that, in spite
  Of poverty and wrong,
Doth here preserve a living light,
  From Hebrew fountains sprung;
That gives this ragged group to cast 45
  Around the dell a gleam
Of Palestine, of glory past,
  And proud Jerusalem!

LI

ON THE POWER OF SOUND

[Composed 1828.—Published 1835.]

ARGUMENT

The Ear addressed, as occupied by a spiritual func-
tionary, in communion with sounds, individual,
or combined in studied harmony.—Sources and
effects of those sounds (to the close of 6th
Stanza).—The power of music, whence proceeding, exemplified in the idiot.—Origin of music,
and its effect in early ages—how produced (to
the middle of 10th Stanza).—The mind recalled
to sounds acting casually and severally.—Wish
uttered (11th Stanza) that these could be united
into a scheme or system for moral interests and
intellectual contemplation.—(Stanza 12th).—
The Pythagorean theory of numbers and music,
with their supposed power over the motions of
the universe—imaginations consonant with such
a theory.—Wish expressed (in 11th Stanza)
realized, in some degree, by the representation
of all sounds under the form of thanksgiving to
the Creator.—(Last Stanza) the destruction o
earth and the planetary system—the survival of
audible harmony, and its support in the Divine
Nature, as revealed in Holy Writ.

I

THY functions are ethereal,
As if within thee dwelt a glancing mind,
Organ of vision! And a Spirit aërial
Informs the cell of Hearing, dark and blind;
Intricate labyrinth, more dread for thought
To enter than oracular cave;   6
Strict passage, through which sighs are
  brought,
And whispers for the heart, their slave;
And shrieks, that revel in abuse
Of shivering flesh; and warbled air,   10
Whose piercing sweetness can unloose
The chains of frenzy, or entice a smile
Into the ambush of despair;
Hosannas pealing down the long-drawn
  aisle,
And requiems answered by the pulse that
  beats   15
Devoutly, in life's last retreats!

II

The headlong streams and fountains
Serve Thee, invisible Spirit, with untired
  powers;
Cheering the wakeful tent on Syrian
  mountains,
They lull perchance ten thousand thou-
  sand flowers.   20
That roar, the prowling lion's *Here I am*,
How fearful to the desert wide!
That bleat, how tender! of the dam
Calling a straggler to her side.
Shout, cuckoo!—let the vernal soul   25
Go with thee to the frozen zone;
Toll from thy loftiest perch, lone bell-
  bird, toll!
At the still hour to Mercy dear,
Mercy from her twilight throne
Listening to nun's faint throb of holy fear,
To sailor's prayer breathed from a darken-
  ing sea,   31
Or widow's cottage-lullaby.

III

Ye Voices, and ye Shadows
And Images of voice—to hound and horn
From rocky steep and rock-bestudded
  meadows   35
Flung back, and, in the sky's blue caves,
  reborn—
On with your pastime! till the church-
  tower bells
A greeting give of measured glee;
And milder echoes from their cells
Repeat the bridal symphony.   40
Then, or far earlier, let us rove
Where mists are breaking up or gone,
And from aloft look down into a cove
Besprinkled with a careless quire,
Happy milk-maids, one by one   45
Scattering a ditty each to her desire,
A liquid conceit matchless by nice Art,
A stream as if from one full heart.

POEMS OF THE IMAGINATION

IV

Blest be the song that brightens
The blind man's gloom, exalts the vete-
   ran's mirth;   50
Unscorned the peasant's whistling breath,
   that lightens
His duteous toil of furrowing the green
   earth.
For the tired slave, Song lifts the languid
   oar,
And bids it aptly fall, with chime
That beautifies the fairest shore,   55
And mitigates the harshest clime.
Yon pilgrims see—in lagging file
They move; but soon the appointed way
A choral *Ave Marie* shall beguile,
And to their hope the distant shrine   60
Glisten with a livelier ray:
Nor friendless he, the prisoner of the
   mine,
Who from the well-spring of his own
   clear breast
Can draw, and sing his griefs to rest.

V

When civic renovation   65
Dawns on a kingdom, and for needful
   haste
Best eloquence avails not, Inspiration
Mounts with a tune, that travels like a
   blast
Piping through cave and battlemented
   tower;
Then starts the sluggard, pleased to meet
That voice of Freedom, in its power 71
Of promises, shrill, wild, and sweet!
Who, from a martial *pageant*, spreads
Incitements of a battle-day,
Thrilling the unweaponed crowd with
   plumeless heads?—   75
Even She whose Lydian airs inspire
Peaceful striving, gentle play
Of timid hope and innocent desire
Shot from the dancing Graces, as they
   move
Fanned by the plausive wings of Love. 80

VI

How oft along thy mazes,
Regent of sound, have dangerous Passions
   trod!
O Thou, through whom the temple rings
   with praises,
And blackening clouds in thunder speak
   of God,
Betray not by the cozenage of sense   85
Thy votaries, wooingly resigned
To a voluptuous influence
That taints the purer, better, mind;
But lead sick Fancy to a harp
That hath in noble tasks been tried;   90
And, if the virtuous feel a pang too sharp;
Soothe it into patience—stay
The uplifted arm of Suicide;

And let some mood of thine in firm array
Knit every thought the impending issue
   needs,   95
Ere martyr burns, or patriot bleeds!

VII

As Conscience, to the centre
Of being, smites with irresistible pain,
So shall a solemn cadence, if it enter
The mouldy vaults of the dull idiot's
   brain,   100
Transmute him to a wretch from quiet
   hurled—
Convulsed as by a jarring din;
And then aghast, as at the world
Of reason partially let in
By concords winding with a sway   105
Terrible for sense and soul!
Or awed he weeps, struggling to quell
   dismay.
Point not these mysteries to an Art
Lodged above the starry pole;
Pure modulations flowing from the heart
Of divine Love, where Wisdom, Beauty,
   Truth   111
With Order dwell, in endless youth?

VIII

Oblivion may not cover
All treasures hoarded by the miser, Time.
Orphean Insight! truth's undaunted
   lover,   115
To the first leagues of tutored passion
   climb,
When Music deigned within this grosser
   sphere
Her subtle essence to enfold,
And voice and shell drew forth a tear
Softer than Nature's self could mould.
Yet *strenuous* was the infant Age: 121
Art, daring because souls could feel,
Stirred nowhere but an urgent equipage
Of rapt imagination sped her march
Through the realms of woe and weal: 125
Hell to the lyre bowed low; the upper
   arch
Rejoiced that clamorous spell and magic
   verse
Her wan disasters could disperse.

IX

The GIFT to king Amphion
That walled a city with its melody   130
Was for belief no dream:—thy skill, Arion!
Could humanize the creatures of the sea,
Where men were monsters. A last grace
   he craves,
Leave for one chant;—the dulcet sound
Steals from the deck o'er willing waves,
And listening dolphins gather round.
Self-cast, as with a desperate course, 137
'Mid that strange audience, he bestrides
A proud One docile as a managed horse;
And singing, while the accordant hand

Sweeps his harp, the Master rides;   141
So shall he touch at length a friendly
    strand,
And he, with his preserver, shine star-
    bright
In memory, through silent night.

X

The pipe of Pan, to shepherds   145
Couched in the shadow of Mænalian
    pines,
Was passing sweet; the eyeballs of the
    leopards,
That in high triumph drew the Lord of
    vines,
How did they sparkle to the cymbal's
    clang!
While Fauns and Satyrs beat the ground
In cadence,—and Silenus swang   151
This way and that, with wild-flowers
    crowned.
To life, to *life* give back thine ear:
Ye who are longing to be rid
Of fable, though to truth subservient,
    hear   155
The little sprinkling of cold earth that fell
Echoed from the coffin-lid;
The convict's summons in the steeple's
    knell;
'The vain distress-gun,' from a leeward
    shore,
Repeated—heard, and heard no more!

XI

For terror, joy, or pity,   161
Vast is the compass and the swell of notes:
From the babe's first cry to voice of regal
    city,
Rolling a solemn sea-like bass, that floats
Far as the woodlands—with the trill to
    blend   165
Of that shy songstress, whose love-tale
Might tempt an angel to descend,
While hovering o'er the moonlight vale.
Ye wandering Utterances, has earth no
    scheme,
No scale of moral music—to unite   170
Powers that survive but in the faintest
    dream
Of memory?—O that ye might stoop to
    bear
Chains, such precious chains of sight
As laboured minstrelsies through ages
    wear!
O for a balance fit the truth to tell   175
Of the Unsubstantial, pondered well!

XII

By one pervading spirit
Of tones and numbers all things are con-
    trolled,
As sages taught, where faith was found
    to merit
Initiation in that mystery old.   180

The heavens, whose aspect makes our
    minds as still
As they themselves appear to be,
Innumerable voices fill
With everlasting harmony;
The towering headlands, crowned with
    mist,   185
Their feet among the billows, know
That Ocean is a mighty harmonist;
Thy pinions, universal Air,
Ever waving to and fro,
Are delegates of harmony, and bear   190
Strains that support the Seasons in their
    round;
Stern Winter loves a dirge-like sound.

XIII

Break forth into thanksgiving,
Ye banded instruments of wind and
    chords;
Unite, to magnify the Ever-living,   195
Your inarticulate notes with the voice of
    words!
Nor hushed be service from the lowing
    mead,
Nor mute the forest hum of noon;
Thou too be heard, lone eagle! freed
From snowy peak and cloud, attune   200
Thy hungry barkings to the hymn
Of joy, that from her utmost walls
The six-days' Work by flaming Seraphim
Transmits to Heaven! As Deep to Deep
Shouting through one valley calls,   205
All worlds, all natures, mood and measure
    keep
For praise and ceaseless gratulation,
    poured
Into the ear of God, their Lord!

XIV

A Voice to Light gave Being;
To Time, and Man his earth-born chro-
    nicler;   210
A Voice shall finish doubt and dim fore-
    seeing,
And sweep away life's visionary stir;
The trumpet (we, intoxicate with pride,
Arm at its blast for deadly wars)
To archangelic lips applied,   215
The grave shall open, quench the stars.
O Silence! are Man's noisy years
No more than moments of thy life?
Is Harmony, blest queen of smiles and
    tears,
With her smooth tones and discords just,
Tempered into rapturous strife,   221
Thy destined bond-slave? No! though
    earth be dust
And vanish, though the heavens dissolve,
    her stay
Is in the WORD, that shall not pass
    away.

PETER BELL

A TALE

[Composed 1798.—Published 1819.]

'What's in a *Name?*'
'Brutus will start a Spirit as soon as Cæsar!'

TO ROBERT SOUTHEY, ESQ., P.L., ETC., ETC.

MY DEAR FRIEND,

The Tale of Peter Bell, which I now introduce to your notice, and to that of the Public, has, in its Manuscript state, nearly survived its *minority*:—for it first saw the light in the summer of 1798. During this long interval, pains have been taken at different times to make the production less unworthy of a favourable reception; or rather to fit it for filling *permanently* a station, however humble, in the Literature of our Country. This has, indeed, been the aim of all my endeavours in Poetry, which, you know, have been sufficiently laborious to prove that I deem the Art not lightly to be approached; and that the attainment of excellence in it may laudably be made the principal object of intellectual pursuit by any man, who, with reasonable consideration of circumstances, has faith in his own impulses.

The Poem of Peter Bell, as the Prologue will show, was composed under a belief that the Imagination not only does not require for its exercise the intervention of supernatural agency, but that, though such agency be excluded, the faculty may be called forth as imperiously, and for kindred results of pleasure, by incidents within the compass of poetic probability, in the humblest departments of daily life. Since that Prologue was written, *you* have exhibited most splendid effects of judicious daring in the opposite and usual course. Let this acknowledgment make my peace with the lovers of the supernatural; and I am persuaded it will be admitted that to you, as a Master in that province of the art, the following Tale, whether from contrast or congruity, is not an unappropriate offering. Accept it, then, as a public testimony of affectionate admiration from one with whose name yours has been often coupled (to use your own words) for evil and for good; and believe me to be, with earnest wishes that life and health may be granted you to complete the many important works in which you are engaged, and with high respect,

Most faithfully yours,
WILLIAM WORDSWORTH.

RYDAL MOUNT,
April 7, 1819.

PROLOGUE

THERE'S something in a flying horse,
There's something in a huge balloon;
But through the clouds I'll never float
Until I have a little Boat,
Shaped like the crescent-moon.   5

And now I *have* a little Boat,
In shape a very crescent-moon:
Fast through the clouds my Boat can sail;
But if perchance your faith should fail,
Look up—and you shall see me soon!   10

The woods, my Friends, are round you
          roaring,
Rocking and roaring like a sea;
The noise of danger's in your ears,
And ye have all a thousand fears
Both for my little Boat and me!   15

Meanwhile untroubled I admire
The pointed horns of my canoe;
And, did not pity touch my breast
To see how ye are all distrest,
Till my ribs ached I'd laugh at you!   20

Away we go, my Boat and I—
Frail man ne'er sate in such another;
Whether among the winds we strive,
Or deep into the clouds we dive,
Each is contented with the other.   25

Away we go—and what care we
For treasons, tumults, and for wars?
We are as calm in our delight
As is the crescent-moon so bright
Among the scattered stars.   30

Up goes my Boat among the stars
Through many a breathless field of light,
Through many a long blue field of ether,
Leaving ten thousand stars beneath her:
Up goes my little Boat so bright!   35

The Crab, the Scorpion, and the Bull—
We pry among them all; have shot
High o'er the red-haired race of Mars,
Covered from top to toe with scars;
Such company I like it not!   40

The towns in Saturn are decayed,
And melancholy Spectres throng them;—
The Pleiads, that appear to kiss
Each other in the vast abyss,
With joy I sail among them.   45

Swift Mercury resounds with mirth,
Great Jove is full of stately bowers;
But these, and all that they contain,
What are they to that tiny grain,
That little Earth of ours?   50

Then back to Earth, the dear green
      Earth:—
Whole ages if I here should roam,
The world for my remarks and me
Would not a whit the better be;
I've left my heart at home.   55

See! there she is, the matchless Earth!
There spreads the famed Pacific Ocean!
Old Andes thrusts yon craggy spear
Through the grey clouds; the Alps are
      here,
Like waters in commotion!   60

Yon tawny slip is Libya's sands;
That silver thread the river Dnieper;
And look, where clothed in brightest green
Is a sweet Isle, of isles the Queen;
Ye fairies, from all evil keep her!   65

And see the town where I was born!
Around those happy fields we span
In boyish gambols;—I was lost
Where I have been, but on this coast
I feel I am a man.   70

Never did fifty things at once
Appear so lovely, never, never;
How tunefully the forests ring!
To hear the earth's soft murmuring
Thus could I hang for ever!   75

'Shame on you!' cried my little Boat,
'Was ever such a homesick Loon,
Within a living Boat to sit,
And make no better use of it;   79
A Boat twin-sister of the crescent-moon!

'Ne'er in the breast of full-grown Poet
Fluttered so faint a heart before;—
Was it the music of the spheres
That overpowered your mortal ears?
—Such din shall trouble them no more.

'These nether precincts do not lack   86
Charms of their own;—then come with
      me,
I want a comrade, and for you
There's nothing that I would not do;
Nought is there that you shall not see.   90

'Haste! and above Siberian snows
We'll sport amid the boreal morning;
Will mingle with her lustres gliding
Among the stars, the stars now hiding,
And now the stars adorning.   95

'I know the secrets of a land
Where human foot did never stray;
Fair is that land as evening skies,
And cool, though in the depth it lies
Of burning Africa.   100

'Or we'll into the realm of Faery,
Among the lovely shades of things;
The shadowy forms of mountains bare,
And streams, and bowers, and ladies fair,
The shades of palaces and kings!   105

'Or, if you thirst with hardy zeal
Less quiet regions to explore,
Prompt voyage shall to you reveal
How earth and heaven are taught to feel
The might of magic lore!'   110

'My little vagrant Form of light,
My gay and beautiful Canoe,
Well have you played your friendly part;
As kindly take what from my heart
Experience forces—then adieu!   115

'Temptation lurks among your words;
But, while these pleasures you're pur-
      suing
Without impediment or let,
No wonder if you quite forget
What on the earth is doing.   120

'There was a time when all mankind
Did listen with a faith sincere
To tuneful tongues in mystery versed;
Then Poets fearlessly rehearsed
The wonders of a wild career.   125

'Go—(but the world's a sleepy world,
And 'tis, I fear, an age too late)
Take with you some ambitious Youth!
For, restless Wanderer! I, in truth,
Am all unfit to be your mate.   130

'Long have I loved what I behold,
The night that calms, the day that cheers;
The common growth of mother-earth
Suffices me—her tears, her mirth,
Her humblest mirth and tears.   135

'The dragon's wing, the magic ring,
I shall not covet for my dower,
If I along that lowly way
With sympathetic heart may stray,
And with a soul of power.   140

'These given, what more need I desire
To stir, to soothe, or elevate?
What nobler marvels than the mind
May in life's daily prospect find,
May find or there create?   145

'A potent wand doth Sorrow wield;
What spell so strong as guilty Fear!
Repentance is a tender Sprite;
If aught on earth have heavenly might,
'Tis lodged within her silent tear.   150

'But grant my wishes,—let us now
Descend from this ethereal height;
Then take thy way, adventurous Skiff,
More daring far than Hippogriff,
And be thy own delight!   155

'To the stone-table in my garden,
Loved haunt of many a summer hour,
The Squire is come: his daughter Bess
Beside him in the cool recess
Sits blooming like a flower.   160

'With these are many more convened;
They know not I have been so far;—
I see them there, in number nine,
Beneath the spreading Weymouth-pine!
I see them—there they are!   165

'There sits the Vicar and his Dame;
And there my good friend, Stephen Otter;
And, ere the light of evening fail,
To them I must relate the Tale
Of Peter Bell the Potter.'   170

Off flew the Boat—away she flees,
Spurning her freight with indignation!
And I, as well as I was able,
On two poor legs, toward my stone-table
Limped on with sore vexation.   175

'O, here he is!' cried little Bess—
She saw me at the garden-door;
'We've waited anxiously and long,'
They cried, and all around me throng,
Full nine of them or more!   180

'Reproach me not—your fears be still—
Be thankful we again have met;—
Resume, my Friends! within the shade
Your seats, and quickly shall be paid
The well-remembered debt.'   185

I spake with faltering voice, like one
Not wholly rescued from the pale
Of a wild dream, or worse illusion;
But straight, to cover my confusion,
Began the promised Tale.   190

PART FIRST

ALL by the moonlight river-side
Groaned the poor Beast—alas! in vain;
The staff was raised to loftier height,
And the blows fell with heavier weight
As Peter struck—and struck again.   195

'Hold!' cried the Squire, 'against the rules
Of common sense you're surely sinning;
This leap is for us all too bold;
Who Peter was, et that be told,
And start from the beginning.'   200

——'A Potter,[1] Sir, he was by trade,'
Said I, becoming quite collected;
'And wheresoever he appeared,
Full twenty times was Peter feared
For once that Peter was respected.   205

He, two-and-thirty years or more
Had been a wild and woodland rover;
Had heard the Atlantic surges roar
On farthest Cornwall's rocky shore,
And trod the cliffs of Dover.   210

[1] In the dialect of the North, a hawker of earthen-ware is thus designated.

'And he had seen Caernarvon's towers,
And well he knew the spire of Sarum;
And he had been where Lincoln bell
Flings o'er the fen that ponderous knell—
A far-renowned alarum!   215

'At Doncaster, at York, and Leeds,
And merry Carlisle had he been;
And all along the Lowlands fair,
All through the bonny shire of Ayr;
And far as Aberdeen.   220

'And he had been at Inverness;
And Peter, by the mountain-rills,
Had danced his round with Highland lasses;
And he had lain beside his asses
On lofty Cheviot Hills: 225

'And he had trudged through Yorkshire dales,
Among the rocks and winding *scars;*
Where deep and low the hamlets lie
Beneath their little patch of sky
And little lot of stars: 230

'And all along the indented coast,
Bespattered with the salt-sea foam;
Where'er a knot of houses lay
On headland, or in hollow bay;—
Sure never man like him did roam!   235

'As well might Peter in the Fleet
Have been fast bound, a begging debtor;—
He travelled here, he travelled there;—
But not the value of a hair
Was heart or head the better.   240

'He roved among the vales and streams,
In the green wood and hollow dell;
They were his dwellings night and day,—
But nature ne'er could find the way
Into the heart of Peter Bell.   245

'In vain, through every changeful year,
Did Nature lead him as before;
A primrose by a river's brim
A yellow primrose was to him,
And it was nothing more.   250

'Small change it made in Peter's heart
To see his gentle panniered train
With more than vernal pleasure feeding,
Where'er the tender grass was leading
Its earliest green along the lane.   255

'In vain, through water, earth, and air,
The soul of happy sound was spread,
When Peter on some April morn,
Beneath the broom or budding thorn,
Made the warm earth his lazy bed.   260

'At noon, when, by the forest's edge
He lay beneath the branches high,
The soft blue sky did never melt
Into his heart; he never felt
The witchery of the soft blue sky!   265

'On a fair prospect some have looked
And felt, as I have heard them say,
As if the moving time had been
A thing as steadfast as the scene
On which they gazed themselves away.

'Within the breast of Peter Bell   271
These silent raptures found no place;
He was a Carl as wild and rude
As ever hue-and-cry pursued,
As ever ran a felon's race.   275

'Of all that lead a lawless life,
Of all that love their lawless lives,
In city or in village small,
He was the wildest far of all;—
He had a dozen wedded wives.   280

'Nay, start not!—wedded wives—and
    twelve!
But how one wife could e'er come near
    him,
In simple truth I cannot tell;
For, be it said of Peter Bell,
To see him was to fear him.   285

'Though Nature could not touch his heart
By lovely forms, and silent weather,
And tender sounds, yet you might see
At once that Peter Bell and she
Had often been together.   290

'A savage wildness round him hung
As of a dweller out of doors;
In his whole figure and his mien
A savage character was seen
Of mountains and of dreary moors.   295

'To all the unshaped half-human thoughts
Which solitary Nature feeds
'Mid summer storms or winter's ice,
Had Peter joined whatever vice
The cruel city breeds.   300

'His face was keen as is the wind
That cuts along the hawthorn-fence:
Of courage you saw little there,
But, in its stead, a medley air
Of cunning and of impudence.   305

'He had a dark and sidelong walk,
And long and slouching was his gait;
Beneath his looks so bare and bold,
You might perceive, his spirit cold
Was playing with some inward bait.   310

'His forehead wrinkled was and furred;
A work, one half of which was done
By thinking of his "*whens*" and "*hows;*"
And half, by knitting of his brows
Beneath the glaring sun.   315

'There was a hardness in his cheek,
There was a hardness in his eye,
As if the man had fixed his face,
In many a solitary place,
Against the wind and open sky!'   320

ONE NIGHT, (and now, my little Bess!
We've reached at last the promised Tale;)
One beautiful November night,
When the full moon was shining bright
Upon the rapid river Swale,   325

Along the river's winding banks
Peter was travelling all alone;—
Whether to buy or sell, or led
By pleasure running in his head,
To me was never known.   330

He trudged along through copse and
    brake
He trudged along o'er hill and dale;
Nor for the moon cared he a tittle,
And for the stars he cared as little,
And for the murmuring river Swale.   335

But, chancing to espy a path
That promised to cut short the way;
As many a wiser man hath done,
He left a trusty guide for one
That might his steps betray.   340

To a thick wood he soon is brought
Where cheerily his course he weaves,
And whistling loud may yet be heard,
Though often buried like a bird
Darkling, among the boughs and leaves.

But quickly Peter's mood is changed,   346
And on he drives with cheeks that burn
In downright fury and in wrath;—
There's little sign the treacherous path
Will to the road return!   350

The path grows dim, and dimmer still;
Now up, now down, the Rover wends,
With all the sail that he can carry,
Till brought to a deserted quarry—
And there the pathway ends.   355

He paused—for shadows of strange shape,
Massy and black, before him lay;
But through the dark, and through the
    cold,
And through the yawning fissures old,
Did Peter boldly press his way   360

Right through the quarry;—and behold
A scene of soft and lovely hue!
Where blue and grey, and tender green,
Together make as sweet a scene
As ever human eye did view.   365

Beneath the clear blue sky he saw
A little field of meadow ground;
But field or meadow name it not;
Call it of earth a small green plot,
With rocks encompassed round.   370

The Swale flowed under the grey rocks,
But he flowed quiet and unseen:—
You need a strong and stormy gale
To bring the noises of the Swale
To that green spot, so calm and green!

And is there no one dwelling here, 376
No hermit with his beads and glass?
And does no little cottage look
Upon this soft and fertile nook?
Does no one live near this green grass?

Across the deep and quiet spot 381
Is Peter driving through the grass—
And now has reached the skirting trees;
When, turning round his head, he sees
A solitary Ass. 385

'A prize!' cries Peter—but he first
Must spy about him far and near:
There's not a single house in sight,
No woodman's hut, no cottage light—
Peter, you need not fear! 390

There's nothing to be seen but woods,
And rocks that spread a hoary gleam,
And this one Beast, that from the bed
Of the green meadow hangs his head
Over the silent stream. 395

His head is with a halter bound;
The halter seizing, Peter leapt
Upon the Creature's back, and plied
With ready heels his shaggy side;
But still the Ass his station kept. 400

Then Peter gave a sudden jerk,
A jerk that from a dungeon-floor
Would have pulled up an iron ring;
But still the heavy-headed Thing
Stood just as he had stood before! 405

Quoth Peter, leaping from his seat,
'There is some plot against me laid;'
Once more the little meadow-ground
And all the hoary cliffs around
He cautiously surveyed. 410

All, all is silent—rocks and woods,
All still and silent—far and near!
Only the Ass, with motion dull,
Upon the pivot of his skull
Turns round his long left ear. 415

Thought Peter. What can mean all this?
Some ugly witchcraft must be here!
—Once more the Ass, with motion dull,
Upon the pivot of his skull
Turned round his long left ear. 420

Suspicion ripened into dread;
Yet, with deliberate action slow,
His staff high-raising, in the pride
Of skill, upon the sounding hide
He dealt a sturdy blow. 425

The poor Ass staggered with the shock;
And then, as if to take his ease,
In quiet uncomplaining mood,
Upon the spot where he had stood, 429
Dropped gently down upon his knees;

As gently on his side he fell;
And by the river's brink did lie;
And, while he lay like one that mourned,
The patient Beast on Peter turned
His shining hazel eye. 435

'Twas but one mild, reproachful look,
A look more tender than severe;
And straight in sorrow, not in dread,
He turned the eye-ball in his head
Towards the smooth river deep and clear.

Upon the Beast the sapling rings; 441
His lank sides heaved, his limbs they
stirred;
He gave a groan, and then another,
Of that which went before the brother,
And then he gave a third. 445

All by the moonlight river side
He gave three miserable groans;
And not till now hath Peter seen
How gaunt the Creature is,—how lean
And sharp his staring bones! 450

With legs stretched out and stiff he lay:—
No word of kind commiseration
Fell at the sight from Peter's tongue;
With hard contempt his heart was wrung,
With hatred and vexation. 455

The meagre beast lay still as death;
And Peter's lips with fury quiver;
Quoth he, 'You little mulish dog,
I'll fling your carcass like a log
Head-foremost down the river!' 460

An impious oath confirmed the threat—
Whereat from the earth on which he lay
To all the echoes, south and north,
And east and west, the Ass sent forth
A long and clamorous bray! 465

This outcry, on the heart of Peter,
Seems like a note of joy to strike,—
Joy at the heart of Peter knocks;
But in the echo of the rocks
Was something Peter did not like. 470

Whether to cheer his coward breast,
Or that he could not break the chain,
In this serene and solemn hour,
Twined round him by demoniac power,
To the blind work he turned again. 475

Among the rocks and winding crags;
Among the mountains far away;
Once more the Ass did lengthen out
More ruefully a deep-drawn shout,
The hard dry see-saw of his horrible bray!

What is there now in Peter's heart! 481
Or whence the might of this strange sound?
The moon uneasy looked and dimmer,
The broad blue heavens appeared to
glimmer, 484
And the rocks staggered all around—

From Peter's hand the sapling dropped!
Threat has he none to execute;
'If any one should come and see
That I am here, they'll think,' quoth he,
'I'm helping this poor dying brute.'   490

He scans the Ass from limb to limb,
And ventures now to uplift his eyes;
More steady looks the moon, and clear,
More like themselves the rocks appear
And touch more quiet skies.   495

His scorn returns—his hate revives;
He stoops the Ass's neck to seize
With malice—that again takes flight;
For in the pool a startling sight
Meets him, among the inverted trees.   500

Is it the moon's distorted face?
The ghost-like image of a cloud?
Is it a gallows there portrayed?
Is Peter of himself afraid?
Is it a coffin,—or a shroud?   505

A grisly idol hewn in stone?
Or imp from witch's lap let fall?
Perhaps a ring of shining fairies?
Such as pursue their feared vagaries
In sylvan bower, or haunted hall?   510

Is it a fiend that to a stake
Of fire his desperate self is tethering?
Or stubborn spirit doomed to yell
In solitary ward or cell,
Ten thousand miles from all his brethren?

Never did pulse so quickly throb,   516
And never heart so loudly panted;
He looks, he cannot choose but look;
Like some one reading in a book—
A book that is enchanted.   520

Ah, well-a-day for Peter Bell!
He will be turned to iron soon,
Meet Statue for the court of Fear!
His hat is up—and every hair
Bristles, and whitens in the moon!   525

He looks, he ponders, looks again;
He sees a motion—hears a groan;
His eyes will burst—his heart will break—
He gives a loud and frightful shriek,
And back he falls, as if his life were flown!

PART SECOND

WE left our Hero in a trance,   531
Beneath the alders, near the river;
The Ass is by the river-side,
And, where the feeble breezes glide,
Upon the stream the moonbeams quiver.

A happy respite! but at length   536
He feels the glimmering of the moon;
Wakes with glazed eye, and feebly sigh-
ing—
To sink, perhaps, where he is lying,
Into a second swoon!   540

He lifts his head, he sees his staff:
He touches—'tis to him a treasure!
Faint recollection seems to tell
That he is yet where mortals dwell—
A thought received with languid pleasure!

His head upon his elbow propped,   546
Becoming less and less perplexed,
Sky-ward he looks—to rock and wood—
And then—upon the glassy flood
His wandering eye is fixed.   550

Thought he, that is the face of one
In his last sleep securely bound!
So toward the stream his head he bent,
And downward thrust his staff, intent
The river's depth to sound.   555

Now—like a tempest-shattered bark,
That overwhelmed and prostrate lies,
And in a moment to the verge
Is lifted of a foaming surge—
Full suddenly the Ass doth rise!   560

His staring bones all shake with joy,
And close by Peter's side he stands:
While Peter o'er the river bends,
The little Ass his neck extends,
And fondly licks his hands.   565

Such life is in the Ass's eyes,
Such life is in his limbs and ears;
That Peter Bell, if he had been
The veriest coward ever seen,
Must now have thrown aside his fears.   570

The Ass looks on—and to his work
Is Peter quietly resigned;
He touches here—he touches there—
And now among the dead man's hair
His sapling Peter has entwined.   575

He pulls—and looks—and pulls again;
And he whom the poor Ass had lost,
The man who had been four days dead,
Head-foremost from the river's bed
Uprises like a ghost!   580

And Peter draws him to dry land;
And through the brain of Peter pass
Some poignant twitches, fast and faster;
'No doubt,' quoth he, 'he is the Master
Of this poor miserable Ass!'   585

The meagre shadow that looks on—
What would he now? what is he doing?
His sudden fit of joy is flown,—
He on his knees hath laid him down,
As if he were his grief renewing;   590

But no—that Peter on his back
Must mount, he shows well as he can:
Thought Peter then, come weal or woe,
I'll do what he would have me do,
In pity to this poor drowned man.   595

With that resolve he boldly mounts
Upon the pleased and thankful Ass;
And then, without a moment's stay,
That earnest Creature turned away,
Leaving the body on the grass.   600

Intent upon his faithful watch,
The Beast four days and nights had past;
A sweeter meadow ne'er was seen,
And there the Ass four days had been,
Nor ever once did break his fast: 605

Yet firm his step, and stout his heart;
The mead is crossed—the quarry's mouth
Is reached; but there the trusty guide
Into a thicket turns aside,
And deftly ambles towards the south.   610

When hark a burst of doleful sound!
And Peter honestly might say,
The like came never to his ears,
Though he has been, full thirty years,
A rover—night and day!   615

'Tis not a plover of the moors,
'Tis not a bittern of the fen;
Nor can it be a barking fox,
Nor night-bird chambered in the rocks,
Nor wild-cat in a woody glen!   620

The Ass is startled—and stops short
Right in the middle of the thicket;
And Peter, wont to whistle loud
Whether alone or in a crowd,
Is silent as a silent cricket.   625

What ails you now, my little Bess?
Well may you tremble and look grave!
This cry—that rings along the wood,
This cry—that floats adown the flood,
Comes from the entrance of a cave: 630

I see a blooming Wood-boy there,
And if I had the power to say
How sorrowful the wanderer is,
Your heart would be as sad as his
Till you had kissed his tears away!   635

Grasping a hawthorn branch in hand,
All bright with berries ripe and red,
Into the cavern's mouth he peeps;
Thence back into the moonlight creeps;
Whom seeks he—whom?—the silent
     dead: 640

His father!—Him doth he require—
Him hath he sought with fruitless pains,
Among the rocks, behind the trees;
Now creeping on his hands and knees,
Now running o'er the open plains.   645

And hither is he come at last,
When he through such a day has gone,
By this dark cave to be distrest
Like a poor bird—her plundered nest
Hovering around with dolorous moan!

Of that intense and piercing cry   651
The listening Ass conjectures well;
Wild as it is, he there can read
Some intermingled notes that plead
With touches irresistible.   655

But Peter—when he saw the Ass
Not only stop but turn, and change
The cherished tenor of his pace
That lamentable cry to chase—
It wrought in him conviction strange;   660

A faith that for the dead man's sake,
And this poor slave who loved him well,
Vengeance upon his head will fall,
Some visitation worse than all
Which ever till this night befell.   665

Meanwhile the Ass to reach his home
Is striving stoutly as he may;
But, while he climbs the woody hill,
The cry grows weak—and weaker still;
And now at last it dies away.   670

So with his freight the Creature turns
Into a gloomy grove of beech,
Along the shade with footsteps true
Descending slowly, till the two
The open moonlight reach.   675

And there, along the narrow dell,
A fair smooth pathway you discern,
A length of green and open road—
As if it from a fountain flowed—
Winding away between the fern.   680

The rocks that tower on either side
Build up a wild fantastic scene;
Temples like those among the Hindoos,
And mosques, and spires, and abbey-win-
     dows,
And castles all with ivy green!   685

And while the Ass pursues his way
Along this solitary dell,
As pensively his steps advance,
The mosques and spires change counte-
     nance,
And look at Peter Bell!   690

That unintelligible cry
Hath left him high in preparation,—
Convinced that he, or soon or late,
This very night will meet his fate—
And so he sits in expectation: 695

The strenuous Animal hath clomb
With the green path; and now he wends
Where, shining like the smoothest sea,
In undisturbed immensity
A level plain extends.   700

But whence this faintly-rustling sound
By which the journeying pair are chased?
—A withered leaf is close behind,
Light plaything for the sportive wind
Upon that solitary waste.   705

When Peter spied the moving thing,
It only doubled his distress;
'Where there is not a bush or tree,
The very leaves they follow me—
So huge hath been my wickedness!'   710

To a close lane they now are come,
Where, as before, the enduring Ass
Moves on without a moment's stop,
Nor once turns round his head to crop
A bramble-leaf or blade of grass.   715

Between the hedges as they go,
The white dust sleeps upon the lane;
And Peter, ever and anon
Back-looking, sees, upon a stone,
Or in the dust, a crimson stain.   720

A stain—as of a drop of blood
By moonlight made more faint and wan;
Ha! why these sinkings of despair?
He knows not how the blood comes
    there—
And Peter is a wicked man.   725

At length he spies a bleeding wound,
Where he had struck the Ass's head;
He sees the blood, knows what it is,—
A glimpse of sudden joy was his,
But then it quickly fled;   730

Of him whom sudden death had seized
He thought,—of thee, O faithful Ass!
And once again those ghastly pains,
Shoot to and fro through heart and reins,
And through his brain like lightning
    pass.   735

PART THIRD

I'VE heard of one, a gentle Soul,
Though given to sadness and to gloom,
And for the fact will vouch,—one night
It chanced that by a taper's light
This man was reading in his room;   740

Bending, as you or I might bend
At night o'er any pious book,
When sudden blackness overspread
The snow-white page on which he read,
And made the good man round him look.

The chamber walls were dark all round,—
And to his book he turned again;   747
—The light had left the lonely taper,
And formed itself upon the paper
Into large letters—bright and plain!   750

The godly book was in his hand—
And on the page, more black than coal,
Appeared, set forth in strange array,
A word—which to his dying day
Perplexed the good man's gentle soul.   755

The ghostly word, thus plainly seen,
Did never from his lips depart;
But he hath said, poor gentle wight!
It brought full many a sin to light
Out of the bottom of his heart.   760

Dread Spirits! to confound the meek
Why wander from your course so far,
Disordering colour, form, and stature!
—Let good men feel the soul of nature,
And see things as they are.   765

Yet, potent Spirits! well I know,
How ye, that play with soul and sense,
Are not unused to trouble friends
Of goodness, for most gracious ends—
And this I speak in reverence!   770

But might I give advice to you,
Whom in my fear I love so well;
From men of pensive virtue go,
Dread Beings! and your empire show
On hearts like that of Peter Bell.   775

Your presence often have I felt
In darkness and the stormy night;
And with like force, if need there be,
Ye can put forth your agency   779
When earth is calm, and heaven is bright.

Then coming from the wayward world,
That powerful world in which we dwell,
Come, Spirits of the Mind! and try,
To-night, beneath the moonlight sky,
What may be done with Peter Bell!   785

—O, would that some more skilful voice
My further labour might prevent!
Kind Listeners, that around me sit,
I feel that I am all unfit
For such high argument.   790

I've played, I've danced, with my nar-
    ration;
I loitered long ere I began:
Ye waited then on my good pleasure;
Pour out indulgence still, in measure
As liberal as ye can!   795

Our Travellers, ye remember well,
Are thridding a sequestered lane;
And Peter many tricks is trying,
And many anodynes applying,
To ease his conscience of its pain.   800

By this his heart is lighter far;
And, finding that he can account
So snugly for that crimson stain,
His evil spirit up again
Does like an empty bucket mount.   805

And Peter is a deep logician
Who hath no lack of wit mercurial;
'Blood drops—leaves rustle—yet,' quoth
    he,
'This poor man never but for me
Could have had Christian burial.   810

'And, say the best you can, 'tis plain,
That here has been some wicked dealing;
No doubt the devil in me wrought;
I'm not the man who could have thought
An Ass like this was worth the steal-
    ing!'   815

So from his pocket Peter takes
His shining horn tobacco-box;
And in a light and careless way,
As men who with their purpose play,
Upon the lid he knocks.   820

Let them whose voice can stop the clouds,
Whose cunning eye can see the wind,
Tell to a curious world the cause
Why, making here a sudden pause,
The Ass turned round his head and
    grinned.   825

Appalling process! I have marked
The like on heath, in lonely wood;
And, verily, have seldom met
A spectacle more hideous—yet
It suited Peter's present mood.   830

And, grinning in his turn, his teeth
He in jocose defiance showed—
When, to upset his spiteful mirth,
A murmur, pent within the earth,
In the dead earth beneath the road,   835

Rolled audibly!—it swept along,
A muffled noise—a rumbling sound!—
'Twas by a troop of miners made,
Plying with gunpowder their trade,
Some twenty fathoms under ground.   840

Small cause of dire effect! for, surely,
If ever mortal, King or Cotter,
Believed that earth was charged to quake
And yawn for his unworthy sake,
'Twas Peter Bell the Potter.   845

But as an oak in breathless air
Will stand though to the centre hewn;
Or as the weakest things, if frost
Have stiffened them, maintain their post;
So he, beneath the gazing moon!—   850

The Beast bestriding thus, he reached
A spot where, in a sheltering cove,
A little chapel stands alone,
With greenest ivy overgrown,
And tufted with an ivy grove;   855

Dying insensibly away
From human thoughts and purposes,
It seemed—wall, window, roof and
    tower—
To bow to some transforming power,
And blend with the surrounding trees.   860

As ruinous a place it was,
Thought Peter, in the shire of Fife
That served my turn, when following still
From land to land a reckless will
I married my sixth wife!   865

The unheeding Ass moves slowly on,
And now is passing by an inn
Brim-full of a carousing crew,
That make, with curses not a few,
An uproar and a drunken din.   870

I cannot well express the thoughts
Which Peter in those noises found;—
A stifling power compressed his frame,
While-as a swimming darkness came
Over that dull and dreary sound.   875

For well did Peter know the sound;
The language of those drunken joys
To him, a jovial soul, I ween
But a few hours ago, had been
A gladsome and a welcome noise.   880

Now, turned adrift into the past,
He finds no solace in his course;
Like planet-stricken men of yore,
He trembles, smitten to the core
By strong compunction and remorse.   885

But, more than all, his heart is stung
To think of one, almost a child;
A sweet and playful Highland girl,
As light and beauteous as a squirrel,
As beauteous and as wild!   890

Her dwelling was a lonely house,
A cottage in a heathy dell;
And she put on her gown of green,
And left her mother at sixteen,
And followed Peter Bell.   895

But many good and pious thoughts
Had she; and, in the kirk to pray,
Two long Scotch miles, through rain or
    snow,
To kirk she had been used to go,
Twice every Sabbath-day.   900

And, when she followed Peter Bell,
It was to lead an honest life;
For he, with tongue not used to falter,
Had pledged his troth before the altar
To love her as his wedded wife.   905

A mother's hope is hers;—but soon
She drooped and pined like one forlorn;
From Scripture she a name did borrow;
Benoni, or the child of sorrow,
She called her babe unborn.   910

For she had learned how Peter lived,
And took it in most grievous part;
She to the very bone was worn,
And, ere that little child was born,
Died of a broken heart.   915

And now the Spirits of the Mind
Are busy with poor Peter Bell;
Upon the rights of visual sense
Usurping, with a prevalence
More terrible than magic spell.   920

Close by a brake of flowering furze
(Above it shivering aspens play)
He sees an unsubstantial creature,
His very self in form and feature,   924
Not four yards from the broad highway:

And stretched beneath the furze he sees
The Highland girl—it is no other;
And hears her crying as she cried,
The very moment that she died,
'My mother! oh my mother!'   930

The sweat pours down from Peter's face,
So grievous is his heart's contrition;
With agony his eye-balls ache
While he beholds by the furze-brake
This miserable vision!   935

Calm is the well-deserving brute,
His peace hath no offence betrayed;
But now, while down that slope he wends,
A voice to Peter's ear ascends,
Resounding from the woody glade: 940

The voice, though clamorous as a horn
Re-echoed by a naked rock,
Comes from that tabernacle—List!
Within, a fervent Methodist
Is preaching to no heedless flock!   945

'Repent! repent!' he cries aloud,
'While yet ye may find mercy;—strive
To love the Lord with all your might;
Turn to him, seek him day and night,
And save your souls alive!   950

'Repent! repent! though ye have gone,
Through paths of wickedness and woe,
After the Babylonian harlot;
And though your sins be red as scarlet,
They shall be white as snow!'   955

Even as he passed the door, these words
Did plainly come to Peter's ears;
And they such joyful tidings were,
The joy was more than he could bear!—
He melted into tears.   960

Sweet tears of hope and tenderness!
And fast they fell, a plenteous shower!
His nerves, his sinews seemed to melt;
Through all his iron frame was felt
A gentle, a relaxing power!   965

Each fibre of his frame was weak;
Weak all the animal within;
But, in its helplessness, grew mild
And gentle as an infant child,
An infant that has known no sin.   970

'Tis said, meek Beast! that, through Hea-
    ven's grace,
He not unmoved did notice now
The cross upon thy shoulder scored,
For lasting impress, by the Lord
To whom all human-kind shall bow;   975

Memorial of his touch—that day
When Jesus humbly deigned to ride,
Entering the proud Jerusalem,
By an immeasurable stream
Of shouting people deified!   980

Meanwhile the persevering Ass
Turned towards a gate that hung in view
Across a shady lane; his chest
Against the yielding gate he pressed
And quietly passed through.   985

And up the stony lane he goes;
No ghost more softly ever trod;
Among the stones and pebbles he
Sets down his hoofs inaudibly,
As if with felt his hoofs were shod.   990

Along the lane the trusty Ass
Went twice two hundred yards or more,
And no one could have guessed his aim,—
Till to a lonely house he came,
And stopped beside the door.   995

Thought Peter, 'tis the poor man's home!
He listens—not a sound is heard
Save from the trickling household rill;
But, stepping o'er the cottage-sill,
Forthwith a little Girl appeared.   1000

She to the Meeting-house was bound
In hopes some tidings there to gather:
No glimpse it is, no doubtful gleam;
She saw—and uttered with a scream,
'My father! here's my father!'   1005

The very word was plainly heard,
Heard plainly by the wretched Mother—
Her joy was like a deep affright:
And forth she rushed into the light,
And saw it was another!   1010

And instantly upon the earth,
Beneath the full moon shining bright,
Close to the Ass's feet she fell;
At the same moment Peter Bell
Dismounts in most unhappy plight.   1015

As he beheld the Woman lie
Breathless and motionless, the mind
Of Peter sadly was confused;
But, though to such demands unused,
And helpless almost as the blind,   1020

He raised her up; and while he held
Her body propped against his knee,
The Woman waked—and when she spied
The poor Ass standing by her side,
She moaned most bitterly.   1025

'Oh! God be praised—my heart's at
    ease—
For he is dead—I know it well!'
—At this she wept a bitter flood;
And, in the best way that he could,
His tale did Peter tell.   1030

He trembles—he is pale as death;
His voice is weak with perturbation;
He turns aside his head, he pauses;
Poor Peter from a thousand causes
Is crippled sore in his narration.   1035

At length she learned how he espied
The Ass in that small meadow-ground;
And that her Husband now lay dead,
Beside that luckless river's bed
In which he had been drowned.   1040

A piercing look the Widow cast
Upon the Beast that near her stands;
She sees 'tis he, that 'tis the same;
She calls the poor Ass by his name,
And wrings, and wrings her hands.   1045

'O wretched loss—untimely stroke!
If he had died upon his bed!
He knew not one forewarning pain;
He never will come home again—
Is dead, for ever dead!'   1050

Beside the Woman Peter stands;
His heart is opening more and more;
A holy sense pervades his mind;
He feels what he for human-kind
Has never felt before.   1055

At length, by Peter's arm sustained,
The Woman rises from the ground—
'Oh, mercy! something must be done,
My little Rachel, you must run,—
Some willing neighbour must be found.

'Make haste—my little Rachel—do,   1061
The first you meet with—bid him come,
Ask him to lend his horse to-night,
And this good Man whom Heaven requite,
Will help to bring the body home.'   1065

Away goes Rachel weeping loud;—
An Infant, waked by her distress,
Makes in the house a piteous cry;
And Peter hears the Mother sigh,
'Seven are they, and all fatherless!' 1070

And now is Peter taught to feel
That man's heart is a holy thing;
And Nature, through a world of death,
Breathes into him a second breath,
More searching than the breath of spring.

Upon a stone the Woman sits   1076
In agony of silent grief—
From his own thoughts did Peter start;
He longs to press her to his heart,
From love that cannot find relief.   1080

But roused, as if through every limb
Had past a sudden shock of dread,
The Mother o'er the threshold flies,
And up the cottage stairs she hies,
And on the pillow lays her burning
        head.   1085

And Peter turns his steps aside
Into a shade of darksome trees,
Where he sits down, he knows not how,
With his hands pressed against his brow,
His elbows on his tremulous knees.   1090

There, self-involved, does Peter sit
Until no sign of life he makes,
As if his mind were sinking deep
Through years that have been long asleep!
The trance is passed away—he wakes;

He lifts his head—and sees the Ass   1096
Yet standing in the clear moonshine;
'When shall I be as good as thou?
Oh! would, poor beast, that I had now
A heart but half as good as thine!'   1100

But *He*—who deviously hath sought
His Father through the lonesome woods,
Hath sought, proclaiming to the ear
Of night his grief and sorrowful fear—
He comes, escaped from fields and
        floods;—   1105

With weary pace is drawing nigh;
He sees the Ass—and nothing living
Had ever such a fit of joy
As hath this little orphan Boy,
For he has no misgiving!   1110

Forth to the gentle Ass he springs,
And up about his neck he climbs;
In loving words he talks to him,
He kisses, kisses face and limb,—
He kisses him a thousand times!   1115

This Peter sees, while in the shade
He stood beside the cottage-door;
And Peter Bell, the ruffian wild,
Sobs loud, he sobs even like a child,
'Oh! God, I can endure no more!'   1120

—Here ends my Tale: for in a trice
Arrived a neighbour with his horse;
Peter went forth with him straightway;
And, with due care, ere break of day,
Together they brought back the Corse.

And many years did this poor Ass,   1126
Whom once it was my luck to see
Cropping the shrubs of Leming-Lane,
Help by his labour to maintain
The Widow and her family.   1130

And Peter Bell, who, till that night,
Had been the wildest of his clan,
Forsook his crimes, renounced his folly,
And, after ten months' melancholy,
Became a good and honest man.   1135

MISCELLANEOUS SONNETS

DEDICATION

TO ——

[Composed 1826 (?).—Published 1827.]

Happy the feeling from the bosom thrown
In perfect shape (whose beauty Time shall spare
Though a breath made it) like a bubble blown
For summer pastime into wanton air;
Happy the thought best likened to a stone   5
Of the sea-beach, when, polished with nice care,
Veins it discovers exquisite and rare,
Which for the loss of that moist gleam atone
That tempted first to gather it. That here,
O chief of Friends! such feelings I present   10
To thy regard, with thoughts so fortunate,
Were a vain notion; but the hope is dear
That thou, if not with partial joy elate,
Wilt smile upon this gift with more than mild content!

PART I

I

[Composed (?).—Published 1807.]

Nuns fret not at their convent's narrow
    room;
And hermits are contented with their
    cells;
And students with their pensive citadels;
Maids at the wheel, the weaver at his
    loom,
Sit blithe and happy; bees that soar for
    bloom,   5
High as the highest Peak of Furness-fells,
Will murmur by the hour in foxglove
    bells:
In truth the prison, unto which we doom
Ourselves, no prison is: and hence for me,
In sundry moods, 'twas pastime to be
    bound   10
Within the Sonnet's scanty plot of ground;
Pleased if some Souls (for such there needs
    must be)
Who have felt the weight of too much
    liberty,
Should find brief solace there, as I have
    found.

II

ADMONITION

Intended more particularly for the perusal of those
who may have happened to be enamoured of
some beautiful place of Retreat, in the Country
of the Lakes.

[Composed (?).—Published 1807.]

Well may'st thou halt—and gaze with
    brightening eye!
The lovely Cottage in the guardian nook
Hath stirred thee deeply; with its own
    dear brook,
Its own small pasture, almost its own sky!
But covet not the Abode;—forbear to
    sigh,   5
As many do, repining while they look;
Intruders—who would tear from Nature's
    book
This precious leaf, with harsh impiety.
Think what the Home must be if it were
    thine,
Even thine, though few thy wants!—Roof,
    window, door,   10
The very flowers are sacred to the Poor,
The roses to the porch which they entwine:
Yea, all, that now enchants thee, from the
    day
On which it should be touched, would
    melt away.

III

[Composed (?).—Published 1807.]

'Beloved Vale!' I said, 'when I shall con
Those many records of my childish years,
Remembrance of myself and of my peers
Will press me down: to think of what is
    gone
Will be an awful thought, if life have one.'
But, when into the Vale I came, no fears
Distressed me; from mine eyes escaped no
    tears;   7
Deep thought, or dread remembrance, had
    I none.
By doubts and thousand petty fancies crost
I stood, of simple shame the blushing
    Thrall;   10
So narrow seemed the brooks, the fields
    so small!
A Juggler's balls old Time about him
    tossed;
I looked, I stared, I smiled, I laughed; and
    all
The weight of sadness was in wonder lost.

IV

AT APPLETHWAITE, NEAR KESWICK

[Composed 1804.—Published 1842.]

Beaumont! it was thy wish that I should
    rear
A seemly Cottage in this sunny Dell,
On favoured ground, thy gift, where I
    might dwell
In neighbourhood with One to me most
    dear,
That undivided we from year to year   5
Might work in our high Calling—a bright
    hope
To which our fancies, mingling, gave free
    scope
Till checked by some necessities severe.

And should these slacken, honoured
  BEAUMONT! still
Even then we may perhaps in vain implore
Leave of our fate thy wishes to fulfil.   11
Whether this boon be granted us or not,
Old Skiddaw will look down upon the Spot
With pride, the Muses love it evermore.

V

[Composed 1801.—Published 1815.]

PELION and Ossa flourish side by side,
Together in immortal books enrolled:
His ancient dower Olympus hath not sold;
And that inspiring Hill, which 'did divide
Into two ample horns his forehead wide,'
Shines with poetic radiance as of old;   6
While not an English Mountain we behold
By the celestial Muses glorified.
Yet round our sea-girt shore they rise in
  crowds:
What was the great Parnassus' self to
  Thee,   10
Mount Skiddaw? In his natural sove-
  reignty
Our British Hill is nobler far; he shrouds
His double front among Atlantic clouds,
And pours forth streams more sweet than
  Castaly.

VI

[Composed 1801.—Published 1820.]

THERE is a little unpretending Rill
Of limpid water, humbler far than aught
That ever among Men or Naiads sought
Notice or name!—It quivers down the hill,
Furrowing its shallow way with dubious
  will;   5
Yet to my mind this scanty Stream is
  brought
Oftener than Ganges or the Nile; a
  thought
Of private recollection sweet and still!
Months perish with their moons; year
  treads on year;
But, faithful Emma! thou with me canst
  say   10
That, while ten thousand pleasures dis-
  appear,
And flies their memory fast almost as they;
The immortal Spirit of one happy day
Lingers beside that Rill, in vision clear.

VII

[Composed (?).—Published 1827.]

HER only pilot the soft breeze, the boat
Lingers, but Fancy is well satisfied;
With keen-eyed Hope, with Memory, at
  her side,
And the glad Muse at liberty to note
All that to each is precious, as we float   5
Gently along; regardless who shall chide
If the heavens smile, and leave us free to
  glide,

Happy Associates breathing air remote
From trivial cares. But, Fancy and the
  Muse,
Why have I crowded this small bark with
  you   10
And others of your kind, ideal crew!
While here sits One whose brightness
  owes its hues
To flesh and blood; no Goddess from
  above,
No fleeting Spirit, but my own true Love?

VIII

[Composed (?).—Published 1815.]

THE fairest, brightest, hues of ether fade;
The sweetest notes must terminate and die;
O Friend! thy flute has breathed a har-
  mony
Softly resounded through this rocky glade;
Such strains of rapture as[1] the Genius
  played   5
In his still haunt on Bagdad's summit
  high;
He who stood visible to Mirza's eye,
Never before to human sight betrayed.
Lo, in the vale, the mists of evening spread!
The visionary Arches are not there,   10
Nor the green Islands, nor the shining
  Seas;
Yet sacred is to me this Mountain's head,
Whence I have risen, uplifted on the breeze
Of harmony, above all earthly care.

IX

UPON THE SIGHT OF A BEAUTIFUL PICTURE,

Painted by Sir G. H. Beaumont, Bart.

[Composed August, 1811.—Published 1815.]

PRAISED be the Art whose subtle power
  could stay
Yon cloud, and fix it in that glorious shape;
Nor would permit the thin smoke to
  escape,
Nor those bright sunbeams to forsake the
  day;
Which stopped that band of travellers on
  their way,   5
Ere they were lost within the shady wood;
And showed the Bark upon the glassy
  flood
For ever anchored in her sheltering bay.
Soul-soothing Art! whom Morning,
  Noontide, Even,
Do serve with all their changeful
  pageantry;   10
Thou, with ambition modest yet sublime,
Here, for the sight of mortal man, hast
  given
To one brief moment caught from fleeting
  time
The appropriate calm of blest eternity.

   [1] See the 'Vision of Mirza' in the 'Spectator.'

X

[Composed (?).—Published 1827.]

'WHY, Minstrel, these untuneful murmur-
    ings—
Dull, flagging notes that with each other
    jar?'
'Think, gentle Lady, of a Harp so far
From its own country, and forgive the
    strings.'   4
A simple answer! but even so forth springs,
From the Castalian fountain of the heart,
The Poetry of Life, and all *that* Art
Divine of words quickening insensate
    things.
From the submissive necks of guiltless
    men
Stretched on the block the glittering axe
    recoils;   10
Sun, moon, and stars, all struggle in the
    toils
Of mortal sympathy; what wonder then
That the poor Harp distempered music
    yields
To its sad Lord, far from his native fields?

XI

[Composed (?).—Published 1819.[1]]

AERIAL Rock—whose solitary brow
From this low threshold daily meets my
    sight;
When I step forth to hail the morning
    light;
Or quit the stars with a lingering fare-
    well—how   4
Shall Fancy pay to thee a grateful vow?
How, with the Muse's aid, her love attest?
—By planting on thy naked head the crest
Of an imperial Castle, which the plough
Of ruin shall not touch. Innocent scheme!
That doth presume no more than to sup-
    ply   10
A grace the sinuous vale and roaring
    stream
Want, through neglect of hoar Antiquity.
Rise, then, ye votive Towers! and catch a
    gleam
Of golden sunset, ere it fade and die.

XII

TO SLEEP

[Composed (?).—Published 1807.]

O GENTLE Sleep! do they belong to thee,
These twinklings of oblivion? Thou dost
    love
To sit in meekness, like the brooding
    Dove,

[1] This, and eleven other Sonnets here marked
simply '1819', appeared in the vol. containing *The
Waggoner*, which was published in the summer of
1819 shortly after *Peter Bell.*—ED.

A captive never wishing to be free.
This tiresome night, O Sleep! thou art
    to me   5
A Fly, that up and down himself doth
    shove
Upon a fretful rivulet, now above,
Now on the water vexed with mockery.
I have no pain that calls for patience, no;
Hence am I cross and peevish as a child:
Am pleased by fits to have thee for my foe,
Yet ever willing to be reconciled: 12
O gentle Creature! do not use me so,
But once and deeply let me be beguiled.

XIII

TO SLEEP

[Composed (?).—Published 1807.]

FOND words have oft been spoken to thee,
    Sleep!
And thou hast had thy store of tenderest
    names;
The very sweetest Fancy culls or frames,
When thankfulness of heart is strong and
    deep!
Dear Bosom-child we call thee, that dost
    steep   5
In rich reward all suffering; Balm that
    tames
All anguish; Saint that evil thoughts and
    aims
Takest away, and into souls dost creep,
Like to a breeze from heaven. Shall I
    alone,
I surely not a man ungently made,   10
Call thee worst Tyrant by which Flesh is
    crost?
Perverse, self-willed to own and to disown,
Mere slave of them who never for thee
    prayed,
Still last to come where thou art wanted
    most!

XIV

TO SLEEP

[Composed (?).—Published 1807.]

A FLOCK of sheep that leisurely pass by,
One after one; the sound of rain, and bees
Murmuring; the fall of rivers, winds and
    seas,
Smooth fields, white sheets of water, and
    pure sky;
I have thought of all by turns, and yet
    do lie   5
Sleepless! and soon the small birds'
    melodies
Must hear, first uttered from my orchard
    trees;
And the first cuckoo's melancholy cry.
Even thus last night, and two nights more,
    I lay
And could not win thee, Sleep! by any
    stealth: 10

MISCELLANEOUS SONNETS

So do not let me wear to-night away:
Without Thee what is all the morning's
    wealth?
Come, blessed barrier between day and
    day,
Dear mother of fresh thoughts and joyous
    health!

XV

THE WILD DUCK'S NEST

[Composed (?).—Published 1819.]

THE imperial Consort of the Fairy-king
Owns not a sylvan bower; or gorgeous cell
With emerald floored, and with purpureal
    shell
Ceilinged and roofed; that is so fair a thing
As this low structure, for the tasks of
    Spring   5
Prepared by one who loves the buoyant
    swell
Of the brisk waves, yet here consents to
    dwell;
And spreads in steadfast peace her brood-
    ing wing.
Words cannot paint the oer'shadowing
    yew-tree bough,
And dimly-gleaming Nest,—a hollow
    crown   10
Of golden leaves inlaid with silver down,
Fine as the mother's softest plumes allow:
I gazed—and, self-accused while gazing,
    sighed
For human-kind, weak slaves of cumbrous
    pride!

XVI

WRITTEN UPON A BLANK LEAF IN 'THE COMPLETE ANGLER'

[Composed (?).—Published 1819.]

WHILE flowing rivers yield a blameless
    sport,
Shall live the name of Walton: Sage
    benign!
Whose pen, the mysteries of the rod and
    line
Unfolding, did not fruitlessly exhort   4
To reverend watching of each still report
That Nature utters from her rural shrine.
Meek, nobly versed in simple discipline—
He found the longest summer day too
    short,
To his loved pastime given by sedgy Lee,
Or down the tempting maze of Shawford
    brook—   10
Fairer than life itself, in this sweet Book,
The cowslip-bank and shady willow-tree;
And the fresh meads—where flowed, from
    every nook
Of his full bosom, gladsome Piety!

XVII

TO THE POET, JOHN DYER

[Composed 1811.—Published 1820.]

BARD of the Fleece, whose skilful genius
    made
That work a living landscape fair and
    bright;
Nor hallowed less with musical delight
Than those soft scenes through which thy
    childhood strayed,
Those southern tracts of Cambria, 'deep
    embayed,   5
With green hills fenced, with ocean's mur-
    mur lulled;'
Though hasty Fame hath many a chaplet
    culled
For worthless brows, while in the pensive
    shade
Of cold neglect she leaves thy head un-
    graced,
Yet pure and powerful minds, hearts
    meek and still,   10
A grateful few, shall love thy modest Lay,
Long as the shepherd's bleating flock
    shall stray
O'er naked Snowdon's wide aerial waste;
Long as the thrush shall pipe on Grongar
    Hill!

XVIII

ON THE DETRACTION WHICH FOLLOWED THE PUBLICATION OF A CERTAIN POEM

[Composed 1820.—Published 1820.]

See Milton's Sonnet, beginning, 'A Book was
    writ of late called "Tetrachordon."'

A BOOK came forth of late, called PETER
    BELL;
Not negligent the style;—the matter?—
    good
As aught that song records of Robin
    Hood;
Or Roy, renowned through many a Scot-
    tish dell;
But some (who brook those hackneyed
    themes full well,   5
Nor heat, at Tam o' Shanter's name, their
    blood)
Waxed wroth, and with foul claws, a
    harpy brood,
On Bard and Hero clamorously fell.
Heed not, wild Rover once through heath
    and glen,
Who mad'st at length the better life thy
    choice,   10
Heed not such onset! nay, if praise of men
To thee appear not an unmeaning voice,
Lift up that grey-haired forehead and
    rejoice
In the just tribute of thy Poet's pen!

XIX

[Composed (?).—Published 1819.]

GRIEF, thou hast lost an ever-ready friend
Now that the cottage Spinning-wheel is
　　mute;
And Care—a comforter that best could
　　suit
Her froward mood, and softliest repre-
　　hend;
And Love—a charmer's voice, that used
　　to lend,　　　　　　　　　　　　5
More efficaciously than aught that flows
From harp or lute, kind influence to com-
　　pose
The throbbing pulse—else troubled with-
　　out end:
Even Joy could tell, Joy craving truce and
　　rest
From her own overflow, what power
　　sedate　　　　　　　　　　　　10
On those revolving motions did await
Assiduously—to soothe her aching breast;
And, to a point of just relief, abate
The mantling triumphs of a day too blest.

XX

TO S. H.

[Composed (?).—Published 1827.]

EXCUSE is needless when with love sincere
Of occupation, not by fashion led,
Thou turn'st the Wheel that slept with
　　dust o'erspread;
My nerves from no such murmur shrink,—
　　tho' near,
Soft as the Dorhawk's to a distant ear,　5
When twilight shades darken the moun-
　　tain's head.
Even She who toils to spin our vital thread
Might smile on work, O Lady, once so
　　dear
To household virtues. Venerable Art,
Torn from the Poor! yet shall kind Heaven
　　protect　　　　　　　　　　　　10
Its own; though Rulers, with undue
　　respect,
Trusting to crowded factory and mart
And proud discoveries of the intellect,
Heed not the pillage of man's ancient
　　heart.

XXI

COMPOSED IN ONE OF THE VALLEYS OF
WESTMORELAND, ON EASTER SUNDAY

[Composed (?).—Published 1819.]

WITH each recurrence of this glorious
　　morn
That saw the Saviour in his human frame
Rise from the dead, erewhile the Cottage-
　　dame

Put on fresh raiment—till that hour un-
　　worn:
Domestic hands the home-bred wool had
　　shorn,　　　　　　　　　　　　5
And she who span it culled the daintiest
　　fleece,
In thoughtful reverence to the Prince of
　　Peace,
Whose temples bled beneath the platted
　　thorn.
A blest estate when piety sublime
These humble props disdained not! O
　　green dales!　　　　　　　　　　10
Sad may *I* be who heard your sabbath
　　chime
When Art's abused inventions were un-
　　known;
Kind Nature's various wealth was all
　　your own;
And benefits were weighed in Reason's
　　scales!

XXII

DECAY OF PIETY

[Composed (?).—Published 1827.]

OFT have I seen, ere Time had ploughed
　　my cheek,
Matrons and Sires—who, punctual to the
　　call
Of their loved Church, on fast or festival
Through the long year the House of
　　Prayer would seek:
By Christmas snows, by visitation bleak
Of Easter winds, unscared, from hut or
　　hall　　　　　　　　　　　　6
They came to lowly bench or sculptured
　　stall,
But with one fervour of devotion meek.
I see the places where they once were
　　known,
And ask, surrounded even by kneeling
　　crowds,　　　　　　　　　　　10
Is ancient Piety for ever flown?
Alas! even then they seemed like fleecy
　　clouds
That, struggling through the western sky,
　　have won
Their pensive light from a departed sun!

XXIII

COMPOSED ON THE EVE OF THE MARRIAGE
OF A FRIEND[1] IN THE VALE OF GRASMERE,
1812

[Composed 1812.—Published 1815.]

WHAT need of clamorous bells, or ribands
　　gay,
These humble nuptials to proclaim or
　　grace?
Angels of love, look down upon the place;

---

[1] The poet's wife's brother, Thomas Hutchinson,
who married Mary Monkhouse, November 1, 1812.
—ED.

MISCELLANEOUS SONNETS

Shed on the chosen vale a sun-bright day!
Yet no proud gladness would the Bride
   display   5
Even for such promise:—serious is her
   face,
Modest her mien; and she, whose thoughts
   keep pace
With gentleness, in that becoming way
Will thank you. Faultless does the Maid
   appear;   9
No disproportion in her soul, no strife:
But, when the closer view of wedded life
Hath shown that nothing human can
   be clear
From frailty, for that insight may the Wife
To her indulgent Lord become more dear.

XXIV

FROM THE ITALIAN OF MICHAEL ANGELO

I

[Composed 1805.—Published 1807.]

YES! hope may with my strong desire keep
   pace,
And I be undeluded, unbetrayed;
For if of our affections none finds grace
In sight of Heaven, then, wherefore hath
   God made   4
The world which we inhabit? Better plea
Love cannot have than that in loving thee
Glory to that eternal Peace is paid,
Who such divinity to thee imparts
As hallows and makes pure all gentle
   hearts.
His hope is treacherous only whose love
   dies   10
With beauty, which is varying every hour;
But in chaste hearts, uninfluenced by the
   power
Of outward change, there blooms a death-
   less flower,
That breathes on earth the air of paradise.

XXV

FROM THE SAME

II

[Composed probably 1805.—Published 1807.]

No mortal object did these eyes behold
When first they met the placid light of
   thine,
And my Soul felt her destiny divine,
And hope of endless peace in me grew
   bold:
Heaven-born, the Soul a heavenward
   course must hold;   5
Beyond the visible world she soars to seek
(For what delights the sense is false and
   weak)
Ideal Form, the universal mould.
The wise man, I affirm, can find no rest
In that which perishes: nor will he lend

His heart to aught which doth on time
   depend.   11
'Tis sense, unbridled will, and not true
   love,
That kills the soul: love betters what is
   best,
Even here below, but more in heaven
   above.

XXVI

FROM THE SAME. TO THE SUPREME BEING

III

[Composed 1805.—Published 1807.]

THE prayers I make will then be sweet
   indeed
If Thou the spirit give by which I pray:
My unassisted heart is barren clay,
That of its native self can nothing feed:
Of good and pious works Thou art the
   seed,   5
That quickens only where Thou say'st it
   may:
Unless Thou show to us thine own true
   way
No man can find it: Father! Thou must
   lead.
Do Thou, then, breathe those thoughts
   into my mind   9
By which such virtue may in me be bred
That in thy holy footsteps I may tread;
The fetters of my tongue do Thou unbind,
That I may have the power to sing of Thee,
And sound thy praises everlastingly.

XXVII

[Composed later than June, 1812.—Published
1815.]

SURPRISED by joy—impatient as the Wind
I turned to share the transport—Oh! with
   whom
But Thee,[1] deep buried in the silent tomb,
That spot which no vicissitude can find?
Love, faithful love, recalled thee to my
   mind—   5
But how could I forget thee? Through
   what power,
Even for the least division of an hour,
Have I been so beguiled as to be blind
To my most grievous loss!—That thought's
   return   9
Was the worst pang that sorrow ever bore,
Save one, one only, when I stood forlorn,
Knowing my heart's best treasure was no
   more;
That neither present time, nor years un-
   born
Could to my sight that heavenly face
   restore.

[1] Catherine, the poet's second daughter, born September 6, 1808, died June 5, 1812. See the poem, *Characteristics of a Child Three Years Old*, page 63. —ED.

XXVIII

I

[Composed (?).—Published 1807.]

METHOUGHT I saw the footsteps of a
   throne
Which mists and vapours from mine eyes
   did shroud—
Nor view of who might sit thereon al-
   lowed;
But all the steps and ground about were
   strown
With sights the ruefullest that flesh and
   bone   5
Ever put on; a miserable crowd,
Sick, hale, old, young, who cried before
   that cloud,
'Thou art our king, O Death! to thee we
   groan.'
Those steps I clomb; the mists before me
   gave
Smooth way; and I beheld the face of one
Sleeping alone within a mossy cave,   11
With her face up to heaven; that seemed
   to have
Pleasing remembrance of a thought fore-
   gone;
A lovely Beauty in a summer grave!

XXIX

NOVEMBER, 1836

II

[Composed November, 1836.—Published 1837.]

EVEN so for me a Vision sanctified
The sway of Death; long ere mine eyes
   had seen
Thy countenance—the still rapture of thy
   mien—
When thou, dear Sister! wert become
   Death's Bride:
No trace of pain or languor could abide
That change:—age on thy brow was
   smoothed—thy cold   6
Wan cheek at once was privileged to
   unfold
A loveliness to living youth denied.
Oh! if within me hope should e'er decline,
The lamp of faith, lost Friend! too faintly
   burn;   10
Then may that heaven-revealing smile of
   thine,
The bright assurance, visibly return:
And let my spirit in that power divine
Rejoice, as, through that power, it ceased
   to mourn.

XXX

[Composed August, 1802.—Published 1807.]

IT is a beauteous evening, calm and free,
The holy time is quiet as a Nun
Breathless with adoration; the broad sun
Is sinking down in its tranquillity;

MISCELLANEOUS SONNETS

The gentleness of heaven broods o'er the
   Sea: 5
Listen! the mighty Being is awake,
And doth with his eternal motion make
A sound like thunder—everlastingly.
Dear Child! dear Girl! that walkest with
   me here,
If thou appear untouched by solemn
   thought,   10
Thy nature is not therefore less divine:
Thou liest in Abraham's bosom all the
   year;
And worshipp'st at the Temple's inner
   shrine,
God being with thee when we know it not.

XXXI

[Composed (?).—Published 1807.]

WHERE lies the Land to which yon Ship
   must go?
Fresh as a lark mounting at break of day,
Festively she puts forth in trim array;
Is she for tropic suns, or polar snow?
What boots the enquiry?—Neither friend
   nor foe   5
She cares for; let her travel where she
   may,
She finds familiar names, a beaten way
Ever before her, and a wind to blow.
Yet still I ask, what haven is her mark?
And, almost as it was when ships were
   rare   10
(From time to time, like Pilgrims, here
   and there
Crossing the waters) doubt, and some-
   thing dark,
Of the old Sea some reverential fear,
Is with me at thy farewell, joyous Bark!

XXXII

[Composed (?).—Published 1807.]

WITH Ships the sea was sprinkled far and
   nigh,
Like stars in heaven, and joyously it
   showed;
Some lying fast at anchor in the road,
Some veering up and down, one knew not
   why.
A goodly Vessel did I then espy   5
Come like a giant from a haven broad;
And lustily along the bay she strode,
Her tackling rich, and of apparel high.
This Ship was nought to me, nor I to her,
Yet I pursued her with a Lover's look;   10
This Ship to all the rest did I prefer:
When she will turn, and whither? She
   will brook
No tarrying; where She comes the winds
   must stir:
On went She, and due north her journey
   took.

MISCELLANEOUS SONNETS

XXXIII

[Composed (?).—Published 1807.]

THE world is too much with us; late and
  soon,
Getting and spending, we lay waste our
  powers:
Little we see in Nature that is ours;
We have given our hearts away, a sordid
  boon!
This Sea that bares her bosom to the
  moon;   5
The winds that will be howling at all hours,
And are up-gathered now like sleeping
  flowers;
For this, for everything, we are out of
  tune;
It moves us not.—Great God! I'd rather
  be
A Pagan suckled in a creed outworn;   10
So might I, standing on this pleasant lea,
Have glimpses that would make me less
  forlorn;
Have sight of Proteus rising from the sea;
Or hear old Triton blow his wreathèd
  horn.

XXXIV

[Composed (?).—Published 1823 (Joanna Baillie's
  Poetic Miscellanies); ed. 1827.]

A VOLANT Tribe of Bards on earth are
  found,
Who, while the flattering Zephyrs round
  them play,
On 'coignes of vantage' hang their nests
  of clay;
How quickly from that aery hold un-
  bound,
Dust for oblivion! To the solid ground   5
Of nature trusts the Mind that builds
  for aye;
Convinced that there, there only, she can
  lay
Secure foundations. As the year runs
  round,
Apart she toils within the chosen ring;
While the stars shine, or while day's purple
  eye   10
Is gently closing with the flowers of spring;
Where even the motion of an Angel's wing
Would interrupt the intense tranquillity
Of silent hills, and more than silent sky.

XXXV

[Composed probably 1815.—Published 1815.]

'WEAK is the will of Man, his judgment
  blind;
Remembrance persecutes, and Hope betrays;
Heavy is woe;—and joy, for human-kind,
A mournful thing, so transient is the
  blaze!'   4

Thus might *he* paint our lot of mortal days
Who wants the glorious faculty assigned
To elevate the more-than-reasoning Mind,
And colour life's dark cloud with orient
  rays.
Imagination is that sacred power,
Imagination lofty and refined: 10
'Tis hers to pluck the amaranthine flower
Of Faith, and round the sufferer's temples
  bind
Wreaths that endure affliction's heaviest
  shower,
And do not shrink from sorrow's keenest
  wind.

XXXVI

TO THE MEMORY OF RAISLEY CALVERT

[Composed (?).—Published 1807.]

CALVERT! it must not be unheard by
  them
Who may respect my name that I to thee
Owed many years of early liberty.
This care was thine when sickness did
  condemn
Thy youth to hopeless wasting, root and
  stem—   5
That I, if frugal and severe, might stray
Where'er I liked; and finally array
My temples with the Muse's diadem.
Hence, if in freedom I have loved the
  truth;
If there be aught of pure, or good, or
  great,   10
In my past verse; or shall be, in the lays
Of higher mood, which now I meditate;—
It gladdens me, O worthy, short-lived,
  Youth!
To think how much of this will be thy
  praise.

PART II

I

[Composed (?).—Published 1827.]

SCORN not the Sonnet; Critic, you have
  frowned,
Mindless of its just honours; with this
  key
Shakspeare unlocked his heart; the
  melody
Of this small lute gave ease to Petrarch's
  wound;
A thousand times this pipe did Tasso
  sound;   5
With it Camöens soothed an exile's grief;
The Sonnet glittered a gay myrtle leaf
Amid the cypress with which Dante
  crowned
His visionary brow: a glow-worm lamp,

It cheered mild Spenser, called from
　　Faery-land　　　　　　　10
To struggle through dark ways; and when
　　a damp
Fell round the path of Milton, in his hand
The Thing became a trumpet; whence he
　　blew
Soul-animating strains—alas, too few!

II

[Composed December 1806.—Published 1807.]

How sweet it is, when mother Fancy rocks
The wayward brain, to saunter through a
　　wood!
An old place, full of many a lovely brood,
Tall trees, green arbours, and ground-
　　flowers in flocks;
And wild rose tip-toe upon hawthorn
　　stocks,　　　　　　　　　　　5
Like a bold Girl, who plays her agile
　　pranks
At Wakes and Fairs with wandering
　　Mountebanks,—
When she stands cresting the Clown's
　　head, and mocks
The crowd beneath her. Verily I think,
Such place to me is sometimes like a
　　dream　　　　　　　　　　10
Or map of the whole world: thoughts,
　　link by link,
Enter through ears and eyesight, with
　　such gleam
Of all things, that at last in fear I shrink,
And leap at once from the delicious
　　stream.

III

TO B. R. HAYDON

[Composed December 1815.—Published February
4, 1816 (*The Champion*); March 31, 1816 (*The
Examiner*); vol. of 1816.]

HIGH is our calling, Friend!—Creative
　　Art
(Whether the instrument of words she use,
Or pencil pregnant with ethereal hues,)
Demands the service of a mind and heart,
Though sensitive, yet, in their weakest
　　part,　　　　　　　　　　　5
Heroically fashioned—to infuse
Faith in the whispers of the lonely Muse,
While the whole world seems adverse to
　　desert.
And, oh! when Nature sinks, as oft she
　　may,
Through long-lived pressure of obscure
　　distress,　　　　　　　　　10
Still to be strenuous for the bright reward,
And in the soul admit of no decay,
Brook no continuance of weak-minded-
　　ness—
Great is the glory, for the strife is hard!

MISCELLANEOUS SONNETS

IV

[Composed 1814.—Published 1815.]

FROM the dark chambers of dejection
　　freed,
Spurning the unprofitable yoke of care,
Rise, GILLIES, rise: the gales of youth shall
　　bear
Thy genius forward like a wingèd steed.
Though bold Bellerophon (so Jove de-
　　creed　　　　　　　　　　　5
In wrath) fell headlong from the fields of
　　air,
Yet a rich guerdon waits on minds that
　　dare,
If aught be in them of immortal seed,
And reason govern that audacious flight
Which heavenward they direct.—Then
　　droop not thou,　　　　　　10
Erroneously renewing a sad vow
In the low dell 'mid Roslin's faded grove:
A cheerful life is what the Muses love,
A soaring spirit is their prime delight.

V

[Composed (?).—Published 1827.]

FAIR Prime of life! were it enough to gild
With ready sunbeams every straggling
　　shower;
And, if an unexpected cloud should lower,
Swiftly thereon a rainbow arch to build
For Fancy's errands,—then, from fields
　　half-tilled　　　　　　　　　5
Gathering green weeds to mix with poppy
　　flower,
Thee might thy Minions crown, and chant
　　thy power,
Unpitied by the wise, all censure stilled.
Ah! show that worthier honours are thy
　　due;
Fair Prime of life! arouse the deeper
　　heart;　　　　　　　　　　10
Confirm the Spirit glorying to pursue
Some path of steep ascent and lofty aim;
And, if there be a joy that slights the claim
Of grateful memory, bid that joy depart.

VI

[Composed (?).—Published 1819.]

I WATCH, and long have watched, with
　　calm regret
Yon slowly-sinking star—immortal Sire
(So might he seem) of all the glittering
　　quire!
Blue ether still surrounds him—yet—and
　　yet;
But now the horizon's rocky parapet　　5
Is reached, where, forfeiting his bright
　　attire,
He burns—transmuted to a dusky fire—
Then pays submissively the appointed
　　debt

MISCELLANEOUS SONNETS

To the flying moments, and is seen no
  more.
Angels and gods! We struggle with our
  fate,   10
While health, power, glory, from their
  height decline,
Depressed; and then extinguished: and
  our state,
In this, how different, lost Star, from thine,
That no to-morrow shall our beams restore!

VII

[Composed (?).—Published 1819.]

I HEARD (alas! 'twas only in a dream)
Strains—which, as sage Antiquity be-
  lieved,
By waking ears have sometimes been
  received
Wafted adown the wind from lake or
  stream;
A most melodious requiem, a supreme   5
And perfect harmony of notes, achieved
By a fair Swan on drowsy billows heaved,
O'er which her pinions shed a silver gleam.
For is she not the votary of Apollo?
And knows she not, singing as he in-
  spires,   10
That bliss awaits her which the ungenial
  Hollow[1]
Of the dull earth partakes not, nor desires?
Mount, tuneful Bird, and join the im-
  mortal quires!
She soared—and I awoke, struggling in
  vain to follow.

VIII

RETIREMENT

[Composed (?).—Published 1827.]

IF the whole weight of what we think and
  feel,
Save only far as thought and feeling blend
With action, were as nothing, patriot
  Friend!
From thy remonstrance would be no
  appeal;
But to promote and fortify the weal   5
Of her own Being is her paramount end;
A truth which they alone shall comprehend
Who shun the mischief which they cannot
  heal.
Peace in these feverish times is sovereign
  bliss:
Here, with no thirst but what the stream
  can slake,   10
And startled only by the rustling brake,
Cool air I breathe; while the unincum-
  bered Mind,
By some weak aims at services assigned
To gentle Natures, thanks not Heaven
  amiss.

[1] See the 'Phædo' of Plato, by which this Sonnet
was suggested.

IX

[Composed (?).—Published 1823 (Joanna Baillie's
  Poetic Miscellanies); ed. 1827.]

NOT Love, not War, nor the tumultuous
  swell
Of civil conflict, nor the wrecks of change,
Nor Duty struggling with afflictions
  strange—
Not these *alone* inspire the tuneful shell;
But where untroubled peace and concord
  dwell,   5
There also is the Muse not loth to range,
Watching the twilight smoke of cot or
  grange,
Skyward ascending from a woody dell.
Meek aspirations please her, lone endea-
  vour,
And sage content, and placid melancholy;
She loves to gaze upon a crystal river— 11
Diaphanous because it travels slowly;
Soft is the music that would charm for
  ever;
The flower of sweetest smell is shy and
  lowly.

X

[Composed (?).—Published 1815.]

MARK the concentred hazels that en-
  close
Yon old grey Stone, protected from the
  ray
Of noontide suns:—and even the beams
  that play
And glance, while wantonly the rough
  wind blows,
Are seldom free to touch the moss that
  grows   5
Upon that roof, amid embowering gloom,
The very image framing of a Tomb,
In which some ancient Chieftain finds
  repose
Among the lonely mountains.—Live, ye
  trees!
And thou, grey Stone, the pensive like-
  ness keep   10
Of a dark chamber where the Mighty sleep:
For more than Fancy to the influence
  bends
When solitary Nature condescends
To mimic Time's forlorn humanities.

XI

COMPOSED AFTER A JOURNEY ACROSS THE
HAMBLETON HILLS, YORKSHIRE

[Composed October 4, 1802.—Published 1807.]

DARK and more dark the shades of evening fell;
The wished-for point was reached—but at
  an hour
When little could be gained from that
  rich dower
Of prospect, whereof many thousands tell.

208

Yet did the glowing west with marvellous
    power   5
Salute us; there stood Indian citadel,
Temple of Greece, and minster with its
    tower
Substantially expressed—a place for bell
Or clock to toll from! Many a tempting
    isle,
With groves that never were imagined, lay
'Mid seas how steadfast! objects all for
    the eye   11
Of silent rapture; but we felt the while
We should forget them; they are of the
    sky,
And from our earthly memory fade away.

XII

[Composed (?).—Published 1807.]

—'they are of the sky,
And from our earthly memory fade away.'

THOSE words were uttered as in pensive
    mood
We turned, departing from that solemn
    sight:
A contrast and reproach to gross delight,
And life's unspiritual pleasures daily
    wooed!
But now upon this thought I cannot
    brood;   5
It is unstable as a dream of night;
Nor will I praise a cloud, however bright,
Disparaging Man's gifts, and proper food.
Grove, isle, with every shape of sky-built
    dome,
Though clad in colours beautiful and
    pure,   10
Find in the heart of man no natural home:
The immortal Mind craves objects that
    endure:
These cleave to it; from these it cannot
    roam,
Nor they from it: their fellowship is
    secure.

XIII

SEPTEMBER, 1815

[Composed December, 1815.—Published February 11, 1816 (*The Examiner*); vol. of 1816.]

WHILE not a leaf seems faded; while the
    fields,
With ripening harvest prodigally fair,
In brightest sunshine bask; this nipping
    air,
Sent from some distant clime where
    Winter wields
His icy scimitar, a foretaste yields   5
Of bitter change, and bids the flowers
    beware;
And whispers to the silent birds, 'Pre-
    pare
Against the threatening foe your trustiest
    shields.'

For me, who under kindlier laws belong
To Nature's tuneful quire, this rustling
    dry   10
Through leaves yet green, and yon crystal-
    line sky,
Announce a season potent to renew,
'Mid frost and snow, the instinctive joys
    of song,
And nobler cares than listless summer
    knew.

XIV

NOVEMBER 1

[Composed December, 1815.—Published January 28, 1816 (*The Examiner*); vol. of 1816.]

How clear, how keen, how marvellously
    bright
The effluence from yon distant mountain's
    head,
Which, strewn with snow smooth as the
    sky can shed,
Shines like another sun—on mortal sight
Uprisen, as if to check approaching Night,
And all her twinkling stars. Who now
    would tread,   6
If so he might, yon mountain's glittering
    head—
Terrestrial, but a surface, by the flight
Of sad mortality's earth-sullying wing,
Unswept, unstained? Nor shall the aerial
    Powers   10
Dissolve that beauty, destined to endure,
White, radiant, spotless, exquisitely pure,
Through all vicissitudes, till genial Spring
Has filled the laughing vales with wel-
    come flowers.

XV

COMPOSED DURING A STORM

[Composed February, 1819.—Published in *Peter Bell* vol., 1819.]

ONE who was suffering tumult in his soul
Yet failed to seek the sure relief of prayer,
Went forth—his course surrendering to
    the care
Of the fierce wind, while mid-day light-
    nings prowl
Insidiously, untimely thunders growl;   5
While trees, dim-seen, in frenzied num-
    bers, tear
The lingering remnant of their yellow hair,
And shivering wolves, surprised with
    darkness, howl
As if the sun were not. He raised his eye
Soul-smitten; for, that instant did appear
Large space ('mid dreadful clouds) of
    purest sky,   11
An azure disc—shield of Tranquillity;
Invisible, unlooked-for, minister
Of providential goodness ever nigh!

MISCELLANEOUS SONNETS

XVI

TO A SNOWDROP

[Composed (?).—Published 1819.]

LONE Flower, hemmed in with snows, and white as they
But hardier far, once more I see thee bend
Thy forehead as if fearful to offend,
Like an unbidden guest. Though day by day
Storms, sallying from the mountain-tops, waylay 5
The rising sun, and on the plains descend;
Yet art thou welcome, welcome as a friend
Whose zeal outruns his promise! Blue-eyed May
Shall soon behold this border thickly set
With bright jonquils, their odours lavishing 10
On the soft west-wind and his frolic peers;
Nor will I then thy modest grace forget,
Chaste Snowdrop, venturous harbinger of Spring,
And pensive monitor of fleeting years!

XVII

TO THE LADY MARY LOWTHER

With a selection from the Poems of Anne, Countess of Winchilsea; and extracts of similar character from other Writers; transcribed by a female friend.

[Composed (?).—Published 1820.]

LADY! I rifled a Parnassian Cave
(But seldom trod) of mildly-gleaming ore;
And culled, from sundry beds a lucid store
Of genuine crystals, pure as those that pave
The azure brooks, where Dian joys to lave
Her spotless limbs; and ventured to explore 6
Dim shades—for reliques, upon Lethe's shore,
Cast up at random by the sullen wave.
To female hands the treasures were resigned;
And lo this Work!—a grotto bright and clear 10
From stain or taint; in which thy blameless mind
May feed on thoughts though pensive not austere;
Or, if thy deeper spirit be inclined
To holy musing, it may enter here.

XVIII

TO LADY BEAUMONT

[Composed January or February, 1807.—Published 1807.]

LADY! the songs of Spring were in the grove
While I was shaping beds for winter flowers;
While I was planting green unfading bowers,
And shrubs—to hang upon the warm alcove,
And sheltering wall; and still, as Fancy wove 5
The dream, to time and nature's blended powers
I gave this paradise for winter hours,
A labyrinth, Lady! which your feet shall rove.
Yes! when the sun of life more feebly shines,
Becoming thoughts, I trust, of solemn gloom 10
Or of high gladness you shall hither bring;
And these perennial bowers and murmuring pines
Be gracious as the music and the bloom
And all the mighty ravishment of spring.

XIX

[Composed (?).—Published 1827.]

THERE is a pleasure in poetic pains
Which only Poets know;—'t was rightly said;
Whom could the Muses else allure to tread
Their smoothest paths, to wear their lightest chains?
When happiest Fancy has inspired the strains, 5
How oft the malice of one luckless word
Pursues the Enthusiast to the social board,
Haunts him belated on the silent plains!
Yet he repines not, if his thought stand clear,
At last, of hindrance and obscurity, 10
Fresh as the star that crowns the brow of morn;
Bright, speckless, as a softly-moulded tear
The moment it has left the virgin's eye,
Or rain-drop lingering on the pointed thorn.

XX

[Composed (?).—Published 1815.]

THE Shepherd, looking eastward, softly said,
'Bright is thy veil, O Moon, as thou art bright!'
Forthwith that little cloud, in ether spread
And penetrated all with tender light,
She cast away, and showed her fulgent head 5
Uncovered; dazzling the Beholder's sight
As if to vindicate her beauty's right,
Her beauty thoughtlessly disparagèd.
Meanwhile that veil, removed or thrown aside,
Went floating from her, darkening as it went; 10
And a huge mass, to bury or to hide,
Approached this glory of the firmament;
Who meekly yields, and is obscured—content
With one calm triumph of a modest pride.

XXI

[Composed not later than 1819.—Published 1820.]

WHEN haughty expectations prostrate lie,
And grandeur crouches like a guilty thing,
Oft shall the lowly weak, till nature bring
Mature release, in fair society
Survive, and Fortune's utmost anger try;
Like these frail snowdrops that together
   cling,   6
And nod their helmets, smitten by the wing
Of many a furious whirl-blast sweeping by.
Observe the faithful flowers! if small to
   great
May lead the thoughts, thus struggling
   used to stand   10
The Emathian phalanx, nobly obstinate;
And so the bright immortal Theban band,
Whom onset, fiercely urged at Jove's
   command,
Might overwhelm, but could not separate!

XXII

[Composed (?).—Published 1815.]

HAIL, Twilight, sovereign of one peaceful
   hour!
Not dull art Thou as undiscerning Night;
But studious only to remove from sight
Day's mutable distinctions.—Ancient
   Power!
Thus did the waters gleam, the moun-
   tains lower,   5
To the rude Briton, when, in wolf-skin vest
Here roving wild, he laid him down to rest
On the bare rock, or through a leafy bower
Looked ere his eyes were closed. By him
   was seen
The self-same Vision which we now be-
   hold,   10
At thy meek bidding, shadowy Power!
   brought forth;
These mighty barriers, and the gulf be-
   tween;
The flood, the stars,—a spectacle as old
As the beginning of the heavens and earth!

XXIII[1]

[Composed perhaps 1802.—Published 1807.]

'WITH how sad steps, O Moon, thou
   climb'st the sky,
How silently, and with how wan a face!'
Where art thou? Thou so often seen on
   high
Running among the clouds a Wood-
   nymph's race!
Unhappy Nuns, whose common breath's
   a sigh   5
Which they would stifle, move at such a
   pace!
The northern Wind, to call thee to the
   chase,

[1] This poem originally consisted of fifteen lines: it
was shortened and classed as a Sonnet in ed. 1820.
See *Supplement*, page 493.—ED.

Must blow to-night his bugle horn. Had I
The power of Merlin, Goddess! this
   should be:
And all the stars, fast as the clouds were
   riven,   10
Should sally forth, to keep thee company,
Hurrying and sparkling through the clear
   blue heaven;
But, Cynthia! should to thee the palm be
   given,
Queen both for beauty and for majesty.

XXIV

[Composed (?).—Published 1815.]

EVEN as a dragon's eye that feels the stress
Of a bedimming sleep, or as a lamp
Sullenly[2] glaring through sepulchral damp,
So burns yon Taper 'mid a black recess
Of mountains, silent, dreary, motionless:
The lake below reflects it not; the sky   6
Muffled in clouds, affords no company
To mitigate and cheer its loneliness.
Yet, round the body of that joyless Thing
Which sends so far its melancholy light,
Perhaps are seated in domestic ring   11
A gay society with faces bright,
Conversing, reading, laughing;—or they
   sing,
While hearts and voices in the song unite.

XXV

[Composed (?).—Published 1820.]

THE stars are mansions built by Nature's
   hand,
And, haply, there the spirits of the blest
Dwell, clothed in radiance, their immortal
   vest;
Huge Ocean shows, within his yellow
   strand,
A habitation marvellously planned,   5
For life to occupy in love and rest;
All that we see—is dome, or vault, or nest,
Or fortress, reared at Nature's sage com-
   mand.
Glad thought for every season! but the
   Spring
Gave it while cares were weighing on my
   heart,   10
'Mid song of birds, and insects murmuring;
And while the youthful year's prolific art—
Of bud, leaf, blade, and flower—was
   fashioning
Abodes where self-disturbance hath no
   part.

[2] The collective edd. of the Poems from 1827 to
1849 read 'suddenly'; edd. 1815, 1820, and the
Sonnet-vol. of 1838 read 'sullenly'. The latter is
undoubtedly the word intended by Wordsworth.
Cf. 'sullen fire', Misc. Son. II. vi. l. 7 (edd. 1819,
1820, 1827); 'sullen star', *Excursion* IV. 487; and
the 'sullen light', i e. the faintly glowing wick of an
extinguished candle, spoken of in Wordsworth's
reply to the letter of *Mathetes* (*The Friend*, iii. 48,
ed. 1818).—ED.

MISCELLANEOUS SONNETS

XXVI

[Composed (?).—Published 1835.]

DESPONDING Father! mark this altered bough,
So beautiful of late, with sunshine warmed,
Or moist with dews; what more unsightly now,
Its blossoms shrivelled, and its fruit, if formed,
Invisible? yet Spring her genial brow   5
Knits not o'er that discolouring and decay
As false to expectation. Nor fret thou
At like unlovely process in the May
Of human life: a Stripling's graces blow,
Fade and are shed, that from their timely fall   10
(Misdeem it not a cankerous change) may grow
Rich mellow bearings, that for thanks shall call:
In all men, sinful is it to be slow
To hope—in Parents, sinful above all.

XXVII

CAPTIVITY.—MARY QUEEN OF SCOTS

[Composed (?).—Published 1819.]

'As the cold aspect of a sunless way
Strikes through the Traveller's frame with deadlier chill,
Oft as appears a grove, or obvious hill,
Glistening with unparticipated ray,
Or shining slope where he must never stray;   5
So joys, remembered without wish or will,
Sharpen the keenest edge of present ill,—
On the crushed heart a heavier burthen lay.
Just Heaven, contract the compass of my mind   9
To fit proportion with my altered state!
Quench those felicities whose light I find
Reflected in my bosom all too late!—
O be my spirit, like my thraldom, strait;
And, like mine eyes that stream with sorrow, blind!'

XXVIII

ST. CATHERINE OF LEDBURY

[Composed (?).—Published 1835.]

WHEN human touch (as monkish books attest)
Nor was applied nor could be, Ledbury bells
Broke forth in concert flung adown the dells,
And upward, high as Malvern's cloudy crest;
Sweet tones, and caught by a noble Lady blest   5
To rapture! Mabel listened at the side
Of her loved mistress: soon the music died,
And Catherine said, Here J set up my rest.
Warned in a dream, the Wanderer long had sought
A home that by such miracle of sound   10
Must be revealed:—she heard it now, or felt
The deep, deep joy of a confiding thought;
And there, a saintly Anchoress, she dwelt
Till she exchanged for heaven that happy ground.

XXIX

[Composed probably 1807.—Published 1807.]

——'gives to airy nothing
A local habitation and a name.'

THOUGH narrow be that old Man's cares, and near,
The poor old Man is greater than he seems:
For he hath waking empire, wide as dreams;
An ample sovereignty of eye and ear.
Rich are his walks with supernatural cheer;   5
The region of his inner spirit teems
With vital sounds and monitory gleams
Of high astonishment and pleasing fear.
He the seven birds hath seen, that never part,
Seen the SEVEN WHISTLERS in their nightly rounds,   10
And counted them: and oftentimes will start—
For overhead are sweeping GABRIEL'S HOUNDS
Doomed, with their impious Lord, the flying Hart
To chase for ever, on aerial grounds!

XXX

[Composed (?).—Published 1835.]

FOUR fiery steeds impatient of the rein
Whirled us o'er sunless ground beneath a sky
As void of sunshine, when, from that wide plain,
Clear tops of far-off mountains we descry,
Like a Sierra of cerulean Spain,   5
All light and lustre. Did no heart reply?
Yes, there was One;—for One, asunder fly
The thousand links of that ethereal chain;
And green vales open out, with grove and field,   9
And the fair front of many a happy Home;
Such tempting spots as into vision come
While Soldiers, weary of the arms they wield,
And sick at heart of strifeful Christendom,
Gaze on the moon by parting clouds revealed.

212

XXXI

[Composed 1806.—Published 1815.]

BROOK! whose society the Poet seeks,
Intent his wasted spirits to renew;
And whom the curious Painter doth
    pursue
Through rocky passes, among flowery
    creeks,
And tracks thee dancing down thy water-
    breaks;   5
If wish were mine some type of thee to
    view,
Thee, and not thee thyself, I would not do
Like Grecian Artists, give thee human
    cheeks,
Channels for tears; no Naiad shouldst
    thou be,—
Have neither limbs, feet, feathers, joints,
    nor hairs: 10
It seems the Eternal Soul is clothed in thee
With purer robes than those of flesh and
    blood,
And hath bestowed on thee a safer good;
Unwearied joy, and life without its cares.

XXXII

COMPOSED ON THE BANKS OF A ROCKY STREAM

[Composed (?).—Published 1820.]

DOGMATIC Teachers, of the snow-white
    fur!
Ye wrangling Schoolmen, of the scarlet
    hood!
Who, with a keenness not to be withstood,
Press the point home, or falter and demur,
Checked in your course by many a teasing
    burr;   5
These natural council-seats your acrid
    blood
Might cool;—and, as the Genius of the
    flood
Stoops willingly to animate and spur
Each lighter function slumbering in the
    brain,
Yon eddying balls of foam, these arrowy
    gleams   10
That o'er the pavement of the surging
    streams
Welter and flash, a synod might detain
With subtle speculations, haply vain,
But surely less so than your far-fetched
    themes!

XXXIII

THIS AND THE TWO FOLLOWING WERE SUGGESTED BY MR. W. WESTALL'S VIEWS OF THE CAVES, ETC., IN YORKSHIRE

[Composed 1818.—Published January, 1819 (*Blackwood's Magazine*); *Peter Bell* vol., 1819.]

PURE element of waters! wheresoe'er
Thou dost forsake thy subterranean
    haunts,
Green herbs, bright flowers, and berry-
    bearing plants,
Rise into life and in thy train appear:
And, through the sunny portion of the
    year,   5
Swift insects shine, thy hovering pursui-
    vants:
And, if thy bounty fail, the forest pants;
And hart and hind and hunter with his
    spear
Languish and droop together. Nor unfelt
In man's perturbèd soul thy sway benign;
And, haply, far within the marble belt 11
Of central earth, where tortured Spirits pine
For grace and goodness lost, thy mur-
    murs melt
Their anguish,—and they blend sweet
    songs with thine.[1]

XXXIV

MALHAM COVE

[Composed 1818.—Published January, 1819 (*Blackwood's Magazine*); *Peter Bell* vol., 1819.]

WAS the aim frustrated by force or guile,
When giants scooped from out the rocky
    ground,
Tier under tier, this semicirque profound?
(Giants—the same who built in Erin's isle
That Causeway with incomparable toil!)—
Oh, had this vast theatric structure wound
With finished sweep into a perfect round,
No mightier work had gained the plausive
    smile
Of all-beholding Phœbus! But, alas,
Vain earth! false world! Foundations
    must be laid   10
In Heaven; for, 'mid the wreck of IS and
    WAS,
Things incomplete and purposes betrayed
Make sadder transits o'er thought's optic
    glass
Than noblest objects utterly decayed.

XXXV

GORDALE

[Composed 1818.—Published January, 1819 (*Blackwood's Magazine*); *Peter Bell* vol., 1819.]

AT early dawn, or rather when the air
Glimmers with fading light, and shadowy
    Eve
Is busiest to confer and to bereave;
Then, pensive Votary! let thy feet repair
To Gordale-chasm, terrific as the lair 5
Where the young lions couch; for so, by
    leave
Of the propitious hour, thou may'st per-
    ceive
The local Deity, with oozy hair

[1] Waters (as Mr. Westall informs us in the letter-press prefixed to his admirable views) are invariably found to flow through these caverns.

MISCELLANEOUS SONNETS

And mineral crown, beside his jagged
     urn,
Recumbent: Him thou may'st behold,
     who hides   10
His lineaments by day, yet there presides,
Teaching the docile waters how to turn,
Or (if need be) impediment to spurn,
And force their passage to the salt-sea
     tides!

XXXVI

COMPOSED UPON WESTMINSTER BRIDGE, SEPTEMBER 3, 1802

[Composed July 31, 1802.—Published 1807.]

EARTH has not anything to show more
     fair:
Dull would he be of soul who could pass by
A sight so touching in its majesty:
This City now doth, like a garment, wear
The beauty of the morning; silent, bare,
Ships, towers, domes, theatres, and tem-
     ples lie   6
Open unto the fields, and to the sky;
All bright and glittering in the smokeless
     air.
Never did sun more beautifully steep
In his first splendour, valley, rock, or
     hill;   10
Ne'er saw I, never felt, a calm so deep!
The river glideth at his own sweet will:
Dear God! the very houses seem asleep;
And all that mighty heart is lying still!

XXXVII

CONCLUSION

TO ——

[Composed probably 1827.—Published 1827.]

IF these brief Records, by the Muses' art
Produced as lonely Nature or the strife
That animates the scenes of public life[1]
Inspired, may in thy leisure claim a part;
And if these Transcripts of the private
     heart   5
Have gained a sanction from thy falling
     tears;
Then I repent not. But my soul hath fears
Breathed from eternity; for, as a dart
Cleaves the blank air, Life flies: now every
     day
Is but a glimmering spoke in the swift
     wheel   10
Of the revolving week. Away, away,
All fitful cares, all transitory zeal!
So timely Grace the immortal wing may
     heal,
And honour rest upon the senseless clay.

[1] This line alludes to Sonnets which will be found
in another Class.

PART III

I

[Composed (?).—Published 1842.]

THOUGH the bold wings of Poesy affect
The clouds, and wheel around the moun-
     tain tops
Rejoicing, from her loftiest height she drops
Well pleased to skim the plain with wild
     flowers deckt,
Or muse in solemn grove whose shades
     protect   5
The lingering dew—there steals along, or
     stops
Watching the least small bird that round
     her hops,
Or creeping worm, with sensitive respect.
Her functions are they therefore less
     divine,
Her thoughts less deep, or void of grave
     intent   10
Her simplest fancies? Should that fear
     be thine,
Aspiring Votary, ere thy hand present
One offering, kneel before her modest
     shrine,
With brow in penitential sorrow bent!

II

OXFORD, MAY 30, 1820

[Composed 1820.—Published 1820.]

YE sacred Nurseries of blooming Youth!
In whose collegiate shelter England's
     Flowers
Expand, enjoying through their vernal
     hours
The air of liberty, the light of truth;
Much have ye suffered from Time's gnaw-
     ing tooth: 5
Yet, O ye spires of Oxford! domes and
     towers!
Gardens and groves! your presence over-
     powers
The soberness of reason; till, in sooth,
Transformed, and rushing on a bold ex-
     change
I slight my own beloved Cam, to range   10
Where silver Isis leads my stripling feet;
Pace the long avenue, or glide adown
The stream-like windings of that glorious
     street—
An eager Novice robed in fluttering gown!

III

OXFORD, MAY 30, 1820

[Composed 1820.—Published 1820.]

SHAME on this faithless heart! that could
     allow
Such transport, though but for a mo-
     ment's space;
Not while—to aid the spirit of the place—

214

The crescent moon clove with its glittering
  prow
The clouds, or night-bird sang from shady
  bough;   5
But in plain daylight:——She, too, at my
  side,
Who, with her heart's experience satisfied,
Maintains inviolate its slightest vow!
Sweet Fancy! other gifts must I receive;
Proofs of a higher sovereignty I claim;   10
Take from *her* brow the withering flowers
  of eve,
And to that brow life's morning wreath
  restore;
Let *her* be comprehended in the frame
Of these illusions, or they please no more.

IV

RECOLLECTION OF THE PORTRAIT OF KING
  HENRY THE EIGHTH, TRINITY LODGE,
  CAMBRIDGE

[Composed (?).—Published 1827.]

THE imperial Stature, the colossal stride,
Are yet before me; yet do I behold
The broad full visage, chest of amplest
  mould,
The vestments 'broidered with barbaric
  pride:
And lo! a poniard, at the Monarch's side,
Hangs ready to be grasped in sympathy   6
With the keen threatenings of that ful-
  gent eye,
Below the white-rimmed bonnet, far-
  descried.
Who trembles now at thy capricious
  mood?
'Mid those surrounding Worthies, haughty
  King,   10
We rather think, with grateful mind
  sedate,
How Providence educeth, from the spring
Of lawless will, unlooked-for streams of
  good,
Which neither force shall check nor time
  abate!

V

ON THE DEATH OF HIS MAJESTY (GEORGE
  THE THIRD)

[Composed 1820.—Published 1820.]

WARD of the Law!—dread Shadow of a
  King!
Whose realm had dwindled to one stately
  room;
Whose universe was gloom immersed in
  gloom,
Darkness as thick as life o'er life could
  fling,
Save haply for some feeble glimmering   5
Of Faith and Hope—if thou, by nature's
  doom,
Gently hast sunk into the quiet tomb,

Why should we bend in grief, to sorrow
  cling,
When thankfulness were best?—Fresh-
  flowing tears,
Or, where tears flow not, sigh succeeding
  sigh,   10
Yield to such after-thought the sole reply
Which justly it can claim. The Nation
  hears
In this deep knell, silent for threescore
  years,
An unexampled voice of awful memory!

VI

JUNE, 1820

[Composed 1820.—Published 1820.]

FAME tells of groves—from England far
  away—
Groves[1] that inspire the Nightingale to
  trill
And modulate, with subtle reach of skill
Elsewhere unmatched, her ever-varying
  lay;
Such bold report I venture to gainsay: 5
For I have heard the quire of Richmond
  hill
Chanting with indefatigable bill,
Strains that recalled to mind a distant
  day;
When, haply under shade of that same
  wood,
And scarcely conscious of the dashing
  oars   10
Plied steadily between those willowy
  shores,
The sweet-souled Poet of the Seasons
  stood—
Listening, and listening long, in raptur-
  ous mood,
Ye heavenly Birds! to your Progenitors.

VII

A PARSONAGE IN OXFORDSHIRE

[Composed 1820.—Published 1822 (*Ecclesiastical
Sketches*, note, p. 121); ed. 1827.]

WHERE holy ground begins, unhallowed
  ends,
Is marked by no distinguishable line;
The turf unites, the pathways intertwine;
And, wheresoe'er the stealing footstep
  tends,
Garden, and that Domain where kindred,
  friends,   5
And neighbours rest together, here con-
  found
Their several features, mingled like the
  sound
Of many waters, or as evening blends
With shady night. Soft airs, from shrub
  and flower,

---

[1] Wallachia is the country alluded to.

215

MISCELLANEOUS SONNETS

Waft fragrant greetings to each silent
    grave;   10
And while those lofty poplars gently wave
Their tops, between them comes and goes
    a sky
Bright as the glimpses of eternity,
To saints accorded in their mortal hour.

VIII

COMPOSED AMONG THE RUINS OF A CASTLE
IN NORTH WALES

[Composed probably September, 1824.—Published
1827.]

THROUGH shattered galleries, 'mid roof-
    less halls,
Wandering with timid footsteps oft be-
    trayed,
The Stranger sighs, nor scruples to up-
    braid
Old Time, though he, gentlest among the
    Thralls   4
Of Destiny, upon these wounds hath laid
His lenient touches, soft as light that falls,
From the wan Moon, upon the towers and
    walls,
Light deepening the profoundest sleep of
    shade.
Relic of Kings! Wreck of forgotten wars,
To winds abandoned and the prying stars,
Time *loves* Thee! at his call the Seasons
    twine   11
Luxuriant wreaths around thy forehead
    hoar;
And, though past pomp no changes can
    restore,
A soothing recompense, his gift, is thine!

IX

TO THE LADY E. B. AND THE HON. MISS P.

[Composed September, 1824.—Published 1827.]

Composed in the Grounds of Plass Newidd, near
Llangollen, 1824.

A STREAM, to mingle with your favourite
    Dee,
Along the VALE OF MEDITATION[1] flows;
So styled by those fierce Britons, pleased
    to see
In Nature's face the expression of repose;
Or haply there some pious hermit chose   5
To live and die, the peace of heaven his
    aim;
To whom the wild sequestered region owes,
At this late day, its sanctifying name.
GLYN CAFAILLGAROCH, in the Cambrian
    tongue,
In ours, the VALE OF FRIENDSHIP, let *this*
    spot   10
Be named; where, faithful to a low-roofed
    Cot,

[1] Glyn Myrvr.

On Deva's banks, ye have abode so long;
Sisters in love, a love allowed to climb,
Even on this earth, above the reach of
    Time!

X

TO THE TORRENT AT THE DEVIL'S BRIDGE,
NORTH WALES, 1824

[Composed September, 1824.—Published 1827.]

How art thou named? In search of what
    strange land,
From what huge height, descending? Can
    such force
Of waters issue from a British source,
Or hath not Pindus fed thee, where the
    band
Of Patriots scoop their freedom out, with
    hand   5
Desperate as thine? Or come the inces-
    sant shocks
From that young Stream, that smites the
    throbbing rocks,
Of Viamala? There I seem to stand,
As in life's morn; permitted to behold,
From the dread chasm, woods climbing
    above woods,   10
In pomp that fades not; everlasting snows;
And skies that ne'er relinquish their
    repose:
Such power possess the family of floods
Over the minds of Poets, young or old!

XI

IN THE WOODS OF RYDAL

[Composed (?).—Published 1827.]

WILD Redbreast! hadst thou at Jemima's
    lip
Pecked, as at mine, thus boldly, Love
    might say,
A half-blown rose had tempted thee to sip
Its glistening dews; but hallowed is the
    clay
Which the Muse warms; and I, whose
    head is grey,   5
Am not unworthy of thy fellowship;
Nor could I let one thought—one motion
    —slip
That might thy sylvan confidence betray.
For are we not all His without whose care
Vouchsafed no sparrow falleth to the
    ground?   10
Who gives his Angels wings to speed
    through air,
And rolls the planets through the blue
    profound;
Then peck or perch, fond Flutterer! nor
    forbear
To trust a Poet in still musings bound.

216

XII

[Composed (?).—Published 1827.]

WHEN Philoctetes in the Lemnian isle
Like a Form sculptured on a monument
Lay couched; on him or his dread bow
    unbent
Some wild Bird oft might settle and
    beguile
The rigid features of a transient smile,   5
Disperse the tear, or to the sigh give vent,
Slackening the pains of ruthless banish-
    ment
From his loved home, and from heroic
    toil.
And trust that spiritual Creatures round
    us move,   9
Griefs to allay which Reason cannot heal;
Yea, veriest reptiles have sufficed to prove
To fettered wretchedness that no Bastille
Is deep enough to exclude the light of love,
Though man for brother man has ceased
    to feel.

XIII

[Composed (?).—Published 1827.]

WHILE Anna's peers and early playmates
    tread,
In freedom, mountain-turf and river's
    marge;
Or float with music in the festal barge;
Rein the proud steed, or through the
    dance are led;
Her doom it is to press a weary bed—   5
Till oft her guardian Angel, to some
    charge
More urgent called, will stretch his wings
    at large,
And friends too rarely prop the languid
    head.
Yet, helped by Genius—untired com-
    forter,
The presence even of a stuffed Owl for
    her   10
Can cheat the time; sending her fancy out
To ivied castles and to moonlight skies,
Though he can neither stir a plume, nor
    shout;
Nor veil, with restless film, his staring
    eyes.

XIV

TO THE CUCKOO

[Composed (?).—Published 1827.]

NOT the whole warbling grove in concert
    heard
When sunshine follows shower, the breast
    can thrill
Like the first summons, Cuckoo! of thy
    bill,
With its twin notes inseparably paired.
The captive 'mid damp vaults unsunned,
    unaired,   5

Measuring the periods of his lonely doom,
That cry can reach; and to the sick man's
    room
Sends gladness, by no languid smile
    declared.
The lordly eagle-race through hostile
    search
May perish; time may come when never
    more   10
The wilderness shall hear the lion roar;
But, long as cock shall crow from house-
    hold perch
To rouse the dawn, soft gales shall speed
    thy wing,
And thy erratic voice be faithful to the
    Spring!

XV

TO ——

[Composed (?).—Published 1835.]

'Miss not the occasion: by the forelock take
That subtle Power, the never-halting Time,
Lest a mere moment's putting-off should make
Mischance almost as heavy as a crime.'

'WAIT, prithee, wait!' this answer Lesbia
    threw
Forth to her Dove, and took no further
    heed.
Her eye was busy, while her fingers flew
Across the harp, with soul-engrossing
    speed;
But from that bondage when her thoughts
    were freed   5
She rose, and toward the close-shut case-
    ment drew,
Whence the poor unregarded Favourite,
    true
To old affections, had been heard to plead
With flapping wing for entrance. What a
    shriek
Forced from that voice so lately tuned to
    a strain   10
Of harmony!—a shriek of terror, pain,
And self-reproach! for, from aloft, a Kite
Pounced,—and the Dove, which from its
    ruthless beak
She could not rescue, perished in her
    sight!

XVI

THE INFANT M—— M——

[Composed (?).—Published 1827.]

UNQUIET Childhood here by special grace
Forgets her nature, opening like a flower
That neither feeds nor wastes its vital
    power
In painful struggles. Months each other
    chase,
And nought untunes that Infant's voice;
    no trace   5

MISCELLANEOUS SONNETS

Of fretful temper sullies her pure cheek;
Prompt, lively, self-sufficing, yet so meek
That one enrapt with gazing on her face
(Which even the placid innocence of death
Could scarcely make more placid, heaven
    more bright)   10
Might learn to picture, for the eye of faith,
The Virgin, as she shone with kindred
    light;
A nursling couched upon her mother's
    knee,
Beneath some shady palm of Galilee.

XVII

TO ——, IN HER SEVENTIETH YEAR

[Composed 1824.—Published 1827.]

SUCH age how beautiful! O Lady bright,
Whose mortal lineaments seem all refined
By favouring Nature and a saintly Mind
To something purer and more exquisite
Than flesh and blood; whene'er thou
    meet'st my sight,   5
When I behold thy blanched unwithered
    cheek,
Thy temples fringed with locks of gleam-
    ing white,
And head that droops because the soul
    is meek,
Thee with the welcome Snowdrop I com-
    pare;
That child of winter, prompting thoughts
    that climb   10
From desolation toward the genial prime;
Or with the Moon conquering earth's
    misty air,
And filling more and more with crystal
    light
As pensive Evening deepens into night.

XVIII

TO ROTHA Q——

[Composed some years after 1822.—Published
1827.]

ROTHA, my Spiritual Child! this head was
    grey
When at the sacred font for thee I stood;
Pledged till thou reach the verge of
    womanhood,
And shalt become thy own sufficient stay:
Too late, I feel, sweet Orphan! was the day
For steadfast hope the contract to fulfil; 6
Yet shall my blessing hover o'er thee still,
Embodied in the music of this Lay,
Breathed forth beside the peaceful moun-
    tain Stream[1]
Whose murmur soothed thy languid
    Mother's ear   10

[1] The river Rotha, that flows into Windermere
from the Lakes of Grasmere and Rydal.

After her throes, this Stream of name
    more dear
Since thou dost bear it,—a memorial
    theme
For others; for thy future self, a spell
To summon fancies out of Time's dark
    cell.

XIX

A GRAVESTONE UPON THE FLOOR IN THE
CLOISTERS OF WORCESTER CATHEDRAL

[Composed probably 1828.—Published 1829 (*The
Keepsake*); ed. 1832.]

'MISERRIMUS!' and neither name nor
    date,
Prayer, text, or symbol, graven upon the
    stone;
Nought but that word assigned to the
    unknown,
That solitary word—to separate
From all, and cast a cloud around the fate
Of him who lies beneath. Most wretched
    one,   6
Who chose his epitaph?—Himself alone
Could thus have dared the grave to agitate,
And claim, among the dead, this awful
    crown;
Nor doubt that He marked also for his
    own   10
Close to these cloistral steps a burial-place,
That every foot might fall with heavier
    tread,
Trampling upon his vileness. Stranger,
    pass
Softly!—To save the contrite, Jesus bled.

XX

ROMAN ANTIQUITIES DISCOVERED AT
BISHOPSTONE, HEREFORDSHIRE

[Composed (?).—Published 1835.]

WHILE poring Antiquarians search the
    ground
Upturned with curious pains, the Bard, a
    Seer,
Takes fire:—The men that have been
    reappear;
Romans for travel girt, for business
    gowned;
And some recline on couches, myrtle-
    crowned,   5
In festal glee: why not? For fresh and
    clear,
As if its hues were of the passing year,
Dawns this time-buried pavement. From
    that mound
Hoards may come forth of Trajans, Maxi-
    mins,
Shrunk into coins with all their warlike
    toil: 10

Or a fierce impress issues with its foil
Of tenderness—the Wolf, whose suckling
   Twins
The unlettered ploughboy pities when he
   wins
The casual treasure from the furrowed
   soil.

XXI
1830

[Composed November, 1830.—Published 1835.]

CHATSWORTH! thy stately mansion, and
   the pride
Of thy domain, strange contrast do present
To house and home in many a craggy rent
Of the wild Peak; where new-born waters
   glide
Through fields whose thrifty occupants
   abide   5
As in a dear and chosen banishment,
With every semblance of entire content;
So kind is simple Nature, fairly tried!
Yet He whose heart in childhood gave her
   troth
To pastoral dales, thin-set with modest
   farms,   10
May learn, if judgment strengthen with
   his growth,
That, not for Fancy only, pomp hath
   charms;
And, strenuous to protect from lawless
   harms
The extremes of favoured life, may honour
   both.

XXII

A TRADITION OF OKER HILL IN DARLEY DALE, DERBYSHIRE

[Composed probably 1828.—Published 1829 (*The Keepsake*); ed. 1832.]

'TIS said that to the brow of yon fair hill
Two Brothers clomb, and, turning face
   from face,
Nor one look more exchanging, grief to
   still
Or feed, each planted on that lofty place
A chosen Tree; then, eager to fulfil   5
Their courses, like two new-born rivers,
   they
In opposite directions urged their way
Down from the far-seen mount. No blast
   might kill
Or blight that fond memorial;—the trees
   grew,
And now entwine their arms; but ne'er
   again   10
Embraced those Brothers upon earth's
   wide plain;
Nor aught of mutual joy or sorrow knew
Until their spirits mingled in the sea
That to itself takes all, Eternity.

XXIII

FILIAL PIETY[1]

[Composed probably 1828.—Published 1829 (*The Casket*); ed. 1832.]

On the Wayside between Preston and Liverpool.

UNTOUCHED through all severity of cold;
Inviolate, whate'er the cottage hearth
Might need for comfort, or for festal
   mirth;
That Pile of Turf is half a century old:
Yes, Traveller! fifty winters have been
   told   5
Since suddenly the dart of death went
   forth
'Gainst him who raised it,—his last work
   on earth:
Thence has it, with the Son, so strong a
   hold
Upon his Father's memory, that his hands,
Through reverence, touch it only to re-
   pair   10
Its waste.—Though crumbling with each
   breath of air,
In annual renovation thus it stands—
Rude Mausoleum! but wrens nestle there,
And red-breasts warble when sweet sounds
   are rare.

XXIV

TO THE AUTHOR'S PORTRAIT

[Painted at Rydal Mount, by W. Pickersgill, Esq., for St. John's College, Cambridge.]

[Composed probably 1832.—Published 1835.]

Go, faithful Portrait! and where long hath
   knelt
Margaret, the saintly Foundress, take thy
   place;
And, if Time spare the colours for the
   grace
Which to the work surpassing skill hath
   dealt,
Thou, on thy rock reclined, though kingdoms melt   5
And states be torn up by the roots, wilt
   seem
To breathe in rural peace, to hear the
   stream,
And think and feel as once the Poet felt.
Whate'er thy fate, those features have not
   grown
Unrecognised through many a household
   tear   10
More prompt, more glad, to fall than
   drops of dew

---

[1] Thomas Scarisbrick was killed by a stroke of lightning while building a turf-stack between Ormskirk and Preston in 1779. His son James finished the stack, and while he lived kept it in constant repair in memory of the father. James died in 1824, leaving to his grandchildren goblets and decanters cut with a turf-stack between two trees. (See Mr. J. Bromley's letter to the *Athenæum*, May 17, 1890.) —ED.

MISCELLANEOUS SONNETS

By morning shed around a flower half-
blown;
Tears of delight, that testified how true
To life thou art, and, in thy truth, how
dear!

XXV

[Composed 1832 or 1833.—Published 1835.]

WHY art thou silent! Is thy love a plant
Of such weak fibre that the treacherous
air
Of absence withers what was once so fair?
Is there no debt to pay, no boon to grant?
Yet have my thoughts for thee been
vigilant—   5
Bound to thy service with unceasing care,
The mind's least generous wish a mendi-
cant
For nought but what thy happiness could
spare.
Speak—though this soft warm heart, once
free to hold
A thousand tender pleasures, thine and
mine,   10
Be left more desolate, more dreary cold
Than a forsaken bird's-nest filled with
snow
'Mid its own bush of leafless eglantine—
Speak, that my torturing doubts their end
may know!

XXVI

TO B. R. HAYDON, ON SEEING HIS PICTURE
OF NAPOLEON BUONAPARTE ON THE
ISLAND OF ST. HELENA

[Composed June 11, 1831.—Published 1832.]

HAYDON! let worthier judges praise the
skill
Here by thy pencil shown in truth of lines
And charm of colours; *I* applaud those
signs
Of thought, that give the true poetic thrill;
That unencumbered whole of blank and
still,   5
Sky without cloud—ocean without a
wave;
And the one Man that laboured to enslave
The World, sole-standing high on the bare
hill—
Back turned, arms folded, the unapparent
face
Tinged, we may fancy, in this dreary
place   10
With light reflected from the invisible sun
Set, like his fortunes; but not set for aye
Like them. The unguilty Power pursues
his way,
And before *him* doth dawn perpetual run.

XXVII

[Composed (?).—Published: vol. of 1842.]

A *POET!*—He hath put his heart to
school,
Nor dares to move unpropped upon the
staff
Which Art hath lodged within his hand—
must laugh
By precept only, and shed tears by rule.
Thy Art be Nature; the live current quaff,
And let the groveller sip his stagnant pool,
In fear that else, when Critics grave and
cool   7
Have killed him, Scorn should write his
epitaph.
How does the Meadow-flower its bloom
unfold?
Because the lovely little flower is free   10
Down to its root, and, in that freedom,
bold;
And so the grandeur of the Forest-tree
Comes not by casting in a formal mould,
But from its *own* divine vitality.

XXVIII

[Composed (?).—Published: vol. of 1842.]

THE most alluring clouds that mount the
sky
Owe to a troubled element their forms,
Their hues to sunset. If with raptured eye
We watch their splendour, shall we covet
storms,
And wish the Lord of day his slow decline
Would hasten, that such pomp may float
on high?   6
Behold, already they forget to shine,
Dissolve—and leave to him who gazed a
sigh.
Not loth to thank each moment for its
boon
Of pure delight, come whensoe'er it may,
Peace let us seek,—to steadfast things
attune   11
Calm expectations, leaving to the gay
And volatile their love of transient bowers,
The house that cannot pass away be ours.

XXIX

ON A PORTRAIT OF THE DUKE OF WELLING-
TON UPON THE FIELD OF WATERLOO, BY
HAYDON

[Composed August 31, 1840.—Published: vol. of
1842.]

BY Art's bold privilege Warrior and War-
horse stand
On ground yet strewn with their last
battle's wreck;
Let the Steed glory while his Master's hand
Lies fixed for ages on his conscious neck;
But by the Chieftain's look, though at his
side   5

220

Hangs that day's treasured sword, how
    firm a check
Is given to triumph and all human pride!
Yon trophied Mound shrinks to a sha-
    dowy speck
In his calm presence! Him the mighty
    deed
Elates not, brought far nearer the grave's
    rest,   10
As shows that time-worn face, for he such
    seed
Has sown as yields, we trust, the fruit of
    fame
In Heaven; hence no one blushes for thy
    name,
Conqueror, 'mid some sad thoughts, di-
    vinely blest!

XXX

COMPOSED ON A MAY MORNING, 1838

[Composed May, 1838.—Published: Sonnet-vol.
of 1838.]

LIFE with yon Lambs, like day, is just
    begun,
Yet Nature seems to them a heavenly guide.
Does joy approach? they meet the coming
    tide;
And sullenness avoid, as now they shun
Pale twilight's lingering glooms,—and in
    the sun   5
Couch near their dams, with quiet satis-
    fied;
Or gambol—each with his shadow at his
    side,
Varying its shape wherever he may run.
As they from turf yet hoar with sleepy dew
All turn, and court the shining and the
    green,   10
Where herbs look up, and opening flowers
    are seen;
Why to God's goodness cannot We be
    true,
And so, His gifts and promises between,
Feed to the last on pleasures ever new?

XXXI

[Composed (?).—Published: vol. of 1842.]

Lo! where she stands fixed in a saint-like
    trance,
One upward hand, as if she needed rest
From rapture, lying softly on her breast!
Nor wants her eyeball an ethereal glance;
But not the less—nay more—that counte-
    nance,   5
While thus illumined, tells of painful
    strife
For a sick heart made weary of this life
By love, long crossed with adverse circum-
    stance.
—Would She were now as when she hoped
    to pass

At God's appointed hour to them who
    tread   10
Heaven's sapphire pavement, yet breathed
    well content,
Well pleased, her foot should print earth's
    common grass,
Lived thankful for day's light, for daily
    bread,
For health, and time in obvious duty
    spent.

XXXII

TO A PAINTER

[Composed 1840.—Published: vol. of 1842.]

ALL praise the Likeness by thy skill por-
    trayed;
But 'tis a fruitless task to paint for me
Who, yielding not to changes Time has
    made,
By the habitual light of memory see
Eyes unbedimmed, see bloom that cannot
    fade,   5
And smiles that from their birthplace
    ne'er shall flee
Into the land where ghosts and phantoms
    be;
And, seeing this, own nothing in its stead.
Couldst thou go back into far-distant
    years,
Or share with me, fond thought! that
    inward eye,   10
Then, and then only, Painter! could thy
    Art
The visual powers of Nature satisfy,
Which hold, whate'er to common sight
    appears,
Their sovereign empire in a faithful heart.

XXXIII

ON THE SAME SUBJECT

[Composed 1840.—Published: vol. of 1842.]

THOUGH I beheld at first with blank sur-
    prise
This Work, I now have gazed on it so long
I see its truth with unreluctant eyes;
O, my Belovèd! I have done thee wrong,
Conscious of blessedness, but, whence it
    sprung,   5
Ever too heedless, as I now perceive:
Morn into noon did pass, noon into eve,
And the old day was welcome as the
    young,
As welcome, and as beautiful—in sooth
More beautiful, as being a thing more
    holy: 10
Thanks to thy virtues, to the eternal youth
Of all thy goodness, never melancholy;
To thy large heart and humble mind, that
    cast
Into one vision, future, present, past.

MISCELLANEOUS SONNETS

XXXIV

[Composed 1838.—Published: Sonnet-vol. of 1838.]

HARK! 'tis the Thrush, undaunted, unde-
    prest,
By twilight premature of cloud and rain;
Nor does that roaring wind deaden his
    strain
Who carols thinking of his Love and nest,
And seems, as more incited, still more
    blest.   5
Thanks; thou hast snapped a fireside
    Prisoner's chain,
Exulting Warbler! eased a fretted brain,
And in a moment charmed my cares to
    rest.
Yes, I will forth, bold Bird! and front the
    blast,
That we may sing together, if thou wilt,
So loud, so clear, my Partner through
    life's day,   11
Mute in her nest love-chosen, if not love-
    built
Like thine, shall gladden, as in seasons
    past,
Thrilled by loose snatches of the social
    Lay.

XXXV

[Composed 1838.—Published: Sonnet-vol. of 1838.]

'TIS He whose yester-evening's high dis-
    dain
Beat back the roaring storm—but how
    subdued
His day-break note, a sad vicissitude!
Does the hour's drowsy weight his glee
    restrain?
Or, like the nightingale, her joyous vein   5
Pleased to renounce, does this dear Thrush
    attune
His voice to suit the temper of yon Moon
Doubly depressed, setting, and in her
    wane?
Rise, tardy Sun! and let the Songster
    prove
(The balance trembling between night and
    morn)   10
No longer) with what ecstasy upborne
He can pour forth his spirit. In heaven
    above,
And earth below, they best can serve true
    gladness
Who meet most feelingly the calls of
    sadness.

XXXVI

[Composed 1837.—Published: Sonnet-vol. of 1838.]

OH what a Wreck! how changed in mien
    and speech!
Yet—though dread Powers, that work in
    mystery, spin

Entanglings of the brain; though shadows
    stretch
O'er the chilled heart—reflect; far, far
    within
Hers is a holy Being, freed from Sin.   5
She is not what she seems, a forlorn
    wretch,
But delegated Spirits comforts fetch
To Her from heights that Reason may
    not win.
Like Children, She is privileged to hold
Divine communion; both do live and
    move,   10
Whate'er to shallow Faith their ways
    unfold,
Inly illumined by Heaven's pitying love;
Love pitying innocence, not long to last,
In them—in Her our sins and sorrows past.

XXXVII

[Composed March 8, 1842.—Published: vol. of 1842.]

INTENT on gathering wool from hedge and
    brake
Yon busy Little-ones rejoice that soon
A poor old Dame will bless them for the
    boon:
Great is their glee while flake they add to
    flake
With rival earnestness; far other strife   5
Than will hereafter move them, if they
    make
Pastime their idol, give their day of life
To pleasure snatched for reckless plea-
    sure's sake.
Can pomp and show allay one heart-born
    grief?
Pains which the World inflicts can she
    requite?   10
Not for an interval however brief;
The silent thoughts that search for stead-
    fast light,
Love from her depths, and Duty in her
    might,
And Faith—these only yield secure relief.

XXXVIII

A PLEA FOR AUTHORS

[Composed May, 1838.—Published: Sonnet-vol. of 1838.]

FAILING impartial measure to dispense
To every suitor, Equity is lame;
And social Justice, stript of reverence
For natural rights, a mockery and a
    shame;
Law but a servile dupe of false pretence,
If, guarding grossest things from common
    claim   6
Now and for ever, She, to works that came
From mind and spirit, grudge a short-
    lived fence.

'What! lengthened privilege, a lineal tie,
For *Books!*' Yes, heartless Ones, or be it
  proved   10
That 'tis a fault in Us to have lived and
  loved
Like others, with like temporal hopes to
  die;
No public harm that Genius from her
  course
Be turned; and streams of truth dried up,
  even at their source!

XXXIX

VALEDICTORY SONNET

Closing the Volume of Sonnets published in 1838

[Composed 1838.—Published: Sonnet-vol. of
1838.]

SERVING no haughty Muse, my hands have
  here
Disposed some cultured Flowerets (drawn
  from spots
Where they bloomed singly, or in scat-
  tered knots,)
Each kind in several beds of one parterre;
Both to allure the casual Loiterer,   5
And that, so placed, my Nurslings may
  requite
Studious regard with opportune delight,
Nor be unthanked, unless I fondly err.
But metaphor dismissed, and thanks
  apart,
Reader, farewell! My last words let them
  be—   10
If in this book Fancy and Truth agree;
If simple Nature trained by careful Art
Through It have won a passage to thy
  heart;
Grant me thy love, I crave no other fee!

XL

TO THE REV. CHRISTOPHER WORDSWORTH, D.D., MASTER OF HARROW SCHOOL

After the perusal of his 'Theophilus Anglicanus,'
recently published

[Composed December 11, 1843.—Published 1845.]

ENLIGHTENED Teacher, gladly from thy
  hand
Have I received this proof of pains be-
  stowed
By Thee to guide thy Pupils on the road
That, in our native isle, and every land,
The Church, when trusting in divine com-
  mand   5
And in her Catholic attributes, hath trod:
O may these lessons be with profit scanned
To thy heart's wish, thy labour blest by
  God!
So the bright faces of the young and gay

Shall look more bright—the happy,
  happier still;   10
Catch, in the pauses of their keenest play,
Motions of thought which elevate the will
And, like the Spire that from your classic
  Hill
Points heavenward, indicate the end and
  way.

XLI

TO THE PLANET VENUS

Upon its approximation (as an Evening Star) to
the Earth, January, 1838

[Composed January, 1838.—Published: Sonnet-
vol. of 1838.]

WHAT strong allurement draws, what
  spirit guides,
Thee, Vesper! brightening still, as if the
  nearer
Thou com'st to man's abode the spot grew
  dearer
Night after night? True is it Nature hides
Her treasures less and less.—Man now
  presides   5
In power, where once he trembled in his
  weakness;
Science advances with gigantic strides;
But are we aught enriched in love and
  meekness?
Aught dost thou see, bright Star! of pure
  and wise
More than in humbler times graced human
  story;   10
That makes our hearts more apt to sym-
  pathize
With heaven, our souls more fit for future
  glory,
When earth shall vanish from our closing
  eyes,
Ere we lie down in our last dormitory?

XLII

[Composed December 24, 1842.—Published 1845.]

WANSFELL![1] this Household has a favoured
  lot,
Living with liberty on thee to gaze,
To watch while Morn first crowns thee
  with her rays,
Or when along thy breast serenely float
Evening's angelic clouds. Yet ne'er a
  note   5
Hath sounded (shame upon the Bard!) thy
  praise
For all that thou, as if from heaven, hast
  brought
Of glory lavished on our quiet days.
Bountiful Son of Earth! when we are gone

[1] The Hill that rises to the south-east, above
Ambleside.

223

MISCELLANEOUS SONNETS

From every object dear to mortal sight,
As soon we shall be, may these words
    attest   11
How oft, to elevate our spirits, shone
Thy visionary majesties of light,
How in thy pensive glooms our hearts
    found rest.

XLIII

[Composed January 1, 1843.—Published 1845.]

WHILE beams of orient light shoot wide
    and high,
Deep in the vale a little rural Town[1]
Breathes forth a cloud-like creature of its
    own,
That mounts not toward the radiant
    morning sky,
But, with a less ambitious sympathy,   5
Hangs o'er its Parent waking to the cares,
Troubles and toils that every day pre-
    pares.
So Fancy, to the musing Poet's eye,
Endears that Lingerer. And how blest
    her sway,
(Like influence never may my soul reject),
If the calm Heaven, now to its zenith
    decked   11
With glorious forms in numberless array,
To the lone shepherd on the hills disclose
Gleams from a world in which the saints
    repose.

XLIV

[Composed (?).—Published 1827.]

IN my mind's eye a Temple, like a cloud
Slowly surmounting some invidious hill,
Rose out of darkness: the bright Work
    stood still;
And might of its own beauty have been
    proud,
But it was fashioned and to God was
    vowed   5
By Virtues that diffused, in every part,
Spirit divine through forms of human art:
Faith had her arch—her arch, when winds
    blow loud,
Into the consciousness of safety thrilled;
And Love her towers of dread foundation
    laid   10
Under the grave of things; Hope had her
    spire
Star-high, and pointing still to some-
    thing higher:
Trembling I gazed, but heard a voice—it
    said,
'Hell-gates are powerless Phantoms when
    we build.'

[1] Ambleside.

XLV

ON THE PROJECTED KENDAL AND
WINDERMERE RAILWAY

[Composed October 12, 1844.—Published in pam-
phlet *Kendal and Windermere Railway*, 1844;
ed. 1845.]

Is then no nook of English ground secure
From rash assault?[2] Schemes of retire-
    ment sown
In youth, and 'mid the busy world kept
    pure
As when their earliest flowers of hope
    were blown,
Must perish;—how can they this blight
    endure?   5
And must he too the ruthless change be-
    moan
Who scorns a false utilitarian lure
'Mid his paternal fields at random thrown?
Baffle the threat, bright Scene, from Or-
    rest-head
Given to the pausing traveller's rapturous
    glance: 10
Plead for thy peace, thou beautiful romance
Of nature; and, if human hearts be dead,
Speak, passing winds; ye torrents, with
    your strong
And constant voice, protest against the
    wrong.

XLVI

[Composed 1844.—Published along with XLV.]

PROUD were ye, Mountains, when, in times
    of old,
Your patriot sons, to stem invasive war,
Intrenched your brows; ye gloried in
    each scar:
Now, for your shame, a Power, the Thirst
    of Gold,
That rules o'er Britain like a baneful star,
Wills that your peace, your beauty, shall
    be sold,   6
And clear way made for her triumphal car
Through the beloved retreats your arms
    enfold!
Hear YE that Whistle? As her long-linked
    Train
Swept onwards, did the vision cross your
    view?   10
Yes, ye were startled;—and, in balance true,
Weighing the mischief with the promised
    gain,
Mountains, and Vales, and Floods, I call
    on you
To share the passion of a just disdain.

[2] The degree and kind of attachment which many
of the yeomanry feel to their small inheritances can
scarcely be over-rated. Near the house of one of
them stands a magnificent tree, which a neighbour
of the owner advised him to fell for profit's sake.
'Fell it!' exclaimed the yeoman, 'I had rather fall
on my knees and worship it.' It happens, I believe,
that the intended railway would pass through this
little property, and I hope that an apology for the
answer will not be thought necessary by one who
enters into the strength of the feeling.

XLVII

AT FURNESS ABBEY

[Composed probably 1845.—Published 1845.]

HERE, where, of havoc tired and rash
    undoing,
Man left this Structure to become Time's
    prey,
A soothing spirit follows in the way
That Nature takes, her counter-work pur-
    suing.
See how her ivy clasps the sacred Ruin, 5
Fall to prevent or beautify decay;
And, on the mouldered walls, how bright,
    how gay,
The flowers in pearly dews their bloom
    renewing!
Thanks to the place, blessings upon the
    hour;
Even as I speak the rising Sun's first smile
Gleams on the grass-crowned top of yon
    tall Tower, 11
Whose cawing occupants with joy pro-
    claim
Prescriptive title to the shattered pile,
Where, Cavendish, *thine* seems nothing
    but a name!

XLVIII

AT FURNESS ABBEY

[Composed June 21, 1845.—Published 1845.]

WELL have yon Railway Labourers to
    THIS ground
Withdrawn for noontide rest. They sit,
    they walk
Among the Ruins, but no idle talk
Is heard; to grave demeanour all are bound;
And from one voice a Hymn with tuneful
    sound 5
Hallows once more the long-deserted
    Quire
And thrills the old sepulchral earth,
    around.
Others look up, and with fixed eyes admire
That wide-spanned arch, wondering how
    it was raised,
To keep, so high in air, its strength and
    grace: 10
All seem to feel the spirit of the place,
And by the general reverence God is
    praised:
Profane Despoilers, stand ye not reproved,
While thus these simple-hearted men are
    moved?

MEMORIALS OF
A TOUR IN SCOTLAND, 1803

I

DEPARTURE

FROM THE VALE OF GRASMERE.
AUGUST, 1803

[Composed 1811.[1]—Published 1827.]

THE gentlest Shade that walked Elysian
    plains
Might sometimes covet dissoluble chains;
Even for the tenants of the zone that lies
Beyond the stars, celestial Paradise,
Methinks 'twould heighten joy, to over-
    leap 5
At will the crystal battlements, and peep
Into some other region, though less fair,
To see how things are made and managed
    there.
Change for the worse might please, in-
    cursion bold 9
Into the tracts of darkness and of cold:
O'er Limbo lake with aery flight to steer,
And on the verge of Chaos hang in fear.

[1] Originally the opening lines of the *Epistle to
Sir George Beaumont*. See p. 408.—ED.

Such animation often do I find,
Power in my breast, wings growing in my
    mind,
Then, when some rock or hill is overpast,
Perchance without one look behind me
    cast, 16
Some barrier with which Nature, from the
    birth
Of things, has fenced this fairest spot on
    earth.
O pleasant transit, Grasmere! to resign
Such happy fields, abodes so calm as thine;
Not like an outcast with himself at strife;
The slave of business, time, or care for life,
But moved by choice: or, if constrained
    in part,
Yet still with Nature's freedom at the
    heart;— 24
To cull contentment upon wildest shores,
And luxuries extract from bleakest moors;
With prompt embrace all beauty to enfold,
And having rights in all that we behold.
—Then why these lingering steps?—A
    bright adieu,
For a brief absence, proves that love is
    true; 30
Ne'er can the way be irksome or forlorn
That winds into itself for sweet return.

225

II

AT THE GRAVE OF BURNS
1803

SEVEN YEARS AFTER HIS DEATH

[Composed partly before 1807.—Published: vol.
of 1842.]

I SHIVER, Spirit fierce and bold,
At thought of what I now behold:
As vapours breathed from dungeons cold
    Strike pleasure dead,
So sadness comes from out the mould   5
    Where Burns is laid.

And have I then thy bones so near,
And thou forbidden to appear?
As if it were thyself that's here
    I shrink with pain;   10
And both my wishes and my fear
    Alike are vain.

Off weight—nor press on weight!—away
Dark thoughts!—they came, but not to
    stay;
With chastened feelings would I pay   15
    The tribute due
To him, and aught that hides his clay
    From mortal view.

Fresh as the flower, whose modest worth
He sang, his genius 'glinted' forth,   20
Rose like a star that touching earth,
    For so it seems,
Doth glorify its humble birth
    With matchless beams.

The piercing eye, the thoughtful brow,   25
The struggling heart, where be they now?—
Full soon the Aspirant of the plough,
    The prompt, the brave,
Slept, with the obscurest, in the low
    And silent grave.   30

I mourned with thousands, but as one
More deeply grieved, for He was gone
Whose light I hailed when first it shone,
    And showed my youth   34
How Verse may build a princely throne
    On humble truth.

Alas! where'er the current tends,
Regret pursues and with it blends,—
Huge Criffel's hoary top ascends
    By Skiddaw seen,—   40
Neighbours we were, and loving friends
    We might have been;

True friends though diversely inclined;
But heart with heart and mind with mind,
Where the main fibres are entwined,   45
    Through Nature's skill,
May even by contraries be joined
    More closely still.

The tear will start, and let it flow;
Thou 'poor Inhabitant below,'   50
At this dread moment—even so—
    Might we together
Have sate and talked where gowans blow,
    Or on wild heather.

What treasures would have then been
    placed   55
Within my reach; of knowledge graced
By fancy what a rich repast!
    But why go on?—
Oh! spare to sweep, thou mournful blast,
    His grave grass-grown.   60

There, too, a Son, his joy and pride,
(Not three weeks past the Stripling died,)
Lies gathered to his Father's side,
    Soul-moving sight!
Yet one to which is not denied   65
    Some sad delight.

For *he* is safe, a quiet bed
Hath early found among the dead,
Harboured where none can be misled,
    Wronged, or distrest;   70
And surely here it may be said
    That such are blest.

And oh for Thee, by pitying grace
Checked oft-times in a devious race,
May He, who halloweth the place   75
    Where Man is laid,
Receive thy Spirit in the embrace
    For which it prayed!

Sighing I turned away; but ere
Night fell I heard, or seemed to hear,   80
    Music that sorrow comes not near,
    A ritual hymn,
Chanted in love that casts out fear
    By Seraphim.

III

THOUGHTS

SUGGESTED THE DAY FOLLOWING, ON THE
BANKS OF NITH, NEAR THE POET'S
RESIDENCE

[Finished 1839.—Published: vol. of 1842.]

Too frail to keep the lofty vow
That must have followed when his brow
Was wreathed—'The Vision' tells us
    how—
    With holly spray,
He faltered, drifted to and fro,   5
    And passed away.

Well might such thoughts, dear Sister,
    throng
Our minds when, lingering all too long,
Over the grave of Burns we hung
    In social grief—   10
Indulged as if it were a wrong
    To seek relief.

But, leaving each unquiet theme
Where gentlest judgments may misdeem,
And prompt to welcome every gleam   15
    Of good and fair,
Let us beside the limpid Stream
    Breathe hopeful air.

Enough of sorrow, wreck, and blight;
Think rather of those moments bright   20
When to the consciousness of right
    His course was true,
When Wisdom prospered in his sight
    And virtue grew.

Yes, freely let our hearts expand,   25
Freely as in youth's season bland,
When side by side, his Book in hand,
    We wont to stray,
Our pleasure varying at command
    Of each sweet Lay.   30

How oft inspired must he have trod
These pathways, yon far-stretching road!
There lurks his home; in that Abode,
    With mirth elate,
Or in his nobly-pensive mood,   35
    The Rustic sate.

Proud thoughts that Image overawes,
Before it humbly let us pause,
And ask of Nature from what cause
    And by what rules   40
She trained her Burns to win applause
    That shames the Schools.

Through busiest street and loneliest glen
Are felt the flashes of his pen;
He rules 'mid winter snows, and when   45
    Bees fill their hives;
Deep in the general heart of men
    His power survives.

What need of fields in some far clime
Where Heroes, Sages, Bards sublime,   50
And all that fetched the flowing rhyme
    From genuine springs,
Shall dwell together till old Time
    Folds up his wings?

Sweet Mercy! to the gates of Heaven   55
This Minstrel lead, his sins forgiven;
The rueful conflict, the heart riven
    With vain endeavour,
And memory of Earth's bitter leaven,
    Effaced for ever.   60

But why to Him confine the prayer,
When kindred thoughts and yearnings
    bear
On the frail heart the purest share
    With all that live?—
The best of what we do and are,   65
    Just God, forgive![1]

[1] See Note, p. 704.

IV

TO THE SONS OF BURNS,

AFTER VISITING THE GRAVE OF THEIR
FATHER

[Composed partly between June 1805 and
Feb. 1806.—Published 1807.[1]]

'The Poet's grave is in a corner of the churchyard.
We looked at it with melancholy and painful re-
flections, repeating to each other his own verses—
"'Is there a man whose judgment clear," etc.'
    —*Extract from the Journal of
    my Fellow-traveller.*

'MID crowded obelisks and urns
I sought the untimely grave of Burns;
Sons of the Bard, my heart still mourns
    With sorrow true;
And more would grieve, but that it turns
    Trembling to you!   6

Through twilight shades of good and ill
Ye now are panting up life's hill,
And more than common strength and skill
    Must ye display;   10
If ye would give the better will
    Its lawful sway.

Hath Nature strung your nerves to bear
Intemperance with less harm, beware!
But if the Poet's wit ye share,   15
    Like him can speed
The social hour—of tenfold care
    There will be need;

For honest men delight will take
To spare your failings for his sake,   20
Will flatter you,—and fool and rake
    Your steps pursue;
And of your Father's name will make
    A snare for you.

Far from their noisy haunts retire,   25
And add your voices to the quire
That sanctify the cottage fire
    With service meet;
There seek the genius of your Sire,
    His spirit greet;   30

Or where 'mid 'lonely heights and hows,'
He paid to Nature tuneful vows;
Or wiped his honourable brows
    Bedewed with toil,
While reapers strove, or busy ploughs   35
    Upturned the soil;

His judgment with benignant ray
Shall guide, his fancy cheer, your way;
But ne'er to a seductive lay
    Let faith be given;   40
Nor deem that 'light which leads astray
    Is light from Heaven.'

[1] Stanzas ii, iii, iv, viii, published in 1807; stanzas
i, v, vi, vii, published in 1827.—ED.

Let no mean hope your souls enslave;
Be independent, generous, brave;
Your Father such example gave,   45
   And such revere;
But be admonished by his grave,
   And think, and fear!

V

ELLEN IRWIN

OR

THE BRAES OF KIRTLE[1]

[Composed probably 1799 or 1800.—Published
1800.]

FAIR Ellen Irwin, when she sate
Upon the braes of Kirtle,
Was lovely as a Grecian maid
Adorned with wreaths of myrtle;
Young Adam Bruce beside her lay,   5
And there they did beguile the day
With love and gentle speeches,
Beneath the budding beeches.

From many knights and many squires
The Bruce had been selected;   10
And Gordon, fairest of them all,
By Ellen was rejected.
Sad tidings to that noble Youth!
For it may be proclaimed with truth,
If Bruce hath loved sincerely,   15
That Gordon loves as dearly.

But what are Gordon's form and face,
His shattered hopes and crosses,
To them, 'mid Kirtle's pleasant braes,
Reclined on flowers and mosses?   20
Alas that ever he was born!
The Gordon, couched behind a thorn,
Sees them and their caressing;
Beholds them blest and blessing.

Proud Gordon, maddened by the thoughts
That through his brain are travelling,   26
Rushed forth, and at the heart of Bruce
He launched a deadly javelin!
Fair Ellen saw it as it came,
And, starting up to meet the same,   30
Did with her body cover
The Youth, her chosen lover.

And, falling into Bruce's arms,
Thus died the beauteous Ellen,
Thus, from the heart of her True-love,   35
The mortal spear repelling.
And Bruce, as soon as he had slain
The Gordon, sailed away to Spain;
And fought with rage incessant
Against the Moorish crescent.   40

[1] The Kirtle is a river in the southern part of
Scotland, on the banks of which the events here
related took place.

But many days, and many months,
And many years ensuing,
This wretched Knight did vainly seek
The death that he was wooing.
So, coming his last help to crave,   45
Heart-broken, upon Ellen's grave
His body he extended,
And there his sorrow ended.

Now ye, who willingly have heard
The tale I have been telling,   50
May in Kirkconnell churchyard view
The grave of lovely Ellen:
By Ellen's side the Bruce is laid;
And, for the stone upon his head,
May no rude hand deface it,   55
And its forlorn *Hic jacet!*

VI

TO A HIGHLAND GIRL,

AT INVERSNEYDE, UPON LOCH LOMOND

[Composed 1803.—Published 1807.]

SWEET Highland Girl, a very shower
Of beauty is thy earthly dower!
Twice seven consenting years have shed
Their utmost bounty on thy head:
And these grey rocks; that household
   lawn;   5
Those trees, a veil just half withdrawn;
This fall of water that doth make
A murmur near the silent lake;
This little bay; a quiet road
That holds in shelter thy Abode—   10
In truth together do ye seem
Like something fashioned in a dream;
Such Forms as from their covert peep
When earthly cares are laid asleep!
But, O fair Creature! in the light   15
Of common day, so heavenly bright,
I bless Thee, Vision as thou art,
I bless thee with a human heart;
God shield thee to thy latest years!
Thee, neither know I, nor thy peers;   20
And yet my eyes are filled with tears.

With earnest feeling I shall pray
For thee when I am far away:
For never saw I mien, or face,
In which more plainly I could trace   25
Benignity and home-bred sense
Ripening in perfect innocence.
Here scattered, like a random seed,
Remote from men, Thou dost not need
The embarrassed look of shy distress, 30
And maidenly shamefacedness:
Thou wear'st upon thy forehead clear
The freedom of a Mountaineer:
A face with gladness overspread!
Soft smiles, by human kindness bred! 35
And seemliness complete, that sways
Thy courtesies, about thee plays;

With no restraint, but such as springs
From quick and eager visitings
Of thoughts that lie beyond the reach   40
Of thy few words of English speech:
A bondage sweetly brooked, a strife
That gives thy gestures grace and life!
So have I, not unmoved in mind,
Seen birds of tempest-loving kind—   45
Thus beating up against the wind.

What hand but would a garland cull
For thee who art so beautiful?
O happy pleasure! here to dwell
Beside thee in some heathy dell;   50
Adopt your homely ways, and dress,
A Shepherd, thou a Shepherdess!
But I could frame a wish for thee
More like a grave reality:
Thou art to me but as a wave   55
Of the wild sea; and I would have
Some claim upon thee, if I could,
Though but of common neighbourhood.
What joy to hear thee, and to see!
Thy elder Brother I would be,   60
Thy Father—anything to thee!

Now thanks to Heaven! that of its grace
Hath led me to this lonely place.
Joy have I had; and going hence
I bear away my recompense.   65
In spots like these it is we prize
Our Memory, feel that she hath eyes:
Then, why should I be loth to stir?
I feel this place was made for her;
To give new pleasure like the past,   70
Continued long as life shall last.
Nor am I loth, though pleased at heart,
Sweet Highland Girl! from thee to part;
For I, methinks, till I grow old,
As fair before me shall behold,   75
As I do now, the cabin small,
The lake, the bay, the waterfall;
And Thee, the Spirit of them all!

VII

GLEN ALMAIN

OR, THE NARROW GLEN

[Composed probably 1803.—Published 1807.]

IN this still place, remote from men,
Sleeps Ossian, in the NARROW GLEN;
In this still place, where murmurs on
But one meek streamlet, only one:
He sang of battles, and the breath   5
Of stormy war, and violent death;
And should, methinks, when all was past,
Have rightfully been laid at last
Where rocks were rudely heaped, and rent
As by a spirit turbulent;   10
Where sights were rough, and sounds
    were wild,
And everything unreconciled;

In some complaining, dim retreat,
For fear and melancholy meet;
But this is calm; there cannot be   15
A more entire tranquillity.

Does then the Bard sleep here indeed?
Or is it but a groundless creed?
What matters it?—I blame them not
Whose Fancy in this lonely Spot   20
Was moved; and in such way expressed
Their notion of its perfect rest.
A convent, even a hermit's cell,
Would break the silence of this Dell:
It is not quiet, is not ease;   25
But something deeper far than these:
The separation that is here
Is of the grave; and of austere
Yet happy feelings of the dead:
And, therefore, was it rightly said   30
That Ossian, last of all his race!
Lies buried in this lonely place.

VIII

STEPPING WESTWARD

[Composed June 3, 1805.—Published 1807.]

While my Fellow-traveller and I were walking by
the side of Loch Ketterine, one fine evening
after sunset, in our road to a Hut where, in the
course of our Tour, we had been hospitably
entertained some weeks before, we met, in one
of the loneliest parts of that solitary region, two
well-dressed Women, one of whom said to us,
by way of greeting, 'What, you are stepping
westward?'

'*WHAT, you are stepping westward?*'—
    '*Yea.*'
—'Twould be a *wildish* destiny,
If we, who thus together roam
In a strange Land, and far from home,
Were in this place the guests of Chance;
Yet who would stop, or fear to advance,
Though home or shelter he had none,
With such a sky to lead him on?

The dewy ground was dark and cold;
Behind, all gloomy to behold;   10
And stepping westward seemed to be
A kind of *heavenly* destiny:
I liked the greeting; 'twas a sound
Of something without place or bound;
And seemed to give me spiritual right   15
To travel through that region bright.

The voice was soft, and she who spake
Was walking by her native lake:
The salutation had to me
The very sound of courtesy: 20
Its power was felt; and while my eye
Was fixed upon the glowing Sky,
The echo of the voice enwrought
A human sweetness with the thought
Of travelling through the world that lay
Before me in my endless way.   26

IX

THE SOLITARY REAPER

[Composed Nov. 1805.—Published 1807.]

BEHOLD her, single in the field,
Yon solitary Highland Lass!
Reaping and singing by herself;
Stop here, or gently pass!
Alone she cuts and binds the grain,   5
And sings a melancholy strain;
O listen! for the Vale profound
Is overflowing with the sound.

No Nightingale did ever chaunt
More welcome notes to weary bands   10
Of travellers in some shady haunt,
Among Arabian sands:
A voice so thrilling ne'er was heard
In spring-time from the Cuckoo-bird,
Breaking the silence of the seas   15
Among the farthest Hebrides.

Will no one tell me what she sings?—
Perhaps the plaintive numbers flow
For old, unhappy, far-off things,
And battles long ago: 20
Or is it some more humble lay,
Familiar matter of to-day?
Some natural sorrow, loss, or pain,
That has been, and may be again?

Whate'er the theme, the Maiden sang   25
As if her song could have no ending;
I saw her singing at her work,
And o'er the sickle bending;—
I listened, motionless and still;
And, as I mounted up the hill,   30
The music in my heart I bore,
Long after it was heard no more.

X

ADDRESS TO KILCHURN CASTLE, UPON LOCH AWE

[Composed ll. 1–3, 1803; finished 'long after.'—
Published 1827.]

From the top of the hill a most impressive
scene opened upon our view,—a ruined Castle
on an Island (for an Island the flood had made
it) at some distance from the shore, backed by
a Cove of the Mountain Cruachan, down which
came a foaming stream. The Castle occupied
every foot of the Island that was visible to us,
appearing to rise out of the water,—mists rested
upon the mountain side, with spots of sunshine;
there was a mild desolation in the low grounds,
a solemn grandeur in the mountains, and the
Castle was wild, yet stately—not dismantled
of turrets—nor the walls broken down, though
obviously a ruin.'—*Extract from the Journal of
my Companion.*

CHILD of loud-throated War! the moun-
    tain Stream
Roars in thy hearing; but thy hour of rest
Is come, and thou art silent in thy age;
Save when the wind sweeps by and
    sounds are caught

Ambiguous, neither wholly thine nor
    theirs.   5
Oh! there is life that breathes not; Powers
    there are
That touch each other to the quick in
    modes
Which the gross world no sense hath to
    perceive,
No soul to dream of. What art Thou,
    from care
Cast off—abandoned by thy rugged Sire,
Nor by soft Peace adopted; though, in
    place   11
And in dimension, such that thou
    might'st seem
But a mere footstool to yon sovereign
    Lord,
Huge Cruachan, (a thing that meaner hills
Might crush, nor know that it had suffered
    harm;)   15
Yet he, not loth, in favour of thy claims
To reverence, suspends his own; submit-
    ting
All that the God of Nature hath con-
    ferred,
All that he holds in common with the
    stars,
To the memorial majesty of Time   20
Impersonated in thy calm decay!
Take, then, thy seat, Vicegerent unre-
    proved!
Now, while a farewell gleam of evening
    light
Is fondly lingering on thy shattered front,
Do thou, in turn, be paramount; and rule
Over the pomp and beauty of a scene   26
Whose mountains, torrents, lake, and
    woods, unite
To pay thee homage; and with these are
    joined,
In willing admiration and respect,
Two Hearts, which in thy presence might
    be called   30
Youthful as Spring.—Shade of departed
    Power,
Skeleton of unfleshed humanity,
The chronicle were welcome that should
    call
Into the compass of distinct regard
The toils and struggles of thy infant
    years!   35
Yon foaming flood seems motionless as
    ice;
Its dizzy turbulence eludes the eye,
Frozen by distance; so, majestic Pile,
To the perception of this Age, appear
Thy fierce beginnings, softened and sub-
    dued   40
And quieted in character—the strife,
The pride, the fury uncontrollable,
Lost on the aerial heights of the Cru-
    sades![1]

[1] The tradition is, that the Castle was built by a
Lady during the absence of her Lord in Palestine.

XI

ROB ROY'S GRAVE

[Composed between June 1805 and Feb. 1806.—
Published 1807.]

The history of Rob Roy is sufficiently known; his
grave is near the head of Loch Ketterine, in
one of those small pinfold-like Burial-grounds,
of neglected and desolate appearance, which
the traveller meets with in the Highlands of
Scotland.

A FAMOUS man is Robin Hood,
The English ballad-singer's joy!
And Scotland has a thief as good,
An outlaw of as daring mood;
She has her brave ROB ROY!   5
Then clear the weeds from off his Grave,
And let us chant a passing stave,
In honour of that Hero brave!

Heaven gave Rob Roy a dauntless heart
And wondrous length and strength of
        arm: 10
Nor craved he more to quell his foes,
        Or keep his friends from harm.

Yet was Rob Roy as *wise* as brave;
Forgive me if the phrase be strong;—
A Poet worthy of Rob Roy   15
        Must scorn a timid song.

Say, then, that he was wise as brave;
As wise in thought as bold in deed:
For in the principles of things
        He sought his moral creed.   20

Said generous Rob, 'What need of books?
Burn all the statutes and their shelves:
They stir us up against our kind;
        And worse, against ourselves.

'We have a passion—make a law,   25
Too false to guide us or control!
And for the law itself we fight
        In bitterness of soul.

'And, puzzled, blinded thus, we lose
Distinctions that are plain and few: 30
These find I graven on my heart:
        That tells me what to do.

'The creatures see of flood and field,
And those that travel on the wind!
With them no strife can last; they live   35
        In peace, and peace of mind.

'For why?—because the good old rule
Sufficeth them, the simple plan,
That they should take, who have the
        power,
        And they should keep who can.   40

'A lesson that is quickly learned,
A signal this which all can see!
Thus nothing here provokes the strong
        To wanton cruelty

'All freakishness of mind is checked;   45
He tamed, who foolishly aspires;
While to the measure of his might
        Each fashions his desires.

'All kinds, and creatures, stand and fall
By strength of prowess or of wit: 50
'Tis God's appointment who must sway,
        And who is to submit.

'Since, then, the rule of right is plain,
And longest life is but a day;
To have my ends, maintain my rights,   55
        I'll take the shortest way.'

And thus among these rocks he lived,
Through summer heat and winter snow:
The Eagle, he was lord above,
        And Rob was lord below.   60

So was it—*would*, at least, have been
But through untowardness of fate;
For Polity was then too strong—
        He came an age too late;

Or shall we say an age too soon?   65
For, were the bold Man living *now*,
How might he flourish in his pride,
        With buds on every bough!

Then rents and factors, rights of chase,
Sheriffs, and lairds and their domains,   70
Would all have seemed but paltry things,
        Not worth a moment's pains.

Rob Roy had never lingered here,
To these few meagre Vales confined;
But thought how wide the world, the   75
        times
        How fairly to his mind!

And to his Sword he would have said,
'Do Thou my sovereign will enact
From land to land through half the earth!
        Judge thou of law and fact!   80

''Tis fit that we should do our part,
Becoming that mankind should learn
That we are not to be surpassed
        In fatherly concern.

'Of old things all are over old,   85
Of good things none are good enough:—
We'll show that we can help to frame
        A world of other stuff.

'I, too, will have my kings that take
From me the sign of life and death: 90
Kingdoms shall shift about, like clouds,
        Obedient to my breath.'

And, if the word had been fulfilled,
As *might* have been, then, thought of joy!
France would have had her present Boast,
        And we our own Rob Roy!   96

Oh! say not so; compare them not;
I would not wrong thee, Champion brave!
Would wrong thee nowhere; least of all
    Here standing by thy grave.   100

For Thou, although with some wild
    thoughts,
Wild Chieftain of a savage Clan!
Hadst this to boast of; thou didst love
    The *liberty* of man.

And, had it been thy lot to live   105
With us who now behold the light,
Thou wouldst have nobly stirred thyself,
    And battled for the Right.

For thou wert still the poor man's stay,
The poor man's heart, the poor man's
    hand;   110
And all the oppressed, who wanted
    strength,
    Had thine at their command.

Bear witness many a pensive sigh
Of thoughtful Herdsman when he strays
Alone upon Loch Veol's heights,   115
    And by Loch Lomond's braes.

And, far and near, through vale and hill,
Are faces that attest the same;
The proud heart flashing through the eyes,
    At sound of ROB ROY'S name.   120

XII

SONNET

COMPOSED AT ⸺ CASTLE

[Composed September 18, 1803.—Published 1807.]

DEGENERATE Douglas! oh, the unworthy
    Lord!
Whom mere despite of heart could so
    far please,
And love of havoc, (for with such disease
Fame taxes him,) that he could send forth
    word
To level with the dust a noble horde,   5
A brotherhood of venerable Trees,
Leaving an ancient dome, and towers like
    these,
Beggared and outraged!—Many hearts
    deplored
The fate of those old Trees; and oft with
    pain
The traveller, at this day, will stop and
    gaze   10
On wrongs, which Nature scarcely seems
    to heed:
For sheltered places, bosoms, nooks, and
    bays,
And the pure mountains, and the gentle
    Tweed,
And the green silent pastures, yet remain.

XIII

YARROW UNVISITED

[Composed 1803.—Published 1807.]

See the various Poems the scene of which is laid
  upon the banks of the Yarrow; in particular,
  the exquisite Ballad of Hamilton beginning—

  'Busk ye, busk ye, my bonny, bonny Bride,
  Busk ye, busk ye, my winsome Marrow!'

FROM Stirling castle we had seen
The mazy Forth unravelled;
Had trod the banks of Clyde, and Tay,
And with the Tweed had travelled;
And when we came to Clovenford,   5
Then said my '*winsome Marrow*,'
'Whate'er betide, we'll turn aside,
And see the Braes of Yarrow.'

'Let Yarrow folk, *frae* Selkirk town,
Who have been buying, selling,   10
Go back to Yarrow, 'tis their own;
Each maiden to her dwelling!
On Yarrow's banks let herons feed,
Hares couch, and rabbits burrow!
But we will downward with the Tweed,
Nor turn aside to Yarrow.   16

'There's Galla Water, Leader Haughs,
Both lying right before us;
And Dryborough, where with chiming
    Tweed
The lintwhites sing in chorus;   20
There's pleasant Tiviot-dale, a land
Made blithe with plough and harrow:
Why throw away a needful day
To go in search of Yarrow?

'What's Yarrow but a river bare,   25
That glides the dark hills under?
There are a thousand such elsewhere
As worthy of your wonder.'
—Strange words they seemed of slight
    and scorn;
My True-love sighed for sorrow;   30
And looked me in the face, to think
I thus could speak of Yarrow!

'Oh! green,' said I, 'are Yarrow's holms,
And sweet is Yarrow flowing!
Fair hangs the apple frae the rock,[1]   35
But we will leave it growing.
O'er hilly path, and open Strath,
We'll wander Scotland thorough;
But, though so near, we will not turn
Into the dale of Yarrow.   40

'Let beeves and home-bred kine partake
The sweets of Burn-mill meadow;
The swan on still St. Mary's Lake
Float double, swan and shadow!
We will not see them; will not go,   45
To-day, nor yet to-morrow;
Enough if in our hearts we know
There's such a place as Yarrow.

    [1] See Hamilton's Ballad as above.

'Be Yarrow stream unseen, unknown!
It must, or we shall rue it: 50
We have a vision of our own;
Ah! why should we undo it?
The treasured dreams of times long past,
We'll keep them, winsome Marrow!
For when we're there, although 'tis fair,
'Twill be another Yarrow!   56

'If Care with freezing years should come,
And wandering seem but folly,—
Should we be loth to stir from home,
And yet be melancholy;   60
Should life be dull, and spirits low,
'Twill soothe us in our sorrow,
That earth hath something yet to show,
The bonny holms of Yarrow!'

XIV

SONNET

IN THE PASS OF KILLICRANKY

An invasion being expected, October, 1803.

[Composed October, 1803.—Published 1807.]

SIX thousand veterans practised in war's
            game,
Tried men, at Killicranky were arrayed
Against an equal host that wore the plaid,
Shepherds and herdsmen.—Like a whirl-
            wind came
The Highlanders, the slaughter spread
            like flame;   5
And Garry, thundering down his moun-
            tain-road,
Was stopped, and could not breathe
            beneath the load
Of the dead bodies.—'Twas a day of
            shame
For them whom precept and the pedantry
Of cold mechanic battle do enslave.   10
O for a single hour of that Dundee,
Who on that day the word of onset gave!
Like conquest would the Men of England
            see;
And her Foes find a like inglorious grave.

XV

THE MATRON OF JEDBOROUGH
AND HER HUSBAND

[Composed between 1803–1805.—Published 1807.]

At Jedborough, my companion and I went into
private lodgings for a few days; and the following Verses were called forth by the character and
domestic situation of our Hostess.

AGE! twine thy brows with fresh spring
            flowers,
And call a train of laughing Hours;
And bid them dance, and bid them sing;
And thou, too, mingle in the ring!
Take to thy heart a new delight;   5
If not, make merry in despite
That there is One who scorns thy power:—
But dance! for under Jedborough Tower

A Matron dwells who, though she bears
The weight of more than seventy years,
Lives in the light of youthful glee,   11
And she will dance and sing with thee.

Nay! start not at that Figure—there!
Him who is rooted to his chair!
Look at him—look again! for he   15
Hath long been of thy family.
With legs that move not, if they can,
And useless arms, a trunk of man,
He sits, and with a vacant eye;
A sight to make a stranger sigh!   20
Deaf, drooping, that is now his doom:
His world is in this single room:
Is this a place for mirthful cheer?
Can merry-making enter here?

The joyous Woman is the Mate   25
Of him in that forlorn estate!
He breathes a subterraneous damp;
But bright as Vesper shines her lamp:
He is as mute as Jedborough Tower:
She jocund as it was of yore,   30
With all its bravery on; in times
When, all alive with merry chimes,
Upon a sun-bright morn of May,
It roused the Vale to holiday.

I praise thee, Matron! and thy due   35
Is praise, heroic praise, and true!
With admiration I behold
Thy gladness unsubdued and bold:
Thy looks, thy gestures, all present
The picture of a life well spent: 40
This do I see; and something more;
A strength unthought of heretofore!
Delighted am I for thy sake;
And yet a higher joy partake:
Our Human-nature throws away   45
Its second twilight, and looks gay;
A land of promise and of pride
Unfolding, wide as life is wide.

Ah! see her helpless Charge! enclosed
Within himself as seems, composed;   50
To fear of loss, and hope of gain,
The strife of happiness and pain,
Utterly dead! yet in the guise
Of little infants, when their eyes
Begin to follow to and fro   55
The persons that before them go,
He tracks her motions, quick or slow.
Her buoyant spirit can prevail
Where common cheerfulness would fail;
She strikes upon him with the heat   60
Of July suns; he feels it sweet;
An animal delight though dim!
'Tis all that now remains for him!

The more I looked, I wondered more—
And, while I scanned them o'er and o'er,
Some inward trouble suddenly   66
Broke from the Matron's strong black
            eye—

233

A remnant of uneasy light,
A flash of something over-bright!
Nor long this mystery did detain   70
My thoughts;—she told in pensive strain
That she had borne a heavy yoke,
Been stricken by a twofold stroke;
Ill health of body; and had pined
Beneath worse ailments of the mind.   75

So be it!—but let praise ascend
To Him who is our lord and friend!
Who from disease and suffering
Hath called for thee a second spring;
Repaid thee for that sore distress   80
By no untimely joyousness;
Which makes of thine a blissful state;
And cheers thy melancholy Mate!

XVI

[Composed September 25, 1803.—Published 1815.]

FLY, some kind Harbinger, to Grasmere-dale!
Say that we come, and come by this day's light;
Fly upon swiftest wing round field and height,
But chiefly let one Cottage hear the tale;
There let a mystery of joy prevail,   5
The kitten frolic, like a gamesome sprite,
And Rover whine, as at a second sight
Of near-approaching good that shall not fail:
And from that Infant's face let joy appear;
Yea, let our Mary's one companion child—   10
That hath her six weeks' solitude beguiled
With intimations manifold and dear,
While we have wandered over wood and wild—
Smile on his Mother now with bolder cheer.   14

XVII

THE BLIND HIGHLAND BOY

A TALE TOLD BY THE FIRE-SIDE, AFTER RETURNING TO THE VALE OF GRASMERE

[Composed probably December, 1806.—Published 1807.]

Now we are tired of boisterous joy,
Have romped enough, my little Boy!
Jane hangs her head upon my breast,
And you shall bring your stool and rest;
This corner is your own.   5

There! take your seat, and let me see
That you can listen quietly:
And, as I promised, I will tell
That strange adventure which befell
A poor blind Highland Boy.   10

A *Highland* Boy!—why call him so?
Because, my Darlings, ye must know
That, under hills which rise like towers,
Far higher hills than these of ours!
He from his birth had lived.   15

He ne'er had seen one earthly sight;
The sun, the day; the stars, the night;
Or tree, or butterfly, or flower,
Or fish in stream, or bird in bower,
Or woman, man, or child.   20

And yet he neither drooped nor pined,
Nor had a melancholy mind;
For God took pity on the Boy,
And was his friend; and gave him joy
Of which we nothing know.   25

His Mother, too, no doubt, above
Her other children him did love:
For was she here, or was she there,
She thought of him with constant care,
And more than mother's love.   30

And proud she was of heart, when clad
In crimson stockings, tartan plaid,
And bonnet with a feather gay,
To Kirk he on the sabbath day
Went hand in hand with her.   35

A dog, too, had he; not for need,
But one to play with and to feed;
Which would have led him, if bereft
Of company or friends, and left
Without a better guide.   40

And then the bagpipes he could blow—
And thus from house to house would go;
And all were pleased to hear and see,
For none made sweeter melody
Than did the poor blind Boy.   45

Yet he had many a restless dream;
Both when he heard the eagles scream,
And when he heard the torrents roar,
And heard the water beat the shore
Near which their cottage stood.   50

Beside a lake their cottage stood,
Not small like ours, a peaceful flood;
But one of mighty size, and strange;
That, rough or smooth, is full of change,
And stirring in its bed.   55

For to this lake, by night and day,
The great Sea-water finds its way
Through long, long windings of the hills,
And drinks up all the pretty rills
And rivers large and strong: 60

Then hurries back the road it came—
Returns, on errand still the same;
This did it when the earth was new;
And this for evermore will do,
As long as earth shall last.   65

234

And, with the coming of the tide,
Come boats and ships that safely ride
Between the woods and lofty rocks;
And to the shepherds with their flocks
    Bring tales of distant lands.   70

And of those tales, whate'er they were,
The blind Boy always had his share;
Whether of mighty towns, or vales
With warmer suns and softer gales,
    Or wonders of the Deep.   75

Yet more it pleased him, more it stirred,
When from the water-side he heard
The shouting, and the jolly cheers;
The bustle of the mariners
    In stillness or in storm.   80

But what do his desires avail?
For He must never handle sail;
Nor mount the mast, nor row, nor float
In sailor's ship, or fisher's boat,
    Upon the rocking waves.   85

His Mother often thought, and said,
What sin would be upon her head
If she should suffer this: 'My Son,
Whate'er you do, leave this undone;
    The danger is so great.'   90

Thus lived he by Loch Leven's side
Still sounding with the sounding tide,
And heard the billows leap and dance,
Without a shadow of mischance,
    Till he was ten years old.   95

When one day (and now mark me well,
Ye soon shall know how this befell)
He in a vessel of his own
On the swift flood is hurrying down,
    Down to the mighty Sea.   100

In such a vessel never more
May human creature leave the shore!
If this or that way he should stir,
Woe to the poor blind Mariner!
    For death will be his doom.   105

But say what bears him?—Ye have seen
The Indian's bow, his arrows keen,
Rare beasts, and birds with plumage
    bright;
Gifts which, for wonder or delight,
    Are brought in ships from far.   110

Such gifts had those seafaring men
Spread round that haven in the glen;
Each hut, perchance, might have its own;
And to the Boy they all were known—
    He knew and prized them all.   115

The rarest was a Turtle-shell
Which he, poor Child, had studied well;
A shell of ample size, and light
As the pearly car of Amphitrite,
    That sportive dolphins drew.   120

And, as a Coracle that braves
On Vaga's breast the fretful waves,
This shell upon the deep would swim,
And gaily lift its fearless brim
    Above the tossing surge.   125

And this the little blind Boy knew;
And he a story strange yet true
Had heard, how in a shell like this
An English Boy, O thought of bliss!
    Had stoutly launched from shore;   130

Launched from the margin of a bay
Among the Indian isles, where lay
His father's ship, and had sailed far—
To join that gallant ship of war,
    In his delightful shell.   135

Our Highland Boy oft visited
The house that held this prize; and, led
By choice or chance, did thither come
One day when no one was at home,
    And found the door unbarred.   140

While there he sate, alone and blind,
That story flashed upon his mind;—
A bold thought roused him, and he took
The shell from out its secret nook,
    And bore it on his head.   145

He launched his vessel,—and in pride
Of spirit, from Loch Leven's side,
Stepped into it—his thoughts all free
As the light breezes that with glee
    Sang through the adventurer's hair.

A while he stood upon his feet;   151
He felt the motion—took his seat;
Still better pleased as more and more
The tide retreated from the shore,
    And sucked, and sucked him in.   155

And there he is in face of Heaven.
How rapidly the Child is driven!
The fourth part of a mile, I ween,
He thus had gone, ere he was seen
    By any human eye.   160

But when he was first seen, oh me
What shrieking and what misery!
For many saw; among the rest
His Mother, she who loved him best,
    She saw her poor blind Boy.   165

But for the child, the sightless Boy,
It is the triumph of his joy!
The bravest traveller in balloon,
Mounting as if to reach the moon,
    Was never half so blessed.   170

And let him, let him go his way,
Alone, and innocent, and gay!
For, if good Angels love to wait
On the forlorn unfortunate,
    This Child will take no harm.   175

But now the passionate lament,
Which from the crowd on shore was sent,
The cries which broke from old and young
In Gaelic, or the English tongue,
Are stifled—all is still.   180

And quickly with a silent crew
A boat is ready to pursue;
And from the shore their course they take,
And swiftly down the running lake
They follow the blind Boy.   185

But soon they move with softer pace;
So have ye seen the fowler chase
On Grasmere's clear unruffled breast
A youngling of the wild-duck's nest
With deftly-lifted oar;   190

Or as the wily sailors crept
To seize (while on the Deep it slept)
The hapless creature which did dwell
Erewhile within the dancing shell,
They steal upon their prey.   195

With sound the least that can be made,
They follow, more and more afraid,
More cautious as they draw more near;
But in his darkness he can hear,
And guesses their intent.   200

'Lei-gha—Lei-gha'—he then cried out,
'Lei-gha—Lei-gha'—with eager shout;
Thus did he cry, and thus did pray,
And what he meant was 'Keep away,
And leave me to myself!'   205

Alas! and when he felt their hands——
You've often heard of magic wands,
That with a motion overthrow
A palace of the proudest show,
Or melt it into air: 210

So all his dreams—that inward light
With which his soul had shone so bright—
All vanished;—'twas a heartfelt cross
To him, a heavy, bitter loss,
As he had ever known.   215

But hark! a gratulating voice,
With which the very hills rejoice:
'Tis from the crowd, who tremblingly
Have watched the event, and now can see
That he is safe at last.   220

And then, when he was brought to land,
Full sure they were a happy band,
Which, gathering round, did on the banks
Of that great Water give God thanks,
And welcomed the poor Child.   225

And in the general joy of heart
The blind Boy's little dog took part;
He leapt about, and oft did kiss
His master's hands in sign of bliss,
With sound like lamentation.   230

But most of all, his Mother dear,
She who had fainted with her fear,
Rejoiced when waking she espies
The Child; when she can trust her eyes,
And touches the blind Boy.   235

She led him home, and wept amain,
When he was in the house again:
Tears flowed in torrents from her eyes;
She kissed him—how could she chastise?
She was too happy far.   240

Thus, after he had fondly braved
The perilous Deep, the Boy was saved;
And, though his fancies had been wild,
Yet he was pleased and reconciled
To live in peace on shore.   245

And in the lonely Highland dell
Still do they keep the Turtle-shell;
And long the story will repeat
Of the blind Boy's adventurous feat,
And how he was preserved.   250

Note.—It is recorded in 'Dampier's Voyages,'
that a boy, son of the captain of a Man-of-War,
seated himself in a Turtle-shell, and floated in it
from the shore to his father's ship, which lay at
anchor at the distance of half a mile. In deference
to the opinion of a Friend, I have substituted such
a shell for the less elegant vessel in which my
blind Voyager did actually entrust himself to the
dangerous current of Loch Leven, as was related
to me by an eye-witness.

MEMORIALS OF
A TOUR IN SCOTLAND, 1814

I

SUGGESTED BY A BEAUTIFUL RUIN UPON
ONE OF THE ISLANDS OF LOCH LOMOND,
A PLACE CHOSEN FOR THE RETREAT OF
A SOLITARY INDIVIDUAL, FROM WHOM
THIS HABITATION ACQUIRED THE NAME
OF

THE BROWNIE'S CELL

[Composed perhaps 1814.—Published 1820.]

I

To barren heath, bleak moor, and quaking
    fen,
Or depth of labyrinthine glen;
Or into trackless forest set
With trees, whose lofty umbrage met;
World-wearied Men withdrew of yore;   5
(Penance their trust, and prayer their
    store;)
And in the wilderness were bound
To such apartments as they found;
Or with a new ambition raised;
That God might suitably be praised.   10

II

High lodged the *Warrior*, like a bird of
    prey;
Or where broad waters round him lay:
But this wild Ruin is no ghost
Of his devices—buried, lost!
Within this little lonely isle   15
There stood a consecrated Pile;
Where tapers burned, and mass was sung,
For them whose timid Spirits clung
To mortal succour, though the tomb
Had fixed, for ever fixed, their doom!   20

III

Upon those servants of another world
When madding Power her bolts had
    hurled,
Their habitation shook;—it fell,
And perished, save one narrow cell;
Whither, at length, a Wretch retired   25
Who neither grovelled nor aspired:
He, struggling in the net of pride,
The future scorned, the past defied;
Still tempering, from the unguilty forge
Of vain conceit, an iron scourge!   30

IV

Proud Remnant was he of a fearless Race,
Who stood and flourished face to face
With their perennial hills;—but Crime,
Hastening the stern decrees of Time,
Brought low a Power, which from its home
Burst, when repose grew wearisome;   36

And, taking impulse from the sword,
And, mocking its own plighted word,
Had found, in ravage widely dealt,
Its warfare's bourn, its travel's belt!   40

V

All, all were dispossessed, save him whose
    smile
Shot lightning through this lonely Isle!
No right had he but what he made
To this small spot, his leafy shade;
But the ground lay within that ring   45
To which he only dared to cling;
Renouncing here, as worse than dead,
The craven few who bowed the head
Beneath the change; who heard a claim
How loud! yet lived in peace with shame.

VI

From year to year this shaggy Mortal
    went   51
(So seemed it) down a strange descent:
Till they, who saw his outward frame,
Fixed on him an unhallowed name;
Him, free from all malicious taint,   55
And guiding, like the Patmos Saint,
A pen unwearied—to indite,
In his lone Isle, the dreams of night;
Impassioned dreams, that strove to span
The faded glories of his Clan!   60

VII

Suns that through blood their western
    harbour sought,
And stars that in their courses fought;
Towers rent, winds combating with
    woods,
Lands deluged by unbridled floods;
And beast and bird that from the spell   65
Of sleep took import terrible;—
These types mysterious (if the show
Of battle and the routed foe
Had failed) would furnish an array
Of matter for the dawning day!   70

VIII

How disappeared He?—ask the newt and
    toad,
Inheritors of his abode;
The otter crouching undisturbed,
In her dank cleft;—but be thou curbed,
O froward Fancy! 'mid a scene   75
Of aspect winning and serene;
For those offensive creatures shun
The inquisition of the sun!
And in this region flowers delight,
And all is lovely to the sight.   80

IX

Spring finds not here a melancholy breast,
When she applies her annual test
To dead and living; when her breath
Quickens, as now, the withered heath;—
Nor flaunting Summer—when he throws
His soul into the briar-rose;   86
Or calls the lily from her sleep
Prolonged beneath the bordering deep;
Nor Autumn, when the viewless wren
Is warbling near the BROWNIE'S Den.   90

X

Wild Relique! beauteous as the chosen
    spot
In Nysa's isle, the embellished grot;
Whither, by care of Libyan Jove,
(High Servant of paternal Love)
Young Bacchus was conveyed—to lie   95
Safe from his step-dame Rhea's eye;
Where bud, and bloom, and fruitage,
    glowed,
Close-crowding round the infant-god;
All colours—and the liveliest streak
A foil to his celestial cheek!   100

II

COMPOSED AT CORA LINN

IN SIGHT OF WALLACE'S TOWER

[Composed perhaps 1814.—Published 1820.]

'—How Wallace fought for Scotland, left the name
Of Wallace to be found, like a wild flower,
All over his dear Country; left the deeds
Of Wallace, like a family of ghosts,
To people the steep rocks and river banks,
Her natural sanctuaries, with a local soul
Of independence and stern liberty.'—*MS.*

LORD of the vale! astounding Flood;
The dullest leaf in this thick wood
Quakes—conscious of thy power;
The caves reply with hollow moan;
And vibrates, to its central stone,   5
Yon time-cemented Tower!

And yet how fair the rural scene!
For thou, O Clyde, hast ever been
Beneficent as strong;
Pleased in refreshing dews to steep   10
The little trembling flowers that peep
Thy shelving rocks among.

Hence all who love their country, love
To look on thee—delight to rove
Where they thy voice can hear;   15
And, to the patriot-warrior's Shade,
Lord of the vale! to Heroes laid
In dust, that voice is dear!

Along thy banks, at dead of night
Sweeps visibly the Wallace Wight;   20
Or stands, in warlike vest,
Aloft, beneath the moon's pale beam,
A Champion worthy of the stream.
Yon grey tower's living crest!

But clouds and envious darkness hide   25
A Form not doubtfully descried:—
Their transient mission o'er,
O say to what blind region flee
These Shapes of awful phantasy?
To what untrodden shore?   30

Less than divine command they spurn;
But this we from the mountains learn,
And this the valleys show;
That never will they deign to hold
Communion where the heart is cold   35
To human weal and woe.

The man of abject soul in vain
Shall walk the Marathonian plain;
Or thrid the shadowy gloom,
That still invests the guardian Pass,   40
Where stood, sublime, Leonidas
Devoted to the tomb.

And let no Slave his head incline,
Or kneel, before the votive shrine
By Uri's lake, where Tell   45
Leapt, from his storm-vext boat, to land,
Heaven's Instrument, for by his hand
That day the Tyrant fell.

III

EFFUSION

IN THE PLEASURE-GROUND ON THE BANKS
OF THE BRAN, NEAR DUNKELD

[Composed 1814 (?).—Published 1827.]

The waterfall, by a loud roaring, warned us when
we must expect it. We were first, however,
conducted into a small apartment, where the
Gardener desired us to look at a picture of
Ossian, which, while he was telling the history
of the young Artist who executed the work, disappeared, parting in the middle—flying asunder
as by the touch of magic—and lo! we are at
the entrance of a splendid apartment, which
was almost dizzy and alive with waterfalls, that
tumbled in all directions; the great cascade,
opposite the window, which faced us, being
reflected in innumerable mirrors upon the ceiling
and against the walls.'—*Extract from the Journal
of my Fellow-Traveller.*

WHAT He—who, mid the kindred throng
Of Heroes that inspired his song,
Doth yet frequent the hill of storms,
The stars dim-twinkling through their
    forms!
What! Ossian here—a painted Thrall,   5
Mute fixture on a stuccoed wall;
To serve—an unsuspected screen
For show that must not yet be seen;
And, when the moment comes, to part
And vanish by mysterious art;   10
Head, harp, and body, split asunder,
For ingress to a world of wonder:

A gay saloon, with waters dancing
Upon the sight wherever glancing;
One loud cascade in front, and lo!   15
A thousand like it, white as snow—
Streams on the walls, and torrent-foam
As active round the hollow dome,
Illusive cataracts! of their terrors
Not stripped, nor voiceless in the mirrors,
That catch the pageant from the flood   21
Thundering adown a rocky wood.
What pains to dazzle and confound!
What strife of colour, shape and sound
In this quaint medley, that might seem
Devised out of a sick man's dream!   26
Strange scene, fantastic and uneasy
As ever made a maniac dizzy,
When disenchanted from the mood
That loves on sullen thoughts to brood!

O Nature—in thy changeful visions,   31
Through all thy most abrupt transitions
Smooth, graceful, tender, or sublime—
Ever averse to pantomime,
Thee neither do they know nor us   35
Thy servants, who can trifle thus;
Else verily the sober powers
Of rock that frowns, and stream that
    roars,
Exalted by congenial sway
Of Spirits, and the undying Lay,   40
And Names that moulder not away,
Had wakened some redeeming thought
More worthy of this favoured Spot;
Recalled some feeling—to set free
The Bard from such indignity!   45

The Effigies[1] of a valiant Wight
I once beheld, a Templar Knight;
Not prostrate, not like those that rest
On tombs, with palms together prest,
But sculptured out of living stone,   50
And standing upright and alone,
Both hands with rival energy
Employed in setting his sword free
From its dull sheath—stern sentinel
Intent to guard St. Robert's cell;   55
As if with memory of the affray
Far distant, when, as legends say,
The Monks of Fountain's thronged to
    force
From its dear home the Hermit's corse,
That in their keeping it might lie,   60
To crown their abbey's sanctity.
So had they rushed into the grot
Of sense despised, a world forgot,
And torn him from his loved retreat,
Where altar-stone and rock-hewn seat
Still hint that quiet best is found,   66
Even by the *Living*, under ground;
But a bold Knight, the selfish aim
Defeating, put the Monks to shame,
There where you see his Image stand   70

[1] On the banks of the river Nid, near Knares-
borough.

Bare to the sky, with threatening brand
Which lingering NID is proud to show
Reflected in the pool below.

Thus, like the men of earliest days,
Our sires set forth their grateful praise:
Uncouth the workmanship, and rude!   76
But, nursed in mountain solitude,
Might some aspiring artist dare
To seize whate'er, through misty air,
A ghost, by glimpses, may present   80
Of imitable lineament,
And give the phantom an array
That less should scorn the abandoned
    clay;
Then let him hew with patient stroke
An Ossian out of mural rock,   85
And leave the figurative Man—
Upon thy margin, roaring Bran!—
Fixed, like the Templar of the steep,
An everlasting watch to keep;
With local sanctities in trust,   90
More precious than a hermit's dust;
And virtues through the mass infused,
Which old idolatry abused.

What though the Granite would deny
All fervour to the sightless eye;   95
And touch from rising suns in vain
Solicit a Memnonian strain;
Yet, in some fit of anger sharp,
The wind might force the deep-grooved
    harp
To utter melancholy moans   100
Not unconnected with the tones
Of soul-sick flesh and weary bones;
While grove and river notes would lend,
Less deeply sad, with these to blend!

Vain pleasures of luxurious life,   105
For ever with yourselves at strife;
Through town and country both deranged
By affectations interchanged,
And all the perishable gauds
That heaven-deserted man applauds;   110
When will your hapless patrons learn
To watch and ponder—to discern
The freshness, the everlasting youth,
Of admiration sprung from truth;
From beauty infinitely growing   115
Upon a mind with love o'erflowing—
To sound the depths of every Art
That seeks its wisdom through the heart?

Thus (where the intrusive Pile, ill-
    graced
With baubles of theatric taste,   120
O'erlooks the torrent breathing showers
On motley bands of alien flowers
In stiff confusion set or sown,
Till Nature cannot find her own,
Or keep a remnant of the sod   125
Which Caledonian Heroes trod)
I mused; and, thirsting for redress,
Recoiled into the wilderness.

MEMORIALS OF A TOUR IN SCOTLAND, 1814

IV

YARROW VISITED

SEPTEMBER, 1814

[Composed 1814.—Published 1815.]
(See page 292.)

AND is this—Yarrow?—*This* the Stream
Of which my fancy cherished,
So faithfully, a waking dream?
An image that hath perished!
O that some Minstrel's harp were near,　5
To utter notes of gladness,
And chase this silence from the air,
That fills my heart with sadness!

Yet why?—a silvery current flows
With uncontrolled meanderings;　10
Nor have these eyes by greener hills
Been soothed, in all my wanderings.
And, through her depths, Saint Mary's
　Lake
Is visibly delighted;
For not a feature of those hills　15
Is in the mirror slighted.

A blue sky bends o'er Yarrow vale,
Save where that pearly whiteness
Is round the rising sun diffused,
A tender hazy brightness;　20
Mild dawn of promise! that excludes
All profitless dejection;
Though not unwilling here to admit
A pensive recollection.

Where was it that the famous Flower　25
Of Yarrow Vale lay bleeding?
His bed perchance was yon smooth
　mound
On which the herd is feeding:
And haply from this crystal pool,
Now peaceful as the morning,　30
The Water-wraith ascended thrice—
And gave his doleful warning.

Delicious is the Lay that sings
The haunts of happy Lovers,
The path that leads them to the grove,
The leafy grove that covers:　36
And Pity sanctifies the Verse
That paints, by strength of sorrow,
The unconquerable strength of love;
Bear witness, rueful Yarrow!　40

But thou, that didst appear so fair
To fond imagination,
Dost rival in the light of day
Her delicate creation:
Meek loveliness is round thee spread,　45
A softness still and holy;
The grace of forest charms decayed,
And pastoral melancholy.

That region left, the vale unfolds
Rich groves of lofty stature,　50
With Yarrow winding through the pomp
Of cultivated nature;
And, rising from those lofty groves,
Behold a Ruin hoary!
The shattered front of Newark's Towers,
Renowned in Border story.　56

Fair scenes for childhood's opening
　bloom,
For sportive youth to stray in;
For manhood to enjoy his strength;
And age to wear away in!　60
Yon cottage seems a bower of bliss,
A covert for protection
Of tender thoughts, that nestle there—
The brood of chaste affection.

How sweet, on this autumnal day,　65
The wild-wood fruits to gather,
And on my True-love's forehead plant
A crest of blooming heather!
And what if I enwreathed my own!
'Twere no offence to reason;　70
The sober Hills thus deck their brows
To meet the wintry season.

I see—but not by sight alone,
Loved Yarrow, have I won thee;
A ray of fancy still survives—　75
Her sunshine plays upon thee!
Thy ever-youthful waters keep
A course of lively pleasure;
And gladsome notes my lips can breathe,
Accordant to the measure.　80

The vapours linger round the Heights,
They melt, and soon must vanish;
One hour is theirs, nor more is mine—
Sad thought, which I would banish,
But that I know, where'er I go,　85
Thy genuine image, Yarrow!
Will dwell with me—to heighten joy,
And cheer my mind in sorrow.

POEMS DEDICATED TO NATIONAL INDEPENDENCE AND LIBERTY

PART I

I

COMPOSED BY THE SEA-SIDE, NEAR CALAIS, AUGUST, 1802

[Composed August, 1802.—Published 1807.]

FAIR Star of evening, Splendour of the west,
Star of my Country!—on the horizon's brink
Thou hangest, stooping, as might seem, to sink
On England's bosom; yet well pleased to rest,
Meanwhile, and be to her a glorious crest   5
Conspicuous to the Nations. Thou, I think,
Shouldst be my Country's emblem; and shouldst wink,
Bright Star! with laughter on her banners, drest
In thy fresh beauty. There! that dusky spot
Beneath thee, that is England; there she lies.   10
Blessings be on you both! one hope, one lot,
One life, one glory!—I, with many a fear
For my dear Country, many a heartfelt sighs,
Among men who do not love her, linger here.

II

CALAIS, AUGUST, 1802

[Composed August, 1802.—Published January 29, 1803 (*Morning Post*[1]); 1807.]

Is it a reed that's shaken by the wind,
Or what is it that ye go forth to see?
Lords, lawyers, statesmen, squires of low degree,
Men known, and men unknown, sick, lame, and blind,
Post forward all, like creatures of one kind,   5
With first-fruit offerings crowd to bend the knee
In France, before the new-born Majesty.
'Tis ever thus. Ye men of prostrate mind,

A seemly reverence may be paid to power;
But that's a loyal virtue, never sown   10
In haste, nor springing with a transient shower:
When truth, when sense, when liberty were flown,
What hardship had it been to wait an hour?
Shame on you, feeble Heads, to slavery prone!

III

COMPOSED NEAR CALAIS, ON THE ROAD LEADING TO ARDRES, AUGUST 7, 1802

[Composed August, 1802.—Published 1807.]

JONES! as from Calais southward you and I
Went pacing side by side, this public Way
Streamed with the pomp of a too-credulous day,[1]
When faith was pledged to new-born Liberty: 4
A homeless sound of joy was in the sky:
From hour to hour the antiquated Earth
Beat like the heart of Man: songs, garlands, mirth,
Banners, and happy faces, far and nigh!
And now, sole register that these things were,
Two solitary greetings have I heard,   10
'Good morrow, Citizen!' a hollow word,
As if a dead man spake it! Yet despair
Touches me not, though pensive as a bird
Whose vernal coverts winter hath laid bare.[2]

IV

1801

[Composed May 21, 1802.—Published September 6, 1802 (*Morning Post*); January 29, 1803 (*Ibid.*); 1807.]

I GRIEVED for Buonaparté, with a vain
And an unthinking grief! The tenderest mood
Of that Man's mind—what can it be? what food
Fed his first hopes? what knowledge could *he* gain?
'Tis not in battles that from youth we train   5
The Governor who must be wise and good,

[1] July 14, 1790.   [2] See Note, p. 705.

And temper with the sternness of the brain
Thoughts motherly, and meek as womanhood.
Wisdom doth live with children round her knees:
Books, leisure, perfect freedom, and the talk   10
Man holds with week-day man in the hourly walk
Of the mind's business: these are the degrees
By which true Sway doth mount; this is the stalk
True Power doth grow on; and her rights are these.

V

CALAIS, AUGUST 15, 1802

[Composed August 15, 1802.—Published February 26, 1803 (*Morning Post*); 1807.]

FESTIVALS have I seen that were not names:
This is young Buonaparté's natal day,
And his is henceforth an established sway—
Consul for life. With worship France proclaims
Her approbation, and with pomps and games.   5
Heaven grant that other Cities may be gay!
Calais is not: and I have bent my way
To the sea-coast, noting that each man frames
His business as he likes. Far other show
My youth here witnessed, in a prouder time;   10
The senselessness of joy was then sublime!
Happy is he, who, caring not for Pope,
Consul, or King, can sound himself to know
The destiny of Man, and live in hope.

VI

ON THE EXTINCTION OF THE VENETIAN REPUBLIC[1]

[Composed probably August, 1802.—Published 1807.]

ONCE did She hold the gorgeous east in fee;
And was the safeguard of the west: the worth
Of Venice did not fall below her birth,
Venice, the eldest Child of Liberty.   4
She was a maiden City, bright and free;
No guile seduced, no force could violate;
And, when she took unto herself a Mate,
She must espouse the everlasting Sea.

[1] By the treaty of Campo Formio, 1797.—ED.

And what if she had seen those glories fade,
Those titles vanish, and that strength decay;   10
Yet shall some tribute of regret be paid
When her long life hath reached its final day:
Men are we, and must grieve when even the Shade
Of that which once was great is passed away.

VII

THE KING OF SWEDEN

[Composed probably August, 1802.—Published 1807.]

THE Voice of song from distant lands shall call
To that great King: shall hail the crownèd Youth
Who, taking counsel of unbending Truth,
By one example hath set forth to all
How they with dignity may stand; or fall,   5
If fall they must. Now, whither doth it tend?
And what to him and his shall be the end?
That thought is one which neither can appal
Nor cheer him; for the illustrious Swede hath done
The thing which ought to be; is raised *above*   10
All consequences: work he hath begun
Of fortitude, and piety, and love,
Which all his glorious ancestors approve:
The heroes bless him, him their rightful son.[1]

VIII

TO TOUSSAINT L'OUVERTURE[2]

[Composed probably August, 1802.—Published February 2, 1803 (*Morning Post*); 1807.]

TOUSSAINT, the most unhappy man of men!
Whether the whistling Rustic tend his plough
Within thy hearing, or thy head be now
Pillowed in some deep dungeon's earless den;—

[1] See note.—W. (The 'crownèd Youth' was Gustavus IV of Sweden: born 1778; crowned 1792; abdicated 1809. See Part II, Sonnets XX, XXI.—ED.)
[2] François Dominique Toussaint, surnamed L'Ouverture, was governor of St. Domingo, and chief of the African slaves enfranchised by the decree of the French Convention (1794). He resisted Napoleon's edict re-establishing slavery in St. Domingo, was arrested and sent to Paris in June, 1802, and there died after ten month's imprisonment in April, 1803.—ED.

O miserable Chieftain! where and when
Wilt thou find patience! Yet die not; do
   thou   6
Wear rather in thy bonds a cheerful brow:
Though fallen thyself, never to rise again,
Live, and take comfort. Thou hast left
   behind
Powers that will work for thee; air, earth,
   and skies;   10
There's not a breathing of the common
   wind
That will forget thee; thou hast great
   allies;
Thy friends are exultations, agonies,
And love, and man's unconquerable mind.

IX

SEPTEMBER 1, 1802

[Composed September 1, 1802.—Published
February 11, 1803 (*Morning Post*); 1807.]

Among the capricious acts of tyranny that disgraced those times, was the chasing of all
Negroes from France by decree of the government: we had a Fellow-passenger who was one
of the expelled.

WE had a female Passenger who came
From Calais with us, spotless in array,—
A white-robed Negro, like a lady gay,
Yet downcast as a woman fearing blame;
Meek, destitute, as seemed, of hope or
   aim   5
She sate, from notice turning not away,
But on all proffered intercourse did lay
A weight of languid speech, or to the same
No sign of answer made by word or face:
Yet still her eyes retained their tropic fire,
That, burning independent of the mind,
Joined with the lustre of her rich attire
To mock the Outcast—O ye Heavens, be
   kind!   13
And feel, thou Earth, for this afflicted
   Race!

X

COMPOSED IN THE VALLEY NEAR DOVER, ON THE DAY OF LANDING

[Composed August 30, 1802.—Published 1807.]

HERE, on our native soil, we breathe once
   more.
The cock that crows, the smoke that curls,
   that sound
Of bells;—those boys who in yon meadow-
   ground
In white-sleeved shirts are playing; and
   the roar
Of the waves breaking on the chalky
   shore;—   5
All, all are English. Oft have I looked
   round
With joy in Kent's green vales; but never
   found

Myself so satisfied in heart before.
Europe is yet in bonds; but let that pass,
Thought for another moment. Thou art
   free,   10
My Country! and 'tis joy enough and pride
For one hour's perfect bliss, to tread the
   grass
Of England once again, and hear and see,
With such a dear Companion at my side.

XI

SEPTEMBER, 1802. NEAR DOVER

[Composed September, 1802.—Published 1807.]

INLAND, within a hollow vale, I stood;
And saw, while sea was calm and air was
   clear,
The coast of France—the coast of France
   how near!
Drawn almost into frightful neighbour-
   hood.
I shrunk; for verily the barrier flood   5
Was like a lake, or river bright and fair,
A span of waters; yet what power is there!
What mightiness for evil and for good!
Even so doth God protect us if we be
Virtuous and wise. Winds blow, and
   waters roll,   10
Strength to the brave, and Power, and
   Deity;
Yet in themselves are nothing! One decree
Spake laws to *them*, and said that by the
   soul
Only, the Nations shall be great and free.

XII

THOUGHT OF A BRITON ON THE SUBJUGA-TION OF SWITZERLAND

[Composed probably early in 1807.—Published
1807.]

Two Voices are there; one is of the sea,
One of the mountains; each a mighty
   Voice:
In both from age to age thou didst rejoice,
They were thy chosen music, Liberty!
There came a Tyrant, and with holy glee
Thou fought'st against him; but hast
   vainly striven: 6
Thou from thy Alpine holds at length art
   driven,
Where not a torrent murmurs heard by
   thee.
Of one deep bliss thine ear hath been
   bereft:
Then cleave, O cleave to that which still
   is left;   10
For, high-souled Maid, what sorrow
   would it be
That Mountain floods should thunder as
   before,
And Ocean bellow from his rocky shore,
And neither awful Voice be heard by thee!

XIII

WRITTEN IN LONDON, SEPTEMBER, 1802

[Composed September, 1802.—Published 1807.]

O FRIEND! I know not which way I must
  look
For comfort, being, as I am, opprest,
To think that now our life is only drest
For show; mean handy-work of crafts-
  man, cook,
Or groom!—We must run glittering like
  a brook   5
In the open sunshine, or we are unblest:
The wealthiest man among us is the best:
No grandeur now in nature or in book
Delights us. Rapine, avarice, expense,
This is idolatry; and these we adore: 10
Plain living and high thinking are no
  more:
The homely beauty of the good old cause
Is gone; our peace, our fearful innocence,
And pure religion breathing household
  laws.

XIV

LONDON, 1802

[Composed September, 1802.—Published 1807.]

MILTON! thou shouldst be living at this
  hour:
England hath need of thee: she is a fen
Of stagnant waters: altar, sword, and pen,
Fireside, the heroic wealth of hall and
  bower,
Have forfeited their ancient English
  dower   5
Of inward happiness. We are selfish men;
Oh! raise us up, return to us again;
And give us manners, virtue, freedom,
  power.
Thy soul was like a Star, and dwelt apart;
Thou hadst a voice whose sound was like
  the sea: 10
Pure as the naked heavens, majestic, free,
So didst thou travel on life's common way,
In cheerful godliness; and yet thy heart
The lowliest duties on herself did lay.

XV

[Composed probably 1802.—Published 1807.]

GREAT men have been among us; hands
  that penned
And tongues that uttered wisdom—better
  none:
The later Sidney, Marvel, Harrington,
Young Vane, and others who called Mil-
  ton friend.
These moralists could act and compre-
  hend: 5
They knew how genuine glory was put on;

Taught us how rightfully a nation shone
In splendour: what strength was, that
  would not bend
But in magnanimous meekness. France,
  'tis strange,
Hath brought forth no such souls as we
  had then.   10
Perpetual emptiness! unceasing change!
No single volume paramount, no code,
No master spirit, no determined road;
But equally a want of books and men!

XVI

[Composed 1802 or 1803.—Published April 16,
1803 (*Morning Post*); 1807.]

IT is not to be thought of that the Flood
Of British freedom, which, to the open sea
Of the world's praise, from dark antiquity
Hath flowed, 'with pomp of waters, un-
  withstood,'   4
Roused though it be full often to a mood
Which spurns the check of salutary bands,
That this most famous Stream in bogs
  and sands
Should perish; and to evil and to good
Be lost for ever. In our halls is hung
Armoury of the invincible Knights of old:
We must be free or die, who speak the
  tongue   11
That Shakspeare spake; the faith and
  morals hold
Which Milton held.—In every thing we
  are sprung
Of Earth's first blood, have titles mani-
  fold.

XVII

[Composed 1802 or 1803.—Published September
17, 1803 (*Morning Post*); 1807.]

WHEN I have borne in memory what has
  tamed
Great Nations, how ennobling thoughts
  depart
When men change swords for ledgers, and
  desert
The student's bower for gold, some fears
  unnamed
I had, my Country—am I to be blamed?
Now, when I think of thee, and what
  thou art,   6
Verily, in the bottom of my heart,
Of those unfilial fears I am ashamed.
For dearly must we prize thee; we who
  find
In thee a bulwark for the cause of men; 10
And I by my affection was beguiled:
What wonder if a Poet now and then,
Among the many movements of his mind,
Felt for thee as a lover or a child!

XVIII
OCTOBER, 1803
[Composed October, 1803.—Published 1807.]

ONE might believe that natural miseries
Had blasted France, and made of it a land
Unfit for men; and that in one great band
Her sons were bursting forth, to dwell at
　　ease.
But 'tis a chosen soil, where sun and
　　breeze　　　　　　　　　　　　　　　5
Shed gentle favours: rural works are
　　there,
And ordinary business without care;
Spot rich in all things that can soothe and
　　please!
How piteous then that there should be
　　such dearth
Of knowledge; that whole myriads should
　　unite　　　　　　　　　　　　　　　10
To work against themselves such fell
　　despite:
Should come in frenzy and in drunken
　　mirth,
Impatient to put out the only light
Of Liberty that yet remains on earth!

XIX
[Composed 1803 (?).—Published 1807.]

THERE is a bondage worse, far worse, to
　　bear
Than his who breathes, by roof, and floor,
　　and wall,
Pent in, a Tyrant's solitary Thrall:
'Tis his who walks about in the open air,
One of a Nation who, henceforth, must
　　wear　　　　　　　　　　　　　　　5
Their fetters in their souls. For who
　　could be,
Who, even the best, in such condition, free
From self-reproach, reproach that he
　　must share
With Human-nature? Never be it ours
To see the sun how brightly it will shine,
And know that noble feelings, manly
　　powers,　　　　　　　　　　　　　　11
Instead of gathering strength, must droop
　　and pine;
And earth with all her pleasant fruits and
　　flowers
Fade, and participate in man's decline.

XX
OCTOBER, 1803
[Composed October, 1803.—Published 1807.]

THESE times strike monied worldlings
　　with dismay:
Even rich men, brave by nature, taint
　　the air
With words of apprehension and despair:
While tens of thousands, thinking on the
　　affray,
Men unto whom sufficient for the day　　5
And minds not stinted or untilled are
　　given,
Sound, healthy, children of the God of
　　heaven,
Are cheerful as the rising sun in May.
What do we gather hence but firmer faith
That every gift of noble origin　　　　　10
Is breathed upon by Hope's perpetual
　　breath;
That virtue and the faculties within
Are vital,—and that riches are akin
To fear, to change, to cowardice, and
　　death?

XXI
[Composed probably 1803.—Published 1807.]

ENGLAND! the time is come when thou
　　shouldst wean
Thy heart from its emasculating food;
The truth should now be better under-
　　stood;
Old things have been unsettled; we have
　　seen
Fair seed-time, better harvest might have
　　been　　　　　　　　　　　　　　　5
But for thy trespasses; and, at this day,
If for Greece, Egypt, India, Africa,
Aught good were destined, thou wouldst
　　step between.
England! all nations in this charge agree:
But worse, more ignorant in love and
　　hate,　　　　　　　　　　　　　　　10
Far—far more abject, is thine Enemy:
Therefore the wise pray for thee, though
　　the freight
Of thy offences be a heavy weight:
Oh grief that Earth's best hopes rest all
　　with Thee!

XXII
OCTOBER, 1803
[Composed October, 1803.—Published 1807.]

WHEN, looking on the present face of
　　things,
I see one man, of men the meanest too!
Raised up to sway the world, to do, undo,
With mighty Nations for his underlings,
The great events with which old story
　　rings　　　　　　　　　　　　　　　5
Seem vain and hollow; I find nothing
　　great:
Nothing is left which I can venerate;
So that a doubt almost within me springs
Of Providence, such emptiness at length
Seems at the heart of all things. But,
　　great God!　　　　　　　　　　　　10
I measure back the steps which I have
　　trod;
And tremble, seeing whence proceeds the
　　strength
Of such poor instruments, with thoughts
　　sublime
I tremble at the sorrow of the time.

POEMS DEDICATED TO NATIONAL

XXIII

TO THE MEN OF KENT. OCTOBER, 1803

[Composed Oct. 1803.—Published 1807.]

VANGUARD of Liberty, ye men of Kent,
Ye children of a Soil that doth advance
Her haughty brow against the coast of
    France,
Now is the time to prove your hardiment!
To France be words of invitation sent!   5
They from their fields can see the coun-
    tenance
Of your fierce war, may ken the glittering
    lance,
And hear you shouting forth your brave
    intent.
Left single, in bold parley, ye, of yore,
Did from the Norman win a gallant
    wreath;   10
Confirmed the charters that were yours
    before;—
No parleying now. In Britain is one
    breath;
We all are with you now from shore to
    shore:—
Ye men of Kent, 'tis victory or death!

XXIV

[Composed (?).—Published 1837.]

WHAT if our numbers barely could defy
The arithmetic of babes, must foreign
    hordes,
Slaves, vile as ever were befooled by words,
Striking through English breasts the
    anarchy
Of Terror, bear us to the ground, and tie
Our hands behind our backs with felon
    cords?   6
Yields every thing to discipline of swords?
Is man as good as man, none low, none
    high?—
Nor discipline nor valour can withstand
The shock, nor quell the inevitable rout,
When in some great extremity breaks
    out   11
A people, on their own beloved Land
Risen, like one man, to combat in the sight
Of a just God for liberty and right.

XXV

LINES ON THE EXPECTED
INVASION

1803

[Composed 1803.—Published: vol. of 1842.]

COME ye—who, if (which Heaven avert!)
    the Land
Were with herself at strife, would take
    your stand,

Like gallant Falkland, by the Monarch's
    side,
And, like Montrose, make Loyalty your
    pride—
Come ye—who, not less zealous, might
    display   5
Banners at enmity with regal sway,
And, like the Pyms and Miltons of that
    day,
Think that a State would live in sounder
    health
If Kingship bowed its head to Common-
    wealth—
Ye too—whom no discreditable fear   10
Would keep, perhaps with many a fruit-
    less tear,
Uncertain what to choose and how to
    steer—
And ye—who might mistake for sober
    sense
And wise reserve the plea of indolence—
Come ye—whate'er your creed—O waken
    all,   15
Whate'er your temper, at your Country's
    call;
Resolving (this a free-born Nation can)
To have one Soul, and perish to a man,
Or save this honoured Land from every
    Lord   19
But British reason and the British sword.

XXVI

ANTICIPATION. OCTOBER, 1803

[Composed October, 1803.—Published 1803 (*The
Poetical Register*, iii. 340); 1804 (*The Anti-
Gallican*); 1807.]

SHOUT, for a mighty Victory is won!
On British ground the Invaders are laid
    low;
The breath of Heaven has drifted them
    like snow,
And left them lying in the silent sun,
Never to rise again!—the work is done.   5
Come forth, ye old men, now in peaceful
    show
And greet your sons! drums beat and
    trumpets blow!
Make merry, wives! ye little children, stun
Your grandame's ears with pleasure of
    your noise!
Clap, infants, clap your hands! Divine
    must be   10
That triumph, when the very worst, the
    pain,
And even the prospect of our brethren
    slain,
Hath something in it which the heart
    enjoys:—
In glory will they sleep and endless
    sanctity.

XXVII

NOVEMBER, 1806

[Composed 1806.—Published 1807.]

ANOTHER year!—another deadly blow!
Another mighty Empire[1] overthrown!
And We are left, or shall be left, alone;
The last that dare to struggle with the
　Foe.
'Tis well! from this day forward we shall
　know　　　　　　　　　　　　　　　5
That in ourselves our safety must be
　sought;
That by our own right hands it must be
　wrought;
That we must stand unpropped, or be
　laid low.
O dastard whom such foretaste doth not
　cheer!
We shall exult, if they who rule the land
Be men who hold its many blessings
　dear,　　　　　　　　　　　　　　　11
Wise, upright, valiant; not a servile band,
Who are to judge of danger which they
　fear,
And honour which they do not under-
　stand.

XXVIII

ODE

I

[Composed probably January, 1816.—Published:
vol. of 1816.]

WHO rises on the banks of Seine,
And binds her temples with the civic
　wreath?
What joy to read the promise of her mien!
How sweet to rest her wide-spread wings
　beneath!
　　But they are ever playing,　　5
　　And twinkling in the light,
　　And, if a breeze be straying,
　　That breeze she will invite;
And stands on tiptoe, conscious she is
　fair,
And calls a look of love into her face,　10
And spreads her arms, as if the general air
Alone could satisfy her wide embrace.
—Melt, Principalities, before her melt!
Her love ye hailed—her wrath have felt!
But She through many a change of form
　hath gone,　　　　　　　　　　　15
And stands amidst you now an armèd
　creature,
Whose panoply is not a thing put on,
But the live scales of a portentous nature;
That, having forced its way from birth to
　birth,
Stalks round—abhorred by Heaven, a
　terror to the Earth!　　　　　　　20

[1] Written after the overthrow of Prussia in the
battle of Jena, October 14, 1806.—ED.

II

I marked the breathings of her dragon
　crest:
My Soul, a sorrowful interpreter,
In many a midnight vision bowed
Before the ominous aspect of her spear;
Whether the mighty beam, in scorn up-
　held,　　　　　　　　　　　　　　25
Threatened her foes,—or, pompously at
　rest,
Seemed to bisect her orbèd shield,
As stretches a blue bar of solid cloud
Across the setting sun and all the fiery
　west.

III

So did she daunt the Earth, and God
　defy!　　　　　　　　　　　　　　30
And, wheresoe'er she spread her sove-
　reignty,
Pollution tainted all that was most pure.
—Have we not known—and live we not
　to tell—
That Justice seemed to hear her final
　knell?
Faith buried deeper in her own deep
　breast　　　　　　　　　　　　　35
Her stores, and sighed to find them
　insecure!
And Hope was maddened by the drops
　that fell
From shades, her chosen place of short-
　lived rest.
Shame followed shame, and woe sup-
　planted woe—
Is this the only change that time can show?
How long shall vengeance sleep? Ye
　patient Heavens, how long?　　41
—Infirm ejaculation! from the tongue
Of Nations wanting virtue to be strong
Up to the measure of accorded might,
And daring not to feel the majesty of
　right!　　　　　　　　　　　　　45

IV

Weak Spirits are there—who would ask,
Upon the pressure of a painful thing,
The lion's sinews, or the eagle's wing;
Or let their wishes loose, in forest-glade,
　Among the lurking powers　　50
　Of herbs and lowly flowers,
Or seek, from saints above, miraculous
　aid—
That Man may be accomplished for a task
Which his own nature hath enjoined;—
　and why?
If, when that interference hath relieved
　him,　　　　　　　　　　　　　　55
　He must sink down to languish
In worse than former helplessness—and lie
　Till the caves roar,—and imbecility
　Again engendering anguish,
The same weak wish returns, that had
　before deceived him.　　　　　　60

V

But Thou, supreme Disposer! may'st
  not speed
The course of things, and change the
  creed
Which hath been held aloft before men's
  sight
Since the first framing of societies,
Whether, as bards have told in ancient
  song,   65
Built up by soft seducing harmonies;
Or prest together by the appetite,
And by the power, of wrong.

PART II

I

ON A CELEBRATED EVENT IN ANCIENT HISTORY[1]

[Composed (?).—Published 1815.]

A ROMAN Master stands on Grecian
  ground,
And to the people at the Isthmian Games
Assembled, He, by a herald's voice, pro-
  claims
THE LIBERTY OF GREECE:—the words
  rebound   4
Until all voices in one voice are drowned;
Glad acclamation by which air was rent!
And birds, high flying in the element,
Dropped to the earth, astonished at the
  sound!
Yet were the thoughtful grieved; and
  still that voice
Haunts, with sad echoes, musing Fancy's
  ear: 10
Ah! that a *Conqueror's* words should be
  so dear:
Ah! that a *boon* could shed such rapturous
  joys!
A gift of that which is not to be given
By all the blended powers of Earth and
  Heaven.

II

UPON THE SAME EVENT

[Composed (?).—Published 1815.

WHEN, far and wide, swift as the beams
  of morn
The tidings passed of servitude repealed,
And of that joy which shook the Isthmian
  Field,
The rough Ætolians smiled with bitter
  scorn.
"Tis known,' cried they, 'that he, who
  would adorn   5
His envied temples with the Isthmian
  crown,

[1] i.e. the proclamation of the Liberty of Greece by
T. Quintius Flamininus, the conqueror of Philip of
Macedon (B.C. 196).—ED.

Must either win, through effort of his own,
The prize, or be content to see it worn
By more deserving brows.—Yet so ye prop,
Sons of the brave who fought at Ma-
  rathon,   10
Your feeble spirits! Greece her head hath
  bowed,
As if the wreath of liberty thereon
Would fix itself as smoothly as a cloud,
Which, at Jove's will, descends on Pe-
  lion's top.'

III

TO THOMAS CLARKSON, ON THE FINAL PASS-ING OF THE BILL FOR THE ABOLITION OF THE SLAVE TRADE. MARCH, 1807

[Composed March, 1807.—Published 1807.]

CLARKSON! it was an obstinate hill to
  climb:
How toilsome—nay, how dire—it was, by
  thee
Is known; by none, perhaps, so feelingly:
But thou, who, starting in thy fervent
  prime,
Didst first lead forth that enterprise sub-
  lime,   5
Hast heard the constant Voice its charge
  repeat,
Which, out of thy young heart's oracular
  seat,
First roused thee.—O true yoke-fellow
  of Time,
Duty's intrepid liegeman, see, the palm
Is won, and by all Nations shall be worn!
The blood-stained Writing is for ever torn;
And thou henceforth wilt have a good
  man's calm,   12
A great man's happiness; thy zeal shall
  find
Repose at length, firm friend of human
  kind!

IV

A PROPHECY
FEBRUARY, 1807

[Composed 1807.—Published 1807.]

HIGH deeds, O Germans, are to come
  from you!
Thus in your books the record shall be
  found,
'A watchword was pronounced, a potent
  sound—
ARMINIUS!—all the people quaked like dew
Stirred by the breeze; they rose, a Nation,
  true,   5
True to herself—the mighty Germany,
She of the Danube and the Northern Sea,
She rose, and off at once the yoke she
  threw.
All power was given her in the dreadful
  trance;

Those new-born Kings[1] she withered like
    a flame.'   10
—Woe to them all! but heaviest woe and
    shame
To that Bavarian who could first advance
His banner in accursed league with
    France,
First open traitor to the German name!

V

COMPOSED BY THE SIDE OF GRASMERE
LAKE

[Composed 1807.—Published 1819.]

CLOUDS, lingering yet, extend in solid bars
Through the grey west; and lo! these
    waters, steeled
By breezeless air to smoothest polish,
    yield
A vivid repetition of the stars;   4
Jove, Venus, and the ruddy crest of Mars
Amid his fellows beauteously revealed
At happy distance from earth's groaning
    field,
Where ruthless mortals wage incessant
    wars.
Is it a mirror?—or the nether Sphere
Opening to view the abyss in which she
    feeds   10
Her own calm fires?—But list! a voice
    is near;
Great Pan himself low-whispering through
    the reeds,
'Be thankful, thou; for, if unholy deeds
Ravage the world, tranquillity is here!'

VI

[Composed (?).—Published 1827.]

Go back to antique ages, if thine eyes
The genuine mien and character would
    trace
Of the rash Spirit that still holds her place,
Prompting the world's audacious vanities!
Go back, and see the Tower of Babel rise;
The pyramid extend its monstrous base,
For some Aspirant of our short-lived race,
Anxious an aery name to immortalize.
There, too, ere wiles and politic dispute
Gave specious colouring to aim and act,
See the first mighty Hunter leave the
    brute—   11
To chase mankind, with men in armies
    packed
For his field-pastime high and absolute,
While, to dislodge his game, cities are
    sacked!

[1] i.e. the heads of twelve sovereign houses of the Empire who, by treaty signed at Paris (July 12, 1806) declared themselves finally severed from Germany, and united into the Confederation of the Rhine under the Protectorate of Napoleon. The *Bavarian* (line 12) was Frederick Augustus, Elector of Saxony, with whom Napoleon (Dec. 11, 1806) concluded a treaty admitting him into the Confederation of the Rhine.—ED.

INDEPENDENCE AND LIBERTY

VII

COMPOSED WHILE THE AUTHOR WAS EN-
GAGED IN WRITING A TRACT OCCASIONED
BY THE CONVENTION OF CINTRA

[Composed November or December, 1808.—
Published 1815.]

NOT 'mid the World's vain objects that
    enslave
The free-born Soul—that World whose
    vaunted skill
In selfish interest perverts the will,
Whose factions lead astray the wise and
    brave—
Not there; but in dark wood and rocky
    cave,   5
And hollow vale which foaming torrents
    fill
With omnipresent murmur as they rave
Down their steep beds, that never shall
    be still:
Here, mighty Nature! in this school
    sublime
I weigh the hopes and fears of suffering
    Spain;   10
For her consult the auguries of time,
And through the human heart explore
    my way;
And look and listen—gathering, whence
    I may,
Triumph, and thoughts no bondage can
    restrain.

VIII

COMPOSED AT THE SAME TIME AND ON THE
SAME OCCASION

[Composed November or December, 1808.—
Published 1815.]

I DROPPED my pen; and listened to the
    Wind
That sang of trees up-torn and vessels
    tost—
A midnight harmony; and wholly lost
To the general sense of men by chains
    confined
Of business, care, or pleasure; or re-
    signed   5
To timely sleep. Thought I, the impas-
    sioned strain,
Which, without aid of numbers, I sus-
    tain,
Like acceptation from the World will find.
Yet some with apprehensive ear shall
    drink
A dirge devoutly breathed o'er sorrows
    past;   10
And to the attendant promise will give
    heed—
The prophecy,—like that of this wild blast,
Which, while it makes the heart with sad-
    ness shrink,
Tells also of bright calms that shall
    succeed.

POEMS DEDICATED TO NATIONAL

IX
HOFER[1]

[Composed 1809.—Published Oct. 26, 1809 (*The Friend*); 1815.]

OF mortal parents is the Hero born
By whom the undaunted Tyrolese are led?
Or is it Tell's great Spirit, from the dead
Returned to animate an age forlorn?
He comes like Phœbus through the gates
   of morn   5
When dreary darkness is discomfited,
Yet mark his modest state! upon his head,
That simple crest, a heron's plume, is worn.
O Liberty! they stagger at the shock
From van to rear—and with one mind
   would flee,   10
But half their host is buried:—rock on
   rock
Descends:—beneath this godlike War-
   rior, see!
Hills, torrents, woods, embodied to bemock
The Tyrant, and confound his cruelty.

X

[Composed 1809.—Published October 26, 1809 (*The Friend*); 1815.]

ADVANCE—come forth from thy Tyrolean
   ground,
Dear Liberty! stern Nymph of soul un-
   tamed;
Sweet Nymph, O rightly of the moun-
   tains named!
Through the long chain of Alps from
   mound to mound
And o'er the eternal snows, like Echo,
   bound;   5
Like Echo, when the hunter train at dawn
Have roused her from her sleep: and
   forest-lawn,
Cliffs, woods and caves, her viewless steps
   resound
And babble of her pastime!—On, dread
   Power!
With such invisible motion speed thy flight,
Through hanging clouds, from craggy
   height to height,   11
Through the green vales and through the
   herdsman's bower—
That all the Alps may gladden in thy might,
Here, there, and in all places at one hour.

XI

FEELINGS OF THE TYROLESE

[Composed 1809.—Published December 21, 1809 (*The Friend*); 1815.]

THE Land we from our fathers had in
   trust,
And to our children will transmit, or die;
This is our maxim, this our piety;

[1] Andreas Hofer, an innkeeper, led the Tyrolese for a time successfully, but was defeated by the Bavarians in October 1809, and tried by court-martial and shot in 1810.—ED.

And God and Nature say that it is just.
That which we *would* perform in arms—
   we must!   5
We read the dictate in the infant's eye;
In the wife's smile; and in the placid sky;
And, at our feet, amid the silent dust
Of them that were before us.—Sing aloud
Old songs, the precious music of the
   heart!   10
Give, herds and flocks, your voices to the
   wind!
While we go forth, a self-devoted crowd,
With weapons grasped in fearless hands,
   to assert
Our virtue, and to vindicate mankind.

XII

[Composed 1809.—Published November 16, 1809 (*The Friend*); 1815.]

ALAS! what boots the long laborious quest
Of moral prudence, sought through good
   and ill;
Or pains abstruse—to elevate the will,
And lead us on to that transcendent rest
Where every passion shall the sway attest
Of Reason, seated on her sovereign hill;
What is it but a vain and curious skill,
If sapient Germany must lie deprest,
Beneath the brutal sword?—Her haughty
   Schools
Shall blush; and may not we with sorrow
   say,   10
A few strong instincts and a few plain rules,
Among the herdsmen of the Alps, have
   wrought
More for mankind at this unhappy day
Than all the pride of intellect and thought?

XIII

[Composed 1809.—Published December 21, 1809 (*The Friend*); 1815.]

AND is it among rude untutored Dales,
There, and there only, that the heart is
   true?
And, rising to repel or to subdue,
Is it by rocks and woods that man prevails?
Ah no! though Nature's dread protection
   fails,   5
There is a bulwark in the soul. This knew
Iberian Burghers when the sword they
   drew
In Zaragoza, naked to the gales
Of fiercely-breathing war. The truth was
   felt
By Palafox, and many a brave compeer,
Like him of noble birth and noble mind;
By ladies, meek-eyed women without
   fear;   12
And wanderers of the street, to whom is
   dealt
The bread which without industry they
   find.

XIV

[Composed 1809.—Published December 21, 1809
(*The Friend*); 1815.]

O'ER the wide earth, on mountain and on
    plain,
Dwells in the affections and the soul of
    man
A Godhead, like the universal PAN;
But more exalted, with a brighter train:
And shall his bounty be dispensed in
    vain,   5
Showered equally on city and on field,
And neither hope nor steadfast promise
    yield
In these usurping times of fear and pain?
Such doom awaits us. Nay, forbid it
    Heaven!
We know the arduous strife, the eternal
    laws   10
To which the triumph of all good is given,
High sacrifice, and labour without pause,
Even to the death:—else wherefore should
    the eye
Of man converse with immortality?

XV

ON THE FINAL SUBMISSION OF THE
TYROLESE

[Composed 1809.—Published December 21, 1809
(*The Friend*); 1815.]

IT was a *moral* end for which they fought;
Else how, when mighty Thrones were put
    to shame,
Could they, poor Shepherds, have pre-
    served an aim,
A resolution, or enlivening thought?
Nor hath that moral good been *vainly*
    sought;   5
For in their magnanimity and fame
Powers have they left, an impulse, and a
    claim
Which neither can be overturned nor
    bought.
Sleep, Warriors, sleep! among your hills
    repose!
We know that ye, beneath the stern
    control   10
Of awful prudence, keep the unvan-
    quished soul:
And when, impatient of her guilt and
    woes,
Europe breaks forth; then, Shepherds!
    shall ye rise
For perfect triumph o'er your Enemies.

XVI

[Composed 1809.—Published 1815.]

HAIL, Zaragoza! If with unwet eye
We can approach, thy sorrow to behold,
Yet is the heart not pitiless nor cold;
Such spectacle demands not tear or sigh.
These desolate remains are trophies high

Of more than martial courage in the breast
Of peaceful civic virtue: they attest
Thy matchless worth to all posterity.
Blood flowed before thy sight without
    remorse;
Disease consumed thy vitals; War up-
    heaved   10
The ground beneath thee with volcanic
    force:
Dread trials! yet encountered and sus-
    tained
Till not a wreck of help or hope remained,
And law was from necessity received.[1]

XVII

[Composed 1809 (?).—Published 1815.]

SAY, what is Honour?—'Tis the finest
    sense
Of *justice* which the human mind can
    frame,
Intent each lurking frailty to disclaim,
And guard the way of life from all offence
Suffered or done. When lawless violence
Invades a Realm, so pressed that in the
    scale   6
Of perilous war her weightiest armies fail,
Honour is hopeful elevation,—whence
Glory, and triumph. Yet with politic skill
Endangered States may yield to terms
    unjust;   10
Stoop their proud heads, but not unto
    the dust—
A Foe's most favourite purpose to fulfil:
Happy occasions oft by self-mistrust
Are forfeited; but infamy doth kill.

XVIII[2]

[Composed October or November, 1809.—
Published 1815.]

THE martial courage of a day is vain,
An empty noise of death the battle's roar,
If vital hope be wanting to restore,
Or fortitude be wanting to sustain,
Armies or kingdoms. We have heard a
    strain   5
Of triumph, how the labouring Danube
    bore
A weight of hostile corses: drenched with
    gore
Were the wide fields, the hamlets heaped
    with slain.
Yet see (the mighty tumult overpast)
Austria a Daughter of her Throne hath
    sold!   10
And her Tyrolean Champion we behold
Murdered, like one ashore by shipwreck
    cast,
Murdered without relief. Oh! blind as bold,
To think that such assurance can stand
    fast!

[1] Saragossa surrendered February 20, 1809.—ED.
[2] Written apparently on the occasion of the Peace
of Vienna, signed Oct. 10, 1809.—ED.

XIX

[Composed after May, 1809.—Published 1815.]

BRAVE Schill[1]! by death delivered, take
　　thy flight
From Prussia's timid region. Go, and rest
With heroes, 'mid the islands of the Blest,
Or in the fields of empyrean light.
A meteor wert thou crossing a dark
　　night:　　　　　　　　　　　　　5
Yet shall thy name, conspicuous and
　　sublime,
Stand in the spacious firmament of time,
Fixed as a star: such glory is thy right.
Alas! it may not be: for earthly fame
Is Fortune's frail dependant; yet there
　　lives　　　　　　　　　　　　　10
A Judge, who, as man claims by merit,
　　gives;
To whose all-pondering mind a noble aim,
Faithfully kept, is as a noble deed;
In whose pure sight all virtue doth suc-
　　ceed.

XX

[Composed 1809.—Published 1815.]

CALL not the royal Swede[2] unfortunate,
Who never did to Fortune bend the knee;
Who slighted fear; rejected steadfastly
Temptation; and whose kingly name and
　　state
Have 'perished by his choice, and not
　　his fate!'　　　　　　　　　　　5
Hence lives He, to his inner self endeared;
And hence, wherever virtue is revered,
He sits a more exalted Potentate,
Throned in the hearts of men. Should
　　Heaven ordain
That this great Servant of a righteous
　　cause　　　　　　　　　　　　10
Must still have sad or vexing thoughts to
　　endure,
Yet may a sympathising spirit pause,
Admonished by these truths, and quench
　　all pain
In thankful joy and gratulation pure.

XXI

[Composed 1809.—Published 1815.]

LOOK now on that Adventurer who hath
　　paid
His vows to Fortune; who, in cruel
　　slight
Of virtuous hope, of liberty, and right,
Hath followed wheresoe'er a way was
　　made
By the blind Goddess,—ruthless, undis-
　　mayed;　　　　　　　　　　　5

[1] Killed at Stralsund, May 31, 1809.—ED.
[2] Gustavus IV (see Part I, Sonnet VII) abdicated
early in 1809. In this and the following Sonnet he
is contrasted with Napoleon. See Wordsworth's note
to Sonnet VII, Part I of this series.—ED.

And so hath gained at length a prosper-
　　ous height,
Round which the elements of worldly
　　might
Beneath his haughty feet, like clouds, are
　　laid.
O joyless power that stands by lawless
　　force!
Curses are his dire portion, scorn, and
　　hate,　　　　　　　　　　　　10
Internal darkness and unquiet breath;
And, if old judgments keep their sacred
　　course,
Him from that height shall Heaven pre-
　　cipitate
By violent and ignominious death.

XXII

[Composed probably 1809.—Published 1815.]

Is there a power that can sustain and
　　cheer
The captive chieftain, by a tyrant's doom,
Forced to descend into his destined
　　tomb—
A dungeon dark! where he must waste
　　the year,
And lie cut off from all his heart holds
　　dear;　　　　　　　　　　　　5
What time his injured country is a stage
Whereon deliberate Valour and the rage
Of righteous Vengeance side by side ap-
　　pear,
Filling from morn to night the heroic scene
With deeds of hope and everlasting
　　praise:—　　　　　　　　　　10
Say can he think of this with mind serene
And silent fetters? Yes, if visions bright
Shine on his soul, reflected from the days
When he himself was tried in open light.

XXIII

1810

[Composed 1810.—Published 1815.]

AH! where is Palafox[1]? Nor tongue nor
　　pen
Reports of him, his dwelling or his grave!
Does yet the unheard-of vessel ride the
　　wave?
Or is she swallowed up, remote from ken
Of pitying human nature? Once again　5
Methinks that we shall hail thee, Cham-
　　pion brave,
Redeemed to baffle that imperial Slave,

[1] Don Joseph Palafox-y-Melzi (1780–1847), famed
for his stubborn defence of Saragossa, on the surrender of that fortress by the general to whom, owing
to illness, he had been compelled to resign the command, was taken prisoner (February, 1809) and sent
to Vincennes, where he was detained for nearly five
years. On the restoration of Ferdinand VII he was
sent back to Madrid, and in 1814 was appointed
Captain-General of Aragon; but soon after retired
into private life, from which he never again emerged.
　　　　　　　　　　　　　　　　—ED

And through all Europe cheer desponding men
With new-born hope. Unbounded is the might
Of martyrdom, and fortitude, and right.
Hark, how thy Country triumphs!—Smilingly   11
The Eternal looks upon her sword that gleams,
Like his own lightning, over mountains high,
On rampart, and the banks of all her streams.

XXIV

[Composed 1810.—Published 1815.]

IN due observance of an ancient rite,
The rude Biscayans, when their children lie
Dead in the sinless time of infancy,
Attire the peaceful corse in vestments white;
And, in like sign of cloudless triumph bright,   5
They bind the unoffending creature's brows
With happy garlands of the pure white rose:
Then do a festal company unite
In choral song; and, while the uplifted cross
Of Jesus goes before, the child is borne
Uncovered to his grave: 'tis closed,—her loss   11
The Mother *then* mourns, as she needs must mourn;
But soon, through Christian faith, is grief subdued:
And joy returns, to brighten fortitude.

XXV

FEELINGS OF A NOBLE BISCAYAN AT ONE OF
THOSE FUNERALS

1810

[Composed 1810.—Published 1815.]

YET, yet, Biscayans! we must meet our Foes
With firmer soul, yet labour to regain
Our ancient freedom: else 'twere worse than vain
To gather round the bier these festal shows.
A garland fashioned of the pure white rose   5
Becomes not one whose father is a slave:
Oh, bear the infant covered to his grave!
These venerable mountains now enclose
A people sunk in apathy and fear.
If this endure, farewell, for us, all good!
The awful light of heavenly innocence   11
Will fail to illuminate the infant's bier;
And guilt and shame, from which is no defence,
Descend on all that issues from our blood.

XXVI

THE OAK OF GUERNICA

[Composed 1810.—Published 1815.]

The ancient oak of Guernica, says Laborde in his account of Biscay, is a most venerable natural monument. Ferdinand and Isabella, in the year 1476, after hearing Mass in the church of Santa Maria de la Antigua, repaired to this tree, under which they swore to the Biscayans to maintain their *fueros* (privileges). What other interest belongs to it in the minds of this people will appear from the following.

SUPPOSED ADDRESS TO THE SAME. 1810

OAK of Guernica! Tree of holier power
Than that which in Dodona did enshrine
(So faith too fondly deemed) a voice divine
Heard from the depths of its aerial bower—
How canst thou flourish at this blighting hour?   5
What hope, what joy can sunshine bring to thee,
Or the soft breezes from the Atlantic sea,
The dews of morn, or April's tender shower?
Stroke merciful and welcome would that be
Which should extend thy branches on the ground,   10
If never more within their shady round
Those lofty-minded Lawgivers shall meet,
Peasant and lord, in their appointed seat,
Guardians of Biscay's ancient liberty.

XXVII

INDIGNATION OF A HIGH-MINDED
SPANIARD

1810

[Composed 1810.—Published 1815.]

WE can endure that He should waste our lands,
Despoil our temples, and by sword and flame
Return us to the dust from which we came;
Such food a Tyrant's appetite demands;
And we can brook the thought that by his hands   5
Spain may be overpowered, and he possess,
For his delight, a solemn wilderness
Where all the brave lie dead. But, when of bands
Which he will break for us he dares to speak,

Of benefits, and of a future day   10
When our enlightened minds shall bless
    his sway;
Then, the strained heart of fortitude
    proves weak;
Our groans, our blushes, our pale cheeks
    declare
That he has power to inflict what we lack
    strength to bear.

XXVIII

[Composed probably 1810.—Published 1815.]

AVAUNT all specious pliancy of mind
In men of low degree, all smooth pretence!
I better like a blunt indifference,
And self-respecting slowness, disinclined
To win me at first sight: and be there
    joined   5
Patience and temperance with this high
    reserve,
Honour that knows the path and will not
    swerve;
Affections which, if put to proof, are kind;
And piety towards God. Such men of old
Were England's native growth; and
    throughout Spain   10
(Thanks to high God) forests of such re-
    main:
Then for that Country let our hopes be
    bold;
For matched with these shall policy prove
    vain,
Her arts, her strength, her iron, and her
    gold.

XXIX

1810

[Composed 1810.—Published 1815.]

O'ERWEENING Statesmen have full long
    relied
On fleets and armies, and external wealth:
But from *within* proceeds a Nation's
    health;
Which shall not fail, though poor men
    cleave with pride
To the paternal floor; or turn aside,   5
In the thronged city, from the walks of gain,
As being all unworthy to detain
A Soul by contemplation sanctified.
There are who cannot languish in this
    strife,
Spaniards of every rank, by whom the
    good   10
Of such high course was felt and under-
    stood;
Who to their Country's cause have bound
    a life
Erewhile, by solemn consecration, given
To labour, and to prayer, to nature, and
    to heaven.[1]

[1] See Laborde's character of the Spanish people;
from him the sentiment of these last two lines is
taken.

XXX

THE FRENCH AND THE SPANISH GUERILLAS

[Composed 1810 or 1811.—Published 1815.]

HUNGER, and sultry heat, and nipping
    blast
From bleak hill-top, and length of march
    by night
Through heavy swamp, or over snow-clad
    height—
These hardships ill-sustained, these dan-
    gers past,
The roving Spanish Bands are reached at
    last,   5
Charged, and dispersed like foam: but as
    a flight
Of scattered quails by signs do reunite,
So these,—and, heard of once again, are
    chased
With combinations of long-practised art
And newly-kindled hope; but they are
    fled—   10
Gone are they, viewless as the buried
    dead:
Where now?—Their sword is at the Foe-
    man's heart!
And thus from year to year his walk they
    thwart,
And hang like dreams around his guilty
    bed.

XXXI

SPANISH GUERILLAS

1811

[Composed 1811.—Published 1815.]

THEY seek, are sought; to daily battle led,
Shrink not, though far outnumbered by
    their Foes,
For they have learnt to open and to close
The ridges of grim war; and at their head
Are captains such as erst their country
    bred   5
Or fostered, self-supported chiefs,—like
    those
Whom hardy Rome was fearful to oppose;
Whose desperate shock the Carthaginian
    fled.
In One who lived unknown a shepherd's
    life
Redoubted Viriathus breathes again;   10
And Mina,[1] nourished in the studious
    shade,
With that great Leader vies, who, sick of
    strife
And bloodshed, longed in quiet to be laid
In some green island of the western main.

[1] Don Esprez y Mina, leader of the Guerillas of
Navarre, had been educated for the priesthood. The
'great Leader' (l. 12) is the Roman general Sertorius,
whose romantic story profoundly stirred Wordsworth's imagination (see Prelude I, ll. 190–202).
Viriathus (l. 10), the renowned shepherd-leader of
the Lusitanians against the arms of Rome.—ED.

XXXII

1811

[Composed 1811.—Published 1815.]

THE power of Armies is a visible thing,
Formal, and circumscribed in time and
    space;
But who the limits of that power shall
    trace
Which a brave People into light can bring
Or hide, at will,—for freedom combating
By just revenge inflamed? No foot may
    chase,   6
No eye can follow, to a fatal place
That power, that spirit, whether on the
    wing
Like the strong wind, or sleeping like the
    wind
Within its awful caves.—From year to
    year   10
Springs this indigenous produce far and
    near;
No craft this subtle element can bind,
Rising like water from the soil, to find
In every nook a lip that it may cheer.

XXXIII

1811

[Composed 1811.—Published 1815.]

HERE pause: the poet claims at least this
    praise,
That virtuous Liberty hath been the scope
Of his pure song, which did not shrink
    from hope
In the worst moment of these evil days;
From hope, the paramount *duty* that
    Heaven lays,   5
For its own honour, on man's suffering
    heart.
Never may from our souls one truth de-
    part—
That an accursed thing it is to gaze
On prosperous tyrants with a dazzled eye;
Nor—touched with due abhorrence of
    their guilt   10
For whose dire ends tears flow, and blood
    is spilt,
And justice labours in extremity—
Forget thy weakness, upon which is built,
O wretched man, the throne of tyranny!

XXXIV

THE FRENCH ARMY IN RUSSIA

1812–13

[Composed Feb., 1816.—Published: vol. of 1816.]

HUMANITY, delighting to behold
A fond reflection of her own decay,
Hath painted Winter like a traveller old,
Propped on a staff, and, through the
    sullen day,

In hooded mantle, limping o'er the plain,
As though his weakness were disturbed
    by pain: 6
Or, if a juster fancy should allow
An undisputed symbol of command,
The chosen sceptre is a withered bough,
Infirmly grasped within a palsied hand.
These emblems suit the helpless and for-
    lorn,   11
But mighty Winter the device shall scorn.

For he it was—dread Winter! who beset,
Flinging round van and rear his ghastly
    net,
That host, when from the regions of the
    Pole   15
They shrunk, insane ambition's barren
    goal—
That host, as huge and strong as e'er
    defied
Their God, and placed their trust in
    human pride!
As fathers persecute rebellious sons,
He smote the blossoms of their warrior
    youth;   20
He called on Frost's inexorable tooth
Life to consume in Manhood's firmest
    hold;
Nor spared the reverend blood that feebly
    runs;
For why—unless for liberty enrolled
And sacred home—ah! why should hoary
    Age be bold?   25
Fleet the Tartar's reinless steed,
But fleeter far the pinions of the Wind,
Which from Siberian caves the Monarch
    freed,
And sent him forth, with squadrons of his
    kind,
And bade the Snow their ample backs
    bestride,   30
    And to the battle ride.
No pitying voice commands a halt,
No courage can repel the dire assault;
Distracted, spiritless, benumbed, and
    blind,
Whole legions sink—and, in one instant,
    find   35
Burial and death: look for them—and
    descry,
When morn returns, beneath the clear
    blue sky,
A soundless waste, a trackless vacancy!

XXXV

ON THE SAME OCCASION

[Composed 1816.—Published 1816.

YE Storms, resound the praises of your
    King!
And ye mild Seasons—in a sunny clime,
Midway on some high hill, while father
    Time
Looks on delighted—meet in festal ring,

255

And loud and long of Winter's triumph
sing! 5
Sing ye, with blossoms crowned, and
fruits, and flowers,
Of Winter's breath surcharged with sleety
showers,
And the dire flapping of his hoary wing!
Knit the blithe dance upon the soft green
grass;
With feet, hands, eyes, looks, lips, report
your gain; 10
Whisper it to the billows of the main,
And to the aerial zephyrs as they pass,
That old decrepit Winter—*He* hath slain
That old Host, which rendered all your boun-
ties vain!

XXXVI

[Composed November or December, 1822.—
Published 1827.]

BY Moscow self-devoted to a blaze
Of dreadful sacrifice; by Russian blood
Lavished in fight with desperate hardi-
hood;
The unfeeling Elements no claim shall
raise
To rob our Human-nature of just praise
For what she did and suffered. Pledges
sure 6
Of a deliverance absolute and pure
She gave, if Faith might tread the beaten
ways
Of Providence. But now did the Most
High
Exalt his still small voice;—to quell that
Host 10
Gathered his power, a manifest ally;
He, whose heaped waves confounded the
proud boast
Of Pharaoh, said to Famine, Snow, and
Frost,
'Finish the strife by deadliest victory!'

XXXVII

THE GERMANS ON THE HEIGHTS OF
HOCHHEIM

[Composed 1820.—Published 1822 (*Memorials of
a Tour*, &c.).]

ABRUPTLY paused the strife;—the field
throughout
Resting upon his arms each warrior stood,
Checked in the very act and deed of blood,
With breath suspended, like a listening
scout.
O Silence! thou wert mother of a shout
That through the texture of yon azure
dome 6
Cleaves its glad way, a cry of harvest
home
Uttered to Heaven in ecstasy devout!
The barrier Rhine hath flashed, through
battle-smoke,

On men who gaze heart-smitten by the
view, 10
As if all Germany had felt the shock!
—Fly, wretched Gauls! ere they the
charge renew
Who have seen—themselves now casting
off the yoke—
The unconquerable Stream his course
pursue.

XXXVIII

NOVEMBER, 1813

[Composed November, 1813.—Published 1815.]

Now that all hearts are glad, all faces
bright,
Our aged Sovereign sits, to the ebb and
flow
Of states and kingdoms, to their joy or
woe,
Insensible. He sits deprived of sight,
And lamentably wrapped in twofold
night, 5
Whom no weak hopes deceived; whose
mind ensued,
Through perilous war, with regal fortitude,
Peace that should claim respect from law-
less Might.
Dread King of Kings, vouchsafe a ray
divine
To his forlorn condition! let thy grace
Upon his inner soul in mercy shine; 11
Permit his heart to kindle, and to embrace
(Though it were only for a moment's
space)
The triumphs of this hour[1]; for they are
THINE!

XXXIX
ODE
1814

[Composed Jan., 1816.—Published: vol. of 1816.]

——————Carmina possumus
Donare, et pretium dicere muneri.
Non incisa notis marmora publicis,
Per quae spiritus et vita redit bonis
Post mortem ducibus,
——————clarius indicant
Laudes, quam————Pierides; neque,
Si chartae sileant quod bene feceris,
Mercedem tuleris.——HOR. Car. 8. Lib. 4. 11 *sq.*

I

WHEN the soft hand of sleep had closed
the latch
On the tired household of corporeal sense,
And Fancy, keeping unreluctant watch,
Was free her choicest favours to dispense;
I saw, in wondrous pérspective displayed,
A landscape more august than happiest
skill 6
Of pencil ever clothed with light and shade;

[1] i.e. the final overthrow of Napoleon at Leipzig,
Oct. 16–19, 1813.—ED.

An intermingled pomp of vale and hill,
City, and naval stream, suburban grove,
And stately forest where the wild deer
  rove;   10
Nor wanted lurking hamlet, dusky towns,
And scattered rural farms of aspect
  bright;
And, here and there, between the pas-
  toral downs,
The azure sea upswelled upon the sight.
Fair prospect, such as Britain only
  shows!   15
But not a living creature could be seen
Through its wide circuit, that, in deep
  repose,
And, even to sadness, lonely and serene,
Lay hushed; till—through a portal in
  the sky
Brighter than brightest loop-hole, in a
  storm,   20
Opening before the sun's triumphant
  eye—
Issued, to sudden view, a glorious Form!
Earthward it glided with a swift descent:
Saint George himself this Visitant must
  be;
And, ere a thought could ask on what
  intent   25
He sought the regions of humanity,
A thrilling voice was heard, that vivified
City and field and flood;—aloud it cried—

'Though from my celestial home,
Like a Champion, armed I come;   30
On my helm the dragon crest,
And the red cross on my breast;
I, the Guardian of this Land,
Speak not now of toilsome duty;
Well obeyed was that command—   35
Whence bright days of festive beauty;
Haste, Virgins, haste!—the flowers which
  summer gave
Have perished in the field;
But the green thickets plenteously shall
  yield
Fit garlands for the brave,   40
That will be welcome, if by you en-
  twined;
Haste, Virgins, haste; and you, ye Ma-
  trons grave,
Go forth with rival youthfulness of mind,
And gather what ye find
Of hardy laurel and wild holly boughs—
To deck your stern Defenders' modest
  brows!   46
Such simple gifts prepare,
Though they have gained a worthier
  meed,
And in due time shall share
Those palms and amaranthine wreaths
Unto their martyred Countrymen de-
  creed,   51
In realms where everlasting freshness
  breathes!'

II

And lo! with crimson banners proudly
  streaming,
And upright weapons innocently gleam-
  ing,
Along the surface of a spacious plain   55
Advance in order the redoubted Bands,
And there receive green chaplets from the
  hands
Of a fair female train—
Maids and Matrons, dight
In robes of dazzling white;   60
While from the crowd bursts forth a
  rapturous noise
By the cloud-capt hills retorted;
And a throng of rosy boys
In loose fashion tell their joys;
And grey-haired sires, on staffs sup-
  ported,   65
Look round, and by their smiling seem to
  say,
'Thus strives a grateful Country to
  display
The mighty debt which nothing can
  repay!'

III

Anon before my sight a palace rose   69
Built of all precious substances,—so pure
And exquisite, that sleep alone bestows
Ability like splendour to endure:
Entered, with streaming thousands,
  through the gate,
I saw the banquet spread beneath a Dome
  of state,
A lofty Dome, that dared to emulate   75
The heaven of sable night
With starry lustre; yet had power to
  throw
Solemn effulgence, clear as solar light,
Upon a princely company below,
While the vault rang with choral har-
  mony,   80
Like some Nymph-haunted grot beneath
  the roaring sea.
—No sooner ceased that peal, than on the
  verge
Of exultation hung a dirge
Breathed from a soft and lonely instru-
  ment,
  That kindled recollections   85
  Of agonised affections;
And, though some tears the strain at-
  tended,
  The mournful passion ended
In peace of spirit, and sublime content!

IV

But garlands wither; festal shows de-
  part,   90
Like dreams themselves; and sweetest
  sound
  (Albeit of effect profound)
  It was—and it is gone!

Victorious England! bid the silent Art
Reflect, in glowing hues that shall not
    fade,   95
Those high achievements; even as she
    arrayed
With second life the deed of Marathon
    Upon Athenian walls;
So may she labour for thy civic halls:
    And be the guardian spaces   100
    Of consecrated places,
As nobly graced by Sculpture's patient
    toil;
And let imperishable Columns rise
Fixed in the depths of this courageous
    soil;   104
Expressive signals of a glorious strife,
And competent to shed a spark divine
Into the torpid breast of daily life;—
Records on which, for pleasure of all eyes,
    The morning sun may shine
With gratulation thoroughly benign!   110

V

And ye, Pierian Sisters, sprung from
    Jove
And sage Mnemosyne,—full long de-
    barred
From your first mansions, exiled all too
    long
From many a hallowed stream and grove,
Dear native regions where ye wont to
    rove,   115
Chanting for patriot heroes the reward
    Of never-dying song!
Now (for, though Truth descending from
    above
The Olympian summit hath destroyed for
    aye   119
Your kindred Deities, Ye live and move,
Spared for obeisance from perpetual love,
For privilege redeemed of godlike sway)
Now, on the margin of some spotless
    fountain,
Or top serene of unmolested mountain,
Strike audibly the noblest of your lyres,
And for a moment meet the soul's de-
    sires!   126
That I, or some more favoured Bard, may
    hear
What ye, celestial Maids! have often
    sung
Of Britain's acts,—may catch it with rapt
    ear,
And give the treasure to our British
    tongue!   130
So shall the characters of that proud page
Support their mighty theme from age
    to age;
And, in the desert places of the earth,
When they to future empires have given
    birth,
So shall the people gather and believe
The bold report, transferred to every
    clime;   136

And the whole world, not envious but
    admiring,
    And to the like aspiring,
Own—that the progeny of this fair Isle
Had power as lofty actions to achieve
As were performed in man's heroic prime;
Nor wanted, when their fortitude had held
Its even tenor, and the foe was quelled,
A corresponding virtue to beguile
The hostile purpose of wide-wasting
    Time—   145
That not in vain they laboured to secure,
For their great deeds, perpetual memory,
And fame as largely spread as land and
    sea,
By Works of spirit high and passion pure!

XL

FEELINGS OF A FRENCH ROYALIST, ON THE
DISINTERMENT OF THE REMAINS OF THE
DUKE D'ENGHIEN.

[Composed 1816.—Published: vol. of 1816.]

DEAR Reliques! from a pit of vilest
    mould
Uprisen—to lodge among ancestral kings;
And to inflict shame's salutary stings
On the remorseless hearts of men grown
    old
In a blind worship; men perversely bold
Even to this hour,—yet, some shall now
    forsake   6
Their monstrous Idol if the dead e'er
    spake,
To warn the living; if truth were ever
    told
By aught redeemed out of the hollow
    grave:
O murdered Prince! meek, loyal, pious,
    brave!   10
The power of retribution once was given:
But 'tis a rueful thought that willow bands
So often tie the thunder-wielding hands
Of Justice sent to earth from highest
    Heaven!

XLI

OCCASIONED BY THE BATTLE OF WATERLOO

(The last six lines intended for an Inscription.)

FEBRUARY, 1816

[Composed 1816.—Published Feb. 4, 1816 (*The
Champion*); vol. of 1816.]

INTREPID sons of Albion! not by you
Is life despised; ah no, the spacious earth
Ne'er saw a race who held, by right of
    birth,
So many objects to which love is due:
Ye slight not life—to God and Nature
    true;   5
But death, becoming death, is dearer far,
When duty bids you bleed in open war:

Hence hath your prowess quelled that impious crew.
Heroes!—for instant sacrifice prepared;
Yet filled with ardour and on triumph bent   10
'Mid direst shocks of mortal accident—
To you who fell, and you whom slaughter spared
To guard the fallen, and consummate the event,
Your Country rears this sacred Monument!

XLII

SIEGE OF VIENNA RAISED BY JOHN
SOBIESKI

FEBRUARY, 1816

[Composed Jan., 1816.—Published Feb. 4, 1816 (*The Champion*); vol. of 1816.]

OH, for a kindling touch from that pure flame
Which ministered, erewhile, to a sacrifice
Of gratitude, beneath Italian skies,
In words like these: 'Up, Voice of song! proclaim
Thy saintly rapture with celestial aim: 5
For lo! the Imperial City stands released
From bondage threatened by the embattled East,
And Christendom respires; from guilt and shame
Redeemed, from miserable fear set free
By one day's feat, one mighty victory.
—Chant the Deliverer's praise in every tongue!   11
The Cross shall spread, the Crescent hath waxed dim;
He conquering, as in joyful Heaven is sung,
HE CONQUERING THROUGH GOD, AND GOD BY HIM'.[1]

XLIII

OCCASIONED BY THE BATTLE OF WATERLOO

FEBRUARY, 1816

[Composed February, 1816.—Published: vol. of 1816.]

THE Bard—whose soul is meek as dawning day,
Yet trained to judgments righteously severe,
Fervid, yet conversànt with holy fear,
As recognising one Almighty sway:
He—whose experienced eye can pierce the array   5
Of past events; to whom, in vision clear,
The aspiring heads of future things appear,
Like mountain-tops whose mists have rolled away—

[1] See Filicaia's Ode.

INDEPENDENCE AND LIBERTY

Assoiled from all encumbrance of our time,[1]   9
He only, if such breathe, in strains devout
Shall comprehend this victory sublime;
Shall worthily rehearse the hideous rout,
The triumph hail, which from their peaceful clime
Angels might welcome with a choral shout!

XLIV

[Composed? (perhaps 1816).—Published 1827.]

EMPERORS and Kings, how oft have temples rung
With impious thanksgiving, the Almighty's scorn!
How oft above their altars have been hung
Trophies that led the good and wise to mourn   4
Triumphant wrong, battle of battle born,
And sorrow that to fruitless sorrow clung!
Now, from Heaven-sanctioned victory, Peace is sprung;
In this firm hour Salvation lifts her horn.
Glory to arms! But, conscious that the nerve
Of popular reason, long mistrusted, freed
Your thrones, ye Powers, from duty fear to swerve!   11
Be just, be grateful; nor, the oppressor's creed
Reviving, heavier chastisement deserve
Than ever forced unpitied hearts to bleed.

XLV

ODE

1815

[Composed 1816.—Published: volume of 1816.]

I

IMAGINATION—ne'er before content,
But aye ascending, restless in her pride
From all that martial feats could yield
To her desires, or to her hopes present—
Stooped to the Victory on that Belgic field   5
Achieved, this closing deed magnificent,
And with the embrace was satisfied.
—Fly, ministers of Fame,
With every help that ye from earth and heaven may claim!
Bear through the world these tidings of delight!   10
—Hours, Days, and Months, *have* borne them in the sight
Of mortals, hurrying like a sudden shower
That landward stretches from the sea,
The morning's splendours to devour;

[1] 'From all this world's encumbrance did himself assoil.'—SPENSER.

But this swift travel scorns the company
Of irksome change, or threats from sad-
dening power.   16
—*The shock is given—the Adversaries
bleed—*
Lo, Justice triumphs! Earth is freed!
Joyful annunciation!—it went forth—
It pierced the caverns of the sluggish
North—   20
It found no barrier on the ridge
Of Andes—frozen gulfs became its
bridge—
The vast Pacific gladdens with the
freight—
Upon the Lakes of Asia 'tis bestowed—
The Arabian desert shapes a willing
road   25
Across her burning breast,
For this refreshing incense from the
West!—
—Where snakes and lions breed,
Where towns and cities thick as stars
appear,
Wherever fruits are gathered, and
where'er   30
The upturned soil receives the hopeful
seed—
While the Sun rules, and cross the shades
of night—
The unwearied arrow hath pursued its
flight!
The eyes of good men thankfully give heed,
And in its sparkling progress read
Of virtue crowned with glory's deathless
meed: 36
Tyrants exult to hear of kingdoms won,
And slaves are pleased to learn that
mighty feats are done;
Even the proud Realm, from whose dis-
tracted borders
This messenger of good was launched
in air,   40
France, humbled France, amid her wild
disorders,
Feels, and hereafter shall the truth
declare,
That she too lacks not reason to rejoice,
And utter England's name with sadly-
plausive voice.

II

O genuine glory, pure renown!   45
And well might it beseem that mighty
Town
Into whose bosom earth's best treasures
flow,
To whom all persecuted men retreat;
If a new Temple lift her votive brow
High on the shore of silver Thames—to
greet   50
The peaceful guest advancing from afar.
Bright be the Fabric, as a star
Fresh risen, and beautiful within!—there
meet

Dependence infinite, proportion just;
A Pile that Grace approves, and Time
can trust   55
With his most sacred wealth, heroic dust.

III

But if the valiant of this land
In reverential modesty demand,
That all observance, due to them, be paid
Where their serene progenitors are laid;
Kings, warriors, high-souled poets, saint-
like sages,   61
England's illustrious sons of long, long
ages;
Be it not unordained that solemn rites,
Within the circuit of those Gothic walls,
Shall be performed at pregnant intervals;
Commemoration holy that unites   66
The living generations with the dead;
By the deep soul-moving sense
Of religious eloquence,—
By visual pomp, and by the tie   70
Of sweet and threatening harmony;
Soft notes, awful as the omen
Of destructive tempests coming,
And escaping from that sadness
Into elevated gladness;   75
While the white-robed choir atten-
dant,
Under mouldering banners pendant,
Provoke all potent symphonies to raise
Songs of victory and praise,
For them who bravely stood unhurt, or
bled   80
With medicable wounds, or found their
graves
Upon the battle field, or under ocean's
waves;
Or were conducted home in single state,
And long procession—there to lie,
Where their sons' sons, and all posterity,
Unheard by them, their deeds shall
celebrate!   86

IV

Nor will the God of peace and love
Such martial service disapprove.
He guides the Pestilence—the cloud
Of locusts travels on his breath;   90
The region that in hope was ploughed
His drought consumes, his mildew taints
with death;
He springs the hushed Volcano's
mine,
He puts the Earthquake on her still design,
Darkens the sun, hath bade the forest sink,
And, drinking towns and cities, still can
drink   96
Cities and towns—'tis Thou—the work is
Thine!—
The fierce Tornado sleeps within Thy
courts—
He hears the word—he flies—
And navies perish in their ports;   100

For Thou art angry with Thine enemies!
  For these, and mourning for our
    errors,
  And sins, that point their terrors,
We bow our heads before Thee, and we
  laud
And magnify Thy name, Almighty God!
But Man is Thy most awful instru-
  ment,   106
  In working out a pure intent;[1]
Thou cloth'st the wicked in their dazzling
  mail,
And for Thy righteous purpose they
  prevail;
  Thine arm from peril guards the
    coasts   110
  Of them who in Thy laws delight:
Thy presence turns the scale of doubtful
  fight,
Tremendous God of battles, Lord of
  Hosts!

V

  Forbear:—to Thee—
Father and Judge of all, with fervent
  tongue,   115
  But in a gentler strain
Of contemplation, by no sense of wrong
(Too quick and keen) incited to disdain
Of pity pleading from the heart in vain—
  To THEE—To THEE,   120
Just God of christianised Humanity,
Shall praises be poured forth, and thanks
  ascend,
That Thou hast brought our warfare to
  an end,
And that we need no second victory!
Blest, above measure blest,   125
If on Thy love our Land her hopes shall
  rest,
And all the Nations labour to fulfil
Thy law, and live henceforth in peace, in
  pure good will.

XLVI
ODE

THE MORNING OF THE DAY APPOINTED FOR
A GENERAL THANKSGIVING. JANUARY 18,
1816.

[Composed January, 1816.—Published: vol. of
1816.]

I

HAIL, orient Conqueror of gloomy Night!
Thou that canst shed the bliss of gratitude
On hearts howe'er insensible or rude;
Whether thy punctual visitations smite
The haughty towers where monarchs
  dwell;   5

[1] Lines 106, 107 were, in 1845, substituted for the
four following lines at which many had stumbled:—
  'But Thy most dreaded instrument,
In working out a pure intent,
Is Man—arrayed for mutual slaughter,
—Yea, Carnage is thy daughter!'—ED.

Or thou, impartial Sun, with presence
  bright
Cheer'st the low threshold of the pea-
  sant's cell!
Not unrejoiced I see thee climb the sky
In naked splendour, clear from mist or
  haze,
Or cloud approaching to divert the rays,
Which even in deepest winter testify 11
  Thy power and majesty,
Dazzling the vision that presumes to gaze.
—Well does thine aspect usher in this
  Day;
As aptly suits therewith that modest pace
  Submitted to the chains   16
That bind thee to the path which God
  ordains
  That thou shalt trace,
Till, with the heavens and earth, thou
  pass away!
Nor less, the stillness of these frosty
  plains,   20
Their utter stillness, and the silent grace
Of yon ethereal summits white with snow,
(Whose tranquil pomp and spotless purity
  Report of storms gone by
  To us who tread below),   25
Do with the service of this Day accord.
—Divinest Object which the uplifted eye
Of mortal man is suffered to behold;
Thou, who upon those snow-clad Heights
  hast poured
Meek lustre, nor forget'st the humble
  Vale;   30
Thou who dost warm Earth's universal
  mould,
And for thy bounty wert not unadored
  By pious men of old;
Once more, heart-cheering Sun, I bid thee
  hail!
Bright be thy course to-day, let not this
  promise fail!   35

II

'Mid the deep quiet of this morning
  hour,
All nature seems to hear me while I speak,
By feelings urged that do not vainly seek
Apt language, ready as the tuneful notes
That stream in blithe succession from the
  throats   40
  Of birds, in leafy bower,
Warbling a farewell to a vernal shower.
—There is a radiant though a short-lived
  flame,   43
That burns for Poets in the dawning east;
And oft my soul hath kindled at the same,
When the captivity of sleep had ceased;
But He who fixed immoveably the frame
Of the round world, and built, by laws as
  strong,
  A solid refuge for distress—
  The towers of righteousness;   50
He knows that from a holier altar came

261

The quickening spark of this day's sacrifice;
Knows that the source is nobler whence
    doth rise
    The current of this matin song;
    That deeper far it lies   55
Than aught dependent on the fickle skies.

III

Have we not conquered?—by the venge-
    ful sword?
Ah no, by dint of Magnanimity;
That curbed the baser passions, and left
    free
A loyal band to follow their liege Lord
Clear-sighted Honour, and his staid Com-
    peers,   61
Along a track of most unnatural years;
In execution of heroic deeds
Whose memory, spotless as the crystal
    beads
Of morning dew upon the untrodden
    meads,   65
Shall live enrolled above the starry
    spheres.
He, who in concert with an earthly string
    Of Britain's acts would sing,
    He with enraptured voice will tell
Of One whose spirit no reverse could
    quell;   70
Of One that 'mid the failing never failed—
Who paints how Britain struggled and
    prevailed
Shall represent her labouring with an eye
    Of circumspect humanity;
Shall show her clothed with strength and
    skill   75
    All martial duties to fulfil;
Firm as a rock in stationary fight;
In motion rapid as the lightning's gleam;
Fierce as a flood-gate bursting at midnight
To rouse the wicked from their giddy
    dream—   80
Woe, woe to all that face her in the field!
Appalled she may not be, and cannot yield.

IV

And thus is *missed* the sole true glory
    That can belong to human story!
    At which they only shall arrive   85
    Who through the abyss of weakness
        dive.
The very humblest are too proud of heart;
And one brief day is rightly set apart
For Him who lifteth up and layeth low;
For that Almighty God to whom we owe,
Say not that we have vanquished—but
    that we survive.   91

V

How dreadful the dominion of the impure!
Why should the Song be tardy to pro-
    claim
That less than power unbounded could
    not tame

That soul of Evil—which, from Hell let
    loose,   95
Had filled the astonished world with such
    abuse
As boundless patience only could endure?
—Wide-wasted regions—cities wrapt in
    flame—
Who sees, may lift a streaming eye
To Heaven;—who never saw, may heave
    a sigh;   100
But the foundation of our nature shakes,
And with an infinite pain the spirit aches,
When desolated countries, towns on fire,
    Are but the avowed attire   104
Of warfare waged with desperate mind
Against the life of virtue in mankind;
    Assaulting without ruth
    The citadels of truth;
While the fair gardens of civility,
    By ignorance defaced,   110
    By violence laid waste,
Perish without reprieve for flower or tree!

VI

A crouching purpose—a distracted
    will—
Opposed to hopes that battened upon
    scorn,
And to desires whose ever-waxing horn
Not all the light of earthly power could
    fill;   116
Opposed to dark, deep plots of patient
    skill,
And to celerities of lawless force;
Which, spurning God, had flung away
    remorse—
What could they gain but shadows of re-
    dress?   120
—So bad proceeded propagating worse;
And discipline was passion's dire excess.
Widens the fatal web, its lines extend,
And deadlier poisons in the chalice blend.
When will your trials teach you to be
    wise?   125
—O prostrate Lands, consult your
    agonies!

VII

No more—the guilt is banished,
And, with the guilt, the shame is fled;
And, with the guilt and shame, the Woe
    hath vanished,
Shaking the dust and ashes from her
    head!   130
—No more—these lingerings of distress
Sully the limpid stream of thankfulness.
What robe can Gratitude employ
So seemly as the radiant vest of Joy?
What steps so suitable as those that move
In prompt obedience to spontaneous
    measures   136
Of glory, and felicity, and love,
Surrendering the whole heart to sacred
    pleasures?

VIII

O Britain! dearer far than life is dear,
　　If one there be　　　　　　140
　　Of all thy progeny
Who can forget thy prowess, never more
Be that ungrateful Son allowed to hear
Thy green leaves rustle or thy torrents
　　roar.
As springs the lion from his den,　145
　　As from a forest-brake
　　Upstarts a glistering snake,
The bold Arch-despot re-appeared;—
　　again
Wide Europe heaves, impatient to be cast,
　　With all her armèd Powers,　150
　　On that offensive soil, like waves
　　upon a thousand shores.
The trumpet blew a universal blast!
But Thou art foremost in the field:—
　　there stand!
Receive the triumph destined to thy hand!
All States have glorified themselves;—
　　their claims　　　　　　155
Are weighed by Providence, in balance
　　even;
And now, in preference to the mightiest
　　names,
To Thee the exterminating sword is given.
Dread mark of approbation, justly gained!
Exalted office, worthily sustained!　160

IX

Preserve, O Lord! within our hearts
　　The memory of Thy favour,
　　That else insensibly departs,
　　And loses its sweet savour!
Lodge it within us!—as the power of
　　light　　　　　　165
Lives inexhaustibly in precious gems,
Fixed on the front of Eastern diadems,
So shine our thankfulness for ever bright!
What offering, what transcendent monu-
　　ment
Shall our sincerity to Thee present?　170
—Not work of hands; but trophies that
　　may reach
To highest Heaven—the labour of the
　　Soul;
That builds, as thy unerring precepts
　　teach,
Upon the internal conquests made by
　　each,
Her hope of lasting glory for the whole.
Yet will not heaven disown nor earth
　　gainsay　　　　　　176
The outward service of this day;
Whether the worshippers entreat
Forgiveness from God's mercy-seat;
Or thanks and praises to His throne
　　ascend　　　　　　180
That He has brought our warfare to an
　　end,
And that we need no second victory!——
Ha! what a ghastly sight for man to see;

And to the heavenly saints in peace who
　　dwell,
For a brief moment, terrible;　185
But, to Thy sovereign penetration, fair,
Before whom all things are, that were,
All judgments that have been, or e'er
　　shall be;
Links in the chain of Thy tranquillity!
Along the bosom of this favoured Nation,
Breathe Thou, this day, a vital undula-
　　tion!　　　　　　191
Let all who do this land inherit
Be conscious of Thy moving spirit!
Oh, 'tis a goodly Ordinance,—the sight,
Though sprung from bleeding war, is one
　　of pure delight;　　　　195
Bless Thou the hour, or ere the hour
　　arrive,
When a whole people shall kneel down in
　　prayer,
And, at one moment, in one rapture,
　　strive
With lip and heart to tell their gratitude
　　For Thy protecting care,　200
Their solemn joy—praising the Eternal
　　Lord
For tyranny subdued,
And for the sway of equity renewed,
For liberty confirmed, and peace restored!

X

But hark—the summons!—down the
　　placid lake　　　　　205
Floats the soft cadence of the church-
　　tower bells;
Bright shines the Sun, as if his beams
　　would wake
The tender insects sleeping in their cells;
Bright shines the Sun—and not a breeze
　　to shake　　　　　209
The drops that tip the melting icicles.
　　O, enter now his Temple gate!
Inviting words—perchance already flung
(As the crowd press devoutly down the
　　aisle
Of some old Minster's venerable pile)
From voices into zealous passion stung,
While the tubed engine feels the inspiring
　　blast,　　　　　　216
And has begun—its clouds of sound to
　　cast
　　Forth towards empyreal Heaven,
　　As if the fretted roof were riven.
Us humbler ceremonies now await;　220
But in the bosom, with devout respect
The banner of our joy we will erect,
And strength of love our souls shall
　　elevate:
For to a few collected in His name,　224
Their heavenly Father will incline an ear
Gracious to service hallowed by its aim;—
Awake! the majesty of God revere!
　　Go—and with foreheads meekly
　　bowed

Present your prayers—go—and rejoice
aloud—
The Holy One will hear!   230
And what, 'mid silence deep, with faith
sincere,
Ye, in your low and undisturbed estate,
Shall simply feel and purely meditate—
Of warnings—from the unprecedented
might,
Which, in our time, the impious have
disclosed;   235

And of more arduous duties thence
imposed
Upon the future advocates of right;
Of mysteries revealed,
And judgments unrepealed,
Of earthly revolution,   240
And final retribution,—
To his omniscience will appear
An offering not unworthy to find place,
On this high DAY of THANKS, before the
Throne of Grace!

MEMORIALS OF
A TOUR ON THE CONTINENT,[1] 1820

DEDICATION

(SENT WITH THESE POEMS, IN MS., TO ——.)

DEAR Fellow-travellers! think not that the Muse,
To You presenting these memorial Lays,
Can hope the general eye thereon would gaze,
As on a mirror that gives back the hues
Of living Nature; no—though free to choose
The greenest bowers, the most inviting ways,
The fairest landscapes and the brightest days—
Her skill she tried with less ambitious views.
For You she wrought: Ye only can supply
The life, the truth, the beauty: she confides
In that enjoyment which with You abides,
Trusts to your love and vivid memory;
Thus far contented, that for You her verse
Shall lack not power the 'meeting soul to pierce!'

W. WORDSWORTH.
RYDAL MOUNT, *Nov.*, 1821.

I

FISH-WOMEN.—ON LANDING AT CALAIS

'TIS said, fantastic ocean doth enfold
The likeness of whate'er on land is seen;
But if the Nereid Sisters and their Queen,
Above whose heads the tide so long hath
rolled,
The Dames resemble whom we here
behold,   5
How fearful were it down through open-
ing waves
To sink, and meet them in their fretted
caves,
Withered, grotesque, immeasurably old,
And shrill and fierce in accent!—Fear it
not:
For they Earth's fairest daughters do
excel;   10
Pure undecaying beauty is their lot;

Their voices into liquid music swell,
Thrilling each pearly cleft and sparry
grot,
The undisturbed abodes where Sea-
nymphs dwell!

II

BRUGÈS

BRUGÈS I saw attired with golden light
(Streamed from the west) as with a robe
of power:
The splendour fled; and now the sunless
hour,
That, slowly making way for peaceful
night,
Best suits with fallen grandeur, to my
sight   5
Offers the beauty, the magnificence,
And sober graces, left her for defence
Against the injuries of time, the spite
Of fortune, and the desolating storms
Of future war. Advance not—spare to
hide,   10
O gentle Power of darkness! these mild
hues;
Obscure not yet these silent avenues
Of stateliest architecture, where the Forms
Of nun-like females, with soft motion,
glide!

III

BRUGÈS

THE Spirit of Antiquity—enshrined
In sumptuous buildings, vocal in sweet
song,
In picture, speaking with heroic tongue,
And with devout solemnities entwined—

---

[1] These *Memorials* were published as a separate volume early in 1822. The poems were mostly written between January and November, 1821, the latest written of all, the *Dedication*, being dated November. To save needless repetition, none of the following poems will be furnished with the usual chronological note, except those to which the preceding observation does not apply. Where the usual note is wanting, the following general note may be taken as appropriate:—Composed 1821.—Published 1822.—Exceptions will be duly noted.—ED.

Mounts to the seat of grace within the
    mind: 5
Hence Forms that glide with swan-like
    ease along,
Hence motions, even amid the vulgar
    throng,
To an harmonious decency confined:
As if the streets were consecrated ground,
The city one vast temple, dedicate 10
To mutual respect in thought and deed;
To leisure, to forbearances sedate;
To social cares from jarring passions
    freed;
A deeper peace than that in deserts found!

IV

INCIDENT AT BRUGÈS

[Composed after July, 1828.—Published: vol.
of 1835.]

IN Brugès town is many a street
    Whence busy life hath fled;
Where, without hurry, noiseless feet
    The grass-grown pavement tread.
There heard we, halting in the shade 5
    Flung from a Convent-tower,
A harp that tuneful prelude made
    To a voice of thrilling power.

The measure, simple truth to tell,
    Was fit for some gay throng; 10
Though from the same grim turret fell
    The shadow and the song.
When silent were both voice and chords,
    The strain seemed doubly dear,
Yet sad as sweet,—for *English* words 15
    Had fallen upon the ear.

It was a breezy hour of eve;
    And pinnacle and spire
Quivered and seemed almost to heave,
    Clothed with innocuous fire; 20
But, where we stood, the setting sun
    Showed little of his state;
And, if the glory reached the Nun,
    'Twas through an iron grate.

Not always is the heart unwise, 25
    Nor pity idly born,
If even a passing Stranger sighs
    For them who do not mourn.
Sad is thy doom, self-solaced dove,
    Captive, whoe'er thou be! 30
Oh! what is beauty, what is love,
    And opening life to thee?

Such feeling pressed upon my soul,
    A feeling sanctified
By one soft trickling tear that stole 35
    From the Maiden at my side;
Less tribute could she pay than this,
    Borne gaily o'er the sea,
Fresh from the beauty and the bliss
    Of English liberty? 40

V

AFTER VISITING THE FIELD OF WATERLOO

A WINGÈD Goddess—clothed in vesture
    wrought
Of rainbow colours; One whose port was
    bold,
Whose overburthened hand could scarcely
    hold
The glittering crowns and garlands which
    it brought—
Hovered in air above the far-famed Spot.
She vanished; leaving prospect blank and
    cold 6
Of wind-swept corn that wide around us
    rolled
In dreary billows, wood, and meagre cot,
And monuments that soon must disap-
    pear:
Yet a dread local recompense we found;
While glory seemed betrayed, while
    patriot-zeal 11
Sank in our hearts, we felt as men *should*
    feel
With such vast hoards of hidden carnage
    near,
And horror breathing from the silent
    ground!

VI

BETWEEN NAMUR AND LIEGE

WHAT lovelier home could gentle Fancy
    choose?
Is this the stream, whose cities, heights,
    and plains,
War's favourite playground, are with
    crimson stains
Familiar, as the Morn with pearly dews?
The Morn, that now, along the silver
    MEUSE, 5
Spreading her peaceful ensigns, calls the
    swains
To tend their silent boats and ringing
    wains,
Or strip the bough whose mellow fruit
    bestrews
The ripening corn beneath it. As mine eyes
Turn from the fortified and threatening
    hill, 10
How sweet the prospect of yon watery
    glade,
With its grey rocks clustering in pensive
    shade—
That, shaped like old monastic turrets, rise
From the smooth meadow-ground, serene
    and still!

VII

AIX-LA-CHAPELLE

WAS it to disenchant, and to undo,
That we approached the Seat of Charle-
    maine?
To sweep from many an old romantic
    strain

That faith which no devotion may renew!
Why does this puny Church present to
view   5
Her feeble columns? and that scanty chair!
This sword that one of our weak times
might wear!
Objects of false pretence, or meanly true!
If from a traveller's fortune I might claim
A palpable memorial of that day,   10
Then would I seek the Pyrenean Breach
That ROLAND clove with huge two-handed
sway,
And to the enormous labour left his name,
Where unremitting frosts the rocky cres-
cent bleach.

VIII

IN THE CATHEDRAL AT COLOGNE

O FOR the help of Angels to complete
This Temple—Angels governed by a plan
Thus far pursued (how gloriously!) by
Man,
Studious that *He* might not disdain the
seat
Who dwells in heaven! But that aspir-
ing heat   5
Hath failed; and now, ye Powers! whose
gorgeous wings
And splendid aspect yon emblazonings
But faintly picture, 'twere an office meet
For you, on these unfinished shafts to try
The midnight virtues of your harmony:—
This vast design might tempt you to
repeat   11
Strains that call forth upon empyreal
ground
Immortal Fabrics, rising to the sound
Of penetrating harps and voices sweet!

IX

IN A CARRIAGE, UPON THE BANKS OF THE RHINE

AMID this dance of objects sadness steals
O'er the defrauded heart—while sweep-
ing by,
As in a fit of Thespian jollity,
Beneath her vine-leaf crown the green
Earth reels:
Backward, in rapid evanescence, wheels
The venerable pageantry of Time,   6
Each beetling rampart, and each tower
sublime,
And what the Dell unwillingly reveals
Of lurking cloistral arch, through trees
espied
Near the bright River's edge. Yet why
repine?   10
To muse, to creep, to halt at will, to gaze—
Such sweet wayfaring—of life's spring
the pride,
Her summer's faithful joy—*that* still is
mine,
And in fit measure cheers autumnal days.

X

HYMN

FOR THE BOATMEN, AS THEY APPROACH
THE RAPIDS UNDER THE CASTLE OF
HEIDELBERG

JESU! bless our slender Boat,
By the current swept along;
Loud its threatenings—let them not
Drown the music of a song
Breathed thy mercy to implore,   5
Where these troubled waters roar!

Saviour, for our warning, seen
Bleeding on that precious Rood;
If, while through the meadows green
Gently wound the peaceful flood,   10
We forgot Thee, do not Thou
Disregard Thy Suppliants now!

Hither, like yon ancient Tower
Watching o'er the River's bed,
Fling the shadow of thy power,   15
Else we sleep among the dead;
Thou who trod'st the billowy sea,
Shield us in our jeopardy!

Guide our Bark among the waves;
Through the rocks our passage smooth;
Where the whirlpool frets and raves   21
Let Thy love its anger soothe:
All our hope is placed in Thee;
Miserere Domine![1]

XI

THE SOURCE OF THE DANUBE

NOT, like his great Compeers, indignantly
Doth DANUBE spring to life![2] The wan-
dering Stream
(Who loves the Cross, yet to the Cres-
cent's gleam
Unfolds a willing breast) with infant glee
Slips from his prison walls: and Fancy, free
To follow in his track of silver light,   6
Mounts on rapt wing, and with a mo-
ment's flight
Hath reached the encincture of that
gloomy sea
Whose waves the Orphean lyre forbad to
meet
In conflict; whose rough winds forgot
their jars   10
To waft the heroic progeny of Greece;
When the first Ship sailed for the Golden
Fleece—
ARGO—exalted for that daring feat
To fix in heaven her shape distinct with
stars.

XII

ON APPROACHING THE STAUB-BACH, LAUTERBRUNNEN

UTTERED by whom, or how inspired—
designed
For what strange service, does this concert reach

[1] See Note, p. 707.   [2] See Note, ibid.

Our ears, and near the dwellings of man-
kind!
'Mid fields familiarised to human
speech?—
No Mermaids warble—to allay the wind
Driving some vessel toward a dangerous
beach—   6
More thrilling melodies; Witch answer-
ing Witch,
To chant a love-spell, never intertwined
Notes shrill and wild with art more
musical:
Alas! that from the lips of abject Want
Or Idleness in tatters mendicant   11
The strain should flow—free Fancy to
enthral,
And with regret and useless pity haunt
This bold, this bright, this sky-born,
WATERFALL!¹

XIII

THE FALL OF THE AAR—HANDEC

FROM the fierce aspect of this River,
throwing
His giant body o'er the steep rock's brink,
Back in astonishment and fear we shrink:
But, gradually a calmer look bestowing,
Flowers we espy beside the torrent grow-
ing;   5
Flowers that peep forth from many a
cleft and chink,
And, from the whirlwind of his anger,
drink
Hues ever fresh, in rocky fortress blowing:
They suck—from breath that, threaten-
ing to destroy,   9
Is more benignant than the dewy eve—
Beauty, and life, and motions as of joy:
Nor doubt but HE to whom yon Pine-
trees nod
Their heads in sign of worship, Nature's
God,
These humbler adorations will receive.

XIV

MEMORIAL

NEAR THE OUTLET OF THE LAKE OF THUN

*'DEM
ANDENKEN
MEINES FREUNDES
ALOYS REDING
MDCCCXVIII.'*

Aloys Reding, it will be remembered, was Captain-
General of the Swiss forces, which, with a
courage and perseverance worthy of the cause,
opposed the flagitious and too successful attempt
of Buonaparte to subjugate their country.

AROUND a wild and woody hill
A gravelled pathway treading,
We reached a votive Stone that bears
The name of Aloys Reding.

¹ See Note, p. 707.

Well judged the Friend who placed it
there   5
For silence and protection;
And haply with a finer care
Of dutiful affection.

The Sun regards it from the West;
And, while in summer glory   10
He sets, his sinking yields a type
Of that pathetic story:

And oft he tempts the patriot Swiss
Amid the grove to linger;
Till all is dim, save this bright Stone 15
Touched by his golden finger.

XV

COMPOSED IN ONE OF THE CATHOLIC CANTONS¹

DOOMED as we are our native dust
To wet with many a bitter shower,
It ill befits us to disdain
The altar, to deride the fane,
Where simple Sufferers bend, in trust   5
To win a happier hour.

I love, where spreads the village lawn,
Upon some knee-worn cell to gaze:
Hail to the firm unmoving cross,
Aloft, where pines their branches toss!
And to the chapel far withdrawn,   11
That lurks by lonely ways!

Where'er we roam—along the brink
Of Rhine—or by the sweeping Po,
Through Alpine vale, or champaign wide,
Whate'er we look on, at our side   16
Be Charity!—to bid us think,
And feel, if we would know.

XVI

AFTER-THOUGHT²

[Composed 1832.—Published 1832.]

OH Life! without thy chequered scene
Of right and wrong, of weal and woe,
Success and failure, could a ground
For magnanimity be found;
For faith, 'mid ruined hopes, serene?   5
Or whence could virtue flow?

[Composed 1837.—Published 1837.]

Pain entered through a ghastly breach—
Nor while sin lasts must effort cease;
Heaven upon earth's an empty boast;
But, for the bowers of Eden lost,   10
Mercy has placed within our reach
A portion of God's peace.

¹ The three stanzas comprised under this title
originally (1822) formed part of the poem No. XXIV
of this series, being the 5th, 4th, and 9th stanzas of
that piece. In 1827 they were detached and arranged
as now to form a separate poem. In 1832 a stanza
(now stanza i of *After-thought*, No. XVI) was added
to them. This again was taken from them in 1837,
and formed, along with a second added stanza, into
the independent poem entitled *After-thought*.—ED.
² See Editor's note to No. XV.

267

XVII
SCENE ON THE LAKE OF BRIENTZ

'WHAT know we of the Blest above
But that they sing and that they love?'
Yet, if they ever did inspire
A mortal hymn, or shaped the choir,
Now, where those harvest-Damsels float
Homeward in their rugged Boat,   6
(While all the ruffling winds are fled—
Each slumbering on some mountain's
        head),
Now, surely, hath that gracious aid
Been felt, that influence is displayed.   10
Pupils of Heaven, in order stand
The rustic Maidens, every hand
Upon a Sister's shoulder laid,—
To chant, as glides the boat along,
A simple, but a touching, song;   15
To chant, as Angels do above,
The melodies of Peace in love!

XVIII
ENGELBERG, THE HILL OF ANGELS[1]

FOR gentlest uses, oft-times Nature takes
The work of Fancy from her willing
        hands;
And such a beautiful creation makes
As renders needless spells and magic
        wands,
And for the boldest tale belief commands.
When first mine eyes beheld that famous
        Hill   6
The sacred ENGELBERG, celestial Bands,
With intermingling motions soft and still,
Hung round its top, on wings that
        changed their hues at will.

Clouds do not name those Visitants;
        they were   10
The very Angels whose authentic lays,
Sung from that heavenly ground in
        middle air,
Made known the spot where piety should
        raise
A holy Structure to the Almighty's praise.
Resplendent Apparition! if in vain   15
My ears did listen, 'twas enough to gaze;
And watch the slow departure of the
        train,
Whose skirts the glowing Mountain
        thirsted to detain.

XIX
OUR LADY OF THE SNOW

MEEK Virgin Mother, more benign
Than fairest Star, upon the height
Of thy own mountain,[2] set to keep
Lone vigils through the hours of sleep,
What eye can look upon thy shrine   5
Untroubled at the sight?

[1] See Note. p. 707.   [2] Mount Righi.

These crowded offerings as they hang
In sign of misery relieved,
Even these, without intent of theirs,
Report of comfortless despairs,   10
Of many a deep and cureless pang
And confidence deceived.

To Thee, in this aerial cleft,
As to a common centre, tend
All sufferers that no more rely   15
On mortal succour—all who sigh
And pine, of human hope bereft,
Nor wish for earthly friend.

And hence, O Virgin Mother mild!
Though plenteous flowers around thee
        blow,   20
Not only from the dreary strife
Of Winter, but the storms of life,
Thee have thy Votaries aptly styled,
OUR LADY OF THE SNOW.

Even for the Man who stops not here,
But down the irriguous valley hies,   26
Thy very name, O Lady! flings,
O'er blooming fields and gushing springs
A tender sense of shadowy fear,
And chastening sympathies!   30

Nor falls that intermingling shade
To summer-gladsomeness unkind:
It chastens only to requite
With gleams of fresher, purer, light;
While, o'er the flower-enamelled glade,
More sweetly breathes the wind.   36

But on!—a tempting downward way,
A verdant path before us lies;
Clear shines the glorious sun above;
Then give free course to joy and love,   40
Deeming 'the evil of the day
Sufficient for the wise.'

XX
EFFUSION

IN PRESENCE OF THE PAINTED TOWER OF
TELL, AT ALTORF

This Tower stands upon the spot where grew the
    Linden Tree against which his Son is said to
    have been placed, when the Father's archery was
    put to proof under circumstances so famous in
    Swiss Story.

WHAT though the Italian pencil wrought
        not here,
Nor such fine skill as did the meed bestow
On Marathonian valour, yet the tear
Springs forth in presence of this gaudy
        show,
While narrow cares their limits overflow.
Thrice happy, burghers, peasants, war-
        riors old,   6
Infants in arms, and ye, that as ye go
Homeward or schoolward, ape what ye
        behold;
Heroes before your time, in frolic fancy
        bold!

And when that calm Spectatress from
    on high   10
Looks down—the bright and solitary
    Moon,
Who never gazes but to beautify;
And snow-fed torrents, which the blaze
    of noon
Roused into fury, murmur a soft tune
That fosters peace, and gentleness recalls;
Then might the passing Monk receive a
    boon   16
Of saintly pleasure from these pictured
    walls,
While on the warlike groups the mellow-
    ing lustre falls.

How blest the souls who when their trials
    come
Yield not to terror or despondency,   20
But face like that sweet Boy their mortal
    doom,
Whose head the ruddy apple tops, while he
Expectant stands beneath the linden tree:
He quakes not like the timid forest game,
But smiles—the hesitating shaft to free;
Assured that Heaven its justice will pro-
    claim,   26
And to his Father give its own unerring
    aim.

XXI
THE TOWN OF SCHWYTZ

BY antique Fancy trimmed—though
    lowly, bred
To dignity—in thee, O SCHWYTZ! are seen
The genuine features of the golden mean;
Equality by Prudence governèd,
Or jealous Nature ruling in her stead;   5
And, therefore, art thou blest with peace,
    serene
As that of the sweet fields and meadows
    green
In unambitious compass round thee spread.
Majestic BERNE, high on her guardian steep,
Holding a central station of command,
Might well be styled this noble body's
    HEAD;   11
Thou, lodged 'mid mountainous entrench-
    ments deep,
Its HEART; and ever may the heroic Land
Thy name, O SCHWYTZ, in happy freedom
    keep![1]

XXII
ON HEARING THE 'RANZ DES VACHES' ON THE TOP OF THE PASS OF ST. GOTHARD

I LISTEN—but no faculty of mine
Avails those modulations to detect,
Which, heard in foreign lands, the Swiss
    affect

[1] Nearly 500 years (says Ebel, speaking of the French Invasion) had elapsed, when, for the first time, foreign soldiers were seen upon the frontiers of this small Canton, to impose upon it the laws of their governors.

With tenderest passion; leaving him to pine
(So fame reports) and die,—his sweet-
    breathed kine   5
Remembering, and green Alpine pastures
    decked
With vernal flowers. Yet may we not
    reject
The tale as fabulous.—Here while I recline,
Mindful how others by this simple Strain
Are moved, for me—upon this Mountain
    named   10
Of God himself from dread pre-
    eminence—
Aspiring thoughts, by memory reclaimed,
Yield to the Music's touching influence;
And joys of distant home my heart en-
    chain.

XXIII
FORT FUENTES

The Ruins of Fort Fuentes form the crest of a rocky eminence that rises from the plain at the head of the lake of Como, commanding views up the Valteline, and toward the town of Chiavenna. The prospect in the latter direction is characterised by melancholy sublimity. We rejoiced at being favoured with a distinct view of those Alpine heights; not, as we had expected from the breaking up of the storm, steeped in celestial glory, yet in communion with clouds floating or stationary—scatterings from heaven. The Ruin is interesting both in mass and in detail. An Inscription, upon elaborately-sculptured marble lying on the ground, records that the Fort had been erected by Count Fuentes in the year 1600, during the reign of Philip the Third; and the Chapel, about twenty years after, by one of his Descendants. Marble pillars of gateways are yet standing, and a considerable part of the Chapel walls: a smooth green turf has taken place of the pavement, and we could see no trace of altar or image; but everywhere something to remind one of former splendour, and of devastation and tumult. In our ascent we had passed abundance of wild vines intermingled with bushes: near the ruins were some ill tended, but growing willingly; and rock, turf, and fragments of the pile, are alike covered or adorned with a variety of flowers, among which the rose-coloured pink was growing in great beauty. While descending, we discovered on the ground, apart from the path, and at a considerable distance from the ruined Chapel, a statue of a Child in pure white marble, uninjured by the explosion that had driven it so far down the hill. 'How little,' we exclaimed, 'are these things valued here! Could we but transport this pretty Image to our own garden!'—Yet it seemed it would have been a pity any one should remove it from its couch in the wilderness, which may be its own for hundreds of years.—*Extract from Journal.*

DREAD hour! when, upheaved by war's
    sulphurous blast,
This sweet-visaged Cherub of Parian
    stone
So far from the holy enclosure was cast,
To couch in this thicket of brambles
    alone,

To rest where the lizard may bask in the palm 5
Of his half-open hand pure from blemish or speck;
And the green, gilded snake, without troubling the calm
Of the beautiful countenance, twine round his neck;
Where haply (kind service to Piety due!)
When winter the grove of its mantle bereaves, 10
Some bird (like our own honoured redbreast) may strew
The desolate Slumberer with moss and with leaves.

FUENTES once harboured the good and the brave,
Nor to her was the dance of soft pleasure unknown:
Her banners for festal enjoyment did wave
While the thrill of her fifes thro' the mountains was blown: 16
Now gads the wild vine o'er the pathless ascent:—
O silence of Nature, how deep is thy sway,
When the whirlwind of human destruction is spent,
Our tumults appeased, and our strifes passed away! 20

XXIV
THE CHURCH OF SAN SALVADOR
SEEN FROM THE LAKE OF LUGANO

This Church was almost destroyed by lightning a few years ago, but the altar and the image of the Patron Saint were untouched. The Mount, upon the summit of which the Church is built, stands amid the intricacies of the Lake of Lugano; and is, from a hundred points of view, its principal ornament, rising to the height of 2,000 feet, and, on one side, nearly perpendicular. The ascent is toilsome; but the traveller who performs it will be amply rewarded. Splendid fertility, rich woods and dazzling waters, seclusion and confinement of view contrasted with sea-like extent of plain fading into the sky; and this again, in an opposite quarter, with an horizon of the loftiest and boldest Alps—unite in composing a prospect more diversified by magnificence, beauty, and sublimity, than perhaps any other point in Europe, of so inconsiderable an elevation, commands.

THOU sacred Pile! whose turrets rise
From yon steep mountain's loftiest stage,
Guarded by lone San Salvador;
Sink (if thou must) as heretofore,
To sulphurous bolts a sacrifice, 5
But ne'er to human rage!

On Horeb's top, on Sinai, deigned
To rest the universal Lord:
Why leap the fountains from their cells
Where everlasting Bounty dwells?— 10
That, while the Creature is sustained,
His God may be adored.

Cliffs, fountains, rivers, seasons, times—
Let all remind the soul of heaven;
Our slack devotion needs them all; 15
And Faith—so oft of sense the thrall,
While she, by aid of Nature, climbs—
May hope to be forgiven.

Glory, and patriotic Love,
And all the Pomps of this frail 'spot 20
Which men call Earth,' have yearned to seek,
Associate with the simply meek,
Religion in the sainted grove,
And in the hallowed grot.

Thither, in time of adverse shocks, 25
Of fainting hopes and backward wills,
Did mighty Tell repair of old—
A Hero cast in Nature's mould,
Deliverer of the steadfast rocks
And of the ancient hills! 30

He, too, of battle-martyrs chief!
Who, to recall his daunted peers,
For victory shaped an open space,
By gathering with a wide embrace,
Into his single breast, a sheaf 35
Of fatal Austrian spears.[1]

XXV
THE ITALIAN ITINERANT, AND THE SWISS GOATHERD
PART I

I

Now that the farewell tear is dried,
Heaven prosper thee, be hope thy guide!
Hope be thy guide, adventurous Boy;
The wages of thy travel, joy!
Whether for London bound—to trill 5
Thy mountain notes with simple skill;
Or on thy head to poise a show
Of Images in seemly row;
The graceful form of milk-white Steed,
Or Bird that soared with Ganymede; 10
Or through our hamlets thou wilt bear
The sightless Milton, with his hair
Around his placid temples curled;
And Shakspeare at his side—a freight,
If clay could think and mind were weight,
For him who bore the world! 16
Hope be thy guide, adventurous Boy;
The wages of thy travel, joy!

II

But thou, perhaps, (alert as free
Though serving sage philosophy), 20
Wilt ramble over hill and dale,
A Vender of the well-wrought Scale,
Whose sentient tube instructs to time
A purpose to a fickle clime:

[1] Arnold Winkelried, at the battle of Sempach, broke an Austrian phalanx in this manner. The event is one of the most famous in the annals of Swiss heroism; and pictures and prints of it are frequent throughout the country.

Whether thou choose this useful part,
Or minister to finer art,   26
Though robbed of many a cherished
    dream,
And crossed by many a shattered scheme,
What stirring wonders wilt thou see
In the proud Isle of liberty!   30
Yet will the Wanderer sometimes pine
With thoughts which no delights can
    chase,
Recall a Sister's last embrace,
His Mother's neck entwine;
Nor shall forget the Maiden coy   35
That *would* have loved the bright-haired
    Boy!

III

My Song, encouraged by the grace
That beams from his ingenuous face,
For this Adventurer scruples not
To prophesy a golden lot;   40
Due recompense, and safe return
To Como's steeps   his happy bourne!
Where he, aloft in garden-glade,
Shall tend, with his own dark-eyed Maid,
The towering maize, and prop the twig
That ill supports the luscious fig;   46
Or feed his eye in paths sun-proof
With purple of the trellis-roof,
That through the jealous leaves escapes
From Cadenabbia's pendent grapes.   50
—Oh might he tempt that Goatherd-child
To share his wanderings! him whose look
Even yet my heart can scarcely brook,
So touchingly he smiled—
As with a rapture caught from heaven—
For unasked alms in pity given.   56

PART II

I

WITH nodding plumes, and lightly drest
Like foresters in leaf-green vest,
The Helvetian Mountaineers, on ground
For Tell's dread archery renowned,   60
Before the target stood—to claim
The guerdon of the steadiest aim.
Loud was the rifle-gun's report—
A startling thunder quick and short!
But, flying through the heights around,
Echo prolonged a tell-tale sound   66
Of hearts and hands alike 'prepared
The treasures they enjoy to guard!'
And, if there be a favoured hour
When Heroes are allowed to quit   70
The tomb, and on the clouds to sit
With tutelary power,
On their Descendants shedding grace—
This was the hour, and that the place.

II

But Truth inspired the Bards of old   75
When of an iron age they told,
Which to unequal laws gave birth,
And drove Astræa from the earth.

—A gentle Boy (perchance with blood
As noble as the best endued,   80
But seemingly a Thing despised;
Even by the sun and air unprized;
For not a tinge or flowery streak
Appeared upon his tender cheek)
Heart-deaf to those rebounding notes,
Apart, beside his silent goats,   86
Sate watching in a forest shed,
Pale, ragged, with bare feet and head;
Mute as the snow upon the hill,
And, as the saint he prays to, still.   90
Ah, what avails heroic deed?
What liberty? if no defence
Be won for feeble Innocence.
Father of all! though wilful Manhood
    read
His punishment in soul-distress,   95
Grant to the morn of life its natural
    blessedness!

XXVI

THE LAST SUPPER, BY LEONARDO DA VINCI,
   IN THE REFECTORY OF THE CONVENT OF
   MARIA DELLA GRAZIA—MILAN[1]

THO' searching damps and many an
    envious flaw
Have marred this Work; the calm ethe-
    real grace,
The love deep-seated in the Saviour's face,
The mercy, goodness, have not failed to
    awe
The Elements; as they do melt and thaw
The heart of the Beholder—and erase   6
(At least for one rapt moment) every trace
Of disobedience to the primal law.
The annunciation of the dreadful truth
Made to the Twelve, survives: lip, fore-
    head, cheek,   10
And hand reposing on the board in ruth
Of what it utters, while the unguilty seek
Unquestionable meanings—still bespeak
A labour worthy of eternal youth!

XXVII

THE ECLIPSE OF THE SUN, 1820

HIGH on her speculative tower
Stood Science waiting for the hour
When Sol was destined to endure
That darkening of his radiant face
Which Superstition strove to chase,   5
Erewhile, with rites impure.

Afloat beneath Italian skies,
Through regions fair as Paradise
We gaily passed,—till Nature wrought
A silent and unlooked-for change,   10
That checked the desultory range
Of joy and sprightly thought.

Where'er was dipped the toiling oar,
The waves danced round us as before,
As lightly, though of altered hue,   15

       [1] See Note, p. 707.

271

'Mid recent coolness, such as falls
At noontide from umbrageous walls
That screen the morning dew.

No vapour stretched its wings; no cloud
Cast far or near a murky shroud; 20
The sky an azure field displayed;
'Twas sunlight sheathed and gently
 charmed,
Of all its sparkling rays disarmed,
And as in slumber laid,—

Or something night and day between, 25
Like moonshine—but the hue was green;
Still moonshine, without shadow, spread
On jutting rock, and curvèd shore,
Where gazed the peasant from his door,
And on the mountain's head. 30

It tinged the Julian steeps—it lay,
Lugano! on thy ample bay;
The solemnising veil was drawn
O'er villas, terraces, and towers;
To Albogasio's olive bowers, 35
Porlezza's verdant lawn.

But Fancy with the speed of fire
Hath past to Milan's loftiest spire,
And there alights 'mid that aerial host
Of Figures human and divine,[1] 40
White as the snows of Apennine
Indúrated by frost.

Awe-stricken she beholds the array
That guards the Temple night and day;
Angels she sees—that might from heaven
 have flown, 45
And Virgin-saints, who not in vain
Have striven by purity to gain
The beatific crown—

Sees long-drawn files, concentric rings
Each narrowing above each;—the wings,
The uplifted palms, the silent marble
 lips 51
The starry zone of sovereign height[2]—
All steeped in this portentous light!
All suffering dim eclipse!

Thus after Man had fallen (if aught 55
These perishable spheres have wrought
May with that issue be compared)
Throngs of celestial visages,
Darkening like water in the breeze,
A holy sadness shared. 60

Lo! while I speak, the labouring Sun
His glad deliverance has begun:
The cypress waves her sombre plume
More cheerily; and town and tower,
The vineyard and the olive-bower, 65
Their lustre re-assume!

O Ye, who guard and grace my home
While in far-distant lands we roam,

[1] See Note, p. 707.
[2] Above the highest circle of figures is a zone of
metallic stars.

What countenance hath this Day put on
 for you?
While we look round with favoured eyes,
Did sullen mists hide lake and skies 71
And mountains from your view?

Or was it given you to behold
Like vision, pensive though not cold,
From the smooth breast of gay Winander-
 mere? 75
Saw ye the soft yet awful veil
Spread over Grasmere's lovely dale,
Helvellyn's brow severe?

I ask in vain—and know far less
If sickness, sorrow, or distress 80
Have spared my Dwelling to this hour;
Sad blindness! but ordained to prove
Our faith in Heaven's unfailing love
And all-controlling power.

XXVIII

THE THREE COTTAGE GIRLS

I

How blest the Maid whose heart—yet
 free
From Love's uneasy sovereignty—
Beats with a fancy running high,
Her simple cares to magnify;
Whom Labour, never urged to toil, 5
Hath cherished on a healthful soil;
Who knows not pomp, who heeds not
 pelf;
Whose heaviest sin it is to look
Askance upon her pretty Self
Reflected in some crystal brook; 10
Whom grief hath spared—who sheds no
 tear
But in sweet pity; and can hear
Another's praise from envy clear.

II

Such (but O lavish Nature! why
That dark unfathomable eye, 15
Where lurks a Spirit that replies
To stillest mood of softest skies,
Yet hints at peace to be o'erthrown,
Another's first, and then her own?)
Such, haply, yon ITALIAN Maid, 20
Our Lady's laggard Votaress,
Halting beneath the chestnut shade
To accomplish there her loveliness:
Nice aid maternal fingers lend;
A Sister serves with slacker hand; 25
Then, glittering like a star, she joins the
 festal band.

III

How blest (if truth may entertain
Coy fancy with a bolder strain)
The HELVETIAN Girl—who daily braves,
In her light skiff, the tossing waves, 30
And quits the bosom of the deep
Only to climb the rugged steep!

—Say whence that modulated shout!
From Wood-nymph of Diana's throng?
Or does the greeting to a rout   35
Of giddy Bacchanals belong?
Jubilant outcry! rock and glade
Resounded—but the voice obeyed
The breath of an Helvetian Maid.

IV

Her beauty dazzles the thick wood;   40
Her courage animates the flood;
Her steps the elastic green-sward meets
Returning unreluctant sweets;
The mountains (as ye heard) rejoice
Aloud, saluted by her voice!   45
Blithe Paragon of Alpine grace,
Be as thou art—for through thy veins
The blood of Heroes runs its race!
And nobly wilt thou brook the chains
That, for the virtuous, Life prepares; 50
The fetters which the Matron wears;
The patriot Mother's weight of anxious
    cares!

V

'Sweet HIGHLAND Girl![1] a very shower
Of beauty was thy earthly dower,'
When thou didst flit before mine eyes,
Gay vision under sullen skies,   56
While Hope and Love around thee played,
Near the rough Falls of Inversneyd!
Have they, who nursed the blossom, seen
No breach of promise in the fruit?   60
Was joy, in following joy, as keen
As grief can be in grief's pursuit?
When youth had flown did hope still bless
Thy goings—or the cheerfulness   64
Of innocence survive to mitigate distress?

VI

But from our course why turn—to tread
A way with shadows overspread;
Where what we gladliest would believe
Is feared as what may most deceive?   69
Bright Spirit, not with amaranth crowned
But heath-bells from thy native ground,
Time cannot thin thy flowing hair,
Nor take one ray of light from Thee;
For in my Fancy thou dost share
The gift of immortality;   75
And there shall bloom, with Thee allied,
The Votaress by Lugano's side;
And that intrepid Nymph, on Uri's steep
    descried!

XXIX

THE COLUMN INTENDED BY BUONAPARTE
    FOR A TRIUMPHAL EDIFICE IN MILAN,
    NOW LYING BY THE WAY-SIDE IN THE
    SIMPLON PASS

AMBITION—following down this far-famed
    slope
Her Pioneer, the snow-dissolving Sun,

[1] See address to a Highland Girl, p. 228.

While clarions prate of kingdoms to be
    won—
Perchance, in future ages, here may stop;
Taught to mistrust her flattering horoscope
By admonition from this prostrate Stone!
Memento uninscribed of Pride o'er-
    thrown,   7
Vanity's hieroglyphic; a choice trope
In Fortune's rhetoric. Daughter of the
    Rock,
Rest where thy course was stayed by
    Power divine!   10
The Soul transported sees, from hint of
    thine,
Crimes which the great Avenger's hand
    provoke,
Hears combats whistling o'er the ensan-
    guined heath:
What groans! what shrieks! what quiet-
    ness in death!

XXX
STANZAS

COMPOSED IN THE SIMPLON PASS

VALLOMBROSA! I longed in thy shadiest
    wood
To slumber, reclined on the moss-covered
    floor,
To listen to ANIO'S precipitous flood,
When the stillness of evening hath
    deepened its roar;
To range through the Temples of PAESTUM,
    to muse   5
In POMPEII preserved by her burial in
    earth;
On pictures to gaze where they drank in
    their hues;
And murmur sweet songs on the ground
    of their birth!

The beauty of Florence, the grandeur of
    Rome,
Could I leave them unseen, and not yield
    to regret?   10
With a hope (and no more) for a season to
    come,
Which ne'er may discharge the magni-
    ficent debt?
Thou fortunate Region! whose Greatness
    inurned
Awoke to new life from its ashes and dust;
Twice-glorified fields! if in sadness I
    turned   15
From your infinite marvels, the sadness
    was just.

Now, risen ere the light-footed Chamois
    retires
From dew-sprinkled grass to heights
    guarded with snow,
Toward the mists that hang over the land
    of my Sires,
From the climate of myrtles contented I
    go.   20

My thoughts become bright like yon
edging of Pines
On the steep's lofty verge: how it blackened the air!
But, touched from behind by the Sun, it
now shines
With threads that seem part of his own
silver hair.

Though the toil of the way with dear
Friends we divide,   25
Though by the same zephyr our temples
be fanned
As we rest in the cool orange-bower side
by side,
A yearning survives which few hearts
shall withstand:
Each step hath its value while homeward
we move;—
O joy when the girdle of England appears!
What moment in life is so conscious of
love,   31
Of love in the heart made more happy by
tears?

XXXI

ECHO, UPON THE GEMMI

WHAT beast of chase hath broken from
the cover?
Stern GEMMI listens to as full a cry,
As multitudinous a harmony
Of sounds as rang the heights of Latmos
over,
When, from the soft couch of her sleeping
Lover,   5
Up-starting, Cynthia skimmed the moun-
tain-dew
In keen pursuit—and gave, where'er she flew,
Impetuous motion to the Stars above her.
A solitary Wolf-dog, ranging on
Through the bleak concave, wakes this
wondrous chime   10
Of aery voices locked in unison,—
Faint — far-off — near — deep — solemn
and sublime!—
So, from the body of one guilty deed,
A thousand ghostly fears, and haunting
thoughts, proceed!

XXXII
PROCESSIONS

SUGGESTED ON A SABBATH MORNING IN
THE VALE OF CHAMOUNY

To appease the Gods; or public thanks to
yield;
Or to solicit knowledge of events,
Which in her breast Futurity concealed;
And that the past might have its true intents
Feelingly told by living monuments—   5
Mankind of yore were prompted to devise
Rites such as yet Persepolis presents
Graven on her cankered walls, solemnities
That moved in long array before admiring
eyes.

The Hebrews thus, carrying in joyful
state   10
Thick boughs of palm, and willows from
the brook,
Marched round the altar—to commemo-
rate
How, when their course they through the
desert took,
Guided by signs which ne'er the sky forsook,
They lodged in leafy tents and cabins
low;   15
Green boughs were borne, while, for the
blast that shook
Down to the earth the walls of Jericho,
Shouts rise, and storms of sound from
lifted trumpets blow!

And thus, in order, 'mid the sacred grove
Fed in the Libyan waste by gushing wells,
The priests and damsels of Ammonian
Jove   21
Provoked responses with shrill canticles;
While, in a ship begirt with silver bells,
They round his altar bore the hornèd God,
Old Cham, the solar Deity, who dwells
Aloft, yet in a tilting vessel rode,   26
When universal sea the mountains over-
flowed.

Why speak of Roman Pomps? the haughty
claims
Of Chiefs triumphant after ruthless wars;
The feast of Neptune—and the Cereal
Games,   30
With images, and crowns, and empty
cars;
The dancing Salii—on the shields of Mars
Smiting with fury; and a deeper dread
Scattered on all sides by the hideous jars
Of Corybantian cymbals, while the head
Of Cybelè was seen, sublimely turreted!

At length a Spirit more subdued and soft
Appeared—to govern Christian pageant-
ries:
The Cross, in calm procession, borne aloft
Moved to the chant of sober litanies.   40
Even such, this day, came wafted on the
breeze
From a long train—in hooded vestments
fair
Enwrapt—and winding, between Alpine
trees
Spiry and dark, around their House of
prayer,   44
Below the icy bed of bright ARGENTIERE.

Still in the vivid freshness of a dream,
The pageant haunts me as it met our eyes!
Still, with those white-robed Shapes—a
living Stream,
The glacier Pillars join in solemn guise[1]
For the same service, by mysterious ties;

[1] See Note, p. 707.

Numbers exceeding credible account   51
Of number, pure and silent Votaries
Issuing or issued from a wintry fount;
The impenetrable heart of that exalted
    Mount!

They, too, who send so far a holy gleam
While they the Church engird with motion
    slow,   56
A product of that awful Mountain seem,
Poured from his vaults of everlasting snow;
Not virgin lilies marshalled in bright row,
Not swans descending with the stealthy
    tide,   60
A livelier sisterly resemblance show
Than the fair Forms, that in long order glide,
Bear to the glacier band—those Shapes
    aloft descried.

Trembling, I look upon the secret springs
Of that licentious craving in the mind   65
To act the God among external things,
To bind, on apt suggestion, or unbind;
And marvel not that antique Faith in-
    clined
To crowd the world with metamorphosis,
Vouchsafed in pity or in wrath assigned;
Such insolent temptations wouldst thou
    miss,   71
Avoid these sights; nor brood o'er Fable's
    dark abyss!

XXXIII
ELEGIAC STANZAS

The lamented Youth, whose untimely death gave
occasion to these elegiac verses, was Frederick
William Goddard, from Boston in North America. He was in his twentieth year, and had
resided for some time with a clergyman in the
neighbourhood of Geneva for the completion
of his education. Accompanied by a fellow-
pupil, a native of Scotland, he had just set out
on a Swiss tour when it was his misfortune to
fall in with a friend of mine who was hastening
to join our party. The travellers, after spending
a day together on the road from Berne and at
Soleure, took leave of each other at night, the
young men having intended to proceed directly
to Zurich. But early in the morning my friend
found his new acquaintances, who were informed of the object of his journey, and the
friends he was in pursuit of, equipped to accompany him. We met at Lucerne the succeeding
evening, and Mr. G. and his fellow-student became in consequence our travelling companions
for a couple of days. We ascended the Righi
together; and, after contemplating the sunrise
from that noble mountain, we separated at an
hour and on a spot well suited to the parting
of those who were to meet no more. Our party
descended through the valley of Our Lady of
the Snow, and our late companions, to Art. We
had hoped to meet in a few weeks at Geneva;
but on the third succeeding day (on the 21st of
August) Mr. Goddard perished, being overset
in a boat while crossing the Lake of Zurich. His
companion saved himself by swimming, and was
hospitably received in the mansion of a Swiss
gentleman (M. Keller) situated on the eastern
coast of the lake. The corpse of poor Goddard

was cast ashore on the estate of the same gentleman, who generously performed all the rites of
hospitality which could be rendered to the dead
as well as to the living. He caused a handsome
mural monument to be erected in the church
of Kü snacht, which records the premature fate
of the young American, and on the shores too of
the lake the traveller may read an inscription
pointing out the spot where the body was deposited by the waves.

LULLED by the sound of pastoral bells,
Rude Nature's Pilgrims did we go,
From the dread summit of the Queen[1]
Of mountains, through a deep ravine,
Where, in her holy chapel, dwells   5
'Our Lady of the Snow.'

The sky was blue, the air was mild;
Free were the streams and green the
    bowers;
As if, to rough assaults unknown,
The genial spot had *ever* shown   10
A countenance that as sweetly smiled—
The face of summer-hours.

And we were gay, our hearts at ease;
With pleasure dancing through the frame
We journeyed; all we knew of care—   15
Our path that straggled here and there;
Of trouble—but the fluttering breeze;
Of Winter—but a name.

If foresight could have rent the veil
Of three short days—but hush—no more!
Calm is the grave, and calmer none   21
Than that to which thy cares are gone,
Thou Victim of the stormy gale;
Asleep on ZURICH'S shore!

Oh   GODDARD!—what   art   thou?—
    a name—   25
A sunbeam followed by a shade!
Nor more, for aught that time supplies,
The great, the experienced, and the wise:
Too much from this frail earth we claim,
And therefore are betrayed.   30

We met, while festive mirth ran wild,
Where, from a deep lake's mighty urn,
Forth slips, like an enfranchised slave,
A sea-green river, proud to lave,
With current swift and undefiled,   35
The towers of old LUCERNE.

We parted upon solemn ground
Far-lifted towards the unfading sky;
But all our thoughts were *then* of Earth,
That gives to common pleasures birth;
And nothing in our hearts we found   41
That prompted even a sigh.

Fetch, sympathising Powers of air,
Fetch, ye that post o'er seas and lands,
Herbs moistened by Virginian dew,   45
A most untimely grave to strew,
Whose turf may never know the care
Of *kindred* human hands!

[1] Mount Righi—Regina Montium.

Beloved by every gentle Muse
He left his Transatlantic home: 50
Europe, a realised romance,
Had opened on his eager glance;
What present bliss!—what golden views!
What stores for years to come!

Though lodged within no vigorous frame,
His soul her daily tasks renewed, 56
Blithe as the lark on sun-gilt wings
High poised—or as the wren that sings
In shady places, to proclaim
Her modest gratitude. 60

Not vain is sadly-uttered praise;
The words of truth's memorial vow
Are sweet as morning fragrance shed
From flowers 'mid GOLDAU's ruins bred;
As evening's fondly-lingering rays, 65
On RIGHI's silent brow.

Lamented youth! to thy cold clay
Fit obsequies the Stranger paid;
And piety shall guard the Stone
Which hath not left the spot unknown
Where the wild waves resigned their
prey— 71
And *that* which marks thy bed.

And, when thy Mother weeps for Thee,
Lost Youth! a solitary Mother;
This tribute from a casual Friend 75
A not unwelcome aid may lend,
To feed the tender luxury,
The rising pang to smother.[1]

XXXIV

SKY-PROSPECT—FROM THE PLAIN OF FRANCE

Lo! in the burning west, the craggy nape
Of a proud Ararat! and, thereupon,
The Ark, her melancholy voyage done!
Yon rampant cloud mimics a lion's shape;
There, combats a huge crocodile—agape
A golden spear to swallow! and that
brown 6
And massy grove, so near yon blazing
town,
Stirs and recedes—destruction to escape!
Yet all is harmless—as the Elysian shades
Where Spirits dwell in undisturbed re-
pose— 10
Silently disappears, or quickly fades:
Meek Nature's evening comment on the
shows
That for oblivion take their daily birth
From all the fuming vanities of Earth!

[1] The persuasion here expressed was not groundless. The first human consolation that the afflicted
Mother felt was derived from this tribute to her son's
memory, a fact which the author learned, at his own
residence, from her Daughter, who visited Europe
some years afterwards.—Goldau is one of the villages
desolated by the fall of part of the Mountain Rossberg.

XXXV

ON BEING STRANDED NEAR THE HARBOUR OF BOULOGNE[1]

WHY cast ye back upon the Gallic shore,
Ye furious waves! a patriotic Son
Of England—who in hope her coast had
won,
His project crowned, his pleasant travel
o'er?
Well—let him pace this noted beach once
more, 5
That gave the Roman his triumphal shells;
That saw the Corsican his cap and bells
Haughtily shake, a dreaming Con-
queror!—
Enough: my Country's cliffs I can behold,
And proudly think, beside the chafing
sea, 10
Of checked ambition, tyranny controlled,
And folly cursed with endless memory:
These local recollections ne'er can cloy;
Such ground I from my very heart enjoy!

XXXVI

AFTER LANDING—THE VALLEY OF DOVER NOVEMBER, 1820

WHERE be the noisy followers of the game
Which faction breeds? the turmoil where,
that passed
Through Europe, echoing from the news-
man's blast,
And filled our hearts with grief for
England's shame?
Peace greets us;—rambling on without
an aim 5
We mark majestic herds of cattle, free
To ruminate, couched on the grassy lea;
And hear far-off the mellow horn proclaim
The Season's harmless pastime. Ruder
sound
Stirs not; enrapt I gaze with strange
delight, 10
While consciousnesses, not to be disowned,
Here only serve a feeling to invite
That lifts the spirit to a calmer height,
And makes this rural stillness more pro-
found.

XXXVII

AT DOVER

[Composed 1837.—Published: Sonnet-vol. of
1838; ed. 1845.]

FROM the Pier's head, musing, and with
increase
Of wonder, I have watched this sea-side
Town,
Under the white cliff's battlemented
crown,
Hushed to a depth of more than Sabbath
peace:
The streets and quays are thronged, but
why disown 5

[1] See Note, p. 708.

Their natural utterance? whence this strange release
From social noise—silence elsewhere unknown?—
A Spirit whispered, 'Let all wonder cease;
Ocean's o'erpowering murmurs have set free
Thy sense from pressure of life's common din;   10
As the dread Voice that speaks from out the sea
Of God's eternal Word, the Voice of Time
Doth deaden, shocks of tumult, shrieks of crime,
The shouts of folly, and the groans of sin.'

XXXVIII
DESULTORY STANZAS

UPON RECEIVING THE PRECEDING SHEETS FROM THE PRESS

[Composed 1822.—Published 1822.]

Is then the final page before me spread,
Nor further outlet left to mind or heart?
Presumptuous Book! too forward to be read,
How can I give thee license to depart?
One tribute more: unbidden feelings start   5
Forth from their coverts; slighted objects rise;
My spirit is the scene of such wild art
As on Parnassus rules, when lightning flies,
Visibly leading on the thunder's harmonies.

All that I saw returns upon my view,   10
All that I heard comes back upon my ear,
All that I felt this moment doth renew;
And where the foot with no unmanly fear
Recoiled—and wings alone could travel—there
I move at ease; and meet contending themes   15
That press upon me, crossing the career
Of recollections vivid as the dreams
Of midnight,—cities, plains, forests, and mighty streams.

Where Mortal never breathed I dare to sit
Among the interior Alps, gigantic crew,
Who triumphed o'er diluvian power!—and yet   21
What are they but a wreck and residue,
Whose only business is to perish!—true
To which sad course, these wrinkled Sons of Time
Labour their proper greatness to subdue;   25
Speaking of death alone, beneath a clime
Where life and rapture flow in plenitude sublime.

Fancy hath flung for me an airy bridge
Across thy long deep Valley, furious Rhone!
Arch that *here* rests upon the granite ridge   30
Of Monte Rosa—*there* on frailer stone
Of secondary birth, the Jung-frau's cone;
And, from that arch, down-looking on the Vale
The aspect I behold of every zone;
A sea of foliage, tossing with the gale,   35
Blithe Autumn's purple crown, and Winter's icy mail!

Far as ST. MAURICE, from yon eastern FORKS,[1]
Down the main avenue my sight can range:
And all its branchy vales, and all that lurks
Within them, church, and town, and hut, and grange,   40
For my enjoyment meet in vision strange;
Snows, torrents;—to the region's utmost bound,
Life, Death, in amicable interchange;—
But list! the avalanche—the hush profound
That follows—yet more awful than that awful sound!   45

Is not the chamois suited to his place?
The eagle worthy of her ancestry?
—Let Empires fall; but ne'er shall Ye disgrace
Your noble birthright, ye that occupy
Your council-seats beneath the open sky,
On Sarnen's Mount,[2] there judge of fit and right,   51
In simple democratic majesty;
Soft breezes fanning your rough brows—the might
And purity of nature spread before your sight!

From this appropriate Court renowned LUCERNE   55
Calls me to pace her honoured Bridge[3]—that cheers
The Patriot's heart with pictures rude and stern,
An uncouth Chronicle of glorious years.
Like portraiture, from loftier source, endears
That work of kindred frame, which spans the lake   60
Just at the point of issue, where it fears
The form and motion of a stream to take;
Where it begins to stir, *yet* voiceless as a snake.

Volumes of sound, from the Cathedral rolled,
This long-roofed Vista penetrate—but see,
One after one, its tablets, that unfold
The whole design of Scripture history;

[1] At the head of the Valais. See Note, p. 708.
[2] See Note, p. 708.   [3] See Note, p. 708.

277

From the first tasting of the fatal Tree,
Till the bright Star appeared in eastern
skies,
Announcing, ONE was born mankind to
free;   70
His acts, his wrongs, his final sacrifice;
Lessons for every heart, a Bible for all
eyes.

Our pride misleads, our timid likings kill.
—Long may these homely Works devised
of old,   74
These simple efforts of Helvetian skill,
Aid, with congenial influence, to uphold
The State,—the Country's destiny to
mould;
Turning, for them who pass, the common
dust
Of servile opportunity to gold;

Filling the soul with sentiments august—
The beautiful, the brave, the holy, and
the just!   81

No more; Time halts not in his noiseless
march—
Nor turns, nor winds, as doth the liquid
flood;
Life slips from underneath us, like that
arch
Of airy workmanship whereon we stood,
Earth stretched below, heaven in our
neighbourhood.   86
Go forth, my little Book! pursue thy way;
Go forth, and please the gentle and the
good;
Nor be a whisper stifled, if it say
That treasures, yet untouched, may grace
some future Lay.   90

MEMORIALS OF
A TOUR IN ITALY,[1] 1837

TO HENRY CRABB ROBINSON

COMPANION! by whose buoyant Spirit cheered,
In whose experience trusting, day by day
Treasures I gained with zeal that neither feared
The toils nor felt the crosses of the way,
These records take, and happy should I be
Were but the Gift a meet Return to thee
For kindnesses that never ceased to flow,
And prompt self-sacrifice to which I owe
Far more than any heart but mine can know.
                                    W. WORDSWORTH.

RYDAL MOUNT,
    Feb. 14*th*, 1842.

The Tour of which the following Poems are very
inadequate remembrances was shortened by
report, too well founded, of the prevalence of
Cholera at Naples. To make some amends for
what was reluctantly left unseen in the South of
Italy, we visited the Tuscan Sanctuaries among
the Apennines, and the principal Italian Lakes
among the Alps. Neither of those lakes, nor
of Venice, is there any notice in these Poems,
chiefly because I have touched upon them elsewhere. See, in particular, 'Descriptive Sketches,'
'Memorials of a Tour on the Continent in 1820,'
and a Sonnet upon the extinction of the Vene-
tian Republic.

I
MUSINGS NEAR AQUAPENDENTE
APRIL, 1837
[Composed 1837.—Published: vol. of 1842.]

YE Apennines! with all your fertile vales
Deeply embosomed, and your winding
shores
Of either sea, an Islander by birth,

A Mountaineer by habit, would resound
Your praise, in meet accordance with
your claims   5
Bestowed by Nature, or from man's great
deeds
Inherited:—presumptuous thought!—it
fled
Like vapour, like a towering cloud, dis-
solved.
Not, therefore, shall my mind give way to
sadness;—
Yon snow-white torrent-fall, plumb down
it drops   10
Yet ever hangs or seems to hang in air,
Lulling the leisure of that high-perched
town,
AQUAPENDENTE, in her lofty site
Its neighbour and its namesake—town,
and flood
Forth flashing out of its own gloomy
chasm   15
Bright sunbeams—the fresh verdure of
this lawn
Strewn with grey rocks, and on the
horizon's verge,
O'er intervenient waste, through glimmer-
ing haze,
Unquestionably kenned, that cone-shaped
hill
With fractured summit, no indifferent
sight   20
To travellers, from such comforts as are
thine,

[1] This group of Poems first appeared in the volume entitled *Poems, Chiefly of Early and Late Years,*
published in 1842. The Sonnets all, or almost all, belong to the year, December, 1840—December, 1841.
Where no note recording dates of composition and of publication is given, it is to be assumed that the poem
was written in 1840-1, and published (as described above) in 1842.—ED.

Bleak Radicofani! escaped with joy—
These are before me; and the varied scene
May well suffice, till noon-tide's sultry
   heat
Relax, to fix and satisfy the mind   25
Passive yet pleased. What! with this
   Broom in flower
Close at my side! She bids me fly to greet
Her sisters, soon like her to be attired
With golden blossoms opening at the feet
Of my own Fairfield. The glad greeting
   given,   30
Given with a voice and by a look returned
Of old companionship, Time counts not
   minutes
Ere, from accustomed paths, familiar
   fields,
The local Genius hurries me aloft,   34
Transported over that cloud-wooing hill,
Seat Sandal, a fond suitor of the clouds,
With dream-like smoothness, to Hel-
   vellyn's top,
There to alight upon crisp moss and range,
Obtaining ampler boon, at every step,
Of visual sovereignty—hills multitu-
   dinous,   40
(Not Apennine can boast of fairer), hills
Pride of two nations, wood and lake and
   plains,
And prospect right below of deep coves
   shaped
By skeleton arms, that, from the moun-
   tain's trunk
Extended, clasp the winds, with mutual
   moan   45
Struggling for liberty, while undismayed
The shepherd struggles with them. On-
   ward thence
And downward by the skirt of Greenside
   fell,
And by Glenridding-screes, and low Glen-
   coign,   49
Places forsaken now, though loving still
The Muses, as they loved them in the days
Of the old minstrels and the border
   bards.—
But here am I fast bound; and let it pass,
The simple rapture;—who that travels far
To feed his mind with watchful eyes could
   share   55
Or wish to share it?—One there surely
   was,
'The Wizard of the North,' with anxious
   hope
Brought to this genial climate, when
   disease
Preyed upon body and mind—yet not the
   less
Had his sunk eye kindled at those dear
   words   60
That spake of bards and minstrels; and
   his spirit
Had flown with mine to old Helvellyn's
   brow,

Where once together, in his day of
   strength,
We stood rejoicing, as if earth were free
From sorrow, like the sky above our
   heads.   65

Years followed years, and when, upon
Of his last going from Tweed-side, thought
   turned,
Or by another's sympathy was led,
To this bright land, Hope was for him no
   friend,
Knowledge no help; Imagination shaped
No promise. Still, in more than ear-deep
   seats,   71
Survives for me, and cannot but survive
The tone of voice which wedded borrowed
   words
To sadness not their own, when, with
   faint smile
Forced by intent to take from speech its
   edge,   75
He said, 'When I am there, although 'tis
   fair,
'Twill be another Yarrow.' Prophecy
More than fulfilled, as gay Campania's
   shores
Soon witnessed, and the city of seven hills,
Her sparkling fountains, and her moulder-
   ing tombs;   80
And more than all, that Eminence which
   showed
Her splendours, seen, not felt, the while
   he stood
A few short steps (painful they were) apart
From Tasso's Convent-haven, and retired
   grave.

Peace to their Spirits! why should
   Poesy   85
Yield to the lure of vain regret, and hover
In gloom on wings with confidence out-
   spread
To move in sunshine?—Utter thanks, my
   Soul!
Tempered with awe, and sweetened by
   compassion
For them who in the shades of sorrow
   dwell,   90
That I—so near the term to human life
Appointed by man's common heritage,
Frail as the frailest, one withal (if that
Deserve a thought) but little known to
   fame—
Am free to rove where Nature's loveliest
   looks,   95
Art's noblest relics, history's rich bequests,
Failed to reanimate and but feebly cheered
The whole world's Darling—free to rove
   at will
O'er high and low, and if requiring rest,
Rest from enjoyment only.
              Thanks poured forth   100

MEMORIALS OF A TOUR IN ITALY, 1837

For what thus far hath blessed my wander-
ings, thanks
Fervent but humble as the lips can breathe
Where gladness seems a duty—let me
guard
Those seeds of expectation which the fruit
Already gathered in this favoured Land
Enfolds within its core. The faith be
mine, 106
That He who guides and governs all,
approves
When gratitude, though disciplined to
look
Beyond these transient spheres, doth wear
a crown
Of earthly hope put on with trembling
hand; 110
Nor is least pleased, we trust, when
golden beams,
Reflected through the mists of age, from
hours
Of innocent delight, remote or recent,
Shoot far a little way—'tis all they can—
Into the doubtful future. Who would
keep 115
Power must resolve to cleave to it through
life,
Else it deserts him, surely as he lives.
Saints would not grieve nor guardian
angels frown
If one—while tossed, as was my lot to be,
In a frail bark urged by two slender oars
Over waves rough and deep, that, when
they broke, 121
Dashed their white foam against the
palace walls
Of Genoa the superb—should there be led
To meditate upon his own appointed tasks,
However humble in themselves, with
thoughts 125
Raised and sustained by memory of Him
Who oftentimes within those narrow
bounds
Rocked on the surge, there tried his
spirit's strength
And grasp of purpose, long ere sailed his
ship
To lay a new world open.
Nor less prized 130
Be those impressions which incline the
heart
To mild, to lowly, and to seeming weak,
Bend that way her desires. The dew, the
storm—
The dew whose moisture fell in gentle
drops
On the small hyssop destined to be-
come, 135
By Hebrew ordinance devoutly kept,
A purifying instrument—the storm
That shook on Lebanon the cedar's top,
And as it shook, enabling the blind roots
Further to force their way, endowed its
trunk 140

With magnitude and strength fit to up-
hold
The glorious temple—did alike proceed
From the same gracious will, were both an
offspring
Of bounty infinite.
Between Powers that aim
Higher to lift their lofty heads, im-
pelled 145
By no profane ambition, Powers that
thrive
By conflict, and their opposites, that trust
In lowliness—a mid-way tract there lies
Of thoughtful sentiment for every mind
Pregnant with good. Young, Middle-
aged, and Old, 150
From century on to century, must have
known
The emotion—nay, more fitly were it
said—
The blest tranquillity that sunk so deep
Into my spirit, when I paced, enclosed
In Pisa's Campo Santo, the smooth floor
Of its Arcades paved with sepulchral slabs,
And through each window's open fret-
work looked 157
O'er the blank Area of sacred earth
Fetched from Mount Calvary, or haply
delved
In precincts nearer to the Saviour's tomb,
By hands of men, humble as brave, who
fought 161
For its deliverance—a capacious field
That to descendants of the dead it holds
And to all living mute memento breathes,
More touching far than aught which on
the walls 165
Is pictured, or their epitaphs can speak,
Of the changed City's long-departed
power,
Glory, and wealth, which, perilous as
they are,
Here did not kill, but nourished, Piety.
And, high above that length of cloistral
roof, 170
Peering in air and backed by azure sky,
To kindred contemplations ministers
The Baptistery's dome, and that which
swells
From the Cathedral pile; and with the
twain
Conjoined in prospect mutable or fixed
(As hurry on in eagerness the feet, 176
Or pause) the summit of the Leaning-
tower.
Nor less remuneration waits on him
Who having left the Cemetery stands
In the Tower's shadow, of decline and
fall 180
Admonished not without some sense of
fear,
Fear that soon vanishes before the sight
Of splendour unextinguished, pomp un-
scathed,

And beauty unimpaired. Grand in itself,
And for itself, the assemblage, grand and
    fair   185
To view, and for the mind's consenting
    eye
A type of age in man, upon its front
Bearing the world-acknowledged evidence
Of past exploits, nor fondly after more
Struggling against the stream of destiny,
But with its peaceful majesty content.
—Oh what a spectacle at every turn 192
The Place unfolds, from pavement skin-
    ned with moss,
Or grass-grown spaces, where the heaviest
    foot
Provokes no echoes, but must softly
    tread;   195
Where Solitude with Silence paired stops
    short
Of Desolation, and to Ruin's scythe
Decay submits not.
            But where'er my steps
Shall wander, chiefly let me cull with care
Those images of genial beauty, oft   200
Too lovely to be pensive in themselves
But by reflexion made so, which do best
And fitliest serve to crown with fragrant
    wreaths
Life's cup when almost filled with years,
    like mine.
—How lovely robed in forenoon light
    and shade,   205
Each ministering to each, didst thou
    appear
Savona, Queen of territory fair
As aught that marvellous coast thro' all
    its length
Yields to the Stranger's eye. Remem-
    brance holds
As a selected treasure thy one cliff,   210
That, while it wore for melancholy crest
A shattered Convent, yet rose proud to
    have
Clinging to its steep sides a thousand herbs
And shrubs, whose pleasant looks gave
    proof how kind
The breath of air can be where earth had
    else   215
Seemed churlish. And behold, both far
    and near,
Garden and field all decked with orange
    bloom,
And peach and citron, in Spring's mild-
    est breeze
Expanding; and, along the smooth shore
    curved
Into a natural port, a tideless sea,   220
To that mild breeze with motion and with
    voice
Softly responsive; and, attuned to all
Those vernal charms of sight and sound,
    appeared
Smooth space of turf which from the
    guardian fort

Sloped seaward, turf whose tender April
    green,   225
In coolest climes too fugitive, might even
    here
Plead with the sovereign Sun for longer stay
Than his unmitigated beams allow,
Nor plead in vain, if beauty could pre-
    serve,
From mortal change, aught that is born
    on earth   230
Or doth on time depend.
            While on the brink
Of that high Convent-crested cliff I stood,
Modest Savona! over all did brood
A pure poetic Spirit—as the breeze,
Mild—as the verdure, fresh—the sun-
    shine, bright—   235
Thy gentle Chiabrera!—not a stone,
Mural or level with the trodden floor,
In Church or Chapel, if my curious quest
Missed not the truth, retains a single name
Of young or old, warrior, or saint, or sage,
To whose dear memories his sepulchral
    verse   241
Paid simple tribute, such as might have
    flowed
From the clear spring of a plain English
    heart,
Say rather, one in native fellowship
With all who want not skill to couple
    grief   245
With praise, as genuine admiration
    prompts.
The grief, the praise, are severed from
    their dust,
Yet in his page the records of that worth
Survive, uninjured;—glory then to words,
Honour to word-preserving Arts, and
    hail   250
Ye kindred local influences that still,
If Hope's familiar whispers merit faith,
Await my steps when they the breezy
    height
Shall range of philosophic Tusculum;
Or Sabine vales explored inspire a wish
To meet the shade of Horace by the side
Of his Bandusian fount; or I invoke   257
His presence to point out the spot where
    once
He sate, and eulogised with earnest pen
Peace, leisure, freedom, moderate de-
    sires;   260
And all the immunities of rural life
Extolled, behind Vacuna's crumbling
    fane.
Or let me loiter, soothed with what is
    given,
Nor asking more, on that delicious Bay,
Parthenope's Domain—Virgilian haunt,
Illustrated with never-dying verse,   266
And, by the Poet's laurel-shaded tomb,
Age after age to Pilgrims from all lands
Endeared.
            And who—if not a man as cold

In heart as dull in brain—while pacing ground 270
Chosen by Rome's legendary Bards, high minds
Out of her early struggles well inspired
To localise heroic acts—could look
Upon the spots with undelighted eye,
Though even to their last syllable the Lays 275
And very names of those who gave them birth
Have perished?—Verily, to her utmost depth,
Imagination feels what Reason fears not
To recognise, the lasting virtue lodged
In those bold fictions that, by deeds assigned 280
To the Valerian, Fabian, Curian Race,
And others like in fame, created Powers
With attributes from History derived,
By Poesy irradiate, and yet graced,
Through marvellous felicity of skill, 285
With something more propitious to high aims
Than either, pent within her separate sphere,
Can oft with justice claim.
                    And not disdaining
Union with those primeval energies
To virtue consecrate, stoop ye from your height 290
Christian Traditions! at my Spirit's call
Descend, and, on the brow of ancient Rome
As she survives in ruin, manifest
Your glories mingled with the brightest hues
Of her memorial halo, fading, fading,
But never to be extinct while Earth endures. 296
O come, if undishonoured by the prayer,
From all her Sanctuaries!—Open for my feet
Ye Catacombs, give to mine eyes a glimpse
Of the Devout, as, 'mid your glooms convened 300
For safety, they of yore enclasped the Cross
On knees that ceased from trembling, or intoned
Their orisons with voices half-suppressed,
But sometimes heard, or fancied to be heard,
Even at this hour.
              And thou Mamertine prison, 305
Into that vault receive me from whose depth
Issues, revealed in no presumptuous vision,
Albeit lifting human to divine,
A Saint, the Church's Rock, the mystic Keys
Grasped in his hand; and lo! with upright sword 310

Prefiguring his own impendent doom,
The Apostle of the Gentiles; both prepared
To suffer pains with heathen scorn and hate
Inflicted;—blessèd Men, for so to Heaven
They follow their dear Lord!
              Time flows—nor winds, 315
Nor stagnates, nor precipitates his course,
But many a benefit borne upon his breast
For human-kind sinks out of sight, is gone,
No one knows how; nor seldom is put forth 319
An angry arm that snatches good away,
Never perhaps to reappear. The Stream
Has to our generation brought and brings
Innumerable gains; yet we, who now
Walk in the light of day, pertain full surely 324
To a chilled age, most pitiably shut out
From that which *is* and actuates, by forms,
Abstractions, and by lifeless fact to fact
Minutely linked with diligence uninspired,
Unrectified, unguided, unsustained,
By godlike insight. To this fate is doomed 330
Science, wide-spread and spreading still as be
Her conquests, in the world of sense made known.
So with the internal mind it fares; and so
With morals, trusting, in contempt or fear
Of vital principle's controlling law, 335
To her purblind guide Expediency; and so
Suffers religious faith. Elate with view
Of what is won, we overlook or scorn
The best that should keep pace with it, and must,
Else more and more the general mind will droop, 340
Even as if bent on perishing. There lives
No faculty within us which the Soul
Can spare, and humblest earthly Weal demands,
For dignity not placed beyond her reach,
Zealous co-operation of all means 345
Given or acquired, to raise us from the mire,
And liberate our hearts from low pursuits.
By gross Utilities enslaved we need 348
More of ennobling impulse from the past,
If to the future aught of good must come
Sounder and therefore holier than the ends
Which, in the giddiness of self-applause,
We covet as supreme. O grant the crown
That Wisdom wears, or take his treacherous staff
From Knowledge!—If the Muse, whom I have served 355
This day, be mistress of a single pearl

Fit to be placed in that pure diadem;
Then, not in vain, under these chestnut
boughs
Reclined, shall I have yielded up my soul
To transports from the secondary founts
Flowing of time and place, and paid to
both   361
Due homage; nor shall fruitlessly have
striven,
By love of beauty moved, to enshrine in
verse
Accordant meditations, which in times
Vexed and disordered, as our own, may
shed   365
Influence, at least among a scattered few,
To soberness of mind and peace of heart
Friendly; as here to my repose hath been
This flowering broom's dear neighbour-
hood, the light
And murmur issuing from yon pendent
flood,   370
And all the varied landscape. Let us now
Rise, and to-morrow greet magnificent
Rome.[1]

II

THE PINE OF MONTE MARIO AT ROME

I SAW far off the dark top of a Pine
Look like a cloud—a slender stem the tie
That bound it to its native earth—poised
high
'Mid evening hues, along the horizon line,
Striving in peace each other to out-
shine.   5
But when I learned the Tree was living there,
Saved from the sordid axe by Beaumont's
care,
Oh, what a gush of tenderness was mine!
The rescued Pine-tree, with its sky so
bright
And cloud-like beauty, rich in thoughts
of home,   10
Death-parted friends, and days too swift
in flight,
Supplanted the whole majesty of Rome
(Then first apparent from the Pincian
Height)
Crowned with St. Peter's everlasting
Dome.[2]

III

AT ROME

Is this, ye Gods, the Capitolian Hill?
Yon petty Steep in truth the fearful Rock,
Tarpeian named of yore, and keeping
still
That name, a local Phantom proud to
mock
The Traveller's expectation?—Could our
Will   5
Destroy the ideal Power within, 'twere done
Thro' what men see and touch,—slaves
wandering on,

[1] See Note, p. 708.   [2] See Note, p. 208.

Impelled by thirst of all but Heaven-
taught skill.
Full oft, our wish obtained, deeply we
sigh;
Yet not unrecompensed are they who
learn,   10
From that depression raised, to mount on
high
With stronger wing, more clearly to discern
Eternal things; and, if need be, defy
Change, with a brow not insolent, though
stern.

IV

AT ROME.—REGRETS.—IN ALLUSION TO
NIEBUHR, AND OTHER MODERN HISTO-
RIANS

THOSE old credulities, to nature dear,
Shall they no longer bloom upon the stock
Of History, stript naked as a rock
'Mid a dry desert? What is it we hear?
The glory of Infant Rome must dis-
appear,   5
Her morning splendours vanish, and their
place
Know them no more. If Truth, who
veiled her face
With those bright beams yet hid it not,
must steer
Henceforth a humbler course perplexed
and slow;   9
One solace yet remains for us who came
Into this world in days when story lacked
Severe research, that in our hearts we
know
How, for exciting youth's heroic flame,
Assent is power, belief the soul of fact.

V

CONTINUED

COMPLACENT Fictions were they, yet the
same
Involved a history of no doubtful sense,
History that proves by inward evidence
From what a precious source of truth it
came.
Ne'er could the boldest Eulogist have
dared   5
Such deeds to paint, such characters to
frame,
But for coeval sympathy prepared
To greet with instant faith their loftiest
claim.
None but a noble people could have loved
Flattery in Ancient Rome's pure-minded
style: 10
Not in like sort the Runic Scald was
moved;
He, nursed 'mid savage passions that
defile
Humanity, sang feats that well might call
For the blood-thirsty mead of Odin's
riotous Hall.

VI

PLEA FOR THE HISTORIAN

FORBEAR to deem the Chronicler unwise,
Ungentle, or untouched by seemly ruth,
Who, gathering up all that Time's en-
    vious tooth
Has spared of sound and grave realities,
Firmly rejects those dazzling flatteries,   5
Dear as they are to unsuspecting Youth,
That might have drawn down Clio from
    the skies
To vindicate the majesty of truth.
Such was her office while she walked with
    men,
A Muse, who, not unmindful of her Sire
All-ruling Jove, whate'er the theme might
    be   11
Revered her Mother, sage Mnemosyne,
And taught her faithful servants how the
    lyre
Should animate, but not mislead, the pen.[1]

VII

AT ROME

THEY—who have seen the noble Roman's
    scorn
Break forth at thought of laying down
    his head,
When the blank day is over, garreted
In his ancestral palace, where, from morn
To night, the desecrated floors are worn
By feet of purse-proud strangers; they—
    who have read   6
In one meek smile, beneath a peasant's
    shed,
How patiently the weight of wrong is
    borne;
They—who have heard some learned
    Patriot treat
Of freedom, with mind grasping the whole
    theme   10
From ancient Rome, downwards through
    that bright dream
Of Commonwealths, each city a starlike
    seat
Of rival glory; they—fallen Italy—
Nor must, nor will, nor can, despair of
    Thee!

VIII

NEAR ROME, IN SIGHT OF ST. PETER'S

LONG has the dew been dried on tree and
    lawn;
O'er man and beast a not unwelcome boon
Is shed, the languor of approaching noon;
To shady rest withdrawing or withdrawn
Mute are all creatures, as this couchant
    fawn,   5
Save insect-swarms that hum in air afloat,
Save that the Cock is crowing, a shrill
    note,

[1] Quem virum——lyra——
    ——sumes celebrare Clio?

Startling and shrill as that which roused
    the dawn.
—Heard in that hour, or when, as now,
    the nerve
Shrinks from the note as from a mis-
    timed thing,   10
Oft for a holy warning may it serve,
Charged with remembrance of *his* sudden
    sting,
His bitter tears, whose name the Papal
    Chair
And yon resplendent Church are proud
    to bear.

IX

AT ALBANO

DAYS passed—and Monte Calvo would
    not clear
His head from mist; and, as the wind
    sobbed through
Albano's dripping Ilex avenue,
My dull forebodings in a Peasant's ear
Found casual vent. She said, 'Be of good
    cheer;   5
Our yesterday's procession did not sue
In vain; the sky will change to sunny
    blue,
Thanks to our Lady's grace.' I smiled
    to hear,
But not in scorn:—the Matron's Faith
    may lack
The heavenly sanction needed to ensure
Fulfilment; but, we trust, her upward
    track   11
Stops not at this low point, nor wants
    the lure
Of flowers the Virgin without fear may
    own,
For by her Son's blest hand the seed was
    sown.

X

NEAR Anio's stream I spied a gentle Dove
Perched on an olive branch, and heard
    her cooing
'Mid new-born blossoms that soft airs
    were wooing,
While all things present told of joy and
    love.
But restless Fancy left that olive grove   5
To hail the exploratory Bird renewing
Hope for the few, who, at the world's
    undoing,
On the great flood were spared to live and
    move.
O bounteous Heaven! signs true as dove
    and bough
Brought to the ark are coming evermore,
Given though we seek them not, but,
    while we plough   11
This sea of life without a visible shore,
Do neither promise ask nor grace implore
In what alone is ours, the living Now.

XI

FROM THE ALBAN HILLS, LOOKING TOWARDS ROME

FORGIVE, illustrious Country! these deep
  sighs,
Heaved less for thy bright plains and hills
  bestrown
With monuments decayed or overthrown,
For all that tottering stands or prostrate
  lies,
Than for like scenes in moral vision
  shown,   5
Ruin perceived for keener sympathies;
Faith crushed, yet proud of weeds, her
  gaudy crown;
Virtues laid low, and mouldering energies.
Yet why prolong this mournful strain?—
  Fallen Power,
Thy fortunes, twice exalted, might pro-
  voke   10
Verse to glad notes prophetic of the hour
When thou, uprisen, shalt break thy
  double yoke,
And enter, with prompt aid from the Most
  High,
On the third stage of thy great destiny.

XII

NEAR THE LAKE OF THRASYMENE

WHEN here with Carthage Rome to con-
  flict came,
An earthquake, mingling with the battle's
  shock,
Checked not its rage; unfelt the ground
  did rock,
Sword dropped not, javelin kept its
  deadly aim.—
Now all is sun-bright peace. Of that day's
  shame,   5
Or glory, not a vestige seems to endure,
Save in this Rill that took from blood the
  name[1]
Which yet it bears, sweet Stream! as
  crystal pure.
So may all trace and sign of deeds aloof
From the true guidance of humanity,   10
Thro' Time and Nature's influence, purify
Their spirit; or, unless they for reproof
Or warning serve, thus let them all, on
  ground
That gave them being, vanish to a sound.

XIII

NEAR THE SAME LAKE

FOR action born, existing to be tried,
Powers manifold we have that intervene
To stir the heart that would too closely
  screen
Her peace from images to pain allied.
What wonder if at midnight, by the side
Of Sanguinetto or broad Thrasymene,   6

[1] Sanguinetto.

The clang of arms is heard, and phantoms
  glide,
Unhappy ghosts in troops by moonlight
  seen;
And singly thine, O vanquished Chief!
  whose corse,
Unburied, lay hid under heaps of slain:
But who is He—the Conqueror? Would
  he force   11
His way to Rome? Ah, no,—round hill
  and plain
Wandering, he haunts, at fancy's strong
  command,
This spot—his shadowy death-cup in his
  hand.

XIV

THE CUCKOO AT LAVERNA

MAY 25, 1837

[Composed June, July, 1837.—Published: vol. of
  1842.]

LIST—'twas the Cuckoo.—O with what
  delight
Heard I that voice! and catch it now,
  though faint,
Far off and faint, and melting into air,
Yet not to be mistaken. Hark again!
Those louder cries give notice that the
  Bird,   5
Although invisible as Echo's self,
Is wheeling hitherward. Thanks, happy
  Creature,
For this unthought-of greeting!
                        While allured
From vale to hill, from hill to vale led on,
We have pursued, through various lands,
  a long   10
And pleasant course; flower after flower
  has blown,
Embellishing the ground that gave them
  birth
With aspects novel to my sight; but still
Most fair, most welcome, when they
  drank the dew
In a sweet fellowship with kinds beloved,
For old remembrance sake. And oft—
  where Spring   16
Displayed her richest blossoms among
  files
Of orange-trees bedecked with glowing
  fruit
Ripe for the hand, or under a thick shade
Of Ilex, or, if better suited to the hour,
The lightsome Olive's twinkling canopy—
Oft have I heard the Nightingale and
  Thrush   22
Blending as in a common English grove
Their love-songs; but, where'er my feet
  might roam,
Whate'er assemblages of new and old,
Strange and familiar, might beguile the
  way,   26
A gratulation from that vagrant Voice
Was wanting;—and most happily till now.

For see, Laverna! mark the far-famed
Pile,
High on the brink of that precipitous
rock,   30
Implanted like a Fortress, as in truth
It is, a Christian Fortress, garrisoned
In faith and hope, and dutiful obedience,
By a few Monks, a stern society,
Dead to the world and scorning earth-
born joys.   35
Nay—though the hopes that drew, the
fears that drove,
St. Francis, far from Man's resort, to abide
Among these sterile heights of Apennine,
Bound him, nor, since he raised yon
House, have ceased   39
To bind his spiritual Progeny, with rules
Stringent as flesh can tolerate and live;
His milder Genius (thanks to the good God
That made us) over those severe restraints
Of mind, that dread heart-freezing disci-
pline,
Doth sometimes here predominate, and
works   45
By unsought means for gracious purposes;
For earth through heaven, for heaven, by
changeful earth,
Illustrated, and mutually endeared.

Rapt though He were above the power
of sense,
Familiarly, yet out of the cleansed heart
Of that once sinful Being overflowed 51
On sun, moon, stars, the nether elements,
And every shape of creature they sustain,
Divine affections; and with beast and bird
(Stilled from afar—such marvel story
tells—   55
By casual outbreak of his passionate
words,
And from their own pursuits in field or
grove
Drawn to his side by look or act of love
Humane, and virtue of his innocent life)
He wont to hold companionship so free,
So pure, so fraught with knowledge and
delight,   61
As to be likened in his Followers' minds
To that which our first Parents, ere the fall
From their high state darkened the Earth
with fear,
Held with all Kinds in Eden's blissful
bowers.   65

Then question not that, 'mid the austere
Band,
Who breathe the air he breathed, tread
where he trod,
Some true Partakers of his loving spirit
Do still survive, and, with those gentle
hearts
Consorted, Others, in the power, the
faith,   70
Of a baptized imagination, prompt

To catch from Nature's humblest monitors
Whate'er they bring of impulses sublime.

Thus sensitive must be the Monk,
though pale
With fasts, with vigils worn, depressed by
years,   75
Whom in a sunny glade I chanced to see,
Upon a pine-tree's storm-uprooted trunk,
Seated alone, with forehead sky-ward
raised,
Hands clasped above the crucifix he wore
Appended to his bosom, and lips closed
By the joint pressure of his musing mood
And habit of his vow. That ancient
Man—   82
Nor haply less the Brother whom I
marked,
As we approached the Convent gate, aloft
Looking far forth from his aerial cell, 85
A young Ascetic—Poet, Hero, Sage,
He might have been, Lover belike he was—
If they received into a conscious ear
The notes whose first faint greeting
startled me,
Whose sedulous iteration thrilled with
joy   90
My heart—may have been moved like me
to think,
Ah! not like me who walk in the world's
ways,
On the great Prophet, styled *the Voice
of One*
Crying amid the wilderness, and given,
Now that their snows must melt, their
herbs and flowers   95
Revive, their obstinate winter pass away,
That awful name to Thee, thee, simple
Cuckoo,
Wandering in solitude, and evermore
Foretelling and proclaiming, ere thou
leave   99
This thy last haunt beneath Italian skies
To carry thy glad tidings over heights
Still loftier, and to climes more near the
Pole.

Voice of the Desert, fare-thee-well;
sweet Bird!
If that substantial title please thee more,
Farewell!—but go thy way, no need hast
thou   105
Of a good wish sent after thee; from bower
To bower as green, from sky to sky as
clear,
Thee gentle breezes waft—or airs that
meet
Thy course and sport around thee softly
fan—
Till Night, descending upon hill and vale,
Grants to thy mission a brief term of
silence,   111
And folds thy pinions up in blest repose.

XV

AT THE CONVENT OF CAMALDOLI

GRIEVE for the Man who hither came
    bereft,
And seeking consolation from above;
Nor grieve the less that skill to him was left
To paint this picture of his lady-love:
Can she, a blessèd saint, the work ap-
    prove?   5
And O, good Brethren of the cowl, a thing
So fair, to which with peril he must cling,
Destroy in pity, or with care remove.
That bloom—those eyes—can they assist
    to bind
Thoughts that would stray from Heaven?
    The dream must cease   10
To be; by Faith, not sight, his soul must
    live;
Else will the enamoured Monk too surely
    find
How wide a space can part from inward
    peace
The most profound repose his cell can give.

XVI

CONTINUED

THE world forsaken, all its busy cares
And stirring interests shunned with
    desperate flight,
All trust abandoned in the healing might
Of virtuous action; all that courage dares,
Labour accomplishes, or patience bears—
Those helps rejected, they, whose minds
    perceive   6
How subtly works man's weakness, sighs
    may heave
For such a One beset with cloistral snares.
Father of Mercy! rectify his view,
If with his vows this object ill agree;   10
Shed over it Thy grace, and thus subdue
Imperious passion in a heart set free:—
That earthly love may to herself be true,
Give him a soul that cleaveth unto Thee.[1]

XVII

AT THE EREMITE OR UPPER CONVENT
OF CAMALDOLI

WHAT aim had they, the Pair of Monks,
    in size
Enormous, dragged, while side by side
    they sate,
By panting steers up to this convent gate?
How, with empurpled cheeks and pam-
    pered eyes,
Dare they confront the lean austerities   5
Of Brethren who, here fixed, on Jesu wait
In sackcloth, and God's anger deprecate
Through all that humbles flesh and mor-
    tifies?
Strange contrast!—verily the world of
    dreams,

[1] See Note, p. 709.

Where mingle, as for mockery combined,
Things in their very essences at strife,   11
Shows not a sight incongruous as the
    extremes
That everywhere, before the thoughtful
    mind,
Meet on the solid ground of waking life.[1]

XVIII

AT VALLOMBROSA

Thick as autumnal leaves that strew the brooks
In Vallombrosa, where Etrurian shades
High over-arch'd embower.[2]
                            PARADISE LOST.

'VALLOMBROSA—I longed in thy shadiest
    wood
To slumber, reclined on the moss-covered
    floor!'
Fond wish that was granted at last, and
    the Flood,
That lulled me asleep, bids me listen once
    more.
Its murmur how soft! as it falls down the
    steep,   5
Near that Cell—yon sequestered Retreat
    high in air—
Where our Milton was wont lonely vigils
    to keep
For converse with God, sought through
    study and prayer.

The Monks still repeat the tradition with
    pride,
And its truth who shall doubt? for his
    Spirit is here;   10
In the cloud-piercing rocks doth her
    grandeur abide,
In the pines pointing heavenward her
    beauty austere;
In the flower-besprent meadows his genius
    we trace
Turned to humbler delights, in which
    youth might confide,
That would yield him fit help while pre-
    figuring that Place   15
Where, if Sin had not entered, Love never
    had died.

When with life lengthened out came a
    desolate time,
And darkness and danger had compassed
    him round,
With a thought he would flee to these
    haunts of his prime,
And here once again a kind shelter be
    found.   20
And let me believe that when nightly the
    Muse
Did waft him to Sion, the glorified hill,
Here also, on some favoured height, he
    would choose
To wander, and drink inspiration at will.

[1] See Note, p. 709.
[2] See for the two *first lines*, 'Stanzas composed in
the Simplon Pass', p. 273.

Vallombrosa! of thee I first heard in the page 25
Of that holiest of Bards, and the name for my mind
Had a musical charm, which the winter of age
And the changes it brings had no power to unbind.
And now, ye Miltonian shades! under you
I repose, nor am I forced from sweet fancy to part, 30
While your leaves I behold and the brooks they will strew,
And the realised vision is clasped to my heart.

Even so, and unblamed, we rejoice as we may
In Forms that must perish, frail objects of sense;
Unblamed—if the Soul be intent on the day 35
When the Being of Beings shall summon her hence.
For he and he only with wisdom is blest
Who, gathering true pleasures wherever they grow,
Looks up in all places, for joy or for rest,
To the Fountain whence Time and Eternity flow. 40

XIX

AT FLORENCE

UNDER the shadow of a stately Pile,
The dome of Florence, pensive and alone,
Nor giving heed to aught that passed the while,
I stood, and gazed upon a marble stone,
The laurelled Dante's favourite seat. A throne, 5
In just esteem, it rivals; though no style
Be there of decoration to beguile
The mind, depressed by thought of greatness flown.
As a true man, who long had served the lyre,
I gazed with earnestness, and dared no more. 10
But in his breast the mighty Poet bore
A Patriot's heart, warm with undying fire.
Bold with the thought, in reverence I sate down,
And, for a moment, filled that empty Throne.

XX

BEFORE THE PICTURE OF THE BAPTIST, BY RAPHAEL, IN THE GALLERY AT FLORENCE

THE Baptist might have been ordained to cry
Forth from the towers of that huge Pile, wherein
His Father served Jehovah; but how win

Due audience, how for aught but scorn defy
The obstinate pride and wanton revelry
Of the Jerusalem below, her sin 6
And folly, if they with united din
Drown not at once mandate and prophecy?
Therefore the Voice spake from the Desert, thence
To Her, as to her opposite in peace, 10
Silence, and holiness, and innocence,
To Her and to all Lands its warning sent,
Crying with earnestness that might not cease,
'Make straight a highway for the Lord—repent!'

XXI

AT FLORENCE.—FROM MICHAEL ANGELO[1]

RAPT above earth by power of one fair face,
Hers in whose sway alone my heart delights,
I mingle with the blest on those pure heights
Where Man, yet mortal, rarely finds a place.
With Him who made the Work that Work accords 5
So well, that by its help and through His grace
I raise my thoughts, inform my deeds and words,
Clasping her beauty in my soul's embrace.
Thus, if from two fair eyes mine cannot turn,
I feel how in their presence doth abide 10
Light which to God is both the way and guide;
And, kindling at their lustre, if I burn,
My noble fire emits the joyful ray
That through the realms of glory shines for aye.

XXII

AT FLORENCE.—FROM MICHAEL ANGELO

ETERNAL Lord! eased of a cumbrous load,
And loosened from the world, I turn to Thee;
Shun, like a shattered bark, the storm, and flee
To Thy protection for a safe abode.
The crown of thorns, hands pierced upon the tree, 5

---

[1] This and the following Sonnet may possibly have been two of the fifteen Sonnets which in 1805 Wordsworth essayed to translate from the Italian of Michael Angelo. A rough draft of No. XXII is given by Mr. Dykes Campbell from a notebook belonging to S. T. Coleridge. See *Coleridge's Poetical Works*, p. 474. Mr. Campbell, unfortunately, does not give the date of the entry, or of the note-book.—ED.

The meek, benign, and lacerated face,
To a sincere repentance promise grace,
To the sad soul give hope of pardon free.
With justice mark not Thou, O Light divine,
My fault, nor hear it with Thy sacred ear;   10
Neither put forth that way Thy arm severe;
Wash with Thy blood my sins; thereto incline
More readily the more my years require
Help, and forgiveness speedy and entire.

XXIII

AMONG THE RUINS OF A CONVENT IN THE APENNINES

YE Trees! whose slender roots entwine
Altars that piety neglects;
Whose infant arms enclasp the shrine
Which no devotion now respects;
If not a straggler from the herd   5
Here ruminate, nor shrouded bird,
Chanting her low-voiced hymn, take pride
In aught that ye would grace or hide—
How sadly is your love misplaced,
Fair Trees, your bounty run to waste!   10

Ye, too, wild Flowers! that no one heeds,
And ye—full often spurned as weeds—
In beauty clothed, or breathing sweetness
From fractured arch and mouldering wall—
Do but more touchingly recall   15
Man's headstrong violence and Time's fleetness,
Making the precincts ye adorn
Appear to sight still more forlorn.

XXIV

IN LOMBARDY

SEE, where his difficult way that Old Man wins
Bent by a load of Mulberry leaves!—most hard
Appears *his* lot, to the small Worm's compared,
For whom his toil with early day begins.
Acknowledging no task-master, at will   5
(As if her labour and her ease were twins)
She seems to work, at pleasure to lie still;—
And softly sleeps within the thread she spins.
So fare they—the Man serving as her Slave.
Ere long their fates do each to each conform: 10
Both pass into new being,—but the Worm,
Transfigured, sinks into a hopeless grave;
His volant Spirit will, he trusts, ascend
To bliss unbounded, glory without end.

XXV

AFTER LEAVING ITALY

FAIR Land! Thee all men greet with joy; how few,
Whose souls take pride in freedom, virtue, fame,
Part from thee without pity dyed in shame:
I could not—while from Venice we withdrew,
Led on till an Alpine strait confined our view   5
Within its depths, and to the shore we came
Of Lago Morto, dreary sight and name,
Which o'er sad thoughts a sadder colouring threw.
Italia! on the surface of thy spirit,
(Too aptly emblemed by that torpid lake)
Shall a few partial breezes only creep?—   11
Be its depths quickened; what thou dost inherit
Of the world's hopes, dare to fulfil; awake,
Mother of Heroes, from thy death-like sleep!

XXVI

CONTINUED

As indignation mastered grief, my tongue
Spake bitter words; words that did ill agree
With those rich stores of Nature's imagery,
And divine Art, that fast to memory clung—   4
Thy gifts, magnificent Region, ever young
In the sun's eye, and in his sister's sight
How beautiful! how worthy to be sung
In strains of rapture, or subdued delight!
I feign not; witness that unwelcome shock
That followed the first sound of German speech,   10
Caught the far-winding barrier Alps among.
In that announcement, greeting seemed to mock
Parting; the casual word had power to reach
My heart, and filled that heart with conflict strong.

XXVII

COMPOSED AT RYDAL ON MAY MORNING, 1838

[Composed May 1, 1838.—Published: Sonnet-vol. of 1838; vol. of 1842.]

IF with old love of you, dear Hills! I share
New love of many a rival image brought
From far, forgive the wanderings of my thought:
Nor art thou wronged, sweet May! when I compare
Thy present birth-morn with thy last, so fair,   5

So rich to me in favours. For my lot
Then was, within the famed Egerian Grot
To sit and muse, fanned by its dewy air
Mingling with thy soft breath! That
    morning too, 9
Warblers I heard their joy unbosoming
Amid the sunny, shadowy, Colosseum;
Heard them, unchecked by aught of sad-
    dening hue,
For victories there won by flower-crowned
    Spring,
Chant in full choir their innocent Te
    Deum.

XXVIII

THE PILLAR OF TRAJAN

[Composed 1825.—Published 1827.[1]]

WHERE towers are crushed, and unfor-
    bidden weeds
O'er mutilated arches shed their seeds;
And temples, doomed to milder change,
    unfold
A new magnificence that vies with old;
Firm in its pristine majesty hath stood 5
A votive Column, spared by fire and
    flood:—
And, though the passions of man's fretful
    race
Have never ceased to eddy round its base,
Not injured more by touch of meddling
    hands 9
Than a lone obelisk, 'mid Nubian sands,
Or aught in Syrian deserts left to save
From death the memory of the good and
    brave.
Historic figures round the shaft embost
Ascend, with lineaments in air not lost:
Still as he turns, the charmed spectator
    sees 15
Group winding after group with dream-
    like ease;
Triumphs in sun-bright gratitude dis-
    played,
Or softly stealing into modest shade.
—So, pleased with purple clusters to en-
    twine
Some lofty elm-tree, mounts the daring
    vine; 20
The woodbine so, with spiral grace, and
    breathes
Wide-spreading odours from her flowery
    wreaths.

Borne by the Muse from rills in shep-
    herds' ears
Murmuring but one smooth story for all
    years,

[1] Included among *Poems of Sentiment and Reflection* in edd. 1827–43. First placed in this Series in
ed. 1845. The preceding Sonnet (xxvii) was included
amongst the *Miscellaneous Sonnets* in the volume of
1842, and first found its present place in ed. 1845.
    —ED.

I gladly commune with the mind and
    heart 25
Of him who thus survives by classic art,
His actions witness, venerate his mien,
And study Trajan as by Pliny seen;
Behold how fought the Chief whose con-
    quering sword
Stretched far as earth might own a single
    lord; 30
In the delight of moral prudence schooled,
How feelingly at home the Sovereign
    ruled;
Best of the good—in pagan faith allied
To more than Man, by virtue deified.

Memorial Pillar! 'mid the wrecks of
    Time 35
Preserve thy charge with confidence
    sublime—
The exultations, pomps, and cares of
    Rome,
Whence half the breathing world received
    its doom;
Things that recoil from language; that,
    if shown 39
By apter pencil, from the light had flown.
A Pontiff, Trajan *here* the Gods implores,
There greets an Embassy from Indian
    shores;
Lo! he harangues his cohorts—*there* the
    storm
Of battle meets him in authentic form!
Unharnessed, naked, troops of Moorish
    horse 45
Sweep to the charge; more high, the
    Dacian force,
To hoof and finger mailed;—yet, high or
    low,
None bleed, and none lie prostrate but
    the foe;
In every Roman, through all turns of
    fate,
Is Roman dignity inviolate; 50
Spirit in him pre-eminent, who guides,
Supports, adorns, and over all presides;
Distinguished only by inherent state
From honoured Instruments that round
    him wait;
Rise as he may, his grandeur scorns the
    test 55
Of outward symbol, nor will deign to rest
On aught by which another is deprest.
—Alas! that One thus disciplined could
    toil
To enslave whole nations on their native
    soil;
So emulous of Macedonian fame, 60
That, when his age was measured with his
    aim,
He drooped, 'mid else unclouded victories,
And turned his eagles back with deep-
    drawn sighs:
O weakness of the Great! O folly of the
    Wise!

Where now the haughty Empire that
  was spread   65
With such fond hope? her very speech is
  dead;
Yet glorious Art the power of Time
  defies,
And Trajan still, through various enterprise,

Mounts, in this fine illusion, toward the
  skies:
Still are we present with the imperial
  Chief,   70
Nor cease to gaze upon the bold Relief
Till Rome, to silent marble unconfined,
Becomes with all her years a vision of the
  Mind.

THE EGYPTIAN MAID

OR

THE ROMANCE OF THE WATER LILY

[Composed 1830.—Published 1835.]

For the names and persons in the following poem see the 'History of the renowned Prince Arthur and his Knights of the Round Table;' for the rest the Author is answerable; only it may be proper to add that the Lotus, with the bust of the Goddess appearing to rise out of the full-blown flower, was suggested by the beautiful work of ancient art, once included among the Townley Marbles, and now in the British Museum.

WHILE Merlin paced the Cornish sands,
Forth-looking toward the rocks of
  Scilly,
The pleased Enchanter was aware
Of a bright Ship that seemed to hang in
  air,
Yet was she work of mortal hands,   5
And took from men her name—THE
  WATER LILY.

Soft was the wind, that landward blew;
And, as the Moon, o'er some dark hill
  ascendant,
Grows from a little edge of light
To a full orb, this Pinnace bright   10
Became, as nearer to the coast she drew,
More glorious, with spread sail and
  streaming pendant.

Upon this wingèd Shape so fair
Sage Merlin gazed with admiration:
Her lineaments, thought he, surpass
Aught that was ever shown in magic
  glass;   16
Was ever built with patient care;
Or, at a touch, produced by happiest
  transformation.

Now, though a Mechanist, whose skill
Shames the degenerate grasp of modern
  science,   20
Grave Merlin (and belike the more
For practising occult and perilous lore)
Was subject to a freakish will
That sapped good thoughts, or scared
  them with defiance.

Provoked to envious spleen, he cast
An altered look upon the advancing
  Stranger   26
Whom he had hailed with joy, and cried,

'My Art shall help to tame her pride—'
Anon the breeze became a blast,
And the waves rose, and sky portended
  danger.   30

With thrilling word, and potent sign
Traced on the beach, his work the Sor-
  cerer urges;
The clouds in blacker clouds are lost,
Like spiteful Fiends that vanish, crossed
By Fiends of aspect more malign;   35
And the winds roused the Deep with
  fiercer scourges.

But worthy of the name she bore
Was this Sea-flower, this buoyant
  Galley;
Supreme in loveliness and grace
Of motion, whether in the embrace   40
Of trusty anchorage, or scudding o'er
The main flood roughened into hill and
  valley.

Behold, how wantonly she laves
Her sides, the Wizard's craft confound-
  ing;
Like something out of Ocean sprung
To be for ever fresh and young,   46
Breasts the sea-flashes, and huge waves
Top-gallant high, rebounding and re-
  bounding!

But Ocean under magic heaves,
And cannot spare the Thing he
  cherished: 50
Ah! what avails that she was fair,
Luminous, blithe, and debonair?
The storm has stripped her of her
  leaves;
The Lily floats no longer!—She hath
  perished.

Grieve for her, she deserves no less; 55
So like, yet so unlike, a living Creature!
No heart had she, no busy brain;
Though loved, she could not love again;
Though pitied, *feel* her own distress;
Nor aught that troubles us, the fools of
Nature. 60

Yet is there cause for gushing tears;
So richly was this Galley laden,
A fairer than herself she bore,
And, in her struggles, cast ashore;
A lovely One, who nothing hears 65
Of wind or wave—a meek and guileless
Maiden.

Into a cave had Merlin fled
From mischief, caused by spells himself
had muttered;
And while, repentant all too late,
In moody posture there he sate, 70
He heard a voice, and saw, with half-
raised head,
A Visitant by whom these words were
uttered:—

'On Christian service this frail Bark
Sailed' (hear me, Merlin!) 'under high
protection,
Though on her prow a sign of heathen
power 75
Was carved—a Goddess with a Lily
flower,
The old Egyptian's emblematic mark
Of joy immortal and of pure affection.

'Her course was for the British strand;
Her freight, it was a Damsel peerless;
God reigns above, and Spirits strong
May gather to avenge this wrong 82
Done to the Princess, and her Land
Which she in duty left, sad but not cheer-
less.

'And to Caerleon's loftiest tower 85
Soon will the Knights of Arthur's Table
A cry of lamentation send;
And all will weep who there attend,
To grace that Stranger's bridal hour,
For whom the sea was made unnavigable.

'Shame! should a Child of royal line
Die through the blindness of thy
malice?' 92
Thus to the Necromancer spake
Nina, the Lady of the Lake,
A gentle Sorceress, and benign, 95
Who ne'er embittered any good man's
chalice.

'What boots,' continued she, 'to
mourn?
To expiate thy sin endeavour: 98
From the bleak isle where she is laid,
Fetched by our art, the Egyptian Maid
May yet to Arthur's court be borne
Cold as she is, ere life be fled for ever.

'My pearly Boat, a shining Light, 103
That brought me down that sunless river,
Will bear me on from wave to wave,
And back with her to this sea-cave;—
Then Merlin! for a rapid flight
Through air, to thee my Charge will I
deliver.

'The very swiftest of thy cars 109
Must, when my part is done, be ready;
Meanwhile, for further guidance, look
Into thy own prophetic book;
And, if that fail, consult the Stars
To learn thy course; farewell! be prompt
and steady.'

This scarcely spoken, she again 115
Was seated in her gleaming shallop,
That, o'er the yet-distempered Deep,
Pursued its way with bird-like sweep,
Or like a steed, without a rein,
Urged o'er the wilderness in sportive
gallop. 120

Soon did the gentle Nina reach
That Isle without a house or haven;
Landing, she found not what she
sought,
Nor saw of wreck or ruin aught 124
But a carved Lotus cast upon the beach
By the fierce waves, a flower in marble
graven.

Sad relique, but how fair the while!
For gently each from each retreating
With backward curve, the leaves re-
vealed 129
The bosom half, and half concealed,
Of a Divinity, that seemed to smile
On Nina, as she passed, with hopeful
greeting.

No quest was hers of vague desire,
Of tortured hope and purpose shaken!
Following the margin of a bay, 135
She spied the lonely Cast-away,
Unmarred, unstripped of her attire,
But with closed eyes,—of breath and
bloom forsaken.

Then Nina, stooping down, embraced,
With tenderness and mild emotion, 140
The Damsel, in that trance embound;
And, while she raised her from the
ground,
And in the pearly shallop placed,
Sleep fell upon the air, and stilled the ocean.

The turmoil hushed, celestial springs
Of music opened, and there came a
blending 146
Of fragrance, underived from earth,
With gleams that owed not to the sun
their birth,
And that soft rustling of invisible wings
Which Angels make, on works of love
descending. 150

And Nina heard a sweeter voice
Than if the Goddess of the flower had
    spoken:
'Thou hast achieved, fair Dame! what
    none
Less pure in spirit could have done;
Go, in thy enterprise rejoice!   155
Air, earth, sea, sky, and heaven, success
    betoken.'

So cheered, she left that Island bleak,
A bare rock of the Scilly cluster;
And, as they traversed the smooth brine,
The self-illumined Brigantine   160
Shed, on the Slumberer's cold wan cheek
And pallid brow, a melancholy lustre.

Fleet was their course, and when they
    came
To the dim cavern, whence the river
Issued into the salt-sea flood,   165
Merlin, as fixed in thought he stood,
Was thus accosted by the Dame:
'Behold to thee my Charge I now deliver!

'But where attends thy chariot—
    where?'—   169
Quoth Merlin, 'Even as I was bidden,
So have I done; as trusty as thy barge
My vehicle shall prove—O precious
    Charge!
If this be sleep, how soft! if death, how
    fair!
Much have my books disclosed, but the
    end is hidden.'

He spake; and gliding into view   175
Forth from the grotto's dimmest
    chamber
Came two mute Swans, whose plumes
    of dusky white
Changed, as the pair approached the
    light,
Drawing an ebon car, their hue
(Like clouds of sunset) into lucid amber.

Once more did gentle Nina lift   181
The Princess, passive to all changes:
The car received her:—then up-went
Into the ethereal element
The Birds with progress smooth and
    swift   185
As thought, when through bright regions
    memory ranges.

Sage Merlin, at the Slumberer's side,
Instructs the Swans their way to mea-
    sure;
And soon Caerleon's towers appeared,
And notes of minstrelsy were heard
From rich pavilions spreading wide,
For some high day of long-expected plea-
    sure.   192

Awe-stricken stood both Knights and
    Dames
Ere on firm ground the car alighted;
Eftsoons astonishment was past,   195

For in that face they saw the last
Last lingering look of clay, that tames
All pride; by which all happiness is
    blighted.

Said Merlin: 'Mighty King, fair Lords,
Away with feast and tilt and tourney!
Ye saw, throughout this royal House,
Ye heard, a rocking marvellous   202
Of turrets, and a clash of swords
Self-shaken, as I closed my airy journey.

Lo! by a destiny well known   205
To mortals, joy is turned to sorrow;
This is the wished-for Bride, the Maid
Of Egypt, from a rock conveyed
Where she by shipwreck had been
    thrown;
Ill sight! but grief may vanish ere the
    morrow.'   210

'Though vast thy power, thy words are
    weak,'
Exclaimed the King, 'a mockery hate-
    ful;
Dutiful Child, her lot how hard!
Is this her piety's reward?
Those watery locks, that bloodless
    cheek!   215
O winds without remorse! O shore un-
    grateful!

'Rich robes are fretted by the moth;
Towers, temples, fall by stroke of
    thunder;
Will that, or deeper thoughts, abate
A Father's sorrow for her fate?   220
He will repent him of his troth;
His brain will burn, his stout heart split
    asunder.

'Alas! and I have caused this woe;
For, when my prowess from invading
    Neighbours   224
Had freed his Realm, he plighted word
That he would turn to Christ our Lord,
And his dear Daughter on a Knight
    bestow
Whom I should choose for love and
    matchless labours.

'Her birth was heathen; but a fence
Of holy Angels round her hovered: 230
A Lady added to my court
So fair, of such divine report
And worship, seemed a recompense
For fifty kingdoms by my sword re-
    covered.

'Ask not for whom, O Champions true!
She was reserved by me her life's be-
    trayer;   236
She who was meant to be a bride
Is now a corse: then put aside
Vain thoughts, and speed ye, with
    observance due
Of Christian rites, in Christian ground to
    lay her.'   240

'The tomb,' said Merlin, 'may not
  close
Upon her yet, earth hide her beauty;
Not froward to thy sovereign will
Esteem me, Liege! if I, whose skill
Wafted her hither, interpose   245
To check this pious haste of erring duty.

'My books command me to lay bare
The secret thou art bent on keeping:
Here must a high attest be given,
What Bridegroom was for her ordained
  by Heaven: 250
And in my glass significants there are
Of things that may to gladness turn this
  weeping.

'For this, approaching, One by One,
Thy Knights must touch the cold hand
  of the Virgin;
So, for the favoured One, the Flower
  may bloom   255
Once more: but, if unchangeable her
  doom,
If life departed be for ever gone,
Some blest assurance, from this cloud
  emerging,

'May teach him to bewail his loss;
Not with a grief that, like a vapour,
  rises   260
And melts; but grief devout that shall
  endure,
And a perpetual growth secure
Of purposes which no false thought
  shall cross,
A harvest of high hopes and noble enter-
  prises.'

'So be it,' said the King;—'anon,   265
Here, where the Princess lies, begin the
  trial;
Knights each in order as ye stand
Step forth.'—To touch the pallid hand
Sir Agravaine advanced; no sign he
  won
From Heaven or earth;—Sir Kaye had
  like denial.   270

Abashed, Sir Dinas turned away;
Even for Sir Percival was no disclo-
  sure;
Though he, devoutest of all Champions,
  ere
He reached that ebon car, the bier
Whereon diffused like snow the Damsel
  lay,   275
Full thrice had crossed himself in meek
  composure.

Imagine (but ye Saints! who can?)
How in still air the balance trembled—
The wishes, peradventure the despites
That overcame some not ungenerous
  Knights;   280

And all the thoughts that lengthened
  out a span
Of time to Lords and Ladies thus assembled.

What patient confidence was here!
And there how many bosoms panted!
While drawing toward the car Sir
  Gawaine, mailed   285
For tournament, his beaver vailed,
And softly touched; but, to his princely
  cheer
And high expectancy, no sign was
  granted.

Next, disencumbered of his harp,
Sir Tristram, dear to thousands as a
  brother,   290
Came to the proof, nor grieved that
  there ensued
No change;—the fair Izonda he had
  wooed
With love too true, a love with pangs
  too sharp,
From hope too distant, not to dread
  another.

Not so Sir Launcelot;—from Heaven's
  grace   295
A sign he craved, tired slave of vain
  contrition;
The royal Guinever looked passing glad
When his touch failed.—Next came
  Sir Galahad;
He paused, and stood entranced by that
  still face
Whose features he had seen in noontide
  vision.   300

For late, as near a murmuring stream
He rested 'mid an arbour green and
  shady,
Nina, the good Enchantress, shed
A light around his mossy bed;
And, at her call, a waking dream   305
Prefigured to his sense the Egyptian Lady.

Now, while his bright-haired front he
  bowed,
And stood, far-kenned by mantle
  furred with ermine,
As o'er the insensate Body hung
The enrapt, the beautiful, the young,
Belief sank deep into the crowd   311
That he the solemn issue would deter-
  mine.

Nor deem it strange; the Youth had
  worn
That very mantle on a day of glory,
The day when he achieved that match-
  less feat,   315
The marvel of the PERILOUS SEAT,
Which whosoe'er approached of
  strength was shorn,
Though King or Knight the most re-
  nowned in story.

He touched with hesitating hand—
And lo! those Birds, far-famed through
  Love's dominions,   320
The Swans, in triumph clap their
  wings;
And their necks play, involved in rings,
Like sinless snakes in Eden's happy
  land;—
'Mine is she,' cried the Knight;—again
  they clapped their pinions.

'Mine was she—mine she is, though
  dead,   325
And to her name my soul shall cleave
  in sorrow;'
Whereat a tender twilight streak
Of colour dawned upon the Damsel's
  cheek;
And her lips, quickening with uncertain
  red,
Seemed from each other a faint warmth
  to borrow.   330

Deep was the awe, the rapture high,
Of love emboldened, hope with dread
  entwining,
When, to the mouth, relenting Death
Allowed a soft and flower-like breath,
Precursor to a timid sigh,   335
To lifted eyelids, and a doubtful shining.

In silence did King Arthur gaze
Upon the signs that pass away or tarry;
In silence watched the gentle strife
Of Nature leading back to life;   340
Then eased his soul at length by praise
Of God, and Heaven's pure Queen—the
  blissful Mary.

Then said he, 'Take her to thy heart,
Sir Galahad! a treasure, that God
  giveth,
Bound by indissoluble ties to thee 345
Through mortal change and immortality;
Be happy and unenvied, thou who art
A goodly Knight that hath no peer that
  liveth!'

Not long the Nuptials were delayed;
And sage tradition still rehearses   350
The pomp, the glory of that hour
When toward the altar from her bower
King Arthur led the Egyptian Maid,
And Angels carolled these far-echoed
  verses;—

Who shrinks not from alliance   355
Of evil with good Powers
To God proclaims defiance,
And mocks whom he adores.

A Ship to Christ devoted
From the Land of Nile did go;   360
Alas! the bright Ship floated,
An Idol at her prow.

By magic domination,
The Heaven-permitted vent
Of purblind mortal passion,   365
Was wrought her punishment.

The Flower, the Form within it,
What served they in her need?
Her port she could not win it,
Nor from mishap be freed.   370

The tempest overcame her,
And she was seen no more;
But gently, gently blame her—
She cast a Pearl ashore.

The Maid to Jesu hearkened,   375
And kept to Him her faith,
Till sense in death was darkened,
Or sleep akin to death.

But Angels round her pillow
Kept watch, a viewless band;   380
And, billow favouring billow,
She reached the destined strand.

Blest Pair! whate'er befall you,
Your faith in Him approve
Who from frail earth can call you
To bowers of endless love!   386

THE RIVER DUDDON

A SERIES OF SONNETS[1]

[Composed between 1806-1820.—Published 1820.]

The River Duddon rises upon Wrynose Fell, on the confines of Westmoreland, Cumberland, and Lancashire; and, having served as a boundary to the two last Counties for the space of about twenty-five miles, enters the Irish Sea, between the Isle of Walney and the Lordship of Millum.

TO THE REV. DR. WORDSWORTH

(WITH THE SONNETS TO THE RIVER DUDDON, AND OTHER POEMS IN THIS COLLECTION, 1820).

[Composed Christmastide, 1819.—Published 1820.]

The Minstrels played their Christmas tune
To-night beneath my cottage-eaves;
While, smitten by a lofty moon,
The encircling laurels, thick with leaves,
Gave back a rich and dazzling sheen, 5
That overpowered their natural green.

Through hill and valley every breeze
Had sunk to rest with folded wings:
Keen was the air, but could not freeze,
Nor check, the music of the strings; 10
So stout and hardy were the band
That scraped the chords with strenuous hand!

And who but listened?—till was paid
Respect to every Inmate's claim:
The greeting given, the music played, 15
In honour of each household name,
Duly pronounced with lusty call,
And 'Merry Christmas' wished to all!

O Brother! I revere the choice
That took thee from thy native hills; 20
And it is given thee to rejoice:
Though public care full often tills
(Heaven only witness of the toil)
A barren and ungrateful soil.

Yet, would that Thou, with me and mine, 25
Hadst heard this never-failing rite;
And seen on other faces shine
A true revival of the light
Which Nature and these rustic Powers,
In simple childhood, spread through ours! 30

For pleasure hath not ceased to wait
On these expected annual rounds;
Whether the rich man's sumptuous gate
Call forth the unelaborate sounds,
Or they are offered at the door 35
That guards the lowliest of the poor.

How touching, when, at midnight, sweep
Snow-muffled winds, and all is dark,
To hear—and sink again to sleep!
Or, at an earlier call, to mark, 40
By blazing fire, the still suspense
Of self-complacent innocence;

The mutual nod,—the grave disguise
Of hearts with gladness brimming o'er;
And some unbidden tears that rise 45
For names once heard, and heard no more;
Tears brightened by the serenade
For infant in the cradle laid.

Ah! not for emerald fields alone,
With ambient streams more pure and bright 50
Than fabled Cytherea's zone
Glittering before the Thunderer's sight,
Is to my heart of hearts endeared
The ground where we were born and reared!

Hail, ancient Manners! sure defence, 55
Where they survive, of wholesome laws;
Remnants of love whose modest sense
Thus into narrow room withdraws;
Hail, Usages of pristine mould,
And ye that guard them, Mountains old! 60

Bear with me, Brother! quench the thought
That slights this passion, or condemns;
If thee fond Fancy ever brought
From the proud margin of the Thames,
And Lambeth's venerable towers, 65
To humbler streams, and greener bowers.

Yes, they can make, who fail to find,
Short leisure even in busiest days;
Moments, to cast a look behind,
And profit by those kindly rays 70
That through the clouds do sometimes steal,
And all the far-off past reveal.

Hence, while the imperial City's din
Beats frequent on thy satiate ear,
A pleased attention I may win 75
To agitations less severe,
That neither overwhelm nor cloy,
But fill the hollow vale with joy!

I

NOT envying Latian shades—if yet they throw
A grateful coolness round that crystal Spring,
Bandusia, prattling as when long ago
The Sabine Bard was moved her praise to sing;
Careless of flowers that in perennial blow
Round the moist marge of Persian fountains cling; 6

[1] These Sonnets (No. XXVII excepted) appeared early in 1820, in a volume entitled *The River Duddon, A Series of Sonnets: Vaudracour and Julia: and other Poems. To which is annexed A Topographical Description of the Country of the Lakes, in the North of England.* They were written at various intervals between 1806 and 1820. Sonnet No. XIV (*O Mountain Stream!*) was written before April 1807, when it first appeared amongst the *Miscellaneous Sonnets* of *Poems in Two Volumes*; and Sonnet No. XXVII (*Fallen, and diffused*) was published in 1819, along with *The Waggoner*; included, in the collective (4 vol.) ed. of 1820, amongst the *Miscellaneous Sonnets*; and, in ed. 1827, transferred to its present place in this Series.—ED.

Heedless of Alpine torrents thundering
Through ice-built arches radiant as
    heaven's bow;
I seek the birthplace of a native Stream.—
All hail, ye mountains! hail, thou morn-
    ing light!   10
Better to breathe at large on this clear
    height
Than toil in needless sleep from dream to
    dream:
Pure flow the verse, pure, vigorous, free,
    and bright,
For Duddon, long-loved Duddon, is my
    theme!

II

CHILD of the clouds! remote from every
    taint
Of sordid industry thy lot is cast;
Thine are the honours of the lofty waste;
Not seldom, when with heat the valleys
    faint,
Thy handmaid Frost with spangled tissue
    quaint   5
Thy cradle decks;—to chant thy birth,
    thou hast
No meaner Poet than the whistling Blast,
And Desolation is thy Patron-saint!
She guards thee, ruthless Power! who
    would not spare
Those mighty forests, once the bison's
    screen,   10
Where stalked the huge deer to his shaggy
    lair[1]
Through paths and alleys roofed with
    darkest green;
Thousands of years before the silent air
Was pierced by whizzing shaft of hunter
    keen!

III

How shall I paint thee?—Be this naked
    stone
My seat, while I give way to such intent;
Pleased could my verse, a speaking monu-
    ment,
Make to the eyes of men thy features
    known.   4
But as of all those tripping lambs not one
Outruns his fellows, so hath Nature lent
To thy beginning nought that doth pre-
    sent
Peculiar ground for hope to build upon.
To dignify the spot that gives thee birth
No sign of hoar Antiquity's esteem   10
Appears, and none of modern Fortune's
    care;
Yet thou thyself hast round thee shed
    a gleam
Of brilliant moss, instinct with freshness
    rare;
Prompt offering to thy Foster-mother,
    Earth!

[1] The deer alluded to is the Leigh, a gigantic
species long since extinct.

IV

TAKE, cradled Nursling of the mountain,
    take
This parting glance, no negligent adieu!
A Protean change seems wrought while I
    pursue
The curves, a loosely-scattered chain doth
    make;
Or rather thou appear'st a glistering snake,
Silent, and to the gazer's eye untrue,   6
Thridding with sinuous lapse the rushes,
    through
Dwarf willows gliding, and by ferny brake.
Starts from a dizzy steep the undaunted
    Rill
Robed instantly in garb of snow-white
    foam;   10
And laughing dares the Adventurer, who
    hath clomb
So high, a rival purpose to fulfil;
Else let the dastard backward wend, and
    roam,
Seeking less bold achievement, where he
    will!

V

SOLE listener, Duddon! to the breeze that
    played
With thy clear voice, I caught the fitful
    sound
Wafted o'er sullen moss and craggy
    mound—
Unfruitful solitudes, that seemed to up-
    braid
The sun in heaven!—but now, to form a
    shade   5
For Thee, green alders have together
    wound
Their foliage; ashes flung their arms
    around;
And birch-trees risen in silver colonnade.
And thou hast also tempted here to rise,
'Mid sheltering pines, this Cottage rude
    and grey;   10
Whose ruddy children, by the mother's
    eyes
Carelessly watched, sport through the
    summer day,
Thy pleased associates:—light as endless
    May
On infant bosoms lonely Nature lies.

VI

FLOWERS

ERE yet our course was graced with social
    trees
It lacked not old remains of hawthorn
    bowers,
Where small birds warbled to their para-
    mours;
And, earlier still, was heard the hum of
    bees;
I saw them ply their harmless robberies,

THE RIVER DUDDON

And caught the fragrance which the sundry flowers, 6
Fed by the stream with soft perpetual showers,
Plenteously yielded to the vagrant breeze.
There bloomed the strawberry of the wilderness;
The trembling eyebright showed her sapphire blue, 10
The thyme her purple, like the blush of Even;
And if the breath of some to no caress
Invited, forth they peeped so fair to view,
All kinds alike seemed favourites of Heaven.

VII

'CHANGE me, some God, into that breathing rose!'
The love-sick Stripling fancifully sighs,
The envied flower beholding, as it lies
On Laura's breast, in exquisite repose;
Or he would pass into her bird, that throws 5
The darts of song from out its wiry cage;
Enraptured,—could he for himself engage
The thousandth part of what the Nymph bestows;
And what the little careless innocent
Ungraciously receives. Too daring choice!
There are whose calmer mind it would content 11
To be an unculled floweret of the glen,
Fearless of plough and scythe; or darkling wren
That tunes on Duddon's banks her slender voice.

VIII

WHAT aspect bore the Man who roved or fled,
First of his tribe, to this dark dell—who first
In this pellucid Current slaked his thirst?
What hopes came with him? what designs were spread
Along his path? His unprotected bed 5
What dreams encompassed? Was the intruder nursed
In hideous usages, and rites accursed,
That thinned the living and disturbed the dead?
No voice replies;—both air and earth are mute;
And Thou, blue Streamlet, murmuring yield'st no more 10
Than a soft record, that, whatever fruit
Of ignorance thou might'st witness heretofore,
Thy function was to heal and to restore,
To soothe and cleanse, not madden and pollute!

IX
THE STEPPING-STONES

THE struggling Rill insensibly is grown
Into a Brook of loud and stately march,
Crossed ever and anon by plank or arch;
And, for like use, lo! what might seem a zone
Chosen for ornament—stone matched with stone 5
In studied symmetry, with interspace
For the clear waters to pursue their race
Without restraint. How swiftly have they flown,
Succeeding—still succeeding! Here the Child
Puts, when the high-swoln Flood runs fierce and wild, 10
His budding courage to the proof; and here
Declining Manhood learns to note the sly
And sure encroachments of infirmity,
Thinking how fast time runs, life's end how near!

X
THE SAME SUBJECT

NOT so that Pair whose youthful spirits dance
With prompt emotion, urging them to pass;
A sweet confusion checks the Shepherd-lass;
Blushing she eyes the dizzy flood askance;
To stop ashamed—too timid to advance;
She ventures once again—another pause!
His outstretched hand He tauntingly withdraws— 7
She sues for help with piteous utterance!
Chidden she chides again; the thrilling touch
Both feel, when he renews the wished-for aid: 10
Ah! if their fluttering hearts should stir too much,
Should beat too strongly, both may be betrayed.
The frolic Loves, who, from yon high rock, see
The struggle, clap their wings for victory!

XI
THE FAERY CHASM

No fiction was it of the antique age:
A sky-blue stone, within this sunless cleft,
Is of the very footmarks unbereft
Which tiny Elves impressed;—on that smooth stage
Dancing with all their brilliant equipage
In secret revels—haply after theft 6
Of some sweet Babe—Flower stolen, and coarse Weed left
For the distracted Mother to assuage

Her grief with, as she might!—But, where,
oh! where
Is traceable a vestige of the notes   10
That ruled those dances wild in charac-
ter?—
Deep underground? Or in the upper air,
On the shrill wind of midnight? or where
floats
O'er twilight fields the autumnal gossa-
mer?

XII

HINTS FOR THE FANCY

ON, loitering Muse—the swift Stream
chides us—on!
Albeit his deep-worn channel doth im-
mure
Objects immense portrayed in miniature,
Wild shapes for many a strange compari-
son!
Niagaras, Alpine passes, and anon   5
Abodes of Naiads, calm abysses pure,
Bright liquid mansions, fashioned to en-
dure
When the broad oak drops, a leafless
skeleton,
And the solidities of mortal pride,
Palace and tower, are crumbled into
dust!—   10
The Bard who walks with Duddon for his
guide,
Shall find such toys of fancy thickly set:
Turn from the sight, enamoured Muse—
we must;
And, if thou canst, leave them without
regret!

XIII

OPEN PROSPECT

HAIL to the fields—with Dwellings
sprinkled o'er,
And one small hamlet, under a green hill
Clustering, with barn and byre, and
spouting mill!
A glance suffices;—should we wish for
more,
Gay June would scorn us. But when
bleak winds roar   5
Through the stiff lance-like shoots of
pollard ash,
Dread swell of sound! loud as the gusts
that lash
The matted forests of Ontario's shore
By wasteful steel unsmitten—then would I
Turn into port; and, reckless of the
gale,   10
Reckless of angry Duddon sweeping by,
While the warm hearth exalts the mantling
ale,
Laugh with the generous household
heartily
At all the merry pranks of Donnerdale!

XIV

[Comp. before April, 1807 (1806?).—Pub. 1807.[1]]

O MOUNTAIN Stream! the Shepherd and
his Cot
Are privileged Inmates of deep solitude;
Nor would the nicest Anchorite exclude
A field or two of brighter green, or plot
Of tillage-ground, that seemeth like a
spot   5
Of stationary sunshine:—thou hast viewed
These only, Duddon! with their paths
renewed
By fits and starts, yet this contents thee
not.
Thee hath some awful Spirit impelled to
leave,
Utterly to desert, the haunts of men,   10
Though simple thy companions were and
few;
And through this wilderness a passage
cleave
Attended but by thy own voice, save when
The clouds and fowls of the air thy way
pursue!

XV

FROM this deep chasm, where quivering
sunbeams play
Upon its loftiest crags, mine eyes behold
A gloomy NICHE, capacious, blank, and
cold;
A concave free from shrubs and mosses
grey;
In semblance fresh, as if, with dire
affray,   5
Some Statue, placed amid these regions old
For tutelary service, thence had rolled,
Startling the flight of timid Yesterday!
Was it by mortals sculptured?—weary
slaves
Of slow endeavour! or abruptly cast   10
Into rude shape by fire, with roaring blast
Tempestuously let loose from central
caves?
Or fashioned by the turbulence of waves,
Then, when o'er highest hills the Deluge
passed?

XVI

AMERICAN TRADITION

SUCH fruitless questions may not long
beguile
Or plague the fancy 'mid the sculptured
shows
Conspicuous yet where Oroonoko flows;
There would the Indian answer with a
smile
Aimed at the White Man's ignorance the
while,   5
Of the GREAT WATERS telling how they
rose,
Covered the plains, and, wandering where
they chose,

[1] See Editor's note, p. 296.

THE RIVER DUDDON

Mounted through every intricate defile,
Triumphant.—Inundation wide and deep,
O'er which his Fathers urged, to ridge
    and steep   10
Else unapproachable, their buoyant way;
And carved, on mural cliff's undreaded
    side,
Sun, moon, and stars, and beast of chase
    or prey;
Whate'er they sought, shunned, loved, or
    deified![1]

XVII
RETURN

A DARK plume fetch me from yon blasted
    yew,
Perched on whose top the Danish Raven
    croaks;
Aloft, the imperial Bird of Rome invokes
Departed ages, shedding where he flew
Loose fragments of wild wailing, that
    bestrew   5
The clouds and thrill the chambers of the
    rocks;
And into silence hush the timorous flocks,
That, calmly couching while the nightly dew
Moistened each fleece, beneath the twink-
    ling stars
Slept amid that lone Camp on Hardknot's
    height,[2]   10
Whose Guardians bent the knee to Jove
    and Mars;
Or near that mystic Round of Druid frame
Tardily sinking by its proper weight
Deep into patient Earth, from whose
    smooth breast it came!

XVIII
SEATHWAITE CHAPEL

SACRED Religion! 'mother of form and
    fear,'
Dread arbitress of mutable respect,
New rites ordaining when the old are
    wrecked,
Or cease to please the fickle worshipper;
Mother of Love! (that name best suits
    thee here)   5
Mother of Love! for this deep vale,
    protect
Truth's holy lamp, pure source of bright
    effect,
Gifted to purge the vapoury atmosphere
That seeks to stifle it;—as in those days
When this low Pile[3] a Gospel Teacher
    knew,   10
Whose good works formed an endless
    retinue:
A Pastor such as Chaucer's verse portrays;
Such as the heaven-taught skill of Herbert
    drew;
And tender Goldsmith crowned with
    deathless praise!

[1] See Humboldt's Personal Narrative.
[2] See Note, p. 710.   [3] See Note, p. 711.

XIX
TRIBUTARY STREAM

MY frame hath often trembled with de-
    light
When hope presented some far-distant
    good,
That seemed from heaven descending,
    like the flood
Of yon pure waters, from their aery
    height   4
Hurrying, with lordly Duddon to unite;
Who, 'mid a world of images imprest
On the calm depth of his transparent
    breast,
Appears to cherish most that Torrent
    white,   8
The fairest, softest, liveliest of them all!
And seldom hath ear listened to a tune
More lulling than the busy hum of Noon,
Swoln by that voice—whose murmur
    musical
Announces to the thirsty fields a boon
Dewy and fresh, till showers again shall
    fall.

XX
THE PLAIN OF DONNERDALE

THE old inventive Poets, had they seen,
Or rather felt, the entrancement that
    detains
Thy waters, Duddon! 'mid these flowery
    plains;
The still repose, the liquid lapse serene,
Transferred to bowers imperishably
    green,   5
Had beautified Elysium! But these
    chains
Will soon be broken;—a rough course
    remains,
Rough as the past; where Thou, of placid
    mien,
Innocuous as a firstling of the flock,
And countenanced like a soft cerulean
    sky,   10
Shalt change thy temper; and, with many
    a shock
Given and received in mutual jeopardy,
Dance, like a Bacchanal, from rock to rock,
Tossing her frantic thyrsus wide and
    high!

XXI

WHENCE that low voice?—A whisper
    from the heart,
That told of days long past, when here
    I roved
With friends and kindred tenderly be-
    loved;
Some who had early mandates to depart,
Yet are allowed to steal my path athwart
By Duddon's side; once more do we
    unite,   6
Once more beneath the kind Earth's
    tranquil light;

And smothered joys into new being start.
From her unworthy seat, the cloudy stall
Of Time, breaks forth triumphant Me-
    mory;   10
Her glistening tresses bound, yet light
    and free
As golden locks of birch, that rise and fall
On gales that breathe too gently to recall
Aught of the fading year's inclemency!

XXII

TRADITION

A LOVE-LORN Maid, at some far-distant
    time,
Came to this hidden pool, whose depths
    surpass
In crystal clearness Dian's looking-glass;
And, gazing, saw that Rose, which from
    the prime
Derives its name, reflected as the chime   5
Of echo doth reverberate some sweet
    sound:
The starry treasure from the blue pro-
    found
She longed to ravish;—shall she plunge,
    or climb
The humid precipice, and seize the guest
Of April, smiling high in upper air?   10
Desperate alternative! what fiend could
    dare
To prompt the thought?—Upon the steep
    rock's breast
The lonely Primrose yet renews its bloom,
Untouched memento of her hapless
    doom!

XXIII

SHEEP-WASHING

SAD thoughts, avaunt!—partake we their
    blithe cheer
Who gathered in betimes the unshorn
    flock
To wash the fleece, where haply bands of
    rock,
Checking the stream, make a pool smooth
    and clear
As this we look on. Distant Mountains
    hear,   5
Hear and repeat, the turmoil that unites
Clamour of boys with innocent despites
Of barking dogs, and bleatings from
    strange fear.
And what if Duddon's spotless flood
    receive
Unwelcome mixtures as the uncouth
    noise   10
Thickens, the pastoral River will forgive
Such wrong; nor need *we* blame the
    licensed joys,
Though false to Nature's quiet equipoise:
Frank are the sports, the stains are
    fugitive.

XXIV

THE RESTING-PLACE

MID-NOON is past;—upon the sultry mead
No zephyr breathes, no cloud its shadow
    throws:
If we advance unstrengthened by repose,
Farewell the solace of the vagrant reed!
This Nook—with woodbine hung and
    straggling weed,   5
Tempting recess as ever pilgrim chose,
Half grot, half arbour—proffers to enclose
Body and mind, from molestation freed,
In narrow compass—narrow as itself:
Or if the Fancy, too industrious Elf,   10
Be loth that we should breathe awhile
    exempt
From new incitements friendly to our
    task,
Here wants not stealthy prospect, that
    may tempt
Loose Idless to forego her wily mask.

XXV

METHINKS 'twere no unprecedented feat
Should some benignant Minister of air
Lift, and encircle with a cloudy chair,
The One for whom my heart shall ever
    beat
With tenderest love;—or, if a safer seat
Atween his downy wings be furnished,
    there   6
Would lodge her, and the cherished bur-
    den bear
O'er hill and valley to this dim retreat!
Rough ways my steps have trod;—too
    rough and long
For her companionship; here dwells soft
    ease: 10
With sweets that she partakes not some
    distaste
Mingles, and lurking consciousness of
    wrong;
Languish the flowers; the waters seem to
    waste
Their vocal charm; their sparklings cease
    to please.

XXVI

RETURN, Content! for fondly I pursued,
Even when a child, the Streams—unheard,
    unseen;
Through tangled woods, impending rocks
    between;
Or, free as air, with flying inquest viewed
The sullen reservoirs whence their bold
    brood—   5
Pure as the morning, fretful, boisterous,
    keen,
Green as the salt-sea billows, white and
    green—
Poured down the hills, a choral multi-
    tude!

THE RIVER DUDDON

Nor have I tracked their course for scant,
    gains;
They taught me random cares and truant
    joys,   10
That shield from mischief and preserve
    from stains
Vague minds, while men are growing out
    of boys;
Maturer Fancy owes to their rough noise
Impetuous thoughts that brook not servile
    reins.

XXVII

[Composed probably between 1815 and 1819.—
    Published 1819.[1]]

FALLEN, and diffused into a shapeless heap,
Or quietly self-buried in earth's mould,
Is that embattled House, whose massy
    Keep
Flung from yon cliff a shadow large and
    cold.
There dwelt the gay, the bountiful, the
    bold;   5
Till nightly lamentations, like the sweep
Of winds—though winds were silent—
    struck a deep
And lasting terror through that ancient
    Hold.
Its line of Warriors fled;—they shrunk
    when tried
By ghostly power:—but Time's unsparing
    hand   10
Hath plucked such foes, like weeds, from
    out the land;
And now, if men with men in peace abide,
All other strength the weakest may with-
    stand,
All worse assaults may safely be defied.

XXVIII

JOURNEY RENEWED

I ROSE while yet the cattle, heat-opprest,
Crowded together under rustling trees
Brushed by the current of the water-
    breeze;
And for *their* sakes, and love of all that
    rest,
On Duddon's margin, in the sheltering
    nest;   5
For all the startled scaly tribes that slink
Into his coverts, and each fearless link
Of dancing insects forged upon his breast;
For these, and hopes and recollections
    worn
Close to the vital seat of human clay;   10
Glad meetings, tender partings, that up-
    stay
The drooping mind of absence, by vows
    sworn
In his pure presence near the trysting
    thorn—
I thanked the Leader of my onward way.

[1] See Editor's note, p. 296.

XXIX

No record tells of lance opposed to lance,
Horse charging horse, 'mid these retired
    domains;
Tells that their turf drank purple from
    the veins
Of heroes, fallen, or struggling to advance,
Till doubtful combat issued in a trance
Of victory, that struck through heart and
    reins   6
Even to the inmost seat of mortal pains,
And lightened o'er the pallid countenance.
Yet, to the loyal and the brave, who lie
In the blank earth, neglected and forlorn,
The passing Winds memorial tribute pay;
The Torrents chant their praise, inspiring
    scorn   12
Of power usurped; with proclamation
    high,
And glad acknowledgment, of lawful
    sway.

XXX

WHO swerves from innocence, who makes
    divorce
Of that serene companion—a good name,
Recovers not his loss; but walks with
    shame,
With doubt, with fear, and haply with
    remorse:
And oft-times he—who, yielding to the
    force   5
Of chance-temptation, ere his journey end,
From chosen comrade turns, or faithful
    friend—
In vain shall rue the broken intercourse.
Not so with such as loosely wear the chain
That binds them, pleasant River! to thy
    side:—   10
Through the rough copse wheel thou with
    hasty stride;
I choose to saunter o'er the grassy plain,
Sure, when the separation has been tried,
That we, who part in love, shall meet
    again.

XXXI

THE KIRK OF ULPHA to the pilgrim's eye
Is welcome as a star, that doth present
Its shining forehead through the peaceful
    rent
Of a black cloud diffused o'er half the sky:
Or as a fruitful palm-tree towering high
O'er the parched waste beside an Arab's
    tent;   6
Or the Indian tree whose branches, down-
    ward bent,
Take root again, a boundless canopy.
How sweet were leisure! could it yield no
    more
Than 'mid that wave-washed Churchyard
    to recline,   10
From pastoral graves extracting thoughts
    divine;

Or there to pace, and mark the summits hoar
Of distant moon-lit mountains faintly shine,
Soothed by the unseen River's gentle roar.

XXXII

NOT hurled precipitous from steep to steep;
Lingering no more 'mid flower-enamelled lands
And blooming thickets; nor by rocky bands
Held; but in radiant progress toward the Deep
Where mightiest rivers into powerless sleep   5
Sink, and forget their nature—*now* expands
Majestic Duddon, over smooth flat sands
Gliding in silence with unfettered sweep!
Beneath an ampler sky a region wide
Is opened round him:—hamlets, towers, and towns,   10
And blue-topped hills, behold him from afar;
In stately mien to sovereign Thames allied
Spreading his bosom under Kentish downs,
With commerce freighted, or triumphant war.

XXXIII

CONCLUSION

BUT here no cannon thunders to the gale;
Upon the wave no haughty pendants cast
A crimson splendour: lowly is the mast
That rises here, and humbly spread, the sail;
While, less disturbed than in the narrow Vale   5

Through which with strange vicissitudes he passed,
The Wanderer seeks that receptacle vast
Where all his unambitious functions fail.
And may thy Poet, cloud-born Stream! be free—
The sweets of earth contentedly resigned,
And each tumultuous working left behind   11
At seemly distance—to advance like Thee;
Prepared, in peace of heart, in calm of mind
And soul, to mingle with Eternity!

XXXIV

AFTER-THOUGHT

I THOUGHT of Thee, my partner and my guide,
As being past away.—Vain sympathies!
For, backward, Duddon! as I cast my eyes,
I see what was, and is, and will abide;
Still glides the Stream, and shall for ever glide;   5
The Form remains, the Function never dies;
While we, the brave, the mighty, and the wise,
We Men, who in our morn of youth defied
The elements, must vanish;—be it so!
Enough, if something from our hands have power   10
To live, and act, and serve the future hour;
And if, as toward the silent tomb we go,
Through love, through hope, and faith's transcendent dower,
We feel that we are greater than we know.

YARROW REVISITED

AND OTHER POEMS

COMPOSED (TWO EXCEPTED) DURING A TOUR IN SCOTLAND, AND ON THE
ENGLISH BORDER, IN THE AUTUMN OF 1831.[1]

TO

SAMUEL ROGERS, ESQ.,

AS A TESTIMONY OF FRIENDSHIP
AND ACKNOWLEDGMENT OF INTELLECTUAL OBLIGATIONS
THESE MEMORIALS ARE AFFECTIONATELY INSCRIBED

RYDAL MOUNT, *Dec.* 11, 1834.

The following Stanzas are a memorial of a day passed with Sir Walter Scott and other Friends visiting the Banks of the Yarrow under his guidance, immediately before his departure from Abbotsford, for Naples.

The title 'Yarrow Revisited' will stand in no need of explanation for Readers acquainted with the Author's previous poems suggested by that celebrated Stream.

I

THE gallant Youth, who may have gained,
　Or seeks, a 'winsome Marrow,'
Was but an Infant in the lap
　When first I looked on Yarrow;
Once more, by Newark's Castle-gate　　5
　Long left without a warder,
I stood, looked, listened, and with Thee,
　Great Minstrel of the Border!

Grave thoughts ruled wide on that sweet day,
　Their dignity installing　　　　10
In gentle bosoms, while sere leaves
　Were on the bough, or falling;
But breezes played, and sunshine gleamed—
　The forest to embolden;
Reddened the fiery hues, and shot　　15
　Transparence through the golden.

For busy thoughts the Stream flowed on
　In foamy agitation;
And slept in many a crystal pool
　For quiet contemplation:　　　　20
No public and no private care
　The freeborn mind enthralling,
We made a day of happy hours,
　Our happy days recalling.

Brisk Youth appeared, the Morn of Youth,　　25
　With freaks of graceful folly,—

Life's temperate Noon, her sober Eve,
　Her Night not melancholy;
Past, present, future, all appeared
　In harmony united,　　　　　30
Like guests that meet, and some from far,
　By cordial love invited.

And if, as Yarrow, through the woods
　And down the meadow ranging,
Did meet us with unaltered face,　　35
　Though we were changed and changing;
If, *then*, some natural shadows spread
　Our inward prospect over,
The soul's deep valley was not slow
　Its brightness to recover.　　　40

Eternal blessings on the Muse,
　And her divine employment!
The blameless Muse, who trains her Sons
　For hope and calm enjoyment;
Albeit sickness, lingering yet,　　45
　Has o'er their pillow brooded;
And Care waylays their steps—a Sprite
　Not easily eluded.

For thee, O SCOTT! compelled to change
　Green Eildon-hill and Cheviot　　50
For warm Vesuvio's vine-clad slopes;
　And leave thy Tweed and Tiviot
For mild Sorento's breezy waves;
　May classic Fancy, linking
With native Fancy her fresh aid,　　55
　Preserve thy heart from sinking!

Oh! while they minister to thee,
　Each vying with the other,
May Health return to mellow Age,
　With Strength, her venturous brother;
And Tiber, and each brook and rill　　61
　Renowned in song and story,
With unimagined beauty shine,
　Nor lose one ray of glory!

---

[1] The poems of this series, with two exceptions (conjectured by Prof. Knight to be Nos. xv and xvii), were written during the autumn of 1831, and first published in the vol. of 1835 entitled, *Yarrow Revisited, and Other Poems.* In order to avoid needless repetition, separate chronological notes will not be added to the individual poems of the series, save where the particulars of composition or publication differ in some respect from those now given.—ED.

For Thou, upon a hundred streams,   65
  By tales of love and sorrow,
Of faithful love, undaunted truth,
  Hast shed the power of Yarrow;
And streams unknown, hills yet unseen,
  Wherever they invite Thee,   70
At parent Nature's grateful call,
  With gladness must requite Thee.   .

A gracious welcome shall be thine,
  Such looks of love and honour
As thy own Yarrow gave to me   75
  When first I gazed upon her;
Beheld what I had feared to see,
  Unwilling to surrender
Dreams treasured up from early days,
  The holy and the tender.   80

And what, for this frail world, were all
  That mortals do or suffer,
Did no responsive harp, no pen,
  Memorial tribute offer?
Yea, what were mighty Nature's self?   85
  Her features, could they win us,
Unhelped by the poetic voice
  That hourly speaks within us?

Nor deem that localised Romance
  Plays false with our affections;   90
Unsanctifies our tears—made sport
  For fanciful dejections:
Ah, no! the visions of the past
  Sustain the heart in feeling
Life as she is—our changeful Life,   95
  With friends and kindred dealing.

Bear witness, Ye, whose thoughts that day
  In Yarrow's groves were centred;
Who through the silent portal arch
  Of mouldering Newark entered;   100
And clomb the winding stair that once
  Too timidly was mounted
By the 'last Minstrel,' (not the last!)
  Ere he his Tale recounted.

Flow on for ever, Yarrow Stream!   105
  Fulfil thy pensive duty,
Well pleased that future Bards should chant
  For simple hearts thy beauty;
To dream-light dear while yet unseen,
  Dear to the common sunshine,   110
And dearer still, as now I feel,
  To memory's shadowy moonshine!

II

ON THE DEPARTURE OF SIR WALTER SCOTT
FROM ABBOTSFORD, FOR NAPLES

[Composed September, 1831.—Published 1833
(*Literary Souvenir* of Alaric Watts); vol. of 1835.]

A TROUBLE, not of clouds, or weeping rain,
Nor of the setting sun's pathetic light
Engendered, hangs o'er Eildon's triple
  height:
Spirits of Power, assembled there, complain
For kindred Power departing from their
  sight;   5

While Tweed, best pleased in chanting a
  blithe strain,
Saddens his voice again, and yet again.
Lift up your hearts, ye Mourners! for the
  might
Of the whole world's good wishes with
  him goes;
Blessings and prayers in nobler retinue
Than sceptred king or laurelled conqueror
  knows,   11
Follow this wondrous Potentate. Be true,
Ye winds of ocean, and the midland sea,
Wafting your Charge to soft Parthenope!

III

A PLACE OF BURIAL IN THE SOUTH OF
SCOTLAND

PART fenced by man, part by a rugged steep
That curbs a foaming brook, a Grave-
  yard lies;
The hare's best couching-place for fear-
  less sleep;
Which moonlit elves, far seen by credulous
  eyes,   4
Enter in dance. Of church, or sabbath ties,
No vestige now remains; yet thither creep
Bereft Ones, and in lowly anguish weep
Their prayers out to the wind and naked
  skies.
Proud tomb is none; but rudely-sculp-
  tured knights,
By humble choice of plain old times, are
  seen   10
Level with earth, among the hillocks green:
Union not sad, when sunny daybreak
  smites
The spangled turf, and neighbouring
  thickets ring
With *jubilate* from the choirs of spring!

IV

ON THE SIGHT OF A MANSE IN THE SOUTH
OF SCOTLAND

SAY, ye far-travelled clouds, far-seeing
  hills—
Among the happiest-looking homes of men
Scattered all Britain over, through deep glen,
On airy upland, and by forest rills,
And o'er wide plains cheered by the lark
  that trills   5
His sky-born warblings—does aught meet
  your ken
More fit to animate the Poet's pen,
Aught that more surely by its aspect fills
Pure minds with sinless envy, than the
  Abode
Of the good Priest: who, faithful through
  all hours   10
To his high charge, and truly serving God,
Has yet a heart and hand for trees and
  flowers,
Enjoys the walks his predecessors trod,
Nor covets lineal rights in lands and towers.

YARROW REVISITED, ETC.

V

COMPOSED IN ROSLIN CHAPEL DURING A STORM

THE wind is now thy organist;—a clank
(We know not whence) ministers for a
    bell
To mark some change of service. As the
    swell
Of music reached its height, and even
    when sank
The notes, in prelude, ROSLIN! to a
    blank   5
Of silence, how it thrilled thy sumptuous
    roof,
Pillars, and arches,—not in vain time-
    proof,
Though Christian rites be wanting! From
    what bank
Came those live herbs? by what hand
    were they sown
Where dew falls not, where rain-drops
    seem unknown?   10
Yet in the Temple they a friendly niche
Share with their sculptured fellows, that,
    green-grown,
Copy their beauty more and more, and
    preach,
Though mute, of all things blending into
    one.

VI

THE TROSACHS

THERE's not a nook within this solemn
    Pass
But were an apt confessional for One
Taught by his summer spent, his autumn
    gone,
That Life is but a tale of morning grass
Withered at eve. From scenes of art
    which chase   5
That thought away, turn, and with watch-
    ful eyes
Feed it 'mid Nature's old felicities,
Rocks, rivers, and smooth lakes more
    clear than glass
Untouched, unbreathed upon. Thrice
    happy quest,
If from a golden perch of aspen spray   10
(October's workmanship to rival May)
The pensive warbler of the ruddy breast
That moral sweeten by a heaven-taught
    lay,
Lulling the year, with all its cares, to rest!

VII

THE pibroch's note, discountenanced or
    mute;
The Roman kilt, degraded to a toy
Of quaint apparel for a half-spoilt boy;
The target mouldering like ungathered
    fruit;
The smoking steam-boat eager in pur-
    suit,   5

As eagerly pursued; the umbrella spread
To weather-fend the Celtic herdsman's
    head—
All speak of manners withering to the
    root,
And of old honours, too, and passions
    high:
Then may we ask, though pleased that
    thought should range   10
Among the conquests of civility,
Survives imagination—to the change
Superior? Help to virtue does she give?
If not, O Mortals, better cease to live!

VIII

COMPOSED IN THE GLEN OF LOCH ETIVE

'THIS Land of Rainbows spanning glens
    whose walls,
Rock-built, are hung with rainbow-
    coloured mists—
Of far-stretched Meres whose salt flood
    never rests—
Of tuneful Caves and playful Waterfalls—
Of Mountains varying momently their
    crests—   5
Proud be this Land! whose poorest huts
    are halls
Where Fancy entertains becoming guests;
While native song the heroic Past recalls.'
Thus, in the net of her own wishes caught,
The Muse exclaimed; but Story now must
    hide   10
Her trophies, Fancy crouch; the course
    of pride
Has been diverted, other lessons taught,
That make the Patriot-spirit bow her head
Where the all-conquering Roman feared
    to tread.

IX

EAGLES
[Composed at Dunollie Castle in the bay of Oban.]

DISHONOURED Rock and Ruin! that, by law
Tyrannic, keep the Bird of Jove em-
    barred
Like a lone criminal whose life is spared.
Vexed is he, and screams loud. The last
    I saw
Was on the wing; stooping, he struck
    with awe   5
Man, bird, and beast; then, with a consort
    paired,
From a bold headland, their loved aery's
    guard,
Flew high above Atlantic waves, to draw
Light from the fountain of the setting sun.
Such was this Prisoner once; and when
    his plumes   10
The sea-blast ruffles as the storm comes on,
Then, for a moment, he, in spirit, resumes
His rank 'mong freeborn creatures that
    live free,
His power, his beauty, and his majesty.

X

IN THE SOUND OF MULL

TRADITION, be thou mute! Oblivion, throw
Thy veil in mercy o'er the records, hung
Round strath and mountain, stamped by the ancient tongue
On rock and ruin darkening as we go,—
Spots where a word, ghost-like, survives to show   5
What crimes from hate, or desperate love, have sprung;
From honour misconceived, or fancied wrong,
What feuds, not quenched but fed by mutual woe.
Yet, though a wild vindictive Race, untamed
By civil arts and labours of the pen,   10
Could gentleness be scorned by those fierce Men,
Who, to spread wide the reverence they claimed
For patriarchal occupations, named
Yon towering Peaks, 'Shepherds of Etive Glen?'[1]

XI

SUGGESTED AT TYNDRUM IN A STORM

ENOUGH of garlands, of the Arcadian crook,
And all that Greece and Italy have sung
Of Swains reposing myrtle groves among!
Ours couch on naked rocks,—will cross a brook
Swoln with chill rains, nor ever cast a look   5
This way or that, or give it even a thought
More than by smoothest pathway may be brought
Into a vacant mind. Can written book
Teach what *they* learn? Up, hardy Mountaineer!
And guide the Bard, ambitious to be One   11
Of Nature's privy council, as thou art,
On cloud-sequestered heights, that see and hear
To what dread Powers He delegates his part
On Earth, who works in the heaven of heavens, alone.

XII

THE EARL OF BREADALBANE'S RUINED MANSION, AND FAMILY BURIAL-PLACE, NEAR KILLIN.

WELL sang the Bard who called the grave, in strains
Thoughtful and sad, the 'narrow house.'
No style
Of fond sepulchral flattery can beguile

[1] In Gaelic, *Buachaill Eite.*

Grief of her sting; nor cheat, where he detains
The sleeping dust, stern Death. How reconcile   5
With truth, or with each other, decked remains
Of a once warm Abode, and that *new* Pile,
For the departed, built with curious pains
And mausolean pomp? Yet here they stand
Together,—'mid trim walks and artful bowers,   10
To be looked down upon by ancient hills,
That, for the living and the dead, demand
And prompt a harmony of genuine powers;
Concord that elevates the mind, and stills.

XIII

'REST AND BE THANKFUL'

[At the Head of Glencroe.]

DOUBLING and doubling with laborious walk,
Who, that has gained at length the wished-for Height,
This brief this simple wayside Call can slight,
And rests not thankful? Whether cheered by talk
With some loved friend, or by the unseen hawk   5
Whistling to clouds and sky-born streams, that shine
At the sun's outbreak, as with light divine,
Ere they descend to nourish root and stalk
Of valley flowers. Nor, while the limbs repose,
Will we forget that, as the fowl can keep
Absolute stillness, poised aloft in air,   11
And fishes front, unmoved, the torrent's sweep,—
So may the Soul, through powers that Faith bestows,
Win rest, and ease, and peace, with bliss that Angels share.

XIV

HIGHLAND HUT

SEE what gay wild flowers deck this earth-built Cot,
Whose smoke, forth-issuing whence and how it may,
Shines in the greeting of the sun's first ray
Like wreaths of vapour without stain or blot.
The limpid mountain-rill avoids it not;
And why shouldst thou? If rightly trained and bred,   6
Humanity is humble, finds no spot

307

Which her Heaven-guided feet refuse to
    tread.
The walls are cracked, sunk is the flowery
    roof,
Undressed the pathway leading to the
    door;   10
But love, as Nature loves, the lonely Poor;
Search, for their worth, some gentle heart
    wrong-proof,
Meek, patient, kind, and, were its trials
    fewer,
Belike less happy.—Stand no more aloof![1]

XV

THE HIGHLAND BROACH

The exact resemblance which the old Broach (still
in use, though rarely met with, among the Highlanders) bears to the Roman Fibula must strike
every one, and concurs with the plaid and kilt
to recall to mind the communication which the
ancient Romans had with this remote country.

IF to Tradition faith be due,
And echoes from old verse speak true,
Ere the meek Saint, Columba, bore
Glad tidings to Iona's shore,
No common light of nature blessed   5
The mountain region of the west,
A land where gentle manners ruled
O'er men in dauntless virtues schooled,
That raised, for centuries, a bar
Impervious to the tide of war: 10
Yet peaceful Arts did entrance gain
Where haughty Force had striven in vain;
And, 'mid the works of skilful hands,
By wanderers brought from foreign lands
And various climes, was not unknown   15
The clasp that fixed the Roman Gown;
The Fibula, whose shape, I ween,
Still in the Highland Broach is seen,
The silver Broach of massy frame,
Worn at the breast of some grave Dame
On road or path, or at the door   21
Of fern-thatched hut on heathy moor:
But delicate of yore its mould,
And the material finest gold;
As might beseem the fairest Fair,   25
Whether she graced a royal chair,
Or shed, within a vaulted hall,
No fancied lustre on the wall
Where shields of mighty heroes hung,
While Fingal heard what Ossian sung.   30

The heroic Age expired—it slept
Deep in its tomb:—the bramble crept
O'er Fingal's hearth; the grassy sod
Grew on the floors his sons had trod:
Malvina! where art thou? Their state 35
The noblest-born must abdicate;
The fairest, while with fire and sword
Come Spoilers—horde impelling horde,
Must walk the sorrowing mountains, drest
By ruder hands in homelier vest.   40

[1] See Note, p. 716.

Yet still the female bosom lent,
And loved to borrow, ornament;
Still was its inner world a place
Reached by the dews of heavenly grace;
Still pity to this last retreat   45
Clove fondly; to his favourite seat
Love wound his way by soft approach,
Beneath a massier Highland Broach.

When alternations came of rage
Yet fiercer, in a darker age;   50
And feuds, where, clan encountering clan,
The weaker perished to a man;
For maid and mother, when despair
Might else have triumphed, baffling
    prayer,
One small possession lacked not power,
Provided in a calmer hour,   56
To meet such need as might befall—
Roof, raiment, bread, or burial:
For woman, even of tears bereft,
The hidden silver Broach was left.   60

As generations come and go,
Their arts, their customs, ebb and flow;
Fate, fortune, sweep strong powers away,
And feeble, of themselves, decay;
What poor abodes the heirloom hide,   65
In which the castle once took pride!
Tokens, once kept as boasted wealth,
If saved at all, are saved by stealth.
Lo! ships, from seas by nature barred,
Mount along ways by man prepared;   70
And in far-stretching vales, whose streams
Seek other seas, their canvas gleams.
Lo! busy towns spring up, on coasts
Thronged yesterday by airy ghosts;
Soon, like a lingering star forlorn   75
Among the novelties of morn,
While young delights on old encroach,
Will vanish the last Highland Broach.

But when, from out their viewless bed,
Like vapours, years have rolled and
    spread;   80
And this poor verse, and worthier lays,
Shall yield no light of love or praise;
Then, by the spade, or cleaving plough,
Or torrent from the mountain's brow,
Or whirlwind, reckless what his might 85
Entombs, or forces into light;
Blind Chance, a volunteer ally,
That oft befriends Antiquity,
And clears Oblivion from reproach,   89
May render back the Highland Broach.[1]

[1] How much the Broach is sometimes prized by
persons in humble stations may be gathered from
an occurrence mentioned to me by a female friend.
She had had an opportunity of benefiting a poor old
woman in her own hut, who, wishing to make a return, said to her daughter in Erse, in a tone of plaintive earnestness, 'I would give anything I have, but
I *hope* she does not wish for my Broach!' and, uttering these words, she put her hand upon the Broach
which fastened her kerchief, and which she imagined,
had attracted the eye of her benefactress.

308

XVI

THE BROWNIE

Upon a small island, not far from the head of Loch Lomond, are some remains of an ancient building, which was for several years the abode of a solitary Individual, one of the last survivors of the clan of Macfarlane, once powerful in that neighbourhood. Passing along the shore opposite this island in the year 1814, the Author learned these particulars, and that this person then living there had acquired the appellation of 'The Brownie.' See 'The Brownie's Cell', to which the following is a sequel.

'How disappeared he?' Ask the newt
   and toad;
Ask of his fellow-men, and they will tell
How he was found, cold as an icicle,
Under an arch of that forlorn abode;
Where he, unpropped, and by the gather-
   ing flood   5
Of years hemmed round, had dwelt, pre-
   pared to try
Privation's worst extremities, and die
With no one near save the omnipresent
   God.
Verily so to live was an awful choice—
A choice that wears the aspect of a doom;
But in the mould of mercy all is cast   11
For Souls familiar with the eternal Voice;
And this forgotten Taper to the last
Drove from itself, we trust, all frightful
   gloom.

XVII

TO THE PLANET VENUS, AN EVENING STAR

[Composed at Loch Lomond.]

THOUGH joy attend Thee orient at the
   birth
Of dawn, it cheers the lofty spirit most
To watch thy course when Daylight, fled
   from earth,
In the grey sky hath left his lingering
   Ghost,
Perplexed as if between a splendour lost
And splendour slowly mustering. Since
   the Sun,   6
The absolute, the world-absorbing One,
Relinquished half his empire to the host
Emboldened by thy guidance, holy Star,
Holy as princely, who that looks on thee
Touching, as now, in thy humility   11
The mountain-borders of this seat of care,
Can question that thy countenance is
   bright,
Celestial Power, as much with love as
   light?

XVIII

BOTHWELL CASTLE

[Passed unseen, on account of stormy weather.]

IMMURED in Bothwell's towers, at times
   the Brave
(So beautiful is Clyde) forgot to mourn
The liberty they lost at Bannockburn.

Once on those steeps *I* roamed at large,
   and have   4
In mind the landscape, as if still in sight;
The river glides, the woods before me
   wave;
Then why repine that now in vain I crave
Needless renewal of an old delight?
Better to thank a dear and long-past day
For joy its sunny hours were free to give
Than blame the present, that our wish
   hath crost.   11
Memory, like sleep, hath powers which
   dreams obey,
Dreams, vivid dreams, that are not
   fugitive;
How little that she cherishes is lost!

XIX

PICTURE OF DANIEL IN THE LIONS' DEN, AT HAMILTON PALACE

AMID a fertile region green with wood
And fresh with rivers, well did it become
The ducal Owner, in his palace-home
To naturalise this tawny Lion brood;
Children of Art, that claim strange
   brotherhood   5
(Couched in their den) with those that
   roam at large
Over the burning wilderness, and charge
The wind with terror while they roar for
   food.
Satiate are *these;* and stilled to eye and
   ear;
Hence, while we gaze, a more enduring
   fear!   10
Yet is the Prophet calm, nor would the
   cave
Daunt him—if his Companions, now
   bedrowsed
Outstretched and listless, were by hunger
   roused:
Man placed him here, and God, he knows,
   can save.

XX

THE AVON

(A feeder of the Annan.)

AVON—a precious, an immortal name!
Yet is it one that other rivulets bear
Like this unheard-of, and their channels
   wear
Like this contented, though unknown to
   Fame:
For great and sacred is the modest claim
Of Streams to Nature's love, where'er
   they flow;   6
And ne'er did Genius slight them, as they
   go,
Tree, flower, and green herb, feeding
   without blame.
But Praise can waste her voice on work
   of tears,

Anguish, and death: full oft where innocent blood 10
Has mixed its current with the limpid flood,
Her heaven-offending trophies Glory rears:
Never for like distinction may the good
Shrink from *thy* name, pure Rill, with unpleased ears.

XXI

SUGGESTED BY A VIEW FROM AN EMINENCE IN INGLEWOOD FOREST

THE forest huge of ancient Caledon
Is but a name, no more is Inglewood,
That swept from hill to hill, from flood to flood:
On her last thorn the nightly moon has shone;
Yet still, though unappropriate Wild be none, 5
Fair parks spread wide where Adam Bell might deign
With Clym o' the Clough, were they alive again,
To kill for merry feast their venison.
Nor wants the holy Abbot's gliding Shade
His church with monumental wreck bestrown; 10
The feudal Warrior-chief, a Ghost unlaid,
Hath still his castle, though a skeleton,
That he may watch by night, and lessons con
Of power that perishes, and rights that fade.

XXII

HART'S-HORN TREE, NEAR PENRITH

HERE stood an Oak, that long had borne affixed
To his huge trunk, or, with more subtle art,
Among its withering topmost branches mixed,
The palmy antlers of a hunted Hart,
Whom the Dog Hercules pursued—his part 5
Each desperately sustaining, till at last
Both sank and died, the life-veins of the chased
And chaser bursting here with one dire smart.
Mutual the victory, mutual the defeat!
High was the trophy hung with pitiless pride; 10
Say, rather, with that generous sympathy
That wants not, even in rudest breasts, a seat;
And, for this feeling's sake, let no one chide
Verse that would guard thy memory, HART'S-HORN TREE![1]

[1] See Note, p. 718.

XXIII

FANCY AND TRADITION

[Composed 1833.—Published 1835.]

THE Lovers took within this ancient grove
Their last embrace; beside those crystal springs
The Hermit saw the Angel spread his wings
For instant flight; the Sage in yon alcove
Sate musing; on that hill the Bard would rove, 5
Not mute, where now the linnet only sings:
Thus everywhere to truth Tradition clings,
Or Fancy localises Powers we love.
Were only History licensed to take note
Of things gone by, her meagre monuments 10
Would ill suffice for persons and events:
There is an ampler page for man to quote,
A readier book of manifold contents,
Studied alike in palace and in cot.

XXIV

COUNTESS' PILLAR

On the roadside between Penrith and Appleby, there stands a pillar with the following inscription:—

'This pillar was erected, in the year 1656, by Anne Countess Dowager of Pembroke, &c. for a memorial of her last parting with her pious mother, Margaret Countess Dowager of Cumberland, on the 2d of April, 1616; in memory whereof she hath left an annuity of £4 to be distributed to the poor of the parish of Brougham, every 2d day of April for ever, upon the stone table placed hard by. Laus Deo!'

WHILE the Poor gather round, till the end of time
May this bright flower of Charity display
Its bloom, unfolding at the appointed day;
Flower than the loveliest of the vernal prime
Lovelier—transplanted from heaven's purest clime! 5
'Charity never faileth:' on that creed,
More than on written testament or deed,
The pious Lady built with hope sublime.
Alms on this stone to be dealt out, *for ever*!
'LAUS DEO.' Many a Stranger passing by 10
Has with that Parting mixed a filial sigh,
Blest its humane Memorial's fond endeavour;
And, fastening on those lines an eye tearglazed,
Has ended, though no Clerk, with 'God be praised!'

XXV

ROMAN ANTIQUITIES

(From the Roman Station at Old Penrith.)

How profitless the relics that we cull,
Troubling the last holds of ambitious
　　Rome,
Unless they chasten fancies that presume
Too high, or idle agitations lull!
Of the world's flatteries if the brain be
　　full,　　　　　　　　　　　　　5
To have no seat for thought were better
　　doom,
Like this old helmet, or the eyeless skull
Of him who gloried in its nodding plume.
Heaven out of view, our wishes what are
　　they?
Our fond regrets tenacious in their grasp?
The Sage's theory? the Poet's lay?—　11
Mere Fibulæ without a robe to clasp;
Obsolete lamps, whose light no time
　　recalls;
Urns without ashes, tearless lacrymals!

XXVI

APOLOGY

FOR THE FOREGOING POEMS

No more: the end is sudden and abrupt,
Abrupt—as without preconceived design
Was the beginning; yet the several Lays
Have moved in order, to each other bound
By a continuous and acknowledged tie
Though unapparent—like those Shapes
　　distinct　　　　　　　　　　　　6
That yet survive ensculptured on the walls
Of palaces, or temples, 'mid the wreck
Of famed Persepolis; each following each,
As might beseem a stately embassy,　　10
In set array; these bearing in their hands

Ensign of civil power, weapon of war,
Or gift to be presented at the throne
Of the Great King; and others, as they go
In priestly vest, with holy offerings
　　charged,　　　　　　　　　　　　15
Or leading victims drest for sacrifice.
Nor will the Power we serve, that sacred
　　Power,
The Spirit of humanity, disdain
A ministration humble but sincere,
That from a threshold loved by every
　　Muse　　　　　　　　　　　　　20
Its impulse took—that sorrow-stricken
　　door,
Whence, as a current from its fountain-
　　head,
Our thoughts have issued, and our feelings
　　flowed,
Receiving, willingly or not, fresh strength
From kindred sources; while around us
　　sighed　　　　　　　　　　　　25
(Life's three first seasons having passed
　　away)
Leaf-scattering winds; and hoar-frost
　　sprinklings fell
(Foretaste of winter) on the moorland
　　heights;
And every day brought with it tidings new
Of rash change, ominous for the public
　　weal.　　　　　　　　　　　　30
Hence, if dejection has too oft encroached
Upon that sweet and tender melancholy
Which may itself be cherished and
　　caressed
More than enough; a fault so natural
(Even with the young, the hopeful, or the
　　gay)　　　　　　　　　　　　35
For prompt forgiveness will not sue in
　　vain.

THE WHITE DOE OF RYLSTONE

OR

THE FATE OF THE NORTONS

[Composed 1807–1808.—Published 1815 (4to); collective ed. 1820.]

ADVERTISEMENT

During the Summer of 1807 I visited, for the first time, the beautiful country that surrounds Bolton Priory in Yorkshire; and the Poem of 'The White Doe,' founded upon a Tradition connected with that place, was composed at the close of the same year.

DEDICATION

In trellised shed with clustering roses gay,
And, Mary! oft beside our blazing fire,
When years of wedded life were as a day
Whose current answers to the heart's desire,
Did we together read in Spenser's Lay　　5
How Una, sad of soul—in sad attire,
The gentle Una, of celestial birth,
To seek her Knight went wandering o'er the earth.

Ah, then, Belovèd! pleasing was the smart,
And the tear precious in compassion shed　　10
For Her, who, pierced by sorrow's thrilling dart,
Did meekly bear the pang unmerited;
Meek as that emblem of her lowly heart
The milk-white Lamb which in a line she led,—
And faithful, loyal in her innocence,　　15
Like the brave Lion slain in her defence.

THE WHITE DOE OF RYLSTONE

Notes could we hear as of a faery shell
Attuned to words with sacred wisdom fraught;
Free Fancy prized each specious miracle,
And all its finer inspiration caught;   20
Till in the bosom of our rustic Cell
We by a lamentable change were taught
That 'bliss with mortal Man may not abide:'
How nearly joy and sorrow are allied!

For us the stream of fiction ceased to flow,   25
For us the voice of melody was mute.
—But, as soft gales dissolve the dreary snow,
And give the timid herbage leave to shoot,
Heaven's breathing influence failed not to bestow
A timely promise of unlooked-for fruit,   30
Fair fruit of pleasure and serene content
From blossoms wild of fancies innocent.

It soothed us—it beguiled us—then, to hear
Once more of troubles wrought by magic spell;
And griefs whose aery motion comes not near   35
The pangs that tempt the Spirit to rebel:
Then, with mild Una in her sober cheer,
High over hill and low adown the dell
Again we wandered, willing to partake
All that she suffered for her dear Lord's sake.   40

Then, too, this Song *of mine* once more could
      please,
Where anguish, strange as dreams of restless sleep,
Is tempered and allayed by sympathies
Aloft ascending, and descending deep,
Even to the inferior Kinds; whom forest-trees   45
Protect from beating sunbeams, and the sweep
Of the sharp winds;—fair Creatures!—to whom
      Heaven
A calm and sinless life, with love, hath given.

This tragic Story cheered us; for it speaks
Of female patience winning firm repose;   50
And, of the recompense that conscience seeks,
A bright, encouraging, example shows;
Needful when o'er wide realms the tempest breaks,
Needful amid life's ordinary woes;—
Hence not for them unfitted who would bless   55
A happy hour with holier happiness.

He serves the Muses erringly and ill,
Whose aim is pleasure light and fugitive:
O, that my mind were equal to fulfil
The comprehensive mandate which they give—
Vain aspiration of an earnest will!   61
Yet in this moral Strain a power may live.
Belovèd Wife! such solace to impart
As it hath yielded to thy tender heart.

RYDAL MOUNT, WESTMORELAND,
      April 20, 1815.

'Action is transitory—a step, a blow,
The motion of a muscle—this way or that—
'Tis done; and in the after-vacancy
We wonder at ourselves like men betrayed:
Suffering is permanent, obscure and dark,
And has the nature of infinity.[1]
Yet through that darkness (infinite though it seem
And irremoveable) gracious openings lie,
By which the soul—with patient steps of thought
Now toiling, wafted now on wings of prayer—
May pass in hope, and, though from mortal bonds
Yet undelivered, rise with sure ascent
Even to the fountain-head of peace divine.'

[1] These six lines ('Action is transitory . . . infinity')
are quoted from the Tragedy of *The Borderers*, Act
III, Scene v (ll. 1539–1544). The entire passage ('Action . . . divine') was added in 1837.—ED.

'They that deny a God destroy Man's nobility:
for certainly Man is of kin to the Beast by his
Body, and if he be not of kin to God by his Spirit,
he is a base ignoble Creature. It destroys likewise
Magnanimity, and the raising of humane Nature:
for take an example of a Dog, and mark what a
generosity and courage he will put on, when he
finds himself maintained by a Man, who to him
is instead of a God, or Melior Natura. Which
courage is manifestly such as that Creature without that confidence of a better Nature than his
own could never attain. So Man, when he rest-
eth and assureth himself upon Divine protection
and favour, gathereth a force and faith which
human Nature in itself could not obtain.'

                                                  LORD BACON.

CANTO FIRST

FROM Bolton's old monastic tower
The bells ring loud with gladsome power;
The sun shines bright; the fields are gay
With people in their best array
Of stole and doublet, hood and scarf,   5
Along the banks of crystal Wharf,
Through the Vale retired and lowly,
Trooping to that summons holy.
And, up among the moorlands, see
What sprinklings of blithe company!   10
Of lasses and of shepherd grooms,
That down the steep hills force their way,
Like cattle through the budded brooms;
Path, or no path, what care they?
And thus in joyous mood they hie   15
To Bolton's mouldering Priory.

What would they there?—full fifty
      years
That sumptuous Pile, with all its peers,
Too harshly hath been doomed to taste
The bitterness of wrong and waste: 20
Its courts are ravaged; but the tower
Is standing with a voice of power,
That ancient voice which wont to call
To mass or some high festival;
And in the shattered fabric's heart   25
Remaineth one protected part;
A Chapel, like a wild-bird's nest,
Closely embowered and trimly drest;
And thither young and old repair,
This Sabbath-day, for praise and prayer.

Fast the churchyard fills;—anon   31
Look again, and they all are gone;
The cluster round the porch, and the folk
Who sate in the shade of the Prior's Oak!
And scarcely have they disappeared   35
Ere the prelusive hymn is heard:—
With one consent the people rejoice,
Filling the church with a lofty voice!
They sing a service which they feel:
For 'tis the sunrise now of zeal;   40
Of a pure faith the vernal prime—
In great Eliza's golden time.

A moment ends the fervent din,
And all is hushed, without and within;
For though the priest, more tranquilly,
Recites the holy liturgy,   46

312

The only voice which you can hear
Is the river murmuring near.
—When soft!—the dusky trees between,
And down the path through the open
   green,   50
Where is no living thing to be seen;
And through yon gateway, where is found,
Beneath the arch with ivy bound,
Free entrance to the churchyard ground—
Comes gliding in with lovely gleam, 55
Comes gliding in serene and slow,
Soft and silent as a dream,
A solitary Doe!
White she is as lily of June,
And beauteous as the silver moon 60
When out of sight the clouds are driven
And she is left alone in heaven;
Or like a ship some gentle day
In sunshine sailing far away,
A glittering ship, that hath the plain 65
Of ocean for her own domain.

Lie silent in your graves, ye dead!
Lie quiet in your churchyard bed!
Ye living, tend your holy cares;
Ye multitude, pursue your prayers; 70
And blame not me if my heart and sight
Are occupied with one delight!
'Tis a work for sabbath hours
If I with this bright Creature go:
Whether she be of forest bowers, 75
From the bowers of earth below;
Or a Spirit for one day given,
A pledge of grace from purest heaven.

What harmonious pensive changes
Wait upon her as she ranges 80
Round and through this Pile of state
Overthrown and desolate!
Now a step or two her way
Leads through space of open day,
Where the enamoured sunny light 85
Brightens her that was so bright;
Now doth a delicate shadow fall,
Falls upon her like a breath,
From some lofty arch or wall,
As she passes underneath: 90
Now some gloomy nook partakes
Of the glory that she makes,—
High-ribbed vault of stone, or cell,
With perfect cunning framed as well
Of stone, and ivy, and the spread 95
Of the elder's bushy head;
Some jealous and forbidding cell,
That doth the living stars repel,
And where no flower hath leave to dwell.

The presence of this wandering Doe
Fills many a damp obscure recess 101
With lustre of a saintly show;
And, reappearing, she no less
Sheds on the flowers that round her blow
A more than sunny liveliness. 105
But say, among these holy places,
Which thus assiduously she paces,

Comes she with a votary's task,
Rite to perform, or boon to ask?
Fair Pilgrim! harbours she a sense 110
Of sorrow, or of reverence?
Can she be grieved for quire or shrine,
Crushed as if by wrath divine?
For what survives of house where God
Was worshipped, or where Man abode;
For old magnificence undone; 116
Or for the gentler work begun
By Nature, softening and concealing,
And busy with a hand of healing?
Mourns she for lordly chamber's hearth
That to the sapling ash gives birth; 121
For dormitory's length laid bare
Where the wild rose blossoms fair;
Or altar, whence the cross was rent,
Now rich with mossy ornament? 125
—She sees a warrior carved in stone,
Among the thick weeds, stretched alone;
A warrior, with his shield of pride
Cleaving humbly to his side,
And hands in resignation prest, 130
Palm to palm, on his tranquil breast;
As little she regards the sight
As a common creature might:
If she be doomed to inward care,
Or service, it must lie elsewhere. 135
—But hers are eyes serenely bright,
And on she moves—with pace how light!
Nor spares to stoop her head, and taste
The dewy turf with flowers bestrown;
And thus she fares, until at last 140
Beside the ridge of a grassy grave
In quietness she lays her down;
Gentle as a weary wave
Sinks, when the summer breeze hath
   died,
Against an anchored vessel's side; 145
Even so, without distress, doth she
Lie down in peace, and lovingly.

The day is placid in its going,
To a lingering motion bound,
Like the crystal stream now flowing 150
With its softest summer sound:
So the balmy minutes pass,
While this radiant Creature lies
Couched upon the dewy grass,
Pensively with downcast eyes. 155
—But now again the people raise
With awful cheer a voice of praise;
It is the last, the parting song;
And from the temple forth they throng,
And quickly spread themselves abroad,
While each pursues his several road. 161
But some—a variegated band
Of middle-aged, and old, and young,
And little children by the hand
Upon their leading mothers hung— 165
With mute obeisance gladly paid
Turn towards the spot where, full in view,
The white Doe, to her service true,
Her sabbath couch has made.

THE WHITE DOE OF RYLSTONE

It was a solitary mound; 170
Which two spears' length of level ground
Did from all other graves divide:
As if in some respect of pride;
Or melancholy's sickly mood,
Still shy of human neighbourhood; 175
Or guilt, that humbly would express
A penitential loneliness.

'Look, there she is, my Child! draw
near;
She fears not, wherefore should we fear?
She means no harm;'—but still the Boy,
To whom the words were softly said, 181
Hung back, and smiled, and blushed for
joy,
A shame-faced blush of glowing red!
Again the Mother whispered low,
'Now you have seen the famous Doe; 185
From Rylstone she hath found her way
Over the hills this sabbath day;
Her work, whate'er it be, is done,
And she will depart when we are gone;
Thus doth she keep, from year to year,
Her sabbath morning, foul or fair.' 191

Bright was the Creature, as in dreams
The Boy had seen her, yea, more bright;
But is she truly what she seems?
He asks with insecure delight, 195
Asks of himself, and doubts,—and still
The doubt returns against his will:
Though he, and all the standers-by,
Could tell a tragic history
Of facts divulged, wherein appear 200
Substantial motive, reason clear,
Why thus the milk-white Doe is found
Couchant beside that lonely mound;
And why she duly loves to pace
The circuit of this hallowed place. 205
Nor to the Child's enquiring mind
Is such perplexity confined:
For, spite of sober Truth that sees
A world of fixed remembrances
Which to this mystery belong, 210
If, undeceived, my skill can trace
The characters of every face,
There lack not strange delusion here,
Conjecture vague, and idle fear,
And superstitious fancies strong, 215
Which do the gentle Creature wrong.

That bearded, staff-supported Sire—
Who in his boyhood often fed
Full cheerily on convent-bread
And heard old tales by the convent-fire,
And to his grave will go with scars, 221
Relics of long and distant wars—
That Old Man, studious to expound
The spectacle, is mounting high
To days of dim antiquity; 225
When Lady Aäliza mourned
Her Son, and felt in her despair
The pang of unavailing prayer;

Her Son in Wharf's abysses drowned,
The noble Boy of Egremound. 230
From which affliction—when the grace
Of God had in her heart found place—
A pious structure, fair to see,
Rose up, this stately Priory!
The Lady's work;—but now laid low;
To the grief of her soul that doth come
and go, 236
In the beautiful form of this innocent
Doe:
Which, though seemingly doomed in its
breast to sustain
A softened remembrance of sorrow and
pain,
Is spotless, and holy, and gentle, and
bright; 240
And glides o'er the earth like an angel of
light.

Pass, pass who will, yon chantry
door;
And through the chink in the fractured
floor
Look down, and see a griesly sight;
A vault where the bodies are buried
upright! 245
There, face by face, and hand by hand,
The Claphams and Mauleverers stand;
And, in his place, among son and sire,
Is John de Clapham, that fierce Esquire,
A valiant man, and a name of dread
In the ruthless wars of the White and
Red; 251
Who dragged Earl Pembroke from
Banbury church
And smote off his head on the stones of
the porch!
Look down among them, if you dare;
Oft does the White Doe loiter there, 255
Prying into the darksome rent;
Nor can it be with good intent:
So thinks that Dame of haughty air,
Who hath a Page her book to hold,
And wears a frontlet edged with gold.
Harsh thoughts with her high mood
agree— 261
Who counts among her ancestry
Earl Pembroke, slain so impiously!

That slender Youth, a scholar pale,
From Oxford come to his native vale,
He also hath his own conceit: 266
It is, thinks he, the gracious Fairy,
Who loved the Shepherd-lord to meet
In his wanderings solitary:
Wild notes she in his hearing sang, 270
A song of Nature's hidden powers;
That whistled like the wind, and rang
Among the rocks and holly bowers.
'Twas said that She all shapes could wear;
And oftentimes before him stood, 275
Amid the trees of some thick wood,
In semblance of a lady fair;

314

And taught him signs, and showed him
 sights,
In Craven's dens, on Cumbrian heights;
When under cloud of fear he lay, 280
A shepherd clad in homely grey;
Nor left him at his later day.
And hence when he, with spear and
 shield,
Rode full of years to Flodden-field,
His eye could see the hidden spring, 285
And how the current was to flow;
The fatal end of Scotland's King,
And all that hopeless overthrow.
But not in wars did he delight,
This Clifford wished for worthier might;
Nor in broad pomp, or courtly state; 291
Him his own thoughts did elevate,—
Most happy in the shy recess
Of Barden's lowly quietness.
And choice of studious friends had he
Of Bolton's dear fraternity; 296
Who, standing on this old church tower,
In many a calm propitious hour,
Perused, with him, the starry sky;
Or, in their cells, with him did pry 300
For other lore,—by keen desire
Urged to close toil with chemic fire;
In quest belike of transmutations
Rich as the mine's most bright creations.
But they and their good works are fled,
And all is now disquieted— 306
And peace is none, for living or dead!

Ah, pensive Scholar, think not so,
But look again at the radiant Doe!
What quiet watch she seems to keep, 310
Alone, beside that grassy heap!
Why mention other thoughts unmeet
For vision so composed and sweet?
While stand the people in a ring,
Gazing, doubting, questioning; 315
Yea, many overcome in spite
Of recollections clear and bright;
Which yet do unto some impart
An undisturbed repose of heart.
And all the assembly own a law 320
Of orderly respect and awe;
But see—they vanish one by one,
And last, the Doe herself is gone.

Harp! we have been full long beguiled
By vague thoughts, lured by fancies
 wild; 325
To which, with no reluctant strings,
Thou hast attuned thy murmurings;
And now before this Pile we stand
In solitude, and utter peace:
But, Harp! thy murmurs may not cease—
A Spirit, with his angelic wings, 331
In soft and breeze-like visitings,
Has touched thee—and a Spirit's hand:
A voice is with us—a command
To chant, in strains of heavenly glory,
A tale of tears, a mortal story! 336

THE WHITE DOE OF RYLSTONE
CANTO SECOND

THE Harp in lowliness obeyed;
And first we sang of the greenwood shade
And a solitary Maid;
Beginning, where the song must end, 340
With her, and with her sylvan Friend;
The Friend, who stood before her sight,
Her only unextinguished light;
Her last companion in a dearth
Of love, upon a hopeless earth. 345

For She it was—this Maid, who
 wrought
Meekly, with foreboding thought,
In vermeil colours and in gold
An unblest work; which, standing by,
Her Father did with joy behold,— 350
Exulting in its imagery;
A Banner, fashioned to fulfil
Too perfectly his headstrong will:
For on this Banner had her hand 354
Embroidered (such her Sire's command)
The sacred Cross; and figured there
The five dear wounds our Lord did bear;
Full soon to be uplifted high,
And float in rueful company!

It was the time when England's Queen
Twelve years had reigned, a Sovereign
 dread; 361
Nor yet the restless crown had been
Disturbed upon her virgin head;
But now the inly-working North
Was ripe to send its thousands forth, 365
A potent vassalage, to fight
In Percy's and in Neville's right,
Two Earls fast leagued in discontent,
Who gave their wishes open vent;
And boldly urged a general plea, 370
The rites of ancient piety
To be triumphantly restored,
By the stern justice of the sword!
And that same Banner, on whose breast
The blameless Lady had exprest 375
Memorials chosen to give life
And sunshine to a dangerous strife;
That Banner, waiting for the Call,
Stood quietly in Rylstone-hall.

It came; and Francis Norton said, 380
'O Father! rise not in this fray—
The hairs are white upon your head;
Dear Father, hear me when I say
It is for you too late a day!
Bethink you of your own good name: 386
A just and gracious Queen have we,
A pure religion, and the claim
Of peace on our humanity.—
'Tis meet that I endure your scorn;
I am your son, your eldest born; 390
But not for lordship or for land,
My Father, do I clasp your knees;
The Banner touch not, stay your hand,
This multitude of men disband,

And live at home in blameless ease;   395
For these my brethren's sake, for me;
And, most of all, for Emily!'

Tumultuous noises filled the hall;
And scarcely could the Father hear
That name—pronounced with a dying
    fall—   400
The name of his only Daughter dear,
As on the banner which stood near
He glanced a look of holy pride,
And his moist eyes were glorified;
Then did he seize the staff, and say: 405
'Thou, Richard, bear'st thy father's name,
Keep thou this ensign till the day
When I of thee require the same:
Thy place be on my better hand;—
And seven as true as thou, I see,   410
Will cleave to this good cause and me.'
He spake, and eight brave sons straight-
    way
All followed him, a gallant band!

Thus, with his sons, when forth he came
The sight was hailed with loud acclaim
And din of arms and minstrelsy,   416
From all his warlike tenantry,
All horsed and harnessed with him to
    ride,—
A voice to which the hills replied!

But Francis, in the vacant hall,   420
Stood silent under dreary weight,—
A phantasm, in which roof and wall
Shook, tottered, swam before his sight;
A phantasm like a dream of night!
Thus overwhelmed, and desolate,   425
He found his way to a postern-gate;
And, when he waked, his languid eye
Was on the calm and silent sky;
With air about him breathing sweet, 429
And earth's green grass beneath his feet;
Nor did he fail ere long to hear
A sound of military cheer,
Faint—but it reached that sheltered spot;
He heard, and it disturbed him not.

There stood he, leaning on a lance   435
Which he had grasped unknowingly,
Had blindly grasped in that strong trance,
That dimness of heart-agony;
There stood he, cleansed from the despair
And sorrow of his fruitless prayer.   440
The past he calmly hath reviewed:
But where will be the fortitude
Of this brave man, when he shall see
That Form beneath the spreading tree,
And know that it is Emily?   445

He saw her where in open view
She sate beneath the spreading yew—
Her head upon her lap, concealing
In solitude her bitter feeling:
'Might ever son *command* a sire,   450
The act were justified to-day.'

This to himself—and to the Maid,
Whom now he had approached, he said—
'Gone are they,—they have their desire;
And I with thee one hour will stay,   455
To give thee comfort if I may.'

She heard, but looked not up, nor
    spake;
And sorrow moved him to partake
Her silence; then his thoughts turned
    round,
And fervent words a passage found.   460

'Gone are they, bravely, though misled;
With a dear Father at their head!
The Sons obey a natural lord;
The Father had given solemn word
To noble Percy; and a force   465
Still stronger, bends him to his course.
This said, our tears to-day may fall
As at an innocent funeral.
In deep and awful channel runs
This sympathy of Sire and Sons: 470
Untried our Brothers have been loved
With heart by simple nature moved;
And now their faithfulness is proved:
For faithful we must call them, bearing
That soul of conscientious daring.   475
—There were they all in circle—there
Stood Richard, Ambrose, Christopher,
John with a sword that will not fail,
And Marmaduke in fearless mail,
And those bright Twins were side by side;
And there, by fresh hopes beautified, 481
Stood He, whose arm yet lacks the power
Of man, our youngest, fairest flower!
I, by the right of eldest born,
And in a second father's place,   485
Presumed to grapple with their scorn,
And meet their pity face to face;
Yea, trusting in God's holy aid,
I to my Father knelt and prayed;
And one, the pensive Marmaduke,   490
Methought, was yielding inwardly,
And would have laid his purpose by,
But for a glance of his Father's eye,
Which I myself could scarcely brook.

'Then be we, each and all, forgiven! 495
Thou, chiefly thou, my Sister dear,
Whose pangs are registered in heaven—
The stifled sigh, the hidden tear,
And smiles, that dared to take their place,
Meek filial smiles, upon thy face,   500
As that unhallowed Banner grew
Beneath a loving old Man's view.
Thy part is done—thy painful part;
Be thou then satisfied in heart!
A further, though far easier, task   505
Than thine hath been, my duties ask;
With theirs my efforts cannot blend,
I cannot for such cause contend;
Their aims I utterly forswear;
But I in body will be there.   510

Unarmed and naked will I go,
Be at their side, come weal or woe:
On kind occasions I may wait,
See, hear, obstruct, or mitigate.
Bare breast I take and an empty hand[1].'—
Therewith he threw away the lance,
Which he had grasped in that strong
    trance;
Spurned it, like something that would
    stand
Between him and the pure intent
Of love on which his soul was bent. 520

'For thee, for thee, is left the sense
Of trial past without offence
To God or man; such innocence,
Such consolation, and the excess
Of an unmerited distress; 525
In that thy very strength must lie.
—O Sister, I could prophesy!
The time is come that rings the knell
Of all we loved, and loved so well:
Hope nothing, if I thus may speak 530
To thee, a woman, and thence weak:
Hope nothing, I repeat; for we
Are doomed to perish utterly:
'Tis meet that thou with me divide
The thought while I am by thy side, 535
Acknowledging a grace in this,
A comfort in the dark abyss.
But look not for me when I am gone,
And be no farther wrought upon:
Farewell all wishes, all debate, 540
All prayers for this cause, or for that!
Weep, if that aid thee; but depend
Upon no help of outward friend;
Espouse thy doom at once, and cleave
To fortitude without reprieve. 545
For we must fall, both we and ours—
This Mansion and these pleasant bowers,
Walks, pools, and arbours, homestead,
    hall—
Our fate is theirs, will reach them all;
The young horse must forsake his manger,
And learn to glory in a Stranger; 551
The hawk forget his perch; the hound
Be parted from his ancient ground:
The blast will sweep us all away—
One desolation, one decay! 555
And even this Creature!' which words
    saying,
He pointed to a lovely Doe,
A few steps distant, feeding, straying;
Fair creature, and more white than
    snow!
'Even she will to her peaceful woods 560
Return, and to her murmuring floods,
And be in heart and soul the same
She was before she hither came;
Ere she had learned to love us all,
Herself beloved in Rylstone-hall. 565
—But thou, my Sister, doomed to be
The last leaf on a blasted tree;

[1] See the Old Ballad,—'The Rising of the North.

If not in vain we breathed the breath
Together of a purer faith;
If hand in hand we have been led, 570
And thou, (O happy thought this day!)
Not seldom foremost in the way;
If on one thought our minds have fed,
And we have in one meaning read;
If, when at home our private weal 575
Hath suffered from the shock of zeal,
Together we have learned to prize
Forbearance and self-sacrifice;
If we like combatants have fared,
And for this issue been prepared; 580
If thou art beautiful, and youth
And thought endue thee with all truth—
Be strong;—be worthy of the grace
Of God, and fill thy destined place:
A Soul, by force of sorrows high, 585
Uplifted to the purest sky
Of undisturbed humanity!'

He ended,—or she heard no more;
He led her from the yew-tree shade,
And at the mansion's silent door, 590
He kissed the consecrated Maid;
And down the valley then pursued,
Alone, the armèd Multitude.

CANTO THIRD

Now joy for you who from the towers
Of Brancepeth look in doubt and fear,
Telling melancholy hours! 596
Proclaim it, let your Masters hear
That Norton with his band is near!
The watchmen from their station high
Pronounced the word,—and the Earls
    descry, 600
Well-pleased, the armèd Company
Marching down the banks of Were.

Said fearless Norton to the pair
Gone forth to greet him on the plain—
'This meeting, noble Lords! looks fair,
I bring with me a goodly train; 606
Their hearts are with you: hill and dale
Have helped us: Ure we crossed, and
    Swale,
And horse and harness followed—see
The best part of their Yeomanry! 610
—Stand forth, my Sons!—these eight are
    mine,
Whom to this service I commend;
Which way soe'er our fate incline,
These will be faithful to the end; 614
They are my all'—voice failed him here—
'My all save one, a Daughter dear!
Whom I have left, Love's mildest birth,
The meekest Child on this blessed earth.
I had—but these are by my side,
These Eight, and this is a day of pride!
The time is ripe. With festive din 621
Lo! how the people are flocking in,—
Like hungry fowl to the feeder's hand
When snow lies heavy upon the land.'

317

THE WHITE DOE OF RYLSTONE

He spake bare truth; for far and near
From every side came noisy swarms 626
Of Peasants in their homely gear;
And, mixed with these, to Brancepeth
came
Grave Gentry of estate and name,
And Captains known for worth in arms;
And prayed the Earls in self-defence 631
To rise, and prove their innocence.—
'Rise, noble Earls, put forth your might
For holy Church, and the People's right!'

The Norton fixed, at this demand, 635
His eye upon Northumberland,
And said; 'The Minds of Men will own
No loyal rest while England's Crown
Remains without an Heir, the bait
Of strife and factions desperate; 640
Who, paying deadly hate in kind
Through all things else, in this can find
A mutual hope, a common mind;
And plot, and pant to overwhelm
All ancient honour in the realm. 645
—Brave Earls! to whose heroic veins
Our noblest blood is given in trust,
To you a suffering State complains,
And ye must raise her from the dust.
With wishes of still bolder scope 650
On you we look, with dearest hope;
Even for our Altars—for the prize
In Heaven, of life that never dies;
For the old and holy Church we mourn,
And must in joy to her return. 655
Behold!'—and from his Son whose stand
Was on his right, from that guardian
hand
He took the Banner, and unfurled
The precious folds—'behold,' said he,
'The ransom of a sinful world; 660
Let this your preservation be;
The wounds of hands and feet and side,
And the sacred Cross on which Jesus died.
—This bring I from an ancient hearth,
These Records wrought in pledge of love
By hands of no ignoble birth, 666
A Maid o'er whom the blessed Dove
Vouchsafed in gentleness to brood
While she the holy work pursued.'
'Uplift the Standard!' was the cry 670
From all the listeners that stood round,
'Plant it,—by this we live or die.'
The Norton ceased not for that sound,
But said; 'The prayer which ye have
heard,
Much injured Earls! by these preferred,
Is offered to the Saints, the sigh 676
Of tens of thousands, secretly.'
'Uplift it!' cried once more the Band,
And then a thoughtful pause ensued:
'Uplift it!' said Northumberland— 680
Whereat from all the multitude
Who saw the Banner reared on high
In all its dread emblazonry
A voice of uttermost joy brake out:

The transport was rolled down the river
of Were, 685
And Durham, the time-honoured Durham, did hear,
And the towers of Saint Cuthbert were
stirred by the shout!

Now was the North in arms:—they
shine
In warlike trim from Tweed to Tyne,
At Percy's voice: and Neville sees 690
His Followers gathering in from Tees,
From Were, and all the little rills
Concealed among the forkèd hills—
Seven hundred Knights, Retainers all
Of Neville, at their Master's call 695
Had sate together in Raby Hall!
Such strength that Earldom held of yore;
Nor wanted at this time rich store
Of well-appointed chivalry.
—Not loth the sleepy lance to wield, 700
And greet the old paternal shield,
They heard the summons;—and, further-
more,
Horsemen and Foot of each degree,
Unbound by pledge of fealty,
Appeared, with free and open hate 705
Of novelties in Church and State;
Knight, burgher, yeoman, and esquire,
And Romish priest, in priest's attire.
And thus, in arms, a zealous Band
Proceeding under joint command, 710
To Durham first their course they bear;
And in Saint Cuthbert's ancient seat
Sang mass,—and tore the book of
prayer,—
And trod the bible beneath their feet.

Thence marching southward smooth
and free 715
'They mustered their host at Wetherby,
Full sixteen thousand fair to see;'[1]
The Choicest Warriors of the North!
But none for beauty and for worth 719
Like those eight Sons—who, in a ring,
(Ripe men, or blooming in life's spring)
Each with a lance, erect and tall,
A falchion, and a buckler small, 723
Stood by their Sire, on Clifford-moor,
To guard the Standard which he bore.
On foot they girt their Father round;
And so will keep the appointed ground
Where'er their march: no steed will he
Henceforth bestride;—triumphantly
He stands upon the grassy sod, 730
Trusting himself to the earth, and God.
Rare sight to embolden and inspire!
Proud was the field of Sons and Sire;
Of him the most; and, sooth to say,
No shape of man in all the array 735
So graced the sunshine of that day.
The monumental pomp of age
Was with this goodly Personage;

[1] From the Old Ballad.

A stature undepressed in size,
Unbent, which rather seemed to rise, 740
In open victory o'er the weight
Of seventy years, to loftier height;
Magnific limbs of withered state;
A face to fear and venerate; 744
Eyes dark and strong; and on his head
Bright locks of silver hair, thick spread,
Which a brown morion half-concealed,
Light as a hunter's of the field;
And thus, with girdle round his waist,
Whereon the Banner-staff might rest 750
At need, he stood, advancing high
The glittering, floating Pageantry.

Who sees him?—thousands see, and
One
With unparticipated gaze;
Who, 'mong those thousands, friend hath
none, 755
And treads in solitary ways.
He, following wheresoe'er he might,
Hath watched the Banner from afar,
As shepherds watch a lonely star,
Or mariners the distant light 760
That guides them through a stormy night.
And now, upon a chosen plot
Of rising ground, yon heathy spot!
He takes alone his far-off stand,
With breast unmailed, unweaponed hand.
Bold is his aspect; but his eye 766
Is pregnant with anxiety,
While, like a tutelary Power,
He there stands fixed from hour to hour:
Yet sometimes in more humble guise 770
Upon the turf-clad height he lies
Stretched, herdsman-like, as if to bask
In sunshine were his only task,
Or by his mantle's help to find
A shelter from the nipping wind: 775
And thus, with short oblivion blest,
His weary spirits gather rest.
Again he lifts his eyes; and lo!
The pageant glancing to and fro;
And hope is wakened by the sight, 780
He thence may learn, ere fall of night,
Which way the tide is doomed to flow.

To London were the Chieftains bent;
But what avails the bold intent?
A Royal army is gone forth 785
To quell the RISING OF THE NORTH;
They march with Dudley at their head,
And, in seven days' space, will to York
be led!—
Can such a mighty host be raised
Thus suddenly, and brought so near? 790
The Earls upon each other gazed,
And Neville's cheek grew pale with fear;
For, with a high and valiant name,
He bore a heart of timid frame;
And bold if both had been, yet they 795
'Against so many may not stay.'[1]

[1] From the Old Ballad.

Back therefore will they hie to seize
A strong Hold on the banks of Tees;
There wait a favourable hour,
Until Lord Dacre with his power 800
From Naworth come; and Howard's aid
Be with them openly displayed.

While through the Host, from man to
man,
A rumour of this purpose ran,
The Standard trusting to the care 805
Of him who heretofore did bear
That charge, impatient Norton sought
The Chieftains to unfold his thought,
And thus abruptly spake;—'We yield
(And can it be?) an unfought field!—
How oft has strength, the strength of
heaven, 811
To few triumphantly been given!
Still do our very children boast
Of mitred Thurston—what a Host
He conquered!—Saw we not the Plain
(And flying shall behold again) 816
Where faith was proved?—while to battle
moved
The Standard, on the Sacred Wain
That bore it, compassed round by a bold
Fraternity of Barons old; 820
And with those grey-haired champions
stood,
Under the saintly ensigns three,
The infant Heir of Mowbray's blood—
All confident of victory!— 824
Shall Percy blush, then, for his name?
Must Westmoreland be asked with shame
Whose were the numbers, where the loss,
In that other day of Neville's Cross?
When the Prior of Durham with holy hand
Raised, as the Vision gave command, 830
Saint Cuthbert's Relic—far and near
Kenned on the point of a lofty spear;
While the Monks prayed in Maiden's
Bower
To God descending in his power.
Less would not at our need be due 835
To us, who war against the Untrue;—
The delegates of Heaven we rise,
Convoked the impious to chastise:
We, we, the sanctities of old
Would re-establish and uphold', 840
Be warned'—His zeal the Chiefs con-
founded,
But word was given, and the trumpet
sounded:
Back through the melancholy Host
Went Norton, and resumed his post.
Alas! thought he, and have I borne 845
This Banner raised with joyful pride,
This hope of all posterity,
By those dread symbols sanctified;
Thus to become at once the scorn
Of babbling winds as they go by, 850
A spot of shame to the sun's bright eye,
To the light clouds a mockery!

—'Even these poor eight of mine would
    stem—'
Half to himself, and half to them   854
He spake—'would stem, or quell, a force
Ten times their number, man and horse;
This by their own unaided might,
Without their father in their sight,
Without the Cause for which they fight;
A Cause, which on a needful day   860
Would breed us thousands brave as they.'
—So speaking, he his reverend head
Raised toward that Imagery once more:
But the familiar prospect shed
Despondency unfelt before: 865
A shock of intimations vain,
Dismay, and superstitious pain,
Fell on him, with the sudden thought
Of her by whom the work was wrought:—
Oh! wherefore was her countenance
    bright   870
With love divine and gentle light?
She would not, could not, disobey,
But her Faith leaned another way.
Ill tears she wept; I saw them fall,
I overheard her as she spake   875
Sad words to that mute Animal,
The White Doe, in the hawthorn brake;
She steeped, but not for Jesu's sake,
This Cross in tears: by her, and One
Unworthier far we are undone—   880
Her recreant Brother—he prevailed
Over that tender Spirit—assailed
Too oft, alas! by her whose head
In the cold grave hath long been laid:
She first in reason's dawn beguiled   885
Her docile, unsuspecting Child:
Far back—far back my mind must go
To reach the well-spring of this woe!

While thus he brooded, music sweet
Of border tunes was played to cheer   890
The footsteps of a quick retreat;
But Norton lingered in the rear,
Stung with sharp thoughts; and, ere the
    last
From his distracted brain was cast,
Before his Father, Francis stood,   895
And spake in firm and earnest mood.

'Though here I bend a suppliant knee
In reverence, and unarmed, I bear
In your indignant thoughts my share;
Am grieved this backward march to see
So careless and disorderly.   901
I scorn your Chiefs—men who would lead,
And yet want courage at their need:
Then look at them with open eyes!
Deserve they further sacrifice?—   905
If—when they shrink, nor dare oppose
In open field their gathering foes,
(And fast, from this decisive day,
Yon multitude must melt away;)
If now I ask a grace not claimed   910
While ground was left for hope; unblamed

Be an endeavour that can do
No injury to them or you.
My Father! I would help to find
A place of shelter, till the rage   915
Of cruel men do like the wind
Exhaust itself and sink to rest;
Be Brother now to Brother joined!
Admit me in the equipage
Of your misfortunes, that at least,   920
Whatever fate remain behind,
I may bear witness in my breast
To your nobility of mind!'

'Thou Enemy, my bane and blight!
Oh! bold to fight the Coward's fight   925
Against all good'—but why declare,
At length, the issue of a prayer
Which love had prompted, yielding scope
Too free to one bright moment's hope?
Suffice it that the Son, who strove   930
With fruitless effort to allay
That passion, prudently gave way;
Nor did he turn aside to prove
His Brothers' wisdom or their love—
But calmly from the spot withdrew;   935
His best endeavours to renew,
Should e'er a kindlier time ensue.

CANTO FOURTH

'TIS night: in silence looking down,
The Moon from cloudless ether sees
A Camp, and a beleaguered Town,   940
And Castle like a stately crown
On the steep rocks of winding Tees;—
And southward far, with moor between,
Hill-top, and flood, and forest green,   944
The bright Moon sees that valley small
Where Rylstone's old sequestered Hall
A venerable image yields
Of quiet to the neighbouring fields;
While from one pillared chimney breathes
The smoke, and mounts in silver wreaths.
—The courts are hushed;—for timely
    sleep   951
The greyhounds to their kennel creep;
The peacock in the broad ash-tree
Aloft is roosted for the night,
He who in proud prosperity   955
Of colours manifold and bright
Walked round, affronting the daylight;
And higher still, above the bower
Where he is perched, from yon lone
    Tower
The hall-clock in the clear moonshine   960
With glittering finger points at nine.

Ah! who could think that sadness here
Hath any sway? or pain, or fear?
A soft and lulling sound is heard
Of streams inaudible by day;   965
The garden pool's dark surface, stirred
By the night insects in their play,
Breaks into dimples small and bright;
A thousand, thousand rings of light

That shape themselves and disappear
Almost as soon as seen:—and lo!   971
Not distant far, the milk-white Doe—
The same who quietly was feeding
On the green herb, and nothing heeding,
When Francis, uttering to the Maid   975
His last words in the yew-tree shade,
Involved whate'er by love was brought
Out of his heart, or crossed his thought,
Or chance presented to his eye,
In one sad sweep of destiny—   980
The same fair Creature, who hath found
Her way into forbidden ground;
Where now—within this spacious plot
For pleasure made, a goodly spot,
With lawns and beds of flowers, and   985
    shades
Of trellis-work in long arcades,
And cirque and crescent framed by wall
Of close-clipt foliage green and tall,
Converging walks, and fountains gay,
And terraces in trim array—   990
Beneath yon cypress spiring high,
With pine and cedar spreading wide
Their darksome boughs on either side,
In open moonlight doth she lie;
Happy as others of her kind,   995
That, far from human neighbourhood,
Range unrestricted as the wind,
Through park, or chase, or savage wood.

But see the consecrated Maid
Emerging from a cedar shade   1000
To open moonshine, where the Doe
Beneath the cypress-spire is laid;
Like a patch of April snow—
Upon a bed of herbage green,
Lingering in a woody glade   1005
Or behind a rocky screen—
Lonely relic! which, if seen
By the shepherd, is passed by
With an inattentive eye.
Nor more regard doth She bestow   1010
Upon the uncomplaining Doe
Now couched at ease, though oft this day
Not unperplexed nor free from pain,
When she had tried, and tried in vain,
Approaching in her gentle way,   1015
To win some look of love, or gain
Encouragement to sport or play;
Attempts which still the heart-sick Maid
Rejected, or with slight repaid.   1019

Yet Emily is soothed;—the breeze
Came fraught with kindly sympathies.
As she approached yon rustic Shed
Hung with late-flowering woodbine, spread
Along the walls and overhead,
The fragrance of the breathing flowers
Revived a memory of those hours   1026
When here, in this remote alcove,
(While from the pendent woodbine came
Like odours, sweet as if the same)

A fondly-anxious Mother strove   1030
To teach her salutary fears
And mysteries above her years.
Yes, she is soothed: an Image faint,
And yet not faint—a presence bright
Returns to her—that blessèd Saint   1035
Who with mild looks and language mild
Instructed here her darling Child,
While yet a prattler on the knee,
To worship in simplicity
The invisible God, and take for guide
The faith reformed and purified.   1041

'Tis flown—the Vision, and the sense
Of that beguiling influence;
'But oh! thou Angel from above,
Mute Spirit of maternal love,   1045
That stood'st before my eyes, more clear
Than ghosts are fabled to appear
Sent upon embassies of fear;
As thou thy presence hast to me
Vouchsafed, in radiant ministry   1050
Descend on Francis; nor forbear
To greet him with a voice, and say;—
"If hope be a rejected stay,
Do thou, my christian Son, beware
Of that most lamentable snare,   1055
The self-reliance of despair!"'

Then from within the embowered
    retreat
Where she had found a grateful seat
Perturbed she issues. She will go!
Herself will follow to the war,   1060
And clasp her Father's knees;—ah, no!
She meets the insuperable bar,
The injunction by her Brother laid;
His parting charge—but ill obeyed—
That interdicted all debate,   1065
All prayer for this cause or for that;
All efforts that would turn aside
The headstrong current of their fate:
Her duty is to stand and wait;
In resignation to abide   1070
The shock, AND FINALLY SECURE
O'ER PAIN AND GRIEF A TRIUMPH PURE.
—She feels it, and her pangs are checked.
But now, as silently she paced
The turf, and thought by thought was
    chased,   1075
Came One who, with sedate respect,
Approached, and, greeting her, thus
    spake;
'An old man's privilege I take:
Dark is the time—a woeful day!
Dear daughter of affliction, say   1080
How can I serve you? point the way.'

'Rights have you, and may well be bold:
You with my Father have grown old
In friendship—strive—for his sake go—
Turn from us all the coming woe: 1085
This would I beg; but on my mind
A passive stillness is enjoined.

321   M

THE WHITE DOE OF RYLSTONE

On you, if room for mortal aid
Be left, is no restriction laid;
You not forbidden to recline   1090
With hope upon the Will divine.'

'Hope,' said the old Man, 'must abide
With all of us, whate'er betide.
In Craven's Wilds is many a den,
To shelter persecuted men: 1095
Far under ground is many a cave,
Where they might lie as in the grave,
Until this storm hath ceased to rave:
Or let them cross the River Tweed,
And be at once from peril freed!'   1100

'Ah tempt me not!' she faintly sighed;
'I will not counsel nor exhort,
With my condition satisfied;
But you, at least, may make report
Of what befalls,—be this your task—
This may be done;—'tis all I ask!'   1106

She spake—and from the Lady's sight
The Sire, unconscious of his age,
Departed promptly as a Page
Bound on some errand of delight.   1110
—The noble Francis—wise as brave,
Thought he, may want not skill to save.
With hopes in tenderness concealed,
Unarmed he followed to the field;   1114
Him will I seek: the insurgent Powers
Are now besieging Barnard's Towers,—
'Grant that the Moon which shines this
        night
May guide them in a prudent flight!'

But quick the turns of chance and
        change,   1119
And knowledge has a narrow range;
Whence idle fears, and needless pain,
And wishes blind, and efforts vain.—
The Moon may shine, but cannot be
Their guide in flight—already she
Hath witnessed their captivity.   1225
She saw the desperate assault
Upon that hostile castle made;—
But dark and dismal is the vault
Where Norton and his sons are laid!
Disastrous issue!—he had said   1130
'This night yon faithless Towers must
        yield,
Or we for ever quit the field.
—Neville is utterly dismayed,
For promise fails of Howard's aid;
And Dacre to our call replies   1135
That *he* is unprepared to rise.
My heart is sick;—this weary pause
Must needs be fatal to our cause.
The breach is open—on the wall,
This night,—the Banner shall be planted!'
—'Twas done: his Sons were with him—
        all;   1141
They belt him round with hearts un-
        daunted

And others follow;—Sire and Son
Leap down into the court;—"'Tis won'—
They shout aloud—but Heaven decreed
That with their joyful shout should close
The triumph of a desperate deed
Which struck with terror friends and
        foes!
The friend shrinks back—the foe recoils
From Norton and his filial band;   1150
But they, now caught within the toils,
Against a thousand cannot stand;—
The foe from numbers courage drew,
And overpowered that gallant few.
'A rescue for the Standard!' cried   1155
The Father from within the walls;
But, see, the sacred Standard falls!—
Confusion through the Camp spread
        wide:
Some fled; and some their fears detained:
But ere the Moon had sunk to rest   1160
In her pale chambers of the west,
Of that rash levy nought remained.

CANTO FIFTH

HIGH on a point of rugged ground
Among the wastes of Rylstone Fell,
Above the loftiest ridge or mound   1165
Where foresters or shepherds dwell,
An edifice of warlike frame
Stands single—Norton Tower its name—
It fronts all quarters, and looks round
O'er path and road, and plain and dell,
Dark moor, and gleam of pool and stream,
Upon a prospect without bound.

The summit of this bold ascent—
Though bleak and bare, and seldom free
As Pendle-hill or Pennygent   1175
From wind, or frost, or vapours wet—
Had often heard the sound of glee
When there the youthful Nortons met,
To practise games and archery: 1179
How proud and happy they! the crowd
Of Lookers-on how pleased and proud!
And from the scorching noon-tide sun,
From showers, or when the prize was won,
They to the Tower withdrew, and there
Would mirth run round, with generous
        fare;   1185
And the stern old Lord of Rylstone-hall
Was happiest, proudest, of them all!

But now, his Child, with anguish pale,
Upon the height walks to and fro;
'Tis well that she hath heard the tale,
Received the bitterness of woe: 1191
For she *had* hoped, had hoped and feared,
Such rights did feeble nature claim;
And oft her steps had hither steered,
Though not unconscious of self-blame;
For she her brother's charge revered,   1196
His farewell words; and by the same,
Yea, by her brother's very name,
Had, in her solitude, been cheered.   1199

Beside the lonely watch-tower stood
That grey-haired Man of gentle blood,
Who with her Father had grown old
In friendship; rival hunters they,
And fellow warriors in their day;
To Rylstone he the tidings brought; 1205
Then on this height the Maid had sought,
And, gently as he could, had told
The end of that dire Tragedy,
Which it had been his lot to see.

To him the Lady turned; 'You said
That Francis lives, *he* is not dead?' 1211

'Your noble brother hath been spared;
To take his life they have not dared;
On him and on his high endeavour 1214
The light of praise shall shine for ever!
Nor did he (such Heaven's will) in vain
His solitary course maintain;
Not vainly struggled in the might
Of duty, seeing with clear sight;
He was their comfort to the last, 1220
Their joy till every pang was past.

'I witnessed when to York they came—
What, Lady, if their feet were tied;
They might deserve a good Man's blame;
But marks of infamy and shame— 1225
These were their triumph, these their pride;
Nor wanted 'mid the pressing crowd
Deep feeling, that found utterance loud,
"Lo, Francis comes," there were who cried,
"A Prisoner once, but now set free! 1230
'Tis well, for he the worst defied
Through force of natural piety;
He rose not in this quarrel, he,
For concord's sake and England's good,
Suit to his Brothers often made 1235
With tears, and of his Father prayed—
And when he had in vain withstood
Their purpose—then did he divide,
He parted from them; but at their side
Now walks in unanimity." 1240
Then peace to cruelty and scorn,
While to the prison they are borne,
Peace, peace to all indignity!"

'And so in Prison were they laid—
Oh hear me, hear me, gentle Maid, 1245
For I am come with power to bless,
By scattering gleams, through your distress,
Of a redeeming happiness.
Me did a reverent pity move
And privilege of ancient love; 1250
And, in your service making bold,
Entrance I gained to that strong-hold.

'Your Father gave me cordial greeting;
But to his purposes, that burned
Within him, instantly returned: 1255
He was commanding and entreating,
And said—"We need not stop, my Son!
Thoughts press, and time is hurrying on"—
And so to Francis he renewed 1259
His words, more calmly thus pursued.

'"Might this our enterprise have sped,
Change wide and deep the Land had seen,
A renovation from the dead,
A spring-tide of immortal green: 1264
The darksome altars would have blazed
Like stars when clouds are rolled away;
Salvation to all eyes that gazed,
Once more the Rood had been upraised
To spread its arms, and stand for aye.
Then, then—had I survived to see 1270
New life in Bolton Priory,
The voice restored, the eye of Truth
Re-opened that inspired my youth;
To see her in her pomp arrayed—
This Banner (for such vow I made) 1275
Should on the consecrated breast
Of that same Temple have found rest:
I would myself have hung it high,
Fit offering of glad victory! 1279

'"A shadow of such thought remains
To cheer this sad and pensive time;
A solemn fancy yet sustains
One feeble Being—bids me climb
Even to the last—one effort more
To attest my Faith, if not restore. 1285

'"Hear then," said he, "while I impart,
My Son, the last wish of my heart.
The Banner strive thou to regain;
And, if the endeavour prove not vain,
Bear it—to whom if not to thee 1290
Shall I this lonely thought consign?—
Bear it to Bolton Priory,
And lay it on Saint Mary's shrine;
To wither in the sun and breeze
'Mid those decaying sanctities. 1295
There let at least the gift be laid,
The testimony there displayed;
Bold proof that with no selfish aim,
But for lost Faith and Christ's dear name,
I helmeted a brow though white, 1300
And took a place in all men's sight;
Yea, offered up this noble Brood,
This fair unrivalled Brotherhood,
And turned away from thee, my Son!
And left—but be the rest unsaid, 1305
The name untouched, the tear unshed;—
My wish is known, and I have done:
Now promise, grant this one request,
This dying prayer, and be thou blest!"

'Then Francis answered—"Trust thy Son, 1310
For, with God's will, it shall be done!"—

'The pledge obtained, the solemn word
Thus scarcely given, a noise was heard,

THE WHITE DOE OF RYLSTONE

And Officers appeared in state
To lead the prisoners to their fate.   1315
They rose, oh! wherefore should I fear
To tell, or, Lady, you to hear?
They rose—embraces none were given—
They stood like trees when earth and
      heaven   1319
Are calm; they knew each other's worth,
And reverently the Band went forth.
They met, when they had reached the
      door,
One with profane and harsh intent
Placed there—that he might go before
And, with that rueful Banner borne   1325
Aloft in sign of taunting scorn,
Conduct them to their punishment:
So cruel Sussex, unrestrained
By human feeling, had ordained.
The unhappy Banner Francis saw,   1330
And, with a look of calm command
Inspiring universal awe,
He took it from the soldier's hand;
And all the people that stood round   1334
Confirmed the deed in peace profound.
—High transport did the Father shed
Upon his Son—and they were led,
Led on, and yielded up their breath;
Together died, a happy death!—
But Francis, soon as he had braved   1340
That insult, and the Banner saved,
Athwart the unresisting tide
Of the spectators occupied
In admiration or dismay,
Bore instantly his Charge away.'   1345

These things, which thus had in the
      sight
And hearing passed of Him who stood
With Emily, on the Watch-tower height,
In Rylstone's woeful neighbourhood,
He told; and oftentimes with voice   1350
Of power to comfort or rejoice;
For deepest sorrows that aspire
Go high, no transport ever higher.
'Yes—God is rich in mercy,' said
The old Man to the silent Maid,   1355
'Yet, Lady! shines, through this black
      night,
One star of aspect heavenly bright;
Your brother lives—he lives—is come
Perhaps already to his home;
Then let us leave this dreary place.'   1360
She yielded, and with gentle pace,
Though without one uplifted look,
To Rylstone-hall her way she took.

CANTO SIXTH

WHY comes not Francis?—From the
      doleful City   1364
He fled,—and, in his flight, could hear
The death-sounds of the Minster-bell:
That sullen stroke pronounced farewell
To Marmaduke, cut off from pity!
To Ambrose that! and then a knell

For him, the sweet half-opened Flower!
For all—all dying in one hour!   1371
—Why comes not Francis? Thoughts of
      love
Should bear him to his Sister dear
With the fleet motion of a dove;
Yea, like a heavenly messenger   1375
Of speediest wing, should he appear.
Why comes he not?—for westward fast
Along the plain of York he past;
Reckless of what impels or leads,
Unchecked he hurries on;—nor heeds
The sorrow, through the Villages,   1381
Spread by triumphant cruelties
Of vengeful military force,
And punishment without remorse.
He marked not, heard not, as he fled;
All but the suffering heart was dead   1386
For him abandoned to blank awe,
To vacancy, and horror strong:
And the first object which he saw,
With conscious sight, as he swept along—
It was the Banner in his hand!   1391
He felt—and made a sudden stand.

He looked about like one betrayed:
What hath he done? what promise made?
Oh weak, weak moment! to what end
Can such a vain oblation tend,   1396
And he the Bearer?—Can he go
Carrying this instrument of woe,
And find, find anywhere, a right   1399
To excuse him in his Country's sight?
No; will not all men deem the change
A downward course, perverse and
      strange?
Here is it;—but how? when? must she,
The unoffending Emily,
Again this piteous object see?   1405

Such conflict long did he maintain,
Nor liberty nor rest could gain:
His own life into danger brought
By this sad burden—even that thought,
Exciting self-suspicion strong,   1410
Swayed the brave man to his wrong.
And how—unless it were the sense
Of all-disposing Providence,
Its will unquestionably shown—
How has the Banner clung so fast   1415
To a palsied, and unconscious hand;
Clung to the hand to which it passed
Without impediment? And why
But that Heaven's purpose might be known
Doth now no hindrance meet his eye,
No intervention, to withstand   1421
Fulfilment of a Father's prayer
Breathed to a Son forgiven, and blest
When all resentments were at rest,
And life in death laid the heart bare?—
Then, like a spectre sweeping by,   1426
Rushed through his mind the prophecy
Of utter desolation made
To Emily in the yew-tree shade:

He sighed, submitting will and power
To the stern embrace of that grasping
  hour.   1431
'No choice is left, the deed is mine—
Dead are they, dead!—and I will go,
And, for their sakes, come weal or woe,
Will lay the Relic on the shrine.'   1435

So forward with a steady will
He went, and traversed plain and hill;
And up the vale of Wharf his way
Pursued;—and, at the dawn of day,
Attained a summit whence his eyes   1440
Could see the Tower of Bolton rise.
There Francis for a moment's space
Made halt—but hark! a noise behind
Of horsemen at an eager pace!
He heard, and with misgiving mind.
—'Tis Sir George Bowes who leads the
  Band: 1446
They come, by cruel Sussex sent;
Who, when the Nortons from the hand
Of death had drunk their punishment,
Bethought him, angry and ashamed,   1450
How Francis, with the Banner claimed
As his own charge, had disappeared,
By all the standers-by revered.
His whole bold carriage (which had
  quelled
Thus far the Opposer, and repelled   1455
All censure, enterprise so bright
That even bad men had vainly striven
Against that overcoming light)
Was then reviewed, and prompt word
  given,
That to what place soever fled   1460
He should be seized, alive or dead.

The troop of horse have gained the height
Where Francis stood in open sight.
They hem him round—'Behold the proof,'
They cried, 'the Ensign in his hand!   1465
He did not arm, he walked aloof!
For why?—to save his Father's land;
Worst Traitor of them all is he,
A Traitor dark and cowardly!'

'I am no Traitor,' Francis said,   1470
'Though this unhappy freight I bear;
And must not part with. But beware;—
Err not, by hasty zeal misled,
Nor do a suffering Spirit wrong,
Whose self-reproaches are too strong!'
At this he from the beaten road   1476
Retreated towards a brake of thorn,
That like a place of vantage showed;
And there stood bravely, though forlorn.
In self-defence with warlike brow   1480
He stood,—nor weaponless was now;
He from a Soldier's hand had snatched
A spear,—and, so protected, watched
The Assailants, turning round and round;
But from behind with treacherous wound
A Spearman brought him to the ground.

The guardian lance, as Francis fell,
Dropped from him; but his other hand
The Banner clenched; till, from out the
  Band,
One, the most eager for the prize,   1490
Rushed in; and—while, O grief to tell!
A glimmering sense still left, with eyes
Unclosed the noble Francis lay—
Seized it, as hunters seize their prey;
But not before the warm life-blood   1495
Had tinged more deeply, as it flowed,
The wounds the broidered Banner
  showed,
Thy fatal work, O Maiden, innocent as
  good!

Proudly the Horsemen bore away
The Standard; and where Francis lay
There was he left alone, unwept,   1501
And for two days unnoticed slept.
For at that time bewildering fear
Possessed the country, far and near;
But, on the third day, passing by   1505
One of the Norton Tenantry
Espied the uncovered Corse; the Man
Shrunk as he recognised the face,
And to the nearest homesteads ran
And called the people to the place.   1510
—How desolate is Rylstone-hall!
This was the instant thought of all;
And if the lonely Lady there
Should be; to her they cannot bear
This weight of anguish and despair.   1515
So, when upon sad thoughts had prest
Thoughts sadder still, they deemed it
  best
That, if the Priest should yield assent
And no one hinder their intent,
Then, they, for Christian pity's sake,   1520
In holy ground a grave would make;
And straightway buried he should be
In the Churchyard of the Priory.

Apart, some little space, was made
The grave where Francis must be laid.
In no confusion or neglect   1526
This did they,—but in pure respect
That he was born of gentle blood;
And that there was no neighbourhood
Of kindred for him in that ground: 1530
So to the Churchyard they are bound,
Bearing the body on a bier;
And psalms they sing—a holy sound
That hill and vale with sadness hear.

But Emily hath raised her head,   1535
And is again disquieted;
She must behold!—so many gone,
Where is the solitary One?
And forth from Rylstone-hall stepped
  she,—
To seek her Brother forth she went,   1540
And tremblingly her course she bent
Toward Bolton's ruined Priory.

THE WHITE DOE OF RYLSTONE

She comes, and in the vale hath heard
The funeral dirge;—she sees the knot
Of people, sees them in one spot— 1545
And darting like a wounded bird
She reached the grave, and with her breast
Upon the ground received the rest,—
The consummation, the whole ruth
And sorrow of this final truth! 1550

CANTO SEVENTH

'Powers there are
That touch each other to the quick—in modes
Which the gross world no sense hath to perceive,
No soul to dream of.'[1]

THOU Spirit, whose angelic hand
Was to the harp a strong command,
Called the submissive strings to wake
In glory for this Maiden's sake,
Say, Spirit! whither hath she fled 1555
To hide her poor afflicted head?
What mighty forest in its gloom
Enfolds her?—is a rifted tomb
Within the wilderness her seat?
Some island which the wild waves beat—
Is that the Sufferer's last retreat? 1561
Or some aspiring rock, that shrouds
Its perilous front in mists and clouds?
High-climbing rock, low sunless dale,
Sea, desert, what do these avail? 1565
Oh take her anguish and her fears
Into a deep recess of years!

'Tis done;—despoil and desolation
O'er Rylstone's fair domain have blown;
Pools, terraces, and walks are sown 1570
With weeds; the bowers are overthrown,
Or have given way to slow mutation,
While, in their ancient habitation
The Norton name hath been unknown.
The lordly Mansion of its pride 1575
Is stripped; the ravage hath spread wide
Through park and field, a perishing
That mocks the gladness of the Spring!
And, with this silent gloom agreeing,
Appears a joyless human Being, 1580
Of aspect such as if the waste
Were under her dominion placed.
Upon a primrose bank, her throne
Of quietness, she sits alone;
Among the ruins of a wood, 1585
Erewhile a covert bright and green,
And where full many a brave tree stood,
That used to spread its boughs, and ring
With the sweet bird's carolling.
Behold her, like a virgin Queen, 1590
Neglecting in imperial state
These outward images of fate,
And carrying inward a serene
And perfect sway, through many a
thought
Of chance and change, that hath been
brought 1595

[1] See *Address to Kilchurn Castle* (*Memorials of a Tour in Scotland*, 1803), ll. 6–9.—ED.

To the subjection of a holy,
Though stern and rigorous, melancholy!
The like authority, with grace
Of awfulness, is in her face,—
There hath she fixed it; yet it seems 1600
To o'ershadow by no native right
That face, which cannot lose the gleams,
Lose utterly the tender gleams,
Of gentleness and meek delight,
And loving-kindness ever bright: 1605
Such is her sovereign mien:—her dress
(A vest with woollen cincture tied,
A hood of mountain-wool undyed)
Is homely,—fashioned to express
A wandering Pilgrim's humbleness. 1610

And she *hath* wandered, long and far,
Beneath the light of sun and star;
Hath roamed in trouble and in grief,
Driven forward like a withered leaf,
Yea, like a ship at random blown 1615
To distant places and unknown.
But now she dares to seek a haven
Among her native wilds of Craven;
Hath seen again her Father's roof,
And put her fortitude to proof; 1620
The mighty sorrow hath been borne,
And she is thoroughly forlorn:
Her soul doth in itself stand fast,
Sustained by memory of the past
And strength of Reason; held above
The infirmities of mortal love; 1626
Undaunted, lofty, calm, and stable,
And awfully impenetrable.

And so—beneath a mouldered tree,
A self-surviving leafless oak 1630
By unregarded age from stroke
Of ravage saved—sate Emily.
There did she rest, with head reclined,
Herself most like a stately flower,
(Such have I seen) whom chance of birth
Hath separated from its kind, 1636
To live and die in a shady bower,
Single on the gladsome earth.

When, with a noise like distant thunder,
A troop of deer came sweeping by; 1640
And, suddenly, behold a wonder!
For One, among those rushing deer,
A single One, in mid career
Hath stopped, and fixed her large full eye
Upon the Lady Emily; 1645
A Doe most beautiful, clear-white,
A radiant creature, silver-bright!

Thus checked, a little while it stayed;
A little thoughtful pause it made;
And then advanced with stealth-like
pace, 1650
Drew softly near her, and more near—
Looked round—but saw no cause for
fear;
So to her feet the Creature came,

326

And laid its head upon her knee,
And looked into the Lady's face,   1655
A look of pure benignity,
And fond unclouded memory.
It is, thought Emily, the same,
The very Doe of other years!—
The pleading look the Lady viewed,   1660
And, by her gushing thoughts subdued,
She melted into tears—
A flood of tears that flowed apace
Upon the happy Creature's face.

Oh, moment ever blest! O Pair   1665
Beloved of Heaven, Heaven's chosen care,
This was for you a precious greeting;
And may it prove a fruitful meeting!
Joined are they, and the sylvan Doe
Can she depart? can she forego   1670
The Lady, once her playful peer,
And now her sainted Mistress dear?
And will not Emily receive
This lovely chronicler of things
Long past, delights and sorrowings?
Lone Sufferer! will not she believe   1676
The promise in that speaking face;
And welcome, as a gift of grace,
The saddest thought the Creature brings?

That day, the first of a re-union   1680
Which was to teem with high communion,
That day of balmy April weather,
They tarried in the wood together.
And when, ere fall of evening dew,   1684
She from her sylvan haunt withdrew,
The White Doe tracked with faithful pace
The Lady to her dwelling-place;
That nook where, on paternal ground,
A habitation she had found,
The Master of whose humble board   1690
Once owned her Father for his Lord;
A hut, by tufted trees defended,
Where Rylstone brook with Wharf is
   blended.

When Emily by morning light   1694
Went forth, the Doe stood there in sight.
She shrunk:—with one frail shock of pain
Received and followed by a prayer,
She saw the Creature once again;
Shun will she not, she feels, will bear;—
But, wheresoever she looked round,   1700
All now was trouble-haunted ground;
And therefore now she deems it good
Once more this restless neighbourhood
To leave.—Unwooed, yet unforbidden,
The White Doe followed up the vale,
Up to another cottage, hidden   1706
In the deep fork of Amerdale;
And there may Emily restore
Herself, in spots unseen before.
—Why tell of mossy rock, or tree,   1710
By lurking Dernbrook's pathless side,
Haunts of a strengthening amity
That calmed her, cheered, and fortified?

For she hath ventured now to read
Of time, and place, and thought, and
   deed—   1715
Endless history that lies
In her silent Follower's eyes;
Who with a power like human reason
Discerns the favourable season,
Skilled to approach or to retire,—   1720
From looks conceiving her desire;
From look, deportment, voice, or mien,
That vary to the heart within.
If she too passionately wreathed
Her arms, or over-deeply breathed,   1725
Walked quick or slowly, every mood
In its degree was understood;
Then well may their accord be true,
And kindliest intercourse ensue.
—Oh! surely 'twas a gentle rousing   1730
When she by sudden glimpse espied
The White Doe on the Mountain browsing,
Or in the meadow wandered wide!
How pleased, when down the Straggler
   sank
Beside her, on some sunny bank!   1735
How soothed, when in thick bower en-
   closed,
They, like a nested pair, reposed!
Fair Vision! when it crossed the Maid
Within some rocky cavern laid,
The dark cave's portal gliding by,   1740
White as whitest cloud on high
Floating through the azure sky.
—What now is left for pain or fear?
That Presence, dearer and more dear,
While they, side by side, were straying,
And the shepherd's pipe was playing,
Did now a very gladness yield   1747
At morning to the dewy field,
And with a deeper peace endued
The hour of moonlight solitude.   1750

With her Companion, in such frame
Of mind, to Rylstone back she came;
And, ranging through the wasted groves,
Received the memory of old loves,
Undisturbed and undistrest,   1755
Into a soul which now was blest
With a soft spring-day of holy,
Mild, and grateful, melancholy:
Not sunless gloom or unenlightened,
But by tender fancies brightened.   1760

When the bells of Rylstone played
Their sabbath music—'GOD US AYDE!'
That was the sound they seemed to speak;
Inscriptive legend which I ween
May on these holy bells be seen,   1765
That legend and her Grandsire's name;
And oftentimes the Lady meek
Had in her childhood read the same;
Words which she slighted at that day;
But now, when such sad change was
   wrought,   1770
And of that lonely name she thought,

327

THE WHITE DOE OF RYLSTONE

The bells of Rylstone seemed to say,
While she sate listening in the shade,
With vocal music, 'GOD US AYDE;'
And all the hills were glad to bear   1775
Their part in this effectual prayer.

Nor lacked she Reason's firmest power;
But with the White Doe at her side
Up would she climb to Norton Tower,
And thence look round her far and wide,
Her fate there measuring;—all is stilled,—
The weak One hath subdued her heart;
Behold the prophecy fulfilled,   1783
Fulfilled, and she sustains her part!
But here her Brother's words have failed;
Here hath a milder doom prevailed;   1786
That she, of him and all bereft,
Hath yet this faithful Partner left;
This one Associate that disproves
His words remains for her, and loves.
If tears are shed, they do not fall   1791
For loss of him—for one, or all;
Yet sometimes, sometimes doth she weep
Moved gently in her soul's soft sleep;
A few tears down her cheek descend   1795
For this her last and living Friend.

Bless, tender Hearts, their mutual lot,
And bless for both this savage spot;
Which Emily doth sacred hold
For reasons dear and manifold—   1800
Here hath she, here before her sight,
Close to the summit of this height,
The grassy rock-encircled Pound
In which the Creature first was found.
So beautiful the timid Thrall   1805
(A spotless Youngling white as foam)
Her youngest Brother brought it home;
The youngest, then a lusty boy,
Bore it, or led, to Rylstone-hall
With heart brimful of pride and joy!   1810

But most to Bolton's sacred Pile,
On favouring nights, she loved to go;
There ranged through cloister, court, and
      aisle,
Attended by the soft-paced Doe;
Nor feared she in the still moonshine
To look upon Saint Mary's shrine;   1816
Nor on the lonely turf that showed
Where Francis slept in his last abode.
For that she came; there oft she sate
Forlorn, but not disconsolate: 1820
And when she from the abyss returned
Of thought, she neither shrunk nor
      mourned;
Was happy that she lived to greet
Her mute Companion as it lay
In love and pity at her feet;   1825
How happy in its turn to meet
The recognition! the mild glance
Beamed from that gracious countenance;
Communication, like the ray
Of a new morning, to the nature   1830
And prospects of the inferior Creature!

A mortal Song we sing, by dower
Encouraged of celestial power;
Power which the viewless Spirit shed
By whom we were first visited;   1835
Whose voice we heard, whose hand and
      wings
Swept like a breeze the conscious strings,
When, left in solitude, erewhile
We stood before this ruined Pile,   1839
And, quitting unsubstantial dreams,
Sang in this Presence kindred themes;
Distress and desolation spread
Through human hearts, and pleasure
      dead,—
Dead—but to live again on earth,
A second and yet nobler birth;   1845
Dire overthrow, and yet how high
The re-ascent in sanctity!
From fair to fairer; day by day
A more divine and loftier way!
Even such this blessèd Pilgrim trod,   1850
By sorrow lifted towards her God;
Uplifted to the purest sky
Of undisturbed mortality.
Her own thoughts loved she; and could
      bend
A dear look to her lowly Friend;   1855
There stopped; her thirst was satisfied
With what this innocent spring supplied:
Her sanction inwardly she bore,
And stood apart from human cares:
But to the world returned no more,
Although with no unwilling mind   1861
Help did she give at need, and joined
The Wharfdale peasants in their prayers.
At length, thus faintly, faintly tied
To earth, she was set free, and died.   1865
Thy soul, exalted Emily,
Maid of the blasted family,
Rose to the God from whom it came!
—In Rylstone Church her mortal frame
Was buried by her Mother's side.   1870

Most glorious sunset! and a ray
Survives—the twilight of this day—
In that fair Creature whom the fields
Support, and whom the forest shields;
Who, having filled a holy place,   1875
Partakes, in her degree, Heaven's grace;
And bears a memory and a mind
Raised far above the law of kind;
Haunting the spots with lonely cheer
Which her dear Mistress once held dear:
Loves most what Emily loved most—
The enclosure of this churchyard ground;
Here wanders like a gliding ghost,
And every sabbath here is found;   1884
Comes with the people when the bells
Are heard among the moorland dells,
Finds entrance through yon arch, where
      way
Lies open on the sabbath day;
Here walks amid the mournful waste
Of prostrate altars, shrines defaced.   1890

And floors encumbered with rich show
Of fret-work imagery laid low;
Paces softly, or makes halt,
By fractured cell, or tomb, or vault;
By plate of monumental brass   1895
Dim-gleaming among weeds and grass,
And sculptured Forms of Warriors brave:
But chiefly by that single grave,
That one sequestered hillock green,
The pensive visitant is seen.   1900

There doth the gentle Creature lie
With those adversities unmoved;
Calm spectacle, by earth and sky
In their benignity approved!
And aye, methinks, this hoary Pile,   1905
Subdued by outrage and decay,
Looks down upon her with a smile,
A gracious smile, that seems to say—
'Thou, thou art not a Child of Time,
But Daughter of the Eternal Prime!'   1910

ECCLESIASTICAL SONNETS

IN SERIES [1]

[Composed mostly in 1821.—Published 1822.]

PART I

FROM THE INTRODUCTION OF CHRISTIANITY INTO BRITAIN TO THE
CONSUMMATION OF THE PAPAL DOMINION

'A verse may catch a wandering Soul, that flies
Profounder Tracts, and by a blest surprise
Convert delight into a Sacrifice.'[2]

I

INTRODUCTION

I, WHO accompanied with faithful pace
Cerulean Duddon from its cloud-fed
   spring,
And loved with spirit ruled by his to sing
Of mountain-quiet and boon nature's
   grace;
I, who essayed the nobler Stream to
   trace   5
Of Liberty, and smote the plausive string
Till the checked torrent, proudly triumph-
   ing,
Won for herself a lasting resting-place;
Now seek upon the heights of Time the
   source
Of a HOLY RIVER, on whose banks are
   found   10
Sweet pastoral flowers, and laurels that
   have crowned
Full oft the unworthy brow of lawless
   force;
And, for delight of him who tracks its
   course,
Immortal amaranth and palms abound.

II

CONJECTURES

IF there be prophets on whose spirits rest
Past things, revealed like future, they can
   tell
What Powers, presiding o'er the sacred well
Of Christian Faith, this savage Island
   blessed
With its first bounty. Wandering through
   the west,   5
Did holy Paul[3] a while in Britain dwell,
And call the Fountain forth by miracle,
And with dread signs the nascent Stream
   invest?
Or He, whose bonds dropped off, whose
   prison doors
Flew open, by an Angel's voice unbarred?
Or some of humbler name, to these wild
   shores   11
Storm-driven; who, having seen the cup
   of woe
Pass from their Master, sojourned here to
   guard
The precious Current they had taught to
   flow?

---

[1] The *Ecclesiastical Sonnets* (first so called in 1837; previously *Ecclesiastical Sketches*) were written for the most part in 1821, and published in 1822. Chronological notes are attached only to those sonnets to which this observation does not apply —ED.
[2] This motto, from George Herbert, was added in 1827.—ED.   [3] See Note, p. 721.

ECCLESIASTICAL SONNETS

III

TREPIDATION OF THE DRUIDS

SCREAMS round the Arch-druid's brow the
    sea-mew[1]—white
As Menai's foam; and toward the mystic
    ring
Where Augurs stand, the Future ques-
    tioning,
Slowly the cormorant aims her heavy
    flight,
Portending ruin to each baleful rite   5
That, in the lapse of ages, hath crept o'er
Diluvian truths, and patriarchal lore.
Haughty the Bard: can these meek doc-
    trines blight
His transports? wither his heroic strains?
But all shall be fulfilled;—the Julian spear
A way first opened; and, with Roman
    chains,   11
The tidings come of Jesus crucified;
They come—they spread—the weak, the
    suffering, hear;
Receive the faith, and in the hope abide.

IV

DRUIDICAL EXCOMMUNICATION

MERCY and Love have met thee on thy
    road,
Thou wretched Outcast, from the gift of
    fire
And food cut off by sacerdotal ire,
From every sympathy that Man be-
    stowed!
Yet shall it claim our reverence, that to
    God,   5
Ancient of days! that to the eternal Sire,
These jealous Ministers of law aspire,
As to the one sole fount whence wisdom
    flowed,
Justice, and order. Tremblingly escaped,
As if with prescience of the coming storm,
That intimation when the stars were
    shaped;   11
And still, 'mid yon thick woods, the
    primal truth
Glimmers through many a superstitious
    form
That fills the Soul with unavailing ruth.

V

UNCERTAINTY

DARKNESS surrounds us; seeking, we are
    lost
On Snowdon's wilds, amid Brigantian
    coves,
Or where the solitary shepherd roves
Along the plain of Sarum, by the ghost
Of Time and shadows of Tradition crost;

[1] This water-fowl was, among the Druids, an emblem of those traditions connected with the Deluge
that made an important part of their mysteries. The
Cormorant was a bird of bad omen.

And where the boatman of the Western
    Isles   6
Slackens his course—to mark those holy
    piles
Which yet survive on bleak Iona's coast.
Nor these, nor monuments of eldest name,
Nor Taliesin's unforgotten lays,   10
Nor characters of Greek or Roman fame,
To an unquestionable Source have led;
Enough—if eyes, that sought the foun-
    tain-head
In vain, upon the growing Rill may gaze.

VI

PERSECUTION

LAMENT! for Diocletian's fiery sword
Works busy as the lightning; but instinct
With malice ne'er to deadliest weapon
    linked,
Which God's ethereal storehouses afford:
Against the Followers of the incarnate
    Lord   5
It rages;—some are smitten in the field—
Some pierced to the heart through the
    ineffectual shield
Of sacred home;—with pomp are others
    gored
And dreadful respite. Thus was Alban
    tried,
England's first Martyr, whom no threats
    could shake;   10
Self-offered victim, for his friend he died,
And for the faith; nor shall his name for-
    sake
That Hill, whose flowery platform seems
    to rise
By Nature decked for holiest sacrifice.[2]

VII

RECOVERY

As, when a storm hath ceased, the birds
    regain
Their cheerfulness, and busily retrim
Their nests, or chant a gratulating hymn
To the blue ether and bespangled plain;
Even so, in many a re-constructed fane,   5
Have the survivors of this Storm renewed
Their holy rites with vocal gratitude:
And solemn ceremonials they ordain
To celebrate their great deliverance;
Most feelingly instructed 'mid their
    fear—   10
That persecution, blind with rage ex-
    treme,
May not the less, through Heaven's mild
    countenance,
Even in her own despite, both feed and
    cheer;
For all things are less dreadful than they
    seem.

[2] See Note, p. 721.

VIII

TEMPTATIONS FROM ROMAN REFINEMENTS

WATCH, and be firm! for soul-subduing
   vice,
Heart-killing luxury, on your steps await.
Fair houses, baths, and banquets delicate,
And temples flashing, bright as polar ice,
Their radiance through the woods—may
   yet suffice   5
To sap your hardy virtue, and abate
Your love of Him upon whose forehead
   sate
The crown of thorns; whose life-blood
   flowed, the price
Of your redemption. Shun the insidious
   arts
That Rome provides, less dreading from
   her frown   10
Than from her wily praise, her peaceful
   gown,
Language, and letters;—these, though
   fondly viewed
As humanising graces, are but parts
And instruments of deadliest servitude!

IX

DISSENSIONS

THAT heresies should strike (if truth be
   scanned
Presumptuously) their roots both wide
   and deep,
Is natural as dreams to feverish sleep.
Lo! Discord at the altar dares to stand
Uplifting toward high Heaven her fiery
   brand,   5
A cherished Priestess of the new-baptized!
But chastisement shall follow peace de-
   spised.
The Pictish cloud darkens the enervate land
By Rome abandoned; vain are suppliant
   cries,
And prayers that would undo her forced
   farewell;   10
For she returns not.—Awed by her own
   knell,
She casts the Britons upon strange Allies,
Soon to become more dreaded enemies
Than heartless misery called them to repel.

X

STRUGGLE OF THE BRITONS AGAINST
THE BARBARIANS

RISE!—they *have* risen: of brave Aneurin
   ask
How they have scourged old foes, per-
   fidious friends:
The Spirit of Caractacus descends
Upon the Patriots, animates their task;—
Amazement runs before the towering
   casque   5
Of Arthur, bearing through the stormy field
The virgin sculptured on his Christian
   shield:—

Stretched in the sunny light of victory
   bask
The Host that followed Urien as he strode
O'er heaps of slain;—from Cambrian
   wood and moss   10
Druids descend, auxiliars of the Cross;
Bards, nursed on blue Plinlimmon's still
   abode,
Rush on the fight, to harps preferring
   swords,
And everlasting deeds to burning words!

XI

SAXON CONQUEST

NOR wants the cause the panic-striking aid
Of hallelujahs[1] tost from hill to hill—
For instant victory. But Heaven's high
   will
Permits a second and a darker shade
Of Pagan night. Afflicted and dismayed,
The Relics of the sword flee to the moun-
   tains: 6
O wretched Land! whose tears have
   flowed like fountains;
Whose arts and honours in the dust are
   laid
By men yet scarcely conscious of a care
For other monuments than those of
   Earth;   10
Who, as the fields and woods have given
   them birth,
Will build their savage fortunes only
   there;
Content, if foss, and barrow, and the girth
Of long-drawn rampart, witness what
   they were.

XII

MONASTERY OF OLD BANGOR[2]

THE oppression of the tumult—wrath and
   scorn—
The tribulation—and the gleaming blades—
Such is the impetuous spirit that pervades
The song of Taliesin;—Ours shall mourn
The *unarmed* Host who by their prayers
   would turn   5
The sword from Bangor's walls, and guard
   the store
Of Aboriginal and Roman lore,
And Christian monuments, that now
   must burn
To senseless ashes. Mark! how all things
   swerve
From their known course, or vanish like
   a dream;   10
Another language spreads from coast to
   coast;
Only perchance some melancholy Stream
And some indignant Hills old names pre-
   serve,
When laws, and creeds, and people all are
   lost!

[1] See Note, p. 721.   [2] See Note, ibid.

ECCLESIASTICAL SONNETS

XIII
CASUAL INCITEMENT

A BRIGHT-HAIRED company of youthful
    slaves,
Beautiful strangers, stand within the pale
Of a sad market, ranged for public sale,
Where Tiber's stream the immortal City
    laves:
ANGLI by name; and not an ANGEL waves
His wing who could seem lovelier to
    man's eye   6
Than they appear to holy Gregory;
Who, having learnt that name, salvation
    craves
For Them, and for their Land. The
    earnest Sire,
His questions urging, feels, in slender ties
Of chiming sound, commanding sym-
    pathies;   11
DE-IRIANS—he would save them from
    God's IRE;
Subjects of Saxon ÆLLA—they shall sing
Glad HALLE-lujahs to the eternal King!

XIV
GLAD TIDINGS

FOR ever hallowed be this morning fair,
Blest be the unconscious shore on which
    ye tread,
And blest the silver Cross, which ye, in-
    stead
Of martial banner, in procession bear;
The Cross preceding Him who floats in
    air,   5
The pictured Saviour!—By Augustin led,
They come—and onward travel without
    dread,
Chanting in barbarous ears a tuneful
    prayer—
Sung for themselves, and those whom
    they would free!
Rich conquest waits them:—the tem-
    pestuous sea   10
Of Ignorance, that ran so rough and high
And heeded not the voice of clashing
    swords,
These good men humble by a few bare
    words,
And calm with fear of God's divinity.

XV
PAULINUS[1]

BUT to remote Northumbria's royal Hall,
Where thoughtful Edwin, tutored in the
    school
Of sorrow, still maintains a heathen rule,
Who comes with functions apostolical?
Mark him, of shoulders curved, and sta-
    ture tall,   5

Black hair, and vivid eye, and meagre
    cheek,
His prominent feature like an eagle's
    beak;
A Man whose aspect doth at once appal
And strike with reverence. The Monarch
    leans
Toward the pure truths this Delegate
    propounds,   10
Repeatedly his own deep mind he sounds
With careful hesitation.—then convenes
A synod of his Councillors:—give ear,
And what a pensive Sage doth utter, hear!

XVI
PERSUASION

'MAN'S life is like a Sparrow, mighty
    King!
That—while at banquet with your Chiefs
    you sit
Housed near a blazing fire—is seen to flit
Safe from the wintry tempest. Fluttering,
Here did it enter; there, on hasty wing,   5
Flies out, and passes on from cold to cold;
But whence it came we know not, nor be-
    hold
Whither it goes. Even such, that tran-
    sient Thing,
The human Soul; not utterly unknown
While in the Body lodged, her warm
    abode;   10
But from what world She came, what woe
    or weal
On her departure waits, no tongue hath
    shown;
This mystery if the Stranger can reveal,
His be a welcome cordially bestowed!'[2]

XVII
CONVERSION

PROMPT transformation works the novel
    Lore;
The Council closed, the Priest in full
    career
Rides forth, an armèd man, and hurls a
    spear
To desecrate the Fane which heretofore
He served in folly. Woden falls, and
    Thor   5
Is overturned; the mace, in battle heaved
(So might they dream) till victory was
    achieved,
Drops, and the God himself is seen no
    more.
Temple and Altar sink, to hide their shame
Amid oblivious weeds. '*O come to me*,   10
Ye heavy laden!' such the inviting voice
Heard near fresh streams;[3] and thou-
    sands, who rejoice
In the new Rite—the pledge of sanctity,
Shall, by regenerate life, the promise
    claim.

---

[1] See Note, p. 722.   [2] See Note, p. 722.   [3] See Note, ibid.

332

XVIII

APOLOGY

NOR scorn the aid which Fancy oft doth
　　lend
The Soul's eternal interests to promote:
Death, darkness, danger, are our natural
　　lot;
And evil Spirits *may* our walk attend
For aught the wisest know or compre-
　　hend;　　　　　　　　　　　　　5
Then be *good* Spirits free to breathe a note
Of elevation; let their odours float
Around these Converts; and their glories
　　blend,
The midnight stars outshining, or the
　　blaze
Of the noon-day. Nor doubt that golden
　　cords　　　　　　　　　　　　10
Of good works, mingling with the visions,
　　raise
The Soul to purer worlds: and *who* the line
Shall draw, the limits of the power define,
That even imperfect faith to man affords?

XIX

PRIMITIVE SAXON CLERGY[1]

How beautiful your presence, how be-
　　nign,
Servants of God! who not a thought will
　　share
With the vain world; who, outwardly as
　　bare
As winter trees, yield no fallacious sign
That the firm soul is clothed with fruit
　　divine!　　　　　　　　　　　5
Such Priest, when service worthy of his
　　care
Has called him forth to breathe the com-
　　mon air,
Might seem a saintly Image from its shrine
Descended:—happy are the eyes that
　　meet
The Apparition; evil thoughts are stayed
At his approach, and low-bowed necks
　　entreat　　　　　　　　　　11
A benediction from his voice or hand;
Whence grace, through which the heart
　　can understand,
And vows, that bind the will, in silence
　　made.

XX

OTHER INFLUENCES

AH, when the Body, round which in love
　　we clung,
Is chilled by death, does mutual service
　　fail?
Is tender pity then of no avail?
Are intercessions of the fervent tongue
A waste of hope?—From this sad source
　　have sprung　　　　　　　　　5

[1] See Note, p. 722.

Rites that console the Spirit, under grief
Which ill can brook more rational relief:
Hence, prayers are shaped amiss, and
　　dirges sung
For Souls whose doom is fixed! The way
　　is smooth
For Power that travels with the human
　　heart:　　　　　　　　　　　10
Confession ministers the pang to soothe
In him who at the ghost of guilt doth start.
Ye holy Men, so earnest in your care,
Of your own mighty instruments beware!

XXI

SECLUSION

LANCE, shield, and sword relinquished—
　　at his side
A bead-roll, in his hand a claspèd book,
Or staff more harmless than a shepherd's
　　crook,
The war-worn Chieftain quits the world—
　　to hide
His thin autumnal locks where Monks
　　abide　　　　　　　　　　　5
In cloistered privacy. But not to dwell
In soft repose he comes. Within his cell,
Round the decaying trunk of human pride,
At morn, and eve, and midnight's silent
　　hour,
Do penitential cogitations cling;　　　10
Like ivy, round some ancient elm, they
　　twine
In grisly folds and strictures serpentine;
Yet, while they strangle, a fair growth
　　they bring,
For recompense—their own perennial
　　bower.

XXII

CONTINUED

METHINKS that to some vacant hermitage
My feet would rather turn—to some dry
　　nook
Scooped out of living rock, and near a
　　brook
Hurled down a mountain-cove from stage
　　to stage,
Yet tempering, for my sight, its bustling
　　rage　　　　　　　　　　　　5
In the soft heaven of a translucent pool;
Thence creeping under sylvan arches cool,
Fit haunt of shapes whose glorious equi-
　　page
Would elevate my dreams. A beechen
　　bowl,
A maple dish, my furniture should be;
Crisp, yellow leaves my bed; the hooting
　　owl　　　　　　　　　　　　11
My night-watch: nor should e'er the
　　crested fowl
From thorp or vill his matins sound for
　　me,
Tired of the world and all its industry.

ECCLESIASTICAL SONNETS

XXIII

REPROOF

BUT what if One, through grove or flowery mead,
Indulging thus at will the creeping feet
Of a voluptuous indolence, should meet
Thy hovering Shade, O venerable Bede!
The saint, the scholar, from a circle freed
Of toil stupendous, in a hallowed seat 6
Of learning, where thou heard'st the billows beat
On a wild coast, rough monitors to feed
Perpetual industry. Sublime Recluse!
The recreant soul, that dares to shun the debt 10
Imposed on human kind, must first forget
Thy diligence, thy unrelaxing use
Of a long life; and, in the hour of death,
The last dear service of thy passing breath![1]

XXIV

SAXON MONASTERIES, AND LIGHTS AND SHADES OF THE RELIGION

BY such examples moved to unbought pains,
The people work like congregated bees;
Eager to build the quiet Fortresses
Where Piety, as they believe, obtains
From Heaven a *general* blessing; timely rains 5
Or needful sunshine; prosperous enterprise,
Justice and peace:—bold faith! yet also rise
The sacred Structures for less doubtful gains.
The Sensual think with reverence of the palms
Which the chaste Votaries seek, beyond the grave; 10
If penance be redeemable, thence alms
Flow to the poor, and freedom to the slave;
And if full oft the Sanctuary save
Lives black with guilt, ferocity it calms.

XXV

MISSIONS AND TRAVELS

NOT sedentary all: there are who roam
To scatter seeds of life on barbarous shores;
Or quit with zealous step their knee-worn floors
To seek the general mart of Christendom;
Whence they, like richly-laden merchants, come 5
To their belovèd cells:—or shall we say
That, like the Red-cross Knight, they urge their way,
To lead in memorable triumph home
Truth, their immortal Una? Babylon,

Learnèd and wise, hath perished utterly,
Nor leaves her Speech one word to aid the sigh 11
That would lament her;—Memphis, Tyre, are gone
With all their Arts,—but classic lore glides on
By these Religious saved for all posterity.

XXVI

ALFRED

BEHOLD a pupil of the monkish gown,
The pious ALFRED, King to Justice dear!
Lord of the harp and liberating spear;
Mirror of Princes! Indigent Renown 4
Might range the starry ether for a crown
Equal to *his* deserts, who, like the year,
Pours forth his bounty, like the day doth cheer,
And awes like night with mercy-tempered frown.
Ease from this noble miser of his time
No moment steals; pain narrows not his cares.[2] 10
Though small his kingdom as a spark or gem,
Of Alfred boasts remote Jerusalem,
And Christian India, through her wide-spread clime,
In sacred converse gifts with Alfred shares.

XXVII

HIS DESCENDANTS

WHEN thy great soul was freed from mortal chains,
Darling of England! many a bitter shower
Fell on thy tomb; but emulative power
Flowed in thy line through undegenerate veins. 4
The Race of Alfred covet glorious pains
When dangers threaten, dangers ever new!
Black tempests bursting, blacker still in view!
But manly sovereignty its hold retains;
The root sincere, the branches bold to strive
With the fierce tempest, while, within the round 10
Of their protection, gentle virtues thrive;
As oft, 'mid some green plot of open ground,
Wide as the oak extends its dewy gloom,
The fostered hyacinths spread their purple bloom.

XXVIII

INFLUENCE ABUSED

URGED by Ambition, who with subtlest skill
Changes her means, the Enthusiast as a dupe
Shall soar, and as a hypocrite can stoop,

---

[1] He expired dictating the last words of a translation of St. John's Gospel.

[2] See Note, p. 722.

And turn the instruments of good to ill,
Moulding the credulous people to his will.
Such DUNSTAN:—from its Benedictine
    coop   6
Issues the master Mind, at whose fell swoop
The chaste affections tremble to fulfil
Their purposes. Behold, pre-signified,
The Might of spiritual sway! his thoughts,
    his dreams,   10
Do in the supernatural world abide:
So vaunt a throng of Followers, filled
    with pride
In what they see of virtues pushed to
    extremes,
And sorceries of talent misapplied.

XXIX
DANISH CONQUESTS

WOE to the Crown that doth the Cowl
    obey![1]
Dissension, checking arms that would
    restrain
The incessant Rovers of the northern main,
Helps to restore and spread a Pagan sway:
But Gospel-truth is potent to allay   5
Fierceness and rage; and soon the cruel
    Dane
Feels, through the influence of her gentle
    reign,
His native superstitions melt away.
Thus often, when thick gloom the east
    o'ershrouds,
The full-orbed Moon, slow-climbing, doth
    appear   10
Silently to consume the heavy clouds;
How no one can resolve; but every eye
Around her sees, while air is hushed, a clear
And widening circuit of ethereal sky.

XXX
CANUTE

A PLEASANT music floats along the Mere,
From Monks in Ely chanting service high,
While-as Canùte the King is rowing by:
'My Oarsmen,' quoth the mighty King,
    'draw near,
That we the sweet song of the Monks
    may hear!'   5
He listens (all past conquests and all
    schemes
Of future vanishing like empty dreams)
Heart-touched, and haply not without a
    tear.
The Royal Minstrel, ere the choir is still,
While his free Barge skims the smooth
    flood along,   10
Gives to that rapture an accordant
    Rhyme.[2]
O suffering Earth! be thankful; sternest
    clime
And rudest age are subject to the thrill
Of heaven-descended Piety and Song.

<hr />

[1] See Note, p. 722.   [2] Which is still extant.

XXXI
THE NORMAN CONQUEST

THE woman-hearted Confessor prepares
The evanescence of the Saxon line.
Hark! 'tis the tolling Curfew!—the stars
    shine;
But of the lights that cherish household
    cares
And festive gladness, burns not one that
    dares   5
To twinkle after that dull stroke of thine,
Emblem and instrument, from Thames to
    Tyne,
Of force that daunts, and cunning that
    ensnares!
Yet as the terrors of the lordly bell,
That quench, from hut to palace, lamps
    and fires,   10
Touch not the tapers of the sacred quires;
Even so a thraldom, studious to expel
Old laws, and ancient customs to derange,
To Creed or Ritual brings no fatal change.

XXXII

[Composed (?).—Published 1837.]

COLDLY we spake. The Saxons, over-
    powered
By wrong triumphant through its own
    excess,
From fields laid waste, from house and
    home devoured
By flames, look up to heaven and crave
    redress
From God's eternal justice. Pitiless   5
Though men be, there are angels that can
    feel
For wounds that death alone has power
    to heal,
For penitent guilt, and innocent distress.
And has a Champion risen in arms to try
His Country's virtue, fought, and breathes
    no more;   10
Him in their hearts the people canonize;
And far above the mine's most precious
    ore
The least small pittance of bare mould
    they prize
Scooped from the sacred earth where his
    dear relics lie.

XXXIII
THE COUNCIL OF CLERMONT

'AND shall,' the Pontiff asks, 'profane-
    ness flow
From Nazareth—source of Christian
    piety,
From Bethlehem, from the Mounts of
    Agony
And glorified Ascension? Warriors, go,
With prayers and blessings we your path
    will sow;   5

Like Moses hold our hands erect, till ye
Have chased far off by righteous victory
These sons of Amalek, or laid them
    low!'—
'GOD WILLETH IT,' the whole assembly
    cry;
Shout which the enraptured multitude
    astounds!   10
The Council-roof and Clermont's towers
    reply;—
'God willeth it,' from hill to hill rebounds,
And, in awe-stricken Countries far and
    nigh,
Through 'Nature's hollow arch' that
    voice resounds.[1]

XXXIV
CRUSADES

THE turbaned Race are poured in thicken-
    ing swarms
Along the west; though driven from
    Aquitaine,
The Crescent glitters on the towers of
    Spain;
And soft Italia feels renewed alarms;
The scimitar, that yields not to the
    charms   5
Of ease, the narrow Bosphorus will dis-
    dain;
Nor long (that crossed) would Grecian
    hills detain
Their tents, and check the current of
    their arms.
Then blame not those who, by the
    mightiest lever
Known to the moral world, Imagination,
Upheave, so seems it, from her natural
    station   11
All Christendom:—they sweep along (was
    never
So huge a host!)—to tear from the
    Unbeliever
The precious Tomb, their haven of salva-
    tion.

XXXV
RICHARD I

REDOUBTED King, of courage leonine,
I mark thee, Richard! urgent to equip
Thy warlike person with the staff and
    scrip;
I watch thee sailing o'er the midland
    brine;
In conquered Cyprus see thy Bride
    decline   5
Her blushing cheek, love-vows upon her lip,
And see love-emblems streaming from thy
    ship,
As thence she holds her way to Palestine.
My Song, a fearless homager, would
    attend

[1] The decision of this council was believed to be
instantly known in remote parts of Europe.

Thy thundering battle-axe as it cleaves
    the press   10
Of war, but duty summons her away
To tell—how, finding in the rash distress
Of those Enthusiasts a subservient friend,
To giddier heights hath clomb the Papal
    sway.

XXXVI
AN INTERDICT

REALMS quake by turns: proud Arbitress
    of grace,
The Church, by mandate shadowing forth
    the power
She arrogates o'er heaven's eternal door,
Closes the gates of every sacred place.
Straight from the sun and tainted air's
    embrace   5
All sacred things are covered: cheerful
    morn
Grows sad as night—no seemly garb is
    worn,
Nor is a face allowed to meet a face
With natural smiles of greeting. Bells
    are dumb;
Ditches are graves—funereal rites denied;
And in the churchyard he must take his
    bride   11
Who dares be wedded! Fancies thickly
    come
Into the pensive heart ill fortified,
And comfortless despairs the soul be-
    numb.

XXXVII
PAPAL ABUSES

As with the Stream our voyage we pursue,
The gross materials of this world present
A marvellous study of wild accident;
Uncouth proximities of old and new;   4
And bold transfigurations, more untrue
(As might be deemed) to disciplined intent
Than aught the sky's fantastic element,
When most fantastic, offers to the view.
Saw we not Henry scourged at Becket's
    Shrine?
Lo! John self-stripped of his insignia:—
    crown,   10
Sceptre and mantle, sword and ring, laid
    down
At a proud Legate's feet! The spears that
    line
Baronial halls the opprobrious insult feel;
And angry Ocean roars a vain appeal.

XXXVIII
SCENE IN VENICE

BLACK Demons hovering o'er his mitred
    head,
To Cæsar's Successor the Pontiff spake;
'Ere I absolve thee, stoop! that on thy neck
Levelled with earth this foot of mine may
    tread.'

Then he, who to the altar had been led,
He, whose strong arm the Orient could
  not check, 6
He, who had held the Soldan at his beck,
Stooped, of all glory disinherited,
And even the common dignity of man!—
Amazement strikes the crowd: while
  many turn 10
Their eyes away in sorrow, others burn
With scorn, invoking a vindictive ban
From outraged Nature; but the sense of
  most
In abject sympathy with power is lost.

XXXIX

PAPAL DOMINION

UNLESS to Peter's Chair the viewless wind
Must come and ask permission when to
  blow,
What further empire would it have?
  for now
A ghostly Domination, unconfined
As that by dreaming Bards to Love
  assigned, 5
Sits there in sober truth—to raise the low,
Perplex the wise, the strong to over-
  throw;
Through earth and heaven to bind and to
  unbind!—
Resist—the thunder quails thee!—crouch
  —rebuff
Shall be thy recompense! from land to
  land 10
The ancient thrones of Christendom are
  stuff
For occupation of a magic wand,
And 'tis the Pope that wields it:—whether
  rough
Or smooth his front, our world is in his
  hand!

PART II

TO THE CLOSE OF THE TROUBLES IN THE
REIGN OF CHARLES I

I

[Composed (?).—Published 1845.]

How soon—alas! did Man, created pure—
By Angels guarded, deviate from the line
Prescribed to duty:—woeful forfeiture
He made by wilful breach of law divine.
With like perverseness did the Church
  abjure 5
Obedience to her Lord, and haste to
  twine,
'Mid Heaven-born flowers that shall for
  aye endure,
Weeds on whose front the world had
  fixed her sign.
O Man,—if with thy trials thus it fares,
If good can smooth the way to evil choice,
From all rash censure be the mind kept
  free; 11

He only judges right who weighs, com-
  pares,
And, in the sternest sentence which his
  voice
Pronounces, ne'er abandons Charity.

II

[Composed (?).—Published 1845.]

FROM false assumption rose, and fondly
  hailed
By superstition, spread the Papal power;
Yet do not deem the Autocracy prevailed
Thus only, even in error's darkest hour.
She daunts, forth-thundering from her
  spiritual tower 5
Brute rapine, or with gentle lure she tames.
Justice and Peace through Her uphold
  their claims;
And Chastity finds many a sheltering
  bower.
Realm there is none that if controlled or
  sway'd
By her commands partakes not, in degree,
Of good, o'er manners arts and arms,
  diffused: 11
Yes, to thy domination, Roman See,
Tho' miserably, oft monstrously, abused
By blind ambition, be this tribute paid.

III

CISTERTIAN MONASTERY

'HERE Man more purely lives, less oft
  doth fall,
More promptly rises, walks with stricter
  heed,
More safely rests, dies happier, is freed
Earlier from cleansing fires, and gains
  withal
A brighter crown.'[1]—On yon Cistertian wall
That confident assurance may be read; 6
And, to like shelter, from the world have
  fled
Increasing multitudes. The potent call
Doubtless shall cheat full oft the heart's
  desires;
Yet, while the rugged Age on pliant knee
Vows to rapt Fancy humble fealty, 11
A gentler life spreads round the holy
  spires;
Where'er they rise, the sylvan waste
  retires,
And aery harvests crown the fertile lea.

IV

[Composed (?). Published 1835.]

DEPLORABLE his lot who tills the ground,
His whole life long tills it, with heartless
  toil
Of villain-service, passing with the soil
To each new Master, like a steer or hound,
Or like a rooted tree, or stone earth-
  bound; 5

[1] See Note, p. 722.

But mark how gladly, through their own
domains,
The Monks relax or break these iron
chains;
While Mercy, uttering, through their
voice, a sound
Echoed in Heaven, cries out, 'Ye Chiefs,
abate
These legalized oppressions! Man—whose
name   10
And nature God disdained not; Man—
whose soul
Christ died for—cannot forfeit his high
claim
To live and move exempt from all control
Which fellow-feeling doth not mitigate!'

V

MONKS AND SCHOOLMEN

RECORD we too, with just and faithful pen,
That many hooded Cenobites there are,
Who in their private cells have yet a care
Of public quiet; unambitious Men,
Counsellors for the world, of piercing ken;
Whose fervent exhortations from afar   6
Move Princes to their duty, peace or war;
And oft-times in the most forbidding den
Of solitude, with love of science strong,
How patiently the yoke of thought they
bear!   10
How subtly glide its finest threads along!
Spirits that crowd the intellectual sphere
With mazy boundaries, as the astronomer
With orb and cycle girds the starry throng.

VI

OTHER BENEFITS

AND, not in vain embodied to the sight,
Religion finds even in the stern retreat
Of feudal sway her own appropriate seat;
From the collegiate pomps on Windsor's
height
Down to the humbler altar, which the
Knight   5
And his Retainers of the embattled hall
Seek in domestic oratory small,
For prayer in stillness, or the chanted rite;
Then chiefly dear, when foes are planted
round,
Who teach the intrepid guardians of the
place—   10
Hourly exposed to death, with famine worn,
And suffering under many a perilous
wound—
How sad would be their durance, if forlorn
Of offices dispensing heavenly grace!

VII

CONTINUED

AND what melodious sounds at times
prevail!
And, ever and anon, how bright a gleam
Pours on the surface of the turbid Stream!

What heartfelt fragrance mingles with
the gale
That swells the bosom of our passing sail!
For where, but on *this* River's margin,
blow   6
Those flowers of chivalry, to bind the
brow
Of hardihood with wreaths that shall not
fail?—
Fair Court of Edward! wonder of the
world!
I see a matchless blazonry unfurled   10
Of wisdom, magnanimity, and love;
And meekness tempering honourable
pride;
The lamb is couching by the lion's side,
And near the flame-eyed eagle sits the
dove.

VIII

CRUSADERS

FURL we the sails, and pass with tardy
oars
Through these bright regions, casting
many a glance
Upon the dream-like issues—the romance
Of many-coloured life that Fortune pours
Round the Crusaders, till on distant
shores   5
Their labours end; or they return to lie,
The vow performed, in cross-legged effigy,
Devoutly stretched upon their chancel
floors.
Am I deceived? Or is their requiem
chanted   9
By voices never mute when Heaven unties
Her inmost, softest, tenderest harmonies;
Requiem which Earth takes up with voice
undaunted,
When she would tell how Brave, and
Good, and Wise,
For their high guerdon not in vain have
panted!

IX

[Composed 1842.—Published 1845.]

As faith thus sanctified the warrior's crest
While from the Papal Unity there came,
What feebler means had failed to give,
one aim
Diffused thro' all the regions of the West;
So does her Unity its power attest   5
By works of Art, that shed, on the out-
ward frame
Of worship, glory and grace, which who
shall blame
That ever looked to heaven for final rest?
Hail countless Temples! that so well befit
Your ministry; that, as ye rise and take
Form spirit and character from holy writ,
Give to devotion, wheresoe'er awake,   12
Pinions of high and higher sweep, and
make
The unconverted soul with awe submit.

X

[Composed 1842.—Published 1845.]

WHERE long and deeply hath been fixed
    the root
In the blest soil of gospel truth, the Tree,
(Blighted or scathed tho' many branches
    be,
Put forth to wither, many a hopeful shoot)
Can never cease to bear celestial fruit.   5
Witness the Church that oft-times, with
    effect
Dear to the saints, strives earnestly to
    eject
Her bane, her vital energies recruit.
Lamenting, do not hopelessly repine
When such good work is doomed to be
    undone,   10
The conquests lost that were so hardly
    won:—
All promises vouchsafed by Heaven will
    shine
In light confirmed while years their course
    shall run,
Confirmed alike in progress and decline.

XI

TRANSUBSTANTIATION

ENOUGH! for see, with dim association
The tapers burn; the odorous incense feeds
A greedy flame; the pompous mass pro-
    ceeds;
The Priest bestows the appointed conse-
    cration;   4
And, while the HOST is raised, its elevation
An awe and supernatural horror breeds;
And all the people bow their heads, like
    reeds
To a soft breeze, in lowly adoration.
This Valdo brooks not. On the banks of
    Rhone
He taught, till persecution chased him
    thence,   10
To adore the Invisible, and Him alone.
Nor are his Followers loth to seek defence,
'Mid woods and wilds, on Nature's craggy
    throne,
From rites that trample upon soul and
    sense.

XII

THE VAUDOIS

[Composed (?).—Published 1835.]

BUT whence came they who for the
    Saviour Lord
Have long borne witness as the Scriptures
    teach?—
Ages ere Valdo raised his voice to preach
In Gallic ears the unadulterate Word,
Their fugitive Progenitors explored   5
Subalpine vales, in quest of safe retreats
Where that pure Church survives, though
    summer heats
Open a passage to the Romish sword,
Far as it dares to follow. Herbs self-sown,

And fruitage gathered from the chestnut-
    wood,   10
Nourish the sufferers then; and mists,
    that brood
O'er chasms with new-fallen obstacles
    bestrown,
Protect them; and the eternal snow that
    daunts
Aliens, is God's good winter for their
    haunts.

XIII

[Composed (?).—Published 1835.]

PRAISED be the Rivers, from their moun-
    tain springs
Shouting to Freedom, 'Plant thy banners
    here!'
To harassed Piety, 'Dismiss thy fear,
And in our caverns smooth thy ruffled
    wings!'
Nor be unthanked their final lingerings—
Silent, but not to high-souled Passion's
    ear—   6
'Mid reedy fens wide-spread and marshes
    drear,
Their own creation. Such glad wel-
    comings
As Po was heard to give where Venice
    rose
Hailed from aloft those Heirs of truth
    divine   10
Who near his fountains sought obscure
    repose,
Yet came prepared as glorious lights to
    shine,
Should that be needed for their sacred
    Charge:
Blest Prisoners They, whose spirits were
    at large!

XIV

WALDENSES

THOSE had given earliest notice, as the
    lark
Springs from the ground the morn to
    gratulate;
Or rather rose the day to antedate,
By striking out a solitary spark,
When all the world with midnight gloom
    was dark.—   5
Then followed the Waldensian bands,
    whom Hate
In vain endeavours to exterminate,
Whom Obloquy pursues with hideous
    bark:[1]
But they desist not;—and the sacred fire,
Rekindled thus, from dens and savage
    woods   10
Moves, handed on with never-ceasing care,
Through courts, through camps, o'er
    limitary floods;
Nor lacks this sea-girt Isle a timely share
Of the new Flame, not suffered to expire.

[1] See Note, p. 722.

ECCLESIASTICAL SONNETS

XV
ARCHBISHOP CHICHELEY TO HENRY V

'WHAT beast in wilderness or cultured
  field
The lively beauty of the leopard shows?
What flower in meadow-ground or garden
  grows
That to the towering lily doth not yield?
Let both meet only on thy royal shield! 5
Go forth, great King! claim what thy
  birth bestows;
Conquer the Gallic lily which thy foes
Dare to usurp;—thou hast a sword to
  wield,
And Heaven will crown the right.'—The
  mitred Sire
Thus spake—and lo! a Fleet, for Gaul
  addrest, 10
Ploughs her bold course across the won-
  dering seas;
For, sooth to say, ambition, in the breast
Of youthful heroes, is no sullen fire,
But one that leaps to meet the fanning
  breeze.

XVI
WARS OF YORK AND LANCASTER

THUS is the storm abated by the craft
Of a shrewd Counsellor, eager to protect
The Church, whose power hath recently
  been checked,
Whose monstrous riches threatened. So
  the shaft
Of victory mounts high, and blood is
  quaffed 5
In fields that rival Cressy and Poictiers—
Pride to be washed away by bitter tears!
For deep as hell itself, the avenging
  draught
Of civil slaughter. Yet, while temporal
  power
Is by these shocks exhausted, spiritual
  truth 10
Maintains the else endangered gift of life;
Proceeds from infancy to lusty youth;
And, under cover of this woeful strife,
Gathers unblighted strength from hour
  to hour.

XVII
WICLIFFE

ONCE more the Church is seized with
  sudden fear,
And at her call is Wicliffe disinhumed:
Yea, his dry bones to ashes are consumed
And flung into the brook that travels
  near;
Forthwith that ancient Voice which
  Streams can hear 5
Thus speaks (that Voice which walks upon
  the wind,

Though seldom heard by busy human
  kind)—
'As thou these ashes, little Brook! wilt
  bear
Into the Avon, Avon to the tide
Of Severn, Severn to the narrow seas, 10
Into main Ocean they, this deed accurst
An emblem yields to friends and enemies
How the bold Teacher's Doctrine, sancti-
  fied
By truth, shall spread, throughout the
  world dispersed.'

XVIII
CORRUPTIONS OF THE HIGHER CLERGY

'WOE to you, Prelates! rioting in ease
And cumbrous wealth—the shame of your
  estate;
You, on whose progress dazzling trains
  await
Of pompous horses; whom vain titles
  please;
Who will be served by others on their
  knees, 5
Yet will yourselves to God no service
  pay;
Pastors who neither take nor point the
  way
To Heaven; for, either lost in vanities
Ye have no skill to teach, or if ye know
And speak the word ——' Alas! of
  fearful things 10
'Tis the most fearful when the people's
  eye
Abuse hath cleared from vain imaginings;
And taught the general voice to prophesy
Of Justice armed, and Pride to be laid
  low.

XIX
ABUSE OF MONASTIC POWER

AND what is Penance with her knotted
  thong;
Mortification with the shirt of hair,
Wan cheek, and knees indúrated with
  prayer,
Vigils, and fastings rigorous as long;
If cloistered Avarice scruple not to wrong
The pious, humble, useful Secular, 6
And rob the people of his daily care,
Scorning that world whose blindness
  makes her strong?
Inversion strange! that, unto One who
  lives
For self, and struggles with himself alone,
The amplest share of heavenly favour
  gives; 11
That to a Monk allots, both in the esteem
Of God and man, place higher than to him
Who on the good of others builds his
  own!

XX

MONASTIC VOLUPTUOUSNESS

YET more,—round many a Convent's
    blazing fire
Unhallowed threads of revelry are spun;
There Venus sits disguisèd like a Nun,—
While Bacchus, clothed in semblance of
    a Friar,
Pours out his choicest beverage high and
    higher   5
Sparkling, until it cannot choose but run
Over the bowl, whose silver lip hath won
An instant kiss of masterful desire—
To stay the precious waste. Through
    every brain
The domination of the sprightly juice   10
Spreads high conceits to madding Fancy
    dear,
Till the arched roof, with resolute abuse
Of its grave echoes, swells a choral strain
Whose votive burthen is—'OUR KING-
    DOM'S HERE!'

XXI

DISSOLUTION OF THE MONASTERIES

THREATS come which no submission may
    assuage,
No sacrifice avert, no power dispute;
The tapers shall be quenched, the belfries
    mute,
And, 'mid their choirs unroofed by selfish
    rage,
The warbling wren shall find a leafy cage;
The gadding bramble hang her purple
    fruit;   6
And the green lizard and the gilded newt
Lead unmolested lives, and die of age.
The owl of evening and the woodland fox
For their abode the shrines of Waltham
    choose: 10
Proud Glastonbury can no more refuse
To stoop her head before these desperate
    shocks—
She whose high pomp displaced, as story
    tells,
Arimathean Joseph's wattled cells.

XXII

THE SAME SUBJECT

THE lovely Nun (submissive, but more
    meek
Through saintly habit than from effort
    due
To unrelenting mandates that pursue
With equal wrath the steps of strong and
    weak)
Goes forth—unveiling timidly a cheek   5
Suffused with blushes of celestial hue,
While through the Convent's gate to open
    view
Softly she glides, another home to seek,
Not Iris, issuing from her cloudy shrine,

An Apparition more divinely bright!   10
Not more attractive to the dazzled sight
Those watery glories, on the stormy brine
Poured forth, while summer suns at dis-
    tance shine,
And the green vales lie hushed in sober
    light!

XXIII

CONTINUED

YET many a Novice of the cloistral shade,
And many chained by vows, with eager
    glee
The warrant hail, exulting to be free;
Like ships before whose keels, full long
    embayed
In polar ice, propitious winds have made
Unlooked-for outlet to an open sea,   6
Their liquid world, for bold discovery,
In all her quarters temptingly displayed!
Hope guides the young; but when the old
    must pass
The threshold, whither shall they turn to
    find   10
The hospitality—the alms (alas!
Alms may be needed) which that House
    bestowed?
Can they, in faith and worship, train the
    mind
To keep this new and questionable road?

XXIV

SAINTS

YE, too, must fly before a chasing hand,
Angels and Saints, in every hamlet
    mourned!
Ah! if the old idolatry be spurned,
Let not your radiant Shapes desert the
    Land:
Her adoration was not your demand,   5
The fond heart proffered it—the servile
    heart;
And therefore are ye summoned to de-
    part,
Michael, and thou, St. George, whose
    flaming brand
The Dragon quelled; and valiant Mar-
    garet   9
Whose rival sword a like Opponent slew:
And rapt Cecilia, seraph-haunted Queen
Of harmony; and weeping Magdalene,
Who in the penitential desert met
Gales sweet as those that over Eden blew!

XXV

THE VIRGIN

MOTHER! whose virgin bosom was un-
    crost
With the least shade of thought to sin
    allied;
Woman! above all women glorified,
Our tainted nature's solitary boast;
Purer than foam on central ocean tost;   5

ECCLESIASTICAL SONNETS

Brighter than eastern skies at daybreak strewn
With fancied roses, than the unblemished moon
Before her wane begins on heaven's blue coast;
Thy Image falls to earth. Yet some, I ween,
Not unforgiven the suppliant knee might bend,   10
As to a visible Power, in which did blend
All that was mixed and reconciled in Thee
Of mother's love with maiden purity,
Of high with low, celestial with terrene!

XXVI
APOLOGY

NOT utterly unworthy to endure
Was the supremacy of crafty Rome;
Age after age to the arch of Christendom
Aerial keystone haughtily secure;
Supremacy from Heaven transmitted pure,   5
As many hold; and, therefore, to the tomb
Pass, some through fire—and by the scaffold some—
Like saintly Fisher, and unbending More.
'Lightly for both the bosom's lord did sit
Upon his throne;' unsoftened, undismayed   10
By aught that mingled with the tragic scene
Of pity or fear; and More's gay genius played
With the inoffensive sword of native wit,
Than the bare axe more luminous and keen.

XXVII
IMAGINATIVE REGRETS

DEEP is the lamentation! Not alone
From Sages justly honoured by mankind;
But from the ghostly tenants of the wind,
Demons and Spirits, many a dolorous groan
Issues for that dominion overthrown: 5
Proud Tiber grieves, and far-off Ganges, blind
As his own worshippers: and Nile, reclined
Upon his monstrous urn, the farewell moan
Renews. Through every forest, cave, and den,
Where frauds were hatched of old, hath sorrow past—   10
Hangs o'er the Arabian Prophet's native Waste,
Where once his airy helpers schemed and planned
'Mid spectral lakes bemocking thirsty men,
And stalking pillars built of fiery sand.

XXVIII
REFLECTIONS

GRANT that by this unsparing hurricane
Green leaves with yellow mixed are torn away,
And goodly fruitage with the mother-spray;
'Twere madness—wished we, therefore, to detain,
With hands stretched forth in mollified disdain,   5
The 'trumpery' that ascends in bare display—
Bulls, pardons, relics, cowls black, white, and grey—
Upwhirled, and flying o'er the ethereal plain
Fast bound for Limbo Lake. And yet not choice
But habit rules the unreflecting herd,   10
And airy bonds are hardest to disown;
Hence, with the spiritual sovereignty transferred
Unto itself, the Crown assumes a voice
Of reckless mastery, hitherto unknown.

XXIX
TRANSLATION OF THE BIBLE

BUT, to outweigh all harm, the sacred Book,
In dusty sequestration wrapt too long,
Assumes the accents of our native tongue;
And he who guides the plough, or wields the crook,
With understanding spirit now may look
Upon her records, listen to her song,   6
And sift her laws—much wondering that the wrong,
Which Faith has suffered, Heaven could calmly brook.
Transcendent Boon! noblest that earthly King
Ever bestowed to equalize and bless   10
Under the weight of mortal wretchedness!
But passions spread like plagues, and thousands wild
With bigotry shall tread the Offering
Beneath their feet, detested and defiled.

XXX
THE POINT AT ISSUE
[Composed (?).—Published 1827.]

FOR what contend the wise?—for nothing less
Than that the Soul, freed from the bonds of Sense,
And to her God restored by evidence
Of things not seen, drawn forth from their recess,
Root there, and not in forms, her holiness;—   5

For Faith, which to the Patriarchs did
    dispense
Sure guidance, ere a ceremonial fence
Was needful round men thirsting to trans-
    gress;—
For Faith, more perfect still, with which
    the Lord
Of all, himself a Spirit, in the youth   10
Of Christian aspiration, deigned to fill
The temples of their hearts who, with his
    word
Informed, were resolute to do his will,
And worship him in spirit and in truth.

XXXI

EDWARD VI

'SWEET is the holiness of Youth'—so felt
Time-honoured Chaucer speaking through
    that Lay
By which the Prioress beguiled the way,
And many a Pilgrim's rugged heart did
    melt.
Hadst thou, loved Bard! whose spirit
    often dwelt   5
In the clear land of vision, but foreseen
King, child, and seraph, blended in the
    mien
Of pious Edward kneeling as he knelt
In meek and simple infancy, what joy
For universal Christendom had thrilled
Thy heart! what hopes inspired thy genius,
    skilled,   11
(O great Precursor, genuine morning Star)
The lucid shafts of reason to employ,
Piercing the Papal darkness from afar!

XXXII

EDWARD SIGNING THE WARRANT FOR THE EXECUTION OF JOAN OF KENT

THE tears of man in various measure gush
From various sources; gently overflow
From blissful transport some—from clefts
    of woe
Some with ungovernable impulse rush;
And some, coeval with the earliest blush
Of infant passion, scarcely dare to show 6
Their pearly lustre—coming but to go;
And some break forth when others' sor-
    rows crush
The sympathising heart. Nor these, nor
    yet
The noblest drops to admiration known,
To gratitude, to injuries forgiven—   11
Claim Heaven's regard like waters that
    have wet
The innocent eyes of youthful Monarchs
    driven
To pen the mandates nature doth disown.

343

ECCLESIASTICAL SONNETS

XXXIII

REVIVAL OF POPERY

[Composed (?).—Published 1827.]

THE saintly Youth has ceased to rule,
    discrowned
By unrelenting Death. O People keen
For change, to whom the new looks al-
    ways green!
Rejoicing did they cast upon the ground
Their Gods of wood and stone; and, at
    the sound   5
Of counter-proclamation, now are seen,
(Proud triumph is it for a sullen Queen!)
Lifting them up, the worship to confound
Of the Most High. Again do they invoke
The Creature, to the Creature glory
    give;   10
Again with frankincense the altars smoke
Like those the Heathen served; and mass
    is sung;
And prayer, man's rational prerogative,
Runs through blind channels of an un-
    known tongue.

XXXIV

LATIMER AND RIDLEY

[Composed (?).—Published 1827.]

How fast the Marian death-list is un-
    rolled!
See Latimer and Ridley in the might
Of Faith stand coupled for a common
    flight!
One (like those prophets whom God sent
    of old)
Transfigured,[1] from this kindling hath
    foretold   5
A torch of inextinguishable light;
The Other gains a confidence as bold;
And thus they foil their enemy's despite.
The penal instruments, the shows of
    crime,
Are glorified while this once-mitred pair
Of saintly Friends the 'murtherer's chain
    partake,   11
Corded, and burning at the social stake:'
Earth never witnessed object more sub-
    lime
In constancy, in fellowship more fair!

XXXV

CRANMER

OUTSTRETCHING flameward his upbraided
    hand
(O God of mercy, may no earthly Seat
Of judgment such presumptuous doom
    repeat!)
Amid the shuddering throng doth Cran-
    mer stand;
Firm as the stake to which with iron
    band   5

[1] See Note, p. 722.

His frame is tied; firm from the naked feet
To the bare head. The victory is complete;
The shrouded Body to the Soul's com-
    mand
Answers with more than Indian fortitude,
Through all her nerves with finer sense
    endued,   10
Till breath departs in blissful aspiration:
Then, 'mid the ghastly ruins of the fire,
Behold the unalterable heart entire,
Emblem of faith untouched, miraculous
    attestation![1]

XXXVI

GENERAL VIEW OF THE TROUBLES OF THE REFORMATION

AID, glorious Martyrs, from your fields
    of light,
Our mortal ken! Inspire a perfect trust
(While we look round) that Heaven's de-
    crees are just:
Which few can hold committed to a fight
That shows, ev'n on its better side, the
    might   5
Of proud Self-will, Rapacity, and Lust,
'Mid clouds enveloped of polemic dust,
Which showers of blood seem rather to
    incite
Than to allay. Anathemas are hurled
From both sides; veteran thunders (the
    brute test   10
Of truth) are met by fulminations new—
Tartarean flags are caught at, and un-
    furled—
Friends strike at friends—the flying shall
    pursue—
And Victory sickens, ignorant where to
    rest!

XXXVII

ENGLISH REFORMERS IN EXILE

SCATTERING, like birds escaped the fowl-
    er's net,
Some seek with timely flight a foreign
    strand;
Most happy, re-assembled in a land
By dauntless Luther freed, could they
    forget
Their Country's woes. But scarcely have
    they met,   5
Partners in faith, and brothers in distress,
Free to pour forth their common thank-
    fulness,
Ere hope declines:—their union is beset
With speculative notions rashly sown,
Whence thickly-sprouting growth of poi-
    sonous weeds;   10
Their forms are broken staves; their pas-
    sions, steeds
That master them. How enviably blest
Is he who can, by help of grace, enthrone
The peace of God within his single breast!

[1] For the belief in this fact, see the contemporary Historians.

XXXVIII

ELIZABETH

HAIL, Virgin Queen! o'er many an en-
    vious bar
Triumphant, snatched from many a trea-
    cherous wile!
All hail, sage Lady, whom a grateful Isle
Hath blest, respiring from that dismal
    war
Stilled by thy voice! But quickly from
    afar   5
Defiance breathes with more malignant
    aim;
And alien storms with home-bred fer-
    ments claim
Portentous fellowship. Her silver car,
By sleepless prudence ruled, glides slowly
    on;
Unhurt by violence, from menaced taint
Emerging pure, and seemingly more
    bright: 11
Ah! wherefore yields it to a foul con-
    straint
Black as the clouds its beams dispersed,
    while shone,
By men and angels blest, the glorious
    light?

XXXIX

EMINENT REFORMERS

METHINKS that I could trip o'er heaviest
    soil,
Light as a buoyant bark from wave to
    wave,
Were mine the trusty staff that JEWEL gave
To youthful HOOKER, in familiar style
The gift exalting, and with playful smile:[1]
For thus equipped, and bearing on his
    head   6
The Donor's farewell blessing, can he
    dread
Tempest, or length of way, or weight of
    toil?—
More sweet than odours caught by him
    who sails
Near spicy shores of Araby the blest,   10
A thousand times more exquisitely sweet,
The freight of holy feeling which we meet,
In thoughtful moments, wafted by the gales
From fields where good men walk, or
    bowers wherein they rest.

XL

THE SAME

HOLY and heavenly Spirits as they are,
Spotless in life, and eloquent as wise,
With what entire affection do they prize
Their Church reformed! labouring with
    earnest care
To baffle all that may her strength im-
    pair;   5

[1] See Note, p. 722.

That Church, the unperverted Gospel's
  seat;
In their afflictions a divine retreat;
Source of their liveliest hope, and tender-
  est prayer!—
The truth exploring with an equal mind,
In doctrine and communion they have
  sought   10
Firmly between the two extremes to steer;
But theirs the wise man's ordinary lot,
To trace right courses for the stubborn
  blind,
And prophesy to ears that will not hear.

XLI

DISTRACTIONS

MEN, who have ceased to reverence, soon
  defy
Their forefathers; lo! sects are formed,
  and split
With morbid restlessness:—the ecstatic fit
Spreads wide; though special mysteries
  multiply,
The Saints must govern is their common
  cry;   5
And so they labour, deeming Holy Writ
Disgraced by aught that seems content to
  sit
Beneath the roof of settled Modesty.
The Romanist exults; fresh hope he draws
From the confusion, craftily incites   10
The overweening, personates the mad—
To heap disgust upon the worthier Cause:
Totters the Throne; the new-born Church
  is sad,
For every wave against her peace unites.

XLII

GUNPOWDER PLOT

FEAR hath a hundred eyes that all agree
To plague her beating heart; and there is
  one
(Nor idlest that!) which holds communion
With things that were not, yet were *meant*
  to be.
Aghast within its gloomy cavity   5
That eye (which sees as if fulfilled and
  done
Crimes that might stop the motion of the
  sun)
Beholds the horrible catastrophe
Of an assembled Senate unredeemed
From subterraneous Treason's darkling
  power: 10
Merciless act of sorrow infinite!
Worse than the product of that dismal
  night,
When gushing, copious as a thunder-
  shower,
The blood of Huguenots through Paris
  streamed.

XLIII

ILLUSTRATION

THE JUNG-FRAU AND THE FALL OF THE
RHINE NEAR SCHAFFHAUSEN

THE Virgin-Mountain,[1] wearing like a
  Queen
A brilliant crown of everlasting snow,
Sheds ruin from her sides; and men below
Wonder that aught of aspect so serene
Can link with desolation. Smooth and
  green,   5
And seeming, at a little distance, slow,
The waters of the Rhine; but on they go
Fretting and whitening, keener and more
  keen;
Till madness seizes on the whole wide
  Flood,
Turned to a fearful Thing whose nostrils
  breathe   10
Blasts of tempestuous smoke—wherewith
  he tries
To hide himself, but only magnifies;
And doth in more conspicuous torment
  writhe,
Deafening the region in his ireful mood.

XLIV

TROUBLES OF CHARLES THE FIRST

EVEN such the contrast that, where'er we
  move,
To the mind's eye Religion doth present;
Now with her own deep quietness con-
  tent;
Then, like the mountain, thundering from
  above
Against the ancient pine-trees of the
  grove   5
And the Land's humblest comforts. Now
  her mood
Recalls the transformation of the flood,
Whose rage the gentle skies in vain re-
  prove,
Earth cannot check. O terrible excess
Of headstrong will! Can this be Piety?
No—some fierce Maniac hath usurped her
  name;   11
And scourges England struggling to be
  free:
Her peace destroyed! her hopes a wilder-
  ness!
Her blessings cursed—her glory turned to
  shame!

XLV

LAUD[2]

PREJUDGED by foes determined not to
  spare,
An old weak Man for vengeance thrown
  aside,
Laud, 'in the painful art of dying' tried,

1 The Jung-frau.   2 See Note, p. 723.

ECCLESIASTICAL SONNETS

(Like a poor bird entangled in a snare
Whose heart still flutters, though his
wings forbear   5
To stir in useless struggle) hath relied
On hope that conscious innocence sup-
plied,
And in his prison breathes celestial air.
Why tarries then thy chariot? Wherefore
stay,
O Death! the ensanguined yet triumphant
wheels,   10
Which thou prepar'st, full often, to con-
vey
(What time a State with madding faction
reels)
The Saint or Patriot to the world that
heals
All wounds, all perturbations doth allay?

XLVI
AFFLICTIONS OF ENGLAND

HARP! couldst thou venture, on thy bold-
est string,
The faintest note to echo which the blast
Caught from the hand of Moses as it
passed
O'er Sinai's top, or from the Shepherd-
king,
Early awake, by Siloa's brook, to sing   5
Of dread Jehovah; then should wood and
waste
Hear also of that name, and mercy cast
Off to the mountains, like a covering
Of which the Lord was weary. Weep, oh!
weep,
Weep with the good, beholding King and
Priest   10
Despised by that stern God to whom they
raise
Their suppliant hands; but holy is the
feast
He keepeth; like the firmament his ways:
His statutes like the chambers of the deep.

PART III
FROM THE RESTORATION TO THE PRESENT
TIMES

I

I SAW the figure of a lovely Maid
Seated alone beneath a darksome tree,
Whose fondly-overhanging canopy
Set off her brightness with a pleasing
shade.
No Spirit was she; *that* my heart be-
trayed,   5
For she was one I loved exceedingly;
But while I gazed in tender reverie
(Or was it sleep that with my Fancy
played?)
The bright corporeal presence—form and
face—

Remaining still distinct grew thin and
rare,   10
Like sunny mist;—at length the golden
hair,
Shape, limbs, and heavenly features, keep-
ing pace
Each with the other in a lingering race
Of dissolution, melted into air.

II
PATRIOTIC SYMPATHIES

LAST night, without a voice, that Vision
spake
Fear to my Soul, and sadness which might
seem
Wholly dissevered from our present
theme;
Yet, my belovèd Country! I partake
Of kindred agitations for thy sake;   5
Thou, too, dost visit oft my midnight
dream;
Thy glory meets me with the earliest beam
Of light, which tells that Morning is
awake.
If aught impair thy beauty or destroy,
Or but forbode destruction, I deplore   10
With filial love the sad vicissitude;
If thou hast fallen, and righteous Heaven
restore
The prostrate, then my spring-time is re-
newed,
And sorrow bartered for exceeding joy.

III
CHARLES THE SECOND

WHO comes—with rapture greeted, and
caressed
With frantic love—his kingdom to regain?
Him Virtue's Nurse, Adversity, in vain
Received, and fostered in her iron breast:
For all she taught of hardiest and of best,
Or would have taught, by discipline of
pain
And long privation, now dissolves amain,
Or is remembered only to give zest
To wantonness.—Away, Circean revels!
But for what gain? if England soon must
sink   10
Into a gulf which all distinction levels—
That bigotry may swallow the good name,
And, with that draught, the life-blood:
misery, shame,
By Poets loathed; from which Historians
shrink!

IV
LATITUDINARIANISM

YET Truth is keenly sought for, and the
wind
Charged with rich words poured out in
thought's defence;
Whether the Church inspire that eloquence,

Or a Platonic Piety confined
To the sole temple of the inward mind; 5
And One there is who builds immortal
  lays,
Though doomed to tread in solitary ways,
Darkness before and danger's voice be-
  hind;
Yet not alone, nor helpless to repel
Sad thoughts; for from above the starry
  sphere   10
Come secrets, whispered nightly to his
  ear;
And the pure spirit of celestial light
Shines through his soul—'that he may
  see and tell
Of things invisible to mortal sight.'

V
WALTON'S BOOK OF LIVES

THERE are no colours in the fairest sky
So fair as these. The feather, whence the
  pen
Was shaped that traced the lives of these
  good men,
Dropped from an Angel's wing. With
  moistened eye
We read of faith and purest charity   5
In Statesman, Priest, and humble Citizen:
Oh could we copy their mild virtues, then
What joy to live, what blessedness to die!
Methinks their very names shine still and
  bright;
Apart—like glow-worms on a summer
  night;   10
Or lonely tapers when from far they fling
A guiding ray; or seen—like stars on high,
Satellites burning in a lucid ring
Around meek Walton's heavenly memory.

VI
CLERICAL INTEGRITY

NOR shall the eternal roll of praise reject
Those Unconforming; whom one rigor-
  ous day
Drives from their Cures, a voluntary prey
To poverty, and grief, and disrespect,
And some to want—as if by tempests
  wrecked   5
On a wild coast; how destitute! did They
Feel not that Conscience never can be-
  tray,
That peace of mind is Virtue's sure effect.
Their altars they forego, their homes they
  quit,
Fields which they love, and paths they
  daily trod,   10
And cast the future upon Providence;
As men the dictate of whose inward sense
Outweighs the world; whom self-deceiv-
  ing wit
Lures not from what they deem the cause
  of God.

VII
PERSECUTION OF THE SCOTTISH COVE-
NANTERS

[Composed (?).—Published 1827.]

WHEN Alpine Vales threw forth a sup-
  pliant cry,
The majesty of England interposed
And the sword stopped; the bleeding
  wounds were closed;
And Faith preserved her ancient purity.
How little boots that precedent of good,
Scorned or forgotten, Thou canst testify,
For England's shame, O Sister Realm!
  from wood,
Mountain, and moor, and crowded street,
  where lie
The headless martyrs of the Covenant,
Slain by Compatriot-protestants that
  draw   10
From councils senseless as intolerant
Their warrant. Bodies fall by wild sword-
  law;
But who would force the Soul tilts with a
  straw
Against a Champion cased in adamant.

VIII
ACQUITTAL OF THE BISHOPS

A VOICE, from long-expecting thousands
  sent,
Shatters the air, and troubles tower and
  spire;
For Justice hath absolved the innocent,
And Tyranny is balked of her desire:
Up, down, the busy Thames—rapid as fire 5
Coursing a train of gunpowder—it went,
And transport finds in every street a vent,
Till the whole City rings like one vast quire.
The Fathers urge the People to be still,
With outstretched hands and earnest
  speech—in vain!   10
Yea, many, haply wont to entertain
Small reverence for the mitre's offices,
And to Religion's self no friendly will,
A Prelate's blessing ask on bended knees.

IX
WILLIAM THE THIRD

CALM as an under-current, strong to draw
Millions of waves into itself, and run,
From sea to sea, impervious to the sun
And ploughing storm, the spirit of Nassau
Swerves not, (how blest if by religious awe 5
Swayed, and thereby enabled to contend
With the wide world's commotions) from
  its end
Swerves not—diverted by a casual law.
Had mortal action e'er a nobler scope?
The Hero comes to liberate, not defy; 10
And while he marches on with steadfast hope,
Conqueror beloved! expected anxiously!
The vacillating Bondman of the Pope
Shrinks from the verdict of his steadfast eye.

ECCLESIASTICAL SONNETS

X

OBLIGATIONS OF CIVIL TO RELIGIOUS
LIBERTY

UNGRATEFUL Country, if thou e'er forget
The sons who for thy civil rights have
    bled!
How, like a Roman, Sidney bowed his
    head,
And Russell's milder blood the scaffold
    wet;
But these had fallen for profitless regret
Had not thy holy Church her champions
    bred,   6
And claims from other worlds inspirited
The star of Liberty to rise. Nor yet
(Grave this within thy heart!) if spiritual
    things
Be lost, through apathy, or scorn, or fear,
Shalt thou thy humbler franchises sup-
    port,   11
However hardly won or justly dear:
What came from heaven to heaven by
    nature clings,
And, if dissevered thence, its course is
    short.

XI

SACHEVEREL

[Composed (?).—Published 1827.]

A SUDDEN conflict rises from the swell
Of a proud slavery met by tenets strained
In Liberty's behalf. Fears, true or feigned,
Spread through all ranks; and lo! the
    Sentinel
Who loudest rang his pulpit 'larum bell,
Stands at the Bar, absolved by female
    eyes   6
Mingling their glances with grave flat-
    teries
Lavished on *Him*—that England may
    rebel
Against her ancient virtue. HIGH and
    Low,
Watchwords of Party, on all tongues are
    rife;   10
As if a Church, though sprung from hea-
    ven, must owe
To opposites and fierce extremes her
    life,—
Not to the golden mean, and quiet flow
Of truths that soften hatred, temper strife.

XII

[Composed (?).—Published 1827.]

DOWN a swift Stream, thus far, a bold
    design
Have we pursued, with livelier stir of
    heart
Than his who sees, borne forward by the
    Rhine,
The living landscapes greet him, and
    depart;
Sees spires fast sinking—up again to start!

And strives the towers to number, that
    recline   6
O'er the dark steeps, or on the horizon line
Striding with shattered crests his eye
    athwart.
So have we hurried on with troubled
    pleasure:
Henceforth, as on the bosom of a stream
That slackens, and spreads wide a watery
    gleam,   11
We, nothing loth a lingering course to
    measure,
May gather up our thoughts, and mark at
    leisure
How widely spread the interests of our
    theme.

XIII

ASPECTS OF CHRISTIANITY IN AMERICA

I.—THE PILGRIM FATHERS

[Composed 1842.—Published: vol. of 1842.]

WELL worthy to be magnified are they
Who, with sad hearts, of friends and
    country took
A last farewell, their loved abodes for-
    sook,
And hallowed ground in which their
    fathers lay;
Then to the new-found World explored
    their way,   5
That so a Church, unforced, uncalled to
    brook
Ritual restraints, within some sheltering
    nook
Her Lord might worship and his word
    obey
In freedom. Men they were who could
    not bend;
Blest Pilgrims, surely, as they took for
    guide   10
A will by sovereign Conscience sanctified;
Blest while their Spirits from the woods
    ascend
Along a Galaxy that knows no end,
But in His glory who for Sinners died.

XIV

II.—CONTINUED

[Composed 1842.—Published: vol. of 1842.]

FROM Rite and Ordinance abused they
    fled
To Wilds where both were utterly un-
    known;
But not to them had Providence fore-
    shown
What benefits are missed, what evils bred,
In worship neither raised nor limited   5
Save by Self-will. Lo! from that distant
    shore,
For Rite and Ordinance, Piety is led
Back to the Land those Pilgrims left of
    yore,

Led by her own free choice. So Truth
and Love
By Conscience governed do their steps
retrace.—   10
Fathers! your Virtues, such the power of
grace,
Their spirit, in your Children, thus approve.
Transcendent over time, unbound by
place,
Concord and Charity in circles move.

XV

III.—CONCLUDED.—AMERICAN EPISCOPACY
[Composed 1842.—Published: vol. of 1842.]

PATRIOTS informed with Apostolic light
Were they who, when their Country had
been freed,
Bowing with reverence to the ancient creed,
Fixed on the frame of England's Church
their sight,
And strove in filial love to reunite   5
What force had severed. Thence they
fetched the seed ˙
Of Christian unity, and won a meed
Of praise from Heaven. To Thee, O
saintly WHITE,
Patriarch of a wide-spreading family,
Remotest lands and unborn times shall
turn,   10
Whether they would restore or build—to
Thee,
As one who rightly taught how zeal should
burn,
As one who drew from out Faith's holiest
urn
The purest stream of patient Energy.

XVI

[Composed (?).—Published 1845.]

BISHOPS and Priests, blessèd are ye, if
deep
(As yours above all offices is high)
Deep in your hearts the sense of duty lie;
Charged as ye are by Christ to feed and
keep
From wolves your portion of His chosen
sheep: 5
Labouring as ever in your Master's sight,
Making your hardest task your best de-
light,
What perfect glory ye in Heaven shall
reap!—
But in the solemn Office which ye sought
And undertook premonished, if unsound
Your practice prove, faithless though but
in thought,   11
Bishops and Priests, think what a gulf
profound
Awaits you then, if they were rightly
taught
Who framed the Ordinance by your lives
disowned!

ECCLESIASTICAL SONNETS

XVII

PLACES OF WORSHIP

AS star that shines dependent upon star
Is to the sky while we look up in love;
As to the deep fair ships which though
they move
Seem fixed, to eyes that watch them from
afar;
As to the sandy desert fountains are,   5
With palm-groves shaded at wide inter-
vals,
Whose fruit around the sun-burnt Native
falls
Of roving tired or desultory war—
Such to this British Isle her christian
Fanes,
Each linked to each for kindred services;
Her Spires, her Steeple-towers with glit-
tering vanes   11
Far-kenned, her Chapels lurking among
trees,
Where a few villagers on bended knees
Find solace which a busy world disdains.

XVIII

PASTORAL CHARACTER

A GENIAL hearth, a hospitable board,
And a refined rusticity, belong
To the neat mansion, where, his flock
among,
The learned Pastor dwells, their watchful
Lord.
Though meek and patient as a sheathèd
sword;   5
Though pride's least lurking thought ap-
pear a wrong
To human kind; though peace be on his
tongue,
Gentleness in his heart—can earth afford
Such genuine state, pre-eminence so free,
As when, arrayed in Christ's authority,
He from the pulpit lifts his awful hand;
Conjures, implores, and labours all he can
For re-subjecting to divine command
The stubborn spirit of rebellious man?

XIX

THE LITURGY

YES, if the intensities of hope and fear
Attract us still, and passionate exercise
Of lofty thoughts, the way before us lies
Distinct with signs, through which in set
career,
As through a zodiac, moves the ritual
year   5
Of England's Church; stupendous mys-
teries!
Which whoso travels in her bosom eyes,
As he approaches them, with solemn
cheer.
Upon that circle traced from sacred story
We only dare to cast a transient glance,

349

ECCLESIASTICAL SONNETS

Trusting in hope that Others may advance   11
With mind intent upon the King of Glory,
From his mild advent till his countenance
Shall dissipate the seas and mountains hoary.

XX

BAPTISM

[Composed (?).—Published 1827.]

DEAR be the Church that, watching o'er the needs
Of Infancy, provides a timely shower
Whose virtue changes to a christian Flower
A Growth from sinful Nature's bed of weeds!—
Fitliest beneath the sacred roof proceeds   5
The ministration; while parental Love
Looks on, and Grace descendeth from above
As the high service pledges now, now pleads.
There, should vain thoughts outspread their wings and fly
To meet the coming hours of festal mirth,
The tombs—which hear and answer that brief cry,   11
The Infant's notice of his second birth—
Recall the wandering Soul to sympathy
With what man hopes from Heaven, yet fears from Earth.

XXI

SPONSORS

[Composed (?).—Published 1832.]

FATHER! to God himself we cannot give
A holier name! then lightly do not bear
Both names conjoined, but of thy spiritual care
Be duly mindful: still more sensitive
Do Thou, in truth a second Mother, strive
Against disheartening custom, that by Thee   6
Watched, and with love and pious industry
Tended at need, the adopted Plant may thrive
For everlasting bloom. Benign and pure
This Ordinance, whether loss it would supply,   10
Prevent omission, help deficiency,
Or seek to make assurance doubly sure.
Shame if the consecrated Vow be found
An idle form, the Word an empty sound!

XXII

CATECHISING

FROM Little down to Least, in due degree,
Around the Pastor, each in new-wrought vest,
Each with a vernal posy at his breast,

We stood, a trembling, earnest Company!
With low soft murmur, like a distant bee,
Some spake, by thought-perplexing fears betrayed;   6
And some a bold unerring answer made:
How fluttered then thy anxious heart for me,
Belovèd Mother! Thou whose happy hand
Had bound the flowers I wore, with faithful tie: 10
Sweet flowers! at whose inaudible command
Her countenance, phantom-like, doth reappear:
O lost too early for the frequent tear,
And ill requited by this heartfelt sigh![1]

XXIII

CONFIRMATION

[Composed (?).—Published 1827.]

THE Young-ones gathered in from hill and dale,
With holiday delight on every brow:
'Tis past away; far other thoughts prevail;
For they are taking the baptismal Vow
Upon their conscious selves; their own lips speak   5
The solemn promise. Strongest sinews fail,
And many a blooming, many a lovely, cheek
Under the holy fear of God turns pale;
While on each head his lawn-robed servant lays
An apostolic hand, and with prayer seals
The Covenant. The Omnipotent will raise   11
Their feeble Souls; and bear with *his* regrets,
Who, looking round the fair assemblage, feels
That ere the Sun goes down their childhood sets.

XXIV

CONFIRMATION CONTINUED

[Composed (?).—Published 1827.]

I SAW a Mother's eye intensely bent
Upon a Maiden trembling as she knelt;
In and for whom the pious Mother felt
Things that we judge of by a light too faint:
Tell, if ye may, some star-crowned Muse, or Saint!   5
Tell what rushed in, from what she was relieved—
Then, when her Child the hallowing touch received,

[1] See Bishop Wordsworth's *Memoirs of William Wordsworth*, I. 8; and *The Prelude*, Bk. V, ll. 256-293.—ED.

350

And such vibration through the Mother
    went
That tears burst forth amain. Did gleams
    appear?
Opened a vision of that blissful place   10
Where dwells a Sister-child? And was
    power given
Part of her lost One's glory back to trace
Even to this Rite? For thus *She* knelt,
    and, ere
The summer-leaf had faded, passed to
    Heaven.

XXV

SACRAMENT

[Composed (?).—Published 1827.]

By chain yet stronger must the Soul be
    tied:
One duty more, last stage of this ascent,
Brings to thy food, mysterious Sacra-
    ment!
The Offspring, haply at the Parent's side;
But not till They, with all that do abide
In Heaven, have lifted up their hearts to
    laud   6
And magnify the glorious name of God,
Fountain of Grace, whose Son for sinners
    died.
Ye, who have duly weighed the summons,
    pause
No longer: ye, whom to the saving rite   10
The Altar calls; come early under laws
That can secure for you a path of light
Through gloomiest shade; put on (nor
    dread its weight)
Armour divine, and conquer in your
    cause!

XXVI

THE MARRIAGE CEREMONY

[Composed 1842.—Published 1845.]

The Vested Priest before the Altar stands:
Approach, come gladly, ye prepared, in
    sight
Of God and chosen friends, your troth to
    plight
With the symbolic ring, and willing hands
Solemnly joined. Now sanctify the bands
O Father!—to the Espoused thy blessing
    give,   6
That mutually assisted they may live
Obedient, as here taught, to thy com-
    mands.
So prays the Church, to consecrate a Vow
'The which would endless matrimony
    make;'   10
Union that shadows forth and doth par-
    take
A mystery potent human love to endow
With heavenly, each more prized for the
    other's sake;
Weep not, meek Bride! uplift thy timid
    brow.

XXVII

THANKSGIVING AFTER CHILDBIRTH

[Composed 1842 (?).—Published 1845.]

Woman! the Power who left His throne
    on high,
And deigned to wear the robe of flesh we
    wear,
The Power that thro' the straits of Infancy
Did pass dependent on maternal care,
His own humanity with Thee will share,
Pleased with the thanks that in His
    People's eye   6
Thou offerest up for safe Delivery
From Childbirth's perilous throes. And
    should the Heir
Of thy fond hopes hereafter walk inclined
To courses fit to make a mother rue   10
That ever he was born, a glance of mind
Cast upon this observance may renew
A better will; and, in the imagined view
Of thee thus kneeling, safety he may find.

XXVIII

VISITATION OF THE SICK

[Composed 1842 (?).—Published 1845.]

The Sabbath bells renew the inviting
    peal;
Glad music! yet there be that, worn with
    pain
And sickness, listen where they long have
    lain,
In sadness listen. With maternal zeal
Inspired, the Church sends ministers to
    kneel   5
Beside the afflicted; to sustain with prayer,
And soothe the heart confession hath laid
    bare—
That pardon, from God's throne, may set
    its seal
On a true Penitent. When breath departs
From one disburthened so, so comforted,
His Spirit Angels greet; and ours be hope
That, if the Sufferer rise from his sick-
    bed,   12
Hence he will gain a firmer mind, to cope
With a bad world, and foil the Tempter's
    arts.

XXIX

THE COMMINATION SERVICE

[Composed 1842 (?).—Published 1845.]

Shun not this Rite, neglected, yea ab-
    horred,
By some of unreflecting mind, as calling
Man to curse man, (thought monstrous
    and appalling).
Go thou and hear the threatenings of the
    Lord;
Listening within his Temple see his sword
Unsheathed in wrath to strike the of-
    fender's head,   6
Thy own, if sorrow for thy sin be dead,

Guilt unrepented, pardon unimplored.
Two aspects bears Truth needful for
  salvation;
Who knows not *that?*—yet would this
  delicate age   10
Look only on the Gospel's brighter page:
Let light and dark duly our thoughts
  employ;
So shall the fearful words of Commination
Yield timely fruit of peace and love and
  joy.

XXX

FORMS OF PRAYER AT SEA

[Composed 1842 (?).—Published 1845.]

To kneeling Worshippers no earthly floor
Gives holier invitation than the deck
Of a storm-shattered Vessel saved from
  Wreck
(When all that Man could do availed no
  more)
By Him who raised the Tempest and re-
  strains: 5
Happy the crew who this have felt, and
  pour
Forth for His mercy, as the Church or-
  dains,
Solemn thanksgiving. Nor will *they* im-
  plore
In vain who, for a rightful cause, give
  breath
To words the Church prescribes aiding
  the lip   10
For the heart's sake, ere ship with hostile
  ship
Encounters, armed for work of pain and
  death.
Suppliants! the God to whom your cause
  ye trust
Will listen, and ye know that He is just.

XXXI

FUNERAL SERVICE

[Composed 1842.—Published 1845.]

FROM the Baptismal hour, thro' weal and
  woe,
The Church extends her care to thought
  and deed;
Nor quits the Body when the Soul is
  freed,
The mortal weight cast off to be laid low.
Blest Rite for him who hears in faith,
  'I know   5
That my Redeemer liveth,'—hears each
  word
That follows—striking on some kindred
  chord
Deep in the thankful heart;—yet tears
  will flow.
Man is as grass that springeth up at morn,
Grows green, and is cut down and wither-
  eth   10

Ere nightfall—truth that well may claim
  a sigh,
Its natural echo; but hope comes reborn
At Jesu's bidding. We rejoice, 'O Death,
Where is thy Sting?—O Grave, where is
  thy Victory?'

XXXII

RURAL CEREMONY [1]

CLOSING the sacred Book which long has
  fed
Our meditations, give we to a day
Of annual joy one tributary lay;
This day, when, forth by rustic music
  led,
The village Children, while the sky is red
With evening lights, advance in long
  array   6
Through the still churchyard, each with
  garland gay,
That, carried sceptre-like, o'ertops the
  head
Of the proud Bearer. To the wide church-
  door,
Charged with these offerings which their
  fathers bore   10
For decoration in the Papal time,
The innocent Procession softly moves:—
The spirit of Laud is pleased in heaven's
  pure clime,
And Hooker's voice the spectacle ap-
  proves!

XXXIII

REGRETS

WOULD that our scrupulous Sires had
  dared to leave
Less scanty measure of those graceful
  rites
And usages, whose due return invites
A stir of mind too natural to deceive;
Giving to Memory help when she would
  weave   5
A crown for Hope!—I dread the boasted
  lights
That all too often are but fiery blights,
Killing the bud o'er which in vain we
  grieve.
Go, seek, when Christmas snows discom-
  fort bring,
The counter Spirit found in some gay
  church   10
Green with fresh holly, every pew a
  perch
In which the linnet or the thrush might
  sing,
Merry and loud and safe from prying
  search,
Strains offered only to the genial Spring.

[1] See Note, p. 723.

XXXIV

MUTABILITY

FROM low to high doth dissolution climb,
And sink from high to low, along a scale
Of awful notes, whose concord shall not fail;
A musical but melancholy chime,
Which they can hear who meddle not with crime,   5
Nor avarice, nor over-anxious care.
Truth fails not; but her outward forms that bear
The longest date do melt like frosty rime,
That in the morning whitened hill and plain
And is no more; drop like the tower sublime   10
Of yesterday, which royally did wear
His crown of weeds, but could not even sustain
Some casual shout that broke the silent air,
Or the unimaginable touch of Time.

XXXV

OLD ABBEYS

MONASTIC Domes! following my downward way,
Untouched by due regret I marked your fall!
Now, ruin, beauty, ancient stillness, all
Dispose to judgments temperate as we lay
On our past selves in life's declining day:
For as, by discipline of Time made wise,
We learn to tolerate the infirmities
And faults of others—gently as he may,
So with our own the mild Instructor deals,
Teaching us to forget them or forgive.   10
Perversely curious, then, for hidden ill
Why should we break Time's charitable seals?
Once ye were holy, ye are holy still;
Your spirit freely let me drink, and live.

XXXVI

EMIGRANT FRENCH CLERGY

[Composed (?).—Published 1827.]

EVEN while I speak, the sacred roofs of France
Are shattered into dust; and self-exiled
From altars threatened, levelled, or defiled,
Wander the Ministers of God, as chance
Opens a way for life, or consonance   5
Of faith invites. More welcome to no land
The fugitives than to the British strand,
Where priest and layman with the vigilance
Of true compassion greet them. Creed and test
Vanish before the unreserved embrace
Of catholic humanity:—distrest   11
They came,—and, while the moral tempest roars
Throughout the Country they have left, our shores
Give to their Faith a fearless resting-place.

XXXVII

CONGRATULATION

THUS all things lead to Charity, secured
By THEM who blessed the soft and happy gale
That landward urged the great Deliverer's sail,
Till in the sunny bay his fleet was moored!
Propitious hour! had we, like them, endured   5
Sore stress of apprehension,[1] with a mind
Sickened by injuries, dreading worse designed,
From month to month trembling and unassured,
How had we then rejoiced! But we have felt,
As a loved substance, their futurity: 10
Good, which they dared not hope for, we have seen;
A State whose generous will through earth is dealt;
A State—which, balancing herself between
Licence and slavish order, dares be free.

XXXVIII

NEW CHURCHES

BUT liberty, and triumphs on the Main,
And laurelled armies, not to be withstood—
What serve they? if, on transitory good
Intent, and sedulous of abject gain,
The State (ah, surely not preserved in vain!)   5
Forbear to shape due channels which the Flood
Of sacred truth may enter—till it brood
O'er the wide realm, as o'er the Egyptian plain
The all-sustaining Nile. No more—the time
Is conscious of her want; through England's bounds,   10
In rival haste, the wished-for Temples rise!
I hear their sabbath bells' harmonious chime
Float on the breeze—the heavenliest of all sounds
That vale or hill prolongs or multiplies!

[1] See Note, p. 723.

ECCLESIASTICAL SONNETS

XXXIX
CHURCH TO BE ERECTED

BE this the chosen site; the virgin sod,
Moistened from age to age by dewy eve,
Shall disappear, and grateful earth receive
The corner-stone from hands that build
    to God.
Yon reverend hawthorns, hardened to
    the rod   5
Of winter storms, yet budding cheerfully;
Those forest oaks of Druid memory,
Shall long survive, to shelter the Abode
Of genuine Faith. Where, haply, 'mid
    this band
Of daisies, shepherds sate of yore and
    wove   10
May-garlands, there let the holy altar
    stand
For kneeling adoration;—while—above,
Broods, visibly portrayed, the mystic
    Dove,
That shall protect from blasphemy the
    Land.

XL
CONTINUED

MINE ear has rung, my spirit sunk sub-
    dued,
Sharing the strong emotion of the crowd,
When each pale brow to dread hosannas
    bowed
While clouds of incense mounting veiled
    the rood,
That glimmered like a pine-tree dimly
    viewed   5
Through Alpine vapours. Such appalling
    rite
Our Church prepares not, trusting to the
    might
Of simple truth with grace divine imbued;
Yet will we not conceal the precious
    Cross,
Like men ashamed: the Sun with his
    first smile   10
Shall greet that symbol crowning the low
    Pile:
And the fresh air of incense-breathing
    morn
Shall wooingly embrace it; and green moss
Creep round its arms through centuries
    unborn.

XLI
NEW CHURCHYARD

THE encircling ground, in native turf
    arrayed,
Is now by solemn consecration given
To social interests, and to favouring
    Heaven;
And where the rugged colts their gambols
    played,
And wild deer bounded through the
    forest glade,   5

Unchecked as when by merry Outlaw
    driven,
Shall hymns of praise resound at morn
    and even;
And soon, full soon, the lonely Sexton's
    spade
Shall wound the tender sod. Encincture
    small,
But infinite its grasp of weal and woe!
Hopes, fears, in never-ending ebb and
    flow;—   11
The spousal trembling, and the 'dust to
    dust,'
The prayers, the contrite struggle, and
    the trust
That to the Almighty Father looks
    through all.

XLII
CATHEDRALS, ETC.

OPEN your gates, ye everlasting Piles!
Types of the spiritual Church which God
    hath reared;
Not loth we quit the newly-hallowed
    sward
And humble altar, 'mid your sumptuous
    aisles   4
To kneel, or thrid your intricate defiles,
Or down the nave to pace in motion slow;
Watching, with upward eye, the tall
    tower grow
And mount, at every step, with living
    wiles
Instinct—to rouse the heart and lead the
    will   9
By a bright ladder to the world above.
Open your gates, ye Monuments of love
Divine! thou Lincoln, on thy sovereign
    hill!
Thou, stately York! and Ye, whose
    splendours cheer
Isis and Cam, to patient Science dear!

XLIII
INSIDE OF KING'S COLLEGE CHAPEL
CAMBRIDGE [1]

TAX not the royal Saint with vain ex-
    pense,
With ill-matched aims the Architect who
    planned—
Albeit labouring for a scanty band
Of white-robed Scholars only—this im-
    mense   4
And glorious Work of fine intelligence!
Give all thou canst; high Heaven rejects
    the lore
Of nicely-calculated less or more;
So deemed the man who fashioned for the
    sense

[1] Wordsworth appears to have written one at least
of these sonnets (XLIII–XLV), and perhaps wrote all
three, during a visit to his brother Christopher
(Master of Trinity) at Cambridge, Nov.-Dec., 1820.
—ED.

These lofty pillars, spread that branching roof
Self-poised, and scooped into ten thou-
    sand cells,   10
Where light and shade repose, where music dwells
Lingering—and wandering on as loth to die;
Like thoughts whose very sweetness yield-
    eth proof
That they were born for immortality.

XLIV

THE SAME

WHAT awful pérspective! while from our sight
With gradual stealth the lateral windows hide
Their Portraitures, their stone-work glim-
    mers, dyed
In the soft chequerings of a sleepy light.
Martyr, or King, or sainted Eremite,   5
Whoe'er ye be, that thus, yourselves un-
    seen,
Imbue your prison-bars with solemn sheen,
Shine on, until ye fade with coming Night!—
But, from the arms of silence—list! O list!
The music bursteth into second life;   10
The notes luxuriate, every stone is kissed
By sound, or ghost of sound, in mazy strife;
Heart-thrilling strains, that cast, before the eye
Of the devout, a veil of ecstasy!

XLV

CONTINUED

THEY dreamt not of a perishable home
Who thus could build. Be mine, in hours of fear
Or grovelling thought, to seek a refuge here;
Or through the aisles of Westminster to roam;
Where bubbles burst, and folly's dancing foam   5
Melts, if it cross the threshold; where the wreath
Of awe-struck wisdom droops: or let my path
Lead to that younger Pile, whose sky-
    like dome
Hath typified by reach of daring art
Infinity's embrace; whose guardian crest,

The silent Cross, among the stars shall spread   11
As now, when She hath also seen her breast
Filled with mementos, satiate with its part
Of grateful England's overflowing Dead.

XLVI

EJACULATION

GLORY to God! and to the Power who came
In filial duty, clothed with love divine,
That made His human tabernacle shine
Like Ocean burning with purpureal flame;
Or like the Alpine Mount, that takes its name   5
From roseate hues, far kenned at morn and even,
In hours of peace, or when the storm is driven
Along the nether region's rugged frame!
Earth prompts—Heaven urges; let us seek the light,
Studious of that pure intercourse begun
When first our infant brows their lustre won;   11
So, like the Mountain, may we grow more bright
From unimpeded commerce with the Sun,
At the approach of all-involving night.

XLVII

CONCLUSION

WHY sleeps the future, as a snake en-
    rolled,
Coil within coil, at noon-tide? For the WORD
Yields, if with unpresumptuous faith explored,
Power at whose touch the sluggard shall unfold
His drowsy rings. Look forth!—that Stream behold,   5
THAT STREAM upon whose bosom we have passed
Floating at ease while nations have effaced
Nations, and Death has gathered to his fold
Long lines of mighty Kings—look forth, my Soul!   9
(Nor in this vision be thou slow to trust)
The living Waters, less and less by guilt
Stained and polluted, brighten as they roll,
Till they have reached the eternal City—
    built
For the perfècted Spirits of the just!

EVENING VOLUNTARIES

I

[Composed 1832.—Published 1835.]

CALM is the fragrant air, and loth to
lose
Day's grateful warmth, tho' moist with
falling dews.
Look for the stars, you'll say that there
are none;
Look up a second time, and, one by
one,
You mark them twinkling out with silvery
light,   5
And wonder how they could elude the
sight!
The birds, of late so noisy in their bowers,
Warbled a while with faint and fainter
powers,
But now are silent as the dim-seen flowers:
Nor does the village Church-clock's iron
tone   10
The time's and season's influence dis-
own;
Nine beats distinctly to each other bound
In drowsy sequence—how unlike the
sound
That, in rough winter, oft inflicts a fear
On fireside listeners, doubting what they
hear!   15
The shepherd, bent on rising with the
sun,
Had closed his door before the day was
done,
And now with thankful heart to bed doth
creep,
And joins his little children in their
sleep.
The bat, lured forth where trees the lane
o'ershade,   20
Flits and reflits along the close arcade;
The busy dor-hawk chases the white
moth
With burring note, which Industry and
Sloth
Might both be pleased with, for it suits
them both.
A stream is heard—I see it not, but
know   25
By its soft music whence the waters
flow:
Wheels and the tread of hoofs are heard
no more;
One boat there was, but it will touch the
shore
With the next dipping of its slackened
oar;
Faint sound, that, for the gayest of the
gay,   30
Might give to serious thought a moment's
sway,
As a last token of man's toilsome day!

II

ON A HIGH PART OF THE COAST OF CUMBERLAND

Easter Sunday, April 7.

THE AUTHOR'S SIXTY-THIRD BIRTHDAY

[Composed April 7, 1833.—Published 1835.]

THE Sun, that seemed so mildly to retire,
Flung back from distant climes a stream-
ing fire,
Whose blaze is now subdued to tender
gleams,
Prelude of night's approach with soothing
dreams.
Look round;—of all the clouds not one is
moving;   5
'Tis the still hour of thinking, feeling,
loving.
Silent, and steadfast as the vaulted sky,
The boundless plain of waters seems to
lie:—
Comes that low sound from breezes rust-
ling o'er
The grass-crowned headland that conceals
the shore?   10
No; 'tis the earth-voice of the mighty sea,
Whispering how meek and gentle he *can*
be!

Thou Power supreme! who, arming to
rebuke
Offenders, dost put off the gracious look,
And clothe thyself with terrors like the
flood   15
Of Ocean roused into his fiercest mood,
Whatever discipline thy Will ordain
For the brief course that must for me
remain;
Teach me with quick-eared spirit to
rejoice
In admonitions of thy softest voice!   20
Whate'er the path these mortal feet may
trace,
Breathe through my soul the blessing of
thy grace,
Glad, through a perfect love, a faith
sincere
Drawn from the wisdom that begins with
fear,
Glad to expand; and, for a season, free
From finite cares, to rest absorbed in
Thee!   26

III

(BY THE SEA-SIDE)

[Composed 1833.—Published 1835.]

THE sun is couched, the sea-fowl gone to
rest,
And the wild storm hath somewhere found
a nest;

Air slumbers—wave with wave no longer
strives,
Only a heaving of the deep survives,
A tell-tale motion! soon will it be laid,   5
And by the tide alone the water swayed.
Stealthy withdrawings, interminglings
mild
Of light with shade in beauty reconciled—
Such is the prospect far as sight can range,
The soothing recompense, the welcome
change.   10
Where now the ships that drove before
the blast,
Threatened by angry breakers as they
passed;
And by a train of flying clouds bemocked;
Or, in the hollow surge, at anchor rocked
As on a bed of death? Some lodge in
peace,   15
Saved by His care who bade the tempest
cease;
And some, too heedless of past danger,
court
Fresh gales to waft them to the far-off
port;
But near, or hanging sea and sky between,
Not one of all those wingèd powers is
seen,   20
Seen in her course, nor 'mid this quiet
heard;
Yet oh! how gladly would the air be
stirred
By some acknowledgment of thanks and
praise,
Soft in its temper as those vesper lays
Sung to the Virgin while accordant oars
Urge the slow bark along Calabrian
shores;   26
A sea-born service through the mountains
felt
Till into one loved vision all things melt:
Or like those hymns that soothe with
graver sound   29
The gulfy coast of Norway iron-bound;
And, from the wide and open Baltic, rise
With punctual care, Lutherian harmonies.
Hush, not a voice is here! but why repine,
Now when the star of eve comes forth to
shine
On British waters with that look benign?
Ye mariners, that plough your onward
way,   36
Or in the haven rest, or sheltering bay,
May silent thanks at least to God be given
With a full heart; 'our thoughts are *heard*
in heaven!'

IV

[Composed 1834.—Published 1835.]

NOT in the lucid intervals of life
That come but as a curse to party-strife;
Not in some hour when Pleasure with a
sigh
Of languor puts his rosy garland by;

Not in the breathing-times of that poor
slave   5
Who daily piles up wealth in Mammon's
cave—
Is Nature felt, or can be; nor do words,
Which practised talent readily affords,
Prove that her hand has touched re-
sponsive chords;
Nor has her gentle beauty power to
move   10
With genuine rapture and with fervent love
The soul of Genius, if he dare to take
Life's rule from passion craved for
passion's sake;
Untaught that meekness is the cherished
bent   14
Of all the truly great and all the innocent.

But who *is* innocent? By grace divine,
Not otherwise, O Nature! we are thine,
Through good and evil thine, in just degree
Of rational and manly sympathy.
To all that Earth from pensive hearts is
stealing,   20
And Heaven is now to gladdened eyes
revealing,
Add every charm the Universe can show
Through every change its aspects under-
go—
Care may be respited, but not repealed;
No perfect cure grows on that bounded
field.   25
Vain is the pleasure, a false calm the peace,
If He, through whom alone our conflicts
cease,
Our virtuous hopes without relapse ad-
vance,
Come not to speed the Soul's deliverance;
To the distempered Intellect refuse   30
His gracious help, or give what we abuse.

V

(BY THE SIDE OF RYDAL MERE)

[Composed 1834.—Published 1835.]

THE linnet's warble, sinking towards a
close,
Hints to the thrush 'tis time for their
repose;
The shrill-voiced thrush is heedless, and
again
The monitor revives his own sweet strain;
But both will soon be mastered, and the
copse   5
Be left as silent as the mountain-tops,
Ere some commanding star dismiss to rest
The throng of rooks, that now, from twig
or nest,
(After a steady flight on home-bound
wings,
And a last game of mazy hoverings   10
Around their ancient grove) with cawing
noise
Disturb the liquid music's equipoise.

357

O Nightingale! Who ever heard thy song
Might here be moved, till Fancy grows so strong
That listening sense is pardonably cheated
Where wood or stream by thee was never greeted.   16
Surely, from fairest spots of favoured lands,
Were not some gifts withheld by jealous hands,
This hour of deepening darkness here would be
As a fresh morning for new harmony;   20
And lays as prompt would hail the dawn of Night:
A *dawn* she has both beautiful and bright,
When the East kindles with the full moon's light;
Not like the rising sun's impatient glow
Dazzling the mountains, but an overflow
Of solemn splendour, in mutation slow.

Wanderer by spring with gradual progress led,   27
For sway profoundly felt as widely spread;
To king, to peasant, to rough sailor, dear,
And to the soldier's trumpet-wearied ear;
How welcome wouldst thou be to this green Vale   31
Fairer than Tempe! Yet, sweet Nightingale!
From the warm breeze that bears thee on, alight
At will, and stay thy migratory flight;
Build, at thy choice, or sing, by pool or fount,   35
Who shall complain, or call thee to account?
The wisest, happiest, of our kind are they
That ever walk content with Nature's way,
God's goodness—measuring bounty as it may;
For whom the gravest thought of what they miss,   40
Chastening the fulness of a present bliss,
Is with that wholesome office satisfied,
While unrepining sadness is allied
In thankful bosoms to a modest pride.

VI
[Composed 1834.—Published 1835.]

SOFT as a cloud is yon blue Ridge—the Mere
Seems firm as solid crystal, breathless, clear,
And motionless; and, to the gazer's eye,
Deeper than ocean, in the immensity   4
Of its vague mountains and unreal sky!
But, from the process in that still retreat,
Turn to minuter changes at our feet;
Observe how dewy Twilight has withdrawn
The crowd of daisies from the shaven lawn,

And has restored to view its tender green,   10
That, while the sun rode high, was lost beneath their dazzling sheen.
—An emblem this of what the sober Hour
Can do for minds disposed to feel its power!
Thus oft, when we in vain have wished away
The petty pleasures of the garish day,   15
Meek eve shuts up the whole usurping host
(Unbashful dwarfs each glittering at his post)
And leaves the disencumbered spirit free
To reassume a staid simplicity.

'Tis well—but what are helps of time and place,   20
When wisdom stands in need of nature's grace;
Why do good thoughts, invoked or not, descend,
Like Angels from their bowers, our virtues to befriend;
If yet To-morrow, unbelied, may say,
'I come to open out, for fresh display,
The elastic vanities of yesterday?'   26

VII
[Composed 1834.—Published 1835.]

THE leaves that rustled on this oak-crowned hill,
And sky that danced among those leaves, are still;
Rest smooths the way for sleep; in field and bower
Soft shades and dews have shed their blended power
On drooping eyelid and the closing flower;   5
Sound is there none at which the faintest heart
Might leap, the weakest nerve of superstition start;
Save when the Owlet's unexpected scream
Pierces the ethereal vault; and ('mid the gleam
Of unsubstantial imagery, the dream,   10
From the hushed vale's realities, transferred
To the still lake) the imaginative Bird
Seems, 'mid inverted mountains, not unheard.

Grave Creature!—whether, while the moon shines bright
On thy wings opened wide for smoothest flight,   15
Thou art discovered in a roofless tower,
Rising from what may once have been a lady's bower;
Or spied where thou sitt'st moping in thy mew
At the dim centre of a churchyard yew;

Or from a rifted crag or ivy tod   20
Deep in a forest, thy secure abode,
Thou giv'st, for pastime's sake, by shriek
   or shout,
A puzzling notice of thy whereabout—
May the night never come, nor day be
   seen,
When I shall scorn thy voice or mock thy
   mien!   25
  In classic ages men perceived a soul
Of sapience in thy aspect, headless Owl!
Thee Athens reverenced in the studious
   grove;
And near the golden sceptre grasped by
   Jove,
His Eagle's favourite perch, while round
   him sate   30
The Gods revolving the decrees of Fate,
Thou, too, wert present at Minerva's
   side:—
Hark to that second larum!—far and
   wide
The elements have heard, and rock and
   cave replied.

VIII

[Composed June 8, 1802.—Published 1807; omitted from edd. 1815–1832; republished 1835.]

This *Impromptu* appeared, many years ago, among the Author's poems, from which, in subsequent editions, it was excluded. It is reprinted at the request of the Friend in whose presence the lines were thrown off.

THE sun has long been set,
  The stars are out by twos and threes,
The little birds are piping yet
  Among the bushes and trees;
There's a cuckoo, and one or two
   thrushes,   5
And a far-off wind that rushes,
And a sound of water that gushes,
And the cuckoo's sovereign cry
Fills all the hollow of the sky.
  Who would go 'parading'   10
In London, 'and masquerading,'
On such a night of June
With that beautiful soft half-moon,
And all these innocent blisses?
On such a night as this is!   15

IX

COMPOSED UPON AN EVENING OF EXTRAORDINARY SPLENDOUR AND BEAUTY

[Composed 1818.—Published 1820.]

I

HAD this effulgence disappeared
With flying haste, I might have sent,
Among the speechless clouds, a look
Of blank astonishment;
But 'tis endued with power to stay,   5
And sanctify one closing day,

That frail Mortality may see—
What is?—ah no, but what *can* be!
Time was when field and watery cove
With modulated echoes rang,   10
While choirs of fervent Angels sang
Their vespers in the grove;
Or, crowning, star-like, each some
   sovereign height,
Warbled, for heaven above and earth
   below,
Strains suitable to both.—Such holy rite,
Methinks, if audibly repeated now   16
From hill or valley, could not move
Sublimer transport, purer love,
Than doth this silent spectacle—the
   gleam—
The shadow—and the peace supreme!   20

II

No sound is uttered,—but a deep
And solemn harmony pervades
The hollow vale from steep to steep,
And penetrates the glades.
Far-distant images draw nigh,   25
Called forth by wondrous potency
Of beamy radiance, that imbues
Whate'er it strikes with gem-like hues!
In vision exquisitely clear,
Herds range along the mountain side;   30
And glistening antlers are descried;
And gilded flocks appear.
Thine is the tranquil hour, purpureal
   Eve!
But long as god-like wish, or hope divine,
Informs my spirit, ne'er can I believe   35
That this magnificence is wholly thine!
—From worlds not quickened by the sun
A portion of the gift is won;
An intermingling of Heaven's pomp is
   spread
On ground which British shepherds
   tread!   40

III

And if there be whom broken ties
Afflict, or injuries assail,
Yon hazy ridges to their eyes
Present a glorious scale,
Climbing suffused with sunny air,   45
To stop—no record hath told where!
And tempting Fancy to ascend,
And with immortal Spirits blend!
—Wings at my shoulders seem to play;
But, rooted here, I stand and gaze   50
On those bright steps that heavenward
   raise
Their practicable way.
Come forth, ye drooping old men, look
   abroad,
And see to what fair countries ye are
   bound!
And if some traveller, weary of his road,
Hath slept since noon-tide on the grassy
   ground,   56

EVENING VOLUNTARIES

Ye Genii! to his covert speed;
And wake him with such gentle heed
As may attune his soul to meet the
    dower
Bestowed on this transcendent hour!   60

IV

Such hues from their celestial Urn
Were wont to stream before mine eye,
Where'er it wandered in the morn
Of blissful infancy.
This glimpse of glory, why renewed?   65
Nay, rather speak with gratitude;
For, if a vestige of those gleams
Survived, 'twas only in my dreams.
Dread Power! whom peace and calmness
    serve
No less than Nature's threatening voice,
If aught unworthy be my choice,   71
From THEE if I would swerve;
Oh, let Thy grace remind me of the light
Full early lost, and fruitlessly deplored;
Which, at this moment, on my waking
    sight   75
Appears to shine, by miracle restored;
My soul, though yet confined to earth,
Rejoices in a second birth!
—'Tis past, the visionary splendour fades;
And night approaches with her shades.

Note.—The multiplication of mountain-ridges,
described at the commencement of the third Stanza
of this Ode as a kind of Jacob's Ladder, leading
to Heaven, is produced either by watery vapours,
or sunny haze;—in the present instance by the
latter cause. Allusions to the Ode entitled 'Intimations of Immortality' pervade the last Stanza of
the foregoing Poem.

X

COMPOSED BY THE SEA-SHORE
[Composed 1833.—Published 1845.]

WHAT mischief cleaves to unsubdued
    regret,
How fancy sickens by vague hopes beset;
How baffled projects on the spirit prey,
And fruitless wishes eat the heart away,
The Sailor knows; he best, whose lot is
    cast   5
On the relentless sea that holds him fast
On chance dependent, and the fickle star
Of power, through long and melancholy
    war.
O sad it is, in sight of foreign shores,
Daily to think on old familiar doors,   10
Hearths loved in childhood, and ancestral
    floors;
Or, tossed about along a waste of foam,
To ruminate on that delightful home
Which with the dear Betrothèd *was* to
    come;
Or came and was and is, yet meets the eye
Never but in the world of memory;   16

Or in a dream recalled, whose smoothest
    range
Is crossed by knowledge, or by dread, of
    change,
And if not so, whose perfect joy makes
    sleep
A thing too bright for breathing man to
    keep.   20
Hail to the virtues which that perilous life
Extracts from Nature's elemental strife;
And welcome glory won in battles fought
As bravely as the foe was keenly sought.
But to each gallant Captain and his crew
A less imperious sympathy is due,   26
Such as my verse now yields, while moon-
    beams play
On the mute sea in this unruffled bay;
Such as will promptly flow from every
    breast,
Where good men, disappointed in the
    quest   30
Of wealth and power and honours, long
    for rest;
Or, having known the splendours of
    success,
Sigh for the obscurities of happiness.

XI
[Composed ?—Published: vol. of 1842.]

THE Crescent-moon, the Star of Love,
Glories of evening, as ye there are seen
With but a span of sky between—
Speak one of you, my doubts remove,
Which is the attendant Page and which
    the Queen?   5

XII
TO THE MOON

COMPOSED BY THE SEASIDE,—ON THE
COAST OF CUMBERLAND
[Composed 1835.—Published 1837.]

WANDERER! that stoop'st so low, and
    com'st so near
To human life's unsettled atmosphere;
Who lov'st with Night and Silence to
    partake,
So might it seem, the cares of them that
    wake;
And, through the cottage-lattice softly
    peeping,   5
Dost shield from harm the humblest of
    the sleeping;
What pleasure once encompassed those
    sweet names
Which yet in thy behalf the Poet claims,
An idolizing dreamer as of yore!—
I slight them all; and, on this sea-beat
    shore   10
Sole-sitting, only can to thoughts attend
That bid me hail thee as the SAILOR'S
    FRIEND;

360

So call thee for heaven's grace through
    thee made known
By confidence supplied and mercy shown,
When not a twinkling star or beacon's
    light   15
Abates the perils of a stormy night;
And for less obvious benefits, that find
Their way, with thy pure help, to heart
    and mind;
Both for the adventurer starting in life's
    prime;
And veteran ranging round from clime to
    clime,   20
Long-baffled hope's slow fever in his
    veins,
And wounds and weakness oft his labour's
    sole remains.

    The aspiring Mountains and the wind-
    ing Streams,
Empress of Night! are gladdened by thy
    beams;   24
A look of thine the wilderness pervades,
And penetrates the forest's inmost shades;
Thou, chequering peaceably the minster's
    gloom,
Guid'st the pale Mourner to the lost one's
    tomb;
Canst reach the Prisoner—to his grated
    cell
Welcome, though silent and intangible!—
And lives there one, of all that come and
    go   31
On the great waters toiling to and fro,
One, who has watched thee at some quiet
    hour
Enthroned aloft in undisputed power,
Or crossed by vapoury streaks and clouds
    that move   35
Catching the lustre they in part reprove—
Nor sometimes felt a fitness in thy sway
To call up thoughts that shun the glare
    of day,
And make the serious happier than the
    gay?

    Yes, lovely Moon! if thou so mildly
    bright   40
Dost rouse, yet surely in thy own despite,
To fiercer mood the frenzy-stricken
    brain,
Let me a compensating faith maintain;
That there's a sensitive, a tender, part
Which thou canst touch in every human
    heart,   45
For healing and composure.—But as least
And mightiest billows ever have confessed
Thy domination; as the whole vast Sea
Feels through her lowest depths thy
    sovereignty;
So shines that countenance with especial
    grace   50
On them who urge the keel her *plains* to
    trace

Furrowing its way right onward. The
    most rude,
Cut off from home and country, may have
    stood—
Even till long gazing hath bedimmed his
    eye,
Or the mute rapture ended in a sigh— 55
Touched by accordance of thy placid
    cheer,
With some internal lights to memory
    dear,
Or fancies stealing forth to soothe the
    breast
Tired with its daily share of earth's
    unrest,—
Gentle awakenings, visitations meek; 60
A kindly influence whereof few will speak,
Though it can wet with tears the hardiest
    cheek.

    And when thy beauty in the shadowy
    cave
Is hidden, buried in its monthly grave;
Then, while the Sailor, 'mid an open sea
Swept by a favouring wind that leaves
    thought free,   66
Paces the deck—no star perhaps in sight,
And nothing save the moving ship's own
    light
To cheer the long dark hours of vacant
    night—
Oft with his musings does thy image
    blend,   70
In his mind's eye thy crescent horns
    ascend,
And thou art still, O Moon, that SAILOR's
    FRIEND!

XIII

TO THE MOON

(RYDAL)

[Composed 1835.—Published 1837.]

QUEEN of the stars!—so gentle, so benign,
That ancient Fable did to thee assign,
When darkness creeping o'er thy silver
    brow
Warned thee these upper regions to
    forego,
Alternate empire in the shades below—
A Bard, who, lately near the wide-spread
    sea   6
Traversed by gleaming ships, looked up
    to thee
With grateful thoughts, doth now thy
    rising hail
From the close confines of a shadowy
    vale.
Glory of night, conspicuous yet serene,
Nor less attractive when by glimpses
    seen   11
Through cloudy umbrage, well might that
    fair face,
And all those attributes of modest grace,

EVENING VOLUNTARIES

In days when Fancy wrought unchecked
  by fear,
Down to the green earth fetch thee from
  thy sphere,   15
To sit in leafy woods by fountains clear!

O still beloved (for thine, meek Power,
  are charms
That fascinate the very Babe in arms,
While he, uplifted towards thee, laughs
  outright,
Spreading his little palms in his glad
  Mother's sight)   20
O still beloved, once worshipped! Time,
  that frowns
In his destructive flight on earthly crowns,
Spares thy mild splendour; still those
  far-shot beams
Tremble on dancing waves and rippling
  streams
With stainless touch, as chaste as when
  thy praise   25
Was sung by Virgin-choirs in festal lays;
And through dark trials still dost thou
  explore
Thy way for increase punctual as of yore,
When teeming Matrons—yielding to rude
  faith
In mysteries of birth and life and death
And painful struggle and deliverance—
  prayed   31
Of thee to visit them with lenient aid.
What though the rites be swept away, the
  fanes
Extinct that echoed to the votive strains;
Yet thy mild aspect does not, cannot,
  cease   35
Love to promote and purity and peace;
And Fancy, unreproved, even yet may
  trace
Faint types of suffering in thy beamless
  face.

Then, silent Monitress! let us—not
  blind
To worlds unthought of till the searching
  mind   40
Of Science laid them open to mankind—
Told, also, how the voiceless heavens
  declare
God's glory; and acknowledging thy
  share
In that blest charge; let us—without
  offence
To aught of highest, holiest, influence—
Receive whatever good 'tis given thee to
  dispense,   46
May sage and simple, catching with one
  eye
The moral intimations of the sky,
Learn from thy course, where'er their
  own be taken,
'To look on tempests, and be never
  shaken;'   50

To keep with faithful step the appointed
  way
Eclipsing or eclipsed, by night or day,
And from example of thy monthly range
Gently to brook decline and fatal change;
Meek, patient, steadfast, and with loftier
  scope,   55
Than thy revival yields, for gladsome
  hope!

XIV

TO LUCCA GIORDANO

[Composed 1846.—Published 1850.]

GIORDANO, verily thy Pencil's skill
Hath here portrayed with Nature's
  happiest grace
The fair Endymion couched on Latmos-
  hill;
And Dian gazing on the Shepherd's face
In rapture,—yet suspending her embrace,
As not unconscious with what power the
  thrill   6
Of her most timid touch his sleep would
  chase,
And, with his sleep, that beauty calm and
  still.
Oh may this work have found its last
  retreat
Here in a Mountain-bard's secure abode,
One to whom, yet a School-boy, Cynthia
  showed   11
A face of love which he in love would
  greet,
Fixed, by her smile, upon some rocky
  seat;
Or lured along where green-wood paths
  he trod.

RYDAL MOUNT, 1846.

XV

[Composed 1846.—Published 1850.]

WHO but is pleased to watch the moon on
  high
Travelling where she from time to time
  enshrouds
Her head, and nothing loth her Majesty
Renounces, till among the scattered clouds
One with its kindling edge declares that
  soon   5
Will reappear before the uplifted eye
A Form as bright, as beautiful a moon,
To glide in open prospect through clear
  sky.
Pity that such a promise e'er should prove
False in the issue, that yon seeming space
Of sky should be in truth the steadfast
  face   11
Of a cloud flat and dense, through which
  must move
(By transit not unlike man's frequent
  doom)
The Wanderer lost in more determined
  gloom.

362

XVI

[Composed 1846.—Published 1850.]

WHERE lies the truth? has Man, in
    wisdom's creed,
A pitiable doom; for respite brief
A care more anxious, or a heavier grief?
Is he ungrateful, and doth little heed
God's bounty, soon forgotten; or indeed,
Must Man, with labour born, awake to
    sorrow   6
When Flowers rejoice and Larks with
    rival speed

Spring from their nests to bid the Sun
    good morrow?
They mount for rapture as their songs
    proclaim
Warbled in hearing both of earth and
    sky;   10
But o'er the contrast wherefore heave a
    sigh?
Like those aspirants let us soar—our aim,
Through life's worst trials, whether shocks
    or snares,
A happier, brighter, purer Heaven than
    theirs.

POEMS

COMPOSED OR SUGGESTED DURING A TOUR
IN THE SUMMER OF 1833[1]

Having been prevented by the lateness of the season, in 1831, from visiting Staffa and Iona, the author
made these the principal objects of a short tour in the summer of 1833, of which the following
Series of Poems is a Memorial. The course pursued was down the Cumberland river Derwent,
and to Whitehaven; thence (by the Isle of Man, where a few days were passed) up the Frith of
Clyde to Greenock, then to Oban, Staffa, Iona; and back towards England, by Loch Awe, Inveray,
Loch Goil-head, Greenock, and through parts of Renfrewshire, Ayrshire, and Dumfries-shire, to
Carlisle, and thence up the river Eden, and homewards by Ullswater.

I

ADIEU, Rydalian Laurels! that have
    grown
And spread as if ye knew that days
    might come
When we would shelter in a happy home,
On this fair Mount, a Poet of your own,
One who ne'er ventured for a Delphic
    crown   5
To sue the God; but, haunting your green
    shade
All seasons through, is humbly pleased to
    braid
Ground-flowers, beneath your guardian-
    ship, self-sown.
Farewell! no Minstrels now with harp
    new-strung
For summer wandering quit their house-
    hold bowers;   10
Yet not for this wants Poesy a tongue
To cheer the Itinerant on whom she
    pours
Her spirit, while he crosses lonely moors,
Or musing sits forsaken halls among.

II

WHY should the Enthusiast, journeying
    through this Isle,
Repine as if his hour were come too late?
Not unprotected in her mouldering state,

Antiquity salutes him with a smile,
'Mid fruitful fields that ring with jocund
    toil,   5
And pleasure-grounds where Taste, re-
    fined Co-mate
Of Truth and Beauty, strives to imitate,
Far as she may, primeval Nature's style.
Fair Land! by Time's parental love made
    free,
By Social Order's watchful arms em-
    braced;   10
With unexampled union meet in thee,
For eye and mind, the present and the
    past;
With golden prospect for futurity,
If that be reverenced which ought to
    last.

III

THEY called Thee MERRY ENGLAND, in
    old time;
A happy people won for thee that name
With envy heard in many a distant clime;
And, spite of change, for me thou keep'st
    the same
Endearing title, a responsive chime   5
To the heart's fond belief; though some
    there are
Whose sterner judgments deem that word
    a snare
For inattentive Fancy, like the lime

[1] The Poems of this Series were for the most part composed in 1833, and published for the first time in
the volume of 1835 entitled *Yarrow Revisited, and Other Poems.* Chronological notes are attached only to
those pieces to which this observation does not apply. See Nos. XXVII, XLIII, and XLVI.—ED.

Which foolish birds are caught with.
Can, I ask,
This face of rural beauty be a mask   10
For discontent, and poverty, and crime;
These spreading towns a cloak for lawless
    will?
Forbid it, Heaven!—and MERRY ENG-
    LAND still
Shall be thy rightful name, in prose and
    rhyme!

IV

TO THE RIVER GRETA, NEAR KESWICK

GRETA, what fearful listening! when huge
    stones
Rumble along thy bed, block after block:
Or, whirling with reiterated shock,
Combat, while darkness aggravates the
    groans:
But if thou (like Cocytus from the moans
Heard on his rueful margin) thence wert
    named   6
The Mourner, thy true nature was
    defamed,
And the habitual murmur that atones
For thy worst rage, forgotten. Oft as
    Spring
Decks, on thy sinuous banks, her thou-
    sand thrones,   10
Seats of glad instinct and love's carolling,
The concert, for the happy, then may vie
With liveliest peals of birth-day har-
    mony:
To a grieved heart the notes are benisons.

V

TO THE RIVER DERWENT

AMONG the mountains were we nursed,
    loved Stream!
Thou near the eagle's nest—within brief
    sail,
I, of his bold wing floating on the gale,
Where thy deep voice could lull me!
    Faint the beam
Of human life when first allowed to
    gleam   5
On mortal notice.—Glory of the vale,
Such thy meek outset, with a crown,
    though frail,
Kept in perpetual verdure by the steam
Of thy soft breath!—Less vivid wreath
    entwined
Nemean victor's brow; less bright was
    worn,   10
Meed of some Roman chief—in triumph
    borne
With captives chained; and shedding
    from his car
The sunset splendours of a finished war
Upon the proud enslavers of mankind!

VI

IN SIGHT OF THE TOWN OF COCKER-
MOUTH

(Where the Author was born, and his Father's
remains are laid.)

A POINT of life between my Parent's dust,
And yours, my buried Little-ones! am I;
And to those graves looking habitually
In kindred quiet I repose my trust.
Death to the innocent is more than just,
And, to the sinner, mercifully bent;   6
So may I hope, if truly I repent
And meekly bear the ills which bear I
    must:
And You, my Offspring! that do still
    remain,
Yet may outstrip me in the appointed
    race,   10
If e'er, through fault of mine, in mutual
    pain
We breathed together for a moment's
    space,
The wrong, by love provoked, let love
    arraign,
And only love keep in your hearts a
    place.

VII

ADDRESS FROM THE SPIRIT OF COCKER-
MOUTH CASTLE

'THOU look'st upon me, and dost fondly
    think,
Poet! that, stricken as both are by years,
We, differing once so much, are now
    Compeers,
Prepared, when each has stood his time,
    to sink
Into the dust. Erewhile a sterner link   5
United us; when thou, in boyish play,
Entering my dungeon, didst become a prey
To soul-appalling darkness. Not a blink
Of light was there;—and thus did I, thy
    Tutor,
Make thy young thoughts acquainted
    with the grave;   10
While thou wert chasing the winged
    butterfly
Through my green courts; or climbing, a
    bold suitor,
Up to the flowers whose golden progeny
Still round my shattered brow in beauty
    wave.'

VIII

NUN'S WELL, BRIGHAM

THE cattle crowding round this beverage
    clear
To slake their thirst, with reckless hoofs
    have trod
The encircling turf into a barren clod;
Through which the waters creep, then
    disappear,
Born to be lost in Derwent flowing near;

Yet o'er the brink, and round the lime-
stone cell   6
Of the pure spring (they call it the 'Nun's
Well,'
Name that first struck by chance my
startled ear)
A tender Spirit broods—the pensive
Shade   9
Of ritual honours to this Fountain paid
By hooded Votaresses with saintly cheer;
Albeit oft the Virgin-mother mild
Looked down with pity upon eyes be-
guiled
Into the shedding of 'too soft a tear.'

IX

TO A FRIEND

On the banks of the Derwent.

PASTOR and Patriot!—at whose bidding
rise
These modest walls, amid a flock that
need,
For one who comes to watch them and
to feed,
A fixed Abode—keep down presageful
sighs.
Threats, which the unthinking only can
despise,   5
Perplex the Church; but be thou firm,—
be true
To thy first hope, and this good work
pursue,
Poor as thou art. A welcome sacrifice
Dost Thou prepare, whose sign will be
the smoke
Of thy new hearth; and sooner shall its
wreaths,   10
Mounting while earth her morning in-
cense breathes,
From wandering fiends of air receive a
yoke,
And straightway cease to aspire, than
God disdain
This humble tribute as ill-timed or vain.

X

MARY QUEEN OF SCOTS

Landing at the mouth of the Derwent,
Workington.

DEAR to the Loves, and to the Graces
vowed,
The Queen drew back the wimple that
she wore;
And to the throng, that on the Cumbrian
shore
Her landing hailed, how touchingly she
bowed!
And like a Star (that, from a heavy cloud
Of pine-tree foliage poised in air, forth
darts,   6
When a soft summer gale at evening parts

The gloom that did its loveliness en-
shroud)
She smiled; but Time, the old Saturnian
seer,
Sighed on the wing as her foot pressed
the strand,   10
With step prelusive to a long array
Of woes and degradations hand in hand—
Weeping captivity, and shuddering fear
Stilled by the ensanguined block of
Fotheringay!

XI

STANZAS

SUGGESTED IN A STEAMBOAT OFF SAINT
BEES' HEADS, ON THE COAST OF CUMBER-
LAND

IF Life were slumber on a bed of down,
Toil unimposed, vicissitude unknown,
Sad were our lot: no hunter of the hare
Exults like him whose javelin from the lair
Has roused the lion; no one plucks the
rose,   5
Whose proffered beauty in safe shelter
blows
'Mid a trim garden's summer luxuries,
With joy like his who climbs, on hands
and knees,
For some rare plant, yon Headland of
St. Bees.

This independence upon oar and sail,   10
This new indifference to breeze or gale,
This straight-lined progress, furrowing a
flat lea,
And regular as if locked in certainty—
Depress the hours. Up, Spirit of the
storm!
That Courage may find something to
perform;   15
That Fortitude, whose blood disdains to
freeze
At Danger's bidding, may confront the
seas,
Firm as the towering Headlands of St.
Bees.

Dread cliff of Baruth! that wild wish may
sleep,
Bold as if men and creatures of the Deep
Breathed the same element; too many
wrecks   21
Have struck thy sides, too many ghastly
decks
Hast thou looked down upon, that such
a thought
Should here be welcome, and in verse
enwrought:
With thy stern aspect better far agrees   25
Utterance of thanks that we have past
with ease,
As millions thus shall do, the Headlands
of St. Bees.

365

Yet, while each useful Art augments her store,
What boots the gain if Nature should lose more?
And Wisdom, as she holds a Christian place   30
In man's intelligence sublimed by grace?
When Bega sought of yore the Cumbrian coast,
Tempestuous winds her holy errand crossed:
She knelt in prayer—the waves their wrath appease;
And, from her vow well weighed in Heaven's decrees,   35
Rose, where she touched the strand, the Chantry of St. Bees.

'Cruel of heart were they, bloody of hand,'
Who in these Wilds then struggled for command;
The strong were merciless, without hope the weak;
Till this bright Stranger came, fair as day-break,   40
And as a cresset true that darts its length
Of beamy lustre from a tower of strength;
Guiding the mariner through troubled seas,
And cheering oft his peaceful reveries,
Like the fixed Light that crowns yon Headland of St. Bees.   45

To aid the Votaress, miracles believed
Wrought in men's minds, like miracles achieved;
So piety took root; and Song might tell
What humanizing virtues near her cell
Sprang up, and spread their fragrance wide around;   50
How savage bosoms melted at the sound
Of gospel-truth enchained in harmonies
Wafted o'er waves, or creeping through close trees,
From her religious Mansion of St. Bees.

When her sweet Voice, that instrument of love,
Was glorified, and took its place, above   55
The silent stars, among the angelic quire,
Her chantry blazed with sacrilegious fire,
And perished utterly; but her good deeds
Had sown the spot, that witnessed them, with seeds   60
Which lay in earth expectant, till a breeze
With quickening impulse answered their mute pleas,
And lo! a *statelier* pile, the Abbey of St. Bees.

There are the naked clothed, the hungry fed;
And Charity extendeth to the dead   65

Her intercessions made for the soul's rest
Of tardy penitents; or for the best
Among the good (when love might else have slept,
Sickened, or died) in pious memory kept:
Thanks to the austere and simple Devotees,   70
Who, to that service bound by venial fees,
Keep watch before the altars of St. Bees.

Are not, in sooth, their Requiem's sacred ties
Woven out of passion's sharpest agonies,
Subdued, composed, and formalized by art,   75
To fix a wiser sorrow in the heart?
The prayer for them whose hour is past away
Says to the Living, profit while ye may!
A little part, and that the worst, he sees
Who thinks that priestly cunning holds the keys   80
That best unlock the secrets of St. Bees.

Conscience, the timid being's inmost light,
Hope of the dawn and solace of the night,
Cheers these Recluses with a steady ray
In many an hour when judgment goes astray.   85
Ah! scorn not hastily their rule who try
Earth to despise, and flesh to mortify;
Consume with zeal, in wingèd ecstasies
Of prayer and praise forget their rosaries,
Nor hear the loudest surges of St. Bees.

Yet none so prompt to succour and protect   91
The forlorn traveller, or sailor wrecked
On the bare coast; nor do they grudge the boon
Which staff and cockle hat and sandal shoon
Claim for the pilgrim: and, though chidings sharp   95
May sometimes greet the strolling minstrel's harp,
It is not then when, swept with sportive ease,
It charms a feast-day throng of all degrees,
Brightening the archway of revered St. Bees.

How did the cliffs and echoing hills rejoice   100
What time the Benedictine Brethren's voice,
Imploring, or commanding with meet pride,
Summoned the Chiefs to lay their feuds aside,
And under one blest ensign serve the Lord
In Palestine. Advance, indignant Sword!

Flaming till thou from Paynim hands
  release   106
That Tomb, dread centre of all sanctities
Nursed in the quiet Abbey of St. Bees.

But look we now to them whose minds
  from far
Follow the fortunes which they may not
  share.   110
While in Judea Fancy loves to roam,
She helps to make a Holy-land at home:
The Star of Bethlehem from its sphere
  invites
To sound the crystal depth of maiden
  rights;
And wedded Life, through scriptural
  mysteries,   115
Heavenward ascends with all her chari-
  ties,
Taught by the hooded Celibates of St.
  Bees.

Nor be it e'er forgotten how by skill
Of cloistered Architects, free their souls
  to fill
With love of God, throughout the Land
  were raised   120
Churches, on whose symbolic beauty
  gazed
Peasant and mail-clad Chief with pious
  awe;
As at this day men seeing what they saw,
Or the bare wreck of faith's solemnities,
Aspire to more than earthly destinies;
Witness yon Pile that greets us from St.
  Bees.   126

Yet more; around those Churches,
  gathered Towns
Safe from the feudal Castle's haughty
  frowns;
Peaceful abodes, where Justice might up-
  hold
Her scales with even hand, and culture
  mould   130
The heart to pity, train the mind in care
For rules of life, sound as the Time could
  bear.
Nor dost thou fail, thro' abject love of
  ease,
Or hindrance raised by sordid purposes,
To bear thy part in this good work, St.
  Bees.   135

Who with the ploughshare clove the barren moors,
And to green meadows changed the
  swampy shores?
Thinned the rank woods; and for the
  cheerful grange
Made room where wolf and boar were
  used to range?
Who taught, and showed by deeds, that
  gentler chains   140

Should bind the vassal to his lord's do-
  mains?
The thoughtful Monks, intent their God
  to please,
For Christ's dear sake, by human sym-
  pathies
Poured from the bosom of thy Church,
  St. Bees!

But all availed not; by a mandate given
Through lawless will the Brotherhood
  was driven   146
Forth from their cells; their ancient House
  laid low
In Reformation's sweeping overthrow.
But now once more the local Heart re-
  vives,
The inextinguishable Spirit strives.   150
Oh may that Power who hushed the
  stormy seas,
And cleared a way for the first Votaries,
Prosper the new-born College of St. Bees!

Alas! the Genius of our age, from Schools
Less humble, draws her lessons, aims, and
  rules.   155
To Prowess guided by her insight keen
Matter and Spirit are as one Machine;
Boastful Idolatress of formal skill
She in her own would merge the eternal
  will:
Better, if Reason's triumphs match with
  these,   160
Her flight before the bold credulities
That furthered the first teaching of St.
  Bees.[1]

XII

IN THE CHANNEL, BETWEEN THE COAST OF
CUMBERLAND AND THE ISLE OF MAN

RANGING the heights of Scawfell or Black-
  comb,
In his lone course the Shepherd oft will
  pause,
And strive to fathom the mysterious laws
By which the clouds, arrayed in light or
  gloom,
On Mona settle, and the shapes assume
Of all her peaks and ridges. What he
  draws   6
From sense, faith, reason, fancy, of the
  cause,
He will take with him to the silent tomb.
Or by his fire, a child upon his knee,
Haply the untaught Philosopher may
  speak   10
Of the strange sight, nor hide his theory
That satisfies the simple and the meek,
Blest in their pious ignorance, though
  weak
To cope with Sages undevoutly free.

[1] See 'Excursion', seventh part; and 'Eccleslasti-
cal Sketches', second part, near the beginning.

367

XIII

AT SEA OFF THE ISLE OF MAN

BOLD words affirmed, in days when faith
was strong
And doubts and scruples seldom teased
the brain,
That no adventurer's bark had power to
gain
These shores if he approached them bent
on wrong;
For, suddenly up-conjured from the
Main,   5
Mists rose to hide the Land—that search,
though long
And eager, might be still pursued in vain.
O Fancy, what an age was *that* for song!
That age, when not by *laws* inanimate,
As men believed, the waters were im-
pelled,   10
The air controlled, the stars their courses
held;
But element and orb on *acts* did wait
Of *Powers* endued with visible form, in-
stinct
With will, and to their work by passion
linked.

XIV

DESIRE we past illusions to recall?
To reinstate wild Fancy, would we hide
Truths whose thick veil Science has drawn
aside?
No,—let this Age, high as she may, instal
In her esteem the thirst that wrought
man's fall,   5
The universe is infinitely wide;
And conquering Reason, if self-glorified,
Can nowhere move uncrossed by some
new wall
Or gulf of mystery, which thou alone,
Imaginative Faith! canst overleap,   10
In progress toward the fount of Love,—
the throne
Of Power whose ministers the records
keep
Of periods fixed, and laws established, less
Flesh to exalt than prove its nothingness.

XV

ON ENTERING DOUGLAS BAY, ISLE OF MAN
'Dignum laude virum Musa vetat mori.'

THE feudal Keep, the bastions of Cohorn,
Even when they rose to check or to repel
Tides of aggressive war, oft served as well
Greedy ambition, armed to treat with
scorn
Just limits; but yon Tower, whose smiles
adorn   5
This perilous bay, stands clear of all
offence;
Blest work it is of love and innocence,
A Tower of refuge built for the else for-
lorn.

Spare it, ye waves, and lift the mariner,
Struggling for life, into its saving arms!
Spare, too, the human helpers! Do they
stir   11
'Mid your fierce shock like men afraid to
die?
No; their dread service nerves the heart
it warms,
And they are led by noble HILLARY.[1]

XVI

BY THE SEA-SHORE, ISLE OF MAN

WHY stand we gazing on the sparkling
Brine,
With wonder smit by its transparency,
And all-enraptured with its purity?—
Because the untrained, the clear, the
crystalline,
Have ever in them something of benign;
Whether in gem, in water, or in sky,   6
A sleeping infant's brow, or wakeful eye
Of a young maiden, only not divine.
Scarcely the hand forbears to dip its palm
For beverage drawn as from a mountain-
well.   10
Temptation centres in the liquid Calm;
Our daily raiment seems no obstacle
To instantaneous plunging in, deep Sea!
And revelling in long embrace with thee.[2]

XVII

ISLE OF MAN

A YOUTH too certain of his power to wade
On the smooth bottom of this clear bright
sea,
To sight so shallow, with a bather's glee,
Leapt from this rock, and but for timely aid
He, by the alluring element betrayed,   5
Had perished. Then might Sea-nymphs
(and with sighs
Of self-reproach) have chanted elegies
Bewailing his sad fate, when he was laid
In peaceful earth: for, doubtless, he was
frank,
Utterly in himself devoid of guile;   10
Knew not the double-dealing of a smile;
Nor aught that makes men's promises a
blank,
Or deadly snare: and He survives to bless
The Power that saved him in his strange
distress.

XVIII

ISLE OF MAN

DID pangs of grief for lenient time too
keen,
Grief that devouring waves had caused—
or guilt
Which they had witnessed, sway the man
who built

[1] See Note, p. 725.
[2] The sea-water on the coast of the Isle of Man
is singularly pure and beautiful.

This Homestead, placed where nothing
   could be seen,
Nought heard, of ocean troubled or
   serene?   5
A tired Ship-soldier on paternal land,
That o'er the channel holds august com-
   mand,
The dwelling raised,—a veteran Marine.
He, in disgust, turned from the neigh-
   bouring sea
To shun the memory of a listless life   10
That hung between two callings. May
   no strife
More hurtful here beset him, doomed
   though free,
Self-doomed, to worse inaction, till his eye
Shrink from the daily sight of earth and
   sky!

XIX

BY A RETIRED MARINER

A Friend of the Author.

FROM early youth I ploughed the restless
   Main,
My mind as restless and as apt to change;
Through every clime and ocean did I
   range,
In hope at length a competence to gain;
For poor to Sea I went, and poor I still
   remain.   5
Year after year I strove, but strove in vain,
And hardships manifold did I endure,
For Fortune on me never deigned to
   smile;
Yet I at last a resting-place have found,
With just enough life's comforts to pro-
   cure,   10
In a snug Cove on this our favoured Isle,
A peaceful spot where Nature's gifts
   abound;
Then sure I have no reason to complain,
Though poor to Sea I went, and poor I
   still remain.

XX

AT BALA-SALA, ISLE OF MAN

Supposed to be written by a Friend.

BROKEN in fortune, but in mind entire
And sound in principle, I seek repose
Where ancient trees this convent-pile en-
   close,[1]
In ruin beautiful. When vain desire
Intrudes on peace, I pray the eternal Sire
To cast a soul-subduing shade on me,   6
A grey-haired, pensive, thankful Refugee;
A shade—but with some sparks of hea-
   venly fire
Once to these cells vouchsafed. And
   when I note
The old Tower's brow yellowed as with
   the beams   10
Of sunset ever there, albeit streams

[1] Rushen Abbey.

Of stormy weather-stains that semblance
   wrought,
I thank the silent Monitor, and say
'Shine so, my aged brow, at all hours of
   the day!'

XXI

TYNWALD HILL

ONCE on the top of Tynwald's formal
   mound
(Still marked with green turf circles nar-
   rowing
Stage above stage) would sit this Island's
   King,
The laws to promulgate, enrobed and
   crowned;
While, compassing the little mound
   around,   5
Degrees and Orders stood, each under
   each:
Now, like to things within fate's easiest
   reach,
The power is merged, the pomp a grave
   has found.
Off with yon cloud, old Snafell! that thine
   eye
Over three Realms may take its widest
   range;   10
And let, for them, thy fountains utter
   strange
Voices, thy winds break forth in pro-
   phecy,
If the whole State must suffer mortal
   change,
Like Mona's miniature of sovereignty.

XXII

DESPOND who will—*I* heard a voice ex-
   claim,
'Though fierce the assault, and shattered
   the defence,
It cannot be that Britain's social frame,
The glorious work of time and provi-
   dence,
Before a flying season's rash pretence   5
Should fall; that She, whose virtue put
   to shame,
When Europe prostrate lay, the Con-
   queror's aim,
Should perish, self-subverted. Black and
   dense
The cloud is; but brings *that* a day of
   doom
To Liberty? Her sun is up the while,   10
That orb whose beams round Saxon
   Alfred shone:
Then laugh, ye innocent Vales! ye
   Streams, sweep on,
Nor let one billow of our heaven-blest Isle
Toss in the fanning wind a humbler
   plume.'

XXIII

IN THE FRITH OF CLYDE, AILSA CRAG

During an Eclipse of the Sun, July 17.

SINCE risen from ocean, ocean to defy,
Appeared the Crag of Ailsa, ne'er did morn
With gleaming lights more gracefully
adorn
His sides, or wreathe with mist his fore-
head high:
Now, faintly darkening with the sun's
eclipse,   5
Still is he seen, in lone sublimity,
Towering above the sea and little ships;
For dwarfs the tallest seem while sailing by,
Each for her haven; with her freight of
Care,
Pleasure, or Grief, and Toil that seldom
looks   10
Into the secret of to-morrow's fare;
Though poor, yet rich, without the wealth
of books,
Or aught that watchful Love to Nature
owes
For her mute Powers, fixed Forms, or
transient Shows.

XXIV

ON THE FRITH OF CLYDE

In a Steamboat.

ARRAN! a single-crested Teneriffe,
A St. Helena next—in shape and hue,
Varying her crowded peaks and ridges
blue;
Who but must covet a cloud-seat, or skiff
Built for the air, or wingèd Hippogriff?
That he might fly, where no one could
pursue,   6
From this dull Monster and her sooty
crew;
And, as a God, light on thy topmost cliff.
Impotent wish! which reason would de-
spise
If the mind knew no union of extremes,
No natural bond between the boldest
schemes   11
Ambition frames and heart-humilities.
Beneath stern mountains many a soft vale
lies,
And lofty springs give birth to lowly
streams.

XXV

ON REVISITING DUNOLLY CASTLE

See former Series, p. 306.

THE captive Bird was gone;—to cliff or
moor
Perchance had flown, delivered by the
storm;
Or he had pined, and sunk to feed the
worm:
Him found we not: but, climbing a tall
tower,

There saw, impaved with rude fidelity   5
Of art mosaic, in a roofless floor,
An Eagle with stretched wings, but beam-
less eye—
An Eagle that could neither wail nor soar.
Effigy of the Vanished—(shall I dare
To call thee so?) or symbol of fierce deeds
And of the towering courage which past
times   11
Rejoiced in—take, whate'er thou be, a
share,
Not undeserved, of the memorial rhymes
That animate my way where'er it leads!

XXVI

THE DUNOLLY EAGLE

NOT to the clouds, not to the cliff, he flew;
But when a storm, on sea or mountain
bred,
Came and delivered him, alone he sped
Into the castle-dungeon's darkest mew.
Now near his master's house in open view
He dwells, and hears indignant tempests
howl,   6
Kennelled and chained. Ye tame domestic
fowl,
Beware of him! Thou, saucy cockatoo,
Look to thy plumage and thy life!—The
roe,
Fleet as the west wind, is for *him* no
quarry;   10
Balanced in ether he will never tarry,
Eyeing the sea's blue depths. Poor Bird!
even so
Doth man of brother man a creature make
That clings to slavery for its own sad sake.

XXVII

WRITTEN IN A BLANK LEAF OF
MACPHERSON'S OSSIAN

[Composed 1824.—Published 1827.]

OFT have I caught, upon a fitful breeze,
Fragments of far-off melodies,
With ear not coveting the whole,
A part so charmed the pensive soul:
While a dark storm before my sight   5
Was yielding, on a mountain height
Loose vapours have I watched, that won
Prismatic colours from the sun;
Nor felt a wish that heaven would show
The image of its perfect bow.   10
What need, then, of these finished Strains?
Away with counterfeit Remains!
An abbey in its lone recess,
A temple of the wilderness,
Wrecks though they be, announce with
feeling   15
The majesty of honest dealing.
Spirit of Ossian! if imbound
In language thou may'st yet be found,
If aught (intrusted to the pen
Or floating on the tongues of men,   20

Albeit shattered and impaired)
Subsist thy dignity to guard,
In concert with memorial claim
Of old grey stone, and high-born name
That cleaves to rock or pillared cave   25
Where moans the blast, or beats the wave,
Let Truth, stern arbitress of all,
Interpret that Original,
And for presumptuous wrongs atone;—
Authentic words be given, or none!   30

Time is not blind;—yet He, who spares
Pyramid pointing to the stars,
Hath preyed with ruthless appetite
On all that marked the primal flight
Of the poetic ecstasy   35
Into the land of mystery.
No tongue is able to rehearse
One measure, Orpheus! of thy verse;
Musæus, stationed with his lyre
Supreme among the Elysian quire,   40
Is, for the dwellers upon earth,
Mute as a lark ere morning's birth.
Why grieve for these, though past away
The music, and extinct the lay?
When thousands, by severer doom,   45
Full early to the silent tomb
Have sunk, at Nature's call; or strayed
From hope and promise, self-betrayed;
The garland withering on their brows;
Stung with remorse for broken vows;   50
Frantic—else how might they rejoice?
And friendless, by their own sad choice!

Hail, Bards of mightier grasp! on you
I chiefly call, the chosen Few,
Who cast not off the acknowledged guide,
Who faltered not, nor turned aside;   56
Whose lofty genius could survive
Privation, under sorrow thrive;
In whom the fiery Muse revered
The symbol of a snow-white beard,   60
Bedewed with meditative tears
Dropped from the lenient cloud of years.

Brothers in soul! though distant times
Produced you nursed in various climes,
Ye, when the orb of life had waned,   65
A plenitude of love retained:
Hence, while in you each sad regret
By corresponding hope was met,
Ye lingered among human kind,
Sweet voices for the passing wind;   70
Departing sunbeams, loth to stop,
Though smiling on the last hill-top!
Such to the tender-hearted maid
Even ere her joys begin to fade;
Such, haply, to the rugged chief   75
By fortune crushed, or tamed by grief;
Appears, on Morven's lonely shore,
Dim-gleaming through imperfect lore,
The Son of Fingal; such was blind
Maeonides of ampler mind;   80
Such Milton, to the fountain-head
Of glory by Urania led!

XXVIII
CAVE OF STAFFA

WE saw, but surely, in the motley crowd,
Not One of us has felt the far-famed sight;
How *could* we feel it? each the other's
    blight,
Hurried and hurrying, volatile and loud.
O for those motions only that invite   5
The Ghost of Fingal to his tuneful Cave
By the breeze entered, and wave after wave
Softly embosoming the timid light!
And by *one* Votary who at will might
    stand   9
Gazing and take into his mind and heart,
With undistracted reverence, the effect
Of those proportions where the almighty
    hand
That made the worlds, the sovereign
    Architect,
Has deigned to work as if with human
    Art!

XXIX
CAVE OF STAFFA
After the Crowd had departed.

THANKS for the lessons of this Spot—fit
    school
For the presumptuous thoughts that
    would assign
Mechanic laws to agency divine;
And, measuring heaven by earth, would
    overrule
Infinite Power. The pillared vestibule,   5
Expanding yet precise, the roof embowed,
Might seem designed to humble man,
    when proud
Of his best workmanship by plan and tool.
Down-bearing with his whole Atlantic
    weight
Of tide and tempest on the Structure's
    base,   10
And flashing to that Structure's topmost
    height,
Ocean has proved its strength, and of its
    grace
In calms is conscious, finding for his
    freight
Of softest music some responsive place.

XXX
CAVE OF STAFFA

YE shadowy Beings, that have rights and
    claims
In every cell of Fingal's mystic Grot,
Where are ye? Driven or venturing to
    the spot,
Our fathers glimpses caught of your thin
    Frames,
And, by your mien and bearing, knew
    your names;   5
And they could hear *his* ghostly song
    who trod
Earth, till the flesh lay on him like a load,

371

While he struck his desolate harp without
   hopes or aims.
Vanished ye are, but subject to recall;
Why keep *we* else the instincts whose
   dread law   10
Ruled here of yore, till what men felt
   they saw,
Not by black arts but magic natural!
If eyes be still sworn vassals of belief,
Yon light shapes forth a Bard, that shade
   a Chief.

XXXI
FLOWERS ON THE TOP OF THE PILLARS AT
THE ENTRANCE OF THE CAVE

HOPE smiled when your nativity was cast,
Children of Summer! Ye fresh Flowers
   that brave
What Summer here escapes not, the fierce
   wave,
And whole artillery of the western blast,
Battering the Temple's front, its long-
   drawn nave   5
Smiting, as if each moment were their last.
But ye, bright Flowers, on frieze and
   architrave
Survive, and once again the Pile stands
   fast:
Calm as the Universe, from specular
   towers
Of heaven contemplated by Spirits pure
With mute astonishment, it stands sus-
   tained   11
Through every part in symmetry, to en-
   dure,
Unhurt, the assault of Time with all his
   hours,
As the supreme Artificer ordained.

XXXII
IONA

ON to Iona!—What can she afford
To *us* save matter for a thoughtful sigh,
Heaved over ruin with stability
In urgent contrast? To diffuse the WORD
(Thy Paramount, mighty Nature! and
   Time's Lord)   5
Her Temples rose, 'mid pagan gloom; but
   why,
Even for a moment, has our verse de-
   plored
Their wrongs, since they fulfilled their
   destiny?
And when, subjected to a common doom
Of mutability, those far-famed Piles   10
Shall disappear from both the sister Isles,
Iona's Saints, forgetting not past days,
Garlands shall wear of amaranthine
   bloom,
While heaven's vast sea of voices chants
   their praise.

XXXIII
IONA
Upon Landing.

How sad a welcome! To each voyager
Some ragged child holds up for sale a
   store
Of wave-worn pebbles, pleading on the
   shore
Where once came monk and nun with
   gentle stir,
Blessings to give, news ask, or suit prefer.
Yet is yon neat trim church a grateful
   speck   6
Of novelty amid the sacred wreck
Strewn far and wide. Think, proud
   Philosopher!
Fallen though she be, this Glory of the west,
Still on her sons the beams of mercy
   shine;   10
And 'hopes, perhaps more heavenly
   bright than thine,
A grace by thee unsought and unpossest,
A faith more fixed, a rapture more divine
Shall gild their passage to eternal rest.'

XXXIV
THE BLACK STONES OF IONA
[See Martin's *Voyage among the Western Isles.*]

HERE on their knees men swore: the
   stones were black,
Black in the people's minds and words,
   yet they
Were at that time, as now, in colour grey.
But what is colour, if upon the rack
Of conscience souls are placed by deeds
   that lack   5
Concord with oaths? What differ night
   and day
Then, when before the Perjured on his way
Hell opens, and the heavens in vengeance
   crack
Above his head uplifted in vain prayer
To Saint, or Fiend, or to the Godhead
   whom   10
He had insulted—Peasant, King, or
   Thane?
Fly where the culprit may, guilt meets a
   doom;
And, from invisible worlds at need laid
   bare,
Come links for social order's awful chain.

XXXV

HOMEWARD we turn. Isle of Columba's
   Cell,
Where Christian piety's soul-cheering
   spark
(Kindled from Heaven between the light
   and dark
Of time) shone like the morning-star,
   farewell!—
And fare thee well, to Fancy visible.   5

Remote St. Kilda, lone and loved sea-
    mark
For many a voyage made in her swift
    bark,
When with more hues than in the rainbow
    dwell
Thou a mysterious intercourse dost hold,
Extracting from clear skies and air serene,
And out of sun-bright waves, a lucid veil,
That thickens, spreads, and, mingling fold
    with fold,   12
Makes known, when thou no longer canst
    be seen,
Thy whereabout, to warn the approaching
    sail.

XXXVI
GREENOCK
Per me si va nella Città dolente.

WE have not passed into a doleful City,
We who were led to-day down a grim dell,
By some too boldly named 'the Jaws of
    Hell:'
Where be the wretched ones, the sights
    for pity?
These crowded streets resound no plain-
    tive ditty:—   5
As from the hive where bees in summer
    dwell,
Sorrow seems here excluded; and that
    knell,
It neither damps the gay, nor checks the
    witty.
Alas! too busy Rival of old Tyre,
Whose merchants Princes were, whose
    decks were thrones;   10
Soon may the punctual sea in vain respire
To serve thy need, in union with that
    Clyde
Whose nursling current brawls o'er mossy
    stones,
The poor, the lonely, herdsman's joy and
    pride.

XXXVII

'THERE!' said a Stripling, pointing with
    meet pride
Towards a low roof with green trees half
    concealed,
'Is Mosgiel Farm; and that's the very field
Where Burns ploughed up the Daisy.'
    Far and wide
A plain below stretched seaward, while,
    descried   5
Above sea-clouds, the Peaks of Arran
    rose;
And, by that simple notice, the repose
Of earth, sky, sea, and air, was vivified.
Beneath 'the random bield of clod or
    stone'
Myriads of daisies have shone forth in
    flower   10
Near the lark's nest, and in their natural
    hour

Have passed away; less happy than the
    One
That, by the unwilling ploughshare, died
    to prove
The tender charm of poetry and love.

XXXVIII
THE RIVER EDEN, CUMBERLAND

EDEN! till now thy beauty had I viewed
By glimpses only, and confess with shame
That verse of mine, whate'er its varying
    mood,
Repeats but once the sound of thy sweet
    name:
Yet fetched from Paradise that honour
    came,   5
Rightfully borne; for Nature gives thee
    flowers
That have no rivals among British bowers;
And thy bold rocks are worthy of their
    fame.
Measuring thy course, fair Stream! at
    length I pay
To my life's neighbour dues of neighbour-
    hood;   10
But I have traced thee on thy winding
    way
With pleasure sometimes by this thought
    restrained—
For things far off we toil, while many a
    good
Not sought, because too near, is never
    gained.

XXXIX
MONUMENT OF MRS. HOWARD
(by Nollekens),
In Wetheral Church, near Corby, on the banks
of the Eden.

STRETCHED on the dying Mother's lap,
    lies dead
Her new-born Babe; dire ending of bright
    hope!
But Sculpture here, with the divinest scope
Of luminous faith, heavenward hath
    raised that head
So patiently; and through one hand has
    spread   5
A touch so tender for the insensate
    Child—
(Earth's lingering love to parting recon-
    ciled,
Brief parting, for the spirit is all but
    fled)—
That we, who contemplate the turns of life
Through this still medium, are consoled
    and cheered;   10
Feel with the Mother, think the severed
    Wife
Is less to be lamented than revered;
And own that Art, triumphant over strife
And pain, hath powers to Eternity en-
    deared.

XL

SUGGESTED BY THE FOREGOING

TRANQUILLITY! the sovereign aim wert
  thou
In heathen schools of philosophic lore;
Heart-stricken by stern destiny of yore
The Tragic Muse thee served with thought-
  ful vow;   4
And what of hope Elysium could allow
Was fondly seized by Sculpture, to restore
Peace to the Mourner. But when He who
  wore
The crown of thorns around his bleeding
  brow
Warmed our sad being with celestial light,
Then Arts, which still had drawn a soften-
  ing grace   10
From shadowy fountains of the Infinite,
Communed with that Idea face to face:
And move around it now as planets run,
Each in its orbit round the central Sun.

XLI

NUNNERY

THE floods are roused, and will not soon
  be weary;
Down from the Pennine Alps[1] how fiercely
  sweeps
CROGLIN, the stately Eden's tributary!
He raves, or through some moody passage
  creeps
Plotting new mischief—out again he leaps
Into broad light, and sends, through re-
  gions airy,   6
That voice which soothed the Nuns while
  on the steeps
They knelt in prayer, or sang to blissful
  Mary.
That union ceased: then, cleaving easy
  walks
Through crags, and smoothing paths be-
  set with danger,   10
Came studious Taste; and many a pensive
  stranger
Dreams on the banks, and to the river talks.
What change shall happen next to Nun-
  nery Dell?
Canal, and Viaduct, and Railway, tell!

XLII

STEAMBOATS, VIADUCTS, AND RAILWAYS

MOTIONS and Means, on land and sea at
  war
With old poetic feeling, not for this,
Shall ye, by Poets even, be judged amiss!
Nor shall your presence, howsoe'er it mar
The loveliness of Nature, prove a bar   5
To the Mind's gaining that prophetic sense
Of future change, that point of vision,
  whence
May be discovered what in soul ye are.

[1] The chain of Crossfell.

In spite of all that beauty may disown
In your harsh features, Nature doth em-
  brace   10
Her lawful offspring in Man's art; and
  Time,
Pleased with your triumphs o'er his
  brother Space,
Accepts from your bold hands the prof-
  fered crown
Of hope, and smiles on you with cheer
  sublime.

XLIII

THE MONUMENT COMMONLY CALLED LONG MEG AND HER DAUGHTERS, NEAR THE RIVER EDEN

[Composed 1821.—Published 1822;[2] ed. 1827.]

A WEIGHT of awe, not easy to be borne,
Fell suddenly upon my Spirit—cast
From the dread bosom of the unknown
  past,
When first I saw that family forlorn.
Speak Thou, whose massy strength and
  stature scorn   5
The power of years—pre-eminent, and
  placed
Apart, to overlook the circle vast—
Speak, Giant-mother! tell it to the Morn
While she dispels the cumbrous shades of
  Night:
Let the Moon hear, emerging from a
  cloud;   10
At whose behest uprose on British ground
That Sisterhood, in hieroglyphic round
Forth-shadowing, some have deemed, the
  infinite
The inviolable God, that tames the
  proud![3]

XLIV

LOWTHER

LOWTHER! in thy majestic Pile are seen
Cathedral pomp and grace, in apt accord
With the baronial castle's sterner mien;
Union significant of God adored,
And charters won and guarded by the
  sword   5
Of ancient honour; whence that goodly
  state
Of polity which wise men venerate,
And will maintain, if God his help afford.
Hourly the democratic torrent swells;
For airy promises and hopes suborned
The strength of backward-looking thoughts
  is scorned   11
Fall if ye must, ye Towers and Pinnacles,
With what ye symbolise; authentic Story
Will say, Ye disappeared with England's
  Glory!

[2] In the little book entitled *A Description of the Scenery of the Lakes*, etc.—ED.
[3] See Note, p. 725.

XLV

TO THE EARL OF LONSDALE

'Magistratus indicat virum.'

LONSDALE! it were unworthy of a Guest,
Whose heart with gratitude to thee inclines,
If he should speak, by fancy touched, of
    signs
On thy Abode harmoniously imprest,
Yet be unmoved with wishes to attest   5
How in thy mind and moral frame agree
Fortitude, and that Christian Charity
Which, filling, consecrates the human
    breast.
And if the Motto on thy 'scutcheon teach
With truth, 'THE MAGISTRACY SHOWS
    THE MAN;'   10
That searching test thy public course has
    stood;
As will be owned alike by bad and good,
Soon as the measuring of life's little span
Shall place thy virtues out of Envy's reach.'

XLVI

THE SOMNAMBULIST

[Composed before 1827 (1807–8?).—Published
1835.]

LIST, ye who pass by Lyulph's Tower[2]
  At eve; how softly then
Doth Aira-force, that torrent hoarse,
  Speak from the woody glen!
Fit music for a solemn vale!   5
  And holier seems the ground
To him who catches on the gale
The spirit of a mournful tale,
  Embodied in the sound.

Not far from that fair site whereon   10
  The Pleasure-house is reared,
As story says, in antique days
  A stern-browed house appeared;
Foil to a Jewel rich in light
  There set, and guarded well;   15
Cage for a Bird of plumage bright,
Sweet-voiced, nor wishing for a flight
  Beyond her native dell.

To win this bright Bird from her cage,
  To make this Gem their own,   20
Came Barons bold, with store of gold,
  And Knights of high renown;
But one She prized, and only one;
  Sir Eglamore was he;
Full happy season, when was known,   25
Ye Dales and Hills! to you alone
  Their mutual loyalty—

Known chiefly, Aira! to thy glen,
  Thy brook, and bowers of holly;
Where Passion caught what Nature taught,
  That all but love is folly;   31

[1] See Note, p. 725.
[2] A pleasure-house built by the late Duke of Nor-
folk upon the banks of Ullswater. FORCE is the word
used in the Lake District for Waterfall.

Where Fact with Fancy stooped to play;
  Doubt came not, nor regret—
To trouble hours that winged their way,
As if through an immortal day   35
  Whose sun could never set.

But in old times Love dwelt not long
  Sequestered with repose;
Best throve the fire of chaste desire,
  Fanned by the breath of foes.   40
'A conquering lance is beauty's test,
  And proves the Lover true;'
So spake Sir Eglamore, and pressed
The drooping Emma to his breast,
  And looked a blind adieu.   45

They parted.—Well with him it fared
  Through wide-spread regions errant;
A knight of proof in love's behoof,
  The thirst of fame his warrant:
And She her happiness can build   50
  On woman's quiet hours;
Though faint, compared with spear and
    shield,
The solace beads and masses yield,
  And needlework and flowers.

Yet blest was Emma when she heard   55
  Her Champion's praise recounted;
Though brain would swim, and eyes grow
    dim,
  And high her blushes mounted;
Or when a bold heroic lay
  She warbled from full heart;   60
Delightful blossoms for the *May*
Of absence! but they will not stay,
  Born only to depart.

Hope wanes with her, while lustre fills
  Whatever path he chooses;   65
As if his orb, that owns no curb,
  Received the light hers loses.
He comes not back; an ampler space
  Requires for nobler deeds;
He ranges on from place to place,   70
Till of his doings is no trace,
  But what her fancy breeds.

His fame may spread, but in the past
  Her spirit finds its centre;
Clear sight She has of what he was,   75
  And that would now content her.
'Still is he my devoted Knight?'
  The tear in answer flows;
Month falls on month with heavier weight,
Day sickens round her, and the night   80
  Is empty of repose.

In sleep She sometimes walked abroad,
  Deep sighs with quick words blending,
Like that pale Queen whose hands are seen
  With fancied spots contending;   85
But *she* is innocent of blood,—
  The moon is not more pure
That shines aloft, while through the wood
She thrids her way, the sounding Flood
  Her melancholy lure!   90

While 'mid the fern-brake sleeps the doe,
  And owls alone are waking,
In white arrayed, glides on the Maid
  The downward pathway taking,
That leads her to the torrent's side   95
  And to a holly bower;
By whom on this still night descried?
By whom in that lone place espied?
  By thee, Sir Eglamore!

A wandering Ghost, so thinks the Knight,
  His coming step has thwarted,   101
Beneath the boughs that heard their vows,
  Within whose shade they parted.
Hush, hush, the busy Sleeper see!
  Perplexed her fingers seem,   105
As if they from the holly tree
Green twigs would pluck, as rapidly
  Flung from her to the stream.

What means the Spectre? Why intent
  To violate the Tree,   110
Thought Eglamore, by which I swore
  Unfading constancy?
Here am I, and to-morrow's sun,
  To her I left, shall prove
That bliss is ne'er so surely won   115
As when a circuit has been run
  Of valour, truth, and love.

So from the spot whereon he stood,
  He moved with stealthy pace;
And, drawing nigh, with his living eye,
  He recognised the face;   121
And whispers caught, and speeches small,
  Some to the green-leaved tree,
Some muttered to the torrent-fall;—
'Roar on, and bring him with thy call;
  I heard, and so may He!'   126

Soul-shattered was the Knight, nor knew
  If Emma's Ghost it were,
Or boding Shade, or if the Maid
  Her very self stood there.   130
He touched; what followed who shall tell?
  The soft touch snapped the thread
Of slumber—shrieking back she fell,
And the Stream whirled her down the dell
  Along its foaming bed.   135

In plunged the Knight!—when on firm
    ground
  The rescued Maiden lay,
Her eyes grew bright with blissful light,
  Confusion passed away;
She heard, ere to the throne of grace   140
  Her faithful Spirit flew,
His voice—beheld his speaking face;
And, dying, from his own embrace,
  She felt that he was true.

So was he reconciled to life: 145
  Brief words may speak the rest;
Within the dell he built a cell,
  And there was Sorrow's guest;

In hermits' weeds repose he found,
  From vain temptations free;   150
Beside the torrent dwelling—bound
By one deep heart-controlling sound,
  And awed to piety.

Wild stream of Aira, hold thy course,
  Nor fear memorial lays,   155
Where clouds that spread in solemn shade,
  Are edged with golden rays!
Dear art thou to the light of heaven,
  Though minister of sorrow;
Sweet is thy voice at pensive even;   160
And thou, in lovers' hearts forgiven,
  Shalt take thy place with Yarrow!

XLVII

TO CORDELIA M——

Hallsteads, Ullswater.

NOT in the mines beyond the western main,
You say, Cordelia, was the metal sought,
Which a fine skill, of Indian growth, has
    wrought
Into this flexible yet faithful Chain;
Nor is it silver of romantic Spain;   5
But from our loved Helvellyn's depths
    was brought,
Our own domestic mountain. Thing and
    thought
Mix strangely; trifles light, and partly vain,
Can prop, as you have learnt, our nobler
    being:
Yes, Lady, while about your neck is
    wound   10
(Your casual glance oft meeting) this
    bright cord,
What witchery, for pure gifts of inward
    seeing,
Lurks in it, Memory's Helper, Fancy's
    Lord,
For precious tremblings in your bosom
    found!

XLVIII

MOST sweet it is with unuplifted eyes
To pace the ground, if path be there or
    none,
While a fair region round the traveller lies
Which he forbears again to look upon;
Pleased rather with some soft ideal scene,
The work of Fancy, or some happy tone
Of meditation, slipping in between   7
The beauty coming and the beauty gone.
If Thought and Love desert us, from that
    day
Let us break off all commerce with the
    Muse: 10
With Thought and Love companions of
    our way,
Whate'er the senses take or may refuse,
The Mind's internal heaven shall shed
    her dews
Of inspiration on the humblest lay.

376

POEMS OF
SENTIMENT AND REFLECTION

I
EXPOSTULATION AND REPLY
[Composed 1798.—Published 1798.]

'WHY, William, on that old grey stone,
Thus for the length of half a day,
Why, William, sit you thus alone,
And dream your time away?

'Where are your books?—that light be-
   queathed   5
To Beings else forlorn and blind!
Up! up! and drink the spirit breathed
From dead men to their kind.

'You look round on your Mother Earth,
As if she for no purpose bore you; 10
As if you were her first-born birth,
And none had lived before you!'

One morning thus, by Esthwaite lake,
When life was sweet, I knew not why,
To me my good friend Matthew spake,
And thus I made reply: 16

'The eye—it cannot choose but see;
We cannot bid the ear be still;
Our bodies feel, where'er they be,
Against or with our will.   20

'Nor less I deem that there are Powers
Which of themselves our minds impress;
That we can feed this mind of ours
In a wise passiveness.

'Think you, 'mid all this mighty sum 25
Of things for ever speaking,
That nothing of itself will come,
But we must still be seeking?

'—Then ask not wherefore, here, alone,
Conversing as I may,   30
I sit upon this old grey stone,
And dream my time away.'

II
THE TABLES TURNED
AN EVENING SCENE ON THE SAME SUBJECT
[Composed 1798.—Published 1798.]

UP! up! my Friend, and quit your books;
Or surely you 'll grow double:
Up! up! my Friend, and clear your looks;
Why all this toil and trouble?

The sun, above the mountain's head, 5
A freshening lustre mellow
Through all the long green fields has
   spread,
His first sweet evening yellow.

Books! 'tis a dull and endless strife:
Come, hear the woodland linnet, 10
How sweet his music! on my life,
There's more of wisdom in it.

And hark! how blithe the throstle sings!
He, too, is no mean preacher:
Come forth into the light of things, 15
Let Nature be your Teacher.

She has a world of ready wealth,
Our minds and hearts to bless—
Spontaneous wisdom breathed by health,
Truth breathed by cheerfulness. 20

One impulse from a vernal wood
May teach you more of man,
Of moral evil and of good,
Than all the sages can.

Sweet is the lore which Nature brings;
Our meddling intellect   26
Mis-shapes the beauteous forms of
   things:—
We murder to dissect.

Enough of Science and of Art;
Close up those barren leaves; 30
Come forth, and bring with you a heart
That watches and receives.

III
LINES WRITTEN IN EARLY SPRING
[Composed 1798.—Published 1798.]

I HEARD a thousand blended notes,
While in a grove I sate reclined,
In that sweet mood when pleasant
   thoughts
Bring sad thoughts to the mind.

To her fair works did Nature link 5
The human soul that through me ran;
And much it grieved my heart to think
What man has made of man.

Through primrose tufts, in that green
   bower,
The periwinkle trailed its wreaths; 10
And 'tis my faith that every flower
Enjoys the air it breathes.

The birds around me hopped and played,
Their thoughts I cannot measure:—
But the least motion which they made,
It seemed a thrill of pleasure. 16

The budding twigs spread out their fan,
To catch the breezy air;
And I must think, do all I can,
That there was pleasure there. 20

If this belief from heaven be sent,
If such be Nature's holy plan,
Have I not reason to lament
What man has made of man?

IV
A CHARACTER

[Composed probably September or October, 1800.
—Published 1800.]

I MARVEL how Nature could ever find
    space
For so many strange contrasts in one
    human face:
There's thought and no thought, and
    there's paleness and bloom
And bustle and sluggishness, pleasure
    and gloom.

There's weakness, and strength both
    redundant and vain;   5
Such strength as, if ever affliction and pain
Could pierce through a temper that's soft
    to disease,
Would be rational peace—a philosopher's
    ease.

There's indifference, alike when he fails
    or succeeds,
And attention full ten times as much as
    there needs;   10
Pride where there's no envy, there's so
    much of joy;
And mildness, and spirit both forward
    and coy.

There's freedom, and sometimes a diffi-
    dent stare
Of shame scarcely seeming to know that
    she's there,
There's virtue, the title it surely may
    claim,   15
Yet wants heaven knows what to be
    worthy the name.

This picture from nature may seem to
    depart,
Yet the Man would at once run away
    with your heart;
And I for five centuries right gladly
    would be
Such an odd such a kind happy creature
    as he.   20

V
TO MY SISTER

[Composed 1798.—Published 1798.]

IT is the first mild day of March:
Each minute sweeter than before,
The redbreast sings from the tall larch
That stands beside our door.

There is a blessing in the air,   5
Which seems a sense of joy to yield
To the bare trees, and mountains bare,
And grass in the green field.

My sister! ('tis a wish of mine)
Now that our morning meal is done,   10
Make haste, your morning task resign;
Come forth and feel the sun.

Edward will come with you;—and, pray,
Put on with speed your woodland dress;
And bring no book: for this one day   15
We'll give to idleness.

No joyless forms shall regulate
Our living calendar:
We from to-day, my Friend, will date
The opening of the year.   20

Love, now a universal birth,
From heart to heart is stealing,
From earth to man, from man to earth:
—It is the hour of feeling.

One moment now may give us more   25
Than years of toiling reason:
Our minds shall drink at every pore
The spirit of the season.

Some silent laws our hearts will make,
Which they shall long obey: 30
We for the year to come may take
Our temper from to-day.

And from the blessed power that rolls
About, below, above,
We'll frame the measure of our souls: 35
They shall be tuned to love.

Then come, my Sister! come, I pray,
With speed put on your woodland dress;
And bring no book: for this one day
We'll give to idleness.   40

VI
SIMON LEE

THE OLD HUNTSMAN

With an incident in which he was concerned.
[Composed 1798.—Published 1798.]

IN the sweet shire of Cardigan,
Not far from pleasant Ivor-hall,
An old Man dwells, a little man,—
'Tis said he once was tall.
Full five-and-thirty years he lived   5
A running huntsman merry;
And still the centre of his cheek
Is red as a ripe cherry.

No man like him the horn could sound,
And hill and valley rang with glee   10
When Echo bandied, round and round,
The halloo of Simon Lee.
In those proud days, he little cared
For husbandry or tillage;
To blither tasks did Simon rouse   15
The sleepers of the village.

He all the country could outrun,
Could leave both man and horse behind;
And often, ere the chase was done,
He reeled, and was stone-blind.   20
And still there's something in the world
At which his heart rejoices;
For when the chiming hounds are out,
He dearly loves their voices!

But, oh the heavy change!—bereft   25
Of health, strength, friends, and kindred, see!
Old Simon to the world is left
In liveried poverty.
His Master's dead,—and no one now
Dwells in the Hall of Ivor;   30
Men, dogs, and horses, all are dead;
He is the sole survivor.

And he is lean and he is sick;
His body, dwindled and awry,
Rests upon ankles swoln and thick;   35
His legs are thin and dry.
One prop he has, and only one,
His wife, an aged woman,
Lives with him, near the waterfall,
Upon the village Common.   40

Beside their moss-grown hut of clay,
Not twenty paces from the door,
A scrap of land they have, but they
Are poorest of the poor.
This scrap of land he from the heath   45
Enclosed when he was stronger;
But what to them avails the land
Which he can till no longer?

Oft, working by her Husband's side,
Ruth does what Simon cannot do;   50
For she, with scanty cause for pride,
Is stouter of the two.
And, though you with your utmost skill
From labour could not wean them,
'Tis little, very little—all   55
That they can do between them.

Few months of life has he in store
As he to you will tell,
For still, the more he works, the more
Do his weak ankles swell.   60
My gentle Reader, I perceive
How patiently you've waited,
And now I fear that you expect
Some tale will be related.

O Reader! had you in your mind   65
Such stores as silent thought can bring,
O gentle Reader! you would find
A tale in every thing.
What more I have to say is short,
And you must kindly take it: 70
It is no tale; but, should you think,
Perhaps a tale you'll make it.

One summer-day I chanced to see
This old Man doing all he could
To unearth the root of an old tree,   75
A stump of rotten wood.

The mattock tottered in his hand;
So vain was his endeavour,
That at the root of the old tree
He might have worked for ever.   80

'You're overtasked, good Simon Lee,
Give me your tool,' to him I said;
And at the word right gladly he
Received my proffered aid.
I struck, and with a single blow   85
The tangled root I severed,
At which the poor old Man so long
And vainly had endeavoured.

The tears into his eyes were brought,
And thanks and praises seemed to run
So fast out of his heart, I thought   91
They never would have done.
—I've heard of hearts unkind, kind deeds
With coldness still returning;
Alas! the gratitude of men   95
Hath oftener left me mourning.

VII
WRITTEN IN GERMANY
ON ONE OF THE COLDEST DAYS OF
THE CENTURY
[Composed 1799.—Published 1800.]

The Reader must be apprised that the Stoves in
North Germany generally have the impression
of a galloping horse upon them, this being part
of the Brunswick Arms.

A PLAGUE on your languages, German
   and Norse!
Let me have the song of the kettle;
And the tongs and the poker, instead of
   that horse
That gallops away with such fury and
   force
On this dreary dull plate of black metal.

See that Fly,—a disconsolate creature!
   perhaps   6
A child of the field or the grove;
And, sorrow for him! the dull treacherous
   heat
Has seduced the poor fool from his winter
   retreat,
And he creeps to the edge of my stove.   10

Alas! how he fumbles about the domains
Which this comfortless oven environ!
He cannot find out in what track he must
   crawl,
Now back to the tiles, then in search of
   the wall,
And now on the brink of the iron.   15

Stock-still there he stands like a traveller
   bemazed:
The best of his skill he has tried;
His feelers, methinks, I can see him put
   forth
To the east and the west, to the south
   and the north,
But he finds neither guide-post nor guide.

His spindles sink under him, foot, leg,
and thigh! 21
His eyesight and hearing are lost;
Between life and death his blood freezes
and thaws;
And his two pretty pinions of blue dusky
gauze
Are glued to his sides by the frost. 25

No brother, no mate has he near him—
while I
Can draw warmth from the cheek of my
Love;
As blest and as glad, in this desolate
gloom,
As if green summer grass were the floor
of my room,
And woodbines were hanging above. 30

Yet, God is my witness, thou small help-
less Thing!
Thy life I would gladly sustain
Till summer come up from the south, and
with crowds
Of thy brethren a march thou shouldst
sound through the clouds,
And back to the forests again!

VIII
A POET'S EPITAPH
[Composed 1799.—Published 1800.]

ART thou a Statist in the van
Of public conflicts trained and bred?
—First learn to love one living man;
Then may'st thou think upon the dead.

A Lawyer art thou?—draw not nigh! 5
Go, carry to some fitter place
The keenness of that practised eye,
The hardness of that sallow face.

Art thou a Man of purple cheer?
A rosy Man, right plump to see? 10
Approach; yet, Doctor, not too near,
This grave no cushion is for thee.

Or art thou one of gallant pride,
A Soldier and no man of chaff?
Welcome!—but lay thy sword aside, 15
And lean upon a peasant's staff.

Physician art thou?—one, all eyes,
Philosopher!—a fingering slave,
One that would peep and botanize
Upon his mother's grave? 20

Wrapt closely in thy sensual fleece,
O turn aside,—and take, I pray,
That he below may rest in peace,
Thy ever-dwindling soul, away!

A Moralist perchance appears; 25
Led, Heaven knows how! to this poor
sod:
And he has neither eyes nor ears;
Himself his world, and his own God;

One to whose smooth-rubbed soul can
cling
Nor form, nor feeling, great or small;
A reasoning, self-sufficing thing, 31
An intellectual All-in-all!

Shut close the door; press down the latch;
Sleep in thy intellectual crust;
Nor lose ten tickings of thy watch 35
Near this unprofitable dust

But who is He, with modest looks,
And clad in homely russet brown?
He murmurs near the running brooks
A music sweeter than their own. 40

He is retired as noontide dew,
Or fountain in a noon-day grove;
And you must love him, ere to you
He will seem worthy of your love.

The outward shows of sky and earth, 45
Of hill and valley, he has viewed;
And impulses of deeper birth
Have come to him in solitude.

In common things that round us lie
Some random truths he can impart,—
The harvest of a quiet eye 51
That broods and sleeps on his own heart.

But he is weak; both Man and Boy,
Hath been an idler in the land;
Contented if he might enjoy 55
The things which others understand.

—Come hither in thy hour of strength;
Come, weak as is a breaking wave!
Here stretch thy body at full length;
Or build thy house upon this grave. 60

IX
TO THE DAISY
[Composed 1802.—Published 1807.]

BRIGHT Flower! whose home is every-
where,
Bold in maternal Nature's care,
And all the long year through the heir
Of joy and sorrow;
Methinks that there abides in thee 5
Some concord with humanity,
Given to no other flower I see
The forest thorough!

Is it that Man is soon deprest?
A thoughtless Thing! who, once unblest,
Does little on his memory rest, 11
Or on his reason,
And Thou wouldst teach him how to find
A shelter under every wind,
A hope for times that are unkind 15
And every season?

Thou wander'st the wide world about,
Unchecked by pride or scrupulous doubt
With friends to greet thee, or without,
Yet pleased and willing; 20

Meek, yielding to the occasion's call,
And all things suffering from all,
Thy function apostolical
  In peace fulfilling.

X
MATTHEW

[Composed 1799.—Published 1800.]

In the School of ———— is a tablet, on which
are inscribed, in gilt letters, the Names of the
several persons who have been Schoolmasters
there since the foundation of the School, with
the time at which they entered upon and quitted
their office. Opposite to one of those Names
the Author wrote the following lines.

IF Nature, for a favourite child,
In thee hath tempered so her clay,
That every hour thy heart runs wild,
Yet never once doth go astray,

Read o'er these lines; and then review   5
This tablet, that thus humbly rears
In such diversity of hue
Its history of two hundred years.

—When through this little wreck of fame,
Cipher and syllable! thine eye   10
Has travelled down to Matthew's name,
Pause with no common sympathy.

And if a sleeping tear should wake,
Then be it neither checked nor stayed:
For Matthew a request I make   15
Which for himself he had not made.

Poor Matthew, all his frolics o'er,
Is silent as a standing pool;
Far from the chimney's merry roar,
And murmur of the village school.   20

The sighs which Matthew heaved were
      sighs
Of one tired out with fun and madness;
The tears which came to Matthew's eyes
Were tears of light, the dew of gladness.

Yet sometimes, when the secret cup   25
Of still and serious thought went round,
It seemed as if he drank it up—
He felt with spirit so profound.

—Thou soul of God's best earthly mould!
Thou happy Soul! and can it be   30
That these two words of glittering gold
Are all that must remain of thee?

XI
THE TWO APRIL MORNINGS

[Composed 1799.—Published 1800.]

WE walked along, while bright and red
Uprose the morning sun;
And Matthew stopped, he looked, and
      said,
'The will of God be done!'

A village schoolmaster was he,   5
With hair of glittering grey;
As blithe a man as you could see
On a spring holiday.

And on that morning, through the grass,
And by the steaming rills,   10
We travelled merrily, to pass
A day among the hills.

'Our work,' said I, 'was well begun,
Then from thy breast what thought,
Beneath so beautiful a sun,   15
So sad a sigh has brought?'

A second time did Matthew stop;
And fixing still his eye
Upon the eastern mountain-top,
To me he made reply: 20

'Yon cloud with that long purple cleft
Brings fresh into my mind
A day like this which I have left
Full thirty years behind.

'And just above yon slope of corn   25
Such colours, and no other,
Were in the sky, that April morn,
Of this the very brother.

'With rod and line I sued the sport
Which that sweet season gave,   30
And, to the churchyard come, stopped
      short
Beside my daughter's grave.

'Nine summers had she scarcely seen,
The pride of all the vale;
And then she sang;—she would have
      been   35
A very nightingale.

'Six feet in earth my Emma lay;
And yet I loved her more,
For so it seemed, than till that day
I e'er had loved before.   40

'And, turning from her grave, I met,
Beside the churchyard yew,
A blooming Girl, whose hair was wet
With points of morning dew.

'A basket on her head she bare;   45
Her brow was smooth and white:
To see a child so very fair,
It was a pure delight!

'No fountain from its rocky cave
E'er tripped with foot so free;   50
She seemed as happy as a wave
That dances on the sea.

'There came from me a sigh of pain
Which I could ill confine;
I looked at her, and looked again: 55
And did not wish her mine!'

Matthew is in his grave, yet now,
Methinks, I see him stand,
As at that moment, with a bough
Of wilding in his hand.   60

381

XII
THE FOUNTAIN
A CONVERSATION
[Composed 1799.—Published 1800.]

WE talked with open heart, and tongue
Affectionate and true,
A pair of friends, though I was young,
And Matthew seventy-two.

We lay beneath a spreading oak, 5
Beside a mossy seat;
And from the turf a fountain broke,
And gurgled at our feet.

'Now, Matthew!' said I, 'let us match
This water's pleasant tune 10
With some old border-song, or catch
That suits a summer's noon;

'Or of the church-clock and the chimes
Sing here beneath the shade,
That half-mad thing of witty rhymes 15
Which you last April made!'

In silence Matthew lay, and eyed
The spring beneath the tree;
And thus the dear old Man replied,
The grey-haired man of glee: 20

'No check, no stay, this Streamlet fears;
How merrily it goes!
'Twill murmur on a thousand years,
And flow as now it flows.

'And here, on this delightful day, 25
I cannot choose but think
How oft, a vigorous man, I lay
Beside this fountain's brink.

'My eyes are dim with childish tears,
My heart is idly stirred, 30
For the same sound is in my ears
Which in those days I heard.

'Thus fares it still in our decay:
And yet the wiser mind
Mourns less for what age takes away 35
Than what it leaves behind.

'The blackbird amid leafy trees,
The lark above the hill,
Let loose their carols when they please,
Are quiet when they will. 40

'With Nature never do *they* wage
A foolish strife; they see
A happy youth, and their old age
Is beautiful and free:

'But we are pressed by heavy laws; 45
And often, glad no more,
We wear a face of joy, because
We have been glad of yore.

'If there be one who need bemoan
His kindred laid in earth, 50
The household hearts that were his own;
It is the man of mirth.

'My days, my Friend, are almost gone,
My life has been approved,
And many love me! but by none 55
Am I enough beloved.'

'Now both himself and me he wrongs,
The man who thus complains!
I live and sing my idle songs
Upon these happy plains; 60

'And, Matthew, for thy children dead
I'll be a son to thee!'
At this he grasped my hand, and said,
'Alas! that cannot be.'

We rose up from the fountain-side; 65
And down the smooth descent
Of the green sheep-track did we glide;
And through the wood we went;

And, ere we came to Leonard's rock,
He sang those witty rhymes 70
About the crazy old church-clock,
And the bewildered chimes.

XIII
PERSONAL TALK
[Composed (?).—Published 1807.]

I

I AM not One who much or oft delight
To season my fireside with personal
talk,—
Of friends, who live within an easy walk,
Or neighbours, daily, weekly, in my
sight:
And, for my chance-acquaintance, ladies
bright, 5
Sons, mothers, maidens withering on the
stalk,
These all wear out of me, like Forms with
chalk
Painted on rich men's floors, for one feast-
night.
Better than such discourse doth silence
long,
Long, barren silence, square with my
desire; 10
To sit without emotion, hope, or aim,
In the loved presence of my cottage-fire,
And listen to the flapping of the flame,
Or kettle whispering its faint under-
song.

II

'Yet life,' you say, 'is life; we have seen
and see, 15
And with a living pleasure we describe;
And fits of sprightly malice do but bribe
The languid mind into activity.
Sound sense, and love itself, and mirth
and glee
Are fostered by the comment and the
gibe.' 20

Even be it so: yet still among your tribe,
Our daily world's true Worldlings, rank
   not me!
Children are blest, and powerful; their
   world lies
More justly balanced; partly at their feet,
And part far from them:—sweetest
   melodies   25
Are those that are by distance made
   more sweet;
Whose mind is but the mind of his own
   eyes,
He is a Slave; the meanest we can meet!

III

Wings have we,—and as far as we can go
We may find pleasure: wilderness and
   wood,   30
Blank ocean and mere sky, support that
   mood
Which with the lofty sanctifies the low.
Dreams, books, are each a world; and
   books, we know,
Are a substantial world, both pure and
   good:
Round these, with tendrils strong as flesh
   and blood,   35
Our pastime and our happiness will
   grow.
There find I personal themes, a plenteous
   store,
Matter wherein right voluble I am,
To which I listen with a ready ear;
Two shall be named, pre-eminently
   dear,—   40
The gentle Lady married to the Moor;
And heavenly Una with her milk-white
   Lamb.

IV

Nor can I not believe but that hereby
Great gains are mine; for thus I live
   remote
From evil-speaking; rancour, never
   sought,   45
Comes to me not; malignant truth, or
   lie.
Hence have I genial seasons, hence have I
Smooth passions, smooth discourse, and
   joyous thought:
And thus from day to day my little boat
Rocks in its harbour, lodging peaceably.
Blessings be with them—and eternal
   praise,   51
Who gave us nobler loves, and nobler
   cares—
The Poets, who on earth have made us
   heirs
Of truth and pure delight by heavenly
   lays!
Oh! might my name be numbered among
   theirs,   55
Then gladly would I end my mortal
   days.

XIV

ILLUSTRATED BOOKS AND NEWSPAPERS

[Composed 1846.—Published 1850.]

DISCOURSE was deemed Man's noblest
   attribute,
And written words the glory of his hand;
Then followed Printing with enlarged
   command
For thought—dominion vast and absolute
For spreading truth, and making love
   expand.   5
Now prose and verse sunk into disrepute
Must lacquey a dumb Art that best can suit
The taste of this once-intellectual Land.
A backward movement surely have we
   here,
From manhood—back to childhood; for
   the age—   10
Back towards caverned life's first rude
   career.
Avaunt this vile abuse of pictured page!
Must eyes be all in all, the tongue and ear
Nothing? Heaven keep us from a lower
   stage!

XV

TO THE SPADE OF A FRIEND

(AN AGRICULTURIST)

Composed while we were labouring together in
his pleasure-ground.

[Composed (probably) 1806.—Published 1807.]

SPADE! with which Wilkinson hath tilled
   his lands,
And shaped these pleasant walks by
   Emont's side,
Thou art a tool of honour in my hands;
I press thee, through the yielding soil,
   with pride.   4

Rare master has it been thy lot to know;
Long hast Thou served a man to reason
   true;
Whose life combines the best of high and
   low,
The labouring many and the resting few;

Health, meekness, ardour, quietness
   secure,
And industry of body and of mind;   10
And elegant enjoyments, that are pure
As nature is;—too pure to be refined.

Here often hast Thou heard the Poet sing
In concord with his river murmuring by;
Or in some silent field, while timid spring
Is yet uncheered by other minstrelsy.   16

Who shall inherit Thee when death has laid
Low in the darksome cell thine own dear
   lord?
That man will have a trophy, humble
   Spade!   19
A trophy nobler than a conqueror's sword.

If he be one that feels, with skill to part
False praise from true, or, greater from
the less,
Thee will he welcome to his hand and
heart,
Thou monument of peaceful happiness!

He will not dread with Thee a toilsome
day—   25
Thee his loved servant, his inspiring
mate!
And, when Thou art past service, worn
away,
No dull oblivious nook shall hide thy fate.

His thrift thy uselessness will never scorn;
An *heir-loom* in his cottage wilt Thou
be:—   30
High will he hang thee up, well pleased
to adorn
His rustic chimney with the last of Thee!

XVI
A NIGHT THOUGHT

[Composed (?).—Published 1837 (*The Tribute:
edited by Lord Northampton*); vol. of 1842.]

Lo! where the Moon along the sky
Sails with her happy destiny;
Oft is she hid from mortal eye
Or dimly seen,
But when the clouds asunder fly   5
How bright her mien!

Far different we—a froward race,
Thousands though rich in Fortune's grace
With cherished sullenness of pace
Their way pursue,   10
Ingrates who wear a smileless face
The whole year through.

If kindred humours e'er would make
My spirit droop for drooping's sake,
From Fancy following in thy wake,   15
Bright ship of heaven!
A counter impulse let me take
And be forgiven.

XVII
INCIDENT

CHARACTERISTIC OF A FAVOURITE DOG
[Composed 1805.—Published 1807.]

On his morning rounds the Master
Goes to learn how all things fare;
Searches pasture after pasture,
Sheep and cattle eyes with care;
And, for silence or for talk,   5
He hath comrades in his walk;
Four dogs, each pair of different breed,
Distinguished two for scent, and two for
speed.

See a hare before him started!
—Off they fly in earnest chase;   10
Every dog is eager-hearted,
All the four are in the race:

And the hare whom they pursue,
Knows from instinct what to do;
Her hope is near: no turn she makes;   15
But, like an arrow, to the river takes.

Deep the river was, and crusted
Thinly by a one night's frost;
But the nimble Hare hath trusted
To the ice, and safely crost;   20
She hath crost, and without heed
All are following at full speed,
When, lo! the ice, so thinly spread,
Breaks—and the greyhound, Dart, is
overhead!

Better fate have Prince and Swallow—
See them cleaving to the sport!   26
Music has no heart to follow,
Little Music, she stops short.
She hath neither wish nor heart,
Hers is now another part: 30
A loving creature she, and brave!
And fondly strives her struggling friend
to save.

From the brink her paws she stretches,
Very hands as you would say!
And afflicting moans she fetches,   35
As he breaks the ice away.
For herself she hath no fears,—
Him alone she sees and hears,—
Makes efforts with complainings; nor
gives o'er
Until her fellow sinks to re-appear no
more.   40

XVIII
TRIBUTE

TO THE MEMORY OF THE SAME DOG
[Composed 1805.—Published 1807.]

Lie here, without a record of thy worth,
Beneath a covering of the common earth!
It is not from unwillingness to praise,
Or want of love, that here no Stone we
raise;
More thou deserv'st; but *this* man gives
to man,   5
Brother to brother, *this* is all we can.
Yet they to whom thy virtues made thee
dear
Shall find thee through all changes of the
year:
This Oak points out thy grave; the silent
tree
Will gladly stand a monument of thee.

We grieved for thee, and wished thy
end were past;   11
And willingly have laid thee here at last:
For thou hadst lived till every thing that
cheers
In thee had yielded to the weight of years;
Extreme old age had wasted thee away,
And left thee but a glimmering of the day;

Thy ears were deaf, and feeble were thy
  knees,—
I saw thee stagger in the summer breeze,
Too weak to stand against its sportive
  breath,
And ready for the gentlest stroke of
  death.   20
It came, and we were glad; yet tears were
  shed;
Both man and woman wept when thou
  wert dead;
Not only for a thousand thoughts that
  were,
Old household thoughts, in which thou
  hadst thy share;
But for some precious boons vouchsafed
  to thee,   25
Found scarcely anywhere in like degree!
For love, that comes wherever life and
  sense
Are given by God, in thee was most
  intense;
A chain of heart, a feeling of the mind,
A tender sympathy, which did thee bind
Not only to us Men, but to thy Kind: 31
Yea, for thy fellow-brutes in thee we saw
A soul of love, love's intellectual law:—
Hence, if we wept, it was not done in
  shame;
Our tears from passion and from reason
  came.   35
And, therefore, shalt thou be an honoured
  name!

XIX
FIDELITY

[Composed 1805.—Published 1807.]

A BARKING sound the Shepherd hears,
A cry as of a dog or fox;
He halts—and searches with his eyes
Among the scattered rocks:
And now at distance can discern   5
A stirring in a brake of fern;
And instantly a dog is seen,
Glancing through that covert green.

The Dog is not of mountain breed;
Its motions, too, are wild and shy;   10
With something, as the Shepherd thinks,
Unusual in its cry:
Nor is there any one in sight
All round, in hollow or on height;
Nor shout, nor whistle strikes his ear; 15
What is the creature doing here?

It was a cove, a huge recess,
That keeps, till June, December's snow;
A lofty precipice in front,
A silent tarn[1] below!   20
Far in the bosom of Helvellyn,
Remote from public road or dwelling,
Pathway, or cultivated land;
From trace of human foot or hand.

[1] Tarn is a *small* Mere or Lake, mostly high up
in the mountains.

There sometimes doth a leaping fish   25
Send through the tarn a lonely cheer;
The crags repeat the raven's croak,
In symphony austere;
Thither the rainbow comes—the cloud—
And mists that spread the flying shroud;
And sunbeams; and the sounding blast,
That, if it could, would hurry past;   32
But that enormous barrier holds it fast.

Not free from boding thoughts, a while
The Shepherd stood; then makes his way
O'er rocks and stones, following the Dog
As quickly as he may;   37
Nor far had gone before he found
A human skeleton on the ground;
The appalled Discoverer with a sigh 40
Looks round, to learn the history.

From those abrupt and perilous rocks
The Man had fallen, that place of fear!
At length upon the Shepherd's mind
It breaks, and all is clear: 45
He instantly recalled the name,
And who he was, and whence he came;
Remembered, too, the very day
On which the Traveller passed this way.

But hear a wonder, for whose sake   50
This lamentable tale I tell!
A lasting monument of words
This wonder merits well.
The Dog, which still was hovering nigh,
Repeating the same timid cry,   55
This Dog, had been through three months'
  space
A dweller in that savage place.

Yes, proof was plain that, since the day
When this ill-fated Traveller died,
The Dog had watched about the spot, 60
Or by his master's side:
How nourished here through such long
  time
He knows, who gave that love sublime;
And gave that strength of feeling, great
Above all human estimate!   65

XX
ODE TO DUTY

[Composed 1805.—Published 1807.]

'Jam non consilio bonus, sed more eò perductus,
ut non tantum rectè facere possim, sed nisi rectè
facere non possim.'

STERN Daughter of the Voice of God!
O Duty! if that name thou love
Who art a light to guide, a rod
To check the erring, and reprove;
Thou, who art victory and law   5
When empty terrors overawe;
From vain temptations dost set free;
And calm'st the weary strife of frail
  humanity!

There are who ask not if thine eye
Be on them; who, in love and truth,　10
Where no misgiving is, rely
Upon the genial sense of youth:
Glad Hearts! without reproach or blot;
Who do thy work, and know it not:
Oh! if through confidence misplaced　15
They fail, thy saving arms, dread Power!
　　around them cast.

Serene will be our days and bright,
And happy will our nature be,
When love is an unerring light,
And joy its own security.　20
And they a blissful course may hold
Even now, who, not unwisely bold,
Live in the spirit of this creed;
Yet seek thy firm support, according to
　　their need.

I, loving freedom, and untried;　25
No sport of every random gust,
Yet being to myself a guide,
Too blindly have reposed my trust:
And oft, when in my heart was heard
Thy timely mandate, I deferred　30
The task, in smoother walks to stray;
But thee I now would serve more strictly,
　　if I may.

Through no disturbance of my soul,
Or strong compunction in me wrought,
I supplicate for thy control;　35
But in the quietness of thought:
Me this unchartered freedom tires;
I feel the weight of chance-desires:
My hopes no more must change their
　　name,
I long for a repose that ever is the
　　same.　40

[Yet not the less would I throughout
Still act according to the voice
Of my own wish; and feel past doubt
That my submissiveness was choice:
Not seeking in the school of pride
For 'precepts over dignified,'
Denial and restraint I prize
No farther than they breed a second Will
more wise.[1]]

Stern Lawgiver! yet thou dost wear
The Godhead's most benignant grace;
Nor know we anything so fair
As is the smile upon thy face:
Flowers laugh before thee on their beds
And fragrance in thy footing treads;　46
Thou dost preserve the stars from wrong;
And the most ancient heavens, through
　　Thee, are fresh and strong.

To humbler functions, awful Power!
I call thee: I myself commend　50
Unto thy guidance from this hour;
Oh, let my weakness have an end!

　　　　　[1] In ed. 1807 only.—ED.

Give unto me, made lowly wise,
The spirit of self-sacrifice;
The confidence of reason give;　55
And in the light of truth thy Bondman
　　let me live!

XXI
CHARACTER OF THE HAPPY WARRIOR

[Composed December 1805 or January 1806.—
Published 1807.]

WHO is the happy Warrior? Who is he
That every man in arms should wish
　　to be?
—It is the generous Spirit, who, when
　　brought
Among the tasks of real life, hath
　　wrought
Upon the plan that pleased his boyish
　　thought:　5
Whose high endeavours are an inward
　　light
That makes the path before him always
　　bright:
Who, with a natural instinct to discern
What knowledge can perform, is diligent
　　to learn;
Abides by this resolve, and stops not
　　there,　10
But makes his moral being his prime
　　care;
Who, doomed to go in company with
　　Pain,
And Fear, and Bloodshed, miserable
　　train!
Turns his necessity to glorious gain;
In face of these doth exercise a power　15
Which is our human nature's highest
　　dower;
Controls them and subdues, transmutes,
　　bereaves
Of their bad influence, and their good
　　receives:
By objects, which might force the soul to
　　abate
Her feeling, rendered more compas-
　　sionate;　20
Is placable—because occasions rise
So often that demand such sacrifice;
More skilful in self-knowledge, even more
　　pure,
As tempted more; more able to endure,
As more exposed to suffering and dis-
　　tress;　25
Thence, also, more alive to tenderness.
—'Tis he whose law is reason; who
　　depends
Upon that law as on the best of friends;
Whence, in a state where men are tempted
　　still
To evil for a guard against worse ill,　30
And what in quality or act is best
Doth seldom on a right foundation rest.

He labours good on good to fix, and owes
To virtue every triumph that he knows:
—Who, if he rise to station of command,
Rises by open means; and there will
stand   36
On honourable terms, or else retire,
And in himself possess his own desire;
Who comprehends his trust, and to the
same
Keeps faithful with a singleness of aim;
And therefore does not stoop, nor lie in
wait   41
For wealth, or honours, or for worldly
state;
Whom they must follow; on whose head
must fall,
Like showers of manna, if they come
at all:
Whose powers shed round him in the
common strife,   45
Or mild concerns of ordinary life,
A constant influence, a peculiar grace;
But who, if he be called upon to face
Some awful moment to which Heaven
has joined
Great issues, good or bad for human
kind,   50
Is happy as a Lover; and attired
With sudden brightness, like a Man
inspired;
And, through the heat of conflict, keeps
the law
In calmness made, and sees what he
foresaw;
Or if an unexpected call succeed,   55
Come when it will, is equal to the need:
—He who, though thus endued as with a
sense
And faculty for storm and turbulence,
Is yet a Soul whose master-bias leans
To homefelt pleasures and to gentle
scenes;   60
Sweet images! which, wheresoe'er he be,
Are at his heart; and such fidelity
It is his darling passion to approve;
More brave for this, that he hath much to
love:——   64
'Tis, finally, the Man, who, lifted high,
Conspicuous object in a Nation's eye,
Or left unthought-of in obscurity,—
Who, with a toward or untoward lot,
Prosperous or adverse, to his wish or not—
Plays, in the many games of life, that one
Where what he most doth value must be
won: 71
Whom neither shape of danger can dismay,
Nor thought of tender happiness betray;
Who, not content that former worth
stand fast,
Looks forward, persevering to the last,
From well to better, daily self-surpast: 76
Who, whether praise of him must walk
the earth
For ever, and to noble deeds give birth,

Or he must fall, to sleep without his fame,
And leave a dead unprofitable name— 80
Finds comfort in himself and in his cause;
And, while the mortal mist is gathering,
draws
His breath in confidence of Heaven's
applause:
This is the happy Warrior; this is He 84
That every Man in arms should wish to be.

XXII

THE FORCE OF PRAYER[1]

OR

THE FOUNDING OF BOLTON PRIORY
A TRADITION

[Composed 1807.—Published 1815 (4to, along with
The White Doe of Rylstone); ed. 1815.]

' 𝖂𝖍𝖆𝖙 𝖎𝖘 𝖌𝖔𝖔𝖉 𝖋𝖔𝖗 𝖆 𝖇𝖔𝖔𝖙𝖑𝖊𝖘𝖘 𝖇𝖊𝖓𝖊 ? '
With these dark words begins my Tale;
And their meaning is, whence can comfort
spring
When Prayer is of no avail?
' 𝖂𝖍𝖆𝖙 𝖎𝖘 𝖌𝖔𝖔𝖉 𝖋𝖔𝖗 𝖆 𝖇𝖔𝖔𝖙𝖑𝖊𝖘𝖘 𝖇𝖊𝖓𝖊 ? ' 5
The Falconer to the Lady said;
And she made answer 'ENDLESS SORROW!'
For she knew that her Son was dead.

She knew it by the Falconer's words, 9
And from the look of the Falconer's eye;
And from the love which was in her soul
For her youthful Romilly.

—Young Romilly through Barden woods
Is ranging high and low;
And holds a greyhound in a leash, 15
To let slip upon buck or doe.

The pair have reached that fearful chasm,
How tempting to bestride!
For lordly Wharf is there pent in
With rocks on either side. 20

The striding-place is called THE STRID,
A name which it took of yore:
A thousand years hath it borne that name,
And shall a thousand more.

And hither is young Romilly come, 25
And what may now forbid
That he, perhaps for the hundredth time,
Shall bound across THE STRID?

He sprang in glee,—for what cared he
That the river was strong, and the rocks
were steep?— 30
But the greyhound in the leash hung back,
And checked him in his leap.

The Boy is in the arms of Wharf,
And strangled by a merciless force;
For never more was young Romilly seen
Till he rose a lifeless corse. 36

[1] See 'The White Doe of Rylstone.'

Now there is stillness in the vale,
And long, unspeaking, sorrow:
Wharf shall be to pitying hearts
A name more sad than Yarrow. 40

If for a Lover the Lady wept,
A solace she might borrow
From death, and from the passion of
death:—
Old Wharf might heal her sorrow.

She weeps not for the wedding-day 45
Which was to be to-morrow:
Her hope was a further-looking hope,
And hers is a mother's sorrow.

He was a tree that stood alone,
And proudly did its branches wave; 50
And the root of this delightful tree
Was in her husband's grave!

Long, long in darkness did she sit,
And her first words were, 'Let there be
In Bolton, on the field of Wharf, 55
A stately Priory!'

The stately Priory was reared;
And Wharf, as he moved along,
To matins joined a mournful voice,
Nor failed at even-song. 60

And the Lady prayed in heaviness
That looked not for relief!
But slowly did her succour come,
And a patience to her grief.

Oh! there is never sorrow of heart 65
That shall lack a timely end,
If but to God we turn, and ask
Of Him to be our friend!

XXIII

A FACT, AND AN IMAGINATION

OR

CANUTE AND ALFRED, ON THE SEA-SHORE

[Composed 1816.—Published 1820.]

THE Danish Conqueror, on his royal
chair,
Mustering a face of haughty sovereignty,
To aid a covert purpose, cried—'O ye
Approaching Waters of the deep, that
share
With this green isle my fortunes, come
not where 5
Your Master's throne is set.'—Deaf was
the Sea;
Her waves rolled on, respecting his decree
Less than they heed a breath of wanton
air.
—Then Canute, rising from the invaded
throne,
Said to his servile Courtiers,—'Poor the
reach, 10

The undisguised extent, of mortal sway!
He only is a King, and he alone
Deserves the name (this truth the billows
preach)
Whose everlasting laws, sea, earth, and
heaven obey.'

This just reproof the prosperous Dane
Drew from the influx of the main, 16
For some whose rugged northern mouths
would strain
At oriental flattery;
And Canute (fact more worthy to be
known)
From that time forth did for his brows
disown 20
The ostentatious symbol of a crown;
Esteeming earthly royalty
Contemptible as vain.

Now hear what one of elder days, 24
Rich theme of England's fondest praise,
Her darling Alfred, *might* have spoken;
To cheer the remnant of his host
When he was driven from coast to coast,
Distressed and harassed, but with mind
unbroken:

'My faithful followers, lo! the tide is
spent 30
That rose, and steadily advanced to fill
The shores and channels, working Na-
ture's will
Among the mazy streams that backward
went,
And in the sluggish pools where ships are
pent:
And now, his task performed, the flood
stands still, 35
At the green base of many an inland hill,
In placid beauty and sublime content!
Such the repose that sage and hero find;
Such measured rest the sedulous and good
Of humbler name; whose souls do, like
the flood 40
Of Ocean, press right on; or gently wind,
Neither to be diverted nor withstood
Until they reach the bounds by Heaven
assigned.'

XXIV

[Composed 1816.—Published 1820.]

'*A LITTLE onward lend thy guiding hand
To these dark steps, a little further on!*'
—What trick of memory to *my* voice hath
brought
This mournful iteration? For though
Time,
The Conqueror, crowns the Conquered,
on this brow 5
Planting his favourite silver diadem,
Nor he, nor minister of his—intent
To run before him, hath enrolled me yet,

388

Though not unmenaced, among those
    who lean
Upon a living staff, with borrowed sight.
—O my own Dora, my belovèd child!   11
Should that day come—but hark! the
    birds salute
The cheerful dawn, brightening for me
    the east;
For me, thy natural leader, once again
Impatient to conduct thee, not as erst   15
A tottering infant, with compliant stoop
From flower to flower supported; but to
    curb
Thy nymph-like step swift-bounding o'er
    the lawn,
Along the loose rocks, or the slippery
    verge
Of foaming torrents.—From thy orisons
Come forth; and, while the morning air
    is yet   21
Transparent as the soul of innocent youth,
Let me, thy happy guide, now point thy
    way,
And now precede thee, winding to and fro,
Till we by perseverance gain the top   25
Of some smooth ridge, whose brink pre-
    cipitous
Kindles intense desire for powers withheld
From this corporeal frame; whereon who
    stands
Is seized with strong incitement to push
    forth
His arms, as swimmers use, and plunge—
    dread thought,   30
For pastime plunge—into the 'abrupt
    abyss,'
Where ravens spread their plumy vans,
    at ease!

And yet more gladly thee would I con-
    duct
Through woods and spacious forests,—to
    behold
There how the Original of human art,   35
Heaven-prompted Nature, measures and
    erects
Her temples, fearless for the stately work,
Though waves, to every breeze, its high-
    arched roof,
And storms the pillars rock. But we such
    schools
Of reverential awe will chiefly seek   40
In the still summer noon, while beams of
    light,
Reposing here, and in the aisles beyond
Traceably gliding through the dusk, recall
To mind the living presences of nuns;
A gentle, pensive, white-robed sisterhood,
Whose saintly radiance mitigates the
    gloom   46
Of those terrestrial fabrics, where they
    serve,
To Christ, the Sun of righteousness, es-
    poused.

Now also shall the page of classic lore,
To these glad eyes from bondage freed,
    again   50
Lie open; and the book of Holy Writ,
Again unfolded, passage clear shall yield
To heights more glorious still, and into
    shades
More awful, where, advancing hand in hand,
We may be taught, O Darling of my care!
To calm the affections, elevate the soul,
And consecrate our lives to truth and love.

XXV
ODE TO LYCORIS
MAY, 1817
[Composed May, 1817.—Published 1820.]

I

AN age hath been when Earth was proud
Of lustre too intense
To be sustained; and Mortals bowed
The front in self-defence.
Who *then*, if Dian's crescent gleamed,   5
Or Cupid's sparkling arrow streamed
While on the wing the Urchin played,
Could fearlessly approach the shade?
—Enough for one soft vernal day,
If I, a bard of ebbing time,   10
And nurtured in a fickle clime,
May haunt this hornèd bay;
Whose amorous water multiplies
The flitting halcyon's vivid dyes;   14
And smooths her liquid breast—to show
These swan-like specks of mountain snow,
White as the pair that slid along the plains
Of heaven, when Venus held the reins!

II

In youth we love the darksome lawn
Brushed by the owlet's wing;   20
Then, Twilight is preferred to Dawn,
And Autumn to the Spring.
Sad fancies do we then affect,
In luxury of disrespect
To our own prodigal excess   25
Of too familiar happiness.
Lycoris (if such name befit
Thee, thee my life's celestial sign!)
When Nature marks the year's decline,
Be ours to welcome it;   30
Pleased with the harvest hope that runs
Before the path of milder suns;
Pleased while the sylvan world displays
Its ripeness to the feeding gaze;
Pleased when the sullen winds resound
    the knell
Of the resplendent miracle.

III

But something whispers to my heart
That, as we downward tend,
Lycoris! life requires an *art*
To which our souls must bend;   40

A skill—to balance and supply;
And, ere the flowing fount be dry,
As soon it must, a sense to sip,
Or drink, with no fastidious lip.
Then welcome, above all, the Guest 45
Whose smiles, diffused o'er land and sea,
Seem to recall the Deity
Of youth into the breast:
May pensive Autumn ne'er present
A claim to her disparagement! 50
While blossoms and the budding spray
Inspire us in our own decay;
Still, as we nearer draw to life's dark goal,
Be hopeful Spring the favourite of the
    Soul!

XXVI
TO THE SAME

[Composed 1817.—Published 1820.]

ENOUGH of climbing toil!—Ambition
    treads
Here, as 'mid busier scenes, ground steep
    and rough,
Or slippery even to peril! and each step,
As we for most uncertain recompense
Mount toward the empire of the fickle
    clouds, 5
Each weary step, dwarfing the world
    below,
Induces, for its old familiar sights,
Unacceptable feelings of contempt,
With wonder mixed—that Man could
    e'er be tied,
In anxious bondage, to such nice array 10
And formal fellowship of petty things!
—Oh! 'tis the *heart* that magnifies this
    life,
Making a truth and beauty of her own;
And moss-grown alleys, circumscribing
    shades, 14
And gurgling rills, assist her in the work
More efficaciously than realms outspread,
As in a map, before the adventurer's
    gaze—
Ocean and Earth contending for regard.

The umbrageous woods are left—how
    far beneath!
But lo! where darkness seems to guard
    the mouth 20
Of yon wild cave, whose jaggèd brows are
    fringed
With flaccid threads of ivy, in the still
And sultry air, depending motionless.
Yet cool the space within, and not un-
    cheered
(As whoso enters shall ere long perceive)
By stealthy influx of the timid day 26
Mingling with night, such twilight to
    compose
As Numa loved; when, in the Egerian
    grot,

From the sage Nymph appearing at his
    wish
He gained whate'er a regal mind might
    ask, 30
Or need, of counsel breathed through lips
    divine.

Long as the heat shall rage, let that
    dim cave
Protect us, there deciphering as we may
Diluvian records; or the sighs of Earth
Interpreting; or counting for old Time 35
His minutes, by reiterated drops,
Audible tears, from some invisible source
That deepens upon fancy—more and more
Drawn toward the centre whence those
    sighs creep forth
To awe the lightness of humanity. 40
Or, shutting up thyself within thyself,
There let me see thee sink into a mood
Of gentler thought, protracted till thine
    eye
Be calm as water when the winds are gone,
And no one can tell whither. Dearest
    Friend! 45
We two[1] have known such happy hours
    together
That, were power granted to replace them
    (fetched
From out the pensive shadows where they
    lie)
In the first warmth of their original sun-
    shine,
Loth should I be to use it: passing sweet
Are the domains of tender memory! 51

XXVII
SEPTEMBER, 1819

[Composed September, 1819.—Published 1820.]

THE sylvan slopes with corn-clad fields
Are hung, as if with golden shields,
Bright trophies of the sun!
Like a fair sister of the sky,
Unruffled doth the blue lake lie, 5
The mountains looking on.

And, sooth to say, yon vocal grove,
Albeit uninspired by love,
By love untaught to ring,
May well afford to mortal ear 10
An impulse more profoundly dear
Than music of the Spring.

For *that* from turbulence and heat
Proceeds, from some uneasy seat
In nature's struggling frame, 15
Some region of impatient life:
And jealousy, and quivering strife,
Therein a portion claim.

    [1] 'We two': edd. 1820–1843; 'we too': edd.
1845, 1849–50.—ED.

390

This, this is holy;—while I hear
These vespers of another year, 20
This hymn of thanks and praise,
My spirit seems to mount above
The anxieties of human love,
And earth's precarious days.

But list!—though winter storms be nigh,
Unchecked is that soft harmony: 26
There lives Who can provide
For all His creatures; and in Him,
Even like the radiant Seraphim,
These choristers confide. 30

XXVIII
UPON THE SAME OCCASION
[Composed September, 1819.—Published 1820.]

DEPARTING summer hath assumed
An aspect tenderly illumed,
The gentlest look of spring;
That calls from yonder leafy shade
Unfaded, yet prepared to fade, 5
A timely carolling.

No faint and hesitating trill,
Such tribute as to winter chill
The lonely redbreast pays!
Clear, loud, and lively is the din, 10
From social warblers gathering in
Their harvest of sweet lays.

Nor doth the example fail to cheer
Me, conscious that my leaf is sere,
And yellow on the bough:— 15
Fall, rosy garlands, from my head!
Ye myrtle wreaths, your fragrance shed
Around a younger brow!

Yet will I temperately rejoice;
Wide is the range, and free the choice 20
Of undiscordant themes;
Which, haply, kindred souls may prize
Not less than vernal ecstasies,
And passion's feverish dreams.

For deathless powers to verse belong, 25
And they like Demi-gods are strong
On whom the Muses smile;
But some their function have disclaimed,
Best pleased with what is aptliest framed
To enervate and defile. 30

Not such the initiatory strains
Committed to the silent plains
In Britain's earliest dawn:
Trembled the groves, the stars grew pale,
While all-too-daringly the veil 35
Of nature was withdrawn!

Nor such the spirit-stirring note
When the live chords Alcæus smote,
Inflamed by sense of wrong;
Woe! woe to Tyrants! from the lyre 40
Broke threateningly, in sparkles dire
Of fierce vindictive song.

And not unhallowed was the page
By wingèd Love inscribed, to assuage

The pangs of vain pursuit; 45
Love listening while the Lesbian Maid
With finest touch of passion swayed
Her own Æolian lute.

O ye, who patiently explore
The wreck of Herculanean lore, 50
What rapture! could ye seize
Some Theban fragment, or unroll
One precious, tender-hearted, scroll
Of pure Simonides.

That were, indeed, a genuine birth 55
Of poesy; a bursting forth
Of genius from the dust:
What Horace gloried to behold,
What Maro loved, shall we enfold?
Can haughty Time be just! 60

XXIX
MEMORY
[Composed 1823.—Published 1827.]

A PEN—to register; a key—
That winds through secret wards;
Are well assigned to Memory
By allegoric Bards.

As aptly, also, might be given 5
A Pencil to her hand;
That, softening objects, sometimes even
Outstrips the heart's demand;

That smoothes foregone distress, the lines
Of lingering care subdues, 10
Long-vanished happiness refines,
And clothes in brighter hues;

Yet, like a tool of Fancy, works
Those Spectres to dilate
That startle Conscience, as she lurks 15
Within her lonely seat.

O! that our lives, which flee so fast,
In purity were such,
That not an image of the past
Should fear that pencil's touch! 20

Retirement then might hourly look
Upon a soothing scene,
Age steal to his allotted nook
Contented and serene;

With heart as calm as lakes that sleep, 25
In frosty moonlight glistening;
Or mountain rivers, where they creep
Along a channel smooth and deep,
To their own far-off murmurs listening.

XXX
[Composed 1829.—Published 1835.]

THIS Lawn, a carpet all alive
With shadows flung from leaves—to strive
In dance, amid a press
Of sunshine, an apt emblem yields
Of Worldlings revelling in the fields 5
Of strenuous idleness;

Less quick the stir when tide and breeze
Encounter, and to narrow seas
   Forbid a moment's rest;
The medley less when boreal Lights   10
Glance to and fro, like aery Sprites
   To feats of arms addrest!

Yet, spite of all this eager strife,
This ceaseless play, the genuine life
   That serves the steadfast hours,   15
Is in the grass beneath, that grows
Unheeded, and the mute repose
   Of sweetly-breathing flowers.

XXXI
HUMANITY

[Composed 1829.—Published 1835.]

The Rocking-stones, alluded to in the beginning
of the following verses, are supposed to have
been used, by our British ancestors, both for
judicial and religious purposes. Such stones are
not uncommonly found, at this day, both in
Great Britain and in Ireland.

WHAT though the Accused, upon his own
   appeal
To righteous Gods when man has ceased
   to feel,
Or at a doubting Judge's stern command,
Before the STONE OF POWER no longer
   stand—
To take his sentence from the balanced
   Block,   5
As, at his touch, it rocks, or seems to
   rock;
Though, in the depths of sunless groves,
   no more
The Druid-priest the hallowed Oak adore;
Yet, for the Initiate, rocks and whisper-
   ing trees
Do still perform mysterious offices!   10
And functions dwell in beast and bird
   that sway
The reasoning mind, or with the fancy
   play,
Inviting, at all seasons, ears and eyes
To watch for undelusive auguries:—
Not uninspired appear their simplest
   ways;   15
Their voices mount symbolical of praise—
To mix with hymns that Spirits make and
   hear;
And to fallen man their innocence is dear.
Enraptured Art draws from those sacred
   springs
Streams that reflect the poetry of things!
Where Christian Martyrs stand in hues
   portrayed,   21
That, might a wish avail, would never
   fade,
Borne in their hands the lily and the palm
Shed round the altar a celestial calm;

There, too, behold the lamb and guileless
   dove   25
Prest in the tenderness of virgin love
To saintly bosoms!—Glorious is the
   blending
Of right affections climbing or descending
Along a scale of light and life, with cares
Alternate; carrying holy thoughts and
   prayers   30
Up to the sovereign seat of the Most High;
Descending to the worm in charity;
Like those good Angels whom a dream of
   night
Gave, in the field of Luz, to Jacob's sight
All, while *he* slept, treading the pendent
   stairs   35
Earthward or heavenward, radiant mes-
   sengers,
That, with a perfect will in one accord
Of strict obedience, serve the Almighty
   Lord;
And with untired humility forbore
To speed their errand by the wings they
   wore.   40

What a fair world were ours for verse
   to paint,
If Power could live at ease with self-
   restraint!
Opinion bow before the naked sense
Of the great Vision,—faith in Providence;
Merciful over all his creatures, just   45
To the least particle of sentient dust;
But fixing by immutable decrees
Seedtime and harvest for his purposes!
Then would be closed the restless oblique
   eye
That looks for evil like a treacherous spy;
Disputes would then relax, like stormy
   winds   51
That into breezes sink; impetuous minds
By discipline endeavour to grow meek
As Truth herself, whom they profess to
   seek.
Then Genius, shunning fellowship with
   Pride,   55
Would braid his golden locks at Wis-
   dom's side;
Love ebb and flow untroubled by caprice;
And not alone *harsh* tyranny would cease,
But unoffending creatures find release
From qualified oppression, whose de-
   fence   60
Rests on a hollow plea of recompense;
Thought-tempered wrongs, for each hu-
   mane respect
Oft worse to bear, or deadlier in effect.
Witness those glances of indignant scorn
From some high-minded Slave, impelled
   to spurn   65
The kindness that would make him less
   forlorn;
Or, if the soul to bondage be subdued,
His look of pitiable gratitude!

Alas for thee, bright Galaxy of Isles,
Whose day departs in pomp, returns with
  smiles—   70
To greet the flowers and fruitage of a
  land,
As the sun mounts, by sea-born breezes
  fanned;
A land whose azure mountain-tops are
  seats
For Gods in council, whose green vales,
  retreats
Fit for the shades of heroes, mingling
  there   75
To breathe Elysian peace in upper air.

Though cold as winter, gloomy as the
  grave,
Stone-walls a prisoner make, but not a
  slave.
Shall man assume a property in man?
Lay on the moral will a withering ban?
Shame that our laws at distance still pro-
  tect   81
Enormities, which they at home reject!
'Slaves cannot breathe in England'—yet
  that boast
Is but a mockery! when from coast to
  coast,
Though *fettered* slave be none, her floors
  and soil   85
Groan underneath a weight of slavish
  toil,
For the poor Many, measured out by
  rules
Fetched with cupidity from heartless
  schools,
That to an Idol, falsely called 'the Wealth
Of Nations,' sacrifice a People's health,
Body and mind and soul; a thirst so
  keen   91
Is ever urging on the vast machine
Of sleepless Labour, 'mid whose dizzy
  wheels
The Power least prized is that which
  thinks and feels.

Then, for the pastimes of this delicate
  age,   95
And all the heavy or light vassalage
Which for their sakes we fasten, as may
  suit
Our varying moods, on human kind or
  brute,
'Twere well in little, as in great, to pause,
Lest Fancy trifle with eternal laws.   100
Not from his fellows only man may
  learn
Rights to compare and duties to dis-
  cern!
All creatures and all objects, in degree,
Are friends and patrons of humanity.
There are to whom the garden, grove, and
  field,   105
Perpetual lessons of forbearance yield;

Who would not lightly violate the grace
The lowliest flower possesses in its place;
Nor shorten the sweet life, too fugitive,
Which nothing less than Infinite Power
  could give.   110

XXXII

[Composed 1846.—Published 1850.]

THE unremitting voice of nightly streams
That wastes so oft, we think, its tuneful
  powers,
If neither soothing to the worm that
  gleams
Through dewy grass, nor small birds
  hushed in bowers,
Nor unto silent leaves and drowsy
  flowers,—   5
That voice of unpretending harmony
(For who what is shall measure by what
  seems
To be, or not to be,
Or tax high Heaven with prodigality?)
Wants not a healing influence that can
  creep   10
Into the human breast, and mix with sleep
To regulate the motion of our dreams
For kindly issues—as through every clime
Was felt near murmuring brooks in
  earliest time;
As, at this day, the rudest swains who
  dwell   15
Where torrents roar, or hear the tinkling
  knell
Of water-breaks, with grateful heart
  could tell.

XXXIII

THOUGHTS ON THE SEASONS

[Composed 1829.—Published 1835.]

FLATTERED with promise of escape
  From every hurtful blast,
Spring takes, O sprightly May! thy shape,
  Her loveliest and her last.

Less fair is summer riding high   5
  In fierce solstitial power,
Less fair than when a lenient sky
  Brings on her parting hour.

When earth repays with golden sheaves
  The labours of the plough,   10
And ripening fruits and forest leaves
  All brighten on the bough;

What pensive beauty autumn shows,
  Before she hears the sound
Of winter rushing in, to close   15
  The emblematic round!

Such be our Spring, our Summer such;
  So may our Autumn blend
With hoary Winter, and Life touch,   19
  Through heaven-born hope, her end!

XXXIV
TO ——

UPON THE BIRTH OF HER FIRST-BORN
CHILD, MARCH, 1833

[Composed March, 1833.—Published 1835.]

'Tum porro puer, ut saevis projectus ab undis
Navita, nudus humi jacet,' &c.—LUCRETIUS.

LIKE a shipwrecked Sailor tost
By rough waves on a perilous coast,
Lies the Babe, in helplessness
And in tenderest nakedness,
Flung by labouring Nature forth   5
Upon the mercies of the earth.
Can its eyes beseech?—no more
Than the hands are free to implore:
Voice but serves for one brief cry;
Plaint was it? or prophecy   10
Of sorrow that will surely come?
Omen of man's grievous doom!

But, O Mother! by the close
Duly granted to thy throes;
By the silent thanks, now tending   15
Incense-like to Heaven, descending
Now to mingle and to move
With the gush of earthly love,
As a debt to that frail Creature,
Instrument of struggling Nature   20
For the blissful calm, the peace
Known but to this *one* release—
Can the pitying spirit doubt
That for human-kind springs out
From the penalty a sense   25
Of more than mortal recompense?

As a floating summer cloud,
Though of gorgeous drapery proud,
To the sun-burnt traveller,
Or the stooping labourer,   30
Oft-times makes its bounty known
By its shadow round him thrown;
So, by chequerings of sad cheer,
Heavenly Guardians, brooding near,
Of their presence tell—too bright   35
Haply for corporeal sight!
Ministers of grace divine
Feelingly their brows incline
O'er this seeming Castaway
Breathing, in the light of day,   40
Something like the faintest breath
That has power to baffle death—
Beautiful, while very weakness
Captivates like passive meekness.

And, sweet Mother! under warrant   45
Of the universal Parent,
Who repays in season due
Them who have, like thee, been true
To the filial chain let down
From his everlasting throne,   50
Angels hovering round thy couch,
With their softest whispers vouch,
That—whatever griefs may fret,
Cares entangle, sins beset,

This thy First-born, and with tears   55
Stain her cheek in future years—
Heavenly succour, not denied
To the babe, whate'er betide,
Will to the woman be supplied!

Mother! blest be thy calm ease;   60
Blest the starry promises,—
And the firmament benign
Hallowed be it, where they shine!
Yes, for them whose souls have scope
Ample for a wingèd hope,   65
And can earthward bend an ear
For needful listening, pledge is here,
That, if thy new-born Charge shall tread
In thy footsteps, and be led
By that other Guide, whose light   70
Of manly virtues, mildly bright,
Gave him first the wished-for part
In thy gentle virgin heart;
Then, amid the storms of life
Presignified by that dread strife   75
Whence ye have escaped together,
She may look for serene weather;
In all trials sure to find
Comfort for a faithful mind;
Kindlier issues, holier rest,   80
Than even now await her prest,
Conscious Nursling, to thy breast!

XXXV
THE WARNING

A SEQUEL TO THE FOREGOING

[Composed 1833.—Published 1835.]

LIST, the winds of March are blowing;
Her ground-flowers shrink, afraid of
     showing
Their meek heads to the nipping air,
Which ye feel not, happy pair!
Sunk into a kindly sleep.   5
We, meanwhile, our hope will keep;
And if Time leagued with adverse Change
(Too busy fear!) shall cross its range,
Whatsoever check they bring,
Anxious duty hindering,   10
To like hope our prayers will cling.

Thus, while the ruminating spirit feeds
Upon the events of home as life proceeds,
Affections pure and holy in their source
Gain a fresh impulse, run a livelier course;
Hopes that within the Father's heart
     prevail,   16
Are in the experienced Grandsire's slow
     to fail;
And if the harp pleased his gay youth, it
     rings
To his grave touch with no unready
     strings,   50
While thoughts press on, and feelings
     overflow,   20
And quick words round him fall like
     flakes of snow.

Thanks to the Powers that yet main-
tain their sway,
And have renewed the tributary Lay.
Truths of the heart flock in with eager
pace,
And FANCY greets them with a fond
embrace;   25
Swift as the rising sun his beams extends
She shoots the tidings forth to distant
friends;
Their gifts she hails (deemed precious, as
they prove
For the unconscious Babe so prompt a
love!)—
But from this peaceful centre of delight
Vague sympathies have urged her to take
flight: 31
Rapt into upper regions, like the bee
That sucks from mountain-heath her
honey fee,
Or, like the warbling lark intent to shroud
His head in sunbeams or a bowery cloud,
She soars—and here and there her pinions
rest   36
On proud towers, like this humble cot-
tage, blest
With a new visitant, an infant guest—
Towers where red streamers flout the
breezy sky
In pomp foreseen by her creative eye,   40
When feasts shall crowd the hall, and
steeple bells
Glad proclamation make, and heights
and dells
Catch the blithe music as it sinks and
swells,
And harboured ships, whose pride is on
the sea,
Shall hoist their topmost flags in sign of
glee,   45
Honouring the hope of noble ancestry.

But who (though neither reckoning ills
assigned
By Nature, nor reviewing in the mind
The track that was, and is, and must be,
worn   49
With weary feet by all of woman born)—
Shall *now* by such a gift with joy be moved,
Nor feel the fulness of that joy reproved?
Not He, whose last faint memory will
command
The truth that Britain was his native land;
Whose infant soul was tutored to confide
In the cleansed faith for which her mar-
tyrs died;   56
Whose boyish ear the voice of her renown
With rapture thrilled; whose Youth re-
vered the crown
Of Saxon liberty that Alfred wore,
Alfred, dear Babe, thy great Progenitor!
—Not He, who from her mellowed prac-
tice drew   61
His social sense of just, and fair, and true;

And saw, thereafter, on the soil of France
Rash Polity begin her maniac dance,
Foundations broken up, the deeps run
wild,   65
Nor grieved to see (himself not unbe-
guiled)—
Woke from the dream, the dreamer to
upbraid,
And learn how sanguine expectations fade
When novel trusts by folly are betrayed,—
To see Presumption, turning pale, refrain
From further havoc, but repent in vain,—
Good aims lie down, and perish in the
road   72
Where guilt had urged them on with
ceaseless goad,
Proofs thickening round her that on
public ends
Domestic virtue vitally depends,   75
That civic strife can turn the happiest
hearth
Into a grievous sore of self-tormenting
earth.

Can such a One, dear Babe! though
glad and proud
To welcome thee, repel the fears that
crowd
Into his English breast, and spare to quake
Less for his own than for thy innocent
sake?   81
Too late—or, should the providence of
God
Lead, through dark ways by sin and sor-
row trod,
Justice and peace to a secure abode,
Too soon—thou com'st into this breath-
ing world;   85
Ensigns of mimic outrage are unfurled,
Who shall preserve or prop the tottering
Realm?
What hand suffice to govern the state-
helm?
If in the aims of men the surest test
Of good or bad (whate'er be sought for or
profest)   90
Lie in the means required, or ways or-
dained,
For compassing the end, else never gained;
Yet governors and governed both are
blind
To this plain truth, or fling it to the wind;
If to expedience principle must bow;   95
Past, future, shrinking up beneath the
incumbent Now;
If cowardly concession still must feed
The thirst for power in men who ne'er
concede;
Nor turn aside, unless to shape a way
For domination at some riper day;   100
If generous Loyalty must stand in awe
Of subtle Treason, in his mask of law,
Or with bravado insolent and hard,
Provoking punishment, to win reward;

If office help the factious to conspire, 105
And they who *should* extinguish, fan the
   fire—
Then, will the sceptre be a straw, the
   crown
Sit loosely, like the thistle's crest of down;
To be blown off at will, by Power that
   spares it
In cunning patience, from the head that
   wears it. 110

Lost people, trained to theoretic feud!
Lost above all, ye labouring multitude!
Bewildered whether ye, by slanderous
   tongues
Deceived, mistake calamities for wrongs;
And over fancied usurpations brood, 115
Oft snapping at revenge in sullen mood;
Or, from long stress of real injuries fly
To desperation for a remedy;
In bursts of outrage spread your judg-
   ments wide,
And to your wrath cry out, 'Be thou our
   guide;' 120
Or, bound by oaths, come forth to tread
   earth's floor
In marshalled thousands, darkening street
   and moor
With the worst shape mock-patience ever
   wore;
Or, to the giddy top of self-esteem
By Flatterers carried, mount into a dream
Of boundless suffrage, at whose sage
   behest 126
Justice shall rule, disorder be supprest,
And every man sit down as Plenty's
   Guest!
—O for a bridle bitted with remorse
To stop your Leaders in their headstrong
   course! 130
Oh may the Almighty scatter with His
   grace
These mists, and lead you to a safer place,
By paths no human wisdom can foretrace!
May He pour round you, from worlds far
   above
Man's feverish passions, His pure light of
   love, 135
That quietly restores the natural mien
To hope, and makes truth willing to be
   seen!
Else shall your blood-stained hands in
   frenzy reap
Fields gaily sown when promises were
   cheap.— 139
Why is the Past belied with wicked art,
The Future made to play so false a part,
Among a people famed for strength of
   mind,
Foremost in freedom, noblest of man-
   kind?
We act as if we joyed in the sad tune
Storms make in rising, valued in the
   moon 145

Nought but her changes. Thus, ungrate-
   ful Nation!
If thou persist, and, scorning moderation,
Spread for thyself the snares of tribula-
   tion,
Whom, then, shall meekness guard? What
   saving skill
Lie in forbearance, strength in standing
   still? 150
—Soon shall the widow (for the speed of
   Time
Nought equals when the hours are winged
   with crime)
Widow, or wife, implore on tremulous
   knee,
From him who judged her lord, a like
   decree;
The skies will weep o'er old men deso-
   late: 155
Ye little-ones! Earth shudders at your fate,
Outcasts and homeless orphans——

But turn, my Soul, and from the sleep-
   ing pair
Learn thou the beauty of omniscient care!
Be strong in faith, bid anxious thoughts
   lie still; 160
Seek for the good and cherish it—the ill
Oppose, or bear with a submissive will.

XXXVI

[Composed 1833.—Published 1835.]

IF this great world of joy and pain
   Revolve in one sure track;
If freedom, set, will rise again,
   And virtue, flown, come back;
Woe to the purblind crew who fill 5
   The heart with each day's care;
Nor gain, from past or future, skill
   To bear, and to forbear!

XXXVII
THE LABOURER'S NOON-DAY HYMN

[Composed 1834.—Published 1835.]

UP to the throne of God is borne
The voice of praise at early morn,
And he accepts the punctual hymn
Sung as the light of day grows dim:

Nor will he turn his ear aside 5
From holy offerings at noontide.
Then here reposing let us raise
A song of gratitude and praise.

What though our burthen be not light
We need not toil from morn to night; 10
The respite of the mid-day hour
Is in the thankful Creature's power.

Blest are the moments, doubly blest,
That, drawn from this one hour of rest,
Are with a ready heart bestowed 15
Upon the service of our God!

Each field is then a hallowed spot,
An altar is in each man's cot,
A church in every grove that spreads
Its living roof above our heads.   20

Look up to Heaven! the industrious Sun
Already half his race hath run;
He cannot halt nor go astray,
But our immortal Spirits may.

Lord! since his rising in the East,   25
If we have faltered or transgressed,
Guide, from thy love's abundant source,
What yet remains of this day's course:

Help with thy grace, through life's short
    day,
Our upward and our downward way;   30
And glorify for us the west,
When we shall sink to final rest.

XXXVIII
ODE

COMPOSED ON MAY MORNING

[Composed 1826.—Published 1835.]

WHILE from the purpling east departs
    The star that led the dawn,
Blithe Flora from her couch upstarts,
    For May is on the lawn.
A quickening hope, a freshening glee,   5
    Foreran the expected Power,
Whose first-drawn breath from bush and
    tree
    Shakes off that pearly shower.

All Nature welcomes Her whose sway
    Tempers the year's extremes;   10
Who scattereth lustres o'er noon-day,
    Like morning's dewy gleams;
While mellow warble, sprightly trill,
    The tremulous heart excite;
And hums the balmy air to still   15
    The balance of delight.

Time was, blest Power! when youths and
    maids
    At peep of dawn would rise,
And wander forth, in forest glades
    Thy birth to solemnize.   20
Though mute the song—to grace the rite
    Untouched the hawthorn bough,
Thy Spirit triumphs o'er the slight;
    Man changes, but not Thou!

Thy feathered Lieges bill and wings   25
    In love's disport employ;
Warmed by thy influence, creeping things
    Awake to silent joy:
Queen art thou still for each gay plant
    Where the slim wild deer roves;   30
And served in depths where fishes haunt
    Their own mysterious groves.

Cloud-piercing peak, and trackless heath,
    Instinctive homage pay;

Nor wants the dim-lit cave a wreath   35
    To honour thee, sweet May!
Where cities fanned by thy brisk airs
    Behold a smokeless sky,
Their puniest flower-pot-nursling dares
    To open a bright eye.   40

And if, on this thy natal morn,
    The pole, from which thy name
Hath not departed, stands forlorn
    Of song and dance and game;
Still from the village-green a vow   45
    Aspires to thee addrest,
Wherever peace is on the brow,
    Or love within the breast.

Yes! where Love nestles thou canst teach
    The soul to love the more;   50
Hearts also shall thy lessons reach
    That never loved before.
Stript is the haughty one of pride,
    The bashful freed from fear,
While rising, like the ocean-tide,   55
    In flows the joyous year.

Hush, feeble lyre! weak words refuse
    The service to prolong!
To yon exulting thrush the Muse
    Entrusts the imperfect song;   60
His voice shall chant, in accents clear,
    Throughout the live-long day,
Till the first silver star appear,
    The sovereignty of May.

XXXIX
TO MAY

[Composed 1826-34.—Published 1835.]

THOUGH many suns have risen and set
    Since thou, blithe May, wert born,
And Bards, who hailed thee, may forget
    Thy gifts, thy beauty scorn;
There are who to a birthday strain   5
    Confine not harp and voice,
But evermore throughout thy reign
    Are grateful and rejoice!

Delicious odours! music sweet,
    Too sweet to pass away!   10
Oh for a deathless song to meet
    The soul's desire—a lay
That, when a thousand years are told,
    Should praise thee, genial Power!
Through summer heat, autumnal cold,   15
    And winter's dreariest hour.

Earth, sea, thy presence feel—nor less,
    If yon ethereal blue
With its soft smile the truth express,
    The heavens have felt it too.   20
The inmost heart of man if glad
    Partakes a livelier cheer;
And eyes that cannot but be sad
    Let fall a brightened tear.

Since thy return, through days and weeks
  Of hope that grew by stealth,   26
How many wan and faded cheeks
  Have kindled into health!
The Old, by thee revived, have said,
  'Another year is ours;'   30
And wayworn Wanderers, poorly fed,
  Have smiled upon thy flowers.

Who tripping lisps a merry song
  Amid his playful peers?
The tender Infant who was long   35
  A prisoner of fond fears;
But now, when every sharp-edged blast
  Is quiet in its sheath,
His Mother leaves him free to taste
  Earth's sweetness in thy breath.   40

Thy help is with the weed that creeps
  Along the humblest ground;
No cliff so bare but on its steeps
  Thy favours may be found;
But most on some peculiar nook   45
  That our own hands have drest,
Thou and thy train are proud to look,
  And seem to love it best.

And yet how pleased we wander forth
  When May is whispering, 'Come!   50
Choose from the bowers of virgin earth
  The happiest for your home;
Heaven's bounteous love through me is
    spread
From sunshine, clouds, winds, waves,
Drops on the mouldering turret's head,
  And on your turf-clad graves!'   56

Such greeting heard, away with sighs
  For lilies that must fade,
Or 'the rathe primrose as it dies
  Forsaken' in the shade!   60
Vernal fruitions and desires
  Are linked in endless chase;
While, as one kindly growth retires,
  Another takes its place.

And what if thou, sweet May, hast known
  Mishap by worm and blight;   66
If expectations newly blown
  Have perished in thy sight;
If loves and joys, while up they sprung,
  Were caught as in a snare;   70
Such is the lot of all the young,
  However bright and fair.

Lo! Streams that April could not check
  Are patient of thy rule;
Gurgling in foamy water-break,   75
  Loitering in glassy pool:
By thee, thee only, could be sent
  Such gentle mists as glide,
Curling with unconfirmed intent,
  On that green mountain's side.   80

How delicate the leafy veil
  Through which yon house of God

Gleams 'mid the peace of this deep dale
  By few but shepherds trod!
And lowly huts, near beaten ways,   85
  No sooner stand attired
In thy fresh wreaths, than they for praise
  Peep forth, and are admired.

Season of fancy and of hope,
  Permit not for one hour   90
A blossom from thy crown to drop,
  Nor add to it a flower!
Keep, lovely May, as if by touch
  Of self-restraining art,
This modest charm of not too much,   95
  Part seen, imagined part!

XL
LINES

SUGGESTED BY A PORTRAIT FROM THE
PENCIL OF F. STONE
[Composed 1834.—Published 1835.]

BEGUILED into forgetfulness of care
Due to the day's unfinished task; of pen
Or book regardless, and of that fair scene
In Nature's prodigality displayed
Before my window, oftentimes and long   5
I gaze upon a Portrait whose mild gleam
Of beauty never ceases to enrich
The common light; whose stillness charms
    the air,
Or seems to charm it, into like repose;
Whose silence, for the pleasure of the
    ear,   10
Surpasses sweetest music. There she sits
With emblematic purity attired
In a white vest, white as her marble neck
Is, and the pillar of the throat would be
But for the shadow by the drooping chin
Cast into that recess—the tender shade,
The shade and light, both there and every-
    where,   17
And through the very atmosphere she
    breathes,
Broad, clear, and toned harmoniously,
    with skill
That might from nature have been learnt
    in the hour   20
When the lone shepherd sees the morning
    spread
Upon the mountains. Look at her,
    whoe'er
Thou be that, kindling with a poet's soul,
Hast loved the painter's true Promethean
    craft
Intensely—from Imagination take   25
The treasure,—what mine eyes behold see
    thou,
Even though the Atlantic ocean roll
    between.

A silver line, that runs from brow to
    crown
And in the middle parts the braided hair,

Just serves to show how delicate a soil   30
The golden harvest grows in; and those
    eyes,
Soft and capacious as a cloudless sky
Whose azure depth their colour emulates,
Must needs be conversant with upward
    looks,
Prayer's voiceless service; but now, seek-
    ing nought   35
And shunning nought, their own peculiar
    life
Of motion they renounce, and with the
    head
Partake its inclination towards earth
In humble grace, and quiet pensiveness
Caught at the point where it stops short
    of sadness.   40

Offspring of soul-bewitching Art, make
    me
Thy confidant! say, whence derived that
    air
Of calm abstraction? Can the ruling
    thought
Be with some lover far away, or one
Crossed by misfortune, or of doubted
    faith?   45
Inapt conjecture! Childhood here, a moon
Crescent in simple loveliness serene,
Has but approached the gates of woman-
    hood,
Not entered them; her heart is yet un-
    pierced
By the blind Archer-god; her fancy free:
The fount of feeling, if unsought else-
    where,   51
Will not be found.
            Her right hand, as it lies
Across the slender wrist of the left arm
Upon her lap reposing, holds—but mark
How slackly, for the absent mind per-
    mits   55
No firmer grasp—a little wild-flower,
    joined
As in a posy, with a few pale ears
Of yellowing corn, the same that over-
    topped
And in their common birthplace sheltered
    it
Till they were plucked together; a blue
    flower   60
Called by the thrifty husbandman a weed;
But Ceres, in her garland, might have
    worn
That ornament, unblamed. The floweret,
    held
In scarcely conscious fingers, was, she
    knows,
(Her Father told her so) in youth's gay
    dawn   65
Her Mother's favourite; and the orphan
    Girl,
In her own dawn—a dawn less gay and
    bright,

Loves it, while there in solitary peace
She sits, for that departed Mother's sake.
—Not from a source less sacred is derived
(Surely I do not err) that pensive air   71
Of calm abstraction through the face
    diffused
And the whole person.
            Words have something told
More than the pencil can, and verily
More than is needed, but the precious
    Art   75
Forgives their interference—Art divine,
That both creates and fixes, in despite
Of Death and Time, the marvels it hath
    wrought.

Strange contrasts have we in this world
    of ours!   79
That posture, and the look of filial love
Thinking of past and gone, with what is
    left
Dearly united, might be swept away
From this fair Portrait's fleshly Arche-
    type,
Even by an innocent fancy's slightest
    freak
Banished, nor ever, haply, be restored   85
To their lost place, or meet in harmony
So exquisite; but *here* do they abide,
Enshrined for ages. Is not then the Art
Godlike, a humble branch of the divine,
In visible quest of immortality,   90
Stretched forth with trembling hope?—In
    every realm,
From high Gibraltar to Siberian plains,
Thousands, in each variety of tongue
That Europe knows, would echo this
    appeal;
One above all, a Monk who waits on God
In the magnific Convent built of yore   96
To sanctify the Escurial palace. He—
Guiding, from cell to cell and room to
    room,
A British Painter (eminent for truth
In character, and depth of feeling, shown
By labours that have touched the hearts
    of kings,   101
And are endeared to simple cottagers)—
Came, in that service, to a glorious work,
Our Lord's Last Supper, beautiful as
    when first
The appropriate Picture, fresh from
    Titian's hand,   105
Graced the Refectory: and there, while
    both
Stood with eyes fixed upon that master-
    piece,
The hoary Father in the Stranger's ear
Breathed out these words:—'Here daily
    do we sit,
Thanks given to God for daily bread, and
    here   110
Pondering the mischiefs of these restless
    times,

And thinking of my Brethren, dead,
dispersed,
Or changed and changing, I not seldom
gaze
Upon this solemn Company unmoved
By shock of circumstance, or lapse of
years,   115
Until I cannot but believe that they—
They are in truth the Substance, we the
Shadows.'

So spake the mild Jeronymite, his griefs
Melting away within him like a dream
Ere he had ceased to gaze, perhaps to
speak: 120
And I, grown old, but in a happier land,
Domestic Portrait! have to verse con-
signed
In thy calm presence those heart-moving
words:
Words that can soothe, more than they
agitate;
Whose spirit, like the angel that went
down   125
Into Bethesda's pool, with healing virtue
Informs the fountain in the human breast
Which by the visitation was disturbed.
——But why this stealing tear? Com-
panion mute,
On thee I look, not sorrowing; fare thee
well,   130
My Song's Inspirer, once again farewell![1]

XLI

THE FOREGOING SUBJECT
RESUMED

[Composed 1834.—Published 1835.]

AMONG a grave fraternity of Monks,
For One, but surely not for One alone,
Triumphs, in that great work, the
Painter's skill,
Humbling the body, to exalt the soul;
Yet representing, amid wreck and wrong
And dissolution and decay, the warm   6
And breathing life of flesh, as if already
Clothed with impassive majesty, and
graced
With no mean earnest of a heritage
Assigned to it in future worlds. Thou,
too,   10
With thy memorial flower, meek Por-
traiture!
From whose serene companionship I
passed
Pursued by thoughts that haunt me still;
thou also—
Though but a simple object, into light

Called forth by those affections that
endear   15
The private hearth; though keeping thy
sole seat
In singleness, and little tried by time,
Creation, as it were, of yesterday—
With a congenial function art endued
For each and all of us, together joined
In course of nature under a low roof   21
By charities and duties that proceed
Out of the bosom of a wiser vow.
To a like salutary sense of awe
Or sacred wonder, growing with the
power   25
Of meditation that attempts to weigh,
In faithful scales, things and their op-
posites,
Can thy enduring quiet gently raise
A household small and sensitive,—whose
love,
Dependent as in part its blessings are   30
Upon frail ties dissolving or dissolved
On earth, will be revived, we trust, in
heaven.[2]

XLII

[Composed 1844.—Published 1845.]

So fair, so sweet, withal so sensitive,
Would that the little Flowers were born
to live,
Conscious of half the pleasure which they
give;

That to this mountain-daisy's self were
known
The beauty of its star-shaped shadow,
thrown   5
On the smooth surface of this naked
stone!

And what if hence a bold desire should
mount
High as the Sun, that he could take
account
Of all that issues from his glorious
fount!

So might he ken how by his sovereign
aid   10
These delicate companionships are made;
And how he rules the pomp of light and
shade;

[1] The pile of buildings composing the palace and convent of San Lorenzo, has, in common usage, lost its proper name in that of the *Escurial*, a village at the foot of the hill upon which the splendid edifice, built by Philip the Second, stands. It need scarcely be added that Wilkie is the painter alluded to.

[2] In the class entitled 'Musings,' in Mr. Southey's Minor Poems, is one upon his own miniature Picture, taken in childhood, and another upon a landscape painted by Gaspar Poussin. It is possible that every word of the above verses, though similar in subject, might have been written had the author been unacquainted with those beautiful effusions of poetic sentiment. But, for his own satisfaction, he must be allowed thus publicly to acknowledge the pleasure those two Poems of his Friend have given him, and the grateful influence they have upon his mind as often as he reads them, or thinks of them.

And were the Sister-power that shines by
   night
So privileged, what a countenance of
   delight
Would through the clouds break forth on
   human sight!   15

Fond fancies! wheresoe'er shall turn
   thine eye
On earth, air, ocean, or the starry sky,
Converse with Nature in pure sympathy;

All vain desires, all lawless wishes
   quelled,
Be Thou to love and praise alike impelled,   20
Whatever boon is granted or withheld.

XLIII
UPON SEEING A COLOURED DRAWING OF THE BIRD OF PARADISE IN AN ALBUM

[Composed 1835–6.—Published 1837.]

WHO rashly strove thy Image to portray?
Thou buoyant minion of the tropic air;
How could he think of the live creature—
   gay
With a divinity of colours, drest
In all her brightness, from the dancing
   crest   5
Far as the last gleam of the filmy train
Extended and extending to sustain
The motions that it graces—and forbear
To drop his pencil! Flowers of every
   clime
Depicted on these pages smile at time;
And gorgeous insects copied with nice
   care   11
Are here, and likenesses of many a shell
Tossed ashore by restless waves,

Or in the diver's grasp fetched up from
   caves
Where sea-nymphs might be proud to
   dwell: 15
But whose rash hand (again I ask) could
   dare,
'Mid casual tokens and promiscuous
   shows,
To circumscribe this Shape in fixed repose;
Could imitate for indolent survey,
Perhaps for touch profane,   20
Plumes that might catch, but cannot
   keep, a stain;
And, with cloud-streaks lightest and
   loftiest, share
The sun's first greeting, his last farewell
   ray!

Resplendent Wanderer! followed with
   glad eyes
Where'er her course; mysterious Bird! 25
To whom, by wondering Fancy stirred,
Eastern Islanders have given
A holy name   the Bird of Heaven!
And even a title higher still,
The Bird of God! whose blessed will   30
She seems performing as she flies
Over the earth and through the skies
In never-wearied search of Paradise—
Region that crowns her beauty with the
   name
She bears for us—for us how blest,   35
How happy at all seasons, could like aim
Uphold our Spirits urged to kindred flight
On wings that fear no glance of God's
   pure sight,
No tempest from his breath, their pro-
   mised rest
Seeking with indefatigable quest   40
Above a world that deems itself most wise
When most enslaved by gross realities!

SONNETS DEDICATED TO LIBERTY AND ORDER

I
COMPOSED AFTER READING A NEWS-PAPER OF THE DAY

[Composed 1831.—Published 1835.]

'PEOPLE! your chains are severing link
   by link;
Soon shall the Rich be levelled down—the
   Poor
Meet them half way.' Vain boast! for
   These, the more
They thus would rise, must low and lower
   sink
Till, by repentance stung, they fear to
   think;   5
While all lie prostrate, save the tyrant
   few
Bent in quick turns each other to undo,
And mix the poison, they themselves
   must drink.
Mistrust thyself, vain Country! cease to
   cry,
'Knowledge will save me from the
   threatened woe.'   10
For if than other rash ones more thou
   know,
Yet on presumptuous wing as far would
   fly
Above thy knowledge as they dared to go,
Thou wilt provoke a heavier penalty.

SONNETS DEDICATED TO LIBERTY AND ORDER

II

UPON THE LATE GENERAL FAST
MARCH, 1832

[Composed 1832.—Published 1838.]

RELUCTANT call it was; the rite delayed;
And in the Senate some there were who
doffed
The last of their humanity, and scoffed
At providential judgments, undismayed
By their own daring. But the People
prayed 5
As with one voice; their flinty heart grew
soft
With penitential sorrow, and aloft
Their spirit mounted, crying, 'God us aid!'
Oh that with aspirations more intense,
Chastised by self-abasement more pro-
found, 10
This People, once so happy, so renowned
For liberty, would seek from God defence
Against far heavier ill, the pestilence
Of revolution, impiously unbound!

III

[Composed probably 1838.—Published 1838.]

SAID Secrecy to Cowardice and Fraud,
Falsehood and Treachery, in close council
met,
Deep under ground, in Pluto's cabinet,
'The frost of England's pride will soon
be thawed;
Hooded the open brow that overawed 5
Our schemes; the faith and honour, never
yet
By us with hope encountered, be upset;—
For once I burst my bands, and cry,
applaud!'
Then whispered she, 'The Bill is carrying
out!'
They heard, and, starting up, the Brood
of Night 10
Clapped hands, and shook with glee their
matted locks;
All Powers and Places that abhor the light
Joined in the transport, echoed back their
shout,
Hurrah for ——,[1] hugging his Ballot-box!

IV

[Composed 1838.—Published 1838.]

BLEST Statesman He, whose Mind's
unselfish will
Leaves him at ease among grand thoughts:
whose eye
Sees that, apart from magnanimity,
Wisdom exists not; nor the humbler skill
Of Prudence, disentangling good and ill
With patient care. What tho' assaults
run high, 6
They daunt not him who holds his
ministry,

[1] i.e. Grote.—ED.

Resolute, at all hazards, to fulfil
Its duties;—prompt to move, but firm to
wait,—
Knowing, things rashly sought are rarely
found; 10
That, for the functions of an ancient
State—
Strong by her charters, free because
imbound,
Servant of Providence, not slave of Fate—
Perilous is sweeping change, all chance
unsound.

V

IN ALLUSION TO VARIOUS RECENT HIS-
TORIES AND NOTICES OF THE FRENCH
REVOLUTION

[Composed ?—Published 1842.]

PORTENTOUS change when History can
appear
As the cool Advocate of foul device;
Reckless audacity extol, and jeer
At consciences perplexed with scruples
nice!
They who bewail not, must abhor, the
sneer 5
Born of Conceit, Power's blind Idolater;
Or haply sprung from vaunting Cowardice
Betrayed by mockery of holy fear.
Hath it not long been said the wrath of
Man
Works not the righteousness of God? Oh
bend, 10
Bend, ye Perverse! to judgments from
on High,
Laws that lay under Heaven's perpetual
ban
All principles of action that transcend
The sacred limits of humanity.

VI

CONTINUED

[Composed (?).—Published 1842.]

WHO ponders National events shall find
An awful balancing of loss and gain,
Joy based on sorrow, good with ill com-
bined,
And proud deliverance issuing out of pain
And direful throes; as if the All-ruling
Mind, 5
With whose perfection it consists to
ordain
Volcanic burst, earthquake, and hurri-
cane,
Dealt in like sort with feeble human kind
By laws immutable. But woe for him
Who thus deceived shall lend an eager
hand 10
To social havoc. Is not Conscience ours,
And Truth, whose eye guilt only can
make dim;
And Will, whose office, by divine command,
Is to control and check disordered Powers?

402

VII

CONCLUDED

[Composed (?).—Published 1842.]

LONG-FAVOURED England! be not thou
　misled
By monstrous theories of alien growth,
Lest alien frenzy seize thee, waxing
　wroth,
Self-smitten till thy garments reek dyed
　red
With thy own blood, which tears in
　torrents shed　　　　　　　　　　5
Fail to wash out, tears flowing ere thy
　troth
Be plighted, not to ease but sullen sloth,
Or wan despair—the ghost of false hope
　fled
Into a shameful grave. Among thy youth,
My Country! if such warning be held
　dear,　　　　　　　　　　　　　10
Then shall a Veteran's heart be thrilled
　with joy,
One who would gather from eternal truth,
For time and season, rules that work to
　cheer—
Not scourge, to save the People—not
　destroy.

VIII

[Composed 1839.—Published 1842.]

MEN of the Western World! in Fate's
　dark book
Whence these opprobrious leaves of dire
　portent?
Think ye your British Ancestors forsook
Their native Land, for outrage provident;
From unsubmissive necks the bridle
　shook　　　　　　　　　　　　　5
To give, in their Descendants, freer vent
And wider range to passions turbulent,
To mutual tyranny a deadlier look?
Nay, said a voice, soft as the south wind's
　breath,
Dive through the stormy surface of the
　flood　　　　　　　　　　　　　10
To the great current flowing underneath;
Explore the countless springs of silent
　good;
So shall the truth be better understood,
And thy grieved Spirit brighten strong
　in faith.

IX

TO THE PENNSYLVANIANS

[Composed probably January or February, 1845.
　　—Published 1845.]

DAYS undefiled by luxury or sloth,
Firm self-denial, manners grave and staid,
Rights equal, laws with cheerfulness
　obeyed,
Words that require no sanction from an
　oath,
And simple honesty a common growth—

This high repute, with bounteous Nature's
　aid,　　　　　　　　　　　　　6
Won confidence, now ruthlessly betrayed
At will, your power the measure of your
　troth!—
All who revere the memory of Penn
Grieve for the land on whose wild woods
　his name　　　　　　　　　　　10
Was fondly grafted with a virtuous aim,
Renounced, abandoned by degenerate
　Men
For state-dishonour black as ever came
To upper air from Mammon's loathsome
　den.

X

AT BOLOGNA, IN REMEMBRANCE OF THE
LATE INSURRECTIONS, 1837

I

[Composed probably 1837.—Published: vol. of
　　1842.]

AH why deceive ourselves! by no mere fit
Of sudden passion roused shall men attain
True freedom where for ages they have
　lain
Bound in a dark abominable pit,
With life's best sinews more and more
　unknit.　　　　　　　　　　　5
Here, there, a banded few who loathe the
　chain
May rise to break it: effort worse than
　vain
For thee, O great Italian nation, split
Into those jarring fractions.—Let thy
　scope
Be one fixed mind for all; thy rights
　approve　　　　　　　　　　　10
To thy own conscience gradually re-
　newed;
Learn to make Time the father of wise
　Hope;
Then trust thy cause to the arm of Forti-
　tude,
The light of Knowledge, and the warmth
　of Love.

XI

CONTINUED

II

[Composed probably 1837.—Published: vol. of
　　1842.]

HARD task! exclaim the undisciplined,
　to lean
On Patience coupled with such slow en-
　deavour,
That long-lived servitude must last for
　ever.
Perish the grovelling few, who, prest
　between
Wrongs and the terror of redress, would
　wean　　　　　　　　　　　　　5

Millions from glorious aims. Our chains
  to sever
Let us break forth in tempest now or
  never!—
What, is there then no space for golden
  mean
And gradual progress?—Twilight leads
  to day,
And, even within the burning zones of
  earth,   10
The hastiest sunrise yields a temperate
  ray;
The softest breeze to fairest flowers gives
  birth:
Think not that Prudence dwells in dark
  abodes,
She scans the future with the eye of gods.

XII

CONCLUDED

III

[Composed probably 1837.—Published: vol. of
1842.]

As leaves are to the tree whereon they
  grow
And wither, every human generation
Is to the Being of a mighty nation,
Locked in our world's embrace through
  weal and woe;
Thought that should teach the zealot to
  forego   5
Rash schemes, to abjure all selfish agita-
  tion,
And seek through noiseless pains and
  moderation
The unblemished good they only can
  bestow.
Alas! with most, who weigh futurity
Against time present, passion holds the
  scales: 10
Hence equal ignorance of both prevails,
And nations sink; or, struggling to be
  free,
Are doomed to flounder on, like wounded
  whales
Tossed on the bosom of a stormy sea.

XIII

[Composed January or February, 1845.—
Published 1845.]

YOUNG ENGLAND—what is then become
  of Old,
Of dear Old England? Think they she is
  dead,
Dead to the very name? Presumption fed
On empty air! That name will keep its
  hold
In the true filial bosom's inmost fold   5
For ever.—The Spirit of Alfred, at the
  head
Of all who for her rights watched, toiled
  and bled,
Knows that this prophecy is not too bold.
What—how! shall she submit in will and
  deed
To Beardless Boys—an imitative race,   10
The *servum pecus* of a Gallic breed?
Dear Mother! if thou *must* thy steps
  retrace,
Go where at least meek Innocency dwells;
Let Babes and Sucklings be thy oracles.

XIV

[Composed (?).—Published 1842.]

FEEL for the wrongs to universal ken
Daily exposed, woe that unshrouded lies;
And seek the Sufferer in his darkest den,
Whether conducted to the spot by sighs
And moanings, or he dwells (as if the
  wren   5
Taught him concealment) hidden from all
  eyes
In silence and the awful modesties
Of sorrow;—feel for all, as brother Men!
Rest not in hope want's icy chain to thaw
By casual boons and formal charities;   10
Learn to be just, just through impartial
  law;
Far as ye may, erect and equalize;
And, what ye cannot reach by statute,
  draw
Each from his fountain of self-sacrifice!

SONNETS UPON THE PUNISHMENT OF DEATH

IN SERIES

[Composed 1839–40.—Published December, 1841 (*Quarterly Review*); vol. of 1842.]

I

SUGGESTED BY THE VIEW OF LANCASTER
CASTLE (ON THE ROAD FROM THE SOUTH)

THIS Spot—at once unfolding sight so
    fair
Of sea and land, with yon grey towers
    that still
Rise up as if to lord it over air—
Might soothe in human breasts the sense
    of ill,
Or charm it out of memory; yea, might
    fill   5
The heart with joy and gratitude to God
For all his bounties upon man bestowed:
Why bears it then the name of 'Weeping
    Hill'?
Thousands, as toward yon old Lancastrian
    Towers,
A prison's crown, along this way they
    past   10
For lingering durance or quick death
    with shame,
From this bare eminence thereon have
    cast
Their first look—blinded as tears fell in
    showers
Shed on their chains; and hence that
    doleful name.

II

TENDERLY do we feel by Nature's law
For worst offenders: though the heart
    will heave
With indignation, deeply moved we
    grieve,
In after-thought, for Him who stood in
    awe   4
Neither of God nor man, and only saw,
Lost wretch, a horrible device enthroned
On proud temptations, till the victim
    groaned
Under the steel his hand had dared to
    draw.
But O, restrain compassion, if its course,
As oft befalls, prevent or turn aside   10
Judgments and aims and acts whose
    higher source
Is sympathy with the unforewarned, who
    died
Blameless—with them that shuddered
    o'er his grave,
And all who from the law firm safety
    crave.

III

THE Roman Consul doomed his sons to
    die
Who had betrayed their country. The
    stern word
Afforded (may it through all time afford)
A theme for praise and admiration high.
Upon the surface of humanity   5
He rested not; its depths his mind
    explored;
He felt; but his parental bosom's lord
Was Duty,—Duty calmed his agony.
And some, we know, when they by wilful
    act
A single human life have wrongly taken,
Pass sentence on themselves, confess the
    fact,   11
And, to atone for it, with soul unshaken
Kneel at the feet of Justice, and, for faith
Broken with all mankind, solicit death.

IV

Is *Death*, when evil against good has
    fought
With such fell mastery that a man may
    dare
By deeds the blackest purpose to lay
    bare—
Is Death, for one to that condition
    brought,—
For him, or any one,—the thing that
    ought   5
To be *most* dreaded? Lawgivers, beware,
Lest, capital pains remitting till ye spare
The murderer, ye, by sanction to that
    thought,
Seemingly given, debase the general mind;
Tempt the vague will tried standards to
    disown;   10
Nor only palpable restraints unbind,
But upon Honour's head disturb the
    crown,
Whose absolute rule permits not to with-
    stand
In the weak love of life his least command.

V

NOT to the object specially designed,
Howe'er momentous in itself it be,
Good to promote or curb depravity,
Is the wise Legislator's view confined.
His Spirit, when most severe, is oft most
    kind;   5

SONNETS UPON THE PUNISHMENT OF DEATH

As all Authority in earth depends
On Love and Fear, their several powers
 he blends,
Copying with awe the one Paternal
 mind.
Uncaught by processes in show humane,
He feels how far the act would derogate
From even the humblest functions of the
 State;   11
If she, self-shorn of Majesty, ordain
That never more shall hang upon her
 breath
The last alternative of Life or Death.

VI

YE brood of Conscience—Spectres! that
 frequent
The bad man's restless walk, and haunt
 his bed—
Fiends in your aspect, yet beneficent
In act, as hovering Angels when they
 spread
Their wings to guard the unconscious
 Innocent—   5
Slow be the Statutes of the land to share
A laxity that could not but impair
Your power to punish crime, and so
 prevent.
And ye, Beliefs! coiled serpent-like about
The adage on all tongues, 'Murder will
 out,'   10
How shall your ancient warnings work
 for good
In the full might they hitherto have
 shown,
If for deliberate shedder of man's blood
Survive not Judgment that requires his
 own?

VII

BEFORE the world had past her time of
 youth
While polity and discipline were weak,
The precept eye for eye, and tooth for
 tooth,
Came forth—a light, though but as of
 daybreak,
Strong as could then be borne. A Master
 meek   5
Proscribed the spirit fostered by that rule,
Patience *his* law, long-suffering *his* school,
And love the end, which all through
 peace must seek.
But lamentably do they err who strain
His mandates, given rash impulse to
 control   10
And keep vindictive thirstings from the
 soul,
So far that, if consistent in their scheme,
They must forbid the State to inflict a
 pain,
Making of social order a mere dream.

VIII

FIT retribution, by the moral code
Determined, lies beyond the State's
 embrace,
Yet, as she may, for each peculiar case
She plants well-measured terrors in the
 road
Of wrongful acts. Downward it is and
 broad,   5
And, the main fear once doomed to
 banishment,
Far oftener then, bad ushering worse
 event,
Blood would be spilt that in his dark
 abode
Crime might lie better hid. And, should
 the change
Take from the horror due to a foul deed,
Pursuit and evidence so far must fail,   11
And, guilt escaping, passion then might
 plead
In angry spirits for her old free range,
And the 'wild justice of revenge' prevail.

IX

THOUGH to give timely warning and deter
Is one great aim of penalty, extend
Thy mental vision further and ascend
Far higher, else full surely shalt thou err.
What is a State? The wise behold in her
A creature born of time, that keeps one eye
Fixed on the statutes of Eternity,   7
To which her judgments reverently defer.
Speaking through Law's dispassionate
 voice the State
Endues her conscience with external life
And being, to preclude or quell the strife
Of individual will, to elevate   12
The grovelling mind, the erring to recall,
And fortify the moral sense of all.

X

OUR bodily life, some plead, that life the
 shrine
Of an immortal spirit, is a gift
So sacred, so informed with light divine,
That no tribunal, though most wise to sift
Deed and intent, should turn the Being
 adrift   5
Into that world where penitential tear
May not avail, nor prayer have for God's
 ear
A voice—that world whose veil no hand
 can lift
For earthly sight. 'Eternity and Time,'
They urge, 'have interwoven claims and
 rights   10
Not to be jeopardised through foulest
 crime:
The sentence rule by mercy's heaven-born
 lights.'
Even so; but measuring not by finite sense
Infinite Power, perfect Intelligence.

XI

AH, think how one compelled for life to abide
Locked in a dungeon needs must eat the heart
Out of his own humanity, and part
With every hope that mutual cares provide;
And, should a less unnatural doom confide   5
In life-long exile on a savage coast,
Soon the relapsing penitent may boast
Of yet more heinous guilt, with fiercer pride.
Hence thoughtful Mercy, Mercy sage and pure,
Sanctions the forfeiture that Law demands,   10
Leaving the final issue in *His* hands
Whose goodness knows no change, whose love is sure,
Who sees, foresees; who cannot judge amiss,
And wafts at will the contrite soul to bliss.

XII

SEE the Condemned alone within his cell
And prostrate at some moment when remorse
Stings to the quick, and, with resistless force,
Assaults the pride she strove in vain to quell.
Then mark him, him who could so long rebel,   5
The crime confessed, a kneeling Penitent
Before the Altar, where the Sacrament
Softens his heart, till from his eyes outwell
Tears of salvation. Welcome death! while Heaven
Does in this change exceedingly rejoice;
While yet the solemn heed the State hath given   11
Helps him to meet the last Tribunal's voice
In faith, which fresh offences, were he cast
On old temptations, might for ever blast.

XIII

CONCLUSION

YES, though He well may tremble at the sound
Of his own voice, who from the judgment-seat
Sends the pale Convict to his last retreat
In death; though Listeners shudder all around,
They know the dread requital's source profound;   5
Nor is, they feel, its wisdom obsolete—
(Would that it were!) the sacrifice unmeet
For Christian Faith. But hopeful signs abound;
The social rights of man breathe purer air;
Religion deepens her preventive care;   10
Then, moved by needless fear of past abuse,
Strike not from Law's firm hand that awful rod,
But leave it thence to drop for lack of use:
Oh, speed the blessed hour, Almighty God!

XIV

APOLOGY

THE formal World relaxes her cold chain
For One who speaks in numbers; ampler scope
His utterance finds; and, conscious of the gain,
Imagination works with bolder hope
The cause of grateful reason to sustain;   5
And, serving Truth, the heart more strongly beats
Against all barriers which his labour meets
In lofty place, or humble Life's domain.
Enough;—before us lay a painful road,
And guidance have I sought in duteous love   10
From Wisdom's heavenly Father. Hence hath flowed
Patience, with trust that, whatsoe'er the way
Each takes in this high matter, all may move
Cheered with the prospect of a brighter day.

MISCELLANEOUS POEMS

I

EPISTLE

TO SIR GEORGE HOWLAND BEAUMONT, BART.
From the South-west Coast of Cumberland.—1811.
[Composed 1811.—Published: vol. of 1842.]

FAR from our home by Grasmere's quiet
 Lake,
From the Vale's peace which all her
 fields partake,
Here on the bleakest point of Cumbria's
 shore
We sojourn stunned by Ocean's ceaseless
 roar;
While, day by day, grim neighbour! huge
 Black Comb   5
Frowns deepening visibly his native
 gloom,
Unless, perchance rejecting in despite
What on the Plain *we* have of warmth
 and light,
In his own storms he hides himself from
 sight.
Rough is the time; and thoughts, that
 would be free   10
From heaviness, oft fly, dear Friend, to
 thee;
Turn from a spot where neither sheltered
 road
Nor hedge-row screen invites my steps
 abroad;
Where one poor Plane-tree, having as it
 might
Attained a stature twice a tall man's
 height,   15
Hopeless of further growth, and brown
 and sere
Through half the summer, stands with
 top cut sheer,
Like an unshifting weathercock which
 proves
How cold the quarter that the wind best
 loves,
Or like a Centinel that, evermore   20
Darkening the window, ill defends the door
Of this unfinished house—a Fortress bare,
Where strength has been the Builder's
 only care;
Whose rugged walls may still for years
 demand
The final polish of the Plasterer's hand.
—This Dwelling's Inmate more than three
 weeks' space   26
And oft a Prisoner in the cheerless place,
I—of whose touch the fiddle would com-
 plain,
Whose breath would labour at the flute in
 vain,
In music all unversed, nor blessed with
 skill   30
A bridge to copy, or to paint a mill,

Tired of my books, a scanty company!
And tired of listening to the boisterous
 sea—
Pace between door and window mutter-
 ing rhyme,
An old resource to cheat a froward time!
Though these dull hours (mine is it, or
 their shame?)   36
Would tempt me to renounce that humble
 aim.
—But if there be a Muse who, free to
 take
Her seat upon Olympus, doth forsake
Those heights (like Phœbus when his
 golden locks   40
He veiled, attendant on Thessalian flocks)
And, in disguise, a Milkmaid with her pail
Trips down the pathways of some winding
 dale;
Or, like a Mermaid, warbles on the shores
To fishers mending nets beside their
 doors;   45
Or, Pilgrim-like, on forest moss reclined,
Gives plaintive ditties to the heedless
 wind,
Or listens to its play among the boughs
Above her head and so forgets her vows—
If such a Visitant of Earth there be   50
And she would deign this day to smile
 on me
And aid my verse, content with local
 bounds
Of natural beauty and life's daily rounds,
Thoughts, chances, sights, or doings,
 which we tell
Without reserve to those whom we love
 well—   55
Then haply, Beaumont! words in current
 clear
Will flow, and on a welcome page appear
Duly before thy sight, unless they perish
 here.

What shall I treat of? News from
 Mona's Isle?
Such have we, but unvaried in its style;
No tales of Runagates fresh landed,
 whence   61
And wherefore fugitive or on what pre-
 tence;
Of feasts, or scandal, eddying like the
 wind
Most restlessly alive when most confined.
Ask not of me, whose tongue can best
 appease   65
The mighty tumults of the HOUSE OF
 KEYS;
The last year's cup whose Ram or Heifer
 gained,
What slopes are planted, or what mosses
 drained:

An eye of fancy only can I cast
On that proud pageant now at hand or
past,   70
When full five hundred boats in trim
array,
With nets and sails outspread and
streamers gay,
And chanted hymns and stiller voice of
prayer,
For the old Manx-harvest to the Deep
repair,
Soon as the herring-shoals at distance
shine   75
Like beds of moonlight shifting on the
brine.

Mona from our Abode is daily seen,
But with a wilderness of waves between;
And by conjecture only can we speak
Of aught transacted there in bay or creek;
No tidings reach us thence from town or
field,   81
Only faint news her mountain-sunbeams
yield,
And some we gather from the misty air,
And some the hovering clouds, our tele-
graph, declare.
But these poetic mysteries I withhold; 85
For Fancy hath her fits both hot and
cold,
And should the colder fit with You be on
When You might read, my credit would
be gone.

Let more substantial themes the pen
engage,
And nearer interests culled from the
opening stage   90
Of our migration.—Ere the welcome dawn
Had from the east her silver star with-
drawn,
The Wain stood ready, at our Cottage-
door,
Thoughtfully freighted with a various
store;
And long or ere the uprising of the Sun
O'er dew-damped dust our journey was
begun,   96
A needful journey, under favouring skies,
Through peopled Vales; yet something
in the guise
Of those old Patriarchs when from well
to well
They roamed through Wastes where now
the tented Arabs dwell.   100

Say first, to whom did we the charge
confide,
Who promptly undertook the Wain to
guide
Up many a sharply-twining road and
down,
And over many a wide hill's craggy
crown,

Through the quick turns of many a hollow
nook,   105
And the rough bed of many an unbridged
brook?
A blooming Lass—who in her better hand
Bore a light switch, her sceptre of com-
mand
When, yet a slender Girl, she often led,
Skilful and bold, the horse and burthened
sled[1]   110
From the peat-yielding Moss on Gowdar's
head.
What could go wrong with such a
Charioteer
For goods and chattels, or those Infants
dear,
A Pair who smilingly sat side by side,
Our hope confirming that the salt-sea
tide,   115
Whose free embraces we were bound to
seek,
Would their lost strength restore and
freshen the pale cheek?
Such hope did either Parent entertain
Pacing behind along the silent lane.

Blithe hopes and happy musings soon
took flight,   120
For lo! an uncouth melancholy sight—
On a green bank a creature stood forlorn
Just half protruded to the light of morn,
Its hinder part concealed by hedge-row
thorn.
The Figure called to mind a beast of prey
Stript of its frightful powers by slow
decay,   126
And, though no longer upon rapine bent,
Dim memory keeping of its old intent.
We started, looked again with anxious
eyes,
And in that griesly object recognise   130
The Curate's Dog—his long-tried friend,
for they,
As well we knew, together had grown
grey.
The Master died, his drooping servant's
grief
Found at the Widow's feet some sad
relief;
Yet still he lived in pining discontent,
Sadness which no indulgence could pre-
vent;   136
Hence whole day wanderings, broken
nightly sleeps
And lonesome watch that out of doors he
keeps;
Not oftentimes, I trust, as we, poor brute!
Espied him on his legs sustained, blank,
mute,   140
And of all visible motion destitute,
So that the very heaving of his breath
Seemed stopt, though by some other
power than death.

[1] A local word for sledge.

409

Long as we gazed upon the form and face,
A mild domestic pity kept its place,   145
Unscared by thronging fancies of strange
hue
That haunted us in spite of what we
knew.
Even now I sometimes think of him as lost
In second-sight appearances, or crost
By spectral shapes of guilt, or to the
ground,   150
On which he stood, by spells unnatural
bound,
Like a gaunt shaggy Porter forced to wait
In days of old romance at Archimago's
gate.

Advancing Summer, Nature's law ful-
filled,   154
The choristers in every grove had stilled;
But we, we lacked not music of our own,
For lightsome Fanny had thus early
thrown,
Mid the gay prattle of those infant
tongues,
Some notes prelusive, from the round of
songs
With which, more zealous than the live-
liest bird   160
That in wild Arden's brakes was ever
heard,
Her work and her work's partners she
can cheer,
The whole day long, and all days of the
year.

Thus gladdened from our own dear
Vale we pass
And soon approach Diana's Looking-
glass!   165
To Loughrigg-tarn, round clear and bright
as heaven,
Such name Italian fancy would have
given,
Ere on its banks the few grey cabins rose
That yet disturb not its concealed repose
More than the feeblest wind that idly
blows.   170

Ah, Beaumont! when an opening in
the road
Stopped me at once by charm of what it
showed,
The encircling region vividly exprest
Within the mirror's depth, a world at
rest—
Sky streaked with purple, grove and
craggy *bield*,[1]   175
And the smooth green of many a pendent
field,
And, quieted and soothed, a torrent
small,
A little daring would-be waterfall,

[1] A word common in the country, signifying shelter, as in Scotland.

One chimney smoking and its azure
wreath,
Associate all in the calm Pool beneath,
With here and there a faint imperfect
gleam   181
Of water-lilies veiled in misty steam—
What wonder at this hour of stillness
deep,
A shadowy link 'tween wakefulness and
sleep,
When Nature's self, amid such blending,
seems   185
To render visible her own soft dreams,
If, mixed with what appeared of rock,
lawn, wood,
Fondly embosomed in the tranquil flood,
A glimpse I caught of that Abode, by
Thee
Designed to rise in humble privacy,   190
A lowly Dwelling, here to be outspread,
Like a small Hamlet, with its bashful
head
Half hid in native trees. Alas 'tis not,
Nor ever was; I sighed, and left the spot
Unconscious of its own untoward lot,
And thought in silence, with regret too
keen,   196
Of unexperienced joys that might have
been;
Of neighbourhood and intermingling arts,
And golden summer days uniting cheer-
ful hearts.
But time, irrevocable time, is flown,   200
And let us utter thanks for blessings
sown
And reaped—what hath been, and what
is, our own.

Not far we travelled ere a shout of glee,
Startling us all, dispersed my reverie;
Such shout as many a sportive echo meet-
ing   205
Oft-times from Alpine *chalets* sends a
greeting.
Whence the blithe hail? behold a Peasant
stand
On high, a kerchief waving in her hand!
Not unexpectant that by early day
Our little Band would thrid this moun-
tain-way,   210
Before her cottage on the bright hill-side
She hath advanced with hope to be de-
scried.
Right gladly answering signals we dis-
played,
Moving along a tract of morning shade,
And vocal wishes sent of like good will
To our kind Friend high on the sunny
hill—   216
Luminous region, fair as if the prime
Were tempting all astir to look aloft or
climb;
Only the centre of the shining cot
With door left open makes a gloomy spot,

Emblem of those dark corners sometimes found 221
Within the happiest breast on earthly ground.

Rich prospect left behind of stream and vale,
And mountain-tops, a barren ridge we scale;
Descend and reach, in Yewdale's depths, a plain 225
With haycocks studded, striped with yellowing grain—
An area level as a Lake and spread
Under a rock too steep for man to tread,
Where sheltered from the north and bleak north-west
Aloft the Raven hangs a visible nest, 230
Fearless of all assaults that would her brood molest.
Hot sunbeams fill the steaming vale; but hark,
At our approach, a jealous watch-dog's bark,
Noise that brings forth no liveried Page of state,
But the whole household, that our coming wait. 235
With Young and Old warm greetings we exchange,
And jocund smiles, and toward the lowly Grange
Press forward by the teasing dogs unscared.
Entering, we find the morning meal prepared:
So down we sit, though not till each had cast 240
Pleased looks around the delicate repast—
Rich cream, and snow-white eggs fresh from the nest,
With amber honey from the mountain's breast;
Strawberries from lane or woodland, offering wild 244
Of children's industry, in hillocks piled;
Cakes for the nonce, and butter fit to lie
Upon a lordly dish; frank hospitality
Where simple art with bounteous nature vied,
And cottage comfort shunned not seemly pride.

Kind Hostess! Handmaid also of the feast, 250
If thou be lovelier than the kindling East,
Words by thy presence unrestrained may speak
Of a perpetual dawn from brow and cheek
Instinct with light whose sweetest promise lies, 254
Never retiring, in thy large dark eyes,
Dark but to every gentle feeling true,
As if their lustre flowed from ether's purest blue.

Let me not ask what tears may have been wept
By those bright eyes, what weary vigils kept,
Beside that hearth what sighs may have been heaved 260
For wounds inflicted, nor what toil relieved
By fortitude and patience, and the grace
Of heaven in pity visiting the place.
Not unadvisedly those secret springs
I leave unsearched: enough that memory clings, 265
Here as elsewhere, to notices that make
Their own significance for hearts awake,
To rural incidents, whose genial powers
Filled with delight three summer morning hours.

More could my pen report of grave or gay 270
That through our gipsy travel cheered the way;
But, bursting forth above the waves, the Sun
Laughs at my pains, and seems to say,
'Be done.'
Yet, Beaumont, thou wilt not, I trust, reprove
This humble offering made by Truth to Love, 275
Nor chide the Muse that stooped to break a spell
Which might have else been on me yet:—
FAREWELL.

UPON PERUSING THE FOREGOING EPISTLE THIRTY YEARS AFTER ITS COMPOSITION

[Composed 1841.—Published: vol. of 1842.]

SOON did the Almighty Giver of all rest
Take those dear young Ones to a fearless nest;
And in Death's arms has long reposed the Friend
For whom this simple Register was penned.
Thanks to the moth that spared it for our eyes; 5
And Strangers even the slighted Scroll may prize,
Moved by the touch of kindred sympathies.
For—save the calm repentance sheds o'er strife
Raised by remembrances of misused life,
The light from past endeavours purely willed 10
And by Heaven's favour happily fulfilled;
Save hope that we, yet bound to Earth, may share
The joys of the Departed—what so fair

As blameless pleasure, not without some
tears,
Reviewed through Love's transparent veil
of years?   15

Note.—LOUGHRIGG TARN, alluded to in the foregoing Epistle, resembles, though much smaller in
compass, the Lake Nemi, or *Speculum Dianæ* as
it is often called, not only in its clear waters and
circular form, and the beauty immediately surrounding it, but also as being overlooked by the
eminence of Langdale Pikes as Lake Nemi is by
that of Monte Calvo. Since this Epistle was written
Loughrigg Tarn has lost much of its beauty by the
felling of many natural clumps of wood, relics of
the old forest, particularly upon the farm called
'The Oaks,' from the abundance of that tree which
grew there.

It is to be regretted, upon public grounds, that
Sir George Beaumont did not carry into effect his
intention of constructing here a Summer Retreat
in the style I have described; as his taste would
have set an example how buildings, with all the
accommodations modern society requires, might
be introduced even into the most secluded parts
of this country without injuring their native
character. The design was not abandoned from
failure of inclination on his part, but in consequence of local untowardness which need not be
particularised.

II
GOLD AND SILVER FISHES IN A VASE

[Composed 1829.—Published 1835.]

THE soaring lark is blest as proud
    When at heaven's gate she sings;
The roving bee proclaims aloud
    Her flight by vocal wings;
While Ye, in lasting durance pent,   5
    Your silent lives employ
For something more than dull content,
    Though haply less than joy.

Yet might your glassy prison seem
    A place where joy is known,   10
Where golden flash and silver gleam
    Have meanings of their own;
While, high and low, and all about,
    Your motions, glittering Elves!
Ye weave—no danger from without,   15
    And peace among yourselves.

Type of a sunny human breast
    Is your transparent cell;
Where Fear is but a transient guest,
    No sullen Humours dwell;   20
Where, sensitive of every ray
    That smites this tiny sea,
Your scaly panoplies repay
    The loan with usury.

How beautiful!—Yet none knows why
    This ever-graceful change,   26
Renewed—renewed incessantly—
    Within your quiet range.

Is it that ye with conscious skill
    For mutual pleasure glide;   30
And sometimes, not without your will,
    Are dwarfed, or magnified?

Fays, Genii of gigantic size!
    And now, in twilight dim,
Clustering like constellated eyes   35
    In wings of Cherubim,
When the fierce orbs abate their glare;—
    Whate'er your forms express,
Whate'er ye seem, whate'er ye are—
    All leads to gentleness.   40

Cold though your nature be, 'tis pure;
    Your birthright is a fence
From all that haughtier kinds endure
    Through tyranny of sense.
Ah! not alone by colours bright   45
    Are Ye to heaven allied,
When, like essential Forms of light,
    Ye mingle, or divide.

For day-dreams soft as e'er beguiled
    Day-thoughts while limbs repose;   50
For moonlight fascinations mild,
    Your gift, ere shutters close—
Accept, mute Captives! thanks and praise;
    And may this tribute prove
That gentle admirations raise   55
    Delight resembling love.

III
LIBERTY

SEQUEL TO THE PRECEDING

Addressed to a friend; the gold and silver fishes
having been removed to a pool in the pleasure-
ground of Rydal Mount.

'The liberty of a people consists in being governed by laws which they have made for themselves,
under whatever form it be of government. The
liberty of a private man, in being master of his
own time and actions, as far as may consist with
the laws of God and of his country. Of this latter
we are here to discourse.'—COWLEY.

[Composed 1829.—Published 1835.]

THOSE breathing Tokens of your kind
    regard,
(Suspect not, Anna, that their fate is
    hard;
Not soon does aught to which mild fancies
    cling
In lonely spots, become a slighted thing;)
Those silent Inmates now no longer share,
Nor do they need, our hospitable care,   6
Removed in kindness from their glassy
    Cell
To the fresh waters of a living Well—
An elfin pool so sheltered that its rest
No winds disturb; the mirror of whose
    breast   10
Is smooth as clear, save where with
    dimples small
A fly may settle, or a blossom fall.

—*There* swims, of blazing sun and beating
  shower
Fearless (but how obscured!) the golden
  Power,   14
That from his bauble prison used to cast
Gleams by the richest jewel unsurpast;
And near him, darkling like a sullen
  Gnome,
The silver Tenant of the crystal dome;
Dissevered both from all the mysteries
Of hue and altering shape that charmed
  all eyes.   20
Alas! they pined, they languished while
  they shone;
And, if not so, what matters beauty gone
And admiration lost, by change of place
That brings to the inward creature no
  disgrace?
But if the change restore his birthright,
  then,   25
Whate'er the difference, boundless is the
  gain.
Who can divine what impulses from God
Reach the caged lark, within a town-
  abode,
From his poor inch or two of daisied sod?
O yield him back his privilege!—No sea
Swells like the bosom of a man set free;
A wilderness is rich with liberty. 32
Roll on, ye spouting whales, who die or
  keep
Your independence in the fathomless
  Deep!
Spread, tiny nautilus, the living sail; 35
Dive, at thy choice, or brave the freshening
  gale!
If unreproved the ambitious eagle mount
Sunward to seek the daylight in its fount,
Bays, gulfs, and ocean's Indian width,
  shall be,   39
Till the world perishes, a field for thee!

While musing here I sit in shadow cool,
And watch these mute Companions, in
  the pool,
(Among reflected boughs of leafy trees)
By glimpses caught—disporting at their
  ease,
Enlivened, braced, by hardy luxuries, 45
I ask what warrant fixed them (like a
  spell
Of witchcraft fixed them) in the crystal
  cell;
To wheel with languid motion round and
  round,
Beautiful, yet in mournful durance bound.
Their peace, perhaps, our lightest footfall
  marred;   50
On their quick sense our sweetest music
  jarred;
And whither could they dart, if seized
  with fear?
No sheltering stone, no tangled root was
  near.

When fire or taper ceased to cheer the
  room,
They wore away the night in starless
  gloom;   55
And when the sun first dawned upon the
  streams,
How faint their portion of his vital beams!
Thus, and unable to complain, they fared,
While not one joy of ours by them was
  shared.

Is there a cherished bird (I venture
  now   60
To snatch a sprig from Chaucer's reverend
  brow)—
Is there a brilliant fondling of the cage,
Though sure of plaudits on his costly
  stage,
Though fed with dainties from the snow-
  white hand
Of a kind mistress, fairest of the land, 65
But gladly would escape; and, if need
  were,
Scatter the colours from the plumes that
  bear
The emancipated captive through blithe
  air
Into strange woods, where he at large
  may live
On best or worst which they and Nature
  give?   70
The beetle loves his unpretending track,
The snail the house he carries on his
  back;
The far-fetched worm with pleasure would
  disown
The bed we give him, though of softest
  down;
A noble instinct; in all kinds the same,
All ranks! What Sovereign, worthy of
  the name,   76
If doomed to breathe against his lawful
  will
An element that flatters him—to kill,
But would rejoice to barter outward
  show
For the least boon that freedom can
  bestow?   80

But most the Bard is true to inborn
  right,
Lark of the dawn, and Philomel of night,
Exults in freedom, can with rapture vouch
For the dear blessings of a lowly couch,
A natural meal—days, months, from
  Nature's hand;   85
Time, place, and business, all at his com-
  mand!—
Who bends to happier duties, who more
  wise
Than the industrious Poet, taught to
  prize,
Above all grandeur, a pure life uncrossed
By cares in which simplicity is lost? 90

That life—the flowery path that winds by
    stealth—
Which Horace needed for his spirit's
    health;
Sighed for, in heart and genius, overcome
By noise and strife, and questions weari-
    some,
And the vain splendours of Imperial
    Rome?— 95
Let easy mirth his social hours inspire,
And fiction animate his sportive lyre,
Attuned to verse that, crowning light
    Distress
With garlands, cheats her into happiness;
Give *me* the humblest note of those sad
    strains 100
Drawn forth by pressure of his gilded
    chains,
As a chance-sunbeam for his memory
    fell
Upon the Sabine farm he loved so well;
Or when the prattle of Bandusia's spring
Haunted his ear—he only listening— 105
He proud to please, above all rivals, fit
To win the palm of gaiety and wit;
He, doubt not, with involuntary dread,
Shrinking from each new favour to be
    shed,
By the world's Ruler, on his honoured
    head! 110

In a deep vision's intellectual scene,
Such earnest longings and regrets as keen
Depressed the melancholy Cowley, laid
Under a fancied yew-tree's luckless
    shade;
A doleful bower for penitential song, 115
Where Man and Muse complained of
    mutual wrong;
While Cam's ideal current glided by,
And antique towers nodded their fore-
    heads high,
Citadels dear to studious privacy.
But Fortune, who had long been used to
    sport 120
With this tried Servant of a thankless
    Court,
Relenting met his wishes; and to you
The remnant of his days at least was true;
You, whom, though long deserted, he
    loved best;
You, Muses, books, fields, liberty, and
    rest! 125

Far happier they who, fixing hope and
    aim
On the humanities of peaceful fame,
Enter betimes with more than martial fire
The generous course, aspire, and still
    aspire;
Upheld by warnings heeded not too late
Stifle the contradictions of their fate, 131
And to one purpose cleave, their Being's
    godlike mate!

Thus, gifted Friend, but with the placid
    brow
That woman ne'er should forfeit, keep *thy*
    vow;
With modest scorn reject whate'er would
    blind 135
The ethereal eyesight, cramp the wingèd
    mind!
Then, with a blessing granted from above
To every act, word, thought, and look of
    love,
Life's book for Thee may lie unclosed, till
    age
Shall with a thankful tear bedrop its latest
    page.[1] 140

IV
POOR ROBIN [2]

[Composed March, 1840.—Published: vol. of
1842.]

Now when the primrose makes a splendid
    show,
And lilies face the March-winds in full
    blow,
And humbler growths as moved with one
    desire
Put on, to welcome spring, their best attire,
Poor Robin is yet flowerless; but how
    gay 5
With his red stalks upon this sunny day!
And, as his tufts of leaves he spreads,
    content
With a hard bed and scanty nourishment,
Mixed with the green, some shine not
    lacking power
To rival summer's brightest scarlet flower;
And flowers they well might seem to
    passers-by 11
If looked at only with a careless eye;
Flowers—or a richer produce (did it suit
The season) sprinklings of ripe strawberry
    fruit.

But while a thousand pleasures come
    unsought, 15
Why fix upon his wealth or want a
    thought?

[1] There is now, alas! no possibility of the anticipation, with which the above Epistle concludes, being
realised: nor were the verses ever seen by the Individual for whom they were intended. She accompanied
her husband, the Rev. Wm. Fletcher, to India, and
died of cholera, at the age of thirty-two or thirty-
three years, on her way from Shalapore to Bombay,
deeply lamented by all who knew her.
    Her enthusiasm was ardent, her piety steadfast;
and her great talents would have enabled her to be
eminently useful in the difficult path of life to which
she had been called. The opinion she entertained of
her own performances, given to the world under her
maiden name, Jewsbury, was modest and humble,
and, indeed, far below their merits; as is often the
case with those who are making trial of their powers,
with a hope to discover what they are best fitted for.
In one quality, viz. quickness in the motions of her
mind, she had, within the range of the Author's
acquaintance, no equal.
[2] The small wild Geranium known by that term.

Is the string touched in prelude to a lay
Of pretty fancies that would round him
    play
When all the world acknowledged elfin
    sway?   19
Or does it suit our humour to commend
Poor Robin as a sure and crafty friend,
Whose practice teaches, spite of names to
    show
Bright colours whether they deceive or
    no?—
Nay, we would simply praise the free
    good-will
With which, though slighted, he, on naked
    hill   25
Or in warm valley, seeks his part to fill;
Cheerful alike if bare of flowers as now,
Or when his tiny gems shall deck his brow:
Yet more, we wish that men by men
    despised,
And such as lift their foreheads over-
    prized,   30
Should sometimes think, where'er they
    chance to spy
This child of Nature's own humility,
What recompense is kept in store or left
For all that seem neglected or bereft;
With what nice care equivalents are given,
How just, how bountiful, the hand of
    Heaven.   36

V

THE GLEANER

SUGGESTED BY A PICTURE

[Composed 1828.—Published, as 'The Country
Girl,' 1829 (*The Keepsake*); ed. 1832.]

THAT happy gleam of vernal eyes,
Those locks from summer's golden skies,
    That o'er thy brow are shed;
That cheek—a kindling of the morn,
That lip—a rose-bud from the thorn,   5
    I saw; and Fancy sped
To scenes Arcadian, whispering, through
    soft air,
Of bliss that grows without a care,
And happiness that never flies—
(How can it where love never dies?)   10
Whispering of promise, where no blight
Can reach the innocent delight;
Where pity, to the mind conveyed
In pleasure, is the darkest shade
That Time, unwrinkled grandsire, flings
From his smoothly gliding wings.   16

What mortal form, what earthly face
Inspired the pencil, lines to trace,
And mingle colours, that should breed
Such rapture, nor want power to feed;   20
For had thy charge been idle flowers,
Fair Damsel! o'er my captive mind,
To truth and sober reason blind,

'Mid that soft air, those long-lost bowers,
The sweet illusion might have hung, for
    hours.   25

Thanks to this tell-tale sheaf of corn,
That touchingly bespeaks thee born
Life's daily tasks with them to share
Who, whether from their lowly bed
They rise, or rest the weary head,   30
Ponder the blessing they entreat
From Heaven, and *feel* what they repeat,
While they give utterance to the prayer
That asks for daily bread.

VI

TO A REDBREAST

(IN SICKNESS)

[Composed (?). —Published: vol. of 1842.]

STAY, little cheerful Robin! stay,
    And at my casement sing,
Though it should prove a farewell lay
    And this our parting spring.

Though I, alas! may ne'er enjoy   5
    The promise in thy song;
A charm, *that* thought can not destroy,
    Doth to thy strain belong.

Methinks that in my dying hour
    Thy song would still be dear,   10
And with a more than earthly power
    My passing Spirit cheer.

Then, little Bird, this boon confer,
    Come, and my requiem sing,
Nor fail to be the harbinger   15
    Of everlasting Spring.

        S. H.

VII

[Composed 1846.—Published 1850.]

I KNOW an aged Man constrained to dwell
In a large house of public charity,
Where he abides, as in a Prisoner's cell,
With numbers near, alas! no company.

When he could creep about, at will,
    though poor   5
And forced to live on alms, this old Man
    fed
A Redbreast, one that to his cottage door
Came not, but in a lane partook his bread.

There, at the root of one particular tree,
An easy seat this worn-out Labourer
    found   10
While Robin pecked the crumbs upon his
    knee
Laid one by one, or scattered on the
    ground.

415

Dear intercourse was theirs, day after
day;
What signs of mutual gladness when they
met!
Think of their common peace, their
simple play, 15
The parting moment and its fond regret.

Months passed in love that failed not to
fulfil,
In spite of season's change, its own
demand,
By fluttering pinions here and busy bill;
There by caresses from a tremulous hand.

Thus in the chosen spot a tie so strong 21
Was formed between the solitary pair,
That when his fate had housed him 'mid
a throng
The Captive shunned all converse prof-
fered there.

Wife, children, kindred, they were dead
and gone; 25
But, if no evil hap his wishes crossed,
One living Stay was left, and on that
one
Some recompense for all that he had lost.

O that the good old Man had power to
prove,
By message sent through air or visible
token, 30
That still he loves the Bird, and still
must love;
That friendship lasts though fellowship
is broken!

VIII
SONNET

TO AN OCTOGENARIAN
[Composed 1846.—Published 1850.]

AFFECTIONS lose their object; Time brings
forth
No successors; and, lodged in memory,
If love exist no longer, it must die,—
Wanting accustomed food, must pass
from earth,
Or never hope to reach a second birth. 5
This sad belief, the happiest that is left
To thousands, share not Thou; howe'er
bereft,
Scorned, or neglected, fear not such a
dearth.
Though poor and destitute of friends thou
art,
Perhaps the sole survivor of thy race, 10
One to whom Heaven assigns that mourn-
ful part
The utmost solitude of age to face,
Still shall be left some corner of the heart
Where Love for living Thing can find a
place.

IX
FLOATING ISLAND

These lines are by the Author of the Address to
the Wind, &c., published heretofore along with
my poems. Those to a Redbreast are by a deceased female Relative.

[Composed ?—Published: vol. of 1842.]

HARMONIOUS Powers with Nature work
On sky, earth, river, lake and sea;
Sunshine and cloud, whirlwind and
breeze,
All in one duteous task agree.

Once did I see a slip of earth 5
(By throbbing waves long undermined)
Loosed from its hold; how, no one knew,
But all might see it float, obedient to the
wind;

Might see it, from the mossy shore
Dissevered, float upon the Lake, 10
Float with its crest of trees adorned
On which the warbling birds their
pastime take.

Food, shelter, safety, there they find;
There berries ripen, flowerets bloom;
There insects live their lives, and die; 15
A peopled world it is; in size a tiny
room.

And thus through many seasons' space
This little Island may survive;
But Nature, though we mark her not,
Will take away, may cease to give. 20

Perchance when you are wandering forth
Upon some vacant sunny day,
Without an object, hope, or fear,
Thither your eyes may turn—the Isle is
passed away;

Buried beneath the glittering Lake, 25
Its place no longer to be found;
Yet the lost fragments shall remain
To fertilise some other ground.
                                        D. W.

X
[Composed (?).—Published 1850.]

How beautiful the Queen of Night, on
high
Her way pursuing among scattered clouds,
Where, ever and anon, her head she
shrouds
Hidden from view in dense obscurity.
But look, and to the watchful eye 5
A brightening edge will indicate that
soon
We shall behold the struggling Moon
Break forth,—again to walk the clear blue
sky.

XI

'Late, late yestreen I saw the new moone
Wi' the auld moone in hir arme.'
Ballad of Sir Patrick Spence,
Percy's Reliques.

[Composed 1826.—Published 1827.]

ONCE I could hail (howe'er serene the sky)
The Moon re-entering her monthly
round,
No faculty yet given me to espy
The dusky Shape within her arms im-
bound,
That thin memento of effulgence lost   5
Which some have named her Prede-
cessor's ghost.

Young, like the Crescent that above me
shone,
Nought I perceived within it dull or dim;
All that appeared was suitable to One
Whose fancy had a thousand fields to
skim;   10
To expectations spreading with wild
growth,
And hope that kept with me her plighted
troth.

I saw (ambition quickening at the view)
A silver boat launched on a boundless
flood;
A pearly crest, like Dian's when it threw
Its brightest splendour round a leafy
wood;   16
But not a hint from under-ground, no sign
Fit for the glimmering brow of Proserpine.

Or was it Dian's self that seemed to
move
Before me?—nothing blemished the fair
sight;   20
On her I looked whom jocund Fairies
love,
Cynthia, who puts the *little* stars to flight,
And by that thinning magnifies the great,
For exaltation of her sovereign state.

And when I learned to mark the spectral
Shape   25
As each new Moon obeyed the call of
Time,
If gloom fell on me, swift was my escape;
Such happy privilege hath life's gay
Prime,
To see or not to see, as best may please
A buoyant Spirit, and a heart at ease. 30

Now, dazzling Stranger! when thou
meet'st my glance,
Thy dark Associate ever I discern;
Emblem of thoughts too eager to advance
While I salute my joys, thoughts sad or
stern;
Shades of past bliss, or phantoms that, to
gain   35
Their fill of promised lustre, wait in vain.

So changes mortal Life with fleeting
years;
A mournful change, should Reason fail
to bring
The timely insight that can temper fears,
And from vicissitude remove its sting; 40
While Faith aspires to seats in that
domain
Where joys are perfect—neither wax nor
wane.

XII

TO THE LADY FLEMING

ON SEEING THE FOUNDATION PREPARING
FOR THE ERECTION OF RYDAL CHAPEL,
WESTMORELAND

[Composed 1823.—Published 1827.]

I

BLEST is this Isle—our native Land;
Where battlement and moated gate
Are objects only for the hand
Of hoary Time to decorate;
Where shady hamlet, town that breathes
Its busy smoke in social wreaths,   6
No rampart's stern defence require,
Nought but the heaven-directed spire,
And steeple tower (with pealing bells
Far-heard)—our only citadels.   10

II

O Lady! from a noble line
Of chieftains sprung, who stoutly bore
The spear, yet gave to works divine
A bounteous help in days of yore,
(As records mouldering in the Dell   15
Of Nightshade[1] haply yet may tell;)
Thee kindred aspirations moved
To build, within a vale beloved,
For Him upon whose high behests
All peace depends, all safety rests.   20

III

How fondly will the woods embrace
This daughter of thy pious care,
Lifting her front with modest grace
To make a fair recess more fair;
And to exalt the passing hour;   25
Or soothe it with a healing power
Drawn from the Sacrifice fulfilled,
Before this rugged soil was tilled,
Or human habitation rose
To interrupt the deep repose!   30

IV

Well may the villagers rejoice!
Nor heat, nor cold, nor weary ways,
Will be a hindrance to the voice
That would unite in prayer and praise;
More duly shall wild wandering Youth
Receive the curb of sacred truth,   36

[1] Bekangs Ghyll—or the dell of Nightshade—in
which stands St. Mary's Abbey in Low Furness.

Shall tottering Age, bent earthward, hear
The Promise, with uplifted ear;
And all shall welcome the new ray
Imparted to their sabbath-day.   40

V

Nor deem the Poet's hope misplaced,
His fancy cheated—that can see
A shade upon the future cast,
Of time's pathetic sanctity;
Can hear the monitory clock   45
Sound o'er the lake with gentle shock
At evening, when the ground beneath
Is ruffled o'er with cells of death;
Where happy generations lie,
Here tutored for eternity.   50

VI

Lives there a man whose sole delights
Are trivial pomp and city noise,
Hardening a heart that loathes or slights
What every natural heart enjoys?
Who never caught a noon-tide dream   55
From murmur of a running stream;
Could strip, for aught the prospect yields
To him, their verdure from the fields;
And take the radiance from the clouds
In which the sun his setting shrouds.   60

VII

A soul so pitiably forlorn,
If such do on this earth abide,
May season apathy with scorn,
May turn indifference to pride;
And still be not unblest—compared   65
With him who grovels, self-debarred
From all that lies within the scope
Of holy faith and Christian hope;
Or, shipwrecked, kindles on the coast
False fires, that others may be lost.   70

VIII

Alas! that such perverted zeal
Should spread on Britain's favoured
    ground!
That public order, private weal,
Should e'er have felt or feared a wound
From champions of the desperate law 75
Which from their own blind hearts they
    draw;
Who tempt their reason to deny
God, whom their passions dare defy,
And boast that they alone are free
Who reach this dire extremity!   80

IX

But turn we from these 'bold bad' men;
The way, mild Lady! that hath led
Down to their 'dark opprobrious den,'
Is all too rough for Thee to tread.
Softly as morning vapours glide   85
Down Rydal-cove from Fairfield's side,

Should move the tenor of *his* song
Who means to charity no wrong;
Whose offering gladly would accord
With this day's work, in thought and
    word.   90

X

Heaven prosper it! may peace, and love,
And hope, and consolation, fall,
Through its meek influence, from above,
And penetrate the hearts of all;
All who, around the hallowed Fane, 95
Shall sojourn in this fair domain;
Grateful to Thee, while service pure,
And ancient ordinance, shall endure,
For opportunity bestowed   99
To kneel together, and adore their God!

XIII
ON THE SAME OCCASION

Oh! gather whencesoe'er ye safely may
The help which slackening Piety requires;
Nor deem that he perforce must go astray
Who treads upon the footmarks of his sires.

Our churches, invariably perhaps, stand east and
west, but *why* is by few persons *exactly* known;
nor, that the degree of deviation from *due* east
often noticeable in the ancient ones was determined, in each particular case, by the point in
the horizon, at which the sun rose upon the day
of the saint to whom the church was dedicated.
These observances of our ancestors, and the
causes of them, are the subject of the following
stanzas.

[Composed 1823.—Published 1827.]

WHEN in the antique age of bow and spear
And feudal rapine clothed with iron mail,
Came ministers of peace, intent to rear
The Mother Church in yon sequestered
    vale;

Then, to her Patron Saint a previous rite
Resounded with deep swell and solemn
    close,   6
Through unremitting vigils of the night,
Till from his couch the wished-for Sun
    uprose.

He rose, and straight—as by divine com-
    mand,
They, who had waited for that sign to
    trace   10
Their work's foundation, gave with care-
    ful hand
To the high altar its determined place;

Mindful of Him Who in the Orient born
There lived, and on the cross His life
    resigned,
And Who, from out the regions of the
    morn,   15
Issuing in pomp, shall come to judge
    mankind.

418

So taught *their* creed;—nor failed the
  eastern sky,
'Mid these more awful feelings, to infuse
The sweet and natural hopes that shall
  not die,
Long as the sun his gladsome course
  renews.   20

For us hath such prelusive vigil ceased;
Yet still we plant, like men of elder days
Our Christian altar faithful to the east,
Whence the tall window drinks the morn-
  ing rays;

That obvious emblem giving to the eye
Of meek devotion, which erewhile it gave,
That symbol of the day-spring from on
  high,   27
Triumphant o'er the darkness of the grave.

XIV
THE HORN OF EGREMONT CASTLE

[Composed 1806.—Published 1807.]

ERE the Brothers through the gateway
Issued forth with old and young,
To the Horn Sir Eustace pointed
Which for ages there had hung.
Horn it was which none could sound, 5
No one upon living ground,
Save He who came as rightful Heir
To Egremont's Domains and Castle fair.

Heirs from times of earliest record
Had the House of Lucie born,   10
Who of right had held the Lordship
Claimed by proof upon the Horn:
Each at the appointed hour
Tried the Horn,—it owned his power;
He was acknowledged: and the blast, 15
Which good Sir Eustace sounded, was
  the last.

With his lance Sir Eustace pointed,
And to Hubert thus said he,
'What I speak this Horn shall witness
For thy better memory.   20
Hear, then, and neglect me not!
At this time, and on this spot,
The words are uttered from my heart,
As my last earnest prayer ere we depart.

'On good service we are going   25
Life to risk by sea and land,
In which course if Christ our Saviour
Do my sinful soul demand,
Hither come thou back straightway,
Hubert, if alive that day;   30
Return, and sound the Horn, that we
May have a living House still left in thee!'

'Fear not,' quickly answered Hubert;
'As I am thy Father's son,
What thou askest, noble Brother,   35
With God's favour shall be done.'

So were both right well content:
Forth they from the Castle went,
And at the head of their Array
To Palestine the Brothers took their way.

Side by side they fought (the Lucies 41
Were a line for valour famed)
And where'er their strokes alighted,
There the Saracens were tamed.
Whence, then, could it come—the
  thought—   45
By what evil spirit brought?
Oh! can a brave Man wish to take
His Brother's life, for Lands' and Castle's
  sake?

'Sir!' the Ruffians said to Hubert,
'Deep he lies in Jordan flood.'   50
Stricken by this ill assurance,
Pale and trembling Hubert stood.
'Take your earnings.'—Oh! that I
Could have *seen* my Brother die!
It was a pang that vexed him then; 55
And oft returned, again, and yet again.

Months passed on, and no Sir Eustace!
Nor of him were tidings heard;
Wherefore, bold as day, the Murderer
Back again to England steered.   60
To his Castle Hubert sped;
Nothing has he now to dread.
But silent and by stealth he came,
And at an hour which nobody could name.

None could tell if it were night-time, 65
Night or day, at even or morn;
No one's eye had seen him enter,
No one's ear had heard the Horn.
But bold Hubert lives in glee:
Months and years went smilingly; 70
With plenty was his table spread;
And bright the Lady is who shares his bed.

Likewise he had sons and daughters;
And, as good men do, he sate
At his board by these surrounded, 75
Flourishing in fair estate.
And while thus in open day
Once he sate, as old books say,
A blast was uttered from the Horn,
Where by the Castle-gate it hung forlorn.

'Tis the breath of good Sir Eustace! 81
He is come to claim his right:
Ancient castle, woods, and mountains
Hear the challenge with delight.
Hubert! though the blast be blown 85
He is helpless and alone:
Thou hast a dungeon, speak the word!
And there he may be lodged, and thou
  be Lord.

Speak!—astounded Hubert cannot;
And, if power to speak he had, 90
All are daunted, all the household
Smitten to the heart, and sad.

'Tis Sir Eustace; if it be
Living man, it must be he!
Thus Hubert thought in his dismay,   95
And by a postern-gate he slunk away.

Long, and long was he unheard of:
To his Brother then he came,
Made confession, asked forgiveness,
Asked it by a brother's name,   100
And by all the saints in heaven;
And of Eustace was forgiven:
Then in a convent went to hide
His melancholy head, and there he died.

But Sir Eustace, whom good angels   105
Had preserved from murderers' hands,
And from Pagan chains had rescued,
Lived with honour on his lands.
Sons he had, saw sons of theirs:
And through ages, heirs of heirs,   110
A long posterity renowned,
Sounded the Horn which they alone could
      sound.

XV
GOODY BLAKE AND HARRY GILL
A TRUE STORY
[Composed 1798.—Published 1798.]

OH! what's the matter? what's the
      matter?
What is't that ails young Harry Gill?
That evermore his teeth they chatter,
Chatter, chatter, chatter still!
Of waistcoats Harry has no lack,   5
Good duffle grey, and flannel fine;
He has a blanket on his back,
And coats enough to smother nine.

In March, December, and in July,
'Tis all the same with Harry Gill;   10
The neighbours tell, and tell you truly,
His teeth they chatter, chatter still.
At night, at morning, and at noon,
'Tis all the same with Harry Gill;
Beneath the sun, beneath the moon,   15
His teeth they chatter, chatter still!

Young Harry was a lusty drover,
And who so stout of limb as he?
His cheeks were red as ruddy clover;
His voice was like the voice of three.   20
Old Goody Blake was old and poor;
Ill fed she was, and thinly clad;
And any man who passed her door
Might see how poor a hut she had.   24

All day she spun in her poor dwelling:
And then her three hours' work at night,
Alas! 'twas hardly worth the telling,
It would not pay for candle-light.
Remote from sheltered village-green,
On a hill's northern side she dwelt,   30
Where from sea-blasts the hawthorns
      lean,
And hoary dews are slow to melt.

By the same fire to boil their pottage,
Two poor old Dames, as I have known,
Will often live in one small cottage;   35
But she, poor Woman! housed alone.
'Twas well enough, when summer came,
The long, warm, lightsome summer-day,
Then at her door the *canty* Dame
Would sit, as any linnet, gay.   40

But when the ice our streams did fetter,
Oh then how her old bones would shake!
You would have said, if you had met her,
'Twas a hard time for Goody Blake.
Her evenings then were dull and dead:
Sad case it was, as you may think,   46
For very cold to go to bed;
And then for cold not sleep a wink.

O joy for her! whene'er in winter
The winds at night had made a rout;   50
And scattered many a lusty splinter
And many a rotten bough about,
Yet never had she, well or sick,
As every man who knew her says,
A pile beforehand, turf or stick,   55
Enough to warm her for three days.

Now, when the frost was past enduring,
And made her poor old bones to ache,
Could any thing be more alluring
Than an old hedge to Goody Blake?   60
And, now and then, it must be said,
When her old bones were cold and chill,
She left her fire, or left her bed,
To seek the hedge of Harry Gill.

Now Harry he had long suspected   65
This trespass of old Goody Blake;
And vowed that she should be detected—
That he on her would vengeance take.
And oft from his warm fire he'd go,
And to the fields his road would take;   70
And there, at night, in frost and snow,
He watched to seize old Goody Blake.

And once, behind a rick of barley,
Thus looking out did Harry stand:
The moon was full and shining clearly,   75
And crisp with frost the stubble land.
—He hears a noise—he's all awake—
Again?—on tip-toe down the hill
He softly creeps—'tis Goody Blake;
She's at the hedge of Harry Gill!   80

Right glad was he when he beheld her:
Stick after stick did Goody pull:
He stood behind a bush of elder,
Till she had filled her apron full.
When with her load she turned about,   85
The by-way back again to take;
He started forward, with a shout,
And sprang upon poor Goody Blake.

And fiercely by the arm he took her,
And by the arm he held her fast,   90
And fiercely by the arm he shook her,
And cried, 'I've caught you then at last!'

Then Goody, who had nothing said,
Her bundle from her lap let fall;
And, kneeling on the sticks, she prayed
To God that is the judge of all.   96

She prayed, her withered hand uprearing,
While Harry held her by the arm—
'God! who art never out of hearing,
O may he never more be warm!'   100
The cold, cold moon above her head,
Thus on her knees did Goody pray;
Young Harry heard what she had said:
And icy cold he turned away.

He went complaining all the morrow   105
That he was cold and very chill:
His face was gloom, his heart was sorrow,
Alas! that day for Harry Gill!
That day he wore a riding-coat,
But not a whit the warmer he: 110
Another was on Thursday brought,
And ere the Sabbath he had three.

'Twas all in vain, a useless matter,
And blankets were about him pinned;
Yet still his jaws and teeth they clatter,
Like a loose casement in the wind.   116
And Harry's flesh it fell away;
And all who see him say, 'tis plain,
That, live as long as live he may,
He never will be warm again.   120

No word to any man he utters,
A-bed or up, to young or old;
But ever to himself he mutters,
'Poor Harry Gill is very cold.'
A-bed or up, by night or day;   125
His teeth they chatter, chatter still.
Now think, ye farmers all, I pray,
Of Goody Blake and Harry Gill!

XVI
PRELUDE

PREFIXED TO THE VOLUME ENTITLED
'POEMS CHIEFLY OF EARLY AND LATE
YEARS.'

[Composed March, 1842.—Published: vol. of
1842.]

IN desultory walk through orchard
grounds,
Or some deep chestnut grove, oft have
I paused
The while a Thrush, urged rather than
restrained
By gusts of vernal storm, attuned his
song
To his own genial instincts; and was
heard   5
(Though not without some plaintive tones
between)
To utter, above showers of blossom swept
From tossing boughs, the promise of a
calm,

Which the unsheltered traveller might
receive
With thankful spirit. The descant, and
the wind   10
That seemed to play with it in love or
scorn,
Encouraged and endeared the strain of
words
That haply flowed from me, by fits of
silence
Impelled to livelier pace. But now, my
Book!
Charged with those lays, and others of
like mood,   15
Or loftier pitch if higher rose the theme,
Go, single—yet aspiring to be joined
With thy Forerunners that through many
a year
Have faithfully prepared each other's
way—
Go forth upon a mission best fulfilled
When and wherever, in this changeful
world,   21
Power hath been given to please for
higher ends
Than pleasure only; gladdening to pre-
pare
For wholesome sadness, troubling to
refine,
Calming to raise; and, by a sapient Art
Diffused through all the mysteries of our
Being,   26
Softening the toils and pains that have
not ceased
To cast their shadows on our mother Earth
Since the primeval doom. Such is the
grace
Which, though unsued for, fails not to
descend   30
With heavenly inspiration; such the aim
That Reason dictates; and, as even the
wish
Has virtue in it, why should hope to me
Be wanting that sometimes, where fancied
ills
Harass the mind and strip from off the
bowers   35
Of private life their natural pleasantness,
A Voice—devoted to the love whose seeds
Are sown in every human breast, to
beauty
Lodged within compass of the humblest
sight,
To cheerful intercourse with wood and
field,   40
And sympathy with man's substantial
griefs—
Will not be heard in vain? And in those
days
When unforeseen distress spreads far and
wide
Among a People mournfully cast down,
Or into anger roused by venal words   45
In recklessness flung out to overturn

The judgment, and divert the general
heart
From mutual good—some strain of thine,
my Book!
Caught at propitious intervals, may win
Listeners who not unwillingly admit   50
Kindly emotion tending to console
And reconcile; and both with young and
old
Exalt the sense of thoughtful gratitude
For benefits that still survive, by faith
In progress, under laws divine, main-
tained.   55

RYDAL MOUNT, *March* 26, 1842.

XVII

TO A CHILD

WRITTEN IN HER ALBUM

[Composed 1834.—Published 1835.]

SMALL service is true service while it
lasts:
Of humblest Friends, bright Creature!
scorn not one:
The Daisy, by the shadow that it casts,
Protects the lingering dew-drop from the
Sun.

XVIII

LINES

WRITTEN IN THE ALBUM OF THE
COUNTESS OF LONSDALE

[Composed November 5, 1834.—Published 1835.]

LADY! a Pen (perhaps with thy regard,
Among the Favoured, favoured not the
least)
Left, 'mid the Records of this Book
inscribed,
Deliberate traces, registers of thought
And feeling, suited to the place and time
That gave them birth:—months passed,
and still this hand,   6
That had not been too timid to imprint
Words which the virtues of thy Lord
inspired,
Was yet not bold enough to write of
Thee.
And why that scrupulous reserve? In
sooth   10
The blameless cause lay in the Theme
itself.
Flowers are there many that delight to
strive
With the sharp wind, and seem to court
the shower,
Yet are by nature careless of the sun
Whether he shine on them or not; and
some,   15
Where'er he moves along the unclouded
sky,
Turn a broad front full on his flattering
beams:
Others do rather from their notice shrink,

Loving the dewy shade,—a humble band,
Modest and sweet, a progeny of earth,   20
Congenial with thy mind and character,
High-born Augusta!
Witness, Towers and Groves!
And Thou, wild Stream, that giv'st the
honoured name
Of Lowther to this ancient Line, bear
witness
From thy most secret haunts; and ye
Parterres,   25
Which She is pleased and proud to call
her own,
Witness how oft upon my noble Friend
Mute offerings, tribute from an inward
sense
Of admiration and respectful love,
Have waited—till the affections could no
more   30
Endure that silence, and broke out in
song,
Snatches of music taken up and dropt
Like those self-solacing, those under,
notes
Trilled by the redbreast, when autumnal
leaves
Are thin upon the bough. Mine, only
mine,   35
The pleasure was, and no one heard the
praise,
Checked, in the moment of its issue,
checked
And reprehended, by a fancied blush
From the pure qualities that called it
forth.

Thus Virtue lives debarred from Vir-
tue's meed;   40
Thus, Lady, is retiredness a veil
That, while it only spreads a softening
charm
O'er features looked at by discerning eyes,
Hides half their beauty from the common
gaze;
And thus, even on the exposed and
breezy hill   45
Of lofty station, female goodness walks,
When side by side with lunar gentleness,
As in a cloister. Yet the grateful Poor
(Such the immunities of low estate,
Plain Nature's enviable privilege,   50
Her sacred recompense for many wants)
Open their hearts before Thee, pouring
out
All that they think and feel, with tears of
joy;
And benedictions not unheard in heaven:
And friend in the ear of friend, where
speech is free   55
To follow truth, is eloquent as they.

Then let the Book receive in these
prompt lines
A just memorial; and thine eyes consent

To read that they, who mark thy course,
      behold
A life declining with the golden light   60
Of summer, in the season of sere leaves;
See cheerfulness undamped by stealing
      Time;
See studied kindness flow with easy
      stream,
Illustrated with inborn courtesy;
And an habitual disregard of self   65
Balanced by vigilance for others' weal.

And shall the Verse not tell of lighter
      gifts
With these ennobling attributes con-
      joined
And blended, in peculiar harmony,
By Youth's surviving spirit? What agile
      grace!   70
A nymph-like liberty, in nymph-like
      form,
Beheld with wonder; whether floor or
      path
Thou tread; or sweep—borne on the
      managed steed—
Fleet as the shadows, over down or field,
Driven by strong winds at play among
      the clouds.   75

Yet one word more—one farewell
      word—a wish
Which came, but it has passed into a
      prayer—
That, as thy sun in brightness is de-
      clining,
So—at an hour yet distant for *their* sakes
Whose tender love, here faltering on the
      way   80
Of a diviner love, will be forgiven—
So may it set in peace, to rise again
For everlasting glory won by faith.

XIX
GRACE DARLING

[Composed 1843.—Published 1845.]

AMONG the dwellers in the silent fields
The natural heart is touched, and public
      way
And crowded street resound with ballad
      strains,
Inspired by ONE whose very name be-
      speaks
Favour divine, exalting human love;   5
Whom, since her birth on bleak North-
      umbria's coast,
Known unto few but prized as far as
      known,
A single Act endears to high and low
Through the whole land—to Manhood,
      moved in spite
Of the world's freezing cares—to generous
      Youth—   10
To Infancy, that lisps her praise—to Age

Whose eye reflects it, glistening through
      a tear
Of tremulous admiration. Such true fame
Awaits her *now;* but, verily, good deeds
Do no imperishable record find   15
Save in the rolls of heaven, where hers
      may live
A theme for angels, when they celebrate
The high-souled virtues which forgetful
      earth
Has witnessed. Oh! that winds and
      waves could speak
Of things which their united power called
      forth   20
From the pure depths of her humanity!
A Maiden gentle, yet, at duty's call,
Firm and unflinching, as the Lighthouse
      reared
On the Island-rock, her lonely dwelling-
      place;
Or like the invincible Rock itself that
      braves,   25
Age after age, the hostile elements,
As when it guarded holy Cuthbert's cell.

All night the storm had raged, nor
      ceased, nor paused,
When, as day broke, the Maid, through
      misty air,
Espies far off a Wreck, amid the surf,   30
Beating on one of those disastrous isles—
Half of a Vessel, half—no more; the rest
Had vanished, swallowed up with all
      that there
Had for the common safety striven in vain,
Or thither thronged for refuge. With
      quick glance   35
Daughter and Sire through optic-glass
      discern,
Clinging about the remnant of this Ship,
Creatures—how precious in the Maiden's
      sight!
For whom, belike, the old Man grieves
      still more
Than for their fellow-sufferers engulfed
Where every parting agony is hushed,   41
And hope and fear mix not in further strife.
'But courage, Father! let us out to sea—
A few may yet be saved.' The Daughter's
      words,
Her earnest tone, and look beaming with
      faith,   45
Dispel the Father's doubts: nor do they
      lack
The noble-minded Mother's helping hand
To launch the boat; and with her blessing
      cheered,
And inwardly sustained by silent prayer,
Together they put forth, Father and Child!
Each grasps an oar, and struggling on
      they go—   51
Rivals in effort; and, alike intent
Here to elude and there surmount, they
      watch

423

The billows lengthening, mutually crossed
And shattered, and re-gathering their
    might;   55
As if the tumult, by the Almighty's will
Were, in the conscious sea, roused and
    prolonged
That woman's fortitude—so tried, so
    proved—
May, brighten more and more!

                 True to the mark,
They stem the current of that perilous
    gorge,   60
Their arms still strengthening with the
    strengthening heart,
Though danger, as the Wreck is neared,
    becomes
More imminent. Not unseen do they
    approach;
And rapture, with varieties of fear
Incessantly conflicting, thrills the frames
Of those who, in that dauntless energy,
Foretaste deliverance; but the least
    perturbed   67
Can scarcely trust his eyes, when he
    perceives
That of the pair—tossed on the waves to
    bring
Hope to the hopeless, to the dying, life—
One is a Woman, a poor earthly sister, 71
Or, be the Visitant other than she seems,
A guardian Spirit sent from pitying
    Heaven,
In woman's shape. But why prolong the
    tale,
Casting weak words amid a host of
    thoughts   75
Armed to repel them? Every hazard
    faced
And difficulty mastered, with resolve
That no one breathing should be left to
    perish,
This last remainder of the crew are all
Placed in the little boat, then o'er the
    deep   80
Are safely borne, landed upon the beach,
And, in fulfilment of God's mercy, lodged
Within the sheltering Lighthouse.—
    Shout, ye Waves!
Send forth a song of triumph. Waves
    and Winds,
Exult in this deliverance wrought through
    faith   85
In Him whose Providence your rage hath
    served!
Ye screaming Sea-mews, in the concert
    join!
And would that some immortal Voice—a
    Voice
Fitly attuned to all that gratitude
Breathes out from floor or couch, through
    pallid lips   90
Of the survivors—to the clouds might
    bear—

Blended with praise of that parental love,
Beneath whose watchful eye the Maiden
    grew
Pious and pure, modest and yet so brave,
Though young so wise, though meek so
    resolute—   95
Might carry to the clouds and to the
    stars,
Yea, to celestial Choirs, GRACE DARLING'S
    name!

XX

THE RUSSIAN FUGITIVE

PART I

[Composed 1830.—Published 1835.]

ENOUGH of rose-bud lips, and eyes
    Like harebells bathed in dew,
Of cheek that with carnation vies,
    And veins of violet hue;
Earth wants not beauty that may scorn 5
    A likening to frail flowers;
Yea, to the stars, if they were born
    For seasons and for hours.

Through Moscow's gates, with gold un-
    barred,
    Stepped One at dead of night,   10
Whom such high beauty could not guard
    From meditated blight;
By stealth she passed, and fled as fast
    As doth the hunted fawn,
Nor stopped, till in the dappling east 15
    Appeared unwelcome dawn.

Seven days she lurked in brake and field,
    Seven nights her course renewed,
Sustained by what her scrip might yield,
    Or berries of the wood;   20
At length, in darkness travelling on,
    When lowly doors were shut,
The haven of her hope she won,
    Her Foster-mother's hut.

'To put your love to dangerous proof 25
    I come,' said she, 'from far;
For I have left my Father's roof,
    In terror of the Czar.'
No answer did the Matron give,
    No second look she cast,   30
But hung upon the Fugitive,
    Embracing and embraced.

She led the Lady to a seat
    Beside the glimmering fire,
Bathed duteously her wayworn feet, 35
    Prevented each desire:—
The cricket chirped, the house-dog dozed,
    And on that simple bed,
Where she in childhood had reposed,
    Now rests her weary head.   40

When she, whose couch had been the sod,
    Whose curtain pine or thorn,
Had breathed a sigh of thanks to God,
    Who comforts the forlorn;

While over her the Matron bent 45
  Sleep sealed her eyes, and stole
Feeling from limbs with travel spent,
  And trouble from the soul.

Refreshed, the Wanderer rose at morn,
  And soon again was dight 50
In those unworthy vestments worn
  Through long and perilous flight;
And 'O beloved Nurse,' she said,
  'My thanks with silent tears
Have unto Heaven and You been paid: 55
  Now listen to my fears!

'Have you forgot'—and here she smiled—
  'The babbling flatteries
You lavished on me when a child
  Disporting round your knees? 60
I was your lambkin, and your bird,
  Your star, your gem, your flower;
Light words, that were more lightly heard
  In many a cloudless hour!

'The blossom you so fondly praised 65
  Is come to bitter fruit;
A mighty One upon me gazed;
  I spurned his lawless suit,
And must be hidden from his wrath:
  You, Foster-father dear, 70
Will guide me in my forward path;
  I may not tarry here!

'I cannot bring to utter woe
  Your proved fidelity.'—
'Dear child, sweet Mistress, say not so!
  For you we both would die.' 76
'Nay, nay, I come with semblance feigned
  And cheek embrowned by art;
Yet, being inwardly unstained,
  With courage will depart.' 80

'But whither would you, could you, flee?
  A poor Man's counsel take;
The Holy Virgin gives to me
  A thought for your dear sake;
Rest, shielded by our Lady's grace, 85
  And soon shall you be led
Forth to a safe abiding-place,
  Where never foot doth tread.'

PART II

THE dwelling of this faithful pair
  In a straggling village stood, 90
For One who breathed unquiet air
  A dangerous neighbourhood;
But wide around lay forest ground
  With thickets rough and blind;
And pine-trees made a heavy shade 95
  Impervious to the wind.

And there, sequestered from the sight,
  Was spread a treacherous swamp,
On which the noonday sun shed light
  As from a lonely lamp; 100

And midway in the unsafe morass,
  A single Island rose
Of firm dry ground, with healthful grass
  Adorned, and shady boughs.

The Woodman knew, for such the craft
  This Russian vassal plied, 106
That never fowler's gun, nor shaft
  Of archer, there was tried;
A sanctuary seemed the spot
  From all intrusion free; 110
And there he planned an artful Cot
  For perfect secrecy.

With earnest pains unchecked by dread
  Of Power's far-stretching hand,
The bold good Man his labour sped 115
  At nature's pure command;
Heart-soothed, and busy as a wren,
  While, in a hollow nook,
She moulds her sight-eluding den
  Above a murmuring brook. 120

His task accomplished to his mind,
  The twain ere break of day
Creep forth, and through the forest wind
  Their solitary way;
Few words they speak, nor dare to slack
  Their pace from mile to mile, 126
Till they have crossed the quaking marsh,
  And reached the lonely Isle.

The sun above the pine-trees showed
  A bright and cheerful face; 130
And Ina looked for her abode,
  The promised hiding-place;
She sought in vain, the Woodman smiled;
  No threshold could be seen,
Nor roof, nor window;—all seemed wild
  As it had ever been. 136

Advancing, you might guess an hour,
  The front with such nice care
Is masked, 'if house it be or bower,'
  But in they entered are; 140
As shaggy as were wall and roof
  With branches intertwined,
So smooth was all within, air-proof,
  And delicately lined:

And hearth was there, and maple dish,
  And cups in seemly rows, 146
And couch—all ready to a wish
  For nurture or repose;
And Heaven doth to her virtue grant
  That there she may abide 150
In solitude, with every want
  By cautious love supplied.

No queen before a shouting crowd
  Led on in bridal state,
E'er struggled with a heart so proud, 155
  Entering her palace gate;
Rejoiced to bid the world farewell,
  No saintly anchoress
E'er took possession of her cell
  With deeper thankfulness. 160

'Father of all, upon thy care
　And mercy am I thrown;
Be thou my safeguard!'—such her prayer
　When she was left alone,
Kneeling amid the wilderness　　　　165
　When joy had passed away,
And smiles, fond efforts of distress
　To hide what they betray!

The prayer is heard, the Saints have seen,
　Diffused through form and face,　170
Resolves devotedly serene;
　That monumental grace
Of Faith, which doth all passions tame
　That Reason *should* control;
And shows in the untrembling frame　175
　A statue of the soul.

PART III

'Tis sung in ancient minstrelsy
　That Phœbus wont to wear
The leaves of any pleasant tree
　Around his golden hair;　　　　　180
Till Daphne, desperate with pursuit
　Of his imperious love,
At her own prayer transformed, took root,
　A laurel in the grove.

Then did the Penitent adorn　　　185
　His brow with laurel green;
And 'mid his bright locks never shorn
　No meaner leaf was seen;
And poets sage, through every age,
　About their temples wound　　　190
The bay; and conquerors thanked the
　　Gods,
　With laurel chaplets crowned.

Into the mists of fabling Time
　So far runs back the praise
Of Beauty, that disdains to climb　195
　Along forbidden ways;
That scorns temptation; power defies
　Where mutual love is not;
And to the tomb for rescue flies
　When life would be a blot.　　　200

To this fair Votaress a fate
　More mild doth Heaven ordain
Upon her Island desolate;
　And words, not breathed in vain,
Might tell what intercourse she found,
　Her silence to endear;　　　　206
What birds she tamed, what flowers the
　　ground
　Sent forth her peace to cheer.

To one mute Presence, above all,
　Her soothed affections clung,　210
A picture on the cabin wall
　By Russian usage hung—
The Mother-maid, whose countenance
　　bright
　With love abridged the day;
And, communed with by taper-light,　215
　Chased spectral fears away.

And oft, as either Guardian came,
　The joy in that retreat
Might any common friendship shame,
　So high their hearts would beat;　220
And to the lone Recluse, whate'er
　They brought, each visiting
Was like the crowding of the year
　With a new burst of spring.

But when she of her Parents thought,　225
　The pang was hard to bear;
And, if with all things not enwrought,
　That trouble still is near.
Before her flight she had not dared
　Their constancy to prove,　　　230
Too much the heroic Daughter feared
　The weakness of their love.

Dark is the past to them, and dark
　The future still must be,
Till pitying Saints conduct her bark　235
　Into a safer sea—
Or gentle Nature close her eyes,
　And set her Spirit free
From the altar of this sacrifice,
　In vestal purity.　　　　　　　240

Yet, when above the forest-glooms
　The white swans southward passed,
High as the pitch of their swift plumes
　Her fancy rode the blast;
And bore her toward the fields of France,
　Her Father's native land,　　　246
To mingle in the rustic dance,
　The happiest of the band!

Of those belovèd fields she oft
　Had heard her Father tell　　　250
In phrase that now with echoes soft
　Haunted her lonely cell;
She saw the hereditary bowers,
　She heard the ancestral stream;
The Kremlin and its haughty towers　255
　Forgotten like a dream!

PART IV

The ever-changing Moon had traced
　Twelve times her monthly round,
When through the unfrequented Waste
　Was heard a startling sound;　260
A shout thrice sent from one who chased
　At speed a wounded deer,
Bounding through branches interlaced,
　And where the wood was clear.

The fainting creature took the marsh,
　And toward the Island fled,　266
While plovers screamed with tumult
　　harsh
　Above his antlered head;
This, Ina saw; and, pale with fear,
　Shrunk to her citadel;　　　　270
The desperate deer rushed on, and near
　The tangled covert fell.

426

Across the marsh, the game in view,
The Hunter followed fast,
Nor paused, till o'er the stag he blew 275
A death-proclaiming blast;
Then, resting on her upright mind,
Came forth the Maid—'In me
Behold,' she said, 'a stricken Hind
Pursued by destiny! 280

'From your deportment, Sir! I deem
That you have worn a sword,
And will not hold in light esteem
A suffering woman's word;
There is my covert, there perchance 285
I might have lain concealed,
My fortunes hid, my countenance
Not even to you revealed.

'Tears might be shed, and I might
pray,
Crouching and terrified, 290
That what has been unveiled to-day,
You would in mystery hide;
But I will not defile with dust
The knee that bends to adore
The God in heaven;—attend, be just; 295
This ask I, and no more!

'I speak not of the winter's cold
For summer's heat exchanged,
While I have lodged in this rough hold,
From social life estranged; 300
Nor yet of trouble and alarms;
High Heaven is my defence;
And every season has soft arms
For injured Innocence.

'From Moscow to the Wilderness 305
It was my choice to come,
Lest virtue should be harbourless,
And honour want a home;
And happy were I, if the Czar
Retain his lawless will, 310
To end life here like this poor deer,
Or a lamb on a green hill.'

'Are you the Maid,' the Stranger cried,
'From Gallic parents sprung,
Whose vanishing was rumoured wide,
Sad theme for every tongue; 316
Who foiled an Emperor's eager quest?
You, Lady, forced to wear
These rude habiliments, and rest
Your head in this dark lair!' 320

But wonder, pity, soon were quelled;
And in her face and mien
The soul's pure brightness he beheld
Without a veil between:

He loved, he hoped,—a holy flame 325
Kindled 'mid rapturous tears;
The passion of a moment came
As on the wings of years.

'Such bounty is no gift of chance,'
Exclaimed he: 'righteous Heaven, 330
Preparing your deliverance,
To me the charge hath given.
The Czar full oft in words and deeds
Is stormy and self-willed;
But, when the Lady Catherine pleads, 335
His violence is stilled.

'Leave open to my wish the course,
And I to her will go;
From that humane and heavenly source
Good, only good, can flow.' 340
Faint sanction given, the Cavalier
Was eager to depart,
Though question followed question, dear
To the Maiden's filial heart.

Light was his step,—his hopes, more light,
Kept pace with his desires; 346
And the fifth morning gave him sight
Of Moscow's glittering spires.
He sued:—heart-smitten by the wrong,
To the lorn Fugitive 350
The Emperor sent a pledge as strong
As sovereign power could give.

O more than mighty change! If e'er
Amazement rose to pain,
And joy's excess produced a fear 355
Of something void and vain;
'Twas when the Parents, who had
mourned
So long the lost as dead,
Beheld their only Child returned
The household floor to tread. 360

Soon gratitude gave way to love
Within the Maiden's breast;
Delivered and Deliverer move
In bridal garments drest;
Meek Catherine had her own reward; 565
The Czar bestowed a dower;
And universal Moscow shared
The triumph of that hour.

Flowers strewed the ground; the nuptial
feast
Was held with costly state; 370
And there, 'mid many a noble guest,
The Foster-parents sate;
Encouraged by the imperial eye,
They shrank not into shade;
Great was their bliss, the honour high
To them and nature paid! 376

INSCRIPTIONS

I

IN THE GROUNDS OF COLEORTON, THE SEAT OF SIR GEORGE BEAUMONT, BART., LEICESTERSHIRE
[Composed 1808.—Published 1815.]

THE embowering rose, the acacia, and the
    pine,
Will not unwillingly their place resign;
If but the Cedar thrive that near them
    stands,
Planted by Beaumont's and by Words-
    worth's hands.
One wooed the silent Art with studious
    pains: 5
These groves have heard the Other's
    pensive strains;
Devoted thus, their spirits did unite
By interchange of knowledge and delight.
May Nature's kindliest powers sustain
    the Tree,
And Love protect it from all injury!   10
And when its potent branches, wide out-
    thrown,
Darken the brow of this memorial Stone,
Here may some Painter sit in future days,
Some future Poet meditate his lays;   14
Not mindless of that distant age renowned
When Inspiration hovered o'er this
    ground,
The haunt of him who sang how spear and
    shield
In civil conflict met on Bosworth-field;
And of that famous Youth, full soon
    removed
From earth, perhaps by Shakespeare's
    self approved,   20
Fletcher's Associate, Jonson's Friend
    beloved.

II

IN A GARDEN OF THE SAME
[Composed 1811 (?).—Published 1815.]

OFT is the medal faithful to its trust
When temples, columns, towers, are laid
    in dust;
And 'tis a common ordinance of fate
That things obscure and small outlive the
    great:
Hence, when yon mansion and the flowery
    trim   5
Of this fair garden, and its alleys dim,
And all its stately trees, are passed away,
This little Niche, unconscious of decay,
Perchance may still survive. And be it
    known
That it was scooped within the living
    stone,—   10
Not by the sluggish and ungrateful pains
Of labourer plodding for his daily gains,

But by an industry that wrought in love;
With help from female hands, that proudly
    strove
To aid the work, what time these walks
    and bowers   15
Were shaped to cheer dark winter's lonely
    hours.

III

WRITTEN AT THE REQUEST OF SIR GEORGE BEAUMONT, BART., AND IN HIS NAME, FOR AN URN, PLACED BY HIM AT THE TERMINATION OF A NEWLY-PLANTED AVENUE, IN THE SAME GROUNDS
[Composed November, 1811.—Published 1815.]

YE Lime-trees, ranged before this hal-
    lowed Urn,
Shoot forth with lively power at Spring's
    return;
And be not slow a stately growth to rear
Of pillars, branching off from year to year,
Till they have learned to frame a dark-
    some aisle;—   5
That may recall to mind that awful Pile
Where Reynolds, 'mid our country's
    noblest dead,
In the last sanctity of fame is laid.
—There, though by right the excelling
    Painter sleep
Where Death and Glory a joint sabbath
    keep,   10
Yet not the less his Spirit would hold dear
Self-hidden praise, and Friendship's
    private tear:
Hence, on my patrimonial grounds, have I
Raised this frail tribute to his memory;
From youth a zealous follower of the Art
That he professed; attached to him in
    heart;   16
Admiring, loving, and with grief and pride
Feeling what England lost when Reynolds
    died.

IV

FOR A SEAT IN THE GROVES OF COLEORTON
[Composed November 19, 1811.—Published 1815.]

BENEATH yon eastern ridge, the craggy
    bound,
Rugged and high, of Charnwood's forest
    ground,
Stand yet, but, Stranger! hidden from
    thy view,
The ivied Ruins of forlorn GRACE DIEU!
Erst a religious House, which day and night
With hymns resounded, and the chanted
    rite: 6
And when those rites had ceased, the Spot
    gave birth
To honourable Men of various worth:

There, on the margin of a streamlet wild,
Did Francis Beaumont sport, an eager
   child;   10
There, under shadow of the neighbouring
   rocks,
Sang youthful tales of shepherds and
   their flocks;
Unconscious prelude to heroic themes,
Heart-breaking tears, and melancholy
   dreams
Of slighted love, and scorn, and jealous
   rage,   15
With which his genius shook the buskined
   stage.
Communities are lost, and Empires die,
And things of holy use unhallowed lie;
They perish;—but the Intellect can raise,
From airy words alone, a Pile that ne'er
   decays.   20

V

WRITTEN WITH A PENCIL UPON A STONE
IN THE WALL OF THE HOUSE (AN OUT-
HOUSE), ON THE ISLAND AT GRASMERE

[Composed 1800.—Published 1800.]

RUDE is this Edifice, and Thou hast seen
Buildings, albeit rude, that have main-
   tained
Proportions more harmonious, and ap-
   proached
To closer fellowship with ideal grace.
But take it in good part:—alas! the
   poor   5
Vitruvius of our village had no help
From the great City; never, upon leaves
Of red Morocco folio saw displayed,
In long succession, pre-existing ghosts
Of Beauties yet unborn—the rustic Lodge
Antique, and Cottage with verandah
   graced,   11
Nor lacking, for fit company, alcove,
Green-house, shell-grot, and moss-lined
   hermitage.
Thou see'st a homely Pile, yet to these
   walls
The heifer comes in the snow-storm, and
   here   15
The new-dropped lamb finds shelter from
   the wind.
And hither does one Poet sometimes row
His pinnace, a small vagrant barge, up-
   piled
With plenteous store of heath and
   withered fern,
(A lading which he with his sickle cuts,
Among the mountains) and beneath this
   roof   21
He makes his summer couch, and here at
   noon
Spreads out his limbs, while, yet unshorn,
   the Sheep,
Panting beneath the burthen of their wool,

Lie round him, even as if they were a
   part   25
Of his own Household: nor, while from
   his bed
He looks, through the open door-place,
   toward the lake
And to the stirring breezes, does he want
Creations lovely as the work of sleep—
Fair sights, and visions of romantic joy!

VI

WRITTEN WITH A SLATE PENCIL ON A
STONE, ON THE SIDE OF THE MOUN-
TAIN OF BLACK COMB

[Composed 1813.—Published 1815.]

STAY, bold Adventurer; rest awhile thy
   limbs
On this commodious Seat! for much
   remains
Of hard ascent before thou reach the top
Of this huge Eminence,—from blackness
   named,
And, to far-travelled storms of sea and
   land,   5
A favourite spot of tournament and war!
But thee may no such boisterous visit-
   ants
Molest; may gentle breezes fan thy brow;
And neither cloud conceal, nor misty
   air   9
Bedim, the grand terraqueous spectacle,
From centre to circumference, unveiled!
Know, if thou grudge not to prolong thy
   rest,
That on the summit whither thou art
   bound,
A geographic Labourer pitched his tent,
With books supplied and instruments of
   art,   15
To measure height and distance; lonely
   task,
Week after week pursued!—To him was
   given
Full many a glimpse (but sparingly be-
   stowed
On timid man) of Nature's processes
Upon the exalted hills. He made re-
   port   20
That once, while there he plied his
   studious work
Within that canvass Dwelling, colours,
   lines,
And the whole surface of the out-spread
   map,
Became invisible: for all around
Had darkness fallen—unthreatened, un-
   proclaimed—   25
As if the golden day itself had been
Extinguished in a moment; total gloom,
In which he sate alone, with unclosed
   eyes,
Upon the blinded mountain's silent top!

INSCRIPTIONS

VII

WRITTEN WITH A SLATE PENCIL UPON
A STONE, THE LARGEST OF A HEAP
LYING NEAR A DESERTED QUARRY,
UPON ONE OF THE ISLANDS AT RYDAL
[Composed 1800.—Published 1800.]

STRANGER! this hillock of mis-shapen
    stones
Is not a Ruin spared or made by time,
Nor, as perchance thou rashly deem'st,
    the Cairn
Of some old British Chief: 'tis nothing
    more
Than the rude embryo of a little Dome 5
Or Pleasure-house, once destined to be
    built
Among the birch-trees of this rocky isle.
But, as it chanced, Sir William having
    learned
That from the shore a full-grown man
    might wade,   9
And make himself a freeman of this spot
At any hour he chose, the prudent Knight
Desisted, and the quarry and the mound
Are monuments of his unfinished task.
The block on which these lines are traced,
    perhaps,
Was once selected as the corner-stone 15
Of that intended Pile, which would have
    been
Some quaint odd plaything of elaborate
    skill,
So that, I guess, the linnet and the
    thrush,
And other little builders who dwell here,
Had wondered at the work. But blame
    him not,   20
For old Sir William was a gentle Knight,
Bred in this vale, to which he appertained
With all his ancestry. Then peace to him,
And for the outrage which he had devised
Entire forgiveness!—But if thou art one
On fire with thy impatience to become
An inmate of these mountains,—if, dis-
    turbed   27
By beautiful conceptions, thou hast hewn
Out of the quiet rock the elements
Of thy trim Mansion destined soon to
    blaze   30
In snow-white splendour,—think again;
    and, taught
By old Sir William and his quarry, leave
Thy fragments to the bramble and the
    rose;
There let the vernal slow-worm sun him-
    self,
And let the redbreast hop from stone to
    stone.   35

VIII

[Composed 1830 (? 1831).—Published 1835.]

IN these fair vales hath many a Tree
    At Wordsworth's suit been spared;

And from the builder's hand this Stone,
For some rude beauty of its own,
    Was rescued by the Bard: 5
So let it rest; and time will come
    When here the tender-hearted
May heave a gentle sigh for him,
    As one of the departed.

IX

[Composed 1826.—Published 1835.]

THE massy Ways, carried across these
    heights
By Roman perseverance, are destroyed,
Or hidden under ground, like sleeping
    worms.
How venture then to hope that Time will
    spare
This humble Walk? Yet on the moun-
    tain's side   5
A POET'S hand first shaped it; and the
    steps
Of that same Bard—repeated to and fro
At morn, at noon, and under moonlight
    skies
Through the vicissitudes of many a year—
Forbade the weeds to creep o'er its grey
    line.   10
No longer, scattering to the heedless winds
The vocal raptures of fresh poesy,
Shall he frequent these precincts; locked
    no more
In earnest converse with belovèd Friends,
Here will he gather stores of ready bliss,
As from the beds and borders of a garden
Choice flowers are gathered! But, if
    Power may spring
Out of a farewell yearning—favoured
    more
Than kindred wishes mated suitably
With vain regrets—the Exile would con-
    sign   20
This Walk, his loved possession, to the
    care
Of those pure Minds that reverence the
    Muse.

X

INSCRIPTIONS SUPPOSED TO BE FOUND
IN AND NEAR A HERMIT'S CELL

[This group (X–XIV) was composed 1818.—
Published 1820.]

I

HOPES what are they?—Beads of morning
Strung on slender blades of grass;
Or a spider's web adorning
In a strait and treacherous pass.

What are fears but voices airy?   5
Whispering harm where harm is not;
And deluding the unwary
Till the fatal bolt is shot!

430

What is glory?—in the socket
See how dying tapers fare!   10
What is pride?—a whizzing rocket
That would emulate a star.

What is friendship?—do not trust her,
Nor the vows which she has made;
Diamonds dart their brightest lustre   15
From a palsy-shaken head.

What is truth?—a staff rejected;
Duty?—an unwelcome clog;
Joy?—a moon by fits reflected
In a swamp or watery bog;   20

Bright, as if through ether steering,
To the Traveller's eye it shone:
He hath hailed it re-appearing—
And as quickly it is gone;

Such is Joy—as quickly hidden,   25
Or mis-shapen to the sight,
And by sullen weeds forbidden
To resume its native light.

What is youth?—a dancing billow,
(Winds behind, and rocks before!)   30
Age?—a drooping, tottering willow
On a flat and lazy shore.

What is peace?—when pain is over,
And love ceases to rebel,
Let the last faint sigh discover   35
That precedes the passing-knell!

XI

INSCRIBED UPON A ROCK

II

PAUSE, Traveller! whosoe'er thou be
Whom chance may lead to this retreat,
Where silence yields reluctantly
Even to the fleecy straggler's bleat;

Give voice to what my hand shall trace,   5
And fear not lest an idle sound
Of words unsuited to the place
Disturb its solitude profound.

I saw this Rock, while vernal air
Blew softly o'er the russet heath,   10
Uphold a Monument as fair
As church or abbey furnisheth.

Unsullied did it meet the day,
Like marble, white, like ether, pure;
As if, beneath, some hero lay,   15
Honoured with costliest sepulture.

My fancy kindled as I gazed;
And, ever as the sun shone forth,
The flattered structure glistened, blazed,
And seemed the proudest thing on earth.

But frost had reared the gorgeous Pile 21
Unsound as those which Fortune builds—
To undermine with secret guile,
Sapped by the very beam that gilds.

And, while I gazed, with sudden shock
Fell the whole Fabric to the ground;   26
And naked left this dripping Rock,
With shapeless ruin spread around!

XII

III

HAST thou seen, with flash incessant,
Bubbles gliding under ice,
Bodied forth and evanescent,
No one knows by what device?

Such are thoughts!—A wind-swept
          meadow   5
Mimicking a troubled sea,
Such is life; and death a shadow
From the rock eternity!

XIII

NEAR THE SPRING OF THE HERMITAGE

IV

TROUBLED long with warring notions
Long impatient of Thy rod,
I resign my soul's emotions
Unto Thee, mysterious God!

What avails the kindly shelter   5
Yielded by this craggy rent,
If my spirit toss and welter
On the waves of discontent?

Parching Summer hath no warrant
To consume this crystal Well;   10
Rains, that make each rill a torrent,
Neither sully it nor swell.

Thus, dishonouring not her station,
Would my Life present to Thee,
Gracious God, the pure oblation   15
Of divine tranquillity!

XIV

V

NOT seldom, clad in radiant vest,
Deceitfully goes forth the Morn;
Not seldom Evening in the west
Sinks smilingly forsworn.

The smoothest seas will sometimes prove,
To the confiding Bark, untrue;   6
And, if she trust the stars above
They can be treacherous too.

The umbrageous Oak, in pomp outspread,
Full oft, when storms the welkin rend,
Draws lightning down upon the head   11
It promised to defend.

But Thou art true, incarnate Lord,
Who didst vouchsafe for man to die;
Thy smile is sure, Thy plighted word 15
No change can falsify!

I bent before Thy gracious throne,
And asked for peace on suppliant knee;
And peace was given,—nor peace alone,
But faith sublimed to ecstasy!   20

INSCRIPTIONS

XV

FOR THE SPOT WHERE THE HERMITAGE
STOOD ON ST. HERBERT'S ISLAND,
DERWENT-WATER

[Composed 1800.—Published 1800.]

IF thou in the dear love of some one
   Friend
Hast been so happy that thou know'st
   what thoughts
Will sometimes in the happiness of love
Make the heart sink, then wilt thou
   reverence
This quiet spot; and, Stranger! not un-
   moved   5
Wilt thou behold this shapeless heap of
   stones,
The desolate ruins of St. Herbert's Cell.
Here stood his threshold; here was spread
   the roof
That sheltered him, a self-secluded Man,
After long exercise in social cares   10
And offices humane, intent to adore
The Deity, with undistracted mind,
And meditate on everlasting things,
In utter solitude.—But he had left
A Fellow-labourer, whom the good Man
   loved   15
As his own soul. And, when with eye
   upraised
To heaven he knelt before the crucifix,
While o'er the lake the cataract of
   Lodore
Pealed to his orisons, and when he paced
Along the beach of this small isle and
   thought   20
Of his Companion, he would pray that
   both
(Now that their earthly duties were
   fulfilled)
Might die in the same moment. Nor in
   vain
So prayed he:—as our chronicles report,
Though here the Hermit numbered his
   last day   25
Far from St. Cuthbert his belovèd Friend,
Those holy Men both died in the same
   hour.

XVI

ON THE BANKS OF A ROCKY STREAM
[Composed (?).—Published 1850.]

BEHOLD an emblem of our human mind
Crowded with thoughts that need a settled
   home,
Yet, like to eddying balls of foam
Within this whirlpool, they each other
   chase
Round and round, and neither find   5
An outlet nor a resting-place!
Stranger, if such disquietude be thine,
Fall on thy knees and sue for help divine.

SELECTIONS FROM CHAUCER

MODERNISED

I

THE PRIORESS' TALE

'Call up him who left half told
The story of Cambuscan bold.'

In the following Poem no further deviation from the original has been made than was necessary for
the fluent reading and instant understanding of the Author: so much, however, is the language
altered since Chaucer's time, especially in pronunciation, that much was to be removed, and its
place supplied with as little incongruity as possible. The ancient accent has been retained in a few
conjunctions, as *alsò* and *alwày*, from a conviction that such sprinklings of antiquity would be
admitted, by persons of taste, to have a graceful accordance with the subject. The fierce bigotry of
the Prioress forms a fine background for her tender-hearted sympathies with the Mother and Child;
and the mode in which the story is told amply atones for the extravagance of the miracle.

[Written 1801.—Published 1820.]

I

'O LORD, our Lord! how wondrously,'
   (quoth she)
'Thy name in this large world is spread
   abroad!
For not alone by men of dignity
Thy worship is performed and precious
   laud;
But by the mouths of children, gracious
   God!   5
Thy goodness is set forth; they when they
   lie
Upon the breast Thy name do glorify.

II

'Wherefore in praise, the worthiest that
   I may,
Jesu! of Thee, and the white Lily-flower
Which did Thee bear, and is a Maid for
   aye,   10

432

To tell a story I will use my power;
Not that I may increase her honour's dower,
For she herself is honour, and the root
Of goodness, next her Son, our soul's best boot.

III

'O Mother Maid! O Maid and Mother free!   15
O bush unburnt! burning in Moses' sight!
That down didst ravish from the Deity,
Through humbleness, the Spirit that did alight
Upon thy heart, whence, through that glory's might,
Conceivèd was the Father's sapience,   20
Help me to tell it in thy reverence!

IV

'Lady! thy goodness, thy magnificence,
Thy virtue, and thy great humility,
Surpass all science and all utterance;
For sometimes, Lady! ere men pray to thee   25
Thou goest before in thy benignity,
The light to us vouchsafing of thy prayer,
To be our guide unto thy Son so dear.

V

'My knowledge is so weak, O blissful Queen!
To tell abroad thy mighty worthiness,   30
That I the weight of it may not sustain;
But as a child of twelvemonths old or less,
That laboureth his language to express,
Even so fare I; and therefore, I thee pray,
Guide thou my song which I of thee shall say.   35

VI

'There was in Asia, in a mighty town,
'Mong Christian folk, a street where Jews might be,
Assigned to them and given them for their own
By a great Lord, for gain and usury,
Hateful to Christ and to His company;
And through this street who list might ride and wend;   41
Free was it, and unbarred at either end.

VII

'A little school of Christian people stood
Down at the farther end, in which there were
A nest of children come of Christian blood,   45
That learnèd in that school from year to year
Such sort of doctrine as men usèd there,
That is to say, to sing and read alsò,
As little children in their childhood do.

VIII

'Among these children was a Widow's son,   50
A little scholar,[1] scarcely seven years old,
Who day by day unto this school hath gone,
And eke, when he the image did behold
Of Jesu's Mother, as he had been told,
This Child was wont to kneel adown and say   55
Ave Marie, as he goeth by the way.

IX

'This Widow thus her little Son hath taught
Our blissful Lady, Jesu's Mother dear,
To worship aye, and he forgat it not;
For simple[2] infant hath a ready ear.   60
Sweet is the holiness of youth: and hence,
Calling to mind this matter when I may,
Saint Nicholas in my presence standeth aye,
For he so young to Christ did reverence.

X

'This little Child, while in the school he sate   65
His Primer conning with an earnest cheer,
The whilst the rest their anthem-book repeat
The Alma Redemptoris did he hear;
And as he durst he drew him near and near,
And hearkened to the words and to the note,   70
Till the first verse he learned it all by rote.

XI

'This Latin knew he nothing what it said,
For he too tender was of age to know;
But to his comrade he repaired, and prayed
That he the meaning of this song would show,   75
And unto him declare why men sing so;
This oftentimes, that he might be at ease,
This child did him beseech on his bare knees.

XII

'His Schoolfellow, who elder was than he,
Answered him thus:—"This song, I have heard say,   80
Was fashioned for our blissful Lady free;
Her to salute, and also her to pray
To be our help upon our dying day:
If there is more in this, I know it not;
Song do I learn,—small grammar I have got."   85

---

[1] *Clergeon* (Chaucer); i.e. chorister.—ED.
[2] *Sely* (Chaucer); i.e. happy. Line 61 was interpolated by Wordsworth.—ED.

XIII

'"And is this song fashioned in reverence
Of Jesu's Mother?" said this Innocent;
"Now, certès, I will use my diligence
To con it all ere Christmas-tide be spent;
Although I for my Primer shall be shent,
And shall be beaten three times in an
hour,   91
Our Lady I will praise with all my power."

XIV

'His Schoolfellow, whom he had so be-
sought,
As they went homeward taught him
privily
And then he sang it well and fearlessly,
From word to word according to the
note: 96
Twice in a day it passèd through his
throat;
Homeward and schoolward whensoe'er he
went,
On Jesu's Mother fixed was his intent.

XV

'Through all the Jewry (this before
said I)   100
This little Child, as he came to and fro,
Full merrily then would he sing and cry,
O *Alma Redemptoris!* high and low:
The sweetness of Christ's Mother piercèd
so
His heart, that her to praise, to her to
pray,   105
He cannot stop his singing by the way.

XVI

'The Serpent, Satan, our first foe, that
hath
His wasp's nest in Jew's heart, upswelled
—"O woe,
O Hebrew people!" said he in his wrath,
"Is it an honest thing? Shall this be so?
That such a Boy where'er he lists shall go
In your despite, and sing his hymns and
saws,
Which is against the reverence of our
laws!"

XVII

'From that day forward have the Jews
conspired   114
Out of the world this Innocent to chase;
And to this end a Homicide they hired,
That in an alley had a privy place,
And, as the Child 'gan to the school to
pace,
This cruel Jew him seized, and held him
fast
And cut his throat, and in a pit him
cast.   120

XVIII

'I say that him into a pit they threw,
A loathsome pit, whence noisome scents
exhale;
O cursèd folk! away, ye Herods new!
What may your ill intentions you avail?
Murder will out; certès it will not fail;
Know, that the honour of high God may
spread,   126
The blood cries out on your accursèd deed.

XIX

'O Martyr 'stablished in virginity!
Now may'st thou sing for aye before the
throne,
Following the Lamb celestial,' quoth
she,   130
'Of which the great Evangelist, Saint
John,
In Patmos wrote, who saith of them that
go
Before the Lamb singing continually,
That never fleshly woman they did know.

XX

'Now this poor Widow waiteth all that
night   135
After her little Child, and he came not;
For which, by earliest glimpse of morning
light,
With face all pale with dread and busy
thought,
She at the School and elsewhere him hath
sought,
Until thus far she learned, that he had
been   140
In the Jews' street, and there he last was
seen.

XXI

'With Mother's pity in her breast en-
closed
She goeth, as she were half out of her
mind,
To every place wherein she hath supposed
By likelihood her little Son to find;   145
And ever on Christ's Mother meek and
kind
She cried, till to the Jewry she was
brought,
And him among the accursèd Jews she
sought.

XXII

'She asketh, and she piteously doth pray
To every Jew that dwelleth in that place
To tell her if her child had passed that
way;   151
They all said—Nay; but Jesu of His grace
Gave to her thought, that in a little space
She for her Son in that same spot did cry
Where he was cast into a pit hard by.   155

XXIII

'O Thou great God that dost perform
Thy laud
By mouths of Innocents, lo! here Thy
might;
This gem of chastity, this emerald,
And eke of martyrdom this ruby bright,
There, where with mangled throat he lay
upright,   160
The *Alma Redemptoris* 'gan to sing
So loud, that with his voice the place did
ring.

XXIV

'The Christian folk that through the
Jewry went
Come to the spot in wonder at the thing;
And hastily they for the Provost sent;
Immediately he came, not tarrying,   166
And praiseth Christ that is our heavenly
King,
And eke His Mother, honour of Mankind:
Which done, he bade that they the Jews
should bind.

XXV

'This Child with piteous lamentation
then   170
Was taken up, singing his song alwày;
And with procession great and pomp of
men
To the next Abbey him they bare away;
His Mother swooning by the body lay:
And scarcely could the people that were
near   175
Remove this second Rachel from the
bier.

XXVI

'Torment and shameful death to every
one
This Provost doth for those bad Jews
prepare
That of this murder wist, and that anon:
Such wickedness his judgments cannot
spare;   180
Who will do evil, evil shall he bear;
Them therefore with wild horses did he
draw,
And after that he hung them by the law.

XXVII

'Upon his bier this Innocent doth lie
Before the altar while the Mass doth
last: 185
The Abbot with his convent's company
Then sped themselves to bury him full
fast;
And, when they holy water on him cast,
Yet spake this Child when sprinkled was
the water;   189
And sang, O *Alma Redemptoris Mater!*

XXVIII

'This Abbot, for he was a holy man,
As all Monks are, or surely ought to be,
In supplication to the Child began
Thus saying, "O dear Child! I summon
thee
In virtue of the holy Trinity   195
Tell me the cause why thou dost sing this
hymn,
Since that thy throat is cut, as it doth
seem."

XXIX

'"My throat is cut unto the bone, I
trow,"
Said this young Child, "and by the law of
kind
I should have died, yea many hours ago;
But Jesus Christ, as in the books ye
find,   201
Will that His glory last, and be in mind;
And, for the worship of His Mother dear,
Yet may I sing, O *Alma!* loud and clear.

XXX

'"This well of mercy, Jesu's Mother
sweet,   205
After my knowledge I have loved alwày;
And in the hour when I my death did
meet
To me she came, and thus to me did
say,
'Thou in thy dying sing this holy lay,'
As ye have heard; and soon as I had
sung   210
Methought she laid a grain upon my
tongue.

XXXI

'"Wherefore I sing, nor can from song
refrain,
In honour of that blissful Maiden free,
Till from my tongue off-taken is the grain;
And after that thus said she unto me;   215
'My little Child, then will I come for
thee
Soon as the grain from off thy tongue they
take;
Be not dismayed, I will not thee forsake!'"

XXXII

'This holy Monk, this Abbot—him
mean I,
Touched then his tongue, and took away
the grain;   220
And he gave up the ghost full peacefully;
And, when the Abbot had this wonder
seen,
His salt tears trickled down like showers
of rain;
And on his face he dropped upon the
ground,
And still he lay as if he had been bound.

XXXIII

'Eke the whole Convent on the pavement lay,   226
Weeping and praising Jesu's Mother dear;
And after that they rose, and took their way,
And lifted up this Martyr from the bier,
And in a tomb of precious marble clear
Enclosed his uncorrupted body sweet.[1]—
Where'er he be, God grant us him to meet!

XXXIV

'Young Hew of Lincoln! in like sort laid low
By cursèd Jews—thing well and widely known,
For it was done a little while ago—   235
Pray also thou for us, while here we tarry
Weak sinful folk, that God, with pitying eye,
In mercy would His mercy multiply
On us, for reverence of His Mother Mary!'

II

THE CUCKOO AND THE NIGHTINGALE

[Written 1801.—Published 1841 (R. H. Horne's *The Poems of Geoffrey Chaucer, Modernised*); vol. of 1842.]

I

THE God of Love—*ah, benedicite!*
How mighty and how great a Lord is he!
For he of low hearts can make high, of high
He can make low, and unto death bring nigh;
And hard hearts he can make them kind and free.   5

II

Within a little time, as hath been found,
He can make sick folk whole and fresh and sound;
Them who are whole in body and in mind,
He can make sick,—bind can he and unbind
All that he will have bound, or have unbound.   10

III

To tell his might my wit may not suffice;
Foolish men he can make them out of wise;—
For he may do all that he will devise;
Loose livers he can make abate their vice,
And proud hearts can make tremble in a trice.   15

[1] *Enclosèd they his little body sweet* (Chaucer). —ED.

IV

In brief, the whole of what he will, he may;
Against him dare not any wight say nay;
To humble or afflict whome'er he will,
To gladden or to grieve, he hath like skill;
But most his might he sheds on the eve of May.   20

V

For every true heart, gentle heart and free,
That with him is, or thinketh so to be,
Now against May shall have some stirring—whether
To joy, or be it to some mourning; never
At other time, methinks, in like degree.

VI

For now when they may hear the small birds' song,   26
And see the budding leaves the branches throng,
This unto their remembrance doth bring
All kinds of pleasure mix'd with sorrowing;
And longing of sweet thoughts that ever long.   30

VII

And of that longing heaviness doth come,
Whence oft great sickness grows of heart and home;
Sick are they all for lack of their desire;
And thus in May their hearts are set on fire,
So that they burn forth in great martyrdom.   35

VIII

In sooth, I speak from feeling, what though now
Old am I, and to genial pleasure slow;
Yet have I felt of sickness through the May,
Both hot and cold, and heart-aches every day,—
How hard, alas! to bear, I only know.   40

IX

Such shaking doth the fever in me keep
Through all this May that I have little sleep;
And also 'tis not likely unto me,
That any living heart should sleepy be
In which Love's dart its fiery point doth steep.   45

X

But tossing lately on a sleepless bed,
I of a token thought which Lovers heed;
How among them it was a common tale,
That it was good to hear the Nightingale,
Ere the vile Cuckoo's note be utterèd.   50

XI

And then I thought anon as it was day,
I gladly would go somewhere to essay
If I perchance a Nightingale might hear,
For yet had I heard none, of all that year,
And it was then the third night of the
    May.   55

XII

And soon as I a glimpse of day espied,
No longer would I in my bed abide,
But straight way to a wood that was hard
    by,
Forth did I go, alone and fearlessly,
And held the pathway down by a brook-
    side;   60

XIII

Till to a lawn I came all white and green,
I in so fair a one had never been.
The ground was green, with daisy
    powdered over;
Tall were the flowers, the grove a lofty
    cover,[1]
All green and white; and nothing else was
    seen.   65

XIV

There sate I down among the fair fresh
    flowers,
And saw the birds come tripping from
    their bowers,
Where they had rested them all night;
    and they,
Who were so joyful at the light of day,
Began to honour May with all their
    powers.   70

XV

Well did they know that service all by
    rote,
And there was many and many a lovely
    note,
Some, singing loud, as if they had com-
    plained;
Some with their notes another manner
    feigned;
And some did sing all out with the full
    throat.   75

XVI

They pruned themselves, and made them-
    selves right gay,
Dancing and leaping light upon the spray;
And ever two and two together were,
The same as they had chosen for the year,
Upon Saint Valentine's returning day.   80

XVII

Meanwhile the stream, whose bank I sate
    upon,
Was making such a noise as it ran on
Accordant to the sweet Birds' harmony;
Methought that it was the best melody
Which ever to man's ear a passage won.

[1] *The flowers and the grass alike all high* (Chaucer);
i.e. grass and daisies being of equal height.—ED.

XVIII

And for delight, but how I never wot,   86
I in a slumber and a swoon was caught,
Not all asleep and yet not waking wholly;
And as I lay, the Cuckoo, bird unholy,
Broke silence, or I heard him in my
    thought.   90

XIX

And that was right upon a tree fast by,
And who was then ill satisfied but I?
Now, God, quoth I, that died upon the
    rood,
From thee and thy base throat, keep all
    that's good,
Full little joy have I now of thy cry.   95

XX

And, as I with the Cuckoo thus 'gan chide,
In the next bush that was me fast beside,
I heard the lusty Nightingale so sing,
That her clear voice made a loud rioting,
Echoing thorough all the green wood
    wide.   100

XXI

Ah! good sweet Nightingale! for my
    heart's cheer,
Hence hast thou stayed a little while too
    long;
For we have had the sorry Cuckoo here,
And she hath been before thee with her
    song;
Evil light on her! she hath done me
    wrong.   105

XXII

But hear you now a wondrous thing, I
    pray;
As long as in that swooning-fit I lay,
Methought I wist right well what these
    birds meant,
And had good knowing both of their
    intent,
And of their speech, and all that they
    would say.   110

XXIII

The Nightingale thus in my hearing
    spake:—
Good Cuckoo, seek some other bush or
    brake,
And, prithee, let us that can sing dwell
    here;
For every wight eschews thy song to hear,
Such uncouth singing verily dost thou
    make.   115

XXIV

What! quoth she then, what is 't that ails
    thee now?
It seems to me I sing as well as thou;
For mine 's a song that is both true and
    plain,—
Although I cannot quaver so in vain
As thou dost in thy throat, I wot not
    how.   120

CHAUCER MODERNISED

XXV

All men may understanding have of me,
But, Nightingale, so may they not of thee;
For thou hast many a foolish and quaint
   cry:—
Thou say'st OSEE, OSEE, then how may I
Have knowledge, I thee pray, what this
   may be?   125

XXVI

Ah, fool! quoth she, wist thou not what
   it is?
Oft as I say OSEE, OSEE, I wis,
Then mean I, that I should be wonderous
   fain
That shamefully they one and all were
   slain,   129
Whoever against Love mean aught amiss.

XXVII

And also would I that they all were dead,
Who do not think in love their life to lead;
For who is loth the God of Love to obey,
Is only fit to die, I dare well say,
And for that cause OSEE I cry; take
   heed!   135

XXVIII

Ay, quoth the Cuckoo, that is a quaint
   law,
That all must love or die; but I withdraw,
And take my leave of all such company,
For mine intent it neither is to die,
Nor ever while I live Love's yoke to
   draw.   140

XXIX

For lovers, of all folk that be alive,
The most disquiet have and least do
   thrive;
Most feeling have of sorrow, woe and care,
And the least welfare cometh to their
   share;
What need is there against the truth to
   strive?   145

XXX

What! quoth she, thou art all out of thy
   mind,
That in thy churlishness a cause canst
   find
To speak of Love's true Servants in this
   mood;
For in this world no service is so good
To every wight that gentle is of kind. 150

XXXI

For thereof comes all goodness and all
   worth;
All gentless and honour thence come
   forth;
Thence worship comes, content and true
   heart's pleasure,
And full-assurèd trust, joy without
   measure,   154
And jollity, fresh cheerfulness, and mirth;

XXXII

And bounty, lowliness, and courtesy,
And seemliness, and faithful company,
And dread of shame that will not do amiss;
For he that faithfully Love's servant is,
Rather than be disgraced, would chuse
   to die.   160

XXXIII

And that the very truth it is which I
Now say—in such belief I'll live and die;
And Cuckoo, do thou so, by my advice.
Then, quoth she, let me never hope for
   bliss,
If with that counsel I do e'er comply. 165

XXXIV

Good Nightingale! thou speakest wondrous fair,
Yet for all that, the truth is found elsewhere;
For Love in young folk is but rage, I
   wis;
And Love in old folk a great dotage is;
Who most it useth, him 'twill most
   impair.   170

XXXV

For thereof come all contraries to glad-
   ness;
Thence sickness comes, and overwhelm-
   ing sadness,
Mistrust and jealousy, despite, debate,
Dishonour, shame, envy importunate,
Pride, anger, mischief, poverty, and mad-
   ness.   175

XXXVI

Loving is aye an office of despair,
And one thing is therein which is not
   fair;
For whoso gets of love a little bliss,
Unless it alway stay with him, I wis
He may full soon go with an old man's
   hair.   180

XXXVII

And, therefore, Nightingale! do thou
   keep nigh,
For trust me well, in spite of thy quaint
   cry,
If long time from thy mate thou be, or
   far,
Thou'lt be as others that forsaken are;
Then shalt thou raise a clamour as do I.

XXXVIII

Fie, quoth she, on thy name, Bird ill
   beseen!   186
The God of Love afflict thee with all
   teen,
For thou art worse than mad a thousand
   fold;
For many a one hath virtues manifold,
Who had been nought, if Love had never
   been.   190

438

XXXIX

For evermore his servants Love amendeth,
And he from every blemish them de-
fendeth;
And maketh them to burn, as in a fire,
In loyalty, and worshipful desire,
And, when it likes him, joy enough them
sendeth.   195

XL

Thou Nightingale! the Cuckoo said, be
still,
For Love no reason hath but his own
will;—
For to th' untrue he oft gives ease and joy;
True lovers doth so bitterly annoy,
He lets them perish through that grievous
ill.   200

XLI

With such a master would I never be;[1]
For he, in sooth, is blind, and may not
see,
And knows not when he hurts and when
he heals;
Within this court full seldom Truth
avails,
So diverse in his wilfulness is he.   205

XLII

Then of the Nightingale did I take note,
How from her inmost heart a sigh she
brought,
And said, Alas! that ever I was born,
Not one word have I now, I am so
forlorn,—
And with that word, she into tears burst
out.   210

XLIII

Alas, alas! my very heart will break,
Quoth she, to hear this churlish bird thus
speak
Of Love, and of his holy services;
Now, God of Love! thou help me in
some wise,
That vengeance on this Cuckoo I may
wreak.   215

XLIV

And so methought I started up anon,
And to the brook I ran and got a stone,
Which at the Cuckoo hardily I cast,
And he for dread did fly away full fast;
And glad, in sooth, was I when he was
gone.   220

XLV

And as he flew, the Cuckoo, ever and aye,
Kept crying, 'Farewell!—farewell, Pop-
injay!'
As if in scornful mockery of me;
And on I hunted him from tree to tree,
Till he was far, all out of sight, away.

[1] From a manuscript in the Bodleian, as are also
stanzas 44 and 45, which are necessary to complete
the sense.

XLVI

Then straightway came the Nightingale
to me,   226
And said, Forsooth, my friend, do I
thank thee,
That thou wert near to rescue me; and
now,
Unto the God of Love I make a vow,
That all this May I will thy songstress
be.   230

XLVII

Well satisfied, I thanked her, and she
said,
By this mishap no longer be dismayed,
Though thou the Cuckoo heard, ere thou
heard'st me;
Yet if I live it shall amended be,
When next May comes, if I am not
afraid.   235

XLVIII

And one thing will I counsel thee also,
The Cuckoo trust not thou, nor his Love's
saw;
All that she said is an outrageous lie.
Nay, nothing shall me bring thereto,
quoth I,
For Love, and it hath done me mighty
woe.   240

XLIX

Yea, hath it? use, quoth she, this
medicine;
This May-time, every day before thou dine,
Go look on the fresh daisy; then say I,
Although for pain thou may'st be like to
die,
Thou wilt be eased, and less wilt droop
and pine.   245

L

And mind always that thou be good and
true,
And I will sing one song, of many new,
For love of thee, as loud as I may cry;
And then did she begin this song full high,
'Beshrew all them that are in love un-
true.'   250

LI

And soon as she had sung it to the end,
Now farewell, quoth she, for I hence
must wend;
And, God of Love, that can right well
and may,
Send unto thee as mickle joy this day,
As ever he to Lover yet did send.   255

LII

Thus takes the Nightingale her leave of
me;
I pray to God with her always to be,
And joy of love to send her evermore;
And shield us from the Cuckoo and her
lore,
For there is not so false a bird as she.   260

LIII

Forth then she flew, the gentle Nightingale,
To all the Birds that lodged within that
dale,
And gathered each and all into one
place;
And them besought to hear her doleful
case,
And thus it was that she began her tale.

LIV

The Cuckoo—'tis not well that I should
hide   266
How she and I did each the other chide,
And without ceasing, since it was day-
light;
And now I pray you all to do me right
Of that false Bird whom Love can not
abide.   270

LV

Then spake one Bird, and full assent all
gave;
This matter asketh counsel good as grave,
For birds we are—all here together
brought;
And, in good sooth, the Cuckoo here is
not;   274
And therefore we a Parliament will have.

LVI

And thereat shall the Eagle be our Lord,
And other Peers whose names are on
record;
A summons to the Cuckoo shall be sent,
And judgment there be given; or that
intent
Failing, we finally shall make accord. 280

LVII

And all this shall be done, without a nay,
The morrow after Saint Valentine's day,
Under a maple that is well beseen,
Before the chamber-window of the Queen,
At Woodstock, on the meadow green and
gay.   285

LVIII

She thankèd them; and then her leave
she took,
And flew into a hawthorn by that brook;
And there she sate and sung—upon that
tree—
'For term of life Love shall have hold
of me'—
So loudly, that I with that song awoke.

Unlearned Book and rude, as well I
know,   291
For beauty thou hast none, nor elo-
quence,
Who did on thee the hardiness bestow
To appear before my Lady? but a sense
Thou surely hast of her benevolence, 295

Whereof her hourly bearing proof doth
give;
For of all good she is the best alive.

Alas, poor Book! for thy unworthiness,
To show to her some pleasant meanings
writ
In winning words, since through her
gentiless,   300
Thee she accepts as for her service fit!
Oh! it repents me I have neither wit
Nor leisure unto thee more worth to give;
For of all good she is the best alive.

Beseech her meekly with all lowliness, 305
Though I be far from her I reverence,
To think upon my truth and steadfastness,
And to abridge my sorrow's violence,
Caused by the wish, as knows your
sapience,
She of her liking proof to me would give;
For of all good she is the best alive. 311

L'ENVOY

Pleasure's Aurora, Day of gladsomeness!
Luna by night, with heavenly influence
Illumined! root of beauty and goodnesse,
Write, and allay by your beneficence 315
My sighs breathed forth in silence,—
comfort give!
Since of all good you are the best alive.

EXPLICIT

III

TROILUS AND CRESIDA

[Written 1801.—Same dates of publication as II.]

NEXT morning Troilus began to clear
His eyes from sleep, at the first break of
day,
And unto Pandarus, his own Brother dear,
For love of God, full piteously did say,
We must the Palace see of Cresida;   5
For since we yet may have no other feast,
Let us behold her Palace at the least!

And therewithal to cover his intent[1]
A cause he found into the Town to go,
And they right forth to Cresid's Palace
went;   10
But, Lord, this simple Troilus was woe,
Him thought his sorrowful heart would
break in two;
For when he saw her doors fast bolted all,
Well nigh for sorrow down he 'gan to fall.

Therewith when this true Lover 'gan
behold,   15
How shut was every window of the place,
Like frost he thought his heart was icy
cold;

---

[1] *His meiny for to blend* (Chaucer); i.e. to hood-
wink his followers.—ED.

For which, with changèd, pale, and
deadly face,
Without word uttered, forth he 'gan to
pace;
And on his purpose bent so fast to ride,
That no wight his continuance[1] espied. 21

Then said he thus,—O Palace desolate!
O house of houses, once so richly dight!
O Palace empty and disconsolate!
Thou lamp of which extinguished is the
light; 25
O Palace whilom day that now art night,
Thou ought'st to fall and I to die; since
she
Is gone who held us both in sovereignty.

O, of all houses once the crownèd boast!
Palace illumined with the sun of bliss; 30
O ring of which the ruby now is lost,
O cause of woe, that cause has been of
bliss:
Yet, since I may no better, would I kiss
Thy cold doors; but I dare not for this
rout;
Farewell, thou shrine of which the Saint
is out! 35

Therewith he cast on Pandarus an eye,
With changèd face, and piteous to behold;
And when he might his time aright espy,
Aye as he rode, to Pandarus he told
Both his new sorrow and his joys of old,
So piteously, and with so dead a hue, 41
That every wight might on his sorrow rue.

Forth from the spot he rideth up and
down,
And everything to his rememberànce
Came as he rode by places of the town
Where he had felt such perfect pleasure
once. 46
Lo, yonder saw I mine own Lady dance,
And in that Temple she with her bright
eyes,
My Lady dear, first bound me captive-
wise.

And yonder with joy-smitten heart have I
Heard my own Cresid's laugh; and once
at play 51
I yonder saw her eke full blissfully;
And yonder once she unto me 'gan say—
Now, my sweet Troilus, love me well, I
pray!
And there so graciously did me behold,
That hers unto the death my heart I
hold. 56

And at the corner of that self-same house
Heard I my most belovèd Lady dear,
So womanly, with voice melodious 59
Singing so well, so goodly, and so clear,
That in my soul methinks I yet do hear

The blissful sound; and in that very
place
My Lady first me took unto her grace.

O blissful God of Love! then thus he
cried,
When I the process have in memory, 65
How thou hast wearied me on every side,
Men thence a book might make, a history;
What need to seek a conquest over me,
Since I am wholly at thy will? what joy
Hast thou thy own liege subjects to de-
stroy? 70

Dread Lord! so fearful when provoked,
thine ire
Well hast thou wreaked on me by pain
and grief;
Now mercy, Lord! thou know'st well I
desire
Thy grace above all pleasures first and
chief;
And live and die I will in thy belief; 75
For which I ask for guerdon but one
boon,
That Cresida again thou send me soon.

Constrain her heart as quickly to return,
As thou dost mine with longing her to see,
Then know I well that she would not
sojourn. 80
Now, blissful Lord, so cruel do not be
Unto the blood of Troy, I pray of thee,
As Juno was unto the Theban blood,
From whence to Thebes came griefs in
multitude.

And after this he to the gate did go 85
Whence Cresid rode, as if in haste she
was;
And up and down there went, and to
and fro,
And to himself full oft he said, alas!
From hence my hope and solace forth
did pass.
O would the blissful God now for his joy,
I might her see again coming to Troy! 91

And up to yonder hill was I her guide;
Alas, and there I took of her my leave;
Yonder I saw her to her Father ride,
For very grief of which my heart shall
cleave;— 95
And hither home I came when it was eve;
And here I dwell an outcast from all joy,
And shall, unless I see her soon in Troy.

And of himself did he imagine oft,
That he was blighted, pale, and waxen less
Than he was wont; and that in whispers
soft 101
Men said, what may it be, can no one
guess
Why Troilus hath all this heaviness?
All which he of himself conceited wholly
Out of his weakness and his melancholy.

---

[1] *Countenance* (Chaucer).—ED.

Another time he took into his head, 106
That every wight, who in the way passed
   by,
Had of him ruth, and fancied that they
   said,
I am right sorry Troilus will die:
And thus a day or two drove wearily; 110
As ye have heard; such life 'gan he to
   lead
As one that standeth betwixt hope and
   dread.

For which it pleased him in his songs to
   show
The occasion of his woe, as best he might;
And made a fitting song, of words but
   few, 115
Somewhat his woeful heart to make more
   light;
And when he was removed from all men's
   sight,
With a soft voice, he of his Lady dear,
That absent was, 'gan sing as ye may hear.

O star, of which I lost have all the light,
With a sore heart well ought I to bewail,
That ever dark in torment, night by night,
Toward my death with wind I steer and
   sail;[1]
For which upon the tenth night if thou fail
With thy bright beams to guide me but
   one hour, 125
My ship and me Charybdis will devour.

As soon as he this song had thus sung
   through,
He fell again into his sorrows old;
And every night, as was his wont to do,
Troilus stood the bright moon to behold;
And all his trouble to the moon he told,
And said: I wis, when thou art horn'd
   anew,
I shall be glad if all the world be true.

Thy horns were old as now upon that
   morrow,
When hence did journey my bright Lady
   dear, 135
That cause is of my torment and my
   sorrow;

[1] *With wind in stern I sail* (Chaucer).—Ed.

For which, oh, gentle Luna, bright and
   clear,
For love of God, run fast above thy
   sphere;
For when thy horns begin once more to
   spring,
Then shall she come, that with her bliss
   may bring. 140

The day is more, and longer every night
Than they were wont to be—for he
   thought so;
And that the sun did take his course not
   right,
By longer way than he was wont to go;
And said, I am in constant dread I trow,
That Phäeton his son is yet alive, 146
His too fond father's car amiss to drive.

Upon the walls fast also would he walk,
To the end that he the Grecian host might
   see; 149
And ever thus he to himself would talk:—
Lo! yonder is my own bright Lady free;
Or yonder is it that the tents must be;
And thence does come this air which is so
   sweet,
That in my soul I feel the joy of it.

And certainly this wind, that more and
   more 155
By moments thus increaseth in my
   face,
Is of my Lady's sighs heavy and sore;
I prove it thus; for in no other space
Of all this town, save only in this place,
Feel I a wind, that soundeth so like
   pain; 160
It saith, Alas, why severed are we twain?

A weary while in pain he tosseth thus,
Till fully passed and gone was the ninth
   night;
And ever at his side stood Pandarus,
Who busily made use of all his might 165
To comfort him, and make his heart more
   light;
Giving him always hope, that she the
   morrow
Of the tenth day will come, and end his
   sorrow.

POEMS REFERRING TO THE PERIOD OF OLD AGE

I

THE OLD CUMBERLAND BEGGAR

The class of Beggars, to which the Old Man here described belongs, will probably soon be extinct. It consisted of poor, and, mostly, old and infirm persons, who confined themselves to a stated round in their neighbourhood, and had certain fixed days, on which, at different houses, they regularly received alms, sometimes in money, but mostly in provisions.

[Composed 1797.—Published 1800.]

I saw an aged Beggar in my walk;
And he was seated, by the highway side,
On a low structure of rude masonry
Built at the foot of a huge hill, that they
Who lead their horses down the steep rough road   5
May thence remount at ease. The aged Man
Had placed his staff across the broad smooth stone
That overlays the pile; and, from a bag
All white with flour, the dole of village dames,
He drew his scraps and fragments, one by one;   10
And scanned them with a fixed and serious look
Of idle computation. In the sun,
Upon the second step of that small pile,
Surrounded by those wild unpeopled hills,
He sat, and ate his food in solitude: 15
And ever, scattered from his palsied hand,
That, still attempting to prevent the waste,
Was baffled still, the crumbs in little showers
Fell on the ground; and the small mountain birds,
Not venturing yet to peck their destined meal,   20
Approached within the length of half his staff.

Him from my childhood have I known; and then
He was so old, he seems not older now;
He travels on, a solitary Man,
So helpless in appearance, that for him
The sauntering Horseman throws not with a slack   26
And careless hand his alms upon the ground,
But stops,—that he may safely lodge the coin
Within the old Man's hat; nor quits him so,
But still, when he has given his horse the rein,   30
Watches the aged Beggar with a look
Sidelong, and half-reverted. She who tends
The toll-gate, when in summer at her door
She turns her wheel, if on the road she sees
The aged Beggar coming, quits her work,
And lifts the latch for him that he may pass.   36
The post-boy, when his rattling wheels o'ertake
The aged Beggar in the woody lane,
Shouts to him from behind; and, if thus warned
The old man does not change his course, the boy   40
Turns with less noisy wheels to the road-side,
And passes gently by, without a curse
Upon his lips or anger at his heart.

He travels on, a solitary Man;
His age has no companion. On the ground   45
His eyes are turned, and, as he moves along,
They move along the ground; and, ever-more,
Instead of common and habitual sight
Of fields with rural works, of hill and dale,
And the blue sky, one little span of earth
Is all his prospect. Thus, from day to day,   51
Bow-bent, his eyes for ever on the ground,
He plies his weary journey; seeing still,
And seldom knowing that he sees, some straw,
Some scattered leaf, or marks which, in one track,   55
The nails of cart or chariot-wheel have left
Impressed on the white road,—in the same line,
At distance still the same. Poor Traveller!
His staff trails with him; scarcely do his feet
Disturb the summer dust; he is so still   60
In look and motion, that the cottage curs,
Ere he has passed the door, will turn away,
Weary of barking at him. Boys and girls,
The vacant and the busy, maids and youths,

And urchins newly breeched—all pass
him by: 65
Him even the slow-paced waggon leaves
behind.

But deem not this Man useless.—States-
men! ye
Who are so restless in your wisdom, ye
Who have a broom still ready in your
hands
To rid the world of nuisances; ye proud,
Heart-swoln, while in your pride ye con-
template   71
Your talents, power, or wisdom, deem
him not
A burthen of the earth! 'Tis Nature's law
That none, the meanest of created things,
Of forms created the most vile and
brute,   75
The dullest or most noxious, should exist
Divorced from good—a spirit and pulse
of good,
A life and soul, to every mode of being
Inseparably linked. Then be assured
That least of all can aught—that ever
owned   80
The heaven-regarding eye and front sub-
lime
Which man is born to—sink, howe'er
depressed,
So low as to be scorned without a sin;
Without offence to God cast out of view;
Like the dry remnant of a garden-flower
Whose seeds are shed, or as an imple-
ment   86
Worn out and worthless. While from
door to door,
This old Man creeps, the villagers in him
Behold a record which together binds
Past deeds and offices of charity,   90
Else unremembered, and so keeps alive
The kindly mood in hearts which lapse of
years,
And that half-wisdom half-experience
gives,
Make slow to feel, and by sure steps
resign
To selfishness and cold oblivious cares.
Among the farms and solitary huts,   96
Hamlets and thinly-scattered villages,
Where'er the aged Beggar takes his
rounds,
The mild necessity of use compels
To acts of love; and habit does the work
Of reason; yet prepares that after-joy
Which reason cherishes. And thus the
soul,   102
By that sweet taste of pleasure unpursued,
Doth find herself insensibly disposed
To virtue and true goodness.
                                Some there are,
By their good works exalted, lofty minds,
And meditative, authors of delight
And happiness, which to the end of time

Will live, and spread, and kindle: even
such minds   109
In childhood, from this solitary Being,
Or from like wanderer, haply have re-
ceived
(A thing more precious far than all that
books
Or the solicitudes of love can do!)
That first mild touch of sympathy and
thought,
In which they found their kindred with
a world   115
Where want and sorrow were. The easy
man
Who sits at his own door,—and, like the
pear
That overhangs his head from the green
wall,
Feeds in the sunshine; the robust and
young,
The prosperous and unthinking, they who
live   120
Sheltered, and flourish in a little grove
Of their own kindred;—all behold in
him
A silent monitor, which on their minds
Must needs impress a transitory thought
Of self-congratulation, to the heart   125
Of each recalling his peculiar boons,
His charters and exemptions; and, per-
chance,
Though he to no one give the fortitude
And circumspection needful to preserve
His present blessings, and to husband up
The respite of the season, he, at least, 131
And 'tis no vulgar service, makes them
felt.

Yet further.——Many, I believe, there
are
Who live a life of virtuous decency,
Men who can hear the Decalogue and
feel   135
No self-reproach; who of the moral law
Established in the land where they abide
Are strict observers; and not negligent
In acts of love to those with whom they
dwell,
Their kindred, and the children of their
blood.   140
Praise be to such, and to their slumbers
peace!
—But of the poor man ask, the abject
poor;
Go, and demand of him, if there be here
In this cold abstinence from evil deeds,
And these inevitable charities,   145
Wherewith to satisfy the human soul?
No—man is dear to man; the poorest poor
Long for some moments in a weary life
When they can know and feel that they
have been,
Themselves, the fathers and the dealers-
out   150

Of some small blessings; have been kind to such
As needed kindness, for this single cause,
That we have all of us one human heart.
—Such pleasure is to one kind Being known,
My neighbour, when with punctual care, each week,   155
Duly as Friday comes, though pressed herself
By her own wants, she from her store of meal
Takes one unsparing handful for the scrip
Of this old Mendicant, and, from her door
Returning with exhilarated heart,   160
Sits by her fire, and builds her hope in heaven.

Then let him pass, a blessing on his head!
And while in that vast solitude to which
The tide of things has borne him, he appears   164
To breathe and live but for himself alone,
Unblamed, uninjured, let him bear about
The good which the benignant law of Heaven
Has hung around him: and, while life is his,
Still let him prompt the unlettered villagers
To tender offices and pensive thoughts.
—Then let him pass, a blessing on his head!   171
And, long as he can wander, let him breathe
The freshness of the valleys; let his blood
Struggle with frosty air and winter snows;
And let the chartered wind that sweeps the heath   175
Beat his grey locks against his withered face.
Reverence the hope whose vital anxiousness
Gives the last human interest to his heart.
May never House, misnamed of Industry,
Make him a captive!—for that pent-up din,   180
Those life-consuming sounds that clog the air,
Be his the natural silence of old age!
Let him be free of mountain solitudes;
And have around him, whether heard or not,
The pleasant melody of woodland birds.
Few are his pleasures: if his eyes have now   186
Been doomed so long to settle upon earth
That not without some effort they behold
The countenance of the horizontal sun,
Rising or setting, let the light at least
Find a free entrance to their languid orbs,   191

And let him, *where* and *when* he will, sit down
Beneath the trees, or on a grassy bank
Of highway side, and with the little birds
Share his chance-gathered meal; and, finally,   195
As in the eye of Nature he has lived,
So in the eye of Nature let him die!

II

THE FARMER OF TILSBURY VALE

[Composed 1800.—Published July 21, 1800 (*Morning Post*); ed. 1815.]

'Tis not for the unfeeling, the falsely refined,
The squeamish in taste, and the narrow of mind,
And the small critic wielding his delicate pen,
That I sing of old Adam, the pride of old men.

He dwells in the centre of London's wide Town;   5
His staff is a sceptre—his grey hairs a crown;
And his bright eyes look brighter, set off
by the streak
Of the unfaded rose that still blooms on his cheek.

'Mid the dews, in the sunshine of morn,—
'mid the joy
Of the fields, he collected that bloom, when a boy;   10
That countenance there fashioned, which, spite of a stain
That his life hath received, to the last will remain.

A Farmer he was; and his house far and near
Was the boast of the country for excellent cheer:
How oft have I heard in sweet Tilsbury Vale   15
Of the silver-rimmed horn whence he dealt his mild ale!

Yet Adam was far as the farthest from ruin,
His fields seemed to know what their Master was doing;
And turnips, and corn-land, and meadow, and lea,
All caught the infection—as generous as he.   20

Yet Adam prized little the feast and the bowl,—
The fields better suited the ease of his soul:
He strayed through the fields like an indolent wight,
The quiet of nature was Adam's delight.

For Adam was simple in thought; and
the poor,   25
Familiar with him, made an inn of his
door:
He gave them the best that he had; or,
to say
What less may mislead you, they took it
away.

Thus thirty smooth years did he thrive
on his farm:
The Genius of plenty preserved him from
harm: 30
At length, what to most is a season of
sorrow,
His means are run out,—he must beg, or
must borrow.

To the neighbours he went,—all were free
with their money;
For his hive had so long been replenished
with honey,
That they dreamt not of dearth;—He
continued his rounds,   35
Knocked here—and knocked there,
pounds still adding to pounds.

He paid what he could with his ill-gotten
pelf,
And something, it might be, reserved for
himself:
Then (what is too true) without hinting a
word,
Turned his back on the country—and off
like a bird.   40

You lift up your eyes!—but I guess that
you frame
A judgment too harsh of the sin and the
shame;
In him it was scarcely a business of art,
For this he did all in the *ease* of his
heart.

To London—a sad emigration I ween—
With his grey hairs he went from the
brook and the green;   46
And there, with small wealth but his legs
and his hands,
As lonely he stood as a crow on the sands.

All trades, as need was, did old Adam
assume,—
Served as stable-boy, errand-boy, porter,
and groom;   50
But nature is gracious, necessity kind,
And, in spite of the shame that may lurk
in his mind,

He seems ten birthdays younger, is green
and is stout;
Twice as fast as before does his blood run
about;
You would say that each hair of his beard
was alive,   55
And his fingers as busy as bees in a hive.

For he's not like an Old Man that leisurely
goes
About work that he knows, in a track
that he knows;
But often his mind is compelled to demur,
And you guess that the more then his
body must stir.   60

In the throng of the town like a stranger
is he,
Like one whose own country's far over
the sea;
And Nature, while through the great city
he hies,
Full ten times a day takes his heart by
surprise.

This gives him the fancy of one that is
young,   65
More of soul in his face than of words on
his tongue;
Like a maiden of twenty he trembles and
sighs,
And tears of fifteen will come into his
eyes.

What's a tempest to him, or the dry
parching heats?
Yet he watches the clouds that pass over
the streets;   70
With a look of such earnestness often will
stand,
You might think he'd twelve reapers at
work in the Strand.

Where proud Covent-garden, in desolate
hours
Of snow and hoar-frost, spreads her fruits
and her flowers,
Old Adam will smile at the pains that
have made   75
Poor winter look fine in such strange
masquerade.

'Mid coaches and chariots, a waggon of
straw,
Like a magnet, the heart of old Adam
can draw;
With a thousand soft pictures his memory
will teem,
And his hearing is touched with the
sounds of a dream.   80

Up the Haymarket hill he oft whistles his
way,
Thrusts his hands in a waggon, and smells
at the hay;
He thinks of the fields he so often hath
mown,
And is happy as if the rich freight were
his own.

But chiefly to Smithfield he loves to
repair,—   85
If you pass by at morning, you'll meet
with him there.

The breath of the cows you may see him
 inhale,
And his heart all the while is in Tilsbury
 Vale.

Now farewell, old Adam! when low thou
 art laid,
May one blade of grass spring up over
 thy head;   90
And I hope that thy grave, wheresoever
 it be,
Will hear the wind sigh through the leaves
 of a tree.

III

THE SMALL CELANDINE

[Composed 1804.—Published 1807.]

THERE is a Flower, the lesser Celandine,
That shrinks, like many more, from cold
 and rain;
And, the first moment that the sun may
 shine,
Bright as the sun himself, 'tis out again!

When hailstones have been falling, swarm
 on swarm,   5
Or blasts the green field and the trees
 distrest,
Oft have I seen it muffled up from harm,
In close self-shelter, like a Thing at rest.

But lately, one rough day, this Flower I
 passed
And recognised it, though an altered
 form,   10
Now standing forth an offering to the
 blast,
And buffeted at will by rain and storm.

I stopped, and said with inly-muttered
 voice,
'It doth not love the shower, nor seek
 the cold:
This neither is its courage nor its choice,
But its necessity in being old.   16

'The sunshine may not cheer it, nor the
 dew;
It cannot help itself in its decay;
Stiff in its members, withered, changed
 of hue.'
And, in my spleen, I smiled that it was
 grey.   20

To be a Prodigal's Favourite—then, worse
 truth,
A Miser's Pensioner—behold our lot!
O Man, that from thy fair and shining
 youth
Age might but take the things Youth
 needed not!

IV

THE TWO THIEVES

OR

THE LAST STAGE OF AVARICE

[Composed 1800.—Published 1800.]

O NOW that the genius of Bewick were
 mine,
And the skill which he learned on the
 banks of the Tyne,
Then the Muses might deal with me just
 as they chose,
For I'd take my last leave both of verse
 and of prose.

What feats would I work with my magical
 hand!   5
Book-learning and books should be
 banished the land:
And, for hunger and thirst and such
 troublesome calls,
Every ale-house should then have a feast
 on its walls.

The traveller would hang his wet clothes
 on a chair;
Let them smoke, let them burn, not a
 straw would he care!   10
For the Prodigal Son, Joseph's Dream
 and his sheaves,
Oh, what would they be to my tale of two
 Thieves?

The One, yet unbreeched, is not three
 birthdays old,
His Grandsire that age more than thirty
 times told;
There are ninety good seasons of fair and
 foul weather   15
Between them, and both go a-pilfering
 together.

With chips is the carpenter strewing his
 floor?
Is a cart-load of turf at an old woman's
 door?
Old Daniel his hand to the treasure will
 slide!
And his Grandson's as busy at work by
 his side.   20

Old Daniel begins; he stops short—and
 his eye,
Through the lost look of dotage, is cunning and sly:
'Tis a look which at this time is hardly
 his own,
But tells a plain tale of the days that are
 flown.

He once had a heart which was moved by
 the wires   25
Of manifold pleasures and many desires:
And what if he cherished his purse?
 'Twas no more
Than treading a path trod by thousands
 before.

447

'Twas a path trod by thousands; but
Daniel is one
Who went something farther than others
have gone,   30
And now with old Daniel you see how it
fares;
You see to what end he has brought his
grey hairs.

The pair sally forth hand in hand: ere
the sun
Has peered o'er the beeches, their work is
begun:
And yet, into whatever sin they may
fall,   35
This child but half knows it, and that not
at all.

They hunt through the streets with
deliberate tread,
And each, in his turn, becomes leader or
led;
And, wherever they carry their plots and
their wiles,
Every face in the village is dimpled with
smiles.   40

Neither checked by the rich nor the needy
they roam;
For the grey-headed Sire has a daughter
at home,
Who will gladly repair all the damage
that's done;
And three, were it asked, would be
rendered for one.

Old Man! whom so oft I with pity have
eyed,   45
I love thee, and love the sweet Boy at thy
side:
Long yet may'st thou live! for a teacher
we see
That lifts up the veil of our nature in thee.

V

ANIMAL TRANQUILLITY AND DECAY

[Composed 1798 (? 1797).—Published 1798.]

THE little hedgerow birds,
That peck along the road, regard him
not.
He travels on, and in his face, his step,
His gait, is one expression: every limb,
His look and bending figure, all bespeak
A man who does not move with pain, but
moves   6
With thought.—He is insensibly subdued
To settled quiet: he is one by whom
All effort seems forgotten; one to whom
Long patience hath such mild composure
given,   10
That patience now doth seem a thing of
which
He hath no need. He is by nature led
To peace so perfect that the young behold
With envy, what the Old Man hardly
feels.

EPITAPHS AND ELEGIAC PIECES

EPITAPHS

TRANSLATED FROM CHIABRERA

I

[Composed (?).—Published 1837.]

WEEP not, belovèd Friends! nor let the
air
For me with sighs be troubled. Not from
life
Have I been taken; this is genuine life
And this alone—the life which now I live
In peace eternal; where desire and joy   5
Together move in fellowship without
end.—
Francesco Ceni willed that, after death,
His tombstone thus should speak for him.
And surely
Small cause there is for that fond wish of
ours
Long to continue in this world; a world
That keeps not faith, nor yet can point a
hope   11
To good, whereof itself is destitute.

II

[Composed 1809 or 1810.—Published February 22,
1810 (The Friend); ed. 1815.]

PERHAPS some needful service of the State
Drew TITUS from the depth of studious
bowers,
And doomed him to contend in faithless
courts,
Where gold determines between right and
wrong.
Yet did at length his loyalty of heart   5
And his pure native genius, lead him
back
To wait upon the bright and gracious
Muses,
Whom he had early loved. And not in
vain
Such course he held! Bologna's learnèd
schools
Were gladdened by the Sage's voice, and
hung   10
With fondness on those sweet Nestorian
strains.

There pleasure crowned his days; and all
 his thoughts
A roseate fragrance breathed.[1]—O human
 life,
That never art secure from dolorous
 change!
Behold a high injunction suddenly 15
To Arno's side hath brought him, and he
 charmed
A Tuscan audience: but full soon was
 called
To the perpetual silence of the grave.
Mourn, Italy, the loss of him who stood
A Champion steadfast and invincible, 20
To quell the rage of literary War!

III

[Composed 1809 or 1810.—Published February 22,
1810 (*The Friend*); ed. 1815.]

O THOU who movest onward with a mind
Intent upon thy way, pause, though in
 haste!
'Twill be no fruitless moment. I was
 born
Within Savona's walls, of gentle blood.
On Tiber's banks my youth was dedicate
To sacred studies; and the Roman Shep-
 herd 6
Gave to my charge Urbino's numerous
 flock.
Well did I watch, much laboured, nor
 had power
To escape from many and strange indig-
 nities;
Was smitten by the great ones of the
 world, 10
But did not fall; for Virtue braves all
 shocks,
Upon herself resting immovably.
Me did a kindlier fortune then invite
To serve the glorious Henry, King of
 France,
And in his hands I saw a high reward 15
Stretched out for my acceptance,—but
 Death came.
Now, Reader, learn from this my fate,
 how false,
How treacherous to her promise, is the
 world;
And trust in God—to whose eternal doom
Must bend the sceptred Potentates of
 earth. 20

IV

[Composed 1809.—Published December 28, 1809
(*The Friend*); ed. 1815.]

THERE never breathed a man who, when
 his life
Was closing, might not of that life relate
Toils long and hard.—The warrior will
 report

---

[1] Ivi vivea giocondo e i suoi pensieri
  Erano tutti rose.
 The Translator had not skill to come nearer to his
original.

Of wounds, and bright swords flashing in
 the field,
And blast of trumpets. He who hath
 been doomed 5
To bow his forehead in the courts of kings,
Will tell of fraud and never-ceasing hate,
Envy and heart-inquietude, derived
From intricate cabals of treacherous
 friends.
I, who on shipboard lived from earliest
 youth, 10
Could represent the countenance horrible
Of the vexed waters, and the indignant
 rage
Of Auster and Boötes. Fifty years
Over the well-steered galleys did I rule:—
From huge Pelorus to the Atlantic
 pillars, 15
Rises no mountain to mine eyes unknown;
And the broad gulfs I traversed oft and
 oft.
Of every cloud which in the heavens
 might stir
I knew the force; and hence the rough
 sea's pride
Availed not to my Vessel's overthrow. 20
What noble pomp and frequent have
 not I
On regal decks beheld! yet in the end
I learned that one poor moment can
 suffice
To equalize the lofty and the low.
We sail the sea of life—a *Calm* One
 finds, 25
And One a *Tempest*—and, the voyage o'er,
Death is the quiet haven of us all.
If more of my condition ye would know,
Savona was my birthplace, and I sprang
Of noble parents: seventy years and three
Lived I—then yielded to a slow disease.

V

[Composed (?).—Published 1837.]

TRUE is it that Ambrosio Salinero
With an untoward fate was long involved
In odious litigation; and full long,
Fate harder still! had he to endure as-
 saults
Of racking malady. And true it is 5
That not the less a frank courageous heart
And buoyant spirit triumphed over pain;
And he was strong to follow in the steps
Of the fair Muses. Not a covert path
Leads to the dear Parnassian forest's
 shade, 10
That might from him be hidden; not a
 track
Mounts to pellucid Hippocrene, but he
Had traced its windings.—This Savona
 knows,
Yet no sepulchral honours to her Son
She paid, for in our age the heart is ruled

EPITAPHS AND ELEGIAC PIECES

Only by gold. And now a simple stone
Inscribed with this memorial here is
raised   17
By his bereft, his lonely, Chiabrera.
Think not, O Passenger! who read'st the
lines
That an exceeding love hath dazzled me;
No—he was One whose memory ought to
spread   21
Where'er Permessus bears an honoured
name,
And live as long as its pure stream shall
flow.

VI

[Composed 1809.—Published December 28, 1809
(*The Friend*); ed. 1815.]

DESTINED to war from very infancy
Was I, Roberto Dati, and I took
In Malta the white symbol of the Cross:
Nor in life's vigorous season did I shun
Hazard or toil; among the sands was seen
Of Lybia; and not seldom, on the banks
Of wide Hungarian Danube, 'twas my lot
To hear the sanguinary trumpet sounded.
So lived I, and repined not at such fate:
This only grieves me, for it seems a
wrong,   10
That stripped of arms I to my end am
brought
On the soft down of my paternal home.
Yet haply Arno shall be spared all cause
To blush for me. Thou, loiter not nor halt
In thy appointed way, and bear in mind
How fleeting and how frail is human life!

VII

[Composed (?).—Published 1837.]

O FLOWER of all that springs from gentle
blood,
And all that generous nurture breeds to
make
Youth amiable; O friend so true of soul
To fair Aglaia; by what envy moved,
Lelius! has death cut short thy brilliant
day   5
In its sweet opening? and what dire
mishap
Has from Savona torn her best delight?
For thee she mourns, nor e'er will cease
to mourn;
And, should the out-pourings of her eyes
suffice not
For her heart's grief, she will entreat
Sebeto   10
Not to withhold his bounteous aid, Sebeto
Who saw thee, on his margin, yield to
death,
In the chaste arms of thy belovèd Love!
What profit riches? what does youth
avail?
Dust are our hopes;—I, weeping bitterly,

Penned these sad lines, nor can forbear
to pray   16
That every gentle Spirit hither led
May read them not without some bitter
tears.

VIII

[Composed 1809.—Published January 4, 1810
(*The Friend*); ed. 1815.]

NOT without heavy grief of heart did He
On whom the duty fell (for at that time
The father sojourned in a distant land)
Deposit in the hollow of this tomb
A brother's Child, most tenderly beloved!
FRANCESCO was the name the Youth had
borne,   6
POZZOBONNELLI his illustrious house;
And, when beneath this stone the Corse
was laid,
The eyes of all Savona streamed with tears.
Alas! the twentieth April of his life   10
Had scarcely flowered: and at this early
time,
By genuine virtue he inspired a hope
That greatly cheered his country: to his
kin
He promised comfort; and the flattering
thoughts
His friends had in their fondness enter-
tained,[1]   15
He suffered not to languish or decay.
Now is there not good reason to break
forth
Into a passionate lament?—O Soul!
Short while a Pilgrim in our nether world,
Do thou enjoy the calm empyreal air; 20
And round this earthly tomb let roses rise,
An everlasting spring! in memory
Of that delightful fragrance which was
once
From thy mild manners quietly exhaled.

IX

[Composed 1809.—Published January 4, 1810
(*The Friend*); ed. 1815.]

PAUSE, courteous Spirit!—Baldi suppli-
cates
That Thou, with no reluctant voice, for
him
Here laid in mortal darkness, wouldst
prefer
A prayer to the Redeemer of the world.
This to the dead by sacred right belongs;
All else is nothing.—Did occasion suit 6
To tell his worth, the marble of this tomb
Would ill suffice: for Plato's lore sublime,
And all the wisdom of the Stagyrite,
Enriched and beautified his studious
mind: 10

[1] In justice to the Author, I subjoin the original:
——— e degli amici
Non lasciava languire i bei pensieri.

450

With Archimedes also he conversed
As with a chosen friend; nor did he leave
Those laureat wreaths ungathered which
    the Nymphs
Twine near their loved Permessus.—
    Finally,
Himself above each lower thought up-
    lifting,   15
His ears he closed to listen to the songs
Which Sion's Kings did consecrate of old;
And his Permessus found on Lebanon.
A blessèd Man! who of protracted days
Made not, as thousands do, a vulgar
    sleep;   20
But truly did *He* live his life. Urbino,
Take pride in him!—O Passenger, fare-
    well!

I

[Composed (?).—Published 1835.]

By a blest Husband guided, Mary came
From nearest kindred, Vernon her new
    name;
She came, though meek of soul, in seemly
    pride
Of happiness and hope, a youthful Bride.
O dread reverse! if aught *be* so, which
    proves   5
That God will chasten whom he dearly
    loves.
Faith bore her up through pains in mercy
    given,
And troubles that were each a step to
    Heaven:
Two Babes were laid in earth before she
    died;
A third now slumbers at the Mother's
    side;   10
Its Sister-twin survives, whose smiles
    afford
A trembling solace to her widowed Lord.

Reader! if to thy bosom cling the pain
Of recent sorrow combated in vain;
Or if thy cherished grief have failed to
    thwart   15
Time still intent on his insidious part,
Lulling the mourner's best good thoughts
    asleep,
Pilfering regrets we would, but cannot,
    keep;
Bear with Him—judge *Him* gently who
    makes known
His bitter loss by this memorial Stone; 20
And pray that in his faithful breast the
    grace
Of resignation find a hallowed place.

II

[Composed 1812 (?).—Published 1837.]

Six months to six years added he re-
    mained
Upon this sinful earth, by sin unstained:

O blessèd Lord! whose mercy then re-
    moved
A Child whom every eye that looked on
    loved;
Support us, teach us calmly to resign
What we possessed, and now is wholly
    thine!

III

CENOTAPH

In affectionate remembrance of Frances Fermor,
whose remains are deposited in the church of
Claines, near Worcester, this stone is erected by
her sister, Dame Margaret, wife of Sir George
Beaumont, Bart., who, feeling not less than the
love of a brother for the deceased, commends
this memorial to the care of his heirs and successors in the possession of this place.

[Composed 1824.—Published 1842.]

By vain affections unenthralled,
Though resolute when duty called
To meet the world's broad eye,
Pure as the holiest cloistered nun
That ever feared the tempting sun,   5
Did Fermor live and die.
This Tablet, hallowed by her name,
One heart-relieving tear may claim;
But if the pensive gloom
Of fond regret be still thy choice,   10
Exalt thy spirit, hear the voice
Of Jesus from her tomb!
'I AM THE WAY, THE TRUTH, AND THE
    LIFE.'

IV

EPITAPH

IN THE CHAPEL-YARD OF LANGDALE,
WESTMORELAND

[Composed 1841.—Published: vol. of 1842.]

By playful smiles, (alas! too oft
A sad heart's sunshine) by a soft
And gentle nature, and a free
Yet modest hand of charity,
Through life was OWEN LLOYD endeared
To young and old; and how revered   6
Had been that pious spirit, a tide
Of humble mourners testified,
When, after pains dispensed to prove
The measure of God's chastening love,
Here, brought from far, his corse found
    rest,—   11
Fulfilment of his own request:—
Urged less for this Yew's shade, though he
Planted with such fond hope the tree;
Less for the love of stream and rock,   15
Dear as they were, than that his Flock,
When they no more their Pastor's voice
Could hear to guide them in their choice
Through good and evil, help might have,
Admonished, from his silent grave,   20
Of righteousness, of sins forgiven,
For peace on earth and bliss in heaven.

V

ADDRESS TO THE SCHOLARS OF THE VILLAGE SCHOLARS OF——

[Composed 1798.—Published: vol. of 1842.]

I COME, ye little noisy Crew,
Not long your pastime to prevent;
I heard the blessing which to you
Our common Friend and Father sent.
I kissed his cheek before he died;   5
And when his breath was fled,
I raised, while kneeling by his side,
His hand:—it dropped like lead.
Your hands, dear Little-ones, do all
That can be done, will never fall   10
Like his till they are dead.
By night or day, blow foul or fair,
Ne'er will the best of all your train
Play with the locks of his white hair,
Or stand between his knees again.   15

Here did he sit confined for hours;
But he could see the woods and plains,
Could hear the wind and mark the showers
Come streaming down the streaming panes.
Now stretched beneath his grass-green mound   20
He rests a prisoner of the ground.
He loved the breathing air,
He loved the sun, but if it rise
Or set, to him where now he lies,
Brings not a moment's care.   25
Alas! what idle words; but take
The Dirge which for our Master's sake
And yours, love prompted me to make.
The rhymes so homely in attire
With learnèd ears may ill agree,   30
But chanted by your Orphan Quire
Will make a touching melody.

DIRGE

Mourn, Shepherd, near thy old grey stone;
Thou Angler, by the silent flood;
And mourn when thou art all alone,   35
Thou Woodman, in the distant wood!

Thou one blind Sailor, rich in joy
Though blind, thy tunes in sadness hum;
And mourn, thou poor half-witted Boy!
Born deaf, and living deaf and dumb.   40

Thou drooping sick Man, bless the Guide
Who checked or turned thy headstrong youth,
As he before had sanctified
Thy infancy with heavenly truth.

Ye Striplings, light of heart and gay,   45
Bold settlers on some foreign shore,
Give, when your thoughts are turned this way,
A sigh to him whom we deplore.

For us who here in funeral strain
With one accord our voices raise,   50
Let sorrow overcharged with pain
Be lost in thankfulness and praise.

And when our hearts shall feel a sting
From ill we meet or good we miss,
May touches of his memory bring   55
Fond healing, like a mother's kiss.

BY THE SIDE OF THE GRAVE SOME YEARS AFTER

Long time his pulse hath ceased to beat;
But benefits, his gift, we trace—
Expressed in every eye we meet
Round this dear Vale, his native place.   60

To stately Hall and Cottage rude
Flowed from his life what still they hold,
Light pleasures, every day renewed;
And blessings half a century old.

Oh true of heart, of spirit gay,   65
Thy faults, where not already gone
From memory, prolong their stay
For charity's sweet sake alone.

Such solace find we for our loss;
And what beyond this thought we crave
Comes in the promise from the Cross,   71
Shining upon thy happy grave.[1]

VI

ELEGIAC STANZAS

SUGGESTED BY A PICTURE OF PEELE CASTLE, IN A STORM, PAINTED BY SIR GEORGE BEAUMONT

[Composed 1805.—Published 1807.]

I WAS thy neighbour once, thou rugged Pile!
Four summer weeks I dwelt in sight of thee:
I saw thee every day; and all the while
Thy Form was sleeping on a glassy sea.

So pure the sky, so quiet was the air!   5
So like, so very like, was day to day!
Whene'er I looked, thy Image still was there;
It trembled, but it never passed away.

How perfect was the calm! it seemed no sleep;
No mood, which season takes away, or brings: 10
I could have fancied that the mighty Deep
Was even the gentlest of all gentle Things.

Ah! then, if mine had been the Painter's hand,
To express what then I saw; and add the gleam,   14
The light that never was, on sea or land,
The consecration, and the Poet's dream;

[1] See upon the subject of the three foregoing pieces 'Matthew,' &c., &c., pp. 381, 382.

I would have planted thee, thou hoary
  Pile
Amid a world how different from this!
Beside a sea that could not cease to smile;
On tranquil land, beneath a sky of bliss.

Thou shouldst have seemed a treasure-
  house divine   21
Of peaceful years; a chronicle of
  heaven;—
Of all the sunbeams that did ever shine
The very sweetest had to thee been given.

A Picture had it been of lasting ease, 25
Elysian quiet, without toil or strife;
No motion but the moving tide, a breeze,
Or merely silent Nature's breathing life.

Such, in the fond illusion of my heart,
Such Picture would I at that time have
  made: 30
And seen the soul of truth in every part,
A steadfast peace that might not be
  betrayed.

So once it would have been,—'tis so no
  more;
I have submitted to a new control:
A power is gone, which nothing can
  restore;   35
A deep distress hath humanised my Soul.

Not for a moment could I now behold
A smiling sea, and be what I have been:
The feeling of my loss will ne'er be old;
This, which I know, I speak with mind
  serene.   40

Then, Beaumont, Friend! who would
  have been the Friend,
If he had lived, of Him whom I deplore,
This work of thine I blame not, but com-
  mend;
This sea in anger, and that dismal shore.

O 'tis a passionate Work!—yet wise and
  well,   45
Well chosen is the spirit that is here;
That Hulk which labours in the deadly
  swell,
This rueful sky, this pageantry of fear!

And this huge Castle, standing here
  sublime,
I love to see the look with which it
  braves,   50
Cased in the unfeeling armour of old
  time,
The lightning, the fierce wind, and trampling waves.

Farewell, farewell the heart that lives
  alone,
Housed in a dream, at distance from the
  Kind!
Such happiness, wherever it be known,
Is to be pitied; for 'tis surely blind. 56

But welcome fortitude, and patient cheer,
And frequent sights of what is to be
  borne!
Such sights, or worse, as are before me
  here.—
Not without hope we suffer and we
  mourn.   60

VII

TO THE DAISY

[Composed 1805.—Published 1815.]

SWEET Flower! belike one day to have
A place upon thy Poet's grave,
I welcome thee once more:
But He, who was on land, at sea,
My Brother, too, in loving thee,   5
Although he loved more silently,
Sleeps by his native shore.

Ah! hopeful, hopeful was the day
When to that Ship he bent his way,
To govern and to guide: 10
His wish was gained: a little time
Would bring him back in manhood's
  prime
And free for life, these hills to climb,
With all his wants supplied.

And full of hope day followed day 15
While that stout Ship at anchor lay
Beside the shores of Wight;
The May had then made all things green;
And, floating there, in pomp serene,
That Ship was goodly to be seen, 20
His pride and his delight!

Yet then, when called ashore, he sought
The tender peace of rural thought:
In more than happy mood
To your abodes, bright daisy Flowers! 25
He then would steal at leisure hours,
And loved you glittering in your bowers,
A starry multitude.

But hark the word!—the ship is gone;—
Returns from her long course:—anon 30
Sets sail:—in season due,
Once more on English earth they stand:
But, when a third time from the land
They parted, sorrow was at hand
For Him and for his crew.   35

Ill-fated Vessel!—ghastly shock!
—At length delivered from the rock,
The deep she hath regained;
And through the stormy night they steer;
Labouring for life, in hope and fear, 40
To reach a safer shore—how near,
Yet not to be attained!

'Silence!' the brave Commander cried;
To that calm word a shriek replied,
It was the last death-shriek.   45
—A few (my soul oft sees that sight)
Survive upon the tall mast's height;
But one dear remnant of the night—
For Him in vain I seek.

EPITAPHS AND ELEGIAC PIECES

Six weeks beneath the moving sea 50
He lay in slumber quietly;
Unforced by wind or wave
To quit the Ship for which he died,
(All claims of duty satisfied;)
And there they found him at her side; 55
And bore him to the grave.

Vain service! yet not vainly done
For this, if other end were none,
That He, who had been cast
Upon a way of life unmeet 60
For such a gentle Soul and sweet,
Should find an undisturbed retreat
Near what he loved, at last—

That neighbourhood of grove and field
To Him a resting-place should yield, 65
A meek man and a brave!
The birds shall sing and ocean make
A mournful murmur for *his* sake;
And Thou, sweet Flower, shalt sleep and
wake
Upon his senseless grave. 70

VIII
ELEGIAC VERSES
IN MEMORY OF MY BROTHER, JOHN WORDSWORTH

Commander of the E. I. Company's ship, the Earl of Abergavenny, in which he perished by calamitous shipwreck, Feb. 6th, 1805. Composed near the Mountain track, that leads from Grasmere through Grisdale Hawes, where it descends towards Patterdale.

[Composed 1805.—Published: vol. of 1842.]

I

THE Sheep-boy whistled loud, and lo!
That instant, startled by the shock,
The Buzzard mounted from the rock
Deliberate and slow:
Lord of the air, he took his flight; 5
Oh! could he on that woeful night
Have lent his wing, my Brother dear,
For one poor moment's space to Thee,
And all who struggled with the Sea,
When safety was so near. 10

II

Thus in the weakness of my heart
I spoke (but let that pang be still)
When rising from the rock at will,
I saw the Bird depart.
And let me calmly bless the Power 15
That meets me in this unknown Flower,
Affecting type of him I mourn!
With calmness suffer and believe,
And grieve, and know that I must grieve,
Not cheerless, though forlorn. 20

III

Here did we stop; and here looked round
While each into himself descends,

For that last thought of parting Friends
That is not to be found. 24
Hidden was Grasmere Vale from sight,
Our home and his, his heart's delight,
His quiet heart's selected home.
But time before him melts away,
And he hath feeling of a day
Of blessedness to come. 30

IV

Full soon in sorrow did I weep,
Taught that the mutual hope was dust,
In sorrow, but for higher trust,
How miserably deep!
All vanished in a single word, 35
A breath, a sound, and scarcely heard.
Sea—Ship—drowned—Shipwreck—so it
came,
The meek, the brave, the good, was gone;
He who had been our living John
Was nothing but a name. 40

V

That was indeed a parting! oh,
Glad am I, glad that it is past;
For there were some on whom it cast
Unutterable woe.
But they as well as I have gains;— 45
From many a humble source, to pains
Like these, there comes a mild release;
Even here I feel it, even this Plant
Is in its beauty ministrant
To comfort and to peace. 50

VI

He would have loved thy modest grace,
Meek Flower! To Him I would have
said,
'It grows upon its native bed
Beside our Parting-place;
There, cleaving to the ground, it lies 55
With multitude of purple eyes,
Spangling a cushion green like moss;
But we will see it, joyful tide!
Some day, to see it in its pride,
The mountain will we cross.' 60

VII

—Brother and friend, if verse of mine
Have power to make thy virtues known,
Here let a monumental Stone
Stand—sacred as a Shrine;
And to the few who pass this way, 65
Traveller or Shepherd, let it say,
Long as these mighty rocks endure,—
Oh do not Thou too fondly brood,
Although deserving of all good,
On any earthly hope, however pure![1] 70

[1] The plant alluded to is the Moss Campion (Silene acaulis, of Linnæus). See Note, p. 925. See among the Poems on the 'Naming of Places', No. VI.

IX
SONNET

[Composed 1846.—Published 1850.]

WHY should we weep or mourn, Angelic
    boy,
For such thou wert ere from our sight
    removed,
Holy, and ever dutiful—beloved
From day to day with never-ceasing joy,
And hopes as dear as could the heart
    employ   5
In aught to earth pertaining? Death has
    proved
His might, nor less his mercy, as
    behoved—
Death conscious that he only could
    destroy
The bodily frame. That beauty is laid low
To moulder in a far-off field of Rome; 10
But Heaven is now, blest Child, thy
    Spirit's home:
When such divine communion, which we
    know,
Is felt, thy Roman burial-place will be
Surely a sweet remembrancer of Thee.

X
LINES

Composed at Grasmere, during a walk one Evening, after a stormy day, the Author having just
read in a Newspaper that the dissolution of
Mr. Fox was hourly expected.

[Composed September (?), 1806.—Published 1807.]

LOUD is the Vale! the Voice is up
With which she speaks when storms are
    gone,
A mighty unison of streams!
Of all her Voices, One!

Loud is the Vale;—this inland Depth 5
In peace is roaring like the Sea;
Yon star upon the mountain-top
Is listening quietly.

Sad was I, even to pain deprest,
Importunate and heavy load![1]   10
The Comforter hath found me here,
Upon this lonely road;

And many thousands now are sad—
Wait the fulfilment of their fear;
For he must die who is their stay, 15
Their glory disappear.

A Power is passing from the earth
To breathless Nature's dark abyss;
But when the great and good depart
What is it more than this—   20

That Man, who is from God sent forth,
Doth yet again to God return?—
Such ebb and flow must ever be,
Then wherefore should we mourn?

[1] Importuna e grave salma.
            MICHAEL ANGELO.

EPITAPHS AND ELEGIAC PIECES
XI
INVOCATION TO THE EARTH
FEBRUARY, 1816

[Composed February, 1816.—Published 1816.]

I

'REST, rest, perturbèd Earth!
O rest, thou doleful Mother of Man-
    kind!'
A Spirit sang in tones more plaintive than
    the wind:
'From regions where no evil thing has
    birth
I come—thy stains to wash away, 5
Thy cherished fetters to unbind,
And open thy sad eyes upon a milder
    day.
The Heavens are thronged with martyrs
    that have risen
From out thy noisome prison;
The penal caverns groan   10
With tens of thousands rent from off the
    tree
Of hopeful life,—by battle's whirlwind
    blown
Into the deserts of Eternity.
Unpitied havoc! Victims unlamented!
But not on high, where madness is
    resented,   15
And murder causes some sad tears to
    flow,
Though, from the widely-sweeping blow,
The choirs of Angels spread, triumphantly
    augmented.

II

'False Parent of Mankind!
Obdurate, proud, and blind,   20
I sprinkle thee with soft celestial dews,
Thy lost, maternal heart to re-infuse!
Scattering this far-fetched moisture from
    my wings,
Upon the act a blessing I implore, 24
Of which the rivers in their secret springs,
The rivers stained so soft with human gore,
Are conscious;—may the like return no
    more!
May Discord—for a Seraph's care
Shall be attended with a bolder prayer—
May she, who once disturbed the seats of
    bliss   30
These mortal spheres above,
Be chained for ever to the black abyss!
And thou, O rescued Earth, by peace and
    love,
And merciful desires, thy sanctity ap-
    prove!'   34
The Spirit ended his mysterious rite,
And the pure vision closed in darkness
    infinite.

EPITAPHS AND ELEGIAC PIECES

XII
LINES

WRITTEN ON A BLANK LEAF IN A COPY OF THE AUTHOR'S POEM 'THE EXCURSION,' UPON HEARING OF THE DEATH OF THE LATE VICAR OF KENDAL

[Composed November 13, 1814.—Published 1815.]

To public notice, with reluctance strong,
Did I deliver this unfinished Song;
Yet for one happy issue;—and I look
With self-congratulation on the Book
Which self, pious, learned, MURFITT saw and
   read;— 5
Upon my thoughts his saintly Spirit fed;
He conned the new-born Lay with grateful heart—
Foreboding not how soon he must
   depart;
Unweeting that to him the joy was given
Which good men take with them from
   earth to heaven. 10

XIII
ELEGIAC STANZAS

(ADDRESSED TO SIR G. H. B. UPON THE DEATH OF HIS SISTER-IN-LAW)

[Composed probably Dec. 1824.—Published 1827.]

O FOR a dirge! But why complain?
Ask rather a triumphal strain
When FERMOR'S race is run;
A garland of immortal boughs
To twine around the Christian's brows, 5
Whose glorious work is done.

We pay a high and holy debt;
No tears of passionate regret
Shall stain this votive lay;
Ill-worthy, Beaumont! were the grief 10
That flings itself on wild relief
When Saints have passed away.

Sad doom, at Sorrow's shrine to kneel,
For ever covetous to feel,
And impotent to bear! 15
Such once was hers—to think and think
On severed love, and only sink
From anguish to despair!

But nature to its inmost part
Faith had refined; and to her heart 20
A peaceful cradle given:
Calm as the dew-drop's, free to rest
Within a breeze-fanned rose's breast
Till it exhales to Heaven.

Was ever Spirit that could bend 25
So graciously?—that could descend,
Another's need to suit,
So promptly from her lofty throne?—
In works of love, in these alone,
How restless, how minute! 30

Pale was her hue; yet mortal cheek
Ne'er kindled with a livelier streak
When aught had suffered wrong,—
When aught that breathes had felt a
   wound;
Such look the Oppressor might confound,
However proud and strong. 36

But hushed be every thought that springs
From out the bitterness of things;
Her quiet is secure;
No thorns can pierce her tender feet, 40
Whose life was, like the violet, sweet,
As climbing jasmine, pure—

As snowdrop on an infant's grave,
Or lily heaving with the wave
That feeds it and defends; 45
As Vesper, ere the star hath kissed
The mountain top, or breathed the mist
That from the vale ascends.

Thou takest not away, O Death!
Thou strikest—absence perisheth, 50
Indifference is no more;
The future brightens on our sight;
For on the past hath fallen a light
That tempts us to adore.

XIV
ELEGIAC MUSINGS

IN THE GROUNDS OF COLEORTON HALL, THE SEAT OF THE LATE SIR G. H. BEAUMONT, BART.

In these grounds stands the Parish Church, wherein is a mural monument bearing an Inscription which, in deference to the earnest request of the deceased, is confined to name, dates, and these words:—'Enter not into judgment with thy servant, O Lord!'

[Composed November, 1830.—Published 1835.]

WITH copious eulogy in prose or rhyme
Graven on the tomb we struggle against
   Time,
Alas, how feebly! but our feelings rise
And still we struggle when a good man
   dies.
Such offering BEAUMONT dreaded and
   forbade, 5
A spirit meek in self-abasement clad.
Yet here at least, though few have
   numbered days
That shunned so modestly the light of
   praise,
His graceful manners, and the temperate
   ray
Of that arch fancy which would round
   him play, 10
Brightening a converse never known to
   swerve
From courtesy and delicate reserve;
That sense, the bland philosophy of life,

Which checked discussion ere it warmed
    to strife;
Those rare accomplishments, and varied
    powers,   15
Might have their record among sylvan
    bowers.
Oh, fled for ever! vanished like a blast
That shook the leaves in myriads as it
    passed;—
Gone from this world of earth, air, sea,
    and sky,
From all its spirit-moving imagery,   20
Intensely studied with a painter's eye,
A poet's heart; and, for congenial view,
Portrayed with happiest pencil, not
    untrue
To common recognitions while the line
Flowed in a course of sympathy divine;—
Oh! severed, too abruptly, from delights
That all the seasons shared with equal
    rights;—
Rapt in the grace of undismantled age,
From soul-felt music, and the treasured
    page
Lit by that evening lamp which loved to
    shed   30
Its mellow lustre round thy honoured
    head;
While Friends beheld thee give with eye,
    voice, mien,
More than theatric force to Shakspeare's
    scene;—
If thou hast heard me—if thy Spirit know
Aught of these bowers and whence their
    pleasures flow;   35
If things in our remembrance held so
    dear,
And thoughts and projects fondly
    cherished here,
To thy exalted nature only seem
Time's vanities, light fragments of earth's
    dream—
Rebuke us not!—The mandate is obeyed
That said, 'Let praise be mute where
    I am laid;'   41
The holier deprecation, given in trust
To the cold marble, waits upon thy dust;
Yet have we found how slowly genuine
    grief
From *silent* admiration wins relief.   45
Too long abashed thy Name is like a rose
That doth 'within itself its sweetness
    close;'
A drooping daisy changed into a cup
In which her bright-eyed beauty is shut up.
Within these groves, where still are
    flitting by   50
Shades of the Past, oft noticed with a sigh,
Shall stand a votive Tablet, haply free,
When towers and temples fall, to speak
    of Thee!
If sculptured emblems of our mortal doom
Recall not there the wisdom of the Tomb,
Green ivy risen from out the cheerful earth

Will fringe the lettered stone; and herbs
    spring forth,
Whose fragrance, by soft dews and rain
    unbound,
Shall penetrate the heart without a wound;
While truth and love their purposes fulfil,
Commemorating genius, talent, skill,   61
That could not lie concealed where Thou
    wert known;
Thy virtues *He* must judge, and He alone,
The God upon whose mercy they are
    thrown.

XV

WRITTEN AFTER THE DEATH OF CHARLES LAMB

[Composed November, 1835.—Published 1837.]

To a good Man of most dear memory
This Stone is sacred. Here he lies apart
From the great city where he first drew
    breath,
Was reared and taught; and humbly
    earned his bread,
To the strict labours of the merchant's
    desk   5
By duty chained. Not seldom did those
    tasks
Tease, and the thought of time so spent
    depress,
His spirit, but the recompense was high;
Firm Independence, Bounty's rightful
    sire;
Affections, warm as sunshine, free as air;
And when the precious hours of leisure
    came,   11
Knowledge and wisdom, gained from
    converse sweet
With books, or while he ranged the
    crowded streets
With a keen eye, and overflowing heart:
So genius triumphed over seeming wrong,
And poured out truth in works by
    thoughtful love   16
Inspired—works potent over smiles and
    tears.
And as round mountain-tops the lightning
    plays,
Thus innocently sported, breaking forth
As from a cloud of some grave sympathy,
Humour and wild instinctive wit, and all
The vivid flashes of his spoken words. 22
From the most gentle creature nursed in
    fields
Had been derived the name he bore—
    a name,
Wherever Christian altars have been
    raised,   25
Hallowed to meekness and to innocence;
And if in him meekness at times gave way,
Provoked out of herself by troubles
    strange,
Many and strange, that hung about his
    life;

Still, at the centre of his being, lodged　30
A soul by resignation sanctified:
And if too often, self-reproached, he felt
That innocence belongs not to our kind,
A power that never ceased to abide in
　him,
Charity, 'mid the multitude of sins　35
That she can cover, left not his exposed
To an unforgiving judgment from just
　Heaven.
O, he was good, if e'er a good Man lived!
. . . .
From a reflecting mind and sorrowing
　heart
Those simple lines flowed with an earnest
　wish,　40
Though but a doubting hope, that they
　might serve
Fitly to guard the precious dust of him
Whose virtues called them forth. That
　aim is missed;
For much that truth most urgently
　required
Had from a faltering pen been asked in
　vain:　45
Yet, haply, on the printed page received,
The imperfect record, there, may stand
　unblamed
As long as verse of mine shall breathe the
　air
Of memory, or see the light of love.

Thou wert a scorner of the fields, my
　Friend,　50
But more in show than truth; and from
　the fields,
And from the mountains, to thy rural
　grave
Transported, my soothed spirit hovers o'er
Its green untrodden turf, and blowing
　flowers;
And taking up a voice shall speak (tho'
　still　55
Awed by the theme's peculiar sanctity
Which words less free presumed not even
　to touch)
Of that fraternal love, whose heaven-lit
　lamp
From infancy, through manhood, to the
　last
Of threescore years, and to thy latest
　hour,　60
Burnt on with ever-strengthening light,
　enshrined
Within thy bosom.
　　　　　'Wonderful' hath been
The love established between man and
　man,
'Passing the love of women;' and between
Man and his help-mate in fast wedlock
　joined　65
Through God, is raised a spirit and soul
　of love
Without whose blissful influence Paradise

Had been no Paradise; and earth were now
A waste where creatures bearing human
　form,
Direst of savage beasts, would roam in
　fear,　70
Joyless and comfortless. Our days glide on;
And let him grieve who cannot choose
　but grieve
That he hath been an Elm without his
　Vine,
And her bright dower of clustering
　charities,
That, round his trunk and branches,
　might have clung　75
Enriching and adorning. Unto thee,
Not so enriched, not so adorned, to thee
Was given (say rather thou of later birth
Wert given to her) a Sister—'tis a word
Timidly uttered, for she *lives*, the meek,
The self-restraining, and the ever-kind;
In whom thy reason and intelligent heart
Found—for all interests, hopes, and
　tender cares,
All softening, humanising, hallowing
　powers,
Whether withheld, or for her sake un-
　sought—　85
More than sufficient recompense!
　　　　　　　　Her love
(What weakness prompts the voice to tell
　it here?)
Was as the love of mothers; and when
　years,
Lifting the boy to man's estate, had called
The long-protected to assume the part　90
Of a protector, the first filial tie
Was undissolved; and, in or out of sight,
Remained imperishably interwoven
With life itself. Thus, 'mid a shifting
　world,
Did they together testify of time　95
And season's difference—a double tree
With two collateral stems sprung from
　one root;
Such were they—such thro' life they *might*
　have been
In union, in partition only such;
Otherwise wrought the will of the Most
　High;　100
Yet, thro' all visitations and all trials,
Still they were faithful; like two vessels
　launched
From the same beach one ocean to explore
With mutual help, and sailing—to their
　league
True, as inexorable winds, or bars　105
Floating or fixed of polar ice, allow.

But turn we rather, let my spirit turn
With thine, O silent and invisible Friend!
To those dear intervals, nor rare nor brief,
When reunited, and by choice withdrawn
From miscellaneous converse, ye were
　taught　111

That the remembrance of foregone distress,
And the worse fear of future ill (which oft
Doth hang around it, as a sickly child
Upon its mother) may be both alike 115
Disarmed of power to unsettle present good
So prized, and things inward and outward held
In such an even balance, that the heart
Acknowledges God's grace, his mercy feels,
And in its depth of gratitude is still. 120

O gift divine of quiet sequestration!
The hermit, exercised in prayer and praise,
And feeding daily on the hope of heaven,
Is happy in his vow, and fondly cleaves
To life-long singleness; but happier far
Was to your souls, and, to the thoughts of others, 126
A thousand times more beautiful appeared,
Your *dual* lonelincss. The sacred tie
Is broken; yet why grieve? for Time but holds
His moiety in trust, till Joy shall lead 130
To the blest world where parting is unknown.

XVI
EXTEMPORE EFFUSION UPON THE DEATH OF JAMES HOGG

[Composed November, 1835.—Published December 12, 1835 (*The Athenæum*); ed. 1837.]

When first, descending from the moor-lands,
I saw the Stream of Yarrow glide
Along a bare and open valley,
The Ettrick Shepherd was my guide.

When last along its banks I wandered, 5
Through groves that had begun to shed
Their golden leaves upon the pathways,
My steps the Border-minstrel led.

The mighty Minstrel breathes no longer,
'Mid mouldering ruins low he lies; 10
And death upon the braes of Yarrow,
Has closed the Shepherd-poet's eyes:

Nor has the rolling year twice measured,
From sign to sign, its steadfast course,
Since every mortal power of Coleridge 15
Was frozen at its marvellous source;

The rapt One, of the godlike forehead,
The heaven-eyed creature sleeps in earth:
And Lamb, the frolic and the gentle,
Has vanished from his lonely hearth. 20

Like clouds that rake the mountain-summits,
Or waves that own no curbing hand,
How fast has brother followed brother,
From sunshine to the sunless land!

Yet I, whose lids from infant slumber 25
Were earlier raised, remain to hear
A timid voice, that asks in whispers,
'Who next will drop and disappear?'

Our haughty life is crowned with darkness,
Like London with its own black wreath,
On which with thee, O Crabbe! forth-looking, 31
I gazed from Hampstead's breezy heath.

As if but yesterday departed,
Thou too art gone before; but why,
O'er ripe fruit, seasonably gathered, 35
Should frail survivors heave a sigh?

Mourn rather for that holy Spirit,
Sweet as the spring, as ocean deep;
For Her who, ere her summer faded,
Has sunk into a breathless sleep. 40

No more of old romantic sorrows,
For slaughtered Youth or love-lorn Maid!
With sharper grief is Yarrow smitten,
And Ettrick mourns with her their Poet dead.[1]

XVII
INSCRIPTION

FOR A MONUMENT IN CROSTHWAITE CHURCH, IN THE VALE OF KESWICK

[Composed 1843.—Published 1845.]

Ye vales and hills whose beauty hither drew
The poet's steps, and fixed him here, on you
His eyes have closed! And ye, lov'd books, no more
Shall Southey feed upon your precious lore,
To works that ne'er shall forfeit their renown, 5
Adding immortal labours of his own—
Whether he traced historic truth, with zeal
For the State's guidance, or the Church's weal,
Or Fancy, disciplined by studious art,
Inform'd his pen, or wisdom of the heart,
Or judgments sanctioned in the Patriot's mind 11
By reverence for the rights of all man-kind.
Wide were his aims, yet in no human breast
Could private feelings meet for holier rest.
His joys, his griefs, have vanished like a cloud 15
From Skiddaw's top; but he to heaven was vowed
Through his industrious life, and Christian faith
Calmed in his soul the fear of change and death.

[1] See Note, p. 726.

459

ODE

INTIMATIONS OF IMMORTALITY FROM RECOLLECTIONS OF EARLY CHILDHOOD

The Child is father of the Man;
And I could wish my days to be
Bound each to each by natural piety.

[Composed 1803 (? 1802)–1806.—Published 1807.]

I

THERE was a time when meadow, grove, and stream,
The earth, and every common sight,
To me did seem
Apparelled in celestial light,
The glory and the freshness of a dream.
It is not now as it hath been of yore;—
Turn wheresoe'er I may,
By night or day,
The things which I have seen I now can see no more.

II

The Rainbow comes and goes,   10
And lovely is the Rose,
The Moon doth with delight
Look round her when the heavens are bare,
Waters on a starry night
Are beautiful and fair;   15
The sunshine is a glorious birth;
But yet I know, where'er I go,
That there hath past away a glory from the earth.

III

Now, while the birds thus sing a joyous song,
And while the young lambs bound   20
As to the tabor's sound,
To me alone there came a thought of grief:
A timely utterance gave that thought relief,
And I again am strong:
The cataracts blow their trumpets from the steep;   25
No more shall grief of mine the season wrong;
I hear the Echoes through the mountains throng,
The Winds come to me from the fields of sleep,
And all the earth is gay;
Land and sea   30
Give themselves up to jollity,
And with the heart of May
Doth every Beast keep holiday;—
Thou Child of Joy,
Shout round me, let me hear thy shouts, thou happy Shepherd-boy!   35

IV

Ye blessèd Creatures, I have heard the call
Ye to each other make; I see
The heavens laugh with you in your jubilee;
My heart is at your festival,
My head hath its coronal,   40
The fulness of your bliss, I feel—I feel it all.
Oh evil day! if I were sullen
While Earth herself is adorning,
This sweet May-morning,
And the Children are culling   45
On every side,
In a thousand valleys far and wide,
Fresh flowers; while the sun shines warm,
And the Babe leaps up on his Mother's arm:—
I hear, I hear, with joy I hear!   50
—But there's a Tree, of many, one,
A single Field which I have looked upon,
Both of them speak of something that is gone:
The Pansy at my feet
Doth the same tale repeat: 55
Whither is fled the visionary gleam?
Where is it now, the glory and the dream?

V

Our birth is but a sleep and a forgetting:
The Soul that rises with us, our life's Star,
Hath had elsewhere its setting,   60
And cometh from afar:
Not in entire forgetfulness,
And not in utter nakedness,
But trailing clouds of glory do we come
From God, who is our home: 65
Heaven lies about us in our infancy!
Shades of the prison-house begin to close
Upon the growing Boy
But He beholds the light, and whence it flows,
He sees it in his joy;   70
The Youth, who daily farther from the east
Must travel, still is Nature's Priest,
And by the vision splendid
Is on his way attended;   74
At length the Man perceives it die away,
And fade into the light of common day.

460

VI

Earth fills her lap with pleasures of her own;
Yearnings she hath in her own natural kind,
And, even with something of a Mother's mind,
And no unworthy aim, 80
The homely Nurse doth all she can
To make her Foster-child, her Inmate Man,
Forget the glories he hath known,
And that imperial palace whence he came.

VII

Behold the Child among his new-born blisses,
A six years' Darling of a pigmy size! 85
See, where 'mid work of his own hand he lies,
Fretted by sallies of his mother's kisses,
With light upon him from his father's eyes!
See, at his feet, some little plan or chart,
Some fragment from his dream of human life, 91
Shaped by himself with newly-learned art;
    A wedding or a festival,
    A mourning or a funeral;
    And this hath now his heart, 95
    And unto this he frames his song:
      Then will he fit his tongue
To dialogues of business, love, or strife;
    But it will not be long
    Ere this be thrown aside, 100
    And with new joy and pride
The little Actor cons another part;
Filling from time to time his 'humorous stage'
With all the Persons, down to palsied Age,
That Life brings with her in her equipage;
    As if his whole vocation 106
    Were endless imitation.

VIII

Thou, whose exterior semblance doth belie
    Thy Soul's immensity;
Thou best Philosopher, who yet dost keep 110
Thy heritage, thou Eye among the blind,
That, deaf and silent, read'st the eternal deep,
Haunted for ever by the eternal mind,—
    Mighty Prophet! Seer blest!
    On whom those truths do rest, 115
Which we are toiling all our lives to find,
In darkness lost, the darkness of the grave;
Thou, over whom thy Immortality
Broods like the Day, a Master o'er a Slave,
A Presence which is not to be put by; 120
    [To whom the grave

Is but a lonely bed without the sense or sight
    Of day or the warm light,
A place of thought where we in waiting lie;[1]]
Thou little Child, yet glorious in the might 125
Of heaven-born freedom on thy being's height,
Why with such earnest pains dost thou provoke
The years to bring the inevitable yoke,
Thus blindly with thy blessedness at strife?
Full soon thy Soul shall have her earthly freight, 130
And custom lie upon thee with a weight,
Heavy as frost, and deep almost as life!

IX

    O joy! that in our embers
    Is something that doth live,
    That nature yet remembers 135
    What was so fugitive!
The thought of our past years in me doth breed
Perpetual benediction: not indeed
For that which is most worthy to be blest;
Delight and liberty, the simple creed 140
Of Childhood, whether busy or at rest,
With new-fledged hope still fluttering in his breast:—
    Not for these I raise
    The song of thanks and praise;
But for those obstinate questionings
Of sense and outward things, 146
Fallings from us, vanishings;
Blank misgivings of a Creature
Moving about in worlds not realised,
High instincts before which our mortal Nature 150
Did tremble like a guilty Thing surprised:
    But for those first affections,
    Those shadowy recollections,
    Which, be they what they may, 154
Are yet the fountain-light of all our day,
Are yet a master-light of all our seeing;
    Uphold us, cherish, and have power to make
Our noisy years seem moments in the being
Of the eternal Silence: truths that wake,
    To perish never: 160
Which neither listlessness, nor mad endeavour,
    Nor Man nor Boy,
Nor all that is at enmity with joy,
Can utterly abolish or destroy!

[1] Found in edd. 1807 and 1815; omitted from ed. 1820 and all subsequent issues in consequence of Coleridge's adverse criticism. See *Biographia Literaria*, chap. xxii.—ED.

461

ODE

Hence in a season of calm weather
    Though inland far we be,   166
Our Souls have sight of that immortal
    sea
    Which brought us hither,
    Can in a moment travel thither,
And see the Children sport upon the
    shore,   170
And hear the mighty waters rolling ever-
    more.

X

Then sing, ye Birds, sing, sing a joyous
    song!
    And let the young Lambs bound
    As to the tabor's sound!
We in thought will join your throng, 175
    Ye that pipe and ye that play,
    Ye that through your hearts to-
    day
    Feel the gladness of the May!
What though the radiance which was
    once so bright
Be now for ever taken from my sight, 180
    Though nothing can bring back the
    hour
Of splendour in the grass, of glory in the
    flower;
    We will grieve not, rather find
    Strength in what remains behind;
    In the primal sympathy   185
    Which having been must ever be;
    In the soothing thoughts that spring
    Out of human suffering;

In the faith that looks through death,
In years that bring the philosophic mind.

XI

And O, ye Fountains, Meadows, Hills,
    and Groves,   191
Forebode not any severing of our loves!
Yet in my heart of hearts I feel your
    might;
I only have relinquished one delight
To live beneath your more habitual sway.
I love the Brooks which down their
    channels fret,   196
Even more than when I tripped lightly
    as they;
The innocent brightness of a new-born
    Day
    Is lovely yet;
The Clouds that gather round the setting
    sun   200
Do take a sober colouring from an eye
That hath kept watch o'er man's mor-
    tality;
Another race hath been, and other palms
    are won.
Thanks to the human heart by which we
    live,
Thanks to its tenderness, its joys, and
    fears,   205
To me the meanest flower that blows can
    give
Thoughts that do often lie too deep for
    tears.

APPENDIX: POEMS OF 1793[1]

AN EVENING WALK

REPRINTED FROM THE QUARTO OF 1793

AN EVENING WALK. AN EPISTLE; IN VERSE. ADDRESSED TO A YOUNG LADY, FROM THE LAKES OF THE NORTH OF ENGLAND. BY W. WORDSWORTH, B.A., OF ST. JOHN'S, CAMBRIDGE. LONDON: PRINTED FOR J. JOHNSON, ST. PAUL'S CHURCHYARD. 1793.

ARGUMENT

General Sketch of the Lakes.—Author's Regret of his Youth passed amongst them.—Short description of Noon.—Cascade Scene.—Noontide Retreat.—Precipice and Sloping Lights.—Face of Nature as the Sun declines.—Mountain Farm, and the Cock.—Slate Quarry.—Sunset.—Superstition of the Country, connected with that Moment.—Swans.—Female Beggar.—Twilight Objects.—Twilight Sounds.—Western Lights.—Spirits.—Night.—Moonlight.—Hope.—Night Sounds.—Conclusion.

FAR from my dearest friend, 'tis mine to
    rove
Thro' bare grey dell, high wood, and
    pastoral cove;
His wizard course where hoary Derwent
    takes
Thro' craggs, and forest glooms, and
    opening lakes,

Staying his silent waves, to hear the
    roar   5
That stuns the tremulous cliffs of high
    Lodore:
Where silver rocks the savage prospect
    chear
Of giant yews that frown on Rydale's
    mere;

[1] The *Errata* of these Poems are here rectified in the text.—ED.

Where peace to Grasmere's lonely island
  leads,
To willowy hedgerows, and to emerald
  meads;   10
Leads to her bridge, rude church, and
  cottag'd grounds,
Her rocky sheepwalks, and her woodland
  bounds;
Where, bosom'd deep, the shy Winander[1]
  peeps
'Mid clust'ring isles, and holly-sprinkl'd
  steeps;
Where twilight glens endear my Esthwaite's shore,   15
And memory of departed pleasures, more.

Fair scenes! with other eyes, than once,
  I gaze,
The ever-varying charm your round
  displays,
Than when, erewhile, I taught, 'a happy
  child,'
The echoes of your rocks my carols
  wild: 20
Then did no ebb of chearfulness demand
Sad tides of joy from Melancholy's hand;
In youth's wild eye the livelong day was
  bright,
The sun at morning, and the stars of
  night,
Alike, when first the vales the bittern
  fills,   25
Or the first woodcocks[2] roam'd the moon-
  light hills.

Return Delights! with whom my road
  begun,
When Life rear'd laughing up her morn-
  ing sun;
When Transport kiss'd away my april tear,
'Rocking as in a dream the tedious
  year;'   30
When link'd with thoughtless Mirth I
  cours'd the plain,
And hope itself was all I knew of pain.
For then, ev'n then, the little heart would
  beat
At times, while young Content forsook
  her seat,
And wild Impatience, panting upward,
  show'd   35
Where tipp'd with gold the mountain-
  summits glow'd.
Alas! the idle tale of man is found
Depicted in the dial's moral round;
With Hope Reflexion blends her social
  rays
To gild the total tablet of his days;   40

Yet still, the sport of some malignant
  Pow'r,
He knows but from its shade the present
  hour.

While, Memory at my side, I wander here,
Starts at the simplest sight th' unbidden
  tear,   44
A form discover'd at the well-known seat,
A spot, that angles at the riv'let's feet,
The ray the cot of morning trav'ling nigh,
And sail that glides the well-known alders
  by.
But why, ungrateful, dwell on idle pain?
To shew her yet some joys to me remain,
Say, will my friend, with soft affection's
  ear,
The history of a poet's ev'ning hear?

When, in the south, the wan noon brood-
  ing still,
Breath'd a pale steam around the glaring
  hill,
And shades of deep embattl'd clouds were
  seen   55
Spotting the northern cliffs with lights
  between;
Gazing the tempting shades to them
  deny'd,
When stood the shorten'd herds amid the
  tide,
Where, from the barren wall's unshelter'd
  end,
Long rails into the shallow lake extend;
When schoolboys stretch'd their length
  upon the green   61
And round the humming elm, a glimmer-
  ing scene!
In the brown park, in flocks, the troubl'd
  deer
Shook the still twinkling tail and glancing
  ear;
When horses in the wall-girt intake[3]
  stood,   65
Unshaded, eying far below, the flood,
Crouded behind the swain, in mute
  distress,
With forward neck the closing gate to
  press;
And long, with wistful gaze, his walk
  survey'd,
Till dipp'd his pathway in the river
  shade;   70
—Then Quiet led me up the huddling rill,
Bright'ning with water-breaks the som-
  brous gill[4];
To where, while thick above the branches
  close,
In dark-brown bason its wild waves
  repose,

[1] These lines are only applicable to the middle part of that lake.

[2] In the beginning of winter, these mountains, in the moonlight nights, are covered with immense quantities of woodcocks; which, in the dark nights, retire into the woods.

[3] The word *intake* is local, and signifies a mountain-inclosure.

[4] Gill is also, I believe, a term confined to this country. Glen, gill, and dingle, have the same meaning.

Inverted shrubs, and moss of darkest
green,   75
Cling from the rocks, with pale wood-
weeds between;
Save that, atop, the subtle sunbeams
shine,
On wither'd briars that o'er the craggs
recline;
Sole light admitted here, a small cascade,
Illumes with sparkling foam the twilight
shade.   80
Beyond, along the visto of the brook,
Where antique roots its bustling path
o'erlook,
The eye reposes on a secret bridge[1]
Half grey, half shagg'd with ivy to its
ridge.
—Sweet rill, farewel! To-morrow's noon
again,   85
Shall hide me wooing long thy wildwood
strain;
But now the sun has gain'd his western
road,
And eve's mild hour invites my steps
abroad.

While, near the midway cliff, the silver'd
kite
In many a whistling circle wheels her
flight;   90
Slant wat'ry lights, from parting clouds
a-pace,
Travel along the precipice's base;
Chearing its naked waste of scatter'd
stone
By lychens grey, and scanty moss o'ergrown,
Where scarce the foxglove peeps, and
thistle's beard,   95
And desert stone-chat, all day long, is
heard.

How pleasant, as the yellowing sun
declines,
And with long rays and shades the landscape shines;
To mark the birches' stems all golden
light,
That lit the dark slant woods with silvery
white!   100
The willows weeping trees, that twinkling hoar,
Glanc'd oft upturn'd along the breezy
shore,
Low bending o'er the colour'd water, fold
Their moveless boughs and leaves like
threads of gold;
The skiffs with naked masts at anchor
laid,   105
Before the boat-house peeping thro' the
shade;

Th' unwearied glance of woodman's
echo'd stroke;
And curling from the trees the cottage
smoke.

Their pannier'd train a groupe of potters
goad,
Winding from side to side up the steep
road;   110
The peasant from yon cliff of fearful edge
Shot, down the headlong pathway darts
his sledge;
Bright beams the lonely mountain horse
illume,
Feeding 'mid purple heath, 'green rings[2],'
and broom;
While the sharp slope the slacken'd team
confounds,   115
Downward[3] the pond'rous timber-wain
resounds;
Beside their sheltering cross[4] of wall, the
flock
Feeds on in light, nor thinks of winter's
shock;
In foamy breaks the rill, with merry
song,
Dash'd down the rough rock, lightly leaps
along;   120
From lonesome chapel at the mountain's
feet,
Three humble bells their rustic chime
repeat;
Sounds from the water-side the hammer'd
boat;
And blasted quarry thunders heard
remote.

Ev'n here, amid the sweep of endless
woods,   125
Blue pomp of lakes, high cliffs, and falling floods,
Not undelightful are the simplest charms
Found by the verdant door of mountain
farms.

Sweetly[5] ferocious round his native walks,
Gaz'd by his sister-wives, the monarch
stalks;   130
Spur clad his nervous feet, and firm his
tread,
A crest of purple tops his warrior head.
Bright sparks his black and haggard eye-
ball hurls
Afar, his tail he closes and unfurls;
Whose state, like pine-trees, waving to
and fro,   135

[1] The reader, who has made the tour of this country, will recognize, in this description, the features
which characterize the lower waterfall in the gardens
of Rydale.

[2] 'Vivid rings of green.' GREENWOOD'S Poem on
Shooting.
[3] 'Down the rough slope the pond'rous waggon
rings.' BEATTIE.
[4] These rude structures, to protect the flocks, are
frequent in this country: the traveller may recollect
one in Withburne, another upon Whinlatter.
[5] 'Dolcemente feroce.'—TASSO.
In this description of the cock, I remembered a
spirited one of the same animal in the l'Agriculture.
ou Les Georgiques Françoises of M. Rossuet.

Droops, and o'er canopies his regal brow,
On tiptoe rear'd he blows his clarion
throat,
Threaten'd by faintly answering farms
remote.

Bright'ning the cliffs between where
sombrous pine,
And yew-trees o'er the silver rocks
recline,   140
I love to mark the quarry's moving trains,
Dwarf pannier'd steeds, and men, and
numerous wains:
How busy the enormous hive within,
While Echo dallies with the various din!
Some hardly heard their chissel's clink-
ing sound,   145
Toil, small as pigmies, in the gulph pro-
found;
Some, dim between th' aëreal cliffs
descry'd,
O'erwalk the viewless plank from side to
side;
These by the pale-blue rocks that cease-
less ring
Glad from their airy baskets hang and
sing.   150

Hung o'er a cloud, above the steep that
rears
It's edge all flame, the broad'ning sun
appears;
A long blue bar it's ægis orb divides,
And breaks the spreading of it's golden
tides;
And now it touches on the purple steep
That flings his shadow on the pictur'd
deep.   156
Cross the calm lake's blue shades the cliffs
aspire,
With tow'rs and woods a 'prospect all on
fire;'
The coves and secret hollows thro' a ray
Of fainter gold a purple gleam betray;
The gilded turf arrays in richer green   161
Each speck of lawn the broken rocks
between;
Deep yellow beams the scatter'd boles
illume,
Far in the level forest's central gloom;
Waving his hat, the shepherd in the vale
Directs his winding dog the cliffs to scale,
That, barking busy 'mid the glittering
rocks,
Hunts, where he points, the intercepted
flocks;
Where oaks o'erhang the road the
radiance shoots
On tawny earth, wild weeds, and twisted
roots;   170
The Druid[1] stones their lighted fane
unfold,

And all the babbling brooks are liquid
gold;
Sunk[2] to a curve the day-star lessens
still,
Gives one bright glance, and sinks behind
the hill.

In these lone vales, if aught of faith may
claim,   175
Thin silver hairs, and ancient hamlet
fame;
When up the hills, as now, retreats the
light,
Strange apparitions mock the village
sight.

A desperate form appears, that spurs his
steed,
Along the midway cliffs with violent
speed;   180
Unhurt pursues his lengthen'd flight,
while all
Attend, at every stretch, his headlong
fall.
Anon, in order mounts a gorgeous show
Of horsemen shadows winding to and
fro;
And now the van is gilt with evening's
beam,   185
The rear thro' iron brown betrays a sullen
gleam;
Lost[3] gradual o'er the heights in pomp
they go,
While silent stands th' admiring vale
below;
Till, but the lonely beacon all is fled,
That tips with eve's last gleam his spiry
head.   190
Now while the solemn evening Shadows
sail,
On red slow-waving pinions down the
vale,
And, fronting the bright west in stronger
lines,
The oak its dark'ning boughs and foliage
twines,
I love beside the glowing lake to stray,
Where winds the road along the secret
bay;   196
By rills that tumble down the woody
steeps,
And run in transport to the dimpling
deeps;
Along the 'wild meand'ring' shore to
view,
Obsequious Grace the winding swan
pursue.   200

may fall into the hands of some curious traveller,
who may thank me for informing him, that up the
Duddon, the river which forms the æstuary at
Broughton, may be found some of the most romantic
scenery of these mountains.

[2] From Thomson: see Scott's Critical Essays.
[3] See a description of an appearance of this kind
in Clark's 'Survey of the Lakes,' accompanied with
vouchers of its veracity that may amuse the reader.

[1] Not far from Broughton is a Druid monument,
of which I do not recollect that any tour descriptive
of this country makes mention. Perhaps this poem

He swells his lifted chest, and backward flings
His bridling neck between his tow'ring wings;
Stately, and burning in his pride, divides
And glorying looks around, the silent tides:
On as he floats, the silver'd waters glow,
Proud of the varying arch and moveless form of snow. 206
While tender Cares and mild domestic Loves,
With furtive watch pursue her as she moves;
The female with a meeker charm succeeds,
And her brown little ones around her leads, 210
Nibbling the water lilies as they pass,
Or playing wanton with the floating grass:
She in a mother's care, her beauty's pride
Forgets, unweary'd watching every side,
She calls them near, and with affection sweet 215
Alternately relieves their weary feet;
Alternately[1] they mount her back, and rest
Close by her mantling wings' embraces prest.

Long may ye roam these hermit waves that sleep,
In birch besprinkl'd cliffs embosom'd deep; 220
These fairy holms untrodden, still, and green,
Whose shades protect the hidden wave serene;
Whence fragrance scents the water's desart gale,
The violet, and the lily[2] of the vale;
Where, tho' her far-off twilight ditty steal, 225
They not the trip of harmless milkmaid feel.

Yon tuft conceals your home, your cottage bow'r,
Fresh water rushes strew the verdant floor;
Long grass and willows form the woven wall,
And swings above the roof the poplar tall. 230
Thence issuing oft, unwieldly as ye stalk,
Ye crush with broad black feet your flow'ry walk;
Safe from your door ye hear at breezy morn,
The hound, the horse's tread, and mellow horn;

At peace inverted your lithe necks ye lave, 235
With the green bottom strewing o'er the wave;
No ruder sound your desart haunts invades,
Than waters dashing wild, or rocking shades.
Ye ne'er, like hapless human wanderers, throw
Your young on winter's winding sheet of snow. 240

Fair swan! by all a mother's joys caress'd,
Haply some wretch has ey'd, and call'd thee bless'd;
Who faint, and beat by summer's breathless ray,
Hath dragg'd her babes along this weary way;
While arrowy fire extorting feverish groans, 245
Shot stinging through her stark o'er-labour'd bones.
—With backward gaze, lock'd joints, and step of pain,
Her seat scarce left, she strives, alas! in vain,
To teach their limbs along the burning road
A few short steps to totter with their load, 250
Shakes her numb arm that slumbers with its weight,
And eyes through tears the mountain's shadeless height;
And bids her soldier come her woes to share,
Asleep on Bunker's charnel hill[3] afar;
For hope's deserted well why wistful look? 255
Chok'd is the pathway, and the pitcher broke.

I see her now, deny'd to lay her head,
On cold blue nights, in hut or straw-built shed;
Turn to a silent smile their sleepy cry,
By pointing to a shooting star on high:
I hear, while in the forest depth he sees,
The Moon's fix'd gaze between the opening trees,
In broken sounds her elder grief demand,
And skyward lift, like one that prays, his hand,
If, in that country, where he dwells afar, 265
His father views that good, that kindly star;
—Ah me! all light is mute amid the gloom,
The interlunar cavern of the tomb.

[1] This is a fact of which I have been an eye-witness.
[2] The lily of the valley is found in great abundance in the smaller islands of Winandermere.

[3] Substituted in *Errata* for the words of the text:—'Minden's charnel plain.'—ED.

—When low-hung clouds each star of
    summer hide,
And fireless are the valleys far and wide,
Where the brook brawls along the painful
    road,   271
Dark with bat haunted ashes stretching
    broad,
The distant clock forgot, and chilling dew,
Pleas'd thro' the dusk their breaking
    smiles to view,
Oft has she taught them on her lap to play
Delighted, with the glow-worm's harm-
    less ray   276
Toss'd light from hand to hand; while
    on the ground
Small circles of green radiance gleam
    around.

Oh! when the bitter showers her path
    assail,
And roars between the hills the torrent
    gale,   280
—No more her breath can thaw their
    fingers cold,
Their frozen arms her neck no more can
    fold;
Scarce heard, their chattering lips her
    shoulder chill,
And her cold back their colder bosoms
    thrill;
All blind she wilders o'er the lightless
    heath,   285
Led by Fear's cold wet hand, and dogg'd
    by Death;
Death, as she turns her neck the kiss to
    seek,
Breaks off the dreadful kiss with angry
    shriek.
Snatch'd from her shoulder with despair-
    ing moan,
She clasps them at that dim-seen roofless
    stone.—   290
'Now ruthless Tempest launch thy dead-
    liest dart!
Fall fires—but let us perish heart to heart.'
Weak roof a cow'ring form two babes to
    shield,
And faint the fire a dying heart can yield;
Press the sad kiss, fond mother! vainly
    fears   295
Thy flooded cheek to wet them with its
    tears;
Soon shall the Light'ning hold before thy
    head
His torch, and shew them slumbering in
    their bed,
No tears can chill them, and no bosom
    warms,
Thy breast their death-bed, coffin'd in
    thine arms.   300
Sweet are the sounds that mingle from
    afar,
Heard by calm lakes, as peeps the folding
    star,

Where the duck dabbles 'mid the rustling
    sedge,
And feeding pike starts from the water's
    edge,
Or the swan stirs the reeds, his neck and
    bill   305
Wetting, that drip upon the water still;
And heron, as resounds the trodden shore,
Shoots upward, darting his long neck
    before.
While, by the scene compos'd, the breast
    subsides,
Nought wakens or disturbs it's tranquil
    tides;   310
Nought but the char that for the may-fly
    leaps,
And breaks the mirror of the circling
    deeps;
Or clock, that blind against the wanderer
    born,
Drops at his feet, and stills his droning
    horn.
—The whistling swain that plods his ring-
    ing way   315
Where the slow waggon winds along the
    bay;
The sugh[1] of swallow flocks that twittering
    sweep,
The solemn curfew swinging long and
    deep;
The talking boat that moves with pensive
    sound,
Or drops his anchor down with plunge
    profound;   320
Of boys that bathe remote the faint
    uproar,
And restless piper wearying out the shore;
These all to swell the village murmurs
    blend,
That soften'd from the water-head
    descend.
While in sweet cadence rising small and
    still   325
The far-off minstrels of the haunted hill,
As the last bleating of the fold expires,
Tune in the mountain dells their water
    lyres.

Now with religious awe the farewell light
Blends with the solemn colouring of the
    night;   330
'Mid groves of clouds that crest the
    mountain's brow,
And round the West's proud lodge their
    shadows throw,
Like Una[2] shining on her gloomy way,
The half seen form of Twilight roams
    astray;

[1] 'Sugh', a Scotch word, expressive, as Mr. Gilpin explains it, of the sound of the motion of a stick through the air, or of the wind passing through the trees. See Burns' Cotter's Saturday Night.
[2] Alluding to this passage of Spenser—
              'Her angel face
As the great eye of Heaven shined bright,
And made a sunshine in that shady place.'

Thence, from three paly loopholes mild
    and small,   335
Slow lights upon the lake's still bosom
    fall,
Beyond the mountain's giant reach that
    hides
In deep determin'd gloom his subject
    tides. -
—'Mid the dark steeps repose the shadowy
    streams,
As touch'd with dawning moonlight's
    hoary gleams,   340
Long streaks of fairy light the wave
    illume
With bordering lines of intervening gloom,
Soft o'er the surface creep the lustres
    pale
Tracking with silvering path the change-
    ful gale.
—'Tis restless magic all; at once the
    bright   345
Breaks on the shade, the shade upon the
    light,
Fair Spirits are abroad; in sportive chase
Brushing with lucid wands the water's
    face,
While music stealing round the glimmer-
    ing deeps
Charms the tall circle of th' enchanted
    steeps.   350
—As thro' th' astonish'd woods the notes
    ascend,
The mountain streams their rising song
    suspend;
Below Eve's listening Star the sheep walk
    stills
It's drowsy tinklings on th' attentive
    hills;
The milkmaid stops her ballad, and her
    pail   355
Stays it's low murmur in th' unbreathing
    vale;
No night-duck clamours for his wilder'd
    mate,
Aw'd, while below the Genii hold their
    state.
—The pomp is fled, and mute the won-
    drous strains,
No wrack of all the pageant scene
    remains,   360
So[1] vanish those fair Shadows, human
    joys,
But Death alone their vain regret destroys.
Unheeded Night has overcome the vales,
On the dark earth the baffl'd vision fails,
If peep between the clouds a star on
    high,   365
There turns for glad repose the weary
    eye;
The latest lingerer of the forest train,
The lone black fir, forsakes the faded
    plain;

Last evening sight, the cottage smoke no
    more,
Lost in the deepen'd darkness, glimmers
    hoar;   370
High towering from the sullen dark-
    brown mere,
Like a black wall, the mountain steeps
    appear,
Thence red from different heights with
    restless gleam
Small cottage lights across the water
    stream,
Nought else of man or life remains
    behind   375
To call from other worlds the wilder'd
    mind,
Till pours the wakeful bird her solemn
    strains
Heard[2] by the night-calm of the wat'ry
    plains.
—No purple prospects now the mind
    employ
Glowing in golden sunset tints of joy, 380
But o'er the sooth'd accordant heart we
    feel
A sympathetic twilight slowly steal,
And ever, as we fondly muse, we find
The soft gloom deep'ning on the tranquil
    mind.
Stay! pensive, sadly-pleasing, visions,
    stay!   385
Ah no! as fades the vale, they fade away.
Yet still the tender, vacant gloom remains,
Still the cold cheek its shuddering tear
    retains.
The bird, with fading light who ceas'd to
    thread
Silent the hedge or steaming rivulet's
    bed,   390
From his grey re-appearing tower shall
    soon
Salute with boding note the rising moon,
Frosting with hoary light the pearly
    ground,
And pouring deeper blue to Æther's
    bound;
Rejoic'd her solemn pomp of clouds to
    fold   395
In robes of azure, fleecy white, and
    gold,
While rose and poppy, as the glow-worm
    fades,
Cheequer with paler red the thicket
    shades.
    Now o'er the eastern hill, where Dark-
    ness broods
O'er all its vanish'd dells, and lawns, and
    woods   400
Where but a mass of shade the sight can
    trace,
She lifts in silence up her lovely face;

---

[1] 'So break those glittering shadows, human joys.'
                                          YOUNG.

[2] 'Charming the night-calm with her powerful
song.' A line of one of our older poets.

Above the gloomy valley flings her light,
Far to the western slopes with hamlets
  white;
And gives, where woods the checquer'd
  upland strew,   405
To the green corn of summer autumn's
  hue.
Thus Hope, first pouring from her
  blessed horn
Her dawn, far lovelier than the Moon's
  own morn;
'Till higher mounted, strives in vain to
  chear
The weary hills, impervious, black'ning
  near;   410
—Yet does she still, undaunted, throw the
  while
On darling spots remote her tempting
  smile.
—Ev'n now she decks for me a distant
  scene,
(For dark and broad the gulph of time
  between)
Gilding that cottage with her fondest ray,
(Sole bourn, sole wish, sole object of my
  way;   416
How fair it's lawn and silvery woods
  appear!
How sweet it's streamlet murmurs in
  mine ear!)
Where we, my friend, to golden days
  shall rise,
'Till our small share of hardly-paining sighs
(For sighs will ever trouble human breath)
Creep hush'd into the tranquil breast of
  Death.
But now the clear-bright Moon her
  zenith gains,
And rimy without speck extend the
  plains;

The deepest dell the mountain's breast
  displays,   425
Scarce hides a shadow from her searching
  rays;
From the dark-blue 'faint silvery threads'
  divide
The hills, while gleams below the azure
  tide;
The scene is waken'd, yet its peace
  unbroke,
By silver'd wreaths of quiet charcoal
  smoke,   430
That, o'er the ruins of the fallen wood,
Steal down the hills, and spread along
  the flood.
The song of mountain streams unheard by
  day,
Now hardly heard, beguiles my home-
  ward way.
All air is, as the sleeping water, still,   435
List'ning th' aëreal music of the hill,
Broke only by the slow clock tolling
  deep,
Or shout that wakes the ferry-man from
  sleep,
Soon follow'd by his hollow-parting oar,
And echo'd hoof approaching the far
  shore;   440
Sound of clos'd gate, across the water
  born,
Hurrying the feeding hare thro' rustling
  corn;
The tremulous sob of the complaining
  owl;
And at long intervals the mill-dog's
  howl;
The distant forge's swinging thump
  profound;   445
Or yell in the deep woods of lonely
  hound.

DESCRIPTIVE SKETCHES

REPRINTED FROM THE QUARTO OF 1793

DESCRIPTIVE SKETCHES. IN VERSE. TAKEN DURING A PEDESTRIAN TOUR IN THE ITALIAN, GRISON, SWISS, AND SAVOYARD ALPS. BY W. WORDSWORTH, B.A., OF ST. JOHN'S, CAMBRIDGE. 'LOCA PASTORUM DESERTA ATQUE OTIA DIA.'—*Lucret.* 'CASTELLA IN TUMULIS—ET LONGE SALTUS LATEQUE VACANTES.'—*Virgil.* LONDON: PRINTED FOR J. JOHNSON, ST. PAUL'S CHURCHYARD. 1793.

TO THE REV. ROBERT JONES, FELLOW OF ST. JOHN'S COLLEGE, CAMBRIDGE

DEAR SIR,—However desirous I might have been of giving you proofs of the high place you hold in my esteem, I should have been cautious of wounding your delicacy by thus publicly addressing you, had not the circumstance of my having accompanied you amongst the Alps, seemed to give this dedication a propriety sufficient to do away any scruples which your modesty might otherwise have suggested.

In inscribing this little work to you I consult my heart. You know well how great is the difference between two companions lolling in a post chaise, and two travellers plodding slowly along the road, side by side, each with his little knapsack of necessaries upon his shoulders. How much more of heart between the two latter!

I am happy in being conscious I shall have one reader who will approach the conclusion of these few pages with regret. You they must certainly interest, in reminding you of moments to which you can hardly look back without a pleasure not the less dear from a shade of melancholy. You will meet with few images without recollecting the spot where we observed them together, consequently, whatever is feeble in my design, or spiritless in my colouring, will be amply supplied by your own memory.

With still greater propriety I might have inscribed to you a description of some of the features of your native mountains, through which we have wandered together, in the same manner, with so much pleasure. But the sea-sunsets which give such splendour to the vale of Clwyd, Snowdon, the chair of Idris, the quiet village of Bethkelert, Menai and her druids, the Alpine steeps of the Conway, and the still more interesting windings of the wizard stream of the Dee remain yet untouched. Apprehensive that my pencil may never be exercised on these subjects, I cannot let slip this opportunity of thus publicly assuring you with how much affection and esteem, I am, Dear Sir, Your most obedient very humble servant. W. WORDSWORTH.

ARGUMENT

Happiness (if she had been to be found on Earth) amongst the Charms of Nature.—Pleasures of the pedestrian Traveller.—Author crosses France to the Alps.—Present state of the Grande Chartreuse. —Lake of Como.—Time, Sunset.—Same Scene, Twilight.—Same Scene, Morning, it's Voluptuous Character; Old Man and Forest Cottage Music.—River Tusa.—Via Mala and Grison Gypsey.— Valley of Sckellenenthal.—Lake of Uri.—Stormy Sunset.—Chapel of William Tell.—Force of Local Emotion.—Chamois Chaser.—View of the higher Alps.—Manner of Life of a Swiss Mountaineer interspersed with Views of the higher Alps.—Golden Age of the Alps.—Life and Views continued.— Ranz des Vaches, famous Swiss Air.—Abbey of Einsiedlen and it's Pilgrims.—Valley of Chamouny. —Mont Blanc.—Slavery of Savoy.—Influence of Liberty on Cottage Happiness.—France.—Wish for the Extirpation of Slavery.—Conclusion.

WERE there, below, a spot of holy ground,
By Pain and her sad family unfound,
Sure, Nature's GOD that spot to man had giv'n,
Where murmuring rivers join the song of ev'n;
Where falls the purple morning far and wide 5
In flakes of light upon the mountain-side;
Where summer Suns in ocean sink to rest,
Or moonlight Upland lifts her hoary breast;
Where Silence, on her night of wing, o'er-broods
Unfathom'd dells and undiscover'd woods;
Where rocks and groves the power of waters shakes 11
In cataracts, or sleeps in quiet lakes.
But doubly pitying Nature loves to show'r
Soft on his wounded heart her healing pow'r,
Who plods o'er hills and vales his road forlorn, 15
Wooing her varying charms from eve to morn.
No sad vacuities his heart annoy,
Blows not a Zephyr but it whispers joy;
For him lost flowers their idle sweets exhale;
He tastes the meanest note that swells the gale; 20
For him sod-seats the cottage-door adorn,
And peeps the far-off spire, his evening bourn!
Dear is the forest frowning o'er his head,
And dear the green-sward to his velvet tread;
Moves there a cloud o'er mid-day's flaming eye? 25

Upward he looks—and calls it luxury;
Kind Nature's charities his steps attend,
In every babbling brook he finds a friend,
While chast'ning thoughts of sweetest use, bestow'd
By Wisdom, moralize his pensive road.
Host of his welcome inn, the noon-tide bow'r, 31
To his spare meal he calls the passing poor;
He views the Sun uprear his golden fire,
Or sink, with heart alive like Memnon's[1] lyre;
Blesses the Moon that comes with kindest ray 35
To light him shaken by his viewless way.
With bashful fear no cottage children steal
From him, a brother at the cottage meal,
His humble looks no shy restraint impart,
Around him plays at will the virgin heart.
While unsuspended wheels the village dance, 41
The maidens eye him with inquiring glance,
Much wondering what sad stroke of crazing Care
Or desperate Love could lead a wanderer there.
Me, lur'd by hope her sorrows to remove, 45
A heart, that could not much itself approve,
O'er Gallia's wastes of corn dejected led,
Her[2] road elms rustling thin above my head,

[1] The lyre of Memnon is reported to have emitted melancholy or cheerful tones, as it was touched by the sun's evening or morning rays.
[2] There are few people whom it may be necessary to inform, that the sides of many of the post-roads in France are planted with a row of trees.

Or through her truant pathway's native
   charms,
By secret villages and lonely farms,   50
To where the Alps, ascending white in
   air,
Toy with the Sun, and glitter from afar.
  Ev'n now I sigh at hoary Chartreuse'
   doom
Weeping beneath his chill of mountain
   gloom.
Where now is fled that Power whose frown
   severe   55
Tam'd 'sober Reason' till she crouch'd
   in fear?
That breath'd a death-like peace these ⎫
   woods around,   ⎪
Broke only by th' unvaried torrent's   ⎬
   sound,   ⎪
Or prayer-bell by the dull cicada   ⎭
   drown'd.
The cloister startles at the gleam of arms,
And Blasphemy the shuddering fane
   alarms;   61
Nod the cloud-piercing pines their
   troubl'd heads,
Spires, rocks, and lawns, a browner night
   o'erspreads.
Strong terror checks the female peasant's
   sighs,
And start th' astonish'd shades at female
   eyes.   65
The thundering tube the aged angler hears,
And swells the groaning torrent with his
   tears.
From Bruno's forest screams the frighted
   jay,
And slow th' insulted eagle wheels away.
The cross with hideous laughter Demons
   mock,   70
By angels[1] planted on the aëreal rock.
The 'parting Genius' sighs with hollow
   breath
Along the mystic streams of Life and
   Death,[2]
Swelling the outcry dull, that long
   resounds
Portentous, thro' her old woods' trackless
   bounds,   75
Deepening her echoing torrents' awful
   peal
And bidding paler shades her form con-
   ceal,
Vallombre,[3] 'mid her falling fanes,
   deplores,
For ever broke, the sabbath of her bow'rs.
  More pleas'd, my foot the hidden
   margin roves   80
Of Como bosom'd deep in chestnut
   groves.

No meadows thrown between, the giddy
   steeps
Tower, bare or silvan, from the narrow
   deeps.
To towns, whose shades of no rude sound
   complain,
To ringing team unknown and grating
   wain,   85
To flat-roof'd towns, that touch the
   water's bound,
Or lurk in woody sunless glens profound,
Or from the bending rocks obtrusive
   cling,
And o'er the whiten'd wave their shadows
   fling;
Wild round the steeps the little[4] path-
   way twines,   90
And Silence loves it's purple roof of vines.
The viewless lingerer hence, at evening,
   sees
From rock-hewn steps the sail between
   the trees;
Or marks, mid opening cliffs, fair dark-
   ey'd maids
Tend the small harvest of their garden
   glades,   95
Or, led by distant warbling notes,
   surveys,
With hollow ringing ears and darkening
   gaze,
Binding the charmed soul in powerless
   trance,
Lip-dewing Song and ringlet-tossing
   Dance,
Where sparkling eyes and breaking smiles
   illume   100
The bosom'd cabin's lyre-enliven'd
   gloom;
Or stops the solemn mountain-shades to
   view
Stretch, o'er their pictur'd mirror, broad
   and blue,
Tracking the yellow sun from steep to
   steep,
As up th' opposing hills, with tortoise
   foot, they creep.   105
Here half a village shines, in gold array'd,
Bright as the moon, half hides itself in
   shade.
From the dark sylvan roofs the restless
   spire,
Inconstant glancing, mounts like spring-
   ing fire,   109
There, all unshaded, blazing forests throw
Rich golden verdure on the waves below.
Slow glides the sail along th' illumined
   shore,
And steals into the shade the lazy oar.

---

[1] Alluding to crosses seen on the tops of the spiry rocks of the Chartreuse, which have every appearance of being inaccessible.
[2] Names of rivers at the Chartreuse.
[3] Name of one of the vallies of the Chartreuse.

[4] If any of my readers should ever visit the Lake of Como, I recommend it to him to take a stroll along this charming little pathway; he must chuse the evening, as it is on the western side of the lake. We pursued it from the foot of the water to its head: it is once interrupted by a ferry.

Soft bosoms breathe around contagious
    sighs,
And amourous music on the water dies.
Heedless how Pliny, musing here, sur-
    vey'd
Old Roman boats and figures thro' the
    shade,
Pale Passion, overpower'd, retires and
    woos
The thicket, where th' unlisten'd stock-
    dove coos.
    How bless'd, delicious Scene! the eye
    that greets   120
Thy open beauties, or thy lone retreats;
Th' unwearied sweep of wood thy cliffs
    that scales,
The never-ending waters of thy vales;
The cots, those dim religious groves
    embow'r,
Or, under rocks that from the water tow'r
Insinuated, sprinkling all the shore,   126
Each with his household boat beside the
    door,
Whose flaccid sails in forms fantastic
    droop,
Bright'ning the gloom where thick the
    forests stoop;
—Thy torrents shooting from the clear-
    blue sky,   130
Thy towns, like swallows' nests that
    cleave on high;
That glimmer hoar in eve's last light,
    descry'd
Dim from the twilight water's shaggy
    side,
Whence lutes and voices down th'
    enchanted woods
Steal, and compose the oar-forgotten
    floods,   135
While Evening's solemn bird melodious
    weeps,
Heard, by star-spotted bays, beneath the
    steeps;
—Thy lake, mid smoking woods, that
    blue and grey
Gleams, streak'd or dappled, hid from
    morning's ray
Slow-travelling down the western hills, to
    fold   140
It's green-ting'd margin in a blaze of gold;
From thickly-glittering spires the matin-
    bell
Calling the woodman from his desert cell,
A summons to the sound of oars, that pass,
Spotting the steaming deeps, to early
    mass;   145
Slow swells the service o'er the water
    born,
While fill each pause the ringing woods of
    morn.
    Farewel! those forms that, in thy
    noon-tide shade,
Rest, near their little plots of wheaten
    glade;

Those steadfast eyes, that beating breasts
    inspire   150
To throw the 'sultry ray' of young
    Desire;
Those lips, whose tides of fragrance come,
    and go,
Accordant to the cheek's unquiet glow;
Those shadowy breasts in love's soft light
    array'd,
And rising, by the moon of passion
    sway'd.   155
—Thy fragrant gales and lute-resounding
    streams,
Breathe o'er the failing soul voluptuous
    dreams;
While Slavery, forcing the sunk mind to
    dwell
On joys that might disgrace the captive's
    cell,
Her shameless timbrel shakes along thy
    marge,   160
And winds between thine isles the vocal
    barge.
Yet, arts are thine that rock th' un-
    sleeping heart,
And smiles to Solitude and Want impart.
I lov'd, mid thy most desert woods astray,
With pensive step to measure my slow
    way,[1]   165
By lonely, silent cottage-doors to roam,
The far-off peasant's day-deserted home;
Once did I pierce to where a cabin stood,
The redbreast peace had bury'd it in
    wood,
There, by the door a hoary-headed sire
Touch'd with his wither'd hand an aged
    lyre;   171
Beneath an old-grey oak as violets lie,
Stretch'd at his feet with steadfast, up-
    ward eye,
His children's children join'd the holy
    sound,
A hermit—with his family around.   175
Hence shall we seek where fair Locarno
    smiles
Embower'd in walnut slopes and citron
    isles,
Or charms that smile on Tusa's evening
    stream,
While mid dim towers and woods her[2]
    waters gleam:
From the bright wave, in solemn gloom,
    retire   180
The dull-red steeps, and darkening still,
    aspire,
To where afar rich orange lustres glow
Round undistinguish'd clouds, and rocks,
    and snow;

1   'Solo, e pensoso i più deserti campi
    Vò misurando à passi tardi, e lenti.'—
                               PETRARCH.
2 The river along whose banks you descend in
crossing the Alps by the Semplon pass. From the
striking contrast of it's features, this pass I should
imagine to be the most interesting among the Alps.

Or, led where Viamala's chasms confine
Th' indignant waters of the infant Rhine,
Bend o'er th' abyss?—the else impervious
    gloom   186
His burning eyes with fearful light
    illume.
The Grison gypsey here her tent has
    plac'd,
Sole human tenant of the piny waste;
Her tawny skin, dark eyes, and glossy
    locks,   190
Bend o'er the smoke that curls beneath
    the rocks.

—The mind condemn'd, without reprieve,
    to go
O'er life's long deserts with it's charge of
    woe,
With sad congratulation joins the ⎱
    train,
Where beasts and men together o'er
    the plain   195
Move on,—a mighty caravan of
    pain;
Hope, strength, and courage, social suffer-
    ing brings,
Freshening the waste of sand with shades
    and springs.
—She solitary through the desert drear
Spontaneous wanders, hand in hand with
    Fear.   200
A giant moan along the forest swells
Protracted, and the twilight storm fore-
    tells,
And, ruining from the cliffs their deafen-
    ing load
Tumbles, the wildering Thunder slips
    abroad;
On the high summits Darkness comes
    and goes,   205
Hiding their fiery clouds, their rocks, and
    snows;
The torrent, travers'd by the lustre broad,
Starts like a horse beside the flashing road;
In the roof'd[1] bridge, at that despairing
    hour,
She seeks a shelter from the battering
    show'r.   210
—Fierce comes the river down; the crash-
    ing wood
Gives way, and half it's pines torment
    the flood;
Fearful,[2] beneath, the Water-spirits call,
And the bridge vibrates, tottering to its
    fall.
—Heavy, and dull, and cloudy is the
    night,   215
No star supplies the comfort of it's light,

---

[1] Most of the bridges among the Alps are of wood
and covered: these bridges have a heavy appearance,
and rather injure the effect of the scenery in some
places.
[2] 'Red came the river down, and loud, and oft
The angry Spirit of the water shriek'd.'
                HOME'S *Douglas.*

Glimmer the dim-lit Alps, dilated, round,
And one sole light shifts in the vale pro-
    found;
While, opposite, the waning moon hangs
    still,
And red, above her melancholy hill. 220
By the deep quiet gloom appall'd, she
    sighs,
Stoops her sick head, and shuts her weary
    eyes.
—Breaking th' ascending roar of desert
    floods,
And insect buzz, that stuns the sultry
    woods,
She hears, upon the mountain forest's
    brow,   225
The death-dog, howling loud and long,
    below;
On viewless fingers counts the valley-
    clock,
Followed by drowsy crow of midnight
    cock.
—Bursts from the troubl'd Larch's giant
    boughs
The pie, and chattering breaks the night's
    repose.   230
Low barks the fox: by Havoc rouz'd the
    bear,
Quits, growling, the white bones that
    strew his lair;
The dry leaves stir as with the serpent's
    walk,
And, far beneath, Banditti voices talk;
Behind her hill the Moon, all crimson,
    rides,   235
And his red eyes the slinking water hides;
Then all is hushed; the bushes rustle near,
And with strange tinglings sings her
    fainting ear.
—Vex'd by the darkness, from the piny
    gulf
Ascending, nearer howls the famish'd
    wolf,   240
While thro' the stillness scatters wild
    dismay,
Her babe's small cry, that leads him to
    his prey.
Now, passing Urseren's open vale
    serene,
Her quiet streams, and hills of downy
    green,
Plunge with the Russ embrown'd by
    Terror's breath,   245
Where danger roofs the narrow walks of
    death;
By floods, that, thundering from their
    dizzy height,
Swell more gigantic on the steadfast sight;
Black drizzling craggs, that beaten by
    the din,
Vibrate, as if a voice complain'd within;
Bare steeps, where Desolation stalks,
    afraid,   251
Unsteadfast, by a blasted yew upstay'd;

By cells[1] whose image, trembling as he
    prays,
Awe struck, the kneeling peasant scarce
    surveys;
Loose-hanging rocks the Day's bless'd
    eye that hide,   255
And crosses[2] rear'd to Death on every
    side,
Which with cold kiss Devotion planted
    near,
And, bending, water'd with the human
    tear,
Soon fading 'silent' from her upward
    eye,
Unmov'd with each rude form of Danger
    nigh,   260
Fix'd on the anchor left by him who saves
Alike in whelming snows and roaring
    waves.
    On as we move, a softer prospect opes,
Calm huts, and lawns between, and sylvan
    slopes.
While mists, suspended on th' expiring
    gale,   265
Moveless o'er-hang the deep secluded
    vale,
The beams of evening, slipping soft
    between,
Light up of tranquil joy a sober scene;
Winding it's dark-green wood and
    emerald glade,
The still vale lengthens underneath the
    shade;   270
While in soft gloom the scattering bowers
    recede,
Green dewy lights adorn the freshen'd
    mead,
Where solitary forms illumin'd stray
Turning with quiet touch the valley's
    hay,
On the low[3] brown wood-huts delighted
    sleep   275
Along the brighten'd gloom reposing
    deep.
While pastoral pipes and streams the
    landscape lull,
And bells of passing mules that tinkle
    dull,
In solemn shapes before th' admiring eye
Dilated hang the misty pines on high,
Huge convent domes with pinnacles and
    tow'rs,   281
And antique castles seen thro' drizzling
    show'rs.
    From such romantic dreams my soul
    awake,

Lo! Fear looks silent down on Uri's lake,
By whose unpathway'd margin still and
    dread   285
Was never heard the plodding peasant's
    tread.
Tower like a wall the naked rocks, or
    reach
Far o'er the secret water dark with beach,
More high, to where creation seems to
    end,
Shade above shade the desert pines
    ascend,   290
And still, below, where mid the savage
    scene
Peeps out a little speck of smiling green,
There with his infants man undaunted
    creeps
And hangs his small wood-hut upon the
    steeps.
A garden-plot the desert air perfumes,
'Mid the dark pines a little orchard
    blooms,   296
A zig-zag path from the domestic skiff
Threading the painful cragg surmounts
    the cliff.
—Before those hermit doors, that never
    know   299
The face of traveller passing to and fro,
No peasant leans upon his pole, to tell
For whom at morning toll'd the funeral
    bell,
Their watch-dog ne'er his angry bark for-
    goes,
Touch'd by the beggar's moan of human
    woes,
The grassy seat beneath their casement
    shade   305
The pilgrim's wistful eye hath never
    stay'd.
—There, did the iron Genius not disdain
The gentle Power that haunts the myrtle
    plain,
There might the love-sick maiden sit, and
    chide
Th' insuperable rocks and severing tide,
There watch at eve her lover's sun-gilt
    sail   311
Approaching, and upbraid the tardy gale,
There list at midnight till is heard no
    more,
Below, the echo of his parting oar,
There hang in fear, when growls the
    frozen stream,   315
To guide his dangerous tread the taper's
    gleam.
'Mid stormy vapours ever driving by,
Where ospreys, cormorants, and herons
    cry,
Where hardly giv'n the hopeless waste to
    chear
Deny'd the bread of life the foodful ear,
Dwindles the pear on autumn's latest
    spray,   321
And apple sickens pale in summer's ray,

---

[1] The Catholic religion prevails here. These cells are, as is well known, very common in the Catholic countries, planted, like Roman tombs, along the road side.
[2] Crosses commemorative of the deaths of travellers by the fall of snow, and other accidents very common along this dreadful road.
[3] The houses in the more retired Swiss valleys are all built of wood.

Ev'n here Content has fix'd her smiling reign
With Independence child of high Disdain.
Exulting mid the winter of the skies, ⎫
Shy as the jealous chamois, Freedom flies,   326 ⎬
And often grasps her sword, and often eyes, ⎭
Her crest a bough of Winter's bleakest pine,
Strange 'weeds' and alpine plants her helm entwine,
And wildly-pausing oft she hangs aghast,
While thrills the 'Spartan fife' between the blast.   331
'Tis storm; and hid in mist from hour to hour
All day the floods a deeper murmur pour,
And mournful sounds, as of a Spirit lost,
Pipe wild along the hollow-blustering coast,   335
'Till the Sun walking on his western field
Shakes from behind the clouds his flashing shield.
Triumphant on the bosom of the storm,
Glances the fire-clad eagle's wheeling form;
Eastward, in long perspective glittering, shine   340
The wood-crown'd cliffs that o'er the lake recline;
Wide o'er the Alps a hundred streams unfold,
At once to pillars turn'd that flame with gold;
Behind his sail the peasant strives to shun
The west that burns like one dilated sun,
Where in a mighty crucible expire   346
The mountains, glowing hot, like coals of fire[1].
But lo! the boatman, over-aw'd, before
The pictur'd fane of Tell suspends his oar;
Confused the Marathonian tale appears,
While burn in his full eyes the glorious tears.   351

[1] I had once given to these sketches the title of Picturesque; but the Alps are insulted in applying to them that term. Whoever, in attempting to describe their sublime features, should confine himself to the cold rules of painting would give his reader but a very imperfect idea of those emotions which they have the irresistible power of communicating to the most impassive imaginations. The fact is, that controuling influence, which distinguishes the Alps from all other scenery, is derived from images which disdain the pencil. Had I wished to make a picture of this scene I had thrown much less light into it. But I consulted nature and my feelings. The ideas excited by the stormy sunset I am here describing owed their sublimity to that deluge of light, or rather of fire, in which nature had wrapped the immense forms around me; any intrusion of shade, by destroying the unity of the impression, had necessarily diminished it's grandeur.

And who but feels a power of strong controul,
Felt only there, oppress his labouring soul,
Who walks, where honour'd men of ancient days
Have wrought with god-like arm the deeds of praise?   355
Say, who, by thinking on Canadian hills,
Or wild Aosta lull'd by Alpine rills,
On Zutphen's plain; or where with soften'd gaze
The old grey stones the plaided chief surveys,
Can guess the high resolve, the cherish'd pain   360
Of him whom passion rivets to the plain,
Where breath'd the gale that caught Wolfe's happiest sigh,
And the last sun-beam fell on Bayard's eye,
Where bleeding Sydney from the cup retir'd,
And glad Dundee in 'faint huzza's' expir'd.   365
But now with other soul I stand alone
Sublime upon this far-surveying cone,
And watch from pike[2] to pike amid the sky
Small as a bird the chamois-chaser fly.
'Tis his with fearless step at large to roam
Thro' wastes, of Spirits wing'd the solemn home,   371
Thro'[3] vacant worlds where Nature never gave
A brook to murmur or a bough to wave,
Which unsubstantial Phantoms sacred keep;
Thro' worlds where Life and Sound, and Motion sleep,   375
Where Silence still her death-like reign extends,
Save when the startling cliff unfrequent rends:
In the deep snow the mighty ruin drown'd,
Mocks the dull ear of Time with deaf abortive sound;
—To mark a planet's pomp and steady light   380
In the least star of scarce-appearing night,
And neighbouring moon, that coasts the vast profound,
Wheel pale and silent her diminish'd round,
While far and wide the icy summits blaze
Rejoicing in the glory of her rays;   385
The star of noon that glitters small and bright,
Shorn of his beams, insufferably white,

[2] Pike is a word very commonly used in the north of England, to signify a high mountain of the conic form, as Langdale pike, &c.
[3] For most of the images in the next sixteen verses I am indebted to M. Raymond's interesting observations annexed to his translation of Coxe's Tour in Switzerland.

And flying fleet behind his orb to view
Th' interminable sea of sable blue.
—Of cloudless suns no more ye frost-
    built spires   390
Refract in rainbow hues the restless fires!
Ye dewy mists the arid rocks o'er-spread
Whose slippery face derides his deathful
    tread!
—To wet the peak's impracticable sides
He opens of his feet the sanguine tides,
Weak and more weak the issuing current
    eyes   396
Lapp'd by the panting tongue of thirsty
    skies.[1]
—At once bewildering mists around him
    close,
And cold and hunger are his least of
    woes;   399
The Demon of the snow with angry roar
Descending, shuts for aye his prison door.
Craz'd by the strength of hope at morn
    he eyes
As sent from heav'n the raven of the skies,
Then with despair's whole weight his
    spirits sink,
No bread to feed him, and the snow his
    drink,   405
While ere his eyes can close upon the
    day,
The eagle of the Alps o'ershades his prey.
—Meanwhile his wife and child with
    cruel hope
All night the door at every moment ope;
Haply that child in fearful doubt may
    gaze,   410
Passing his father's bones in future days,
Start at the reliques of that very thigh,
On which so oft he prattled when a boy.
    Hence shall we turn where, heard with
    fear afar,
Thunders thro' echoing pines the head-
    long Aar?   415
Or rather stay to taste the mild delights
Of pensive Underwalden's[2] pastoral
    heights?
—Is there who mid these awful wilds
    has seen
The native Genii walk the mountain
    green?
Or heard, while other worlds their
    charms reveal,   420
Soft music from th' aëreal summit steal?
While o'er the desert, answering every
    close,
Rich steam of sweetest perfume comes
    and goes.

—And sure there is a secret Power that
    reigns
Here, where no trace of man the spot
    profanes,   425
Nought but the herds that pasturing
    upward creep,
Hung dim-discover'd from the dangerous
    steep,
Or summer hamlet,[3] flat and bare, on high
Suspended, mid the quiet of the sky.   429
How still! no irreligious sound or sight
Rouzes the soul from her severe delight.
An idle voice the sabbath region fills
Of Deep that calls to Deep across the hills,
Broke only by the melancholy sound
Of drowsy bells for ever tinkling round;
Faint wail of eagle melting into blue   436
Beneath the cliffs, and pine-woods steady
    sugh;[4]
The solitary heifer's deepen'd low;
Or rumbling heard remote of falling snow.
Save that, the stranger seen below, the
    boy   440
Shouts from the echoing hills with savage
    joy.
When warm from myrtle bays and
    tranquil seas,
Comes on. to whisper hope, the vernal
    breeze,[5]
When hums the mountain bee in May's
    glad ear,
And emerald isles to spot the heights
    appear,   445
When shouts and lowing herds the valley
    fill,
And louder torrents stun the noon-tide
    hill,
When fragrant scents beneath th' en-
    chanted tread
Spring up, his little all around him spread,
The pastoral Swiss begins the cliffs to
    scale,   450
To silence leaving the deserted vale,
Up the green mountain tracking Sum-
    mer's feet,
Each twilight earlier call'd the Sun to
    meet,
With earlier smile the ray of morn to view
Fall on his shifting hut that gleams mid
    smoking dew;   455
Bless'd with his herds, as in the patriarch's
    age,
The summer long to feed from stage to
    stage;
O'er azure pikes serene and still, they go,
And hear the rattling thunder far below;

[1] The rays of the sun drying the rocks frequently produce on their surface a dust so subtile and slippery, that the wretched chamois-chasers are obliged to bleed themselves in the legs and feet in order to secure a footing.
[2] The people of this Canton are supposed to be of a more melancholy disposition than the other inhabitants of the Alps: this, if true, may proceed from their living more secluded.

[3] These summer hamlets are most probably (as I have seen observed by a critic in the *Gentleman's Magazine*) what Virgil alludes to in the expression 'Castella in tumulis'.
[4] Sugh, a Scotch word expressive of the sound of the wind through the trees.
[5] This wind, which announces the spring to the Swiss, is called in their language FOEN; and is according to M. Raymond the Syroco of the Italians.

Or lost at eve in sudden mist the day   460
Attend, or dare with minute-steps their
    way;
Hang from the rocks that tremble o'er
    the steep,
And tempt the icy valley yawning deep,
O'er-walk the chasmy torrent's foam-lit
    bed,
Rock'd on the dizzy larch's narrow tread,
Whence Danger leans, and pointing
    ghastly, joys   466
To mock the mind with 'desperation's
    toys';
Or steal beneath loose mountains, half-
    deterr'd,
That sigh and shudder to the lowing
    herd.
—I see him, up the midway cliff he creeps
To where a scanty knot of verdure
    peeps,
Thence down the steep a pile of grass he
    throws
The fodder of his herds in winter snows.
Far different life to what tradition hoar
Transmits of days more bless'd in times
    of yore. [1]   475
Then Summer lengthen'd out his season
    bland,
And with rock-honey flow'd the happy
    land.
Continual fountains welling chear'd the
    waste,
And plants were wholesome, now of
    deadly taste.
Nor Winter yet his frozen stores had
    pil'd   480
Usurping where the fairest herbage
    smil'd;
Nor Hunger forc'd the herbs from
    pastures bare
For scanty food the treacherous cliffs to
    dare.
Then the milk-thistle bad those herds
    demand
Three times a day the pail and welcome
    hand.   485
But human vices have provok'd the rod
Of angry Nature to avenge her God.
Thus does the father to his sons relate,
On the lone mountain top, their chang'd
    estate.   489
Still, Nature, ever just, to him imparts
Joys only given to uncorrupted hearts.
—'Tis morn: with gold the verdant
    mountain glows,

[1] This tradition of the golden age of the Alps, as
M. Raymond observes, is highly interesting, interesting not less to the philosopher than to the poet.
Here I cannot help remarking, that the superstitions
of the Alps appear to be far from possessing that
poetical character which so eminently distinguishes
those of Scotland and the other mountainous
northern countries. The Devil with his horns, &c.,
seems to be, in their idea, the principal agent that
brings about the sublime natural revolutions that
take place daily before their eyes.

More high, the snowy peaks with hues of
    rose.
Far stretch'd beneath the many-tinted
    hills,
A mighty waste of mist the valley fills,
A solemn sea! whose vales and mountains
    round   496
Stand motionless, to awful silence bound.
A gulf of gloomy blue, that opens wide
And bottomless, divides the midway tide.
Like leaning masts of stranded ships
    appear   500
The pines that near the coast their sum-
    mits rear
Of cabins, woods, and lawns a pleasant
    shore
Bounds calm and clear the chaos still
    and hoar;
Loud thro' that midway gulf ascending,
    sound
Unnumber'd streams with hollow roar
    profound.   505
Mounts thro' the nearer mist the chaunt
    of birds,
And talking voices, and the low of herds,
The bark of dogs, the drowsy tinkling bell,
And wild-wood mountain lutes of saddest
    swell.
Think not, suspended from the cliff on
    high   510
He looks below with undelighted eye.
—No vulgar joy is his, at even tide
Stretch'd on the scented mountain's
    purple side.
For as the pleasures of his simple day
Beyond his native valley hardly stray,   515
Nought round it's darling precincts can
    he find
But brings some past enjoyment to his
    mind,
While Hope that ceaseless leans on
    Pleasure's urn
Binds her wild wreathes, and whispers
    his return.
    Once Man entirely free, alone and
    wild,   520
Was bless'd as free—for he was Nature's
    child.
He, all superior but his God disdain'd,
Walk'd none restraining, and by none
    restrain'd,
Confess'd no law but what his reason
    taught,
Did all he wish'd, and wish'd but what he
    ought.   525
As Man in his primæval dower array'd
The image of his glorious sire display'd,
Ev'n so, by vestal Nature guarded, here
The traces of primæval Man appear.
The native dignity no forms debase,   530
The eye-sublime, and surly lion-grace.
The slave of none, of beasts alone the lord,
He marches with his flute, his book, and
    sword,

477

Well taught by that to feel his rights,
prepar'd
With this 'the blessings he enjoys to
guard.'   535
And as on glorious ground he draws his
breath,
Where Freedom oft, with Victory and
Death,
Hath seen in grim array amid their
Storms
Mixed with auxiliar Rocks, three hundred
Forms;[1]
While twice ten thousand corselets at the
view   540
Dropp'd loud at once, Oppression
shriek'd, and flew.
Oft as those sainted Rocks before him
spread,
An unknown power connects him with
the dead.
For images of other worlds are there,
Awful the light, and holy is the air.   545
Uncertain thro' his fierce uncultur'd soul
Like lighted tempests troubled transports
roll;
To viewless realms his Spirit towers
amain,
Beyond the senses and their little reign.
And oft, when pass'd that solemn vision
by,   550
He holds with God himself communion
high,
When the dread peal of swelling torrents
fills
The sky-roof'd temple of the eternal hills,
And savage Nature humbly joins the
rite,
While flash her upward eyes severe
delight.   555
Or gazing from the mountain's silent
brow,
Bright stars of ice and azure worlds of
snow,
Where needle peaks of granite shooting
bare
Tremble in ever-varying tints of air,
Great joy by horror tam'd dilates his
heart,   560
And the near heav'ns their own delights
impart.
—When the Sun bids the gorgeous scene
farewell,
Alps overlooking Alps their state up-
swell;

Huge Pikes of Darkness named, of Fear[2]
and Storms,
Lift, all serene, their still, illumin'd
forms,   565
In sea-like reach of prospect round him
spread,
Ting'd like an angel's smile all rosy red.
When downward to his winter hut he
goes,
Dear and more dear the lessening circle
grows,
The hut which from the hills his eyes
employs   570
So oft, the central point of all his joys.
And as a swift by tender cares oppress'd
Peeps often ere she dart into her nest,
So to th' untrodden floor, where round
him looks
His father helpless as the babe he rocks,
Oft he descends to nurse the brother
pair,   576
Till storm and driving ice blockade him
there;
There hears, protected by the woods
behind,
Secure, the chiding of the baffled wind,
Hears Winter, calling all his Terrors
round,   580
Rush down the living rocks with whirl-
wind sound.
Thro' Nature's vale his homely pleasures
glide
Unstain'd by envy, discontent, and pride,
The bound of all his vanity to deck
With one bright bell a favourite heifer's
neck;   585
Content upon some simple annual feast,
Remember'd half the year, and hop'd the
rest,
If dairy produce, from his inner hoard,
Of thrice ten summers consecrate the
board.
—Alas! in every clime a flying ray   590
Is all we have to chear our wintry way,
Condemn'd, in mists and tempests ever
rife,
To pant slow up the endless Alp of life.
'Here,' cried a swain, whose venerable
head
Bloom'd with the snow-drops of Man's
narrow bed,   595
Last night, while by his dying fire, as
clos'd
The day, in luxury my limbs repos'd,
'Here Penury oft from misery's mount
will guide
Ev'n to the summer door his icy tide,
And here the avalanche of Death destroy
The little cottage of domestic Joy.   601
But, ah! th' unwilling mind may more
than trace
The general sorrows of the human race:

[1] Alluding to several battles which the Swiss in
very small numbers have gained over their oppressors, the house of Austria; and in particular, to
one fought at Naeffels near Glarus, where three
hundred and thirty men defeated an army of between
fifteen and twenty thousand Austrians. Scattered
over the valley are to be found eleven stones, with
this inscription 1388, the year the battle was fought,
marking out as I was told upon the spot, the several
places where the Austrians attempting to make a
stand were repulsed anew.

[2] As Schreck-Horn, the pike of terror. Wetter-
Horn the pike of storms, &c., &c.

The churlish gales, that unremitting blow
Cold from necessity's continual snow, 605
To us the gentle groups of bliss deny
That on the noon-day bank of leisure lie.
Yet more; the tyrant Genius, still at strife
With all the tender Charities of life,
When close and closer they begin to
    strain, 610
No fond hand left to staunch th' unclosing
    vein,
Tearing their bleeding ties leaves Age to
    groan
On his wet bed, abandon'd and alone.
For ever, fast as they of strength become
To pay the filial debt, for food to roam,
The father forc'd by Powers that only
    deign 616
That solitary Man disturb their reign,
From his bare nest amid the storms of
    heaven
Drives, eagle-like, his sons as he was
    driven,
His last dread pleasure! watches to the
    plain— 620
And never, eagle-like, beholds again.'
    When the poor heart has all its joys
    resign'd,
Why does their sad remembrance cleave
    behind?
Lo! by the lazy Seine the exile roves,
Or where thick sails illume Batavia's
    groves; 625
Soft o'er the waters mournful measures
    swell,
Unlocking bleeding Thought's 'memorial
    cell;'
At once upon his heart Despair has set
Her seal, the mortal tear his cheek has wet;
Strong poison not a form of steel can
    brave 630
Bows his young hairs with sorrow to the
    grave.[1]
    Gay lark of hope thy silent song
    resume!
Fair smiling lights the purpled hills illume!
Soft gales and dews of life's delicious
    morn,
And thou! lost fragrance of the heart
    return! 635
Soon[2] flies the little joy to man allow'd,
And tears before him travel like a cloud.
For come Diseases on, and Penury's rage,
Labour, and Pain, and Grief, and joyless
    Age,
And Conscience dogging close his bleed-
    ing way 640
Cries out, and leads her Spectres to their
    prey,

'Till Hope-deserted, long in vain his
    breath
Implores the dreadful untried sleep of
    Death.
—Mid savage rocks and seas of snow that
    shine
Between interminable tracts of pine, 645
Round a lone fane the human Genii
    mourn,
Where fierce the rays of woe collected
    burn.
—From viewless lamps a ghastly dimness
    falls,
And ebbs uncertain on the troubled walls,
Dim dreadful faces thro' the gloom
    appear, 650
Abortive Joy, and Hope that works in
    fear,
While strives a secret Power to hush the
    croud,
Pain's wild rebellious burst proclaims her
    rights aloud.
    Oh give not me that eye of hard dis-
    dain
That views undimm'd Einsiedlen's
    wretched fane.[3] 655
Mid muttering prayers all sounds of
    torment meet,
Dire clap of hands, distracted chase of
    feet,
While loud and dull ascends the weeping
    cry,
Surely in other thoughts contempt may
    die.
If the sad grave of human ignorance
    bear 660
One flower of hope—Oh pass and leave it
    there.
—The tall Sun, tip-toe on an Alpine
    spire,
Flings o'er the desert blood-red streams
    of fire.
At such an hour there are who love to
    stray,
And meet the gladdening pilgrims on
    their way. 665
—Now with joy's tearful kiss each other
    greet,
Nor longer naked be your way-worn feet,
For ye have reach'd at last the happy
    shore,
Where the charm'd worm of pain shall
    gnaw no more.
How gayly murmur and how sweetly 670
    taste
The fountains[4] rear'd for you amid the
    waste!

---

[1] The effect of the famous air, called in French Ranz des Vaches, upon the Swiss troops removed from their native country is well known, as also the injunction of not playing it on pain of death, before the regiments of that nation, in the service of France and Holland.
[2] Optima quaeque dies, &c.

[3] This shrine is resorted to, from a hope of relief, by multitudes, from every corner of the Catholick world, labouring under mental or bodily afflictions.
[4] Rude fountains built and covered with sheds for the accommodation of the pilgrims, in their ascent of the mountain. Under those sheds the sentimental traveller and the philosopher may find interesting sources of meditation.

Yes I will see you when ye first behold
Those turrets tipp'd by hope with morn-
    ing gold,
And watch, while on your brows the cross
    ye make,
Round your pale eyes a wintry lustre
    wake.   675
—Without one hope her written griefs to
    blot,
Save in the land where all things are
    forgot,
My heart, alive to transports long
    unknown,
Half wishes your delusion were it's
    own.
Last let us turn to where Chamouny[1]
    shields,   680
Bosom'd in gloomy woods, her golden
    fields,
Five streams of ice amid her cots de-
    scend,
And with wild flowers and blooming
    orchards blend,
A scene more fair than what the Grecian
    feigns
Of purple lights and ever vernal plains.
Here lawns and shades by breezy rivulets
    fann'd,   686
Here all the Seasons revel hand in hand.
—Red stream the cottage lights; the
    landscape fades,
Erroneous wavering mid the twilight
    shades.
Alone ascends that mountain nam'd of
    white[2]   690
That dallies with the Sun the summer
    night.
Six thousand years amid his lonely bounds
The voice of Ruin, day and night, re-
    sounds.
Where Horror-led his sea of ice assails,
Havoc and Chaos blast a thousand vales,
In waves, like two enormous serpents,
    wind   696
And drag their length of deluge train
    behind.
Between the pine's enormous boughs
    descry'd
Serene he towers, in deepest purple dy'd;
Glad Day-light laughs upon his top of
    snow,   700
Glitter the stars above, and all is black
    below.
  At such an hour I heav'd the human
    sigh,
When roar'd the sullen Arve in anger by,
That not for thee, delicious vale! unfold
Thy reddening orchards, and thy fields of
    gold;   705

That thou, the slave of slaves,[3] art
    doom'd to pine,
While no Italian arts their charms com-
    bine
To teach the skirt of thy dark cloud to
    shine;
For thy poor babes that, hurrying from
    the door,
With pale-blue hands, and eyes that fix'd
    implore,   710
Dead muttering lips, and hair of hungry
    white,
Besiege the traveller whom they half
    affright.
—Yes, were it mine, the cottage meal to
    share
Forc'd from my native mountains bleak
    and bare;
O'er Anet's[4] hopeless seas of marsh to
    stray,   715
Her shrill winds roaring round my lonely
    way;
To scent the sweets of Piedmont's breath-
    ing rose,
And orange gale that o'er Lugano blows;
In the wide range of many a weary
    round,
Still have my pilgrim feet unfailing
    found,   720
As despot courts their blaze of gems
    display,
Ev'n by the secret cottage far away
The lily of domestic joy decay;
While Freedom's farthest hamlets bless-
    ings share,
Found still beneath her smile, and only
    there.   725
The casement shade more luscious wood-
    bine binds,
And to the door a neater pathway winds,
At early morn the careful housewife, led
To cull her dinner from it's garden bed,
Of weedless herbs a healthier prospect
    sees,   730
While hum with busier joy her happy
    bees;
In brighter rows her table wealth as-
    pires,
And laugh with merrier blaze her evening
    fires;
Her infant's cheeks with fresher roses
    glow,
And wilder graces sport around their
    brow;   735
By clearer taper lit a cleanlier board
Receives at supper hour her tempting
    hoard;
The chamber hearth with fresher boughs
    is spread,
And whiter is the hospitable bed.

---

[1] This word is pronounced upon the spot Chàmouny, I have taken the liberty of reading it long
thinking it more musical
[2] It is only from the higher part of the valley of
Chàmouny that Mont Blanc is visible.

[3] It is scarce necessary to observe that these lines
were written before the emancipation of Savoy.
[4] A vast extent of marsh so called near the lake
of Neufchatel.

—And thou! fair favoured region! which
   my soul   740
Shall love, 'till Life has broke her golden
   bowl,
Till Death's cold touch her cistern-wheel
   assail,
And vain regret and vain desire shall fail;
Tho' now, where erst the grey-clad peasant
   stray'd,
To break the quiet of the village shade
Gleam war's[1] discordant habits thro' the
   trees,   746
And the red banner mock the sullen
   breeze;
'Tho' now no more thy maids their voices
   suit
To the low-warbled breath of twilight lute,
And heard, the pausing village hum
   between,   750
No solemn songstress lull the fading green,
Scared by the fife, and rumbling drum's
   alarms,
And the short thunder, and the flash of
   arms;
While, as Night bids the startling uproar
   die,
Sole sound, the sourd[2] renews his mourn-
   ful cry: 755
—Yet, hast thou found that Freedom
   spreads her pow'r
Beyond the cottage hearth, the cottage
   door:
All nature smiles; and owns beneath her
   eyes
Her fields peculiar, and peculiar skies.
Yes, as I roam'd where Loiret's[3] waters
   glide   760

[1] This, as may be supposed, was written before France became the seat of war.
[2] An insect so called, which emits a short, melancholy cry, heard, at the close of the summer evenings, on the banks of the Loire.
[3] The river Loiret, which has the honour of giving name to a department, rises out of the earth at a place, called La Source, a league and a half south-east of Orleans, and taking at once the character of a considerable stream, winds under a most delicious bank on its left, with a flat country of meadows, woods, and vineyards on its right, till it falls into the Loire about three or four leagues below Orleans. The hand of false taste has committed on its banks those outrages which the Abbé de Lille so pathetically deprecates in those charming verses descriptive of the Seine, visiting in secret the retreat of his friend Watelet. Much as the Loiret, in its short course, suffers from injudicious ornament, yet are there spots to be found upon its banks as soothing as meditation could wish for: the curious traveller may meet with some of them where it loses itself among the mills in the neighbourhood of the villa called La Fontaine. The walks of La Source, where it takes its rise, may, in the eyes of some people, derive an additional interest from the recollection that they were the retreat of Bolingbroke during his exile, and that here it was that his philosophical works were chiefly composed. The inscriptions of which he speaks in one of his letters to Swift descriptive of this spot, are not, I believe, now extant. The gardens have been modelled within these twenty years according to a plan evidently not dictated by the taste of the friend of Pope.

Thro' rustling aspins heard from side to
   side,
When from october clouds a milder
   light
Fell, where the blue flood rippled into
   white,
Methought from every cot the watchful
   bird
Crowed with ear-piercing power 'till then
   unheard;   765
Each clacking mill, that broke the
   murmuring streams,
Rock'd the charm'd thought in more
   delightful dreams,
Chasing those long long dreams the fall-
   ing leaf
Awoke a fainter pang of moral grief;
The measured echo of the distant flail 770
Winded in sweeter cadence down the vale;
A more majestic tide the water[1] roll'd
And glowed the sun-gilt groves in richer
   gold:
—Tho' Liberty shall soon, indignant, raise
Red on his hills his beacon's comet
   blaze;   775
Bid from on high his lonely cannon
   sound,
And on ten thousand hearths his shout
   rebound;
His larum-bell from village-tow'r to tow'r
Swing on th' astounded ear it's dull
   undying roar:
Yet, yet rejoice, tho' Pride's perverted ire
Rouze Hell's own aid, and wrap thy hills
   in fire.   781
Lo! from th' innocuous flames, a lovely
   birth!
With it's own Virtues springs another
   earth:
Nature, as in her prime, her virgin reign
Begins, and Love and Truth compose her
   train;   785
With pulseless hand, and fix'd unwearied
   gaze,
Unbreathing Justice her still beam
   surveys:
No more, along thy vales and viny groves,
Whole hamlets disappearing as he moves,
With cheeks o'erspread by smiles of bale-
   ful glow,   790
On his pale horse shall fell Consumption
   go.
Oh give, great God, to Freedom's
   waves to ride
Sublime o'er Conquest, Avarice, and
   Pride,
To break, the vales where Death with
   Famine scow'rs,
And dark Oppression builds her thick-
   ribb'd tow'rs;   795

[1] The duties upon many of the French rivers were so exorbitant that the poorer people, deprived of the benefit of water carriage, were obliged to transport their goods by land.

Where Machination her fell soul resigns,
Fled panting to the centre of her mines;
Where Persecution decks with ghastly
	smiles
Her bed, his mountains mad Ambition
	piles;
Where Discord stalks dilating, every
	hour,								800
And crouching fearful at the feet of
	Pow'r,
Like Lightnings eager for th' almighty
	word,
Look up for sign of havoc, Fire and
	Sword,[1]

¹ ————————And, at his heels,
Leash'd in like hounds, should Famine, Sword,
	and Fire,
Crouch for employment.

—Give them, beneath their breast while
	Gladness springs,
To brood the nations o'er with Nile-like
	wings;								805
And grant that every sceptred child of
	clay,
Who cries, presumptuous, 'here their
	tides shall stay,'
Swept in their anger from th' affrighted
	shore,
With all his creatures sink—to rise no
	more.
To-night, my friend, within this humble
	cot								810
Be the dead load of mortal ills forgot,
Renewing, when the rosy summits glow
At morn, our various journey, sad and
	slow.

SUPPLEMENT

OF PIECES NOT APPEARING IN THE EDITION
OF 1849–50

ARRANGED IN CHRONOLOGICAL ORDER

I
LINES

WRITTEN AS A SCHOOL EXERCISE AT
HAWKSHEAD, ANNO ÆTATIS 14

[Composed 1784–5.—Published 1851 (*Memoirs
of W.*)]

'I was called upon, among other scholars,' Wordsworth says, 'to write verses upon the completion
of the second centenary from the foundation of
the school in 1585, by Archbishop Sandys. The
verses were much admired, far more than they
deserved, for they were but a tame imitation of
Pope's versification, and a little in his style. This
exercise, however, put it into my head to compose verses from the impulse of my own mind,
and I wrote, while yet a schoolboy, a long poem
running upon my own adventures, and the
scenery of the country in which I was brought
up. The only part of that poem which has been
preserved is the conclusion of it, which stands
at the beginning of my collected Poems.' (See
Extract from the Conclusion of a Poem, &c.,
page 1.)—ED.

'AND has the Sun his flaming chariot
	driven
Two hundred times around the ring of
	heaven,
Since Science first, with all her sacred
	train,
Beneath yon roof began her heavenly
	reign?
While thus I mused, methought, before
	mine eyes,							5

The Power of EDUCATION seemed to
	rise;
Not she whose rigid precepts trained the
	boy
Dead to the sense of every finer joy;
Nor that vile wretch who bade the tender
	age
Spurn Reason's law and humour Passion's
	rage;							10
But she who trains the generous British
	youth
In the bright paths of fair majestic Truth:
Emerging slow from Academus' grove
In heavenly majesty she seem'd to move.
Stern was her forehead, but a smile serene
"Soften'd the terrors of her awful mien."
Close at her side were all the powers,
	design'd
To curb, exalt, reform the tender mind:
With panting breast, now pale as winter
	snows,							19
Now flush'd as Hebe, Emulation rose;
Shame follow'd after with reverted eye,
And hue far deeper than the Tyrian dye;
Last Industry appear'd with steady pace,
A smile sat beaming on her pensive face.
I gazed upon the visionary train,			25
Threw back my eyes, return'd, and gazed
	again.
When lo! the heavenly goddess thus
	began,
Through all my frame the pleasing accents
	ran.

482

'"When Superstition left the golden
light
And fled indignant to the shades of night;
When pure Religion rear'd the peaceful
   breast   31
And lull'd the warring passions into
   rest,
Drove far away the savage thoughts that
   roll
In the dark mansions of the bigot's soul,
Enlivening Hope display'd her cheerful
   ray,   35
And beam'd on Britain's sons a brighter
   day;
So when on Ocean's face the storm sub-
   sides,
Hush'd are the winds and silent are the
   tides;
The God of day, in all the pomp of light,
Moves through the vault of heaven, and
   dissipates the night;   40
Wide o'er the main a trembling lustre
   plays,
The glittering waves reflect the dazzling
   blaze;
Science with joy saw Superstition fly
Before the lustre of Religion's eye;
With rapture she beheld Britannia smile,
Clapp'd her strong wings, and sought the
   cheerful isle,   46
The shades of night no more the soul
   involve,
She sheds her beam, and, lo! the shades
   dissolve;
No jarring monks, to gloomy cell con-
   fined,   49
With mazy rules perplex the weary mind;
No shadowy forms entice the soul aside,
Secure she walks, Philosophy her guide.
Britain, who long her warriors had adored,
And deem'd all merit centred in the sword;
Britain, who thought to stain the field was
   fame,   55
Now honour'd Edward's less than Bacon's
   name.
Her sons no more in listed fields advance
To ride the ring, or toss the beamy lance;
No longer steel their indurated hearts
To the mild influence of the finer arts; 60
Quick to the secret grotto they retire
To court majestic truth, or wake the
   golden lyre;
By generous Emulation taught to rise,
The seats of learning brave the distant
   skies.
Then noble Sandys, inspir'd with great
   design,   65
Reared Hawkshead's happy roof, and
   call'd it mine.
There have I loved to show the tender age
The golden precepts of the classic page;
To lead the mind to those Elysian plains
Where, throned in gold, immortal Science
   reigns;   70

Fair to the view is sacred Truth display'd,
In all the majesty of light array'd,
To teach, on rapid wings, the curious soul
To roam from heaven to heaven, from
   pole to pole,
From thence to search the mystic cause of
   things   75
And follow Nature to her secret springs;
Nor less to guide the fluctuating youth
Firm in the sacred paths of moral truth,
To regulate the mind's disordered frame,
And quench the passions kindling into
   flame;   80
The glimmering fires of Virtue to enlarge,
And purge from Vice's dross my tender
   charge.
Oft have I said, the paths of Fame pursue,
And all that Virtue dictates, dare to do;
Go to the world, peruse the book of man,
And learn from thence thy own defects to
   scan;   86
Severely honest, break no plighted trust,
But coldly rest not here—be more than
   just;
Join to the rigours of the sires of Rome
The gentler manners of the private dome;
When Virtue weeps in agony of woe, 91
Teach from the heart the tender tear to
   flow;
If Pleasure's soothing song thy soul
   entice,
Or all the gaudy pomp of splendid Vice,
Arise superior to the Siren's power, 95
The wretch, the short-lived vision of an
   hour;
Soon fades her cheek, her blushing
   beauties fly,
As fades the chequer'd bow that paints
   the sky.

'"So shall thy sire, whilst hope his
   breast inspires,
And wakes anew life's glimmering
   trembling fires,   100
Hear Britain's sons rehearse thy praise
   with joy,
Look up to heaven, and bless his darling
   boy.
If e'er these precepts quell'd the passions'
   strife,
If e'er they smooth'd the rugged walks of
   life,
If e'er they pointed forth the blissful way
That guides the spirit to eternal day, 106
Do thou, if gratitude inspire thy breast,
Spurn the soft fetters of lethargic rest.
Awake, awake! and snatch the slumbering
   lyre,
Let this bright morn and Sandys the song
   inspire."   110

'I look'd obedience: the celestial Fair
Smiled like the morn, and vanish'd into
   air.'

483

SUPPLEMENT OF PIECES

II

SONNET, ON SEEING MISS HELEN MARIA WILLIAMS WEEP AT A TALE OF DISTRESS

[Composed 1787.—Published March, 1787 (*The European Magazine*, Vol. XI, p. 202); never reprinted by W.]

SHE wept.—Life's purple tide began to
flow
In languid streams through every thrilling
vein;
Dim were my swimming eyes—my pulse
beat slow,
And my full heart was swell'd to dear
delicious pain. 4
Life left my loaded heart, and closing eye;
A sigh recall'd the wanderer to my breast;
Dear was the pause of life, and dear the
sigh
That call'd the wanderer home, and home
to rest.
That tear proclaims—in thee each virtue
dwells,
And bright will shine in misery's midnight
hour; 10
As the soft star of dewy evening tells
What radiant fires were drown'd by day's
malignant pow'r,
That only wait the darkness of the night
To cheer the wand'ring wretch with
hospitable light.

AXIOLOGUS.

III

THE BIRTH OF LOVE

[Composed 1795 (?).—Published 1795.]

Reprinted from a vol. entitled *Poems by Francis Wrangham, M.A.* A translation (signed *Words-worth*) of some French stanzas signed *Anon.;* never reprinted by Wordsworth.—ED.

WHEN Love was born of heavenly line,
What dire intrigues disturbed *Cythera's*
joy!
Till VENUS cried, 'A mother's heart is
mine;
None but myself shall nurse my boy.'

But, infant as he was, the child 5
In that divine embrace enchanted lay;
And, by the beauty of the vase beguil'd,
Forgot the beverage—and pin'd away.

'And must my offspring languish in my
sight?'
(Alive to all a mother's pain, 10
The Queen of Beauty thus her court
address'd)
'No: Let the most discreet of all my
train
Receive him to her breast:
Think all, he is the God of young
delight.' 14

Then TENDERNESS with CANDOUR join'd,
And GAIETY the charming office sought;
Nor even DELICACY stayed behind:
But none of those fair Graces brought
Wherewith to nurse the child—and still he
pin'd.
Some fond hearts to COMPLIANCE seem'd
inclin'd; 20
But she had surely spoil'd the boy:
And sad experience forbade a thought
On the wild Goddess of VOLUPTUOUS
JOY.

Long undecided lay th' important choice,
Till of the beauteous court, at length, a
voice 25
Pronounced the name of HOPE:—The
conscious child
Stretched forth his little arms and smil'd.

'Tis said ENJOYMENT (who averr'd
The charge belong'd to her alone)
Jealous that HOPE had been preferr'd 30
Laid snares to make the babe her own.

Of INNOCENCE the garb she took,
The blushing mien and downcast look;
And came her services to proffer:
And HOPE (what has not HOPE believ'd!)
By that seducing air deceiv'd, 36
Accepted of the offer.

It happen'd that, to sleep inclin'd,
Deluded HOPE for one short hour
To that false INNOCENCE'S power 40
Her little charge consign'd.

The Goddess then her lap with sweetmeats
fill'd
And gave, in handfuls gave, the treacherous store:
A wild delirium first the infant thrill'd;
But soon upon her breast he sunk—to
wake no more. 45

IV

THE CONVICT

[Composed (?).—Published 1798; never reprinted by W.]

THE glory of evening was spread through
the west;
—On the slope of a mountain I stood,
While the joy that precedes the calm
season of rest
Rang loud through the meadow and
wood.

'And must we then part from a dwelling
so fair?' 5
In the pain of my spirit I said,
And with a deep sadness I turned, to
repair
To the cell where the convict is laid.

The thick-ribbèd walls that o'ershadow
  the gate
Resound; and the dungeons unfold: 10
I pause; and at length, through the
  glimmering grate,
That outcast of pity behold.

His black matted hair on his shoulder is
  bent,
And deep is the sigh of his breath,
And with steadfast dejection his eyes are
  intent 15
On the fetters that link him to death.

'Tis sorrow enough on that visage to gaze,
  That body dismiss'd from his care;
Yet my fancy has pierced to his heart, and
  pourtrays
More terrible images there. 20

His bones are consumed, and his life-
  blood is dried,
With wishes the past to undo;
And his crime, through the pains that o'er-
  whelm him, descried,
Still blackens and grows on his view.

When from the dark synod, or blood-
  reeking field, 25
To his chamber the monarch is led,
All soothers of sense their soft virtue shall
  yield,
And quietness pillow his head.

But if grief, self-consumed, in oblivion
  would doze,
And conscience her tortures appease,
'Mid tumult and uproar this man must
  repose; 31
In the comfortless vault of disease.

When his fetters at night have so press'd
  on his limbs,
That the weight can no longer be borne,
If, while a half-slumber his memory
  bedims, 35
The wretch on his pallet should turn,

While the jail-mastiff howls at the dull
  clanking chain,
From the roots of his hair there shall
  start
A thousand sharp punctures of cold-
  sweating pain,
And terror shall leap at his heart. 40

But now he half-raises his deep-sunken
  eye,
And the motion unsettles a tear;
The silence of sorrow it seems to supply,
And asks of me why I am here.

'Poor victim! no idle intruder has stood
  With o'erweening complacence our
  state to compare, 46
But one, whose first wish is the wish to be
  good,
  Is come as a brother thy sorrows to
  share.

'At thy name though compassion her
  nature resign,
Though in virtue's proud mouth thy
  report be a stain, 50
My care, if the arm of the mighty were
  mine,
Would plant thee where yet thou
  might'st blossom again.'

V

ANDREW JONES

[Composed probably 1800.—Published 1800, 1802,
1805 (*Lyrical Ballads*); ed. 1815; omitted from
edd. 1820—1849-50.]

I HATE that Andrew Jones: he'll breed
His children up to waste and pillage.
I wish the press-gang or the drum
Would, with its rattling music, come,
And sweep him from the village! 5

I said not this, because he loves
Through the long day to swear and tipple;
But for the poor dear sake of one
To whom a foul deed he had done,
A friendless Man, a travelling Cripple! 10

For this poor crawling helpless wretch
Some Horseman who was passing by,
A penny on the ground had thrown;
But the poor Cripple was alone
And could not stoop—no help was nigh.

Inch-thick the dust lay on the ground 16
For it had long been droughty weather;
So with his staff the Cripple wrought
Among the dust till he had brought
The halfpennies together. 20

It chanc'd that Andrew pass'd that way
Just at the time; and there he found
The Cripple in the mid-day heat
Standing alone, and at his feet
He saw the penny on the ground. 25

He stooped and took the penny up:
And when the Cripple nearer drew,
Quoth Andrew, 'Under half-a-crown,
What a man finds is all his own,
And so, my Friend, good-day to you.'

And *hence* I say, that Andrew's boys 31
Will all be train'd to waste and pillage;
And wish'd the press-gang, or the drum
Would, with its rattling music, come,
And sweep him from the village! 35

VI

'ON NATURE'S INVITATION DO
I COME'

[Composed probably in 1800.—Published 1851.]

ON Nature's invitation do I come,
By Reason sanctioned. Can the choice
  mislead,
That made the calmest, fairest spot on
  earth,
With all its unappropriated good,

485

My own; and not mine only, for with me
Entrenched—say rather peacefully em-
bowered—   6
Under yon orchard, in yon humble cot,
A younger orphan of a Home extinct,
The only daughter of my parents dwells:
Aye, think on that, my heart, and cease to
stir;   10
Pause upon that, and let the breathing
frame
No longer breathe, but all be satisfied.
Oh, if such silence be not thanks to God
For what hath been bestowed, then where,
where then
Shall gratitude find rest? Mine eyes did
ne'er   15
Fix on a lovely object, nor my mind
Take pleasure in the midst of happy
thoughts,
But either she, whom now I have, who now
Divides with me this loved abode, was
there,
Or not far off. Where'er my footsteps
turned,   20
Her voice was like a hidden Bird that sang;
The thought of her was like a flash of light
Or an unseen companionship, a breath
Or fragrance independent of the wind.
In all my goings, in the new and old   25
Of all my meditations, and in this
Favourite of all, in this the most of all. . . .
Embrace me then, ye hills, and close me in.
Now in the clear and open day I feel   29
Your guardianship: I take it to my heart;
'Tis like the solemn shelter of the night.
But I would call thee beautiful; for mild,
And soft, and gay, and beautiful thou art,
Dear valley, having in thy face a smile,
Though peaceful, full of gladness. Thou
art pleased,   35
Pleased with thy crags, and woody steeps,
thy Lake,
Its one green Island, and its winding shores,
The multitude of little rocky hills,
Thy Church, and cottages of mountain-
stone
Clustered like stars some few, but single
most,   40
And lurking dimly in their shy retreats,
Or glancing at each other cheerful looks,
Like separated stars with clouds between.

VII[1]

'BLEAK SEASON WAS IT, TURBU-
LENT AND WILD'

[Composed (possibly) in 1800.—Published 1851.]

BLEAK season was it, turbulent and wild,
When hitherward we journeyed, side by
side,

---

[1] Nos. VI and VII are extracts, given by Bishop
Wordsworth in his *Memoirs* of the poet (1851), from
The Recluse, Book I, Part I, Home at Grasmere:—
a poem which, being copyright, is not included in
this volume. For two other extracts from the same

Through bursts of sunshine and through
flying showers,
Paced the long Vales, how long they were,
and yet
How fast that length of way was left
behind,   5
Wensley's rich Vale and Sedbergh's naked
heights.
The frosty wind, as if to make amends
For its keen breath, was aiding to our
steps,
And drove us onward as two ships at sea;
Or, like two birds, companions in mid-air,
Parted and reunited by the blast.   11
Stern was the face of nature; we rejoiced
In that stern countenance; for our souls
thence drew
A feeling of their strength. The naked
trees,
The icy brooks, as on we passed, appeared
To question us, 'Whence come ye? To
what end?'   16

VIII

AMONG ALL LOVELY THINGS MY
LOVE HAD BEEN

[Composed April 12, 1802.—Published 1807;
never reprinted by W.]

AMONG all lovely things my Love had
been;
Had noted well the stars, all flowers that
grew
About her home; but she had never seen
A Glow-worm, never one, and this I
knew.

While riding near her home one stormy
night   5
A single Glow-worm did I chance to espy;
I gave a fervent welcome to the sight,
And from my Horse I leapt; great joy
had I.

Upon a leaf the Glow-worm did I lay,
To bear it with me through the stormy
night: 10
And, as before, it shone without dismay;
Albeit putting forth a fainter light.

When to the Dwelling of my Love I came,
I went into the Orchard quietly;
And left the Glow-worm, blessing it by
name,   15
Laid safely by itself, beneath a Tree.

The whole next day, I hoped, and hoped
with fear;
At night the Glow-worm shone beneath
the Tree:
I led my Lucy to the spot, 'Look here!'
Oh! joy it was for her, and joy for me![1]

---

poem see *Water-Fowl*, page 174, and the *Preface to
The Excursion.*—ED.
[1] The incident described in this poem took place
in 1795—probably at Racedown—between the poet
and his sister Dorothy.—ED.

IX
SONNET[1]

[Composed (?).—Published October 10, 1803
(*Morning Post*); never reprinted by W.]

I FIND it written of Simonides
  That travelling in strange countries
    once he found
A corpse that lay expos'd upon the
    ground,
For which, with pains, he caused due
    obsequies
To be performed, and paid all holy fees. 5
Soon after, this man's Ghost unto him
    came
And told him not to sail as was his aim,
On board a ship then ready for the seas.
Simonides, admonished by the ghost,
Remained behind; the ship the following
    day   10
Set sail, was wrecked, and all on board
    were lost.
Thus was the tenderest Poet that could be,
Who sang in ancient Greece his moving
    lay,
Saved out of many by his piety.

X
GEORGE AND SARAH GREEN[2]

[Composed 1808.—Published September. 1839
(*Tait's Edinburgh Magazine*); never reprinted by
W.]

WHO weeps for strangers? Many wept
  For George and Sarah Green;
Wept for that pair's unhappy fate,
  Whose grave may here be seen.

By night, upon these stormy fells,   5
  Did wife and husband roam;
Six little ones at home had left,
  And could not find that home.

For *any* dwelling-place of man
  As vainly did they seek.   10
He perish'd; and a voice was heard—
  The widow's lonely shriek.

Not many steps, and she was left
  A body without life—
A few short steps were the chain that
    bound   15
  The husband to the wife.

Now do those sternly-featured hills
  Look gently on this grave;
And quiet *now* are the depths of air,
  As a sea without a wave.   20

[1] This sonnet bears no signature in the *Morning Post*, but Coleridge, in an unpublished letter, assigns it to Wordsworth. Cf. line 12 with line 53 of the Poem, No. II, on *September*, 1819 (*Poems of Sentiment*, XXVIII; p. 498), and with a passage in the *Essay on Epitaphs* (page 729) in which the story of this sonnet is related in prose.—ED.
[2] See De Quincey's *Early Memorials of Grasmere*.—ED.

But deeper lies the heart of peace
  In quiet more profound;
The heart of quietness is here
  Within this churchyard bound.

And from all agony of mind   25
  It keeps them safe, and far
From fear and grief, and from all need
  Of sun or guiding star.

O darkness of the grave! how deep,
  After that living night—   30
That last and dreary living one
  Of sorrow and affright?

O sacred marriage-bed of death,
  That keeps them side by side
In bond of peace, in bond of love,   3
  That may not be untied!

XI
TRANSLATION OF PART OF THE
FIRST BOOK OF THE ÆNEID

[Written c. 1816.—Published 1832 (*The Philologica Museum*); not reprinted by W.]

TO THE EDITORS OF THE 'PHILOLOGICAL MUSEUM'

Your letter, reminding me of an expectation I some time since held out to you of allowing some specimens of my translation from the Æneid to be printed in the 'Philological Museum,' was not very acceptable; for I had abandoned the thought of ever sending into the world any part of that experiment—for it was nothing more—an experiment begun for amusement, and I now think a less fortunate one than when I first named it to you. Having been displeased in modern translations with the additions of incongruous matter, I began to translate with a resolve to keep clear of that fault, by adding nothing; but I became convinced that a spirited translation can scarcely be accomplished in the English language without admitting a principle of compensation. On this point, however, I do not wish to insist, and merely send the following passage, taken at random, from a wish to comply with your request.—W. W.

BUT Cytherea, studious to invent
Arts yet untried, upon new counsels bent,
Resolves that Cupid, chang'd in form and
    face
To young Ascanius, should assume his
    place;
Present the maddening gifts, and kindle
    heat   5
Of passion at the bosom's inmost seat.
She dreads the treacherous house, the
    double tongue;
She burns, she frets—by Juno's rancour
    stung;
The calm of night is powerless to remove
These cares, and thus she speaks to winged
    Love: 10
'O son, my strength, my power! who
    dost despise
(What, save thyself, none dares through
    earth and skies)

SUPPLEMENT OF PIECES

The giant-quelling bolts of Jove, I flee,
O son, a suppliant to thy deity!
What perils meet Æneas in his course, 15
How Juno's hate with unrelenting force
Pursues thy brother—this to thee is
known;
And oft-times hast thou made my griefs
thine own.
Him now the generous Dido by soft chains
Of bland entreaty at her court detains; 20
Junonian hospitalities prepare
Such apt occasion that I dread a snare.
Hence, ere some hostile God can inter-
vene,
Would I, by previous wiles, inflame the
queen
With passion for Æneas, such strong love
That at my beck, mine only, she shall
move. 26
Hear, and assist;—the father's mandate
calls
His young Ascanius to the Tyrian walls;
He comes, my dear delight,—and costliest
things
Preserv'd from fire and flood for presents
brings. 30
Him will I take, and in close covert keep,
'Mid groves Idalian, lull'd to gentle sleep,
Or on Cythera's far-sequestered steep,
That he may neither know what hope is
mine,
Nor by his presence traverse the design.
Do thou, but for a single night's brief
space, 36
Dissemble; be that boy in form and face.
And when enraptured Dido shall receive
Thee to her arms, and kisses interweave
With many a fond embrace, while joy runs
high, 40
And goblets crown the proud festivity,
Instil thy subtle poison, and inspire,
At every touch, an unsuspected fire.'

Love, at the word, before his mother's
sight
Puts off his wings, and walks, with proud
delight, 45
Like young Iulus; but the gentlest dews
Of slumber Venus sheds, to circumfuse
The true Ascanius steep'd in placid rest;
Then wafts him, cherish'd on her careful
breast,
Through upper air to an Idalian glade, 50
Where he on soft *amaracus* is laid,
With breathing flowers embraced, and
fragrant shade.
But Cupid, following cheerily his guide
Achates, with the gifts to Carthage hied;
And, as the hall he entered, there, between
The sharers of her golden couch, was seen
Reclin'd in festal pomp the Tyrian queen.
The Trojans too (Æneas at their head),
On couches lie, with purple overspread:
Meantime in canisters is heap'd the bread,

Pellucid water for the hands is borne, 61
And napkins of smooth texture, finely
shorn.
Within are fifty handmaids, who prepare,
As they in order stand, the dainty fare;
And fume the household deities with store
Of odorous incense; while a hundred more
Match'd with an equal number of like age,
But each of manly sex, a docile page,
Marshal the banquet, giving with due
grace
To cup or viand its appointed place. 70
The Tyrians rushing in, an eager band,
Their painted couches seek, obedient to
command.
They look with wonder on the gifts—they
gaze
Upon Iulus, dazzled with the rays
That from his ardent countenance are
flung, 75
And charm'd to hear his simulating
tongue;
Nor pass unprais'd the robe and veil
divine,
Round which the yellow flowers and
wandering foliage twine.
But chiefly Dido, to the coming ill
Devoted, strives in vain her vast desires to
fill; 80
She views the gifts; upon the child then
turns
Insatiable looks, and gazing burns.
To ease a father's cheated love he hung
Upon Æneas, and around him clung;
Then seeks the queen; with her his arts he
tries; 85
She fastens on the boy enamour'd eyes,
Clasps in her arms, nor weens (O lot
unblest!)
How great a God, incumbent o'er her
breast,
Would fill it with his spirit. He, to please
His Acidalian mother, by degrees 90
Blots out Sichæus, studious to remove
The dead, by influx of a living love,
By stealthy entrance of a perilous guest,
Troubling a heart that had been long at
rest.

Now when the viands were withdrawn,
and ceas'd 95
The first division of the splendid feast,
While round a vacant board the chiefs
recline,
Huge goblets are brought forth; they
crown the wine.
Voices of gladness roll the walls around;
Those gladsome voices from the courts
rebound; 100
From gilded rafters many a blazing light
Depends, and torches overcome the night.
The minutes fly—till, at the queen's com-
mand,
A bowl of state is offered to her hand:

488

Then she, as Belus wont, and all the line
From Belus, filled it to the brim with
   wine;   106
Silence ensued. 'O Jupiter, whose care
Is hospitable dealing, grant my prayer!
Productive day be ʰthis of lasting joy
To Tyrians, and these exiles driven from
   Troy;   110
A day to future generations dear!
Let Bacchus, donor of soul-quick'ning
   cheer,
Be present; kindly Juno, be thou near!
And, Tyrians, may your choicest favours
   wait
Upon this hour, the bond to celebrate!'
She spake and shed an offering on the
   board;   116
Then sipp'd the bowl whence she the wine
   had pour'd
And gave to Bitias, urging the prompt lord;
He rais'd the bowl, and took a long deep
   draught;
Then every chief in turn the beverage
   quaff'd.   120

Graced with redundant hair, Iopas sings
The lore of Atlas, to resounding strings,
The labours of the Sun, the lunar wander-
   ings;
Whence human kind, and brute; what
   natural powers
Engender lightning, whence are falling
   showers.   125
He chaunts Arcturus,—that fraternal
   twain
The glittering Bears,—the Pleiads fraught
   with rain;
—Why suns in winter, shunning heaven's
   steep heights
Post seaward,—what impedes the tardy
   nights.
The learned song from Tyrian hearers
   draws   130
Loud shouts,—the Trojans echo the
   applause.
—But, lengthening out the night with
   converse new,
Large draughts of love unhappy Dido
   drew;
Of Priam ask'd, of Hector,—o'er and
   o'er—
What arms the son of bright Aurora
   wore;—   135
What steeds the car of Diomed could
   boast;
Among the leaders of the Grecian host
How looked Achilles—their dread paramount—
'But nay—the fatal wiles, O guest,
   recount,
Retrace the Grecian cunning from its
   source,   140
Your own grief and your friends'—your
   wandering course;

For now, till this seventh summer have
   ye rang'd
The sea, or trod the earth, to peace
   estrang'd.'

XII

SONNET

AUTHOR'S VOYAGE DOWN THE RHINE
(THIRTY YEARS AGO)

[Composed probably 1821.—Published 1822 (*Memorials of a Tour on the Continent*, 1820); never
reprinted by W.]

THE confidence of Youth our only Art,
And Hope gay Pilot of the bold design,
We saw the living Landscapes of the
   Rhine,
Reach after reach, salute us and depart;
Slow sink the Spires,—and up again they
   start!   5
But who shall count the Towers as they
   recline
O'er the dark steeps, or on the horizon
   line
Striding, with shattered crests, the eye
   athwart?
More touching still, more perfect was the
   pleasure,
When hurrying forward till the slack'ning
   stream   10
Spread like a spacious Mere, we there
   could measure
A smooth free course along the watery
   gleam
Think calmly on the past, and mark at
   leisure
Features which else had vanished like
   a dream.

XIII

A CENTO MADE BY WORDSWORTH

[Published 1835 (*Yarrow Revisited and other
Poems*); never reprinted by W.]

For printing [the following piece] some reason
should be given, as not a word of it is original:
it is simply a fine stanza of Akenside, connected
with a still finer from Beattie, by a couplet from
Thomson. This practice, in which the author
sometimes indulges, of linking together, in his
own mind, favourite passages from different
authors, seems in itself unobjectionable: but, as
the *publishing* such compilations might lead to
confusion in literature, he should deem himself
inexcusable in giving this specimen, were it not
from a hope that it might open to others a harmless source of *private* gratification.—W. W.

THRONED in the Sun's descending car
What Power unseen diffuses far
This tenderness of mind?
What Genius smiles on yonder flood?
What God in whispers from the wood 5
Bids every thought be kind?

SUPPLEMENT OF PIECES

O ever pleasing Solitude,
Companion of the wise and good,
Thy shades, thy silence, now be mine,
Thy charms my only theme;   10
My haunt the hollow cliff whose Pine
Waves o'er the gloomy stream;
Whence the scared Owl on pinions grey
Breaks from the rustling boughs,
And down the lone vale sails away   15
To more profound repose!

XIV

INSCRIPTION ON A ROCK AT RYDAL MOUNT. (1838)

WOULDST thou be gathered to Christ's
chosen flock,
Shun the broad way too easily explored,
And let thy path be hewn out of the Rock,
The living Rock of God's eternal Word.

XV

PROTEST AGAINST THE BALLOT (1838)

[Composed 1838.—Published 1838 (collected vol.
of *Sonnets*); 1839 (Supplement to ed. 1842);
afterwards omitted by W.]

FORTH rushed from Envy sprung and
Self-conceit,
A Power misnamed the SPIRIT of REFORM,
And through the astonished Island swept
in storm,
Threatening to lay all Orders at her feet
That crossed her way. Now stoops she to
entreat   5
Licence to hide at intervals her head
Where she may work, safe, undisquieted,
In a close Box, covert for Justice meet.
St. George of England! keep a watchful
eye
Fixed on the Suitor; frustrate her re-
quest—   10
Stifle her hope; for, if the State comply,
From such Pandorian gift may come a
Pest
Worse than the Dragon that bowed low
his crest,
Pierced by thy spear in glorious victory.

XVI

A POET TO HIS GRANDCHILD

SEQUEL TO 'A PLEA FOR AUTHORS'[1]

[Composed 1838.—Same dates and mode of publication as XV; omitted from edd. 1843—1849—
50.]

'SON of my buried Son, while thus thy
hand
Is clasping mine, it saddens me to think

[1] See page 222.—ED.

How Want may press thee down, and with
thee sink
Thy Children left unfit, through vain
demand
Of culture, even to feel or understand   5
My simplest Lay that to their memory
May cling;—hard fate! which haply need
not be
Did Justice mould the Statutes of the
Land.
A Book time-cherished and an honoured
name
Are high rewards; but bound they
Nature's claim   10
Or Reason's? No—hopes spun in timid
line
From out the bosom of a modest home
Extend through unambitious years to
come,
My careless Little-one, for thee and thine!'
May 23, 1838.

XVII

ON A PORTRAIT OF I. F. [ISABELLA FENWICK], PAINTED BY MARGA-RET GILLIES[1]

WE gaze—nor grieve to think that we
must die,
But that the precious love this friend hath
sown
Within our hearts, the love whose flower
hath blown
Bright as if heaven were ever in its eye,
Will pass so soon from human memory;   5
And not by strangers to our blood alone,
But by our best descendants be unknown,
Unthought of—this may surely claim a
sigh.
Yet, blessed Art, we yield not to dejection;
Thou against Time so feelingly dost strive.
Where'er, preserved in this most true
reflection,   11
An image of her soul is kept alive,
Some lingering fragrance of the pure
affection,
Whose flower with us will vanish, must
survive.
RYDAL MOUNT, *New Year's Day*, 1840.

XVIII

TO I. F.

THE star which comes at close of day to
shine
More heavenly bright than when it leads
the morn,
Is Friendship's emblem, whether the
forlorn
She visiteth, or, shedding light benign

[1] XVII and XVIII were first published (1851) in
the *Memoirs of William Wordsworth*, by his nephew,
the late Bishop of Lincoln.—ED.

490

Through shades that solemnize Life's
    calm decline,   5
Doth make the happy happier. This have
    we
Learnt, Isabel, from thy society,
Which now we too unwillingly resign
Though for brief absence. But farewell!
    the page
Glimmers before my sight through thank-
    ful tears,   10
Such as start forth, not seldom, to approve
Our truth, when we, old yet unchilled by
    age,
Call thee, though known but for a few
    fleet years,
The heart-affianced sister of our love!

RYDAL MOUNT, *Feb.* 1840.

XIX
'WHEN SEVERN'S SWEEPING FLOOD HAD OVERTHROWN'

In 1842 a bazaar was held in Cardiff Castle to raise funds for the building of a Church. Wordsworth assisted by contributing this Sonnet, which was printed and sold along with verses by James Montgomery and others (cf. Prof. Knight's note, in his edition of the *Poems*, Vol. VIII).—ED.

WHEN Severn's sweeping flood had over-
    thrown
St. Mary's Church, the preacher then
    would cry:—
'Thus, Christian people, God his might
    hath shown
That ye to him your love may testify;
Haste, and rebuild the pile.'—But not
    a stone   5
Resumed its place. Age after age went by,
And Heaven still lacked its due, though
    piety
In secret did, we trust, her loss bemoan.
But now her Spirit hath put forth its
    claim   9
In Power, and Poesy would lend her voice;
Let the new Church be worthy of its aim,
That in its beauty Cardiff may rejoice!
Oh! in the past if cause there was for
    shame,
Let not our times halt in their better
    choice.

RYDAL MOUNT, *Jan.* 23, 1842.

XX
THE EAGLE AND THE DOVE

[Composed 1842 (?).—Published 1842 (*La Petite Chouannerie ou Histoire d'un Collège Breton sous l'Empire*. By A. F. Rio).]

SHADE of Caractacus, if spirits love
The cause they fought for in their earthly
    home,
To see the Eagle ruffled by the Dove
May soothe thy memory of the chains of
    Rome.

These children claim thee for their sire;
    the breath   5
Of thy renown, from Cambrian mountains,
    fans
A flame within them that despises death
And glorifies the truant youth of Vannes.
With thy own scorn of tyrants they
    advance,
But truth divine has sanctified their rage,
A silver cross enchased with Flowers of
    France   11
Their badge, attests the holy fight they
    wage.
The shrill defiance of the young crusade
Their veteran foes mock as an idle noise;
But unto Faith and Loyalty comes aid   15
From Heaven, gigantic force to beardless
    boys.

XXI
LINES

INSCRIBED IN A COPY OF HIS POEMS SENT TO
THE QUEEN FOR THE ROYAL LIBRARY AT
WINDSOR

DEIGN, Sovereign Mistress! to accept a
    lay,
No Laureate offering of elaborate art;
But salutation taking its glad way
    From deep recesses of a loyal heart.

Queen, Wife and Mother! may All-
    judging Heaven   5
    Shower with a bounteous hand on Thee
        and Thine
Felicity that only can be given
    On earth to goodness blest by grace
        divine.

Lady! devoutly honoured and beloved
    Through every realm confided to thy
        sway;   10
May'st thou pursue thy course by God
    approved,
    And He will teach thy people to obey.

As thou art wont, thy sovereignty adorn
    With woman's gentleness, yet firm and
        staid;
So shall that earthly crown thy brows have
    worn   15
    Be changed for one whose glory cannot
        fade.

And now by duty urged, I lay this Book
    Before thy Majesty, in humble trust
That on its simplest pages thou wilt look
    With a benign indulgence more than
    just.   20

Nor wilt thou blame an aged Poet's
    prayer,
    That issuing hence may steal into thy
        mind
Some solace under weight of royal care,
    Or grief—the inheritance of human-
        kind.

SUPPLEMENT OF PIECES

For know we not ┤that from celestial
    spheres,   25
When Time was young, an inspiration
    came
(Oh were it mine!) to hallow saddest tears,
And help life onward in its noblest aim,
                W. W.
January 9th, 1846.

XXII

ODE ON THE INSTALLATION OF HIS ROYAL HIGHNESS PRINCE ALBERT AS CHANCELLOR OF THE UNIVERSITY OF CAMBRIDGE, JULY, 1847 [1]

[Composed 1847.—Published 1847.]

For thirst of power that Heaven dis-
    owns,
For temples, towers, and thrones
Too long insulted by the Spoiler's shock,
Indignant Europe cast
    Her stormy foe at last   5
To reap the whirlwind on a Libyan rock.
    War is passion's basest game
    Madly played to win a name:
Up starts some tyrant, Earth and Heaven
    to dare,
    The servile million bow;   10
But will the Lightning glance aside to
    spare
    The Despot's laurelled brow?

War is mercy, glory, fame,
Waged in Freedom's holy cause,
Freedom, such as man may claim 15
Under God's restraining laws.
Such is Albion's fame and glory,
Let rescued Europe tell the story.
But lo! what sudden cloud has darkened
    all
    The land as with a funeral pall? 20
The Rose of England suffers blight,
The Flower has drooped, the Isle's delight;
    Flower and bud together fall;
A Nation's hopes lie crushed in Clare-
    mont's desolate Hall.

Time a chequered mantle wears— 25
    Earth awakes from wintry sleep:
Again the Tree a blossom bears;
    Cease, Britannia, cease to weep!
Hark to the peals on this bright May-
    morn!
They tell that your future Queen is born.
    A Guardian Angel fluttered 31
    Above the babe, unseen;
    One word he softly uttered,
    It named the future Queen; 34
And a joyful cry through the Island rang,
As clear and bold as the trumpet's clang,

[1] The poet's nephew Christopher (late Bishop of Lincoln) aided in the composition of this 'commanded' Ode.—Ed.

As bland as the reed of peace:
    'VICTORIA be her name!'
For righteous triumphs are the base
Whereon Britannia rests her peaceful
    fame.   40

Time, in his mantle's sunniest fold
Uplifted in his arms the child,
And while the fearless infant smiled,
Her happier destiny foretold:—
    'Infancy, by Wisdom mild, 45
    Trained to health and artless beauty;
    Youth, by pleasure unbeguiled
    From the lore of lofty duty;
    Womanhood in pure renown,
    Seated on her lineal throne; 50
    Leaves of myrtle in her Crown,
    Fresh with lustre all their own.
Love, the treasure worth possessing
More than all the world beside,
This shall be her choicest blessing, 55
Oft to royal hearts denied.'

That eve, the Star of Brunswick shone
    With steadfast ray benign
On Gotha's ducal roof, and on
    The softly flowing Leine, 60
Nor failed to gild the spires of Bonn,
    And glittered on the Rhine.
Old Camus, too, on that prophetic night
    Was conscious of the ray;
And his willows whispered in its light, 65
    Not to the Zephyr's sway,
But with a Delphic life, in sight
    Of this auspicious day—
This day, when Granta hails her chosen
    Lord,
    And, proud of her award, 70
    Confiding in that Star serene,
Welcomes the Consort of a happy Queen.

Prince, in these collegiate bowers,
Where science, leagued with holier
    truth,
Guards the sacred heart of youth, 75
Solemn monitors are ours.
These reverend aisles, these hallowed
    towers,
Raised by many a hand august,
Are haunted by majestic Powers,
The Memories of the Wise and Just, 80
Who, faithful to a pious trust,
Here, in the Founder's Spirit sought
To mould and stamp the ore of thought
In that bold form and impress high
That best betoken patriot loyalty. 85
Not in vain those Sages taught,—
True disciples, good as great,
Have pondered here their country's
    weal,
Weighed the Future by the Past,
Learned how social frames may last, 90
And how a Land may rule its fate
By constancy inviolate,
Though worlds to their foundations reel
The sport of factious Hate or godless Zeal.

492

Albert, in thy race we cherish 95
A Nation's strength that will not perish
While England's sceptred Line
True to the King of Kings is found;
Like that Wise ancestor of thine
Who threw the Saxon shield o'er Luther's
  life 100
When first, above the yells of bigot strife,
  The trumpet of the Living Word
Assumed a voice of deep portentous
  sound,
From gladdened Elbe to startled Tiber
  heard.
What shield more sublime 105
E'er was blazoned or sung?
And the PRINCE whom we greet
From its Hero is sprung.
  Resound, resound the strain
  That hails him for our own! 110
Again, again, and yet again,
For the Church, the State, the Throne!
And that Presence fair and bright,
Ever blest wherever seen,
Who deigns to grace our festal rite, 115
The Pride of the Islands, VICTORIA
  THE QUEEN!

XXIII

QUINZAIN

CONJECTURALLY ASSIGNED TO WORDS-
WORTH

[Composed (?).—Published 1802 (*Morning Post*);
  never reprinted by W.]

A writer (E. H. C.) in the *Athenæum* of November 4, 1893, suggests that the following lines, which
appeared in the *Morning Post* on February 9, 1802,
were probably composed by Wordsworth. 'It may
be remembered,' writes E. H. C., 'that the phrase
"monthly grave" is to be found in *Lines to the
Moon* (1835); and in one of Wordsworth's latest
sonnets, that *To Lucca Giordano*, the aged poet
turns with pleasure to the delightful vision of
"young Endymion, couched on Latmos Hill."'
The suggestion is undoubtedly a happy one. The

rhyme-arrangement of these lines resembles that
of the piece beginning, *With how sad steps, O
Moon, thou climb'st the Sky*, which first appeared
in *Poems in Two Volumes* (1807), but may have
been written in or about 1802. Both pieces appear
to be experiments in metre. They are neither
sonnets nor quatorzains, but *quinzains*, or stanzas
consisting of fifteen lines each; though that published in 1807 was subsequently curtailed by one
line and placed amongst the *Miscellaneous Sonnets*
(1815 onwards). Moreover, the turn of the sentence in lines 8 and 9—the repetition of the substantive (*Nymphs*) in apposition, qualified by an
adjective or adjectival phrase—is of frequent
occurrence in Wordsworth's poetry. Cf. *Misc.
Son.*, Part II, xx, ll. 7, 8:—

  'As if to vindicate her beauty's right,
  Her beauty thoughtlessly disparaged.'—ED.[1]

WRITTEN IN A GROTTO

O MOON! if e'er I joyed when thy soft light
  Danc'd to the murmuring rill on
    Lomond's wave,
Or sighed for thy sweet presence some
    dark night,
  When thou wert hidden in thy monthly
    grave;
If e'er, on wings which active fancy gave,
  I sought thy golden vale with dancing
    flight, 6
Then, stretcht at ease in some sequestered
    cave,
  Gaz'd on thy lovely Nymphs with fond
    delight,
Thy Nymphs with more than earthly
    beauty bright;
If e'er thy beam, as Smyrna's shepherds
    tell, 10
  Soft as the gentle kiss of amorous maid
On the closed eyes of young Endymion
    fell,
  That he might wake to clasp thee in the
    shade:
Each night, while I recline within this cell,
Guide hither, O sweet Moon, the maid I
  love so well. 15

[1] [Mr. T. E. Casson points out (1926) that there is no very close resemblance between the rhyme-
arrangement of the above and that of the piece beginning *With how sad steps* in its original form of fifteen
lines, now subjoined for comparison (for the 14 line form see p. 211):

    'With how sad steps, O Moon, thou climb'st the sky,
    How silently, and with how wan a face!'
    Where art thou? Thou whom I have seen on high
    Running among the clouds a Wood-nymph's race?
    Unhappy Nuns, whose common breath's a sigh
    Which they would stifle, move at such a pace!
    The Northern Wind, to call thee to the chace,
    Must blow tonight his bugle horn. Had I
    The power of Merlin, Goddess! this should be:
    And all the Stars, now shrouded up in heaven,
    Should sally forth to keep thee company.
    What strife would then be yours, fair Creatures, driv'n
    Now up, now down, and sparkling in your glee!
    But, Cynthia, should to Thee the palm be giv'n.
    Queen both for beauty and for majesty.]

THE PRELUDE

OR

GROWTH OF A POET'S MIND

AN AUTOBIOGRAPHICAL POEM

ADVERTISEMENT

[BY THE EDITOR OF 1850.]

THE following Poem was commenced in the beginning of the year 1799, and completed in the summer of 1805.[1]

The design and occasion of the work are described by the Author in his Preface to the 'Excursion,' first published in 1814, where he thus speaks:—

'Several years ago, when the Author retired to his native mountains with the hope of being enabled to construct a literary work that might live, it was a reasonable thing that he should take a review of his own mind, and examine how far Nature and Education had qualified him for such an employment.

'As subsidiary to this preparation, he undertook to record, in verse, the origin and progress of his own powers, as far as he was acquainted with them.

'That work, addressed to a dear friend, most distinguished for his knowledge and genius, and to whom the Author's intellect is deeply indebted, has been long finished; and the result of the investigation which gave rise to it, was a determination to compose a philosophical Poem, containing views of Man, Nature, and Society, and to be entitled the "Recluse;" as having for its principal subject the sensations and opinions of a poet living in retirement.

'The preparatory poem is biographical, and conducts the history of the Author's mind to the point when he was emboldened to hope that his faculties were sufficiently matured for entering upon the arduous labour which he had proposed to himself; and the two works have the same kind of relation to each other, if he may so express himself, as the Ante-chapel has to the body of a Gothic Church. Continuing this allusion, he may be permitted to add, that his minor pieces, which have been long before the public, when they shall be properly arranged, will be found by the attentive reader to have such connection with the main work as may give them claim to be likened to the little cells, oratories, and sepulchral recesses, ordinarily included in those edifices.'

Such was the Author's language in the year 1814.

It will thence be seen, that the present Poem was intended to be introductory to the 'Recluse,' and that the 'Recluse,' if completed, would have consisted of Three Parts. Of these, the Second Part alone, viz. the 'Excursion,' was finished, and given to the world by the Author.

The First Book of the First Part of the 'Recluse' still [1850] remains in manuscript; but the Third Part was only planned. The materials of which it would have been formed have, however, been incorporated, for the most part, in the Author's other Publications, written subsequently to the 'Excursion.'

The Friend, to whom the present Poem is addressed, was the late SAMUEL TAYLOR COLERIDGE, who was resident in Malta, for the restoration of his health, when the greater part of it was composed.

Mr. Coleridge read a considerable portion of the Poem while he was abroad; and his feelings, on hearing it recited by the Author (after his return to his own country), are recorded in his Verses, addressed to Mr. Wordsworth, which will be found in the 'Sibylline Leaves,' p. 197, ed. 1817, or 'Poetical Works, by S. T. Coleridge,' vol. i., p. 206.

RYDAL MOUNT,
July 13th, 1850.

[1] For further information regarding the dates of composition of the several Books of *The Prelude* see *The Prelude,* ed. by E. de Selincourt, 2nd ed., 1928.

THE PRELUDE

BOOK FIRST

INTRODUCTION—CHILDHOOD AND SCHOOL-TIME

Oh there is blessing in this gentle breeze,
A visitant that while it fans my cheek
Doth seem half-conscious of the joy it
   brings
From the green fields, and from yon
   azure sky.
Whate'er its mission, the soft breeze can
   come   5
To none more grateful than to me;
   escaped
From the vast city, where I long had
   pined
A discontented sojourner: now free,
Free as a bird to settle where I will.
What dwelling shall receive me? in what
   vale   10
Shall be my harbour? underneath what
   grove
Shall I take up my home? and what
   clear stream
Shall with its murmur lull me into rest?
The earth is all before me. With a heart
Joyous, nor scared at its own liberty,   15
I look about; and should the chosen
   guide
Be nothing better than a wandering cloud,
I cannot miss my way. I breathe again!
Trances of thought and mountings of the
   mind
Come fast upon me: it is shaken off,   20
That burthen of my own unnatural self,
The heavy weight of many a weary day
Not mine, and such as were not made for
   me.
Long months of peace (if such bold word
   accord
With any promises of human life),   25
Long months of ease and undisturbed
   delight
Are mine in prospect; whither shall I
   turn,
By road or pathway, or through trackless
   field,
Up hill or down, or shall some floating
   thing   29
Upon the river point me out my course?

Dear Liberty! Yet what would it avail
But for a gift that consecrates the joy?
For I, methought, while the sweet breath
   of heaven
Was blowing on my body, felt within
A correspondent breeze, that gently
   moved   35
With quickening virtue, but is now
   become

A tempest, a redundant energy,
Vexing its own creation. Thanks to both,
And their congenial powers, that, while
   they join
In breaking up a long-continued frost,   40
Bring with them vernal promises, the
   hope
Of active days urged on by flying hours,—
Days of sweet leisure, taxed with patient
   thought
Abstruse, nor wanting punctual service
   high,   44
Matins and vespers of harmonious verse!

   Thus far, O Friend! did I, not used to
   make
A present joy the matter of a song,
Pour forth that day my soul in measured
   strains
That would not be forgotten, and are
   here
Recorded: to the open fields I told   50
A prophecy: poetic numbers came
Spontaneously to clothe in priestly robe
A renovated spirit singled out,
Such hope was mine, for holy services.
My own voice cheered me, and, far more,
   the mind's   55
Internal echo of the imperfect sound;
To both I listened, drawing from them
   both
A cheerful confidence in things to come.

   Content and not unwilling now to give
A respite to this passion, I paced on   60
With brisk and eager steps; and came,
   at length,
To a green shady place, where down I
   sate
Beneath a tree, slackening my thoughts
   by choice,
And settling into gentler happiness.
'Twas autumn, and a clear and placid day,
With warmth, as much as needed, from a
   sun   66
Two hours declined towards the west;
   a day
With silver clouds, and sunshine on the
   grass,
And in the sheltered and the sheltering
   grove
A perfect stillness. Many were the
   thoughts   70
Encouraged and dismissed, till choice
   was made
Of a known Vale, whither my feet should
   turn,

495

Nor rest till they had reached the very
  door
Of the one cottage which methought I
  saw.   74
No picture of mere memory ever looked
So fair; and while upon the fancied scene
I gazed with growing love, a higher power
Than Fancy gave assurance of some work
Of glory there forthwith to be begun,
Perhaps too there performed. Thus long
  I mused,   80
Nor e'er lost sight of what I mused upon,
Save when, amid the stately grove of oaks,
Now here, now there, an acorn, from its
  cup
Dislodged, through sere leaves rustled, or
  at once
To the bare earth dropped with a start-
  ling sound.   85
From that soft couch I rose not, till the
  sun
Had almost touched the horizon; casting
  then
A backward glance upon the curling
  cloud
Of city smoke, by distance ruralised;
Keen as a Truant or a Fugitive,   90
But as a Pilgrim resolute, I took,
Even with the chance equipment of that
  hour,
The road that pointed toward the chosen
  Vale.
It was a splendid evening, and my soul
Once more made trial of her strength,
  nor lacked   95
Æolian visitations; but the harp
Was soon defrauded, and the banded
  host
Of harmony dispersed in straggling
  sounds,
And lastly utter silence! 'Be it so;
Why think of anything but present
  good?'   100
So, like a home-bound labourer, I pursued
My way beneath the mellowing sun, that
  shed
Mild influence; nor left in me one wish
Again to bend the Sabbath of that time
To a servile yoke. What need of many
  words?   105
A pleasant loitering journey, through
  three days
Continued, brought me to my hermitage.
I spare to tell of what ensued, the life
In common things—the endless store of
  things,
Rare, or at least so seeming, every day
Found all about me in one neighbour-
  hood—   111
The self-congratulation, and, from morn
To night, unbroken cheerfulness serene.
But speedily an earnest longing rose
To brace myself to some determined aim,
Reading or thinking; either to lay up

New stores, or rescue from decay the old
By timely interference: and therewith
Came hopes still higher, that with out-
  ward life
I might endue some airy phantasies   120
That had been floating loose about for
  years,
And to such beings temperately deal
  forth
The many feelings that oppressed my
  heart.
That hope hath been discouraged; wel-
  come light
Dawns from the east, but dawns to dis-
  appear   125
And mock me with a sky that ripens not
Into a steady morning: if my mind,
Remembering the bold promise of the
  past,
Would gladly grapple with some noble
  theme,
Vain is her wish; where'er she turns she
  finds   130
Impediments from day to day renewed.

    And now it would content me to yield
  up
Those lofty hopes awhile, for present
  gifts
Of humbler industry. But, oh, dear
  Friend!
The Poet, gentle creature as he is,   135
Hath, like the Lover, his unruly times;
His fits when he is neither sick nor well,
Though no distress be near him but his
  own
Unmanageable thoughts: his mind, best
  pleased
While she as duteous as the mother dove
Sits brooding, lives not always to that
  end,   141
But like the innocent bird, hath goadings
  on
That drive her as in trouble through the
  groves;
With me is now such passion, to be
  blamed
No otherwise than as it lasts too long.

    When, as becomes a man who would
  prepare   146
For such an arduous work, I through
  myself
Make rigorous inquisition, the report
Is often cheering; for I neither seem
To lack that first great gift, the vital soul,
Nor general Truths, which are them-
  selves a sort   151
Of Elements and Agents, Under-powers,
Subordinate helpers of the living mind:
Nor am I naked of external things,
Forms, images, nor numerous other aids
Of less regard, though won perhaps with
  toil   156

And needful to build up a Poet's praise.
Time, place, and manners do I seek, and these
Are found in plenteous store, but nowhere such   159
As may be singled out with steady choice;
No little band of yet remembered names
Whom I, in perfect confidence, might hope
To summon back from lonesome banishment,
And make them dwellers in the hearts of men
Now living, or to live in future years.   165
Sometimes the ambitious Power of choice, mistaking
Proud spring-tide swellings for a regular sea,
Will settle on some British theme, some old
Romantic tale by Milton left unsung;
More often turning to some gentle place
Within the groves of Chivalry, I pipe 171
To shepherd swains, or seated harp in hand,
Amid reposing knights by a river side
Or fountain, listen to the grave reports
Of dire enchantments faced and overcome   175
By the strong mind, and tales of warlike feats,
Where spear encountered spear, and sword with sword
Fought, as if conscious of the blazonry
That the shield bore, so glorious was the strife;
Whence inspiration for a song that winds
Through ever-changing scenes of votive quest   181
Wrongs to redress, harmonious tribute paid
To patient courage and unblemished truth,
To firm devotion, zeal unquenchable,
And Christian meekness hallowing faithful loves.   185
Sometimes, more sternly moved, I would relate
How vanquished Mithridates northward passed,
And, hidden in the cloud of years, became
Odin, the Father of a race by whom
Perished the Roman Empire: how the friends   190
And followers of Sertorius, out of Spain
Flying, found shelter in the Fortunate Isles,
And left their usages, their arts and laws,
To disappear by a slow gradual death,
To dwindle and to perish one by one,   195
Starved in those narrow bounds: but not the soul
Of Liberty, which fifteen hundred years
Survived, and, when the European came

With skill and power that might not be withstood,
Did, like a pestilence, maintain its hold
And wasted down by glorious death that race   201
Of natural heroes: or I would record
How, in tyrannic times, some high-souled man,
Unnamed among the chronicles of kings,
Suffered in silence for Truth's sake; or tell,   205
How that one Frenchman,[1] through continued force
Of meditation on the inhuman deeds
Of those who conquered first the Indian Isles,
Went single in his ministry across   209
The Ocean; not to comfort the oppressed,
But, like a thirsty wind, to roam about
Withering the Oppressor: how Gustavus sought
Help at his need in Dalecarlia's mines:
How Wallace fought for Scotland; left the name
Of Wallace to be found, like a wild flower,
All over his dear Country; left the deeds   216
Of Wallace, like a family of Ghosts,
To people the steep rocks and river banks,
Her natural sanctuaries, with a local soul
Of independence and stern liberty.   220
Sometimes it suits me better to invent
A tale from my own heart, more near akin
To my own passions and habitual thoughts;
Some variegated story, in the main
Lofty, but the unsubstantial structure melts   225
Before the very sun that brightens it,
Mist into air dissolving! Then a wish,
My last and favourite aspiration, mounts
With yearning toward some philosophic song
Of Truth that cherishes our daily life; 230
With meditations passionate from deep
Recesses in man's heart, immortal verse
Thoughtfully fitted to the Orphean lyre;
But from this awful burthen I full soon
Take refuge and beguile myself with trust   235
That mellower years will bring a riper mind
And clearer insight. Thus my days are past
In contradiction; with no skill to part
Vague longing, haply bred by want of power,
From paramount impulse not to be withstood,   240
A timorous capacity from prudence,
From circumspection, infinite delay.

[1] Dominique de Gourgues, who in 1567 sailed to Florida to avenge the massacre of the French by the Spaniards.—ED. of 1850.

Humility and modest awe themselves
Betray me, serving often for a cloak 244
To a more subtle selfishness; that now
Locks every function up in blank reserve,
Now dupes me, trusting to an anxious
    eye
That with intrusive restlessness beats off
Simplicity and self-presented truth.
Ah! better far than this, to stray about
Voluptuously through fields and rural
    walks,   251
And ask no record of the hours, resigned
To vacant musing, unreproved neglect
Of all things, and deliberate holiday. 254
Far better never to have heard the name
Of zeal and just ambition, than to live
Baffled and plagued by a mind that every
    hour
Turns recreant to her task; takes heart
    again,
Then feels immediately some hollow
    thought
Hang like an interdict upon her hopes.
This is my lot; for either still I find 261
Some imperfection in the chosen theme,
Or see of absolute accomplishment
Much wanting, so much wanting, in my-
    self,
That I recoil and droop, and seek repose
In listlessness from vain perplexity, 266
Unprofitably travelling toward the grave,
Like a false steward who hath much
    received
And renders nothing back.
                          Was it for this
That one, the fairest of all rivers, loved
To blend his murmurs with my nurse's
    song,   271
And, from his alder shades and rocky falls,
And from his fords and shallows, sent a
    voice
That flowed along my dreams? For this,
    didst thou,   274
O Derwent! winding among grassy holms
Where I was looking on, a babe in arms,
Make ceaseless music that composed my
    thoughts
To more than infant softness, giving me
Amid the fretful dwellings of mankind
A foretaste, a dim earnest, of the calm
That Nature breathes among the hills
    and groves.   281

When he had left the mountains and
    received
On his smooth breast the shadow of those
    towers
That yet survive, a shattered monument
Of feudal sway, the bright blue river
    passed   285
Along the margin of our terrace walk;
A tempting playmate whom we dearly
    loved.
Oh, many a time have I, a five years' child,

In a small mill-race severed from his
    stream,
Made one long bathing of a summer's
    day;   290
Basked in the sun, and plunged and
    basked again
Alternate, all a summer's day, or scoured
The sandy fields, leaping through flowery
    groves
Of yellow ragwort; or when rock and
    hill,
The woods, and distant Skiddaw's lofty
    height,   295
Were bronzed with deepest radiance,
    stood alone
Beneath the sky, as if I had been born
On Indian plains, and from my mother's
    hut
Had run abroad in wantonness, to sport,
A naked savage, in the thunder shower.

Fair seed-time had my soul, and I grew
    up   301
Fostered alike by beauty and by fear:
Much favoured in my birthplace, and no
    less
In that belovèd Vale to which erelong
We were transplanted—there were we let
    loose   305
For sports of wider range. Ere I had
    told
Ten birth-days, when among the
    mountain-slopes
Frost, and the breath of frosty wind, had
    snapped
The last autumnal crocus, 'twas my joy
With store of springes o'er my shoulder
    hung   310
To range the open heights where wood-
    cocks run
Among the smooth green turf. Through
    half the night,
Scudding away from snare to snare, I
    plied
That anxious visitation;—moon and stars
Were shining o'er my head. I was alone,
And seemed to be a trouble to the peace
That dwelt among them. Sometimes it
    befell   317
In these night wanderings, that a strong
    desire
O'erpowered my better reason, and the
    bird
Which was the captive of another's toil
Became my prey; and when the deed was
    done   321
I heard among the solitary hills
Low breathings coming after me, and
    sounds
Of undistinguishable motion, steps
Almost as silent as the turf they trod. 325

    Nor less when spring had warmed the
        cultured Vale,

Roved we as plunderers where the mother-
  bird
Had in high places built her lodge;
  though mean
Our object and inglorious, yet the end
Was not ignoble. Oh! when I have hung
Above the raven's nest, by knots of grass
And half-inch fissures in the slippery
  rock
But ill sustained, and almost (so it
  seemed)
Suspended by the blast that blew amain,
Shouldering the naked crag, oh, at that
  time   335
While on the perilous ridge I hung alone,
With what strange utterance did the loud
  dry wind
Blow through my ear! the sky seemed not
  a sky
Of earth—and with what motion moved
  the clouds!

    Dust as we are, the immortal spirit
      grows   340
Like harmony in music; there is a dark
Inscrutable workmanship that reconciles
Discordant elements, makes them cling
  together
In one society. How strange that all
The terrors, pains, and early miseries, 345
Regrets, vexations, lassitudes interfused
Within my mind, should e'er have borne
  a part,
And that a needful part, in making up
The calm existence that is mine when I
Am worthy of myself! Praise to the end!
Thanks to the means which Nature
  deigned to employ;   351
Whether her fearless visitings, or those
That came with soft alarm, like hurtless
  light
Opening the peaceful clouds; or she may
  use
Severer interventions, ministry   355
More palpable, as best might suit her aim.

    One summer evening (led by her) I
      found
A little boat tied to a willow tree
Within a rocky cave, its usual home.
Straight I unloosed her chain, and step-
  ping in   360
Pushed from the shore. It was an act of
  stealth
And troubled pleasure, nor without the
  voice
Of mountain-echoes did my boat move on;
Leaving behind her still, on either side,
Small circles glittering idly in the moon,
Until they melted all into one track   366
Of sparkling light. But now, like one who
  rows,
Proud of his skill, to reach a chosen point
With an unswerving line, I fixed my view
Upon the summit of a craggy ridge,   370

The horizon's utmost boundary; for
  above
Was nothing but the stars and the grey
  sky.
She was an elfin pinnace; lustily
I dipped my oars into the silent lake,
And, as I rose upon the stroke, my boat
Went heaving through the water like a
  swan;   376
When, from behind that craggy steep till
  then
The horizon's bound, a huge peak, black
  and huge,
As if with voluntary power instinct
Upreared its head. I struck and struck
  again,   380
And growing still in stature the grim
  shape
Towered up between me and the stars,
  and still,
For so it seemed, with purpose of its own
And measured motion like a living thing,
Strode after me. With trembling oars I
  turned,   385
And through the silent water stole my
  way
Back to the covert of the willow tree;
There in her mooring-place I left my
  bark,—
And through the meadows homeward
  went, in grave   389
And serious mood; but after I had seen
That spectacle, for many days, my brain
Worked with a dim and undetermined
  sense
Of unknown modes of being; o'er my
  thoughts   393
There hung a darkness, call it solitude
Or blank desertion. No familiar shapes
Remained, no pleasant images of trees,
Of sea or sky, no colours of green fields;
But huge and mighty forms, that do not
  live
Like living men, moved slowly through
  the mind
By day, and were a trouble to my dreams.

    Wisdom and Spirit of the universe! 401
Thou Soul that art the eternity of thought,
That givest to forms and images a breath
And everlasting motion, not in vain
By day or star-light thus from my first
  dawn   405
Of childhood didst thou intertwine for me
The passions that build up our human
  soul;
Not with the mean and vulgar works of
  man,
But with high objects, with enduring
  things—
With life and nature—purifying thus   410
The elements of feeling and of thought,
And sanctifying, by such discipline,
Both pain and fear, until we recognise

A grandeur in the beatings of the heart.
Nor was this fellowship vouchsafed to me
With stinted kindness. In November
    days,   416
When vapours rolling down the valley
    made
A lonely scene more lonesome, among
    woods,
At noon and 'mid the calm of summer
    nights,
When, by the margin of the trembling
    lake,   420
Beneath the gloomy hills homeward I
    went
In solitude, such intercourse was mine;
Mine was it in the fields both day and
    night,
And by the waters, all the summer long.

And in the frosty season, when the sun
Was set, and visible for many a mile   426
The cottage windows blazed through
    twilight gloom,
I heeded not their summons: happy time
It was indeed for all of us—for me
It was a time of rapture! Clear and loud
The village clock tolled six,—I wheeled
    about,   431
Proud and exulting like an untired horse
That cares not for his home. All shod
    with steel,
We hissed along the polished ice in games
Confederate, imitative of the chase   435
And woodland pleasures,—the resound-
    ing horn,
The pack loud chiming, and the hunted
    hare.
So through the darkness and the cold we
    flew,
And not a voice was idle; with the din
Smitten, the precipices rang aloud;   440
The leafless trees and every icy crag
Tinkled like iron; while far distant hills
Into the tumult sent an alien sound
Of melancholy not unnoticed, while the
    stars
Eastward were sparkling clear, and in the
    west   445
The orange sky of evening died away.
Not seldom from the uproar I retired
Into a silent bay, or sportively
Glanced sideway, leaving the tumultuous
    throng,
To cut across the reflex of a star   450
That fled, and, flying still before me,
    gleamed
Upon the glassy plain; and oftentimes,
When we had given our bodies to the
    wind,
And all the shadowy banks on either side
Came sweeping through the darkness,
    spinning still   455
The rapid line of motion, then at once
Have I, reclining back upon my heels,

Stopped short; yet still the solitary cliffs
Wheeled by me—even as if the earth had
    rolled
With visible motion her diurnal round!
Behind me did they stretch in solemn
    train,   461
Feebler and feebler, and I stood and
    watched
Till all was tranquil as a dreamless sleep.

Ye Presences of Nature in the sky
And on the earth! Ye Visions of the
    hills!   465
And Souls of lonely places! can I think
A vulgar hope was yours when ye em-
    ployed
Such ministry, when ye through many
    a year
Haunting me thus among my boyish
    sports,
On caves and trees, upon the woods and
    hills,   470
Impressed upon all forms the characters
Of danger or desire; and thus did make
The surface of the universal earth
With triumph and delight, with hope and
    fear,
Work like a sea?
            Not uselessly employed,
Might I pursue this theme through every
    change   476
Of exercise and play, to which the year
Did summon us in his delightful round.

We were a noisy crew; the sun in
    heaven
Beheld not vales more beautiful than
    ours;   480
Nor saw a band in happiness and joy
Richer, or worthier of the ground they
    trod.
I could record with no reluctant voice
The woods of autumn, and their hazel
    bowers
With milk-white clusters hung; the rod
    and line,   485
True symbol of hope's foolishness, whose
    strong
And unreproved enchantment led us on
By rocks and pools shut out from every
    star,
All the green summer, to forlorn cascades
Among the windings hid of mountain
    brooks.   490
—Unfading recollections! at this hour
The heart is almost mine with which I
    felt,
From some hill-top on sunny afternoons,
The paper kite high among fleecy clouds
Pull at her rein like an impetuous courser;
Or, from the meadows sent on gusty
    days,   496
Beheld her breast the wind, then suddenly
Dashed headlong, and rejected by the
    storm.

Ye lowly cottages wherein we dwelt,
A ministration of your own was yours;
Can I forget you, being as you were 501
So beautiful among the pleasant fields
In which ye stood? or can I here forget
The plain and seemly countenance with
    which
Ye dealt out your plain comforts? Yet
    had ye 505
Delights and exultations of your own.
Eager and never weary we pursued
Our home-amusements by the warm peat-
    fire
At evening, when with pencil, and smooth
    slate
In square divisions parcelled out and all
With crosses and with cyphers scribbled
    o'er, 511
We schemed and puzzled, head opposed
    to head
In strife too humble to be named in verse:
Or round the naked table, snow-white
    deal,
Cherry or maple, sate in close array, 515
And to the combat, Loo or Whist, led on
A thick-ribbed army; not, as in the world,
Neglected and ungratefully thrown by
Even for the very service they had
    wrought,
But husbanded through many a long
    campaign. 520
Uncouth assemblage was it, where no few
Had changed their functions; some,
    plebeian cards
Which Fate, beyond the promise of their
    birth,
Had dignified, and called to represent
The persons of departed potentates. 525
Oh, with what echoes on the board they
    fell!
Ironic diamonds,—clubs, hearts, dia-
    monds, spades,
A congregation piteously akin!
Cheap matter offered they to boyish wit,
Those sooty knaves, precipitated down
With scoffs and taunts, like Vulcan out
    of heaven: 531
The paramount ace, a moon in her eclipse,
Queens gleaming through their splen-
    dour's last decay,
And monarchs surly at the wrongs sus-
    tained
By royal visages. Meanwhile abroad 535
Incessant rain was falling, or the frost
Raged bitterly, with keen and silent tooth;
And, interrupting oft that eager game,
From under Esthwaite's splitting fields of
    ice
The pent-up air, struggling to free itself,
Gave out to meadow-grounds and hills a
    loud 541
Protracted yelling, like the noise of
    wolves
Howling in troops along the Bothnic Main.

Nor, sedulous as I have been to trace
How Nature by extrinsic passion first 545
Peopled the mind with forms sublime or
    fair,
And made me love them, may I here omit
How other pleasures have been mine, and
    joys
Of subtler origin; how I have felt,
Not seldom even in that tempestuous time,
Those hallowed and pure motions of the
    sense 551
Which seem, in their simplicity, to own
An intellectual charm; that calm delight
Which, if I err not, surely must belong
To those first-born affinities that fit 555
Our new existence to existing things,
And, in our dawn of being, constitute
The bond of union between life and joy.

Yes, I remember when the changeful
    earth,
And twice five summers on my mind had
    stamped 560
The faces of the moving year, even then
I held unconscious intercourse with beauty
Old as creation, drinking in a pure
Organic pleasure from the silver wreaths
Of curling mist, or from the level plain 565
Of waters coloured by impending clouds.

The sands of Westmoreland, the creeks
    and bays
Of Cumbria's rocky limits, they can tell
How, when the Sea threw off his evening
    shade 569
And to the shepherd's hut on distant hills
Sent welcome notice of the rising moon,
How I have stood, to fancies such as these
A stranger, linking with the spectacle 573
No conscious memory of a kindred sight,
And bringing with me no peculiar sense
Of quietness or peace; yet have I stood,
Even while mine eye hath moved o'er
    many a league
Of shining water, gathering as it seemed,
Through every hair-breadth in that field
    of light, 579
New pleasure like a bee among the flowers.

Thus oft amid those fits of vulgar joy
Which, through all seasons, on a child's
    pursuits
Are prompt attendants, 'mid that giddy
    bliss
Which, like a tempest, works along the
    blood
And is forgotten; even then I felt 585
Gleams like the flashing of a shield;—the
    earth
And common face of Nature spake to me
Rememberable things; sometimes, 'tis
    true,
By chance collisions and quaint accidents
(Like those ill-sorted unions, work sup-
    posed 590

Of evil-minded fairies), yet not vain
Nor profitless, if haply they impressed
Collateral objects and appearances,   593
Albeit lifeless then, and doomed to sleep
Until maturer seasons called them forth
To impregnate and to elevate the mind.
—And if the vulgar joy by its own weight
Wearied itself out of the memory,
The scenes which were a witness of that
    joy
Remained in their substantial lineaments
Depicted on the brain, and to the eye   601
Were visible, a daily sight; and thus
By the impressive discipline of fear,
By pleasure and repeated happiness,
So frequently repeated, and by force   605
Of obscure feelings representative
Of things forgotten, these same scenes so
    bright,
So beautiful, so majestic in themselves,
Though yet the day was distant, did
    become
Habitually dear, and all their forms   610
And changeful colours by invisible links
Were fastened to the affections.
                                 I began
My story early—not misled, I trust,
By an infirmity of love for days
Disowned by memory—ere the breath of
    spring   615
Planting my snowdrops among winter
    snows:
Nor will it seem to thee, O Friend! so
    prompt
In sympathy, that I have lengthened out
With fond and feeble tongue a tedious tale.
Meanwhile, my hope has been, that I
    might fetch   620
Invigorating thoughts from former years;
Might fix the wavering balance of my
    mind,

And haply meet reproaches too, whose
    power
May spur me on, in manhood now
    mature,
To honourable toil. Yet should these
    hopes   625
Prove vain, and thus should neither I be
    taught
To understand myself, nor thou to know
With better knowledge how the heart
    was framed
Of him thou lovest; need I dread from
    thee
Harsh judgments, if the song be loth to
    quit   630
Those recollected hours that have the
    charm
Of visionary things, those lovely forms
And sweet sensations that throw back
    our life,
And almost make remotest infancy
A visible scene, on which the sun is
    shining?   635

One end at least hath been attained; my
    mind
Hath been revived, and if this genial mood
Desert me not, forthwith shall be brought
    down
Through later years the story of my life.
The road lies plain before me;—'tis a
    theme   640
Single and of determined bounds; and
    hence
I choose it rather at this time, than work
Of ampler or more varied argument,
Where I might be discomfited and lost:
And certain hopes are with me, that to
    thee   645
This labour will be welcome, honoured
    Friend!

BOOK SECOND

SCHOOL-TIME (*continued*)

THUS far, O Friend! have we, though
    leaving much
Unvisited, endeavoured to retrace
The simple ways in which my childhood
    walked;
Those chiefly that first led me to the love
Of rivers, woods, and fields. The passion
    yet   5
Was in its birth, sustained as might befall
By nourishment that came unsought; for
    still
From week to week, from month to
    month, we lived
A round of tumult. Duly were our games
Prolonged in summer till the day-light
    failed: 10

No chair remained before the doors; the
    bench
And threshold steps were empty; fast
    asleep
The labourer, and the old man who had
    sate
A later lingerer; yet the revelry
Continued and the loud uproar: at last,
When all the ground was dark, and
    twinkling stars   16
Edged the black clouds, home and to bed
    we went,
Feverish with weary joints and beating
    minds.
Ah! is there one who ever has been
    young,

502

Nor needs a warning voice to tame the
　　pride   20
Of intellect and virtue's self-esteem?
One is there, though the wisest and the
　　best
Of all mankind, who covets not at times
Union that cannot be;—who would not
　　give,
If so he might, to duty and to truth   25
The eagerness of infantine desire?
A tranquillising spirit presses now
On my corporeal frame, so wide appears
The vacancy between me and those days
Which yet have such self-presence in my
　　mind,   30
That, musing on them, often do I seem
Two consciousnesses, conscious of myself
And of some other Being. A rude mass
Of native rock, left midway in the square
Of our small market village, was the
　　goal
Or centre of these sports; and when,
　　returned   36
After long absence, thither I repaired,
Gone was the old grey stone, and in its
　　place
A smart Assembly-room usurped the
　　ground
That had been ours. There let the fiddle
　　scream,   40
And be ye happy! Yet, my Friends! I
　　know
That more than one of you will think with
　　me
Of those soft starry nights, and that old
　　Dame
From whom the stone was named, who
　　there had sate,
And watched her table with its huckster's
　　wares   45
Assiduous, through the length of sixty
　　years.

We ran a boisterous course; the year
　　span round
With giddy motion. But the time ap-
　　proached
That brought with it a regular desire
For calmer pleasures, when the winning
　　forms   50
Of Nature were collaterally attached
To every scheme of holiday delight
And every boyish sport, less grateful else
And languidly pursued.
　　　　　　　When summer came,
Our pastime was, on bright half-holidays,
To sweep along the plain of Windermere
With rival oars; and the selected bourne
Was now an Island musical with birds
That sang and ceased not; now a Sister
　　Isle
Beneath the oaks' umbrageous covert,
　　sown   60
With lilies of the valley like a field;

And now a third small Island, where
　　survived
In solitude the ruins of a shrine
Once to Our Lady dedicate, and served
Daily with chaunted rites. In such a
　　race   65
So ended, disappointment could be none,
Uneasiness, or pain, or jealousy:
We rested in the shade, all pleased alike,
Conquered and conqueror. Thus the
　　pride of strength,
And the vain-glory of superior skill,   70
Were tempered; thus was gradually pro-
　　duced
A quiet independence of the heart;
And to my Friend who knows me I may
　　add,
Fearless of blame, that hence for future
　　days
Ensued a diffidence and modesty,   75
And I was taught to feel, perhaps too
　　much,
The self-sufficing power of Solitude.

Our daily meals were frugal, Sabine
　　fare!
More than we wished we knew the bless-
　　ing then
Of vigorous hunger—hence corporeal
　　strength   80
Unsapped by delicate viands; for, exclude
A little weekly stipend, and we lived
Through three divisions of the quartered
　　year
In penniless poverty. But now to school
From the half-yearly holidays returned,
We came with weightier purses, that
　　sufficed   86
To furnish treats more costly than the
　　Dame
Of the old grey stone, from her scant
　　board, supplied.
Hence rustic dinners on the cool green
　　ground,
Or in the woods, or by a river side   90
Or shady fountain, while among the
　　leaves
Soft airs were stirring, and the mid-day sun
Unfelt shone brightly round us in our joy.
Nor is my aim neglected if I tell
How sometimes, in the length of those
　　half-years,   95
We from our funds drew largely;—proud
　　to curb,
And eager to spur on, the galloping steed;
And with the cautious inn-keeper, whose
　　stud
Supplied our want, we haply might
　　employ
Sly subterfuge, if the adventure's bound
Were distant: some famed temple where
　　of yore   101
The Druids worshipped, or the antique
　　walls

503

Of that large abbey, where within the Vale
Of Nightshade, to St. Mary's honour built,
Stands yet a mouldering pile with fractured arch, 105
Belfry, and images, and living trees;
A holy scene!—Along the smooth green turf
Our horses grazed. To more than inland peace,
Left by the west wind sweeping overhead
From a tumultuous ocean, trees and towers 110
In that sequestered valley may be seen,
Both silent and both motionless alike;
Such the deep shelter that is there, and such
The safeguard for repose and quietness.

Our steeds remounted and the summons given, 115
With whip and spur we through the chauntry flew
In uncouth race, and left the cross-legged knight,
And the stone-abbot, and that single wren
Which one day sang so sweetly in the nave
Of the old church, that—though from recent showers 120
The earth was comfortless, and, touched by faint
Internal breezes, sobbings of the place
And respirations, from the roofless walls
The shuddering ivy dripped large drops—yet still
So sweetly 'mid the gloom the invisible bird 125
Sang to herself, that there I could have made
My dwelling-place, and lived for ever there
To hear such music. Through the walls we flew
And down the valley, and, a circuit made
In wantonness of heart, through rough and smooth 130
We scampered homewards. Oh, ye rocks and streams,
And that still spirit shed from evening air!
Even in this joyous time I sometimes felt
Your presence, when with slackened step we breathed
Along the sides of the steep hills, or when
Lighted by gleams of moonlight from the sea 136
We beat with thundering hoofs the level sand.

Midway on long Winander's eastern shore,
Within the crescent of a pleasant bay,

A tavern stood; no homely-featured house, 140
Primeval like its neighbouring cottages,
But 'twas a splendid place, the door beset
With chaises, grooms, and liveries, and within
Decanters, glasses, and the blood-red wine.
In ancient times, or ere the Hall was built 145
On the large island, had this dwelling been
More worthy of a poet's love, a hut,
Proud of its one bright fire and sycamore shade.
But—though the rhymes were gone that once inscribed
The threshold, and large golden characters, 150
Spread o'er the spangled sign-board, had dislodged
The old Lion and usurped his place, in slight
And mockery of the rustic painter's hand—
Yet, to this hour, the spot to me is dear
With all its foolish pomp. The garden lay 155
Upon a slope surmounted by a plain
Of a small bowling-green; beneath us stood
A grove, with gleams of water through the trees
And over the tree-tops; nor did we want
Refreshment, strawberries and mellow cream. 160
There, while through half an afternoon we played
On the smooth platform, whether skill prevailed
Or happy blunder triumphed, bursts of glee
Made all the mountains ring. But, ere nightfall,
When in our pinnace we returned at leisure 165
Over the shadowy lake, and to the beach
Of some small island steered our course with one,
The Minstrel of the Troop, and left him there,
And rowed off gently, while he blew his flute 169
Alone upon the rock—oh, then, the calm
And dead still water lay upon my mind
Even with a weight of pleasure, and the sky,
Never before so beautiful, sank down
Into my heart, and held me like a dream!
Thus were my sympathies enlarged, and thus 175
Daily the common range of visible things
Grew dear to me: already I began
To love the sun; a boy I loved the sun,
Not as I since have loved him, as a pledge

And surety of our earthly life, a light 180
Which we behold and feel we are alive;
Nor for his bounty to so many worlds—
But for this cause, that I had seen him
    lay
His beauty on the morning hills, had seen
The western mountain touch his setting
    orb,   185
In many a thoughtless hour, when, from
    excess
Of happiness, my blood appeared to flow
For its own pleasure, and I breathed with
    joy.
And, from like feelings, humble though
    intense,
To patriotic and domestic love   190
Analogous, the moon to me was dear;
For I could dream away my purposes,
Standing to gaze upon her while she hung
Midway between the hills, as if she knew
No other region, but belonged to thee, 195
Yea, appertained by a peculiar right
To thee and thy grey huts, thou one dear
    Vale!

   Those incidental charms which first
       attached
My heart to rural objects, day by day
Grew weaker, and I hasten on to tell 200
How Nature, intervenient till this time
And secondary, now at length was sought
For her own sake. But who shall parcel
    out
His intellect by geometric rules,
Split like a province into round and
    square?   205
Who knows the individual hour in which
His habits were first sown, even as a seed?
Who that shall point as with a wand and
    say
'This portion of the river of my mind
Came from yon fountain?' Thou, my
    Friend! art one   210
More deeply read in thy own thoughts;
    to thee
Science appears but what in truth she is,
Not as our glory and our absolute boast,
But as a succedaneum, and a prop
To our infirmity. No officious slave 215
Art thou of that false secondary power
By which we multiply distinctions, then
Deem that our puny boundaries are things
That we perceive, and not that we have
    made.
To thee, unblinded by these formal arts,
The unity of all hath been revealed, 221
And thou wilt doubt, with me less aptly
    skilled
Than many are to range the faculties
In scale and order, class the cabinet
Of their sensations, and in voluble phrase
Run through the history and birth of
    each   226
As of a single independent thing.

Hard task, vain hope, to analyse the
    mind,
If each most obvious and particular
    thought,
Not in a mystical and idle sense,   230
But in the words of Reason deeply
    weighed,
Hath no beginning.
                   Blest the infant Babe,
(For with my best conjecture I would
    trace
Our Being's earthly progress,) blest the
    Babe,
Nursed in his Mother's arms, who sinks
    to sleep,   235
Rocked on his Mother's breast; who with
    his soul
Drinks in the feelings of his Mother's
    eye!
For him, in one dear Presence, there
    exists
A virtue which irradiates and exalts
Objects through widest intercourse of
    sense.   240
No outcast he, bewildered and depressed:
Along his infant veins are interfused
The gravitation and the filial bond
Of nature that connect him with the
    world.
Is there a flower, to which he points with
    hand   245
Too weak to gather it, already love
Drawn from love's purest earthly fount
    for him
Hath beautified that flower; already
    shades
Of pity cast from inward tenderness
Do fall around him upon aught that bears
Unsightly marks of violence or harm. 251
Emphatically such a Being lives,
Frail creature as he is, helpless as frail,
An inmate of this active universe:
For feeling has to him imparted power
That through the growing faculties of
    sense   256
Doth like an agent of the one great Mind
Create, creator and receiver both,
Working but in alliance with the works
Which it beholds.—Such, verily, is the
    first   260
Poetic spirit of our human life,
By uniform control of after years,
In most, abated or suppressed; in some,
Through every change of growth and of
    decay,
Pre-eminent till death.
                       From early days, 265
Beginning not long after that first time
In which, a Babe, by intercourse of touch
I held mute dialogues with my Mother's
    heart,
I have endeavoured to display the means
Whereby this infant sensibility,   270
Great birthright of our being, was in me

Augmented and sustained. Yet is a path
More difficult before me; and I fear
That in its broken windings we shall need
The chamois' sinews, and the eagle's
    wing: 275
For now a trouble came into my mind
From unknown causes. I was left alone
Seeking the visible world, nor knowing
    why.
The props of my affections were removed,
And yet the building stood, as if sustained
By its own spirit! All that I beheld 281
Was dear, and hence to finer influxes
The mind lay open, to a more exact
And close communion. Many are our
    joys 284
In youth, but oh! what happiness to live
When every hour brings palpable access
Of knowledge, when all knowledge is
    delight,
And sorrow is not there! The seasons
    came,
And every season wheresoe'er I moved
Unfolded transitory qualities, 290
Which, but for this most watchful power
    of love,
Had been neglected; left a register
Of permanent relations, else unknown.
Hence life, and change, and beauty, soli-
    tude
More active even than 'best society'—
Society made sweet as solitude 296
By silent inobtrusive sympathies,
And gentle agitations of the mind
From manifold distinctions, difference
Perceived in things, where, to the un-
    watchful eye, 300
No difference is, and hence, from the
    same source,
Sublimer joy; for I would walk alone,
Under the quiet stars, and at that time
Have felt whate'er there is of power in
    sound 304
To breathe an elevated mood, by form
Or image unprofaned; and I would stand,
If the night blackened with a coming
    storm,
Beneath some rock, listening to notes
    that are
The ghostly language of the ancient earth,
Or make their dim abode in distant
    winds. 310
Thence did I drink the visionary power;
And deem not profitless those fleeting
    moods
Of shadowy exultation: not for this,
That they are kindred to our purer mind
And intellectual life; but that the soul,
Remembering how she felt, but what she
    felt 316
Remembering not, retains an obscure
    sense
Of possible sublimity, whereto
With growing faculties she doth aspire,

With faculties still growing, feeling still
That whatsoever point they gain, they
    yet 321
Have something to pursue.
                        And not alone,
'Mid gloom and tumult, but no less 'mid
    fair
And tranquil scenes, that universal power
And fitness in the latent qualities 325
And essences of things, by which the mind
Is moved with feelings of delight, to me
Came strengthened with a superadded
    soul,
A virtue not its own. My morning walks
Were early;—oft before the hours of
    school 330
I travelled round our little lake, five
    miles
Of pleasant wandering. Happy time!
    more dear
For this, that one was by my side, a
    Friend,[1]
Then passionately loved; with heart how
    full
Would he peruse these lines! For many
    years 335
Have since flowed in between us, and,
    our minds
Both silent to each other, at this time
We live as if those hours had never been.
Nor seldom did I lift our cottage latch
Far earlier, ere one smoke-wreath had
    risen 340
From human dwelling, or the vernal
    thrush
Was audible; and sate among the woods
Alone upon some jutting eminence,
At the first gleam of dawn-light, when the
    Vale,
Yet slumbering, lay in utter solitude. 345
How shall I seek the origin? where find
Faith in the marvellous things which then
    I felt?
Oft in these moments such a holy calm
Would overspread my soul, that bodily
    eyes
Were utterly forgotten, and what I saw
Appeared like something in myself, a
    dream, 351
A prospect in the mind.
                        'Twere long to tell
What spring and autumn, what the winter
    snows,
And what the summer shade, what day
    and night,
Evening and morning, sleep and waking
    thought, 355
From sources inexhaustible, poured forth
To feed the spirit of religious love
In which I walked with Nature. But let
    this
Be not forgotten, that I still retained

[1] Rev. John Fleming, of Rayrigg, Windermere.—
Ed. of 1850.

My first creative sensibility; 360
That by the regular action of the world
My soul was unsubdued. A plastic power
Abode with me; a forming hand, at times
Rebellious, acting in a devious mood;
A local spirit of his own, at war 365
With general tendency, but, for the most,
Subservient strictly to external things
With which it communed. An auxiliar
  light
Came from my mind, which on the setting
  sun
Bestowed new splendour; the melodious
  birds, 370
The fluttering breezes, fountains that run
  on
Murmuring so sweetly in themselves,
  obeyed
A like dominion, and the midnight storm
Grew darker in the presence of my eye:
Hence my obeisance, my devotion hence,
And hence my transport.
          Nor should this, perchance,
Pass unrecorded, that I still had loved
The exercise and produce of a toil,
Than analytic industry to me
More pleasing, and whose character I
  deem 380
Is more poetic as resembling more
Creative agency. The song would speak
Of that interminable building reared
By observation of affinities
In objects where no brotherhood exists
To passive minds. My seventeenth year
  was come; 386
And, whether from this habit rooted now
So deeply in my mind, or from excess
In the great social principle of life
Coercing all things into sympathy, 390
To unorganic natures were transferred
My own enjoyments; or the power of
  truth
Coming in revelation, did converse
With things that really are; I, at this time,
Saw blessings spread around me like a sea.
Thus while the days flew by, and years
  passed on, 396
From Nature and her overflowing soul
I had received so much, that all my
  thoughts
Were steeped in feeling; I was only then
Contented, when with bliss ineffable 400
I felt the sentiment of Being spread
O'er all that moves and all that seemeth
  still;
O'er all that, lost beyond the reach of
  thought
And human knowledge, to the human eye
Invisible, yet liveth to the heart; 405
O'er all that leaps and runs, and shouts
  and sings,
Or beats the gladsome air; o'er all that
  glides
Beneath the wave, yea, in the wave itself,

And mighty depth of waters. Wonder not
If high the transport, great the joy I felt
Communing in this sort through earth
  and heaven 411
With every form of creature, as it looked
Towards the Uncreated with a counten-
  ance
Of adoration, with an eye of love. 414
One song they sang, and it was audible,
Most audible, then, when the fleshly ear,
O'ercome by humblest prelude of that
  strain,
Forgot her functions, and slept undis-
  turbed.

If this be error, and another faith
Find easier access to the pious mind, 420
Yet were I grossly destitute of all
Those human sentiments that make this
  earth
So dear, if I should fail with grateful voice
To speak of you, ye mountains, and ye
  lakes
And sounding cataracts, ye mists and
  winds 425
That dwell among the hills where I was
  born.
If in my youth I have been pure in heart,
If, mingling with the world, I am content
With my own modest pleasures, and have
  lived
With God and Nature communing, re-
  moved 430
From little enmities and low desires,
The gift is yours; if in these times of fear
This melancholy waste of hopes o'er-
  thrown,
If, 'mid indifference and apathy, 434
And wicked exultation when good men
On every side fall off, we know not how,
To selfishness, disguised in gentle names
Of peace and quiet and domestic love,
Yet mingled not unwillingly with sneers
On visionary minds; if, in this time 440
Of dereliction and dismay, I yet
Despair not of our nature, but retain
A more than Roman confidence, a faith
That fails not, in all sorrow my support,
The blessing of my life; the gift is yours,
Ye winds and sounding cataracts! 'tis
  yours, 446
Ye mountains! thine, O Nature! Thou
  hast fed
My lofty speculations; and in thee,
For this uneasy heart of ours, I find
A never-failing principle of joy 450
And purest passion.
          Thou, my Friend! wert reared
In the great city, 'mid far other scenes;
But we, by different roads, at length have
  gained
The self-same bourne. And for this cause
  to thee
I speak, unapprehensive of contempt, 455

The insinuated scoff of coward tongues,
And all that silent language which so
    oft
In conversation between man and man
Blots from the human countenance all
    trace
Of beauty and of love. For thou hast
    sought   460
The truth in solitude, and, since the days
That gave thee liberty, full long desired,

To serve in Nature's temple, thou hast been
The most assiduous of her ministers;   464
In many things my brother, chiefly here
In this our deep devotion.
                            Fare thee well!
Health and the quiet of a healthful mind
Attend thee! seeking oft the haunts of men,
And yet more often living with thyself,
And for thyself, so haply shall thy days
Be many, and a blessing to mankind. 471

BOOK THIRD

RESIDENCE AT CAMBRIDGE

IT was a dreary morning when the wheels
Rolled over a wide plain o'erhung with
    clouds,
And nothing cheered our way till first
    we saw
The long-roofed chapel of King's College
    lift
Turrets and pinnacles in answering files,
Extended high above a dusky grove.   6

    Advancing, we espied upon the road
A student clothed in gown and tasselled
    cap,
Striding along as if o'ertasked by Time,
Or covetous of exercise and air;   10
He passed—nor was I master of my eyes
Till he was left an arrow's flight behind.
As near and nearer to the spot we drew,
It seemed to suck us in with an eddy's
    force.
Onward we drove beneath the Castle;
    caught,   15
While crossing Magdalene Bridge, a
    glimpse of Cam;
And at the *Hoop* alighted, famous Inn.

    My spirit was up, my thoughts were
    full of hope;
Some friends I had, acquaintances who
    there
Seemed friends, poor simple schoolboys,
    now hung round   20
With honour and importance: in a world
Of welcome faces up and down I roved;
Questions, directions, warnings and advice,
Flowed in upon me, from all sides; fresh
    day   24
Of pride and pleasure! to myself I seemed
A man of business and expense, and went
From shop to shop about my own affairs,
To Tutor or to Tailor, as befell,
From street to street with loose and care-
    less mind.

    I was the Dreamer, they the Dream;
    I roamed   30
Delighted through the motley spectacle;

Gowns grave, or gaudy, doctors, students,
    streets,
Courts, cloisters, flocks of churches, gate-
    ways, towers:
Migration strange for a stripling of the
    hills,
A northern villager.
                        As if the change   35
Had waited on some Fairy's wand, at once
Behold me rich in monies, and attired
In splendid garb, with hose of silk, and
    hair
Powdered like rimy trees, when frost is
    keen.
My lordly dressing-gown, I pass it by,   40
With other signs of manhood that sup-
    plied
The lack of beard.—The weeks went
    roundly on,
With invitations, suppers, wine and fruit,
Smooth housekeeping within, and all
    without
Liberal, and suiting gentleman's array. 45

    The Evangelist St. John my patron was:
Three Gothic courts are his, and in the
    first
Was my abiding-place, a nook obscure;
Right underneath, the College kitchens
    made
A humming sound, less tuneable than
    bees,   50
But hardly less industrious; with shrill
    notes
Of sharp command and scolding inter-
    mixed.
Near me hung Trinity's loquacious clock,
Who never let the quarters, night or day,
Slip by him unproclaimed, and told the
    hours   55
Twice over with a male and female voice.
Her pealing organ was my neighbour too;
And from my pillow, looking forth by
    light
Of moon or favouring stars, I could be-
    hold

The antechapel where the statue stood   60
Of Newton with his prism and silent face,
The marble index of a mind for ever
Voyaging through strange seas of Thought,
    alone.

Of College labours, of the Lecturer's
    room
All studded round, as thick as chairs
    could stand,   65
With loyal students faithful to their books,
Half-and-half idlers, hardy recusants,
And honest dunces—of important days,
Examinations, when the man was weighed
As in a balance! of excessive hopes,   70
Tremblings withal and commendable
    fears,
Small jealousies, and triumphs good or
    bad—
Let others that know more speak as they
    know.
Such glory was but little sought by me,
And little won. Yet from the first crude
    days   75
Of settling time in this untried abode,
I was disturbed at times by prudent
    thoughts,
Wishing to hope without a hope, some
    fears
About my future worldly maintenance,
And, more than all, a strangeness in the
    mind,   80
A feeling that I was not for that hour,
Nor for that place. But wherefore be
    cast down?
For (not to speak of Reason and her pure
Reflective acts to fix the moral law
Deep in the conscience, nor of Christian
    Hope,   85
Bowing her head before her sister Faith
As one far mightier), hither I had come,
Bear witness Truth, endowed with holy
    powers
And faculties, whether to work or feel.
Oft when the dazzling show no longer new
Had ceased to dazzle, ofttimes did I quit
My comrades, leave the crowd, buildings
    and groves,
And as I paced alone the level fields
Far from those lovely sights and sounds
    sublime
With which I had been conversant, the
    mind   95
Drooped not; but there into herself return-
    ing,
With prompt rebound seemed fresh as
    heretofore.
At least I more distinctly recognised
Her native instincts: let me dare to speak
A higher language, say that now I felt
What independent solaces were mine,   101
To mitigate the injurious sway of place
Or circumstance, how far soever changed
In youth, or *to* be changed in after years.

As if awakened, summoned, roused, con-
    strained,   105
I looked for universal things; perused
The common countenance of earth and
    sky:
Earth, nowhere unembellished by some
    trace
Of that first Paradise whence man was
    driven;
And sky, whose beauty and bounty are
    expressed   110
By the proud name she bears—the name
    of Heaven.
I called on both to teach me what they
    might;
Or turning the mind in upon herself,
Pored, watched, expected, listened, spread
    my thoughts
And spread them with a wider creeping;
    felt   115
Incumbencies more awful, visitings
Of the Upholder of the tranquil soul,
That tolerates the indignities of Time,
And, from the centre of Eternity
All finite motions overruling, lives   120
In glory immutable. But peace! enough
Here to record that I was mounting now
To such community with highest truth—
A track pursuing, not untrod before,
From strict analogies by thought sup-
    plied   125
Or consciousnesses not to be subdued.
To every natural form, rock, fruit, or
    flower,
Even the loose stones that cover the high-
    way,
I gave a moral life: I saw them feel,
Or linked them to some feeling: the great
    mass   130
Lay bedded in a quickening soul, and all
That I beheld respired with inward mean-
    ing.
Add that whate'er of Terror or of Love
Or Beauty, Nature's daily face put on
From transitory passion, unto this   135
I was as sensitive as waters are
To the sky's influence; in a kindred mood
Of passion was obedient as a lute
That waits upon the touches of the wind.
Unknown, unthought of, yet I was most
    rich—   140
I had a world about me—'twas my own;
I made it, for it only lived to me,
And to the God who sees into the heart.
Such sympathies, though rarely, were
    betrayed   144
By outward gestures and by visible looks:
Some called it madness—so indeed it was,
If child-like fruitfulness in passing joy,
If steady moods of thoughtfulness
    matured
To inspiration, sort with such a name;
If prophecy be madness; if things viewed
By poets in old time, and higher up   151

By the first men, earth's first inhabitants,
May in these tutored days no more be
    seen
With undisordered sight. But leaving this,
It was no madness, for the bodily eye 155
Amid my strongest workings evermore
Was searching out the lines of difference
As they lie hid in all external forms,
Near or remote, minute or vast; an eye
Which, from a tree, a stone, a withered
    leaf,   160
To the broad ocean and the azure heavens
Spangled with kindred multitudes of
    stars,
Could find no surface where its power
    might sleep;
Which spake perpetual logic to my soul,
And by an unrelenting agency   165
Did bind my feelings even as in a chain.

And here, O Friend! have I retraced
    my life
Up to an eminence, and told a tale
Of matters which not falsely may be
    called
The glory of my youth. Of genius,
    power,   170
Creation and divinity itself
I have been speaking, for my theme has
    been
What passed within me. Not of outward
    things
Done visibly for other minds, words, signs,
Symbols or actions, but of my own heart
Have I been speaking, and my youthful
    mind.   176
O Heavens! how awful is the might of
    souls,
And what they do within themselves while
    yet
The yoke of earth is new to them, the
    world
Nothing but a wild field where they were
    sown.   180
This is, in truth, heroic argument,
This genuine prowess, which I wished to
    touch
With hand however weak, but in the main
It lies far hidden from the reach of words.
Points have we all of us within our souls
Where all stand single; this I feel, and
    make   186
Breathings for incommunicable powers;
But is not each a memory to himself?—
And, therefore, now that we must quit
    this theme,
I am not heartless, for there's not a man
That lives who hath not known his god-
    like hours,   191
And feels not what an empire we inherit
As natural beings in the strength of
    Nature.

    No more: for now into a populous
    plain

We must descend. A Traveller I am, 195
Whose tale is only of himself; even so,
So be it, if the pure of heart be prompt
To follow, and if thou, my honoured
    Friend!
Who in these thoughts art ever at my
    side,
Support, as heretofore, my fainting steps.

    It hath been told, that when the first
    delight   201
That flashed upon me from this novel
    show
Had failed, the mind returned into her-
    self;
Yet true it is, that I had made a change
In climate, and my nature's outward coat
Changed also slowly and insensibly. 206
Full oft the quiet and exalted thoughts
Of loneliness gave way to empty noise
And superficial pastimes; now and then
Forced labour, and more frequently
    forced hopes;   210
And, worst of all, a treasonable growth
Of indecisive judgments, that impaired
And shook the mind's simplicity.—And
    yet
This was a gladsome time. Could I be-
    hold—
Who, less insensible than sodden clay 215
In a sea-river's bed at ebb of tide,
Could have beheld,—with undelighted
    heart,
So many happy youths, so wide and fair
A congregation in its budding-time
Of health, and hope, and beauty, all at
    once   220
So many divers samples from the growth
Of life's sweet season—could have seen
    unmoved
That miscellaneous garland of wild flowers
Decking the matron temples of a place
So famous through the world? To me, at
    least,   225
It was a goodly prospect: for, in sooth,
Though I had learnt betimes to stand
    unpropped,
And independent musings pleased me so
That spells seemed on me when I was
    alone,
Yet could I only cleave to solitude   230
In lonely places; if a throng was near
That way I leaned by nature; for my
    heart
Was social, and loved idleness and joy.

    Not seeking those who might partici-
    pate
My deeper pleasures (nay, I had not once,
Though not unused to mutter lonesome
    songs,   236
Even with myself divided such delight,
Or looked that way for aught that might
    be clothed
In human language), easily I passed

From the remembrances of better things,
And slipped into the ordinary works 241
Of careless youth, unburdened, un-
    alarmed.
Caverns there were within my mind which
    sun
Could never penetrate, yet did there not
Want store of leafy *arbours* where the
    light   245
Might enter in at will. Companionships,
Friendships, acquaintances, were welcome
    all.
We sauntered, played, or rioted; we
    talked
Unprofitable talk at morning hours;
Drifted about along the streets and
    walks,   250
Read lazily in trivial books, went forth
To gallop through the country in blind
    zeal
Of senseless horsemanship, or on the
    breast
Of Cam sailed boisterously, and let the
    stars
Come forth, perhaps without one quiet
    thought.   255

Such was the tenour of the second act
In this new life. Imagination slept,
And yet not utterly. I could not print
Ground where the grass had yielded to
    the steps
Of generations of illustrious men,   260
Unmoved. I could not always lightly
    pass
Through the same gateways, sleep where
    they had slept,
Wake where they waked, range that in-
    closure old,
That garden of great intellects, undis-
    turbed.
Place also by the side of this dark sense
Of nobler feeling, that those spiritual
    men,   266
Even the great Newton's own ethereal
    self,
Seemed humbled in these precincts thence
    to be
The more endeared. Their several me-
    mories here
(Even like their persons in their portraits
    clothed   270
With the accustomed garb of daily life)
Put on a lowly and a touching grace
Of more distinct humanity, that left
All genuine admiration unimpaired.

Beside the pleasant Mill of Tromping-
    ton   275
I laughed with Chaucer; in the hawthorn
    shade
Heard him, while birds were warbling,
    tell his tales
Of amorous passion. And that gentle
    Bard,

Chosen by the Muses for their Page of
    State—
Sweet Spenser, moving through his
    clouded heaven   280
With the moon's beauty and the moon's
    soft pace,
I called him Brother, Englishman, and
    Friend!
Yea, our blind Poet, who, in his later day,
Stood almost single; uttering odious
    truth—
Darkness before, and danger's voice be-
    hind,   285
Soul awful—if the earth has ever lodged
An awful soul—I seemed to see him here
Familiarly, and in his scholar's dress
Bounding before me, yet a stripling
    youth—
A boy, no better, with his rosy cheeks 290
Angelical, keen eye, courageous look,
And conscious step of purity and pride.
Among the band of my compeers was one
Whom chance had stationed in the very
    room
Honoured by Milton's name. O temperate
    Bard!   295
Be it confest that, for the first time, seated
Within thy innocent lodge and oratory,
One of a festive circle, I poured out
Libations, to thy memory drank, till pride
And gratitude grew dizzy in a brain   300
Never excited by the fumes of wine
Before that hour, or since. Then, forth
    I ran
From the assembly; through a length of
    streets,
Ran, ostrich-like, to reach our chapel door
In not a desperate or opprobrious time,
Albeit long after the importunate bell 306
Had stopped, with wearisome Cassandra
    voice
No longer haunting the dark winter night.
Call back, O Friend! a moment to thy
    mind,   309
The place itself and fashion of the rites.
With careless ostentation shouldering up
My surplice, through the inferior throng
    I clove
Of the plain Burghers, who in audience
    stood
On the last skirts of their permitted
    ground,
Under the pealing organ. Empty
    thoughts!   315
I am ashamed of them: and that great
    Bard,
And thou, O Friend! who in thy ample
    mind
Hast placed me high above my best
    deserts,
Ye will forgive the weakness of that hour,
In some of its unworthy vanities,   320
Brother to many more.
                    In this mixed sort

511

The months passed on, remissly, not given
    up
To wilful alienation from the right,   323
Or walks of open scandal, but in vague
And loose indifference, easy likings, aims
Of a low pitch—duty and zeal dismissed,
Yet Nature, or a happy course of things
Not doing in their stead the needful work.
The memory languidly revolved, the heart
Reposed in noontide rest, the inner pulse
Of contemplation almost failed to beat.
Such life might not inaptly be compared
To a floating island, an amphibious spot
Unsound, of spongy texture, yet withal
Not wanting a fair face of water-weeds
And pleasant flowers. The thirst of living
    praise,   336
Fit reverence for the glorious Dead, the
    sight
Of those long vistas, sacred catacombs,
Where mighty *minds* lie visibly entombed,
Have often stirred the heart of youth,
    and bred   340
A fervent love of rigorous discipline.—
Alas! such high emotion touched not
    me.
Look was there none within these walls
    to shame
My easy spirits, and discountenance   344
Their light composure, far less to instil
A calm resolve of mind, firmly addressed
To puissant efforts. Nor was this the
    blame
Of others but my own; I should, in truth,
As far as doth concern my single self,
Misdeem most widely, lodging it else-
    where: 350
For I, bred up 'mid Nature's luxuries,
Was a spoiled child, and, rambling like
    the wind,
As I had done in daily intercourse
With those crystalline rivers, solemn
    heights,
And mountains, ranging like a fowl of
    the air,   355
I was ill-tutored for captivity;
To quit my pleasure, and, from month to
    month,
Take up a station calmly on the perch
Of sedentary peace. Those lovely forms
Had also left less space within my mind,
Which, wrought upon instinctively, had
    found   361
A freshness in those objects of her love,
A winning power, beyond all other power.
Not that I slighted books,—that were to
    lack
All sense,—but other passions in me
    ruled,   365
Passions more fervent, making me less
    prompt
To in-door study than was wise or well,
Or suited to those years. Yet I, though
    used

In magisterial liberty to rove,
Culling such flowers of learning as might
    tempt   370
A random choice, could shadow forth a
    place
(If now I yield not to a flattering dream)
Whose studious aspect should have bent
    me down
To instantaneous service; should at once
Have made me pay to science and to arts
And written lore, acknowledged my liege
    lord,   376
A homage frankly offered up, like that
Which I had paid to Nature. Toil and
    pains
In this recess, by thoughtful Fancy built,
Should spread from heart to heart; and
    stately groves,   380
Majestic edifices, should not want
A corresponding dignity within.
The congregating temper that pervades
Our unripe years, not wasted, should be
    taught
To minister to works of high attempt—
Works which the enthusiast would per-
    form with love.   386
Youth should be awed, religiously pos-
    sessed
With a conviction of the power that waits
On knowledge, when sincerely sought and
    prized   389
For its own sake, on glory and on praise
If but by labour won, and fit to endure.
The passing day should learn to put aside
Her trappings here, should strip them off
    abashed
Before antiquity and steadfast truth
And strong book-mindedness; and over
    all   395
A healthy sound simplicity should reign,
A seemly plainness, name it what you
    will,
Republican or pious.
                        If these thoughts
Are a gratuitous emblazonry
That mocks the recreant age *we* live in,
    then   400
Be Folly and False-seeming free to affect
Whatever formal gait of discipline
Shall raise them highest in their own
    esteem—
Let them parade among the Schools at
    will,
But spare the House of God. Was ever
    known   405
The witless shepherd who persists to
    drive
A flock that thirsts not to a pool disliked?
A weight must surely hang on days begun
And ended with such mockery. Be wise,
Ye Presidents and Deans, and, till the
    spirit   410
Of ancient times revive, and youth be
    trained

At home in pious service, to your bells
Give seasonable rest, for 'tis a sound
Hollow as ever vexed the tranquil air;
And your officious doings bring disgrace
On the plain steeples of our English
    Church,   416
Whose worship. 'mid remotest village
    trees,
Suffers for this. Even Science, too, at
    hand
In daily sight of this irreverence,
Is smitten thence with an unnatural taint,
Loses her just authority, falls beneath
Collateral suspicion, else unknown.   422
This truth escaped me not, and I confess,
That having 'mid my native hills given
    loose
To a schoolboy's vision, I had raised a
    pile   425
Upon the basis of the coming time,
That fell in ruins round me. Oh, what
    joy
To see a sanctuary for our country's youth
Informed with such a spirit as might be
Its own protection; a primeval grove,   430
Where, though the shades with cheerful-
    ness were filled,
Nor indigent of songs warbled from
    crowds
In under-coverts, yet the countenance
Of the whole place should bear a stamp
    of awe;
A habitation sober and demure   435
For ruminating creatures; a domain
For quiet things to wander in; a haunt
In which the heron should delight to feed
By the shy rivers, and the pelican   439
Upon the cypress spire in lonely thought
Might sit and sun himself.—Alas! alas!
In vain for such solemnity I looked;
Mine eyes were crossed by butterflies,
    ears vexed
By chattering popinjays; the inner heart
Seemed trivial, and the impresses without
Of a too gaudy region.
                    Different sight   446
Those venerable Doctors saw of old,
When all who dwelt within these famous
    walls
Led in abstemiousness a studious life;
When, in forlorn and naked chambers
    cooped   450
And crowded, o'er the ponderous books
    they hung
Like caterpillars eating out their way
In silence, or with keen devouring noise
Not to be tracked or fathered. Princes
    then
At matins froze, and couched at curfew-
    time,   455
Trained up through piety and zeal to
    prize
Spare diet, patient labour, and plain
    weeds.

O seat of Arts! renowned throughout the
    world!
Far different service in those homely days
The Muses' modest nurslings underwent
From their first childhood: in that
    glorious time   461
When Learning, like a stranger come
    from far,
Sounding through Christian lands her
    trumpet, roused
Peasant and king; when boys and youths,
    the growth
Of ragged villages and crazy huts,   465
Forsook their homes, and, errant in the
    quest
Of Patron, famous school or friendly
    nook,
Where, pensioned, they in shelter might
    sit down,
From town to town and through wide
    scattered realms
Journeyed with ponderous folios in their
    hands;   470
And often, starting from some covert
    place,
Saluted the chance comer on the road,
Crying, 'An obolus, a penny give
To a poor scholar!'—when illustrious
    men,   474
Lovers of truth, by penury constrained,
Bucer, Erasmus, or Melancthon, read
Before the doors or windows of their
    cells
By moonshine through mere lack of taper
    light.

But peace to vain regrets! We see but
    darkly
Even when we look behind us, and best
    things   480
Are not so pure by nature that they needs
Must keep to all, as fondly all believe,
Their highest promise. If the mariner,
When at reluctant distance he hath
    passed
Some tempting island, could but know
    the ills   485
That must have fallen upon him had he
    brought
His bark to land upon the wished-for
    shore,
Good cause would oft be his to thank the
    surf
Whose white belt scared him thence, or
    wind that blew
Inexorably adverse: for myself   490
I grieve not; happy is the gownèd youth,
Who only misses what I missed, who falls
No lower than I fell.
                    I did not love,
Judging not ill perhaps, the timid course
Of our scholastic studies; could have
    wished   495
To see the river flow with ampler range

513

And freer pace; but more, far more, I
     grieved
To see displayed among an eager few,
Who in the field of contest persevered,
Passions unworthy of youth's generous
     heart   500
And mounting spirit, pitiably repaid,
When so disturbed, whatever palms are
     won.
From these I turned to travel with the
     shoal
Of more unthinking natures, easy minds
And pillowy; yet not wanting love that
     makes   505
The day pass lightly on, when foresight
     sleeps,
And wisdom and the pledges inter-
     changed
With our own inner being are forgot.

Yet was this deep vacation not given up
To utter waste. Hitherto I had stood   510
In my own mind remote from social life,
(At least from what we commonly so
     name,)
Like a lone shepherd on a promontory
Who lacking occupation looks far forth
Into the boundless sea, and rather makes
Than finds what he beholds. And sure
     it is,   516
That this first transit from the smooth
     delights
And wild outlandish walks of simple
     youth
To something that resembles an approach
Towards human business, to a privileged
     world   520
Within a world, a midway residence
With all its intervenient imagery,
Did better suit my visionary mind,
Far better, than to have been bolted
     forth,   524
Thrust out abruptly into Fortune's way
Among the conflicts of substantial life;
By a more just gradation did lead on
To higher things; more naturally matured,
For permanent possession, better fruits,
Whether of truth or virtue, to ensue.   530
In serious mood, but oftener, I confess,
With playful zest of fancy, did we note
(How could we less?) the manners and the
     ways
Of those who lived distinguished by the
     badge
Of good or ill report; or those with whom
By frame of Academic discipline   536
We were perforce connected, men whose
     sway
And known authority of office served
To set our minds on edge, and did no
     more.
Nor wanted we rich pastime of this kind,
Found everywhere, but chiefly in the
     ring   541

Of the grave Elders, men unscoured,
     grotesque
In character, tricked out like agèd trees
Which through the lapse of their infirmity
Give ready place to any random seed 545
That chooses to be reared upon their
     trunks.

Here on my view, confronting vividly
Those shepherd swains whom I had lately
     left,
Appeared a different aspect of old age;
How different! yet both distinctly marked,
Objects embossed to catch the general
     eye,   551
Or portraitures for special use designed,
As some might seem, so aptly do they
     serve
To illustrate Nature's book of rudiments—
That book upheld as with maternal care
When she would enter on her tender
     scheme   556
Of teaching comprehension with delight,
And mingling playful with pathetic
     thoughts.

The surfaces of artificial life
And manners finely wrought, the delicate
     race   560
Of colours, lurking, gleaming up and
     down
Through that state arras woven with silk
     and gold;
This wily interchange of snaky hues,
Willingly or unwillingly revealed,
I neither knew nor cared for; and as
     such   565
Were wanting here, I took what might be
     found
Of less elaborate fabric. At this day
I smile, in many a mountain solitude
Conjuring up scenes as obsolete in freaks
Of character, in points of wit as broad,
As aught by wooden images performed
For entertainment of the gaping crowd
At wake or fair. And oftentimes do flit
Remembrances before me of old men—
Old humourists, who have been long in
     their graves,   575
And having almost in my mind put off
Their human names, have into phantoms
     passed
Of texture midway between life and books.

I play the loiterer: 'tis enough to note
That here in dwarf proportions were
     expressed   580
The limbs of the great world; its eager
     strifes
Collaterally pourtrayed, as in mock fight,
A tournament of blows, some hardly dealt
Though short of mortal combat; and
     whate'er   584
Might in this pageant be supposed to hit
An artless rustic's notice, this way less,

More that way, was not wasted upon
    me—
And yet the spectacle may well demand
A more substantial name, no mimic
    show,
Itself a living part of a live whole,   590
A creek in the vast sea; for, all degrees
And shapes of spurious fame and short-
    lived praise
Here sate in state, and fed with daily
    alms
Retainers won away from solid good;
And here was Labour, his own bond-
    slave; Hope,   595
That never set the pains against the
    prize;
Idleness halting with his weary clog,
And poor misguided Shame, and witless
    Fear,
And simple Pleasure foraging for Death;
Honour misplaced, and Dignity astray;
Feuds, factions, flatteries, enmity, and
    guile,   601
Murmuring submission, and bald govern-
    ment,
(The idol weak as the idolater),
And Decency and Custom starving Truth,
And blind Authority beating with his
    staff   605
The child that might have led him;
    Emptiness
Followed as of good omen, and meek
    Worth
Left to herself unheard of and unknown.

Of these and other kindred notices
I cannot say what portion is in truth   610
The naked recollection of that time,
And what may rather have been called to
    life
By after-meditation. But delight
That, in an easy temper lulled asleep,
Is still with Innocence its own reward, 615
This was not wanting. Carelessly I
    roamed
As through a wide museum from whose
    stores
A casual rarity is singled out
And has its brief perusal, then gives way
To others, all supplanted in their turn;
Till 'mid this crowded neighbourhood of
    things   621
That are by nature most unneighbourly,
The head turns round and cannot right
    itself;
And though an aching and a barren sense
Of gay confusion still be uppermost,   625
With few wise longings and but little love,
Yet to the memory something cleaves at
    last,
Whence profit may be drawn in times to
    come.

Thus in submissive idleness, my Friend!
The labouring time of autumn, winter,
    spring,   630
Eight months! rolled pleasingly away;
    the ninth
Came and returned me to my native hills.

BOOK FOURTH

SUMMER VACATION

BRIGHT was the summer's noon when
    quickening steps
Followed each other till a dreary moor
Was crossed, a bare ridge clomb, upon
    whose top
Standing alone, as from a rampart's edge,
I overlooked the bed of Windermere,   5
Like a vast river, stretching in the sun.
With exultation, at my feet I saw
Lake, islands, promontories, gleaming
    bays,
A universe of Nature's fairest forms
Proudly revealed with instantaneous
    burst,   10
Magnificent, and beautiful, and gay.
I bounded down the hill shouting amain
For the old Ferryman; to the shout the
    rocks
Replied, and when the Charon of the
    flood
Had staid his oars, and touched the
    jutting pier,   15
I did not step into the well-known boat

Without a cordial greeting. Thence with
    speed
Up the familiar hill I took my way
Towards that sweet Valley[1] where I had
    been reared;
'Twas but a short hour's walk, ere veering
    round   20
I saw the snow-white church upon her hill
Sit like a thronèd Lady, sending out
A gracious look all over her domain.
Yon azure smoke betrays the lurking
    town;
With eager footsteps I advance and reach
The cottage threshold where my journey
    closed.   26
Glad welcome had I, with some tears,
    perhaps,
From my old Dame, so kind and motherly,
While she perused me with a parent's
    pride.
The thoughts of gratitude shall fall like
    dew   30

    [1] Hawkshead.

515

Upon thy grave, good creature! While
my heart
Can beat never will I forget thy name.
Heaven's blessing be upon thee where
thou liest
After thy innocent and busy stir   34
In narrow cares, thy little daily growth
Of calm enjoyments, after eighty years,
And more than eighty, of untroubled life,
Childless, yet by the strangers to thy
blood
Honoured with little less than filial love.
What joy was mine to see thee once
again,   40
Thee and thy dwelling, and a crowd of
things
About its narrow precincts all beloved,
And many of them seeming yet my own!
Why should I speak of what a thousand
hearts
Have felt, and every man alive can
guess?   45
The rooms, the court, the garden were not
left
Long unsaluted, nor the sunny seat
Round the stone table under the dark
pine,
Friendly to studious or to festive hours;
Nor that unruly child of mountain birth,
The froward brook, who, soon as he was
boxed   51
Within our garden, found himself at once,
As if by trick insidious and unkind,
Stripped of his voice and left to dimple
down
(Without an effort and without a will)   55
A channel paved by man's officious care.
I looked at him and smiled, and smiled
again,
And in the press of twenty thousand
thoughts,
'Ha,' quoth I, 'pretty prisoner, are you
there!'
Well might sarcastic Fancy then have
whispered,   60
'An emblem here behold of thy own life;
In its late course of even days with all
Their smooth enthralment;' but the
heart was full,
Too full for that reproach. My aged
Dame
Walked proudly at my side: she guided
me;   65
I willing, nay—nay, wishing to be led.
—The face of every neighbour whom
I met
Was like a volume to me; some were
hailed
Upon the road, some busy at their work,
Unceremonious greetings interchanged
With half the length of a long field
between.   71
Among my schoolfellows I scattered
round

Like recognitions, but with some con-
straint
Attended, doubtless, with a little pride,
But with more shame, for my habili-
ments,   75
The transformation wrought by gay
attire.
Not less delighted did I take my place
At our domestic table: and, dear Friend!
In this endeavour simply to relate
A Poet's history, may I leave untold   80
The thankfulness with which I laid me
down
In my accustomed bed, more welcome
now
Perhaps than if it had been more desired
Or been more often thought of with
regret;
That lowly bed whence I had heard the
wind   85
Roar, and the rain beat hard; where I so
oft
Had lain awake on summer nights to
watch
The moon in splendour couched among
the leaves
Of a tall ash, that near our cottage stood;
Had watched her with fixed eyes while to
and fro   90
In the dark summit of the waving tree
She rocked with every impulse of the
breeze.

Among the favourites whom it pleased
me well   93
To see again, was one by ancient right
Our inmate, a rough terrier of the hills;
By birth and call of nature pre-ordained
To hunt the badger and unearth the fox
Among the impervious crags, but having
been
From youth our own adopted, he had
passed   99
Into a gentler service. And when first
The boyish spirit flagged, and day by day
Along my veins I kindled with the stir,
The fermentation, and the vernal heat
Of poesy, affecting private shades
Like a sick Lover, then this dog was
used   105
To watch me, an attendant and a friend,
Obsequious to my steps early and late,
Though often of such dilatory walk
Tired, and uneasy at the halts I made.
A hundred times when, roving high and
low,   110
I have been harassed with the toil of
verse,
Much pains and little progress, and at
once
Some lovely Image in the song rose up
Full-formed, like Venus rising from the
sea;   114
Then have I darted forwards to let loose

My hand upon his back with stormy joy,
Caressing him again and yet again.
And when at evening on the public way
I sauntered, like a river murmuring
And talking to itself when all things
    else   120
Are still, the creature trotted on before;
Such was his custom; but whene'er he
    met
A passenger approaching, he would turn
To give me timely notice, and straight-
    way,
Grateful for that admonishment, I hushed
My voice, composed my gait, and, with
    the air   126
And mien of one whose thoughts are free,
    advanced
To give and take a greeting that might
    save
My name from piteous rumours, such as
    wait
On men suspected to be crazed in brain.

    Those walks well worthy to be prized
        and loved—   131
Regretted!—that word, too, was on my
    tongue,
But they were richly laden with all good,
And cannot be remembered but with
    thanks
And gratitude, and perfect joy of heart—
Those walks in all their freshness now
    came back   136
Like a returning Spring. When first I
    made
Once more the circuit of our little lake,
If ever happiness hath lodged with man,
That day consummate happiness was
    mine,   140
Wide-spreading, steady, calm, contem-
    plative.
The sun was set, or setting, when I left
Our cottage door, and evening soon
    brought on
A sober hour, not winning or serene,
For cold and raw the air was, and un-
    tuned;   145
But as a face we love is sweetest then
When sorrow damps it, or, whatever look
It chance to wear, is sweetest if the heart
Have fulness in herself; even so with me
It fared that evening. Gently did my
    soul   150
Put off her veil, and, self-transmuted,
    stood
Naked, as in the presence of her God.
While on I walked, a comfort seemed to
    touch
A heart that had not been disconsolate:
Strength came where weakness was not
    known to be,   155
At least not felt; and restoration came
Like an intruder knocking at the door
Of unacknowledged weariness. I took

The balance, and with firm hand weighed
    myself.
—Of that external scene which round me
    lay,   160
Little, in this abstraction, did I see;
Remembered less; but I had inward
    hopes
And swellings of the spirit, was rapt and
    soothed,
Conversed with promises, had glimmer-
    ing views   164
How life pervades the undecaying mind;
How the immortal soul with God-like
    power
Informs, creates, and thaws the deepest
    sleep
That time can lay upon her; how on
    earth
Man, if he do but live within the light
Of high endeavours, daily spreads abroad
His being armed with strength that can-
    not fail.   171
Nor was there want of milder thoughts,
    of love,
Of innocence, and holiday repose;
And more than pastoral quiet, 'mid the
    stir   174
Of boldest projects, and a peaceful end
At last, or glorious, by endurance won.
Thus musing, in a wood I sate me down
Alone, continuing there to muse: the
    slopes
And heights meanwhile were slowly over-
    spread
With darkness, and before a rippling
    breeze   180
The long lake lengthened out its hoary
    line,
And in the sheltered coppice where I
    sate,
Around me from among the hazel leaves,
Now here, now there, moved by the
    straggling wind,   184
Came ever and anon a breath-like sound,
Quick as the pantings of the faithful dog,
The off and on companion of my walk;
And such, at times, believing them to
    be,
I turned my head to look if he were there;
Then into solemn thought I passed once
    more.   190

    A freshness also found I at this time
In human Life, the daily life of those
Whose occupations really I loved;
The peaceful scene oft filled me with
    surprise
Changed like a garden in the heat of
    spring,   195
After an eight-days' absence. For (to
    omit
The things which were the same and yet
    appeared
Far otherwise) amid this rural solitude,

A narrow Vale where each was known to all,
'Twas not indifferent to a youthful mind
To mark some sheltering bower or sunny nook,   201
Where an old man had used to sit alone,
Now vacant; pale-faced babes whom I had left
In arms, now rosy prattlers at the feet
Of a pleased grandame tottering up and down;   205
And growing girls whose beauty, filched away
With all its pleasant promises, was gone
To deck some slighted playmate's homely cheek.

Yes, I had something of a subtler sense,
And often looking round was moved to smiles   210
Such as a delicate work of humour breeds;
I read, without design, the opinions, thoughts,
Of those plain-living people now observed
With clearer knowledge; with another eye
I saw the quiet woodman in the woods,
The shepherd roam the hills. With new delight,   216
This chiefly, did I note my grey-haired Dame;
Saw her go forth to church or other work
Of state, equipped in monumental trim;
Short velvet cloak, (her bonnet of the like),   220
A mantle such as Spanish Cavaliers
Wore in old time. Her smooth domestic life,
Affectionate without disquietude,
Her talk, her business, pleased me; and no less
Her clear though shallow stream of piety
That ran on Sabbath days a fresher course;   226
With thoughts unfelt till now I saw her read
Her Bible on hot Sunday afternoons,
And loved the book, when she had dropped asleep
And made of it a pillow for her head.   230

Nor less do I remember to have felt,
Distinctly manifested at this time,
A human-heartedness about my love
For objects hitherto the absolute wealth
Of my own private being and no more;
Which I had loved, even as a blessed spirit   236
Or Angel, if he were to dwell on earth,
Might love in individual happiness.
But now there opened on me other thoughts
Of change, congratulation or regret,   240
A pensive feeling! It spread far and wide;

The trees, the mountains shared it, and the brooks,
The stars of Heaven, now seen in their old haunts—
White Sirius glittering o'er the southern crags,
Orion with his belt, and those fair Seven,
Acquaintances of every little child,   246
And Jupiter, my own beloved star!
Whatever shadings of mortality,
Whatever imports from the world of death
Had come among these objects heretofore,   250
Were, in the main, of mood less tender: strong,
Deep, gloomy were they, and severe; the scatterings
Of awe or tremulous dread, that had given way
In later youth to yearnings of a love
Enthusiastic, to delight and hope.   255

As one who hangs down-bending from the side
Of a slow-moving boat, upon the breast
Of a still water, solacing himself
With such discoveries as his eye can make
Beneath him in the bottom of the deep,
Sees many beauteous sights—weeds, fishes, flowers,   261
Grots, pebbles, roots of trees, and fancies more,
Yet often is perplexed and cannot part
The shadow from the substance, rocks and sky,
Mountains and clouds, reflected in the depth   265
Of the clear flood, from things which there abide
In their true dwelling; now is crossed by gleam
Of his own image, by a sunbeam now,
And wavering motions sent he knows not whence,
Impediments that make his task more sweet;   270
Such pleasant office have we long pursued
Incumbent o'er the surface of past time
With like success, nor often have appeared
Shapes fairer or less doubtfully discerned
Than these to which the Tale, indulgent Friend!   275
Would now direct thy notice. Yet in spite
Of pleasure won, and knowledge not withheld,
There was an inner falling off—I loved,
Loved deeply all that had been loved before,
More deeply even than ever: but a swarm   280

Of heady schemes jostling each other,
    gawds,
And feast and dance, and public revelry,
And sports and games (too grateful in
    themselves,
Yet in themselves less grateful, I believe,
Than as they were a badge glossy and
    fresh   285
Of manliness and freedom) all conspired
To lure my mind from firm habitual
    quest
Of feeding pleasures, to depress the zeal
And damp those yearnings which had
    once been mine—
A wild, unworldly-minded youth, given
    up   290
To his own eager thoughts. It would
    demand
Some skill, and longer time than may be
    spared,
To paint these vanities, and how they
    wrought
In haunts where they, till now, had been
    unknown.
It seemed the very garments that I wore
Preyed on my strength, and stopped the
    quiet stream   296
Of self-forgetfulness.
                    Yes, that heartless chase
Of trivial pleasures was a poor exchange
For books and nature at that early age.
'Tis true, some casual knowledge might
    be gained   300
Of character or life; but at that time,
Of manners put to school I took small
    note,
And all my deeper passions lay else-
    where.
Far better had it been to exalt the mind
By solitary study, to uphold   305
Intense desire through meditative peace;
And yet, for chastisement of these
    regrets,
The memory of one particular hour
Doth here rise up against me. 'Mid a
    throng
Of maids and youths, old men, and
    matrons staid,   310
A medley of all tempers, I had passed
The night in dancing, gaiety, and mirth,
With din of instruments and shuffling
    feet,
And glancing forms, and tapers glittering,
And unaimed prattle flying up and down;
Spirits upon the stretch, and here and
    there   316
Slight shocks of young love-liking inter-
    spersed,
Whose transient pleasure mounted to the
    head,
And tingled through the veins. Ere we
    retired,
The cock had crowed, and now the
    eastern sky   320

Was kindling, nor unseen, from humble
    copse
And open field, through which the path-
    way wound,
And homeward led my steps. Magni-
    ficent
The morning rose, in memorable pomp,
Glorious as e'er I had beheld—in front,
The sea lay laughing at a distance; near,
The solid mountains shone, bright as the
    clouds,   327
Grain-tinctured, drenched in empyrean
    light;
And in the meadows and the lower
    grounds
Was all the sweetness of a common
    dawn—   330
Dews, vapours, and the melody of birds,
And labourers going forth to till the
    fields.
Ah! need I say, dear Friend! that to
    the brim
My heart was full; I made no vows, but
    vows
Were then made for me; bond unknown
    to me   335
Was given, that I should be, else sinning
    greatly,
A dedicated Spirit. On I walked
In thankful blessedness, which yet sur-
    vives.

Strange rendez-vous my mind was at
    that time,
A parti-coloured show of grave and gay,
Solid and light, short-sighted and pro-
    found;   341
Of inconsiderate habits and sedate,
Consorting in one mansion unreproved.
The worth I knew of powers that I
    possessed,
Though slighted and too oft misused,
    Besides,   345
That summer, swarming as it did with
    thoughts
Transient and idle, lacked not intervals
When Folly from the frown of fleeting
    Time
Shrunk, and the mind experienced in
    herself
Conformity as just as that of old   350
To the end and written spirit of God's
    works,
Whether held forth in Nature or in Man,
Through pregnant vision, separate or
    conjoined.

When from our better selves we have
    too long
Been parted by the hurrying world, and
    droop,   355
Sick of its business, of its pleasures tired,
How gracious, how benign, is Solitude;
How potent a mere image of her sway;

Most potent when impressed upon the
mind
With an appropriate human centre—
hermit,   360
Deep in the bosom of the wilderness;
Votary (in vast cathedral, where no foot
Is treading, where no other face is seen)
Kneeling at prayers; or watchman on
the top   364
Of lighthouse, beaten by Atlantic waves;
Or as the soul of that great Power is met
Sometimes embodied on a public road,
When, for the night deserted, it assumes
A character of quiet more profound
Than pathless wastes.
　　　Once, when those summer
months   370
Were flown, and autumn brought its
annual show
Of oars with oars contending, sails with
sails,
Upon Winander's spacious breast, it
chanced
That—after I had left a flower-decked
room
(Whose in-door pastime, lighted up,
survived   375
To a late hour), and spirits overwrought
Were making night do penance for a
day
Spent in a round of strenuous idleness—
My homeward course led up a long
ascent,
Where the road's watery surface, to the
top   380
Of that sharp rising, glittered to the moon
And bore the semblance of another
stream
Stealing with silent lapse to join the
brook
That murmured in the vale. All else
was still;
No living thing appeared in earth or air,
And, save the flowing water's peaceful
voice,   386
Sound there was none—but, lo! an un-
couth shape,
Shown by a sudden turning of the road,
So near that, slipping back into the shade
Of a thick hawthorn, I could mark him
well,
Myself unseen. He was of stature tall,   390
A span above man's common measure,
tall,
Stiff, lank, and upright; a more meagre
man
Was never seen before by night or day.
　ong were his arms, pallid his hands;
his mouth   395
Looked ghastly in the moonlight: from
behind,
A mile-stone propped him; I could also
　ken
That he was clothed in military garb,

Though faded, yet entire. Companion-
less,   399
No dog attending, by no staff sustained,
He stood, and in his very dress appeared
A desolation, a simplicity,
To which the trappings of a gaudy world
Make a strange back-ground. From his
lips, ere long,
Issued low muttered sounds, as if of
pain   405
Or some uneasy thought; yet still his
form
Kept the same awful steadiness—at his
feet
His shadow lay, and moved not. From
self-blame
Not wholly free, I watched him thus; at
length   409
Subduing my heart's specious cowardice,
I left the shady nook where I had stood
And hailed him. Slowly from his resting-
place
He rose, and with a lean and wasted arm
In measured gesture lifted to his head
Returned my salutation; then resumed
His station as before; and when I asked
His history, the veteran, in reply,   417
Was neither slow nor eager; but, un-
moved,
And with a quiet uncomplaining voice,
A stately air of mild indifference,   420
He told in few plain words a soldier's
tale—
That in the Tropic Islands he had served,
Whence he had landed scarcely three
weeks past;
That on his landing he had been dis-
missed,
And now was travelling towards his
native home.   425
This heard, I said, in pity, 'Come with
me.'
He stooped, and straightway from the
ground took up
An oaken staff by me yet unobserved—
A staff which must have dropt from his
slack hand
And lay till now neglected in the grass.
Though weak his step and cautious, he
appeared   431
To travel without pain, and I beheld,
With an astonishment but ill suppressed,
His ghostly figure moving at my side;
Nor could I, while we journeyed thus,
forbear   435
To turn from present hardships to the
past,
And speak of war, battle, and pestilence,
Sprinkling this talk with questions, better
spared,
On what he might himself have seen or
felt.   439
He all the while was in demeanour calm,
Concise in answer; solemn and sublime

He might have seemed, but that in all he
said
There was a strange half-absence, as of one
Knowing too well the importance of his
theme,   444
But feeling it no longer. Our discourse
Soon ended, and together on we passed
In silence through a wood gloomy and
still.
Up-turning, then, along an open field,
We reached a cottage. At the door I
knocked,
And earnestly to charitable care   450
Commended him as a poor friendless
man,
Belated and by sickness overcome.
Assured that now the traveller would
repose
In comfort, I entreated that henceforth
He would not linger in the public ways,
But ask for timely furtherance and help

Such as his state required. At this re-
proof,   457
With the same ghastly mildness in his
look,
He said, 'My trust is in the God of
Heaven,
And in the eye of him who passes me!'

The cottage door was speedily unbarred,
And now the soldier touched his hat once
more   462
With his lean hand, and in a faltering
voice,
Whose tone bespake reviving interests
Till then unfelt, he thanked me; I re-
turned   465
The farewell blessing of the patient man,
And so we parted. Back I cast a look,
And lingered near the door a little space,
Then sought with quiet heart my distant
home.

BOOK FIFTH

BOOKS

WHEN Contemplation, like the night-
calm felt
Through earth and sky, spreads widely,
and sends deep
Into the soul its tranquillising power,
Even then I sometimes grieve for thee,
O Man,
Earth's paramount Creature! not so much
for woes   5
That thou endurest; heavy though that
weight be,
Cloud-like it mounts, or touched with
light divine
Doth melt away; but for those palms
achieved,
Through length of time, by patient
exercise
Of study and hard thought; there, there,
it is   10
That sadness finds its fuel. Hitherto,
In progress through this Verse, my mind
hath looked
Upon the speaking face of earth and
heaven
As her prime teacher, intercourse with
man
Established by the sovereign Intellect,   15
Who through that bodily image hath
diffused,
As might appear to the eye of fleeting
time,
A deathless spirit. Thou also, man! hast
wrought,
For commerce of thy nature with herself,
Things that aspire to unconquerable life;

And yet we feel—we cannot choose but
feel—   21
That they must perish. Tremblings of
the heart
It gives, to think that our immortal
being
No more shall need such garments; and
yet man,
As long as he shall be the child of earth,
Might almost 'weep to have' what he
may lose,   26
Nor be himself extinguished, but survive,
Abject, depressed, forlorn, disconsolate.
A thought is with me sometimes, and I
say,—
Should the whole frame of earth by inward
throes   30
Be wrenched, or fire come down from far
to scorch
Her pleasant habitations, and dry up
Old Ocean, in his bed left singed and
bare,
Yet would the living Presence still subsist
Victorious, and composure would ensue,
And kindlings like the morning—presage
sure   36
Of day returning and of life revived.
But all the meditations of mankind,
Yea, all the adamantine holds of truth
By reason built, or passion, which itself
Is highest reason in a soul sublime;   41
The consecrated works of Bard and Sage,
Sensuous or intellectual, wrought by men,
Twin labourers and heirs of the same
hopes;

521

Where would they be? Oh! why hath not
  the Mind   45
Some element to stamp her image on
In nature somewhat nearer to her own?
Why, gifted with such powers to send
  abroad
Her spirit, must it lodge in shrines so
  frail?

One day, when from my lips a like
  complaint   50
Had fallen in presence of a studious
  friend,
He with a smile made answer, that in
  truth
'Twas going far to seek disquietude;
But on the front of his reproof confessed
That he himself had oftentimes given
  way   55
To kindred hauntings. Whereupon I told,
That once in the stillness of a summer's
  noon,
While I was seated in a rocky cave
By the sea-side, perusing, so it chanced,
The famous history of the errant knight
Recorded by Cervantes, these same
  thoughts   61
Beset me, and to height unusual rose,
While listlessly I sate, and, having closed
The book, had turned my eyes toward
  the wide sea.
On poetry and geometric truth,   65
And their high privilege of lasting life,
From all internal injury exempt,
I mused; upon these chiefly: and at
  length,
My senses yielding to the sultry air,
Sleep seized me, and I passed into a
  dream.   70
I saw before me stretched a boundless
  plain
Of sandy wilderness, all black and void,
And as I looked around, distress and fear
Came creeping over me, when at my side,
Close at my side, an uncouth shape
  appeared   75
Upon a dromedary, mounted high,
He seemed an Arab of the Bedouin
  tribes:
A lance he bore, and underneath one arm
A stone, and in the opposite hand a shell
Of a surpassing brightness. At the sight
Much I rejoiced, not doubting but a
  guide   81
Was present, one who with unerring skill
Would through the desert lead me; and
  while yet
I looked and looked, self-questioned what
  this freight
Which the new-comer carried through
  the waste   85
Could mean, the Arab told me that the
  stone
(To give it in the language of the dream)

Was 'Euclid's Elements;' and 'This,' said
  he,
'Is something of more worth;' and at
  the word
Stretched forth the shell, so beautiful in
  shape,   90
In colour so resplendēnt, with command
That I should hold it to my ear. I did so,
And heard that instant in an unknown
  tongue,
Which yet I understood, articulate sounds,
A loud prophetic blast of harmony;   95
An Ode, in passion uttered, which fore-
  told
Destruction to the children of the earth
By deluge, now at hand. No sooner
  ceased
The song, than the Arab with calm look
  declared
That all would come to pass of which the
  voice   100
Had given forewarning, and that he
  himself
Was going then to bury those two books:
The one that held acquaintance with the
  stars,
And wedded soul to soul in purest bond
Of reason, undisturbed by space or time;
The other that was a god, yea many gods,
Had voices more than all the winds, with
  power   107
To exhilarate the spirit, and to soothe,
Through every clime, the heart of human
  kind.
While this was uttering, strange as it
  may seem,   110
I wondered not, although I plainly saw
The one to be a stone, the other a shell;
Nor doubted once but that they both were
  books,
Having a perfect faith in all that passed.
Far stronger, now, grew the desire I felt
To cleave unto this man; but when I
  prayed   116
To share his enterprise, he hurried on
Reckless of me: I followed, not unseen,
For oftentimes he cast a backward look,
Grasping his twofold treasure.—Lance in
  rest,   120
He rode, I keeping pace with him; and
  now
He, to my fancy, had become the knight
Whose tale Cervantes tells; yet not the
  knight,
But was an Arab of the desert too;
Of these was neither, and was both at
  once.   125
His countenance, meanwhile, grew more
  disturbed;
And, looking backwards when he looked,
  mine eyes
Saw, over half the wilderness diffused,
A bed of glittering light: I asked the
  cause:

'It is,' said he, 'the waters of the deep
Gathering upon us;' quickening then
  the pace   131
Of the unwieldy creature he bestrode,
He left me: I called after him aloud;
He heeded not; but, with his twofold
  charge   134
Still in his grasp, before me, full in view,
Went hurrying o'er the illimitable waste,
With the fleet waters of a drowning
  world
In chase of him; whereat I waked in
  terror,
And saw the sea before me, and the book,
In which I had been reading, at my side.

  Full often, taking from the world of
  sleep   141
This Arab phantom, which I thus beheld,
This semi-Quixote, I to him have given
A substance, fancied him a living man,
A gentle dweller in the desert, crazed 145
By love and feeling, and internal thought
Protracted among endless solitudes;
Have shaped him wandering upon this
  quest!
Nor have I pitied him; but rather felt
Reverence was due to a being thus em-
  ployed;   150
And thought that, in the blind and awful
  lair
Of such a madness, reason did lie couched.
Enow there are on earth to take in charge
Their wives, their children, and their
  virgin loves,   154
Or whatsoever else the heart holds dear;
Enow to stir for these; yea, will I say,
Contemplating in soberness the approach
Of an event so dire, by signs in earth
Or heaven made manifest, that I could
  share
That maniac's fond anxiety, and go 160
Upon like errand. Oftentimes at least
Me hath such strong entrancement over-
  come,
When I have held a volume in my hand,
Poor earthly casket of immortal verse,
Shakespeare, or Milton, labourers divine!

  Great and benign, indeed, must be the
  power   166
Of living nature, which could thus so
  long
Detain me from the best of other guides
And dearest helpers, left unthanked, un-
  praised.
Even in the time of lisping infancy, 170
And later down, in prattling childhood,
  even
While I was travelling back among those
  days,
How could I ever play an ingrate's part?
Once more should I have made those
  bowers resound,

By intermingling strains of thankfulness
With their own thoughtless melodies; at
  least   176
It might have well beseemed me to repeat
Some simply fashioned tale, to tell again,
In slender accents of sweet verse, some
  tale
That did bewitch me then, and soothes
  me now.   180
O Friend! O Poet! brother of my soul,
Think not that I could pass along un-
  touched
By these remembrances. Yet wherefore
  speak?
Why call upon a few weak words to say
What is already written in the hearts 185
Of all that breathe?—what in the path of
  all
Drops daily from the tongue of every
  child,
Wherever man is found? The trickling tear
Upon the cheek of listening Infancy
Proclaims it, and the insuperable look 190
That drinks as if it never could be full.

  That portion of my story I shall leave
There registered: whatever else of power
Or pleasure sown, or fostered thus, may be
Peculiar to myself, let that remain 195
Where still it works, though hidden from
  all search
Among the depths of time. Yet is it just
That here, in memory of all books which
  lay
Their sure foundations in the heart of
  man,
Whether by native prose, or numerous
  verse,   200
That in the name of all inspirèd souls—
From Homer the great Thunderer, from
  the voice
That roars along the bed of Jewish song,
And that more varied and elaborate,
Those trumpet-tones of harmony that
  shake   205
Our shores in England,—from those
  loftiest notes
Down to the low and wren-like warblings,
  made
For cottagers and spinners at the wheel,
And sun-burnt travellers resting their
  tired limbs,
Stretched under wayside hedge-rows,
  ballad tunes,   210
Food for the hungry ears of little ones,
And of old men who have survived their
  joys—
'Tis just that in behalf of these, the works,
And of the men that framed them,
  whether known,
Or sleeping nameless in their scattered
  graves,   215
That I should here assert their rights,
  attest

Their honours, and should, once for all,
    pronounce
Their benediction; speak of them as
    Powers
For ever to be hallowed; only less,
For what we are and what we may
    become,   220
Than Nature's self, which is the breath of
    God,
Or His pure Word by miracle revealed.

Rarely and with reluctance would I
    stoop
To transitory themes; yet I rejoice,
And, by these thoughts admonished, will
    pour out   225
Thanks with uplifted heart, that I was
    reared
Safe from an evil which these days have
    laid
Upon the children of the land, a pest
That might have dried me up, body and
    soul.   229
This verse is dedicate to Nature's self,
And things that teach as Nature teaches:
    then,
Oh! where had been the Man, the Poet
    where,
Where had we been, we two, belovèd
    Friend!
If in the season of unperilous choice,
In lieu of wandering, as we did, through
    vales   235
Rich with indigenous produce, open
    ground
Of Fancy, happy pastures ranged at
    will,
We had been followed, hourly watched,
    and noosed,
Each in his several melancholy walk
Stringed like a poor man's heifer at its
    feed,   240
Led through the lanes in forlorn servi-
    tude;
Or rather like a stallèd ox debarred
From touch of growing grass, that may
    not taste
A flower till it have yielded up its sweets
A prelibation to the mower's scythe.   245

Behold the parent hen amid her brood,
Though fledged and feathered, and well
    pleased to part
And straggle from her presence, still a
    brood,
And she herself from the maternal bond
Still undischarged; yet doth she little
    more   250
Than move with them in tenderness and
    love,
A centre to the circle which they make;
And now and then, alike from need of
    theirs
And call of her own natural appetites,

She scratches, ransacks up the earth for
    food,   255
Which they partake at pleasure. Early
    died
My honoured Mother, she who was the
    heart
And hinge of all our learnings and our
    loves:
She left us destitute, and, as we might,
Trooping together. Little suits it me   260
To break upon the sabbath of her rest
With any thought that looks at others'
    blame;
Nor would I praise her but in perfect love.
Hence am I checked: but let me boldly
    say,
In gratitude, and for the sake of truth,
Unheard by her, that she, not falsely
    taught,   266
Fetching her goodness rather from times
    past,
Than shaping novelties for times to come,
Had no presumption, no such jealousy,
Nor did by habit of her thoughts mis-
    trust   270
Our nature, but had virtual faith that He
Who fills the mother's breast with in-
    nocent milk,
Doth also for our nobler part provide,
Under His great correction and control,
As innocent instincts, and as innocent
    food;   275
Or draws for minds that are left free to
    trust
In the simplicities of opening life
Sweet honey out of spurned or dreaded
    weeds.
This was her creed, and therefore she was
    pure
From anxious fear of error or mishap,
And evil, overweeningly so called;   281
Was not puffed up by false unnatural
    hopes,
Nor selfish with unnecessary cares,
Nor with impatience from the season
    asked
More than its timely produce; rather
    loved   285
The hours for what they are, than from
    regard
Glanced on their promises in restless
    pride.
Such was she—not from faculties more
    strong
Than others have, but from the times,
    perhaps,
And spot in which she lived, and through
    a grace   290
Of modest meekness, simple-mindedness,
A heart that found benignity and hope,
Being itself benign.
                    My drift I fear
Is scarcely obvious; but, that common
    sense

May try this modern system by its fruits,
Leave let me take to place before her
   sight   296
A specimen pourtrayed with faithful
   hand.
Full early trained to worship seemliness,
This model of a child is never known
To mix in quarrels; that were far beneath
Its dignity; with gifts he bubbles o'er
As generous as a fountain; selfishness
May not come near him, nor the little
   throng
Of flitting pleasures tempt him from his
   path;
The wandering beggars propagate his
   name,   305
Dumb creatures find him tender as a nun,
And natural or supernatural fear,
Unless it leap upon him in a dream,
Touches him not. To enhance the wonder,
   see
How arch his notices, how nice his sense
Of the ridiculous; not blind is he   311
To the broad follies of the licensed world,
Yet innocent himself withal, though
   shrewd,
And can read lectures upon innocence;
A miracle of scientific lore,   315
Ships he can guide across the pathless
   sea,
And tell you all their cunning; he can
   read
The inside of the earth, and spell the
   stars;
He knows the policies of foreign lands;
Can string you names of districts, cities,
   towns,   320
The whole world over, tight as beads of
   dew
Upon a gossamer thread; he sifts, he
   weighs;
All things are put to question; he must
   live
Knowing that he grows wiser every day
Or else not live at all, and seeing too 325
Each little drop of wisdom as it falls
Into the dimpling cistern of his heart:
For this unnatural growth the trainer
   blame,
Pity the tree.—Poor human vanity,
Wert thou extinguished, little would be
   left   330
Which he could truly love; but how
   escape?
For, ever as a thought of purer birth
Rises to lead him toward a better clime,
Some intermeddler still is on the watch
To drive him back, and pound him, like
   a stray,   335
Within the pinfold of his own conceit.
Meanwhile old grandame earth is grieved
   to find
The playthings, which her love designed
   for him,

Unthought of: in their woodland beds
   the flowers   339
Weep, and the river sides are all forlorn.
Oh! give us once again the wishing-cap
Of Fortunatus, and the invisible coat
Of Jack the Giant-killer, Robin Hood,
And Sabra in the forest with St. George!
The child, whose love is here, at least,
   doth reap   345
One precious gain, that he forgets himself.

These mighty workmen of our later age,
Who, with a broad highway, have over-
   bridged
The froward chaos of futurity,
Tamed to their bidding; they who have
   the skill   350
To manage books, and things, and make
   them act
On infant minds as surely as the sun
Deals with a flower; the keepers of our
   time,
The guides and wardens of our faculties,
Sages who in their prescience would
   control   355
All accidents, and to the very road
Which they have fashioned would confine
   us down,
Like engines; when will their presump-
   tion learn,
That in the unreasoning progress of the
   world
A wiser spirit is at work for us,   360
A better eye than theirs, most prodigal
Of blessings, and most studious of our
   good,
Even in what seem our most unfruitful
   hours?

There was a Boy[1]: ye knew him well,
   ye cliffs   364
And islands of Winander!—many a time
At evening, when the earliest stars began
To move along the edges of the hills,
Rising or setting, would he stand alone
Beneath the trees or by the glimmering lake,
And there, with fingers interwoven, both
   hands   370
Pressed closely palm to palm, and to his
   mouth
Uplifted, he, as through an instrument,
Blew mimic hootings to the silent owls,
That they might answer him; and they
   would shout
Across the watery vale, and shout again,
Responsive to his call, with quivering
   peals,   376
And long halloos and screams, and echoes
   loud,
Redoubled and redoubled, concourse wild
Of jocund din; and, when a lengthened
   pause
Of silence came and baffled his best skill,

                    [1] See page 145.

Then sometimes, in that silence while he
    hung   381
Listening, a gentle shock of mild surprise
Has carried far into his heart the voice
Of mountain torrents; or the visible scene
Would enter unawares into his mind, 385
With all its solemn imagery, its rocks,
Its woods, and that uncertain heaven,
    received
Into the bosom of the steady lake.

    This Boy was taken from his mates,
    and died
In childhood, ere he was full twelve years
    old.   390
Fair is the spot, most beautiful the vale
Where he was born; the grassy church-
    yard hangs
Upon a slope above the village school,
And through that churchyard when my
    way has led   394
On summer evenings, I believe that there
A long half hour together I have stood
Mute, looking at the grave in which he
    lies!
Even now appears before the mind's clear
    eye
That self-same village church; I see her
    sit
(The thronèd Lady whom erewhile we
    hailed)   400
On her green hill, forgetful of this Boy
Who slumbers at her feet,—forgetful, too,
Of all her silent neighbourhood of graves,
And listening only to the gladsome sounds
That, from the rural school ascending,
    play   405
Beneath her and about her. May she long
Behold a race of young ones like to those
With whom I herded!—(easily, indeed,
We might have fed upon a fatter soil
Of arts and letters—but be that for-
    given)—   410
A race of real children; not too wise,
Too learned, or too good; but wanton,
    fresh,
And bandied up and down by love and
    hate;
Not unresentful where self-justified;
Fierce, moody, patient, venturous, modest,
    shy;   415
Mad at their sports like withered leaves
    in winds;
Though doing wrong and suffering, and
    full oft
Bending beneath our life's mysterious
    weight
Of pain, and doubt, and fear, yet yielding
    not
In happiness to the happiest upon earth.
Simplicity in habit, truth in speech, 421
Be these the daily strengtheners of their
    minds;
May books and Nature be their early joy!

And knowledge, rightly honoured with
    that name—
Knowledge not purchased by the loss of
    power!   425

    Well do I call to mind the very week
When I was first intrusted to the care
Of that sweet Valley; when its paths, its
    shores,
And brooks were like a dream of novelty
To my half-infant thoughts; that very
    week,   430
While I was roving up and down alone,
Seeking I knew not what, I chanced to cross
One of those open fields, which, shaped
    like ears,
Make green peninsulas on Esthwaite's
    Lake:
Twilight was coming on, yet through the
    gloom   435
Appeared distinctly on the opposite shore
A heap of garments, as if left by one
Who might have there been bathing.
    Long I watched,
But no one owned them; meanwhile the
    calm lake
Grew dark with all the shadows on its
    breast,   440
And, now and then, a fish up-leaping
    snapped
The breathless stillness. The succeeding
    day,
Those unclaimed garments telling a plain
    tale
Drew to the spot an anxious crowd; some
    looked
In passive expectation from the shore,
While from a boat others hung o'er the
    deep,   446
Sounding with grappling irons and long
    poles.
At last, the dead man, 'mid that beauteous
    scene
Of trees and hills and water, bolt upright
Rose, with his ghastly face, a spectre
    shape   450
Of terror; yet no soul-debasing fear,
Young as I was, a child not nine years old,
Possessed me, for my inner eye had seen
Such sights before, among the shining
    streams
Of faery land, the forest of romance. 455
Their spirit hallowed the sad spectacle
With decoration of ideal grace;
A dignity, a smoothness, like the works
Of Grecian art, and purest poesy.

    A precious treasure had I long pos-
    sessed,   460
A little yellow, canvas-covered book,
A slender abstract of the Arabian tales;
And, from companions in a new abode,
When first I learnt, that this dear prize
    of mine

Was but a block hewn from a mighty
     quarry—   465
That there were four large volumes, laden
     all
With kindred matter, 'twas to me, in
     truth,
A promise scarcely earthly. Instantly,
With one not richer than myself, I made
A covenant that each should lay aside
The moneys he possessed, and hoard up
     more,   471
Till our joint savings had amassed enough
To make this book our own. Through
     several months,
In spite of all temptation, we preserved
Religiously that vow; but firmness failed,
Nor were we ever masters of our wish.

     And when thereafter to my father's
     house   477
The holidays returned me, there to find
That golden store of books which I had
     left,
What joy was mine! How often in the
     course   480
Of those glad respites, though a soft west
     wind
Ruffled the waters to the angler's wish,
For a whole day together, have I lain
Down by thy side, O Derwent! murmur-
     ing stream,   484
On the hot stones, and in the glaring sun,
And there have read, devouring as I read,
Defrauding the day's glory, desperate!
Till with a sudden bound of smart
     reproach,
Such as an idler deals with in his shame,
I to the sport betook myself again.   490

     A gracious spirit o'er this earth pre-
     sides,
And o'er the heart of man: invisibly
It comes, to works of unreproved delight,
And tendency benign, directing those
Who care not, know not, think not what
     they do.   495
The tales that charm away the wakeful
     night
In Araby, romances; legends penned
For solace by dim light of monkish lamps;
Fictions, for ladies of their love, devised
By youthful squires; adventures endless,
     spun   500
By the dismantled warrior in old age,
Out of the bowels of those very schemes
In which his youth did first extravagate;
These spread like day, and something in
     the shape
Of these will live till man shall be no
     more.   505
Dumb yearnings, hidden appetites, are
     ours,
And *they must* have their food. Our
     childhood sits,

Our simple childhood, sits upon a throne
That hath more power than all the ele-
     ments.   509
I guess not what this tells of Being past,
Nor what it augurs of the life to come;
But so it is, and, in that dubious hour,
That twilight when we first begin to see
This dawning earth, to recognise, expect,
And, in the long probation that ensues,
The time of trial, ere we learn to live
In reconcilement with our stinted powers;
To endure this state of meagre vassalage,
Unwilling to forego, confess, submit,
Uneasy and unsettled, yoke-fellows   520
To custom, mettlesome, and not yet tamed
And humbled down;—oh! then we feel,
     we feel,
We know where we have friends. Ye
     dreamers, then,
Forgers of daring tales! we bless you then,
Impostors, drivellers, dotards, as the ape
Philosophy will call you: *then* we feel
With what, and how great might ye are
     in league,   527
Who make our wish our power, our
     thought a deed,
An empire, a possession,—ye whom time
And seasons serve; all Faculties;—to
     whom   530
Earth crouches, the elements are potter's
     clay,
Space like a heaven filled up with northern
     lights,
Here, nowhere, there, and everywhere at
     once.

     Relinquishing this lofty eminence
For ground, though humbler, not the less
     a tract   535
Of the same isthmus, which our spirits
     cross
In progress from their native continent
To earth and human life, the Song might
     dwell
On that delightful time of growing youth
When craving for the marvellous gives
     way   540
To strengthening love for things that we
     have seen;
When sober truth and steady sympathies,
Offered to notice by less daring pens,
Take firmer hold of us, and words them-
     selves
Move us with conscious pleasure.
                        I am sad
At thought of raptures now for ever
     flown;   546
Almost to tears I sometimes could be
     sad
To think of, to read over, many a page,
Poems withal of name, which at that time
Did never fail to entrance me, and are
     now   550
Dead in my eyes, dead as a theatre

Fresh emptied of spectators. Twice five
    years
Or less I might have seen, when first my
    mind
With conscious pleasure opened to the
    charm
Of words in tuneful order, found them
    sweet   555
For their own *sakes*, a passion, and a
    power;
And phrases pleased me chosen for de-
    light,
For pomp, or love. Oft, in the public
    roads
Yet unfrequented, while the morning
    light
Was yellowing the hill tops, I went
    abroad   560
With a dear friend, and for the better
    part
Of two delightful hours we strolled along
By the still borders of the misty lake,
Repeating favourite verses with one voice,
Or conning more, as happy as the birds
That round us chaunted. Well might we
    be glad,   566
Lifted above the ground by airy fancies,
More bright than madness or the dreams
    of wine;
And, though full oft the objects of our
    love
Were false, and in their splendour over-
    wrought,   570
Yet was there surely then no vulgar
    power
Working within us,—nothing less, in
    truth,
Than that most noble attribute of man,
Though yet untutored and inordinate,
That wish for something loftier, more
    adorned,   575

Than is the common aspect, daily garb,
Of human life. What wonder, then, if
    sounds
Of exultation echoed through the groves!
For, images, and sentiments, and words,
And everything encountered or pursued
In that delicious world of poesy,   581
Kept holiday, a never-ending show,
With music, incense, festival, and flowers!

Here must we pause: this only let me
    add,
From heart-experience, and in humblest
    sense   585
Of modesty, that he, who in his youth
A daily wanderer among woods and fields
With living Nature hath been intimate,
Not only in that raw unpractised time
Is stirred to ecstasy, as others are,   590
By glittering verse; but further, doth
    receive,
In measure only dealt out to himself,
Knowledge and increase of enduring joy
From the great Nature that exists in
    works
Of mighty Poets. Visionary power   595
Attends the motions of the viewless winds,
Embodied in the mystery of words:
There, darkness makes abode, and all the
    host
Of shadowy things work endless changes,
    —there,   599
As in a mansion like their proper home,
Even forms and substances are circum-
    fused
By that transparent veil with light divine,
And, through the turnings intricate of
    verse,
Present themselves as objects recognised,
In flashes, and with glory not their
    own.   605

BOOK SIXTH

CAMBRIDGE AND THE ALPS

The leaves were fading when to Esth-
    waite's banks
And the simplicities of cottage life
I bade farewell; and, one among the
    youth
Who, summoned by that season, reunite
As scattered birds troop to the fowler's
    lure,   5
Went back to Granta's cloisters, not so
    prompt
Or eager, though as gay and undepressed
In mind, as when I thence had taken flight
A few short months before. I turned my
    face
Without repining from the coves and
    heights   10

Clothed in the sunshine of the withering
    fern;
Quitted, not loth, the mild magnifi-
    cence
Of calmer lakes and louder streams; and
    you,
Frank-hearted maids of rocky Cumber-
    land,
You and your not unwelcome days of
    mirth   15
Relinquished, and your nights of revelry,
And in my own unlovely cell sate down
In lightsome mood—such privilege has
    youth
That cannot take long leave of pleasant
    thoughts.

The bonds of indolent society   20
Relaxing in their hold, henceforth I lived
More to myself. Two winters may be
    passed
Without a separate notice: many books
Were skimmed, devoured, or studiously
    perused,
But with no settled plan. I was detached
Internally from academic cares;   26
Yet independent study seemed a course
Of hardy disobedience towards friends
And kindred, proud rebellion and unkind.
This spurious virtue, rather let it bear 30
A name it more deserves, this cowardice,
Gave treacherous sanction to that over-
    love
Of freedom which encouraged me to turn
From regulations even of my own
As from restraints and bonds. Yet who
    can tell—   35
Who knows what thus may have been
    gained, both then
And at a later season, or preserved;
What love of nature, what original
    strength
Of contemplation, what intuitive truths,
The deepest and the best, what keen
    research,   40
Unbiassed, unbewildered, and unawed?

The Poet's soul was with me at that
    time;
Sweet meditations, the still overflow
Of present happiness, while future years
Lacked not anticipations, tender dreams,
No few of which have since been realised;
And some remain, hopes for my future
    life.   47
Four years and thirty, told this very
    week,
Have I been now a sojourner on earth,
By sorrow not unsmitten; yet for me 50
Life's morning radiance hath not left the
    hills,
Her dew is on the flowers. Those were
    the days
Which also first emboldened me to trust
With firmness, hitherto but lightly
    touched
By such a daring thought, that I might
    leave   55
Some monument behind me which pure
    hearts
Should reverence. The instinctive hum-
    bleness,
Maintained even by the very name and
    thought
Of printed books and authorship, began
To melt away; and further, the dread
    awe   60
Of mighty names was softened down and
    seemed
Approachable, admitting fellowship
Of modest sympathy. Such aspect now,

Though not familiarly, my mind put on,
Content to observe, to achieve, and to
    enjoy.   65

    All winter long, whenever free to
    choose,
Did I by night frequent the College
    groves
And tributary walks; the last, and oft
The only one, who had been lingering
    there
Through hours of silence, till the porter's
    bell,   70
A punctual follower on the stroke of nine,
Rang with its blunt unceremonious voice,
Inexorable summons! Lofty elms,
Inviting shades of opportune recess,
Bestowed composure on a neighbourhood
Unpeaceful in itself. A single tree 76
With sinuous trunk, boughs exquisitely
    wreathed,
Grew there; an ash which Winter for
    himself
Decked as in pride, and with outlandish
    grace:
Up from the ground, and almost to the
    top,   80
The trunk and every master branch were
    green
With clustering ivy, and the lightsome
    twigs
And outer spray profusely tipped with
    seeds
That hung in yellow tassels, while the air
Stirred them, not voiceless. Often have
    I stood   85
Foot-bound uplooking at this lovely tree
Beneath a frosty moon. The hemisphere
Of magic fiction, verse of mine perchance
May never tread; but scarcely Spenser's
    self
Could have more tranquil visions in his
    youth,   90
Or could more bright appearances create
Of human forms with superhuman
    powers,
Than I beheld loitering on calm clear
    nights
Alone, beneath this fairy work of earth.

    On the vague reading of a truant youth
'Twere idle to descant. My inner judg-
    ment   96
Not seldom differed from my taste in
    books,
As if it appertained to another mind,
And yet the books which then I valued
    most
Are dearest to me now; for, having
    scanned,   100
Not heedlessly, the laws, and watched
    the forms
Of Nature, in that knowledge I possessed
A standard, often usefully applied,

529

Even when unconsciously, to things
removed
From a familiar sympathy.—In fine,   105
I was a better judge of thoughts than
words,
Misled in estimating words, not only
By common inexperience of youth,
But by the trade in classic niceties,
The dangerous craft of culling term and
phrase   110
From languages that want the living voice
To carry meaning to the natural heart;
To tell us what is passion, what is truth,
What reason, what simplicity and sense.

Yet may we not entirely overlook   115
The pleasure gathered from the rudi-
ments
Of geometric science. Though advanced
In these enquiries, with regret I speak,
No farther than the threshold, there I
found
Both elevation and composed delight:
With Indian awe and wonder, ignorance
pleased   121
With its own struggles, did I meditate
On the relation those abstractions bear
To Nature's laws, and by what process led,
Those immaterial agents bowed their
heads   125
Duly to serve the mind of earth-born man;
From star to star, from kindred sphere to
sphere,
From system on to system without end.

More frequently from the same source
I drew
A pleasure quiet and profound, a sense
Of permanent and universal sway,   131
And paramount belief; there, recognised
A type, for finite natures, of the one
Supreme Existence, the surpassing life
Which—to the boundaries of space and
time,   135
Of melancholy space and doleful time,
Superior, and incapable of change,
Nor touched by welterings of passion—is,
And hath the name of, God. Transcen-
dent peace
And silence did await upon these thoughts
That were a frequent comfort to my
youth.   141

'Tis told by one whom stormy waters
threw,
With fellow-sufferers by the shipwreck
spared,
Upon a desert coast, that having brought
To land a single volume, saved by chance,
A treatise of Geometry, he wont,   146
Although of food and clothing destitute,
And beyond common wretchedness de-
pressed,
To part from company and take this book

(Then first a self-taught pupil in its
truths)   150
To spots remote, and draw his diagrams
With a long staff upon the sand, and thus
Did oft beguile his sorrow, and almost
Forget his feeling: so (if like effect
From the same cause produced, 'mid
outward things   155
So different, may rightly be compared),
So was it then with me, and so will be
With Poets ever. Mighty is the charm
Of those abstractions to a mind beset
With images, and haunted by herself,
And specially delightful unto me   161
Was that clear synthesis built up aloft
So gracefully; even then when it appeared
Not more than a mere plaything, or a toy
To sense embodied: not the thing it is
In verity, an independent world,   166
Created out of pure intelligence.

Such dispositions then were mine un-
earned
By aught, I fear, of genuine desert—
Mine, through heaven's grace and inborn
aptitudes.   170
And not to leave the story of that time
Imperfect, with these habits must be
joined
Moods melancholy, fits of spleen, that
loved
A pensive sky, sad days, and piping winds,
The twilight more than dawn, autumn
than spring;   175
A treasured and luxurious gloom of choice
And inclination mainly, and the mere
Redundancy of youth's contentedness.
—To time thus spent, add multitudes of
hours
Pilfered away, by what the Bard who
sang   180
Of the Enchanter Indolence hath called
'Good-natured lounging,' and behold a
map
Of my collegiate life—far less intense
Than duty called for, or, without regard
To duty, *might* have sprung up of itself
By change of accidents, or even, to
speak   186
Without unkindness, in another place.
Yet why take refuge in that plea?—the
fault,
This I repeat, was mine; mine be the
blame.

In summer, making quest for works of
art,   190
Or scenes renowned for beauty, I explored
That streamlet whose blue current works
its way
Between romantic Dovedale's spiry rocks;
Pried into Yorkshire dales, or hidden
tracts

Of my own native region, and was blest
Between these sundry wanderings with
    a joy   196
Above all joys, that seemed another morn
Risen on mid noon; blest with the
    presence, Friend!
Of that sole Sister, her who hath been long
Dear to thee also, thy true friend and
    mine,   200
Now, after separation desolate,
Restored to me—such absence that she
    seemed
A gift then first bestowed. The varied
    banks
Of Emont, hitherto unnamed in song,
And that monastic castle, 'mid tall trees,
Low-standing by the margin of the stream,
A mansion visited (as fame reports) 207
By Sidney, where, in sight of our Helvellyn,
Or stormy Cross-fell, snatches he might
    pen
Of his Arcadia, by fraternal love   210
Inspired;—that river and those moulder-
    ing towers
Have seen us side by side, when, having
    clomb
The darksome windings of a broken stair,
And crept along a ridge of fractured wall,
Not without trembling, we in safety
    looked   215
Forth, through some Gothic window's
    open space,
And gathered with one mind a rich reward
From the far-stretching landscape, by
    the light
Of morning beautified, or purple eve;
Or, not less pleased, lay on some turret's
    head,   220
Catching from tufts of grass and hare-
    bell flowers
Their faintest whisper to the passing
    breeze,
Given out while mid-day heat oppressed
    the plains.

Another maid there was, who also shed
A gladness o'er that season, then to me,
By her exulting outside look of youth
And placid under-countenance, first en-
    deared;   227
That other spirit, Coleridge! who is now
So near to us, that meek confiding heart,
So reverenced by us both. O'er paths and
    fields   230
In all that neighbourhood, through nar-
    row lanes
Of eglantine, and through the shady
    woods,
And o'er the Border Beacon, and the
    waste
Of naked pools, and common crags that
    lay
Exposed on the bare fell, were scattered
    love,   235

The spirit of pleasure, and youth's golden
    gleam.
O Friend! we had not seen thee at that
    time,
And yet a power is on me, and a strong
Confusion, and I seem to plant thee there.
Far art thou wandered now in search of
    health   240
And milder breezes,—melancholy lot!
But thou art with us, with us in the
    past,
The present, with us in the times to come.
There is no grief, no sorrow, no despair,
No languor, no dejection, no dismay, 245
No absence scarcely can there be, for those
Who love as we do. Speed thee well!
    divide
With us thy pleasure; thy returning
    strength,
Receive it daily as a joy of ours;
Share with us thy fresh spirits, whether
    gift   250
Of gales Etesian or of tender thoughts.

I, too, have been a wanderer; but, alas!
How different the fate of different men.
Though mutually unknown, yea, nursed
    and reared   254
As if in several elements, we were framed
To bend at last to the same discipline,
Predestined, if two beings ever were,
To seek the same delights, and have one
    health,
One happiness. Throughout this narra-
    tive,
Else sooner ended, I have borne in mind
For whom it registers the birth, and
    marks the growth,   261
Of gentleness, simplicity, and truth,
And joyous loves, that hallow innocent
    days
Of peace and self-command. Of rivers,
    fields,
And groves I speak to thee, my Friend!
    to thee,   265
Who, yet a liveried schoolboy, in the
    depths
Of the huge city, on the leaded roof
Of that wide edifice, thy school and home,
Wert used to lie and gaze upon the clouds
Moving in heaven; or, of that pleasure
    tired,   270
To shut thine eyes, and by internal light
See trees, and meadows, and thy native
    stream,
Far distant, thus beheld from year to year
Of a long exile. Nor could I forget,
In this late portion of my argument, 275
That scarcely, as my term of pupilage
Ceased, had I left those academic bowers
When thou wert thither guided. From
    the heart
Of London, and from cloisters there, thou
    camest,

And didst sit down in temperance and
    peace,   280
A rigorous student. What a stormy
    course
Then followed. Oh! it is a pang that calls
For utterance, to think what easy change
Of circumstances might to thee have
    spared
A world of pain, ripened a thousand
    hopes,   285
For ever withered. Through this retro-
    spect
Of my collegiate life I still have had
Thy after-sojourn in the self-same place
Present before my eyes, have played with
    times
And accidents as children do with cards,
Or as a man, who, when his house is
    built,   291
A frame locked up in wood and stone,
    doth still,
As impotent fancy prompts, by his fire-
    side,
Rebuild it to his liking. I have thought
Of thee, thy learning, gorgeous eloquence,
And all the strength and plumage of thy
    youth,   296
Thy subtle speculations, toils abstruse
Among the schoolmen, and Platonic forms
Of wild ideal pageantry, shaped out
From things well-matched or ill, and
    words for things,   300
The self-created sustenance of a mind
Debarred from Nature's living images,
Compelled to be a life unto herself,
And unrelentingly possessed by thirst
Of greatness, love, and beauty. Not alone,
Ah! surely not in singleness of heart   306
Should I have seen the light of evening
    fade
From smooth Cam's silent waters: had
    we met,
Even at that early time, needs must I
    trust
In the belief, that my maturer age,   310
My calmer habits, and more steady voice,
Would with an influence benign have
    soothed,
Or chased away, the airy wretchedness
That battened on thy youth. But thou
    hast trod
A march of glory, which doth put to
    shame   315
These vain regrets; health suffers in thee,
    else
Such grief for thee would be the weakest
    thought
That ever harboured in the breast of man.

    A passing word erewhile did lightly
    touch
On wanderings of my own, that now
    embraced   320
With livelier hope a region wider far.

When the third summer freed us from
    restraint,
A youthful friend, he too a mountaineer,
Not slow to share my wishes, took his
    staff,
And sallying forth, we journeyed side by
    side,   325
Bound to the distant Alps. A hardy slight
Did this unprecedented course imply
Of college studies and their set rewards;
Nor had, in truth, the scheme been formed
    by me   329
Without uneasy forethought of the pain,
The censures, and ill-omening of those
To whom my worldly interests were dear.
But Nature then was sovereign in my
    mind,
And mighty forms, seizing a youthful
    fancy,   334
Had given a charter to irregular hopes.
In any age of uneventful calm
Among the nations, surely would my
    heart
Have been possessed by similar desire;
But Europe at that time was thrilled with
    joy,
France standing on the top of golden
    hours,   340
And human nature seeming born again.

    Lightly equipped, and but a few brief
    looks
Cast on the white cliffs of our native shore
From the receding vessel's deck, we
    chanced
To land at Calais on the very eve   345
Of that great federal day; and there we
    saw,
In a mean city, and among a few,
How bright a face is worn when joy of one
Is joy for tens of millions. Southward
    thence
We held our way, direct through hamlets,
    towns,   350
Gaudy with reliques of that festival,
Flowers left to wither on triumphal arcs,
And window-garlands. On the public
    roads,
And, once, three days successively,
    through paths
By which our toilsome journey was
    abridged,   355
Among sequestered villages we walked
And found benevolence and blessedness
Spread like a fragrance everywhere, when
    spring
Hath left no corner of the land un-
    touched:
Where elms for many and many a league
    in files   360
With their thin umbrage, on the stately
    roads
Of that great kingdom, rustled o'er our
    heads,

For ever near us as we paced along:
How sweet at such a time, with such
    delight
On every side, in prime of youthful
    strength,   365
To feed a Poet's tender melancholy
And fond conceit of sadness, with the
    sound
Of undulations varying as might please
The wind that swayed them; once, and
    more than once,
Unhoused beneath the evening star we
    saw   370
Dances of liberty, and, in late hours
Of darkness, dances in the open air
Deftly prolonged, though grey-haired
    lookers on
Might waste their breath in chiding.
                        Under hills—
The vine-clad hills and slopes of Bur-
    gundy,   375
Upon the bosom of the gentle Saone
We glided forward with the flowing
    stream.
Swift Rhone! thou wert the *wings* on
    which we cut
A winding passage with majestic ease
Between thy lofty rocks. Enchanting
    show   380
Those woods and farms and orchards did
    present,
And single cottages and lurking towns,
Reach after reach, succession without end
Of deep and stately vales! A lonely pair
Of strangers, till day closed, we sailed
    along,   385
Clustered together with a merry crowd
Of those emancipated, a blithe host
Of travellers, chiefly delegates returning
From the great spousals newly solemnized
At their chief city, in the sight of Heaven.
Like bees they swarmed, gaudy and gay
    as bees;   391
Some vapoured in the unruliness of joy,
And with their swords flourished as if to
    fight
The saucy air. In this proud company
We landed—took with them our evening
    meal,   395
Guests welcome almost as the angels were
To Abraham of old. The supper done,
With flowing cups elate and happy
    thoughts
We rose at signal given, and formed a
    ring
And, hand in hand, danced round and
    round the board;   400
All hearts were open, every tongue was
    loud
With amity and glee; we bore a name
Honoured in France, the name of English-
    men,
And hospitably did they give us hail,
As their forerunners in a glorious course;

And round and round the board we
    danced again.   406
With these blithe friends our voyage we
    renewed
At early dawn. The monastery bells
Made a sweet jingling in our youthful
    ears;   409
The rapid river flowing without noise,
And each uprising or receding spire
Spake with a sense of peace, at intervals
Touching the heart amid the boisterous
    crew
By whom we were encompassed. Taking
    leave
Of this glad throng, foot-travellers side
    by side,   415
Measuring our steps in quiet, we pursued
Our journey, and ere twice the sun had
    set
Beheld the Convent of Chartreuse, and
    there
Rested within an awful *solitude*:   419
Yes; for even then no other than a place
Of soul-affecting *solitude* appeared
That far-famed region, though our eyes
    had seen,
As toward the sacred mansion we ad-
    vanced,
Arms flashing, and a military glare   424
Of riotous men commissioned to expel
The blameless inmates, and belike subvert
That frame of social being, which so long
Had bodied forth the ghostliness of
    things
In silence visible and perpetual calm.
—'Stay, stay your sacrilegious hands!'—
        The voice   430
Was Nature's, uttered from her Alpine
    throne;
I heard it then, and seem to hear it now—
'Your impious work forbear: perish what
    may,
Let this one temple last, be this one spot
Of earth devoted to eternity!'   435
She ceased to speak, but while St. Bruno's
    pines
Waved their dark tops, not silent as they
    waved,
And while below, along their several beds,
Murmured the sister streams of Life and
    Death,
Thus by conflicting passions pressed, my
    heart   440
Responded; 'Honour to the patriot's zeal!
Glory and hope to new-born Liberty!
Hail to the mighty projects of the time!
Discerning sword that Justice wields, do
    thou
Go forth and prosper; and, ye purging
    fires,   445
Up to the loftiest towers of Pride ascend,
Fanned by the breath of angry Provi-
    dence.
But oh! if Past and Future be the wings

On whose support harmoniously con-
joined
Moves the great spirit of human know-
ledge, spare   450
These courts of mystery, where a step
advanced
Between the portals of the shadowy rocks
Leaves far behind life's treacherous vani-
ties,
For penitential tears and trembling hopes
Exchanged—to equalise in God's pure
sight   455
Monarch and peasant: be the house
redeemed
With its unworldly votaries, for the sake
Of conquest over sense, hourly achieved
Through faith and meditative reason,
resting
Upon the word of heaven-imparted truth,
Calmly triumphant; and for humbler
claim   461
Of that imaginative impulse sent
From these majestic floods, yon shining
cliffs,
The untransmuted shapes of many worlds,
Cerulean ether's pure inhabitants,   465
These forests unapproachable by death,
That shall endure as long as man endures,
To think, to hope, to worship, and to feel,
To struggle, to be lost within himself
In trepidation, from the blank abyss   470
To look with bodily eyes, and be con-
soled.'
Not seldom since that moment have I
wished
That thou, O Friend! the trouble or the
calm
Hadst shared, when, from profane regards
apart,
In sympathetic reverence we trod   475
The floors of those dim cloisters, till that
hour,
From their foundation, strangers to the
presence
Of unrestricted and unthinking man.
Abroad, how cheeringly the sunshine lay
Upon the open lawns! Vallombre's groves
Entering, we fed the soul with darkness;
thence   481
Issued, and with uplifted eyes beheld,
In different quarters of the bending sky,
The cross of Jesus stand erect, as if
Hands of angelic powers had fixed it
there,   485
Memorial reverenced by a thousand
storms;
Yet then, from the undiscriminating
sweep
And rage of one State-whirlwind, in-
secure.

'Tis not my present purpose to retrace
That variegated journey step by step. 490
A march it was of military speed,

And Earth did change her images and
forms
Before us, fast as clouds are changed in
heaven.
Day after day, up early and down late,
From hill to vale we dropped, from vale
to hill   495
Mounted—from province on to province
swept,
Keen hunters in a chase of fourteen weeks,
Eager as birds of prey, or as a ship
Upon the stretch, when winds are blow-
ing fair: 499
Sweet coverts did we cross of pastoral life,
Enticing valleys, greeted them and left
Too soon, while yet the very flash and
gleam
Of salutation were not passed away.
Oh! sorrow for the youth who could have
seen
Unchastened, unsubdued, unawed, un-
raised   505
To patriarchal dignity of mind,
And pure simplicity of wish and will,
Those sanctified abodes of peaceful man,
Pleased (though to hardship born, and
compassed round
With danger, varying as the seasons
change),   510
Pleased with his daily task, or, if not
pleased,
Contented, from the moment that the
dawn
(Ah! surely not without attendant gleams
Of soul-illumination) calls him forth
To industry, by glistenings flung on rocks,
Whose evening shadows lead him to re-
pose.   516

Well might a stranger look with bound-
ing heart
Down on a green recess, the first I saw
Of those deep haunts, an aboriginal vale,
Quiet and lorded over and possessed 520
By naked huts, wood-built, and sown like
tents
Or Indian cabins over the fresh lawns
And by the river side.
                       That very day,
From a bare ridge we also first beheld
Unveiled the summit of Mont Blanc, and
grieved   525
To have a soulless image on the eye
That had usurped upon a living thought
That never more could be. The wondrous
Vale
Of Chamouny stretched far below, and
soon
With its dumb cataracts and streams of
ice,   530
A motionless array of mighty waves,
Five rivers broad and vast, made rich
amends,
And reconciled us to realities;

There small birds warble from the leafy trees,
The eagle soars high in the element, 535
There doth the reaper bind the yellow sheaf, ·
The maiden spread the haycock in the sun,
While Winter like a well-tamed lion walks,
Descending from the mountain to make sport 539
Among the cottages by beds of flowers.

Whate'er in this wide circuit we beheld,
Or heard, was fitted to our unripe state
Of intellect and heart. With such a book
Before our eyes, we could not choose but read
Lessons of genuine brotherhood, the plain
And universal reason of mankind, 546
The truths of young and old. Nor, side by side
Pacing, two social pilgrims, or alone
Each with his humour, could we fail to abound
In dreams and fictions, pensively composed: 550
Dejection taken up for pleasure's sake,
·And gilded sympathies, the willow wreath,
And sober posies of funereal flowers,
Gathered among those solitudes sublime
From formal gardens of the lady Sorrow,
Did sweeten many a meditative hour. 556

Yet still in me with those soft luxuries
Mixed something of stern mood, an underthirst
Of vigour seldom utterly allayed:
And from that source how different a sadness 560
Would issue, let one incident make known.
When from the Vallais we had turned, and clomb
Along the Simplon's steep and rugged road,
Following a band of muleteers, we reached
A halting-place, where all together took
Their noon-tide meal. Hastily rose our guide, 566
Leaving us at the board; awhile we lingered,
Then paced the beaten downward way that led
Right to a rough stream's edge, and there broke off;
The only track now visible was one 570
That from the torrent's further brink held forth
Conspicuous invitation to ascend
A lofty mountain. After brief delay
Crossing the unbridged stream, that road we took,
And clomb with eagerness, till anxious fears 575
Intruded, for we failed to overtake

Our comrades gone before. By fortunate chance,
While every moment added doubt to doubt,
A peasant met us, from whose mouth we learned
That to the spot which had perplexed us first 580
We must descend, and there should find the road,
Which in the stony channel of the stream
Lay a few steps, and then along its banks;
And, that our future course, all plain to sight,
Was downwards, with the current of that stream. 585
Loth to believe what we so grieved to hear,
For still we had hopes that pointed to the clouds,
We questioned him again, and yet again;
But every word that from the peasant's lips
Came in reply, translated by our feelings,
Ended in this,—*that we had crossed the Alps.* 591

Imagination—here the Power so called
Through sad incompetence of human speech,
That awful Power rose from the mind's abyss 594
Like an unfathered vapour that enwraps,
At once, some lonely traveller. I was lost;
Halted without an effort to break through;
But to my conscious soul I now can say—
'I recognise thy glory:' in such strength
Of usurpation, when the light of sense
Goes out, but with a flash that has revealed 601
The invisible world, doth greatness make abode,
There harbours; whether we be young or old,
Our destiny, our being's heart and home,
Is with infinitude, and only there; 605
With hope it is, hope that can never die,
Effort, and expectation, and desire,
And something evermore about to be.
Under such banners militant, the soul
Seeks for no trophies, struggles for no spoils 610
That may attest her prowess, blest in thoughts
That are their own perfection and reward,
Strong in herself and in beatitude
That hides her, like the mighty flood of Nile
Poured from his fount of Abyssinian clouds 615
To fertilise the whole Egyptian plain.

The melancholy slackening that ensued
Upon those tidings by the peasant given
Was soon dislodged. Downwards we hurried fast,

And, with the half-shaped road which we
    had missed,   620
Entered a narrow chasm. ¹The brook and
    road
Were fellow-travellers in this gloomy
    strait,
And with them did we journey several
    hours
At a slow pace. The immeasurable height
Of woods decaying, never to be decayed,
The stationary blasts of waterfalls, 626
And in the narrow rent at every turn
Winds thwarting winds, bewildered and
    forlorn,
The torrents shooting from the clear blue
    sky,
The rocks that muttered close upon our
    ears,   630
Black drizzling crags that spake by the
    way-side
As if a voice were in them, the sick sight
And giddy prospect of the raving stream,
The unfettered clouds and region of the
    Heavens,
Tumult and peace, the darkness and the
    light—   635
Were all like workings of one mind, the
    features
Of the same face, blossoms upon one tree;
Characters of the great Apocalypse,
The types and symbols of Eternity,
Of first, and last, and midst, and without
    end.   640

    That night our lodging was a house that
    stood
Alone, within the valley, at a point
Where, tumbling from aloft, a torrent
    swelled
The rapid stream whose margin we had
    trod;
A dreary mansion, large beyond all need,
With high and spacious rooms, deafened
    and stunned   646
By noise of waters, making innocent sleep
Lie melancholy among weary bones.

    Uprisen betimes, our journey we re-
    newed,
Led by the stream, ere noon-day magni-
    fied   650
Into a lordly river, broad and deep,
Dimpling along in silent majesty,
With mountains for its neighbours, and
    in view
Of distant mountains and their snowy
    tops,
And thus proceeding to Locarno's Lake,
Fit resting-place for such a visitant. 656
Locarno! spreading out in width like
    Heaven,
How dost thou cleave to the poetic heart,
Bask in the sunshine of the memory;

    ¹ See page 147.

And Como! thou, a treasure whom the
    earth   660
Keeps to herself, confined as in a depth
Of Abyssinian privacy. I spake
Of thee, thy chestnut woods, and garden
    plots
Of Indian corn tended by dark-eyed
    maids;
Thy lofty steeps, and pathways roofed
    with vines,   665
Winding from house to house, from town
    to town,
Sole link that binds them to each other;
    walks,
League after league, and cloistral avenues,
Where silence dwells if music be not there:
While yet a youth undisciplined in verse,
Through fond ambition of that hour, I
    strove   671
To chant your praise; nor can approach
    you now
Ungreeted by a more melodious Song,
Where tones of Nature smoothed by
    learned Art
May flow in lasting current. Like a
    breeze   675
Or sunbeam over your domain I passed
In motion without pause; but ye have left
Your beauty with me, a serene accord
Of forms and colours, passive, yet en-
    dowed
In their submissiveness with power as
    sweet   680
And gracious, almost might I dare to say,
As virtue is, or goodness; sweet as love,
Or the remembrance of a generous deed,
Or mildest visitations of pure thought,
When God, the giver of all joy, is thanked
Religiously, in silent blessedness;   686
Sweet as this last herself, for such it is.

    With those delightful pathways we ad-
    vanced,
For two days' space, in presence of the
    Lake,
That, stretching far among the Alps,
    assumed   690
A character more stern. The second
    night,
From sleep awakened, and misled by
    sound
Of the church clock telling the hours with
    strokes
Whose import then we had not learned,
    we rose
By moonlight, doubting not that day was
    nigh,   695
And that meanwhile, by no uncertain
    path,
Along the winding margin of the lake,
Led, as before, we should behold the
    scene,
Hushed in profound repose. We left the
    town

536

Of Gravedona with this hope; but soon
Were lost, bewildered among woods immense,   701
And on a rock sate down, to wait for day.
An open place it was, and overlooked,
From high, the sullen water far beneath,
On which a dull red image of the moon
Lay bedded, changing oftentimes its form
Like an uneasy snake. From hour to hour
We sate and sate, wondering as if the night
Had been ensnared by witchcraft. On the rock
At last we stretched our weary limbs for sleep,   710
But *could not* sleep, tormented by the stings
Of insects, which with noise like that of noon
Filled all the woods: the cry of unknown birds;
The mountains more by blackness visible
And their own size, than any outward light;   715
The breathless wilderness of clouds; the clock
That told, with unintelligible voice,
The widely parted hours; the noise of streams,
And sometimes rustling motions nigh at hand,
That did not leave us free from personal fear;   720
And, lastly, the withdrawing moon, that set
Before us, while she still was high in heaven;—
These were our food; and such a summer's night
Followed that pair of golden days that shed
On Como's Lake, and all that round it lay,   725
Their fairest, softest, happiest influence.

But here I must break off, and bid farewell
To days, each offering some new sight, or fraught
With some untried adventure, in a course
Prolonged till sprinklings of autumnal snow   730
Checked our unwearied steps. Let this alone
Be mentioned as a parting word, that not
In hollow exultation, dealing out
Hyperboles of praise comparative;   734
Not rich one moment to be poor for ever;
Not prostrate, overborne, as if the mind

Herself were nothing, a mere pensioner
On outward forms—did we in presence stand
Of that magnificent region. On the front
Of this whole Song is written that my heart   740
Must, in such Temple, needs have offered up
A different worship. Finally, whate'er
I saw, or heard, or felt, was but a stream
That flowed into a kindred stream; a gale,
Confederate with the current of the soul,
To speed my voyage; every sound or sight,   746
In its degree of power, administered
To grandeur or to tenderness,—to the one
Directly, but to tender thoughts by means
Less often instantaneous in effect;   750
Led me to these by paths that, in the main,
Were more circuitous, but not less sure
Duly to reach the point marked out by Heaven.

Oh, most belovèd Friend! a glorious time,
A happy time that was; triumphant looks
Were then the common language of all eyes;   756
As if awaked from sleep, the Nations hailed
Their great expectancy: the fife of war
Was then a spirit-stirring sound indeed,
A blackbird's whistle in a budding grove.
We left the Swiss exulting in the fate 761
Of their near neighbours; and, when shortening fast
Our pilgrimage, nor distant far from home,
We crossed the Brabant armies on the fret
For battle in the cause of Liberty.   765
A stripling, scarcely of the household then
Of social life, I looked upon these things
As from a distance; heard, and saw, and felt,
Was touched, but with no intimate concern;   769
I seemed to move along them, as a bird
Moves through the air, or as a fish pursues
Its sport, or feeds in its proper element;
I wanted not that joy, I did not need
Such help; the ever-living universe,
Turn where I might, was opening out its glories,   775
And the independent spirit of pure youth
Called forth, at every season, new delights
Spread round my steps like sunshine o'er green fields.

BOOK SEVENTH

RESIDENCE IN LONDON

Six changeful years have vanished since
    I first
Poured out (saluted by that quickening
    breeze
Which met me issuing from the City's
    walls)
A glad preamble to this Verse: I sang
Aloud, with fervour irresistible   5
Of short-lived transport, like a torrent
    bursting,
From a black thunder-cloud, down
    Scafell's side
To rush and disappear. But soon broke
    forth
(So willed the Muse) a less impetuous
    stream,
That flowed awhile with unabating
    strength,   10
Then stopped for years; not audible again
Before last primrose-time. Belovèd Friend!
The assurance which then cheered some
    heavy thoughts
On thy departure to a foreign land
Has failed; too slowly moves the promised
    work.   15
Through the whole summer have I been
    at rest,
Partly from voluntary holiday,
And part through outward hindrance.
    But I heard,
After the hour of sunset yester-even,
Sitting within doors between light and
    dark,   20
A choir of redbreasts gathered somewhere
    near
My threshold,—minstrels from the distant
    woods
Sent in on Winter's service, to announce,
With preparation artful and benign,
That the rough lord had left the surly
    North   25
On his accustomed journey. The delight,
Due to this timely notice, unawares
Smote me, and, listening, I in whispers
    said,
'Ye heartsome Choristers, ye and I will
    be
Associates, and, unscared by blustering
    winds,   30
Will chant together.' Thereafter, as the
    shades
Of twilight deepened, going forth, I spied
A glow-worm underneath a dusky plume
Or canopy of yet unwithered fern,
Clear-shining, like a hermit's taper seen
Through a thick forest. Silence touched
    me here   36
No less than sound had done before; the
    child

Of Summer, lingering, shining, by her-
    self,
The voiceless worm on the unfrequented
    hills,
Seemed sent on the same errand with the
    choir   40
Of Winter that had warbled at my door,
And the whole year breathed tenderness
    and love.

The last night's genial feeling over-
    flowed
Upon this morning, and my favourite
    grove,
Tossing in sunshine its dark boughs
    aloft,   45
As if to make the strong wind visible,
Wakes in me agitations like its own,
A spirit friendly to the Poet's task,
Which we will now resume with lively
    hope,   49
Nor checked by aught of tamer argument,
That lies before us, needful to be told.

Returned from that excursion,[1] soon I
    bade
Farewell for ever to the sheltered seats
Of gownèd students, quitted hall and
    bower,
And every comfort of that privileged
    ground,   55
Well pleased to pitch a vagrant tent
    among
The unfenced regions of society.

Yet, undetermined to what course of
    life
I should adhere, and seeming to possess
A little space of intermediate time   60
At full command, to London first I turned,
In no disturbance of excessive hope,
By personal ambition unenslaved,
Frugal as there was need, and, though self-
    willed,
From dangerous passions free. Three
    years had flown   65
Since I had felt in heart and soul the shock
Of the huge town's first presence, and had
    paced
Her endless streets, a transient visitant:
Now, fixed amid that concourse of man-
    kind   69
Where Pleasure whirls about incessantly,
And life and labour seem but one, I filled
An idler's place; an idler well content
To have a house (what matter for a home?)
That owned him; living cheerfully abroad
With unchecked fancy ever on the stir,   75
And all my young affections out of doors.

[1] See page 532

There was a time when whatsoe'er is
   feigned
Of airy palaces, and gardens built
By Genii of romance; or hath in grave
Authentic history been set forth of Rome,
Alcairo, Babylon, or Persepolis;   81
Or given upon report by pilgrim friars,
Of golden cities ten months' journey deep
Among Tartarian wilds—fell short, far
   short,
Of what my fond simplicity believed   85
And thought of London—held me by a
   chain
Less strong of wonder and obscure de-
   light.
Whether the bolt of childhood's Fancy
   shot
For me beyond its ordinary mark,
'Twere vain to ask; but in our flock of
   boys   90
Was One, a cripple from his birth, whom
   chance
Summoned from school to London; for-
   tunate
And envied traveller! When the Boy
   returned,
After short absence, curiously I scanned
His mien and person, nor was free, in
   sooth,   95
From disappointment, not to find some
   change
In look and air, from that new region
   brought,
As if from Fairy-land. Much I questioned
   him;
And every word he uttered, on my ears
Fell flatter than a cagèd parrot's note,   100
That answers unexpectedly awry,
And mocks the prompter's listening.
   Marvellous things
Had vanity (quick Spirit that appears
Almost as deeply seated and as strong
In a Child's heart as fear itself) conceived
For my enjoyment. Would that I could
   now   106
Recall what then I pictured to myself,
Of mitred Prelates, Lords in ermine clad,
The King, and the King's Palace, and,
   not last,
Nor least, Heaven bless him! the re-
   nowned Lord Mayor: 110
Dreams not unlike to those which once
   begat
A change of purpose in young Whitting-
   ton,
When he, a friendless and a drooping boy,
Sate on a stone, and heard the bells speak
   out   114
Articulate music. Above all, one thought
Baffled my understanding: how men lived
Even next-door neighbours, as we say, yet
   still
Strangers, not knowing each the other's
   name.

O, wond'rous power of words, by simple
   faith   119
Licensed to take the meaning that we love!
Vauxhall and Ranelagh! I then had heard
Of your green groves, and wilderness of
   lamps
Dimming the stars, and fireworks magical,
And gorgeous ladies, under splendid
   domes,
Floating in dance, or warbling high in
   air   125
The songs of spirits! Nor had Fancy fed
With less delight upon that other class
Of marvels, broad-day wonders perma-
   nent:
The River proudly bridged; the dizzy top
And Whispering Gallery of St. Paul's;
   the tombs   130
Of Westminster; the Giants of Guild-
   hall;
Bedlam, and those carved maniacs at the
   gates,
Perpetually recumbent; Statues—man,
And the horse under him—in gilded pomp
Adorning flowery gardens, 'mid vast
   squares;   135
The Monument, and that Chamber of the
   Tower
Where England's sovereigns sit in long
   array,
Their steeds bestriding,—every mimic
   shape
Cased in the gleaming mail the monarch
   wore,
Whether for gorgeous tournament ad-
   dressed,   140
Or life or death upon the battle-field.
Those bold imaginations in due time
Had vanished, leaving others in their
   stead:
And now I looked upon the living scene;
Familiarly perused it; oftentimes,   145
In spite of strongest disappointment,
   pleased
Through courteous self-submission, as a
   tax
Paid to the object by prescriptive right.

Rise up, thou monstrous ant-hill on the
   plain
Of a too busy world! Before me flow,
Thou endless stream of men and moving
   things!   151
Thy every-day appearance, as it strikes—
With wonder heightened, or sublimed by
   awe—
On strangers, of all ages; the quick dance
Of colours, lights, and forms; the deafen-
   ing din;   155
The comers and the goers face to face,
Face after face; the string of dazzling
   wares,
Shop after shop, with symbols, blazoned
   names,

And all the tradesman's honours over-
head:
Here, fronts of houses, like a title-page,
With letters huge inscribed from top to
toe;   161
Stationed above the door, like guardian
saints,
There, allegoric shapes, female or male,
Or physiognomies of real men.
Land-warriors, kings, or admirals of the
sea,   165
Boyle, Shakspeare, Newton, or the attrac-
tive head
Of some quack-doctor, famous in his
day.

Meanwhile the roar continues, till at
length,
Escaped as from an enemy, we turn
Abruptly into some sequestered nook,
Still as a sheltered place when winds blow
loud!   171
At leisure, thence, through tracts of thin
resort,
And sights and sounds that come at
intervals,
We take our way. A raree-show is here,
With children gathered round; another
street   175
Presents a company of dancing dogs,
Or dromedary, with an antic pair
Of monkeys on his back; a minstrel band
Of Savoyards; or, single and alone,   179
An English ballad-singer. Private courts,
Gloomy as coffins, and unsightly lanes
Thrilled by some female vendor's scream,
belike
The very shrillest of all London cries,
May then entangle our impatient steps;
Conducted through those labyrinths, un-
awares,   185
To privileged regions and inviolate,
Where from their airy lodges studious
lawyers
Look out on waters, walks, and gardens
green.

Thence back into the throng, until we
reach,
Following the tide that slackens by
degrees,   190
Some half-frequented scene, where wider
streets
Bring straggling breezes of suburban air.
Here files of ballads dangle from dead
walls;
Advertisements, of giant-size, from high
Press forward, in all colours, on the sight;
These, bold in conscious merit, lower
down;   196
That, fronted with a most imposing word,
Is, peradventure, one in masquerade.
As on the broadening causeway we ad-
vance,

Behold, turned upwards, a face hard and
strong   200
In lineaments, and red with over-toil.
'Tis one encountered here and every-
where;
A travelling cripple, by the trunk cut short,
And stumping on his arms. In sailor's
garb
Another lies at length, beside a range
Of well-formed characters, with chalk in-
scribed   206
Upon the smooth flat stones: the Nurse
is here,
The Bachelor, that loves to sun himself,
The military Idler, and the Dame,
That field-ward takes her walk with decent
steps.   210

Now homeward through the thickening
hubbub, where
See, among less distinguishable shapes,
The begging scavenger, with hat in hand;
The Italian, as he thrids his way with care,
Steadying, far-seen, a frame of images
Upon his head; with basket at his breast
The Jew; the stately and slow-moving
Turk,   217
With freight of slippers piled beneath his
arm!

Enough;—the mighty concourse I sur-
veyed
With no unthinking mind, well pleased
to note   220
Among the crowd all specimens of man,
Through all the colours which the sun
bestows,
And every character of form and face:
The Swede, the Russian; from the genial
south,
The Frenchman and the Spaniard; from
remote   225
America, the Hunter-Indian; Moors,
Malays, Lascars, the Tartar; the Chinese,
And Negro Ladies in white muslin gowns.

At leisure, then, I viewed, from day to
day,
The spectacles within doors,—birds and
beasts   230
Of every nature, and strange plants con-
vened
From every clime; and, next, those sights
that ape
The absolute presence of reality,
Expressing, as in mirror, sea and land,
And what earth is, and what she has to
show.   235
I do not here allude to subtlest craft,
By means refined attaining purest ends,
But imitations, fondly made in plain
Confession of man's weakness and his
loves.
Whether the Painter, whose ambitious
skill   240

Submits to nothing less than taking in
A whole horizon's circuit, do with power,
Like that of angels or commissioned
    spirits,
Fix us upon some lofty pinnacle,
Or in a ship on waters, with a world   245
Of life, and life-like mockery beneath,
Above, behind, far stretching and before;
Or more mechanic artist represent
By scale exact, in model, wood or clay,
From blended colours also borrowing
    help,   250
Some miniature of famous spots or
    things,—
St. Peter's Church; or, more aspiring aim,
In microscopic vision, Rome herself;
Or, haply, some choice rural haunt,—the
    Falls
Of Tivoli; and, high upon that steep,   255
The Sibyl's mouldering Temple! every
    tree,
Villa, or cottage, lurking among rocks
Throughout the landscape; tuft, stone,
    scratch minute—
All that the traveller sees when he is
    there.   259

Add to these exhibitions, mute and still,
Others of wider scope, where living men,
Music, and shifting pantomimic scenes,
Diversified the allurement. Need I fear
To mention by its name, as in degree,
Lowest of these and humblest in attempt,
Yet richly graced with honours of her own,
Half-rural Sadler's Wells? Though at that
    time   267
Intolerant, as is the way of youth
Unless itself be pleased, here more than
    once
Taking my seat, I saw (nor blush to add,
With ample recompense) giants and
    dwarfs,   271
Clowns, conjurors, posture-masters, har-
    lequins,
Amid the uproar of the rabblement,
Perform their feats. Nor was it mean
    delight
To watch crude Nature work in untaught
    minds;   275
To note the laws and progress of belief;
Though obstinate on this way, yet on that
How willingly we travel, and how far!
To have, for instance, brought upon the
    scene   279
The champion, Jack the Giant-killer: Lo!
He dons his coat of darkness: on the stage
Walks, and achieves his wonders, from
    the eye
Of living Mortal covert, 'as the moon
Hid in her vacant interlunar cave.'
Delusion bold! and how can it be wrought?
The garb he wears is black as death, the
    word   286
'*Invisible*' flames forth upon his chest.

Here, too, were 'forms and pressures
    of the time,'
Rough, bold, as Grecian comedy displayed
When Art was young; dramas of living
    men,   290
And recent things yet warm with life;
    a sea-fight,
Shipwreck, or some domestic incident
Divulged by Truth and magnified by
    Fame;
Such as the daring brotherhood of late
Set forth, too serious theme for that light
    place—   295
I mean, O distant Friend! a story drawn
From our own ground,—the Maid of
    Buttermere,—
And how, unfaithful to a virtuous wife
Deserted and deceived, the Spoiler came
And wooed the artless daughter of the
    hills,   300
And wedded her, in cruel mockery
Of love and marriage bonds. These words
    to thee
Must needs bring back the moment when
    we first,
Ere the broad world rang with the maiden's
    name,   304
Beheld her serving at the cottage inn;
Both stricken, as she entered or with-
    drew
With admiration of her modest mien
And carriage, marked by unexampled
    grace.
We since that time not unfamiliarly
Have seen her,—her discretion have
    observed,   310
Her just opinions, delicate reserve,
Her patience, and humility of mind
Unspoiled by commendation and the
    excess
Of public notice—an offensive light
To a meek spirit suffering inwardly.   315

From this memorial tribute to my theme
I was returning, when, with sundry forms
Commingled—shapes which met me in
    the way
That we must tread—thy image rose
    again,
Maiden of Buttermere! She lives in peace
Upon the spot where she was born and
    reared;   321
Without contamination doth she live
In quietness, without anxiety:
Beside the mountain-chapel, sleeps in
    earth
Her new-born infant, fearless as a lamb
That, thither driven from some unshel-
    tered place,   326
Rests underneath the little rock-like pile
When storms are raging. Happy are they
    both—
Mother and child!—These feelings, in
    themselves

Trite, do yet scarcely seem so when I
   think   330
On those ingenuous moments of our
   youth
Ere we have learnt by use to slight the
   crimes
And sorrows of the world. Those simple
   days
Are now my theme; and, foremost of the
   scenes,   334
Which yet survive in memory, appears
One, at whose centre sate a lovely Boy,
A sportive infant, who, for six months'
   space,
Not more, had been of age to deal about
Articulate prattle—Child as beautiful
As ever clung around a mother's neck,
Or father fondly gazed upon with pride.
There, too, conspicuous for stature tall
And large dark eyes, beside her infant
   stood
The mother; but, upon her cheeks dif-
   fused,
False tints too well accorded with the
   glare   345
From play-house lustres thrown without
   reserve
On every object near. The Boy had been
The pride and pleasure of all lookers-on
In whatsoever place, but seemed in this
A sort of alien scattered from the clouds.
Of lusty vigour, more than infantine   351
He was in limb, in cheek a summer rose
Just three parts blown—a cottage-child—
   if e'er,
By cottage-door on breezy mountain-side,
Or in some sheltering vale, was seen a
   babe   355
By Nature's gift so favoured. Upon a
   board
Decked with refreshments had this child
   been placed,
His little stage in the vast theatre,
And there he sate surrounded with a
   throng
Of chance spectators, chiefly dissolute
   men   360
And shameless women, treated and
   caressed;
Ate, drank, and with the fruit and glasses
   played,
While oaths and laughter and indecent
   speech
Were rife about him as the songs of birds
Contending after showers. The mother
   now   365
Is fading out of memory, but I see
The lovely Boy as I beheld him then
Among the wretched and the falsely
   gay,
Like one of those who walked with hair
   unsinged
Amid the fiery furnace. Charms and
   spells   370

Muttered on black and spiteful instiga-
   tion
Have stopped, as some believe, the kind-
   liest growths.
Ah, with how different spirit might a
   prayer
Have been preferred, that this fair crea-
   ture, checked
By special privilege of Nature's love, 375
Should in his childhood be detained for
   ever!
But with its universal freight the tide
Hath rolled along, and this bright in-
   nocent,
Mary! may now have lived till he could
   look
With envy on thy nameless babe that
   sleeps,   380
Beside the mountain-chapel, undisturbed.

Four rapid years had scarcely then
   been told
Since, travelling southward from our
   pastoral hills,
I heard, and for the first time in my life,
The voice of woman utter blasphemy—
Saw woman as she is, to open shame 386
Abandoned, and the pride of public vice;
I shuddered, for a barrier seemed at once
Thrown in, that from humanity divorced
Humanity, splitting the race of man 390
In twain, yet leaving the same outward
   form.
Distress of mind ensued upon the sight,
And ardent meditation. Later years
Brought to such spectacle a milder sad-
   ness,
Feelings of pure commiseration, grief 395
For the individual and the overthrow
Of her soul's beauty; farther I was then
But seldom led, or wished to go; in truth
The sorrow of the passion stopped me
   there.

But let me now, less moved, in order
   take   400
Our argument. Enough is said to show
How casual incidents of real life,
Observed where pastime only had been
   sought,
Outweighed, or put to flight, the set
   events
And measured passions of the stage,
   albeit   405
By Siddons trod in the fulness of her
   power.
Yet was the theatre my dear delight;
The very gilding, lamps and painted
   scrolls,
And all the mean upholstery of the place,
Wanted not animation, when the tide
Of pleasure ebbed but to return as fast
With the ever-shifting figures of the
   scene,   412

Solemn or gay: whether some beauteous
 dame
Advanced in radiance through a deep
 recess
Of thick entangled forest, like the moon
Opening the clouds; or sovereign king,
 announced   416
With flourishing trumpet, came in full-
 blown state
Of the world's greatness, winding round
 with train
Of courtiers, banners, and a length of
 guards;
Or captive led in abject weeds, and
 jingling   420
His slender manacles; or romping girl
Bounced, leapt, and pawed the air; or
 mumbling sire,
A scare-crow pattern of old age dressed up
In all the tatters of infirmity
All loosely put together, hobbled in,   425
Stumping upon a cane with which he
 smites,
From time to time, the solid boards, and
 makes them
Prate somewhat loudly of the whereabout
Of one so overloaded with his years.
But what of this! the laugh, the grin,
 grimace,   430
The antics striving to outstrip each other,
Were all received, the least of them not
 lost,
With an unmeasured welcome. Through
 the night,
Between the show, and many-headed
 mass   434
Of the spectators, and each several nook
Filled with its fray or brawl, how eagerly
And with what flashes, as it were, the
 mind
Turned this way—that way! sportive and
 alert
And watchful, as a kitten when at play,
While winds are eddying round her,
 among straws   440
And rustling leaves. Enchanting age and
 sweet!
Romantic almost, looked at through a
 space,
How small, of intervening years! For
 then,
Though surely no mean progress had been
 made
In meditations holy and sublime,   445
Yet something of a girlish child-like gloss
Of novelty survived for scenes like these;
Enjoyment haply handed down from
 times
When at a country-playhouse, some rude
 barn
Tricked out for that proud use, if I per-
 chance   450
Caught, on a summer evening through a
 chink

In the old wall, an unexpected glimpse
Of daylight, the bare thought of where I
 was
Gladdened me more than if I had been
 led
Into a dazzling cavern of romance,   455
Crowded with Genii busy among works
Not to be looked at by the common sun.

The matter that detains us now may
 seem,
To many, neither dignified enough
Nor arduous, yet will not be scorned by
 them,   460
Who, looking inward, have observed the
 ties
That bind the perishable hours of life
Each to the other, and the curious props
By which the world of memory and
 thought
Exists and is sustained.   More lofty
 themes,   465
Such as at least do wear a prouder face,
Solicit our regard; but when I think
Of these, I feel the imaginative power
Languish within me; even then it slept,
When, pressed by tragic sufferings, the
 heart   470
Was more than full; amid my sobs and
 tears
It slept, even in the pregnant season of
 youth.
For though I was most passionately moved
And yielded to all changes of the scene
With an obsequious promptness, yet the
 storm   475
Passed not beyond the suburbs of the
 mind;
Save when realities of act and mien,
The incarnation of the spirits that move
In harmony amid the Poet's world,   479
Rose to ideal grandeur, or, called forth
By power of contrast, made me recognise,
As at a glance, the things which I had
 shaped,
And yet not shaped, had seen and scarcely
 seen,
When, having closed the mighty Shak-
 speare's page,
I mused, and thought, and felt, in soli-
 tude.   485

Pass we from entertainments, that are
 such
Professedly, to others titled higher,
Yet, in the estimate of youth at least,
More near akin to those than names
 imply,—
I mean the brawls of lawyers in their
 courts   490
Before the ermined judge, or that great
 stage
Where senators, tongue-favoured men,
 perform,

Admired and envied. Oh! the beating
      heart,
When one among the prime of these rose
      up,—
One, of whose name from childhood we
      had heard   495
Familiarly, a household term, like those,
The Bedfords, Glosters, Salisburys, of
      old
Whom the fifth Harry talks of. Silence!
      hush!
This is no trifler, no short-flighted wit,
No stammerer of a minute, painfully   500
Delivered. No! the Orator hath yoked
The Hours, like young Aurora, to his car:
Thrice welcome Presence! how can pa-
      tience e'er
Grow weary of attending on a track
That kindles with such glory! All are
      charmed,   505
Astonished; like a hero in romance,
He winds away his never-ending horn;
Words follow words, sense seems to follow
      sense:
What memory and what logic! till the
      strain   509
Transcendent, superhuman as it seemed,
Grows tedious even in a young man's ear.

      Genius of Burke! forgive the pen
      seduced
By specious wonders, and too slow to tell
Of what the ingenuous, what bewildered
      men,
Beginning to mistrust their boastful
      guides,   515
And wise men, willing to grow wiser,
      caught,
Rapt auditors! from thy most eloquent
      tongue—
Now mute, for ever mute in the cold grave.
I see him,—old, but vigorous in age,—
Stand like an oak whose stag-horn
      branches start   520
Out of its leafy brow, the more to awe
The younger brethren of the grove. But
      some—
While he forewarns, denounces, launches
      forth,
Against all systems built on abstract rights,
Keen ridicule; the majesty proclaims   525
Of Institutes and Laws, hallowed by time;
Declares the vital power of social ties
Endeared by Custom; and with high
      disdain,
Exploding upstart Theory, insists
Upon the allegiance to which men are
      born—   530
Some—say at once a froward multitude—
Murmur (for truth is hated, where not
      loved)
As the winds fret within the Æolian cave,
Galled by their monarch's chain. The
      times were big

With ominous change, which, night by
      night, provoked   535
Keen struggles, and black clouds of
      passion raised;
But memorable moments intervened,
When Wisdom, like the Goddess from
      Jove's brain,
Broke forth in armour of resplendent
      words,
Startling the Synod. Could a youth, and
      one   540
In ancient story versed, whose breast had
      heaved
Under the weight of classic eloquence,
Sit, see, and hear, unthankful, uninspired?

      Nor did the Pulpit's oratory fail
To achieve its higher triumph. Not un-
      felt   545
Were its admonishments, nor lightly
      heard
The awful truths delivered thence by
      tongues
Endowed with various power to search
      the soul;
Yet ostentation, domineering, oft
Poured forth harangues, how sadly out of
      place!—   550
There have I seen a comely bachelor,
Fresh from a toilette of two hours, ascend
His rostrum, with seraphic glance look up,
And, in a tone elaborately low
Beginning, lead his voice through many
      a maze   555
A minuet course; and, winding up his
      mouth,
From time to time, into an orifice
Most delicate, a lurking eyelet, small,
And only not invisible, again
Open it out, diffusing thence a smile   560
Of rapt irradiation, exquisite.
Meanwhile the Evangelists, Isaiah, Job,
Moses, and he who penned, the other day,
The Death of Abel, Shakspeare, and the
      Bard
Whose genius spangled o'er a gloomy
      theme   565
With fancies thick as his inspiring stars,
And Ossian (doubt not—'tis the naked
      truth)
Summoned from streamy Morven—each
      and all
Would, in their turns, lend ornaments
      and flowers
To entwine the crook of eloquence that
      helped   570
This pretty Shepherd, pride of all the
      plains,
To rule and guide his captivated flock.

      I glance but at a few conspicuous marks,
Leaving a thousand others, that, in hall,
Court, theatre, conventicle, or shop,   575
In public room or private, park or street,

Each fondly reared on his own pedestal,
Looked out for admiration. Folly, vice,
Extravagance in gesture, mien, and dress,
And all the strife of singularity,   580
Lies to the ear, and lies to every sense—
Of these, and of the living shapes they wear,
There is no end. Such candidates for regard,
Although well pleased to be where they were found,
I did not hunt after, nor greatly prize, 585
Nor made unto myself a secret boast
Of reading them with quick and curious eye;
But, as a common produce, things that are
To-day, to-morrow will be, took of them
Such willing note, as, on some errand bound   590
That asks not speed, a traveller might bestow
On sea-shells that bestrew the sandy beach,
Or daisies swarming through the fields of June.

But foolishness and madness in parade,
Though most at home in this their dear domain,   595
Are scattered everywhere, no rarities,
Even to the rudest novice of the Schools.
Me, rather, it employed, to note, and keep
In memory, those individual sights
Of courage, or integrity, or truth,   600
Or tenderness, which there, set off by foil,
Appeared more touching. One will I select;
A Father—for he bore that sacred name—
Him saw I, sitting in an open square,
Upon a corner-stone of that low wall, 605
Wherein were fixed the iron pales that fenced
A spacious grass-plot; there, in silence, sate
This One Man, with a sickly babe outstretched
Upon his knee, whom he had thither brought
For sunshine, and to breathe the fresher air.   610
Of those who passed, and me who looked at him,
He took no heed; but in his brawny arms
(The Artificer was to the elbow bare,
And from his work this moment had been stolen)
He held the child, and, bending over it,
As if he were afraid both of the sun   616
And of the air, which he had come to seek,
Eyed the poor babe with love unutterable.

As the black storm upon the mountain-top
Sets off the sunbeam in the valley, so 620

That huge fermenting mass of human-kind
Serves as a solemn background, or relief,
To single forms and objects, whence they draw,
For feeling and contemplative regard, 624
More than inherent liveliness and power.
How oft, amid those overflowing streets,
Have I gone forward with the crowd, and said
Unto myself, 'The face of every one
That passes by me is a mystery!'
Thus have I looked, nor ceased to look, oppressed   630
By thoughts of what and whither, when and how,
Until the shapes before my eyes became
A second-sight procession, such as glides
Over still mountains, or appears in dreams;
And once, far-travelled in such mood, beyond   635
The reach of common indication, lost
Amid the moving pageant, I was smitten
Abruptly, with the view (a sight not rare)
Of a blind Beggar, who, with upright face,
Stood, propped against a wall, upon his chest   640
Wearing a written paper, to explain
His story, whence he came, and who he was.
Caught by the spectacle my mind turned round
As with the might of waters; an apt type
This label seemed of the utmost we can know,   645
Both of ourselves and of the universe;
And, on the shape of that unmoving man,
His steadfast face and sightless eyes, I gazed,
As if admonished from another world.

Though reared upon the base of outward things,   650
Structures like these the excited spirit mainly
Builds for herself; scenes different there are,
Full-formed, that take, with small internal help,
Possession of the faculties,—the peace
That comes with night; the deep solemnity   655
Of nature's intermediate hours of rest,
When the great tide of human life stands still;
The business of the day to come, unborn,
Of that gone by, locked up, as in the grave;
The blended calmness of the heavens and earth,   660
Moonlight and stars, and empty streets, and sounds

Unfrequent as in deserts; at late hours
Of winter evenings, when unwholesome
    rains
Are falling hard, with people yet astir,
The feeble salutation from the voice 665
Of some unhappy woman, now and then
Heard as we pass, when no one looks
    about,
Nothing is listened to. But these, I fear,
Are falsely catalogued; things that are,
    are not,
As the mind answers to them, or the
    heart   670
Is prompt, or slow, to feel. What say
    you, then,
To times, when half the city shall break
    out
Full of one passion, vengeance, rage, or
    fear?
To executions, to a street on fire,
Mobs, riots, or rejoicings? From these
    sights   675
Take one,—that ancient festival, the Fair,
Holden where martyrs suffered in past
    time,
And named of St. Bartholomew; there,
    see
A work completed to our hands, that lays,
If any spectacle on earth can do,   680
The whole creative powers of man
    asleep!—
For once, the Muse's help will we implore,
And she shall lodge us, wafted on her
    wings,
Above the press and danger of the crowd,
Upon some showman's platform. What
    a shock   685
For eyes and ears! what anarchy and
    din,
Barbarian and infernal,—a phantasma,
Monstrous in colour, motion, shape, sight,
    sound!
Below, the open space, through every
    nook
Of the wide area, twinkles, is alive   690
With heads; the midway region, and
    above,
Is thronged with staring pictures and huge
    scrolls,
Dumb proclamations of the Prodigies;
With chattering monkeys, dangling from
    their poles,
And children whirling in their round-
    abouts;   695
With those that stretch the neck and
    strain the eyes,
And crack the voice in rivalship, the
    crowd
Inviting; with buffoons against buffoons
Grimacing, writhing, screaming,—him
    who grinds
The hurdy-gurdy, at the fiddle weaves,
Rattles the salt-box thumps the kettle-
    drum,   701

And him who at the trumpet puffs his
    cheeks,
The silver-collared Negro with his timbrel,
Equestrians, tumblers, women, girls, and
    boys,
Blue-breeched, pink-vested, with high-
    towering plumes.—   705
All moveables of wonder, from all parts,
Are here—Albinos, painted Indians,
    Dwarfs,
The Horse of knowledge, and the learned
    Pig,
The Stone-eater, the man that swallows
    fire,
Giants, Ventriloquists, the Invisible Girl,
The Bust that speaks and moves its
    goggling eyes,   711
The Wax-work, Clock-work, all the mar-
    vellous craft
Of modern Merlins, Wild Beasts, Puppet-
    shows,
All out-o'-the-way, far-fetched, perverted
    things,
All freaks of nature, all Promethean
    thoughts   715
Of man, his dulness, madness, and their
    feats
All jumbled up together, to compose
A Parliament of Monsters. Tents and
    Booths
Meanwhile, as if the whole were one vast
    mill,
Are vomiting, receiving on all sides, 720
Men, Women, three-years' Children,
    Babes in arms.

Oh, blank confusion! true epitome
Of what the mighty City is herself,
To thousands upon thousands of her sons,
Living amid the same perpetual whirl 725
Of trivial objects, melted and reduced
To one identity, by differences
That have no law, no meaning, and no
    end—
Oppression, under which even highest
    minds
Must labour, whence the strongest are
    not free.   730
But though the picture weary out the eye,
By nature an unmanageable sight,
It is not wholly so to him who looks
In steadiness, who hath among least
    things   734
An under-sense of greatest; sees the parts
As parts, but with a feeling of the whole.
This, of all acquisitions, first awaits
On sundry and most widely different
    modes
Of education, nor with least delight
On that through which I passed. Atten-
    tion springs,   740
And comprehensiveness and memory flow,
From early converse with the works of
    God

Among all regions; chiefly where appear
Most obviously simplicity and power.
Think, how the everlasting streams and
      woods,   745
Stretched and still stretching far and wide,
      exalt
The roving Indian, on his desert sands:
What grandeur not unfelt, what pregnant
      show
Of beauty, meets the sun-burnt Arab's
      eye:
And, as the sea propels, from zone to
      zone,   750
Its currents; magnifies its shoals of life
Beyond all compass; spreads, and sends
      aloft
Armies of clouds,—even so, its powers
      and aspects
Shape for mankind, by principles as fixed,
The views and aspirations of the soul   755

To majesty. Like virtue have the forms
Perennial of the ancient hills; nor less
The changeful language of their coun-
      tenances
Quickens the slumbering mind, and aids
      the thoughts,
However multitudinous, to move   760
With order and relation. This, if still,
As hitherto, in freedom I may speak,
Not violating any just restraint,
As may be hoped, of real modesty,—
This did I feel, in London's vast do-
      main.   765
The Spirit of Nature was upon me there;
The soul of Beauty and enduring Life
Vouchsafed her inspiration, and diffused,
Through meagre lines and colours, and
      the press
Of self-destroying, transitory things,   770
Composure, and ennobling Harmony.

BOOK EIGHTH

RETROSPECT.—LOVE OF NATURE LEADING TO LOVE OF MAN

WHAT sounds are those, Helvellyn, that
      are heard
Up to thy summit, through the depth of
      air
Ascending, as if distance had the power
To make the sounds more audible? What
      crowd
Covers, or sprinkles o'er, yon village
      green?   5
Crowd seems it, solitary hill! to thee,
Though but a little family of men,
Shepherds and tillers of the ground—be-
      times
Assembled with their children and their
      wives,
And here and there a stranger inter-
      spersed.   10
They hold a rustic fair—a festival,
Such as, on this side now, and now on
      that,
Repeated through his tributary vales,
Helvellyn, in the silence of his rest,
Sees annually, if clouds towards either
      ocean   15
Blown from their favourite resting-place,
      or mists
Dissolved, have left him an unshrouded
      head.
Delightful day it is for all who dwell
In this secluded glen, and eagerly
They give it welcome. Long ere heat of
      noon,   20
From byre or field the kine were brought;
      the sheep
Are penned in cotes; the chaffering is
      begun.

The heifer lows, uneasy at the voice
Of a new master; bleat the flocks aloud.
Booths are there none; a stall or two is
      here;   25
A lame man or a blind, the one to beg,
The other to make music; hither, too,
From far, with basket, slung upon her
      arm,
Of hawker's wares—books, pictures,
      combs, and pins—
Some agèd woman finds her way again, 30
Year after year, a punctual visitant!
There also stands a speech-maker by rote,
Pulling the strings of his boxed raree-
      show;
And in the lapse of many years may come
Prouder itinerant, mountebank, or he 35
Whose wonders in a covered wain lie
      hid.
But one there is, the loveliest of them all,
Some sweet lass of the valley, looking out
For gains, and who that sees her would
      not buy?
Fruits of her father's orchard are her
      wares,   40
And with the ruddy produce she walks
      round
Among the crowd, half pleased with, half
      ashamed
Of her new office, blushing restlessly.
The children now are rich, for the old to-
      day
Are generous as the young; and, if con-
      tent   45
With looking on, some ancient wedded
      pair

547

Sit in the shade together, while they gaze,
'A cheerful smile unbends the wrinkled
　　brow,
The days departed start again to life,
And all the scenes of childhood reappear,
Faint, but more tranquil, like the chang-
　　ing sun   51
To him who slept at noon and wakes at
　　eve.'[1]
Thus gaiety and cheerfulness prevail,
Spreading from young to old, from old to
　　young,
And no one seems to want his share.—
　　Immense   55
Is the recess, the circumambient world
Magnificent, by which they are embraced:
They move about upon the soft green
　　turf:
How little they, they and their doings,
　　seem,
And all that they can further or obstruct!
Through utter weakness pitiably dear,   61
As tender infants are: and yet how great!
For all things serve them; them the
　　morning light
Loves, as it glistens on the silent rocks;
And them the silent rocks, which now
　　from high   65
Look down upon them; the reposing
　　clouds;
The wild brooks prattling from invisible
　　haunts;
And old Helvellyn, conscious of the stir
Which animates this day their calm
　　abode.   69

With deep devotion, Nature, did I feel,
In that enormous City's turbulent world
Of men and things, what benefit I owed
To thee, and those domains of rural peace,
Where to the sense of beauty first my
　　heart
Was opened; tract more exquisitely fair
Than that famed paradise of ten thousand
　　trees,   76
Or Gehol's matchless gardens, for delight
Of the Tartarian dynasty composed
(Beyond that mighty wall, not fabulous,
China's stupendous mound) by patient
　　toil   80
Of myriads and boon nature's lavish help;
There, in a clime from widest empire
　　chosen,
Fulfilling (could enchantment have done
　　more?)
A sumptuous dream of flowery lawns, with
　　domes
Of pleasure sprinkled over, shady dells 85
For eastern monasteries, sunny mounts
With temples crested, bridges, gondolas,
Rocks, dens, and groves of foliage taught
　　to melt
Into each other their obsequious hues,

[1] From the *Malvern Hills* of Joseph Cottle.

Vanished and vanishing in subtle chase,
Too fine to be pursued; or standing forth
In no discordant opposition, strong
And gorgeous as the colours side by side
Bedded among rich plumes of tropic
　　birds;
And mountains over all, embracing all; 95
And all the landscape, endlessly enriched
With waters running, falling, or asleep.

But lovelier far than this, the paradise
Where I was reared; in Nature's primi-
　　tive gifts
Favoured no less, and more to every
　　sense   100
Delicious, seeing that the sun and sky,
The elements, and seasons as they change,
Do find a worthy fellow-labourer there—
Man free, man working for himself, with
　　choice
Of time, and place, and object; by his
　　wants,   105
His comforts, native occupations, cares,
Cheerfully led to individual ends
Or social, and still followed by a train
Unwooed, unthought-of even—simpli-
　　city,
And beauty, and inevitable grace.   110

Yea, when a glimpse of those imperial
　　bowers
Would to a child be transport over-great,
When but a half-hour's roam through such
　　a place
Would leave behind a dance of images,
That shall break in upon his sleep for
　　weeks;   115
Even then the common haunts of the
　　green earth,
And ordinary interests of man,
Which they embosom, all without regard
As both may seem, are fastening on the
　　heart
Insensibly, each with the other's help. 120
For me, when my affections first were led
From kindred, friends, and playmates, to
　　partake
Love for the human creature's absolute
　　self,
That noticeable kindliness of heart
Sprang out of fountains, there abounding
　　most,   125
Where sovereign Nature dictated the
　　tasks
And occupations which her beauty
　　adorned,
And Shepherds were the men that pleased
　　me first;
Not such as Saturn ruled 'mid Latian
　　wilds,
With arts and laws so tempered, that
　　their lives   130
Left, even to us toiling in this late day,
A bright tradition of the golden age;
Not such as, 'mid Arcadian fastnesses

Sequestered, handed down among them-
selves
Felicity, in Grecian song renowned; 135
Nor such as—when an adverse fate had
driven,
From house and home, the courtly band
whose fortunes
Entered, with Shakspeare's genius, the
wild woods
Of Arden—amid sunshine or in shade
Culled the best fruits of Time's uncounted
hours,   140
Ere Phœbe sighed for the false Gany-
mede;
Or there where Perdita and Florizel
Together danced, Queen of the feast, and
King;
Nor such as Spenser fabled. True it is,
That I had heard (what he perhaps had
seen)   145
Of maids at sunrise bringing in from far
Their May-bush, and along the street in
flocks
Parading with a song of taunting rhymes,
Aimed at the laggards slumbering within
doors;
Had also heard, from those who yet re-
membered,   150
Tales of the May-pole dance, and wreaths
that decked
Porch, door-way, or kirk-pillar; and of
youths,
Each with his maid, before the sun was
up,
By annual custom, issuing forth in troops,
To drink the waters of some sainted well,
And hang it round with garlands. Love
survives;   156
But, for such purpose, flowers no longer
grow:
The times, too sage, perhaps too proud,
have dropped
These lighter graces; and the rural ways
And manners which my childhood looked
upon   160
Were the unluxuriant produce of a life
Intent on little but substantial needs,
Yet rich in beauty, beauty that was felt.
But images of danger and distress,
Man suffering among awful Powers and
Forms;   165
Of this I heard, and saw enough to make
Imagination restless; nor was free
Myself from frequent perils; nor were
tales
Wanting,—the tragedies of former times,
Hazards and strange escapes, of which
the rocks   170
Immutable, and everflowing streams,
Where'er I roamed, were speaking monu-
ments.

Smooth life had flock and shepherd in
old time,

Long springs and tepid winters, on the
banks
Of delicate Galesus; and no less   175
Those scattered along Adria's myrtle
shores:
Smooth life had herdsman, and his snow-
white herd
To triumphs and to sacrificial rites
Devoted, on the inviolable stream
Of rich Clitumnus; and the goat-herd
lived   180
As calmly, underneath the pleasant brows
Of cool Lucretilis, where the pipe was
heard
Of Pan, Invisible God, thrilling the rocks
With tutelary music, from all harm
The fold protecting. I myself, mature
In manhood then, have seen a pastoral
tract   186
Like one of these, where Fancy might
run wild,
Though under skies less generous, less
serene:
There, for her own delight had Nature
framed
A pleasure-ground, diffused a fair ex-
panse   190
Of level pasture, islanded with groves
And banked with woody risings; but the
Plain
Endless, here opening widely out, and
there
Shut up in lesser lakes or beds of lawn
And intricate recesses, creek or bay 195
Sheltered within a shelter, where at large
The shepherd strays, a rolling hut his
home.
Thither he comes with spring-time, there
abides
All summer, and at sunrise ye may hear
His flageolet to liquid notes of love 200
Attuned, or sprightly fife resounding far.
Nook is there none, nor tract of that vast
space
Where passage opens, but the same shall
have
In turn its visitant, telling there his hours
In unlaborious pleasure, with no task
More toilsome than to carve a beechen
bowl   206
For spring or fountain, which the traveller
finds,
When through the region he pursues at
will
His devious course. A glimpse of such
sweet life
I saw when, from the melancholy walls
Of Goslar, once imperial, I renewed 211
My daily walk along that wide cham-
paign,
That, reaching to her gates, spreads east
and west,
And northwards, from beneath the moun-
tainous verge

Of the Hercynian forest. Yet, hail to
you   215
Moors, mountains, headlands, and ye
hollow vales,
Ye long deep channels for the Atlantic's
voice,
Powers of my native region! Ye that
seize
The heart with firmer grasp! Your snows
and streams   219
Ungovernable, and your terrifying winds,
That howl so dismally for him who treads
Companionless your awful solitudes!
There, 'tis the shepherd's task the winter
long
To wait upon the storms: of their
approach
Sagacious, into sheltering coves he drives
His flock, and thither from the homestead
bears   226
A toilsome burden up the craggy ways,
And deals it out, their regular nourish-
ment
Strewn on the frozen snow. And when
the spring
Looks out, and all the pastures dance
with lambs,   230
And when the flock, with warmer weather,
climbs
Higher and higher, him his office leads
To watch their goings, whatsoever track
The wanderers choose. For this he quits
his home
At day-spring, and no sooner doth the
sun   235
Begin to strike him with a fire-like heat,
Than he lies down upon some shining
rock,
And breakfasts with his dog. When they
have stolen,
As is their wont, a pittance from strict
time,
For rest not needed or exchange of love,
Then from his couch he starts; and now
his feet   241
Crush out a livelier fragrance from the
flowers
Of lowly thyme, by Nature's skill en-
wrought
In the wild turf: the lingering dews of
morn
Smoke round him, as from hill to hill he
hies,   245
His staff protending like a hunter's spear,
Or by its aid leaping from crag to crag,
And o'er the brawling beds of unbridged
streams.
Philosophy, methinks, at Fancy's call,
Might deign to follow him through what
he does   250
Or sees in his day's march; himself he
feels,
In those vast regions where his service
lies,

A freeman, wedded to his life of hope
And hazard, and hard labour inter-
changed
With that majestic indolence so dear 255
To native man. A rambling schoolboy,
thus
I felt his presence in his own domain,
As of a lord and master, or a power,
Or genius, under Nature, under God,
Presiding; and severest solitude   260
Had more commanding looks when he
was there.
When up the lonely brooks on rainy days
Angling I went, or trod the trackless hills
By mists bewildered, suddenly mine eyes
Have glanced upon him distant a few
steps,   265
In size a giant, stalking through thick
fog,
His sheep like Greenland bears; or, as he
stepped
Beyond the boundary line of some hill-
shadow,
His form hath flashed upon me, glorified
By the deep radiance of the setting sun:
Or him have I descried in distant sky, 271
A solitary object and sublime,
Above all height! like an aerial cross
Stationed alone upon a spiry rock
Of the Chartreuse, for worship. Thus
was man   275
Ennobled outwardly before my sight,
And thus my heart was early introduced
To an unconscious love and reverence
Of human nature; hence the human form
To me became an index of delight,   280
Of grace and honour, power and worthi-
ness.
Meanwhile this creature—spiritual almost
As those of books, but more exalted far;
Far more of an imaginative form
Than the gay Corin of the groves, who
lives   285
For his own fancies, or to dance by the
hour,
In coronal, with Phyllis in the midst—
Was, for the purposes of kind, a man
With the most common; husband, father;
learned,
Could teach, admonish; suffered with the
rest   290
From vice and folly, wretchedness and
fear;
Of this I little saw, cared less for it,
But something must have felt.
               Call ye these appearances—
Which I beheld of shepherds in my
youth,
This sanctity of Nature given to man—
A shadow, a delusion, ye who pore   296
On the dead letter, miss the spirit of
things;
Whose truth is not a motion or a shape
Instinct with vital functions, but a block

Or waxen image which yourselves have
  made,   300
And ye adore! But blessèd be the God
Of Nature and of Man that this was so;
That men before my inexperienced eyes
Did first present themselves thus purified,
Removed, and to a distance that was fit;
And so we all of us in some degree 306
Are led to knowledge, wheresoever led,
And howsoever; were it otherwise,
And we found evil fast as we find good
In our first years, or think that it is found,
How could the innocent heart bear up
  and live!   311
But doubly fortunate my lot; not here
Alone, that something of a better life
Perhaps was round me than it is the
  privilege
Of most to move in, but that first I looked
At man through objects that were great
  or fair;   316
First communed with him by their help.
  And thus
Was founded a sure safeguard and de-
  fence
Against the weight of meanness, selfish
  cares,
Coarse manners, vulgar passions, that
  beat in   320
On all sides from the ordinary world
In which we traffic. Starting from this
  point
I had my face turned toward the truth,
  began
With an advantage furnished by that
  kind
Of prepossession, without which the soul
Receives no knowledge that can bring
  forth good,   326
No genuine insight ever comes to her.
From the restraint of over-watchful eyes
Preserved, I moved about, year after
  year,
Happy, and now most thankful that my
  walk   330
Was guarded from too early intercourse
With the deformities of crowded life,
And those ensuing laughters and con-
  tempts,
Self-pleasing, which, if we would wish to
  think
With a due reverence on earth's rightful
  lord,   335
Here placed to be the inheritor of heaven,
Will not permit us; but pursue the mind,
That to devotion willingly would rise,
Into the temple and the temple's heart.

Yet deem not, Friend! that human
  kind with me   340
Thus early took a place pre-eminent;
Nature herself was, at this unripe time,
But secondary to my own pursuits
And animal activities, and all

Their trivial pleasures; and when these
  had drooped   345
And gradually expired, and Nature,
  prized
For her own sake, became my joy, even
  then—
And upwards through late youth, until
  not less
Than two-and-twenty summers had been
  told—
Was Man in my affections and regards
Subordinate to her, her visible forms 351
And viewless agencies: a passion, she,
A rapture often, and immediate love
Ever at hand; he, only a delight
Occasional, an accidental grace,   355
His hour being not yet come. Far less
  had then
The inferior creatures, beast or bird,
  attuned
My spirit to that gentleness of love
(Though they had long been carefully
  observed),   359
Won from me those minute obeisances
Of tenderness, which I may number
  now
With my first blessings. Nevertheless,
  on these
The light of beauty did not fall in vain,
Or grandeur circumfuse them to no end.

But when that first poetic faculty 365
Of plain Imagination and severe,
No longer a mute influence of the soul,
Ventured, at some rash Muse's earnest
  call,
To try her strength among harmonious
  words;
And to book-notions and the rules of art
Did knowingly conform itself; there
  came   371
Among the simple shapes of human life
A wilfulness of fancy and conceit:
And Nature and her objects beautified
These fictions, as in some sort, in their
  turn,   375
They burnished her. From touch of this
  new power
Nothing was safe: the elder-tree that
  grew
Beside the well-known charnel-house had
  then
A dismal look; the yew-tree had its
  ghost,   379
That took his station there for ornament:
The dignities of plain occurrence then
Were tasteless, and truth's golden mean,
  a point
Where no sufficient pleasure could be
  found.
Then, if a widow, staggering with the
  blow
Of her distress, was known to have turned
  her steps   385

To the cold grave in which her husband
  slept,
One night, or haply more than one,
  through pain
Or half-insensate impotence of mind,
The fact was caught at greedily, and there
She must be visitant the whole year
  through,   390
Wetting the turf with never-ending tears.

      Through quaint obliquities I might
        pursue
These cravings; when the foxglove, one
  by one,
Upwards through every stage of the tall
  stem,   394
Had shed beside the public way its bells,
And stood of all dismantled, save the last
Left at the tapering ladder's top, that
  seemed
To bend as doth a slender blade of grass
Tipped with a rain-drop, Fancy loved to
  seat,
Beneath the plant despoiled, but crested
  still   400
With this last relic, soon itself to fall,
Some vagrant mother, whose arch little
  ones,
All unconcerned by her dejected plight,
Laughed as with rival eagerness their
  hands
Gathered the purple cups that round
  them lay,   405
Strewing the turf's green slope.
              A diamond light
(Whene'er the summer sun, declining,
  smote
A smooth rock wet with constant springs)
  was seen
Sparkling from out a copse-clad bank
  that rose
Fronting our cottage. Oft beside the
  hearth   410
Seated, with open door, often and long
Upon this restless lustre have I gazed,
That made my fancy restless as itself.
'Twas now for me a burnished silver
  shield   414
Suspended over a knight's tomb, who lay
Inglorious, buried in the dusky wood:
An entrance now into some magic cave
Or palace built by fairies of the rock;
Nor could I have been bribed to disen-
  chant
The spectacle, by visiting the spot.   420
Thus wilful Fancy, in no hurtful mood,
Engrafted far-fetched shapes on feelings
  bred
By pure Imagination: busy Power
She was, and with her ready pupil turned
Instinctively to human passions, then
Least understood. Yet, 'mid the fervent
  swarm   426
Of these vagaries, with an eye so rich

As mine was through the bounty of a
  grand
And lovely region, I had forms distinct
To steady me: each airy thought re-
  volved   430
Round a substantial centre, which at
  once
Incited it to motion, and controlled.
I did not pine like one in cities bred,
As was thy melancholy lot, dear Friend!
Great Spirit as thou art, in endless
  dreams   435
Of sickliness, disjoining, joining, things
Without the light of knowledge. Where
  the harm,
If, when the woodman languished with
  disease
Induced by sleeping nightly on the
  ground   439
Within his sod-built cabin, Indian-wise,
I called the pangs of disappointed love,
And all the sad etcetera of the wrong,
To help him to his grave? Meanwhile the
  man,
If not already from the woods retired
To die at home, was haply as I knew,
Withering by slow degrees, 'mid gentle
  airs,   446
Birds, running streams, and hills so
  beautiful
On golden evenings, while the charcoal
  pile
Breathed up its smoke, an image of his
  ghost
Or spirit that full soon must take her
  flight.   450
Nor shall we not be tending towards that
  point
Of sound humanity to which our Tale
Leads, though by sinuous ways, if here I
  show
How Fancy, in a season when she wove
Those slender cords, to guide the uncon-
  scious Boy   455
For the Man's sake, could feed at Nature's
  call
Some pensive musings which might well
  beseem
Maturer years.
          A grove there is whose boughs
Stretch from the western marge of Thur-
  ston-mere,
With length of shade so thick, that whoso
  glides   460
Along the line of low-roofed water, moves
As in a cloister. Once—while, in that
  shade
Loitering, I watched the golden beams of
  light
Flung from the setting sun, as they
  reposed
In silent beauty on the naked ridge   465
Of a high eastern hill—thus flowed my
  thoughts

In a pure stream of words fresh from the heart:
Dear native Regions, wheresoe'er shall close
By mortal course, there will I think on you;   469
Dying, will cast on you a backward look;
Even as this setting sun (albeit the Vale
Is no where touched by one memorial gleam)
Doth with the fond remains of his last power
Still linger, and a farewell lustre sheds
On the dear mountain-tops where first he rose.   475

Enough of humble arguments; recall,
My Song! those high emotions which thy voice
Has heretofore made known; that bursting forth
Of sympathy, inspiring and inspired,
When everywhere a vital pulse was felt,
And all the several frames of things, like stars,   481
Through every magnitude distinguishable,
Shone mutually indebted, or half lost
Each in the other's blaze, a galaxy
Of life and glory. In the midst stood Man,
Outwardly, inwardly contemplated,   486
As, of all visible natures, crown, though born
Of dust, and kindred to the worm; a Being,
Both in perception and discernment, first
In every capability of rapture,   490
Through the divine effect of power and love;
As, more than anything we know, instinct
With godhead, and, by reason and by will,
Acknowledging dependency sublime.

Ere long, the lonely mountains left, I moved,   495
Begirt, from day to day, with temporal shapes
Of vice and folly thrust upon my view,
Objects of sport, and ridicule, and scorn,
Manners and characters discriminate,
And little bustling passions that eclipse,
As well they might, the impersonated thought,   501
The idea, or abstraction of the kind.

An Idler among academic bowers,
Such was my new condition, as at large
Has been set forth; yet here the vulgar light   505
Of present, actual, superficial life,
Gleaming through colouring of other times,
Old usages and local privilege,
Was welcome, softened, if not solemnised.

This notwithstanding, being brought more near   510
To vice and guilt, forerunning wretchedness,
I trembled,—thought, at times, of human life
With an indefinite terror and dismay,
Such as the storms and angry elements
Had bred in me; but gloomier far, a dim
Analogy to uproar and misrule,   516
Disquiet, danger, and obscurity.

It might be told (but wherefore speak of things
Common to all?) that, seeing, I was led
Gravely to ponder—judging between good
And evil, not as for the mind's delight
But for her guidance—one who was to act,
As sometimes to the best of feeble means
I did, by human sympathy impelled;
And, through dislike and most offensive pain,   525
Was to the truth conducted; of this faith
Never forsaken, that, by acting well,
And understanding, I should learn to love
The end of life, and everything we know.

Grave Teacher, stern Preceptress! for at times   530
Thou canst put on an aspect most severe;
London, to thee I willingly return.
Erewhile my verse played idly with the flowers
Enwrought upon thy mantle; satisfied
With that amusement, and a simple look
Of child-like inquisition now and then
Cast upwards on thy countenance, to detect
Some inner meanings which might harbour there.
But how could I in mood so light indulge,
Keeping such fresh remembrance of the day,   540
When, having thridded the long labyrinth
Of the suburban villages, I first
Entered thy vast dominion? On the roof
Of an itinerant vehicle I sate,
With vulgar men about me, trivial forms
Of houses, pavement, streets, of men and things,—   546
Mean shapes on every side: but, at the instant,
When to myself it fairly might be said,
The threshold now is overpast, (how strange
That aught external to the living mind
Should have such mighty sway! yet so it was),   551
A weight of ages did at once descend
Upon my heart; no thought embodied, no
Distinct remembrances, but weight and power,—
Power growing under weight: alas! I feel   555

That I am trifling: 'twas a moment's
pause,—
All that took place within me came and
went
As in a moment; yet with Time it dwells,
And grateful memory, as a thing divine.

The curious traveller, who, from open
day,   560
Hath passed with torches into some huge
cave,
The Grotto of Antiparos, or the Den
In old time haunted by that Danish Witch,
Yordas; he looks around and sees the
vault
Widening on all sides; sees, or thinks he
sees,   565
Erelong, the massy roof above his head,
That instantly unsettles and recedes,—
Substance and shadow, light and dark-
ness, all
Commingled, making up a canopy
Of shapes and forms and tendencies to
shape   570
That shift and vanish, change and inter-
change
Like spectres,—ferment silent and sub-
lime!
That after a short space works less and
less,
Till, every effort, every motion gone,
The scene before him stands in perfect
view   575
Exposed, and lifeless as a written book!—
But let him pause awhile, and look again,
And a new quickening shall succeed, at
first
Beginning timidly, then creeping fast,
Till the whole cave, so late a senseless
mass,   580
Busies the eye with images and forms
Boldly assembled,—here is shadowed
forth
From the projections, wrinkles, cavities,
A variegated landscape,—there the shape
Of some gigantic warrior clad in mail,   585
The ghostly semblance of a hooded monk,
Veiled nun, or pilgrim resting on his
staff:
Strange congregation! yet not slow to
meet
Eyes that perceive through minds that
can inspire.

Even in such sort had I at first been
moved,   590
Nor otherwise continued to be moved,
As I explored the vast metropolis,
Fount of my country's destiny and the
world's;
That great emporium, chronicle at once
And burial-place of passions, and their
home   595
Imperial, their chief living residence.

With strong sensations teeming as it
did
Of past and present, such a place must
needs
Have pleased me, seeking knowledge at
that time
Far less than craving power; yet know-
ledge came,   600
Sought or unsought, and influxes of
power
Came, of themselves, or at her call de-
rived
In fits of kindliest apprehensiveness,
From all sides, when whate'er was in
itself
Capacious found, or seemed to find, in
me   605
A correspondent amplitude of mind;
Such is the strength and glory of our
youth!
The human nature unto which I felt
That I belonged, and reverenced with
love,
Was not a punctual presence, but a spirit
Diffused through time and space, with
aid derived   611
Of evidence from monuments, erect,
Prostrate, or leaning towards their com-
mon rest
In earth, the widely scattered wreck sub-
lime
Of vanished nations, or more clearly
drawn   615
From books and what they picture and
record.

'Tis true, the history of our native land,
With those of Greece compared and
popular Rome,
And in our high-wrought modern narra-
tives
Stript of their harmonising soul, the life
Of manners and familiar incidents,   621
Had never much delighted me. And
less
Than other intellects had mine been used
To lean upon extrinsic circumstance
Of record or tradition; but a sense   625
Of what in the Great City had been done
And suffered, and was doing, suffering,
still,
Weighed with me, could support the test
of thought;
And, in despite of all that had gone by,
Or was departing never to return.   630
There I conversed with majesty and power
Like independent natures. Hence the
place
Was thronged with impregnations like
the Wilds
In which my early feelings had been
nursed—
Bare hills and valleys, full of caverns,
rocks,   635

And audible seclusions, dashing lakes,
Echoes and waterfalls, and pointed crags
That into music touch the passing
    wind.
Here then my young imagination found
No uncongenial element; could here 640
Among new objects serve or give com-
    mand,
Even as the heart's occasions might re-
    quire,
To forward reason's else too scrupulous
    march.
The effect was, still more elevated views
Of human nature. Neither vice nor guilt,
Debasement undergone by body or mind,
Nor all the misery forced upon my sight,
Misery not lightly passed, but sometimes
    scanned   648
Most feelingly, could overthrow my trust
In what we *may* become; induce belief
That I was ignorant, had been falsely
    taught,   651
A solitary, who with vain conceits
Had been inspired, and walked about in
    dreams.
From those sad scenes when meditation
    turned,
Lo! everything that was indeed divine
Retained its purity inviolate,   656
Nay brighter shone, by this portentous
    gloom
Set off; such opposition as aroused
The mind of Adam, yet in Paradise
Though fallen from bliss, when in the
    East he saw   660
Darkness ere day's mid course, and morn-
    ing light

More orient in the western cloud, that
    drew
O'er the blue firmament a radiant white,
Descending slow with something heavenly
    fraught.   664
Add also, that among the multitudes
Of that huge city, oftentimes was seen
Affectingly set forth, more than else-
    where
Is possible, the unity of man,
One spirit over ignorance and vice
Predominant in good and evil hearts;
One sense for moral judgments, as one
    eye   671
For the sun's light. The soul when
    smitten thus
By a sublime *idea*, whencesoe'er
Vouchsafed for union or communion,
    feeds
On the pure bliss, and takes her rest with
    God.   675
    Thus from a very early age, O Friend!
My thoughts by slow gradations had
    been drawn
To human-kind, and to the good and ill
Of human life: Nature had led me on;
And oft amid the 'busy hum' I seemed
To travel independent of her help,   681
As if I had forgotten her; but no,
The world of human-kind outweighed not
    hers
In my habitual thoughts; the scale of love,
Though filling daily, still was light, com-
    pared   685
With that in which *her* mighty objects
    lay.

BOOK NINTH

RESIDENCE IN FRANCE

EVEN as a river,—partly (it might seem)
Yielding to old remembrances, and
    swayed
In part by fear to shape a way direct,
That would engulph him soon in the
    ravenous sea—
Turns, and will measure back his course,
    far back,   5
Seeking the very regions which he crossed
In his first outset; so have we, my Friend!
Turned and returned with intricate delay.
Or as a traveller, who has gained the brow
Of some aerial Down, while there he halts
For breathing-time, is tempted to review
The region left behind him; and, if aught
Deserving notice have escaped regard,
Or been regarded with too careless eye,
Strives, from that height, with one and
    yet one more   15

Last look, to make the best amends he
    may:
So have we lingered. Now we start
    afresh
With courage, and new hope risen on our
    toil.
Fair greetings to this shapeless eagerness,
Whene'er it comes! needful in work so
    long,   20
Thrice needful to the argument which
    now
Awaits us! Oh, how much unlike the
    past!
    Free as a colt at pasture on the hill,
I ranged at large, through London's wide
    domain,
Month after month. Obscurely did I
    live,   25

Not seeking frequent intercourse with
men,
By literature, or elegance, or rank,
Distinguished. Scarcely was a year thus
      spent
Ere I forsook the crowded solitude,   29
With less regret for its luxurious pomp,
And all the nicely-guarded shows of art,
Than for the humble book-stalls in the
      streets,
Exposed to eye and hand where'er I
      turned.

France lured me forth; the realm that
      I had crossed
So lately, journeying toward the snow-
      clad Alps.   35
But now, relinquishing the scrip and staff,
And all enjoyment which the summer sun
Sheds round the steps of those who meet
      the day
With motion constant as his own, I went
Prepared to sojourn in a pleasant town,
Washed by the current of the stately
      Loire.   41

Through Paris lay my readiest course,
      and there
Sojourning a few days, I visited
In haste, each spot of old or recent fame,
The latter chiefly; from the field of Mars
Down to the suburbs of St. Antony,   46
And from Mont Martre southward to
      the Dome
Of Geneviève. In both her clamorous
      Halls,
The National Synod and the Jacobins,
I saw the Revolutionary Power   50
Toss like a ship at anchor, rocked by
      storms;
The Arcades I traversed, in the Palace
      huge
Of Orleans; coasted round and round the
      line
Of Tavern, Brothel, Gaming-house, and
      Shop,
Great rendezvous of worst and best, the
      walk   55
Of all who had a purpose, or had not;
I stared and listened, with a stranger's
      ears,
To Hawkers and Haranguers, hubbub
      wild!
And hissing Factionists with ardent eyes,
In knots, or pairs, or single. Not a look
Hope takes, or Doubt or Fear is forced
      to wear,   61
But seemed there present; and I scanned
      them all,
Watched every gesture uncontrollable,
Of anger, and vexation, and despite,
All side by side, and struggling face to
      face,   65
With gaiety and dissolute idleness.

Where silent zephyrs sported with the
      dust
Of the Bastille, I sate in the open sun,
And from the rubbish gathered up a stone,
And pocketed the relic, in the guise   70
Of an enthusiast; yet, in honest truth,
I looked for something that I could not
      find,
Affecting more emotion than I felt;
For 'tis most certain, that these various
      sights,
However potent their first shock, with me
Appeared to recompense the traveller's
      pains   76
Less than the painted Magdalene of Le
      Brun,
A beauty exquisitely wrought, with hair
Dishevelled, gleaming eyes, and rueful
      cheek
Pale and bedropped with everflowing
      tears.   80

But hence to my more permanent abode
I hasten; there, by novelties in speech,
Domestic manners, customs, gestures,
      looks,
And all the attire of ordinary life,
Attention was engrossed; and, thus
      amused,   85
I stood, 'mid those concussions, uncon-
      cerned,
Tranquil almost, and careless as a flower
Glassed in a greenhouse, or a parlour
      shrub
That spreads its leaves in unmolested
      peace,
While every bush and tree, the country
      through,   90
Is shaking to the roots: indifference this
Which may seem strange: but I was un-
      prepared
With needful knowledge, had abruptly
      passed
Into a theatre, whose stage was filled
And busy with an action far advanced.
Like others, I had skimmed, and some-
      times read   96
With care, the master-pamphlets of the
      day;
Nor wanted such half-insight as grew
      wild
Upon that meagre soil, helped out by
      talk   99
And public news; but having never seen
A chronicle that might suffice to show
Whence the main organs of the public
      power
Had sprung, their transmigrations, when
      and how
Accomplished, giving thus unto events
A form and body; all things were to me
Loose and disjointed, and the affections
      left   106
Without a vital interest. At that time,

Moreover, the first storm was overblown,
And the strong hand of outward violence
Locked up in quiet. For myself, I fear
Now in connection with so great a theme
To speak (as I must be compelled to do)
Of one so unimportant; night by night
Did I frequent the formal haunts of men,
Whom, in the city, privilege of birth   115
Sequestered from the rest, societies
Polished in arts, and in punctilio versed;
Whence, and from deeper causes, all dis-
    course
Of good and evil of the time was shunned
With scrupulous care; but these restric-
    tions soon   120
Proved tedious, and I gradually with-
    drew
Into a noisier world, and thus ere long
Became a patriot; and my heart was all
Given to the people, and my love was
    theirs.

A band of military Officers,   125
Then stationed in the city, were the chief
Of my associates: some of these wore
    swords
That had been seasoned in the wars, and
    all
Were men well-born; the chivalry of
    France.
In age and temper differing, they had yet
One spirit ruling in each heart; alike   131
(Save only one, hereafter to be named)
Were bent upon undoing what was done:
This was their rest and only hope; there-
    with
No fear had they of bad becoming worse,
For worst to them was come; nor would
    have stirred,   136
Or deemed it worth a moment's thought
    to stir,
In anything, save only as the act
Looked thitherward. One, reckoning by
    years,
Was in the prime of manhood, and ere-
    while   140
He had sate lord in many tender hearts;
Though heedless of such honours now,
    and changed:
His temper was quite mastered by the
    times,
And they had blighted him, had eaten
    away
The beauty of his person, doing wrong
Alike to body and to mind: his port,   146
Which once had been erect and open, now
Was stooping and contracted, and a face,
Endowed by Nature with her fairest gifts
Of symmetry and light and bloom, ex-
    pressed,   150
As much as any that was ever seen,
A ravage out of season, made by thoughts
Unhealthy and vexatious. With the hour,
That from the press of Paris duly brought

Its freight of public news, the fever
    came,   155
A punctual visitant, to shake this man,
Disarmed his voice and fanned his yellow
    cheek
Into a thousand colours; while he read,
Or mused, his sword was haunted by his
    touch
Continually, like an uneasy place   160
In his own body. 'Twas in truth an hour
Of universal ferment; mildest men
Were agitated; and commotions, strife
Of passions and opinions, filled the walls
Of peaceful houses with unquiet sounds.
The soil of common life, was, at that
    time,   166
Too hot to tread upon. Oft said I then,
And not then only, 'What a mockery
    this
Of history, the past and that to come!
Now do I feel how all men are deceived,
Reading of nations and their works, in
    faith,   171
Faith given to vanity and emptiness;
Oh! laughter for the page that would
    reflect
To future times the face of what now is!'
The land all swarmed with passion, like
    a plain   175
Devoured by locusts,—Carra, Gorsas,—
    add
A hundred other names, forgotten now,
Nor to be heard of more; yet, they were
    powers,
Like earthquakes, shocks repeated day
    by day,
And felt through every nook of town and
    field.   180

Such was the state of things. Mean-
    while the chief
Of my associates stood prepared for flight
To augment the band of emigrants in
    arms
Upon the borders of the Rhine, and
    leagued
With foreign foes mustered for instant
    war.   185
This was their undisguised intent, and
    they
Were waiting with the whole of their
    desires
The moment to depart.

                                An Englishman,
Born in a land whose very name appeared
To license some unruliness of mind;   190
A stranger, with youth's further privilege,
And the indulgence that a half-learnt
    speech
Wins from the courteous; I, who had
    been else
Shunned and not tolerated, freely lived
With these defenders of the Crown, and
    talked,   195

557

And heard their notions; nor did they
disdain
The wish to bring me over to their cause.

But though untaught by thinking or by
books
To reason well of polity or law,
And nice distinctions, then on every
tongue, 200
Of natural rights and civil; and to acts
Of nations and their passing interests,
(If with unworldly ends and aims com-
pared)
Almost indifferent, even the historian's
tale 204
Prizing but little otherwise than I prized
Tales of the poets, as it made the heart
Beat high, and filled the fancy with fair
forms,
Old heroes and their sufferings and their
deeds;
Yet in the regal sceptre, and the pomp
Of orders and degrees, I nothing found
Then, or had ever, even in crudest youth,
That dazzled me, but rather what I
mourned 212
And ill could brook, beholding that the
best
Ruled not, and feeling that they ought to
rule.

For, born in a poor district, and which
yet 215
Retaineth more of ancient homeliness,
Than any other nook of English ground,
It was my fortune scarcely to have seen,
Through the whole tenour of my school-
day time,
The face of one, who, whether boy or
man, 220
Was vested with attention or respect
Through claims of wealth or blood; nor
was it least
Of many benefits, in later years
Derived from academic institutes
And rules, that they held something up
to view 225
Of a Republic, where all stood thus far
Upon equal ground; that we were brothers
all
In honour, as in one community,
Scholars and gentlemen; where, further-
more,
Distinction open lay to all that came, 230
And wealth and titles were in less esteem
Than talents, worth, and prosperous in-
dustry.
Add unto this, subservience from the first
To presences of God's mysterious power
Made manifest in Nature's sovereignty,
And fellowship with venerable books, 236
To sanction the proud workings of the
soul,
And mountain liberty. It could not be

But that one tutored thus should look
with awe
Upon the faculties of man, receive 240
Gladly the highest promises, and hail,
As best, the government of equal rights
And individual worth. And hence, O
Friend!
If at the first great outbreak I rejoiced
Less than might well befit my youth, the
cause 245
In part lay here, that unto me the events
Seemed nothing out of nature's certain
course,
A gift that was come rather late than
soon.
No wonder, then, if advocates like these,
Inflamed by passion, blind with pre-
judice, 250
And stung with injury, at this riper day,
Were impotent to make my hopes put on
The shape of theirs, my understanding
bend
In honour to their honour: zeal, which
yet 254
Had slumbered, now in opposition burst
Forth like a Polar summer: every word
They uttered was a dart, by counter-
winds
Blown back upon themselves; their reason
seemed
Confusion-stricken by a higher power
Than human understanding, their dis-
course 260
Maimed, spiritless: and, in their weakness
strong,
I triumphed.
          Meantime, day by day, the roads
Were crowded with the bravest youth of
France,
And all the promptest of her spirits,
linked 264
In gallant soldiership, and posting on
To meet the war upon her frontier bounds.
Yet at this very moment do tears start
Into mine eyes: I do not say I weep—
I wept not then,—but tears have dimmed
my sight,
In memory of the farewells of that time,
Domestic severings, female fortitude 271
At dearest separation, patriot love
And self-devotion, and terrestrial hope,
Encouraged with a martyr's confidence;
Even files of strangers merely seen but
once, 275
And for a moment, men from far with
sound
Of music, martial tunes, and banners
spread,
Entering the city, here and there a face,
Or person singled out among the rest,
Yet still a stranger and beloved as such;
Even by these passing spectacles my
heart 281
Was oftentimes uplifted, and they seemed

Arguments sent from Heaven to prove
  the cause
Good, pure, which no one could stand up
  against,
Who was not lost, abandoned, selfish,
  proud,   285
Mean, miserable, wilfully depraved,
Hater perverse of equity and truth.

Among that band of Officers was one,
Already hinted at,[1] of other mould—
A patriot, thence rejected by the rest, 290
And with an oriental loathing spurned,
As of a different caste. A meeker man
Than this lived never, nor a more benign,
Meek though enthusiastic. Injuries
Made *him* more gracious, and his nature
  then   295
Did breathe its sweetness out most sen-
  sibly,
As aromatic flowers on Alpine turf,
When foot hath crushed them. He
  through the events
Of that great change wandered in perfect
  faith,
As through a book, an old romance, or
  tale   300
Of Fairy, or some dream of actions
  wrought
Behind the summer clouds. By birth he
  ranked
With the most noble, but unto the poor
Among mankind he was in service bound,
As by some tie invisible, oaths professed
To a religious order. Man he loved   306
As man; and, to the mean and the obscure,
And all the homely in their homely works,
Transferred a courtesy which had no air
Of condescension; but did rather seem
A passion and a gallantry, like that 311
Which he, a soldier, in his idler day
Had paid to woman: somewhat vain he
  was,
Or seemed so, yet it was not vanity,
But fondness, and a kind of radiant joy
Diffused around him, while he was intent
On works of love or freedom, or revolved
Complacently the progress of a cause,
Whereof he was a part: yet this was meek
And placid, and took nothing from the man
That was delightful. Oft in solitude   321
With him did I discourse about the end
Of civil government, and its wisest forms;
Of ancient loyalty, and chartered rights,
Custom and habit, novelty and change;
Of self-respect, and virtue in the few 326
For patrimonial honour set apart,
And ignorance in the labouring multitude.
For he, to all intolerance indisposed,
Balanced these contemplations in his
  mind;   330
And I, who at that time was scarcely
  dipped

Into the turmoil, bore a sounder judgment
Than later days allowed; carried about me,
With less alloy to its integrity,
The experience of past ages, as, through
  help   335
Of books and common life, it makes sure
  way
To youthful minds, by objects over near
Not pressed upon, nor dazzled or misled
By struggling with the crowd for present
  ends.

But though not deaf, nor obstinate to
  find   340
Error without excuse upon the side
Of them who strove against us, more
  delight
We took, and let this freely be confessed,
In painting to ourselves the miseries 344
Of royal courts, and that voluptuous life
Unfeeling, where the man who is of soul
The meanest thrives the most; where
  dignity,
True personal dignity, abideth not;
A light, a cruel, and vain world cut off
From the natural inlets of just sentiment,
From lowly sympathy and chastening
  truth: 351
Where good and evil interchange their
  names,
And thirst for bloody spoils abroad is
  paired
With vice at home. We added dearest
  themes—
Man and his noble nature, as it is   355
The gift which God has placed within his
  power,
His blind desires and steady faculties
Capable of clear truth, the one to break
Bondage, the other to build liberty
On firm foundations, making social life,
Through knowledge spreading and im-
  perishable,   361
As just in regulation, and as pure
As individual in the wise and good.

We summoned up the honourable deeds
Of ancient Story, thought of each bright
  spot,   365
That would be found in all recorded time,
Of truth preserved and error passed away;
Of single spirits that catch the flame from
  Heaven,
And how the multitudes of men will feed
And fan each other; thought of sects, how
  keen   370
They are to put the appropriate nature on,
Triumphant over every obstacle
Of custom, language, country, love, or
  hate,
And what they do and suffer for their
  creed;
How far they travel, and how long endure;
How quickly mighty Nations have been
  formed,   376

From least beginnings; how, together
locked
By new opinions, scattered tribes have
made
One body, spreading wide as clouds in
heaven.
To aspirations then of our own minds 380
Did we appeal; and, finally, beheld
A living confirmation of the whole
Before us, in a people from the depth
Of shameful imbecility uprisen,
Fresh as the morning star. Elate we
looked   385
Upon their virtues; saw, in rudest men,
Self-sacrifice the firmest; generous love,
And continence of mind, and sense of
right,
Uppermost in the midst of fiercest strife.

Oh, sweet it is, in academic groves, 390
Or such retirement, Friend! as we have
known
In the green dales beside our Rotha's
stream,
Greta, or Derwent, or some nameless rill,
To ruminate, with interchange of talk,
On rational liberty, and hope in man, 395
Justice and peace. But far more sweet
such toil—
Toil, say I, for it leads to thoughts ab-
struse—
If nature then be standing on the brink
Of some great trial, and we hear the voice
Of one devoted,—one whom circumstance
Hath called upon to embody his deep
sense   401
In action, give it outwardly a shape,
And that of benediction, to the world.
Then doubt is not, and truth is more than
truth,—
A hope it is, and a desire; a creed   405
Of zeal, by an authority Divine
Sanctioned, of danger, difficulty, or death.
Such conversation, under Attic shades,
Did Dion hold with Plato; ripened thus
For a deliverer's glorious task,—and such
He, on that ministry already bound,   411
Held with Eudemus and Timonides,
Surrounded by adventurers in arms,
When those two vessels with their daring
freight,
For the Sicilian Tyrant's overthrow,   415
Sailed from Zacynthus,—philosophic war,
Led by Philosophers. With harder fate,
Though like ambition, such was he, O
Friend!
Of whom I speak. So BEAUPUY (let the
name
Stand near the worthiest of Antiquity)
Fashioned his life; and many a long dis-
course,   421
With like persuasion honoured, we main-
tained:
He, on his part, accoutred for the worst,

He perished fighting, in supreme com-
mand,
Upon the borders of the unhappy Loire,[1]
For liberty, against deluded men,   426
His fellow country-men; and yet most
blessed
In this, that he the fate of later times
Lived not to see, nor what we now behold,
Who have as ardent hearts as he had
then.[2]   430

Along that very Loire, with festal mirth
Resounding at all hours, and innocent yet
Of civil slaughter, was our frequent walk;
Or in wide forests of continuous shade,
Lofty and over-arched, with open space
Beneath the trees, clear footing many
a mile—   436
A solemn region. Oft amid those haunts,
From earnest dialogues I slipped in
thought,
And let remembrance steal to other times,
When o'er those interwoven roots, moss-
clad,   440
And smooth as marble or a waveless sea,
Some Hermit, from his cell forth-strayed,
might pace
In sylvan meditation undisturbed;
As on the pavement of a Gothic church
Walks a lone Monk, when service hath
expired,   445
In peace and silence. But if e'er was
heard,—
Heard, though unseen,—a devious tra-
veller,
Retiring or approaching from afar
With speed and echoes loud of trampling
hoofs
From the hard floor reverberated, then
It was Angelica thundering through the
woods   451
Upon her palfrey, or that gentle maid
Erminia, fugitive as fair as she.
Sometimes methought I saw a pair of
knights
Joust underneath the trees, that as in
storm   455
Rocked high above their heads; anon,
the din
Of boisterous merriment, and music's
roar,
In sudden proclamation, burst from haunt
Of Satyrs in some viewless glade, with
dance
Rejoicing o'er a female in the midst, 460
A mortal beauty, their unhappy thrall.
The width of those huge forests, unto me
A novel scene, did often in this way
Master my fancy while I wandered on

[1] An error. Beaupuy died at Emmendingen, shot
while in command of a division of the Army of the
Rhine and the Moselle.—ED.
[2] For the story of W's. relations with Beaupuy,
see Le Général Michel Beaupuy, by MM. Georges
Bussière and Emile Legouis: Chap. II.—ED.

With that revered companion. And some-
times—   465
When to a convent in a meadow green,
By a brook-side, we came, a roofless pile,
And not by reverential touch of Time
Dismantled, but by violence abrupt—
In spite of those heart-bracing colloquies,
In spite of real fervour, and of that   471
Less genuine and wrought up within my-
self—
I could not but bewail a wrong so harsh,
And for the Matin-bell to sound no more
Grieved, and the twilight taper, and the
cross   475
High on the topmost pinnacle, a sign
(How welcome to the weary traveller's
eyes!)
Of hospitality and peaceful rest.
And when the partner of those varied
walks
Pointed upon occasion to the site   480
Of Romorentin, home of ancient kings,
To the imperial edifice of Blois,
Or to that rural castle, name now slipped
From my remembrance, where a lady
lodged,
By the first Francis wooed, and bound to
him   485
In chains of mutual passion, from the
tower,
As a tradition of the country tells,
Practised to commune with her royal
knight
By cressets and love-beacons, intercourse
'Twixt her high-seated residence and his
Far off at Chambord on the plain beneath;
Even here, though less than with the peace-
ful house
Religious, 'mid those frequent monuments
Of Kings, their vices and their better
deeds,
Imagination, potent to inflame   495
At times with virtuous wrath and noble
scorn,
Did also often mitigate the force
Of civic prejudice, the bigotry,
So call it, of a youthful patriot's mind;
And on these spots with many gleams I
looked   500
Of chivalrous delight. Yet not the less,
Hatred of absolute rule, where will of one
Is law for all, and of that barren pride
In them who, by immunities unjust,
Between the sovereign and the people
stand,   505
His helper and not theirs, laid stronger
hold
Daily upon me, mixed with pity too
And love; for where hope is, there love
will be
For the abject multitude. And when we
chanced
One day to meet a hunger-bitten girl,   510
Who crept along fitting her languid gait

Unto a heifer's motion, by a cord
Tied her arm, and picking thus from
the lane
Its sustenance, while the girl with pallid
hands   514
Was busy knitting in a heartless mood
Of solitude, and at the sight my friend
In agitation said, ''Tis against *that*
That we are fighting,' I with him believed
That a benignant spirit was abroad
Which might not be withstood, that
poverty   520
Abject as this would in a little time
Be found no more, that we should see the
earth
Unthwarted in her wish to recompense
The meek, the lowly, patient child of
toil,
All institutes for ever blotted out   525
That legalised exclusion, empty pomp
Abolished, sensual state and cruel power,
Whether by edict of the one or few;
And finally, as sum and crown of all,
Should see the people having a strong
hand   530
In framing their own laws; whence better
days
To all mankind. But, these things set
apart,
Was not this single confidence enough
To animate the mind that ever turned
A thought to human welfare,—that,
henceforth   535
Captivity by mandate without law
Should cease; and open accusation lead
To sentence in the hearing of the world,
And open punishment, if not the air
Be free to breathe in, and the heart of
man   540
Dread nothing? From this height I shall
not stoop
To humbler matter that detained us oft
In thought or conversation, public acts,
And public persons, and emotions
wrought
Within the breast, as ever-varying winds
Of record or report swept over us;   546
But I might here, instead, repeat a tale,[1]
Told by my Patriot friend, of sad events,
That prove to what low depth had struck
the roots,
How widely spread the boughs, of that
old tree   550
Which, as a deadly mischief, and a foul
And black dishonour, France was weary
of.

O, happy time of youthful lovers, (thus
The story might begin,) oh, balmy time,
In which a love-knot on a lady's brow,
Is fairer than the fairest star in Heaven!
So might—and with that prelude *did*
begin   557

[1] *Vaudracour and Julia*, p. 96.—Ed.

The record; and, in faithful verse, was
given
The doleful sequel.
               But our little bark
On a strong river boldly hath been
launched;   560
And from the driving current should we
turn
To loiter wilfully within a creek,
Howe'er attractive, Fellow voyager!
Wouldst thou not chide? Yet deem not
my pains lost:
For Vaudracour and Julia (so were
named   565
The ill-fated pair) in that plain tale will
draw
Tears from the hearts of others, when
their own
Shall beat no more. Thou, also, there
may'st read,
At leisure, how the enamoured youth was
driven,   569
By public power abased, to fatal crime,
Nature's rebellion against monstrous law;

How, between heart and heart, oppres-
sion thrust
Her mandates, severing whom true love
had joined,
Harassing both; until he sank and pressed
The couch his fate had made for him;
supine,   575
Save when the stings of viperous re-
morse,
Trying their strength, enforced him to
start up,
Aghast and prayerless. Into a deep wood
He fled, to shun the haunts of human
kind;
There dwelt, weakened in spirit more
and more;   580
Nor could the voice of Freedom, which
through France
Full speedily resounded, public hope,
Or personal memory of his own worst
wrongs,
Rouse him; but, hidden in those gloomy
shades,   584
His days he wasted,—an imbecile mind.

BOOK TENTH

RESIDENCE IN FRANCE—(Continued)

It was a beautiful and silent day
That overspread the countenance of earth,
Then fading with unusual quietness,—
A day as beautiful as e'er was given
To soothe regret, though deepening what
it soothed,   5
When by the gliding Loire I paused, and
cast
Upon his rich domains, vineyard and
tilth,
Green meadow-ground, and many-
coloured woods,
Again, and yet again, a farewell look;
Then from the quiet of that scene passed
on,   10
Bound to the fierce Metropolis. From
his throne
The King had fallen, and that invading
host—
Presumptuous cloud, on whose black
front was written
The tender mercies of the dismal wind
That bore it—on the plains of Liberty 15
Had burst innocuous. Say in bolder
words,
They—who had come elate as eastern
hunters
Banded beneath the Great Mogul, when
he
Erewhile went forth from Agra or Lahore,
Rajahs and Omrahs in his train, intent 20
To drive their prey enclosed within a ring
Wide as a province, but, the signal given,

Before the point of the life-threatening
spear
Narrowing itself by moments—they, rash
men,
Had seen the anticipated quarry turned
Into avengers, from whose wrath they
fled   26
In terror. Disappointment and dismay
Remained for all whose fancies had run
wild
With evil expectations; confidence 29
And perfect triumph for the better cause.

    The State, as if to stamp the final seal
On her security, and to the world
Show what she was, a high and fearless
soul,
Exulting in defiance, or heart-stung 34
By sharp resentment, or belike to taunt
With spiteful gratitude the baffled League,
That had stirred up her slackening facul-
ties
To a new transition, when the King was
crushed,
Spared not the empty throne, and in
proud haste
Assumed the body and venerable name
Of a Republic. Lamentable crimes, 41
'Tis true, had gone before this hour, dire
work
Of massacre, in which the senseless sword
Was prayed to as a judge; but these were
past

Earth free from them for ever, as was
 thought,—   45
Ephemeral monsters, to be seen but once!
Things that could only show themselves
 and die.

Cheered with this hope, to Paris I
 returned,
And ranged, with ardour heretofore un-
 felt,
The spacious city, and in progress passed
The prison where the unhappy Monarch
 lay,   51
Associate with his children and his wife
In bondage; and the palace, lately
 stormed
With roar of cannon by a furious host. 54
I crossed the square (an empty area then!)
Of the Carrousel, where so late had lain
The dead, upon the dying heaped, and
 gazed
On this and other spots, as doth a man
Upon a volume whose contents he knows
Are memorable, but from him locked
 up,   60
Being written in a tongue he cannot read,
So that he questions the mute leaves with
 pain,
And half upbraids their silence. But
 that night
I felt most deeply in what world I was,
What ground I trod on, and what air I
 breathed.   65
High was my room and lonely, near the
 roof
Of a large mansion or hotel, a lodge
That would have pleased me in more
 quiet times;
Nor was it wholly without pleasure then.
With unextinguished taper I kept watch,
Reading at intervals; the fear gone by 71
Pressed on me almost like a fear to come.
I thought of those September massacres,
Divided from me by one little month,
Saw them and touched: the rest was con-
 jured up   75
From tragic fictions or true history,
Remembrances and dim admonishments.
The horse is taught his manage, and no
 star
Of wildest course but treads back his own
 steps;
For the spent hurricane the air provides
As fierce a successor; the tide retreats 81
But to return out of its hiding-place
In the great deep; all things have second
 birth;
The earthquake is not satisfied at once;
And in this way I wrought upon myself,
Until I seemed to hear a voice that cried,
To the whole city, 'sleep no more.' The
 trance
Fled with the voice to which it had given
 birth;

But vainly comments of a calmer mind
Promised soft peace and sweet forgetful-
 ness.   90
The place, all hushed and silent as it was,
Appeared unfit for the repose of night,
Defenceless as a wood where tigers roam.

With early morning towards the Palace-
 walk
Of Orleans eagerly I turned; as yet 95
The streets were still; not so those long
 Arcades;
There, 'mid a peal of ill-matched sounds
 and cries,
That greeted me on entering, I could
 hear
Shrill voices from the hawkers in the
 throng,
Bawling, 'Denunciation of the Crimes 100
Of Maximilian Robespierre;' the hand,
Prompt as the voice, held forth a printed
 speech,
The same that had been recently pro-
 nounced,
When Robespierre, not ignorant for what
 mark
Some words of indirect reproof had
 been   105
Intended, rose in hardihood, and dared
The man who had an ill surmise of him
To bring his charge in openness; whereat,
When a dead pause ensued, and no one
 stirred,
In silence of all present, from his seat 110
Louvet walked single through the avenue,
And took his station in the Tribune, say-
 ing,
'I, Robespierre, accuse thee!' Well is
 known
The inglorious issue of that charge, and
 how
He, who had launched the startling thun-
 derbolt,   115
The one bold man, whose voice the attack
 had sounded,
Was left without a follower to discharge
His perilous duty, and retire lamenting
That Heaven's best aid is wasted upon
 men
Who to themselves are false.
      But these are things 120
Of which I speak, only as they were storm
Or sunshine to my individual mind,
No further. Let me then relate that
 now—
In some sort seeing with my proper eyes
That Liberty, and Life, and Death would
 soon   125
To the remotest corners of the land
Lie in the arbitrement of those who ruled
The capital City; what was struggled for,
And by what combatants victory must be
 won;
The indecision on their part whose aim

Seemed best, and the straightforward
path of those 131
Who in attack or in defence were strong
Through their impiety—my inmost soul
Was agitated; yea, I could almost
Have prayed that throughout earth upon
all men, 135
By patient exercise of reason made
Worthy of liberty, all spirits filled
With zeal expanding in Truth's holy light,
The gift of tongues might fall, and power
arrive
From the four quarters of the winds to
do 140
For France, what without help she could
not do,
A work of honour; think not that to this
I added, work of safety: from all doubt
Or trepidation for the end of things
Far was I, far as angels are from guilt. 145

Yet did I grieve, nor only grieved, but
thought
Of opposition and of remedies:
An insignificant stranger and obscure,
And one, moreover, little graced with
power
Of eloquence even in my native speech,
And all unfit for tumult or intrigue, 151
Yet would I at this time with willing
heart
Have undertaken for a cause so great
Service however dangerous. I revolved,
How much the destiny of Man had
still 155
Hung upon single persons; that there
was,
Transcendent to all local patrimony,
One nature, as there is one sun in heaven;
That objects, even as they are great,
thereby
Do come within the reach of humblest
eyes; 160
That Man is only weak through his mis-
trust
And want of hope where evidence divine
Proclaims to him that hope should be
most sure;
Nor did the inexperience of my youth
Preclude conviction, that a spirit strong
In hope, and trained to noble aspirations,
A spirit thoroughly faithful to itself, 167
Is for Society's unreasoning herd
A domineering instinct, serves at once
For way and guide, a fluent receptacle 170
That gathers up each petty straggling rill
And vein of water, glad to be rolled on
In safe obedience; that a mind, whose
rest
Is where it ought to be, in self-restraint,
In circumspection and simplicity, 175
Falls rarely in entire discomfiture
Below its aim, or meets with, from with-
out,

A treachery that foils it or defeats;
And, lastly, if the means on human will
Frail human will, dependent should be-
tray 180
Him who too boldly trusted them, I felt
That 'mid the loud distractions of the
world
A sovereign voice subsists within the soul,
Arbiter undisturbed of right and wrong,
Of life and death, in majesty severe 185
Enjoining, as may best promote the aims
Of truth and justice, utter sacrifice,
From whatsoever region of our cares
Or our infirm affections Nature pleads,
Earnest and blind, against the stern
decree. 190

On the other side, I called to mind
those truths
That are the commonplaces of the
schools—
(A theme for boys, too hackneyed for
their sires,)
Yet, with a revelation's liveliness,
In all their comprehensive bearings known
And visible to philosophers of old, 196
Men who, to business of the world un-
trained,
Lived in the shade; and to Harmodius
known
And his compeer Aristogiton, known
To Brutus—that tyrannic power is weak,
Hath neither gratitude, nor faith, nor
love, 201
Nor the support of good or evil men
To trust in; that the godhead which is
ours
Can never utterly be charmed or stilled;
That nothing hath a natural right to last
But good and reason; that all else 206
Meets foes irreconcilable, and at best
Lives only by variety of disease.

Well might my wishes be intense, my
thoughts
Strong and perturbed, not doubting at
that time 210
But that the virtue of one paramount
mind
Would have abashed those impious
crests—have quelled
Outrage and bloody power, and—in de-
spite
Of what the People long had been and
were
Through ignorance and false teaching,
sadder proof 215
Of immaturity, and—in the teeth
Of desperate opposition from without—
Have cleared a passage for just govern-
ment,
And left a solid birthright to the State,
Redeemed, according to example given
By ancient lawgivers.

In this frame of mind,
Dragged by a chain of harsh necessity,
So seemed it,—now I thankfully acknow-
ledge,
Forced by the gracious providence of
Heaven,—
To England I returned, else (though
assured   225
That I both was and must be of small
weight,
No better than a landsman on the deck
Of a ship struggling with a hideous storm)
Doubtless, I should have then made
common cause
With some who perished; haply perished
too,   230
A poor mistaken and bewildered offer-
ing,—
Should to the breast of Nature have gone
back,
With all my resolutions, all my hopes,
A Poet only to myself, to men
Useless, and even, beloved Friend! a
soul   235
To thee unknown!
          Twice had the trees let fall
Their leaves, as often Winter had put on
His hoary crown, since I had seen the
surge
Beat against Albion's shore, since ear of
mine
Had caught the accents of my native
speech   240
Upon our native country's sacred ground.
A patriot of the world, how could I glide
Into communion with her sylvan shades,
Erewhile my tuneful haunt? It pleased
me more   244
To abide in the great City, where I found
The general air still busy with the stir
Of that first memorable onset made
By a strong levy of humanity
Upon the traffickers in Negro blood;
Effort which, though defeated, had re-
called   250
To notice old forgotten principles,
And through the nation spread a novel
heat
Of virtuous feeling. For myself, I own
That this particular strife had wanted
power
To rivet my affections; nor did now   255
Its unsuccessful issue much excite
My sorrow; for I brought with me the
faith
That, if France prospered, good men
would not long
Pay fruitless worship to humanity,
And this most rotten branch of human
shame,   260
Object, so seemed it, of superfluous pains,
Would fall together with its parent tree.
What, then, were my emotions, when in
arms

Britain put forth her freeborn strength
in league,
Oh, pity and shame! with those confede-
rate Powers!   265
Not in my single self alone I found,
But in the minds of all ingenuous youth,
Change and subversion from that hour.
No shock
Given to my moral nature had I known
Down to that very moment; neither lapse
Nor turn of sentiment that might be
named   271
A revolution, save at this one time;
All else was progress on the self-same path
On which, with a diversity of pace,
I had been travelling: this a stride at
once   275
Into another region. As a light
And pliant harebell, swinging in the
breeze
On some grey rock—its birthplace—so
had I
Wantoned, fast rooted on the ancient
tower
Of my belovèd country, wishing not   280
A happier fortune than to wither there:
Now was I from that pleasant station torn
And tossed about in whirlwind. I re-
joiced,
Yea, afterwards—truth most painful to
record!—
Exulted, in the triumph of my soul,   285
When Englishmen by thousands were
o'erthrown,
Left without glory on the field, or driven,
Brave hearts! to shameful flight. It was
a grief,—
Grief call it not, 'twas anything but
that,—   289
A conflict of sensations without name,
Of which *he* only, who may love the sight
Of a village steeple, as I do, can judge,
When, in the congregation bending all
To their great Father, prayers were offered
up,
Or praises for our country's victories;
And, 'mid the simple worshippers, per-
chance   296
I only, like an uninvited guest
Whom no one owned, sate silent, shall
I add,
Fed on the day of vengeance yet to come.

Oh! much have they to account for, who
could tear,   300
By violence, at one decisive rent,
From the best youth in England their dear
pride,
Their joy, in England; this, too, at a
time
In which worst losses easily might wear
The best of names, when patriotic love
Did of itself in modesty give way,   306
Like the Precursor when the Deity

Is come Whose harbinger he was; a time
In which apostasy from ancient faith
Seemed but conversion to a higher creed;
Withal a season dangerous and wild,   311
A time when sage Experience would have
    snatched
Flowers out of any hedge-row to compose
A chaplet in contempt of his grey locks.

When the proud fleet that bears the
    red-cross flag   315
In that unworthy service was prepared
To mingle, I beheld the vessels lie,
A brood of gallant creatures, on the deep;
I saw them in their rest, a sojourner
Through a whole month of calm and glassy
    days   320
In that delightful island which protects
Their place of convocation—there I heard,
Each evening, pacing by the still sea-
    shore,
A monitory sound that never failed,—
The sunset cannon. While the orb went
    down   325
In the tranquillity of nature, came
That voice, ill requiem! seldom-heard by
    me
Without a spirit overcast by dark
Imaginations, sense of woes to come,
Sorrow for human kind, and pain of
    heart.   330

    In France, the men, who, for their
    desperate ends,
Had plucked up mercy by the roots, were
    glad
Of this new enemy. Tyrants, strong
    before
In wicked pleas, were strong as demons
    now;
And thus, on every side beset with foes,
The goaded land waxed mad; the crimes
    of few   336
Spread into madness of the many; blasts
From hell came sanctified like airs from
    heaven.
The sternness of the just, the faith of
    those
Who doubted not that Providence had
    times   340
Of vengeful retribution, theirs who
    throned
The human Understanding paramount
And made of that their God, the hopes
    of men
Who were content to barter short-lived
    pangs
For a paradise of ages, the blind rage 345
Of insolent tempers, the light vanity
Of intermeddlers, steady purposes
Of the suspicious, slips of the indiscreet,
And all the accidents of life were pressed
Into one service, busy with one work. 350
The Senate stood aghast, her prudence
    quenched,

Her wisdom stifled, and her justice scared,
Her frenzy only active to extol
Past outrages, and shape the way for new,
Which no one dared to oppose or mitigate.

    Domestic carnage now filled the whole
    year   356
With feast-days; old men from the
    chimney-nook,
The maiden from the bosom of her love,
The mother from the cradle of her babe,
The warrior from the field—all perished,
    all—   360
Friends, enemies, of all parties, ages,
    ranks,
Head after head, and never heads enough
For those that bade them fall. They
    found their joy,
They made it proudly, eager as a child,
(If like desires of innocent little ones 365
May with such heinous appetites be com-
    pared),
Pleased in some open field to exercise
A toy that mimics with revolving wings
The motion of a wind-mill; though the
    air
Do of itself blow fresh, and make the
    vanes   370
Spin in his eyesight, *that* contents him
    not,
But, with the plaything at arm's length,
    he sets
His front against the blast, and runs
    amain,
That it may whirl the faster.
                        Amid the depth
Of those enormities, even thinking minds
Forgot, at seasons, whence they had their
    being;   376
Forgot that such a sound was ever heard
As Liberty upon earth: yet all beneath
Her innocent authority was wrought,
Nor could have been, without her blessèd
    name.   380
The illustrious wife of Roland, in the
    hour
Of her composure, felt that agony,
And gave it vent in her last words. O
    Friend!
It was a lamentable time for man,
Whether a hope had e'er been his or not;
A woeful time for them whose hopes
    survived   386
The shock; most woeful for those few
    who still
Were flattered, and had trust in human
    kind:
They had the deepest feeling of the grief.
Meanwhile the Invaders fared as they
    deserved: 390
The Herculean Commonwealth had put
    forth her arms,
And throttled with an infant godhead's
    might

The snakes about her cradle; that was
  well,
And as it should be; yet no cure for them
Whose souls were sick with pain of what
  would be   395
Hereafter brought in charge against man-
  kind.
Most melancholy at that time, O Friend!
Were my day-thoughts,—my nights were
  miserable;
Through months, through years, long
  after the last beat
Of those atrocities, the hour of sleep   400
To me came rarely charged with natural
  gifts,
Such ghastly visions had I of despair
And tyranny, and implements of death;
And innocent victims sinking under fear,
And momentary hope, and worn-out
  prayer,   405
Each in his separate cell, or penned in
  crowds
For sacrifice, and struggling with forced
  mirth
And levity in dungeons, where the dust
Was laid with tears. Then suddenly the
  scene
Changed, and the unbroken dream en-
  tangled me   410
In long orations, which I strove to plead
Before unjust tribunals,—with a voice
Labouring, a brain confounded, and a
  sense,
Death-like, of treacherous desertion, felt
In the last place of refuge—my own soul.

When I began in youth's delightful
  prime   416
To yield myself to Nature, when that
  strong
And holy passion overcame me first,
Nor day nor night, evening or morn, was
  free
From its oppression. But, O Power
  Supreme!   420
Without Whose care this world would
  cease to breathe,
Who from the Fountain of Thy grace dost
  fill
The veins that branch through every
  frame of life,
Making man what he is, creature divine,
In single or in social eminence,   425
Above the rest raised infinite ascents
When reason that enables him to be
Is not sequestered—what a change is
  here!
How different ritual for this after-worship,
What countenance to promote this second
  love!   430
The first was service paid to things which
  lie
Guarded within the bosom of Thy will.
Therefore to serve was high beatitude;

Tumult was therefore gladness, and the
  fear
Ennobling, venerable; sleep secure,   435
And waking thoughts more rich than
  happiest dreams.

But as the ancient Prophets, borne
  aloft
In vision, yet constrained by natural laws
With them to take a troubled human
  heart,
Wanted not consolations, nor a creed 440
Of reconcilement, then when they de-
  nounced,
On towns and cities, wallowing in the
  abyss
Of their offences, punishment to come;
Or saw, like other men, with bodily eyes,
Before them, in some desolated place, 445
The wrath consummate and the threat
  fulfilled;
So, with devout humility be it said,
So, did a portion of that spirit fall
On me uplifted from the vantage-ground
Of pity and sorrow to a state of being
That through the time's exceeding fierce-
  ness saw   451
Glimpses of retribution, terrible,
And in the order of sublime behests:
But, even if that were not, amid the awe
Of unintelligible chastisement,   455
Not only acquiescences of faith
Survived, but daring sympathies with
  power,
Motions not treacherous or profane, else
  why
Within the folds of no ungentle breast
Their dread vibration to this hour pro-
  longed?   460
Wild blasts of music thus could find their
  way
Into the midst of turbulent events;
So that worst tempests might be listened
  to.
Then was the truth received into my
  heart,
That, under heaviest sorrow earth can
  bring,   465
If from the affliction somewhere do not
  grow
Honour which could not else have been,
  a faith,
An elevation, and a sanctity,
If new strength be not given nor old
  restored,
The blame is ours, not Nature's. When
  a taunt   470
Was taken up by scoffers in their pride,
Saying, 'Behold the harvest that we reap
From popular government and equality,'
I clearly saw that neither these nor aught
Of wild belief engrafted on their names
By false philosophy had caused the woe,
But a terrific reservoir of guilt   477

And ignorance filled up from age to age,
That could no longer hold its loathsome
    charge,
But burst and spread in deluge through
    the land.   480

    And as the desert hath green spots, the
        sea
Small islands scattered amid stormy waves
So *that* disastrous period did not want
Bright sprinklings of all human excellence,
To which the silver wands of saints in
    Heaven   485
Might point with rapturous joy. Yet not
    the less,
For those examples, in no age surpassed,
Of fortitude and energy and love,
And human nature faithful to herself
Under worst trials, was I driven to think
Of the glad times when first I traversed
    France   491
A youthful pilgrim; above all reviewed
That eventide, when under windows bright
With happy faces and with garlands hung,
And through a rainbow-arch that spanned
    the street,   495
Triumphal pomp for liberty confirmed,
I paced, a dear companion at my side,
The town of Arras, whence with promise
    high
Issued, on delegation to sustain
Humanity and right, *that* Robespierre, 500
He who thereafter, and in how short time!
Wielded the sceptre of the Atheist crew.
When the calamity spread far and wide—
And this same city, that did then appear
To outrun the rest in exultation, groaned
Under the vengeance of her cruel son, 506
As Lear reproached the winds—I could
    almost
Have quarrelled with that blameless
    spectacle
For lingering yet an image in my mind
To mock me under such a strange re-
    verse.   510

    O Friend! few happier moments have
        been mine
Than that which told the downfall of this
    Tribe
So dreaded, so abhorred. The day de-
    serves
A separate record. Over the smooth sands
Of Leven's ample estuary lay   515
My journey, and beneath a genial sun,
With distant prospect among gleams of sky
And clouds, and intermingling mountain-
    tops,
In one inseparable glory clad,
Creatures of one ethereal substance met
In consistory, like a diadem   521
Or crown of burning seraphs as they sit
In the empyrean. Underneath that pomp
Celestial, lay unseen the pastoral vales

Among whose happy fields I had grown
    up   525
From childhood. On the fulgent spec-
    tacle,
That neither passed away nor changed, I
    gazed
Enrapt; but brightest things are wont to
    draw
Sad opposites out of the inner heart,
As even their pensive influence drew from
    mine.   530
How could it otherwise? for not in vain
That very morning had I turned aside
To seek the ground where, 'mid a throng
    of graves,
An honoured teacher of my youth was
    laid,
And on the stone were graven by his
    desire   535
Lines from the churchyard elegy of Gray.
This faithful guide, speaking from his
    death-bed,
Added no farewell to his parting counsel,
But said to me, 'My head will soon lie
    low;'
And when I saw the turf that covered
    him,   540
After the lapse of full eight years, those
    words,
With sound of voice and countenance of
    the Man,
Came back upon me, so that some few
    tears
Fell from me in my own despite. But
    now
I thought, still traversing that widespread
    plain,   545
With tender pleasure of the verses graven
Upon his tombstone, whispering to my-
    self:
He loved the Poets, and, if now alive,
Would have loved me, as one not desti-
    tute
Of promise, nor belying the kind hope
That he had formed, when I, at his com-
    mand,   551
Began to spin, with toil, my earliest
    songs.

    As I advanced, all that I saw or felt
Was gentleness and peace. Upon a small
And rocky island near, a fragment stood
(Itself like a sea rock) the low remains 556
(With shells encrusted, dark with briny
    weeds)
Of a dilapidated structure, once
A Romish chapel, where the vested priest
Said matins at the hour that suited those
Who crossed the sands with ebb of morn-
    ing tide.   561
Not far from that still ruin all the plain
Lay spotted with a variegated crowd
Of vehicles and travellers, horse and
    foot,

Wading beneath the conduct of their
   guide   565
In loose procession through the shallow
   stream
Of inland waters; the great sea meanwhile
Heaved at safe distance, far retired. I
   paused,
Longing for skill to paint a scene so bright
And cheerful, but the foremost of the
   band   570
As he approached, no salutation given
In the familiar language of the day,
Cried, 'Robespierre is dead!'—nor was
   a doubt,
After strict question, left within my mind
That he and his supporters all were
   fallen.   575

   Great was my transport, deep my
     gratitude
To everlasting Justice, by this fiat
Made manifest. 'Come now, ye golden
   times,'
Said I forth-pouring on those open sands
A hymn of triumph: 'as the morning
   comes   580
From out the bosom of the night, come ye:
Thus far our trust is verified; behold!
They who with clumsy desperation
   brought
A river of Blood, and preached that
   nothing else

Could cleanse the Augean stable, by the
   might   585
Of their own helper have been swept
   away;
Their madness stands declared and
   visible;
Elsewhere will safety now be sought, and
   earth
March firmly towards righteousness and
   peace.'—
Then schemes I framed more calmly,
   when and how   590
The madding factions might be tran-
   quillised,
And how through hardships manifold and
   long
The glorious renovation would proceed.
Thus interrupted by uneasy bursts
Of exultation, I pursued my way   595
Along that very shore which I had
   skimmed
In former days, when—spurring from the
   Vale
Of Nightshade, and St. Mary's moulder-
   ing fane,
And the stone abbot, after circuit made
In wantonness of heart, a joyous band
Of schoolboys hastening to their distant
   home   601
Along the margin of the moonlight sea—
We beat with thundering hoofs the level
   sand.

BOOK ELEVENTH

FRANCE—(CONCLUDED)

FROM that time forth, Authority in France
Put on a milder face; Terror had ceased,
Yet everything was wanting that might
   give
Courage to them who looked for good by
   light
Of rational Experience, for the shoots 5
And hopeful blossoms of a second spring:
Yet, in me, confidence was unimpaired;
The Senate's language, and the public acts
And measures of the Government, though
   both
Weak, and of heartless omen, had not
   power   10
To daunt me; in the People was my trust,
And in the virtues which mine eyes had
   seen.
I knew that wound external could not
   take
Life from the young Republic; that new
   foes
Would only follow, in the path of shame,
Their brethren, and her triumphs be in
   the end   16
Great, universal, irresistible.

This intuition led me to confound
One victory with another, higher far,—
Triumphs of unambitious peace at home,
And noiseless fortitude. Beholding still
Resistance strong as heretofore, I thought
That what was in degree the same was
   likewise
The same in quality,—that, as the worse
Of the two spirits then at strife remained
Untired, the better, surely, would pre-
   serve   26
The heart that first had roused him.
   Youth maintains,
In all conditions of society,
Communion more direct and intimate
With Nature,—hence, ofttimes, with
   reason too—   30
Than age or manhood, even. To Nature,
   then,
Power had reverted: habit, custom, law,
Had left an interregnum's open space
For *her* to move about in, uncontrolled.
Hence could I see how Babel-like their
   task,   35
Who, by the recent deluge stupefied,

With their whole souls went culling from the day
Its petty promises, to build a tower
For their own safety; laughed with my compeers
At gravest heads, by enmity to France
Distempered, till they found, in every blast   41
Forced from the street-disturbing newsman's horn,
For her great cause record or prophecy
Of utter ruin. How might we believe
That wisdom could, in any shape, come near   45
Men clinging to delusions so insane?
And thus, experience proving that no few
Of our opinions had been just, we took
Like credit to ourselves where less was due,
And thought that other notions were as sound,   50
Yea, could not but be right, because we saw
That foolish men opposed them.
                          To a strain
More animated I might here give way,
And tell, since juvenile errors are my theme,
What in those days through Britain was performed   55
To turn *all* judgments out of their right course;
But this is passion over-near ourselves,
Reality too close and too intense,
And intermixed with something, in my mind,
Of scorn and condemnation personal, 60
That would profane the sanctity of verse.
Our Shepherds, this say merely, at that time
Acted, or seemed at least to act, like men
Thirsting to make the guardian crook of law
A tool of murder; they who ruled the State,—   65
Though with such awful proof before their eyes
That he, who would sow death, reaps death, or worse,
And can reap nothing better,—child-like longed
To imitate, not wise enough to avoid;
Or left (by mere timidity betrayed) 70
The plain straight road, for one no better chosen
Than if their wish had been to undermine
Justice, and make an end of Liberty.

But from these bitter truths I must return
To my own history. It hath been told 75
That I was led to take an eager part
In arguments of civil polity,
Abruptly, and indeed before my time:

I had approached, like other youths, the shield
Of human nature from the golden side,
And would have fought, even to the death, to attest   81
The quality of the metal which I saw.
What there is best in individual man,
Of wise in passion, and sublime in power,
Benevolent in small societies,   85
And great in large ones, I had oft revolved,
Felt deeply, but not thoroughly understood
By reason: nay, far from it; they were yet,
As cause was given me afterwards to learn,
Not proof against the injuries of the day;   90
Lodged only at the sanctuary's door,
Not safe within its bosom. Thus prepared,
And with such general insight into evil,
And of the bounds which sever it from good,
As books and common intercourse with life   95
Must needs have given—to the inexperienced mind,
When the world travels in a beaten road,
Guide faithful as is needed—I began
To meditate with ardour on the rule
And management of nations; what it is
And ought to be; and strove to learn how far   101
Their power or weakness, wealth or poverty,
Their happiness or misery, depends
Upon their laws, and fashion of the State.

O pleasant exercise of hope and joy![1]
For mighty were the auxiliars which then stood   106
Upon our side, us who were strong in love!
Bliss was it in that dawn to be alive,
But to be young was very Heaven! O times,
In which the meagre, stale, forbidding ways   110
Of custom, law, and statute, took at once
The attraction of a country in romance!
When Reason seemed the most to assert her rights
When most intent on making of herself
A prime enchantress—to assist the work,
Which then was going forward in her name!   116
Not favoured spots alone, but the whole Earth,
The beauty wore of promise—that which sets
(As at some moments might not be unfelt
Among the bowers of Paradise itself) 120
                    [1] See page 165.—ED.

The budding rose above the rose full
  blown.
What temper at the prospect did not wake
To happiness unthought of? The inert
Were roused, and lively natures rapt
  away!
They who had fed their childhood upon
  dreams,   125
The play-fellows of fancy, who had made
All powers of swiftness, subtilty, and
  strength
Their ministers,—who in lordly wise had
  stirred
Among the grandest objects of the sense,
And dealt with whatsoever they found
  there   130
As if they had within some lurking right
To wield it;—they, too, who of gentle
  mood
Had watched all gentle motions, and to
  these
Had fitted their own thoughts, schemers
  more mild,
And in the region of their peaceful
  selves;—   135
Now was it that *both* found, the meek
  and lofty
Did both find, helpers to their hearts'
  desire,
And stuff at hand, plastic as they could
  wish,—
Were called upon to exercise their skill,
Not in Utopia,—subterranean fields,—
Or some secreted island, Heaven knows
  where!   141
But in the very world, which is the world
Of all of us,—the place where, in the end,
We find our happiness, or not at all!

Why should I not confess that Earth
  was then   145
To me, what an inheritance, new-fallen,
Seems, when the first time visited, to one
Who thither comes to find in it his home?
He walks about and looks upon the spot
With cordial transport, moulds it and
  remoulds,   150
And is half pleased with things that are
  amiss,
'Twill be such joy to see them disappear.

An active partisan, I thus convoked
From every object pleasant circumstance
To suit my ends; I moved among man-
  kind   155
With genial feelings still predominant;
When erring, erring on the better part,
And in the kinder spirit; placable,
Indulgent, as not uninformed that men
See as they have been taught—Antiquity
Gives rights to error; and aware, no less,
That throwing off oppression must be
  work
As well of License as of Liberty;

And above all—for this was more than
  all—   164
Not caring if the wind did now and then
Blow keen upon an eminence that gave
Prospect so large into futurity;
In brief, a child of Nature, as at first,
Diffusing only those affections wider
That from the cradle had grown up with
  me,   170
And losing, in no other way than light
Is lost in light, the weak in the more
  strong.

In the main outline, such it might be
  said
Was my condition, till with open war
Britain opposed the liberties of France.
This threw me first out of the pale of
  love;   176
Soured and corrupted, upwards to the
  source,
My sentiments; was not, as hitherto,
A swallowing up of lesser things in great,
But change of them into their contraries;
And thus a way was opened for mis-
  takes   181
And false conclusions, in degree as gross,
In kind more dangerous. What had been
  a pride,
Was now a shame; my likings and my
  loves
Ran in new channels, leaving old ones
  dry;   185
And hence a blow that, in maturer age,
Would but have touched the judgment,
  struck more deep
Into sensations near the heart: mean-
  time,
As from the first, wild theories were
  afloat,
To whose pretensions, sedulously urged,
I had but lent a careless ear, assured   191
That time was ready to set all things
  right,
And that the multitude, so long op-
  pressed,
Would be oppressed no more.
                 But when events
Brought less encouragement, and unto
  these   195
The immediate proof of principles no
  more
Could be entrusted, while the events
  themselves,
Worn out in greatness, stripped of novelty,
Less occupied the mind, and sentiments
Could through my understanding's natural
  growth   200
No longer keep their ground, by faith
  maintained
Of inward consciousness, and hope that
  laid
Her hand upon her object—evidence
Safer, of universal application, such

As could not be impeached, was sought
    elsewhere.   205

But now, become oppressors in their
    turn,
Frenchmen had changed a war of self-
    defence
For one of conquest, losing sight of all
Which they had struggled for: up mounted
    now,   209
Openly in the eye of earth and heaven,
The scale of liberty. I read her doom,
With anger vexed, with disappointment
    sore,
But not dismayed, nor taking to the
    shame
Of a false prophet. While resentment
    rose
Striving to hide, what nought could heal,
    the wounds   215
Of mortified presumption, I adhered
More firmly to old tenets, and, to prove
Their temper, strained them more; and
    thus, in heat
Of contest, did opinions every day
Grow into consequence, till round my
    mind   220
They clung, as if they were its life, nay
    more,
The very being of the immortal soul.

    This was the time, when, all things
        tending fast
To depravation, speculative schemes—
That promised to abstract the hopes of
    Man   225
Out of his feelings, to be fixed thence-
    forth
For ever in a purer element—
Found ready welcome. Tempting region
    that
For Zeal to enter and refresh herself,
Where passions had the privilege to work,
And never hear the sound of their own
    names.   231
But, speaking more in charity, the dream
Flattered the young, pleased with ex-
    tremes, nor least
With that which makes our Reason's
    naked self
The object of its fervour. What delight!
How glorious! in self-knowledge and self-
    rule,   236
To look through all the frailties of the
    world,
And, with a resolute mastery shaking off
Infirmities of nature, time, and place,
Build social upon personal Liberty,   240
Which, to the blind restraints of general
    laws
Superior, magisterially adopts
One guide, the light of circumstances,
    flashed
Upon an independent intellect.

Thus expectation rose again; thus hope,
From her first ground expelled, grew
    proud once more.   246
Oft, as my thoughts were turned to
    human kind,
I scorned indifference; but, inflamed with
    thirst
Of a secure intelligence, and sick   249
Of other longing, I pursued what seemed
A more exalted nature; wished that Man
Should start out of his earthly, worm-like
    state,
And spread abroad the wings of Liberty,
Lord of himself, in undisturbed delight—
A noble aspiration! *yet* I feel   255
(Sustained by worthier as by wiser
    thoughts)
The aspiration, nor shall ever cease
To feel it;—but return we to our course.

    Enough, 'tis true—could such a plea
        excuse
Those aberrations—had the clamorous
    friends   260
Of ancient Institutions said and done
To bring disgrace upon their very names;
Disgrace, of which, custom and written
    law,
And sundry moral sentiments as props
Or emanations of those institutes,   265
Too justly bore a part. A veil had been
Uplifted; why deceive ourselves? in sooth,
'Twas even so; and sorrow for the man
Who either had not eyes wherewith to
    see,
Or, seeing, had forgotten! A strong shock
Was given to old opinions; all men's
    minds   271
Had felt its power, and mine was both let
    loose,
Let loose and goaded. After what hath
    been
Already said of patriotic love,
Suffice it here to add, that, somewhat   275
In temperament, withal a happy man,
And therefore bold to look on painful
    things,
Free likewise of the world, and thence
    more bold,
I summoned my best skill, and toiled,
    intent
To anatomise the frame of social life;
Yea, the whole body of society   281
Searched to its heart. Share with me,
    Friend! the wish
That some dramatic tale, endued with
    shapes
Livelier, and flinging out less guarded
    words
Than suit the work we fashion, might set
    forth   285
What then I learned, or think I learned,
    of truth,

And the errors into which I fell, betrayed
By present objects, and by reasonings
    false
From their beginnings, inasmuch as
    drawn   289
Out of a heart that had been turned aside
From Nature's way by outward accidents,
And which was thus confounded, more
    and more
Misguided, and misguiding. So I fared,
Dragging all precepts, judgments, maxims,
    creeds,   294
Like culprits to the bar; calling the mind,
Suspiciously, to establish in plain day
Her titles and her honours; now believ-
    ing,
Now disbelieving; endlessly perplexed
With impulse, motive, right and wrong,
    the ground   299
Of obligation, what the rule and whence
The sanction; till, demanding formal
    proof,
And seeking it in everything, I lost
All feeling of conviction, and, in fine,
Sick, wearied out with contrarieties,   304
Yielded up moral questions in despair.

    This was the crisis of that strong disease,
This the soul's last and lowest ebb; I
    drooped,
Deeming our blessèd reason of least use
Where wanted most: 'The lordly at-
    tributes   309
Of will and choice,' I bitterly exclaimed,
'What are they but a mockery of a Being
Who hath in no concerns of his a test
Of good and evil; knows not what to fear
Or hope for, what to covet or to shun;
And who, if those could be discerned,
    would yet   315
Be little profited, would see, and ask
Where is the obligation to enforce?
And, to acknowledged law rebellious, still,
As selfish passion urged, would act amiss;
The dupe of folly, or the slave of crime.'

    Depressed, bewildered thus, I did not
    walk   321
With scoffers, seeking light and gay re-
    venge
From indiscriminate laughter, nor sate
    down
In reconcilement with an utter waste
Of intellect; such sloth I could not brook,
(Too well I loved, in that my spring of
    life,   326
Pains-taking thoughts, and truth, their
    dear reward)
But turned to abstract science, and there
    sought
Work for the reasoning faculty enthroned
Where the disturbances of space and
    time—   330
Whether in matter's various properties

Inherent, or from human will and power
Derived—find no admission. Then it
    was—
Thanks to the bounteous Giver of all
    good!—
That the belovèd Sister in whose sight
Those days were passed, now speaking in
    a voice   336
Of sudden admonition—like a brook
That did but *cross* a lonely road, and now
Is seen, heard, felt, and caught at every
    turn,
Companion never lost through many a
    league—   340
Maintained for me a saving intercourse
With my true self; for, though bedimmed
    and changed
Much, as it seemed, I was no further
    changed
Than as a clouded and a waning moon:
She whispered still that brightness would
    return,   345
She, in the midst of all, preserved me still
A Poet, made me seek beneath that name,
And that alone, my office upon earth;
And, lastly, as hereafter will be shown,
If willing audience fail not, Nature's self,
By all varieties of human love   351
Assisted, led me back through opening
    day
To those sweet counsels between head
    and heart
Whence grew that genuine knowledge,
    fraught with peace,
Which, through the later sinkings of this
    cause,   355
Hath still upheld me, and upholds me now
In the catastrophe (for so they dream,
And nothing less), when, finally to close
And seal up all the gains of France, a
    Pope
Is summoned in to crown an Emperor—
This last opprobrium, when we see a
    people,   361
That once looked up in faith, as if to
    Heaven
For manna, take a lesson from the dog
Returning to his vomit; when the sun
That rose in splendour, was alive, and
    moved   365
In exultation with a living pomp
Of clouds—his glory's natural retinue—
Hath dropped all functions by the gods
    bestowed,
And, turned into a gewgaw, a machine,
Sets like an Opera phantom.
                        Thus, O Friend!
Through times of honour and through
    times of shame   371
Descending, have I faithfully retraced
The perturbations of a youthful mind
Under a long-lived storm of great events—
A story destined for thy ear, who now,
Among the fallen of nations, dost abide

Where Etna, over hill and valley, casts
His shadow stretching towards Syracuse,
The city of Timoleon! Righteous Heaven!
How are the mighty prostrated! They
first,   380
They first of all that breathe should have
awaked
When the great voice was heard from out
the tombs
Of ancient heroes. If I suffered grief
For ill-requited France, by many deemed
A trifler only in her proudest day;   385
Have been distressed to think of what
she once
Promised, now is; a far more sober cause
Thine eyes must see of sorrow in a land,
To the reanimating influence lost
Of memory, to virtue lost and hope,   390
Though with the wreck of loftier years
bestrewn.

But indignation works where hope is
not,
And thou, O Friend! wilt be refreshed.
There is
One great society alone on earth:
The noble Living and the noble Dead.   395

Thine be such converse strong and
sanative,
A ladder for thy spirit to reascend
To health and joy and pure contented-
ness;
To me the grief confined, that thou art
gone
From this last spot of earth, where Free-
dom now   400
Stands single in her only sanctuary;
A lonely wanderer art gone, by pain
Compelled and sickness, at this latter day,
This sorrowful reverse for all mankind.
I feel for thee, must utter what I feel: 405
The sympathies erewhile in part dis-
charged,
Gather afresh, and will have vent again:
My own delights do scarcely seem to me
My own delights; the lordly Alps them-
selves,
Those rosy peaks, from which the Morn-
ing looks   410
Abroad on many nations, are no more
For me that image of pure gladsomeness
Which they were wont to be. Through
kindred scenes,
For purpose, at a time, how different!
Thou tak'st thy way, carrying the heart
and soul   415
That Nature gives to Poets, now by
thought
Matured, and in the summer of their
strength.
Oh! wrap him in your shades, ye giant
woods,
On Etna's side; and thou, O flowery field

Of Enna! is there not some nook of thine,
From the first playtime of the infant
world   421
Kept sacred to restorative delight,
When from afar invoked by anxious love?

Child of the mountains, among shep-
herds reared,
Ere yet familiar with the classic page, 425
I learnt to dream of Sicily; and lo,
The gloom, that, but a moment past, was
deepened
At thy command, at her command gives
way;
A pleasant promise, wafted from her
shores,
Comes o'er my heart: in fancy I behold
Her seas yet smiling, her once happy
vales;   431
Nor can my tongue give utterance to a
name
Of note belonging to that honoured isle,
Philosopher or Bard, Empedocles,
Or Archimedes, pure abstracted soul! 435
That doth not yield a solace to my grief:
And, O Theocritus,[1] so far have some
Prevailed among the powers of heaven
and earth,
By their endowments, good or great, that
they
Have had, as thou reportest, miracles
Wrought for them in old time: yea, not
unmoved,   441
When thinking on my own beloved friend,
I hear thee tell how bees with honey fed
Divine Comates, by his impious lord
Within a chest imprisoned; how they
came   445
Laden from blooming grove or flowery
field,
And fed him there, alive, month after
month,
Because the goatherd, blessed man: had
lips
Wet with the Muses' nectar.
                        Thus I soothe
The pensive moments by this calm fire-
side,   450
And find a thousand bounteous images
To cheer the thoughts of those I love, and
mine.
Our prayers have been accepted; thou
wilt stand
On Etna's summit, above earth and sea,
Triumphant, winning from the invaded
heavens   455
Thoughts without bound, magnificent de-
signs,
Worthy of poets who attuned their harps
In wood or echoing cave, for discipline
Of heroes; or, in reverence to the gods,
'Mid temples, served by sapient priests,
and choirs   460
    [1] *Theocrit. Idyll.* vii. 78.—ED.

Of virgins crowned with roses. Not in
vain
Those temples, where they in their ruins
yet
Survive for inspiration, shall attract
Thy solitary steps: and on the brink 464
Thou wilt recline of pastoral Arethuse;

Or, if that fountain be in truth no more,
Then, near some other spring—which by
the name
Thou gratulatest, willingly deceived—
I see thee linger a glad votary,   469
And not a captive pining for his home.

BOOK TWELFTH

IMAGINATION AND TASTE, HOW IMPAIRED AND
RESTORED

LONG time have human ignorance and
guilt
Detained us, on what spectacles of woe
Compelled to look, and inwardly op-
pressed
With sorrow, disappointment, vexing
thoughts,
Confusion of the judgment, zeal decayed,
And, lastly, utter loss of hope itself   6
And things to hope for! Not with these
began
Our song, and not with these our song
must end.—
Ye motions of delight, that haunt the
sides
Of the green hills; ye breezes and soft
airs,   10
Whose subtle intercourse with breathing
flowers,
Feelingly watched, might teach Man's
haughty race
How without injury to take, to give
Without offence; ye who, as if to show
The wondrous influence of power gently
used,   15
Bend the complying heads of lordly pines,
And, with a touch, shift the stupendous
clouds
Through the whole compass of the sky;
ye brooks,
Muttering along the stones, a busy noise
By day, a quiet sound in silent night; 20
Ye waves, that out of the great deep steal
forth
In a calm hour to kiss the pebbly shore,
Not mute, and then retire, fearing no
storm;
And you, ye groves, whose ministry it is
To interpose the covert of your shades, 25
Even as a sleep, between the heart of man
And outward troubles, between man him-
self,
Not seldom, and his own uneasy heart:
Oh! that I had a music and a voice
Harmonious as your own, that I might
tell   30
What ye have done for me. The morning
shines,

Nor heedeth Man's perverseness; Spring
returns,—
I saw the Spring return, and could rejoice,
In common with the children of her love,
Piping on boughs, or sporting on fresh
fields,   35
Or boldly seeking pleasure nearer heaven
On wings that navigate cerulean skies.
So neither were complacency, nor peace,
Nor tender yearnings, wanting for my
good
Through these distracted times; in
Nature still   40
Glorying, I found a counterpoise in her,
Which, when the spirit of evil reached its
height,
Maintained for me a secret happiness.

This narrative, my Friend! hath chiefly
told
Of intellectual power, fostering love, 45
Dispensing truth, and, over men and
things,
Where reason yet might hesitate, diffusing
Prophetic sympathies of genial faith:
So was I favoured—such my happy lot—
Until that natural graciousness of mind
Gave way to overpressure from the times
And their disastrous issues. What availed,
When spells forbade the voyager to land,
That fragrant notice of a pleasant shore
Wafted, at intervals, from many a bower
Of blissful gratitude and fearless love? 56
Dare I avow that wish was mine to see,
And hope that future times *would* surely
see,
The man to come, parted, as by a gulph,
From him who had been; that I could no
more   60
Trust the elevation which had made me
one
With the great family that still survives
To illuminate the abyss of ages past,
Sage, warrior, patriot, hero; for it seemed
That their best virtues were not free from
taint   65
Of something false and weak, that could
not stand

575

THE PRELUDE [BOOK XII]

The open eye of Reason. Then I said,
'Go to the Poets, they will speak to thee
More perfectly of purer creatures;—yet
If reason be nobility in man,   70
Can aught be more ignoble than the man
Whom they delight in, blinded as he is
By prejudice, the miserable slave
Of low ambition or distempered love?'

In such strange passion, if I may once
more   75
Review the past, I warred against my-
self—
A bigot to a new idolatry—
Like a cowled monk who hath forsworn
the world,
Zealously laboured to cut off my heart
From all the sources of her former
strength;   80
And as, by simple waving of a wand,
The wizard instantaneously dissolves
Palace or grove, even so could I unsoul
As readily by syllogistic words
Those mysteries of being which have
made,   85
And shall continue evermore to make
Of the whole human race one brother-
hood.

What wonder, then, if, to a mind so far
Perverted, even the visible Universe
Fell under the dominion of a taste   90
Less spiritual, with microscopic view
Was scanned, as I had scanned the moral
world?

O Soul of Nature! excellent and fair!
That didst rejoice with me, with whom I,
too,
Rejoiced through early youth, before the
winds   95
And roaring waters, and in lights and
shades
That marched and countermarched about
the hills
In glorious apparition, Powers on whom
I daily waited, now all eye and now   99
All ear; but never long without the heart
Employed, and man's unfolding intellect:
O Soul of Nature! that, by laws divine
Sustained and governed, still dost over-
flow
With an impassioned life, what feeble
ones
Walk on this earth! how feeble have I
been   105
When thou wert in thy strength! Nor
this through stroke
Of human suffering, such as justifies
Remissness and inaptitude of mind,
But through presumption; even in plea-
sure pleased   109
Unworthily, disliking here, and there
Liking; by rules of mimic art transferred

To things above all art; but more,—for
this,
Although a strong infection of the age,
Was never much my habit—giving way
To a comparison of scene with scene,   115
Bent overmuch on superficial things,
Pampering myself with meagre novelties
Of colour and proportion; to the moods
Of time and season, to the moral power,
The affections and the spirit of the place,
Insensible. Nor only did the love   121
Of sitting thus in judgment interrupt
My deeper feelings, but another cause,
More subtle and less easily explained,
That almost seems inherent in the crea-
ture,   125
A twofold frame of body and of mind.
I speak in recollection of a time
When the bodily eye, in every stage of
life
The most despotic of our senses, gained
Such strength in *me* as often held my
mind   130
In absolute dominion. Gladly here,
Entering upon abstruser argument,
Could I endeavour to unfold the means
Which Nature studiously employs to
thwart
This tyranny, summons all the senses
each   135
To counteract the other, and themselves,
And makes them all, and the objects with
which all
Are conversant, subservient in their turn
To the great ends of Liberty and Power.
But leave we this: enough that my
delights   140
(Such as they were) were sought insati-
ably.
Vivid the transport, vivid though not
profound;
I roamed from hill to hill, from rock to
rock,
Still craving combinations of new forms,
New pleasure, wider empire for the sight,
Proud of her own endowments, and re-
joiced   146
To lay the inner faculties asleep.
Amid the turns and counterturns, the
strife
And various trials of our complex being,
As we grow up, such thraldom of that
sense   150
Seems hard to shun. And yet I knew a
maid
A young enthusiast, who escaped these
bonds;
Her eye was not the mistress of her
heart;
Far less did rules prescribed by passive
taste,
Or barren intermeddling subtleties,   155
Perplex her mind; but, wise as women
are

576

When genial circumstance hath favoured
   them,
She welcomed what was given, and craved
   no more;
Whate'er the scene presented to her view
That was the best, to that she was attuned
By her benign simplicity of life,   161
And through a perfect happiness of soul,
Whose variegated feelings were in this
Sisters, that they were each some new
   delight.
Birds in the bower, and lambs in the
   green field,   165
Could they have known her, would have
   loved; methought
Her very presence such a sweetness
   breathed,
That flowers, and trees, and even the
   silent hills,
And everything she looked on, should
   have had
An intimation how she bore herself   170
Towards them and to all creatures. God
   delights
In such a being; for, her common thoughts
Are piety, her life is gratitude.

   Even like this maid, before I was called
   forth   174
From the retirement of my native hills,
I loved whate'er I saw: nor lightly loved,
But most intensely; never dreamt of
   aught
More grand, more fair, more exquisitely
   framed
Than those few nooks to which my happy
   feet
Were limited. I had not at that time
Lived long enough, nor in the least sur-
   vived   181
The first diviner influence of this world,
As it appears to unaccustomed eyes.
Worshipping then among the depth of
   things,
As piety ordained; could I submit   185
To measured admiration, or to aught
That should preclude humility and love?
I felt, observed, and pondered; did not
   judge,
Yea, never thought of judging; with the
   gift
Of all this glory filled and satisfied.   190
And afterwards, when through the gor-
   geous Alps
Roaming, I carried with me the same
   heart:
In truth, the degradation—howsoe'er
Induced, effect, in whatsoe'er degree,
Of custom that prepares a partial scale
In which the little oft outweighs the
   great;   196
Or any other cause that hath been
   named;
Or lastly, aggravated by the times

And their impassioned sounds, which
   well might make   199
The milder minstrelsies of rural scenes
Inaudible—was transient; I had known
Too forcibly, too early in my life,
Visitings of imaginative power
For this to last: I shook the habit off
Entirely and for ever, and again   205
In Nature's presence stood, as now I
   stand,
A sensitive being, a *creative* soul.

   There are in our existence spots of time,
That with distinct pre-eminence retain
A renovating virtue, whence, depressed
By false opinion and contentious thought,
Or aught of heavier or more deadly
   weight,
In trivial occupations, and the round
Of ordinary intercourse, our minds   214
Are nourished and invisibly repaired;
A virtue, by which pleasure is enhanced,
That penetrates, enables us to mount,
When high, more high, and lifts us up
   when fallen.
This efficacious spirit chiefly lurks
Among those passages of life that give
Profoundest knowledge to what point,
   and how,   221
The mind is lord and master—outward
   sense
The obedient servant of her will. Such
   moments
Are scattered everywhere, taking their
   date
From our first childhood. I remember
   well,   225
That once, while yet my inexperienced
   hand
Could scarcely hold a bridle, with proud
   hopes
I mounted, and we journeyed towards
   the hills:
An ancient servant of my father's house
Was with me, my encourager and guide:
We had not travelled long, ere some mis-
   chance   231
Disjoined me from my comrade; and,
   through fear
Dismounting, down the rough and stony
   moor
I led my horse, and, stumbling on, at
   length
Came to a bottom, where in former times
A murderer had been hung in iron chains.
The gibbet-mast had mouldered down,
   the bones   237
And iron case were gone; but on the
   turf,
Hard by, soon after that fell deed was
   wrought,
Some unknown hand had carved the
   murderer's name.   240
The monumental letters were inscribed

In times long past; but still, from year to year,
By superstition of the neighbourhood,
The grass is cleared away, and to this hour
The characters are fresh and visible: 245
A casual glance had shown them, and I fled,
Faltering and faint, and ignorant of the road:
Then, reascending the bare common, saw
A naked pool that lay beneath the hills,
The beacon on the summit, and, more near,   250
A girl, who bore a pitcher on her head,
And seemed with difficult steps to force her way
Against the blowing wind. It was, in truth,
An ordinary sight; but I should need
Colours and words that are unknown to man,   255
To paint the visionary dreariness
Which, while I looked all round for my lost guide,
Invested moorland waste, and naked pool,
The beacon crowning the lone eminence,
The female and her garments vexed and tossed   260
By the strong wind. When, in the blessèd hours
Of early love, the loved one at my side,
I roamed, in daily presence of this scene,
Upon the naked pool and dreary crags,
And on the melancholy beacon, fell 265
A spirit of pleasure and youth's golden gleam;
And think ye not with radiance more sublime
For these remembrances, and for the power
They had left behind? So feeling comes in aid
Of feeling, and diversity of strength 270
Attends us, if but once we have been strong.
Oh! mystery of man, from what a depth
Proceed thy honours. I am lost, but see
In simple childhood something of the base
On which thy greatness stands; but this I feel,   275
That from thyself it comes, that thou must give,
Else never canst receive. The days gone by
Return upon me almost from the dawn
Of life: the hiding-places of man's power
Open; I would approach them, but they close.   280
I see by glimpses now; when age comes on,
May scarcely see at all; and I would give,
While yet we may, as far as words can give,

Substance and life to what I feel, enshrining,
Such is my hope, the spirit of the Past
For future restoration.—Yet another 286
Of these memorials:—
                    One Christmas-time,
On the glad eve of its dear holidays,
Feverish, and tired, and restless, I went forth
Into the fields, impatient for the sight
Of those led palfreys that should bear us home;   291
My brothers and myself. There rose a crag,
That, from the meeting-point of two highways
Ascending, overlooked them both, far stretched;
Thither, uncertain on which road to fix
My expectation, thither I repaired, 296
Scout-like, and gained the summit; 'twas a day
Tempestuous, dark, and wild, and on the grass
I sate half-sheltered by a naked wall;
Upon my right hand crouched a single sheep,   300
Upon my left a blasted hawthorn stood;
With those companions at my side, I watched,
Straining my eyes intensely, as the mist
Gave intermitting prospect of the copse
And plain beneath. Ere we to school returned,—   305
That dreary time,—ere we had been ten days
Sojourners in my father's house, he died,
And I and my three brothers, orphans then,
Followed his body to the grave. The event,
With all the sorrow that it brought, appeared   310
A chastisement; and when I called to mind
That day so lately past, when from the crag
I looked in such anxiety of hope;
With trite reflections of morality, 314
Yet in the deepest passion, I bowed low
To God, Who thus corrected my desires;
And, afterwards, the wind and sleety rain,
And all the business of the elements,
The single sheep, and the one blasted tree,
And the bleak music from that old stone wall,   320
The noise of wood and water, and the mist
That on the line of each of those two roads
Advanced in such indisputable shapes;
All these were kindred spectacles and sounds
To which I oft repaired, and thence would drink,   325

As at a fountain; and on winter nights,
Down to this very time, when storm and
    rain
Beat on my roof, or, haply, at noon
    day,
While in a grove I walk, whose lofty trees,
Laden with summer's thickest foliage,
    rock   330

In a strong wind, some working of the
    spirit,
Some inward agitations thence are
    brought,
Whate'er their office, whether to beguile
Thoughts over busy in the course they
    took,
Or animate an hour of vacant ease.   335

BOOK THIRTEENTH

IMAGINATION AND TASTE, HOW IMPAIRED AND RESTORED.—(CONCLUDED).

FROM Nature doth emotion come, and
    moods
Of calmness equally are Nature's gift:
This is her glory; these two attributes
Are sister horns that constitute her
    strength.
Hence Genius, born to thrive by inter-
    change   5
Of peace and excitation, finds in her
His best and purest friend; from her
    receives
That energy by which he seeks the truth,
From her that happy stillness of the mind
Which fits him to receive it when un-
    sought.   10

    Such benefit the humblest intellects
Partake of, each in their degree; 'tis mine
To speak, what I myself have known and
    felt;
Smooth task! for words find easy way,
    inspired
By gratitude, and confidence in truth. 15
Long time in search of knowledge did I
    range
The field of human life, in heart and mind
Benighted; but, the dawn beginning now
To re-appear, 'twas proved that not in
    vain
I had been taught to reverence a Power
That is the visible quality and shape 21
And image of right reason; that matures
Her processes by steadfast laws; gives
    birth
To no impatient or fallacious hopes,
No heat of passion or excessive zeal, 25
No vain conceits; provokes to no quick
    turns
Of self-applauding intellect; but trains
To meekness, and exalts by humble faith;
Holds up before the mind intoxicate 29
With present objects, and the busy dance
Of things that pass away, a temperate
    show
Of objects that endure; and by this course
Disposes her, when over-fondly set
On throwing off incumbrances, to seek
In man, and in the frame of social life, 35

Whate'er there is desirable and good
Of kindred permanence, unchanged in
    form
And function, or, through strict vicissi-
    tude
Of life and death, revolving. Above all
Were re-established now those watchful
    thoughts   40
Which, seeing little worthy or sublime
In what the Historian's pen so much de-
    lights
To blazon—power and energy detached
From moral purpose—early tutored me
To look with feelings of fraternal love 45
Upon the unassuming things that hold
A silent station in this beauteous world.

    Thus moderated, thus composed, I
    found
Once more in Man an object of delight,
Of pure imagination, and of love; 50
And, as the horizon of my mind enlarged,
Again I took the intellectual eye
For my instructor, studious more to see
Great truths, than touch and handle
    little ones.
Knowledge was given accordingly; my
    trust   55
Became more firm in feelings that had
    stood
The test of such a trial; clearer far
My sense of excellence—of right and
    wrong:
The promise of the present time retired
Into its true proportion; sanguine schemes,
Ambitious projects, pleased me less; I
    sought   61
For present good in life's familiar face,
And built thereon my hopes of good to
    come.

    With settling judgments now of what
    would last
And what would disappear; prepared to
    find   65
Presumption, folly, madness, in the men
Who thrust themselves upon the passive
    world

As Rulers of the world; to see in these,
Even when the public welfare is their
    aim,
Plans without thought, or built on theories
Vague and unsound; and having brought
    the books   71
Of modern statists to their proper test,
Life, human life, with all its sacred claims
Of sex and age, and heaven-descended
    rights,
Mortal, or those beyond the reach of
    death;   75
And having thus discerned how dire a
    thing
Is worshipped in that idol proudly named
'The Wealth of Nations,' *where* alone
    that wealth
Is lodged, and how increased; and having
    gained
A more judicious knowledge of the worth
And dignity of individual man,   81
No composition of the brain, but man
Of whom we read, the man whom we be-
    hold
With our own eyes—I could not but
    enquire—
Not with less interest than heretofore, 85
But greater, though in spirit more sub-
    dued—
Why is this glorious creature to be found
One only in ten thousand? What one is,
Why may not millions be? What bars
    are thrown
By Nature in the way of such a hope? 90
Our animal appetites and daily wants,
Are these obstructions insurmountable?
If not, then others vanish into air.
'Inspect the basis of the social pile:
Enquire,' said I, 'how much of mental
    power   95
And genuine virtue they possess who live
By bodily toil, labour exceeding far
Their due proportion, under all the weight
Of that injustice which upon ourselves
Ourselves entail.' Such estimate to frame
I chiefly looked (what need to look
    beyond?)   101
Among the natural abodes of men,
Fields with their rural works; recalled to
    mind
My earliest notices; with these compared
The observations made in later youth,
And to that day continued.—For, the
    time   106
Had never been when throes of mighty
    Nations
And the world's tumult unto me could
    yield,
How far soe'er transported and possessed,
Full measure of content; but still I craved
An intermingling of distinct regards 111
And truths of individual sympathy
Nearer ourselves. Such often might be
    gleaned

From the great City, else it must have
    proved
To me a heart-depressing wilderness; 115
But much was wanting: therefore did I
    turn
To you, ye pathways, and ye lonely roads;
Sought you enriched with everything I
    prized,
With human kindnesses and simple joys.

Oh! next to one dear state of bliss,
    vouchsafed   120
Alas! to few in this untoward world,
The bliss of walking daily in life's prime
Through field or forest with the maid we
    love,
While yet our hearts are young, while yet
    we breathe   124
Nothing but happiness, in some lone nook,
Deep vale, or anywhere, the home of
    both,
From which it would be misery to stir:
Oh! next to such enjoyment of our youth,
In my esteem, next to such dear delight,
Was that of wandering on from day to
    day   130
Where I could meditate in peace, and cull
Knowledge that step by step might lead
    me on
To wisdom; or, as lightsome as a bird
Wafted upon the wind from distant lands,
Sing notes of greeting to strange fields or
    groves,   135
Which lacked not voice to welcome me in
    turn:
And, when that pleasant toil had ceased
    to please,
Converse with men, where if we meet a
    face
We almost meet a friend, on naked heaths
With long long ways before, by cottage
    bench,   140
Or well-spring where the weary traveller
    rests.

Who doth not love to follow with his eye
The windings of a public way? the sight,
Familiar object as it is, hath wrought
On my imagination since the morn 145
Of childhood, when a disappearing line,
One daily present to my eyes, that crossed
The naked summit of a far-off hill
Beyond the limits that my feet had trod,
Was like an invitation into space 150
Boundless, or guide into eternity.
Yes, something of the grandeur which
    invests
The mariner who sails the roaring sea
Through storm and darkness, early in my
    mind
Surrounded, too, the wanderers of the
    earth;   155
Grandeur as much, and loveliness far
    more.

Awed have I been by strolling Bedlam-
ites;
From many other uncouth vagrants
(passed
In fear) have walked with quicker step;
but why
Take note of this? When I began to
enquire,   160
To watch and question those I met, and
speak
Without reserve to them, the lonely roads
Were open schools in which I daily read
With most delight the passions of man-
kind,
Whether by words, looks, sighs, or tears,
revealed;   165
There saw into the depth of human souls,
Souls that appear to have no depth at all
To careless eyes. And—now convinced
at heart
How little those formalities, to which
With overweening trust alone we give
The name of Education, have to do   171
With real feeling and just sense; how vain
A correspondence with the talking world
Proves to the most; and called to make
good search
If man's estate, by doom of Nature yoked
With toil, be therefore yoked with igno-
rance;   176
If virtue be indeed so hard to rear,
And intellectual strength so rare a boon—
I prized such walks still more, for there
I found
Hope to my hope, and to my pleasure
peace   180
And steadiness, and healing and repose.
To every angry passion. There I heard,
From mouths of men obscure and lowly,
truths
Replete with honour; sounds in unison
With loftiest promises of good and fair.

There are who think that strong
affection, love   186
Known by whatever name, is falsely
deemed
A gift, to use a term which they would
use,
Of vulgar nature; that its growth requires
Retirement, leisure, language purified
By manners studied and elaborate;   191
That whoso feels such passion in its
strength
Must live within the very light and air
Of courteous usages refined by art.
True is it, where oppression worse than
death   195
Salutes the being at his birth, where grace
Of culture hath been utterly unknown,
And poverty and labour in excess
From day to day pre-occupy the ground
Of the affections, and to Nature's self   200
Oppose a deeper nature; there, indeed,

Love cannot be; nor does it thrive with
ease
Among the close and overcrowded haunts
Of cities, where the human heart is sick,
And the eye feeds it not, and cannot
feed.   205
—Yes, in those wanderings deeply did
I feel
How we mislead each other; above all,
How books mislead us, seeking their
reward
From judgments of the wealthy Few,
who see
By artificial lights; how they debase   210
The Many for the pleasure of those Few;
Effeminately level down the truth
To certain general notions, for the sake
Of being understood at once, or else
Through want of better knowledge in the
heads   215
That framed them; flattering self-conceit
with words,
That, while they most ambitiously set
forth
Extrinsic differences, the outward marks
Whereby society has parted man
From man, neglect the universal heart.

Here, calling up to mind what then I
saw,   221
A youthful traveller, and see daily now
In the familiar circuit of my home,
Here might I pause, and bend in reverence
To Nature, and the power of human
minds,   225
To men as they are men within them-
selves.
How oft high service is performed within,
When all the external man is rude in
show,—
Not like a temple rich with pomp and
gold,
But a mere mountain-chapel, that pro-
tects   230
Its simple worshippers from sun and
shower.
Of these, said I, shall be my song; of
these,
If future years mature me for the task,
Will I record the praises, making verse
Deal boldly with substantial things; in
truth   235
And sanctity of passion, speak of these,
That justice may be done, obeisance paid
Where it is due: thus haply shall I teach,
Inspire; through unadulterated ears
Pour rapture, tenderness, and hope,—my
theme   240
No other than the very heart of man,
As found among the best of those who
live—
Not unexalted by religious faith,
Nor uninformed by books, good books,
though few—   244

In Nature's presence: thence may I select
Sorrow, that is not sorrow, but delight;
And miserable love, that is not pain
To hear of, for the glory that redounds
Therefrom to human kind, and what we
    are.
Be mine to follow with no timid step   250
Where knowledge leads me: it shall be
    my pride
That I have dared to tread this holy
    ground,
Speaking no dream, but things oracular;
Matter not lightly to be heard by those
Who to the letter of the outward promise
Do read the invisible soul; by men adroit
In speech, and for communion with the
    world   257
Accomplished; minds whose faculties are
    then
Most active when they are most eloquent,
And elevated most when most admired.
Men may be found of other mould than
    these,   261
Who are their own upholders, to them-
    selves
Encouragement, and energy, and will,
Expressing liveliest thoughts in lively
    words   264
As native passion dictates. Others, too,
There are among the walks of homely life
Still higher, men for contemplation
    framed,
Shy, and unpractised in the strife of
    phrase:
Meek men, whose very souls perhaps
    would sink
Beneath them, summoned to such inter-
    course: 270
Theirs is the language of the heavens, the
    power,
The thought, the image, and the silent joy;
Words are but under-agents in their souls;
When they are grasping with their greatest
    strength,
They do not breathe among them: this
    I speak   275
In gratitude to God, Who feeds our hearts
For His own service; knoweth, loveth us,
When we are unregarded by the world.

Also, about this time did I receive
Convictions still more strong than hereto-
    fore,   280
Not only that the inner frame is good,
And graciously composed, but that, no
    less,
Nature for all conditions wants not
    power
To consecrate, if we have eyes to see,
The outside of her creatures, and to
    breathe   285
Grandeur upon the very humblest face
Of human life. I felt that the array
Of act and circumstance, and visible form,

Is mainly to the pleasure of the mind
What passion makes them; that mean-
    while the forms   290
Of Nature have a passion in themselves,
That intermingles with those works of
    man
To which she summons him; although
    the works
Be mean, have nothing lofty of their own;
And that the Genius of the Poet hence
May boldly take his way among mankind
Wherever Nature leads; that he hath
    stood
By Nature's side among the men of old,
And so shall stand for ever. Dearest
    Friend!
If thou partake the animating faith 300
That Poets, even as Prophets, each with
    each
Connected in a mighty scheme of truth,
Have each his own peculiar faculty,
Heaven's gift, a sense that fits him to
    perceive
Objects unseen before, thou wilt not
    blame   305
The humblest of this band who dares to
    hope
That unto him hath also been vouchsafed
An insight that in some sort he possesses,
A privilege whereby a work of his,
Proceeding from a source of untaught
    things,   310
Creative and enduring, may become
A power like one of Nature's. To a hope
Not less ambitious once among the wilds
Of Sarum's Plain, my youthful spirit was
    raised;
There, as I ranged at will the pastoral
    downs   315
Trackless and smooth, or paced the bare
    white roads
Lengthening in solitude their dreary line,
Time with his retinue of ages fled
Backwards, nor checked his flight until I
    saw
Our dim ancestral Past in vision clear;
Saw multitudes of men, and, here and
    there,   321
A single Briton clothed in wolf-skin vest,
With shield and stone-axe, stride across
    the wold;
The voice of spears was heard, the rattling
    spear
Shaken by arms of mighty bone, in
    strength,   325
Long mouldered, of barbaric majesty.
I called on Darkness—but before the word
Was uttered, midnight darkness seemed
    to take
All objects from my sight; and lo! again
The Desert visible by dismal flames; 330
It is the sacrificial altar, fed
With living men—how deep the groans!
    the voice

Of those that crowd the giant wicker
    thrills
The monumental hillocks, and the pomp
Is for both worlds, the living and the dead.
At other moments—(for through that
    wide waste   336
Three summer days I roamed) where'er
    the Plain
Was figured o'er with circles, lines, or
    mounds,
That yet survive, a work, as some divine,
Shaped by the Druids, so to represent
Their knowledge of the heavens, and
    image forth   341
The constellations—gently was I charmed
Into a waking dream, a reverie
That, with believing eyes, where'er I
    turned,
Beheld long-bearded teachers, with white
    wands   345
Uplifted, pointing to the starry sky,
Alternately, and plain below, while breath
Of music swayed their motions, and the
    waste
Rejoiced with them and me in those sweet
    sounds.

    This for the past, and things that may
    be viewed   350
Or fancied in the obscurity of years
From monumental hints: and thou, O
    Friend!

Pleased with some unpremeditated strains
That served those wanderings to beguile,
    hast said
That then and there my mind had exer-
    cised   355
Upon the vulgar forms of present things,
The actual world of our familiar days,
Yet higher power; had caught from them
    a tone,
An image, and a character, by books
Not hitherto reflected. Call we this   360
A partial judgment—and yet why? for
    then
We were as strangers; and I may not
    speak
Thus wrongfully of verse, however rude,
Which on thy young imagination, trained
In the great City, broke like light from far.
Moreover, each man's Mind is to herself
Witness and judge; and I remember well
That in life's every-day appearances
I seemed about this time to gain clear sight
Of a new world—a world, too, that was fit
To be transmitted, and to other eyes   371
Made visible; as ruled by those fixed laws
Whence spiritual dignity originates,
Which do both give it being and maintain
A balance, an ennobling interchange   375
Of action from without and from within;
The excellence, pure function, and best
    power
Both of the object seen, and eye that sees.

BOOK FOURTEENTH

CONCLUSION

IN one of those excursions (may they ne'er
Fade from remembrance!) through the
    Northern tracts
Of Cambria ranging with a youthful
    friend,
I left Bethgelert's huts at couching-time,
And westward took my way, to see the
    sun   5
Rise, from the top of Snowdon. To the
    door
Of a rude cottage at the mountain's base
We came, and roused the shepherd who
    attends
The adventurous stranger's steps, a trusty
    guide;
Then, cheered by short refreshment, sal-
    lied forth.   10

    It was a close, warm, breezeless summer
    night,
Wan, dull, and glaring, with a dripping
    fog
Low-hung and thick that covered all the
    sky;
But, undiscouraged, we began to climb

The mountain-side. The mist soon girt
    us round,   15
And, after ordinary travellers' talk
With our conductor, pensively we sank
Each into commerce with his private
    thoughts:
Thus did we breast the ascent, and by
    myself
Was nothing either seen or heard that
    checked   20
Those musings or diverted, save that once
The shepherd's lurcher, who, among the
    crags,
Had to his joy unearthed a hedgehog,
    teased
His coiled-up prey with barkings turbu-
    lent.
This small adventure, for even such it
    seemed   25
In that wild place and at the dead of
    night,
Being over and forgotten, on we wound
In silence as before. With forehead bent
Earthward, as if in opposition set
Against an enemy, I panted up   30

With eager pace, and no less eager thoughts.
Thus might we wear a midnight hour away,
Ascending at loose distance each from each,
And I, as chanced, the foremost of the band;
When at my feet the ground appeared to brighten, 35
And with a step or two seemed brighter still;
Nor was time given to ask or learn the cause,
For instantly a light upon the turf
Fell like a flash, and lo! as I looked up,
The Moon hung naked in a firmament 40
Of azure without cloud, and at my feet
Rested a silent sea of hoary mist.
A hundred hills their dusky backs upheaved
All over this still ocean; and beyond,
Far, far beyond, the solid vapours stretched, 45
In headlands, tongues, and promontory shapes,
Into the main Atlantic, that appeared
To dwindle, and give up his majesty,
Usurped upon far as the sight could reach.
Not so the ethereal vault; encroachment none 50
Was there, nor loss; only the inferior stars
Had disappeared, or shed a fainter light
In the clear presence of the full-orbed Moon,
Who, from her sovereign elevation, gazed
Upon the billowy ocean, as it lay 55
All meek and silent, save that through a rift—
Not distant from the shore whereon we stood,
A fixed, abysmal, gloomy, breathing-place—
Mounted the roar of waters, torrents, streams
Innumerable, roaring with one voice! 60
Heard over earth and sea, and, in that hour,
For so it seemed, felt by the starry heavens.

When into air had partially dissolved
That vision, given to spirits of the night
And three chance human wanderers, in calm thought 65
Reflected, it appeared to me the type
Of a majestic intellect, its acts
And its possessions, what it has and craves,
What in itself it is, and would become.
There I beheld the emblem of a mind 70
That feeds upon infinity, that broods
Over the dark abyss, intent to hear
Its voices issuing forth to silent light

In one continuous stream; a mind sustained
By recognitions of transcendent power,
In sense conducting to ideal form, 76
In soul of more than mortal privilege.
One function, above all, of such a mind
Had Nature shadowed there, by putting forth,
'Mid circumstances awful and sublime, 80
That mutual domination which she loves
To exert upon the face of outward things,
So moulded, joined, abstracted, so endowed
With interchangeable supremacy,
That men, least sensitive, see, hear, perceive, 85
And cannot choose but feel. The power, which all
Acknowledge when thus moved, which Nature thus
To bodily sense exhibits, is the express
Resemblance of that glorious faculty
That higher minds bear with them as their own. 90
This is the very spirit in which they deal
With the whole compass of the universe:
They from their native selves can send abroad
Kindred mutations; for themselves create
A like existence; and, whene'er it dawns
Created for them, catch it, or are caught
By its inevitable mastery, 97
Like angels stopped upon the wing by sound
Of harmony from Heaven's remotest spheres.
Them the enduring and the transient both 100
Serve to exalt; they build up greatest things
From least suggestions; ever on the watch,
Willing to work and to be wrought upon,
They need not extraordinary calls
To rouse them; in a world of life they live, 105
By sensible impressions not enthralled,
But by their quickening impulse made more prompt
To hold fit converse with the spiritual world,
And with the generations of mankind
Spread over time, past, present, and to come, 110
Age after age, till Time shall be no more.
Such minds are truly from the Deity,
For they are Powers; and hence the highest bliss
That flesh can know is theirs—the consciousness
Of Whom they are, habitually infused
Through every image and through every thought, 116
And all affections by communion raised

From earth to heaven, from human to
divine;
Hence endless occupation for the Soul,
Whether discursive or intuitive;   120
Hence cheerfulness for acts of daily life,
Emotions which best foresight need not
fear,
Most worthy then of trust when most
intense.
Hence, amid ills that vex and wrongs that
crush
Our hearts—if here the words of Holy
Writ   125
May with fit reverence be applied—that
peace
Which passeth understanding, that repose
In moral judgments which from this pure
source
Must come, or will by man be sought in
vain.

Oh! who is he that hath his whole life
long   130
Preserved, enlarged, this freedom in him-
self?
For this alone is genuine liberty:
Where is the favoured being who hath
held
That course unchecked, unerring, and
untired,
In one perpetual progress smooth and
bright?—   135
A humbler destiny have we retraced,
And told of lapse and hesitating choice,
And backward wanderings along thorny
ways:
Yet—compassed round by mountain soli-
tudes,
Within whose solemn temple I received
My earliest visitations, careless then 141
Of what was given me; and which now I
range,
A meditative, oft a suffering, man—
Do I declare—in accents which, from
truth
Deriving cheerful confidence, shall blend
Their modulation with these vocal
streams—   146
That, whatsoever falls my better mind,
Revolving with the accidents of life,
May have sustained, that, howsoe'er mis-
led,
Never did I, in quest of right and wrong,
Tamper with conscience from a private
aim;   151
Nor was in any public hope the dupe
Of selfish passions; nor did ever yield
Wilfully to mean cares or low pursuits,
But shrunk with apprehensive jealousy
From every combination which might aid
The tendency, too potent in itself,
Of use and custom to bow down the soul
Under a growing weight of vulgar sense,
And substitute a universe of death 160

For that which moves with light and life
informed,
Actual, divine, and true. To fear and love,
To love as prime and chief, for there fear
ends,
Be this ascribed; to early intercourse,
In presence of sublime or beautiful forms,
With the adverse principles of pain and
joy—   166
Evil as one is rashly named by men
Who know not what they speak. By love
subsists
All lasting grandeur, by pervading love;
That gone, we are as dust.—Behold the
fields   170
In balmy spring-time full of rising flowers
And joyous creatures; see that pair, the
lamb
And the lamb's mother, and their tender
ways
Shall touch thee to the heart; thou callest
this love,
And not inaptly so, for love it is,   175
Far as it carries thee. In some green
bower
Rest, and be not alone, but have thou
there
The One who is thy choice of all the
world:
There linger, listening, gazing, with de-
light
Impassioned, but delight how pitiable!
Unless this love by a still higher love 181
Be hallowed, love that breathes not with-
out awe;
Love that adores, but on the knees of
prayer,
By heaven inspired; that frees from
chains the soul,
Lifted, in union with the purest, best, 185
Of earth-born passions, on the wings of
praise
Bearing a tribute to the Almighty's
Throne.

This spiritual Love acts not nor can
exist
Without Imagination, which, in truth,
Is but another name for absolute power
And clearest insight, amplitude of mind,
And Reason in her most exalted mood.
This faculty hath been the feeding source
Of our long labour: we have traced the
stream
From the blind cavern whence is faintly
heard   195
Its natal murmur; followed it to light
And open day; accompanied its course
Among the ways of Nature, for a time
Lost sight of it bewildered and engulphed;
Then given it greeting as it rose once
more   200
In strength, reflecting from its placid
breast

The works of man and face of human life;
And lastly, from its progress have we
    drawn
Faith in life endless, the sustaining thought
Of human Being, Eternity, and God. 205

Imagination having been our theme,
So also hath that intellectual Love,
For they are each in each, and cannot
    stand
Dividually.—Here must thou be, O Man!
Power to thyself; no Helper hast thou
    here;   210
Here keepest thou in singleness thy state:
No other can divide with thee this work:
No secondary hand can intervene
To fashion this ability; 'tis thine,
The prime and vital principle is thine 215
In the recesses of thy nature, far
From any reach of outward fellowship,
Else is not thine at all. But joy to him,
Oh, joy to him who here hath sown, hath
    laid   219
Here, the foundation of his future years!
For all that friendship, all that love can do,
All that a darling countenance can look
Or dear voice utter, to complete the man,
Perfect him, made imperfect in himself,
All shall be his: and he whose soul hath
    risen   225
Up to the height of feeling intellect
Shall want no humbler tenderness; his
    heart
Be tender as a nursing mother's heart;
Of female softness shall his life be full,
Of humble cares and delicate desires, 230
Mild interests and gentlest sympathies.

Child of my parents! Sister of my soul!
Thanks in sincerest verse have been else-
    where
Poured out for all the early tenderness
Which I from thee imbibed: and 'tis
    most true   235
That later seasons owed to thee no less;
For, spite of thy sweet influence and the
    touch
Of kindred hands that opened out the
    springs
Of genial thought in childhood, and in
    spite
Of all that unassisted I had marked 240
In life or nature of those charms minute
That win their way into the heart by
    stealth,
Still, to the very going-out of youth,
I too exclusively esteemed *that* love,
And sought *that* beauty, which, as Milton
    sings,   245
Hath terror in it. Thou didst soften down
This over-sternness; but for thee, dear
    Friend!
My soul, too reckless of mild grace, had
    stood

In her original self too confident,
Retained too long a countenance severe;
A rock with torrents roaring, with the
    clouds   251
Familiar, and a favourite of the stars:
But thou didst plant its crevices with
    flowers,
Hang it with shrubs that twinkle in the
    breeze,
And teach the little birds to build their
    nests   255
And warble in its chambers. At a time
When Nature, destined to remain so long
Foremost in my affections, had fallen
    back
Into a second place, pleased to become
A handmaid to a nobler than herself, 260
When every day brought with it some
    new sense
Of exquisite regard for common things,
And all the earth was budding with these
    gifts
Of more refined humanity, thy breath,
Dear Sister! was a kind of gentler spring
That went before my steps. Thereafter
    came   266
One whom with thee friendship had early
    paired;
She came, no more a phantom to adorn
A moment, but an inmate of the heart,
And yet a spirit, there for me enshrined
To penetrate the lofty and the low;   271
Even as one essence of pervading light
Shines in the brightest of ten thousand
    stars,
And the meek worm that feeds her lonely
    lamp
Couched in the dewy grass.
                           With such a theme,
Coleridge! with this my argument, of
    thee   276
Shall I be silent? O capacious Soul!
Placed on this earth to love and under-
    stand,
And from thy presence shed the light of
    love,
Shall I be mute, ere thou be spoken of?
Thy kindred influence to my heart of
    hearts   281
Did also find its way. Thus fear relaxed
Her overweening grasp; thus thoughts
    and things
In the self-haunting spirit learned to take
More rational proportions; mystery, 285
The incumbent mystery of sense and soul,
Of life and death, time and eternity,
Admitted more habitually a mild
Interposition—a serene delight
In closelier gathering cares, such as be-
    come   290
A human creature, howsoe'er endowed,
Poet, or destined for a humbler name;
And so the deep enthusiastic joy,
The rapture of the hallelujah sent

From all that breathes and is, was chas-
    tened, stemmed   295
And balanced by pathetic truth, by trust
In hopeful reason, leaning on the stay
Of Providence; and in reverence for duty,
Here, if need be, struggling with storms,
    and there
Strewing in peace life's humblest ground
    with herbs,   300
At every season green, sweet at all hours.

And now, O Friend! this history is
    brought
To its appointed close: the discipline
And consummation of a Poet's mind,
In everything that stood most prominent,
Have faithfully been pictured; we have
    reached   306
The time (our guiding object from the
    first)
When we may, not presumptuously, I
    hope,
Suppose my powers so far confirmed, and
    such   309
My knowledge, as to make me capable
Of building up a Work that shall endure.
Yet much hath been omitted, as need
    was;
Of books how much! and even of the
    other wealth
That is collected among woods and fields,
Far more: for Nature's secondary grace
Hath hitherto been barely touched upon,
The charm more superficial that attends
Her works, as they present to Fancy's
    choice
Apt illustrations of the moral world,
Caught at a glance, or traced with curi-
    ous pains.   320

Finally, and above all, O Friend! (I
    speak
With due regret) how much is overlooked
In human nature and her subtle ways,
As studied first in our own hearts, and
    then   324
In life among the passions of mankind,
Varying their composition and their hue,
Where'er we move, under the diverse
    shapes
That individual character presents
To an attentive eye. For progress meet,
Along this intricate and difficult path,
Whate'er was wanting, something had I
    gained,   331
As one of many schoolfellows compelled,
In hardy independence, to stand up
Amid conflicting interests, and the shock
Of various tempers; to endure and note
What was not understood, though known
    to be;   336
Among the mysteries of love and hate,
Honour and shame, looking to right and
    left,

Unchecked by innocence too delicate,
And moral notions too intolerant,   340
Sympathies too contracted. Hence, when
    called
To take a station among men, the step
Was easier, the transition more secure,
More profitable also; for the mind   344
Learns from such timely exercise to keep
In wholesome separation the two natures,
The one that feels, the other that observes

Yet one word more of personal con-
    cern;—
Since I withdrew unwillingly from France,
I led an undomestic wanderer's life,   350
In London chiefly harboured, whence I
    roamed,
Tarrying at will in many a pleasant spot
Of rural England's cultivated vales
Or Cambrian solitudes. A youth—(he
    bore
The name of Calvert—it shall live, if
    words   355
Of mine can give it life,) in firm belief
That by endowments not from me with-
    held
Good might be furthered—in his last
    decay
By a bequest sufficient for my needs
Enabled me to pause for choice, and
    walk   360
At large and unrestrained, nor damped
    too soon
By mortal cares. Himself no Poet, yet
Far less a common follower of the world,
He deemed that my pursuits and labours
    lay
Apart from all that leads to wealth, or
    even   365
A necessary maintenance insures,
Without some hazard to the finer sense;
He cleared a passage for me, and the
    stream
Flowed in the bent of Nature.
                    Having now
Told what best merits mention, further
    pains   370
Our present purpose seems not to require,
And I have other tasks. Recall to mind
The mood in which this labour was begun,
O Friend! The termination of my course
Is nearer now, much nearer; yet even
    then,   375
In that distraction and intense desire,
I said unto the life which I had lived,
Where art thou? Hear I not a voice from
    thee
Which 'tis reproach to hear? Anon I rose
As if on wings, and saw beneath me
    stretched   380
Vast prospect of the world which I had
    been
And was; and hence this Song, which like
    a lark

I have protracted, in the unwearied
heavens
Singing, and often with more plaintive
voice
To earth attempered and her deep-drawn
sighs,   385
Yet centring all in love, and in the end
All gratulant, if rightly understood.

Whether to me shall be allotted life,
And, with life, power to accomplish aught
of worth,
That will be deemed no insufficient plea
For having given the story of myself, 391
Is all uncertain: but, beloved Friend!
When, looking back, thou seest, in clearer
view
Than any liveliest sight of yesterday,
That summer, under whose indulgent
skies,   395
Upon smooth Quantock's airy ridge we
roved
Unchecked, or loitered 'mid her sylvan
combs,
Thou in bewitching words, with happy
heart,
Didst chaunt the vision of that Ancient
Man,
The bright-eyed Mariner, and rueful woes
Didst utter of the Lady Christabel;   401
And I, associate with such labour, steeped
In soft forgetfulness the livelong hours,
Murmuring of him who, joyous hap, was
found,
After the perils of his moonlight ride, 405
Near the loud waterfall; or her who sate
In misery near the miserable Thorn;—
When thou dost to that summer turn thy
thoughts,
And hast before thee all which then we
were,
To thee, in memory of that happiness,
It will be known, by thee at least, my
Friend!   411
Felt, that the history of a Poet's mind
Is labour not unworthy of regard:
To thee the work shall justify itself.

The last and later portions of this gift
Have been prepared, not with the buoy-
ant spirits   416
That were our daily portion when we
first
Together wantoned in wild Poesy,

But, under pressure of a private grief,
Keen and enduring, which the mind and
heart,   420
That in this meditative history
Have been laid open, needs must make
me feel
More deeply, yet enable me to bear
More firmly; and a comfort now hath
risen
From hope that thou art near, and wilt
be soon   425
Restored to us in renovated health;
When, after the first mingling of our tears
'Mong other consolations, we may draw
Some pleasure from this offering of my
love.

Oh! yet a few short years of useful life,
And all will be complete, thy race be
run,   431
Thy monument of glory will be raised;
Then, though (too weak to tread the ways
of truth)
This age fall back to old idolatry,   434
Though men return to servitude as fast
As the tide ebbs, to ignominy and shame
By nations sink together, we shall still
Find solace—knowing what we have
learnt to know,
Rich in true happiness if allowed to be
Faithful alike in forwarding a day   440
Of firmer trust, joint labourers in the
work
(Should Providence such grace to us
vouchsafe)
Of their deliverance, surely yet to come.
Prophets of Nature, we to them will
speak
A lasting inspiration, sanctified   445
By reason, blest by faith: what we have
loved,
Others will love, and we will teach them
how;
Instruct them how the mind of man
becomes
A thousand times more beautiful than
the earth
On which he dwells, above this frame of
things   450
(Which, 'mid all revolution in the hopes
And fears of men, doth still remain un-
changed)
In beauty exalted, as it is itself
Of quality and fabric more divine.

THE EXCURSION

TO THE RIGHT HONOURABLE

WILLIAM, EARL OF LONSDALE, K.G.

ETC., ETC.

OFT, through thy fair domains, illustrious Peer!
In youth I roamed, on youthful pleasures bent;
And mused in rocky cell or sylvan tent,
Beside swift-flowing Lowther's current clear.
—Now, by thy care befriended, I appear
Before thee, LONSDALE, and this Work present,
A token (may it prove a monument!)
Of high respect and gratitude sincere.
Gladly would I have waited till my task
Had reached its close; but Life is insecure,
And Hope full oft fallacious as a dream:
Therefore, for what is here produced, I ask
Thy favour; trusting that thou wilt not deem
The offering, though imperfect, premature.

WILLIAM WORDSWORTH.

RYDAL MOUNT, WESTMORELAND,
July 29, 1814.

PREFACE TO THE EDITION OF 1814

THE Title-page announces that this is only a portion of a poem; and the Reader must be here apprised that it belongs to the second part of a long and laborious Work, which is to consist of three parts.— The Author will candidly acknowledge that, if the first of these had been completed, and in such a manner as to satisfy his own mind, he should have preferred the natural order of publication, and have given that to the world first; but, as the second division of the Work was designed to refer more to passing events, and to an existing state of things, than the others were meant to do, more continuous exertion was naturally bestowed upon it, and greater progress made here than in the rest of the poem; and as this part does not depend upon the preceding, to a degree which will materially injure its own peculiar interest, the Author, complying with the earnest entreaties of some valued Friends, presents the following pages to the Public.

It may be proper to state whence the poem, of which 'The Excursion' is a part, derives its Title of THE RECLUSE.—Several years ago, when the Author retired to his native mountains, with the hope of being enabled to construct a literary Work that might live, it was a reasonable thing that he should take a review of his own mind, and examine how far Nature and Education had qualified him for such employment. As subsidiary to this preparation, he undertook to record, in verse, the origin and progress of his own powers, as far as he was acquainted with them. That Work, addressed to a dear Friend, most distinguished for his knowledge and genius, and to whom the Author's Intellect is deeply indebted, has been long finished; and the result of the investigation which gave rise to it was a determination to compose a philosophical poem, containing views of Man, Nature, and Society; and to be entitled, 'The Recluse;' as having for its principal subject the sensations and opinions of a poet living in retirement.—The preparatory poem is biographical, and conducts the history of the Author's mind to the point when he was emboldened to hope that his faculties were sufficiently matured for entering upon the arduous labour which he had proposed to himself; and the two Works have the same kind of relation to each other, if he may so express himself, as the ante-chapel has to the body of a gothic church. Continuing this allusion, he may be permitted to add, that his minor Pieces, which have been long before the Public, when they shall be properly arranged, will be found by the attentive Reader to have such connection with the main Work as may give them claim to be likened to the little cells, oratories, and sepulchral recesses, ordinarily included in those edifices.

The Author would not have deemed himself justified in saying, upon this occasion, so much of performances either unfinished, or unpublished, if he had not thought that the labour bestowed by him upon what he has heretofore and now laid before the Public, entitled him to candid attention for such a statement as he thinks necessary to throw light upon his endeavours to please and, he would hope, to benefit his countrymen.—Nothing further need be added, than that the first and third parts of 'The Recluse' will consist chiefly of meditations in the Author's own person; and that in the intermediate part ('The Excursion') the intervention of characters speaking is employed, and something of a dramatic form adopted.

It is not the Author's intention formally to announce a system: it was more animating to him to proceed in a different course; and if he shall succeed in conveying to the mind clear thoughts, lively images, and strong feelings, the Reader will have no difficulty in extracting the system for himself. And in the meantime the following passage, taken from the conclusion of the first book of 'The Recluse,' may be acceptable as a kind of *Prospectus* of the design and scope of the whole Poem.

PREFACE TO THE EDITION OF 1814

'On Man, on Nature, and on Human Life,
Musing in solitude, I oft perceive
Fair trains of imagery before me rise,
Accompanied by feelings of delight
Pure, or with no unpleasing sadness mixed,   5
And I am conscious of affecting thoughts
And dear remembrances, whose presence soothes
Or elevates the Mind, intent to weigh
The good and evil of our mortal state.
—To these emotions, whencesoe'er they come, 10
Whether from breath of outward circumstance,
Or from the Soul—an impulse to herself—
I would give utterance in numerous verse.
Of Truth, of Grandeur, Beauty, Love, and Hope,
And melancholy Fear subdued by Faith;   15
Of blessèd consolations in distress;
Of moral strength, and intellectual Power;
Of joy in widest commonalty spread;
Of the individual Mind that keeps her own
Inviolate retirement, subject there   20
To Conscience only, and the law supreme
Of that Intelligence which governs all—
I sing:—"fit audience let me find though few!"

'So prayed, more gaining than he asked, the
   Bard—
In holiest mood. Urania, I shall need   25
Thy guidance, or a greater Muse, if such
Descend to earth or dwell in highest heaven!
For I must tread on shadowy ground, must sink
Deep—and, aloft ascending, breathe in worlds
To which the heaven of heavens is but a veil. 30
All strength—all terror, single or in bands,
That ever was put forth in personal form—
Jehovah—with his thunder, and the choir
Of shouting Angels, and the empyreal thrones—
I pass them unalarmed. Not Chaos, not   35
The darkest pit of lowest Erebus,
Nor aught of blinder vacancy, scooped out
By help of dreams—can breed such fear and awe
As fall upon us often when we look
Into our Minds, into the Mind of Man—   40
My haunt, and the main region of my song.
—Beauty—a living Presence of the earth,
Surpassing the most fair ideal Forms
Which craft of delicate Spirits hath composed
From earth's materials—waits upon my steps; 45
Pitches her tents before me as I move,
An hourly neighbour. Paradise, and groves
Elysian, Fortunate Fields—like those of old
Sought in the Atlantic Main—why should they be
A history only of departed things,   50
Or a mere fiction of what never was?
For the discerning intellect of Man,
When wedded to this goodly universe

In love and holy passion, shall find these
A simple produce of the common day.   55
—I, long before the blissful hour arrives,
Would chant, in lonely peace, the spousal verse
Of this great consummation:—and, by words
Which speak of nothing more than what we
   are,
Would I arouse the sensual from their sleep 60
Of Death, and win the vacant and the vain
To noble raptures; while my voice proclaims
How exquisitely the individual Mind
(And the progressive powers perhaps no less
Of the whole species) to the external World 65
Is fitted:—and how exquisitely, too—
Theme this but little heard of among men—
The external World is fitted to the Mind;
And the creation (by no lower name
Can it be called) which they with blended might
Accomplish:—this is our high argument.   71
—Such grateful haunts foregoing, if I oft
Must turn elsewhere—to travel near the tribes
And fellowships of men, and see ill sights
Of madding passions mutually inflamed; 75
Must hear Humanity in fields and groves
Pipe solitary anguish; or must hang
Brooding above the fierce confederate storm
Of sorrow, barricadoed evermore
Within the walls of cities—may these sounds 80
Have their authentic comment; that even these
Hearing, I be not downcast or forlorn!—
Descend, prophetic Spirit! that inspir'st
The human Soul of universal earth,
Dreaming on things to come; and dost possess
A metropolitan temple in the hearts   86
Of mighty Poets: upon me bestow
A gift of genuine insight; that my Song
With star-like virtue in its place may shine,
Shedding benignant influence, and secure, 90
Itself, from all malevolent effect
Of those mutations that extend their sway
Throughout the nether sphere!—And if with this
I mix more lowly matter; with the thing
Contemplated, describe the Mind and Man 95
Contemplating; and who, and what he was—
The transitory Being that beheld
This Vision; when and where, and how he lived;—
Be not this labour useless. If such theme
May sort with highest objects, then—dread Power!
Whose gracious favour is the primal source 101
Of all illumination,—may my Life
Express the image of a better time,
More wise desires, and simpler manners;—nurse
My Heart in genuine freedom:—all pure thoughts
Be with me;—so shall thy unfailing love 106
Guide, and support, and cheer me to the end!'

THE EXCURSION

BOOK FIRST

THE WANDERER

ARGUMENT

A summer forenoon.—The Author reaches a ruined Cottage upon a Common, and there meets with a revered Friend, the Wanderer, of whose education and course of life he gives an account.— The Wanderer, while resting under the shade of the Trees that surround the Cottage, relates the History of its last Inhabitant.

'Twas summer, and the sun had mounted
    high:
Southward the landscape indistinctly
    glared
Through a pale steam; but all the northern
    downs,
In clearest air ascending, showed far off
A surface dappled o'er with shadows
    flung   5
From brooding clouds; shadows that lay
    in spots
Determined and unmoved, with steady
    beams
Of bright and pleasant sunshine inter-
    posed;
To him most pleasant who on soft cool
    moss
Extends his careless limbs along the
    front   10
Of some huge cave, whose rocky ceiling
    casts
A twilight of its own, an ample shade,
Where the wren warbles, while the dream-
    ing man,
Half conscious of the soothing melody,
With side-long eye looks out upon the
    scene,   15
By power of that impending covert,
    thrown
To finer distance. Mine was at that hour
Far other lot, yet with good hope that
    soon
Under a shade as grateful I should find
Rest, and be welcomed there to livelier
    joy.   20
Across a bare wide Common I was toiling
With languid steps that by the slippery
    turf
Were baffled; nor could my weak arm
    disperse
The host of insects gathering round my
    face,
And ever with me as I paced along.   25

Upon that open moorland stood a grove,
The wished-for port to which my course
    was bound.
Thither I came, and there, amid the
    gloom
Spread by a brotherhood of lofty elms,

Appeared a roofless Hut; four naked
    walls   30
That stared upon each other!—I looked
    round,
And to my wish and to my hope espied
The Friend I sought; a Man of reverend
    age,
But stout and hale, for travel unimpaired.
There was he seen upon the cottage-
    bench,   35
Recumbent in the shade, as if asleep;
An iron-pointed staff lay at his side.

Him had I marked the day before—
    alone
And stationed in the public way, with
    face
Turned toward the sun then setting, while
    that staff   40
Afforded, to the figure of the man
Detained for contemplation or repose,
Graceful support; his countenance as he
    stood
Was hidden from my view, and he re-
    mained
Unrecognised; but, stricken by the sight,
With slackened footsteps I advanced, and
    soon   46
A glad congratulation we exchanged
At such unthought-of meeting.—For the
    night
We parted, nothing willingly; and now
He by appointment waited for me here, 50
Under the covert of these clustering elms.

We were tried Friends: amid a pleasant
    vale,
In the antique market-village where was
    passed
My school-time, an apartment he had
    owned,
To which at intervals the Wanderer drew,
And found a kind of home or harbour
    there.   56
He loved me; from a swarm of rosy boys
Singled out me, as he in sport would say,
For my grave looks, too thoughtful for
    my years.
As I grew up, it was my best delight   60
To be his chosen comrade. Many a time,

On holidays, we rambled through the
   woods:
We sate—we walked; he pleased me with
   report
Of things which he had seen; and often
   touched
Abstrusest matter, reasonings of the
   mind   65
Turned inward; or at my request would
   sing
Old songs, the product of his native hills;
A skilful distribution of sweet sounds,
Feeding the soul, and eagerly imbibed
As cool refreshing water, by the care   70
Of the industrious husbandman, diffused
Through a parched meadow-ground, in
   time of drought.
Still deeper welcome found his pure
   discourse:
How precious when in riper days I
   learned
To weigh with care his words, and to
   rejoice   75
In the plain presence of his dignity!

Oh! many are the Poets that are sown
By Nature; men endowed with highest
   gifts,
The vision and the faculty divine;
Yet wanting the accomplishment of verse,
(Which, in the docile season of their
   youth,   81
It was denied them to acquire, through
   lack
Of culture and the inspiring aid of books,
Or haply by a temper too severe,
Or a nice backwardness afraid of shame)
Nor having e'er, as life advanced, been
   led   86
By circumstance to take unto the height
The measure of themselves, these favoured
   Beings,
All but a scattered few, live out their
   time,
Husbanding that which they possess
   within,   90
And go to the grave, unthought of.
   Strongest minds
Are often those of whom the noisy world
Hears least; else surely this Man had not
   left
His graces unrevealed and unproclaimed.
But, as the mind was filled with inward
   light,   95
So not without distinction had he lived,
Beloved and honoured—far as he was
   known.
And some small portion of his eloquent
   speech,
And something that may serve to set in
   view
The feeling pleasures of his loneliness,
His observations, and the thoughts his
   mind   101

Had dealt with—I will here record in
   verse;
Which, if with truth it correspond, and
   sink
Or rise as venerable Nature leads,   104
The high and tender Muses shall accept
With gracious smile, deliberately pleased,
And listening Time reward with sacred
   praise.

Among the hills of Athol he was born;
Where, on a small hereditary farm,
An unproductive slip of rugged ground,
His Parents, with their numerous off-
   spring, dwelt;   111
A virtuous household, though exceeding
   poor!
Pure livers were they all, austere and
   grave,
And fearing God; the very children
   taught
Stern self-respect, a reverence for God's
   word,   115
And an habitual piety, maintained
With strictness scarcely known on Eng-
   lish ground.

From his sixth year, the Boy of whom
   I speak,
In summer, tended cattle on the hills;
But, through the inclement and the
   perilous days   120
Of long-continuing winter, he repaired,
Equipped with satchel, to a school, that
   stood
Sole building on a mountain's dreary edge,
Remote from view of city spire, or sound
Of minster clock! From that bleak tene-
   ment   125
He, many an evening, to his distant home
In solitude returning, saw the hills .
Grow larger in the darkness; all alone
Beheld the stars come out above his head,
And travelled through the wood, with no
   one near   130
To whom he might confess the things he
   saw.

So the foundations of his mind were
   laid.
In such communion, not from terror free,
While yet a child, and long before his
   time,
Had he perceived the presence and the
   power   135
Of greatness; and deep feelings had
   impressed
So vividly great objects that they lay
Upon his mind like substances, whose
   presence
Perplexed the bodily sense. He had
   received
A precious gift; for, as he grew in years,
With these impressions would he still
   compare   141

All his remembrances, thoughts, shapes,
    and forms;
And, being still unsatisfied with aught
Of dimmer character, he thence attained
An active power to fasten images   145
Upon his brain; and on their pictured
    lines
Intensely brooded, even till they acquired
The liveliness of dreams. Nor did he fail,
While yet a child, with a child's eager-
    ness
Incessantly to turn his ear and eye   150
On all things which the moving seasons
    brought
To feed such appetite—nor this alone
Appeased his yearning:—in the after-day
Of boyhood, many an hour in caves
    forlorn,
And 'mid the hollow depths of naked
    crags   155
He sate, and even in their fixed linea-
    ments,
Or from the power of a peculiar eye,
Or by creative feeling overborne,
Or by predominance of thought op-
    pressed,
Even in their fixed and steady linea-
    ments   160
He traced an ebbing and a flowing mind,
Expression ever varying!
                        Thus informed,
He had small need of books; for many a
    tale
Traditionary round the mountains hung,
And many a legend, peopling the dark
    woods,   165
Nourished Imagination in her growth,
And gave the Mind that apprehensive
    power
By which she is made quick to recognise
The moral properties and scope of things.
But eagerly he read, and read again,   170
Whate'er the minister's old shelf sup-
    plied;
The life and death of martyrs, who
    sustained,
With will inflexible, those fearful pangs
Triumphantly displayed in records left
Of persecution, and the Covenant—times
Whose echo rings through Scotland to
    this hour!   176
And there, by lucky hap, had been pre-
    served
A straggling volume, torn and incomplete,
That left half-told the preternatural tale,
Romance of giants, chronicle of fiends,
Profuse in garniture of wooden cuts   181
Strange and uncouth; dire faces, figures
    dire,
Sharp-kneed, sharp-elbowed, and lean-
    ankled too,
With long and ghostly shanks—forms
    which once seen   184
Could never be forgotten!

                          In his heart,
Where Fear sate thus, a cherished visitant,
Was wanting yet the pure delight of love
By sound diffused, or by the breathing air,
Or by the silent looks of happy things,
Or flowing from the universal face   190
Of earth and sky. But he had felt the
    power
Of Nature, and already was prepared,
By his intense conceptions, to receive
Deeply the lesson deep of love which he,
Whom Nature, by whatever means, has
    taught   195
To feel intensely, cannot but receive.

Such was the Boy—but for the growing
    Youth
What soul was his, when, from the naked
    top
Of some bold headland, he beheld the sun
Rise up, and bathe the world in light!
    He looked—   200
Ocean and earth, the solid frame of earth
And ocean's liquid mass, in gladness lay
Beneath him:—Far and wide the clouds
    were touched,
And in their silent faces could he read
Unutterable love. Sound needed none,
Nor any voice of joy; his spirit drank
The spectacle: sensation, soul, and form,
All melted into him; they swallowed up
His animal being; in them did he live,
And by them did he live; they were his
    life.   210
In such access of mind, in such high hour
Of visitation from the living God,
Thought was not; in enjoyment it expired.
No thanks he breathed, he proffered no
    request;   214
Rapt into still communion that transcends
The imperfect offices of prayer and praise,
His mind was a thanksgiving to the power
That made him; it was blessedness and
    love!

A Herdsman on the lonely mountain-
    tops,   219
Such intercourse was his, and in this sort
Was his existence oftentimes *possessed.*
O then how beautiful, how bright, ap-
    peared
The written promise! Early had he
    learned
To reverence the volume that displays
The mystery, the life which cannot die;
But in the mountains did he *feel* his
    faith.   226
All things, responsive to the writing, there
Breathed immortality, revolving life,
And greatness still revolving; infinite:
There littleness was not; the least of
    things   230
Seemed infinite; and there his spirit
    shaped

Her prospects, nor did he believe,—he *saw*.
What wonder if his being thus became
Sublime and comprehensive! Low desires,
Low thoughts had there no place; yet was
    his heart   235
Lowly; for he was meek in gratitude,
Oft as he called those ecstasies to mind,
And whence they flowed; and from them
    he acquired
Wisdom, which works thro' patience;
    thence he learned   239
In oft-recurring hours of sober thought
To look on Nature with a humble heart,
Self-questioned where it did not under-
    stand,
And with a superstitious eye of love.

    So passed the time; yet to the nearest
        town
He duly went with what small overplus
His earnings might supply, and brought
    away   246
The book that most had tempted his
    desires
While at the stall he read. Among the
    hills
He gazed upon that mighty orb of song,
The divine Milton. Lore of different kind,
The annual savings of a toilsome life,   251
His Schoolmaster supplied; books that
    explain
The purer elements of truth involved
In lines and numbers, and, by charm
    severe,
(Especially perceived where nature droops
And feeling is suppressed) preserve the
    mind   256
Busy in solitude and poverty.
These occupations oftentimes deceived
The listless hours, while in the hollow vale,
Hollow and green, he lay on the green
    turf   260
In pensive idleness. What could he do,
Thus daily thirsting, in that lonesome life,
With blind endeavours? Yet, still upper-
    most,
Nature was at his heart as if he felt,
Though yet he knew not how, a wasting
    power   265
In all things that from her sweet influence
Might tend to wean him. Therefore with
    her hues,
Her forms, and with the spirit of her
    forms,
He clothed the nakedness of austere truth.
While yet he lingered in the rudiments
Of science, and among her simplest laws,
His triangles—they were the stars of
    heaven,
The silent stars! Oft did he take delight
To measure the altitude of some tall crag
That is the eagle's birthplace, or some
    peak   275
Familiar with forgotten years, that shows

Inscribed upon its visionary sides,
The history of many a winter storm,
Or obscure records of the path of fire.

    And thus before his eighteenth year
        was told,   280
Accumulated feelings pressed his heart
With still increasing weight; he was o'er-
    powered
By Nature; by the turbulence subdued
Of his own mind; by mystery and hope,
And the first virgin passion of a soul   285
Communing with the glorious universe.
Full often wished he that the winds might
    rage
When they were silent: far more fondly
    now
Than in his earlier season did he love
Tempestuous nights—the conflict and the
    sounds   290
That live in darkness. From his intellect
And from the stillness of abstracted
    thought
He asked repose; and, failing oft to win
The peace required, he scanned the laws
    of light
Amid the roar of torrents, where they
    send   295
From hollow clefts up to the clearer air
A cloud of mist, that smitten by the sun
Varies its rainbow hues. But vainly thus,
And vainly by all other means, he strove
To mitigate the fever of his heart.   300

    In dreams, in study, and in ardent
        thought,
Thus was he reared; much wanting to
    assist
The growth of intellect, yet gaining more,
And every moral feeling of his soul
Strengthened and braced, by breathing in
    content   305
The keen, the wholesome, air of poverty,
And drinking from the well of homely life.
—But, from past liberty, and tried re-
    straints,
He now was summoned to select the
    course   309
Of humble industry that promised best
To yield him no unworthy maintenance.
Urged by his Mother, he essayed to teach
A village-school—but wandering thoughts
    were then
A misery to him; and the Youth resigned
A task he was unable to perform.   315

    That stern yet kindly Spirit, who con-
        strains
The Savoyard to quit his naked rocks,
The freeborn Swiss to leave his narrow
    vales,
(Spirit attached to regions mountainous
Like their own steadfast clouds) did now
    impel   320

His restless mind to look abroad with
　hope.
—An irksome drudgery seems it to plod
　on,
Through hot and dusty ways, or pelting
　storm,
A vagrant Merchant under a heavy load
Bent as he moves, and needing frequent
　rest;   325
Yet do such travellers find their own
　delight;
And their hard service, deemed debasing
　now,
Gained merited respect in simpler times;
When squire, and priest, and they who
　round them dwelt
In rustic sequestration—all dependent
Upon the PEDLAR'S toil—supplied their
　wants,   331
Or pleased their fancies, with the wares
　he brought.
Not ignorant was the Youth that still no
　few
Of his adventurous countrymen were led
By perseverance in this track of life   335
To competence and ease:—to him it
　offered
Attractions manifold;—and this he chose.
—His Parents on the enterprise bestowed
Their farewell benediction, but with hearts
Foreboding evil. From his native hills
He wandered far; much did he see of
　men,[1]   341
Their manners, their enjoyments, and
　pursuits,
Their passions and their feelings; chiefly
　those
Essential and eternal in the heart,
That, 'mid the simpler forms of rural life,
Exist more simple in their elements,   346
And speak a plainer language. In the
　woods,
A lone Enthusiast, and among the fields,
Itinerant in this labour, he had passed
The better portion of his time; and there
Spontaneously had his affections thriven
Amid the bounties of the year, the peace
And liberty of nature; there he kept
In solitude and solitary thought
His mind in a just equipoise of love.   355
Serene it was, unclouded by the cares
Of ordinary life; unvexed, unwarped
By partial bondage. In his steady course,
No piteous revolutions had he felt,
No wild varieties of joy and grief.   360
Unoccupied by sorrow of its own,
His heart lay open; and, by nature tuned
And constant disposition of his thoughts
To sympathy with man, he was alive
To all that was enjoyed where'er he
　went,   365
And all that was endured; for, in himself
Happy, and quiet in his cheerfulness,

[1] See Note, p. 727.

He had no painful pressure from without
That made him turn aside from wretched-
　ness
With coward fears. He could *afford* to
　suffer   370
With those whom he saw suffer. Hence
　it came
That in our best experience he was rich,
And in the wisdom of our daily life.
For hence, minutely, in his various rounds,
He had observed the progress and decay
Of many minds, of minds and bodies too;
The history of many families;
How they had prospered; how they were
　o'erthrown
By passion or mischance, or such misrule
Among the unthinking masters of the
　earth   380
As makes the nations groan.
　　　　　　　　This active course
He followed till provision for his wants
Had been obtained;—the Wanderer then
　resolved
To pass the remnant of his days, untasked
With needless services, from hardship
　free.   385
His calling laid aside, he lived at ease:
But still he loved to pace the public roads
And the wild paths; and, by the sum-
　mer's warmth
Invited, often would he leave his home
And journey far, revisiting the scenes   390
That to his memory were most endeared.
—Vigorous in health, of hopeful spirits,
　undamped
By worldly-mindedness or anxious care;
Observant, studious, thoughtful, and re-
　freshed
By knowledge gathered up from day to
　day;   395
Thus had he lived a long and innocent
　life.

The Scottish Church, both on himself
　and those
With whom from childhood he grew up,
　had held
The strong hand of her purity; and still
Had watched him with an unrelenting eye.
This he remembered in his riper age 401
With gratitude, and reverential thoughts.
But by the native vigour of his mind,
By his habitual wanderings out of doors,
By loneliness, and goodness, and kind
　works,   405
Whate'er, in docile childhood or in youth,
He had imbibed of fear or darker thought
Was melted all away; so true was this,
That sometimes his religion seemed to me
Self-taught, as of a dreamer in the woods;
Who to the model of his own pure heart
Shaped his belief, as grace divine inspired,
And human reason dictated with awe.
—And surely never did there live on earth

A man of kindlier nature. The rough
    sports   415
And teasing ways of children vexed not
    him;
Indulgent listener was he to the tongue
Of garrulous age; nor did the sick man's
    tale,
To his fraternal sympathy addressed,
Obtain reluctant hearing.
          Plain his garb;   420
Such as might suit a rustic Sire, prepared
For sabbath duties; yet he was a man
Whom no one could have passed without
    remark.
Active and nervous was his gait; his
    limbs
And his whole figure breathed intelli-
    gence.   425
Time had compressed the freshness of his
    cheek
Into a narrower circle of deep red,
But had not tamed his eye; that, under
    brows
Shaggy and grey, had meanings which it
    brought
From years of youth; which, like a Being
    made   430
Of many Beings, he had wondrous skill
To blend with knowledge of the years to
    come,
Human, or such as lie beyond the grave.

    So was He framed; and such his course
    of life   434
Who now, with no appendage but a staff,
The prized memorial of relinquished toils,
Upon that cottage-bench reposed his
    limbs,
Screened from the sun. Supine the Wan-
    derer lay,
His eyes as if in drowsiness half shut,
The shadows of the breezy elms above
Dappling his face. He had not heard the
    sound   441
Of my approaching steps, and in the shade
Unnoticed did I stand some minutes'
    space.
At length I hailed him, seeing that his
    hat
Was moist with water-drops, as if the
    brim   445
Had newly scooped a running stream. He
    rose,
And ere our lively greeting into peace
Had settled, ''Tis,' said I, 'a burning day:
My lips are parched with thirst, but you,
    it seems,
Have somewhere found relief.' He, at
    the word,   450
Pointing towards a sweet-briar, bade me
    climb
The fence where that aspiring shrub
    looked out

Upon the public way. It was a plot
Of garden ground run wild, its matted
    weeds
Marked with the steps of those, whom,
    as they passed,   455
The gooseberry trees that shot in long
    lank slips,
Or currants, hanging from their leafless
    stems,
In scanty strings, had tempted to o'erleap
The broken wall. I looked around, and
    there,
Where two tall hedge-rows of thick alder
    boughs   460
Joined in a cold damp nook, espied a
    well
Shrouded with willow-flowers and plumy
    fern.
My thirst I slaked, and, from the cheer-
    less spot
Withdrawing, straightway to the shade
    returned
Where sate the old Man on the cottage-
    bench;   465
And, while, beside him, with uncovered
    head,
I yet was standing, freely to respire,
And cool my temples in the fanning air,
Thus did he speak. 'I see around me
    here
Things which you cannot see: we die, my
    Friend,   470
Nor we alone, but that which each man
    loved
And prized in his peculiar nook of earth
Dies with him, or is changed; and very
    soon
Even of the good is no memorial left.   474
—The Poets, in their elegies and songs
Lamenting the departed, call the groves,
They call upon the hills and streams to
    mourn,
And senseless rocks; nor idly; for they
    speak,
In these their invocations, with a voice
Obedient to the strong creative power 480
Of human passion. Sympathies there are
More tranquil, yet perhaps of kindred
    birth,
That steal upon the meditative mind,
And grow with thought. Beside yon
    spring I stood,
And eyed its waters till we seemed to feel
One sadness, they and I. For them a
    bond   486
Of brotherhood is broken: time has been
When, every day, the touch of human
    hand
Dislodged the natural sleep that binds
    them up
In mortal stillness; and they ministered
To human comfort. Stooping down to
    drink,   491
Upon the slimy foot-stone I espied

The useless fragment of a wooden bowl,
Green with the moss of years, and subject
    only
To the soft handling of the elements: 495
There let it lie—how foolish are such
    thoughts!
Forgive them;—never—never did my
    steps
Approach this door but she who dwelt
    within
A daughter's welcome gave me, and I
    loved her
As my own child. Oh, Sir! the good die
    first,   500
And they whose hearts are dry as summer
    dust
Burn to the socket. Many a passenger
Hath blessed poor Margaret for her
    gentle looks,
When she upheld the cool refreshment
    drawn
From that forsaken spring; and no one
    came   505
But he was welcome; no one went away
But that it seemed she loved him. She is
    dead,
The light extinguished of her lonely hut,
The hut itself abandoned to decay,
And she forgotten in the quiet grave. 510

    'I speak,' continued he, 'of One whose
    stock
Of virtues bloomed beneath this lowly
    roof.
She was a Woman of a steady mind,
Tender and deep in her excess of love;
Not speaking much, pleased rather with
    the joy   515
Of her own thoughts: by some especial
    care
Her temper had been framed, as if to
    make
A Being, who by adding love to peace
Might live on earth a life of happiness.
Her wedded Partner lacked not on his
    side   520
The humble worth that satisfied her
    heart:
Frugal, affectionate, sober, and withal
Keenly industrious. She with pride would
    tell
That he was often seated at his loom, 524
In summer, ere the mower was abroad
Among the dewy grass,—in early spring,
Ere the last star had vanished.—They who
    passed
At evening, from behind the garden fence
Might hear his busy spade, which he
    would ply,
After his daily work, until the light   530
Had failed, and every leaf and flower were
    lost
In the dark hedges. So their days were
    spent

In peace and comfort; and a pretty boy
Was their best hope, next to the God in
    heaven.

    'Not twenty years ago, but you I think
Can scarcely bear it now in mind, there
    came   536
Two blighting seasons, when the fields
    were left
With half a harvest. It pleased Heaven
    to add
A worse affliction in the plague of war:
This happy Land was stricken to the
    heart!   540
A Wanderer then among the cottages,
I, with my freight of winter raiment,
    saw
The hardships of that season: many rich
Sank down, as in a dream, among the
    poor;
And of the poor did many cease to be,
And their place knew them not. Mean-
    while, abridged   546
Of daily comforts, gladly reconciled
To numerous self-denials, Margaret
Went struggling on through those cala-
    mitous years
With cheerful hope, until the second
    autumn,   550
When her life's Helpmate on a sick-bed
    lay,
Smitten with perilous fever. In disease
He lingered long; and, when his strength
    returned,
He found the little he had stored, to meet
The hour of accident or crippling age, 555
Was all consumed. A second infant now
Was added to the troubles of a time
Laden, for them and all of their degree,
With care and sorrow: shoals of artisans
From ill-requited labour turned adrift 560
Sought daily bread from public charity,
They, and their wives and children—hap-
    pier far
Could they have lived as do the little birds
That peck along the hedge-rows, or the
    kite
That makes her dwelling on the mountain
    rocks!   565

    'A sad reverse it was for him who long
Had filled with plenty, and possessed in
    peace,
This lonely Cottage. At the door he stood,
And whistled many a snatch of merry
    tunes
That had no mirth in them; or with his
    knife   570
Carved uncouth figures on the heads of
    sticks—
Then, not less idly, sought, through every
    nook
In house or garden, any casual work
Of use or ornament; and with a strange,

Amusing, yet uneasy, novelty, 575
He mingled, where he might, the various
  tasks
Of summer, autumn, winter, and of
  spring.
But this endured not; his good humour
  soon
Became a weight in which no pleasure
  was:
And poverty brought on a petted mood
And a sore temper: day by day he
  drooped, 581
And he would leave his work—and to the
  town
Would turn without an errand his slack
  steps;
Or wander here and there among the
  fields.
One while he would speak lightly of his
  babes, 585
And with a cruel tongue: at other times
He tossed them with a false unnatural
  joy:
And 'twas a rueful thing to see the looks
Of the poor innocent children. "Every
  smile,"
Said Margaret to me, here beneath these
  trees, 590
"Made my heart bleed."'
          At this the Wanderer paused;
And, looking up to those enormous elms,
He said, ''Tis now the hour of deepest
  noon.
At this still season of repose and peace,
This hour when all things which are not
  at rest 595
Are cheerful; while this multitude of flies
With tuneful hum is filling all the air;
Why should a tear be on an old Man's
  cheek?
Why should we thus, with an untoward
  mind,
And in the weakness of humanity, 600
From natural wisdom turn our hearts
  away;
To natural comfort shut our eyes and ears;
And, feeding on disquiet, thus disturb
The calm of nature with our restless
  thoughts?'

HE spake with somewhat of a solemn
  tone: 605
But, when he ended, there was in his face
Such easy cheerfulness, a look so mild,
That for a little time it stole away
All recollection; and that simple tale
Passed from my mind like a forgotten
  sound. 610
A while on trivial things we held dis-
  course,
To me soon tasteless. In my own despite,
I thought of that poor Woman as of one

Whom I had known and loved. He had
  rehearsed 614
Her homely tale with such familiar power,
With such an active countenance, an eye
So busy, that the things of which he spake
Seemed present; and, attention now
  relaxed,
A heart-felt chillness crept along my veins.
I rose; and, having left the breezy shade,
Stood drinking comfort from the warmer
  sun, 621
That had not cheered me long—ere, look-
  ing round
Upon that tranquil Ruin, I returned,
And begged of the old Man that, for my
  sake,
He would resume his story.

                          He replied, 625
'It were a wantonness, and would de-
  mand
Severe reproof, if we were men whose
  hearts
Could hold vain dalliance with the misery
Even of the dead; contented thence to
  draw
A momentary pleasure, never marked
By reason, barren of all future good. 631
But we have known that there is often
  found
In mournful thoughts, and always might
  be found,
A power to virtue friendly; were 't not so,
I am a dreamer among men, indeed 635
An idle dreamer! 'Tis a common tale,
An ordinary sorrow of man's life,
A tale of silent suffering, hardly clothed
In bodily form.—But without further
  bidding
I will proceed.
              While thus it fared with them,
To whom this cottage, till those hapless
  years, 641
Had been a blessèd home, it was my
  chance
To travel in a country far remote;
And when these lofty elms once more
  appeared
What pleasant expectations lured me on
O'er the flat Common!—With quick step
  I reached 646
The threshold, lifted with light hand the
  latch;
But, when I entered, Margaret looked at
  me
A little while; then turned her head
  away
Speechless,—and, sitting down upon a
  chair, 650
Wept bitterly. I wist not what to do,
Nor how to speak to her. Poor Wretch!
  at last
She rose from off her seat, and then,—
  O Sir!

I cannot *tell* how she pronounced my
   name:—
With fervent love, and with a face of
   grief   655
Unutterably helpless, and a look
That seemed to cling upon me, she
   enquired
If I had seen her husband. As she spake
A strange surprise and fear came to my
   heart,
Nor had I power to answer ere she told
That he had disappeared—not two months
   gone.   661
He left his house: two wretched days had
   past,
And on the third, as wistfully she raised
Her head from off her pillow, to look
   forth,   664
Like one in trouble, for returning light,
Within her chamber-casement she espied
A folded paper, lying as if placed
To meet her waking eyes. This trem-
   blingly
She opened—found no writing, but beheld
Pieces of money carefully enclosed,   670
Silver and gold. "I shuddered at the
   sight,"
Said Margaret, "for I knew it was his
   hand
That must have placed it there; and ere
   that day
Was ended, that long anxious day, I
   learned,
From one who by my husband had been
   sent   675
With the sad news, that he had joined
   a troop
Of soldiers, going to a distant land.
—He left me thus—he could not gather
   heart
To take a farewell of me; for he feared
That I should follow with my babes, and
   sink   680
Beneath the misery of that wandering
   life."

   'This tale did Margaret tell with many
   tears:
And, when she ended, I had little power
To give her comfort, and was glad to take
Such words of hope from her own mouth
   as served   685
To cheer us both. But long we had not
   talked
Ere we built up a pile of better thoughts,
And with a brighter eye she looked around
As if she had been shedding tears of joy.
We parted.—'Twas the time of early
   spring;   690
I left her busy with her garden tools;
And well remember, o'er that fence she
   looked,
And, while I paced along the foot-way
   path,

Called out, and sent a blessing after me,
With tender cheerfulness, and with a
   voice   695
That seemed the very sound of happy
   thoughts.

   'I roved o'er many a hill and many a
   dale,
With my accustomed load; in heat and
   cold,
Through many a wood and many an open
   ground,
In sunshine and in shade, in wet and
   fair,   700
Drooping or blithe of heart, as might
   befall;
My best companions now the driving
   winds,
And now the "trotting brooks" and whis-
   pering trees,
And now the music of my own sad steps,
With many a short-lived thought that
   passed between,   705
And disappeared.
                    I journeyed back this way,
When, in the warmth of midsummer, the
   wheat
Was yellow; and the soft and bladed grass,
Springing afresh, had o'er the hay-field
   spread
Its tender verdure. At the door arrived,
I found that she was absent. In the
   shade,   711
Where now we sit, I waited her return.
Her cottage, then a cheerful object, wore
Its customary look,—only, it seemed,
The honeysuckle, crowding round the
   porch,   715
Hung down in heavier tufts; and that
   bright weed,
The yellow stone-crop, suffered to take
   root
Along the window's edge, profusely grew
Blinding the lower panes. I turned aside,
And strolled into her garden. It appeared
To lag behind the season, and had lost
Its pride of neatness. Daisy-flowers and
   thrift
Had broken their trim border-lines, and
   straggled
O'er paths they used to deck: carnations,
   once   724
Prized for surpassing beauty, and no less
For the peculiar pains they had required,
Declined their languid heads, wanting
   support.
The cumbrous bind-weed, with its wreaths
   and bells,
Had twined about her two small rows of
   peas,
And dragged them to the earth.
                              Ere this an hour
Was wasted.—Back I turned my restless
   steps;   731

A stranger passed; and, guessing whom
I sought,
He said that she was used to ramble far.—
The sun was sinking in the west; and now
I sate with sad impatience. From within
Her solitary infant cried aloud;   736
Then, like a blast that dies away self-
stilled,
The voice was silent. From the bench I
rose;
But neither could divert nor soothe my
thoughts.   739
The spot, though fair, was very desolate—
The longer I remained, more desolate:
And, looking round me, now I first
observed
The corner stones, on either side the
porch,
With dull red stains discoloured, and
stuck o'er
With tufts and hairs of wool, as if the
sheep,   745
That fed upon the Common, thither came
Familiarly, and found a couching-place
Even at her threshold. Deeper shadows
fell
From these tall elms; the cottage-clock
struck eight;—
I turned, and saw her distant a few steps.
Her face was pale and thin—her figure,
too,   751
Was changed. As she unlocked the door,
she said,
"It grieves me you have waited here so
long,
But, in good truth, I've wandered much
of late,
And, sometimes—to my shame I speak—
have need   755
Of my best prayers to bring me back
again."
While on the board she spread our evening
meal,
She told me—interrupting not the work
Which gave employment to her listless
hands—
That she had parted with her elder child;
To a kind master on a distant farm   761
Now happily apprenticed.—"I perceive
You look at me, and you have cause;
to-day
I have been travelling far; and many days
About the fields I wander, knowing
this   765
Only, that what I seek I cannot find;
And so I waste my time: for I am changed;
And to myself," said she, "have done
much wrong
And to this helpless infant. I have slept
Weeping, and weeping have I waked; my
tears   770
Have flowed as if my body were not such
As others are; and I could never die.
But I am now in mind and in my heart

More easy; and I hope," said she, "that
God
Will give me patience to endure the
things   775
Which I behold at home."
                    It would have grieved
Your very soul to see her. Sir, I feel
The story linger in my heart; I fear
'Tis long and tedious; but my spirit clings
To that poor Woman:—so familiarly   780
Do I perceive her manner, and her look,
And presence; and so deeply do I feel
Her goodness, that, not seldom, in my
walks
A momentary trance comes over me;   784
And to myself I seem to muse on One
By sorrow laid asleep; or borne away,
A human being destined to awake
To human life, or something very near
To human life, when he shall come again
For whom she suffered. Yes, it would
have grieved   790
Your very soul to see her: evermore
Her eyelids drooped, her eyes downward
were cast;
And, when she at her table gave me
food,
She did not look at me. Her voice was
low,   794
Her body was subdued. In every act
Pertaining to her house-affairs, appeared
The careless stillness of a thinking mind
Self-occupied; to which all outward
things
Are like an idle matter. Still she sighed,
But yet no motion of the breast was seen,
No heaving of the heart. While by the
fire   801
We sate together, sighs came on my ear,
I knew not how, and hardly whence they
came.

'Ere my departure, to her care I gave,
For her son's use, some tokens of regard,
Which with a look of welcome she re-
ceived;   806
And I exhorted her to place her trust
In God's good love, and seek his help by
prayer.
I took my staff, and, when I kissed her
babe,
The tears stood in her eyes. I left her
then   810
With the best hope and comfort I could
give:
She thanked me for my wish;—but for my
hope
It seemed she did not thank me.
                    I returned,
And took my rounds along this road again
When on its sunny bank the primrose
flower   815
Peeped forth, to give an earnest of the
Spring.

I found her sad and drooping: she had
    learned
No tidings of her husband; if he lived,
She knew not that he lived; if he were
    dead,
She knew not he was dead. She seemed
    the same   820
In person and appearance; but her house
Bespake a sleepy hand of negligence;
The floor was neither dry nor neat, the
    hearth
Was comfortless, and her small lot of
    books,
Which, in the cottage-window, heretofore
Had been piled up against the corner
    panes   826
In seemly order, now, with straggling
    leaves
Lay scattered here and there, open or shut,
As they had chanced to fall. Her infant
    Babe
Had from its mother caught the trick of
    grief,   830
And sighed among its playthings. I
    withdrew,
And once again entering the garden saw,
More plainly still, that poverty and grief
Were now come nearer to her: weeds
    defaced
The hardened soil, and knots of withered
    grass: 835
No ridges there appeared of clear black
    mould,
No winter greenness; of her herbs and
    flowers,
It seemed the better part were gnawed
    away
Or trampled into earth; a chain of straw,
Which had been twined about the slender
    stem   840
Of a young apple-tree, lay at its root;
The bark was nibbled round by truant
    sheep.
—Margaret stood near, her infant in her
    arms,
And, noting that my eye was on the tree,
She said, "I fear it will be dead and gone
Ere Robert come again." When to the
    House   846
We had returned together, she enquired
If I had any hope:—but for her babe
And for her little orphan boy, she said,
She had no wish to live, that she must
    die   850
Of sorrow. Yet I saw the idle loom
Still in its place; his Sunday garments
    hung
Upon the self-same nail; his very staff
Stood undisturbed behind the door.
                              And when,
In bleak December, I retraced this way,
She told me that her little babe was dead,
And she was left alone.' She now, released
From her maternal cares, had taken up

The employment common through these
    wilds, and gained,
By spinning hemp, a pittance for herself;
And for this end had hired a neighbour's
    boy   861
To give her needful help. That very time
Most willingly she put her work aside,
And walked with me along the miry road,
Heedless how far; and, in such piteous
    sort   865
That any heart had ached to hear her,
    begged
That, wheresoe'er I went, I still would ask
For him whom she had lost. We parted
    then—
Our final parting; for from that time forth
Did many seasons pass ere I returned 870
Into this tract again.
                        Nine tedious years;
From their first separation, nine long
    years,
She lingered in unquiet widowhood;
A Wife and Widow. Needs must it have
    been
A sore heart-wasting! I have heard, my
    Friend,   875
That in yon arbour oftentimes she sate
Alone, through half the vacant sabbath
    day;
And, if a dog passed by, she still would
    quit
The shade, and look abroad. On this old
    bench   879
For hours she sate; and evermore her eye
Was busy in the distance, shaping things
That made her heart beat quick. You see
    that path,
Now faint,—the grass has crept o'er its
    grey line;
There, to and fro, she paced through many
    a day
Of the warm summer, from a belt of hemp
That girt her waist, spinning the long-
    drawn thread   886
With backward steps. Yet ever as there
    passed
A man whose garments showed the sol-
    dier's red,
Or crippled mendicant in sailor's garb,
The little child who sate to turn the wheel
Ceased from his task; and she with falter-
    ing voice   891
Made many a fond enquiry; and when they,
Whose presence gave no comfort, were
    gone by,
Her heart was still more sad. And by yon
    gate,
That bars the traveller's road, she often
    stood,   895
And when a stranger horseman came, the
    latch
Would lift, and in his face look wistfully:
Most happy, if, from aught discovered
    there

Of tender feeling, she might dare repeat
The same sad question. Meanwhile her
  poor Hut   900
Sank to decay; for he was gone, whose
  hand,
At the first nipping of October frost,
Closed up each chink, and with fresh
  bands of straw
Chequered the green-grown thatch. And
  so she lived
Through the long winter, reckless and
  alone;   905
Until her house by frost, and thaw, and
  rain,
Was sapped; and while she slept, the
  nightly damps
Did chill her breast; and in the stormy
  day
Her tattered clothes were ruffled by the
  wind,
Even at the side of her own fire. Yet
  still   910
She loved this wretched spot, nor would
  for worlds
Have parted hence; and still that length
  of road,
And this rude bench, one torturing hope
  endeared,
Fast rooted at her heart: and here, my
  Friend,—
In sickness she remained; and here she
  died,   915
Last human tenant of these ruined walls!'

The old Man ceased: he saw that I was
  moved;
From that low bench, rising instinctively
I turned aside in weakness, nor had power
To thank him for the tale which he had
  told.   920
I stood, and leaning o'er the garden wall
Reviewed that Woman's sufferings; and
  it seemed
To comfort me while with a brother's love
I blessed her in the impotence of grief.
Then towards the cottage I returned; and
  traced   925
Fondly, though with an interest more
  mild,
That secret spirit of humanity
Which, 'mid the calm oblivious tendencies
Of nature, 'mid her plants, and weeds,
  and flowers,
And silent overgrowings, still survived.
The old Man, noting this, resumed, and
  said;   931
'My Friend! enough to sorrow you have
  given,

The purposes of wisdom ask no more:
Nor more would she have craved as due
  to One
Who, in her worst distress, had ofttimes
  felt   935
The unbounded might of prayer; and
  learned, with soul
Fixed on the Cross, that consolation
  springs,
From sources deeper far than deepest
  pain,
For the meek Sufferer. Why then should
  we read
The forms of things with an unworthy
  eye?   940
She sleeps in the calm earth, and peace is
  here.
I well remember that those very plumes,
Those weeds, and the high spear-grass on
  that wall,
By mist and silent rain-drops silvered o'er,
As once I passed, into my heart conveyed
So still an image of tranquillity,   946
So calm and still, and looked so beautiful
Amid the uneasy thoughts which filled
  my mind,
That what we feel of sorrow and despair
From ruin and from change, and all the
  grief   950
That passing shows of Being leave behind,
Appeared an idle dream, that could main-
  tain,
Nowhere, dominion o'er the enlightened
  spirit
Whose meditative sympathies repose
Upon the breast of Faith. I turned
  away,   955
And walked along my road in happiness.'

He ceased. Ere long the sun declining
  shot
A slant and mellow radiance, which began
To fall upon us, while, beneath the trees,
We sate on that low bench: and now we
  felt,   960
Admonished thus, the sweet hour coming
  on.
A linnet warbled from those lofty elms,
A thrush sang loud, and other melodies,
At distance heard, peopled the milder air.
The old Man rose, and, with a sprightly
  mien   965
Of hopeful preparation, grasped his staff;
Together casting then a farewell look
Upon those silent walls, we left the shade;
And, ere the stars were visible, had
  reached   969
A village-inn,—our evening resting-place.

BOOK SECOND

THE SOLITARY

ARGUMENT

The Author describes his travels with the Wanderer, whose character is further illustrated.—Morning scene, and view of a Village Wake.—Wanderer's account of a Friend whom he purposes to visit.—View, from an eminence, of the Valley which his Friend had chosen for his retreat.—Sound of singing from below.—A funeral procession.—Descent into the Valley.—Observations drawn from the Wanderer at sight of a book accidentally discovered in a recess in the Valley.—Meeting with the Wanderer's friend, the Solitary.—Wanderer's description of the mode of burial in this mountainous district.—Solitary contrasts with this, that of the individual carried a few minutes before from the cottage.—The cottage entered.—Description of the Solitary's apartment.—Repast there.—View, from the window, of two mountain summits; and the Solitary's description of the companionship they afford him.—Account of the departed inmate of the cottage.—Description of a grand spectacle upon the mountains, with its effect upon the Solitary's mind.—Leave the house.

In days of yore how fortunately fared
The Minstrel! wandering on from hall to
    hall,
Baronial court or royal; cheered with
    gifts
Munificent, and love, and ladies' praise;
Now meeting on his road an armed
    knight,   5
Now resting with a pilgrim by the side
Of a clear brook;—beneath an abbey's
    roof
One evening sumptuously lodged; the
    next,
Humbly in a religious hospital;
Or with some merry outlaws of the wood;
Or haply shrouded in a hermit's cell.   11
Him, sleeping or awake, the robber
    spared;
He walked—protected from the sword of
    war
By virtue of that sacred instrument
His harp, suspended at the traveller's
    side;   15
His dear companion wheresoe'er he went
Opening from land to land an easy way
By melody, and by the charm of verse.
Yet not the noblest of that honoured Race
Drew happier, loftier, more empassioned,
    thoughts   20
From his long journeyings and eventful
    life,
Than this obscure Itinerant had skill
To gather, ranging through the tamer
    ground
Of these our unimaginative days;
Both while he trod the earth in humblest
    guise   25
Accoutred with his burthen and his staff;
And now, when free to move with lighter
    pace.

What wonder, then, if I, whose favourite
    school
Hath been the fields, the roads, and rural
    lanes,
Looked on this guide with reverential
    love?   30

Each with the other pleased, we now
    pursued
Our journey, under favourable skies.
Turn wheresoe'er we would, he was a
    light
Unfailing: not a hamlet could we pass,
Rarely a house, that did not yield to him
Remembrances; or from his tongue call
    forth   36
Some way-beguiling tale. Nor less regard
Accompanied those strains of apt dis-
    course,
Which nature's various objects might
    inspire;
And in the silence of his face I read   40
His overflowing spirit. Birds and beasts,
And the mute fish that glances in the
    stream,
And harmless reptile coiling in the sun,
And gorgeous insect hovering in the air,
The fowl domestic, and the household
    dog—   45
In his capacious mind, he loved them all:
Their rights acknowledging he felt for all.
Oft was occasion given me to perceive
How the calm pleasures of the pasturing
    herd
To happy contemplation soothed his
    walk;   50
How the poor brute's condition, forced to
    run
Its course of suffering in the public road,
Sad contrast! all too often smote his heart
With unavailing pity. Rich in love
And sweet humanity, he was, himself,   55
To the degree that he desired, beloved.
Smiles of good-will from faces that he
    knew
Greeted us all day long; we took our seats
By many a cottage-hearth, where he
    received
The welcome of an Inmate from afar,   60
And I at once forgot I was a Stranger.
—Nor was he loth to enter ragged huts,
Huts where his charity was blest; his voice
Heard as the voice of an experienced
    friend.

And, sometimes—where the poor man
   held dispute   65
With his own mind, unable to subdue
Impatience through inaptness to perceive
General distress in his particular lot;
Or cherishing resentment, or in vain
Struggling against it; with a soul per-
   plexed,   70
And finding in herself no steady power
To draw the line of comfort that divides
Calamity, the chastisement of Heaven,
From the injustice of our brother men—
To him appeal was made as to a judge;
Who, with an understanding heart, al-
   layed   76
The perturbation; listened to the plea;
Resolved the dubious point; and sentence
   gave
So grounded, so applied, that it was heard
With softened spirit, even when it con-
   demned.   80

   Such intercourse I witnessed, while we
   roved,
Now as his choice directed, now as mine;
Or both, with equal readiness of will,
Our course submitting to the changeful
   breeze
Of accident. But when the rising sun 85
Had three times called us to renew our
   walk,
My Fellow-traveller, with earnest voice,
As if the thought were but a moment old,
Claimed absolute dominion for the day.
We started—and he led me toward the
   hills,   90
Up through an ample vale, with higher
   hills
Before us, mountains stern and desolate;
But, in the majesty of distance, now
Set off, and to our ken appearing fair
Of aspect, with aerial softness clad,   95
And beautified with morning's purple
   beams.

   The wealthy, the luxurious, by the stress
Of business roused, or pleasure, ere their
   time,
May roll in chariots, or provoke the hoofs
Of the fleet coursers they bestride, to raise
From earth the dust of morning, slow to
   rise;   101
And they, if blest with health and hearts
   at ease,
Shall lack not their enjoyment:—but how
   faint
Compared with ours! who, pacing side
   by side,
Could, with an eye of leisure, look on all
That we beheld; and lend the listening
   sense   106
To every grateful sound of earth and air;
Pausing at will—our spirits braced, our
   thoughts

Pleasant as roses in the thickets blown,
And pure as dew bathing their crimson
   leaves.   110

Mount slowly, sun! that we may journey
   long,
By this dark hill protected from thy
   beams!
Such is the summer pilgrim's frequent
   wish;
But quickly from among our morning
   thoughts
'Twas chased away: for, toward the
   western side   115
Of the broad vale, casting a casual glance,
We saw a throng of people;—wherefore
   met?
Blithe notes of music, suddenly let loose
On the thrilled ear, and flags uprising,
   yield
Prompt answer; they proclaim the annual
   Wake,   120
Which the bright season favours.—Tabor
   and pipe
In purpose join to hasten or reprove
The laggard Rustic; and repay with boons
Of merriment a party-coloured knot, 124
Already formed upon the village-green.
—Beyond the limits of the shadow cast
By the broad hill, glistened upon our
   sight
That gay assemblage. Round them and
   above,
Glitter, with dark recesses interposed,
Casement, and cottage-roof, and stems of
   trees   130
Half-veiled in vapoury cloud, the silver
   steam
Of dews fast melting on their leafy boughs
By the strong sunbeams smitten. Like
   a mast
Of gold, the Maypole shines; as if the
   rays
Of morning, aided by exhaling dew,   135
With gladsome influence could re-animate
The faded garlands dangling from its
   sides.

   Said I, 'The music and the sprightly
   scene
Invite us; shall we quit our road, and join
These festive matins?'—He replied, 'Not
   loth   140
To linger I would here with you partake,
Not one hour merely, but till evening's
   close,
The simple pastimes of the day and place.
By the fleet Racers, ere the sun be set,
The turf of yon large pasture will be
   skimmed;   145
There, too, the lusty Wrestlers shall con-
   tend:
But know we not that he, who intermits
The appointed task and duties of the day,

Untunes full oft the pleasures of the
    day;
Checking the finer spirits that refuse 150
To flow, when purposes are lightly
    changed?
A length of journey yet remains untraced:
Let us proceed.' Then, pointing with his
    staff
Raised toward those craggy summits, his
    intent
He thus imparted:—
                'In a spot that lies 155
Among yon mountain fastnesses con-
    cealed,
You will receive, before the hour of noon,
Good recompense, I hope, for this day's
    toil,
From sight of One who lives secluded
    there,
Lonesome and lost: of whom, and whose
    past life,   160
(Not to forestall such knowledge as may
    be
More faithfully collected from himself)
This brief communication shall suffice.

'Though now sojourning there, he, like
    myself,   164
Sprang from a stock of lowly parentage
Among the wilds of Scotland, in a tract
Where many a sheltered and well-tended
    plant
Bears, on the humblest ground of social
    life,
Blossoms of piety and innocence.
Such grateful promises his youth dis-
    played: 170
And, having shown in study forward
    zeal,
He to the Ministry was duly called;
And straight, incited by a curious mind
Filled with vague hopes, he undertook
    the charge
Of Chaplain to a military troop   175
Cheered by the Highland bagpipe, as they
    marched
In plaided vest,—his fellow-countrymen.
This office filling, yet by native power
And force of native inclination made
An intellectual ruler in the haunts   180
Of social vanity, he walked the world,
Gay, and affecting graceful gaiety;
Lax, buoyant—less a pastor with his flock
Than a soldier among soldiers—lived and
    roamed
Where Fortune led:—and Fortune, who
    oft proves   185
The careless wanderer's friend, to him
    made known
A blooming Lady—a conspicuous flower,
Admired for beauty, for her sweetness
    praised;
Whom he had sensibility to love,
Ambition to attempt, and skill to win. 190

'For this fair Bride, most rich in gifts
    of mind,
Nor sparingly endowed with worldly
    wealth,
His office he relinquished; and retired
From the world's notice to a rural home.
Youth's season yet with him was scarcely
    past,   195
And she was in youth's prime. How free
    their love,
How full their joy! Till, pitiable doom!
In the short course of one undreaded year,
Death blasted all. Death suddenly o'er-
    threw
Two lovely Children—all that they
    possessed!   200
The Mother followed:—miserably bare
The one Survivor stood; he wept, he
    prayed
For his dismissal, day and night, com-
    pelled
To hold communion with the grave, and
    face
With pain the regions of eternity.   205
An uncomplaining apathy displaced
This anguish; and, indifferent to delight,
To aim and purpose, he consumed his
    days,
To private interest dead, and public care.
So lived he; so he might have died.
                                But now,
To the wide world's astonishment, ap-
    peared   211
A glorious opening, the unlooked-for
    dawn,
That promised everlasting joy to France!
Her voice of social transport reached even
    him!
He broke from his contracted bounds,
    repaired   215
To the great City, an emporium then
Of golden expectations, and receiving
Freights every day from a new world of
    hope.
Thither his popular talents he transferred;
And, from the pulpit, zealously main-
    tained   220
The cause of Christ and civil liberty,
As one, and moving to one glorious end.
Intoxicating service! I might say
A happy service; for he was sincere
As vanity and fondness for applause, 225
And new and shapeless wishes, would
    allow.

'That righteous cause (such power hath
    freedom) bound,
For one hostility, in friendly league,
Ethereal natures and the worst of slaves;
Was served by rival advocates that came
From regions opposite as heaven and hell.
One courage seemed to animate them all:
And, from the dazzling conquests daily
    gained

By their united efforts, there arose
A proud and most presumptuous con-
    fidence   235
In the transcendent wisdom of the age,
And her discernment; not alone in rights,
And in the origin and bounds of power
Social and temporal; but in laws divine,
Deduced by reason, or to faith revealed.
An overweening trust was raised; and
    fear   241
Cast out, alike of person and of thing.
Plague from this union spread, whose
    subtle bane
The strongest did not easily escape;
And He, what wonder! took a mortal
    taint.   245
How shall I trace the change, how bear
    to tell
That he broke faith with them whom he
    had laid
In earth's dark chambers, with a Chris-
    tian's hope!
An infidel contempt of holy writ
Stole by degrees upon his mind; and
    hence   250
Life, like that Roman Janus, double-
    faced;
Vilest hypocrisy—the laughing, gay
Hypocrisy, not leagued with fear, but
    pride.
Smooth words he had to wheedle simple
    souls;
But, for disciples of the inner school, 255
Old freedom was old servitude, and they
The wisest whose opinions stooped the
    least
To known restraints; and who most
    boldly drew
Hopeful prognostications from a creed,
That, in the light of false philosophy, 260
Spread like a halo round a misty moon,
Widening its circle as the storms advance.

'His sacred function was at length
    renounced;
And every day and every place enjoyed
The unshackled layman's natural liberty;
Speech, manners, morals, all without dis-
    guise.   266
I do not wish to wrong him; though the
    course
Of private life licentiously displayed
Unhallowed actions—planted like a
    crown
Upon the insolent aspiring brow   270
Of spurious notions—worn as open signs
Of prejudice subdued—still he retained,
'Mid much abasement, what he had
    received
From nature, an intense and glowing
    mind.
Wherefore, when humbled Liberty grew
    weak,   275
And mortal sickness on her face appeared,

He coloured objects to his own desire
As with a lover's passion. Yet his moods
Of pain were keen as those of better men,
Nay keener, as his fortitude was less: 280
And he continued, when worse days were
    come,
To deal about his sparkling eloquence,
Struggling against the strange reverse
    with zeal
That showed like happiness. But, in
    despite
Of all this outside bravery, within,   285
He neither felt encouragement nor hope:
For moral dignity, and strength of mind,
Were wanting; and simplicity of life;
And reverence for himself; and, last and
    best,
Confiding thoughts, through love and fear
    of Him   290
Before whose sight the troubles of this
    world
Are vain, as billows in a tossing sea.

    'The glory of the times fading away—
The splendour, which had given a festal
    air
To self-importance, hallowed it, and
    veiled   295
From his own sight—this gone, he for-
    feited
All joy in human nature; was consumed,
And vexed, and chafed, by levity and
    scorn,
And fruitless indignation; galled by pride;
Made desperate by contempt of men who
    throve   300
Before his sight in power or fame, and
    won,
Without desert, what he desired; weak
    men,
Too weak even for his envy or his hate!
Tormented thus, after a wandering course
Of discontent, and inwardly opprest 305
With malady—in part, I fear, provoked
By weariness of life—he fixed his home,
Or, rather say, sate down by very chance,
Among these rugged hills; where now he
    dwells,
And wastes the sad remainder of his
    hours,   310
Steeped in a self-indulging spleen, that
    wants not
Its own voluptuousness;—on this re-
    solved,
With this content, that he will live and
    die
Forgotten,—at safe distance from "a
    world
Not moving to his mind."'
                        These serious words
Closed the preparatory notices   316
That served my Fellow-traveller to beguile
The way, while we advanced up that wide
    vale.

Diverging now (as if his quest had been
Some secret of the mountains, cavern,
    fall   320
Of water, or some lofty eminence,
Renowned for splendid prospect far and
    wide)
We scaled, without a track to ease our
    steps,
A steep ascent; and reached a dreary
    plain,
With a tumultuous waste of huge hill
    tops   325
Before us; savage region! which I paced
Dispirited: when, all at once, behold!
Beneath our feet, a little lowly vale,
A lowly vale, and yet uplifted high
Among the mountains; even as if the
    spot   330
Had been from eldest time by wish of
    theirs
So placed, to be shut out from all the
    world!
Urn-like it was in shape, deep as an urn;
With rocks encompassed, save that to the
    south
Was one small opening, where a heath-
    clad ridge   335
Supplied a boundary less abrupt and
    close;
A quiet treeless nook, with two green
    fields,
A liquid pool that glittered in the sun,
And one bare dwelling; one abode, no
    more!
It seemed the home of poverty and toil,
Though not of want: the little fields, made
    green   341
By husbandry of many thrifty years,
Paid cheerful tribute to the moorland
    house.
—There crows the cock, single in his
    domain:
The small birds find in spring no thicket
    there   345
To shroud them; only from the neighbour-
    ing vales
The cuckoo, straggling up to the hill tops,
Shouteth faint tidings of some gladder
    place.

Ah! what a sweet Recess, thought I,
    is here!
Instantly throwing down my limbs at
    ease   350
Upon a bed of heath;—full many a spot
Of hidden beauty have I chanced to espy
Among the mountains; never one like
    this;
So lonesome, and so perfectly secure;
Not melancholy—no, for it is green, 355
And bright, and fertile, furnished in itself
With the few needful things that life
    requires.
—In rugged arms how softly does it lie,

How tenderly protected! Far and near
We have an image of the pristine earth,
The planet in its nakedness: were this 361
Man's only dwelling, sole appointed seat,
First, last, and single, in the breathing
    world,
It could not be more quiet: peace is here
Or nowhere; days unruffled by the gale
Of public news or private; years that
    pass   366
Forgetfully; uncalled upon to pay
The common penalties of mortal life,
Sickness, or accident, or grief, or pain.

On these and kindred thoughts intent
    I lay   370
In silence musing by my Comrade's side,
He also silent; when from out the heart
Of that profound abyss a solemn voice,
Or several voices in one solemn sound,
Was heard ascending; mournful, deep,
    and slow   375
The cadence, as of psalms—a funeral
    dirge!
We listened, looking down upon the hut,
But seeing no one: meanwhile from be-
    low
The strain continued, spiritual as before;
And now distinctly could I recognise 380
These words:—'*Shall in the grave thy love
    be known,*
In death thy faithfulness?'—'God rest his
    soul!'
Said the old man, abruptly breaking
    silence,—
'He is departed, and finds peace at last!'

This scarcely spoken, and those holy
    strains   385
Not ceasing, forth appeared in view a
    band
Of rustic persons, from behind the hut
Bearing a coffin in the midst, with which
They shaped their course along the sloping
    side
Of that small valley, singing as they
    moved;   390
A sober company and few, the men
Bare-headed, and all decently attired!
Some steps when they had thus advanced,
    the dirge
Ended; and, from the stillness that ensued
Recovering, to my Friend I said, 'You
    spake,   395
Methought, with apprehension that these
    rites
Are paid to Him upon whose shy retreat
This day we purposed to intrude.'—'I
    did so,
But let us hence, that we may learn the
    truth:
Perhaps it is not he but some one else 400
For whom this pious service is performed;
Some other tenant of the solitude.'

So, to a steep and difficult descent
Trusting ourselves, we wound from crag
    to crag,
Where passage could be won; and, as the
    last   405
Of the mute train, behind the heathy top
Of that off-sloping outlet, disappeared,
I, more impatient in my downward
    course,
Had landed upon easy ground; and there
Stood waiting for my Comrade. When
    behold   410
An object that enticed my steps aside!
A narrow, winding, entry opened out
Into a platform—that lay, sheepfold-wise,
Enclosed between an upright mass of rock
And one old moss-grown wall;—a cool
    recess,   415
And fanciful! For where the rock and
    wall
Met in an angle, hung a penthouse, framed
By thrusting two rude staves into the wall
And overlaying them with mountain sods;
To weather-fend a little turf-built seat 420
Whereon a full-grown man might rest,
    nor dread
The burning sunshine, or a transient
    shower;
But the whole plainly wrought by chil-
    dren's hands!
Whose skill had thronged the floor with
    a proud show
Of baby-houses, curiously arranged; 425
Nor wanting ornament of walks between,
With mimic trees inserted in the turf,
And gardens interposed. Pleased with
    the sight,
I could not choose but beckon to my
    Guide,
Who, entering, round him threw a careless
    glance   430
Impatient to pass on, when I exclaimed,
'Lo! what is here?' and, stooping down,
    drew forth
A book, that, in the midst of stones and
    moss
And wreck of party-coloured earthenware,
Aptly disposed, had lent its help to raise
One of those petty structures. 'His it
    must be!'   436
Exclaimed the Wanderer, 'cannot but be
    his,
And he is gone!' The book, which in my
    hand
Had opened of itself (for it was swoln
With searching damp, and seemingly had
    lain   440
To the injurious elements exposed
From week to week,) I found to be a work
In the French tongue, a Novel of Voltaire,
His famous Optimist. 'Unhappy Man!'
Exclaimed my Friend: 'here then has
    been to him   445
Retreat within retreat, a sheltering-place

Within how deep a shelter! He had fits,
Even to the last, of genuine tenderness,
And loved the haunts of children; here,
    no doubt,
Pleasing and pleased, he shared their
    simple sports,   450
Or sate companionless; and here the book,
Left and forgotten in his careless way,
Must by the cottage-children have been
    found:
Heaven bless them, and their inconsiderate
    work!
To what odd purpose have the darlings
    turned   455
This sad memorial of their hapless friend!'

'Me,' said I, 'most doth it surprise,
    to find
Such book in such a place!'—'A book it
    is,'
He answered, 'to the Person suited well,
Though little suited to surrounding
    things: 460
'Tis strange, I grant; and stranger still had
    been
To see the Man who owned it, dwelling
    here,
With one poor shepherd, far from all the
    world!—
Now, if our errand hath been thrown
    away,   464
As from these intimations I forebode,
Grieved shall I be—less for my sake than
    yours,
And least of all for him who is no more.'

    By this, the book was in the old Man's
    hand;
And he continued, glancing on the leaves
An eye of scorn:—'The lover,' said he,
    'doomed   470
To love when hope hath failed him—
    whom no depth
Of privacy is deep enough to hide,
Hath yet his bracelet or his lock of hair,
And that is joy to him. When change of
    times
Hath summoned kings to scaffolds, do
    but give   475
The faithful servant, who must hide his
    head
Henceforth in whatsoever nook he may,
A kerchief sprinkled with his master's
    blood,
And he too hath his comforter. How
    poor,
Beyond all poverty how destitute,   480
Must that Man have been left, who, hither
    driven,
Flying or seeking, could yet bring with
    him
No dearer relique, and no better stay,
Than this dull product of a scoffer's pen,
Impure conceits discharging from a heart

Hardened by impious pride!—I did not
  fear   486
To tax you with this journey;'—mildly
  said
My venerable Friend, as forth we stepped
Into the presence of the cheerful light—
'For I have knowledge that you do not
  shrink   490
From moving spectacles;—but let us on.'

So speaking, on he went, and at the word
I followed, till he made a sudden stand:
For full in view, approaching through a
  gate
That opened from the enclosure of green
  fields   495
Into the rough uncultivated ground,
Behold the Man whom he had fancied
  dead!
I knew from his deportment, mien, and
  dress,
That it could be no other; a pale face,
A meagre person, tall, and in a garb   500
Not rustic—dull and faded like himself!
He saw us not, though distant but few
  steps;
For he was busy, dealing, from a store
Upon a broad leaf carried, choicest strings
Of red ripe currants; gift by which he
  strove,   505
With intermixture of endearing words,
To soothe a Child, who walked beside
  him, weeping
As if disconsolate.—'They to the grave
Are bearing him, my Little-one,' he said,
'To the dark pit; but he will feel no pain;
His body is at rest, his soul in heaven.' 511

More might have followed—but my
  honoured Friend
Broke in upon the Speaker with a frank
And cordial greeting.—Vivid was the
  light
That flashed and sparkled from the other's
  eyes;   515
He was all fire: no shadow on his brow
Remained, nor sign of sickness on his face.
Hands joined he with his Visitant,—a
  grasp,
An eager grasp; and many moments'
  space—
When the first glow of pleasure was no
  more,   520
And, of the sad appearance which at once
Had vanished, much was come and com-
  ing back—
An amicable smile retained the life
Which it had unexpectedly received,
Upon his hollow cheek. 'How kind,' he
  said,   525
'Nor could your coming have been better
  timed;
For this, you see, is in our narrow world
A day of sorrow. I have here a charge'—

And, speaking thus, he patted tenderly
The sun-burnt forehead of the weeping
  child—   530
'A little mourner, whom it is my task
To comfort;—but how came ye?—if yon
  track   .
(Which doth at once befriend us and
  betray)
Conducted hither your most welcome feet,
Ye could not miss the funeral train—they
  yet   535
Have scarcely disappeared.' 'This bloom-
  ing Child,'
Said the old Man, 'is of an age to weep
At any grave or solemn spectacle,
Inly distressed or overpowered with awe,
He knows not wherefore;—but the boy
  to-day,   540
Perhaps is shedding orphan's tears; you
  also
Must have sustained a loss.'—'The hand
  of Death,'
He answered, 'has been here; but could
  not well
Have fallen more lightly, if it had not
  fallen
Upon myself.'—The other left these
  words   545
Unnoticed, thus continuing.—
                          'From yon crag
Down whose steep sides we dropped into
  the vale,
We heard the hymn they sang—a solemn
  sound
Heard anywhere; but in a place like this
'Tis more than human! Many precious
  rites   550
And customs of our rural ancestry
Are gone, or stealing from us; this, I
  hope,
Will last for ever. Oft on my way have I
Stood still, though but a casual passenger,
So much I felt the awfulness of life,   555
In that one moment when the corse is
  lifted
In silence, with a hush of decency;
Then from the threshold moves with song
  of peace,
And confidential yearnings, tow'rds its
  home,
Its final home on earth. What traveller—
  who—   560
(How far soe'er a stranger) does not own
The bond of brotherhood, when he sees
  them go,
A mute procession on the houseless road;
Or passing by some single tenement
Or clustered dwellings, where again they
  raise   565
The monitory voice? But most of all
It touches, it confirms, and elevates,
Then, when the body, soon to be con-
  signed
Ashes to ashes, dust bequeathed to dust,

Is raised from the church-aisle, and for-
ward borne   570
Upon the shoulders of the next in love,
The nearest in affection or in blood;
Yea, by the very mourners who had knelt
Beside the coffin, resting on its lid
In silent grief their unuplifted heads,   575
And heard meanwhile the Psalmist's
mournful plaint,
And that most awful scripture which
declares
We shall not sleep, but we shall all be
changed!
—Have I not seen—ye likewise may have
seen—
Son, husband, brothers—brothers side by
side,   580
And son and father also side by side,
Rise from that posture:—and in concert
move
On the green turf following the vested
Priest,
Four dear supporters of one senseless
weight,
From which they do not shrink, and under
which   585
They faint not, but advance towards the
open grave—
Step after step—together, with their firm
Unhidden faces: he that suffers most,
He outwardly, and inwardly perhaps,
The most serene, with most undaunted
eye!—   590
Oh! blest are they who live and die like
these,
Loved with such love, and with such sor-
row mourned!'

'That poor Man taken hence to-day,'
replied
The Solitary, with a faint sarcastic smile
Which did not please me, 'must be
deemed, I fear,   595
Of the unblest; for he will surely sink
Into his mother earth without such pomp
Of grief, depart without occasion given
By him for such array of fortitude.
Full seventy winters hath he lived, and
mark!   600
This simple Child will mourn his one short
hour,
And I shall miss him; scanty tribute! yet,
This wanting, he would leave the sight of
men,
If love were his sole claim upon their care,
Like a ripe date which in the desert falls
Without a hand to gather it.'
                            At this   606
I interposed, though loth to speak, and
said,
'Can it be thus among so small a band
As ye must needs be here? in such a place
I would not willingly, methinks, lose
sight   610

Of a departing cloud.'—''Twas not for
love'—
Answered the sick Man with a careless
voice,
'That I came hither; neither have I found
Among associates who have power of
speech,
Nor in such other converse as is here, 615
Temptation so prevailing as to change
That mood, or undermine my first re-
solve.'
Then, speaking in like careless sort, he
said
To my benign Companion,—'Pity 'tis
That fortune did not guide you to this
house   620
A few days earlier; then would you have
seen
What stuff the Dwellers in a solitude,
That seems by Nature hollowed out to be
The seat and bosom of pure innocence,
Are made of; an ungracious matter this!
Which, for truth's sake, yet in remem-
brance too   626
Of past discussions with this zealous
friend
And advocate of humble life, I now
Will force upon his notice; undeterred
By the example of his own pure course,
And that respect and deference which a
soul   631
May fairly claim, by niggard age enriched
In what she most doth value, love of God
And his frail creature Man;—but ye
shall hear.
I talk—and ye are standing in the sun 635
Without refreshment!'
                   Quickly had he spoken,
And, with light steps still quicker than
his words,
Led toward the Cottage. Homely was
the spot;
And, to my feeling, ere we reached the
door,
Had almost a forbidding nakedness;   640
Less fair, I grant, even painfully less fair,
Than it appeared when from the beetling
rock
We had looked down upon it. All within,
As left by the departed company,
Was silent; save the solitary clock   645
That on mine ear ticked with a mournful
sound.—
Following our Guide, we clomb the
cottage-stairs
And reached a small apartment dark and
low,
Which was no sooner entered than our
Host
Said gaily, 'This is my domain, my cell,
My hermitage, my cabin, what you will—
I love it better than a snail his house.
But now ye shall be feasted with our
best.'

So, with more ardour than an unripe girl
Left one day mistress of her mother's stores,   655
He went about his hospitable task.
My eyes were busy, and my thoughts no less,
And pleased I looked upon my grey-haired Friend,
As if to thank him; he returned that look,
Cheered, plainly, and yet serious. What a wreck   660
Had we about us! scattered was the floor,
And, in like sort, chair, window-seat, and shelf,
With books, maps, fossils, withered plants and flowers,
And tufts of mountain moss. Mechanic tools
Lay intermixed with scraps of paper, some   665
Scribbled with verse: a broken angling-rod
And shattered telescope, together linked
By cobwebs, stood within a dusty nook;
And instruments of music, some half-made,
Some in disgrace, hung dangling from the walls.   670
But speedily the promise was fulfilled;
A feast before us, and a courteous Host
Inviting us in glee to sit and eat.
A napkin, white as foam of that rough brook
By which it had been bleached, o'erspread the board;   675
And was itself half-covered with a store
Of dainties,—oaten bread, curd, cheese, and cream;
And cakes of butter curiously embossed,
Butter that had imbibed from meadow-flowers
A golden hue, delicate as their own   680
Faintly reflected in a lingering stream.
Nor lacked, for more delight on that warm day,
Our table, small parade of garden fruits,
And whortle-berries from the mountain side.
The Child, who long ere this had stilled his sobs,   685
Was now a help to his late comforter,
And moved, a willing Page, as he was bid,
Ministering to our need.
                        In genial mood,
While at our pastoral banquet thus we sate
Fronting the window of that little cell,
I could not, ever and anon, forbear   691
To glance an upward look on two huge Peaks,
That from some other vale peered into this.
'Those lusty twins,' exclaimed our host, 'if here

It were your lot to dwell, would soon become   695
Your prized companions.—Many are the notes
Which, in his tuneful course, the wind draws forth
From rocks, woods, caverns, heaths, and dashing shores;
And well those lofty brethren bear their part
In the wild concert—chiefly when the storm   700
Rides high; then all the upper air they fill
With roaring sound, that ceases not to flow,
Like smoke, along the level of the blast,
In mighty current; theirs, too, is the song
Of stream and headlong flood that seldom fails;   705
And, in the grim and breathless hour of noon,
Methinks that I have heard them echo back
The thunder's greeting. Nor have nature's laws
Left them ungifted with a power to yield
Music of finer tone; a harmony,   710
So do I call it, though it be the hand
Of silence, though there be no voice;—
the clouds,
The mist, the shadows, light of golden suns,
Motions of moonlight, all come thither—touch,
And have an answer—thither come, and shape   715
A language not unwelcome to sick hearts
And idle spirits:—there the sun himself,
At the calm close of summer's longest day,
Rests his substantial orb;—between those heights
And on the top of either pinnacle,   720
More keenly than elsewhere in night's blue vault,
Sparkle the stars, as of their station proud.
Thoughts are not busier in the mind of man
Than the mute agents stirring there:—alone
Here do I sit and watch.—'
                        A fall of voice, 725
Regretted like the nightingale's last note,
Had scarcely closed this high-wrought strain of rapture
Ere with inviting smile the Wanderer said:
'Now for the tale with which you threatened us!'
'In truth the threat escaped me unawares:
Should the tale tire you, let this challenge stand   731
For my excuse. Dissevered from mankind,

As to your eyes and thoughts we must
    have seemed
When ye looked down upon us from the
    crag,
Islanders 'mid a stormy mountain sea, 735
We are not so;—perpetually we touch
Upon the vulgar ordinances of the world;
And he, whom this our cottage hath to-
    day
Relinquished, lived dependent for his
    bread
Upon the laws of public charity.   740
The Housewife, tempted by such slender
    gains
As might from that occasion be distilled,
Opened, as she before had done for me,
Her doors to admit this homeless Pen-
    sioner;
The portion gave of coarse but whole-
    some fare   745
Which appetite required—a blind dull
    nook,
Such as she had, the *kennel* of his rest!
This, in itself not ill, would yet have been
Ill borne in earlier life; but his was now
The still contentedness of seventy years.
Calm did he sit under the wide-spread
    tree   751
Of his old age; and yet less calm and meek,
Winningly meek or venerably calm,
Than slow and torpid; paying in this
    wise
A penalty, if penalty it were,   755
For spendthrift feats, excesses of his
    prime.
I loved the old Man, for I pitied him!
A task it was, I own, to hold discourse
With one so slow in gathering up his
    thoughts,
But he was a cheap pleasure to my eyes;
Mild, inoffensive, ready in *his* way,   761
And helpful to his utmost power: and
    there
Our housewife knew full well what she
    possessed!
He was her vassal of all labour, tilled
Her garden, from the pasture fetched her
    kine;   765
And, one among the orderly array
Of hay-makers, beneath the burning sun
Maintained his place; or heedfully pur-
    sued
His course, on errands bound, to other
    vales,
Leading sometimes an inexperienced child
Too young for any profitable task.   771
So moved he like a shadow that per-
    formed
Substantial service. Mark me now, and
    learn
For what reward!—The moon her
    monthly round
Hath not completed since our dame, the
    queen   775

Of this one cottage and this lonely dale,
Into my little sanctuary rushed—-
Voice to a rueful treble humanised,
And features in deplorable dismay.
I treat the matter lightly, but, alas! 780
It is most serious: persevering rain
Had fallen in torrents; all the mountain-
    tops
Were hidden, and black vapours coursed
    their sides;
This had I seen, and saw; but, till she
    spake,
Was wholly ignorant that my ancient
    Friend—   785
Who at her bidding early and alone,
Had clomb aloft to delve the moorland
    turf
For winter fuel—to his noontide meal
Returned not, and now, haply, on the
    heights
Lay at the mercy of this raging storm.
'Inhuman!'—said I, 'was an old Man's
    life   791
Not worth the trouble of a thought?—
    alas!
This notice comes too late.' With joy I
    saw
Her husband enter—from a distant vale.
We sallied forth together; found the
    tools   795
Which the neglected veteran had dropped,
But through all quarters looked for him
    in vain.
We shouted—but no answer! Darkness
    fell
Without remission of the blast or shower,
And fears for our own safety drove us
    home.   800

    'I, who weep little, did, I will confess,
The moment I was seated here alone,
Honour my little cell with some few tears
Which anger and resentment could not
    dry.
All night the storm endured: and, soon
    as help   805
Had been collected from the neighbour-
    ing vale,
With morning we renewed our quest:
    the wind
Was fallen, the rain abated, but the hills
Lay shrouded in impenetrable mist;
And long and hopelessly we sought in
    vain: 810
Till, chancing on that lofty ridge to pass
A heap of ruin—almost without walls
And wholly without roof (the bleached
    remains
Of a small chapel, where, in ancient time,
The peasants of these lonely valleys used
To meet for worship on that central
    height)—   816
We there espied the object of our search,
Lying full three parts buried among tufts

Of heath-plant, under and above him
    strewn,
To baffle, as he might, the watery storm:
And there we found him breathing peace-
    ably,   821
Snug as a child that hides itself in sport
'Mid a green hay-cock in a sunny field.
We spake—he made reply, but would not
    stir
At our entreaty; less from want of power
Than apprehension and bewildering
    thoughts.   826

    'So was he lifted gently from the
        ground,
And with their freight homeward the
    shepherds moved
Through the dull mist, I following—when
    a step,
A single step, that freed me from the
    skirts   830
Of the blind vapour, opened to my view
Glory beyond all glory ever seen
By waking sense or by the dreaming soul!
The appearance, instantaneously dis-
    closed,
Was of a mighty city—boldly say   835
A wilderness of building, sinking far
And self-withdrawn into a boundless
    depth,
Far sinking into splendour—without end!
Fabric it seemed of diamond and of gold,
With alabaster domes, and silver spires,
And blazing terrace upon terrace, high 841
Uplifted; here, serene pavilions bright,
In avenues disposed; there, towers begirt
With battlements that on their restless
    fronts
Bore stars—illumination of all gems! 845
By earthly nature had the effect been
    wrought
Upon the dark materials of the storm
Now pacified; on them, and on the coves
And mountain-steeps and summits,
    whereunto
The vapours had receded, taking there
Their station under a cerulean sky.   851
Oh, 'twas an unimaginable sight!
Clouds, mists, streams, watery rocks and
    emerald turf,
Clouds of all tincture, rocks and sapphire
    sky,
Confused, commingled, mutually in-
    flamed,   855
Molten together, and composing thus,
Each lost in each, that marvellous array
Of temple, palace, citadel, and huge
Fantastic pomp of structure without
    name,
In fleecy folds voluminous, enwrapped.
Right in the midst, where interspace
    appeared   861
Of open court, an object like a throne
Under a shining canopy of state

Stood fixed; and fixed resemblances were
    seen
To implements of ordinary use,   865
But vast in size, in substance glorified;
Such as by Hebrew Prophets were beheld
In vision—forms uncouth of mightiest
    power
For admiration and mysterious awe. 869
This little Vale, a dwelling-place of Man,
Lay low beneath my feet; 'twas visible—
I saw not, but I felt that it was there.
That which I *saw* was the revealed abode
Of Spirits in beatitude: my heart
Swelled in my breast.—"I have been
    dead," I cried,   875
"And now I live! Oh! wherefore *do* I
    live?"
And with that pang I prayed to be no
    more!—
—But I forget our Charge, as utterly
I then forgot him:—there I stood and
    gazed;
The apparition faded not away,   880
And I descended.
                    Having reached the house,
I found its rescued inmate safely lodged,
And in serene possession of himself,
Beside a fire whose genial warmth seemed
    met   884
By a faint shining from the heart, a gleam
Of comfort, spread over his pallid face.
Great show of joy the housewife made,
    and truly
Was glad to find her conscience set at
    ease;
And not less glad, for sake of her good
    name,
That the poor Sufferer had escaped with
    life.   890
But, though he seemed at first to have
    received
No harm, and uncomplaining as before
Went through his usual tasks, a silent
    change
Soon showed itself: he lingered three
    short weeks;
And from the cottage hath been borne
    to-day.   895

    'So ends my dolorous tale, and glad
        I am
That it is ended.' At these words he
    turned—
And, with blithe air of open fellowship,
Brought from the cupboard wine and
    stouter cheer,
Like one who would be merry. Seeing
    this,   900
My grey-haired Friend said courteously—
    'Nay, nay,
You have regaled us as a hermit ought;
Now let us forth into the sun!'—Our Host
Rose, though reluctantly, and forth we
    went.

BOOK THIRD

DESPONDENCY

ARGUMENT

Images in the Valley.—Another Recess in it entered and described.—Wanderer's sensations.—Solitary's excited by the same objects.—Contrast between these.—Despondency of the Solitary gently reproved.—Conversation exhibiting the Solitary's past and present opinions and feelings, till he enters upon his own History at length.—His domestic felicity.—Afflictions.—Dejection.—Roused by the French Revolution.—Disappointment and disgust.—Voyage to America.—Disappointment and disgust pursue him.—His return.—His languor and depression of mind, from want of faith in the great truths of Religion, and want of confidence in the virtue of Mankind.

A HUMMING BEE—a little tinkling rill—
A pair of falcons wheeling on the wing,
In clamorous agitation, round the crest
Of a tall rock, their airy citadel—
By each and all of these the pensive ear   5
Was greeted, in the silence that ensued,
When through the cottage-threshold we
        had passed,
And, deep within that lonesome valley,
        stood
Once more beneath the concave of a blue
And cloudless sky.—Anon exclaimed our
        Host,   10
Triumphantly dispersing with the taunt
The shade of discontent which on his
        brow
Had gathered,—'Ye have left my cell,—
        but see
How Nature hems you in with friendly
        arms!
And by her help ye are my prisoners still.
But which way shall I lead you?—how
        contrive,   16
In spot so parsimoniously endowed,
That the brief hours, which yet remain,
        may reap
Some recompense of knowledge or de-
        light?'
So saying, round he looked, as if per-
        plexed;   20
And, to remove those doubts, my grey-
        haired Friend
Said—'Shall we take this pathway for
        our guide?—
Upward it winds, as if, in summer heats,
Its line had first been fashioned by the
        flock
Seeking a place of refuge at the root   25
Of yon black Yew-tree, whose protruded
        boughs
Darken the silver bosom of the crag,
From which she draws her meagre sus-
        tenance.
There in commodious shelter may we rest.
Or let us trace this streamlet to its source;
Feebly it tinkles with an earthy sound,   31
And a few steps may bring us to the spot
Where, haply, crowned with flowerets
        and green herbs,
The mountain infant to the sun comes
        forth,

Like human life from darkness.'—A quick
        turn   35
Through a strait passage of encumbered
        ground,
Proved that such hope was vain:—for now
        we stood
Shut out from prospect of the open vale,
And saw the water, that composed this
        rill,
Descending, disembodied, and diffused   40
O'er the smooth surface of an ample crag,
Lofty, and steep, and naked as a tower.
All further progress here was barred;—
        And who,
Thought I, if master of a vacant hour,
Here would not linger, willingly de-
        tained?   45
Whether to such wild objects he were led
When copious rains have magnified the
        stream
Into a loud and white-robed waterfall,
Or introduced at this more quiet time.   49

Upon a semicirque of turf-clad ground,
The hidden nook discovered to our view
A mass of rock, resembling, as it lay
Right at the foot of that moist precipice,
A stranded ship, with keel upturned, that
        rests
Fearless of winds and waves. Three
        several stones   55
Stood near, of smaller size, and not unlike
To monumental pillars: and, from these
Some little space disjoined, a pair were
        seen,
That with united shoulders bore aloft   59
A fragment, like an altar, flat and smooth:
Barren the tablet, yet thereon appeared
A tall and shining holly, that had found
A hospitable chink, and stood upright,
As if inserted by some human hand
In mockery, to wither in the sun,   65
Or lay its beauty flat before a breeze,
The first that entered. But no breeze
        did now
Find entrance;—high or low appeared no
        trace
Of motion, save the water that descended,
Diffused adown that barrier of steep rock,
And softly creeping, like a breath of
        air,   71

614

Such as is sometimes seen, and hardly
seen,
To brush the still breast of a crystal lake.

'Behold a cabinet for sages built,
Which kings might envy!'—Praise to
this effect   75
Broke from the happy old Man's reverend
lip;
Who to the Solitary turned, and said,
'In sooth, with love's familiar privilege,
You have decried the wealth which is
your own.
Among these rocks and stones, methinks,
I see   80
More than the heedless impress that
belongs
To lonely nature's casual work: they bear
A semblance strange of power intelligent,
And of design not wholly worn away.
Boldest of plants that ever faced the
wind,   85
How gracefully that slender shrub looks
forth
From its fantastic birthplace! And I
own,
Some shadowy intimations haunt me
here,
That in these shows a chronicle survives
Of purposes akin to those of Man,   90
But wrought with mightier arm than now
prevails.
—Voiceless the stream descends into the
gulf
With timid lapse;—and lo! while in this
strait
I stand—the chasm of sky above my head
Is heaven's profoundest azure; no domain
For fickle, short-lived clouds to occupy,
Or to pass through; but rather an abyss
In which the everlasting stars abide—
And whose soft gloom, and boundless
depth, might tempt
The curious eye to look for them by day.
—Hail, Contemplation! from the stately
towers,   101
Reared by the industrious hand of human
art
To lift thee high above the misty air
And turbulence of murmuring cities vast;
From academic groves, that have for thee
Been planted, hither come and find a
lodge   106
To which thou may'st resort for holier
peace,—
From whose calm centre thou, through
height or depth,
May'st penetrate, wherever truth shall
lead;
Measuring through all degrees, until the
scale   110
Of time and conscious nature disappear,
Lost in unsearchable eternity[1]!'
[1] See Note, p. 727.

A pause ensued; and with minuter care
We scanned the various features of the
scene: 114
And soon the Tenant of that lonely vale
With courteous voice thus spake—
                              'I should have grieved
Hereafter, not escaping self-reproach,
If from my poor retirement ye had gone
Leaving this nook unvisited: but, in sooth,
Your unexpected presence had so roused
My spirits, that they were bent on enter-
prise;   121
And, like an ardent hunter, I forgot,
Or, shall I say?—disdained, the game that
lurks
At my own door. The shapes before our
eyes
And their arrangement, doubtless must
be deemed   125
The sport of Nature, aided by blind
Chance
Rudely to mock the works of toiling Man.
And hence, this upright shaft of unhewn
stone,
From Fancy, willing to set off her stores
By sounding titles, hath acquired the
name   130
Of Pompey's pillar; that I gravely style
My Theban obelisk; and, there, behold
A Druid cromlech!—thus I entertain
The antiquarian humour, and am pleased
To skim along the surfaces of things, 135
Beguiling harmlessly the listless hours.
But if the spirit be oppressed by sense
Of instability, revolt, decay,
And change, and emptiness, these freaks
of Nature
And her blind helper Chance, do *then*
suffice   140
To quicken, and to aggravate—to feed
Pity and scorn, and melancholy pride,
Not less than that huge Pile (from some
abyss
Of mortal power unquestionably sprung)
Whose hoary diadem of pendent rocks
Confines the shrill-voiced whirlwind
round and round   146
Eddying within its vast circumference,
On Sarum's naked plain—than pyramid
Of Egypt, unsubverted, undissolved—
Or Syria's marble ruins towering high 150
Above the sandy desert, in the light
Of sun or moon.—Forgive me, if I say
That an appearance which hath raised
your minds
To an exalted pitch (the self-same cause
Different effect producing) is for me
Fraught rather with depression than
delight,   156
Though shame it were, could I not look
around,
By the reflection of your pleasure, pleased.
Yet happier in my judgment, even than
you

615

With your bright transports fairly may
  be deemed,   160
The wandering Herbalist,—who, clear
  alike
From vain, and, that worse evil, vexing
  thoughts,
Casts, if he ever chance to enter here,
Upon these uncouth Forms a slight
  regard
Of transitory interest, and peeps round
For some rare floweret of the hills, or
  plant   166
Of craggy fountain; what he hopes for
  wins,
Or learns, at least, that 'tis not to be won:
Then, keen and eager, as a fine-nosed
  hound
By soul-engrossing instinct driven along
Through wood or open field, the harmless
  Man   171
Departs, intent upon his onward quest!—
Nor is that Fellow-wanderer, so deem I,
Less to be envied, (you may trace him oft
By scars which his activity has left   175
Beside our roads and pathways, though,
  thank Heaven!
This covert nook reports not of his hand)
He who with pocket-hammer smites the
  edge
Of luckless rock or prominent stone,
  disguised
In weather-stains or crusted o'er by
  Nature   180
With her first growths, detaching by the
  stroke
A chip or splinter—to resolve his doubts;
And, with that ready answer satisfied,
The substance classes by some barbarous
  name,
And hurries on; or from the fragments
  picks   185
His specimen, if but haply intervened
With sparkling mineral, or should crystal
  cube
Lurk in its cells—and thinks himself en-
  riched,
Wealthier, and doubtless wiser, than be-
  fore!
Intrusted safely each to his pursuit,   190
Earnest alike, let both from hill to hill
Range; if it please them, speed from clime
  to clime;
The mind is full—and free from pain
  their pastime.'

'Then,' said I, interposing, 'One is
  near,
Who cannot but possess in your esteem
Place worthier still of envy. May I name,
Without offence, that fair-faced cottage-
  boy?   197
Dame Nature's pupil of the lowest form,
Youngest apprentice in the school of art!
Him, as we entered from the open glen,

You might have noticed, busily engaged,
Heart, soul, and hands,—in mending the
  defects   202
Left in the fabric of a leaky dam
Raised for enabling this penurious stream
To turn a slender mill (that new-made
  plaything)   205
For his delight—the happiest he of all!'

'Far happiest,' answered the despond-
  ing Man,
'If, such as now he is, he might remain!
Ah! what avails imagination high
Or question deep? what profits all that
  earth,   210
Or heaven's blue vault, is suffered to put
  forth
Of impulse or allurement, for the Soul
To quit the beaten track of life, and soar
Far as she finds a yielding element
In past or future; far as she can go   215
Through time or space—if neither in the
  one,
Nor in the other region, nor in aught
That Fancy, dreaming o'er the map of
  things,
Hath placed beyond these penetrable
  bounds,
Words of assurance can be heard; if no-
  where   220
A habitation, for consummate good,
Or for progressive virtue, by the search
Can be attained,—a better sanctuary
From doubt and sorrow, than the sense-
  less grave?'

'Is this,' the grey-haired Wanderer
  mildly said,   225
'The voice, which we so lately overheard,
To that same child, addressing tenderly
The consolations of a hopeful mind?
"*His body is at rest, his soul in heaven.*"
These were your words; and, verily,
  methinks   230
Wisdom is ofttimes nearer when we stoop
Than when we soar.'—
       The Other, not displeased,
Promptly replied—'My notion is the
  same.
And I, without reluctance, could decline
All act of inquisition whence we rise,
And what, when breath hath ceased, we
  may become.   236
Here are we, in a bright and breathing
  world.
Our origin, what matters it? In lack
Of worthier explanation, say at once
With the American (a thought which
  suits   240
The place where now we stand) that
  certain men
Leapt out together from a rocky cave;
And these were the first parents of man-
  kind:

Or, if a different image be recalled
By the warm sunshine, and the jocund
  voice   245
Of insects chirping out their careless lives
On these soft beds of thyme-besprinkled
  turf,
Choose, with the gay Athenian, a conceit
As sound—blithe race! whose mantles
  were bedecked
With golden grasshoppers, in sign that
  they   250
Had sprung, like those bright creatures,
  from the soil
Whereon their endless generations dwelt.
But stop! these theoretic fancies jar
On serious minds: then, as the Hindoos
  draw   254
Their holy Ganges from a skyey fount,
Even so deduce the stream of human life
From seats of power divine; and hope, or
  trust,
That our existence winds her stately
  course
Beneath the sun, like Ganges, to make part
Of a living ocean; or, to sink engulfed,
Like Niger, in impenetrable sands   261
And utter darkness: thought which may
  be faced,
Though comfortless!—
              Not of myself I speak;
Such acquiescence neither doth imply,
In me, a meekly-bending spirit soothed
By natural piety; nor a lofty mind,   266
By philosophic discipline prepared
For calm subjection to acknowledged law;
Pleased to have been, contented not to be.
Such palms I boast not;—no! to me, who
  find,   270
Reviewing my past way, much to con-
  demn,
Little to praise, and nothing to regret,
(Save some remembrances of dream-like
  joys
That scarcely seem to have belonged to
  me)
If I must take my choice between the
  pair   275
That rule alternately the weary hours,
Night is than day more acceptable; sleep
Doth, in my estimate of good, appear
A better state than waking; death than
  sleep:
Feelingly sweet is stillness after storm,
Though under covert of the wormy
  ground!   281

'Yet be it said, in justice to myself,
That in more genial times, when I was
  free
To explore the destiny of human kind
(Not as an intellectual game pursued 285
With curious subtilty, from wish to cheat
Irksome sensations; but by love of truth
Urged on, or haply by intense delight

In feeding thought, wherever thought
  could feed)
I did not rank with those (too dull or
  nice,   290
For to my judgment such they then ap-
  peared,
Or too aspiring, thankless at the best)
Who, in this frame of human life, perceive
An object whereunto their souls are tied
In discontented wedlock; nor did e'er,
From me, those dark impervious shades,
  that hang   296
Upon the region whither we are bound,
Exclude a power to enjoy the vital beams
Of present sunshine.—Deities that float
On wings, angelic Spirits! I could muse
O'er what from eldest time we have been
  told   301
Of your bright forms and glorious facul-
  ties,
And with the imagination rest content,
Not wishing more; repining not to tread
The little sinuous path of earthly care,
By flowers embellished, and by springs
  refreshed.   306
—"Blow winds of autumn!—let your chill-
  ing breath
Take the live herbage from the mead, and
  strip
The shady forest of its green attire,—
And let the bursting clouds to fury rouse
The gentle brooks!—Your desolating
  sway,   311
Sheds," I exclaimed, "no sadness upon me,
And no disorder in your rage I find.
What dignity, what beauty, in this change
From mild to angry, and from sad to gay,
Alternate and revolving! How benign,
How rich in animation and delight,
How bountiful these elements—compared
With aught, as more desirable and fair,
Devised by fancy for the golden age; 320
Or the perpetual warbling that prevails
In Arcady, beneath unaltered skies,
Through the long year in constant quiet
  bound,
Night hushed as night, and day serene as
  day!"
—But why this tedious record?—Age, we
  know,   325
Is garrulous; and solitude is apt
To anticipate the privilege of Age.
From far ye come; and surely with a hope
Of better entertainment:—let us hence!'

Loth to forsake the spot, and still more
  loth   330
To be diverted from our present theme,
I said, 'My thoughts, agreeing, Sir, with
  yours,
Would push this censure farther;—for, if
  smiles
Of scornful pity be the just reward
Of Poesy thus courteously employed 335

In framing models to improve the scheme
Of Man's existence, and recast the world,
Why should not grave Philosophy be
    styled,
Herself, a dreamer of a kindred stock,
A dreamer yet more spiritless and dull?
Yes, shall the fine immunities she boasts
Establish sounder titles of esteem
For her, who (all too timid and reserved
For onset, for resistance too inert,
Too weak for suffering, and for hope too
    tame)   345
Placed, among flowery gardens curtained
    round
With world-excluding groves, the brother-
    hood
Of soft Epicureans, taught—if they
The ends of being would secure, and win
The crown of wisdom—to yield up their
    souls   350
To a voluptuous unconcern, preferring
Tranquillity to all things. Or is she,'
I cried, 'more worthy of regard, the Power,
Who, for the sake of sterner quiet, closed
The Stoic's heart against the vain ap-
    proach   355
Of admiration, and all sense of joy?'

    His countenance gave notice that my
        zeal
Accorded little with his present mind;
I ceased, and he resumed.—'Ah! gentle
    Sir,
Slight, if you will, the *means;* but spare
    to slight   360
The *end* of those, who did, by system, rank,
As the prime object of a wise man's aim,
Security from shock of accident,
Release from fear; and cherished peace-
    ful days
For their own sakes, as mortal life's chief
    good,   365
And only reasonable felicity.
What motive drew, what impulse, I would
    ask,
Through a long course of later ages, drove,
The hermit to his cell in forest wide;
Or what detained him, till his closing
    eyes   370
Took their last farewell of the sun and
    stars,
Fast anchored in the desert?—Not alone
Dread of the persecuting sword, remorse,
Wrongs unredressed, or insults unavenged
And unavengeable, defeated pride,   375
Prosperity subverted, maddening want,
Friendship   betrayed,   affection   un-
    returned,
Love with despair, or grief in agony;—
Not always from intolerable pangs
He fled; but, compassed round by plea-
    sure, sighed   380
For independent happiness; craving
    peace,

The central feeling of all happiness,
Not as a refuge from distress or pain,
A breathing-time, vacation, or a truce,
But for its absolute self; a life of peace,
Stability without regret or fear;   386
That hath been, is, and shall be ever-
    more!—
Such the reward he sought; and wore out
    life,
There, where on few external things his
    heart
Was set, and those his own; or, if not
    his,   390
Subsisting under nature's steadfast law.

    'What other yearning was the master
        tie
Of the monastic brotherhood, upon rock
Aerial, or in green secluded vale,
One after one, collected from afar,   395
An undissolving fellowship?—What but
    this,
The universal instinct of repose,
The longing for confirmed tranquillity,
Inward and outward; humble, yet sub-
    lime:
The life where hope and memory are as
    one;   400
Where earth is quiet and her face un-
    changed
Save by the simplest toil of human hands
Or season's difference; the immortal Soul
Consistent in self-rule; and heaven re-
    vealed
To meditation in that quietness!—   405
Such was their scheme: and though the
    wished-for end
By multitudes was missed, perhaps at-
    tained
By none, they for the attempt, and pains
    employed,
Do, in my present censure, stand redeemed
From the unqualified disdain, that once
Would have been cast upon them by my
    voice   411
Delivering her decisions from the seat
Of forward youth—that scruples not to
    solve
Doubts, and determine questions, by the
    rules   . 414
Of inexperienced judgment, ever prone
To overweening faith; and is inflamed,
By courage, to demand from real life
The test of act and suffering, to provoke
Hostility—how dreadful when it comes,
Whether affliction be the foe, or guilt!

    'A child of earth, I rested, in that
        stage   421
Of my past course to which these thoughts
    advert,
Upon earth's native energies; forgetting
That mine was a condition which required
Nor energy, nor fortitude—a calm   425

Without vicissitude; which, if the like
Had been presented to my view elsewhere,
I might have even been tempted to de-
    spise.
But no—for the serene was also bright;
Enlivened happiness with joy o'erflowing,
With joy, and—oh! that memory should
    survive   431
To speak the word—with rapture! Na-
    ture's boon,
Life's genuine inspiration, happiness
Above what rules can teach, or fancy
    feign;
Abused, as all possessions *are* abused
That are not prized according to their
    worth.   436
And yet, what worth? what good is given
    to men,
More solid than the gilded clouds of
    heaven?
What joy more lasting than a vernal
    flower?—
None! 'tis the general plaint of human
    kind   440
In solitude: and mutually addressed
From each to all, for wisdom's sake:—
    This truth
The priest announces from his holy seat:
And, crowned with garlands in the sum-
    mer grove,
The poet fits it to his pensive lyre.   445
Yet, ere that final resting-place be gained,
Sharp contradictions may arise, by doom
Of this same life, compelling us to grieve
That the prosperities of love and joy
Should be permitted, ofttimes, to endure
So long, and be at once cast down for
    ever.   451
Oh! tremble, ye, to whom hath been as-
    signed
A course of days composing happy
    months,
And they as happy years; the present
    still
So like the past, and both so firm a pledge
Of a congenial future, that the wheels
Of pleasure move without the aid of hope:
For Mutability is Nature's bane;   458
And slighted Hope *will* be avenged; and,
    when
Ye need her favours, ye shall find her not;
But in her stead—fear—doubt—and
    agony!'   461

This was the bitter language of the
    heart:
But, while he spake, look, gesture, tone
    of voice,
Though discomposed and vehement, were
    such
As skill and graceful nature might sug-
    gest   465
To a proficient of the tragic scene
Standing before the multitude, beset

With dark events. Desirous to divert
Or stem the current of the speaker's
    thoughts,   469
We signified a wish to leave that place
Of stillness and close privacy, a nook
That seemed for self-examination made;
Or, for confession, in the sinner's need,
Hidden from all men's view. To our at-
    tempt   474
He yielded not; but, pointing to a slope
Of mossy turf defended from the sun,
And on that couch inviting us to rest,
Full on that tender-hearted Man he
    turned
A serious eye, and his speech thus re-
    newed.

'You never saw, your eyes did never
    look   480
On the bright form of Her whom once I
    loved:—
Her silver voice was heard upon the earth,
A sound unknown to you; else, honoured
    Friend!
Your heart had borne a pitiable share
Of what I suffered, when I wept that loss,
And suffer now, not seldom, from the
    thought   486
That I remember, and can weep no more.—
Stripped as I am of all the golden fruit
Of self-esteem; and by the cutting blasts
Of self-reproach familiarly assailed; 490
Yet would I not be of such wintry bare-
    ness
But that some leaf of your regard should
    hang
Upon my naked branches:—lively
    thoughts
Give birth, full often, to unguarded words;
I grieve that, in your presence, from my
    tongue   495
Too much of frailty hath already dropped;
But that too much demands still more.
                                    You know,
Revered Compatriot—and to you, kind
    Sir,
(Not to be deemed a stranger, as you come
Following the guidance of these welcome
    feet   500
To our secluded vale) it may be told—
That my demerits did not sue in vain
To One on whose mild radiance many
    gazed
With hope, and all with pleasure. This
    fair Bride—
In the devotedness of youthful love, 505
Preferring me to parents, and the choir
Of gay companions, to the natal roof,
And all known places and familiar sights
(Resigned with sadness gently weighing
    down   509
Her trembling expectations, but no more
Than did to her due honour, and to me
Yielded, that day, a confidence sublime

In what I had to build upon)—this Bride,
Young, modest, meek, and beautiful, I led
To a low cottage in a sunny bay,   515
Where the salt sea innocuously breaks,
And the sea breeze as innocently breathes,
On Devon's leafy shores;—a sheltered
      hold,
In a soft clime encouraging the soil   519
To a luxuriant bounty!—As our steps
Approach the embowered abode—our
      chosen seat—
See, rooted in the earth, her kindly bed,
The unendangered myrtle, decked with
      flowers,
Before the threshold stands to welcome
      us!
While, in the flowering myrtle's neigh-
      bourhood,   525
Not overlooked but courting no regard,
Those native plants, the holly and the yew,
Gave modest intimation to the mind
How willingly their aid they would unite
With the green myrtle, to endear the
      hours   530
Of winter, and protect that pleasant place.
—Wild were the walks upon those lonely
      Downs,
Track leading into track; how marked,
      how worn
Into bright verdure, between fern and
      gorse,
Winding away its never-ending line   535
On their smooth surface, evidence was
      none:
But, there, lay open to our daily haunt,
A range of unappropriated earth,
Where youth's ambitious feet might move
      at large;
Whence, unmolested wanderers, we be-
      held   540
The shining giver of the day diffuse
His brightness o'er a tract of sea and land
Gay as our spirits, free as our desires;
As our enjoyments, boundless.—From
      those heights
We dropped, at pleasure, into sylvan
      combs;   545
Where arbours of impenetrable shade,
And mossy seats, detained us side by side,
With hearts at ease, and knowledge in
      our hearts
"That all the grove and all the day was
      ours."

'O happy time! still happier was at
      hand;   550
For Nature called my Partner to resign
Her share in the pure freedom of that life,
Enjoyed by us in common.—To my hope,
To my heart's wish, my tender Mate be-
      came
The thankful captive of maternal bonds;
And those wild paths were left to me
      alone.   556

There could I meditate on follies past;
And, like a weary voyager escaped
From risk and hardship, inwardly retrace
A course of vain delights and thoughtless
      guilt,   560
And self-indulgence—without shame pur-
      sued,
There, undisturbed, could think of and
      could thank
Her whose submissive spirit was to me
Rule and restraint—my guardian—shall
      I say
That earthly Providence, whose guiding
      love   565
Within a port of rest had lodged me safe;
Safe from temptation, and from danger
      far?
Strains followed of acknowledgment ad-
      dressed
To an Authority enthroned above
The reach of sight; from whom, as from
      their source,   570
Proceed all visible ministers of good
That walk the earth—Father of heaven
      and earth,
Father, and king, and judge, adored and
      feared!
These acts of mind, and memory, and
      heart,
And spirit—interrupted and relieved 575
By observations transient as the glance
Of flying sunbeams, or to the outward
      form
Cleaving with power inherent and intense,
As the mute insect fixed upon the plant
On whose soft leaves it hangs, and from
      whose cup   580
It draws its nourishment imperceptibly—
Endeared my wanderings; and the
      mother's kiss
And infant's smile awaited my return.

'In privacy we dwelt, a wedded pair,
Companions daily, often all day long; 585
Not placed by fortune within easy reach
Of various intercourse, nor wishing aught
Beyond the allowance of our own fireside,
The twain within our happy cottage born,
Inmates, and heirs of our united love; 590
Graced mutually by difference of sex,
And with no wider interval of time
Between their several births than served
      for one
To establish something of a leader's sway;
Yet left them joined by sympathy in
      age;   595
Equals in pleasure, fellows in pursuit,
On these two pillars rested as in air
Our solitude.
            It soothes me to perceive,
Your courtesy withholds not from my
      words
Attentive audience. But, oh! gentle
      Friends,   600

As times of quiet and unbroken peace,
Though, for a nation, times of blessedness,
Give back faint echoes from the historian's page;
So, in the imperfect sounds of this discourse,
Depressed I hear, how faithless is the voice					605
Which those most blissful days reverberate.
What special record can, or need, be given
To rules and habits, whereby much was done,
But all within the sphere of little things;
Of humble, though, to us, important cares,
And precious interests? Smoothly did our life					611
Advance, swerving not from the path prescribed;
Her annual, her diurnal, round alike
Maintained with faithful care. And you divine					614
The worst effects that our condition saw
If you imagine changes slowly wrought,
And in their process unperceivable;
Not wished for; sometimes noticed with a sigh,
(Whate'er of good or lovely they might bring)					619
Sighs of regret, for the familiar good
And loveliness endeared which they removed.

'Seven years of occupation undisturbed
Established seemingly a right to hold
That happiness; and use and habit gave
To what an alien spirit had acquired 625
A patrimonial sanctity. And thus,
With thoughts and wishes bounded to this world,
I lived and breathed; most grateful—if to enjoy
Without repining or desire for more,
For different lot, or change to higher sphere,					630
(Only except some impulses of pride
With no determined object, though upheld
By theories with suitable support)—
Most grateful, if in such wise to enjoy
Be proof of gratitude for what we have;
Else, I allow, most thankless.—But, at once,					636
From some dark seat of fatal power was urged
A claim that shattered all.—Our blooming girl,
Caught in the gripe of death, with such brief time
To struggle in as scarcely would allow 640
Her cheek to change its colour, was conveyed
From us to inaccessible worlds, to regions

Where height, or depth, admits not the approach
Of living man, though longing to pursue.
—With even as brief a warning—and how soon,					645
With what short interval of time between,
I tremble yet to think of—our last prop,
Our happy life's only remaining stay—
The brother followed; and was seen no more!

'Calm as a frozen lake when ruthless winds					650
Blow fiercely, agitating earth and sky,
The Mother now remained; as if in her,
Who, to the lowest region of the soul,
Had been erewhile unsettled and disturbed,					654
This second visitation had no power
To shake; but only to bind up and seal;
And to establish thankfulness of heart
In Heaven's determinations, ever just.
The eminence whereon her spirit stood,
Mine was unable to attain. Immense
The space that severed us! But, as the sight					661
Communicates with heaven's ethereal orbs
Incalculably distant; so, I felt
That consolation may descend from far
(And that is intercourse, and union, too,)
While, overcome with speechless gratitude,					666
And, with a holier love inspired, I looked
On her—at once superior to my woes
And partner of my loss.—O heavy change!
Dimness o'er this clear luminary crept 670
Insensibly;—the immortal and divine
Yielded to mortal reflux; her pure glory,
As from the pinnacle of worldly state
Wretched ambition drops astounded, fell
Into a gulf obscure of silent grief,					675
And keen heart-anguish—of itself ashamed,
Yet obstinately cherishing itself:
And, so consumed, she melted from my arms;
And left me, on this earth, disconsolate!

'What followed cannot be reviewed in thought;					680
Much less, retraced in words. If she, of life
Blameless, so intimate with love and joy
And all the tender motions of the soul,
Had been supplanted, could I hope to stand—					684
Infirm, dependent, and now destitute?
I called on dreams and visions, to disclose
That which is veiled from waking thought; conjured
Eternity, as men constrain a ghost
To appear and answer; to the grave I spake

Imploringly;—looked up, and asked the
Heavens   690
If Angels traversed their cerulean floors,
If fixed or wandering star could tidings
yield
Of the departed spirit—what abode
It occupies—what consciousness retains
Of former loves and interests. Then my
soul   695
Turned inward,—to examine of what stuff
Time's fetters are composed; and life was
put
To inquisition, long and profitless!
By pain of heart—now checked—and now
impelled—
The intellectual power, through words
and things,   700
Went sounding on, a dim and perilous
way!
And from those transports, and these toils
abstruse,
Some trace am I enabled to retain
Of time, else lost;—existing unto me
Only by records in myself not found. 705

'From that abstraction I was roused,—
and how?
Even as a thoughtful shepherd by a flash
Of lightning startled in a gloomy cave
Of these wild hills. For, lo! the dread
Bastille,
With all the chambers in its horrid towers,
Fell to the ground:—by violence over-
thrown   711
Of indignation; and with shouts that
drowned
The crash it made in falling! From the
wreck
A golden palace rose, or seemed to rise,
The appointed seat of equitable law 715
And mild paternal sway. The potent
shock
I felt: the transformation I perceived,
As marvellously seized as in that moment
When, from the blind mist issuing, I
beheld
Glory—beyond all glory ever seen,   720
Confusion infinite of heaven and earth,
Dazzling the soul. Meanwhile, prophetic
harps
In every grove were ringing, "War shall
cease;
Did ye not hear that conquest is abjured?
Bring garlands, bring forth choicest
flowers, to deck   725
The tree of Liberty."—My heart re-
bounded;
My melancholy voice the chorus joined;
—"Be joyful all ye nations; in all lands,
Ye that are capable of joy be glad!
Henceforth, whate'er is wanting to your-
selves   730
In others ye shall promptly find;—and all,
Enriched by mutual and reflected wealth,

Shall with one heart honour their common
kind."

'Thus was I reconverted to the world;
Society became my glittering bride, 735
And airy hopes my children.—From the
depths
Of natural passion, seemingly escaped,
My soul diffused herself in wide embrace
Of institutions, and the forms of things;
As they exist, in mutable array,   740
Upon life's surface. What, though in my
veins
There flowed no Gallic blood, nor had I
breathed
The air of France, not less than Gallic
zeal
Kindled and burnt among the sapless
twigs
Of my exhausted heart. If busy men 745
In sober conclave met, to weave a web
Of amity, whose living threads should
stretch
Beyond the seas, and to the farthest pole,
There did I sit, assisting. If, with noise
And acclamation, crowds in open air 750
Expressed the tumult of their minds, my
voice
There mingled, heard or not. The powers
of song
I left not uninvoked; and, in still groves,
Where mild enthusiasts tuned a pensive
lay   754
Of thanks and expectation, in accord
With their belief, I sang Saturnian rule
Returned,—a progeny of golden years
Permitted to descend, and bless mankind.
—With promises the Hebrew Scriptures
teem:
I felt their invitation; and resumed 760
A long-suspended office in the House
Of public worship, where, the glowing
phrase
Of ancient inspiration serving me,
I promised also,—with undaunted trust
Foretold, and added prayer to prophecy;
The admiration winning of the crowd; 766
The help desiring of the pure devout.

'Scorn and contempt forbid me to
proceed!
But History, time's slavish scribe, will
tell
How rapidly the zealots of the cause 770
Disbanded—or in hostile ranks appeared;
Some, tired of honest service; these, out-
done,
Disgusted therefore, or appalled, by aims
Of fiercer zealots—so confusion reigned,
And the more faithful were compelled to
exclaim,   775
As Brutus did to Virtue, "Liberty,
I worshipped thee, and find thee but a
Shade!"

'Such recantation had for me no charm,
Nor would I bend to it; who should have
     grieved
At aught, however fair, that bore the mien
Of a conclusion, or catastrophe.   781
Why then conceal, that, when the simply
     good
In timid selfishness withdrew, I sought
Other support, not scrupulous whence it
     came:
And, by what compromise it stood, not
     nice?   785
Enough if notions seemed to be high-
     pitched,
And qualities determined.—Among men
So charactered did I maintain a strife
Hopeless, and still more hopeless every
     hour;
But, in the process, I began to feel   790
That, if the emancipation of the world
Were missed, I should at least secure my
     own,
And be in part compensated. For rights,
Widely—inveterately usurped upon,
I spake with vehemence; and promptly
     seized   795
All that Abstraction furnished for my
     needs
Or purposes; nor scrupled to proclaim,
And propagate, by liberty of life,
Those new persuasions. Not that I re-
     joiced,
Or even found pleasure, in such vagrant
     course,   800
For its own sake; but farthest from the
     walk
Which I had trod in happiness and peace,
Was most inviting to a troubled mind;
That, in a struggling and distempered
     world,
Saw a seductive image of herself.   805
Yet, mark the contradictions of which
     Man
Is still the sport! Here Nature was my
     guide,
The Nature of the dissolute; but thee,
O fostering Nature! I rejected—smiled
At others' tears in pity; and in scorn
At those, which thy soft influence some-
     times drew   811
From my unguarded heart.—The tranquil
     shores
Of Britain circumscribed me; else, per-
     haps
I might have been entangled among deeds,
Which, now, as infamous, I should
     abhor—
Despise, as senseless: for my spirit re-
     lished   816
Strangely the exasperation of that Land,
Which turned an angry beak against the
     down
Of her own breast; confounded into hope
Of disencumbering thus her fretful wings.

'But all was quieted by iron bonds 821
Of military sway. The shifting aims,
The moral interests, the creative might,
The varied functions and high attributes
Of civil action, yielded to a power   825
Formal, and odious, and contemptible.
—In Britain, ruled a panic dread of
     change;
The weak were praised, rewarded, and
     advanced;
And, from the impulse of a just disdain,
Once more did I retire into myself.   830
There feeling no contentment, I resolved
To fly, for safeguard, to some foreign
     shore,
Remote from Europe; from her blasted
     hopes;
Her fields of carnage, and polluted air.

'Fresh blew the wind, when o'er the
     Atlantic Main   835
The ship went gliding with her thought-
     less crew;
And who among them but an Exile, freed
From discontent, indifferent, pleased to
     sit
Among the busily-employed, not more
With obligation charged, with service
     taxed,   840
Than the loose pendant—to the idle wind
Upon the tall mast streaming. But, ye
     Powers
Of soul and sense mysteriously allied,
O, never let the Wretched, if a choice
Be left him, trust the freight of his dis-
     tress   845
To a long voyage on the silent deep!
For, like a plague, will memory break out;
And, in the blank and solitude of things,
Upon his spirit, with a fever's strength,
Will conscience prey.—Feebly must they
     have felt   850
Who, in old time, attired with snakes and
     whips
The vengeful Furies. *Beautiful* regards
Were turned on me—the face of her I
     loved;
The Wife and Mother pitifully fixing
Tender reproaches, insupportable!   855
Where now that boasted liberty? No
     welcome
From unknown objects I received; and
     those,
Known and familiar, which the vaulted
     sky
Did, in the placid clearness of the night,
Disclose, had accusations to prefer   860
Against my peace. Within the cabin
     stood
That volume—as a compass for the soul—
Revered among the nations. I implored
Its guidance; but the infallible support
Of faith was wanting. Tell me, why
     refused   865

To One by storms annoyed and adverse
  winds;
Perplexed with currents; of his weak-
  ness sick;
Of vain endeavours tired; and by his own,
And by his nature's, ignorance, dismayed!

'Long wished-for sight, the Western
  World appeared;   870
And, when the ship was moored, I leaped
  ashore
Indignantly—resolved to be a man,
Who, having o'er the past no power,
  would live
No longer in subjection to the past,   874
With abject mind—from a tyrannic lord
Inviting penance, fruitlessly endured:
So, like a fugitive, whose feet have cleared
Some boundary, which his followers may
  not cross
In prosecution of their deadly chase,
Respiring I looked round.—How bright
  the sun,   880
The breeze how soft! Can any thing
  produced
In the old World compare, thought I, for
  power
And majesty with this gigantic stream,
Sprung from the desert? And behold a
  city
Fresh, youthful, and aspiring! What are
  these   885
To me, or I to them? As much, at least
As he desires that they should be, whom
  winds
And waves have wafted to this distant
  shore,
In the condition of a damaged seed,
Whose fibres cannot, if they would, take
  root.   890
Here may I roam at large;—my business
  is,
Roaming at large, to observe, and not to
  feel
And, therefore, not to act—convinced
  that all
Which bears the name of action, how-
  soe'er
Beginning, ends in servitude—still pain-
  ful,   895
And mostly profitless. And, sooth to say,
On nearer view, a motley spectacle
Appeared, of high pretensions—unre-
  proved
But by the obstreperous voice of higher
  still;   899
Big passions strutting on a petty stage;
Which a detached spectator may regard
Not unamused.—But ridicule demands
Quick change of objects; and, to laugh
  alone,   903
At a composing distance from the haunts
Of strife and folly, though it be a treat
As choice as musing Leisure can bestow;

Yet, in the very centre of the crowd,
To keep the secret of a poignant scorn,
Howe'er to airy Demons suitable,
Of all unsocial courses, is least fit   910
For the gross spirit of mankind,—the one
That soonest fails to please, and quickliest
  turns
Into vexation.
                 Let us, then, I said,
Leave this unknit Republic to the scourge
Of her own passions; and to regions haste,
Whose shades have never felt the en-
  croaching axe,   916
Or soil endured a transfer in the mart
Of dire rapacity. There, Man abides,
Primeval Nature's child. A creature weak
In combination, (wherefore else driven
  back   920
So far, and of his old inheritance
So easily deprived?) but, for that cause,
More dignified, and stronger in himself;
Whether to act, judge, suffer, or enjoy.
True, the intelligence of social art   925
Hath overpowered his forefathers, and
  soon
Will sweep the remnant of his line away;
But contemplations, worthier, nobler far
Than her destructive energies, attend   929
His independence, when along the side
Of Mississippi, or that northern stream[1]
That spreads into successive seas, he
  walks;
Pleased to perceive his own unshackled
  life,
And his innate capacities of soul,
There imaged: or when, having gained
  the top   935
Of some commanding eminence, which
  yet
Intruder ne'er beheld, he thence surveys
Regions of wood and wide savannah, vast
Expanse of unappropriated earth,
With mind that sheds a light on what he
  sees;   940
Free as the sun, and lonely as the sun,
Pouring above his head its radiance down
Upon a living and rejoicing world!

'So, westward, tow'rd the unviolated
  woods
I bent my way; and, roaming far and
  wide,   945
Failed not to greet the merry Mocking-
  bird;
And, while the melancholy Muccawiss
(The sportive bird's companion in the
  grove)
Repeated o'er and o'er his plaintive cry,
I sympathised at leisure with the sound;
But that pure archetype of human great-
  ness,   951
I found him not. There, in his stead,
  appeared

[1] See Note, p. 727.

A creature, squalid, vengeful, and impure;
Remorseless, and submissive to no law
But superstitious fear, and abject sloth.

'Enough is told! Here am I—ye have
    heard   956
What evidence I seek, and vainly seek;
What from my fellow-beings I require,
And either they have not to give, or I
Lack virtue to receive; what I myself,
Too oft by wilful forfeiture, have lost   961
Nor can regain. How languidly I look
Upon this visible fabric of the world,
May be divined—perhaps it hath been
    said:—   964
But spare your pity, if there be in me
Aught that deserves respect: for I exist,
Within myself, not comfortless.—The
    tenour
Which my life holds, he readily may con-
    ceive
Whoe'er hath stood to watch a mountain
    brook
In some still passage of its course, and
    seen,   970
Within the depths of its capacious breast,
Inverted trees, rocks, clouds, and azure
    sky;

And, on its glassy surface, specks of
    foam,
And conglobated bubbles undissolved,
Numerous as stars; that, by their onward
    lapse,   975
Betray to sight the motion of the stream,
Else imperceptible. Meanwhile, is heard
A softened roar, or murmur; and the
    sound
Though soothing, and the little floating
    isles
Though beautiful, are both by Nature
    charged   980
With the same pensive office; and make
    known
Through what perplexing labyrinths, ab-
    rupt
Precipitations, and untoward straits,
The earth-born wanderer hath passed;
    and quickly,   984
That respite o'er, like traverses and toils
Must he again encounter.—Such a stream
Is human Life; and so the Spirit fares
In the best quiet to her course allowed;
And such is mine,—save only for a hope
That my particular current soon will reach
The unfathomable gulf, where all is
    still!'   991

BOOK FOURTH

DESPONDENCY CORRECTED

ARGUMENT

State of feeling produced by the foregoing Narrative.—A belief in a superintending Providence
the only adequate support under affliction.—Wanderer's ejaculation.—Acknowledges the difficulty
of a lively faith.—Hence immoderate sorrow.—Exhortations.—How received.—Wanderer applies his
discourse to that other cause of dejection in the Solitary's mind.—Disappointment from the French
Revolution.—States grounds of hope, and insists on the necessity of patience and fortitude with
respect to the course of great revolutions.—Knowledge the source of tranquillity.—Rural Solitude
favourable to knowledge of the inferior Creatures; Study of their habits and ways recommended;
exhortation to bodily exertion and communion with Nature.—Morbid Solitude pitiable.—Superstition
better than apathy.—Apathy and destitution unknown in the infancy of society.—The various modes
of Religion prevented it.—Illustrated in the Jewish, Persian, Babylonian, Chaldean, and Grecian
modes of belief.—Solitary interposes.—Wanderer points out the influence of religious and imaginative
feeling in the humble ranks of society, illustrated from present and past times.—These principles
tend to recall exploded superstitions and Popery.—Wanderer rebuts this charge, and contrasts the
dignities of the Imagination with the presumptuous littleness of certain modern Philosophers.—
Recommends other lights and guides.—Asserts the power of the Soul to regenerate herself; Solitary
asks how.—Reply.—Personal appeal.—Exhortation to activity of body renewed.—How to commune
with Nature.—Wanderer concludes with a legitimate union of the imagination, affections, understanding, and reason.—Effect of his discourse.—Evening; Return to the Cottage.

HERE closed the Tenant of that lonely
    vale
His mournful narrative—commenced in
    pain,
In pain commenced, and ended without
    peace:
Yet tempered, not unfrequently, with
    strains
Of native feeling, grateful to our minds;
And yielding surely some relief to his,   6

While we sate listening with compassion
    due.
A pause of silence followed; then, with
    voice
That did not falter though the heart was
    moved,
The Wanderer said:—
                    'One adequate support   1
For the calamities of mortal life
Exists—one only; an assured belief

That the procession of our fate, howe'er
Sad or disturbed, is ordered by a Being
Of infinite benevolence and power;   15
Whose everlasting purposes embrace
All accidents, converting them to good.
—The darts of anguish *fix* not where the
    seat
Of suffering hath been thoroughly fortified
By acquiescence in the Will supreme   20
For time and for eternity; by faith,
Faith absolute in God, including hope,
And the defence that lies in boundless
    love
Of his perfections; with habitual dread
Of aught unworthily conceived, endured
Impatiently, ill-done, or left undone,   26
To the dishonour of his holy name.
Soul of our Souls, and safeguard of the
    world!
Sustain, thou only canst, the sick of heart;
Restore their languid spirits, and recall
Their lost affections unto thee and
    thine!'   31

    Then, as we issued from that covert
        nook,
He thus continued, lifting up his eyes
To heaven:—'How beautiful this dome
    of sky;
And the vast hills, in fluctuation fixed   35
At thy command, how awful! Shall the
    Soul,
Human and rational, report of thee
Even less than these!—Be mute who will,
    who can,
Yet I will praise thee with impassioned
    voice:
My lips, that may forget thee in the
    crowd,   40
Cannot forget thee here; where thou hast
    built,
For thy own glory, in the wilderness!
Me didst thou constitute a priest of thine,
In such a temple as we now behold
Reared for thy presence: therefore am I
    bound   45
To worship, here, and everywhere—as one
Not doomed to ignorance, though forced
    to tread,
From childhood up, the ways of poverty;
From unreflecting ignorance preserved,
And from debasement rescued.—By thy
    grace   50
The particle divine remained unquenched;
And, 'mid the wild weeds of a rugged soil,
Thy bounty caused to flourish deathless
    flowers,
From paradise transplanted: wintry age
Impends; the frost will gather round my
    heart;   55
If the flowers wither, I am worse than
    dead!
—Come, labour, when the worn-out frame
    requires

Perpetual sabbath; come, disease and
    want;
And sad exclusion through decay of
    sense;
But leave me unabated trust in thee—   60
And let thy favour, to the end of life,
Inspire me with ability to seek
Repose and hope among eternal things—
Father of heaven and earth! and I am
    rich,
And will possess my portion in content!

    'And what are things eternal?—powers
        depart,'   66
The grey-haired Wanderer steadfastly
    replied,
Answering the question which himself
    had asked,
'Possessions vanish, and opinions change,
And passions hold a fluctuating seat: 70
But, by the storms of circumstance un-
    shaken,
And subject neither to eclipse nor wane,
Duty exists;—immutably survive,
For our support, the measures and the
    forms,
Which an abstract intelligence supplies;
Whose kingdom is, where time and space
    are not.   76
Of other converse which mind, soul, and
    heart,
Do, with united urgency, require,
What more that may not perish?—Thou,
    dread source,   79
Prime, self-existing cause and end of all
That in the scale of being fill their place;
Above our human region, or below,
Set and sustained;—thou, who didst wrap
    the cloud
Of infancy around us, that thyself,
Therein, with our simplicity awhile   85
Might'st hold, on earth, communion un-
    disturbed;
Who from the anarchy of dreaming sleep,
Or from its death-like void, with punctual
    care,
And touch as gentle as the morning light,
Restor'st us, daily, to the powers of sense
And reason's steadfast rule—thou, thou
    alone   91
Art everlasting, and the blessed Spirits,
Which thou includest, as the sea her
    waves:
For adoration thou endur'st; endure
For consciousness the motions of thy will;
For apprehension those transcendent
    truths   96
Of the pure intellect, that stand as laws
(Submission constituting strength and
    power)
Even to thy Being's infinite majesty!
This universe shall pass away—a work   100
Glorious! because the shadow of thy
    might,

A step, or link, for intercourse with thee
Ah! if the time must come, in which my
      feet
No more shall stray where meditation
      leads,
By flowing stream, through wood, or
      craggy wild,   105
Loved haunts like these; the unim-
      prisoned Mind
May yet have scope to range among her
      own,
Her thoughts, her images, her high desires.
If the dear faculty of sight should fail, 109
Still, it may be allowed me to remember
What visionary powers of eye and soul
In youth were mine; when, stationed on
      the top
Of some huge hill, expectant, I beheld
The sun rise up, from distant climes
      returned
Darkness to chase, and sleep; and bring
      the day   115
His bounteous gift! or saw him toward
      the deep
Sink, with a retinue of flaming clouds
Attended; then, my spirit was entranced
With joy exalted to beatitude;
The measure of my soul was filled with
      bliss,   120
And holiest love; as earth, sea, air, with
      light,
With pomp, with glory, with magni-
      ficence!

'Those fervent raptures are for ever
      flown;
And, since their date, my soul hath under-
      gone   124
Change manifold, for better or for worse:
Yet cease I not to struggle, and aspire
Heavenward; and chide the part of me
      that flags,
Through sinful choice; or dread necessity
On human nature from above imposed.
'Tis, by comparison, an easy task   130
Earth to despise; but, to converse with
      heaven—[1]
This is not easy:—to relinquish all
We have, or hope, of happiness and joy,
And stand in freedom loosened from this
      world,
I deem not arduous; but must needs
      confess   135
That 'tis a thing impossible to frame
Conceptions equal to the soul's desires;
And the most difficult of tasks to *keep*
Heights which the soul is competent to
      gain.
—Man is of dust: ethereal hopes are his,
Which, when they should sustain them-
      selves aloft,   141
Want due consistence; like a pillar of
      smoke,

That with majestic energy from earth
Rises; but, having reached the thinner
      air,
Melts, and dissolves, and is no longer seen.
From this infirmity of mortal kind   146
Sorrow proceeds, which else were not;
      at least,
If grief be something hallowed and or-
      dained,
If, in proportion, it be just and meet,
Yet, through this weakness of the general
      heart,   150
Is it enabled to maintain its hold
In that excess which conscience dis-
      approves.
For who could sink and settle to that
      point
Of selfishness; so senseless who could be
As long and perseveringly to mourn   155
For any object of his love, removed
From this unstable world, if he could fix
A satisfying view upon that state
Of pure, imperishable, blessedness,
Which reason promises, and holy writ   160
Ensures to all believers?—Yet mistrust
Is of such incapacity, methinks,
No natural branch; despondency far less;
And, least of all, is absolute despair.
—And, if there be whose tender frames
      have drooped   165
Even to the dust; apparently, through
      weight
Of anguish unrelieved, and lack of power
An agonizing sorrow to transmute;
Deem not that proof is here of hope with-
      held
When wanted most; a confidence im-
      paired   170
So pitiably, that, having ceased to see
With bodily eyes, they are borne down by
      love
Of what is lost, and perish through regret.
Oh! no, the innocent Sufferer often sees
Too clearly; feels too vividly; and longs
To realize the vision, with intense   176
And over-constant yearning;—there—
      there lies
The excess, by which the balance is de-
      stroyed.
Too, too contracted are these walls of
      flesh,
This vital warmth too cold, these visual
      orbs,   180
Though inconceivably endowed, too dim
For any passion of the soul that leads
To ecstasy; and all the crooked paths
Of time and change disdaining, takes its
      course
Along the line of limitless desires.   185
I, speaking now from such disorder free,
Nor rapt, nor craving, but in settled
      peace,
I cannot doubt that they whom you de-
      plore

627

Are glorified; or, if they sleep, shall wake
From sleep, and dwell with God in end-
less love.   190
Hope, below this, consists not with belief
In mercy, carried infinite degrees
Beyond the tenderness of human hearts:
Hope, below this, consists not with belief
In perfect wisdom, guiding mightiest
power,   195
That finds no limits but her own pure will.

'Here then we rest; not fearing for our
creed
The worst that human reasoning can
achieve,
To unsettle or perplex it: yet with pain
Acknowledging, and grievous self-re-
proach,   200
That, though immovably convinced, we
want
Zeal, and the virtue to exist by faith
As soldiers live by courage; as, by
strength
Of heart, the sailor fights with roaring seas.
Alas! the endowment of immortal power
Is matched unequally with custom, time,[1]
And domineering faculties of sense
In *all;* in most with superadded foes,
Idle temptations; open vanities,
Ephemeral offspring of the unblushing
world;   210
And, in the private regions of the mind,
Ill-governed passions, ranklings of despite,
Immoderate wishes, pining discontent,
Distress and care. What then remains?—
To seek
Those helps for his occasions ever near
Who lacks not will to use them; vows,
renewed   216
On the first motion of a holy thought;
Vigils of contemplation; praise; and
prayer—
A stream, which, from the fountain of
the heart   219
Issuing, however feebly, nowhere flows
Without access of unexpected strength.
But, above all, the victory is most sure
For him, who, seeking faith by virtue,
strives
To yield entire submission to the law
Of conscience—conscience reverenced
and obeyed,   225
As God's most intimate presence in the
soul,
And his most perfect image in the world.
—Endeavour thus to live; these rules
regard;
These helps solicit; and a steadfast seat
Shall then be yours among the happy few
Who dwell on earth, yet breathe empy-
real air,   231
Sons of the morning. For your nobler
part,

<hr>

[1] See Note, p. 728.

Ere disencumbered of her mortal chains,
Doubt shall be quelled and trouble chased
away;
With only such degree of sadness left 235
As may support longings of pure desire;
And strengthen love, rejoicing secretly
In the sublime attractions of the grave.'

While, in this strain, the venerable Sage
Poured forth his aspirations, and an-
nounced   240
His judgments, near that lonely house we
paced
A plot of green-sward, seemingly pre-
served
By nature's care from wreck of scattered
stones,
And from encroachment of encircling
heath:
Small space! but, for reiterated steps,
Smooth and commodious; as a stately
deck   246
Which to and fro the mariner is used
To tread for pastime, talking with his
mates,
Or haply thinking of far-distant friends,
While the ship glides before a steady
breeze.   250
Stillness prevailed around us: and the
voice
That spake was capable to lift the soul
Toward regions yet more tranquil. But,
methought,
That he, whose fixed despondency had
given
Impulse and motive to that strong dis-
course,   255
Was less upraised in spirit than abashed;
Shrinking from admonition, like a man
Who feels that to exhort is to reproach.
Yet not to be diverted from his aim,
The Sage continued:—
                     'For that other loss, 260
The loss of confidence in social man,
By the unexpected transports of our age
Carried so high, that every thought, which
looked
Beyond the temporal destiny of the Kind,
To many seemed superfluous—as, no
cause   265
Could e'er for such exalted confidence
Exist; so, none is now for fixed despair:
The two extremes are equally disowned
By reason: if, with sharp recoil, from
one
You have been driven far as its opposite,
Between them seek the point whereon to
build   271
Sound expectations. So doth he advise
Who shared at first the illusion; but was
soon
Cast from the pedestal of pride by shocks
Which Nature gently gave, in woods and
fields;   275

Nor unreproved by Providence, thus
    speaking
To the inattentive children of the world:
"Vain-glorious Generation! what new
    powers
On you have been conferred? what gifts,
    withheld   279
From your progenitors, have ye received,
Fit recompense of new desert? what claim
Are ye prepared to urge, that my decrees
For you should undergo a sudden change;
And the weak functions of one busy day,
Reclaiming and extirpating, perform 285
What all the slowly-moving years of time,
With their united force, have left undone?
By nature's gradual processes be taught;
By story be confounded! Ye aspire
Rashly, to fall once more; and that false
    fruit,   290
Which, to your overweening spirits,
    yields
Hope of a flight celestial, will produce
Misery and shame. But Wisdom of her
    sons
Shall not the less, though late, be justi-
    fied."

'Such timely warning,' said the Wan-
    derer, 'gave   295
That visionary voice; and, at this day,
When a Tartarean darkness overspreads
The groaning nations; when the impious
    rule,
By will or by established ordinance,
Their own dire agents, and constrain the
    good   300
To acts which they abhor; though I
    bewail
This triumph, yet the pity of my heart
Prevents me not from owning, that the
    law,
By which mankind now suffers, is most
    just.   304
For by superior energies; more strict
Affiance in each other; faith more firm
In their unhallowed principles; the bad
Have fairly earned a victory o'er the weak,
The vacillating, inconsistent good.
Therefore, not unconsoled, I wait—in
    hope   310
To see the moment, when the righteous
    cause
Shall gain defenders zealous and devout
As they who have opposed her; in which
    Virtue
Will, to her efforts, tolerate no bounds
That are not lofty as her rights; aspiring
By impulse of her own ethereal zeal. 316
That spirit only can redeem mankind;
And when that sacred spirit shall appear,
Then shall *our* triumph be complete as
    theirs.
Yet, should this confidence prove vain,
    the wise   320

Have still the keeping of their proper
    peace;
Are guardians of their own tranquillity.
They act, or they recede, observe, and
    feel;
"Knowing the heart of man is set to be[1]
The centre of this world, about the which
Those revolutions of disturbances   326
Still roll; where all the aspects of misery
Predominate; whose strong effects are
    such
As he must bear, being powerless to re-
    dress;
And that unless above himself he can 330
Erect himself, how poor a thing is man[2]*!"*

'Happy is he who lives to understand,
Not human nature only, but explores
All natures,—to the end that he may find
The law that governs each; and where
    begins   335
The union, the partition where, that makes
Kind and degree, among all visible Beings;
The constitutions, powers, and faculties,
Which they inherit,—cannot step be-
    yond,—   339
And cannot fall beneath; that do assign
To every class its station and its office,
Through all the mighty commonwealth of
    things;
Up from the creeping plant to sovereign
    Man.
Such converse, if directed by a meek,
Sincere, and humble spirit, teaches love:
For knowledge is delight; and such de-
    light   346
Breeds love: yet, suited as it rather is
To thought and to the climbing intellect,
It teaches less to love, than to adore;
If that be not indeed the highest love!'

'Yet,' said I, tempted here to inter-
    pose,   351
'The dignity of life is not impaired
By aught that innocently satisfies
The humbler cravings of the heart; and he
Is still a happier man, who, for those
    heights   355
Of speculation not unfit, descends;
And such benign affections cultivates
Among the inferior kinds; not merely
    those
That he may call his own, and which de-
    pend,
As individual objects of regard,   360
Upon his care, from whom he also looks
For signs and tokens of a mutual bond;
But others, far beyond this narrow sphere,
Whom, for the very sake of love, he loves.
Nor is it a mean praise of rural life 365
And solitude, that they do favour most,
Most frequently call forth, and best sus-
    tain,
[1] See Note, p. 728   [2] Daniel.

These pure sensations; that can penetrate
The obstreperous city; on the barren seas
Are not unfelt; and much might recom-
    mend,   370
How much they might inspirit and endear,
The loneliness of this sublime retreat!'

    'Yes,' said the Sage, resuming the dis-
        course
Again directed to his downcast Friend,
'If, with the froward will and grovelling
    soul   375
Of man, offended, liberty is here,
And invitation every hour renewed,
To mark *their* placid state, who never
    heard
Of a command which they have power to
    break,
Or rule which they are tempted to trans-
    gress: 380
These with a soothed or elevated heart,
May we behold; their knowledge register;
Observe their ways; and, free from envy,
    find
Complacence there:—but wherefore this
    to you?
I guess that, welcome to your lonely
    hearth,   385
The redbreast, ruffled up by winter's cold
Into a "feathery bunch," feeds at your
    hand:
A box, perchance, is from your casement
    hung
For the small wren to build in;—not in
    vain,   389
The barriers disregarding that surround
This deep abiding place, before your sight
Mounts on the breeze the butterfly; and
    soars,
Small creature as she is, from earth's
    bright flowers,
Into the dewy clouds. Ambition reigns
In the waste wilderness: the Soul ascends
Drawn towards her native firmament of
    heaven,   396
When the fresh eagle, in the month of
    May,
Upborne, at evening, on replenished wing,
This shaded valley leaves; and leaves the
    dark
Empurpled hills, conspicuously renewing
A proud communication with the sun 401
Low sunk beneath the horizon!—List!—
    I heard,
From yon huge breast of rock, a voice
    sent forth
As if the visible mountain made the cry.
Again!'—The effect upon the soul was
    such   405
As he expressed: from out the mountain's
    heart
The solemn voice appeared to issue,
    startling
The blank air—for the region all around

Stood empty of all shape of life, and silent
Save for that single cry, the unanswer'd
    bleat   410
Of a poor lamb—left somewhere to itself,
The plaintive spirit of the solitude!
He paused, as if unwilling to proceed,
Through consciousness that silence in
    such place
Was best, the most affecting eloquence.
But soon his thoughts returned upon
    themselves,   416
And, in soft tone of speech, thus he re-
    sumed.

    'Ah! if the heart, too confidently raised,
Perchance too lightly occupied, or lulled
Too easily, despise or overlook   420
The vassalage that binds her to the earth,
Her sad dependence upon time, and all
The trepidations of mortality,
What place so destitute and void—but
    there
The little flower her vanity shall check;
The trailing worm reprove her thought-
    less pride?   426

    'These craggy regions, these chaotic
        wilds,
Does that benignity pervade, that warms
The mole contented with her darksome
    walk
In the cold ground; and to the emmet
    gives   430
Her foresight, and intelligence that makes
The tiny creatures strong by social league;
Supports the generations, multiplies
Their tribes, till we behold a spacious
    plain
Or grassy bottom, all, with little hills—
Their labour, covered, as a lake with
    waves;   436
Thousands of cities, in the desert place
Built up of life, and food, and means of
    life!
Nor wanting here, to entertain the
    thought,
Creatures that in communities exist 440
Less, as might seem, for general guardian-
    ship
Or through dependence upon mutual aid,
Than by participation of delight
And a strict love of fellowship, combined.
What other spirit can it be that prompts
The gilded summer flies to mix and weave
Their sports together in the solar beam,
Or in the gloom of twilight hum their
    joy?
More obviously the self-same influence
    rules
The feathered kinds; the fieldfare's pen-
    sive flock,   450
The cawing rooks, and sea-mews from
    afar,
Hovering above these inland solitudes,

By the rough wind unscattered, at whose
    call
Up through the trenches of the long-
    drawn vales
Their voyage was begun: nor is its power
Unfelt among the sedentary fowl   456
That seek yon pool, and there prolong
    their stay
In silent congress; or together roused
Take flight; while with their clang the
    air resounds.
And, over all, in that ethereal vault, 460
Is the mute company of changeful clouds;
Bright apparition, suddenly put forth,
The rainbow smiling on the faded storm;
The mild assemblage of the starry
    heavens;
And the great sun, earth's universal lord!

'How bountiful is Nature! he shall
    find   466
Who seeks not; and to him, who hath
    not asked,
Large measures shall be dealt. Three
    sabbath-days
Are scarcely told, since, on a service bent
Of mere humanity, you clomb those
    heights;   470
And what a marvellous and heavenly
    show
Was suddenly revealed!—the swains
    moved on,
And heeded not: you lingered, you per-
    ceived
And felt, deeply as living man could feel.
There is a luxury in self-dispraise;   475
And inward self-disparagement affords
To meditative spleen a grateful feast.
Trust me, pronouncing on your own
    desert,
You judge unthankfully: distempered
    nerves
Infect the thoughts; the languor of the
    frame   480
Depresses the soul's vigour. Quit your
    couch—
Cleave not so fondly to your moody cell;
Nor let the hallowed powers, that shed
    from heaven
Stillness and rest, with disapproving eye
Look down upon your taper, through a
    watch   485
Of midnight hours, unseasonably twink-
    ling
In this deep Hollow, like a sullen star
Dimly reflected in a lonely pool.
Take courage, and withdraw yourself
    from ways
That run not parallel to nature's course.
Rise with the lark! your matins shall
    obtain   491
Grace be their composition what it may,
If but with hers performed; climb once
    again,

Climb every day, those ramparts; meet
    the breeze
Upon their tops, adventurous as a bee
That from your garden thither soars, to
    feed   496
On new-blown heath; let yon command-
    ing rock
Be your frequented watch-tower; roll the
    stone
In thunder down the mountains; with all
    your might
Chase the wild goat; and if the bold red
    deer   500
Fly to those harbours, driven by hound
    and horn
Loud echoing, add your speed to the
    pursuit;
So, wearied to your hut shall you return,
And sink at evening into sound repose.'

    The Solitary lifted toward the hills 505
A kindling eye:—accordant feelings
    rushed
Into my bosom, whence these words
    broke forth:
'Oh! what a joy it were, in vigorous
    health,
To have a body (this our vital frame
With shrinking sensibility endued,   510
And all the nice regards of flesh and
    blood)
And to the elements surrender it
As if it were a spirit!—How divine,
The liberty, for frail, for mortal, man 514
To roam at large among unpeopled glens
And mountainous retirements, only trod
By devious footsteps; regions consecrate
To oldest time! and, reckless of the storm
That keeps the raven quiet in her nest,
Be as a presence or a motion—one   520
Among the many there; and while the
    mists
Flying, and rainy vapours, call out shapes
And phantoms from the crags and solid
    earth
As fast as a musician scatters sounds
Out of an instrument; and while the
    streams   525
(As at a first creation and in haste
To exercise their untried faculties)
Descending from the region of the clouds,
And starting from the hollows of the
    earth
More multitudinous every moment, rend
Their way before them—what a joy to
    roam   531
An equal among mightiest energies;
And haply sometimes with articulate
    voice,
Amid the deafening tumult, scarcely
    heard
By him that utters it, exclaim aloud, 535
"Rage on, ye elements! let moon and
    stars

Their aspects lend, and mingle in their
  turn
With this commotion (ruinous though it
  be)
From day to night, from night to day,
  prolonged!'''

'Yes,' said the Wanderer, taking from
  my lips   540
The strain of transport, 'whosoe'er in
  youth
Has, through ambition of his soul, given
  way
To such desires, and grasped at such
  delight,
Shall feel congenial stirrings late and long,
In spite of all the weakness that life
  brings,   545
Its cares and sorrows; he, though taught
  to own
The tranquillizing power of time, shall
  wake,
Wake sometimes to a noble restlessness—
Loving the sports which once he gloried
  in.

'Compatriot, Friend, remote are
  Garry's hills,   550
The streams far distant of your native
  glen;
Yet is their form and image here ex-
  pressed
With brotherly resemblance. Turn your
  steps
Wherever fancy leads; by day, by night,
Are various engines working, not the
  same   555
As those with which your soul in youth
  was moved,
But by the great Artificer endowed
With no inferior power. You dwell alone;
You walk, you live, you speculate alone;
Yet doth remembrance, like a sovereign
  prince,   560
For you a stately gallery maintain
Of gay or tragic pictures. You have seen,
Have acted, suffered, travelled far, ob-
  served
With no incurious eye; and books are
  yours,
Within whose silent chambers treasure
  lies   565
Preserved from age to age; more precious
  far
Than that accumulated store of gold
And orient gems, which, for a day of need,
The Sultan hides deep in ancestral tombs.
These hoards of truth you can unlock at
  will: 570
And music waits upon your skilful touch,
Sounds which the wandering shepherd
  from these heights
Hears, and forgets his purpose;—
  furnished thus,

How can you droop, if willing to be upraised?

  'A piteous lot it were to flee from
  Man—   575
Yet not rejoice in Nature. He, whose
  hours
Are by domestic pleasure uncaressed
And unenlivened; who exists whole years
Apart from benefits received or done
'Mid the transactions of the bustling
  crowd;   580
Who neither hears, nor feels a wish to
  hear,
Of the world's interests—such a one hath
  need
Of a quick fancy and an active heart,
That, for the day's consumption, books
  may yield
Food not unwholesome; earth and air
  correct   585
His morbid humour, with delight sup-
  plied
Or solace, varying as the seasons change.
—Truth has her pleasure-grounds, her
  haunts of ease
And easy contemplation; gay parterres,
And labyrinthine walks, her sunny glades
And shady groves in studied contrast—
  each,   591
For recreation, leading into each:
These may he range, if willing to partake
Their soft indulgences, and in due time
May issue thence, recruited for the tasks
And course of service Truth requires from
  those   596
Who tend her altars, wait upon her
  throne,
And guard her fortresses. Who thinks,
  and feels,
And recognises ever and anon
The breeze of nature stirring in his soul,
Why need such man go desperately
  astray,   601
And nurse "the dreadful appetite of
  death"?
If tired with systems, each in its degree
Substantial, and all crumbling in their
  turn,
Let him build systems of his own, and
  smile   605
At the fond work, demolished with a
  touch;
If unreligious, let him be at once,
Among ten thousand innocents, enrolled
A pupil in the many-chambered school,
Where superstition weaves her airy
  dreams.   610

'Life's autumn past, I stand on winter's
  verge;
And daily lose what I desire to keep:
Yet rather would I instantly decline
To the traditionary sympathies

Of a most rustic ignorance, and take 615
A fearful apprehension from the owl
Or death-watch: and as readily rejoice,
If two auspicious magpies crossed my
    way;—
To this would rather bend than see and
    hear
The repetitions wearisome of sense, 620
Where soul is dead, and feeling hath no
    place;
Where knowledge, ill begun in cold
    remark
On outward things, with formal inference
    ends;
Or, if the mind turn inward, she recoils
At once—or, not recoiling, is perplexed—
Lost in a gloom of uninspired research;
Meanwhile, the heart within the heart,
    the seat   627
Where peace and happy consciousness
    should dwell,
On its own axis restlessly revolving,
Seeks, yet can nowhere find, the light of
    truth.   630

    'Upon the breast of new-created earth
Man walked; and when and wheresoe'er
    he moved,
Alone or mated, solitude was not.
He heard, borne on the wind, the articu-
    late voice
Of God; and Angels to his sight ap-
    peared   635
Crowning the glorious hills of paradise;
Or through the groves gliding like morn-
    ing mist
Enkindled by the sun. He sate—and
    talked
With wingèd Messengers; who daily
    brought
To his small island in the ethereal deep
Tidings of joy and love.—From those pure
    heights   641
(Whether of actual vision, sensible
To sight and feeling, or that in this sort
Have condescendingly been shadowed
    forth
Communications spiritually maintained,
And intuitions moral and divine)   646
Fell Human-kind—to banishment con-
    demned
That flowing years repealed not: and
    distress
And grief spread wide; but Man escaped
    the doom
Of destitution;—solitude was not.   650
—Jehovah—shapeless Power above all
    Powers,
Single and one, the omnipresent God,
By vocal utterance, or blaze of light,
Or cloud of darkness, localised in heaven;
On earth, enshrined within the wander-
    ing ark;   655
Or, out of Sion, thundering from his throne

Between the Cherubim—on the chosen
    Race
Showered miracles, and ceased not to
    dispense
Judgments, that filled the land from age
    to age
With hope, and love, and gratitude, and
    fear;   660
And with amazement smote;—thereby
    to assert
His scorned, or unacknowledged, sove-
    reignty.
And when the One, ineffable of name,
Of nature indivisible, withdrew
From mortal adoration or regard,   665
Not then was Deity engulfed; nor Man,
The rational creature, left, to feel the
    weight
Of his own reason, without sense or
    thought
Of higher reason and a purer will,
To benefit and bless, through mightier
    power:—   670
Whether the Persian—zealous to reject
Altar and image, and the inclusive walls
And roofs of temples built by human
    hands—
To loftiest heights ascending, from their
    tops,   674
With myrtle-wreathed tiara on his brow,
Presented sacrifice to moon and stars,
And to the winds and mother elements,
And the whole circle of the heavens, for
    him
A sensitive existence, and a God,
With lifted hands invoked, and songs of
    praise: 680
Or, less reluctantly to bonds of sense
Yielding his soul, the Babylonian framed
For influence undefined a personal shape;
And, from the plain, with toil immense,
    upreared
Tower eight times planted on the top of
    tower,   685
That Belus, nightly to his splendid couch
Descending, there might rest; upon that
    height
Pure and serene, diffused—to overlook
Winding Euphrates, and the city vast
Of his devoted worshippers, far-stretched,
With grove and field and garden inter-
    spersed;   691
Their town, and foodful region for sup-
    port
Against the pressure of beleaguering war.

    'Chaldean Shepherds, ranging track-
    less fields,   694
Beneath the concave of unclouded skies
Spread like a sea, in boundless solitude,
Looked on the polar star, as on a guide
And guardian of their course, that never
    closed
His steadfast eye. The planetary Five

With a submissive reverence they be-
held;   700
Watched, from the centre of their sleep-
ing flocks,
Those radiant Mercuries, that seemed to
move
Carrying through ether, in perpetual
round,
Decrees and resolutions of the Gods;
And, by their aspects, signifying works
Of dim futurity, to Man revealed.   706
—The imaginative faculty was lord
Of observations natural; and, thus
Led on, those shepherds made report of
stars
In set rotation passing to and fro,   710
Between the orbs of our apparent sphere
And its invisible counterpart, adorned
With answering constellations, under
earth,
Removed from all approach of living
sight
But present to the dead; who, so they
deemed,   715
Like those celestial messengers beheld
All accidents, and judges were of all.

'The lively Grecian, in a land of hills,
Rivers and fertile plains, and sounding
shores,—
Under a cope of sky more variable,   720
Could find commodious place for every
God,
Promptly received, as prodigally brought,
From the surrounding countries at the
choice
Of all adventurers. With unrivalled skill,
As nicest observation furnished hints
For studious fancy, his quick hand be-
stowed   726
On fluent operations a fixed shape;
Metal or stone, idolatrously served;
And yet—triumphant o'er this pompous
show
Of art, this palpable array of sense, 730
On every side encountered; in despite
Of the gross fictions chanted in the streets
By wandering Rhapsodists; and in con-
tempt
Of doubt and bold denial hourly urged
Amid the wrangling schools—a SPIRIT
hung,   735
Beautiful region! o'er thy towns and
farms,
Statues and temples, and memorial tombs;
And emanations were perceived; and acts
Of immortality, in Nature's course,   739
Exemplified by mysteries, that were felt
As bonds, on grave philosopher imposed
And armèd warrior; and in every grove
A gay or pensive tenderness prevailed,
When piety more awful had relaxed.
—"Take, running river, take these locks
of mine"—   745

Thus would the Votary say—"this severed
hair,
My vow fulfilling, do I here present,
Thankful for my belovèd child's return.
Thy banks, Cephisus, he again hath trod,
Thy murmurs heard; and drunk the
crystal lymph   750
With which thou dost refresh the thirsty
lip,
And, all day long, moisten these flowery
fields!"
And, doubtless, sometimes, when the hair
was shed
Upon the flowing stream, a thought arose
Of Life continuous, Being unimpaired;
That hath been, is, and where it was and
is   756
There shall endure,—existence unexposed
To the blind walk of mortal accident;
From diminution safe and weakening age;
While man grows old, and dwindles, and
decays;   760
And countless generations of mankind
Depart; and leave no vestige where they
trod.

'We live by Admiration, Hope, and
Love;
And, even as these are well and wisely
fixed,
In dignity of being we ascend.   765
But what is error?'—'Answer he who
can!'
The Sceptic somewhat haughtily ex-
claimed:
'Love, Hope, and Admiration—are they
not
Mad Fancy's favourite vassals? Does not
life   769
Use them, full oft, as pioneers to ruin,
Guides to destruction? Is it well to trust
Imagination's light when reason's fails,
The unguarded taper where the guarded
faints?
—Stoop from those heights, and soberly
declare
What error is; and, of our errors, which
Doth most debase the mind; the genuine
seats   776
Of power, where are they? Who shall
regulate,
With truth, the scale of intellectual rank?'

'Methinks,' persuasively the Sage re-
plied,   779
'That for this arduous office you possess
Some rare advantages. Your early days
A grateful recollection must supply
Of much exalted good by Heaven vouch-
safed
To dignify the humblest state.—Your
voice
Hath, in my hearing, often testified   785
That poor men's children, they, and they
alone,

By their condition taught, can under-
stand
The wisdom of the prayer that daily asks
For daily bread. A consciousness is
yours   789
How feelingly religion may be learned
In smoky cabins, from a mother's
tongue—
Heard while the dwelling vibrates to the
din
Of the contiguous torrent, gathering
strength
At every moment—and, with strength,
increase   794
Of fury; or, while snow is at the door,
Assaulting and defending, and the wind,
A sightless labourer, whistles at his work—
Fearful; but resignation tempers fear,
And piety is sweet to infant minds.
—The Shepherd-lad, that in the sunshine
carves,   800
On the green turf, a dial—to divide
The silent hours; and who to that report
Can portion out his pleasures, and adapt,
Throughout a long and lonely summer's
day   804
His round of pastoral duties, is not left
With less intelligence for *moral* things
Of gravest import. Early he perceives,
Within himself, a measure and a rule,
Which to the sun of truth he can apply,
That shines for him, and shines for all
mankind.   810
Experience daily fixing his regards
On nature's wants, he knows how few
they are,
And where they lie, how answered and
appeared.
This knowledge ample recompense affords
For manifold privations; he refers   815
His notions to this standard; on this rock
Rests his desires; and hence, in after life,
Soul-strengthening patience, and sublime
content.
Imagination—not permitted here
To waste her powers, as in the worldling's
mind,   820
On fickle pleasures, and superfluous cares,
And trivial ostentation—is left free
And puissant to range the solemn walks
Of time and nature, girded by a zone
That, while it binds, invigorates and sup-
ports.   825
Acknowledge, then, that whether by the
side
Of his poor hut, or on the mountain-top,
Or in the cultured field, a Man so bred
(Take from him what you will upon the
score   829
Of ignorance or illusion) lives and breathes
For noble purposes of mind: his heart
Beats to the heroic song of ancient days;
His eye distinguishes, his soul creates,
And those illusions, which excite the scorn

Or move the pity of unthinking minds,
Are they not mainly outward ministers
Of inward conscience? with whose service
charged   837
They came and go, appeared and dis-
appear,
Diverting evil purposes, remorse
Awakening, chastening an intemperate
grief,   840
Or pride of heart abating: and, whene'er
For less important ends those phantoms
move,
Who would forbid them, if their presence
serve,
On thinly-peopled mountains and wild
heaths,
Filling a space, else vacant, to exalt   845
The forms of Nature, and enlarge her
powers?

'Once more to distant ages of the world
Let us revert, and place before our
thoughts
The face which rural solitude might wear
To the unenlightened swains of pagan
Greece.   850
—In that fair clime, the lonely herdsman,
stretched
On the soft grass through half a summer's
day,
With music lulled his indolent repose:
And, in some fit of weariness, if he,
When his own breath was silent, chanced
to hear   855
A distant strain, far sweeter than the
sounds
Which his poor skill could make, his
fancy fetched,
Even from the blazing chariot of the sun,
A beardless Youth, who touched a golden
lute,
And filled the illumined groves with
ravishment.   860
The nightly hunter, lifting a bright eye
Up towards the crescent moon, with
grateful heart
Called on the lovely wanderer who be-
stowed
That timely light, to share his joyous
sport:
And hence, a beaming Goddess with her
Nymphs,   865
Across the lawn and through the dark-
some grove,
Not unaccompanied with tuneful notes
By echo multiplied from rock or cave,
Swept in the storm of chase; as moon and
stars
Glance rapidly along the clouded heaven,
When winds are blowing strong. The
traveller slaked   871
His thirst from rill or gushing fount, and
thanked
The Naiad. Sunbeams, upon distant hills

Gliding apace, with shadows in their train,
Might, with small help from fancy, be
    transformed   875
Into fleet Oreads sporting visibly.
The Zephyrs fanning, as they passed,
    their wings,
Lacked not, for love, fair objects whom
    they wooed
With gentle whisper. Withered boughs
    grotesque,
Stripped of their leaves and twigs by
    hoary age,   880
From depth of shaggy covert peeping
    forth
In the low vale, or on steep mountain-side;
And, sometimes, intermixed with stirring
    horns
Of the live deer, or goat's depending
    beard,—
These were the lurking Satyrs, a wild
    brood   885
Of gamesome Deities; or Pan himself,
The simple shepherd's awe-inspiring
    God!'

The strain was aptly chosen; and I
    could mark
Its kindly influence, o'er the yielding brow
Of our Companion, gradually diffused;
While, listening, he had paced the noise-
    less turf,   891
Like one whose untired ear a murmuring
    stream
Detains; but tempted now to interpose,
He with a smile exclaimed:—
            ''Tis well you speak
At a safe distance from our native land,
And from the mansions where our youth
    was taught.   896
The true descendants of those godly men
Who swept from Scotland, in a flame of
    zeal,
Shrine, altar, image, and the massy piles
That harboured them,—the souls retain-
    ing yet   900
The churlish features of that after-race
Who fled to woods, caverns, and jutting
    rocks,
In deadly scorn of superstitious rites,
Or what their scruples construed to be
    such—
How, think you, would they tolerate this
    scheme   905
Of fine propensities, that tends, if urged
Far as it might be urged, to sow afresh
The weeds of Romish phantasy, in vain
Uprooted; would re-consecrate our wells
To good Saint Fillan and to fair Saint
    Anne;   910
And from long banishment recall Saint
    Giles,
To watch again with tutelary love
O'er stately Edinborough throned on
    crags?

A blessed restoration, to behold
The patron, on the shoulders of his priests,
Once more parading through her crowded
    streets   916
Now simply guarded by the sober powers
Of science, and philosophy, and sense!'

This answer followed.—'You have
    turned my thoughts
Upon our brave Progenitors, who rose
Against idolatry with warlike mind,   921
And shrunk from vain observances, to
    lurk
In woods, and dwell under impending
    rocks
Ill-sheltered, and oft wanting fire and
    food;
Why?—for this very reason that they felt,
And did acknowledge, wheresoe'er they
    moved,   926
A spiritual presence, ofttimes miscon-
    ceived,
But still a high dependence, a divine
Bounty and government, that filled their
    hearts
With joy, and gratitude, and fear, and
    love;   930
And from their fervent lips drew hymns
    of praise,
That through the desert rang. Though
    favoured less,
Far less, than these, yet such, in their
    degree,
Were those bewildered Pagans of old
    time.
Beyond their own poor natures and
    above   935
They looked; were humbly thankful for
    the good
Which the warm sun solicited, and earth
Bestowed; were gladsome,—and their
    moral sense
They fortified with reverence for the
    Gods;
And they had hopes that overstepped the
    Grave.   940

'Now, shall our great Discoverers,' he
    exclaimed,
Raising his voice triumphantly, 'obtain
From sense and reason less than these
    obtained,
Though far misled? Shall men for whom
    our age
Unbaffled powers of vision hath prepared,
To explore the world without and world
    within,   946
Be joyless as the blind? Ambitious
    spirits—
Whom earth, at this late season, hath
    produced
To regulate the moving spheres, and weigh
The planets in the hollow of their hand;
And they who rather dive than soar,
    whose pains   951

636

Have solved the elements, or analysed
The thinking principle—shall they in fact
Prove a degraded Race? and what avails
Renown, if their presumption make them
    such?   955
Oh! there is laughter at their work in
    heaven!
Enquire of ancient Wisdom; go, demand
Of mighty Nature, if 'twas ever meant
That we should pry far off yet be unraised;
That we should pore, and dwindle as we
    pore,   960
Viewing all objects unremittingly
In disconnection dead and spiritless;
And still dividing, and dividing still,
Break down all grandeur, still unsatisfied
With the perverse attempt, while little-
    ness   965
May yet become more little; waging thus
An impious warfare with the very life
Of our own souls!
            And if indeed there be
An all-pervading Spirit, upon whom
Our dark foundations rest, could he de-
    sign   970
That this magnificent effect of power,
The earth we tread, the sky that we be-
    hold
By day, and all the pomp which night
    reveals;
That these—and that superior mystery
Our vital frame, so fearfully devised,
And the dread soul within it—should
    exist   976
Only to be examined, pondered, searched,
Probed, vexed, and criticised?—Accuse
    me not
Of arrogance, unknown Wanderer as I am,
If, having walked with Nature threescore
    years,   980
And offered, far as frailty would allow,
My heart a daily sacrifice to Truth,
I now affirm of Nature and of Truth,
Whom I have served, that their DIVINITY
Revolts, offended at the ways of men
Swayed by such motives, to such ends
    employed;   986
Philosophers, who, though the human soul
Be of a thousand faculties composed,
And twice ten thousand interests, do yet
    prize   989
This soul, and the transcendent universe,
No more than as a mirror that reflects
To proud Self-love her own intelligence;
That one, poor, finite object, in the abyss
Of infinite Being, twinkling restlessly!

'Nor higher place can be assigned to
    him   995
And his compeers—the laughing Sage of
    France.—
Crowned was he, if my memory do not
    err,
With laurel planted upon hoary hairs,

In sign of conquest by his wit achieved
And benefits his wisdom had conferred;
His stooping body tottered with wreaths
    of flowers   1001
Opprest, far less becoming ornaments
Than Spring oft twines about a moulder-
    ing tree;
Yet so it pleased a fond, a vain, old Man.
And a most frivolous people. Him I
    mean   1005
Who penned, to ridicule confiding faith,
This sorry Legend; which by chance we
    found
Piled in a nook, through malice, as might
    seem,
Among more innocent rubbish.'—Speak-
    ing thus,
With a brief notice when, and how, and
    where,   1010
We had espied the book, he drew it forth;
And courteously, as if the act removed,
At once, all traces from the good Man's
    heart
Of unbenign aversion or contempt,   1014
Restored it to its owner. 'Gentle Friend,'
Herewith he grasped the Solitary's hand,
'You have known lights and guides better
    than these.
Ah! let not aught amiss within dispose
A noble mind to practise on herself, 1019
And tempt opinion to support the wrongs
Of passion: whatsoe'er be felt or feared,
From higher judgment-seats make no ap-
    peal
To lower: can you question that the soul
Inherits an allegiance, not by choice
To be cast off, upon an oath proposed
By each new upstart notion? In the
    ports   1026
Of levity no refuge can be found,
No shelter, for a spirit in distress.
He, who by wilful disesteem of life
And proud insensibility to hope,   1030
Affronts the eye of Solitude, shall learn
That her mild nature can be terrible;
That neither she nor Silence lack the
    power
To avenge their own insulted majesty.

'O blest seclusion! when the mind
    admits   1035
The law of duty; and can therefore move
Through each vicissitude of loss and gain,
Linked in entire complacence with her
    choice;
When youth's presumptuousness is mel-
    lowed down,
And manhood's vain anxiety dismissed;
When wisdom shows her seasonable
    fruit,   1041
Upon the boughs of sheltering leisure
    hung
In sober plenty; when the spirit stoops
To drink with gratitude the crystal stream

Of unreproved enjoyment; and is pleased
To muse, and be saluted by the air   1046
Of meek repentance, wafting wallflower
  scents
From out the crumbling ruins of fallen
  pride
And chambers of transgression, now for-
  lorn.
O, calm contented days, and peaceful
  nights!   1050
Who, when such good can be obtained,
  would strive
To reconcile his manhood to a couch
Soft, as may seem, but, under that dis-
  guise,
Stuffed with the thorny substance of the
  past
For fixed annoyance; and full oft be-
  set   1055
With floating dreams, black and dis-
  consolate,
The vapoury phantoms of futurity?

  'Within the soul a faculty abides,
That with interpositions, which would
  hide
And darken, so can deal that they be-
  come   1060
Contingencies of pomp; and serve to
  exalt
Her native brightness. As the ample
  moon,
In the deep stillness of a summer even
Rising behind a thick and lofty grove,
Burns, like an unconsuming fire of light,
In the green trees; and, kindling on all
  sides   1066
Their leafy umbrage, turns the dusky
  veil
Into a substance glorious as her own,
Yea, with her own incorporated, by
  power
Capacious and serene. Like power
  abides   1070
In man's celestial spirit; virtue thus
Sets forth and magnifies herself; thus
  feeds
A calm, a beautiful, and silent fire,
From the encumbrances of mortal life,
From error, disappointment—nay, from
  guilt;   1075
And sometimes, so relenting justice wills,
From palpable oppressions of despair.'

  The Solitary by these words was
  touched
With manifest emotion, and exclaimed;
'But how begin? and whence?—"The
  Mind is free—   1080
Resolve," the haughty Moralist would
  say,
"This single act is all that we demand."
Alas! such wisdom bids a creature fly
Whose very sorrow is, that time hath
  shorn

His natural wings!—To friendship let
  him turn   1085
For succour; but perhaps he sits alone
On stormy waters, tossed in a little boat
That holds but him, and can contain no
  more!
Religion tells of amity sublime
Which no condition can preclude; of
  One   1090
Who sees all suffering, comprehends all
  wants,
All weakness fathoms, can supply all
  needs:
But is that bounty absolute?—His gifts,
Are they not, still, in some degree, rewards
For acts of service? Can his love ex-
  tend   1095
To hearts that own not him? Will showers
  of grace,
When in the sky no promise may be seen,
Fall to refresh a parched and withered
  land?
Or shall the groaning Spirit cast her load
At the Redeemer's feet?'
                    In rueful tone,   1100
With some impatience in his mien, he
  spake:
Back to my mind rushed all that had been
  urged
To calm the Sufferer when his story
  closed;
I looked for counsel as unbending now;
But a discriminating sympathy   1105
Stooped to this apt reply:—
                    'As men from men
Do, in the constitution of their souls,
Differ, by mystery not to be explained;
And as we fall by various ways, and sink
One deeper than another, self-condemned
Through manifold degrees of guilt and
  shame;   1111
So manifold and various are the ways
Of restoration, fashioned to the steps
Of all infirmity, and tending all
To the same point, attainable by all— 1115
Peace in ourselves, and union with our
  God.
For you, assuredly, a hopeful road
Lies open: we have heard from you a
  voice
At every moment softened in its course
By tenderness of heart; have seen your
  eye,   1120
Even like an altar lit by fire from heaven,
Kindle before us.—Your discourse this
  day,
That, like the fabled Lethe, wished to
  flow
In creeping sadness, through oblivious
  shades
Of death and night, has caught at every
  turn   1125
The colours of the sun. Access for you
Is yet preserved to principles of truth,

Which the imaginative Will upholds
In seats of wisdom, not to be approached
By the inferior Faculty that moulds,   1130
With her minute and speculative pains,
Opinion, ever changing!
                        I have seen
A curious child, who dwelt upon a tract
Of inland ground, applying to his ear
The convolutions of a smooth-lipped
    shell;   1135
To which, in silence hushed, his very soul
Listened intensely; and his countenance
    soon
Brightened with joy; for from within
    were heard
Murmurings, whereby the monitor ex-
    pressed
Mysterious union with its native sea. 1140
Even such a shell the universe itself
Is to the ear of Faith; and there are times,
I doubt not, when to you it doth impart
Authentic tidings of invisible things;
Of ebb and flow, and ever-during power;
And central peace, subsisting at the
    heart   1146
Of endless agitation. Here you stand,
Adore, and worship, when you know it
    not;
Pious beyond the intention of your
    thought;
Devout above the meaning of your will.
—Yes, you have felt, and may not cease
    to feel.   1151
The estate of man would be indeed forlorn
If false conclusions of the reasoning power
Made the eye blind, and closed the
    passages
Through which the ear converses with the
    heart.   1155
Has not the soul, the being of your life,
Received a shock of awful consciousness,
In some calm season, when these lofty
    rocks
At night's approach bring down the un-
    clouded sky,   1159
To rest upon their circumambient walls;
A temple framing of dimensions vast,
And yet not too enormous for the sound
Of human anthems,—choral song, or
    burst
Sublime of instrumental harmony,
To glorify the Eternal! What if these 1165
Did never break the stillness that prevails
Here,—if the solemn nightingale be mute,
And the soft woodlark here did never
    chant
Her vespers,—Nature fails not to pro-
    vide
Impulse and utterance. The whispering
    air   1170
Sends inspiration from the shadowy
    heights,
And blind recesses of the caverned rocks;
The little rills, and waters numberless,

Inaudible by daylight, blend their notes
With the loud streams: and often, at the
    hour   1175
When issue forth the first pale stars, is
    heard,
Within the circuit of this fabric huge,
One voice—the solitary raven, flying
Athwart the concave of the dark blue
    dome,
Unseen, perchance above all power of
    sight—   1180
An iron knell! with echoes from afar
Faint—and still fainter—as the cry, with
    which
The wanderer accompanies her flight
Through the calm region, fades upon the
    ear,
Diminishing by distance till it seemed
To expire; yet from the abyss is caught
    again,   1186
And yet again recovered!
                        But descending
From these imaginative heights, that
    yield
Far-stretching views into eternity,
Acknowledge that to Nature's humbler
    power   1190
Your cherished sullenness is forced to
    bend
Even here, where her amenities are sown
With sparing hand. Then trust yourself
    abroad
To range her blooming bowers, and spa-
    cious fields,   1194
Where on the labours of the happy throng
She smiles, including in her wide embrace
City, and town, and tower,—and sea with
    ships
Sprinkled;—be our Companion while we
    track
Her rivers populous with gliding life;
While, free as air, o'er printless sands we
    march,   1200
Or pierce the gloom of her majestic woods;
Roaming, or resting under grateful shade
In peace and meditative cheerfulness;
Where living things, and things inani-
    mate,
Do speak, at Heaven's command, to eye
    and ear,   1205
And speak to social reason's inner sense,
With inarticulate language.
                        For, the Man—
Who, in this spirit, communes with the
    Forms
Of nature, who with understanding heart
Both knows and loves such objects as
    excite   1210
No morbid passions, no disquietude,
No vengeance, and no hatred—needs must
    feel
The joy of that pure principle of love
So deeply, that, unsatisfied with aught
Less pure and exquisite, he cannot choose

But seek for objects of a kindred love
In fellow-natures and a kindred joy.
Accordingly he by degrees perceives
His feelings of aversion softened down;
A holy tenderness pervade his frame. 1220
His sanity of reason not impaired,
Say rather, all his thoughts now flowing
     clear,
From a clear fountain flowing, he looks
     round
And seeks for good; and finds the good
     he seeks:
Until abhorrence and contempt are
     things   1225
He only knows by name; and, if he hear,
From other mouths, the language which
     they speak,
He is compassionate; and has no thought,
No feeling, which can overcome his love.

'And further; by contemplating these
     Forms   1230
In the relations which they bear to man,
He shall discern, how, through the various
     means
Which silently they yield, are multiplied
The spiritual presences of absent things.
Trust me, that for the instructed, time
     will come   1235
When they shall meet no object but may
     teach
Some acceptable lesson to their minds
Of human suffering, or of human joy.
So shall they learn, while all things speak
     of man,
Their duties from all forms; and general
     laws,   1240
And local accidents, shall tend alike
To rouse, to urge; and, with the will,
     confer
The ability to spread the blessings wide
Of true philanthropy. The light of love
Not failing, perseverance from their steps
Departing not, for them shall be con-
     firmed   1246
The glorious habit by which sense is made
Subservient still to moral purposes,
Auxiliar to divine. That change shall
     clothe
The naked spirit, ceasing to deplore 1250
The burthen of existence. Science then
Shall be a precious visitant; and then,
And only then, be worthy of her name:
For then her heart shall kindle; her dull
     eye,   1254
Dull and inanimate, no more shall hang
Chained to its object in brute slavery;
But taught with patient interest to watch
The processes of things, and serve the
     cause
Of order and distinctness, not for this
Shall it forget that its most noble use,
Its most illustrious province, must be
     found   1261

In furnishing clear guidance, a support
Not treacherous, to the mind's *excursive*
     power.
—So build we up the Being that we are;
Thus deeply drinking-in the soul of
     things,   1265
We shall be wise perforce; and, while
     inspired
By choice, and conscious that the Will is
     free,
Shall move unswerving, even as if im-
     pelled
By strict necessity, along the path 1269
Of order and of good. Whate'er we see,
Or feel, shall tend to quicken and refine;
Shall fix, in calmer seats of moral strength,
Earthly desires; and raise, to loftier
     heights
Of divine love, our intellectual soul.'

Here closed the Sage that eloquent
     harangue,   1275
Poured forth with fervour in continuous
     stream,
Such as, remote, 'mid savage wilderness,
An Indian Chief discharges from his
     breast
Into the hearing of assembled tribes, 1279
In open circle seated round, and hushed
As the unbreathing air, when not a leaf
Stirs in the mighty woods.—So did he
     speak:
The words he uttered shall not pass away
Dispersed, like music that the wind takes
     up
By snatches, and lets fall, to be for-
     gotten;   1285
No—they sank into me, the bounteous
     gift
Of one whom time and nature had made
     wise.
Gracing his doctrine with authority
Which hostile spirits silently allow;
Of one accustomed to desires that feed
On fruitage gathered from the tree of
     life;   1291
To hopes on knowledge and experience
     built;
Of one in whom persuasion and belief
Had ripened into faith, and faith become
A passionate intuition; whence the Soul,
Though bound to earth by ties of pity
     and love,   1296
From all injurious servitude was free.

The Sun, before his place of rest were
     reached,
Had yet to travel far, but unto us,
To us who stood low in that hollow
     dell,   1300
He had become invisible,—a pomp
Leaving behind of yellow radiance spread
Over the mountain-sides, in contrast bold
With ample shadows, seemingly, no less

Than those resplendent lights, his rich
    bequest;   1305
A dispensation of his evening power.
—Adown the path that from the glen had
    led
The funeral train, the Shepherd and his
    Mate
Were seen descending:—forth to greet
    them ran
Our little Page: the rustic pair approach;
And in the Matron's countenance may be
    read   1311
Plain indication that the words, which
    told
How that neglected Pensioner was sent
Before his time into a quiet grave,

Had done to her humanity no wrong: 1315
But we are kindly welcomed—promptly
    served
With ostentatious zeal.—Along the floor
Of the small Cottage in the lonely Dell
A grateful couch was spread for our re-
    pose;
Where, in the guise of mountaineers, we
    lay,   1320
Stretched upon fragrant heath, and lulled
    by sound
Of far-off torrents charming the still
    night,
And, to tired limbs and over-busy
    thoughts,
Inviting sleep and soft forgetfulness.

BOOK FIFTH

THE PASTOR

ARGUMENT

Farewell to the Valley.—Reflections.—A large and populous Vale described.—The Pastor's Dwelling, and some account of him.—Church and Monuments.—The Solitary musing, and where.—Roused.— In the Churchyard the Solitary communicates the thoughts which had recently passed through his mind.—Lofty tone of the Wanderer's discourse of yesterday adverted to.—Rite of Baptism, and the professions accompanying it, contrasted with the real state of human life.—Apology for the Rite.— Inconsistency of the best men.—Acknowledgment that practice falls far below the injunctions of duty as existing in the mind.—General complaint of a falling-off in the value of life after the time of youth.— Outward appearances of content and happiness in degree illusive.—Pastor approaches.—Appeal made to him.—His answer.—Wanderer in sympathy with him.—Suggestion that the least ambitious enquirers may be most free from error.—The Pastor is desired to give some portraits of the living or dead from his own observation of life among these Mountains—and for what purpose.—Pastor consents.— Mountain cottage.—Excellent qualities of its Inhabitants.—Solitary expresses his pleasure; but denies the praise of virtue to worth of this kind.—Feelings of the Priest before he enters upon his account of persons interred in the Churchyard.—Graves of unbaptized Infants.—Funeral and sepulchral observances, whence.—Ecclesiastical Establishments, whence derived.—Profession of belief in the doctrine of Immortality.

'FAREWELL, deep Valley, with thy one
    rude House,
And its small lot of life-supporting fields,
And guardian rocks!—Farewell, attrac-
    tive seat!
To the still influx of the morning light
Open, and day's pure cheerfulness, but
    veiled   5
From human observation, as if yet
Primeval forests wrapped thee round with
    dark
Impenetrable shade; once more farewell,
Majestic circuit, beautiful abyss,
By Nature destined from the birth of
    things   10
For quietness profound!'
                    Upon the side
Of that brown ridge, sole outlet of the
    vale
Which foot of boldest stranger would
    attempt,
Lingering behind my comrades, thus I
    breathed   14
A parting tribute to a spot that seemed
Like the fixed centre of a troubled world.

Again I halted with reverted eyes;
The chain that would not slacken, was at
    length
Snapt,—and, pursuing leisurely my way,
How vain, thought I, is it by change of
    place   20
To seek that comfort which the mind
    denies:
Yet trial and temptation oft are shunned
Wisely; and by such tenure do we hold
Frail life's possessions, that even they
    whose fate
Yields no peculiar reason of complaint 25
Might, by the promise that is here, be
    won
To steal from active duties, and embrace
Obscurity, and undisturbed repose.
—Knowledge, methinks, in these disor-
    dered times,
Should be allowed a privilege to have   30
Her anchorites, like piety of old;
Men, who, from faction sacred, and un-
    stained
By war, might, if so minded, turn aside
Uncensured, and subsist, a scattered few

Living to God and nature, and content
With that communion. Consecrated be
The spots where such abide! But happier
      still
The Man, whom, furthermore, a hope
      attends
That meditation and research may guide
His privacy to principles and powers   40
Discovered or invented; or set forth,
Through his acquaintance with the ways
      of truth,
In lucid order; so that, when his course
Is run, some faithful eulogist may say,
He sought not praise, and praise did over-
      look   45
His unobtrusive merit; but his life,
Sweet to himself, was exercised in good
That shall survive his name and memory.

Acknowledgments of gratitude sincere
Accompanied these musings; fervent
      thanks   50
For my own peaceful lot and happy
      choice;
A choice that from the passions of the
      world
Withdrew, and fixed me in a still retreat;
Sheltered, but not to social duties lost,
Secluded, but not buried; and with song
Cheering my days, and with industrious
      thought;   56
With the ever-welcome company of
      books;
With virtuous friendship's soul-sustaining
      aid,
And with the blessings of domestic love.

Thus occupied in mind I paced along,
Following the rugged road, by sledge or
      wheel   61
Worn in the moorland, till I overtook
My two Associates, in the morning sun-
      shine
Halting together on a rocky knoll,
Whence the bare road descended rapidly
To the green meadows of another vale.

Here did our pensive Host put forth his
      hand   67
In sign of farewell. 'Nay,' the old Man
      said,
'The fragrant air its coolness still retains;
The herds and flocks are yet abroad to
      crop   70
The dewy grass; you cannot leave us now,
We must not part at this inviting hour.'
He yielded, though reluctant; for his
      mind
Instinctively disposed him to retire   74
To his own covert; as a billow, heaved
Upon the beach, rolls back into the sea.
—So we descend: and winding round a
      rock
Attain a point that showed the valley—
      stretched

In length before us; and, not distant
      far,
Upon a rising ground a grey church-
      tower,   80
Whose battlements were screened by
      tufted trees.
And towards a crystal Mere, that lay
      beyond
Among steep hills and woods embosomed,
      flowed
A copious stream with boldly-winding
      course;
Here traceable, there hidden—there again
To sight restored, and glittering in the
      sun.   86
On the stream's bank, and everywhere,
      appeared
Fair dwellings, single, or in social knots;
Some scattered o'er the level, others
      perched
On the hill-sides, a cheerful quiet scene,
Now in its morning purity arrayed.   91

'As 'mid some happy valley of the
      Alps,'
Said I, 'once happy, ere tyrannic power,
Wantonly breaking in upon the Swiss,
Destroyed their unoffending common-
      wealth,   95
A popular equality reigns here,
Save for yon stately House beneath whose
      roof
A rural lord might dwell.'—'No feudal
      pomp,
Or power,' replied the Wanderer, 'to
      that House
Belongs, but there in his allotted Home
Abides, from year to year, a genuine
      Priest,   101
The shepherd of his flock; or, as a king
Is styled, when most affectionately
      praised,
The father of his people. Such is he;
And rich and poor, and young and old,
      rejoice   105
Under his spiritual sway. He hath vouch-
      safed
To me some portion of a kind regard;
And something also of his inner mind
Hath he imparted—but I speak of him
As he is known to all.
              The calm delights   110
Of unambitious piety he chose,
And learning's solid dignity; though born
Of knightly race, nor wanting powerful
      friends.
Hither, in prime of manhood, he with-
      drew
From academic bowers. He loved the
      spot—   115
Who does not love his native soil?—he
      prized
The ancient rural character, composed
Of simple manners, feelings unsupprest

And undisguised, and strong and serious
   thought;
A character reflected in himself,   120
With such embellishment as well beseems
His rank and sacred function. This deep
   vale
Winds far in reaches hidden from our
   sight,
And one a turreted manorial hall
Adorns, in which the good Man's an-
   cestors   125
Have dwelt through ages—Patrons of
   this Cure.
To them, and to his own judicious pains,
The Vicar's dwelling, and the whole
   domain,
Owes that presiding aspect which might
   well
Attract your notice; statelier than could
   else   130
Have been bestowed, through course of
   common chance,
On an unwealthy mountain Benefice.'

   This said, oft pausing, we pursued our
   way;
Nor reached the village-churchyard till
   the sun
Travelling at steadier pace than ours, had
   risen   135
Above the summits of the highest hills,
And round our path darted oppressive
   beams.

   As chanced, the portals of the sacred
   Pile
Stood open; and we entered. On my
   frame,
At such transition from the fervid air, 140
A grateful coolness fell, that seemed to
   strike
The heart, in concert with that temperate
   awe
And natural reverence which the place
   inspired.
Not raised in nice proportions was the
   pile,   144
But large and massy; for duration built;
With pillars crowded, and the roof up-
   held
By naked rafters intricately crossed,
Like leafless underboughs, in some thick
   wood,
All withered by the depth of shade above.
Admonitory texts inscribed the walls, 150
Each, in its ornamental scroll, enclosed;
Each also crowned with wingèd heads—
   a pair
Of rudely-painted Cherubim. The floor
Of nave and aisle, in unpretending guise,
Was occupied by oaken benches ranged
In seemly rows; the chancel only showed
Some vain distinctions, marks of earthly
   state   157

By immemorial privilege allowed;
Though with the Encincture's special
   sanctity
But ill according. An heraldic shield,
Varying its tincture with the changeful
   light,   161
Imbued the altar-window; fixed aloft
A faded hatchment hung, and one by
   time
Yet undiscoloured. A capacious pew
Of sculptured oak stood here, with drapery
   lined;   165
And marble monuments were here dis-
   played
Thronging the walls; and on the floor
   beneath
Sepulchral stones appeared, with emblems
   graven
And foot-worn epitaphs, and some with
   small
And shining effigies of brass inlaid.   170

   The tribute by these various records
   claimed,
Duly we paid, each after each, and read
The ordinary chronicle of birth,
Office, alliance, and promotion—all
Ending in dust; of upright magistrates,
Grave doctors strenuous for the mother-
   church,   176
And uncorrupted senators, alike
To king and people true. A brazen plate,
Not easily deciphered, told of one
Whose course of earthly honour was be-
   gun   180
In quality of page among the train
Of the eighth Henry, when he crossed the
   seas
His royal state to show, and prove his
   strength
In tournament, upon the fields of France.
Another tablet registered the death,   185
And praised the gallant bearing, of a
   Knight
Tried in the sea-fights of the second
   Charles.
Near this brave Knight his Father lay
   entombed;
And, to the silent language giving voice,
I read,—how in his manhood's earlier
   day   190
He, 'mid the afflictions of intestine war
And rightful government subverted, found
One only solace—that he had espoused
A virtuous Lady tenderly beloved
For her benign perfections; and yet
   more   195
Endeared to him, for this, that, in her
   state
Of wedlock richly crowned with Heaven's
   regard,
She with a numerous Issue filled his house,
Who throve, like plants, uninjured by the
   storm

That laid their country waste. No need
　　to speak   200
Of less particular notices assigned
To Youth or Maiden gone before their
　　time,
And Matrons and unwedded Sisters old;
Whose charity and goodness were re-
　　hearsed
In modest panegyric.
　　　　　'These dim lines,   205
What would they tell?' said I,—but, from
　　the task
Of puzzling out that faded narrative,
With whisper soft my venerable Friend
Called me; and, looking down the dark-
　　some aisle,
I saw the Tenant of the lonely vale   210
Standing apart; with curvèd arm reclined
On the baptismal font; his pallid face
Upturned, as if his mind were rapt, or
　　lost
In some abstraction;—gracefully he
　　stood,
The semblance bearing of a sculptured
　　form   215
That leans upon a monumental urn
In peace, from morn to night, from year
　　to year.

　　Him from that posture did the Sexton
　　rouse;
Who entered, humming carelessly a tune,
Continuation haply of the notes   220
That had beguiled the work from which
　　he came,
With spade and mattock o'er his shoulder
　　hung;
To be deposited, for future need,
In their appointed place. The pale Re-
　　cluse
Withdrew; and straight we followed,—
　　to a spot   225
Where sun and shade were intermixed;
　　for there
A broad oak, stretching forth its leafy arms
From an adjoining pasture, overhung
Small space of that green churchyard
　　with a light
And pleasant awning. On the moss-
　　grown wall   230
My ancient Friend and I together took
Our seats; and thus the Solitary spake,
Standing before us:—
　　　　　'Did you note the mien
Of that self-solaced, easy-hearted churl,
Death's hireling, who scoops out his
　　neighbour's grave,   235
Or wraps an old acquaintance up in
　　clay,
All unconcerned as he would bind a sheaf,
Or plant a tree. And did you hear his
　　voice?
I was abruptly summoned by the sound
From some affecting images and thoughts,

Which then were silent; but crave utter-
　　ance now.   241

　　'Much,' he continued, with dejected
　　look,
'Much, yesterday, was said in glowing
　　phrase
Of our sublime dependencies, and hopes
For future states of being; and the wings
Of speculation, joyfully outspread,   246
Hovered above our destiny on earth:
But stoop, and place the prospect of the
　　soul
In sober contrast with reality,
And man's substantial life. If this mute
　　earth   250
Of what it holds could speak, and every
　　grave
Were as a volume, shut, yet capable
Of yielding its contents to eye and ear,
We should recoil, stricken with sorrow
　　and shame,
To see disclosed, by such dread proof,
　　how ill   255
That which is done accords with what
　　is known
To reason, and by conscience is enjoined;
How idly, how perversely, life's whole
　　course,
To this conclusion, deviates from the line,
Or of the end stops short, proposed to all
At her aspiring outset.
　　　　　Mark the babe   261
Not long accustomed to this breathing
　　world;
One that hath barely learned to shape
　　a smile,
Though yet irrational of soul, to grasp
With tiny finger—to let fall a tear;   265
And, as the heavy cloud of sleep dis-
　　solves,
To stretch his limbs, bemocking, as might
　　seem,
The outward functions of intelligent man;
A grave proficient in amusive feats
Of puppetry, that from the lap declare
His expectations, and announce his
　　claims   271
To that inheritance which millions rue
That they were ever born to! In due
　　time
A day of solemn ceremonial comes;
When they, who for this Minor hold in
　　trust   275
Rights that transcend the loftiest heritage
Of mere humanity, present their Charge,
For this occasion daintily adorned,
At the baptismal font. And when the
　　pure
And consecrating element hath cleansed
The original stain, the child is there
　　received   281
Into the second ark, Christ's church,
　　with trust

That he, from wrath redeemed, therein
    shall float
Over the billows of this troublesome
    world
To the fair land of everlasting life.   285
Corrupt affections, covetous desires,
Are all renounced; high as the thought
    of man
Can carry virtue, virtue is professed;
A dedication made, a promise given
For due provision to control and guide,
And unremitting progress to ensure   291
In holiness and truth.'
                    'You cannot blame,'
Here interposing fervently I said,
'Rites which attest that Man by nature
    lies
Bedded for good and evil in a gulf   295
Fearfully low; nor will your judgment
    scorn
Those services, whereby attempt is made
To lift the creature toward that eminence
On which, now fallen, erewhile in majesty
He stood; or if not so, whose top serene
At least he feels 'tis given him to descry;
Not without aspirations, evermore   302
Returning, and injunctions from within
Doubt to cast off and weariness; in trust
That what the Soul perceives, if glory
    lost,   305
May be, through pains and persevering
    hope,
Recovered; or, if hitherto unknown,
Lies within reach, and one day shall be
    gained.'

'I blame them not,' he calmly answered
    —'no;   309
The outward ritual and established forms
With which communities of men invest
These inward feelings, and the aspiring
    vows
To which the lips give public utterance
Are both a natural process; and by me
Shall pass uncensured; though the issue
    prove,   315
Bringing from age to age its own reproach,
Incongruous, impotent, and blank.—But,
    oh!
If to be weak is to be wretched—miser-
    able,
As the lost Angel by a human voice
Hath mournfully pronounced, then, in
    my mind,   320
Far better not to move at all than move
By impulse sent from such illusive
    power,—
That finds and cannot fasten down; that
    grasps
And is rejoiced, and loses while it grasps;
That tempts, emboldens—for a time
    sustains,   325
And then betrays; accuses and inflicts
Remorseless punishment; and so retreads

The inevitable circle: better far
Than this, to graze the herb in thought-
    less peace,
By foresight, or remembrance, undis-
    turbed!   330

'Philosophy! and thou more vaunted
    name
Religion! with thy statelier retinue,
Faith, Hope, and Charity—from the
    visible world
Choose for your emblems whatsoe'er ye
    find
Of safest guidance or of firmest trust—
The torch, the star, the anchor; nor
    except   336
The cross itself, at whose unconscious
    feet
The generations of mankind have knelt
Ruefully seized, and shedding bitter tears,
And through that conflict seeking rest—
    of you,   340
High-titled Powers, am I constrained to
    ask,
Here standing, with the unvoyageable sky
In faint reflection of infinitude
Stretched overhead, and at my pensive
    feet
A subterranean magazine of bones,   345
In whose dark vaults my own shall soon
    be laid,
Where are your triumphs? your dominion
    where?
And in what age admitted and con-
    firmed?
—Not for a happy land do I enquire,
Island or grove, that hides a blessed few
Who, with obedience willing and sincere,
To your serene authorities conform;
But whom, I ask, of individual Souls,
Have ye withdrawn from passion's
    crooked ways,
Inspired, and thoroughly fortified?—If
    the heart   355
Could be inspected to its inmost folds
By sight undazzled with the glare of
    praise,
Who shall be named—in the resplendent
    line
Of sages, martyrs, confessors—the man
Whom the best might of faith, wherever
    fixed,   360
For one day's little compass, has pre-
    served
From painful and discreditable shocks
Of contradiction, from some vague de-
    sire
Culpably cherished, or corrupt relapse
To some unsanctioned fear?'
                    'If this be so,   365
And Man,' said I, 'be in his noblest shape
Thus pitiably infirm; then, he who made,
And who shall judge the creature, will
    forgive.

—Yet, in its general tenor, your com-
  plaint
Is all too true; and surely not mis-
  placed: 370
For, from this pregnant spot of ground,
  such thoughts
Rise to the notice of a serious mind
By natural exhalation. With the dead
In their repose, the living in their mirth,
Who can reflect, unmoved, upon the
  round   375
Of smooth and solemnized complacencies,
By which, on Christian lands, from age
  to age
Profession mocks performance? Earth is
  sick,
And Heaven is weary, of the hollow words
Which States and Kingdoms utter when
  they talk   380
Of truth and justice. Turn to private life
And social neighbourhood; look we to
  ourselves;
A light of duty shines on every day
For all; and yet how few are warmed or
  cheered!
How few who mingle with their fellow-
  men   385
And still remain self-governed, and apart,
Like this our honoured Friend; and thence
  acquire
Right to expect his vigorous decline,
That promises to the end a blest old age!'

'Yet,' with a smile of triumph thus
  exclaimed   390
The Solitary, 'in the life of man,
If to the poetry of common speech
Faith may be given, we see as in a glass
A true reflection of the circling year,
With all its seasons. Grant that Spring
  is there,   395
In spite of many a rough untoward blast,
Hopeful and promising with buds and
  flowers;
Yet where is glowing Summer's long rich
  day,
That *ought* to follow faithfully expressed?
And mellow Autumn, charged with
  bounteous fruit,   400
Where is she imaged? in what favoured
  clime
Her lavish pomp, and ripe magnificence?
—Yet, while the better part is missed,
  the worse
In man's autumnal season is set forth
With a resemblance not to be denied, 405
And that contents him; bowers that hear
  no more
The voice of gladness, less and less supply
Of outward sunshine and internal
  warmth;
And, with this change, sharp air and
  falling leaves,   409
Foretelling agèd Winter's desolate sway.

'How gay the habitations that bedeck
This fertile valley! Not a house but seems
To give assurance of content within;
Embosomed happiness, and placid love;
As if the sunshine of the day were met
With answering brightness in the hearts
  of all   416
Who walk this favoured ground. But
  chance-regards,
And notice forced upon incurious ears;
These, if these only, acting in despite
Of the encomiums by my Friend pro-
  nounced   420
On humble life, forbid the judging mind
To trust the smiling aspect of this fair
And noiseless commonwealth. The simple
  race
Of mountaineers (by nature's self removed
From foul temptations, and by constant
  care   425
Of a good shepherd tended, as them-
  selves
Do tend their flocks) partake man's
  general lot
With little mitigation. They escape,
Perchance, the heavier woes of guilt; feel
  not
The tedium of fantastic idleness: 430
Yet life, as with the multitude, with them
Is fashioned like an ill-constructed tale,
That on the outset wastes its gay desires,
Its fair adventures, its enlivening hopes,
And pleasant interests—for the sequel
  leaving   435
Old things repeated with diminished grace;
And all the laboured novelties at best
Imperfect substitutes, whose use and
  power
Evince the want and weakness whence
  they spring.'

While in this serious mood we held
  discourse,   440
The reverend Pastor toward the church-
  yard gate
Approached; and, with a mild respectful
  air
Of native cordiality, our Friend
Advanced to greet him. With a gracious
  mien
Was he received, and mutual joy pre-
  vailed.   445
Awhile they stood in conference, and I
  guess
That he, who now upon the mossy wall
Sate by my side, had vanished, if a wish
Could have transferred him to the flying
  clouds,
Or the least penetrable hiding-place   450
In his own valley's rocky guardianship.
—For me, I looked upon the pair, well
  pleased:
Nature had framed them both, and both
  were marked

By circumstance, with intermixture fine
Of contrast and resemblance. To an oak
Hardy and grand, a weather-beaten oak,
Fresh in the strength and majesty of age,
One might be likened: flourishing ap-
    peared,
Though somewhat past the fulness of his
    prime,
The other—like a stately sycamore, 460
That spreads, in gentle pomp, its honied
    shade.

A general greeting was exchanged;
    and soon
The Pastor learned that his approach had
    given
A welcome interruption to discourse
Grave, and in truth too often sad.—'Is
    Man   465
A child of hope? Do generations press
On generations, without progress made?
Halts the individual, ere his hairs be grey,
Perforce? Are we a creature in whom
    good
Preponderates, or evil? Doth the will
Acknowledge reason's law? A living
    power   471
Is virtue, or no better than a name,
Fleeting as health or beauty, and un-
    sound?
So that the only substance which remains,
(For thus the tenour of complaint hath
    run)   475
Among so many shadows, are the pains
And penalties of miserable life,
Doomed to decay, and then expire in
    dust!
—Our cogitations this way have been
    drawn,
These are the points,' the Wanderer said,
    'on which   480
Our inquest turns.—Accord, good Sir!
    the light
Of your experience to dispel this gloom:
By your persuasive wisdom shall the
    heart
That frets, or languishes, be stilled and
    cheered.'

'Our nature,' said the Priest, in mild
    reply,   485
'Angels may weigh and fathom: they
    perceive,
With undistempered and unclouded spirit,
The object as it is; but, for ourselves,
That speculative height we may not reach.
The good and evil are our own; and we
Are that which we would contemplate
    from far.   491
Knowledge, for us, is difficult to gain—
Is difficult to gain, and hard to keep—
As virtue's self; like virtue is beset
With snares; tried, tempted, subject to
    decay.   495

Love, admiration, fear, desire, and hate,
Blind were we without these: through
    these alone
Are capable to notice or discern
Or to record; we judge, but cannot be
Indifferent judges. 'Spite of proudest
    boast,   500
Reason, best reason, is to imperfect man
An effort only, and a noble aim;
A crown, an attribute of sovereign power,
Still to be courted—never to be won.
—Look forth, or each man dive into him-
    self;   505
What sees he but a creature too per-
    turbed;
That is transported to excess; that yearns,
Regrets, or trembles, wrongly, or too
    much;
Hopes rashly, in disgust as rash recoils;
Battens on spleen, or moulders in despair?
Thus comprehension fails, and truth is
    missed;   511
Thus darkness and delusion round our
    path
Spread, from disease, whose subtle injury
    lurks
Within the very faculty of sight.   514

'Yet for the general purposes of faith
In Providence, for solace and support,
We may not doubt that who can best
    subject
The will to reason's law, can strictliest
    live
And act in that obedience, he shall gain
The clearest apprehension of those
    truths,   520
Which unassisted reason's utmost power
Is too infirm to reach. But, waiving this,
And our regards confining within bounds
Of less exalted consciousness, through
    which
The very multitude are free to range, 525
We safely may affirm that human life
Is either fair and tempting, a soft scene
Grateful to sight, refreshing to the soul,
Or a forbidding tract of cheerless view;
Even as the same is looked at, or ap-
    proached.   530
Thus, when in changeful April fields are
    white
With new-fallen snow, if from the sullen
    north
Your walk conduct you hither, ere the
    sun
Hath gained his noontide height, this
    churchyard, filled
With mounds transversely lying side by
    side   535
From east to west, before you will ap-
    pear
An unillumined, blank, and dreary, plain,
With more than wintry cheerlessness and
    gloom

Saddening the heart. Go forward, and
  look back;
Look, from the quarter whence the lord
  of light,   540
Of life, of love, and gladness doth dis-
  pense
His beams; which, unexcluded in their fall,
Upon the southern side of every grave
Have gently exercised a melting power;
Then will a vernal prospect greet your eye,
All fresh and beautiful, and green and
  bright,   546
Hopeful and cheerful:—vanished is the
  pall
That overspread and chilled the sacred
  turf,
Vanished or hidden; and the whole
  domain,
To some, too lightly minded, might ap-
  pear   550
A meadow carpet for the dancing hours.
—This contrast, not unsuitable to life,
Is to that other state more apposite,
Death and its two-fold aspect! wintry—
  one,
Cold, sullen, blank, from hope and joy
  shut out;   555
The other, which the ray divine hath
  touched,
Replete with vivid promise, bright as
  spring.'

'We see, then, as we feel,' the Wanderer
  thus
With a complacent animation spake,
'And in your judgment, Sir! the mind's
  repose   560
On evidence is not to be ensured
By act of naked reason. Moral truth
Is no mechanic structure, built by rule;
And which, once built, retains a steadfast
  shape
And undisturbed proportions; but a
  thing   565
Subject, you deem, to vital accidents;
And, like the water-lily, lives and thrives,
Whose root is fixed in stable earth, whose
  head
Floats on the tossing waves. With joy
  sincere
I re-salute these sentiments confirmed
By your authority. But how acquire   571
The inward principle that gives effect
To outward argument; the passive will
Meek to admit; the active energy,
Strong and unbounded to embrace, and
  firm   575
To keep and cherish? how shall man unite
With self-forgetting tenderness of heart
An earth-despising dignity of soul?
Wise in that union, and without it blind!'

    'The way,' said I, 'to court, if not
  obtain   580

The ingenuous mind, apt to be set aright;
This, in the lonely dell discoursing, you
Declared at large; and by what exercise
From visible nature, or the inner self
Power may be trained, and renovation
  brought   585
To those who need the gift. But, after all,
Is aught so certain as that man is doomed
To breathe beneath a vault of ignorance?
The natural roof of that dark house in
  which
His soul is pent! How little can be
  known—   590
This is the wise man's sigh; how far we
  err—
This is the good man's not unfrequent
  pang!
And they perhaps err least, the lowly
  class
Whom a benign necessity compels   594
To follow reason's least ambitious course;
Such do I mean who, unperplexed by
  doubt,
And unincited by a wish to look
Into high objects farther than they may,
Pace to and fro, from morn till eventide,
The narrow avenue of daily toil   600
For daily bread.'
              'Yes,' buoyantly exclaimed
The pale Recluse—'praise to the sturdy
  plough,
And patient spade; praise to the simple
  crook,
And ponderous loom—resounding while
  it holds
Body and mind in one captivity;   605
And let the light mechanic tool be hailed
With honour; which, encasing by the
  power
Of long companionship, the artist's hand,
Cuts off that hand, with all its world of
  nerves,
From a too busy commerce with the
  heart!   610
—Inglorious implements of craft and toil,
Both ye that shape and build, and ye
  that force,
By slow solicitation, earth to yield
Her annual bounty, sparingly dealt forth
With wise reluctance; you would I extol,
Not for gross good alone which ye pro-
  duce,   616
But for the impertinent and ceaseless
  strife
Of proofs and reasons ye preclude—in
  those
Who to your dull society are born,
And with their humble birthright rest
  content.   620
—Would I had ne'er renounced it!'
                      A slight flush
Of moral anger previously had tinged
The old Man's cheek; but, at this closing
  turn

Of self-reproach, it passed away. Said he,
'That which we feel we utter; as we
think   625
So have we argued; reaping for our pains
No visible recompense. For our relief
You,' to the Pastor turning thus he spake,
'Have kindly interposed. May I entreat
Your further help? The mine of real
life   630
Dig for us; and present us, in the shape
Of virgin ore, that gold which we, by
pains
Fruitless as those of aery alchemists,
Seek from the torturing crucible. There
lies
Around us a domain where you have long
Watched both the outward course and
inner heart: 636
Give us, for our abstractions, solid facts;
For our disputes, plain pictures. Say
what man
He is who cultivates yon hanging field;
What qualities of mind she bears, who
comes,   640
For morn and evening service, with her
pail,
To that green pasture; place before our
sight
The family who dwell within yon house
Fenced round with glittering laurel; or
in that
Below, from which the curling smoke
ascends.   645
Or rather, as we stand on holy earth,[1]
And have the dead around us, take from
them
Your instances; for they are both best
known,
And by frail man most equitably judged.
Epitomise the life; pronounce, you can,
Authentic epitaphs on some of these   651
Who, from their lowly mansions hither
brought,
Beneath this turf lie mouldering at our
feet:
So, by your records, may our doubts be
solved;
And so, not searching higher, we may learn
*To prize the breath we share with human
kind;*   656
And look upon the dust of man with awe.'

The Priest replied—'An office you
impose
For which peculiar requisites are mine;
Yet much, I feel, is wanting—else the
task   660
Would be most grateful. True indeed it is
That they whom death has hidden from
our sight
Are worthiest of the mind's regard; with
these
The future cannot contradict the past:
———————
[1] See Note, p. 728.

Mortality's last exercise and proof   665
Is undergone; the transit made that shows
The very Soul, revealed as she departs.
Yet, on your first suggestion, will I give,
Ere we descend into these silent vaults,
One picture from the living.
                    You behold,   670
High on the breast of yon dark moun-
tain, dark
With stony barrenness, a shining speck
Bright as a sunbeam sleeping till a shower
Brush it away, or cloud pass over it;
And such it might be deemed—a sleeping
sunbeam;   675
But 'tis a plot of cultivated ground,
Cut off, an island in the dusky waste;
And that attractive brightness is its own.
The lofty site, by nature framed to tempt
Amid a wilderness of rocks and stones
The tiller's hand, a hermit might have
chosen,   681
For opportunity presented, thence
Far forth to send his wandering eye o'er
land
And ocean, and look down upon the
works,
The habitations, and the ways of men,
Himself unseen! But no tradition tells
That ever hermit dipped his maple dish
In the sweet spring that lurks 'mid yon
green fields;
And no such visionary views belong   689
To those who occupy and till the ground,
High on that mountain where they long
have dwelt
A wedded pair in childless solitude.
A house of stones collected on the spot,
By rude hands built, with rocky knolls
in front,
Backed also by a ledge of rock, whose
crest   695
Of birch-trees waves over the chimney-
top;
A rough abode—in colour, shape, and
size,
Such as in unsafe times of border-war
Might have been wished for and con-
trived, to elude
The eye of roving plunderer—for their
need   700
Suffices; and unshaken bears the assault
Of their most dreaded foe, the strong
South-west
In anger blowing from the distant sea.
—Alone within her solitary hut;   704
There, or within the compass of her fields,
At any moment may the Dame be found,
True as the stock-dove to her shallow
nest
And to the grove that holds it. She
beguiles
By intermingled work of house and field
The summer's day, and winter's; with
success   710

Not equal, but sufficient to maintain,
Even at the worst, a smooth stream of
content,
Until the expected hour at which her
Mate
From the far-distant quarry's vault re-
turns;
And by his converse crowns a silent day
With evening cheerfulness. In powers of
mind,   716
In scale of culture, few among my flock
Hold lower rank than this sequestered
pair:
But true humility descends from heaven;
And that best gift of heaven hath fallen
on them;   720
Abundant recompense for every want.
—Stoop from your height, ye proud, and
copy these!
Who, in their noiseless dwelling-place,
can hear
The voice of wisdom whispering scripture
texts
For the mind's government, or temper's
peace;   725
And recommending for their mutual need,
Forgiveness, patience, hope, and charity!'

'Much was I pleased,' the grey-haired
Wanderer said,
'When to those shining fields our notice
first
You turned; and yet more pleased have
from your lips   730
Gathered this fair report of them who
dwell
In that retirement; whither, by such
course
Of evil hap and good as oft awaits
A tired way-faring man, once *I* was
brought
While traversing alone yon mountain-pass.
Dark on my road the autumnal evening
fell,   736
And night succeeded with unusual gloom,
So hazardous that feet and hands became
Guides better than mine eyes—until a
light
High in the gloom appeared, too high,
methought,   740
For human habitation; but I longed
To reach it, destitute of other hope.
I looked with steadiness as sailors look
On the north star, or watch-tower's dis-
tant lamp,
And saw the light—now fixed—and shift-
ing now—   745
Not like a dancing meteor, but in line
Of never-varying motion, to and fro.
It is no night-fire of the naked hills,
Thought I—some friendly covert must be
near.
With this persuasion thitherward my
steps   750

I turn, and reach at last the guiding light;
Joy to myself! but to the heart of her
Who there was standing on the open hill,
(The same kind Matron whom your
tongue hath praised)
Alarm and disappointment! The alarm
Ceased, when she learned through what
mishap I came,   756
And by what help had gained those dis-
tant fields.
Drawn from her cottage, on that aery
height,
Bearing a lantern in her hand she stood,
Or paced the ground—to guide her Hus-
band home,   760
By that unwearied signal, kenned afar;
An anxious duty! which the lofty site,
Traversed but by a few irregular paths,
Imposes, whensoe'er untoward chance
Detains him after his accustomed hour
Till night lies black upon the ground.
"But come,   766
Come," said the Matron, "to our poor
abode;
Those dark rocks hide it!" Entering, I
beheld
A blazing fire—beside a cleanly hearth
Sate down; and to her office, with leave
asked,   770
The Dame returned.
                    Or ere that glowing pile
Of mountain turf required the builder's
hand
Its wasted splendour to repair, the door
Opened, and she re-entered with glad
looks,
Her Helpmate following, Hospitable fare,
Frank conversation, made the evening's
treat: 776
Need a bewildered traveller wish for
more?
But more was given; I studied as we sate
By the bright fire, the good Man's form,
and face
Not less than beautiful; an open brow 780
Of undisturbed humanity; a cheek
Suffused with something of a feminine hue;
Eyes beaming courtesy and mild regard;
But, in the quicker turns of the discourse,
Expression slowly varying, that evinced
A tardy apprehension. From a fount 786
Lost, thought I, in the obscurities of time,
But honoured once, those features and
that mien
May have descended, though I see them
here.
In such a man, so gentle and subdued, 790
Withal so graceful in his gentleness,
A race illustrious for heroic deeds,
Humbled, but not degraded, may expire.
This pleasing fancy (cherished and upheld
By sundry recollections of such fall 795
From high to low, ascent from low to
high,

As books record, and even the careless mind
Cannot but notice among men and things)
Went with me to the place of my repose.

'Roused by the crowing cock at dawn
    of day,   800
I yet had risen too late to interchange
A morning salutation with my Host,
Gone forth already to the far-off seat
Of his day's work. "Three dark mid-
    winter months
Pass," said the Matron, "and I never see,
Save when the sabbath brings its kind
    release,   806
My helpmate's face by light of day. He
    quits
His door in darkness, nor till dusk returns.
And, through Heaven's blessing, thus we
    gain the bread
For which we pray; and for the wants
    provide   810
Of sickness, accident, and helpless age.
Companions have I many; many friends,
Dependants, comforters—my wheel, my
    fire,
All day the house-clock ticking in mine
    ear,
The cackling hen, the tender chicken
    brood,   815
And the wild birds that gather round my
    porch.
This honest sheep-dog's countenance I
    read;
With him can talk; nor blush to waste a
    word
On creatures less intelligent and shrewd.
And if the blustering wind that drives the
    clouds   820
Care not for me, he lingers round my door,
And makes me pastime when our tempers
    suit;—
But, above all, my thoughts are my sup-
    port,
My comfort:—would that they were
    oftener fixed
On what, for guidance in the way that
    leads   825
To heaven, I knew, by my Redeemer
    taught."
The Matron ended—nor could I forbear
To exclaim—"O happy! yielding to the
    law
Of these privations, richer in the main!—
While thankless thousands are opprest
    and clogged   830
By ease and leisure; by the very wealth
And pride of opportunity made poor;
While tens of thousands falter in their
    path,
And sink, through utter want of cheering
    light;   834
For you the hours of labour do not flag;

For you each evening hath its shining star,
And every sabbath-day its golden sun." '

'Yes!' said the Solitary with a smile
That seemed to break from an expanding
    heart,
'The untutored bird may found, and so
    construct,   840
And with such soft materials line, her nest
Fixed in the centre of a prickly brake,
That the thorns wound her not; they
    only guard.
Powers not unjustly likened to those gifts
Of happy instinct which the woodland
    bird
Shares with her species, nature's grace
    sometimes   846
Upon the individual doth confer,
Among her higher creatures born and
    trained
To use of reason. And, I own that, tired
Of the ostentatious world—a swelling
    stage   850
With empty actions and vain passions
    stuffed,
And from the private struggles of man-
    kind
Hoping far less than I could wish to hope,
Far less than once I trusted and be-
    lieved—
I love to hear of those, who, not contend-
    ing   855
Nor summoned to contend for virtue's
    prize,
Miss not the humbler good at which they
    aim,
Blest with a kindly faculty to blunt
The edge of adverse circumstance, and
    turn
Into their contraries the petty plagues
And hindrances with which they stand
    beset.   861
In early youth, among my native hills,
I knew a Scottish Peasant who possessed
A few small crofts of stone-encumbered
    ground;
Masses of every shape and size, that lay
Scattered about under the mouldering
    walls   866
Of a rough precipice; and some, apart,
In quarters unobnoxious to such chance,
As if the moon had showered them down
    in spite.
But he repined not. Though the plough
    was scared   870
By these obstructions, "round the shady
    stones
A fertilising moisture," said the Swain,
"Gathers, and is preserved; and feeding
    dews
And damps, through all the droughty
    summer day
From out their substance issuing, main-
    tain   875

Herbage that never fails: no grass springs
  up
So green, so fresh, so plentiful, as mine!''
But thinly sown these natures; rare, at
  least,
The mutual aptitude of seed and soil
That yields such kindly product. He,
  whose bed   880
Perhaps yon loose sods cover, the poor
  Pensioner
Brought yesterday from our sequestered
  dell
Here to lie down in lasting quiet, he,
If living now, could otherwise report
Of rustic loneliness: that grey-haired
  Orphan—   885
So call him, for humanity to him
No parent was—feelingly could have told,
In life, in death, what solitude can breed
Of selfishness, and cruelty, and vice;
Or, if it breed not, hath not power to cure.
—But your compliance, Sir! with our
  request   891
My words too long have hindered.'
            Undeterred,
Perhaps incited rather, by these shocks,
In no ungracious opposition given
To the confiding spirit of his own   895
Experienced faith, the reverend Pastor
  said,
Around him looking; 'Where shall I
  begin?
Who shall be first selected from my flock
Gathered together in their peaceful fold?'
He paused—and having lifted up his eyes
To the pure heaven, he cast them down
  again   901
Upon the earth beneath his feet; and
  spake:—

'To a mysteriously-united pair
This place is consecrate; to Death and
  Life,
And to the best affections that proceed
From their conjunction; consecrate to
  faith   906
In him who bled for man upon the cross;
Hallowed to revelation; and no less
To reason's mandates; and the hopes
  divine
Of pure imagination;—above all,   910
To charity, and love, that have provided,
Within these precincts, a capacious bed
And receptacle, open to the good
And evil, to the just and the unjust;   914
In which they find an equal resting-place:
Even as the multitude of kindred brooks
And streams, whose murmur fills this
  hollow vale,
Whether their course be turbulent or
  smooth,   918
Their waters clear or sullied, all are lost
Within the bosom of yon crystal Lake,
And end their journey in the same repose!

'And blest are they who sleep; and we
  that know,
While in a spot like this we breathe and
  walk,
That all beneath us by the wings are
  covered
Of motherly humanity, outspread   925
And gathering all within their tender
  shade,
Though loth and slow to come! A battle-
  field,
In stillness left when slaughter is no more,
With this compared, makes a strange
  spectacle!
A dismal prospect yields the wild shore
  strewn   930
With wrecks, and trod by feet of young
  and old
Wandering about in miserable search
Of friends or kindred, whom the angry sea
Restores not to their prayer! Ah! who
  would think
That all the scattered subjects which com-
  pose   935
Earth's melancholy vision through the
  space
Of all her climes—these wretched, these
  depraved,
To virtue lost, insensible of peace,
From the delights of charity cut off, 939
To pity dead, the oppressor and the
  opprest;
Tyrants who utter the destroying word,
And slaves who will consent to be de-
  stroyed—
Were of one species with the sheltered few,
Who, with a dutiful and tender hand,
Lodged, in a dear appropriated spot, 945
This file of infants; some that never
  breathed
The vital air; others, which, though
  allowed
That privilege, did yet expire too soon,
Or with too brief a warning, to admit
Administration of the holy rite   950
That lovingly consigns the babe to the
  arms
Of Jesus, and his everlasting care.
These that in trembling hope are laid
  apart;
And the besprinkled nursling, unrequired
Till he begins to smile upon the breast
That feeds him; and the tottering little-
  one   956
Taken from air and sunshine when the rose
Of infancy first blooms upon his cheek;
The thinking, thoughtless, school-boy; the
  bold youth
Of soul impetuous, and the bashful maid
Smitten while all the promises of life 961
Are opening round her; those of middle
  age,
Cast down while confident in strength
  they stand,

652

Like pillars fixed more firmly, as might
    seem,
And more secure, by very weight of all
That, for support, rests on them; the
    decayed   966
And burthensome; and lastly, that poor
    few
Whose light of reason is with age extinct;
The hopeful and the hopeless, first and
    last,
The earliest summoned and the longest
    spared—   970
Are here deposited, with tribute paid
Various, but unto each some tribute paid;
As if, amid these peaceful hills and groves,
Society were touched with kind concern,
And gentle "Nature grieved, that one
    should die;"[1]   975
Or, if the change demanded no regret,
Observed the liberating stroke—and
    blessed.

    'And whence that tribute? wherefore
    these regards?'[1]
Not from the naked *Heart* alone of Man
(Though claiming high distinction upon
    earth   980
As the sole spring and fountain-head of
    tears,
His own peculiar utterance for distress
Or gladness)—No,' the philosophic Priest
Continued, "'tis not in the vital seat
Of feeling to produce them, without aid
From the pure soul, the soul sublime and
    pure;   986
With her two faculties of eye and ear,
The one by which a creature, whom his
    sins

[1] See Notes, p. 728.

Have rendered prone, can upward look
    to heaven;   989
The other that empowers him to perceive
The voice of Deity, on height and plain,
Whispering those truths in stillness, which
    the WORD,
To the four quarters of the winds, pro-
    claims.
Not without such assistance could the use
Of these benign observances prevail: 995
Thus are they born, thus fostered, thus
    maintained;
And by the care prospective of our wise
Forefathers, who, to guard against the
    shocks,
The fluctuation and decay of things,
Embodied and established these high
    truths   1000
In solemn institutions:—men convinced
That life is love and immortality,
The being one, and one the element.
There lies the channel, and original bed,
From the beginning, hollowed out and
    scooped   1005
For Man's affections—else betrayed and
    lost,
And swallowed up 'mid deserts infinite!
This is the genuine course, the aim, and
    end
Of prescient reason; all conclusions else
Are abject, vain, presumptuous, and per-
    verse.   1010
The faith partaking of those holy times,
Life, I repeat, is energy of love
Divine or human; exercised in pain,
In strife, in tribulation; and ordained,
If so approved and sanctified, to pass,
Through shades and silent rest, to endless
    joy.'   1016

BOOK SIXTH

THE CHURCHYARD AMONG THE MOUNTAINS

ARGUMENT

Poet's Address to the State and Church of England.—The Pastor not inferior to the ancient Worthies of the Church.—He begins his Narratives with an instance of unrequited Love.—Anguish of mind subdued, and how.—The lonely Miner.—An instance of perseverance.—Which leads by contrast to an example of abused talents, irresolution, and weakness.—Solitary, applying this covertly to his own case, asks for an instance of some Stranger, whose dispositions may have led him to end his days here.—Pastor, in answer, gives an account of the harmonising influence of Solitude upon two men of opposite principles, who had encountered agitations in public life.—The rule by which Peace may be obtained expressed, and where.—Solitary hints at an overpowering Fatality.—Answer of the Pastor.—What subjects he will exclude from his Narratives.—Conversation upon this.—Instance of an unamiable character, a Female, and why given.—Contrasted with this, a meek sufferer, from unguarded and betrayed love.—Instance of heavier guilt, and its consequences to the Offender.—With this instance of a Marriage Contract broken is contrasted one of a Widower, evidencing his faithful affection towards his deceased wife by his care of their female Children.

HAIL to the crown by Freedom shaped—
    to gird
An English Sovereign's brow! and to the
    throne
Whereon he sits! Whose deep foundations
    lie

In veneration and the people's love;
Whose steps are equity, whose seat is law.
—Hail to the State of England! And
    conjoin   6
With this a salutation as devout,
Made to the spiritual fabric of her Church;

Founded in truth; by blood of Martyrdom
Cemented; by the hands of Wisdom
reared 10
In beauty of holiness, with ordered pomp,
Decent and unreproved. The voice, that
greets
The majesty of both, shall pray for both;
That, mutually protected and sustained,
They may endure long as the sea sur-
rounds 15
This favoured Land, or sunshine warms
her soil.

And O, ye swelling hills, and spacious
plains!
Besprent from shore to shore with steeple-
towers,
And spires whose 'silent finger points to
heaven;'[1] 19
Nor wanting, at wide intervals, the bulk
Of ancient minster lifted above the cloud
Of the dense air, which town or city
breeds
To intercept the sun's glad beams—may
ne'er
That true succession fail of English
hearts, 24
Who, with ancestral feeling, can perceive
What in those holy structures ye possess
Of ornamental interest, and the charm
Of pious sentiment diffused afar,
And human charity, and social love. 29
—Thus never shall the indignities of time
Approach their reverend graces, un-
opposed;
Nor shall the elements be free to hurt
Their fair proportions; nor the blinder
rage
Of bigot zeal madly to overturn;
And, if the desolating hand of war 35
Spare them, they shall continue to bestow,
Upon the thronged abodes of busy men
(Depraved, and ever prone to fill the mind
Exclusively with transitory things)
An air and mien of dignified pursuit; 40
Of sweet civility, on rustic wilds.

The Poet, fostering for his native land
Such hope, entreats that servants may
abound
Of those pure altars worthy; ministers
Detached from pleasure, to the love of
gain 45
Superior, insusceptible of pride,
And by ambitious longings undisturbed;
Men, whose delight is where their duty
leads
Or fixes them; whose least distinguished
day
Shines with some portion of that heavenly
lustre 50
Which makes the sabbath lovely in the
sight

[1] See Note, p. 733.

Of blessèd angels, pitying human cares.
—And, as on earth it is the doom of truth
To be perpetually attacked by foes
Open or covert, be that priesthood still,
For her defence, replenished with a band
Of strenuous champions, in scholastic arts
Thoroughly disciplined; nor (if in course
Of the revolving world's disturbances
Cause should recur, which righteous
Heaven avert! 60
To meet such trial) from their spiritual
sires
Degenerate; who, constrained to wield
the sword
Of disputation, shrunk not, though as-
sailed
With hostile din, and combating in sight
Of angry umpires, partial and unjust; 65
And did, thereafter, bathe their hands in
fire,
So to declare the conscience satisfied:
Nor for their bodies would accept release;
But, blessing God and praising him, be-
queathed
With their last breath, from out the
smouldering flame, 70
The faith which they by diligence had
earned,
Or, through illuminating grace, received,
For their dear countrymen, and all man-
kind.
O high example, constancy divine!

Even such a Man (inheriting the zeal
And from the sanctity of elder times 76
Not deviating,—a priest, the like of
whom,
If multiplied, and in their stations set,
Would o'er the bosom of a joyful land
Spread true religion and her genuine
fruits) 80
Before me stood that day; on holy
ground
Fraught with the relics of mortality,
Exalting tender themes, by just degrees
To lofty raised; and to the highest, last;
The head and mighty paramount of
truths,— 85
Immortal life, in never-fading worlds,
For mortal creatures, conquered and
secured.

That basis laid, those principles of faith
Announced, as a preparatory act
Of reverence done to the spirit of the
place, 90
The Pastor cast his eyes upon the ground;
Not, as before, like one oppressed with
awe,
But with a mild and social cheerfulness;
Then to the Solitary turned, and spake.

'At morn or eve, in your retired
domain, 95

Perchance you not unfrequently have
   marked
A Visitor—in quest of herbs and flowers;
Too delicate employ, as would appear,
For one, who, though of drooping mien,
   had yet
From nature's kindliness received a frame
Robust as ever rural labour bred.'   101

   The Solitary answered: 'Such a Form
Full well I recollect. We often crossed
Each other's path; but, as the Intruder
   seemed
Fondly to prize the silence which he
   kept,   105
And I as willingly did cherish mine,
We met, and passed, like shadows. I
   have heard,
From my good Host, that being crazed in
   brain
By unrequited love, he scaled the rocks,
Dived into caves, and pierced the matted
   woods,   110
In hope to find some virtuous herb of
   power
To cure his malady!'
               The Vicar smiled,—
'Alas! before to-morrow's sun goes down
His habitation will be here: for him
That open grave is destined.'
             'Died he then   115
Of pain and grief?' the Solitary asked,
'Do not believe it; never could that be!'

'He loved,' the Vicar answered, 'deeply
   loved,
Loved fondly, truly, fervently; and dared
At length to tell his love, but sued in
   vain;   120
Rejected, yea repelled; and, if with scorn
Upon the haughty maiden's brow, 'tis but
A high-prized plume which female Beauty
   wears
In wantonness of conquest, or puts on
To cheat the world, or from herself to
   hide   125
Humiliation, when no longer free.
That he could brook, and glory in;—but
   when
The tidings came that she whom he had
   wooed
Was wedded to another, and his heart
Was forced to rend away its only hope;
Then, Pity could have scarcely found on
   earth   131
An object worthier of regard than he,
In the transition of that bitter hour!
Lost was she, lost; nor could the Sufferer
   say
That in the act of preference he had been
Unjustly dealt with; but the Maid was
   gone!   136
Had vanished from his prospects and
   desires;

Not by translation to the heavenly choir
Who have put off their mortal spoils—
   ah no!   139
She lives another's wishes to complete,—
"Joy be their lot, and happiness," he cried,
"His lot and hers, as misery must be mine!"

   'Such was that strong concussion; but
   the Man,
Who trembled, trunk and limbs, like some
   huge oak   144
By a fierce tempest shaken, soon resumed
The steadfast quiet natural to a mind
Of composition gentle and sedate,
And, in its movements, circumspect and
   slow.
To books, and to the long-forsaken desk,
O'er which enchained by science he had
   loved   150
To bend, he stoutly re-addressed himself,
Resolved to quell his pain, and search for
   truth
With keener appetite (if that might be)
And closer industry. Of what ensued
Within the heart no outward sign ap-
   peared   155
Till a betraying sickliness was seen
To tinge his cheek; and through his frame
   it crept
With slow mutation unconcealable;
Such universal change as autumn makes
In the fair body of a leafy grove   160
Discoloured, then divested.
              'Tis affirmed
By poets skilled in nature's secret ways
That Love will not submit to be controlled
By mastery:—and the good Man lacked
   not friends
Who strove to instil this truth into his
   mind,   165
A mind in all heart-mysteries unversed.
"Go to the hills," said one, "remit a while
This baneful diligence:—at early morn
Court the fresh air, explore the heaths
   and woods;
And, leaving it to others to foretell,   170
By calculations sage, the ebb and flow
Of tides, and when the moon will be
   eclipsed,
Do you, for your own benefit, construct
A calendar of flowers, plucked as they
   blow
Where health abides, and cheerfulness,
   and peace."   175
The attempt was made;—'tis needless to
   report
How hopelessly; but innocence is strong,
And an entire simplicity of mind
A thing most sacred in the eye of Heaven;
That opens, for such sufferers, relief   180
Within the soul, fountains of grace divine;
And doth commend their weakness and
   disease
To Nature's care, assisted in her office

By all the elements that round her wait
To generate, to preserve, and to restore;
And by her beautiful array of forms   186
Shedding sweet influence from above; or
    pure
Delight exhaling from the ground they
    tread.'

'Impute it not to impatience, if,' ex-
    claimed
The Wanderer, 'I infer that he was
    healed   190
By perseverance in the course prescribed.'

'You do not err: the powers, that had
    been lost
By slow degrees, were gradually regained;
The fluttering nerves composed; the beat-
    ing heart
In rest established; and the jarring
    thoughts   195
To harmony restored.—But yon dark
    mould
Will cover him, in the fulness of his
    strength,
Hastily smitten by a fever's force;
Yet not with stroke so sudden as refused
Time to look back with tenderness on
    her   200
Whom he had loved in passion; and to
    send
Some farewell words—with one, but one,
    request;
That, from his dying hand, she would
    accept
Of his possessions that which most he
    prized;
A book, upon whose leaves some chosen
    plants,   205
By his own hand disposed with nicest care,
In undecaying beauty were preserved;
Mute register, to him, of time and place,
And various fluctuations in the breast;
To her, a monument of faithful love   210
Conquered, and in tranquillity retained!

'Close to his destined habitation, lies
One who achieved a humbler victory,
Though marvellous in its kind. A place
    there is
High in these mountains, that allured a
    band   215
Of keen adventurers to unite their pains
In search of precious ore: they tried, were
    foiled—
And all desisted, all, save him alone.
He, taking counsel of his own clear
    thoughts,   219
And trusting only to his own weak hands,
Urged unremittingly the stubborn work,
Unseconded, uncountenanced; then, as
    time
Passed on, while still his lonely efforts
    found

No recompense, derided; and at length,
By many pitied, as insane of mind;   225
By others dreaded as the luckless thrall
Of subterranean Spirits feeding hope
By various mockery of sight and sound;
Hope after hope, encouraged and de-
    stroyed.
—But when the lord of seasons had
    matured   230
The fruits of earth through space of twice
    ten years,
The mountain's entrails offered to his
    view
And trembling grasp the long-deferred
    reward.
Not with more transport did Columbus
    greet
A world, his rich discovery! But our
    Swain,   235
A very hero till his point was gained,
Proved all unable to support the weight
Of prosperous fortune. On the fields he
    looked
With an unsettled liberty of thought,
Wishes and endless schemes; by daylight
    walked   240
Giddy and restless; ever and anon
Quaffed in his gratitude immoderate cups;
And truly might be said to die of joy!
He vanished; but conspicuous to this day
The path remains that linked his cottage-
    door   245
To the mine's mouth; a long and slanting
    track,
Upon the rugged mountain's stony side,
Worn by his daily visits to and from
The darksome centre of a constant hope.
This vestige, neither force of beating rain,
Nor the vicissitudes of frost and thaw 251
Shall cause to fade, till ages pass away;
And it is named, in memory of the event,
The PATH OF PERSEVERANCE.'
                    'Thou from whom
Man has his strength,' exclaimed the
    Wanderer, 'oh!   255
Do thou direct it! To the virtuous grant
The penetrative eye which can perceive
In this blind world the guiding vein of
    hope;
That, like this Labourer, such may dig
    their way,
"Unshaken, unseduced, unterrified;" 260
Grant to the wise his firmness of resolve!'

'That prayer were not superfluous,'
    said the Priest,
'Amid the noblest relics, proudest dust,
That Westminster, for Britain's glory,
    holds
Within the bosom of her awful pile, 265
Ambitiously collected. Yet the sigh,
Which wafts that prayer to heaven, is
    due to all,
Wherever laid, who living fell below

Their virtue's humbler mark; a sigh of
 pain
If to the opposite extreme they sank. 270
How would you pity her who yonder
 rests;
Him, farther off; the pair, who here are
 laid;
But, above all, that mixture of earth's
 mould
Whom sight of this green hillock to my
 mind
Recalls!

   He lived not till his locks were
 nipped   275
By seasonable frost of age; nor died
Before his temples, prematurely forced
To mix the manly brown with silver grey,
Gave obvious instance of the sad effect
Produced, when thoughtless Folly hath
 usurped   280
The natural crown that sage Experience
 wears.
Gay, volatile, ingenious, quick to learn,
And prompt to exhibit all that he pos-
 sessed
Or could perform; a zealous actor, hired
Into the troop of mirth, a soldier, sworn
Into the lists of giddy enterprise— 286
Such was he; yet, as if within his frame
Two several souls alternately had lodged,
Two sets of manners could the Youth
 put on;
And, fraught with antics as the Indian
 bird   290
That writhes and chatters in her wiry cage,
Was graceful, when it pleased him, smooth
 and still
As the mute swan that floats adown the
 stream,
Or, on the waters of the unruffled lake,
Anchors her placid beauty. Not a leaf,
That flutters on the bough, lighter than
 he;   296
And not a flower, that droops in the green
 shade,
More winningly reserved! If ye enquire
How such consummate elegance was bred
Amid these wilds, this answer may suf-
 fice;   300
'Twas Nature's will; who sometimes un-
 dertakes,
For the reproof of human vanity,
Art to outstrip in her peculiar walk.
Hence, for this Favourite—lavishly en-
 dowed
With personal gifts, and bright instinctive
 wit,   305
While both, embellishing each other,
 stood
Yet farther recommended by the charm
Of fine demeanour, and by dance and
 song,
And skill in letters—every fancy shaped

Fair expectations; nor, when to the
 world's   310
Capacious field forth went the Adven-
 turer, there
Were he and his attainments overlooked,
Or scantily rewarded; but all hopes,
Cherished for him, he suffered to depart,
Like blighted buds; or clouds that mi-
 micked land   315
Before the sailor's eye; or diamond drops
That sparkling decked the morning grass;
 or aught
That *was* attractive, and hath ceased to
 be!

  'Yet, when this Prodigal returned, the
 rites
Of joyful greeting were on him bestowed,
Who, by humiliation undeterred, 321
Sought for his weariness a place of rest
Within his Father's gates.—Whence came
 he?—clothed
In tattered garb, from hovels where abides
Necessity, the stationary host 325
Of vagrant poverty; from rifted barns
Where no one dwells but the wide-staring
 owl
And the owl's prey; from these bare
 haunts, to which
He had descended from the proud saloon,
He came, the ghost of beauty and of
 health,   330
The wreck of gaiety! But soon revived
In strength, in power refitted, he renewed
His suit to Fortune; and she smiled again
Upon a fickle Ingrate. Thrice he rose,
Thrice sank as willingly. For he—whose
 nerves   335
Were used to thrill with pleasure, while
 his voice
Softly accompanied the tuneful harp,
By the nice finger of fair ladies touched
In glittering halls—was able to derive
No less enjoyment from an abject choice.
Who happier for the moment—who more
 blithe   341
Than this fallen Spirit? in those dreary
 holds
His talents lending to exalt the freaks
Of merry-making beggars,—now, pro-
 voked   344
To laughter multiplied in louder peals
By his malicious wit; then, all enchained
With mute astonishment, themselves to
 see
In their own arts outdone, their fame
 eclipsed,
As by the very presence of the Fiend
Who dictates and inspires illusive feats,
For knavish purposes! The city, too, 351
(With shame I speak it) to her guilty
 bowers
Allured him, sunk so low in self-respect
As there to linger, there to eat his bread,

Hired minstrel of voluptuous blandish-
ment; 355
Charming the air with skill of hand or
voice,
Listen who would, be wrought upon who
might,
Sincerely wretched hearts, or falsely gay.
—Such the too frequent tenour of his
boast 359
In ears that relished the report;—but all
Was from his Parents happily concealed;
Who saw enough for blame and pitying
love.
They also were permitted to receive
His last, repentant breath; and closed his
eyes, 364
No more to open on that irksome world
Where he had long existed in the state
Of a young fowl beneath one mother
hatched,
Though from another sprung, different in
kind:
Where he had lived, and could not cease
to live,
Distracted in propensity; content 370
With neither element of good or ill;
And yet in both rejoicing; man unblest;
Of contradictions infinite the slave,
Till his deliverance, when Mercy made him
One with himself, and one with them
that sleep.' 375

''Tis strange,' observed the Solitary,
'strange
It seems, and scarcely less than pitiful,
That in a land where charity provides
For all that can no longer feed themselves,
A man like this should choose to bring
his shame 380
To the parental door; and with his sighs
Infect the air which he had freely breathed
In happy infancy. He could not pine
Through lack of converse; no—he must
have found
Abundant exercise for thought and speech,
In his dividual being, self-reviewed, 386
Self-catechised, self-punished. — Some
there are
Who, drawing near their final home, and
much
And daily longing that the same were
reached,
Would rather shun than seek the fellow-
ship 390
Of kindred mould.—Such haply here are
laid?'

'Yes,' said the Priest, 'the Genius of
our hills—
Who seems, by these stupendous barriers
cast
Round his domain, desirous not alone
To keep his own, but also to exclude 395
All other progeny—doth sometimes lure,

Even by his studied depth of privacy.
The unhappy alien hoping to obtain
Concealment, or seduced by wish to find,
In place from outward molestation free,
Helps to internal ease. Of many such 401
Could I discourse; but as their stay was
brief,
So their departure only left behind
Fancies, and loose conjectures. Other
trace
Survives, for worthy mention, of a pair
Who, from the pressure of their several
fates, 406
Meeting as strangers, in a petty town
Whose blue roofs ornament a distant
reach
Of this far-winding vale, remained as
friends
True to their choice; and gave their bones
in trust 410
To this loved cemetery, here to lodge
With unescutcheoned privacy interred
Far from the family vault.—A Chieftain
one
By right of birth; within whose spotless
breast
The fire of ancient Caledonia burned:
He, with the foremost whose impatience
hailed 416
The Stuart, landing to resume, by force
Of arms, the crown which bigotry had
lost,
Aroused his clan; and, fighting at their
head,
With his brave sword endeavoured to
prevent 420
Culloden's fatal overthrow. Escaped
From that disastrous rout, to foreign
shores
He fled; and when the lenient hand of
time
Those troubles had appeased, he sought
and gained,
For his obscured condition, an obscure
Retreat, within this nook of English
ground. 426

'The other, born in Britain's southern
tract,
Had fixed his milder loyalty, and placed
His gentler sentiments of love and hate,
There, where *they* placed them who in
conscience prized 430
The new succession, as a line of kings
Whose oath had virtue to protect the land
Against the dire assaults of papacy
And arbitrary rule. But launch thy bark
On the distempered flood of public life,
And cause for most rare triumph will be
thine 436
If, spite of keenest eye and steadiest hand,
The stream, that bears thee forward,
prove not, soon
Or late, a perilous master. He—who oft,

Beneath the battlements and stately trees
That round his mansion cast a sober
   gloom,   441
Had moralised on this, and other truths
Of kindred import, pleased and satisfied—
Was forced to vent his wisdom with a
   sigh
Heaved from the heart in fortune's bitter-
   ness,   445
When he had crushed a plentiful estate
By ruinous contest, to obtain a seat
In Britain's senate. Fruitless was the
   attempt:
And while the uproar of that desperate
   strife
Continued yet to vibrate on his ear,   450
The vanquished Whig, under a borrowed
   name,
(For the mere sound and echo of his own
Haunted him with sensations of disgust
That he was glad to lose) slunk from the
   world
To the deep shade of those untravelled
   Wilds;   455
In which the Scottish Laird had long
   possessed
An undisturbed abode. Here, then, they
   met,
Two doughty champions; flaming Ja-
   cobite
And sullen Hanoverian! You might think
That losses and vexations, less severe   460
Than those which they had severally sus-
   tained,
Would have inclined each to abate his
   zeal
For his ungrateful cause; no,—I have
   heard
My reverend Father tell that, 'mid the
   calm
Of that small town encountering thus,
   they filled,   465
Daily, its bowling-green with harmless
   strife;
Plagued with uncharitable thoughts the
   church;
And vexed the market-place. But in the
   breasts
Of these opponents gradually was
   wrought,
With little change of general sentiment,
Such leaning towards each other, that
   their days   471
By choice were spent in constant fellow-
   ship;
And if, at times, they fretted with the
   yoke,
Those very bickerings made them love it
   more.

'A favourite boundary to their lengthened walks   475
This Churchyard was. And, whether they
   had come

Treading their path in sympathy and
   linked
In social converse, or by some short space
Discreetly parted to preserve the peace,
One spirit seldom failed to extend its
   sway   480
Over both minds, when they awhile had
   marked
The visible quiet of this holy ground,
And breathed its soothing air;—the spirit
   of hope
And saintly magnanimity; that—spurn-
   ing   484
The field of selfish difference and dispute,
And every care which transitory things,
Earth and the kingdoms of the earth,
   create—
Doth, by a rapture of forgetfulness,
Preclude forgiveness, from the praise de-
   barred,
Which else the Christian virtue might
   have claimed.   490

'There live who yet remember here to
   have seen
Their courtly figures, seated on the stump
Of an old yew, their favourite resting-
   place.
But as the remnant of the long-lived tree
Was disappearing by a swift decay,   495
They, with joint care, determined to erect,
Upon its site, a dial, that might stand
For public use preserved, and thus sur-
   vive
As their own private monument: for this
Was the particular spot, in which they
   wished   500
(And Heaven was pleased to accomplish
   the desire)
That, undivided, their remains should lie.
So, where the mouldered tree had stood,
   was raised
Yon structure, framing, with the ascent
   of steps
That to the decorated pillar lead,   505
A work of art more sumptuous than
   might seem
To suit this place; yet built in no proud
   scorn
Of rustic homeliness; they only aimed
To ensure for it respectful guardianship.
Around the margin of the plate, whereon
The shadow falls to note the stealthy
   hours,   511
Winds an inscriptive legend.'—At these
   words
Thither we turned; and gathered, as we
   read,
The appropriate sense, in Latin numbers
   couched:
'*Time flies; it is his melancholy task*   515
To bring, and bear away, delusive hopes,
And reproduce the troubles he destroys.
But, while his blindness thus is occupied,

Discerning Mortal! do thou serve the will
Of Time's eternal Master, and that peace,
Which the world wants, shall be for thee
*   confirmed!'*   521

'Smooth verse, inspired by no un-
   lettered Muse,'
Exclaimed the Sceptic, 'and the strain of
   thought
Accords with nature's language;—the soft
   voice
Of yon white torrent falling down the
   rocks   525
Speaks, less distinctly, to the same effect.
If, then, their blended influence be not
   lost
Upon our hearts, not wholly lost, I grant,
Even upon mine, the more are we re-
   quired   529
To feel for those among our fellow-men,
Who, offering no obeisance to the world,
Are yet made desperate by "too quick
   a sense
Of constant infelicity," cut off
From peace like exiles on some barren
   rock,
Their life's appointed prison; not more
   free   535
Than sentinels, between two armies, set,
With nothing better, in the chill night
   air,
Than their own thoughts to comfort them.
   Say why
That ancient story of Prometheus chained
To the bare rock, on frozen Caucasus; 540
The vulture, the inexhaustible repast
Drawn from his vitals? Say what meant
   the woes
By Tantalus entailed upon his race,
And the dark sorrows of the line of
   Thebes?
Fictions in form, but in their substance
   truths,   545
Tremendous truths? familiar to the men
Of long-past times, nor obsolete in ours.
Exchange the shepherd's frock of native
   grey
For robes with regal purple tinged; con-
   vert
The crook into a sceptre; give the pomp
Of circumstance; and here the tragic
   Muse   551
Shall find apt subjects for her highest art.
Amid the groves, under the shadowy
   hills,
The generations are prepared; the pangs,
The internal pangs, are ready; the dread
   strife   555
Of poor humanity's afflicted will
Struggling in vain with ruthless destiny.'

'Though,' said the Priest in answer,
   'these be terms
Which a divine philosophy rejects,

We, whose established and unfailing
   trust   560
Is in controlling Providence, admit
That, through all stations, human life
   abounds
With mysteries;—for, if Faith were left
   untried,
How could the might, that lurks within
   her, then
Be shown? her glorious excellence—that
   ranks   565
Among the first of Powers and Virtues—
   proved?
Our system is not fashioned to preclude
That sympathy which you for others ask;
And I could tell, not travelling for my
   theme
Beyond these humble graves, of grievous
   crimes   570
And strange disasters; but I pass them
   by,
Loth to disturb what Heaven hath hushed
   in peace.
—Still less, far less, am I inclined to treat
Of Man degraded in his Maker's sight
By the deformities of brutish vice: 575
For, in such portraits, though a vulgar
   face
And a coarse outside of repulsive life
And unaffecting manners might at once
Be recognised by all—' 'Ah! do not
   think,'
The Wanderer somewhat eagerly ex-
   claimed,   580
'Wish could be ours that you, for such
   poor gain,
(Gain shall I call it?—gain of what?—for
   whom?)
Should breathe a word tending to violate
Your own pure spirit. Not a step we
   look for
In slight of that forbearance and reserve
Which common human-heartedness in-
   spires,   586
And mortal ignorance and frailty claim,
Upon this sacred ground, if nowhere else.'

'True,' said the Solitary, 'be it far
From us to infringe the laws of charity.
Let judgment here in mercy be pro-
   nounced;   591
This, self-respecting Nature prompts, and
   this
Wisdom enjoins; but if the thing we seek
Be genuine knowledge, bear we then in
   mind
How, from his lofty throne, the sun can
   fling   595
Colours as bright on exhalations bred
By weedy pool or pestilential swamp,
As by the rivulet sparkling where it runs,
Or the pellucid lake.'
                       'Small risk,' said I,
'Of such illusion do we here incur;   600

Temptation here is none to exceed the truth;
No evidence appears that they who rest
Within this ground, were covetous of praise,
Or of remembrance even, deserved or not.
Green is the Churchyard, beautiful and green,   605
Ridge rising gently by the side of ridge,
A heaving surface, almost wholly free
From interruption of sepulchral stones,
And mantled o'er with aboriginal turf
And everlasting flowers. These Dalesmen trust   610
The lingering gleam of their departed lives
To oral record, and the silent heart;
Depositories faithful and more kind
Than fondest epitaph: for, if those fail,
What boots the sculptured tomb? And who can blame,   615
Who rather would not envy, men that feel
This mutual confidence; if, from such source,
The practice flow,—if thence, or from a deep
And general humility in death?
Nor should I much condemn it, if it spring   620
From disregard of time's destructive power,
As only capable to prey on things
Of earth, and human nature's mortal part.

'Yet—in less simple districts, where we see
Stone lift its forehead emulous of stone
In courting notice; and the ground all paved   626
With commendations of departed worth;
Reading, where'er we turn, of innocent lives,
Of each domestic charity fulfilled,
And sufferings meekly borne—I, for my part,   630
Though with the silence pleased that here prevails,
Among those fair recitals also range,
Soothed by the natural spirit which they breathe.
And, in the centre of a world whose soil
Is rank with all unkindness, compassed round   635
With such memorials, I have sometimes felt,
It was no momentary happiness
To have *one* Enclosure where the voice that speaks
In envy or detraction is not heard;
Which malice may not enter; where the traces   640
Of evil inclinations are unknown;
Where love and pity tenderly unite

With resignation; and no jarring tone
Intrudes, the peaceful concert to disturb
Of amity and gratitude.'
         'Thus sanctioned,'   645
The Pastor said, 'I willingly confine
My narratives to subjects that excite
Feelings with these accordant; love, esteem,
And admiration; lifting up a veil,
A sunbeam introducing among hearts   650
Retired and covert; so that ye shall have
Clear images before your gladdened eyes
Of nature's unambitious underwood,
And flowers that prosper in the shade.
         And when
I speak of such among my flock as swerved   655
Or fell, those only shall be singled out
Upon whose lapse, or error, something more
Than brotherly forgiveness may attend;
To such will we restrict our notice, else
Better my tongue were mute.
         And yet there are,
I feel, good reasons why we should not leave   661
Wholly untraced a more forbidding way.
For, strength to persevere and to support,
And energy to conquer and repel—
These elements of virtue, that declare   665
The native grandeur of the human soul—
Are ofttimes not unprofitably shown
In the perverseness of a selfish course:
Truth every day exemplified, no less
In the grey cottage by the murmuring stream   670
Than in fantastic conqueror's roving camp,
Or 'mid the factious senate unappalled
Whoe'er may sink, or rise—to sink again,
As merciless proscription ebbs and flows.

'There,' said the Vicar, pointing as he spake,   675
'A woman rests in peace; surpassed by few
In power of mind, and eloquent discourse.
Tall was her stature; her complexion dark
And saturnine; her head not raised to hold
Converse with heaven, nor yet deprest towards earth,   680
But in projection carried, as she walked
For ever musing. Sunken were her eyes;
Wrinkled and furrowed with habitual thought
Was her broad forehead; like the brow of one
Whose visual nerve shrinks from a painful glare   685
Of overpowering light.—While yet a child,
She, 'mid the humble flowerets of the vale,

Towered like the imperial thistle, not
  unfurnished
With its appropriate grace, yet rather
  seeking
To be admired, than coveted and loved.
Even at that age she ruled, a sovereign
  queen,   691
Over her comrades; else their simple
  sports,
Wanting all relish for her strenuous mind,
Had crossed her only to be shunned with
  scorn.
—Oh! pang of sorrowful regret for those
Whom, in their youth, sweet study has
  enthralled,   696
That they have lived for harsher servi-
  tude,
Whether in soul, in body, or estate!
Such doom was hers; yet nothing could
  subdue   699
Her keen desire of knowledge, nor efface
Those brighter images by books imprest
Upon her memory, faithfully as stars
That occupy their places, and, though
  oft
Hidden by clouds, and oft bedimmed by
  haze,
Are not to be extinguished, nor impaired.

  'Two passions, both degenerate, for
    they both   706
Began in honour, gradually obtained
Rule over her, and vexed her daily life;
An unremitting, avaricious thrift;   709
And a strange thraldom of maternal love,
That held her spirit, in its own despite,
Bound—by vexation, and regret, and
  scorn,
Constrained forgiveness, and relenting
  vows,
And tears, in pride suppressed, in shame
  concealed—
To a poor dissolute Son, her only child.
—Her wedded days had opened with
  mishap,   716
Whence dire dependence. What could
  she perform
To shake the burthen off? Ah! there was
  felt,
Indignantly, the weakness of her sex.
She mused, resolved, adhered to her
  resolve;   720
The hand grew slack in alms-giving, the
  heart
Closed by degrees to charity; heaven's
  blessing
Not seeking from that source, she placed
  her trust
In ceaseless pains—and strictest parsi-
  mony
Which sternly hoarded all that could be
  spared,   725
From each day's need, out of each day's
  least gain.

  'Thus all was re-established, and a pile
Constructed, that sufficed for every end,
Save the contentment of the builder's
  mind;
A mind by nature indisposed to aught
So placid, so inactive, as content;   731
A mind intolerant of lasting peace,
And cherishing the pang her heart de-
  plored.
Dread life of conflict! which I oft com-
  pared
To the agitation of a brook that runs   735
Down a rocky mountain, buried now and
  lost
In silent pools, now in strong eddies
  chained;
But never to be charmed to gentleness:
Its best attainment fits of such repose
As timid eyes might shrink from fathom-
  ing.   740

  'A sudden illness seized her in the
    strength
Of life's autumnal season.—Shall I tell
How on her bed of death the Matron lay,
To Providence submissive, so she thought;
But fretted, vexed, and wrought upon,
  almost   745
To anger, by the malady that griped
Her prostrate frame with unrelaxing
  power,
As the fierce eagle fastens on the lamb?
She prayed, she moaned;—her husband's
  sister watched   749
Her dreary pillow, waited on her needs;
And yet the very sound of that kind foot
Was anguish to her ears! "And must she
  rule,"
This was the death-doomed Woman heard
  to say
In bitterness, "and must she rule and
  reign,
Sole Mistress of this house, when I am
  gone?   755
Tend what I tended, calling it her own!"
Enough;—I fear, too much.—One vernal
  evening,
While she was yet in prime of health and
  strength,
I well remember, while I passed her door
Alone, with loitering step, and upward
  eye   760
Turned towards the planet Jupiter that
  hung
Above the centre of the Vale, a voice
Roused me, her voice; it said, "That
  glorious star
In its untroubled element will shine
As now it shines, when we are laid in
  earth   765
And safe from all our sorrows." With a
  sigh
She spake, yet, I believe, not unsustained
By faith in glory that shall far transcend

Aught by these perishable heavens dis-
closed
To sight or mind. Nor less than care
divine   770
Is divine mercy. She, who had rebelled,
Was into meekness softened and subdued;
Did, after trials not in vain prolonged,
With resignation sink into the grave;
And her uncharitable acts, I trust,   775
And harsh unkindnesses are all forgiven,
Tho', in this Vale, remembered with deep
awe.'

———

THE Vicar paused; and toward a seat
advanced,
A long stone-seat, fixed in the Church-
yard wall;   779
Part shaded by cool sycamore, and part
Offering a sunny resting-place to them
Who seek the House of worship, while
the bells
Yet ring with all their voices, or before
The last hath ceased its solitary knoll.
Beneath the shade we all sate down; and
there   785
His office, uninvited, he resumed.

'As on a sunny bank, a tender lamb
Lurks in safe shelter from the winds of
March,
Screened by its parent, so that little
mound
Lies guarded by its neighbour; the small
heap   790
Speaks for itself; an Infant there doth
rest;
The sheltering hillock is the Mother's
grave.
If mild discourse, and manners that con-
ferred
A natural dignity on humblest rank;
If gladsome spirits, and benignant looks,
That for a face not beautiful did more
Than beauty for the fairest face can do;
And if religious tenderness of heart,
Grieving for sin, and penitential tears
Shed when the clouds had gathered and
distained   800
The spotless ether of a maiden life;
If these may make a hallowed spot of
earth
More holy in the sight of God or Man;
Then, o'er that mould, a sanctity shall
brood   804
Till the stars sicken at the day of doom.

'Ah! what a warning for a thoughtless
man,
Could field or grove, could any spot of
earth,
Show to his eye an image of the pangs
Which it hath witnessed; render back
an echo

Of the sad steps by which it hath been
trod!   810
There, by her innocent Baby's precious
grave,
And on the very turf that roofs her own,
The Mother oft was seen to stand, or
kneel
In the broad day, a weeping Magda-
lene.
Now she is not; the swelling turf reports
Of the fresh shower, but of poor Ellen's
tears   816
Is silent; nor is any vestige left
Of the path worn by mournful tread of
her
Who, at her heart's light bidding, once
had moved
In virgin fearlessness, with step that
seemed   820
Caught from the pressure of elastic turf
Upon the mountains gemmed with morn-
ing dew,
In the prime hour of sweetest scents and
airs.
—Serious and thoughtful was her mind;
and yet,
By reconcilement exquisite and rare, 825
The form, port, motions, of this Cottage-
girl
Were such as might have quickened and
inspired
A Titian's hand, addrest to picture forth
Oread or Dryad glancing through the
shade
What time the hunter's earliest horn is
heard   830
Startling the golden hills.

A wide-spread elm
Stands in our valley, named THE JOYFUL
TREE;
From dateless usage which our peasants
hold
Of giving welcome to the first of May
By dances round its trunk.—And if the
sky   835
Permit, like honours, dance and song, are
paid
To the Twelfth Night, beneath the frosty
stars
Or the clear moon. The queen of these
gay sports,
If not in beauty yet in sprightly air,
Was hapless Ellen.—No one touched the
ground   840
So deftly, and the nicest maiden's locks
Less gracefully were braided;—but this
praise,
Methinks, would better suit another place.

'She loved, and fondly deemed herself beloved.
—The road is dim, the current unper-
ceived,   845
The weakness painful and most pitiful,

663

By which a virtuous woman, in pure
youth,
May be delivered to distress and shame.
Such fate was hers.—The last time Ellen
danced,
Among her equals, round THE JOYFUL
TREE,   850
She bore a secret burthen; and full soon
Was left to tremble for a breaking vow,—
Then, to bewail a sternly-broken vow,
Alone, within her widowed Mother's
house.
It was the season of unfolding leaves, 855
Of days advancing toward their utmost
length,
And small birds singing happily to mates
Happy as they. With spirit-saddening
power
Winds pipe through fading woods; but
those blithe notes   859
Strike the deserted to the heart; I speak
Of what I know, and what we feel within.
—Beside the cottage in which Ellen dwelt
Stands a tall ash-tree; to whose topmost
twig
A thrush resorts, and annually chants,
At morn and evening from that naked
perch,   865
While all the undergrove is thick with
leaves,
A time-beguiling ditty, for delight
Of his fond partner, silent in the nest.
—"Ah why," said Ellen, sighing to her-
self,
"Why do not words, and kiss, and solemn
pledge,   870
And nature that is kind in woman's
breast,
And reason that is in man is wise and good,
And fear of him who is a righteous judge
Why do not these prevail for human life,
To keep two hearts together, that began
Their spring-time with one love, and that
have need   876
Of mutual pity and forgiveness, sweet
To grant, or be received; while that poor
bird—
O come and hear him! Thou who hast to
me
Been faithless, hear him, though a lowly
creature,   880
One of God's simple children that yet
know not
The universal Parent, how he sings
As if he wished the firmament of heaven
Should listen, and give back to him the
voice
Of his triumphant constancy and love;
The proclamation that he makes, how
far   886
His darkness doth transcend our fickle
light!"

'Such was the tender passage, not by me

Repeated without loss of simple phrase,
Which I perused, even as the words had
been   890
Committed by forsaken Ellen's hand
To the blank margin of a Valentine,
Bedropped with tears. 'Twill please you
to be told
That, studiously withdrawing from the
eye   894
Of all companionship, the Sufferer yet
In lonely reading found a meek resource:
How thankful for the warmth of summer
days,
When she could slip into the cottage-
barn,
And find a secret oratory there;
Or, in the garden, under friendly veil 900
Of their long twilight, pore upon her book
By the last lingering help of the open sky
Until dark night dismissed her to her bed!
Thus did a waking fancy sometimes lose
The unconquerable pang of despised love.

'A kindlier passion opened on her soul
When that poor Child was born. Upon
its face
She gazed as on a pure and spotless gift
Of unexpected promise, where a grief
Or dread was all that had been thought
of,—joy   910
Far livelier than bewildered traveller feels,
Amid a perilous waste that all night long
Hath harassed him toiling through fear-
ful storm,
When he beholds the first pale speck
serene
Of day-spring, in the gloomy east, re-
vealed,   915
And greets it with thanksgiving. "Till this
hour,"
Thus, in her Mother's hearing Ellen spake,
"There was a stony region in my heart;
But He, at whose command the parchèd
rock
Was smitten, and poured forth a quench-
ing stream,   920
Hath softened that obduracy, and made
Unlooked-for gladness in the desert place,
To save the perishing; and, henceforth, I
breathe
The air with cheerful spirit, for thy sake,
My Infant! and for that good Mother
dear,   925
Who bore me; and hath prayed for me
in vain;—
Yet not in vain; it shall not be in vain."
She spake, nor was the assurance unful-
filled;
And if heart-rending thoughts would oft
return,
They stayed not long.—The blameless
Infant grew;   930
The Child whom Ellen and her Mother
loved

They soon were proud of; tended it and nursed;
A soothing comforter, although forlorn;
Like a poor singing-bird from distant lands;
Or a choice shrub, which he, who passes by
With vacant mind, not seldom may observe   936
Fair-flowering in a thinly-peopled house,
Whose window, somewhat sadly, it adorns.

'Through four months' space the Infant drew its food
From the maternal breast; then scruples rose;   940
Thoughts, which the rich are free from, came and crossed
The fond affection. She no more could bear
By her offence to lay a twofold weight
On a kind parent willing to forget
Their slender means: so, to that parent's care   945
Trusting her child, she left their common home,
And undertook with dutiful content
A Foster-mother's office.
                             'Tis, perchance,
Unknown to you that in these simple vales
The natural feeling of equality   950
Is by domestic service unimpaired;
Yet, though such service be, with us, removed
From sense of degradation, not the less
The ungentle mind can easily find means
To impose severe restraints and laws unjust,   955
Which hapless Ellen now was doomed to feel:
For (blinded by an over-anxious dread
Of such excitement and divided thought
As with her office would but ill accord)
The pair, whose infant she was bound to nurse,   960
Forbad her all communion with her own:
Week after week, the mandate they enforced.
—So near! yet not allowed upon that sight
To fix her eyes—alas! 'twas hard to bear!
But worse affliction must be borne—far worse;   965
For 'tis Heaven's will—that, after a disease
Begun and ended within three days' space,
Her child should die; as Ellen now exclaimed,
Her own—deserted child!—Once, only once,
She saw it in that mortal malady;   970
And, on the burial-day, could scarcely gain
Permission to attend its obsequies.

She reached the house, last of the funeral train;
And some one, as she entered, having chanced
To urge unthinkingly their prompt departure,   975
"Nay," said she, with commanding look, a spirit
Of anger never seen in her before,
"Nay, ye must wait my time!" and down she sate,
And by the unclosed coffin kept her seat
Weeping and looking, looking on and weeping,   980
Upon the last sweet slumber of her Child,
Until at length her soul was satisfied.

'You see the Infant's Grave; and to this spot,
The Mother, oft as she was sent abroad,
On whatsoever errand, urged her steps:
Hither she came; here stood, and sometimes knelt   986
In the broad day, a rueful Magdalene!
So call her; for not only she bewailed
A mother's loss, but mourned in bitterness
Her own transgression; penitent sincere
As ever raised to heaven a streaming eye!
—At length the parents of the foster-child,   992
Noting that in despite of their commands
She still renewed and could not but renew
Those visitations, ceased to send her forth;   995
Or, to the garden's narrow bounds, confined.
I failed not to remind them that they erred;
For holy Nature might not thus be crossed,
Thus wronged in woman's breast: in vain I pleaded—
But the green stalk of Ellen's life was snapped,   1000
And the flower drooped; as every eye could see,
It hung its head in mortal languishment.
—Aided by this appearance, I at length
Prevailed; and, from those bonds released, she went
Home to her mother's house.
                             The Youth was fled;
The rash betrayer could not face the shame   1006
Or sorrow which his senseless guilt had caused;
And little would his presence, or proof given
Of a relenting soul, have now availed;
For, like a shadow, he was passed away
From Ellen's thoughts; had perished   1011
For all concerns of fear, or hope, or love,

Save only those which to their common
    shame,
And to his moral being appertained:
Hope from that quarter would, I know,
    have brought   1015
A heavenly comfort; there she recognised
An unrelaxing bond, a mutual need;
There, and, as seemed, there only.
                            She had built,
Her fond maternal heart had built, a nest
In blindness all too near the river's edge;
That work a summer flood with hasty
    swell   1021
Had swept away; and now her Spirit
    longed
For its last flight to heaven's security.
—The bodily frame wasted from day to
    day;
Meanwhile, relinquishing all other cares,
Her mind she strictly tutored to find
    peace   1026
And pleasure in endurance. Much she
    thought,
And much she read; and brooded feel-
    ingly
Upon her own unworthiness. To me,
As to a spiritual comforter and friend,
Her heart she opened; and no pains were
    spared   1031
To mitigate, as gently as I could,
The sting of self-reproach, with healing
    words.
Meek Saint! through patience glorified
    on earth!
In whom, as by her lonely hearth she
    sate,   1035
The ghastly face of cold decay put on
A sun-like beauty, and appeared divine!
May I not mention—that, within those
    walls,
In due observance of her pious wish,
The congregation joined with me in
    prayer   1040
For her soul's good? Nor was that office
    vain.
—Much did she suffer: but, if any friend,
Beholding her condition, at the sight
Gave way to words of pity or complaint,
She stilled them with a prompt reproof,
    and said,   1045
"He who afflicts me knows what I can
    bear;
And, when I fail, and can endure no more,
Will mercifully take me to himself."
So, through the cloud of death, her Spirit
    passed
Into that pure and unknown world of
    love   1050
Where injury cannot come:—and here is
    laid
The mortal Body by her Infant's side.'

  The Vicar ceased; and downcast looks
    made known

That each had listened with his inmost
    heart.
For me, the emotion scarcely was less
    strong   1055
Or less benign than that which I had felt
When seated near my venerable Friend,
Under those shady elms, from him I
    heard
The story that retraced the slow decline
Of Margaret, sinking on the lonely heath
With the neglected house to which she
    clung.   1061
—I noted that the Solitary's cheek
Confessed the power of nature.—Pleased
    though sad,
More pleased than sad, the grey-haired
    Wanderer sate;
Thanks to his pure imaginative soul 1065
Capacious and serene; his blameless life,
His knowledge, wisdom, love of truth,
    and love
Of human kind! He was it who first broke
The pensive silence, saying:—
                        'Blest are they
Whose sorrow rather is to suffer wrong
Than to do wrong, albeit themselves have
    erred.   1071
This tale gives proof that Heaven most
    gently deals
With such, in their affliction.—Ellen's fate,
Her tender spirit, and her contrite heart,
Call to my mind dark hints which I have
    heard   1075
Of one who died within this vale, by doom
Heavier, as his offence was heavier far.
Where, Sir, I pray you, where are laid the
    bones
Of Wilfred Armathwaite?'
                        The Vicar answered,
'In that green nook, close by the Church-
    yard wall,   1080
Beneath yon hawthorn, planted by myself
In memory and for warning, and in sign
Of sweetness where dire anguish had been
    known,
Of reconcilement after deep offence—
There doth he rest. No theme his fate
    supplies   1085
For the smooth glozings of the indulgent
    world;
Nor need the windings of his devious
    course
Be here retraced;—enough that, by mis-
    hap
And venial error, robbed of competence,
And her obsequious shadow, peace of
    mind,
He craved a substitute in troubled joy;
Against his conscience rose in arms, and,
    braving   1092
Divine displeasure, broke the marriage-
    vow.
That which he had been weak enough to
    do

Was misery in remembrance: he was
    stung,   1095
Stung by his inward thoughts, and by the
    smiles
Of wife and children stung to agony.
Wretched at home, he gained no peace
    abroad;
Ranged through the mountains, slept
    upon the earth,   1099
Asked comfort of the open air, and found
No quiet in the darkness of the night,
No pleasure in the beauty of the day.
His flock he slighted: his paternal fields
Became a clog to him, whose spirit wished
To fly—but whither! And this gracious
    Church,   1105
That wears a look so full of peace and
    hope
And love, benignant mother of the vale,
How fair amid her brood of cottages!
She was to him a sickness and reproach.
Much to the last remained unknown: but
    this   1110
Is sure, that through remorse and grief
    he died;
Though pitied among men, absolved by
    God,
He could not find forgiveness in himself;
Nor could endure the weight of his own
    shame.

'Here rests a Mother. But from her I
    turn   1115
And from her grave.—Behold—upon that
    ridge,
That, stretching boldly from the moun-
    tain side,
Carries into the centre of the vale
Its rocks and woods—the Cottage where
    she dwelt;
And where yet dwells her faithful Partner,
    left   1120
(Full eight years past) the solitary prop
Of many helpless Children. I begin
With words that might be prelude to a
    tale
Of sorrow and dejection; but I feel
No sadness, when I think of what mine
    eyes   1125
See daily in that happy family,
—Bright garland form they for the pen-
    sive brow
Of their undrooping Father's widowhood,
Those six fair Daughters, budding yet—
    not one,
Not one of all the band, a full-blown
    flower.   1130
Deprest, and desolate of soul, as once
That Father was, and filled with anxious
    fear,
Now, by experience taught, he stands
    assured,
That God, who takes away, yet takes not
    half

Of what he seems to take; or gives it back,
Not to our prayer, but far beyond our
    prayer;   1136
He gives it—the boon produce of a soil
Which our endeavours have refused to
    till,
And hope hath never watered. The Abode,
Whose grateful owner can attest these
    truths,   1140
Even were the object nearer to our sight,
Would seem in no distinction to surpass
The rudest habitations. Ye might think
That it had sprung self-raised from earth,
    or grown
Out of the living rock, to be adorned 1145
By nature only; but, if thither led,
Ye would discover, then, a studious work
Of many fancies, prompting many hands.

'Brought from the woods the honey-
    suckle twines
Around the porch, and seems, in that trim
    place,   1150
A plant no longer wild; the cultured rose
There blossoms, strong in health, and will
    be soon
Roof-high; the wild pink crowns the
    garden-wall,
And with the flowers are intermingled
    stones
Sparry and bright, rough scatterings of
    the hills.   1155
These ornaments, that fade not with the
    year,
A hardy Girl continues to provide;
Who, mounting fearlessly the rocky
    heights,
Her Father's prompt attendant, does for
    him
All that a boy could do, but with delight
More keen and prouder daring; yet hath
    she,   1161
Within the garden, like the rest, a bed
For her own flowers and favourite herbs,
    a space,
By sacred charter, holden for her use.
—These, and whatever else the garden
    bears   1165
Of fruit or flower, permission asked or not,
I freely gather; and my leisure draws
A not unfrequent pastime from the hum
Of bees around their range of sheltered
    hives
Busy in that enclosure; while the rill,
That sparkling thrids the rocks, attunes
    his voice   1171
To the pure course of human life which
    there
Flows on in solitude. But, when the
    gloom
Of night is falling round my steps, then
    most
This Dwelling charms me; often I stop
    short,   1175

Who could refrain?) and feed by stealth
    my sight
With prospect of the company within,
Laid open through the blazing window:—
    there
I see the eldest Daughter at her wheel
Spinning amain, as if to overtake   1180
The never-halting time; or, in her turn,
Teaching some Novice of the sisterhood
That skill in this or other household
    work,
Which, from her Father's honoured hand,
    herself,

While she was yet a little-one, had
    learned.   1185
Mild Man! he is not gay, but they are
    gay;
And the whole house seems filled with
    gaiety.
—Thrice happy, then, the Mother may be
    deemed,
The Wife, from whose consolatory grave
I turned, that ye in mind might witness
    where,   1190
And how, her Spirit yet survives on
    earth!'

BOOK SEVENTH

THE CHURCHYARD AMONG THE MOUNTAINS.—(CONTINUED)

ARGUMENT

Impression of these Narratives upon the Author's mind.—Pastor invited to give account of certain
Graves that lie apart.—Clergyman and his Family.—Fortunate influence of change of situation.—
Activity in extreme old age.—Another Clergyman, a character of resolute Virtue.—Lamentations
over mis-directed applause.—Instance of less exalted excellence in a deaf man.—Elevated character
of a blind man.—Reflection upon Blindness.—Interrupted by a Peasant who passes—his animal
cheerfulness and careless vivacity.—He occasions a digression on the fall of beautiful and interesting
Trees.—A female Infant's Grave.—Joy at her Birth.—Sorrow at her Departure.—A youthful Peasant—
his patriotic enthusiasm and distinguished qualities—his untimely death.—Exultation of the Wanderer,
as a patriot, in this Picture.—Solitary how affected.—Monument of a Knight.—Traditions concerning
him.—Peroration of the Wanderer on the transitoriness of things and the revolutions of society.—
Hints at his own past Calling.—Thanks the Pastor.

WHILE thus from theme to theme the
    Historian passed,
The words he uttered, and the scene that
    lay
Before our eyes, awakened in my mind
Vivid remembrance of those long-past
    hours;
When, in the hollow of some shadowy
    vale,   5
(What time the splendour of the setting
    sun
Lay beautiful on Snowdon's sovereign
    brow,
On Cader Idris, or huge Penmanmaur)
A wandering Youth, I listened with de-
    light
To pastoral melody or warlike air,   10
Drawn from the chords of the ancient
    British harp
By some accomplished Master, while he
    sate
Amid the quiet of the green recess,
And there did inexhaustibly dispense
An interchange of soft or solemn tunes, 15
Tender or blithe; now, as the varying
    mood
Of his own spirit urged,—now, as a voice
From youth or maiden, or some honoured
    chief
Of his compatriot villagers (that hung
Around him, drinking in the impassioned
    notes   20

Of the time-hallowed minstrelsy) required
For their heart's ease or pleasure. Strains
    of power
Were they, to seize and occupy the sense;
But to a higher mark than song can reach
Rose this pure eloquence. And, when the
    stream   25
Which overflowed the soul was passed
    away,
A consciousness remained that it had left,
Deposited upon the silent shore
Of memory, images and precious thoughts,
That shall not die, and cannot be de-
    stroyed.   30

'These grassy heaps lie amicably close,'
Said I, 'like surges heaving in the wind
Along the surface of a mountain pool:
Whence comes it, then, that yonder we
    behold
Five graves, and only five, that rise to-
    gether   35
Unsociably sequestered, and encroaching
On the smooth playground of the village-
    school?'

The Vicar answered,—'No disdainful
    pride
In them who rest beneath, nor any course
Of strange or tragic accident, hath helped
To place those hillocks in that lonely
    guise.   41

—Once more look forth, and follow with
    your sight
The length of road that from yon moun-
    tain's base
Through bare enclosures stretches, 'till
    its line
Is lost within a little tuft of trees;   45
Then, reappearing in a moment, quits
The cultured fields; and up the heathy
    waste,
Mounts, as you see, in mazes serpentine,
Led towards an easy outlet of the vale.
That little shady spot, that sylvan tuft, 50
By which the road is hidden, also hides
A cottage from our view; though I discern
(Ye scarcely can) amid its sheltering trees
The smokeless chimney-top.—
                  All unembowered
And naked stood that lowly Parsonage 55
(For such in truth it is, and appertains
To a small Chapel in the vale beyond)
When hither came its last Inhabitant.
Rough and forbidding were the choicest
    roads
By which our northern wilds could then
    be crossed;   60
And into most of these secluded vales
Was no access for wain, heavy or light.
So, at his dwelling-place the Priest arrived
With store of household goods, in pan-
    niers slung
On sturdy horses graced with jingling
    bells,   65
And on the back of more ignoble beast;
That, with like burthen of effects most
    prized
Or easiest carried, closed the motley train.
Young was I then, a schoolboy of eight
    years;
But still, methinks, I see them as they
    passed   70
In order, drawing toward their wished-
    for home.
—Rocked by the motion of a trusty ass
Two ruddy children hung, a well-poised
    freight,
Each in his basket nodding drowsily;
Their bonnets, I remember, wreathed with
    flowers,   75
Which told it was the pleasant month of
    June;
And, close behind, the comely Matron
    rode,
A woman of soft speech and gracious
    smile,
And with a lady's mien.—From far they
    came,
Even from Northumbrian hills; yet theirs
    had been   80
A merry journey, rich in pastime, cheered
By music, prank, and laughter-stirring
    jest;
And freak put on, and arch word dropped
    —to swell

The cloud of fancy and uncouth surmise
That gathered round the slowly-moving
    train.   85
—"Whence do they come? and with what
    errand charged?
Belong they to the fortune-telling tribe
Who pitch their tents under the green-
    wood tree?
Or Strollers are they, furnished to enact
Fair Rosamond, and the Children of the
    Wood,   90
And, by that whiskered tabby's aid, set
    forth
The lucky venture of sage Whittington,
When the next village hears the show
    announced
By blast of trumpet?" Plenteous was the
    growth
Of such conjectures, overheard, or seen 95
On many a staring countenance portrayed
Of boor or burgher, as they marched
    along.
And more than once their steadiness of
    face
Was put to proof, and exercise supplied
To their inventive humour, by stern looks,
And questions in authoritative tone, 101
From some staid guardian of the public
    peace,
Checking the sober steed on which he
    rode,
In his suspicious wisdom; oftener still,
By notice indirect, or blunt demand 105
From traveller halting in his own despite,
A simple curiosity to ease:
Of which adventures, that beguiled and
    cheered
Their grave migration, the good pair
    would tell,
With undiminished glee, in hoary age. 110

   'A Priest he was by function; but his
    course
From his youth up, and high as man-
    hood's noon,
(The hour of life to which he then was
    brought)
Had been irregular, I might say, wild;
By books unsteadied, by his pastoral care
Too little checked.   An active, ardent
    mind;   116
A fancy pregnant with resource and
    scheme
To cheat the sadness of a rainy day;
Hands apt for all ingenious arts and
    games;
A generous spirit, and a body strong 120
To cope with stoutest champions of the
    bowl;
Had earned for him sure welcome, and
    the rights
Of a prized visitant, in the jolly hall
Of country 'squire; or at the statelier
    board

Of duke or earl, from scenes of courtly
   pomp   125
Withdrawn,—to while away the summer
   hours
In condescension among rural guests.

'With these high comrades he had
   revelled long,
Frolicked industriously, a simple Clerk
By hopes of coming patronage beguiled
Till the heart sickened. So, each loftier
   aim   131
Abandoning and all his showy friends,
For a life's stay (slender it was, but sure)
He turned to this secluded chapelry;
That had been offered to his doubtful
   choice   135
By an unthought-of patron. Bleak and
   bare
They found the cottage, their allotted
   home;
Naked without, and rude within; a spot
With which the Cure not long had been
   endowed:
And far remote the chapel stood,—re-
   mote,   140
And, from his Dwelling, unapproachable,
Save through a gap high in the hills, an
   opening
Shadeless and shelterless, by driving
   showers
Frequented, and beset with howling
   winds.
Yet cause was none, whate'er regret might
   hang   145
On his own mind, to quarrel with the
   choice
Or the necessity that fixed him here;
Apart from old temptations, and con-
   strained
To punctual labour in his sacred charge.
See him a constant preacher to the poor!
And visiting, though not with saintly
   zeal,   151
Yet, when need was, with no reluctant
   will,
The sick in body, or distrest in mind;
And, by as salutary change, compelled
To rise from timely sleep, and meet the
   day   155
With no engagement, in his thoughts,
   more proud
Or splendid than his garden could afford,
His fields, or mountains by the heath-
   cock ranged,
Or the wild brooks; from which he now
   returned
Contented to partake the quiet meal 160
Of his own board, where sat his gentle
   Mate
And three fair Children, plentifully fed
Though simply, from their little house-
   hold farm;
Nor wanted timely treat of fish or fowl

By nature yielded to his practised hand;—
To help the small but certain comings-in
Of that spare benefice. Yet not the less
Theirs was a hospitable board, and theirs
A charitable door.
                       So days and years
Passed on;—the inside of that rugged
   house   170
Was trimmed and brightened by the
   Matron's care,
And gradually enriched with things of
   price,
Which might be lacked for use or orna-
   ment.
What, though no soft and costly sofa
   there
Insidiously stretched out its lazy length,
And no vain mirror glittered upon the
   walls,   176
Yet were the windows of the low abode
By shutters weather-fended, which at
   once
Repelled the storm and deadened its loud
   roar.
Their snow-white curtains hung in decent
   folds;   180
Tough moss, and long-enduring mountain-
   plants,
That creep along the ground with sinuous
   trail,
Were nicely braided; and composed a
   work
Like Indian mats, that with appropriate
   grace
Lay at the threshold and the inner doors;
And a fair carpet, woven of homespun
   wool   186
But tinctured daintily with florid hues,
For seemliness and warmth, on festal days,
Covered the smooth blue slabs of moun-
   tain-stone
With which the parlour-floor, in simplest
   guise   190
Of pastoral homesteads, had been long
   inlaid.

   'Those pleasing works the Housewife's
      skill produced:
Meanwhile the unsedentary Master's hand
Was busier with his task—to rid, to plant,
To rear for food, for shelter, and delight;
A thriving covert! And when wishes,
   formed   196
In youth, and sanctioned by the riper
   mind,
Restored me to my native valley, here
To end my days; well pleased was I to
   see
The once-bare cottage, on the mountain-
   side,   200
Screen'd from assault of every bitter
   blast;
While the dark shadows of the summer
   leaves

Danced in the breeze, chequering its
   mossy roof.
Time, which had thus afforded willing
   help
To beautify with nature's fairest growths
This rustic tenement, had gently shed, 206
Upon its Master's frame, a wintry grace;
The comeliness of unenfeebled age.

  'But how could I say, gently? for he
   still
Retained a flashing eye, a burning palm,
A stirring foot, a head which beat at
   nights   211
Upon its pillow with a thousand schemes.
Few likings had he dropped, few plea-
   sures lost;
Generous and charitable, prompt to serve;
And still his harsher passions kept their
   hold—   215
Anger and indignation. Still he loved
The sound of titled names, and talked in
   glee
Of long-past banquetings with high-born
   friends:
Then, from those lulling fits of vain de-
   light   219
Uproused by recollected injury, railed
At their false ways disdainfully,—and oft
In bitterness, and with a threatening eye
Of fire, incensed beneath its hoary brow.
—Those transports, with staid looks of
   pure good-will,
And with soft smile, his consort would
   reprove.   225
She, far behind him in the race of years,
Yet keeping her first mildness, was ad-
   vanced
Far nearer, in the habit of her soul,
To that still region whither all are bound.
Him might we liken to the setting sun 230
As seen not seldom on some gusty day,
Struggling and bold, and shining from
   the west
With an inconstant and unmellowed
   light;
She was a soft attendant cloud, that hung
As if with wish to veil the restless orb;
From which it did itself imbibe a ray 236
Of pleasing lustre.—But no more of this;
I better love to sprinkle on the sod
That now divides the pair, or rather say,
That still unites them, praises, like hea-
   ven's dew,   240
Without reserve descending upon both.

  'Our very first in eminence of years
This old Man stood, the patriarch of the
   Vale!
And, to his unmolested mansion, death
Had never come, through space of forty
   years;   245
Sparing both old and young in that
   abode.

Suddenly then they disappeared: not
   twice
Had summer scorched the fields; not
   twice had fallen,
On those high peaks, the first autumnal
   snow,
Before the greedy visiting was closed, 250
And the long-privileged house left empty
   —swept
As by a plague. Yet no rapacious plague
Had been among them; all was gentle
   death,
One after one, with intervals of peace.
A happy consummation! an accord 255
Sweet, perfect, to be wished for! save that
   here
Was something which to mortal sense
   might sound
Like harshness,—that the old grey-headed
   Sire,
The oldest, he was taken last, survived
When the meek Partner of his age, his
   Son,
His Daughter, and that late and high-
   prized gift,   261
His little smiling Grandchild, were no
   more.

  '"All gone, all vanished! he deprived
   and bare,
How will he face the remnant of his life?
What will become of him?" we said, and
   mused   265
In sad conjectures—"Shall we meet him
   now
Haunting with rod and line the craggy
   brooks?
Or shall we overhear him, as we pass,
Striving to entertain the lonely hours
With music?" (for he had not ceased to
   touch   270
The harp or viol which himself had
   framed,
For their sweet purposes, with perfect
   skill.)
"What titles will he keep? will he remain
Musician, gardener, builder, mechanist,
A planter, and a rearer from the seed? 275
A man of hope and forward-looking mind
Even to the last!"—Such was he, un-
   subdued.
But Heaven was gracious; yet a little
   while,
And this Survivor, with his cheerful
   throng
Of open projects, and his inward hoard
Of unsunned griefs, too many and too
   keen,   281
Was overcome by unexpected sleep,
In one blest moment. Like a shadow
   thrown
Softly and lightly from a passing cloud,
Death fell upon him, while reclined he
   lay   285

For noontide solace on the summer grass,
The warm lap of his mother earth: and so,
Their lenient term of separation past,
That family (whose graves you there be-
hold)
By yet a higher privilege once more 290
Were gathered to each other.'
Calm of mind
And silence waited on these closing
words;
Until the Wanderer (whether moved by
fear
Lest in those passages of life were some
That might have touched the sick heart
of his Friend 295
Too nearly, or intent to reinforce
His own firm spirit in degree deprest
By tender sorrow for our mortal state)
Thus silence broke:—'Behold a thought-
less Man
From vice and premature decay pre-
served 300
By useful habits, to a fitter soil
Transplanted ere too late.—The hermit,
lodged
Amid the untrodden desert, tells his beads,
With each repeating its allotted prayer,
And thus divides and thus relieves the
time; 305
Smooth task, with *his* compared, whose
mind could string,
Not scantily, bright minutes on the
thread
Of keen domestic anguish; and beguile
A solitude, unchosen, unprofessed;
Till gentlest death released him.
Far from us
Be the desire—too curiously to ask 311
How much of this is but the blind result
Of cordial spirits and vital temperament,
And what to higher powers is justly due.
But you, Sir, know that in a neighbouring
vale 315
A Priest abides before whose life such
doubts
Fall to the ground; whose gifts of nature
lie
Retired from notice, lost in attributes
Of reason, honourably effaced by debts
Which her poor treasure-house is content
to owe, 320
And conquests over her dominion gained,
To which her frowardness must needs
submit.
In this one Man is shown a temperance—
proof
Against all trials; industry severe
And constant as the motion of the day;
Stern self-denial round him spread, with
shade 326
That might be deemed forbidding, did
not there
All generous feelings flourish and rejoice;
Forbearance, charity in deed and thought,

And resolution competent to take 330
Out of the bosom of simplicity
All that her holy customs recommend,
And the best ages of the world prescribe.
—Preaching, administering, in every work
Of his sublime vocation, in the walks 335
Of worldly intercourse between man and
man,
And in his humble dwelling, he appears
A labourer, with moral virtue girt,
With spiritual graces, like a glory,
crowned.'

'Doubt can be none,' the Pastor said,
'for whom 340
This portraiture is sketched. The great,
the good,
The well-beloved, the fortunate, the
wise,—
These titles emperors and chiefs have
borne,
Honour assumed or given: and him, the
WONDERFUL,
Our simple shepherds, speaking from the
heart, 345
Deservedly have styled.—From his abode
In a dependent chapelry that lies
Behind yon hill, a poor and rugged wild,
Which in his soul he lovingly embraced,
And, having once espoused, would never
quit; 350
Into its graveyard will ere long be borne
That lowly, great, good Man. A simple
stone
May cover him; and by its help, per-
chance,
A century shall hear his name pro-
nounced,
With images attendant on the sound; 355
Then, shall the slowly-gathering twilight
close
In utter night; and of his course remain
No cognizable vestiges, no more
Than of this breath, which shapes itself
in words
To speak of him, and instantly dissolves.'

The Pastor pressed by thoughts which
round his theme 361
Still linger'd, after a brief pause, resumed;
'Noise is there not enough in doleful war,
But that the heaven-born poet must stand
forth,
And lend the echoes of his sacred shell,
To multiply and aggravate the din? 366
Pangs are there not enough in hopeless
love—
And, in requited passion, all too much
Of turbulence, anxiety, and fear— 369
But that the minstrel of the rural shade
Must tune his pipe, insidiously to nurse
The perturbation in the suffering breast,
And propagate its kind, far as he may?
—Ah who (and with such rapture as befits

The hallowed theme) will rise and cele-
brate　　　　　　　　　　　375
The good man's purposes and deeds;
retrace
His struggles, his discomfitures deplore,
His triumphs hail, and glorify his end;
That virtue, like the fumes and vapoury
clouds
Through fancy's heat redounding in the
brain,　　　　　　　　　　380
And like the soft infections of the heart,
By charm of measured words may spread
o'er field,
Hamlet, and town; and piety survive
Upon the lips of men in hall or bower;
Not for reproof, but high and warm
delight,　　　　　　　　　　385
And grave encouragement, by song in-
spired?
—Vain thought! but wherefore murmur
or repine?
The memory of the just survives in
heaven:
And, without sorrow, will the ground
receive　　　　　　　　　　389
That venerable clay. Meanwhile the best
Of what lies here confines us to degrees
In excellence less difficult to reach,
And milder worth: nor need we travel far
From those to whom our last regards
were paid,
For such example.
　　　　　　　Almost at the root
Of that tall pine, the shadow of whose
bare　　　　　　　　　　396
And slender stem, while here I sit at eve,
Oft stretches toward me, like a long
straight path
Traced faintly in the greensward; there,
beneath
A plain blue stone, a gentle Dalesman
lies,　　　　　　　　　　400
From whom, in early childhood, was
withdrawn
The precious gift of hearing. He grew up
From year to year in loneliness of soul;
And this deep mountain-valley was to him
Soundless, with all its streams. The bird
of dawn　　　　　　　　　　405
Did never rouse this Cottager from sleep
With startling summons; not for his
delight
The vernal cuckoo shouted; not for him
Murmured the labouring bee. When
stormy winds
Were working the broad bosom of the
lake　　　　　　　　　　410
Into a thousand thousand sparkling
waves,
Rocking the trees, or driving cloud on
cloud
Along the sharp edge of yon lofty crags,
The agitated scene before his eye
Was silent as a picture: evermore　　415

Were all things silent, wheresoe'er he
moved.
Yet, by the solace of his own pure
thoughts
Upheld, he duteously pursued the round
Of rural labours; the steep mountain-side
Ascended, with his staff and faithful
dog;　　　　　　　　　　420
The plough he guided, and the scythe he
swayed;
And the ripe corn before his sickle fell
Among the jocund reapers. For himself,
All watchful and industrious as he was.
He wrought not: neither field nor flock
he owned:　　　　　　　　　425
No wish for wealth had place within his
mind;
Nor husband's love, nor father's hope or
care.

'Though born a younger brother, need
was none
That from the floor of his paternal home
He should depart, to plant himself anew.
And when, mature in manhood, he be-
held　　　　　　　　　　431
His parents laid in earth, no loss ensued
Of rights to him; but he remained well
pleased,
By the pure bond of independent love,
An inmate of a second family;　　435
The fellow-labourer and friend of him
To whom the small inheritance had fallen.
—Nor deem that his mild presence was a
weight
That pressed upon his brother's house;
for books
Were ready comrades whom he could not
tire;　　　　　　　　　　440
Of whose society the blameless Man
Was never satiate. Their familiar voice,
Even to old age, with unabated charm
Beguiled his leisure hours; refreshed his
thoughts;
Beyond its natural elevation raised　445
His introverted spirit; and bestowed
Upon his life an outward dignity
Which all acknowledged. The dark
winter night,
The stormy day, each had its own re-
source;
Song of the muses, sage historic tale,　450
Science severe, or word of holy Writ
Announcing immortality and joy
To the assembled spirits of just men
Made perfect, and from injury secure.
—Thus soothed at home, thus busy in the
field,　　　　　　　　　　455
To no perverse suspicion he gave way,
No languor, peevishness, nor vain com-
plaint:
And they, who were about him, did not
fail
In reverence, or in courtesy; they prized

His gentle manners: and his peaceful smiles,   460
The gleams of his slow-varying countenance,
Were met with answering sympathy and love.

'At length, when sixty years and five were told,
A slow disease insensibly consumed
The powers of nature: and a few short steps   465
Of friends and kindred bore him from his home
(Yon cottage shaded by the woody crags)
To the profounder stillness of the grave.
—Nor was his funeral denied the grace
Of many tears, virtuous and thoughtful grief;   470
Heart-sorrow rendered sweet by gratitude.
And now that monumental stone preserves
His name, and unambitiously relates
How long, and by what kindly outward aids,   474
And in what pure contentedness of mind,
The sad privation was by him endured.
—And yon tall pine-tree, whose composing sound
Was wasted on the good Man's living ear,
Hath now its own peculiar sanctity;
And, at the touch of every wandering breeze,   480
Murmurs, not idly, o'er his peaceful grave.

'Soul-cheering Light, most bountiful of things!
Guide of our way, mysterious comforter!
Whose sacred influence, spread through earth and heaven,
We all too thanklessly participate,   485
Thy gifts were utterly withheld from him
Whose place of rest is near yon ivied porch.
Yet, of the wild brooks ask if he complained;
Ask of the channelled rivers if they held
A safer, easier, more determined, course.
What terror doth it strike into the mind
To think of one, blind and alone, advancing   492
Straight toward some precipice's airy brink!
But, timely warned, *He* would have stayed his steps,
Protected, say enlightened, by his ear;
And on the very edge of vacancy   496
Not more endangered than a man whose eye
Beholds the gulf beneath.—No floweret blooms
Throughout the lofty range of these rough hills,
Nor in the woods, that could from him conceal   500

Its birthplace; none whose figure did not live
Upon his touch. The bowels of the earth
Enriched with knowledge his industrious mind;
The ocean paid him tribute from the stores
Lodged in her bosom; and, by science led,   505
His genius mounted to the plains of heaven.
—Methinks I see him—how his eye-balls rolled,
Beneath his ample brow, in darkness paired,—
But each instinct with spirit; and the frame
Of the whole countenance alive with thought,   510
Fancy, and understanding; while the voice
Discoursed of natural or moral truth
With eloquence, and such authentic power,
That, in his presence, humbler knowledge stood
Abashed, and tender pity overawed.'   515

'A noble—and, to unreflecting minds,
A marvellous spectacle,' the Wanderer said,
'Beings like these present! But proof abounds
Upon the earth that faculties, which seem
Extinguished, do not, *therefore*, cease to be.   520
And to the mind among her powers of sense
This transfer is permitted,—not alone
That the bereft their recompense may win;
But for remoter purposes of love   524
And charity; nor last nor least for this,
That to the imagination may be given
A type and shadow of an awful truth;
How, likewise, under sufferance divine,
Darkness is banished from the realms of death,
By man's imperishable spirit, quelled.   530
Unto the men who see not as we see
Futurity was thought, in ancient times,
To be laid open, and they prophesied.
And know we not that from the blind   534
The highest, holiest, raptures of the lyre:
And wisdom married to immortal verse?'

Among the humbler Worthies, at our feet
Lying insensible to human praise,
Love, or regret,—*whose* lineaments would next
Have been portrayed, I guess not; but it chanced   540

That, near the quiet churchyard where we
	sate,
A team of horses, with a ponderous freight
Pressing behind, adown a rugged slope,
Whose sharp descent confounded their
	array,
Came at that moment, ringing noisily. 545

	'Here,' said the Pastor, 'do we muse,
		and mourn
The waste of death; and lo! the giant oak
Stretched on his bier—that massy timber
	wain;
Nor fail to note the Man who guides the
	team.'

He was a peasant of the lowest class:
Grey locks profusely round his temples
	hung	551
In clustering curls, like ivy, which the
	bite
Of winter cannot thin; the fresh air
	lodged
Within his cheek, as light within a cloud;
And he returned our greeting with a
	smile.	555
When he had passed, the Solitary spake;
'A Man he seems of cheerful yesterdays
And confident to-morrows; with a face
Not worldly-minded, for it bears too much
Of Nature's impress,—gaiety and health,
Freedom and hope; but keen, withal, and
	shrewd.	561
His gestures note,—and hark! his tones
	of voice
Are all vivacious as his mien and looks.'

	The Pastor answered, 'You have read
		him well.
Year after year is added to his store	565
With *silent* increase: summers, winters—
	past,
Past or to come; yea, boldly might I say,
Ten summers and ten winters of a space
That lies beyond life's ordinary bounds,
Upon his sprightly vigour cannot fix	570
The obligation of an anxious mind,
A pride in having, or a fear to lose;
Possessed like outskirts of some large
	domain,
By any one more thought of than by him
Who holds the land in fee, its careless
	lord!	575
Yet is the creature rational, endowed
With foresight; hears, too, every sabbath
	day,
The Christian promise with attentive ear;
Nor will, I trust, the Majesty of Heaven
Reject the incense offered up by him,	580
Though of the kind which beasts and
	birds present
In grove or pasture; cheerfulness of soul,
From trepidation and repining free.
How many scrupulous worshippers fall
	down

Upon their knees, and daily homage
	pay	585
Less worthy, less religious even, than his!

'This qualified respect, the old Man's
	due,
Is paid without reluctance; but in truth,'
(Said the good Vicar with a fond half-
	smile)
'I feel at times a motion of despite	590
Towards one, whose bold contrivances
	and skill,
As you have seen, bear such conspicuous
	part
In works of havoc; taking from these
	vales,
One after one, their proudest ornaments.
Full oft his doings leave me to deplore
Tall ash-tree, sown by winds, by vapours
	nursed,	596
In the dry crannies of the pendent rocks;
Light birch, aloft upon the horizon's edge.
A veil of glory for the ascending moon;
And oak whose roots by noontide dew
	were damped,	600
And on whose forehead inaccessible
The raven lodged in safety.—Many a ship
Launched into Morecambe-bay, to *him*
	hath owed
Her strong knee-timbers, and the mast
	that bears
The loftiest of her pendants; He, from
	park	605
Or forest, fetched the enormous axle-tree
That whirls (how slow itself!) ten thou-
	sand spindles:
And the vast engine labouring in the mine,
Content with meaner prowess, must have
	lacked
The trunk and body of its marvellous
	strength,	610
If his undaunted enterprise had failed
Among the mountain coves.
			Yon household fir,
A guardian planted to fence off the blast,
But towering high the roof above, as if
Its humble destination were forgot—	615
That sycamore, which annually holds
Within its shade, as in a stately tent[1]
On all sides open to the fanning breeze,
A grave assemblage, seated while they
	shear
The fleece-encumbered flock—the JOYFUL
	ELM,	620
Around whose trunk the maidens dance
	in May—
And the LORD'S OAK—would plead their
	several rights
In vain, if he were master of their fate;
His sentence to the axe would doom
	them all.
But, green in age and lusty as he is,	625
And promising to keep his hold on earth
---
[1] See Note, p. 733.

Less, as might seem, in rivalship with
    men
Than with the forest's more enduring
    growth,
His own appointed hour will come at
    last;
And, like the haughty Spoilers of the
    world,   630
This keen Destroyer, in his turn, must
    fall.

'Now from the living pass we once
    again:
From Age,' the Priest continued, 'turn
    your thoughts;
From Age, that often unlamented drops,
And mark that daisied hillock, three
    spans long!   635
—Seven lusty Sons sate daily round the
    board
Of Gold-rill side; and, when the hope had
    ceased
Of other progeny, a Daughter then
Was given, the crowning bounty of the
    whole;
And so acknowledged with a tremulous
    joy   640
Felt to the centre of that heavenly calm
With which by nature every mother's soul
Is stricken in the moment when her throes
Are ended, and her ears have heard the
    cry   644
Which tells her that a living child is born;
And she lies conscious, in a blissful rest,
That the dread storm is weathered by
    them both.

'The Father—him at this unlooked-
    for gift
A bolder transport seizes. From the side
Of his bright hearth, and from his open
    door,   650
Day after day the gladness is diffused
To all that come, almost to all that pass;
Invited, summoned, to partake the cheer
Spread on the never-empty board, and
    drink
Health and good wishes to his new-born
    girl,   655
From cups replenished by his joyous
    hand.
—Those seven fair brothers variously were
    moved
Each by the thoughts best suited to his
    years:
But most of all and with most thankful
    mind   659
The hoary grandsire felt himself enriched;
A happiness that ebbed not, but remained
To fill the total measure of his soul!
—From the low tenement, his own abode,
Whither, as to a little private cell,
He had withdrawn from bustle, care, and
    noise,   665

To spend the sabbath of old age in peace,
Once every day he duteously repaired
To rock the cradle of the slumbering babe:
For in that female infant's name he heard
The silent name of his departed wife;
Heart-stirring music! hourly heard that
    name;   671
Full blest he was, "Another Margaret
    Green,"
Oft did he say, "was come to Gold-rill
    side."

'Oh! pang unthought of, as the precious
    boon
Itself had been unlooked-for; oh! dire
    stroke   675
Of desolating anguish for them all!
—Just as the Child could totter on the
    floor,
And, by some friendly finger's help up-
    stayed
Ranged round the garden walk, while she
    perchance
Was catching at some novelty of spring,
Ground-flower, or glossy insect from its
    cell   681
Drawn by the sunshine—at that hopeful
    season
The winds of March, smiting insidiously,
Raised in the tender passage of the throat
Viewless obstruction; whence, all unfore-
    warned,   685
The household lost their pride and soul's
    delight.
—But time hath power to soften all re-
    grets,
And prayer and thought can bring to
    worst distress
Due resignation. Therefore, though some
    tears
Fail not to spring from either Parent's
    eye   690
Oft as they hear of sorrow like their own,
Yet this departed Little-one, too long
The innocent troubler of their quiet, sleeps
In what may now be called a peaceful
    bed.

'On a bright day—so calm and bright,
    it seemed   695
To us, with our sad spirits, heavenly-
    fair—
These mountains echoed to an unknown
    sound;
A volley, thrice repeated o'er the Corse
Let down into the hollow of that grave,
Whose shelving sides are red with naked
    mould.   700
Ye rains of April, duly wet this earth!
Spare, burning sun of midsummer, these
    sods,
That they may knit together, and there-
    with
Our thoughts unite in kindred quietness!

Nor so the Valley shall forget her loss.
Dear Youth, by young and old alike be-
　　loved,　　　　　　　　　　　　706
To me as precious as my own!—Green
　　herbs
May creep (I wish that they would softly
　　creep)
Over thy last abode, and we may pass
Reminded less imperiously of thee;—　710
The ridge itself may sink into the breast
Of earth, the great abyss, and be no more;
Yet shall not thy remembrance leave our
　　hearts,
Thy image disappear!
　　　　　　The Mountain-ash　714
No eye can overlook, when 'mid a grove
Of yet unfaded trees she lifts her head
Decked with autumnal berries, that out-
　　shine
Spring's richest blossoms; and ye may
　　have marked,
By a brook-side or solitary tarn,
How she her station doth adorn: the
　　pool　　　　　　　　　　　　720
Glows at her feet, and all the gloomy
　　rocks
Are brightened round her. In his native
　　vale
Such and so glorious did this Youth
　　appear;
A sight that kindled pleasure in all hearts
By his ingenuous beauty, by the gleam
Of his fair eyes, by his capacious brow,
By all the graces with which nature's hand
Had lavishly arrayed him. As old bards
Tell in their idle songs of wandering gods,
Pan or Apollo, veiled in human form:　730
Yet, like the sweet-breathed violet of the
　　shade,
Discovered in their own despite to sense
Of mortals (if such fables without blame
May find chance-mention on this sacred
　　ground)—
So, through a simple rustic garb's dis-
　　guise,　　　　　　　　　　　　735
And through the impediment of rural
　　cares,
In him revealed a scholar's genius shone;
And so, not wholly hidden from men's
　　sight,
In him the spirit of a hero walked
Our unpretending valley.—How the quoit
Whizzed from the Stripling's arm! If
　　touched by him,　　　　　　　741
The inglorious football mounted to the
　　pitch
Of the lark's flight,—or shaped a rainbow
　　curve,
Aloft, in prospect of the shouting field!
The indefatigable fox had learned　745
To dread his perseverance in the chase.
With admiration would he lift his eyes
To the wide-ruling eagle, and his hand
Was loth to assault the majesty he loved:

Else had the strongest fastnesses proved
　　weak　　　　　　　　　　　　750
To guard the royal brood. The sailing
　　glead,
The wheeling swallow, and the darting
　　snipe,
The sportive sea-gull dancing with the
　　waves,
And cautious water-fowl, from distant
　　climes,
Fixed at their seat, the centre of the
　　Mere,　　　　　　　　　　　　755
Were subject to young Oswald's steady
　　aim,
And lived by his forbearance.
　　　　　　　　　From the coast
Of France a boastful Tyrant hurled his
　　threats;
Our Country marked the preparation vast
Of hostile forces; and she called—with
　　voice　　　　　　　　　　　　760
That filled her plains, that reached her
　　utmost shores,
And in remotest vales was heard—to
　　arms!
—Then, for the first time, here you might
　　have seen
The shepherd's grey to martial scarlet
　　changed,
That flashed uncouthly through the woods
　　and fields.　　　　　　　　　　765
Ten hardy Striplings, all in bright attire,
And graced with shining weapons, weekly
　　marched,
From this lone valley, to a central spot
Where, in assemblage with the flower and
　　choice
Of the surrounding district, they might
　　learn　　　　　　　　　　　　770
The rudiments of war; ten—hardy,
　　strong,
And valiant; but young Oswald, like a
　　chief
And yet a modest comrade, led them forth
From their shy solitude, to face the world,
With a gay confidence and seemly pride;
Measuring the soil beneath their happy
　　feet　　　　　　　　　　　　776
Like Youths released from labour, and
　　yet bound
To most laborious service, though to them
A festival of unencumbered ease;
The inner spirit keeping holiday,　780
Like vernal ground to sabbath sunshine
　　left.

'Oft have I marked him, at some leisure
　　hour,
Stretched on the grass, or seated in the
　　shade,
Among his fellows, while an ample map
Before their eyes lay carefully outspread,
From which the gallant teacher would
　　discourse,　　　　　　　　　　786

Now pointing this way, and now that.
—"Here flows,"
Thus would he say, "the Rhine, that
    famous stream!
Eastward, the Danube toward this inland
    sea,
A mightier river, winds from realm to
    realm;   790
And, like a serpent, shows his glittering
    back
Bespotted—with innumerable isles:
Here reigns the Russian, there the Turk;
    observe
His capital city!" Thence, along a tract
Of livelier interest to his hopes and fears,
His finger moved, distinguishing the
    spots   796
Where wide-spread conflict then most
    fiercely raged;
Nor left unstigmatized those fatal fields
On which the sons of mighty Germany
Were taught a base submission.—"Here
    behold   800
A nobler race, the Switzers, and their land,
Vales deeper far than these of ours, huge
    woods,
And mountains white with everlasting
    snow!"
—And, surely, he, that spake with kind-
    ling brow,
Was a true patriot, hopeful as the best
Of that young peasantry, who, in our
    days,   806
Have fought and perished for Helvetia's
    rights—
Ah, not in vain!—or those who, in old
    time,
For work of happier issue, to the side
Of Tell came trooping from a thousand
    huts,   810
When he had risen alone! No braver
    Youth
Descended from Judean heights, to march
With righteous Joshua; nor appeared in
    arms
When grove was felled, and altar was cast
    down,
And Gideon blew the trumpet, soul-in-
    flamed,   815
And strong in hatred of idolatry.'

    The Pastor, even as if by these last
        words
Raised from his seat within the chosen
    shade,
Moved towards the grave;—instinctively
    his steps
We followed; and my voice with joy
    exclaimed: 820
'Power to the Oppressors of the world
    is given,
A might of which they dream not. Oh!
    the curse,
To be the awakener of divinest thoughts,

Father and founder of exalted deeds;
And, to whole nations bound in servile
    straits,   825
The liberal donor of capacities
More than heroic! this to be, nor yet
Have sense of one connatural wish, nor
    yet
Deserve the least return of human thanks;
Winning no recompense but deadly hate
With pity mixed, astonishment with
    scorn!'   831

    When this involuntary strain had
        ceased,
The Pastor said: 'So Providence is served;
The forkèd weapon of the skies can send
Illumination into deep, dark holds,   835
Which the mild sunbeam hath not power
    to pierce.
Ye Thrones that have defied remorse, and
    cast
Pity away, soon shall ye quake with *fear!*
For, not unconscious of the mighty debt
Which to outrageous wrong the sufferer
    owes,   840
Europe, through all her habitable bounds,
Is thirsting for *their* overthrow, who yet
Survive, as pagan temples stood of yore,
By horror of their impious rites, pre-
    served;
Are still permitted to extend their pride,
Like cedars on the top of Lebanon   846
Darkening the sun.
                    But less impatient thoughts,
And love "all hoping and expecting all,"
This hallowed grave demands, where rests
    in peace
A humble champion of the better cause;
A Peasant-youth, so call him, for he
    asked   851
No higher name; in whom our country
    showed,
As in a favourite son, most beautiful.
In spite of vice, and misery, and disease,
Spread with the spreading of her wealthy
    arts,   855
England, the ancient and the free, ap-
    peared
In him to stand before my swimming
    eyes,
Unconquerably virtuous and secure.
—No more of this, lest I offend his dust:
Short was his life, and a brief tale remains.

    'One day—a summer's day of annual
        pomp   861
And solemn chase—from morn to sultry
    noon
His steps had followed, fleetest of the
    fleet,
The red-deer driven along its native
    heights
With cry of hound and horn; and, from
    that toil   865

Returned with sinews weakened and re-
    laxed,
This generous Youth, too negligent of self,
Plunged—'mid a gay and busy throng
    convened
To wash the fleeces of his Father's flock—
Into the chilling flood. Convulsions dire
Seized him, that self-same night; and
    through the space   871
Of twelve ensuing days his frame was
    wrenched,
Till nature rested from her work in death.
To him, thus snatched away, his com-
    rades paid
A soldier's honours. At his funeral hour
Bright was the sun, the sky a cloudless
    blue—   876
A golden lustre slept upon the hills;
And if by chance a stranger, wandering
    there,
From some commanding eminence had
    looked
Down on this spot, well pleased would
    he have seen   880
A glittering spectacle; but every face
Was pallid: seldom hath that eye been
    moist
With tears, that wept not then; nor were
    the few,
Who from their dwellings came not forth
    to join
In this sad service, less disturbed than
    we.   885
They started at the tributary peal
Of instantaneous thunder, which an-
    nounced,
Through the still air, the closing of the
    Grave;
And distant mountains echoed with a
    sound
Of lamentation, never heard before!'

    The Pastor ceased.—My venerable
    Friend   891
Victoriously upraised his clear bright eye;
And, when that eulogy was ended, stood
Enrapt, as if his inward sense perceived
The prolongation of some still response,
Sent by the ancient Soul of this wide
    land,   896
The Spirit of its mountains and its seas,
Its cities, temples, fields, its awful power,
Its rights and virtues—by that Deity
Descending, and supporting his pure
    heart   900
With patriotic confidence and joy.
And, at the last of those memorial words,
The pining Solitary turned aside;
Whether through manly instinct to con-
    ceal
Tender emotions spreading from the
    heart   905
To his worn cheek; or with uneasy shame
For those cold humours of habitual spleen

That, fondly seeking in dispraise of man
Solace and self-excuse, had sometimes
    urged
To self-abuse a not ineloquent tongue.
—Right toward the sacred Edifice his
    steps   911
Had been directed; and we saw him now
Intent upon a monumental stone,
Whose uncouth form was grafted on the
    wall,
Or rather seemed to have grown into the
    side   915
Of the rude pile; as ofttimes trunks of
    trees,
Where nature works in wild and craggy
    spots,
Are seen incorporate with the living
    rock—
To endure for aye. The Vicar, taking note
Of his employment, with a courteous
    smile   920
Exclaimed—
             'The sagest Antiquarian's eye
That task would foil;' then, letting fall
    his voice
While he advanced, thus spake: 'Tradi-
    tion tells
That, in Eliza's golden days, a Knight
Came on a war-horse sumptuously at-
    tired,   925
And fixed his home in this sequestered
    vale.
'Tis left untold if here he first drew
    breath,
Or as a stranger reached this deep recess,
Unknowing and unknown. A pleasing
    thought
I sometimes entertain, that haply bound
To Scotland's court in service of his
    Queen,   931
Or sent on mission to some northern
    Chief
Of England's realm, this vale he might
    have seen
With transient observation; and thence
    caught
An image fair, which, brightening in his
    soul   935
When joy of war and pride of chivalry
Languished beneath accumulated years,
Had power to draw him from the world,
    resolved
To make that paradise his chosen home
To which his peaceful fancy oft had turned.

    'Vague thoughts are these; but, if belief
    may rest   941
Upon unwritten story fondly traced
From sire to son, in this obscure retreat
The Knight arrived, with spear and shield,
    and borne
Upon a Charger gorgeously bedecked   945
With broidered housings. And the lofty
    Steed—

His sole companion, and his faithful friend,
Whom he, in gratitude, let loose to range
In fertile pastures—was beheld with eyes
Of admiration and delightful awe,   950
By those untravelled Dalesmen. With less pride,
Yet free from touch of envious discontent,
They saw a mansion at his bidding rise,
Like a bright star, amid the lowly band
Of their rude homesteads. Here the Warrior dwelt;   955
And, in that mansion, children of his own,
Or kindred, gathered round him. As a tree
That falls and disappears, the house is gone;
And, through improvidence or want of love
For ancient worth and honourable things,
The spear and shield are vanished, which the Knight   961
Hung in his rustic hall. One ivied arch
Myself have seen, a gateway, last remains
Of that foundation in domestic care
Raised by his hands. And now no trace is left   965
Of the mild-hearted Champion, save this stone,
Faithless memorial! and his family name
Borne by yon clustering cottages, that sprang
From out the ruins of his stately lodge:
These, and the name and title at full length,—   970
$\mathfrak{Sir}$ $\mathfrak{Alfred}$ $\mathfrak{Erthing}$, with appropriate words
Accompanied, still extant, in a wreath
Or posy, girding round the several fronts
Of three clear-sounding and harmonious bells,
That in the steeple hang, his pious gift.'

'So fails, so languishes, grows dim, and dies,'   976
The grey-haired Wanderer pensively exclaimed,
'All that this world is proud of. From their spheres
The stars of human glory are cast down;
Perish the roses and the flowers of kings,[1]
Princes, and emperors, and the crowns and palms   981
Of all the mighty, withered and consumed!
Nor is power given to lowliest innocence
Long to protect her own. The man himself
Departs; and soon is spent the line of those   985
Who, in the bodily image, in the mind,
In heart or soul, in station or pursuit,
      [1] See Note, p. 733.

Did most resemble him. Degrees and ranks,
Fraternities and orders—heaping high
New wealth upon the burthen of the old,
And placing trust in privilege confirmed
And re-confirmed—are scoffed at with a smile
Of greedy foretaste, from the secret stand
Of Desolation, aimed: to slow decline
These yield, and these to sudden overthrow: 995
Their virtue, service, happiness, and state
Expire; and nature's pleasant robe of green,
Humanity's appointed shroud, enwraps
Their monuments and their memory. The vast Frame
Of social nature changes evermore   1000
Her organs and her members, with decay
Restless, and restless generation, powers
And functions dying and produced at need,—
And by this law the mighty whole subsists:
With an ascent and progress in the main;
Yet, oh! how disproportioned to the hopes   1006
And expectations of self-flattering minds!

'The courteous Knight, whose bones are here interred,
Lived in an age conspicuous as our own
For strife and ferment in the minds of men;   1010
Whence alteration in the forms of things,
Various and vast. A memorable age!
Which did to him assign a pensive lot—
To linger 'mid the last of those bright clouds
That, on the steady breeze of honour, sailed   1015
In long procession calm and beautiful.
He who had seen his own bright order fade,
And its devotion gradually decline,
(While war, relinquishing the lance and shield,
Her temper changed, and bowed to other laws)   1020
Had also witnessed, in his morn of life,
That violent commotion, which o'erthrew,
In town and city and sequestered glen,
Altar, and cross, and church of solemn roof,
And old religious house—pile after pile;
And shook their tenants out into the fields,   1026
Like wild beasts without home! Their hour was come;
But why no softening thought of gratitude,
No just remembrance, scruple, or wise doubt?
Benevolence is mild; nor borrows help,

Save at worst need, from bold impetuous
    force,   1031
Fitliest allied to anger and revenge.
But Human-kind rejoices in the might
Of mutability; and airy hopes,
Dancing around her, hinder and disturb
Those meditations of the soul that feed
The retrospective virtues. Festive songs
Break from the maddened nations at the
    sight
Of sudden overthrow; and cold neglect
Is the sure consequence of slow decay.

'Even,' said the Wanderer, 'as that
    courteous Knight,   1041
Bound by his vow to labour for redress
Of all who suffer wrong, and to enact
By sword and lance the law of gentleness,
(If I may venture of myself to speak, 1045

Trusting that not incongruously I blend
Low things with lofty) I too shall be
    doomed
To outlive the kindly use and fair esteem
Of the poor calling which my youth
    embraced
With no unworthy prospect. But enough;
—Thoughts crowd upon me—and 'twere
    seemlier now   1051
To stop, and yield our gracious Teacher
    thanks
For the pathetic records which his voice
Hath here delivered; words of heartfelt
    truth,
Tending to patience when affliction
    strikes;   1055
To hope and love; to confident repose
In God; and reverence for the dust of
    Man.'

BOOK EIGHTH

THE PARSONAGE

ARGUMENT

Pastor's apology and apprehensions that he might have detained his Auditors too long, with the Pastor's invitation to his house.—Solitary disinclined to comply—rallies the Wanderer—and playfully draws a comparison between his itinerant profession and that of the Knight-errant—which leads to Wanderer's giving an account of changes in the Country from the manufacturing spirit.—Favourable effects.—The other side of the picture, and chiefly as it has affected the humbler classes.—Wanderer asserts the hollowness of all national grandeur if unsupported by moral worth.—Physical science unable to support itself.—Lamentations over an excess of manufacturing industry among the humbler Classes of Society.—Picture of a Child employed in a Cotton-mill.—Ignorance and degradation of Children among the agricultural Population reviewed.—Conversation broken off by a renewed Invitation from the Pastor.—Path leading to his House.—Its appearance described.—His Daughter.—His Wife.—His Son (a Boy) enters with his Companion.—Their happy appearance.—The Wanderer how affected by the sight of them.

THE pensive Sceptic of the lonely vale
To those acknowledgments subscribed his
    own,
With a sedate compliance, which the
    Priest
Failed not to notice, inly pleased, and
    said:—
'If ye, by whom invited I began   5
These narratives of calm and humble life,
Be satisfied, 'tis well,—the end is gained;
And in return for sympathy bestowed
And patient listening, thanks accept from
    me.
—Life, death, eternity! momentous
    themes   10
Are they—and might demand a seraph's
    tongue,
Were they not equal to their own support;
And therefore no incompetence of mine
Could do them wrong. The universal
    forms
Of human nature, in a spot like this,   15
Present themselves at once to all men's
    view:

Ye wished for act and circumstance, that
    make
The individual known and understood;
And such as my best judgment could
    select
From what the place afforded, have been
    given;   20
Though apprehensions crossed me that
    my zeal
To his might well be likened, who unlocks
A cabinet stored with gems and pictures—
    draws
His treasures forth, soliciting regard
To this, and this, as worthier than the
    last,   25
Till the spectator, who awhile was pleased
More than the exhibitor himself, becomes
Weary and faint, and longs to be released.
—But let us hence! my dwelling is in sight,
And there—'
                At this the Solitary shrunk   30
With backward will; but, wanting not
    address
That inward motion to disguise, he said

To his Compatriot, smiling as he spake;
—'The peaceable remains of this good
    Knight
Would be disturbed, I fear, with wrathful
    scorn,   35
If consciousness could reach him where
    he lies
That one, albeit of these degenerate times,
Deploring changes past, or dreading
    change
Foreseen, had dared to couple, even in
    thought,
The fine vocation of the sword and lance
With the gross aims and body-bending
    toil   41
Of a poor brotherhood who walk the
    earth
Pitied, and, where they are not known,
    despised.

'Yet, by the good Knight's leave, the
    two estates
Are graced with some resemblance.
    Errant those,   45
Exiles and wanderers—and the like are
    these;
Who, with their burthen, traverse hill
    and dale,
Carrying relief for nature's simple wants.
—What though no higher recompense be
    sought
Than honest maintenance, by irksome
    toil   50
Full oft procured, yet may they claim
    respect,
Among the intelligent, for what this
    course
Enables them to be and to perform.
Their tardy steps give leisure to observe,
While solitude permits the mind to feel;
Instructs, and prompts her to supply
    defects   56
By the division of her inward self
For grateful converse: and to these poor
    men
Nature (I but repeat your favourite boast)
Is bountiful—go wheresoe'er they may;
Kind nature's various wealth is all their
    own.   61
Versed in the characters of men; and
    bound,
By ties of daily interest, to maintain
Conciliatory manners and smooth speech;
Such have been, and still are in their
    degree,   65
Examples efficacious to refine
Rude intercourse; apt agents to expel,
By importation of unlooked-for arts,
Barbarian torpor, and blind prejudice;
Raising, through just gradation, savage
    life   70
To rustic, and the rustic to urbane.
—Within their moving magazines is
    lodged

Power that comes forth to quicken and
    exalt
Affections seated in the mother's breast,
And in the lover's fancy; and to feed   75
The sober sympathies of long-tried friends.
—By these Itinerants, as experienced
    men,
Counsel is given; contention they appease
With gentle language; in remotest wilds,
Tears wipe away, and pleasant tidings
    bring;   80
Could the proud quest of chivalry do
    more?'

'Happy,' rejoined the Wanderer, 'they
    who gain
A panegyric from your generous tongue!
But, if to these Wayfarers once per-
    tained
Aught of romantic interest, it is gone.   85
Their purer service, in this realm at least,
Is past for ever.—An inventive Age
Has wrought, if not with speed of magic,
    yet
To most strange issues. I have lived to
    mark
A new and unforeseen creation rise   90
From out the labours of a peaceful Land
Wielding her potent enginery to frame
And to produce, with appetite as keen
As that of war, which rests not night or
    day,
Industrious to destroy! With fruitless
    pains   95
Might one like me *now* visit many a tract
Which, in his youth, he trod, and trod
    again,
A lone pedestrian with a scanty freight,
Wished-for, or welcome, wheresoe'er he
    came—
Among the tenantry of thorpe and vill;
Or straggling burgh, of ancient charter
    proud,   101
And dignified by battlements and towers
Of some stern castle, mouldering on the
    brow
Of a green hill or bank of rugged stream.
The foot-path faintly marked, the horse-
    track wild,   105
And formidable length of plashy lane,
(Prized avenues ere others had been
    shaped
Or easier links connecting place with
    place)
Have vanished—swallowed up by stately
    roads
Easy and bold, that penetrate the gloom
Of Britain's farthest glens. The Earth
    has lent   111
Her waters, Air her breezes;[1] and the sail
Of traffic glides with ceaseless intercourse,
Glistening along the low and woody dale;
Or, in its progress, on the lofty side 115

[1] See Note, p. 733.

Of some bare hill, with wonder kenned
   from far.

'Meanwhile, at social Industry's com-
   mand,
How quick, how vast an increase! From
   the germ
Of some poor hamlet, rapidly produced
Here a huge town, continuous and com-
   pact,   120
Hiding the face of earth for leagues—and
   there,
Where not a habitation stood before,
Abodes of men irregularly massed
Like trees in forests,—spread through
   spacious tracts,
O'er which the smoke of unremitting fires
Hangs permanent, and plentiful as
   wreaths   126
Of vapour glittering in the morning sun.
And, wheresoe'er the traveller turns his
   steps,
He sees the barren wilderness erased,
Or disappearing; triumph that proclaims
How much the mild Directress of the
   plough   131
Owes to alliance with these new-born
   arts!
—Hence is the wide sea peopled,—hence
   the shores
Of Britain are resorted to by ships
Freighted from every climate of the
   world   135
With the world's choicest produce. Hence
   that sum
Of keels that rest within her crowded
   ports,
Or ride at anchor in her sounds and bays;
That animating spectacle of sails
That, through her inland regions, to and
   fro   140
Pass with the respirations of the tide,
Perpetual, multitudinous! Finally,
Hence a dread arm of floating power, a
   voice
Of thunder daunting those who would
   approach
With hostile purposes the blessèd Isle, 145
Truth's consecrated residence, the seat
Impregnable of Liberty and Peace.

'And yet, O happy Pastor of a flock
Faithfully watched, and, by that loving
   care
And Heaven's good providence, preserved
   from taint!   150
With you I grieve, when on the darker side
Of this great change I look; and there
   behold
Such outrage done to nature as compels
The indignant power to justify herself;
Yea, to avenge her violated rights,   155
For England's bane.—When soothing
   darkness spreads

O'er hill and vale,' the Wanderer thus
   expressed
His recollections, 'and the punctual
   stars,
While all things else are gathering to
   their homes,   159
Advance, and in the firmament of heaven
Glitter—but undisturbing, undisturbed;
As if their silent company were charged
With peaceful admonitions for the heart
Of all-beholding Man, earth's thoughtful
   lord;
Then, in full many a region, once like
   this   165
The assured domain of calm simplicity
And pensive quiet, an unnatural light
Prepared for never-resting Labour's eyes
Breaks from a many-windowed fabric
   huge;   169
And at the appointed hour a bell is heard,
Of harsher import than the curfew-knoll
That spake the Norman Conqueror's stern
   behest—
A local summons to unceasing toil!
Disgorged are now the ministers of day;
And, as they issue from the illumined
   pile,   175
A fresh band meets them, at the crowded
   door—
And in the courts—and where the rum-
   bling stream,
That turns the multitude of dizzy wheels,
Glares, like a troubled spirit, in its bed
Among the rocks below. Men, maidens,
   youths,   180
Mother and little children, boys and girls,
Enter, and each the wonted task resumes
Within this temple, where is offered up
To Gain, the master-idol of the realm,
Perpetual sacrifice. Even thus of old 185
Our ancestors, within the still domain
Of vast cathedral or conventual church,
Their vigils kept; where tapers day and
   night
On the dim altar burned continually,
In token that the House was evermore
Watching to God. Religious men were
   they;   191
Nor would their reason, tutored to aspire
Above this transitory world, allow
That there should pass a moment of the
   year,
When in their land the Almighty's service
   ceased.   195

'Triumph who will in these profaner
   rites
Which we, a generation self-extolled,
As zealously perform! I cannot share
His proud complacency:—yet do I exult,
Casting reserve away, exult to see   200
An intellectual mastery exercised
O'er the blind elements; a purpose given,
A perseverance fed; almost a soul

683

Imparted—to brute matter. I rejoice,
Measuring the force of those gigantic
powers   205
That, by the thinking mind, have been
compelled
To serve the will of feeble-bodied Man.
For with the sense of admiration blends
The animating hope that time may come
When, strengthened, yet not dazzled, by
the might   210
Of this dominion over nature gained,
Men of all lands shall exercise the same
In due proportion to their country's need;
Learning, though late, that all true glory
rests,   214
All praise, all safety, and all happiness,
Upon the moral law. Egyptian Thebes,
Tyre, by the margin of the sounding
waves,
Palmyra, central in the desert, fell;
And the Arts died by which they had
been raised.   219
—Call Archimedes from his buried tomb
Upon the grave of vanished Syracuse,
And feelingly the Sage shall make report
How insecure, how baseless in itself,
Is the Philosophy whose sway depends
On mere material instruments;—how
weak   225
Those arts, and high inventions, if un-
propped
By virtue.—He, sighing with pensive
grief,
Amid his calm abstractions, would admit
That not the slender privilege is theirs
To save themselves from blank forgetful-
ness!'   230

When from the Wanderer's lips these
words had fallen,
I said, 'And, did in truth those vaunted
Arts
Possess such privilege, how could we
escape
Sadness and keen regret, we who revere,
And would preserve as things above all
price,   235
The old domestic morals of the land,
Her simple manners, and the stable worth
That dignified and cheered a low estate?
Oh! where is now the character of peace,
Sobriety, and order, and chaste love, 240
And honest dealing, and untainted speech,
And pure good-will, and hospitable cheer;
That made the very thought of country-
life
A thought of refuge, for a mind detained
Reluctantly amid the bustling crowd? 245
Where now the beauty of the sabbath kept
With conscientious reverence, as a day
By the almighty Lawgiver pronounced
Holy and blest? and where the winning
grace
Of all the lighter ornaments attached

To time and season, as the year rolled
round?'   251

'Fled!' was the Wanderer's passion-
ate response,
'Fled utterly! or only to be traced
In a few fortunate retreats like this;
Which I behold with trembling, when I
think   255
What lamentable change, a year—a
month—
May bring; that brook converting as it
runs
Into an instrument of deadly bane
For those, who, yet untempted to forsake
The simple occupations of their sires, 260
Drink the pure water of its innocent
stream
With lip almost as pure.—Domestic bliss
(Or call it comfort, by a humbler name,)
How art thou blighted for the poor Man's
heart!
Lo! in such neighbourhood, from morn
to eve,   265
The habitations empty! or perchance
The Mother left alone,—no helping hand
To rock the cradle of her peevish babe;
No daughters round her, busy at the
wheel,   269
Or in dispatch of each day's little growth
Of household occupation; no nice arts
Of needle-work; no bustle at the fire,
Where once the dinner was prepared with
pride;
Nothing to speed the day, or cheer the
mind;
Nothing to praise, to teach, or to com-
mand!   275

'The Father, if perchance he still retain
His old employments, goes to field or
wood,
No longer led or followed by the Sons;
Idlers perchance they were,—but in his
sight;
Breathing fresh air, and treading the green
earth;   280
Till their short holiday of childhood
ceased,
Ne'er to return! That birthright now is
lost.
Economists will tell you that the State
Thrives by the forfeiture—unfeeling
thought,
And false as monstrous! Can the mother
thrive   285
By the destruction of her innocent sons
In whom a premature necessity
Blocks out the forms of nature, precon-
sumes
The reason, famishes the heart, shuts up
The infant Being in itself, and makes
Its very spring a season of decay!   291
The lot is wretched, the condition sad,

Whether a pining discontent survive,
And thirst for change; or habit hath sub-
  dued   294
The soul deprest, dejected—even to love
Of her close tasks, and long captivity.

'Oh, banish far such wisdom as con-
  demns
A native Briton to these inward chains,
Fixed in his soul, so early and so deep;
Without his own consent, or knowledge,
  fixed!   300
He is a slave to whom release comes
  not,
And cannot come. The boy, where'er he
  turns,
Is still a prisoner; when the wind is up
Among the clouds, and roars through the
  ancient woods;
Or when the sun is shining in the east,
Quiet and calm. Behold him—in the
  school   306
Of his attainments? no; but with the air
Fanning his temples under heaven's blue
  arch.
His raiment, whitened o'er with cotton-
  flakes
Or locks of wool, announces whence he
  comes.   310
Creeping his gait and cowering, his lip
  pale,
His respiration quick and audible;
And scarcely could you fancy that a
  gleam
Could break from out those languid eyes,
  or a blush
Mantle upon his cheek. Is this the form,
Is that the countenance, and such the
  port,   316
Of no mean Being? One who should be
  clothed
With dignity befitting his proud hope;
Who, in his very childhood, should ap-
  pear
Sublime from present purity and joy! 320
The limbs increase; but liberty of mind
Is gone for ever; and this organic frame,
So joyful in its motions, is become
Dull, to the joy of her own motions dead;
And even the touch, so exquisitely poured
Through the whole body, with a languid
  will   326
Performs its functions; rarely competent
To impress a vivid feeling on the mind
Of what there is delightful in the breeze,
The gentle visitations of the sun,   330
Or lapse of liquid element—by hand,
Or foot, or lip, in summer's warmth—per-
  ceived,
—Can hope look forward to a manhood
  raised
On such foundations?'
                    'Hope is none for him!'
The pale Recluse indignantly exclaimed,

'And tens of thousands suffer wrong as
  deep.   336
Yet be it asked, in justice to our age,
If there were not, before those arts ap-
  peared,
These structures rose, commingling old
  and young,
And unripe sex with sex, for mutual
  taint;   340
If there were not, *then*, in our far-famed
  Isle,
Multitudes, who from infancy had
  breathed
Air unimprisoned, and had lived at large;
Yet walked beneath the sun, in human
  shape,
As abject, as degraded? At this day, 345
Who shall enumerate the crazy huts
And tottering hovels, whence do issue
  forth
A ragged Offspring, with their upright
  hair
Crowned like the image of fantastic Fear;
Or wearing, (shall we say?) in that white
  growth   350
An ill-adjusted turban, for defence
Or fierceness, wreathed around their sun-
  burnt brows,
By savage Nature? Shrivelled are their
  lips;
Naked, and coloured like the soil, the
  feet
On which they stand; as if thereby they
  drew   355
Some nourishment, as trees do by their
  roots,
From earth, the common mother of us all.
Figure and mien, complexion and attire,
Are leagued to strike dismay; but out-
  stretched hand
And whining voice denote them suppli-
  cants   360
For the least boon that pity can bestow.
Such on the breast of darksome heaths
  are found;
And with their parents occupy the skirts
Of furze-clad commons; such are born
  and reared
At the mine's mouth under impending
  rocks;   365
Or dwell in chambers of some natural
  cave;
Or where their ancestors erected huts,
For the convenience of unlawful gain,
In forest purlieus; and the like are bred,
All England through, where nooks and
  slips of ground   370
Purloined, in times less jealous than our
  own,
From the green margin of the public way,
A residence afford them, 'mid the bloom
And gaiety of cultivated fields.   374
Such (we will hope the lowest in the scale)
Do I remember ofttimes to have seen

'Mid Buxton's dreary heights. In earnest watch,
Till the swift vehicle approach, they stand;
Then, following closely with the cloud of dust, 379
An uncouth feat exhibit, and are gone
Heels over head, like tumblers on a stage.
—Up from the ground they snatch the copper coin,
And, on the freight of merry passengers
Fixing a steady eye, maintain their speed;
And spin—and pant—and overhead again, 385
Wild pursuivants! until their breath is lost,
Or bounty tires—and every face, that smiled
Encouragement, hath ceased to look that way.
—But, like the vagrants of the gipsy tribe,
These, bred to little pleasure in themselves, 390
Are profitless to others.

           Turn we then
To Britons born and bred within the pale
Of civil polity, and early trained
To earn, by wholesome labour in the field,
The bread they eat. A sample should I give 395
Of what this stock hath long produced to enrich
The tender age of life, ye would exclaim,
"Is this the whistling plough-boy whose shrill notes
Impart new gladness to the morning air!"
Forgive me if I venture to suspect 400
That many, sweet to hear of in soft verse,
Are of no finer frame. Stiff are his joints;
Beneath a cumbrous frock, that to the knees
Invests the thriving churl, his legs appear,
Fellows to those that lustily upheld 405
The wooden stools for everlasting use,
Whereon our fathers sate. And mark his brow!
Under whose shaggy canopy are set
Two eyes—not dim, but of a healthy stare—
Wide, sluggish, blank, and ignorant, and strange— 410
Proclaiming boldly that they never drew
A look or motion of intelligence
From infant-conning of the Christ-cross-row,
Or puzzling through a primer, line by line,
Till perfect mastery crown the pains at last. 415
—What kindly warmth from touch of fostering hand,
What penetrating power of sun or breeze,
Shall e'er dissolve the crust wherein his soul
Sleeps, like a caterpillar sheathed in ice?
This torpor is no pitiable work 420
Of modern ingenuity; no town
Nor crowded city can be taxed with aught
Of sottish vice or desperate breach of law,
To which (and who can tell where or how soon?)
He may be roused. This Boy the fields produce: 425
His spade and hoe, mattock and glittering scythe,
The carter's whip that on his shoulder rests
In air high-towering with a boorish pomp,
The sceptre of his sway; his country's name,
Her equal rights, her churches and her schools— 430
What have they done for him? And, let me ask,
For tens of thousands uninformed as he?
In brief, what liberty of *mind* is here?'

    This ardent sally pleased the mild good Man,
To whom the appeal couched in its closing words 435
Was pointedly addressed; and to the thoughts
That, in assent or opposition, rose
Within his mind, he seemed prepared to give
Prompt utterance; but the Vicar interposed
With invitation urgently renewed. 440
—We followed, taking as he led, a path
Along a hedge of hollies dark and tall,
Whose flexile boughs low bending with a weight
Of leafy spray, concealed the stems and roots
That gave them nourishment. When frosty winds 445
Howl from the north, what kindly warmth, methought,
Is here—how grateful this impervious screen!
—Not shaped by simple wearing of the foot
On rural business passing to and fro
Was the commodious walk: a careful hand 450
Had marked the line, and strewn its surface o'er
With pure cerulean gravel, from the heights
Fetched by a neighbouring brook.—
Across the vale
The stately fence accompanied our steps;
And thus the pathway, by perennial green 455
Guarded and graced, seemed fashioned to unite,
As by a beautiful yet solemn chain,
The Pastor's mansion with the house of prayer.

Like image of solemnity, conjoined
With feminine allurement soft and fair,
The mansion's self displayed;—a reverend
   pile   461
With bold projections and recesses deep;
Shadowy, yet gay and lightsome as it
   stood
Fronting the noontide sun. We paused
   to admire
The pillared porch, elaborately embossed;
The low wide windows with their mul-
   lions old;   466
The cornice, richly fretted, of grey stone;
And that smooth slope from which the
   dwelling rose,
By beds and banks Arcadian of gay
   flowers
And flowering shrubs, protected and
   adorned: 470
Profusion bright! and every flower as-
   suming
A more than natural vividness of hue
From unaffected contrast with the gloom
Of sober cypress, and the darker foil
Of yew, in which survived some traces,
   here   475
Not unbecoming, of grotesque device
And uncouth fancy. From behind the
   roof
Rose the slim ash and massy sycamore,
Blending their diverse foliage with the
   green
Of ivy, flourishing and thick, that clasped
The huge round chimneys, harbour of
   delight   481
For wren and redbreast,—where they sit
   and sing
Their slender ditties when the trees are
   bare.
Nor must I leave untouched (the picture
   else
Were incomplete) a relique of old times
Happily spared, a little Gothic niche
Of nicest workmanship; that once had
   held
The sculptured image of some patron-
   saint,
Or of the blessèd Virgin, looking down
On all who entered those religious doors.

But lo! where from the rocky garden-
   mount   491
Crowned by its antique summer-house—
   descends,
Light as the silver fawn, a radiant Girl;
For she hath recognised her honoured
   friend,
The Wanderer ever welcome! A prompt
   kiss   495
The gladsome child bestows at his re-
   quest;
And, up the flowery lawn as we advance,
Hangs on the old Man with a happy look,
And with a pretty restless hand of love.

—We enter—by the Lady of the place
Cordially greeted. Graceful was her port:
A lofty stature undepressed by time,
Whose visitation had not wholly spared
The finer lineaments of form and face;
To that complexion brought which pru-
   dence trusts in   505
And wisdom loves.—But when a stately
   ship
Sails in smooth weather by the placid
   coast
On homeward voyage,—what if wind and
   wave,
And hardship undergone in various
   climes,
Have caused her to abate the virgin
   pride,   510
And that full trim of inexperienced hope
With which she left her haven—not for
   this,
Should the sun strike her, and the im-
   partial breeze
Play on her streamers, fails she to assume
Brightness and touching beauty of her
   own,   515
That charm all eyes. So bright, so fair,
   appeared
This goodly Matron, shining in the beams
Of unexpected pleasure.—Soon the board
Was spread, and we partook a plain re-
   past.   519

Here, resting in cool shelter, we beguiled
The mid-day hours with desultory talk;
From trivial themes to general argument
Passing, as accident or fancy led,
Or courtesy prescribed. While question
   rose   524
And answer flowed, the fetters of reserve
Dropping from every mind, the Solitary
Resumed the manners of his happier
   days;
And in the various conversation bore
A willing, nay, at times, a forward part;
Yet with the grace of one who in the
   world   530
Had learned the art of pleasing, and had
   now
Occasion given him to display his skill,
Upon the steadfast 'vantage-ground of
   truth.
He gazed, with admiration unsuppressed,
Upon the landscape of the sun-bright
   vale,   535
Seen, from the shady room in which we
   sate,
In softened pérspective; and more than
   once
Praised the consummate harmony serene
Of gravity and elegance, diffused
Around the mansion and its whole
   domain;   540
Not, doubtless, without help of female
   taste

And female care.—'A blessed lot is
yours!'
The words escaped his lip, with a tender
sigh
Breathed over them: but suddenly the
door
Flew open, and a pair of lusty Boys   545
Appeared, confusion checking their de-
light.
—Not brothers they in feature or attire,
But fond companions, so I guessed, in
field,
And by the river's margin—whence they
come,   549
Keen anglers with unusual spoil elated.
One bears a willow-pannier on his back,
The boy of plainer garb, whose blush
survives
More deeply tinged. Twin might the
other be
To that fair girl who from the garden-
mount
Bounded:—triumphant entry this for
him!   555
Between his hands he holds a smooth
blue stone,
On whose capacious surface see out-
spread
Large store of gleaming crimson-spotted
trouts;
Ranged side by side, and lessening by
degrees
Up to the dwarf that tops the pinnacle.
Upon the board he lays the sky-blue
stone   561
With its rich freight; their number he
proclaims;
Tells from what pool the noblest had
been dragged;
And where the very monarch of the brook,
After long struggle, had escaped at last—
Stealing alternately at them and us   566
(As doth his comrade too) a look of pride:
And, verily, the silent creatures made
A splendid sight, together thus exposed;
Dead—but not sullied or deformed by
death,   570
That seemed to pity what he could not
spare.

But O, the animation in the mien
Of those two boys! yea in the very words
With which the young narrator was in-
spired,
When, as our questions led, he told at
large   575
Of that day's prowess! Him might I com-
pare,
His looks, tones, gestures, eager elo-
quence,
To a bold brook that splits for better
speed,
And at the self-same moment, works its
way
Through many channels, ever and anon
Parted and re-united: his compeer   581
To the still lake, whose stillness is to sight
As beautiful—as grateful to the mind.
—But to what object shall the lovely Girl
Be likened? She whose countenance and
air   585
Unite the graceful qualities of both,
Even as she shares the pride and joy of
both.

My grey-haired Friend was moved; his
vivid eye
Glistened with tenderness; his mind, I
knew,
Was full; and had, I doubted not, re-
turned,   590
Upon this impulse, to the theme—ere-
while
Abruptly broken off. The ruddy boys
Withdrew, on summons to their well-
earned meal;
And He—to whom all tongues resigned
their rights
With willingness, to whom the general
ear   595
Listened with readier patience than to
strain
Of music, lute or harp, a long delight
That ceased not when his voice had
ceased—as One
Who from truth's central point serenely
views   599
The compass of his argument—began
Mildly, and with a clear and steady tone.

BOOK NINTH

DISCOURSE OF THE WANDERER, AND AN EVENING VISIT TO THE LAKE

ARGUMENT

Wanderer asserts that an active principle pervades the Universe, its noblest seat the human soul.—How lively this principle is in Childhood.—Hence the delight in old Age of looking back upon Childhood.—The dignity, powers, and privileges of Age asserted.—These not to be looked for generally but under a just government.—Right of a human Creature to be exempt from being considered as a mere Instrument.—The condition of multitudes deplored.—Former conversation recurred to, and the Wanderer's opinions set in a clearer light.—Truth placed within reach of the humblest.—Equality.—Happy state of the two Boys again adverted to.—Earnest wish expressed for a System of National Education established universally by Government.—Glorious effects of this foretold.—Walk to the Lake.—Grand spectacle from the side of a hill.—Address of Priest to the Supreme Being—in the course of which he contrasts with ancient Barbarism the present appearance of the scene before him. —The change ascribed to Christianity.—Apostrophe to his flock, living and dead.—Gratitude to the Almighty.—Return over the Lake.—Parting with the Solitary.—Under what circumstances.

'To every Form of being is assigned,'
Thus calmly spake the venerable Sage,
'An *active* Principle:—howe'er removed
From sense and observation, it subsists
In all things, in all natures; in the stars 5
Of azure heaven, the unenduring clouds,
In flower and tree, in every pebbly stone
That paves the brooks, the stationary rocks,
The moving waters, and the invisible air.
Whate'er exists hath properties that spread 10
Beyond itself, communicating good,
A simple blessing, or with evil mixed;
Spirit that knows no insulated spot,
No chasm, no solitude; from link to link
It circulates, the Soul of all the worlds. 15
This is the freedom of the universe;
Unfolded still the more, more visible,
The more we know; and yet is reverenced least,
And least respected in the human Mind,
Its most apparent home. The food of hope 20
Is meditated action; robbed of this
Her sole support, she languishes and dies.
We perish also; for we live by hope
And by desire; we see by the glad light
And breathe the sweet air of futurity; 25
And so we live, or else we have no life.
To-morrow—nay perchance this very hour
(For every moment hath its own to-morrow!)
Those blooming Boys, whose hearts are almost sick
With present triumph, will be sure to find 30
A field before them freshened with the dew
Of other expectations;—in which course
Their happy year spins round. The youth obeys

A like glad impulse; and so moves the man
'Mid all his apprehensions, cares, and fears,— 35
Or so he ought to move. Ah! why in age
Do we revert so fondly to the walks
Of childhood—but that there the Soul discerns
The dear memorial footsteps unimpaired
Of her own native vigour; thence can hear 40
Reverberations; and a choral song,
Commingling with the incense that ascends,
Undaunted, toward the imperishable heavens,
From her own lonely altar?
                                Do not think
That good and wise ever will be allowed, 45
Though strength decay, to breathe in such estate
As shall divide them wholly from the stir
Of hopeful nature. Rightly it is said
That Man descends into the VALE of years;
Yet have I thought that we might also speak, 50
And not presumptuously, I trust, of Age,
As of a final EMINENCE; though bare
In aspect and forbidding, yet a point
On which 'tis not impossible to sit
In awful sovereignty; a place of power, 55
A throne, that may be likened unto his,
Who, in some placid day of summer, looks
Down from a mountain-top, —say one of those
High peaks, that bound the vale where now we are. 59
Faint, and diminished to the gazing eye,
Forest and field, and hill and dale appear,
With all the shapes over their surface spread:

689

But, while the gross and visible frame of
    things
Relinquishes its hold upon the sense,
Yea almost on the Mind herself, and
    seems   65
All unsubstantialized,—how loud the
    voice
Of waters, with invigorated peal
From the full river in the vale below,
Ascending! For on that superior height
Who sits, is disencumbered from the press
Of near obstructions, and is privileged 71
To breathe in solitude, above the host
Of ever-humming insects, 'mid thin air
That suits not them. The murmur of the
    leaves
Many and idle, visits not his ear: 75
This he is freed from, and from thousand
    notes
(Not less unceasing, not less vain than
    these,)
By which the finer passages of sense
Are occupied; and the Soul, that would
    incline
To listen, is prevented or deterred.   80

'And may it not be hoped, that, placed
    by age
In like removal, tranquil though severe,
We are not so removed for utter loss;
But for some favour, suited to our need?
What more than that the severing should
    confer   85
Fresh power to commune with the in-
    visible world,
And hear the mighty stream of tendency
Uttering, for elevation of our thought,
A clear sonorous voice, inaudible   89
To the vast multitude; whose doom it is
To run the giddy round of vain delight,
Or fret and labour on the Plain below.

'But, if to such sublime ascent the
    hopes
Of Man may rise, as to a welcome close
And termination of his mortal course;   95
Them only can such hope inspire whose
    minds   .
Have not been starved by absolute neglect;
Nor bodies crushed by unremitting toil;
To whom kind Nature, therefore, may
    afford
Proof of the sacred love she bears for all;
Whose birthright Reason, therefore, may
    ensure.   101
For me, consulting what I feel within
In times when most existence with her-
    self
Is satisfied, I cannot but believe,
That, far as kindly Nature hath free
    scope   105
And Reason's sway predominates; even
    so far,
Country, society, and time itself,

That saps the individual's bodily frame,
And lays the generations low in dust,
Do, by the almighty Ruler's grace, par-
    take   110
Of one maternal spirit, bringing forth
And cherishing with ever-constant love,
That tires not, nor betrays. Our life is
    turned
Out of her course, wherever man is made
An offering, or a sacrifice, a tool   115
Or implement, a passive thing employed
As a brute mean, without acknowledg-
    ment
Of common right or interest in the end;
Used or abused, as selfishness may prompt.
Say, what can follow for a rational soul
Perverted thus, but weakness in all good,
And strength in evil? Hence an after-
    call
For chastisement, and custody, and
    bonds,
And ofttimes Death, avenger of the past,
And the sole guardian in whose hands we
    dare   125
Entrust the future.—Not for these sad
    issues
Was Man created; but to obey the law
Of life, and hope, and action. And 'tis
    known
That when we stand upon our native soil,
Unelbowed by such objects as oppress
Our active powers, those powers them-
    selves become   131
Strong to subvert our noxious qualities:
They sweep distemper from the busy day,
And make the chalice of the big round
    year
Run o'er with gladness; whence the Be-
    ing moves   135
In beauty through the world; and all
    who see
Bless him, rejoicing in his neighbour-
    hood.'

'Then,' said the Solitary, 'by what
    force
Of language shall a feeling heart express
Her sorrow for that multitude in whom
We look for health from seeds that have
    been sown   141
In sickness, and for increase in a power
That works but by extinction? On them-
    selves
They cannot lean, nor turn to their own
    hearts
To know what they must do; their wis-
    dom is   145
To look into the eyes of others, thence
To be instructed what they must avoid:
Or rather, let us say, how least observed,
How with most quiet and most silent
    death,
With the least taint and injury to the
    air   150

The oppressor breathes, their human form
    divine,
And their immortal soul, may waste
    away.'

    The Sage rejoined, 'I thank you—you
    have spared
My voice the utterance of a keen regret,
A wide compassion which with you I
    share.   155
When, heretofore, I placed before your
    sight
A Little-one, subjected to the arts
Of modern ingenuity, and made
The senseless member of a vast machine,
Serving as doth a spindle or a wheel; 160
Think not, that, pitying him, I could
    forget
The rustic Boy, who walks the fields,
    untaught;
The slave of ignorance, and oft of want,
And miserable hunger. Much, too much,
Of this unhappy lot, in early youth   165
We both have witnessed, lot which I my-
    self
Shared, though in mild and merciful
    degree:
Yet was the mind to hinderances exposed,
Through which I struggled, not without
    distress
And sometimes injury, like a lamb en-
    thralled   170
'Mid thorns and brambles; or a bird that
    breaks
Through a strong net, and mounts upon
    the wind,
Though with her plumes impaired. If
    they, whose souls
Should open while they range the richer
    fields   174
Of merry England, are obstructed less
By indigence, their ignorance is not less,
Nor less to be deplored. For who can doubt
That tens of thousands at this day exist
Such as the boy you painted, lineal heirs
Of those who once were vassals of her
    soil,   180
Following its fortunes like the beasts or
    trees
Which it sustained. But no one takes
    delight
In this oppression; none are proud of it;
It bears no sounding name, nor ever bore;
A standing grievance, an indigenous vice
Of every country under heaven. My
    thoughts   186
Were turned to evils that are new and
    chosen,
A bondage lurking under shape of good,—
Arts, in themselves beneficent and kind,
But all too fondly followed and too far;—
To victims, which the merciful can see
Nor think that they are victims—turned
    to wrongs,   192

By women, who have children of their
    own,
Beheld without compassion, yea, with
    praise!
I spake of mischief by the wise diffused
With gladness, thinking that the more it
    spreads   196
The healthier, the securer, we become;
Delusion which a moment may destroy!
Lastly I mourned for those whom I had
    seen
Corrupted and cast down, on favoured
    ground,   200
Where circumstance and nature had com-
    bined
To shelter innocence, and cherish love;
Who, but for this intrusion, would have
    lived,
Possessed of health, and strength, and
    peace of mind;
Thus would have lived, or never have
    been born.   205

    'Alas! what differs more than man
    from man!
And whence that difference? Whence but
    from himself?
For see the universal Race endowed
With the same upright form! The sun is
    fixed,   209
And the infinite magnificence of heaven
Fixed, within reach of every human
    eye;
The sleepless ocean murmurs for all ears;
The vernal field infuses fresh delight
Into all hearts. Throughout the world of
    sense,
Even as an object is sublime or fair,   215
That object is laid open to the view
Without reserve or veil; and as a power
Is salutary, or an influence sweet,
Are each and all enabled to perceive
That power, that influence, by impartial
    law.   220
Gifts nobler are vouchsafed alike to all;
Reason, and, with that reason, smiles and
    tears;
Imagination, freedom in the will;
Conscience to guide and check; and death
    to be
Foretasted, immortality conceived   225
By all,—a blissful immortality,
To them whose holiness on earth shall
    make
The Spirit capable of heaven, assured.
Strange, then, nor less than monstrous,
    might be deemed
The failure, if the Almighty, to this
    point   230
Liberal and undistinguishing, should hide
The excellence of moral qualities
From common understanding; leaving
    truth
And virtue, difficult, abstruse, and dark;

Hard to be won, and only by a few; 235
Strange, should He deal herein with nice
    respects,
And frustrate all the rest! Believe it not:
The primal duties shine aloft—like stars;
The charities that soothe, and heal, and
    bless,
Are scattered at the feet of Man—like
    flowers.   240
The generous inclination, the just rule,
Kind wishes, and good actions, and pure
    thoughts—
No mystery is here! Here is no boon
For high—yet not for low; for proudly
    graced—
Yet not for meek of heart. The smoke
    ascends   245
To heaven as lightly from the cottage-
    hearth
As from the haughtiest palace. He, whose
    soul
Ponders this true equality, may walk
The fields of earth with gratitude and
    hope;
Yet, in that meditation, will he find   250
Motive to sadder grief, as we have found;
Lamenting ancient virtues overthrown,
And for the injustice grieving, that hath
    made
So wide a difference between man and
    man.

'Then let us rather fix our gladdened
    thoughts   255
Upon the brighter scene. How blest that
    pair
Of blooming Boys (whom we beheld even
    now)
Blest in their several and their common
    lot!
A few short hours of each returning day
The thriving prisoners of their village-
    school: 260
And thence let loose, to seek their
    pleasant homes
Or range the grassy lawn in vacancy;
To breathe and to be happy, run and
    shout
Idle,—but no delay, no harm, no loss;
For every genial power of heaven and
    earth,   265
Through all the seasons of the changeful
    year,
Obsequiously doth take upon herself
To labour for them; bringing each in turn
The tribute of enjoyment, knowledge,
    health,
Beauty, or strength! Such privilege is
    theirs,   270
Granted alike in the outset of their course
To both; and, if that partnership must
    cease,
I grieve not,' to the Pastor here he
    turned,

'Much as I glory in that child of yours,
Repine not for his cottage-comrade,
    whom   275
Belike no higher destiny awaits
Than the old hereditary wish fulfilled;
The wish for liberty to live—content
With what Heaven grants, and die—in
    peace of mind,
Within the bosom of his native vale. 280
At least, whatever fate the noon of life
Reserves for either, sure it is that both
Have been permitted to enjoy the dawn;
Whether regarded as a jocund time,
That in itself may terminate, or lead 285
In course of nature to a sober eve.
Both have been fairly dealt with; looking
    back
They will allow that justice has in them
Been shown, alike to body and to mind.'
    He paused, as if revolving in his soul
Some weighty matter; then, with fervent
    voice   291
And an impassioned majesty, exclaimed—

'O for the coming of that glorious time
When, prizing knowledge as her noblest
    wealth   294
And best protection, this imperial Realm,
While she exacts allegiance, shall admit
An obligation, on her part, to *teach*
Them who are born to serve her and obey;
Binding herself by statute to secure[1]
For all the children whom her soil
    maintains   300
The rudiments of letters, and inform
The mind with moral and religious truth,
Both understood and practised,—so that
    none,
However destitute, be left to droop
By timely culture unsustained; or run 305
Into a wild disorder; or be forced
To drudge through a weary life without
    the help
Of intellectual implements and tools;
A savage horde among the civilised,
A servile band among the lordly free! 310
This sacred right, the lisping babe pro-
    claims
To be inherent in him, by Heaven's will,
For the protection of his innocence;
And the rude boy—who, having overpast
The sinless age, by conscience is enrolled,
Yet mutinously knits his angry brow,
And lifts his wilful hand on mischief bent,
Or turns the godlike faculty of speech
To impious use—by process indirect
Declares his due, while he makes known
    his need.   320
—This sacred right is fruitlessly an-
    nounced,
This universal plea in vain addressed,
To eyes and ears of parents who them-
    selves

See Note, p. 733.

Did, in the time of their necessity,
Urge it in vain; and, therefore, like a
    prayer   325
That from the humblest floor ascends to
    heaven,
It mounts to reach the State's parental
    ear;
Who, if indeed she own a mother's heart,
And be not most unfeelingly devoid
Of gratitude to Providence, will grant 330
The unquestionable good—which, Eng-
    land, safe
From interference of external force,
May grant at leisure; without risk in-
    curred
That what in wisdom for herself she doth,
Others shall e'er be able to undo.   335

    'Look! and behold, from Calpe's sun-
        burnt cliffs
To the flat margin of the Baltic sea,
Long-reverenced titles cast away as weeds;
Laws overturned; and territory split,
Like fields of ice rent by the polar wind,
And forced to join in less obnoxious
    shapes   341
Which, ere they gain consistence, by a gust
Of the same breath are shattered and
    destroyed.
Meantime the sovereignty of these fair
    Isles
Remains entire and indivisible: 345
And, if that ignorance were removed,
    which breeds
Within the compass of their several shores
Dark discontent, or loud commotion, each
Might still preserve the beautiful repose
Of heavenly bodies shining in their
    spheres.   350
—The discipline of slavery is unknown
Among us,—hence the more do we re-
    quire
The discipline of virtue; order else
Cannot subsist, nor confidence, nor peace.
Thus, duties rising out of good possest 355
And prudent caution needful to avert
Impending evil, equally require
That the whole people should be taught
    and trained.
So shall licentiousness and black resolve
Be rooted out, and virtuous habits take
Their place; and genuine piety descend,
Like an inheritance, from age to age. 362

    'With such foundations laid, avaunt
        the fear
Of numbers crowded on their native soil,
To the prevention of all healthful growth
Through mutual injury! Rather in the
    law   366
Of increase and the mandate from above
Rejoice!—and ye have special cause for
    joy.
—For, as the element of air affords

An easy passage to the industrious bees
Fraught with their burthens; and a way
    as smooth   371
For those ordained to take their sounding
    flight
From the thronged hive, and settle where
    they list
In fresh abodes—their labour to renew;
So the wide waters, open to the power,
The will, the instincts, and appointed
    needs   376
Of Britain, do invite her to cast off
Her swarms, and in succession send them
    forth;
Bound to establish new communities
On every shore whose aspect favours
    hope   380
Or bold adventure; promising to skill
And perseverance their deserved reward.

    'Yes,' he continued, kindling as he
        spake,
'Change wide, and deep, and silently
    performed,
This Land shall witness; and as days roll
    on,   385
Earth's universal frame shall feel the
    effect;
Even till the smallest habitable rock,
Beaten by lonely billows, hear the songs
Of humanised society; and bloom
With civil arts, that shall breathe forth
    their fragrance,   390
A grateful tribute to all-ruling Heaven.
From culture, unexclusively bestowed
On Albion's noble Race in freedom born,
Expect these mighty issues: from the
    pains   394
And faithful care of unambitious schools
Instructing simple childhood's ready ear:
Thence look for these magnificent results!
—Vast the circumference of hope—and ye
Are at its centre, British Lawgivers;
Ah! sleep not there in shame! Shall Wis-
    dom's voice   400
From out the bosom of these troubled
    times
Repeat the dictates of her calmer mind,
And shall the venerable halls ye fill
Refuse to echo the sublime decree?
Trust not to partial care a general good;
Transfer not to futurity a work   406
Of urgent need.—Your Country must
    complete
Her glorious destiny. Begin even now,
Now, when oppression, like the Egyptian
    plague
Of darkness, stretched o'er guilty Europe,
    makes   410
The brightness more conspicuous that in-
    vests
The happy Island where ye think and act;
Now, when destruction is a prime pur-
    suit,

Show to the wretched nations for what
  end   414
The powers of civil polity were given.'

  Abruptly here, but with a graceful air,
The Sage broke off. No sooner had he
  ceased
Than, looking forth, the gentle Lady said,
'Behold the shades of afternoon have
  fallen
Upon this flowery slope; and see—be-
  yond—   420
The silvery lake is streaked with placid
  blue;
As if preparing for the peace of evening.
How temptingly the landscape shines!
  The air
Breathes invitation; easy is the walk
To the lake's margin, where a boat lies
  moored   425
Under a sheltering tree.'—Upon this hint
We rose together: all were pleased; but
  most
The beauteous girl, whose cheek was
  flushed with joy.
Light as a sunbeam glides along the hills
She vanished—eager to impart the scheme
To her loved brother and his shy com-
  peer.   431
—Now was there bustle in the Vicar's
  house
And earnest preparation.—Forth we went,
And down the vale along the streamlet's
  edge
Pursued our way, a broken company,   435
Mute or conversing, single or in pairs.
Thus having reached a bridge, that over-
  arched
The hasty rivulet where it lay becalmed
In a deep pool, by happy chance we saw
A twofold image; on a grassy bank   440
A snow-white ram, and in the crystal
  flood
Another and the same! Most beautiful,
On the green turf, with his imperial front
Shaggy and bold, and wreathèd horns
  superb,
The breathing creature stood; as beauti-
  ful,   445
Beneath him, showed his shadowy coun-
  terpart.
Each had his glowing mountains, each
  his sky,
And each seemed centre of his own fair
  world:
Antipodes unconscious of each other,
Yet, in partition, with their several
  spheres,   450
Blended in perfect stillness, to our sight!

  'Ah! what a pity were it to disperse,
Or to disturb, so fair a spectacle,
And yet a breath can do it!'
                        These few words

The Lady whispered, while we stood and
  gazed   455
Gathered together, all in still delight,
Not without awe. Thence passing on, she
  said
In like low voice to my particular ear,
'I love to hear that eloquent old Man
Pour forth his meditations, and descant
On human life from infancy to age.   461
How pure his spirit! in what vivid hues
His mind gives back the various forms
  of things,
Caught in their fairest, happiest, atti-
  tude!
While he is speaking, I have power to
  see   465
Even as he sees; but when his voice hath
  ceased,
Then, with a sigh, sometimes I feel, as
  now,
That combinations so serene and bright
Cannot be lasting in a world like ours,
Whose highest beauty, beautiful as it is,
Like that reflected in yon quiet pool,
Seems but a fleeting sunbeam's gift, whose
  peace   472
The sufferance only of a breath of air!'
    More had she said—but sportive shouts
  were heard
Sent from the jocund hearts of those two
  Boys,   475
Who, bearing each a basket on his arm,
Down the green field came tripping after
  us.
With caution we embarked; and now the
  pair
For prouder service were addrest; but
  each,
Wishful to leave an opening for my
  choice,   480
Dropped the light oar his eager hand had
  seized.
Thanks given for that becoming courtesy,
Their place I took—and for a grateful
  office
Pregnant with recollections of the time
When, on thy bosom, spacious Winder-
  mere!   485
A Youth, I practised this delightful art;
Tossed on the waves alone, or 'mid a
  crew
Of joyous comrades. Soon as the reedy
  marge
Was cleared, I dipped, with arms ac-
  cordant, oars
Free from obstruction; and the boat ad-
  vanced   490
Through crystal water, smoothly as a
  hawk,
That, disentangled from the shady boughs
Of some thick wood, her place of covert,
  cleaves
With correspondent wings the abyss of
  air.

—'Observe,' the Vicar said, 'yon rocky
 isle   495
With birch-trees fringed; my hand shall
 guide the helm,
While thitherward we shape our course;
 or while
We seek that other, on the western shore;
Where the bare columns of those lofty
 firs,
Supporting gracefully a massy dome 500
Of sombre foliage, seem to imitate
A Grecian temple rising from the Deep.'

'Turn where we may,' said I, 'we
 cannot err
In this delicious region.'—Cultured slopes,
Wild tracts of forest-ground, and scat-
 tered groves,   505
And mountains bare, or clothed with
 ancient woods,
Surrounded us; and, as we held our way
Along the level of the glassy flood,
They ceased not to surround us; change
 of place,
From kindred features diversely com-
 bined,   510
Producing change of beauty ever new.
—Ah! that such beauty, varying in the light
Of living nature, cannot be portrayed
By words, nor by the pencil's silent skill;
But is the property of him alone 515
Who hath beheld it, noted it with care,
And in his mind recorded it with love!
Suffice it, therefore, if the rural Muse
Vouchsafe sweet influence, while her
 Poet speaks
Of trivial occupations well devised, 520
And unsought pleasures springing up by
 chance;
As if some friendly Genius had ordained
That, as the day thus far had been en-
 riched
By acquisition of sincere delight,
The same should be continued to its
 close.   525

One spirit animating old and young,
A gipsy-fire we kindled on the shore
Of the fair Isle with birch-trees fringed—
 and there,
Merrily seated in a ring, partook
A choice repast—served by our young
 companions   530
With rival earnestness and kindred glee.
Launched from our hands the smooth
 stone skimmed the lake;
With shouts we raised the echoes;—
 stiller sounds
The lovely Girl supplied—a simple song,
Whose low tones reached not to the
 distant rocks   535
To be repeated thence, but gently sank
Into our hearts; and charmed the peace-
 ful flood.

Rapaciously we gathered flowery spoils
From land and water; lilies of each hue—
Golden and white, that float upon the
 waves,   540
And court the wind; and leaves of that
 shy plant,
(Her flowers were shed) the lily of the vale,
That loves the ground, and from the sun
 withholds
Her pensive beauty; from the breeze her
 sweets.

Such product, and such pastime, did
 the place   545
And season yield; but, as we re-embarked,
Leaving, in quest of other scenes, the
 shore
Of that wild spot, the Solitary said
In a low voice, yet careless who might
 hear,
'The fire, that burned so brightly to our
 wish,   550
Where is it now?—Deserted on the
 beach—
Dying, or dead! Nor shall the fanning
 breeze
Revive its ashes. What care we for this,
Whose ends are gained? Behold an
 emblem here
Of one day's pleasure, and all mortal
 joys!   555
And, in this unpremeditated slight
Of that which is no longer needed, see
The common course of human gratitude!'

This plaintive note disturbed not the
 repose
Of the still evening. Right across the lake
Our pinnace moves; then, coasting creek
 and bay,   561
Glades we behold, and into thickets peep,
Where couch the spotted deer; or raised
 our eyes
To shaggy steeps on which the careless
 goat
Browsed by the side of dashing water-
 falls;   565
And thus the bark, meandering with the
 shore,
Pursued her voyage, till a natural pier
Of jutting rock invited us to land.

Alert to follow as the Pastor led,
We clomb a green hill's side; and, as we
 clomb,   570
The Valley, opening out her bosom, gave
Fair prospect, intercepted less and less,
O'er the flat meadows and indented coast
Of the smooth lake, in compass seen:—
 far off,
And yet conspicuous, stood the old
 Church-tower,   575
In majesty presiding over fields
And habitations seemingly preserved

From all intrusion of the restless world
By rocks impassable and mountains huge.

Soft heath this elevated spot supplied,
And choice of moss-clad stones, whereon
  we couched   581
Or sate reclined; admiring quietly
The general aspect of the scene; but each
Not seldom over anxious to make known
His own discoveries; or to favourite
  points   585
Directing notice, merely from a wish
To impart a joy, imperfect while un-
  shared.
That rapturous moment never shall I
  forget
When these particular interests were
  effaced
From every mind!—Already had the
  sun,   590
Sinking with less than ordinary state,
Attained his western bound; but rays of
  light—
Now suddenly diverging from the orb
Retired behind the mountain-tops or
  veiled
By the dense air—shot upwards to the
  crown   595
Of the blue firmament—aloft, and wide:
And multitudes of little floating clouds,
Through their ethereal texture pierced—
  ere we,
Who saw, of change were conscious—had
  become
Vivid as fire; clouds separately poised,—
Innumerable multitude of forms   601
Scattered through half the circle of the
  sky;
And giving back, and shedding each on
  each,
With prodigal communion, the bright
  hues
Which from the unapparent fount of
  glory   605
They had imbibed, and ceased not to
  receive.
That which the heavens displayed, the
  liquid deep
Repeated; but with unity sublime!

While from the grassy mountain's open
  side
We gazed, in silence hushed, with eyes
  intent   610
On the refulgent spectacle, diffused
Through earth, sky, water, and all visible
  space,
The Priest in holy transport thus exclaimed:

'Eternal Spirit! universal God!
Power inaccessible to human thought,
Save by degrees and steps which thou hast
  deigned   616
To furnish; for this effluence of thyself,

To the infirmity of mortal sense
Vouchsafed; this local transitory type
Of thy paternal splendours, and the
  pomp   620
Of those who fill thy courts in highest
  heaven,
The radiant Cherubim;—accept the
  thanks
Which we, thy humble Creatures, here
  convened,
Presume to offer; we, who—from the
  breast   624
Of the frail earth, permitted to behold
The faint reflections only of thy face—
Are yet exalted, and in soul adore!
Such as they are who in thy presence
  stand
Unsullied, incorruptible, and drink
Imperishable majesty streamed forth 630
From thy empyreal throne, the elect of
  earth
Shall be—divested at the appointed hour
Of all dishonour, cleansed from mortal
  stain.
—Accomplish, then, their number; and
  conclude
Time's weary course! Or, if, by thy decree,
The consummation that will come by
  stealth   636
Be yet far distant, let thy Word prevail,
Oh! let thy Word prevail, to take away
The sting of human nature. Spread the
  law,
As it is written in thy holy book,   640
Throughout all lands: let every nation
  hear
The high behest, and every heart obey;
Both for the love of purity, and hope
Which it affords, to such as do thy will
And persevere in good, that they shall
  rise,   645
To have a nearer view of thee, in heaven.
—Father of good! this prayer in bounty
  grant,
In mercy grant it, to thy wretched sons.
Then, nor till then, shall persecution
  cease,
And cruel wars expire. The way is
  marked,   650
The guide appointed, and the ransom
  paid.
Alas! the nations, who of yore received
These tidings, and in Christian temples
  meet
The sacred truth to acknowledge, linger
  still;
Preferring bonds and darkness to a state
Of holy freedom, by redeeming love 656
Proffered to all, while yet on earth de-
  tained.

'So fare the many; and the thoughtful
  few,
Who in the anguish of their souls bewail

This dire perverseness, cannot choose but
　　ask,　　　　　　　　　　660
Shall it endure?—Shall enmity and
　　strife,
Falsehood and guile, be left to sow their
　　seed;
And the kind never perish? Is the hope
Fallacious, or shall righteousness obtain
A peaceable dominion, wide as earth, 665
And ne'er to fail? Shall that blest day
　　arrive
When they, whose choice or lot it is to
　　dwell
In crowded cities, without fear shall live
Studious of mutual benefit; and he,
Whom Morn awakens, among dews and
　　flowers　　　　　　　　　670
Of every clime, to till the lonely field,
Be happy in himself?—The law of faith
Working through love, such conquest
　　shall it gain,
Such triumph over sin and guilt achieve?
Almighty Lord, thy further grace im-
　　part!　　　　　　　　　675
And with that help the wonder shall be
　　seen
Fulfilled, the hope accomplished; and thy
　　praise
Be sung with transport and unceasing joy.

'Once,' and with wild demeanour, as
　　he spake,
On us the venerable Pastor turned　680
His beaming eye that had been raised to
　　Heaven,
'Once, while the Name, Jehovah, was a
　　sound
Within the circuit of this sea-girt isle
Unheard, the savage nations bowed the
　　head
To Gods delighting in remorseless deeds;
Gods which themselves had fashioned, to
　　promote　　　　　　　　686
Ill purposes, and flatter foul desires.
Then, in the bosom of yon mountain-cove,
To those inventions of corrupted man
Mysterious rites were solemnised; and
　　there—　　　　　　　　690
Amid impending rocks and gloomy
　　woods—
Of those terrific Idols some received
Such dismal service, that the loudest voice
Of the swoln cataracts (which now are
　　heard
Soft murmuring) was too weak to over-
　　come,　　　　　　　　　695
Though aided by wild winds, the groans
　　and shrieks
Of human victims, offered up to appease
Or to propitiate. And, if living eyes
Had visionary faculties to see
The thing that hath been as the thing
　　that is,　　　　　　　　700
Aghast we might behold this crystal Mere

Bedimmed with smoke, in wreaths volu-
　　minous,
Flung from the body of devouring fires,
To Taranis erected on the heights
By priestly hands, for sacrifice performed
Exultingly, in view of open day　　706
And full assemblage of a barbarous host;
Or to Andates, female Power! who gave
(For so they fancied) glorious victory.
—A few rude monuments of mountain-
　　stone　　　　　　　　　710
Survive; all else is swept away.—How
　　bright
The appearances of things! From such,
　　how changed
The existing worship; and with those
　　compared,
The worshippers how innocent and blest!
So wide the difference, a willing mind　715
Might almost think, at this affecting hour,
That paradise, the lost abode of man,
Was raised again: and to a happy few,
In its original beauty, here restored.

'Whence but from thee, the true and
　　only God,　　　　　　　720
And from the faith derived through Him
　　who bled
Upon the cross, this marvellous advance
Of good from evil; as if one extreme
Were left, the other gained.—O ye, who
　　come　　　　　　　　　724
To kneel devoutly in yon reverend Pile,
Called to such office by the peaceful sound
Of sabbath bells; and ye, who sleep in
　　earth,
All cares forgotten, round its hallowed
　　walls!
For you, in presence of this little band
Gathered together on the green hill-side,
Your Pastor is emboldened to prefer　731
Vocal thanksgivings to the eternal King;
Whose love, whose counsel, whose com-
　　mands, have made
Your very poorest rich in peace of thought
And in good works; and him, who is
　　endowed　　　　　　　735
With scantiest knowledge, master of all
　　truth
Which the salvation of his soul requires.
Conscious of that abundant favour show-
　　ered
On you, the children of my humble care,
And this dear land, our country, while on
　　earth　　　　　　　　　740
We sojourn, have I lifted up my soul,
Joy giving voice to fervent gratitude.
These barren rocks, your stern inheritance;
These fertile fields, that recompense your
　　pains;
The shadowy vale, the sunny mountain-
　　top;　　　　　　　　　745
Woods waving in the wind their lofty
　　heads,

Or hushed; the roaring waters, and the still—
They see the offering of my lifted hands,
They hear my lips present their sacrifice,
They know if I be silent, morn or even:
For, though in whispers speaking, the full heart   751
Will find a vent; and thought is praise to him,
Audible praise, to thee, omniscient Mind,
From whom all gifts descend, all blessings flow!'

This vesper-service closed, without delay,   755
From that exalted station to the plain
Descending, we pursued our homeward course,
In mute composure, o'er the shadowy lake,
Under a faded sky. No trace remained
Of those celestial splendours; grey the vault—   760
Pure, cloudless, ether; and the star of eve
Was wanting; but inferior lights appeared
Faintly, too faint almost for sight; and some
Above the darkened hills stood boldly forth
In twinkling lustre, ere the boat attained
Her mooring-place; where, to the sheltering tree,   766
Our youthful Voyagers bound fast her prow,
With prompt yet careful hands. This done, we paced
The dewy fields; but ere the Vicar's door
Was reached, the Solitary checked his steps;   770

Then, intermingling thanks, on each bestowed
A farewell salutation; and, the like
Receiving, took the slender path that leads
To the one cottage in the lonely dell:
But turned not without welcome promise made   775
That he would share the pleasures and pursuits
Of yet another summer's day, not loth
To wander with us through the fertile vales,
And o'er the mountain-wastes. 'Another sun,'
Said he, 'shall shine upon us, ere we part;   780
Another sun, and peradventure more;
If time, with free consent, be yours to give,
And season favours.'
              To enfeebled Power,
From this communion with uninjured Minds,
What renovation had been brought; and what   785
Degree of healing to a wounded spirit,
Dejected, and habitually disposed
To seek, in degradation of the Kind,
Excuse and solace for her own defects;
How far those erring notions were reformed;   790
And whether aught, of tendency as good
And pure, from further intercourse ensued;
This—if delightful hopes, as heretofore,
Inspire the serious song, and gentle Hearts
Cherish, and lofty Minds approve the past—   795
My future labours may not leave untold.

NOTES

'If thou indeed derive thy light' (Inscription following title-page). Written (earliest draft) some time after 1813; first printed (amongst *Poems of Sentiment and Reflection*) in ed. 1827. Expanded (1836), and placed in its present position in ed. 1845.—ED.

GUILT AND SORROW
Page 18.

Thirty stanzas (xxii–xxxiv, and xxxviii–l) of *Guilt and Sorrow* were printed in the *Lyrical Ballads* of 1798, under the title of *The Female Vagrant*. This poem of 1798—much altered from time to time, and ultimately cut down to twenty-five stanzas—appeared in successive edd. of the Poetical Works from 1815 to 1843. The whole, as it now stands, was first printed in the vol. entitled *Poems, Chiefly of Early and Late Years* (1842). 'Beside the changes made in these stanzas by Wordsworth from the point of view of poetic art, there are others the object of which seems to be to moderate the force of his indictment of society' (Dowden).—ED.

Page 20, l. 81.

'And, hovering, round it often did a raven fly.' From a short MS. poem read to me when an undergraduate, by my schoolfellow and friend, Charles Farish, long since deceased. The verses were by a brother of his, a man of promising genius, who died young.—W.

THE BORDERERS
Page 29.

This Dramatic Piece, as noticed in its title-page, was composed in 1795–6. It lay nearly from that time till within the last two or three months unregarded among my papers, without being mentioned even to my most intimate friends. Having, however, impressions upon my mind which made me unwilling to destroy the MS., I determined to undertake the responsibility of publishing it during my own life, rather than impose upon my successors the task of deciding its fate. Accordingly it has been revised with some care; but, as it was at first written, and is now published, without any view to its exhibition upon the stage, not the slightest alteration has been made in the conduct of the story, or the composition of the characters; above all, in respect to the two leading Persons of the Drama, I felt no inducement to make any change. The study of human nature suggests this awful truth, that, as in the trials to which life subjects us, sin and crime are apt to start from their very opposite qualities, so are there no limits to the hardening of the heart, and the perversion of the understanding to which they may carry their slaves. During my long residence in France, while the revolution was rapidly advancing to its extreme of wickedness, I had frequent opportunities of being an eye-witness of this process, and it was while that knowledge was fresh upon my memory, that the Tragedy of 'The Borderers' was composed. —W.

TO A BUTTERFLY
Page 62.

The following pseudonyms occur in Wordsworth's poems:—*Emmeline, Emma* = Dorothy, the poet's sister; *Laura* = Dora, his daughter; Edward, in the *Anecdote for Fathers* (p. 67) = little Basil Montagu, in his sister's *Address to a Child* (p. 63) = Johnnie, the poet's eldest son. It had been noted that each of these poetic substitutes, except Emma, is the exact metrical equivalent of the name for which it stands, and it is just possible, though not likely, that Emma may have been used as = Dolly, the name by which Dorothy was sometimes called in her youth. But there is no evidence that the poet ever so called her, and it is more probable that the equivalences were accidental. Anyhow, to argue from them that the Louisa of *I met Louisa in the shade* must be intended for Joanna Hutchinson is quite unjustifiable. This poem, like several if not all of the poems on Lucy, was inspired in part, if not wholly, by his sister Dorothy. It is worth noting, perhaps, that whilst Wordsworth refers to his wife Mary, to his daughter Dora (except in one place where she appears as Laura), and to Sara Hutchinson by their names, the name Dorothy is nowhere found in his poetry.

THE MOTHER'S RETURN
Page 64.

This poem was written by Dorothy Wordsworth at Coleorton, on the eve of the return of Wordsworth and his wife from London where they had spent a month (prob. April) in 1807.—ED.

THE NORMAN BOY
Page 72.

'Among ancient Trees there are few, I believe, at least in France, so worthy of attention as an Oak which may be seen in the "Pays de Caux," about a league from Yvetot, close to the church, and in the burial-ground of Allonville.

'The height of this Tree does not answer to its girth; the trunk, from the roots to the summit, forms a complete cone; and the inside of this cone is hollow throughout the whole of its height.

'Such is the oak of Allonville, in its state of nature. The hand of Man, however, has endeavoured to impress upon it a character still more interesting, by adding a religious feeling to the respect which its age naturally inspires.

'The lower part of its hollow trunk has been transformed into a Chapel of six or seven feet in diameter, carefully wainscotted and paved, and an open iron gate guards the humble Sanctuary.

'Leading to it there is a staircase, which twists round the body of the Tree. At certain seasons of the year divine service is performed in this Chapel.

'The summit has been broken off many years, but there is a surface at the top of the trunk, of the diameter of a very large tree, and from it rises a pointed roof, covered with slates, in the form of a steeple, which is surmounted with an iron Cross, that rises in a picturesque manner from the middle of the leaves, like an ancient Hermitage above the surrounding Wood.

'Over the entrance to the Chapel an Inscription appears, which informs us it was erected by the Abbé du Détroit, Curate of Allonville in the year 1696; and over a door is another, dedicating it "To Our Lady of Peace."'

Vide No. 14, Saturday Magazine.—W.

NOTES

TO ——
Page 87.

No doubt addressed to the Poet's daughter Dora. See *The Longest Day*, stanza xvi.—ED.

THE EMIGRANT MOTHER
Page 95.

This poem was written in the orchard, Townend, Grasmere, in the spring of 1802.—ED.

TO THE DAISY
Page 124.

This poem, and two others to the same flower, were written in the year 1802; which is mentioned, because in some of the ideas, though not in the manner in which those ideas are connected, and likewise even in some of the expressions, there is a resemblance to passages in a poem (lately published) of Mr. Montgomery's, entitled 'A Field Flower.' This being said, Mr. Montgomery will not think any apology due to him; I cannot, however, help addressing him in the words of the Father of English Poets:

> 'Though it happe me to rehersin
> That ye han in your freshe songis saied,
> Forberith me, and beth not ill apaied,
> Sith that ye se I doe it in the honour
> Of Love, and eke in service of the Flour.'
> 1807.—W.

THE SEVEN SISTERS
Page 127.

The story of this poem is from the German of Frederica Brun [*flor.* 1765–1835.—ED.].—W.

THE DANISH BOY
Page 131.

'These stanzas were designed to introduce a Ballad upon the Story of a Danish Prince who had fled from Battle, and, for the sake of the valuables about him, was murdered by the Inhabitant of a Cottage in which he had taken refuge. The House fell under a curse, and the Spirit of the Youth, it was believed, haunted the Valley where the crime had been committed.'—W. 1827.

THE WAGGONER
Page 137.

Several years after the event that forms the subject of the poem, in company with my friend, the late Mr. Coleridge, I happened to fall in with the person to whom the name of Benjamin is given. Upon our expressing regret that we had not, for a long time, seen upon the road either him or his waggon, he said:—'They could not do without me; and as to the man who was put in my place, no good could come out of him; he was a man of no *ideas*.'

The fact of my discarded hero's getting the horses out of a great difficulty with a word, as related in the poem, was told me by an eye-witness.—W.

Page 137, l. 3.

'The buzzing dor-hawk, round and round, is wheeling.' When the poem was first written the note of the bird was thus described:

> 'The Night-hawk is singing his frog-like tune,
> Twirling his watchman's rattle about—'

but from unwillingness to startle the reader at the outset by so bold a mode of expression, the passage was altered as it now stands.—W.

After the line, '*Can any mortal clog come to her,*' (p. 138, l. 28) followed in the MS. an incident which has been kept back. Part of the suppressed verses shall here be given as a gratification of private feeling, which the well-disposed reader will find no difficulty in excusing. They are now printed for the first time.

> Can any mortal clog come to her?
> It can: . . .
>
> . . . .
>
> But Benjamin, in his vexation,
> Possesses inward consolation;
> He knows his ground, and hopes to find
> A spot with all things to his mind,
> An upright mural block of stone,
> Moist with pure water trickling down.
> A slender spring; but kind to man
> It is, a true Samaritan;
> Close to the highway, pouring out
> Its offering from a chink or spout;
> Whence all, howe'er athirst, or drooping
> With toil, may drink, and without stooping.
>
> Cries Benjamin 'Where is it, where?
> Voice it hath none, but must be near.'
> —A star, declining towards the west,
> Upon the watery surface threw
> Its image tremulously imprest,
> That just marked out the object and withdrew
> Right welcome service! . . .
>
> . . . . . .
>
> ROCK OF NAMES![1]
> Light is the strain, but not unjust
> To Thee and Thy memorial-trust
> That once seemed only to express
> Love that was love in idleness;
> Tokens, as year hath followed year
> How changed, alas, in character!
> For they were graven on thy smooth breast
> By hands of those my soul loved best;
> Meek women, men as true and brave
> As ever went to a hopeful grave:
> Their hands and mine, when side by side
> With kindred zeal and mutual pride,
> We worked until the Initials took
> Shapes that defied a scornful look.—
> Long as for us a genial feeling
> Survives, or one in need of healing,
> The power, dear Rock, around thee cast,
> Thy monumental power, shall last
> For me and mine! O thought of pain,
> That would impair it or profane!
> Take all in kindness then, as said
> With a staid heart but playful head;
> And fail not Thou, loved Rock! to keep
> Thy charge when we are laid asleep.—W.

Page 148.

'She was a Phantom of delight.' '*She was a Phantom of delight,* he [Wordsworth] said, was written "on his dear wife".' (Hon. Justice Coleridge in *Memoirs of Wordsworth*, ii. 306.) —ED.

Page 148.

'O Nightingale! thou surely art.' Written probably at Coleorton, in Nov. or Dec., 1806.—ED.

[1] The 'Rock of Names' is at Thirlmere, 'on the right hand of the road a short way past Waterhead.' Upon it were carved the initials of William, Dorothy and John Wordsworth, of S. T. Coleridge, and of Mary and Sarah Hutchinson.—ED.

NOTES

RESOLUTION AND INDEPENDENCE
Page 155.

W. wrote as follows to some friends who had received a copy of *Resolution and Independence* in manuscript:—'I will explain to you in prose my feelings in writing *that* poem. . . . I describe myself as having been exalted to the highest pitch of delight by the joyousness and beauty of nature; and then as depressed, even in the midst of those beautiful objects, to the lowest dejection and despair. A young poet in the midst of the happiness of nature is described as overwhelmed by the thoughts of the miserable reverses which have befallen the happiest of all men, *viz.* poets. I think of this till I am so deeply impressed with it, that I consider the manner in which I was rescued from my dejection and despair almost as an interposition of Providence. A person reading the poem with feelings like mine will have been awed and controlled, expecting something spiritual or supernatural. What is brought forward? A lonely place, "a pond by which an old man *was*, far from all house or home:" not *stood*, nor *sat*, but *was*—the figure presented in the most naked simplicity possible. This feeling of spirituality or supernaturalness is again referred to as being strong in my mind in this passage. How came he here? thought I, or what can he be doing? I then describe him, whether ill or well is not for me to judge with perfect confidence; but this I can confidently affirm, that though I believe God has given me a strong imagination, I cannot conceive a figure more impressive than that of an old man like this, the survivor of a wife and ten children, travelling alone among the mountains and all lonely places, carrying with him his own fortitude, and the necessities which an unjust state of society has laid upon him.'—*Memoirs of Wordsworth,* i. 172, 173.

THE THORN
Page 157.

This Poem ought to have been preceded by an introductory Poem, which I have been prevented from writing by never having felt myself in a mood when it was probable that I should write it well. The character which I have here introduced speaking is sufficiently common. The Reader will perhaps have a general notion of it, if he has ever known a man, a captain of a small trading vessel, for example, who being past the middle age of life, had retired upon an annuity or small independent income to some village or country town of which he was not a native, or in which he had not been accustomed to live. Such men, having little to do, become credulous and talkative from indolence; and from the same cause, and other predisposing causes by which it is probable that such men may have been affected, they are prone to superstition. On which account it appeared to me proper to select a character like this to exhibit some of the general laws by which superstition acts upon the mind. Superstitious men are almost always men of slow faculties and deep feelings; their minds are not loose, but adhesive; they have a reasonable share of imagination, by which word I mean the faculty which produces impressive effects out of simple elements; but they are utterly destitute of fancy, the power by which pleasure and surprise are excited by sudden varieties of situation and by accumulated imagery.

It was my wish in this poem to show the manner in which such men cleave to the same ideas; and to follow the turns of passion, always different, yet not palpably different, by which their conversation is swayed. I had two objects to attain; first, to represent a picture which should not be unimpressive, yet consistent with the character that should describe it; secondly, while I adhered to the style in which such persons describe, to take care that words, which in their minds are impregnated with passion, should likewise convey passion to Readers who are not accustomed to sympathize with men feeling in that manner or using such language. It seemed to me that this might be done by calling in the assistance of Lyrical and rapid Metre. It was necessary that the Poem, to be natural, should in reality move slowly; yet I hoped that, by the aid of the metre, to those who should at all enter into the spirit of the Poem, it would appear to move quickly. The Reader will have the kindness to excuse this note, as I am sensible that an introductory Poem is necessary to give the Poem its full effect.

Upon this occasion I will request permission to add a few words closely connected with 'The Thorn' and many other Poems in these volumes. There is a numerous class of readers who imagine that the same words cannot be repeated without tautology: this is a great error: virtual tautology is much oftener produced by using different words when the meaning is exactly the same. Words, in a Poet's words more particularly, ought to be weighed in the balance of feeling, and not measured by the space which they occupy upon paper. For the Reader cannot be too often reminded that Poetry is passion: it is the history or science of feelings. Now every man must know that an attempt is rarely made to communicate impassioned feelings without something of an accompanying consciousness of the inadequateness of our own powers, or the deficiencies of language. During such efforts there will be a craving in the mind, and as long as it is unsatisfied the speaker will cling to the same words, or words of the same character. There are also various other reasons why repetition and apparent tautology are frequently beauties of the highest kind. Among the chief of these reasons is the interest which the mind attaches to words, not only as symbols of the passion, but as *things*, active and efficient, which are of themselves part of the passion. And further, from a spirit of fondness, exultation, and gratitude, the mind luxuriates in the repetition of words which appear successfully to communicate its feelings. The truth of these remarks might be shown by innumerable passages from the Bible, and from the impassioned poetry of every nation. 'Awake, awake, Deborah!' &c. Judges, chap. v, verses 12th, 27th, and part of 28th. See also the whole of that tumultuous and wonderful Poem.— W. 1800–1805.

SONG AT THE FEAST, &c.
Page 162.

Henry Lord Clifford, &c., &c., who is the subject of this poem, was the son of John Lord Clifford, who was slain at Towton Field, which John Lord Clifford, as is known to the reader of English history, was the person who after the battle of Wakefield slew, in the pursuit, the young Earl of Rutland, son of the Duke of York, who had fallen in the battle, 'in part of revenge' (say the Authors of the 'History of Cumberland and Westmoreland'); 'for the Earl's Father had slain his.' A deed which worthily blemished the author (saith Speed); but who, as he adds, 'dare promise

701

NOTES

anything temperate of himself in the heat of martial fury? chiefly, when it was resolved not to leave any branch of the York line standing; for so one maketh this Lord to speak.' This, no doubt, I would observe by the bye, was an action sufficiently in the vindictive spirit of the times, and yet not altogether so bad as represented; 'for the Earl was no child, as some writers would have him, but able to bear arms, being sixteen or seventeen years of age, as is evident from this, (say the Memoirs of the Countess of Pembroke, who was laudably anxious to wipe away, as far as could be, this stigma from the illustrious name to which she was born,) that he was the next child to King Edward the Fourth, which his mother had by Richard Duke of York, and that King was then eighteen years of age: and for the small distance betwixt her children, see Austin Vincent, in his "Book of Nobility," p. 622, where he writes of them all.' It may further be observed, that Lord Clifford, who was then himself only twenty-five years of age, had been a leading man and commander two or three years together in the army of Lancaster, before this time; and, therefore, would be less likely to think that the Earl of Rutland might be entitled to mercy from his youth.—But independent of this act, at best a cruel and savage one, the family of Clifford had done enough to draw upon them the vehement hatred of the House of York: so that after the Battle of Towton there was no hope for them but in flight and concealment. Henry, the subject of the poem, was deprived of his estate and honours during the space of twenty-four years; all which time he lived as a shepherd in Yorkshire, or in Cumberland, where the estate of his father-in-law (Sir Lancelot Threlkeld) lay. He was restored to his estate and honours in the first year of Henry the Seventh. It is recorded that, 'when called to Parliament, he behaved nobly and wisely; but otherwise came seldom to London or the Court; and rather delighted to live in the country, where he repaired several of his Castles, which had gone to decay during the late troubles.' Thus far is chiefly collected from Nicholson and Burn; and I can add, from my own knowledge, that there is a tradition current in the village of Threlkeld and its neighbourhood, his principal retreat, that, in the course of his shepherd-life, he had acquired great astronomical knowledge. I cannot conclude this note without adding a word upon the subject of those numerous and noble feudal edifices, spoken of in the poem, the ruins of some of which are, at this day, so great an ornament to that interesting country. The Cliffords had always been distinguished for an honourable pride in these Castles; and we have seen that, after the wars of York and Lancaster, they were rebuilt; in the civil wars of Charles the First they were again laid waste, and again restored almost to their former magnificence by the celebrated Lady Anne Clifford, Countess of Pembroke, &c., &c. Not more than twenty-five years after this was done, when the estates of Clifford had passed into the family of Tufton, three of these Castles, namely, Brough, Brougham, and Pendragon, were demolished, and the timber and other materials sold by Thomas Earl of Thanet. We will hope that, when this order was issued, the Earl had not consulted the text of Isaiah, 58th chap. 12th verse, to which the inscription placed over the gate of Pendragon Castle, by the Countess of Pembroke (I believe his grandmother), at the time she repaired that structure, refers the reader:—'*And they that shall be of thee shall build the old waste places: thou shalt raise up the foundations of many generations; and thou shalt*

be called the repairer of the breach, the restorer of paths to dwell in.' The Earl of Thanet, the present possessor of the Estates, with a due respect for the memory of his ancestors, and a proper sense of the value and beauty of these remains of antiquity, has (I am told) given orders that they shall be preserved from all depredations.—W.

Page 162, l. 27.

'Earth helped him with the cry of blood.' This line is from 'The Battle of Bosworth Field,' by Sir John Beaumont (brother to the Dramatist), whose poems are written with much spirit, elegance, and harmony; and have deservedly been reprinted lately in Chalmers' 'Collection of English Poets.'—W.

Page 163, ll. 122, 123.

'And both the undying fish that swim
Through Bowscale-tarn,' &c.]

It is imagined by the people of the country that there are two immortal fish, inhabitants of this tarn, which lies in the mountains not far from Threlkeld.—Blencathara, mentioned before, is the old and proper name of the mountain vulgarly called Saddle-back.—W.

Page 163, ll. 142, 143.

'Armour rusting in his halls
On the blood of Clifford calls.'

The martial character of the Cliffords is well known to the readers of English history; but it may not be improper here to say, by way of comment on these lines and what follows, that besides several others who perished in the same manner, the four immediate progenitors of the person in whose hearing this is supposed to be spoken, all died in the field.—W.

LINES COMPOSED A FEW MILES ABOVE TINTERN ABBEY
Page 163.

I have not ventured to call this Poem an Ode; but it was written with a hope that in the transitions and the impassioned music of the versification, would be found the principal requisites, of that species of composition.—W. 1802-5.

LAODAMIA
Page 166.

In 1827 a change of unique importance—amounting to an absolute reversal of the central motive of the poem—was made in the penultimate stanza of *Laodamia*. In edd. 1815, 1820 the heroine's love, while described as at war with Reason, is expressly declared guiltless; and she is dismissed to the serene region tenanted by happy Ghosts, with a due respect for the memory of his ancestors, 'to gather flowers of blissful quiet,' &c., &c. In 1827 all this is reversed. Love, indulged 'in Reason's spite,' is now declared a crime; and Laodamia, as manifestly guilty, is 'doomed to wander in a grosser clime, Apart from happy Ghosts.' In 1832 the severity of the sentence is mitigated: not now to dateless exile from the presence of her beloved, but to a limited period of exclusion,—an expiatory or purgatorial term of banishment—is she sentenced by 'the just Gods whom no weak pity moves.' Changes made subsequently to 1832 in no way affect the question of Laodamia's doom. The several forms successively assumed by this stanza must now be given:—

NOTES

Ah, judge her gently who so deeply loved!
Her, who, in reason's spite, yet without crime,
Was in a trance of passion thus removed;
Delivered from the galling yoke of time
And these frail elements—to gather flowers
Of blissful quiet 'mid unfading bowers.
Edd. 1815, 1820.

By no weak pity might the Gods be moved;
She who thus perished not without the crime
Of Lovers than in Reason's spite have loved,
Was doomed to wander in a grosser clime
Apart from happy Ghosts—that gather flowers
Of blissful quiet 'mid unfading bowers.
Ed. 1827.

Edd. 1832 and 1836 follow ed. 1827 exactly, except in line 4, which in them runs as follows:—

'Was doomed to wear out her appointed time.'

She—who, though warned, exhorted, and reproved,
Thus died, from passion desperate to a crime—
By the just Gods, whom no weak pity moved,
Was doomed to wear out her appointed time
Apart from happy Ghosts, that gather flowers, &c.
Edd. 1840–1843.

Our text follows the version of edd. 1845 and 1849. In defence of the change effected in 1827, Wordsworth wrote to his nephew John Wordsworth in 1831:—'As first written, the heroine was dismissed to happiness in Elysium. To what purpose then the mission of Protesilaus? He exhorts her to moderate her passion; the exhortation is fruitless, and no punishment follows. So it stood: at present she is placed among unhappy ghosts for disregard of the exhortation. Virgil also places her there; but compare the two passages and give me *your* opinion' (*William Wordsworth*, by Elizabeth Wordsworth, p. 131). Thus Laodamia probably owes the mitigated doom subsequently (ed. 1832) pronounced upon her to the interposition of the poet's nephew John Wordsworth.—Ed.

DION
Page 169.

This poem began with the following stanza, which has been displaced on account of its detaining the reader too long from the subject, and as rather precluding, than preparing for the due effect of the allusion to the genius of Plato:

'Fair is the Swan, whose majesty, prevailing,'
&c., &c., &c.—W.

Page 172, l. 114.

'Living hill.'
'awhile the living hill
Heaved with convulsive throes, and all was still.'
Dr. Darwin.—W.

THE WISHING-GATE DESTROYED
Page 178.

'In the Vale of Grasmere, by the side of the old highway leading to Ambleside, is a gate which, time out of mind, has been called the Wishing-gate.'

Having been told, upon what I thought good authority, that this gate had been destroyed, and the opening, where it hung, walled up, I gave vent immediately to my feelings in these stanzas. But going to the place some time after, I found, with much delight, my old favourite unmolested.—W.

PETER BELL
Page 180.

After line 515 occurred the stanza (immortalised by Shelley) omitted by Wordsworth after 1819:

'Is it a party in a parlour?
Cramm'd just as they on earth were cramm'd—
Some sipping punch, some sipping tea,
But, as you by their faces see,
All silent and all damn'd!'

In Crabb Robinson's Diary, June 6, 1812, we find: 'Mrs. Basil Montagu told me she had no doubt she had suggested this image to Wordsworth by relating to him an anecdote. A person, walking in a friend's garden, looking in at a window, saw a company of ladies at a table near the window with countenances *fixed*. In an instant he was aware of their condition, and broke the window. He saved them from incipient suffocation.'—Ed.

MISCELLANEOUS SONNETS
Page 199.

Through the kindness of the author, Professor Edward Dowden, I am enabled to print at length the following valuable note upon the grouping of the Miscellaneous Sonnets. The note originally appeared in the Aldine Edition of Wordsworth's Poems, vol. iii, p. 327 (ed. 1892).—Ed.

'A group of Miscellaneous Sonnets was first published by Wordsworth in the "Poems in two volumes," 1807. In subsequent editions the number of Sonnets was increased, and the arrangement was altered. It seems to me evident that although these poems were written at various widely-parted times, they were finally arranged so as to illustrate one another, and form not indeed a linked chain of sonnets but a sequence as far as a sequence can be made from disconnected pieces by happy ordering. Let me try to show that this is the case with at least the thirty-six sonnets of Part I.

'I. Prefatory Sonnet on the Sonnet: contentment in limitation.

'II. The cottage of the poor; its beauty and happiness; contentment in limitation.

'III. The native vale of the child; the child's content in limitation altered by growth to manhood.

'IV. A little cottage, but glorified by Skiddaw and by the Muses.

'V. The glory of Skiddaw and its streams, though unsung by the Muses.

'VI. The glory of a little mountain stream sanctified by memory and the affections.

'VII. A mountain lake, glorified even more by human love than by Fancy and the Muses.

'VIII. Vale and mountain glorified by friendship and the art of music.

'IX. Immortality conferred on the beauty of nature by a friend's art of painting.

'X. True art springs from the human heart, and all external things are modified by human affections.

'XI. Fancy and the Muse also deal with outward nature and add a grace and dignity to it.

'XII, XIII, XIV, three sonnets "To Sleep" stand unconnected with what precedes and serve as a resting-place.

'XV. The simplicity of the life of nature; the cumbrous pride of the artificial life.

'XVI. Walton; the happiness of a life "nobly versed in simple discipline."

'XVII. Dyer; the modesty and simplicity of his verse.

'XVIII. "Peter Bell," a poem of nature, ill received in an artificial age.

'XIX. Loss of cottage simplicity and its joys: the decay of spinning.

'XX. Spinning—a lost art: intellectual pride of the age.

703

'XXI. Pious use of the cottage fleece on Easter Sunday: contrast with these days of mechanical progress.

'XXII. Decay of rustic piety: Easter and Christmas church-going.

'XXIII. Piety of rural nuptials: love and religion united.

'XXIV–XXVI. Love and devotion have fitly led up to the sonnets translated from Michael Angelo, on mortal love leading to God.

'XXVII. And here is a fitting place for the contemplation of Death.

'XXVIII, XXIX. Beauty and repose in death a source of faith.

'XXX. But there are glad childlike hearts untouched by great solemnities, yet pure and sacred: mystery of the sea.

'XXXI. The "reverential fear" of the sea, connected with a ship setting forth.

'XXXII. A ship singled out for love.

'XXXIII. How few of these glories and mysteries of Nature are felt by us! The mystery and beauty of the sea.

'XXXIV. The poets of Fashion contrasted with the poet of Nature.

'XXXV. Ennui and misanthropy of the poet of worldlings; how true Imagination transmutes the sorrows of life.

'XXXVI. Memorial Sonnet to Raisley Calvert who enabled the author to live the life poetic.

'The reader who follows and verifies the above analysis can hardly doubt that Wordsworth was studious to arrange his sonnets with a view to their mutual illustration.'

Page 199, Dedication, l. 14.

'Something less than joy, but more than dull content.'

COUNTESS OF WINCHILSEA.—W.

SONNET XI
Page 216.

'Wild Redbreast!' &c. This Sonnet, as Poetry, explains itself, yet the scene of the incident having been a wild wood, it may be doubted, as a point of natural history, whether the bird was aware that his attentions were bestowed upon a human, or even a living, creature. But a Redbreast will perch upon the foot of a gardener at work, and alight on the handle of the spade when his hand is half upon it—this I have seen. And under my own roof I have witnessed affecting instances of the creature's friendly visits to the chambers of sick persons, as described in the verses to the Redbreast, p. 114. One of these welcome intruders used frequently to roost upon a nail in the wall, from which a picture had hung, and was ready, as morning came, to pipe his song in the hearing of the invalid, who had been long confined to her room. These attachments to a particular person, when marked and continued, used to be reckoned ominous; but the superstition is passing away.—W.

AT THE GRAVE OF BURNS
Page 226.

The following is extracted from the journal of my fellow-traveller, to which, as persons acquainted with my poems will know, I have been obliged on other occasions:

'*Dumfries, August,* 1803.

'On our way to the churchyard where Burns is buried, we were accompanied by a bookseller, who showed us the outside of Burns's house, where he had lived the last three years of his life, and where he died. It has a mean appearance, and is in a bye situation; the front whitewashed, dirty about the doors, as most Scotch houses are; flowering plants in the window. Went to visit his grave; he lies in a corner of the churchyard, and his second son, Francis Wallace, beside him. There is no stone to mark the spot; but a hundred guineas have been collected to be expended upon some sort of monument. "There," said the bookseller, pointing to a pompous monument, "lies Mr.—(I have forgotten the name)—a remarkably clever man; he was an attorney, and scarcely ever lost a cause he undertook. Burns made many a lampoon upon him, and there they rest as you see." We looked at Burns's grave with melancholy and painful reflections, repeating to each other his own poet's epitaph:—

'Is there a man,' &c.

'The churchyard is full of gravestones and expensive monuments, in all sorts of fantastic shapes—obelisk-wise, pillar-wise, &c. When our guide had left us we turned again to Burns's grave, and afterwards went to his house, wishing to enquire after Mrs. Burns, who had gone to spend some time by the sea-shore with her children. We spoke to the maid-servant at the door, who invited us forward, and we sate down in the parlour. The walls were coloured with a blue wash; on one side of the fire was a mahogany desk; opposite the window a clock, which Burns mentions, in one of his letters, having received as a present. The house was cleanly and neat in the inside, the stairs of stone scoured white, the kitchen on the right side of the passage, the parlour on the left. In the room above the parlour the poet died, and his son, very lately, in the same room. The servant told us she had lived four years with Mrs. Burns, who was now in great sorrow for the death of Wallace. She said that Mrs. B's youngest son was now at Christ's Hospital. We were glad to leave Dumfries, where we could think of little but poor Burns, and his moving about on that unpoetic ground. In our road to Brownhill, the next stage, we passed Ellisland, at a little distance on our right—his farmhouse. Our pleasure in looking round would have been still greater, if the road had led us nearer the spot.

.   .   .   .   .   .

'I cannot take leave of this country which we passed through to-day, without mentioning that we saw the Cumberland mountains within half-a-mile of Ellisland, Burns's house, the last view we had of them. Drayton has prettily described the connection, which this neighbourhood has with ours, when he makes Skiddaw say,—

"Scruffel, from the sky
That Annandale doth crown, with a most amorous eye
Salutes me every day, or at my pride looks grim,
Oft threatening me with clouds, as I oft threaten him."

These lines came to my brother's memory, as well as the Cumberland saying,—

"If Skiddaw hath a cap
Scruffel wots well of that."

'We talked of Burns, and of the prospect he must have had, perhaps from his own door, of Skiddaw and his companions: indulging ourselves in the fancy that we might have been personally known to each other, and he have looked upon those objects with more pleasure for our sakes.' —W.

NOTES

SONNET COMPOSED AT —— CASTLE
Page 232.

In the MS. copy of this Sonnet which Wordsworth sent to Walter Scott (Oct. 16, 1803) the first line ran as follows:

'Now, as I live, I pity that great Lord
    Whom mere despite,' &c.

'In that original shape,' says Lockhart, 'Scott always recited it [the sonnet], and few lines in the language were more frequently in his mouth.'—ED.

THE BLIND HIGHLAND BOY
Page 234.

In Ed. 1807, the vessel in which the boy embarked was a common wash-tub:

'But say, what was it? Thought of fear!
Well may ye tremble when ye hear!
—A Household Tub, like one of those
Which women use to wash their clothes,
This carried the blind Boy.'

The shell was substituted (in 1815) for the tub, on the suggestion of Coleridge—a change of which Charles Lamb and Barron Field strongly disapproved.—ED.

SONNET III
Page 241.

'Jones! as from Calais southward.'] (See Dedication to Descriptive Sketches, p. 469.)

This excellent Person, one of my earliest and dearest friends, died in the year 1835. We were undergraduates together of the same year, at the same college; and companions in many a delightful ramble through his own romantic Country of North Wales. Much of the latter part of his life he passed in comparative solitude; which I know was often cheered by remembrance of our youthful adventures, and of the beautiful regions which, at home and abroad, we had visited together. Our long friendship was never subject to a moment's interruption,—and while revising these volumes for the last time, I have been so often reminded of my loss, with a not unpleasing sadness, that I trust the Reader will excuse this passing mention of a Man who well deserves from me something more than so brief a notice. Let me only add, that during the middle part of his life he resided many years (as Incumbent of the Living) at a Parsonage in Oxfordshire, which is the subject of the 7th of the 'Miscellaneous Sonnets,' Part 3.—W.

SONNET VII
Page 242.

In this and a succeeding sonnet on the same subject, let me be understood as a Poet availing himself of the situation which the King of Sweden occupied, and of the principles AVOWED IN HIS MANIFESTOES; as laying hold of these advantages for the purpose of embodying moral truths. This remark might, perhaps, as well have been suppressed; for to those who may be in sympathy with the course of these Poems, it will be superfluous; and will, I fear, be thrown away upon that other class, whose besotted admiration of the intoxicated despot hereafter placed in contrast with him, is the most melancholy evidence of degradation in British feeling and intellect which the times have furnished.—W.

NOVEMBER, 1806
Page 247.

'Danger which they fear, and honour which they understand not.' Words in Lord Brooke's Life of Sir P. Sydney.—W.

SONNET XVI
Page 251.

'Zaragoza.'] In this sonnet I am under some obligations to one of an Italian author, to which I cannot refer.—W.

THE GERMANS ON THE HEIGHTS OF HOCHHEIM
Page 256.

The event is thus recorded in the journals of the day:—'When the Austrians took Hochheim, in one part of the engagement they got to the brow of the hill, whence they had their first view of the Rhine. They instantly halted—not a gun was fired —not a voice heard; they stood gazing on the river with those feelings which the events of the last fifteen years at once called up. Prince Schwartzenberg rode up to know the cause of this sudden stop; they then gave three cheers, rushed after the enemy, and drove them into the water.'—W.

THANKSGIVING ODE
Page 261.

Wholly unworthy of touching upon the momentous subject here treated would that Poet be, before whose eyes the present distresses under which this kingdom labours could interpose a veil sufficiently thick to hide, or even to obscure, the splendour of this great moral triumph. If I have given way to exultation, unchecked by these distresses, it might be sufficient to protect me from a charge of insensibility, should I state my own belief that the sufferings will be transitory. Upon the wisdom of a very large majority of the British nation rested that generosity which poured out the treasures of this country for the deliverance of Europe: and in the same national wisdom, presiding in time of peace over an energy not inferior to that which has been displayed in war, *they* confide, who encourage a firm hope, that the cup of our wealth will be gradually replenished. There will, doubtless, be no few ready to indulge in regrets and repinings; and to feed a morbid satisfaction, by aggravating these burthens in imagination; in order that calamity so confidently prophesied, as it has not taken the shape which their sagacity allotted to it, may appear as grievous as possible under another. But the body of the nation will not quarrel with the gain, because it might have been purchased at a less price: and, acknowledging in these sufferings, which they feel to have been in a great degree unavoidable, a consecration of their noble efforts, they will vigorously apply themselves to remedy the evil.

Nor is it at the expense of rational patriotism, or in disregard of sound philosophy, that I have given vent to feelings tending to encourage a martial spirit in the bosoms of my countrymen, at a time when there is a general outcry against the prevalence of these dispositions. The British army, both by its skill and valour in the field, and by the discipline which rendered it, to the inhabitants of the several countries where its operations were carried on, a protection from the violence of their own troops, has performed services that will not allow the language of gratitude and admiration to be suppressed or restrained (whatever be the temper of the public mind) through a scrupulous dread lest the tribute due to the past should prove an injurious incentive for the future. Every man deserving the name of Briton adds his voice to the chorus which extols the exploits of his countrymen, with a consciousness, at times overpowering the effort, that they transcend all praise. But this particular sentiment, thus irresistibly excited, is not sufficient. The nation would err grievously, if she suffered the abuse which other states have made of military power to prevent her from perceiving that no people ever was or can be, independent, free, or secure, much less great, in any sane application of the word, without a cultivation of military virtues. Nor let it be overlooked, that the benefits derivable from these sources are placed within the reach of Great Britain, under conditions peculiarly favourable. The same insular position which, by rendering territorial incorporation impossible, utterly precludes the desire of conquest under the most seductive shape it can assume, enables her to rely, for her defence against foreign foes, chiefly upon a species of armed force from which her own liberties have nothing to fear. Such are the privileges of her situation; and, by permitting, they invite her to give way to the courageous instincts of human nature, and to strengthen and refine them by culture.

But some have more than insinuated that a design exists to subvert the civil character of the English people by unconstitutional applications and unnecessary increase of military power. The advisers and abettors of such a design, were it possible that it should exist, would be guilty of the most heinous crime, which, upon this planet, can be committed. Trusting that this apprehension arises from the delusive influences of an honourable jealousy, let me hope that the martial qualities which I venerate will be fostered by adhering to those good old usages which experience has sanctioned; and by availing ourselves of new means of indisputable promise: particularly by applying, in its utmost possible extent, that system of tuition whose master-spring is a habit of gradually enlightened subordination;—by imparting knowledge, civil, moral, and religious, in such measure that the mind, among all classes of the community, may love, admire, and be prepared and accomplished to defend, that country under whose protection its faculties have been unfolded, and its riches acquired;—by just dealing towards all orders of the state, so that, no members of it being trampled upon, courage may everywhere continue to rest immovably upon its ancient English foundation, personal self-respect;—by adequate rewards, and permanent honours, conferred upon the deserving;—by encouraging athletic exercises and manly sports among the peasantry of the country; —and by especial care to provide and support institutions, in which, during a time of peace, the youth of the country may be instructed in military science.

I have only to add, that I should feel little satisfaction in giving to the world these limited attempts to celebrate the virtues of my country, if I did not encourage a hope that a subject, which it has fallen within my province to treat only in the mass, will by other poets be illustrated in that detail which its importance calls for, and which will allow opportunities to give the merited applause to PERSONS as well as to THINGS.

The ode was published along with other pieces, now interspersed through these volumes.—W.

'Had it been a hymn, uttering the sentiments of a *multitude*, a *stanza* would have been indispensable. But though I have called it a "Thanksgiving Ode," strictly speaking it is not so, but a poem composed, or supposed to be composed, on the morning of the thanksgiving, uttering the sentiments of an *individual* upon that occasion. It is a *dramatised ejaculation*; and this, if anything can, must excuse the irregular frame of the metre' (Letter of Wordsworth to Southey, 1816, in *Memoirs* by Bishop Wordsworth, ii. 60, 61.)—Ed.

Page 262, l. 122.

'Discipline the rule whereof is passion.'
　　　　　　　　　　　　LORD BROOKE.—W.

SONNET I
Page 264.

If in this sonnet I should seem to have borne a little too hard upon the personal appearance of the worthy Poissards of Calais, let me take shelter under the authority of my lamented friend, the late Sir George Beaumont. He, a most accurate observer, used to say of them, that their features and countenances seemed to have conformed to those of the creatures they dealt in; at all events the resemblance was striking.—W.

BRUGÈS
Page 264.

This is not the first poetical tribute which in our times has been paid to this beautiful city. Mr. Southey, in the 'Poet's Pilgrimage,' speaks of it in lines which I cannot deny myself the pleasure of connecting with my own.

'Time hath not wronged her, nor hath ruin sought
　Rudely her splendid structures to destroy,
Save in those recent days, with evil fraught,
　When mutability, in drunken joy
Triumphant, and from all restraint released,
Let loose her fierce and many-headed beast.

But for the scars in that unhappy rage
Inflicted, firm she stands and undecayed;
Like our first Sires, a beautiful old age
Is hers in venerable years arrayed,
And yet, to her, benignant stars may bring,
What fate denies to man,—a second spring.

When I may read of tilts in days of old,
　And tourneys graced by Chieftains of renown,
Fair dames, grave citizens, and warriors bold,
　If fancy would portray some stately town,
Which for such pomp fit theatre should be,
Fair Brugès, I shall then remember thee.'

In this city are many vestiges of the splendour of the Burgundian Dukedom, and the long black mantle universally worn by the females is probably a remnant of the old Spanish connection, which, if I do not much deceive myself, is traceable in the grave deportment of its inhabitants. Brugès is comparatively little disturbed by that curious contest, or rather conflict, of Flemish with French propensities in matters of taste, so conspicuous through other parts of Flanders. The hotel to which we drove at Ghent furnished an odd instance. In the passages were paintings and statues, after the antique, of Hebe and Apollo; and in the garden, a little pond, about a yard and a half in diameter, with a weeping willow bending over it, and under the shade of that tree, in the centre of the pond, a wooden painted statue of a Dutch or Flemish boor, looking ineffably tender upon his mistress, and embracing her. A living duck, tethered at the feet of the sculptured lovers, alternately tormented a miserable eel and itself

NOTES

with endeavours to escape from its bonds and prison. Had we chanced to espy the hostess of the hotel in this quaint rural retreat, the exhibition would have been complete. She was a true Flemish figure, in the dress of the days of Holbein; her symbol of office, a weighty bunch of keys, pendent from her portly waist. In Brussels, the modern taste in costume, architecture, &c. has got the mastery; in Ghent there is a struggle: but in Brugès old images are still paramount, and an air of monastic life among the quiet goings-on of a thinly-peopled city is inexpressibly soothing; a pensive grace seems to be cast over all, even the very children.—*Extract from Journal.*—W.

Page 266.

'Where unremitting frosts the rocky crescent bleach.'] 'Let a wall of rocks be imagined from three to six hundred feet in height, and rising between France and Spain, so as physically to separate the two kingdoms—let us fancy this wall curved like a crescent, with its convexity towards France. Lastly, let us suppose, that in the very middle of the wall, a breach of 300 feet wide has been beaten down by the famous *Roland,* and we may have a good idea of what the mountaineers call the "BRECHE DE ROLAND."'—*Raymond's Pyrenees.*—W.

Page 266.

'Miserere Domine.'] See the beautiful Song in Mr. Coleridge's Tragedy, 'The Remorse.' Why is the harp of Quantock silent?—W.

Page 266.

'Not, like his great Compeers, indignantly Doth Danube spring to life!'] Before this quarter of the Black Forest was inhabited, the source of the Danube might have suggested some of those sublime images which Armstrong has so finely described; at present, the contrast is most striking. The Spring appears in a capacious stone Basin in front of a Ducal palace, with a pleasure-ground opposite; then, passing under the pavement, takes the form of a little, clear, bright, black, vigorous rill, barely wide enough to tempt the agility of a child five years old to leap over it,—and entering the garden, it joins, after a course of a few hundred yards, a stream much more considerable than itself. The *copiousness* of the spring at *Doneschingen* must have procured for it the honour of being named the Source of the Danube.—W.

ON APPROACHING THE STAUB-BACH
Page 266.

'The Staub-bach' is a narrow Stream, which, after a long course on the heights, comes to the sharp edge of a somewhat overhanging precipice, overleaps it with a bound, and, after a fall of 930 feet, forms again a rivulet. The vocal powers of these musical Beggars may seem to be exaggerated; but this wild and savage air was utterly unlike any sounds I had ever heard; the notes reached me from a distance, and on what occasion they were sung I could not guess, only they seemed to belong, in some way or other, to the Waterfall—and reminded me of religious services chanted to Streams and Fountains in Pagan times. Mr. Southey has thus accurately characterised the peculiarity of this music: 'While we were at the Waterfall, some half-score peasants, chiefly women and girls, assembled just out of reach of the Spring, and set up—surely, the wildest chorus that ever was heard by human ears,—a song not of articulate

sounds, but in which the voice was used as a mere instrument of music, more flexible than any which art could produce,—sweet, powerful, and thrilling beyond description.'—See Notes to 'A Tale of Paraguay.'—W.

ENGELBERG
Page 268.

The Convent whose site was pointed out, according to tradition, in this manner, is seated at its base. The architecture of the building is unimpressive, but the situation is worthy of the honour which the imagination of the mountaineers has conferred upon it.—W.

Page 271.

'Tho' searching damps and many an envious flaw
Have marred this Work;']

This picture of the Last Supper has not only been grievously injured by time, but the greatest part of it, if not the whole, is said to have been retouched, or painted over again. These niceties may be left to connoisseurs,—I speak of it as I felt. The copy exhibited in London some years ago, and the engraving by Morghen, are both admirable; but in the original is a power which neither of those works has attained, or even approached. —W.

Page 272.

'Of Figures human and divine.'] The Statues ranged round the spire and along the roof of the Cathedral of Milan, have been found fault with by persons whose exclusive taste is unfortunate for themselves. It is true that the same expense and labour, judiciously directed to purposes more strictly architectural, might have much heightened the general effect of the building; for, seen from the ground, the Statues appear diminutive. But the *coup d'œil,* from the best point of view, which is half way up the spire, must strike an unprejudiced person with admiration; and surely the selection and arrangement of the Figures is exquisitely fitted to support the religion of the country in the imaginations and feelings of the spectator. It was with great pleasure that I saw, during the two ascents which we made, several children, of different ages, tripping up and down the slender spire, and pausing to look around them, with feelings much more animated than could have been derived from these or the finest works of art, if placed within easy reach.—Remember also that you have the Alps on one side, and on the other the Apennines, with the plain of Lombardy between!—W.

Page 274.

'Still, with those white-robed Shapes, a living Stream,
The glacier Pillars join in solemn guise.']

This Procession is a part of the sacramental service performed once a month. In the valley of Engelberg we had the good fortune to be present at the *Grand Festival* of the Virgin—but the Procession on that day, though consisting of upwards of 1,000 persons, assembled from all the branches of the sequestered valley, was much less striking (notwithstanding the sublimity of the surrounding scenery): it wanted both the simplicity of the other and the accompaniment of the Glacier-columns, whose sisterly resemblance to the *moving* Figures gave it a most beautiful and solemn peculiarity. —W.

707

NOTES

ON BEING STRANDED, &c.
Page 276.

Near the town of Boulogne, and overhanging the beach, are the remains of a tower which bears the name of Caligula, who here terminated his western expedition, of which these sea-shells were the boasted spoils. And at no great distance from these ruins, Buonaparte, standing upon a mound of earth, harangued his 'Army of England,' reminding them of the exploits of Cæsar, and pointing towards the white cliffs, upon which their standards *were to float.* He recommended also a subscription to be raised among the Soldiery to erect on that ground, in memory of the foundation of the 'Legion of Honour,' a Column—which was not completed at the time we were there.—W.

Page 276.

'We mark majestic herds of cattle, free
To ruminate.']
This is a most grateful sight for an Englishman returning to his native land. Everywhere one misses in the cultivated grounds abroad, the animated and soothing accompaniment of animals ranging and selecting their own food at will.—W.

Page 277.

'Far as St. Maurice, from yon eastern Forks.']
LES FOURCHES, the point at which the two chains of mountains part, that inclose the Valais, which terminates at ST. MAURICE.—W.

Page 277.

——————'ye that occupy
Your council-seats beneath the open sky,
On Sarnen's Mount.']
Sarnen, one of the two capitals of the Canton of Underwalden; the spot here alluded to is close to the town, and is called the Landenberg, from the tyrant of that name, whose château formerly stood there. On the 1st of January, 1308, the great day which the confederated Heroes had chosen for the deliverance of their country, all the castles of the Governors were taken by force or stratagem; and the Tyrants themselves conducted, with their creatures, to the frontiers, after having witnessed the destruction of their strongholds. From that time the Landenberg has been the place where the Legislators of this division of the Canton assemble. The site, which is well described by Ebel, is one of the most beautiful in Switzerland.—W.

Page 277.

'Calls me to pace her honoured Bridge—.'] The bridges of Lucerne are roofed, and open at the sides, so that the passenger has, at the same time, the benefit of shade and a view of the magnificent country. The pictures are attached to the rafters; those from Scripture History, on the Cathedral Bridge, amount, according to my notes, to 240. Subjects from the Old Testament face the passenger as he goes towards the Cathedral, and those from the New as he returns. The pictures on these bridges, as well as those in most other parts of Switzerland, are not to be spoken of as works of art; but they are instruments admirably answering the purpose for which they were designed.—W.

Page 279, ll. 76, 77.

——————'although 'tis fair,
'Twill be another Yarrow.']
These words were quoted to me from 'Yarrow Unvisited,' by Sir Walter Scott, when I visited him at Abbotsford, a day or two before his departure for Italy: and the affecting condition in which he was when he looked upon Rome from the Janicular Mount, was reported to me by a lady who had the honour of conducting him thither.—W.

Page 281, l. 241.

'His sepulchral verse.'] If any English reader should be desirous of knowing how far I am justified in thus describing the epitaphs of Chiabrera, he will find translated specimens of them on pp. 448–451, under the head of 'Epitaphs and Elegiac Pieces.'—W.

Page 283.

'This flowering broom's dear neighbourhood.'] In the course of this continental tour of 1837, Wordsworth was deeply impressed with the splendour and profusion of the flowering broom in the valleys and the more sheltered heights of the Apennines; and reluctantly owned the inferiority of the English to the French variety in respect of both beauty and fragrance. The note upon the Oxford movement which follows (and which should properly be read at the conclusion of this poem) was written, at the request of the poet, by his friend Frederick Faber.—ED.

It would be ungenerous not to advert to the religious movement that, since the composition of these verses in 1837, has made itself felt, more or less strongly, throughout the English Church;—a movement that takes, for its first principle, a devout deference to the voice of Christian antiquity. It is not my office to pass judgment on questions of theological detail; but my own repugnance to the spirit and system of Romanism has been so repeatedly and, I trust, feelingly expressed, that I shall not be suspected of a leaning that way, if I do not join in the grave charge, thrown out, perhaps in the heat of controversy, against the learned and pious men to whose labours I allude. I speak apart from controversy; but, with strong faith in the moral temper which would elevate the present by doing reverence to the past, I would draw cheerful auguries for the English Church from this movement, as likely to restore among us a tone of piety more earnest and real than that produced by the mere formalities of the understanding, refusing, in a degree which I cannot but lament, that its own temper and judgment shall be controlled by those of antiquity.—W.

THE PINE OF MONTE MARIO
Page 283.

Within a couple of hours of my arrival at Rome, I saw from Monte Pincio, the Pine-tree as described in the sonnet; and, while expressing admiration at the beauty of its appearance, I was told by an acquaintance of my fellow-traveller, who happened to join us at the moment, that a price had been paid for it by the late Sir G. Beaumont, upon condition that the proprietor should not act upon his known intention of cutting it down.—W.

CAMALDOLI
Page 287.

This famous sanctuary was the original establishment of Saint Romualdo (or Rumwald, as our ancestors saxonised the name), in the 11th century, the ground (campo) being given by a Count Maldo. The Camaldolensi, however, have spread wide as a branch of Benedictines, and may therefore be classed among the *gentlemen* of the monastic

NOTES

orders. The society comprehends two orders, monks and hermits; symbolised by their arms, two doves drinking out of the same cup. The monastery in which the monks here reside is beautifully situated, but a large unattractive edifice, not unlike a factory. The hermitage is placed in a loftier and wilder region of the forest. It comprehends between twenty and thirty distinct residences, each including for its single hermit an inclosed piece of ground and three very small apartments. There are days of indulgence when the hermit may quit his cell, and when old age arrives, he descends from the mountain and takes his abode among the monks.

My companion had in the year 1831 fallen in with the monk, the subject of these two sonnets, who showed him his abode among the hermits. It is from him that I received the following particulars. He was then about forty years of age, but his appearance was that of an older man. He had been a painter by profession, but on taking orders changed his name from Santi to Raffaelo, perhaps with an unconscious reference as well to the great Sanzio d'Urbino as to the archangel. He assured my friend that he had been thirteen years in the hermitage and had never known melancholy or ennui. In the little recess for study and prayer, there was a small collection of books. 'I read only,' said he, 'books of asceticism and mystical theology.' On being asked the names of the most famous mystics, he enumerated *Scaramelli, San Giovanni della Croce, Saint Dionysius the Areopagite* (supposing the work which bears his name to be really his), and with peculiar emphasis *Ricardo di San Vittori*. The works of *Saint Theresa* are also in high repute among ascetics. These names may interest some of my readers.

We heard that Raffaelo was then living in the convent; my friend sought in vain to renew his acquaintance with him. It was probably a day of seclusion. The reader will perceive that these sonnets were supposed to be written when he was a young man.—W.

Page 287.

'What aim had they, the Pair of Monks.'] In justice to the Benedictines of Camaldoli, by whom strangers are so hospitably entertained, I feel obliged to notice that I saw among them no other figures at all resembling, in size and complexion, the two Monks described in this Sonnet. What was their office, or the motive which brought them to this place of mortification, which they could not have approached without being carried in this or some other way, a feeling of delicacy prevented me from enquiring. An account has before been given of the hermitage they were about to enter. It was visited by us towards the end of the month of May; yet snow was lying thick under the pine-trees, within a few yards of the gate.—W.

AT VALLOMBROSA
Page 287.

The name of Milton is pleasingly connected with Vallombrosa in many ways. The pride with which the Monk, without any previous question from me, pointed out his residence, I shall not readily forget. It may be proper here to defend the Poet from a charge which has been brought against him, in respect to the passage in 'Paradise Lost,' where this place is mentioned. It is said, that he has erred in speaking of the trees there being deciduous, whereas they are, in fact, pines. The fault-finders are themselves mistaken; the *natural* woods of the region of Vallombrosa *are* deciduous, and spread to a great extent; those near the convent are, indeed, mostly pines; but they are avenues of trees *planted* within a few steps of each other, and thus composing large tracts of wood; plots of which are periodically cut down. The appearance of those narrow avenues, upon steep slopes open to the sky, on account of the height which the trees attain by being *forced* to grow upwards, is often very impressive. My guide, a boy of about fourteen years old, pointed this out to me in several places.—W.

Page 290, ll. 46, 47.

——'more high, the Dacian force,
To hoof and finger mailed;']

Here and infra, see Forsyth.—W.

THE RIVER DUDDON
Page 296.

A Poet[1] whose works are not yet known as they deserve to be thus enters upon his description of the 'Ruins of Rome:'

'The rising Sun
Flames on the ruins in the purer air
Towering aloft;'

and ends thus—

'The setting Sun displays
His visible great round, between you towers,
As through two shady cliffs.'

Mr. Crowe, in his excellent loco-descriptive Poem, 'Lewesdon Hill,' is still more expeditious, finishing the whole on a May-morning, before breakfast.

'To-morrow for severer thought, but now
To breakfast, and keep festival to-day.'

No one believes, or is desired to believe, that those Poems were actually composed within such limits of time; nor was there any reason why a prose statement should acquaint the Reader with the plain fact, to the disturbance of poetic credibility. But, in the present case, I am compelled to mention, that the above series of Sonnets was the growth of many years;—the one which stands the 14th was the first produced; and others were added upon occasional visits to the Stream, or as recollections of the scenes upon its banks awakened in me a wish to describe them. In this manner I had proceeded insensibly, without perceiving that I was trespassing upon ground preoccupied, at least as far as intention went, by Mr. Coleridge; who, more than twenty years ago, used to speak of writing a rural Poem, to be entitled 'The Brook,' of which he has given a sketch in a recent publication. But a particular subject, cannot, I think, much interfere with a general one; and I have been further kept from encroaching upon any right Mr. C. may still wish to exercise, by the restriction which the frame of the Sonnet imposed upon me, narrowing unavoidably the range of thought, and precluding, though not without its advantages, many graces to which a freer movement of verse would naturally have led.

May I not venture, then, to hope, that, instead of being a hindrance, by anticipation of any part of the subject, these Sonnets may remind Mr.

[1] i.e. the Welshman John Dyer (1699–1758), author of *Grongar Hill* (1726), a kind of descriptive ode in octosyllabic verse, and of the two didactic poems in Miltonic blank verse, entitled, *The Ruins of Rome* (1740) and *The Fleece* (1757). *Lewesdon Hill*, by the Rev. William Crowe, went through three editions between 1788 and 1804.—ED.

NOTES

Coleridge of his own more comprehensive design, and induce him to fulfil it?——There is a sympathy in streams,—'one calleth to another;' and I would gladly believe, that 'The Brook' will, ere long, murmur in concert with 'The Duddon.' But, asking pardon for this fancy, I need not scruple to say, that those verses must indeed be ill-fated which can enter upon such pleasant walks of nature, without receiving and giving inspiration. The power of waters over the minds of Poets has been acknowledged from the earliest ages;—through the 'Flumina amem sylvasque inglorius' of Virgil, down to the sublime apostrophe to the great rivers of the earth, by Armstrong, and the simple ejaculation of Burns (chosen, if I recollect right, by Mr. Coleridge, as a motto for his embryo 'Brook'):

'The Muse nae Poet ever fand her,
Till by himsel' he learned to wander,
Adown some trotting burn's meander,
AND NA' THINK LANG.'—W.

SONNET VI

Page 298.

'There bloomed the strawberry of the wilderness; The trembling eyebright showed her sapphire blue.']
These two lines are in a great measure taken from 'The Beauties of Spring, a Juvenile Poem,' by the Rev. Joseph Sympson. He was a native of Cumberland, and was educated in the vale of Grasmere, and at Hawkshead school: his poems are little known, but they contain passages of splendid description; and the versification of his 'Vision of Alfred' is harmonious and animated. In describing the motions of the Sylphs, that constitute the strange machinery of his Poem, he uses the following illustrative simile—

——'Glancing from their plumes
A changeful light the azure vault illumes.
Less varying hues beneath the Pole adorn
The streamy glories of the Boreal morn,
That wavering to and fro their radiance shed
On Bothnia's gulf with glassy ice o'erspread,
Where the lone native, as he homeward glides,
On polished sandals o'er the imprisoned tides,
And still the balance of his frame preserves,
Wheeled on alternate foot in lengthening curves,
Sees at a glance, above him and below,
Two rival heavens with equal splendour glow.
Sphered in the centre of the world he seems;
For all around with soft effulgence gleams;
Stars, moons, and meteors, ray opposed to ray,
And solemn midnight pours the blaze of day.'

He was a man of ardent feeling, and his faculties of mind, particularly his memory, were extraordinary. Brief notices of his life ought to find a place in the History of Westmoreland.—W.

SONNETS XVII AND XVIII

Page 300.

The EAGLE requires a large domain for its support: but several pairs, not many years ago, were constantly resident in this country, building their nests in the steeps of Borrowdale, Wastdale, Ennerdale, and on the eastern side of Helvellyn. Often have I heard anglers speak of the grandeur of their appearance, as they hovered over Red Tarn, in one of the coves of this mountain. The bird frequently returns, but is always destroyed. Not long since, one visited Rydal lake, and remained some hours near its banks: the consternation which it occasioned among the different species of fowl, particularly the herons, was expressed by

loud screams. The horse also is naturally afraid of the eagle.—There were several Roman stations among these mountains; the most considerable seems to have been in a meadow at the head of Windermere, established, undoubtedly, as a check over the Passes of Kirkstone, Dunmail-raise, and of Hardknot and Wrynose. On the margin of Rydal lake, a coin of Trajan was discovered very lately.—The ROMAN FORT here alluded to, called by the country people 'Hardknot Castle,' is most impressively situated half-way down the hill on the right of the road that descends from Hardknot into Eskdale. It has escaped the notice of most antiquarians, and is but slightly mentioned by Lysons. The DRUIDICAL CIRCLE is about half a mile to the left of the road ascending Stone-side from the vale of Duddon: the country people call it *Sunken Church.*

The reader who may have been interested in the foregoing Sonnets (which together may be considered as a Poem), will not be displeased to find in this place a prose account of the Duddon, extracted from Green's comprehensive 'Guide to the Lakes,' lately published. 'The road leading from Coniston to Broughton is over high ground, and commands a view of the river Duddon; which, at high water, is a grand sight, having the beautiful and fertile lands of Lancashire and Cumberland stretching each way from its margin. In this extensive view, the face of nature is displayed in a wonderful variety of hill and dale; wooded grounds and buildings; amongst the latter Broughton Tower, seated on the crown of a hill, rising elegantly from the valley, is an object of extraordinary interest. Fertility on each side is gradually diminished, and lost in the superior heights of Blackcomb, in Cumberland, and the high lands between Kirkby and Ulverstone.'

'The road from Broughton to Seathwaite is on the banks of the Duddon, and on its Lancashire side it is of various elevations. The river is an amusing companion, one while brawling and tumbling over rocky precipices, until the agitated water becomes again calm by arriving at a smoother and less precipitous bed, but its course is soon again ruffled, and the current thrown into every variety of foam which the rocky channel of a river can give to water.'—*Vide Green's Guide to the Lakes,* vol. i, pp. 98-100.

After all, the traveller would be most gratified who should approach this beautiful Stream, neither at its source, as is done in the Sonnets, nor from its termination; but from Coniston over Walna Scar; first descending into a little circular valley, a collateral compartment of the long winding vale through which flows the Duddon. This recess, towards the close of September, when the after-grass of the meadows is still of a fresh green, with the leaves of many of the trees faded, but perhaps none fallen, is truly enchanting. At a point elevated enough to show the various objects in the valley, and not so high as to diminish their importance, the stranger will instinctively halt. On the foreground, a little below the most favourable station, a rude foot-bridge is thrown over the bed of the noisy brook foaming by the way-side. Russet and craggy hills, of bold and varied outline, surround the level valley, which is besprinkled with grey rocks plumed with birch trees. A few homesteads are interspersed, in some places peeping out from among the rocks like hermitages, whose site has been chosen for the benefit of sunshine as well as shelter; in other instances, the dwelling-house, barn, and byre, compose together a cruciform structure, which, with its embowering trees, and

710

the ivy clothing part of the walls and roof like a fleece, call to mind the remains of an ancient abbey. Time, in most cases, and nature everywhere, have given a sanctity to the humble works of man, that are scattered over this peaceful retirement. Hence a harmony of tone and colour, a consummation and perfection of beauty, which would have been marred had aim or purpose interfered with the course of convenience, utility, or necessity. This unvitiated region stands in no need of the veil of twilight to soften or disguise its features. As it glistens in the morning sunshine, it would fill the spectator's heart with gladsomeness. Looking from our chosen station, he would feel an impatience to rove among its pathways, to be greeted by the milkmaid, to wander from house to house, exchanging 'good-morrows' as he passed the open doors; but, at evening, when the sun is set, and a pearly light gleams from the western quarter of the sky, with an answering light from the smooth surface of the meadows; when the trees are dusky, but each kind still distinguishable; when the cool air has condensed the blue smoke rising from the cottage chimneys; when the dark mossy stones seem to sleep in the bed of the foaming brook; *then*, he would be unwilling to move forward, not less from a reluctance to relinquish what he beholds, than from an apprehension of disturbing, by his approach, the quietness beneath him. Issuing from the plain of this valley, the brook descends in a rapid torrent passing by the churchyard of Seathwaite. The traveller is thus conducted at once into the midst of the wild and beautiful scenery which gave occasion to the Sonnets from the 14th to the 20th inclusive. From the point where the Seathwaite brook joins the Duddon, is a view upwards, into the pass through which the river makes its way into the plain of Donnerdale. The perpendicular rock on the right bears the ancient British name of THE PEN; the one opposite is called WALLA-BARROW CRAG, a name that occurs in other places to designate rocks of the same character. The *chaotic* aspect of the scene is well marked by the expression of a stranger, who strolled out while dinner was preparing, and at his return, being asked by his host, 'What way he had been wandering?' replied, 'As far as it is *finished!*'

The bed of the Duddon is here strewn with large fragments of rocks fallen from aloft; which, as Mr. Green truly says, 'are happily adapted to the many-shaped waterfalls' (or rather waterbreaks, for none of them are high), 'displayed in the short space of half a mile.' That there is some hazard in frequenting these desolate places, I myself have had proof; for one night an immense mass of rock fell upon the very spot where, with a friend, I had lingered the day before. 'The concussion,' says Mr. Green, speaking of the event (for he also, in the practice of his art, on that day sat exposed for a still longer time to the same peril), 'was heard, not without alarm, by the neighbouring shepherds.' But to return to Seathwaite Churchyard: it contains the following inscription:—

'In memory of the Reverend Robert Walker, who died the 25th of June, 1802, in the 93d year of his age, and 67th of his curacy at Seathwaite.
'Also, of Anne his wife, who died the 28th of January, in the 93d year of her age.'

In the parish register of Seathwaite Chapel, is this notice:—

'Buried, June 28th, the Rev. Robert Walker. He was curate of Seathwaite sixty-six years. He was a man singular for his temperance, industry, and integrity.'

This individual is the Pastor alluded to, in the eighteenth Sonnet, as a worthy compeer of the country parson of Chaucer, &c. In the Seventh Book of the Excursion, an abstract of his character is given, beginning—

'A Priest abides before whose life such doubts
Fall to the ground;—'

and some account of his life, for it is worthy of being recorded, will not be out of place here.

MEMOIR OF THE REV. ROBERT WALKER

IN the year 1709, Robert Walker was born at Under-crag, in Seathwaite; he was the youngest of twelve children. His eldest brother, who inherited the small family estate, died at Under-crag, aged ninety-four, being twenty-four years older than the subject of this Memoir, who was born of the same mother. Robert was a sickly infant; and, through his boyhood and youth, continuing to be of delicate frame and tender health, it was deemed best, according to the country phrase, to *breed him a scholar;* for it was not likely that he would be able to earn a livelihood by bodily labour. At that period few of these dales were furnished with school-houses; the children being taught to read and write in the chapel; and in the same consecrated building, where he officiated for so many years both as preacher and schoolmaster, he himself received the rudiments of his education. In his youth he became schoolmaster at Loweswater; not being called upon, probably, in that situation to teach more than reading, writing, and arithmetic. But, by the assistance of a 'Gentleman,' in the neighbourhood, he acquired, at leisure hours, a knowledge of the classics, and became qualified for taking holy orders. Upon his ordination, he had the offer of two curacies: the one, Torver, in the vale of Coniston,—the other, Seathwaite, in his native vale. The value of each was the same, *viz.* five pounds *per annum:* but the cure of Seathwaite having a cottage attached to it, as he wished to marry, he chose it in preference. The young person on whom his affections were fixed, though in the condition of a domestic servant, had given promise, by her serious and modest deportment, and by her virtuous dispositions, that she was worthy to become the helpmate of a man entering upon a plan of life such as he had marked out for himself. By her frugality she had stored up a small sum of money, with which they began housekeeping. In 1735 or 1736, he entered upon his curacy; and, nineteen years afterwards, his situation is thus described, in some letters to be found in the Annual Register for 1760, from which the following is extracted:

To Mr. ——.

'CONISTON, *July* 26, 1754.

'SIR,

'I was the other day upon a party of pleasure, about five or six miles from this place, where I met with a very striking object, and of a nature not very common. Going into a clergyman's house (of whom I had frequently heard), I found him sitting at the head of a long square table, such as is commonly used in this country by the lower class of people, dressed in a coarse blue frock, trimmed with black horn buttons; a checked shirt, a leathern strap about his neck for a stock, a coarse apron, and a pair of great wooden-soled shoes plated with iron to preserve them (what we call clogs in these

NOTES

parts), with a child upon his knee, eating his breakfast; his wife, and the remainder of his children, were some of them employed in waiting upon each other, the rest in teazing and spinning wool, at which trade he is a great proficient; and moreover, when it is made ready for sale, will lay it, by sixteen or thirty two pounds' weight, upon his back, and on foot, seven or eight miles, will carry it to the market, even in the depth of winter. I was not much surprised at all this, as you may possibly be, having heard a great deal of it related before. But I must confess myself astonished with the alacrity and the good humour that appeared both in the clergyman and his wife, and more so at the sense and ingenuity of the clergyman himself.' . . .

Then follows a letter from another person, dated 1755, from which an extract shall be given.

'By his frugality and good management, he keeps the wolf from the door, as we say; and if he advances a little in the world, it is owing more to his own care, than to anything else he has to rely upon. I don't find his inclination is running after further preferment. He is settled among the people, that are happy among themselves; and lives in the greatest unanimity and friendship with them; and, I believe, the minister and people are exceedingly satisfied with each other; and indeed how should they be dissatisfied when they have a person of so much worth and probity for their pastor? A man who, for his candour and meekness, his sober, chaste, and virtuous conversation, his soundness in principle and practice, is an ornament to his profession, and an honour to the country he is in; and bear with me if I say, the plainness of his dress, the sanctity of his manners, the simplicity of his doctrine, and the vehemence of his expression, have a sort of resemblance to the pure practice of primitive Christianity.'

We will now give his own account of himself, to be found in the same place.

From the Rev. Robert Walker

'Sir,—Yours of the 26th instant was communicated to me by Mr. C——, and I should have returned an immediate answer, but the hand of Providence, then laying heavy upon an amiable pledge of conjugal endearment, hath since taken from me a promising girl, which the disconsolate mother too pensively laments the loss of; though we have yet eight living, all healthful, hopeful children, whose names and ages are as follows:—Zaccheus, aged almost eighteen years; Elizabeth, sixteen years and ten months; Mary, fifteen; Moses, thirteen years and three months; Sarah, ten years and three months; Mabel, eight years and three months; William Tyson, three years and eight months; and Anne Esther, one year and three months; besides Anne, who died two years and six months ago, and was then aged between nine and ten; and Eleanor, who died the 23rd inst., January, aged six years and ten months. Zaccheus, the eldest child, is now learning the trade of tanner, and has two years and a half of his apprenticeship to serve. The annual income of my chapel at present, as near as I can compute it, may amount to about £17, of which is paid in cash, viz. £5 from the bounty of Queen Anne, and £5 from W. P., Esq., of P——, out of the annual rents, he being lord of the manor, and £3 from the several inhabitants of L——, settled upon the tenements as a rent-charge; the house and gardens I value at £4 yearly, and not worth more; and I believe the surplice fees and voluntary contributions, one year with another, may be worth £3; but as the inhabitants are few in number, and the fees very low,

this last-mentioned sum consists merely in free-will offerings.

'I am situated greatly to my satisfaction with regard to the conduct and behaviour of my auditory, who not only live in the happy ignorance of the follies and vices of the age, but in mutual peace and goodwill with one another, and are seemingly (I hope really too) sincere Christians, and sound members of the established church, not one dissenter of any denomination being amongst them all. I got to the value of £40 for my wife's fortune, but had no real estate of my own, being the youngest son of twelve children, born of obscure parents; and, though my income has been but small, and my family large, yet, by a providential blessing upon my own diligent endeavours, the kindness of friends, and a cheap country to live in, we have always had the necessaries of life. By what I have written (which is a true and exact account, to the best of my knowledge,) I hope you will not think your favour to me, out of the late worthy Dr. Stratford's effects, quite misbestowed, for which I must ever gratefully own myself,

'Sir,
'Your much obliged and most obedient humble Servant,
'R. W., Curate of S——.

'To Mr. C., of Lancaster.'

About the time when this letter was written, the Bishop of Chester recommended the scheme of joining the curacy of Ulpha to the contiguous one of Seathwaite, and the nomination was offered to Mr. Walker; but an unexpected difficulty arising, Mr. W., in a letter to the Bishop, (a copy of which, in his own beautiful handwriting, now lies before me,) thus expresses himself. 'If he,' meaning the person in whom the difficulty originated, 'had suggested any such objection before, I should utterly have declined any attempt to the curacy of Ulpha: indeed, I was always apprehensive it might be disagreeable to my auditory at Seathwaite, as they have been always accustomed to double duty, and the inhabitants of Ulpha despair of being able to support a schoolmaster who is not curate there also; which suppressed all thoughts in me of serving them both.' And in a second letter to the Bishop he writes:—

'My Lord,—I have the favour of yours of the 1st instant, and am exceedingly obliged on account of the Ulpha affair: if that curacy should lapse into your Lordship's hands, I would beg leave rather to decline than embrace it; for the chapels of Seathwaite and Ulpha, annexed together, would be apt to cause a general discontent among the inhabitants of both places; by either thinking themselves slighted, being only served alternately, or neglected in the duty, or attributing it to covetousness in me; all which occasions of murmuring I would willingly avoid.' And in concluding his former letter, he expresses a similar sentiment upon the same occasion, 'desiring, if it be possible, however, as much as in me lieth, to live peaceably with all men.'

The year following, the curacy of Seathwaite was again augmented; and, to effect this augmentation, fifty pounds had been advanced by himself; and, in 1760, lands were purchased with eight hundred pounds. Scanty as was his income, the frequent offer of much better benefices could not tempt Mr. W. to quit a situation where he had been so long happy, with a consciousness of being useful. Among his papers I find the following copy of a letter, dated 1775, twenty years after his refusal

NOTES

of the curacy of Ulpha, which will show what exertions had been made for one of his sons.

'MAY IT PLEASE YOUR GRACE,

'Our remote situation here makes it difficult to get the necessary information for transacting business regularly; such is the reason of my giving your Grace the present trouble.

'The bearer (my son) is desirous of offering himself candidate for deacon's orders at your Grace's ensuing ordination; the first, on the 25th instant, so that his papers could not be transmitted in due time. As he is now fully at age, and I have afforded him education to the utmost of my ability, it would give me great satisfaction (if your Grace would take him, and find him qualified) to have him ordained. His constitution has been tender for some years; he entered the college of Dublin, but his health would not permit him to continue there, or I would have supported him much longer. He has been with me at home above a year, in which time he has gained great strength of body, sufficient, I hope, to enable him for performing the function. Divine Providence, assisted by liberal benefactors, has blest my endeavours, from a small income, to rear a numerous family; and as my time of life renders me now unfit for much future expectancy from this world, I should be glad to see my son settled in a promising way to acquire an honest livelihood for himself. His behaviour, so far in life, has been irreproachable; and I hope he will not degenerate, in principles or practice, from the precepts and pattern of an indulgent parent. Your Grace's favourable reception of this, from a distant corner of the diocese, and an obscure hand, will excite filial gratitude, and a due use shall be made of the obligation vouchsafed thereby to

'Your Grace's very dutiful and most obedient
'Son and Servant,
'ROBERT WALKER.'

The same man, who was thus liberal in the education of his numerous family, was even munificent in hospitality as a parish priest. Every Sunday, were served, upon the long table, at which he has been described sitting with a child upon his knee, messes of broth, for the refreshment of those of his congregation who came from a distance, and usually took their seats as parts of his own household. It seems scarcely possible that this custom could have commenced before the augmentation of his cure; and what would to many have been a high price of self-denial, was paid, by the pastor and his family, for this gratification; as the treat could only be provided by dressing at one time the whole, perhaps, of their weekly allowance of fresh animal food; consequently, for a succession of days, the table was covered with cold victuals only. His generosity in old age may be still further illustrated by a little circumstance relating to an orphan grandson, then ten years of age, which I find in a copy of a letter to one of his sons; he requests that half a guinea may be left for 'little Robert's pocket money,' who was then at school: intrusting it to the care of a lady, who, as he says, 'may sometimes frustrate his squandering it away foolishly,' and promising to send him an equal allowance annually for the same purpose. The conclusion of the same letter is so characteristic, that I cannot forbear to transcribe it. 'We,' meaning his wife and himself, 'are in our wonted state of health, allowing for the hasty strides of old age knocking daily at our door, and threateningly telling us, we are not only mortal, but must expect ere long to take our leave of our ancient cottage, and lie down in our last dormitory. Pray pardon my neglect to answer yours: let us hear sooner from you, to augment the mirth of the Christmas holidays. Wishing you all the pleasures of the approaching season, I am, dear Son, with lasting sincerity, yours affectionately,
'ROBERT WALKER.'

He loved old customs and old usages, and in some instances stuck to them to his own loss; for, having had a sum of money lodged in the hands of a neighbouring tradesman, when long course of time had raised the rate of interest, and more was offered, he refused to accept it; an act not difficult to one, who, while he was drawing seventeen pounds a year from his curacy, declined, as we have seen, to add the profits of another small benefice to his own, lest he should be suspected of cupidity.—From this vice he was utterly free; he made no charge for teaching school; such as could afford to pay, gave him what they pleased. When very young, having kept a diary of his expenses, however trifling, the large amount at the end of the year surprised him; and from that time the rule of his life was to be economical, not avaricious. At his decease he left behind him no less a sum than £2,000; and such a sense of his various excellences was prevalent in the country, that the epithet of WONDERFUL is to this day attached to his name.

There is in the above sketch something so extraordinary as to require further *explanatory* details. —And to begin with his industry: eight hours in each day, during five days in the week, and half of Saturday, except when the labours of husbandry were urgent, he was occupied in teaching. His seat was within the rails of the altar; the communion table was his desk; and, like Shenstone's schoolmistress, the master employed himself at the spinning-wheel, while the children were repeating their lessons by his side. Every evening, after school hours, if not more profitably engaged, he continued the same kind of labour, exchanging, for the benefit of exercise, the small wheel at which he had sate, for the large one on which wool is spun, the spinner stepping to and fro. Thus, was the wheel constantly in readiness to prevent the waste of a moment's time. Nor was his industry with the pen, when occasion called for it, less eager. Intrusted with extensive management of public and private affairs, he acted, in his rustic neighbourhood, as scrivener, writing out petitions, deeds of conveyance, wills, covenants, &c., with pecuniary gain to himself, and to the great benefit of his employers. These labours (at all times considerable) at one period of the year, viz. between Christmas and Candlemas, when money transactions are settled in this country, were often so intense, that he passed great part of the night, and sometimes whole nights, at his desk. His garden also was tilled by his own hand; he had a right of pasturage upon the mountains for a few sheep and a couple of cows, which required his attendance; with this pastoral occupation he joined the labours of husbandry upon a small scale, renting two or three acres in addition to his own less than one acre of glebe; and the humblest drudgery which the cultivation of these fields required was performed by himself.

He also assisted his neighbours in haymaking and shearing their flocks, and in the performance of this latter service he was eminently dexterous. They, in their turn, complimented him with the present of a haycock, or a fleece; less as a recom-

713

pense for this particular service than as a general acknowledgment. The Sabbath was in a strict sense kept holy; the Sunday evenings being devoted to reading the Scripture and family prayer. The principal festivals appointed by the Church were also duly observed; but through every other day in the week, through every week in the year he was incessantly occupied in work of hand or mind; not allowing a moment for recreation, except upon a Saturday afternoon, when he indulged himself with a Newspaper, or sometimes with a Magazine. The frugality and temperance established in his house were as admirable as the industry. Nothing to which the name of luxury could be given was there known; in the latter part of his life, indeed, when tea had been brought into almost general use, it was provided for visitors, and for such of his own family as returned occasionally to his roof, and had been accustomed to this refreshment elsewhere; but neither he nor his wife ever partook of it. The raiment worn by his family was comely and decent, but as simple as their diet; the home-spun materials were made up into apparel by their own hands. At the time of the decease of this thrifty pair, their cottage contained a large store of webs of woollen and linen cloth, woven from thread of their own spinning. And it is remarkable that the pew in the chapel in which the family used to sit, remains neatly lined with woollen cloth spun by the pastor's own hands. It is the only pew in the chapel so distinguished; and I know of no other instance of his conformity to the delicate accommodations of modern times. The fuel of the house, like that of their neighbours, consisted of peat, procured from the mosses by their own labour. The lights by which, in the winter evenings, their work was performed, were of their own manufacture, such as still continue to be used in these cottages; they are made of the pith of rushes dipped in any unctuous substance that the house affords. *White* candles, as tallow candles are here called, were reserved to honour the Christmas festivals, and were perhaps produced upon no other occasions. Once a month, during the proper season, a sheep was drawn from their small mountain flock, and killed for the use of the family; and a cow, towards the close of the year, was salted and dried for winter provision: the hide was tanned to furnish them with shoes.—By these various resources, this venerable clergyman reared a numerous family, not only preserving them, as he affectingly says, 'from wanting the necessaries of life;' but affording them an unstinted education, and the means of raising themselves in society. In this they were eminently assisted by the effects of their father's example, his precepts, and injunctions: he was aware that truth-speaking, as a moral virtue, is best secured by inculcating attention to accuracy of report even on trivial occasions; and so rigid were the rules of honesty by which he endeavoured to bring up his family, that if one of them had chanced to find in the lanes or fields anything of the least use or value without being able to ascertain to whom it belonged, he always insisted upon the child's carrying it back to the place from which it had been brought.

No one it might be thought could, as has been described, convert his body into a machine, as it were, of industry for the humblest uses, and keep his thoughts so frequently bent upon secular concerns, without grievous injury to the more precious parts of his nature. How could the powers of intellect thrive, or its graces be displayed, in the midst of circumstances apparently so unfavourable, and where, to the direct cultivation of the mind,

so small a portion of time was allotted? But, in this extraordinary man, things in their nature adverse were reconciled. His conversation was remarkable, not only for being chaste and pure, but for the degree in which it was fervent and eloquent; his written style was correct, simple, and animated. Nor did his *affections* suffer more than his intellect; he was tenderly alive to all the duties of his pastoral office; the poor and needy 'he never sent empty away,'—the stranger was fed and refreshed in passing that unfrequented vale—the sick were visited; and the feelings of humanity found further exercise among the distresses and embarrassments in the worldly estate of his neighbours, with which his talents for business made him acquainted; and the disinterestedness, impartiality, and uprightness which he maintained in the management of all affairs confided to him, were virtues seldom separated in his own conscience from religious obligation. Nor could such conduct fail to remind those who witnessed it of a spirit nobler than law or custom: they felt convictions which, but for such intercourse, could not have been afforded, that, as in the practice of their pastor, there was no guile, so in his faith there was nothing hollow; and we are warranted in believing, that upon these occasions, selfishness, obstinacy, and discord would often give way before the breathings of his good-will and saintly integrity. It may be presumed also—while his humble congregation were listening to the moral precepts which he delivered from the pulpit, and to the Christian exhortations that they should love their neighbours as themselves, and do as they would be done unto —that peculiar efficacy was given to the preacher's labours by recollections in the minds of his congregation, that they were called upon to do no more than his own actions were daily setting before their eyes.

The afternoon service in the chapel was less numerously attended than that of the morning, but by a more serious auditory; the lesson from the New Testament, on those occasions, was accompanied by Burkitt's Commentaries. These lessons he read with impassioned emphasis, frequently drawing tears from his hearers, and leaving a lasting impression upon their minds. His devotional feelings and the powers of his own mind were further exercised, along with those of his family, in perusing the Scriptures: not only on the Sunday evenings, but on every other evening, while the rest of the household were at work, some one of the children, and in her turn the servant, for the sake of practice in reading, or for instruction, read the Bible aloud; and in this manner the whole was repeatedly gone through. That no common importance was attached to the observance of religious ordinances by his family, appears from the following memorandum by one of his descendants, which I am tempted to insert at length, as it is characteristic, and somewhat curious. 'There is a small chapel in the county palatine of Lancaster, where a certain clergyman has regularly officiated above sixty years, and a few months ago administered the sacrament of the Lord's Supper in the same, to a decent number of devout communicants. After the clergyman had received himself, the first company out of the assembly who approached the altar, and kneeled down to be partakers of the sacred elements, consisted of the parson's wife; to whom he had been married upwards of sixty years; one son and his wife; four daughters, each with her husband; whose ages, all added together, amounted to above 714 years. The several and respective distances from the place of each of their abodes, to the chapel where they all communicated, will measure more than 1,000 English miles. Though the narration will appear surprising, it is without doubt a fact that the same persons, exactly four years before, met at the same place, and all joined in performance of the same venerable duty.'

He was indeed most zealously attached to the doctrine and frame of the Established Church. We have seen him congratulating himself that he had no dissenters in his cure of any denomination. Some allowance must be made for the state of opinion when his first religious impressions were received, before the reader will acquit him of bigotry, when I mention, that at the time of the augmentation of the cure, he refused to invest part of the money in the purchase of an estate offered to him upon advantageous terms, because the proprietor was a Quaker;—whether from scrupulous apprehension that a blessing would not attend a contract framed for the benefit of the church between persons not in religious sympathy with each other; or, as a seeker of peace, he was afraid of the uncompling disposition which at one time was too frequently conspicuous in that sect. Of this an instance had fallen under his own notice; for, while he taught school at Loweswater, certain persons of that denomination had refused to pay annual interest due under the title of Church-stock;[1] a great hardship upon the incumbent, for the curacy of Loweswater was then scarcely less poor than that of Seathwaite. To what degree this prejudice of his was blameable need not be determined;—certain it is, that he was not only desirous, as he himself says, to live in peace, but in love, with all men. He was placable, and charitable in his judgments; and, however correct in conduct and rigorous to himself, he was ever ready to forgive the trespasses of others, and to soften the censure that was cast upon their frailties.—It would be unpardonable to omit that, in the maintenance of his virtues, he received due support from the partner of his long life. She was equally strict, in attending to her share of their joint cares, nor less diligent in her appropriate occupations. A person who had been some time their servant in the latter part of their lives, concluded the panegyric of her mistress by saying to me, 'She was no less excellent than her husband; she was good to the poor; she was good to everything!' He survived for a short time this virtuous companion. When she died, he ordered that her body should be borne to the grave by three of her daughters and one grand-daughter; and, when the corpse was lifted from the threshold, he insisted upon lending his aid, and feeling about, for he was then almost blind, took hold of a napkin fixed to the coffin; and, as a bearer of the body, entered the chapel, a few steps from the lowly parsonage.

What a contrast does the life of this obscurely-seated, and, in point of worldly wealth, poorly-repaid Churchman, present to that of a Cardinal Wolsey!

'O 'tis a burthen, Cromwell, 'tis a burthen
Too heavy for a man who hopes for heaven!'

We have been dwelling upon images of peace in the moral world, that have brought us again to the quiet enclosure of consecrated ground, in which this venerable pair lie interred. The sounding brook, that rolls close by the church-

[1] Mr. Walker's charity being of that kind which 'seeketh not her own,' he would rather forego his rights than distrain for dues which the parties liable refused, as a point of conscience, to pay.

yard, without disturbing feeling or meditation, is now unfortunately laid bare; but not long ago it participated, with the chapel, the shade of some stately ash-trees, which will not spring again. While the spectator from this spot is looking round upon the girdle of stony mountains that encompasses the vale,—masses of rock, out of which monuments for all men that ever existed might have been hewn—it would surprise him to be told, as with truth it might be, that the plain blue slab dedicated to the memory of this aged pair is a production of a quarry in North Wales. It was sent as a mark of respect by one of their descendants from the vale of Festiniog, a region almost as beautiful as that in which it now lies!

Upon the Seathwaite Brook, at a small distance from the parsonage, has been erected a mill for spinning yarn; it is a mean and disagreeable object, though not unimportant to the spectator, as calling to mind the momentous changes wrought by such inventions in the frame of society—changes which have proved especially unfavourable to these mountain solitudes. So much had been effected by those new powers, before the subject of the preceding biographical sketch closed his life, that their operation could not escape his notice, and doubtless excited touching reflections upon the comparatively insignificant results of his own manual industry. But Robert Walker was not a man of times and circumstances: had he lived at a later period, the principle of duty would have produced application as unremitting; the same energy of character would have been displayed, though in many instances with widely-different effects.

With pleasure I annex, as illustrative and confirmatory of the above account, extracts from a paper in the 'Christian Remembrancer,' October, 1819; it bears an assumed signature, but is known to be the work of the Rev. Robert Bamford, vicar of Bishopton, in the county of Durham; a great-grandson of Mr. Walker, whose worth it commemorates, by a record not the less valuable for being written in very early youth.

'His house was a nursery of virtue. All the inmates were industrious, and cleanly, and happy. Sobriety, neatness, quietness, characterised the whole family. No railings, no idleness, no indulgence of passion were permitted. Every child, however young, had its appointed engagements; every hand was busy. Knitting, spinning, reading, writing, mending clothes, making shoes, were by the different children constantly performing. The father himself sitting amongst them, and guiding their thoughts, was engaged in the same occupations. . . .

'He sate up late, and rose early; when the family were at rest, he retired to a little room which he had built on the roof of his house. He had slated it, and fitted it up with shelves for his books, his stock of cloth, wearing apparel, and his utensils. There many a cold winter's night, without fire, while the roof was glazed with ice, did he remain reading or writing till the day dawned. He taught the children in the chapel, for there was no school-house. Yet in that cold, damp place he never had a fire. He used to send the children in parties either to his own fire at home, or make them run up the mountain side.

. . . .

'It may be further mentioned, that he was a passionate admirer of Nature; she was his mother, and he was a dutiful child. While engaged on the mountains, it was his greatest pleasure to view the rising sun; and in tranquil evenings, as it slided behind the hills, he blessed its departure. He was skilled in fossils and plants; a constant observer of the stars and winds: the atmosphere was his delight. He made many experiments on its nature and properties. In summer he used to gather a multitude of flies and insects, and, by his entertaining description, amuse and instruct his children. They shared all his daily employments, and derived many sentiments of love and benevolence from his observations on the works and productions of nature. Whether they were following him in the field, or surrounding him in school, he took every opportunity of storing their minds with useful information.—Nor was the circle of his influence confined to Seathwaite. Many a distant mother has told her child of Mr. Walker, and begged him to be as good a man.

. . . . . .

'Once, when I was very young, I had the pleasure of seeing and hearing that venerable old man in his 90th year, and even then, the calmness, the force, the perspicuity of his sermon, sanctified and adorned by the wisdom of grey hairs, and the authority of virtue, had such an effect upon my mind, that I never see a hoary-headed clergyman, without thinking of Mr. Walker. . . . He allowed no dissenter or methodist to interfere in the instruction of the souls committed to his cure: and so successful were his exertions, that he had not one dissenter of any denomination whatever in the whole parish. Though he avoided all religious controversies, yet when age had silvered his head, and virtuous piety had secured to his appearance reverence and silent honour, no one, however determined in his hatred of apostolic descent, could have listened to his discourse on ecclesiastical history and ancient times, without thinking that one of the beloved apostles had returned to mortality, and in that vale of peace had come to exemplify the beauty of holiness in the life and character of Mr. Walker.

. . . . . .

'Until the sickness of his wife, a few months previous to her death, his health and spirits and faculties were unimpaired. But this misfortune gave him such a shock, that his constitution gradually decayed. His senses, except sight, still preserved their powers. He never preached with steadiness after his wife's death. His voice faltered: he always looked at the seat she had used. He could not pass her tomb without tears. He became, when alone, sad and melancholy, though still among his friends kind and good-humoured. He went to bed about twelve o'clock the night before his death. As his custom was, he went, tottering and leaning upon his daughter's arm, to examine the heavens, and meditate a few moments in the open air. "How clear the moon shines to-night!" He said these words, sighed, and laid down. At six next morning he was found a corpse. Many a tear, and many a heavy heart, and many a grateful blessing followed him to the grave.'

Having mentioned in this narrative the vale of Loweswater as a place where Mr. Walker taught school, I will add a few memoranda from its parish register, respecting a person apparently of desires as moderate, with whom he must have been intimate during his residence there.

'Let him that would, ascend the tottering seat
Of courtly grandeur, and become as great
As are his mounting wishes; but for me,
Let sweet repose and rest my portion be.
'HENRY FOREST, Curate.'

'Honour, the idol which the most adore,
Receives no homage from my knee;
Content in privacy I value more
Than all uneasy dignity.'

'Henry Forest came to Loweswater, 1708, being twenty-five years of age.'
'This curacy was twice augmented by Queen Anne's Bounty. The first payment, with great difficulty, was paid to Mr. John Curwen of London, on the 9th of May, 1724, deposited by me, Henry Forest, Curate of Loweswater. Ye said 9th of May, ye said Mr. Curwen went to the office, and saw my name registered there, &c. This, by the Providence of God, came by lot to this poor place.
'Hæc testor H. FOREST.'

In another place he records, that the sycamore trees were planted in the churchyard in 1710.
He died in 1741, having been curate thirty-four years. It is not improbable that H. Forest was the gentleman who assisted Robert Walker in his classical studies at Loweswater.
To this parish register is prefixed a motto, of which the following verses are a part:—
'Invigilate viri, tacito nam tempora gressu
Diffugiunt, nulloque sono convertitur annus;
Utendum est ætate, cito pede præterit ætas.'—W.

Page 303, last line.

'We feel that we are greater than we know.']
'And feel that I am happier than I know.'
MILTON.

The allusion to the Greek poet will be obvious to the classical reader.—W.

The poet in question is Moschus; the passage of which W. is thinking is from the *Epitaphium Bionis*, ll. 106-111.
The seventh line of the Sonnet is a reminiscence of the following line of Moschus:—
ἄμμες δ', οἱ μεγάλοι καὶ καρτεροὶ ἢ σοφοὶ ἄνδρες.—ED.

HIGHLAND HUT
Page 307.

This Sonnet describes the *exterior* of a Highland hut, as often seen under morning or evening sunshine. To the authoress of the 'Address to the Wind,' and other poems, in these volumes, who was my fellow-traveller in this tour, I am indebted for the following extract from her journal, which accurately describes under particular circumstances, the beautiful appearance of the *interior* of one of these rude habitations.
'On our return from the Trosachs the evening began to darken, and it rained so heavily that we were completely wet before we had come two miles, and it was dark when we landed with our boatman, at his hut upon the banks of Loch Katrine. I was faint from cold: the good woman had provided, according to her promise, a better fire than we had found in the morning; and, indeed, when I sat down in the chimney-corner of her smoky biggin, I thought I had never felt more comfortable in my life: a pan of coffee was boiling for us, and, having put our clothes in the way of drying, we all sat down thankful for a shelter. We could not prevail upon our boatman, the master of the house, to draw near the fire, though he was cold and wet, or to suffer his wife to get him dry clothes till she had served us, which she did most willingly, though not very expeditiously.
'A Cumberland man of the same rank would not have had such a notion of what was fit and right in his own house, or, if he had, one would have accused him of servility; but in the Highlander it

NOTES

only seemed like politeness (however erroneous and painful to us), naturally growing out of the dependence of the inferiors of the clan upon their laird; he did not, however, refuse to let his wife bring out the whisky bottle for his refreshment, at our request. "She keeps a dram," as the phrase is: indeed, I believe there is scarcely a lonely house by the wayside, in Scotland, where travellers may not be accommodated with a dram. We asked for sugar, butter, barley-bread, and milk; and, with a smile and a stare more of kindness than wonder, she replied, "Ye'll get that," bringing each article separately. We caroused our cups of coffee, laughing like children at the strange atmosphere in which we were: the smoke came in gusts, and spread along the walls; and above our heads in the chimney (where the hens were roosting) it appeared like clouds in the sky. We laughed and laughed again, in spite of the smarting of our eyes, yet had a quieter pleasure in observing the beauty of the beams and rafters gleaming between the clouds of smoke: they had been crusted over, and varnished by many winters, till, where the twilight fell upon them, they had become as glossy as black rocks, on a sunny day, cased in ice. When we had eaten our supper we sat about half an hour, and I think I never felt so deeply the blessing of a hospitable welcome and a warm fire. The man of the house repeated from time to time that we should often tell of this night when we got to our homes, and interposed praises of his own lake, which he had more than once, when we were returning in the boat, ventured to say was "bonnier than Loch Lomond." Our companion from the Trosachs, who, it appeared, was an Edinburgh drawing-master going, during the vacation, on a pedestrian tour to John o'Groat's house, was to sleep in the barn with my fellow-travellers, where the man said he had plenty of dry hay. I do not believe that the hay of the Highlands is ever very dry, but this year it had a better chance than usual: wet or dry, however, the next morning they said they had slept comfortably. When I went to bed, the mistress, desiring me to "go ben," attended me with a candle, and assured me that the bed was dry, though not "sic as I had been used to." It was of chaff: there were two others in the room, a cupboard and two chests, upon one of which stood milk in wooden vessels, covered over. The walls of the house were of stone unplastered: it consisted of three apartments, the cowhouse at one end, the kitchen or house in the middle, and the spence at the other end; the rooms were divided not up to the rigging, but only to the beginning of the roof, so that there was a free passage for light and smoke from one end of the house to the other. I went to bed some time before the rest of the family; the door was shut between us, and they had a bright fire, which I could not see, but the light it sent up amongst the varnished rafters and beams, which crossed each other in almost as intricate and fantastic a manner as I have seen the under-boughs of a large beech-tree withered by the depth of shade above, produced the most beautiful effect that can be conceived. It was like what I should suppose an underground cave or temple to be, with a dripping or moist roof, and the moonlight entering in upon it by some means or other; and yet the colours were more like those of melted gems. I lay looking up till the light of the fire faded away, and the man and his wife and child had crept into their bed at the other end of the room: I did not sleep much, but passed a comfortable night; for my bed, though hard, was

warm and clean: the unusualness of my situation prevented me from sleeping. I could hear the waves beat against the shore of the lake; a little rill close to the door made a much louder noise, and, when I sat up in my bed, I could see the lake through an open window-place at the bed's head. Add to this, it rained all night. I was less occupied by remembrance of the Trosachs, beautiful as they were, than the vision of the Highland hut, which I could not get out of my head; I thought of the Faery-land of Spenser, and what I had read in romance at other times; and then what a feast it would be for a London Pantomime-maker could he but transplant it to Drury-lane, with all its beautiful colours!'—*MS.*—W.

Page 309.

'Once on those steeps *I* roamed.'] The following is from the same MS., and gives an account of the visit to Bothwell Castle here alluded to:—

'It was exceedingly delightful to enter thus unexpectedly upon such a beautiful region. The castle stands nobly, overlooking the Clyde. When we came up to it, I was hurt to see that flower-borders had taken place of the natural over-growings of the ruin, the scattered stones, and wild plants. It is a large and grand pile of red freestone, harmonising perfectly with the rocks of the river, from which, no doubt, it has been hewn. When I was a little accustomed to the unnaturalness of a modern garden, I could not help admiring the excessive beauty and luxuriance of some of the plants, particularly the purple-flowered clematis, and a broad-leafed creeping plant without flowers, which scrambled up the castle wall, along with the ivy, and spread its vine-like branches so lavishly that it seemed to be in its natural situation, and one could not help thinking that, though not self-planted among the ruins of this country, it must somewhere have its native abode in such places. If Bothwell Castle had not been close to the Douglas mansion, we should have been disgusted with the possessor's miserable conception of *adorning* such a venerable ruin; but it is so very near to the house, that of necessity the pleasure-grounds must have extended beyond it, and perhaps the neatness of a shaven lawn and the complete desolation natural to a ruin might have made an unpleasing contrast; and, besides being within the precincts of the pleasure-grounds, and so very near to the dwelling of a noble family, it has forfeited, in some degree, its independent majesty, and becomes a tributary to the mansion: its solitude being interrupted, it has no longer the command over the mind in sending it back into past times, or excluding the ordinary feelings which we bear about us in daily life. We had then only to regret that the castle and the house were so near to each other; and it was impossible *not* to regret it; for the ruin presides in state over the river, far from city or town, as if it might have a peculiar privilege to preserve its memorials of past ages, and maintain its own character for centuries to come. We sat upon a bench under the high trees, and had beautiful views of the different reaches of the river, above and below. On the opposite bank, which is finely wooded with elm and other trees, are the remains of a priory built upon a rock; and rock and ruin are so blended, that it is impossible to separate the one from the other. Nothing can be more beautiful than the little remnant of this holy place; elm-trees (for we were near enough to distinguish them by their branches) grow out of the walls, and overshadow a small, but very elegant window. It can scarcely be conceived what a grace

717

NOTES

the castle and priory impart to each other; and the river Clyde flows on, smooth and unruffled below, seeming to my thoughts more in harmony with the sober and stately images of former times, than if it had roared over a rocky channel, forcing its sound upon the ear. It blended gently with the warbling of the smaller birds, and the chattering of the larger ones, that had made their nests in the ruins. In this fortress the chief of the English nobility were confined after the battle of Bannockburn. If a man *is* to be a prisoner, he scarcely could have a more pleasant place to solace his captivity; but I thought that, for close confinement, I should prefer the banks of a lake, or the seaside. The greatest charm of a brook or river is in the liberty to pursue it through its windings: you can then take it in whatever mood you like; silent or noisy, sportive or quiet. The beauties of a brook or river must be sought, and the pleasure is in going in search of them; those of a lake or of the sea come to you of themselves. These rude warriors cared little, perhaps, about either; and yet, if one may judge from the writings of Chaucer, and from the old romances, more interesting passions were connected with natural objects in the days of chivalry than now; though going in search of scenery, as it is called, had not then been thought of. I had previously heard nothing of Bothwell Castle, at least nothing that I remembered; therefore, perhaps, my pleasure was greater, compared with what I received elsewhere, than others might feel.'—*MS. Journal.*—W.

HART'S-HORN TREE
Page 310.

'In the time of the first Robert de Clifford, in the year 1333 or 1334, Edward Baliol king of Scotland came into Westmoreland, and stayed some time with the said Robert at his castles of Appleby, Brougham, and Pendragon. And during that time they ran a stag by a single greyhound out of Whinfell Park to Redkirk, in Scotland, and back again to this place; where, being both spent, the stag leaped over the pales, but died on the other side; and the greyhound, attempting to leap, fell, and died on the contrary side. In memory of this fact the stag's horns were nailed upon a tree just by, and (the dog being named Hercules) this rhythm was made upon them:

'Hercules kill'd Hart a greese,
And Hart a greese killed Hercules.'

The tree to this day bears the name of Hart's-horn Tree. The horns in process of time were almost grown over by the growth of the tree, and another pair was put up in their place.'—*Nicholson and Burns's History of Westmoreland and Cumberland.*

The tree has now disappeared, but I well remember its imposing appearance as it stood, in a decayed state, by the side of the high road leading from Penrith to Appleby. This whole neighbourhood abounds in interesting traditions and vestiges of antiquity, viz. Julian's Bower; Brougham and Penrith Castles; Penrith Beacon, and the curious remains in Penrith Churchyard; Arthur's Round Table, and, close by, Maybrough; the excavation, called the Giant's Cave, on the banks of the Emont; Long Meg and her daughters, near Eden. &c. &c.—W.

THE WHITE DOE OF RYLSTONE
Page 311.

The Poem of the White Doe of Rylstone is founded on a local tradition, and on the Ballad in Percy's Collection, entitled 'The Rising of the North.' The tradition is as follows:—'About this time,' not long after the Dissolution, 'a White Doe,' say the aged people of the neighbourhood, 'long continued to make a weekly pilgrimage from Rylstone over the fells of Bolton, and was constantly found in the Abbey Churchyard during divine service; after the close of which she returned home as regularly as the rest of the congregation.' —DR. WHITAKER'S *History of the Deanery of Craven.*—Rylstone was the property and residence of the Nortons, distinguished in that ill-advised and unfortunate Insurrection; which led me to connect with this tradition the principal circumstances of their fate, as recorded in the Ballad.

'Bolton Priory,' says Dr. Whitaker in his excellent book, 'The History and Antiquities of the Deanery of Craven,' 'stands upon a beautiful curvature of the Wharf, on a level sufficiently elevated ro protect it from inundations, and low enough for every purpose of picturesque effect.

'Opposite to the East window of the Priory Church, the river washes the foot of a rock nearly perpendicular, and of the richest purple, where several of the mineral beds, which break out, instead of maintaining their usual inclination to the horizon, are twisted by some inconceivable process into undulating and spiral lines. To the South all is soft and delicious; the eye reposes upon a few rich pastures, a moderate reach of the river, sufficiently tranquil to form a mirror to the sun, and the bounding hills beyond, neither too near nor too lofty to exclude, even in winter, any portion of his rays.

'But, after all, the glories of Bolton are on the North. Whatever the most fastidious taste could require to constitute a perfect landscape, is not only found here, but in its proper place. In front, and immediately under the eye, is a smooth expanse of park-like enclosure, spotted with native elm, ash, &c., of the finest growth: on the right a skirting oak wood, with jutting points of grey rock; on the left a rising copse. Still forward are seen the aged groves of Bolton Park, the growth of centuries; and farther yet, the barren and rocky distances of Simon-seat and Barden Fell contrasted with the warmth, fertility, and luxuriant foliage of the valley below.

'About half a mile above Bolton the valley closes, and either side of the Wharf is overhung by solemn woods, from which huge perpendicular masses of grey rock jut out at intervals.

'This sequestered scene was almost inaccessible till of late, that ridings have been cut on both sides of the river, and the most interesting points laid open by judicious thinnings in the woods. Here a tributary stream rushes from a waterfall, and bursts through a woody glen to mingle its waters with the Wharf: there the Wharf itself is nearly lost in a deep cleft in the rock, and next becomes a horned flood enclosing a woody island —sometimes it reposes for a moment, and then resumes its native character, lively, irregular, and impetuous.

'The cleft mentioned above is the tremendous STRID. This chasm, being incapable of receiving the winter floods, has formed on either side a broad strand of naked grit-stone full of rockbasins, or "pots of the Linn," which bear witness to the restless impetuosity of so many Northern torrents. But, if here Wharf is lost to the eye, it amply repays another sense by its deep and solemn roar, like "the Voice of the angry Spirit of the Waters," heard far above and beneath, amidst the silence of the surrounding woods.

718

NOTES

'The terminating object of the landscape is the remains of Barden Tower, interesting from their form and situation, and still more so from the recollections which they excite.'—W.

Page 312.

'Action is transitory.'] This and the five lines that follow were either read or recited by me, more than thirty years since, to the late Mr. Hazlitt, who quoted some expressions in them (imperfectly remembered) in a work of his published several years ago.—W.

Page 312, l. 1.

'From Bolton's old monastic Tower.'] It is to be regretted that at the present day Bolton Abbey wants this ornament: but the Poem, according to the imagination of the Poet, is composed in Queen Elizabeth's time. 'Formerly,' says Dr. Whitaker, 'over the Transept was a tower. This is proved not only from the mention of bells at the Dissolution, when they could have had no other place, but from the pointed roof of the choir, which must have terminated westward, in some building of superior height to the ridge.'—W.

Page 312, l. 27.

'A Chapel, like a wild-bird's nest.'] 'The Nave of the Church having been reserved at the Dissolution, for the use of the Saxon Cure, is still a parochial Chapel; and, at this day, is as well kept as the neatest English cathedral.'—W.

Page 312, l. 34.

'Who sate in the shade of the Prior's Oak!'] 'At a small distance from the great gateway stood the Prior's Oak, which was felled about the year 1720, and sold for £70. According to the price of wood at that time, it could scarcely have contained less than 1400 feet of timber.'—W.

Page 314, l. 226.

'When Lady Aäliza mourned.'] The detail of this tradition may be found in Dr. Whitaker's book, and in a Poem of this Collection, 'The Force of Prayer.'—W.

Page 314, l. 242.

'Pass, pass who will, yon chantry door;'] 'At the East end of the North aisle of Bolton Priory Church is a chantry belonging to Bethmesly Hall, and a vault, where, according to tradition, the Claphams' (who inherited this estate, by the female line, from the Mauleverers) 'were interred upright.' John de Clapham, of whom this ferocious act is recorded, was a man of great note in his time: 'he was a vehement partisan of the house of Lancaster, in whom the spirit of his chieftains, the Cliffords, seemed to survive.'—W.

Page 314, l. 268.

'Who loved the Shepherd-lord to meet.'] In the second Volume of these Poems [Collective Edition of 1820.—ED.] will be found one entitled, 'Song at the Feast of Brougham Castle, upon the Restoration of Lord Clifford, the Shepherd, to the Estates and Honours of his Ancestors.' To that Poem is annexed an account of this personage, chiefly extracted from Burns and Nicholson's 'History of Cumberland and Westmoreland.' It gives me pleasure to add these further particulars concerning him, from Dr. Whitaker, who says he 'retired to the solitude of Barden, where he seems to have enlarged the tower out of a common keeper's lodge, and where he found a retreat

equally favourable to taste, to instruction, and to devotion. The narrow limits of his residence show that he had learned to despise the pomp of greatness, and that a small train of servants could suffice him, who had lived to the age of thirty a servant himself. I think this nobleman resided here almost entirely when in Yorkshire, for all his charters which I have seen are dated at Barden.

'His early habits, and the want of those artificial measures of time which even shepherds now possess, had given him a turn for observing the motions of the heavenly bodies; and, having purchased such an apparatus as could then be procured, he amused and informed himself by those pursuits, with the aid of the Canons of Bolton, some of whom are said to have been well versed in what was then known of the science.

'I suspect this nobleman to have been sometimes occupied in a more visionary pursuit, and probably in the same company.

'For, from the family evidences, I have met with two MSS., on the subject of Alchemy, which, from the character, spelling, &c., may almost certainly be referred to the reign of Henry the Seventh. If these were originally deposited with the MSS. of the Cliffords, it might have been for the use of this nobleman. If they were brought from Bolton at the Dissolution, they must have been the work of those Canons whom he almost exclusively conversed with.

'In these peaceful employments Lord Clifford spent the whole reign of Henry the Seventh, and the first years of his son. But in the year 1513, when almost sixty years old, he was appointed to a principal command over the army which fought at Flodden, and showed that the military genius of the family had neither been chilled in him by age, nor extinguished by habits of peace.

'He survived the battle of Flodden ten years, and died April 23rd, 1523, aged about 70. I shall endeavour to appropriate to him a tomb, vault, and chantry, in the choir of the church of Bolton, as I should be sorry to believe that he was deposited, when dead, at a distance from the place which in his lifetime he loved so well.

'By his last will he appointed his body to be interred at Shap, if he died in Westmoreland; or at Bolton, if he died in Yorkshire.'

With respect to the Canons of Bolton, Dr. Whitaker shows from MSS. that not only alchemy but astronomy was a favourite pursuit with them.—W.

Page 317, ll. 594–5.

'Now joy for you who from the towers
Of Brancepeth look in doubt and fear,']

Brancepeth Castle stands near the river Were, a few miles from the city of Durham. It formerly belonged to the Nevilles, Earls of Westmoreland. See Dr. Percy's account.—W.

Page 319, ll. 814–15.

'Of mitred Thurston—what a Host
He conquered!']

See the Historians for the account of this memorable battle, usually denominated the Battle of the Standard.—W.

Page 319, l. 828.

'In that other day of Neville's Cross?'] 'In the night before the battle of Durham was strucken and begun, the 17th day of October, anno 1346, there did appear to John Fosser, then Prior of the Abbey of Durham, a Vision, commanding him to take the holy Corporax-cloth, wherewith St.

Cuthbert did cover the chalice when he used to say mass, and to put the same holy relique like to a banner-cloth upon the point of a spear, and the next morning to go and repair to a place on the west side of the city of Durham, called the Red Hills, where the Maid's Bower wont to be, and there to remain and abide till the end of the battle. To which vision the Prior obeying, and taking the same for a revelation of God's grace and mercy by the mediation of Holy St. Cuthbert, did accordingly the next morning, with the monks of the said abbey, repair to the said Red Hills, and there most devoutly humbling and prostrating themselves in prayer for the victory in the said battle: (a great multitude of the Scots running and pressing by them, with intention to have spoiled them, yet had no power to commit any violence under such holy persons, so occupied in prayer, being protected and defended by the mighty Providence of Almighty God, and by the mediation of Holy St. Cuthbert, and the presence of the holy relique). And, after many conflicts and warlike exploits there had and done between the English men and the King of Scots and his company, the said battle ended, and the victory was obtained, to the great overthrow and confusion of the Scots, their enemies: And then the said Prior and monks accompanied with Ralph Lord Nevil, and John Nevil his son, and the Lord Percy, and many other nobles of England, returned home and went to the abbey church, there joining in hearty prayer and thanksgiving to God and Holy St. Cuthbert for the victory achieved that day.'

The battle was afterwards called the Battle of Neville's Cross from the following circumstance:—

'On the west side of the city of Durham, where two roads pass each other, a most notable, famous, and goodly cross of stonework was erected and set up to the honour of God for the victory there obtained in the field of battle, and known by the name of Nevil's Cross, and built at the sole cost of the Lord Ralph Nevil, one of the most excellent and chief persons in the said battle.' The Relique of St. Cuthbert afterwards became of great importance in military events. For soon after this battle, says the same author, 'The prior caused a goodly and sumptuous banner to be made,' (which is then described at great length), 'and in the midst of the same banner-cloth was the said holy relique and corporax-cloth enclosed, &c. &c., and so sumptuously finished, and absolutely perfected, this banner was dedicated to Holy St. Cuthbert, of intent and purpose that for the future it should be carried to any battle, as occasion should serve; and was never carried and showed at any battle but by the especial grace of God Almighty, and the mediation of Holy St. Cuthbert, it brought home victory; which banner-cloth, after the dissolution of the abbey, fell into the possession of Dean WHITTINGHAM, whose wife, called KATHARINE, being a French woman, (as is most credibly reported by eyewitnesses,) did most injuriously burn the same in her fire, to the open contempt and disgrace of all ancient and goodly reliques.'—Extracted from a book entitled, 'Durham Cathedral, as it stood before the Dissolution of the Monastery.' It appears, from the old metrical History, that the above-mentioned banner was carried by the Earl of Surrey to Flodden Field.—W.

Page 322, ll. 1167–8.
'An edifice of warlike frame
Stands single—Norton Tower its name—']
It is so called to this day, and is thus described

by Dr. Whitaker:—'Rylstone Fell yet exhibits a monument of the old warfare between the Nortons and Cliffords. On a point of very high ground, commanding an immense prospect, and protected by two deep ravines, are the remains of a square tower, expressly said by Dodsworth to have been built by Richard Norton. The walls are of strong grout-work, about four feet thick. It seems to have been three stories high. Breaches have been industriously made in all the sides, almost to the ground, to render it untenable.

'But Norton Tower was probably a sort of pleasure-house in summer, as there are, adjoining to it, several large mounds, (two of them are pretty entire,) of which no other account can be given than that they were butts for large companies of archers.

'The place is savagely wild, and admirably adapted to the uses of a watch tower.'—W.

Page 326, ll. 1568–9.
————'despoil and desolation
O'er Rylstone's fair domain have blown;']
'After the attainder of Richard Norton his estates were forfeited to the crown, where they remained till the 2nd or 3rd of James; they were then granted to Francis Earl of Cumberland.' From an accurate survey, made at that time, several particulars have been extracted by Dr. W. It appears that the 'mansion-house was then in decay. Immediately adjoining is a close, called the Vivery, so called, undoubtedly, from the French Vivier, or modern Latin Vivarium; for there are near the house large remains of a pleasure-ground, such as were introduced in the earlier part of Elizabeth's time, with topiary works, fishponds, and island, &c. The whole township was ranged by an hundred and thirty red deer, the property of the Lord, which, together with the wood, had after the attainder of Mr. Norton, been committed to Sir Stephen Tempest. The wood, it seems, had been abandoned to depredations, before which time it appears that the neighbourhood must have exhibited a forest-like and sylvan scene. In this survey among the old tenants, is mentioned one Richard Kitchen, butler to Mr. Norton, who rose in rebellion with his master, and was executed at Ripon.'—W.

Page 327, l. 1707.
'In the deep fork of Amerdale;']'At the extremity of the parish of Burnsal, the valley of Wharf forks off into two great branches, one of which retains the name of Wharfdale, to the source of the river; the other is usually called Littondale, but more anciently and properly, Amerdale. Dernbrook, which runs along an obscure valley from the N.W., is derived from a Teutonic word, signifying concealment.'—DR. WHITAKER.—W.

Page 327, ll. 1761–2.
'When the bells of Rylstone played
Their sabbath music—" God us ayde"'
On one of the bells of Rylstone Church, which seems coeval with the building of the tower, is this cypher, ' I. A.' for John Norton, and the motto, ' God us ayde.'—W.

Page 328, l. 1803.
'The grassy rock-encircled Pound.'] Which is thus described by Dr. Whitaker:—'On the plain summit of the hill are the foundations of a strong wall stretching from the S.W. to the N.E. corner of the tower, and to the edge of a very deep glen. From this glen, a ditch, several hundred yards long,

720

runs south to another deep and rugged ravine. On the N. and W. where the banks are very steep, no wall or mound is discoverable, paling being the only fence that could stand on such ground.

'From the Minstrelsy of the Scottish Border it appears that such pounds for deer, sheep, &c. were far from being uncommon in the south of Scotland. The principle of them was something like that of a wire mouse-trap. On the declivity of a steep hill, the bottom and sides of which were fenced so as to be impassable, a wall was constructed nearly level with the surface on the outside, yet so high within, that without wings it was impossible to escape in the opposite direction. Care was probably taken that these enclosures should contain better feed than the neighbouring parks or forests; and whoever is acquainted with the habits of these sequacious animals, will easily conceive, that if the leader was once tempted to descend into the snare, a herd would follow.'

I cannot conclude without recommending to the notice of all lovers of beautiful scenery, Bolton Abbey and its neighbourhood. This enchanting spot belongs to the Duke of Devonshire; and the superintendence of it has for some years been entrusted to the Rev. William Carr, who has most skilfully opened out its features; and, in whatever he has added has done justice to the place, by working with an invisible hand of art in the very spirit of nature.—W.

ECCLESIASTICAL SONNETS
Page 329.

During the month of December, 1820, I accompanied a much-beloved and honoured Friend in a walk through different parts of his estate, with a view to fix upon the site of a new Church which he intended to erect. It was one of the most beautiful mornings of a mild season,—our feelings were in harmony with the cherishing influences of the scene; and such being our purpose, we were naturally led to look back upon past events with wonder and gratitude, and on the future with hope. Not long afterwards, some of the Sonnets which will be found towards the close of this series were produced as a private memorial of that morning's occupation.

The Catholic Question, which was agitated in Parliament about that time, kept my thoughts in the same course; and it struck me that certain points in the Ecclesiastical History of our Country might advantageously be presented to view in verse. Accordingly, I took up the subject, and what I now offer to the reader was the result.

When this work was far advanced, I was agreeably surprised to find that my friend, Mr. Southey, had been engaged with similar views in writing a concise History of the Church in England. If our Productions, thus unintentionally coinciding, shall be found to illustrate each other, it will prove a high gratification to me, which I am sure my friend will participate.

W. WORDSWORTH.

RYDAL MOUNT,
January 24, 1822.

For the convenience of passing from one point of the subject to another without shocks of abruptness, this work has taken the shape of a series of Sonnets: but the Reader, it is to be hoped, will find that the pictures are often so closely connected as to have jointly the effect of passages of a poem in a form of stanza to which there is no objection but one that bears upon the Poet only—its difficulty. —W.

Page 329.

'Did Holy Paul,' &c.] Stillingfleet adduces many arguments in support of this opinion, but they are unconvincing. The latter part of this Sonnet refers to a favourite notion of Roman Catholic writers, that Joseph of Arimathea and his companions brought Christianity into Britain, and built a rude church at Glastonbury; alluded to hereafter, in a passage upon the dissolution of monasteries.—W.

Page 330.

'That Hill, whose flowery platform,' &c.]. This hill at St. Alban's must have been an object of great interest to the imagination of the venerable Bede, who thus describes it, with a delicate feeling, delightful to meet with in that rude age, traces of which are frequent in his works:—'Variis herbarum floribus depictus imò usquequaque vestitus, in quo nihil repentè arduum, nihil præceps, nihil abruptum, quem lateribus longè latèque deductum in modum æquoris natura complanat, dignum videlicet eum pro insitâ sibi specie venustatis jam olim reddens, qui beati martyris cruore dicaretur.' —W.

Page 331.

'Nor wants the cause the panic-striking aid Of hallelujahs.']

Alluding to the victory gained under Germanus. —See Bede.—W.

Page 331, XI, ll. 9, 10.

'By men yet scarcely conscious of a care For other monuments than those of Earth;']

The last six lines of this Sonnet are chiefly from the prose of Daniel; and here I will state (though to the Readers whom this Poem will chiefly interest it is unnecessary) that my obligations to other prose writers are frequent,—obligations which, even if I had not a pleasure in courting, it would have been presumptuous to shun, in treating an historical subject. I must, however, particularise Fuller, to whom I am indebted in the Sonnet upon Wicliffe and in other instances. And upon the acquittal of the Seven Bishops I have done little more than versify a lively description of that event in the MS. Memoirs of the first Lord Lonsdale. —W.

SONNET XII
Page 331.

'Ethelforth reached the convent of Bangor, he perceived the Monks, twelve hundred in number, offering prayers for the success of their countrymen: "if they are praying against us," he exclaimed, "they are fighting against us;" and he ordered them to be first attacked: they were destroyed; and, appalled by their fate, the courage of Brocmail wavered, and he fled from the field in dismay. Thus abandoned by their leader, his army soon gave way, and Ethelforth obtained a decisive conquest. Ancient Bangor itself soon fell into his hands, and was demolished; the noble monastery was levelled to the ground; its library, which is mentioned as a large one, the collection of ages, the repository of the most precious monuments of the ancient Britons, was consumed; half ruined walls, gates, and rubbish were all that remained of the magnificent edifice.'—See Turner's valuable history of the Anglo-Saxons.

Taliesin was present at the battle which preceded this desolation.

The account Bede gives of this remarkable event,

NOTES

suggests a most striking warning against National and Religious prejudices.—W.

SONNET XV
Page 332.

The person of Paulinus is thus described by Bede, from the memory of an eye-witness:—'Longæ staturæ, paululum incurvus, nigro capillo, facie macilentâ, naso adunco, pertenui, venerabilis simul et terribilis aspectu.'—W.

Page 332.

'Man's life is like a Sparrow.'] See the original of this speech in Bede.—The Conversion of Edwin, as related by him, is highly interesting—and the breaking up of this Council accompanied with an event so striking and characteristic, that I am tempted to give it at length in a translation. '"Who," exclaimed the King, when the Council was ended, "shall first desecrate the altars and the temples?" "I," answered the Chief Priest; "for who more fit than myself, through the wisdom which the true God hath given me, to destroy, for the good example of others, what in foolishness I worshipped?" Immediately, casting away vain superstition, he besought the King to grant him what the laws did not allow to a priest, arms and a courser (equum emissarium); which mounting, and furnished with a sword and lance, he proceeded to destroy the Idols. The crowd, seeing this, thought him mad—he, however, halted not, but, approaching, he profaned the temple, casting against it the lance which he had held in his hand, and, exulting in acknowledgment of the worship of the true God, he ordered his companions to pull down the temple, with all its enclosures. The place is shown where those Idols formerly stood, not far from York, at the source of the river Derwent, and is at this day called Gormund Gaham, ubi pontifex ille, inspirante Deo vero, polluit ac destruxit eas, quas ipse sacraverat aras.' The last expression is a pleasing proof that the venerable monk of Wearmouth was familiar with the poetry of Virgil.—W.

Page 332.

————'such the inviting voice
Heard near fresh streams;']

The early propagators of Christianity were accustomed to preach near rivers, for the convenience of baptism.—W.

SONNET XIX
Page 333.

Having spoken of the zeal, disinterestedness, and temperance of the clergy of those times, Bede thus proceeds:—'Unde et in magna erat veneratione tempore illo religionis habitus, ita ut ubicunque clericus aliquis, aut monachus adveniret, gaudenter ab omnibus tanquam Dei famulus exciperetur. Etiam si in itinere pergens inveniretur, accurrebant, et flexâ cervice, vel manu signari, vel ore illius se benedici, gaudebant. Verbis quoque horum exhortatoriis diligenter auditum præbebant.' Lib. iii. cap. 26.—W.

Page 334, XXIV, 1. 2.

'The people work like congregated bees.'] See, in Turner's History, vol. iii. p. 528, the account of the erection of Ramsey Monastery. Penances were removable by the performance of acts of charity and benevolence.—W.

Page 334.

————'pain narrows not his cares.'] Through the whole of his life, Alfred was subject to grievous maladies.—W.

Page 335.

'Woe to the Crown that doth the Cowl obey!'] The violent measures carried on under the influence of Dunstan, for strengthening the Benedictine Order, were a leading cause of the second series of Danish invasions.—See Turner.—W.

Page 337.

'Here Man more purely lives,' &c.] Bonum est nos hic esse, quia homo vivit purius, cadit rarius, surgit velocius, incedit cautius, quiescit securius, moritur felicius, purgatur citius, præmiatur copiosius.'—Bernard. 'This sentence,' says Dr. Whitaker, 'is usually inscribed in some conspicuous part of the Cistertian houses.'—W.

Page 339.

'Whom Obloquy pursues with hideous bark.'] The list of foul names bestowed upon those poor creatures is long and curious:—and, as is, alas! too natural, most of the opprobrious appellations are drawn from circumstances into which they were forced by their persecutors, who even consolidated their miseries into one reproachful term, calling them Patarenians, or Paturins, from pati, to suffer.
'Dwellers with wolves, she names them, for the pine
And green oak are their covert; as the gloom
Of night oft foils their enemy's design,
She calls them Riders on the flying broom;
Sorcerers, whose frame and aspect have become
One and the same through practices malign.'—W.

Page 341, XXI, ll. 7, 8.

'And the green lizard and the gilded newt
Lead unmolested lives, and die of age.']

These two lines are adopted from a MS., written about the year 1770, which accidentally fell into my possession. The close of the preceding Sonnet on monastic voluptuousness is taken from the same source, as is the verse, 'Where Venus sits,' &c., and the line, 'Once ye were holy, ye are holy still,' in a subsequent Sonnet.—W.

Page 343.

'One (like those prophets whom God sent of old) Transfigured,' &c.] 'M. Latimer suffered his keeper very quietly to pull off his hose, and his other array, which to looke unto was very simple: and being stripped into his shrowd, he seemed as comely a person to them that were present, as one should lightly see: and whereas in his clothes hee appeared a withered and crooked sillie (weak) olde man, he now stood bold upright, as comely a father as one might lightly behold. . . . Then they brought a faggotte, kindled with fire, and laid the same downe at doctor Ridley's feete. To whome M. Latimer spake in this manner, "Bee of good comfort, master Ridley, and play the man: wee shall this day light such a candle by God's grace in England, as I trust shall never bee put out."' —Fox's Acts, &c.
Similar alterations in the outward figure and deportment of persons brought to like trial were not uncommon. See note to the above passage in Dr. Wordsworth's 'Ecclesiastical Biography,' for an example in an humble Welsh fisherman.—W.

Page 344.

'The gift exalting, and with playful smile:'] 'On foot they went, and took Salisbury in their way,

722

NOTES

purposely to see the good Bishop, who made Mr. Hooker sit at his own table; which Mr. Hooker boasted of with much joy and gratitude when he saw his mother and friends; and at the Bishop's parting with him, the Bishop gave him good counsel and his benediction, but forgot to give him money; which when the Bishop had considered, he sent a servant in all haste to call Richard back to him, and at Richard's return, the Bishop said to him, "Richard, I sent for you back to lend you a horse which hath carried me many a mile, and I thank God with much ease," and presently delivered into his hand a walking-staff, with which he professed he had travelled through many parts of Germany; and he said, "Richard, I do not give, but lend you my horse, be sure you be honest, and bring my horse back to me, at your return this way to Oxford. And I do now give you ten groats to bear your charges to Exeter; and here is ten groats more, which I charge you to deliver to your mother, and tell her I send her a Bishop's benediction with it, and beg the continuance of her prayers for me. And if you bring my horse back to me, I will give you ten groats more to carry you on foot to the college; and so God bless you, good Richard."'
—See WALTON'S *Life of Richard Hooker.*—W.

Page 345, XLI, ll. 10, 11.

————'craftily incites
The overweening, personates the mad—']

A common device in religious and political conflicts.—See Strype in support of this instance.—W.

LAUD

Page 345.

In this age a word cannot be said in praise of Laud, or even in compassion for his fate, without incurring a charge of bigotry; but fearless of such imputation, I concur with Hume, 'that it is sufficient for his vindication to observe that his errors were the most excusable of all those which prevailed during that zealous period.' A key to the right understanding of those parts of his conduct that brought the most odium upon him in his own time, may be found in the following passage of his speech before the bar of the House of Peers:— 'Ever since I came in place, I have laboured nothing more than the external publick worship of God, so much slighted in divers parts of this kingdom, might be preserved, and that with as much decency and uniformity as might be. For I evidently saw that the public neglect of God's service in the outward face of it, and the nasty lying of many places dedicated to that service, *had almost cast a damp upon the true and inward worship of God, which while we live in the body, needs external helps, and all little enough to keep it in any vigour.*'—W.

THE PILGRIM FATHERS

Pages 348, 349.

American episcopacy, in union with the church in England, strictly belongs to the general subject; and I here make my acknowledgments to my American friends, Bishop Doane, and Mr. Henry Reed of Philadelphia, for having suggested to me the propriety of adverting to it, and pointed out the virtues and intellectual qualities of Bishop White, which so eminently fitted him for the great work he undertook. Bishop White was consecrated at Lambeth, Feb. 4, 1787, by Archbishop Moore; and before his long life was closed, twenty-six bishops had been consecrated in America, by

himself. For his character and opinions, see his own numerous Works, and a 'Sermon in commemoration of him, by George Washington Doane, Bishop of New Jersey.'—W.

Page 349, XVIII, ll. 1–3.

'A genial hearth————
And a refined rusticity, belong
To the neat mansion']

Among the benefits arising, as Mr. Coleridge has well observed, from a Church establishment of endowments corresponding with the wealth of the country to which it belongs, may be reckoned as eminently important, the examples of civility and refinement which the clergy stationed at intervals, afford to the whole people. The established clergy in many parts of England have long been, as they continue to be, the principal bulwark against barbarism, and the link which unites the sequestered peasantry with the intellectual advancement of the age. Nor is it below the dignity of the subject to observe, that their taste, as acting upon rural residences and scenery often furnishes models which country gentlemen, who are more at liberty to follow the caprices of fashion, might profit by. The precincts of an old residence must be treated by ecclesiastics with respect, both from prudence and necessity. I remember being much pleased, some years ago, at Rose Castle, the rural seat of the See of Carlisle, with a style of garden and architecture, which, if the place had belonged to a wealthy layman, would no doubt have been swept away. A parsonage-house generally stands not far from the church; this proximity imposes favourable restraints, and sometimes suggests an affecting union of the accommodations and elegancies of life with the outward signs of piety and mortality. With pleasure I recall to mind a happy instance of this in the residence of an old and much-valued friend in Oxfordshire. The house and church stand parallel to each other, at a small distance; a circular lawn or rather grass-plot, spreads between them; shrubs and trees curve from each side of the dwelling, veiling, but not hiding, the church. From the front of this dwelling, no part of the burial-ground is seen; but as you wind by the side of the shrubs towards the steeple-end of the church, the eye catches a single, small, low, monumental headstone, moss-grown, sinking into, and gently inclining towards the earth. Advance, and the churchyard, populous and gay with glittering tombstones, opens upon the view. This humble, and beautiful parsonage called forth a tribute, for which see the seventh of the 'Miscellaneous Sonnets,' Part III.—W.

SONNET XXXII

Page 352.

This is still continued in many churches in Westmoreland. It takes place in the month of July, when the floor of the stalls is strewn with fresh rushes; and hence it is called the 'Rushbearing.'—W.

Page 353, XXXV, l. 10.

'Teaching us to forget them or forgive.'] This is borrowed from an affecting passage in Mr. George Dyer's history of Cambridge.—W.

Page 353, XXXVII, ll. 5, 6.

——'Had we, like them, endured
Sore stress of apprehension.']

See Burnet, who is unusually animated on this subject; the east wind, so anxiously expected and prayed for, was called the 'Protestant wind.'—W.

NOTES

Page 354, XL, ll. 9, 10.

'Yet will we not conceal the precious Cross,
Like men ashamed;']

The Lutherans have retained the Cross within
their churches: it is to be regretted that we have
not done the same.—W.

Page 355, XLVI, ll. 5, 6.

'Or like the Alpine Mount, that takes its name
From roseate hues,' &c.]

Some say that Monte Rosa take its name from
a belt of rock at its summit—a very unpoetical
and scarcely a probable supposition.—W.

Page 359, l. 49.

'Wings at my shoulders seem to play.'] In these
lines I am under obligation to the exquisite picture
of 'Jacob's Dream,' by Mr. Alstone, now in
America. It is pleasant to make this public acknowledgment to a man of genius, whom I have
the honour to rank among my friends.—W.

Page 364, IV, l. 5.

'But if thou, like Cocytus,' &c.] Many years ago,
when I was at Greta Bridge, in Yorkshire, the
hostess of the inn, proud of her skill in etymology,
said, that 'the name of the river was taken from
the bridge, the form of which, as every one must
notice, exactly resembled a great A.' Dr. Whitaker
has derived it from the word of common occurrence
in the North of England, 'to greet;' signifying to
lament aloud, mostly with weeping: a conjecture
rendered more probable from the stony and rocky
channel of both the Cumberland and Yorkshire
rivers. The Cumberland Greta, though it does
not, among the country people, take up that name
till within three miles of its disappearance in the
River Derwent, may be considered as having its
source in the mountain cove of Wythburn, and
flowing through Thirlmere, the beautiful features of
which lake are known only to those who, travelling
between Grasmere and Keswick, have quitted the
main road in the vale of Wythburn, and, crossing
over to the opposite side of the lake, have proceeded
with it on the right hand.

The channel of the Greta, immediately above
Keswick, has, for the purposes of building, been in
a great measure cleared of the immense stones
which, by their concussion in high floods, produced the loud and awful noises described in the
sonnet.

'The scenery upon this river,' says Mr. Southey
in his 'Colloquies,' 'where it passes under the
woody side of Latrigg, is of the finest and most
rememberable kind:—

——' "ambiguo lapsu refluitque fluitque,
Occurrensque sibi venturas aspicit undas." '—W.

Page 365, VIII, l. 11.

'By hooded Votaresses,' &c.] Attached to the
church of Brigham was formerly a chantry, which
held a moiety of the manor; and in the decayed
parsonage some vestiges of monastic architecture
are still to be seen.—W.

MARY QUEEN OF SCOTS LANDING AT WORKINGTON
Page 365.

'The fears and impatience of Mary were so
great,' says Robertson, 'that she got into a fisher-
boat, and with about twenty attendants landed at
Workington, in Cumberland; and thence she was
conducted with many marks of respect to Carlisle.'

The apartment in which the Queen had slept at
Workington Hall (where she was received by Sir
Henry Curwen as became her rank and misfortunes) was long preserved, out of respect to her
memory, as she had left it; and one cannot but
regret that some necessary alterations in the
mansion could not be effected without its destruction.—W.

STANZAS, &c.
Page 365.

St. Bees' Heads, anciently called the Cliff of
Baruth, are a conspicuous sea-mark for all vessels
sailing in the N.E. parts of the Irish Sea. In a bay,
one side of which is formed by the southern headland, stands the village of St. Bees; a place distinguished, from very early times, for its religious
and scholastic foundations.

'St. Bees,' says Nicholson and Burns, 'had its
name from Bega, an holy woman from Ireland, who
is said to have founded here, about the year
of our Lord 650, a small monastery, where afterwards a church was built in memory of her.

'The aforesaid religious house, being destroyed
by the Danes, was restored by William de Meschiens, son of Ranulph, and brother of Ranulph
de Meschiens, first Earl of Cumberland after the
Conquest; and made a cell of a prior and six Benedictine monks to the Abbey of St. Mary at York.'

Several traditions of miracles, connected with
the foundation of the first of these religious
houses, survive among the people of the neighbourhood; one of which is alluded to in these
Stanzas; and another, of a somewhat bolder and
more peculiar character, has furnished the subject of a spirited poem by the Rev. R. Parkinson,
M.A., late Divinity Lecturer of St. Bees' College,
and now Fellow of the Collegiate Church of Man-
chester.

After the dissolution of the monasteries, Archbishop Grindal founded a free school at St. Bees,
from which the counties of Cumberland and
Westmoreland have derived great benefit; and
recently, under the patronage of the Earl of
Lonsdale, a college has been established there for
the education of ministers for the English Church.
The old Conventual Church has been repaired
under the superintendence of the Rev. Dr. Ainger,
the Head of the College; and is well worthy of
being visited by any strangers who might be led
to the neighbourhood of this celebrated spot.

The form of stanza in this Poem, and something in the style of versification, are adopted from
the 'St. Monica,' a poem of much beauty upon a
monastic subject, by Charlotte Smith: a lady to
whom English verse is under greater obligations
than are likely to be either acknowledged or
remembered. She wrote little, and that little unambitiously, but with true feeling for rural nature,
at a time when nature was not much regarded by
English Poets; for in point of time her earlier
writings preceded, I believe, those of Cowper and
Burns.—W.

Page 366, l. 73.

'Are not, in sooth, their Requiem's sacred ties.']
I am aware that I am here treading upon tender
ground; but to the intelligent reader I feel that no
apology is due. The prayers of survivors, during
passionate grief for the recent loss of relatives and
friends, as the object of those prayers could no
longer be the suffering body of the dying, would
naturally be ejaculated for the souls of the departed; the barriers between the two worlds dis-

NOTES

solving before the power of love and faith. The ministers of religion, from their habitual attendance upon sick-beds, would be daily witnesses of these benign results, and hence would be strongly tempted to aim at giving to them permanence, by embodying them in rites and ceremonies, recurring at stated periods. All this, as it was in course of nature, so was it blameless, and even praiseworthy; since some of its effects, in that rude state of society, could not but be salutary. No reflecting person, however, can view without sorrow the abuses which rose out of thus formalising sublime instincts, and disinterested movements of passion, and perverting them into means of gratifying the ambition and rapacity of the priesthood. But, while we deplore and are indignant at these abuses, it would be a great mistake if we imputed the origin of the offices to prospective selfishness on the part of the monks and clergy: *they* were at first sincere in their sympathy, and in their degree dupes rather of their own creed, than artful and designing men. Charity is, upon the whole, the safest guide that we can take in judging our fellow-men, whether of past ages, or of the present time.—W.

Page 368.

'And they are led by noble Hillary.'] The TOWER OF REFUGE, an ornament to Douglas Bay, was erected chiefly through the humanity and zeal of Sir William Hillary; and he also was the founder of the lifeboat establishment at that place; by which, under his superintendence, and often by his exertions at the imminent hazard of his own life, many seamen and passengers have been saved.—W.

BY A RETIRED MARINER
Page 369.

This unpretending sonnet is by a gentleman nearly connected with me, and I hope, as it falls so easily into its place, that both the writer and the reader will excuse its appearance here.—W.

Page 369, XXI, l. 9.

'Off with yon cloud, old Snafell!'] The summit of this mountain is well chosen by Cowley as the scene of the 'Vision,' in which the spectral angel discourses with him concerning the government of Oliver Cromwell. 'I found myself,' says he, 'on the top of that famous hill in the Island Mona, which has the prospect of three great, and not long since most happy, kingdoms. As soon as ever I looked upon them, they called forth the sad representation of all the sins and all the miseries that had overwhelmed them these twenty years.' It is not to be denied that the changes now in progress, and the passions, and the way in which they work, strikingly resemble those which led to the disasters the philosophic writer so feelingly bewails. God grant that the resemblance may not become still more striking as months and years advance!—W.

ON REVISITING DUNOLLY CASTLE
Page 370.

This ingenious piece of workmanship, as I afterwards learned, had been executed for their own amusement by some labourers employed about the place.—W.

SONNET XXIX: CAVE OF STAFFA
Page 371.

The reader may be tempted to exclaim, 'How came this and the two following sonnets to be written, after the dissatisfaction expressed in the preceding one?' In fact, at the risk of incurring the reasonable displeasure of the master of the steamboat, I returned to the cave, and explored it under circumstances more favourable to those imaginative impressions which it is so wonderfully fitted to make upon the mind.—W.

Page 372, XXXI.

'Hope smiled when your nativity was cast, Children of Summer!']

Upon the head of the columns which form the front of the cave, rests a body of decomposed basaltic matter, which was richly decorated with that large bright flower. the ox-eyed daisy. I had noticed the same flower growing with profusion among the bold rocks on the western coast of the Isle of Man, making a brilliant contrast with their black and gloomy surfaces.—W.

IONA. UPON LANDING
Page 372.

The four last lines of this sonnet are adopted from a well-known sonnet of Russel, as conveying my feeling better than any words of my own could do.—W.

THE RIVER EDEN, CUMBERLAND
Page 373.

It is to be feared that there is more of the poet than the sound etymologist in this derivation of the name Eden. On the western coast of Cumberland is a rivulet which enters the sea at Moresby, known also in the neighbourhood by the name of Eden. May not the latter syllable come from the word Dean, *a valley*? Langdale, near Ambleside, is by the inhabitants called Langden. The former syllable occurs in the name Emont, a principal feeder of the Eden; and the stream which flows, when the tide is out, over Cartmel sands, is called the Ea—eau, French—aqua, Latin.—W.

Page 374, XLI, l. 14.

'Canal, and Viaduct, and Railway, tell!'] At Corby, a few miles below Nunnery, the Eden is crossed by a magnificent viaduct; and another of these works is thrown over a deep glen or ravine, at a very short distance from the main stream.—W.

Page 374, XLIII, l. 1.

'A weight of awe, not easy to be borne.'] The daughters of Long Meg, placed in a perfect circle eighty yards in diameter, are seventy-two in number above ground; a little way out of the circle stands Long Meg herself, a single stone, eighteen feet high. When I first saw this monument, as I came upon it by surprise, I might over-rate its importance as an object; but, though it will not bear a comparison with Stonehenge, I must say I have not seen any other relique of those dark ages which can pretend to rival it in singularity and dignity of appearance.—W.

TO THE EARL OF LONSDALE
Page 375.

This sonnet was written immediately after certain trials, which took place at the Cumberland Assizes, when the Earl of Lonsdale, in consequence of repeated and long-continued attacks upon his character, through the local press, had thought it right to prosecute the conductors and proprietors of three several journals. A verdict of libel

NOTES

was given in one case; and, in the others, the prosecutions were withdrawn, upon the individuals retracting and disavowing the charges, expressing regret that they had been made, and promising to abstain from the like in future.—W.

Page 392, l. 32.

'Descending to the worm in charity;'] I am indebted, here, to a passage in one of Mr. Digby's valuable works.—W.

SONNET IV
Page 402, l. 14.

'All change is perilous and all chance unsound.'
SPENSER.—W.

SONNET VIII
Page 403.

These lines were written several years ago, when reports prevailed of cruelties committed in many parts of America, by men making a law of their own passions. A far more formidable, as being a more deliberate mischief, has appeared among those States, which have lately broken faith with the public creditor in a manner so infamous. I cannot, however, but look at both evils under a similar relation to inherent good, and hope that the time is not distant when our brethren of the West will wipe off this stain from their name and nation.—W.

Additional Note.

I am happy to add that this anticipation is already partly realised; and that the reproach addressed to the Pennsylvanians in the next sonnet is no longer applicable to them. I trust that those other States to which it may yet apply will soon follow the example now set them by Philadelphia, and redeem their credit with the world.—W. 1850.

THE HORN OF EGREMONT CASTLE
Page 419.

This story is a Cumberland tradition. I have heard it also related of the Hall of Hutton John, an ancient residence of the Hudlestons, in a sequestered valley upon the river Dacor.—W.

THE RUSSIAN FUGITIVE
Page 424.

Peter Henry Bruce, having given in his entertaining Memoirs the substance of this Tale, affirms that, besides the concurring reports of others, he had the story from the lady's own mouth.
The Lady Catherine, mentioned towards the close, is the famous Catherine, then bearing that name as the acknowledged Wife of Peter the Great.—W.

THE FARMER OF TILSBURY VALE
Page 445.

With this picture, which was taken from real life, compare the imaginative one of 'The Reverie of Poor Susan,' page 149; and see (to make up the deficiencies of this class) 'The Excursion,' passim.—W.

Page 454 n.

Moss Campion (Silene acaulis).] This most beautiful plant is scarce in England, though it is found in great abundance upon the mountains of Scotland. The first specimen I ever saw of it, in its native bed, was singularly fine, the tuft or cushion being at least eight inches in diameter, and the root proportionably thick. I have only met with it in two places among our mountains, in both of which I have since sought for it in vain.
Botanists will not, I hope, take it ill, if I caution them against carrying off, inconsiderately, rare and beautiful plants. This has often been done, particularly from Ingleborough and other mountains in Yorkshire, till the species have totally disappeared, to the great regret of lovers of nature living near the places where they grew.—W.

Page 457, XV, l. 23.

'From the most gentle creature nursed in fields.'] This way of indicating the *name* of my lamented friend has been found fault with; perhaps rightly so; but I may say in justification of the double sense of the word, that similar allusions are not uncommon in epitaphs. One of the best in our language in verse, I ever read, was upon a person who bore the name of Palmer; and the course of the thought, throughout, turned upon the Life of the Departed, considered as a pilgrimage. Nor can I think that the objection in the present case will have much force with any one who remembers Charles Lamb's beautiful sonnet addressed to his own name, and ending,

'No deed of mine shall shame thee, gentle name!'
—W.

EXTEMPORE EFFUSION UPON THE DEATH OF JAMES HOGG
Page 459.

Walter Scott	.	. died 21st Sept., 1832.
S. T. Coleridge	.	. „ 25th July, 1834.
Charles Lamb	.	. „ 27th Dec., 1834.
Geo. Crabbe	.	. „ 3rd Feb., 1832.
Felicia Hemans	.	. „ 16th May, 1835.

—W.

THE PRELUDE

The 1850 text of *The Prelude* has been corrected from the MS. which was sent to the printer, and in some places, where the reading is doubtful, by reference to earlier MSS.

Page 509, Bk. III, l. 104.

'In youth, or *to* be changed in after years.'] So 1857, but 1850 reads:—

'In youth, or to be changed in manhood's prime;
Or for the few who shall be called to look
On the long shadows in our evening years,
Ordained precursors to the night of death.'

There is no MS. authority for the change of l. 104 and the omission of the three lines following, and if there were one, it would have been as valid in 1850 as in 1857. It is probable that the change was made by Bishop Wordsworth on its being pointed out to him that the reading of 1850 was grammatically obscure.

Page 564, Bk. X, l. 187.

'utter.'] Professor Harper's emendation of 1850 'either', which is clearly wrong.

THE EXCURSION. PREFACE
Page 590, ll. 83, 84.

'Descend, prophetic Spirit! that inspir'st The human Soul,' &c.]

'Not mine own fears, nor the prophetic Soul
Of the wide world dreaming on things to come.'
SHAKSPEARE'S *Sonnets.*—W.

NOTES

'—— much did he see of men.'] At the risk of giving a shock to the prejudices of artificial society, I have ever been ready to pay homage to the aristocracy of nature; under a conviction that vigorous human-heartedness is the constituent principle of true taste. It may still, however, be satisfactory to have prose testimony how far a Character, employed for purposes of imagination, is founded upon general fact. I, therefore, subjoin an extract from an author who had opportunities of being well acquainted with a class of men, from whom my own personal knowledge emboldened me to draw this portrait.

'We learn from Cæsar and other Roman Writers, that the travelling merchants who frequented Gaul and other barbarous countries, either newly conquered by the Roman arms, or bordering on the Roman conquests, were ever the first to make the inhabitants of those countries familiarly acquainted with the Roman modes of life, and to inspire them with an inclination to follow the Roman fashions, and to enjoy Roman conveniences. In North America, travelling merchants from the Settlements have done and continue to do much more towards civilizing the Indian natives, than all the missionaries, papist or protestant, who have ever been sent among them.

'It is farther to be observed, for the credit of this most useful class of men, that they commonly contribute, by their personal manners, no less than by the sale of their wares, to the refinement of the people among whom they travel. Their dealings form them to great quickness of wit and acuteness of judgment. Having constant occasion to recommend themselves and their goods, they acquire habits of the most obliging attention, and the most insinuating address. As in their peregrinations they have opportunity of contemplating the manners of various men and various cities, they become eminently skilled in the knowledge of the world. *As they wander, each alone, through thinly-inhabited districts, they form habits of reflection and of sublime contemplation.* With all these qualifications, no wonder, that they should often be, in remote parts of the country, the best mirrors of fashion, and censors of manners; and should contribute much to polish the roughness, and soften the rusticity of our peasantry. It is not more than twenty or thirty years since a young man going from any part of Scotland to England, of purpose *to carry the pack,* was considered as going to lead the life and acquire the fortune of a gentleman. When, after twenty years' absence, in that honourable line of employment, he returned with his acquisitions to his native country, he was regarded as a gentleman to all intents and purposes.'— HERON'S *Journey in Scotland,* vol. i, p. 89.—W.

'Lost in unsearchable eternity!'] Since this paragraph was composed, I have read with so much pleasure, in Burnet's 'Theory of the Earth,' a passage expressing corresponding sentiments, excited by objects of a similar nature, that I cannot forbear to transcribe it.

'Siquod verò Natura nobis dedit spectaculum, in hâc tellure, verè gratum, et philosopho dignum, id semel mihi contigisse arbitror; cùm ex celsissimâ rupe speculabundus ad oram maris Mediterranei, hinc æquor cæruleum, illinc tractus Alpinos prospexi; nihil quidem magis dispar aut dissimile, nec in suo genere, magìs egregium et singulare. Hoc theatrum ego facilè prætulerim

Romanis cunctis, Græcisve; atque id quod natura hîc spectandum exhibet, scenicis ludis omnibus, aut amphitheatri certaminibus. Nihil hîc elegans aut venustum, sed ingens et magnificum, et quod placet magnitudine suâ et quâdam specie immensitatis. Hinc intuebar maris æquabilem superficiem, usque et usque diffusam, quantum maximùm oculorum acies ferri potuit; illinc disruptissimam terræ faciem, et vastas moles variè elevatas aut depressas, erectas, propendentes, reclinatas, coacervatas, omni situ inæquali et turbido. Placuit, ex hâc parte, Naturæ unitas et simplicitas, et inexhausta quædam planities; ex alterâ, multiformis confusio magnorum corporum, et insanæ rerum strages: quas cùm intuebar, non urbis alicujus aut oppidi, sed confracti mundi rudera, ante oculos habere mihi visus sum.

'In singulis ferè montibus erat aliquid insolens et mirabile, sed præ cæteris mihi placebat illa, quâ sedebam, rupes; erat maxima et altissima, et quâ terram respiciebat, molliori ascensu altitudinem suam dissimulabat: quà verò mare, horrendùm præceps, et quasi ad perpendiculum facta, instar parietis. Præstereà facies illa marina adeò erat lævis ac uniformis (quod in rupibus aliquando observare licet) ac si scissa fuisset à summo ad imum, in illo plano; vel terræ motu aliquo, aut fulmine, divulsa.

'Ima pars rupis erat cava, recessusque habuit, et saxeos specus, euntes in vacuum montem; sive naturâ pridem factos, sive exesos mari, et undarum crebris ictibus: In hos enim cum impetu ruebant et fragore, æstuantis maris fluctus; quos iterum spumantes reddidit antrum, et quas i ab imo ventre evomuit.

'Dextrum latus montis erat præruptum, aspero saxo et nudâ caute; sinistrum non adeò neglexerat Natura, arboribus utpote ornatum: et prope pedem montis rivus limpidæ aquæ prorupit; qui cùm vicinam vallem irrigaverat, lento motu serpens, et per varios mæandros, quasi ad protrahendam vitam, in magno mari absorptus subito periit. Denique in summo vertice promontorii, commodè eminebat saxum, cui insidebam contemplabundus. Vale augusta sedes, Rege digna: Augusta rupes, semper mihi memoranda!'—Page 89. *Telluris Theoria sacra, etc. Editio secunda.*—W.

'Of Mississippi, or that northern stream.'] 'A man is supposed to improve by going out into the *World,* by visiting *London.* Artificial man does; he extends with his sphere; but, alas! that sphere is microscopic; it is formed of minutiæ, and he surrenders his genuine vision to the artist, in order to embrace it in his ken. His bodily senses grow acute, even to barren and inhuman pruriency; while his mental become proportionally obtuse. The reverse is the Man of Mind: he who is placed in the sphere of Nature and of God, might be a mock at Tattersall's and Brooks's, and a sneer at St. James's: he would certainly be swallowed alive by the first *Pizarro* that crossed him:—But when he walks along the river of Amazons; when he rests his eye on the unrivalled Andes; when he measures the long and watered savannah; or contemplates, from a sudden promontory, the distant, vast Pacific—and feels himself a freeman in this vast theatre, and commanding each ready produced fruit of this wilderness, and each progeny of this stream—his exaltation is not less than imperial. He is as gentle, too, as he is great: his emotions of tenderness keep pace with his elevation of sentiment; for he says, "These were made by a good Being, who, unsought by me, placed me

727

NOTES

here to enjoy them." He becomes at once a child and a king. His mind is in himself; from hence he argues, and from hence he acts, and he argues unerringly, and acts magisterially; his mind in himself is also in his God; and therefore he loves, and therefore he soars.'—From the notes upon 'The Hurricane,' a Poem, by William Gilbert.

The Reader, I am sure, will thank me for the above quotation, which, though from a strange book, is one of the finest passages of modern English prose.—W.

Page 627.

"'Tis, by comparison, an easy task
Earth to despise,' &c.]

See, upon this subject, Baxter's most interesting review of his own opinions and sentiments in the decline of life. It may be found (lately reprinted) in Dr. Wordsworth's 'Ecclesiastical Biography.'—W.

Page 628.

'Alas! the endowment of immortal power,
Is matched unequally with custom, time,' &c.]

This subject is treated at length in the Ode— 'Intimations of Immortality,' page 587.—W.

Page 629.

'Knowing the heart of man is set to be' &c.] The passage quoted from Daniel is taken from a poem addressed to the Lady Margaret, Countess of Cumberland, and the two last lines, printed in Italics, are by him translated from Seneca. The whole poem is very beautiful. I will transcribe four stanzas from it, as they contain an admirable picture of the state of a wise Man's mind in a time of public commotion.

'Nor is he moved with all the thunder-cracks
Of tyrant's threats, or with the surly brow
Of Power, that proudly sits on others' crimes;
Charged with more crying sins than those he checks.
The storms of sad confusion that may grow
Up in the present for the coming times,
Appal not him; that hath no side at all,
But of himself, and knows the worst can fall.

'Although his heart (so near allied to earth)
Cannot but pity the perplexed state
Of troublous and distressed mortality,
That thus make way unto the ugly birth
Of their own sorrows, and do still beget
Affliction upon Imbecility:
Yet seeing thus the course of things must run,
He looks thereon not strange, but as fore-done.

'And whilst distraught ambition compasses,
And is encompassed, while as craft deceives,
And is deceived: whilst man doth ransack man,
And builds on blood, and rises by distress;
And th' Inheritance of desolation leaves
To great-expecting hopes: He looks thereon,
As from the shore of peace, with unwet eye,
And bears no venture in Impiety.

'Thus, Lady, fares that man that hath prepared
A rest for his desires; and sees all things
Beneath him; and hath learned this book of man,
Full of the notes of frailty; and compared
The best of glory with her sufferings:
By whom, I see, you labour all you can
To plant your heart! and set your thoughts as near
His glorious mansion as your powers can bear.'—W.

Page 649.

'Or rather, as we stand on holy earth
And have the dead around us.']

'*Leo.* You, Sir, could help me to the history
Of half these graves?

Priest.   For eight-score winters past,
With what Eve witnessed, and with what I've
     heard,
Perhaps I might; . . .
By turning o'er these hillocks one by one,
We two could travel, Sir, through a strange round;
Yet all in the broad highway of the world.'
                              See *The Brothers.*—W.

Page 653.

'And gentle "Nature grieved,"' &c.]
'And suffering Nature grieved that one should die.'
                      SOUTHEY'S *Retrospect.*—W.

Page 653.

'And whence that tribute? wherefore these regards?'] The sentiments and opinions here uttered are in unison with those expressed in the following Essay upon Epitaphs, which was furnished by me for Mr. Coleridge's periodical work, 'The Friend;' and as they are dictated by a spirit congenial to that which pervades this and the two succeeding books, the sympathising reader will not be displeased to see the Essay here annexed.—W.

ESSAY UPON EPITAPHS

IT need scarcely be said, that an Epitaph presupposes a Monument, upon which it is to be engraven. Almost all Nations have wished that certain external signs should point out the places where their dead are interred. Among savage tribes unacquainted with letters this has mostly been done either by rude stones placed near the graves, or by mounds of earth raised over them. This custom proceeded obviously from a twofold desire; first, to guard the remains of the deceased from irreverent approach or from savage violation: and, secondly, to preserve their memory. 'Never any,' says Camden, 'neglected burial but some savage nations, as the Bactrians, which cast their dead to the dogs; some varlet philosophers, as Diogenes, who desired to be devoured of fishes; some dissolute courtiers, as Mæcenas, who was wont to say, "Non tumulum curo; sepelit natura relictos."'

'I'm careless of a grave:—Nature her dead will save.'

As soon as nations had learned the use of letters, epitaphs were inscribed upon these monuments; in order that their intention might be more surely and adequately fulfilled. I have derived monuments and epitaphs from two sources of feeling: but these do in fact resolve themselves into one. The invention of epitaphs, Weever, in his 'Discourse of Funeral Monuments,' says rightly, 'proceeded from the presage or fore-feeling of immortality, implanted in all men naturally, and is referred to the scholars of Linus the Theban poet, who flourished about the year of the world two thousand seven hundred; who first bewailed this Linus their Master, when he was slain, in doleful verses, then called of him Œlina, afterwards Epitaphia, for that they were first sung at burials, after engraved upon the sepulchres.'

And, verily, without the consciousness of a principle of immortality in the human soul, Man could never have had awakened in him the desire to live in the remembrance of his fellows: mere love, or the yearning of kind towards kind, could not have produced it. The dog or horse perishes in the field, or in the stall, by the side of his companions, and is incapable of anticipating the sorrow with which his surrounding associates shall bemoan his death, or pine for his loss; he cannot pre-conceive this regret, he can form no thought of it; and therefore cannot possibly have a desire to leave such regret or remembrance behind him. Add to the principle of love which exists in the inferior animals, the faculty of reason which exists in Man alone; will the conjunction of these account for the desire? Doubtless it is a necessary consequence of this conjunction; yet not I think as a direct result, but only to be come at through an intermediate thought, viz. that of an intimation or assurance within us, that some part of our nature is imperishable. At least the precedence, in order of birth, of one feeling to the other, is unquestionable. If we look back upon the days of childhood, we shall find that the time is not in remembrance when, with respect to our own individual Being, the mind was without this assurance; whereas, the wish to be remembered by our friends or kindred after death, or even in absence, is, as we shall discover, a sensation that does not form itself till the *social* feelings have been developed, and the Reason has connected itself with a wide range of objects. Forlorn, and cut off from communication with the best part of his nature, must that man be, who should derive the sense of immortality, as it exists in the mind of a child, from the same unthinking gaiety or liveliness of animal spirits with which the lamb in the meadow, or any other irrational creature is endowed; who should ascribe it, in short, to blank ignorance in the child; to an inability arising from the imperfect state of his faculties to come, in any point of his being, into contact with a notion of death; or to an unreflecting acquiescence in what had been instilled into him! Has such an unfolder of the mysteries of nature, though he may have forgotten his former self, ever noticed the early, obstinate, and unappeasable inquisitiveness of children upon the subject of origination? This single fact proves outwardly the monstrousness of those suppositions: for, if we had no direct external testimony that the minds of very young children meditate feelingly upon death and immortality, these enquiries, which we all know they are perpetually making concerning the *whence*, do necessarily include correspondent habits of interrogation concerning the *whither*. Origin and tendency are notions inseparably co-relative. Never did a child stand by the side of a running stream, pondering within himself what power was the feeder of the perpetual current, from what never-wearied sources the body of water was supplied, but he must have been inevitably propelled to follow this question by another: 'Towards what abyss is it in progress? what receptacle can contain the mighty influx?' And the spirit of the answer must have been, though the word might be sea or ocean, accompanied perhaps with an image gathered from a map, or from the real object in nature—these might have been the *letter*, but the *spirit* of the answer must have been *as* inevitably,—a receptacle without bounds or dimensions;—nothing less than infinity. We may, then, be justified in asserting, that the sense of immortality, if not a co-existent and twin birth with Reason, is among the earliest of her offspring: and we may further assert, that from these conjoined, and under their countenance, the human affections are gradually formed and opened out. This is not the place to enter into the recesses of these investigations; but the subject requires me here to make a plain avowal, that, for my own part, it is to me inconceivable, that the sympathies of love towards each other, which grow with our growth, could ever attain any new strength, or even preserve the old, after we had

received from the outward senses the impression of death, and were in the habit of having that impression daily renewed and its accompanying feeling brought home to ourselves, and to those we love; if the same were not counteracted by those communications with our internal Being, which are anterior to all these experiences, and with which revelation coincides, and has through that coincidence alone (for otherwise it could not possess it) a power to affect us. I confess, with me the conviction is absolute, that, if the impression and sense of death were not thus counterbalanced, such a hollowness would pervade the whole system of things, such a want of correspondence and consistency, a disproportion so astounding betwixt means and ends, that there could be no repose, no joy. Were we to grow up unfostered by this genial warmth, a frost would chill the spirit, so penetrating and powerful, that there could be no motions of the life of love; and infinitely less could we have any wish to be remembered after we had passed away from a world in which each man had moved about like a shadow.—If, then, in a creature endowed with the faculties of foresight and reason, the social affections could not have unfolded themselves uncountenanced by the faith that Man is an immortal being; and if, consequently, neither could the individual dying have had a desire to survive in the remembrance of his fellows, nor on their side could they have felt a wish to preserve for future times vestiges of the departed; it follows, as a final inference, that without the belief in immortality, wherein these several desires originate, neither monuments nor epitaphs, in affectionate or laudatory commemoration of the deceased, could have existed in the world.

Simonides, it is related, upon landing in a strange country, found the corse of an unknown person lying by the sea-side; he buried it, and was honoured throughout Greece for the piety of that act. Another ancient Philosopher, chancing to fix his eyes upon a dead body, regarded the same with slight, if not with contempt; saying, 'See the shell of the flown bird!' But it is not to be supposed that the moral and tender-hearted Simonides was incapable of the lofty movements of thought, to which that other Sage gave way at the moment while his soul was intent only upon the indestructible being; nor, on the other hand, that he, in whose sight a lifeless human body was of no more value than the worthless shell from which the living fowl had departed, would not, in a different mood of mind, have been affected by those earthly considerations which had incited the philosophic Poet to the performance of that pious duty. And with regard to this latter we may be assured that, if he had been destitute of the capability of communing with the more exalted thoughts that appertain to human nature, he would have cared no more for the corse of the stranger than for the dead body of a seal or porpoise which might have been cast up by the waves. We respect the corporeal frame of Man, not merely because it is the habitation of a rational, but of an immortal Soul. Each of these Sages was in sympathy with the best feelings of our nature; feelings which, though they seem opposite to each other, have another and a finer connection than that of contrast.—It is a connection formed through the subtle progress by which, both in the natural and the moral world, qualities pass insensibly into their contraries, and things revolve upon each other. As, in sailing upon the orb of this planet, a voyage towards the regions where the sun sets, conducts gradually to the quarter where we have been accustomed to behold it come forth at its rising; and, in like manner, a voyage towards the east, the birthplace in our imagination of the morning, leads finally to the quarter where the sun is last seen when he departs from our eyes; so the contemplative Soul, travelling in the direction of mortality, advances to the country of everlasting life; and, in like manner, may she continue to explore those cheerful tracts, till she is brought back, for her advantage and benefit, to the land of transitory things—of sorrow and of tears.

On a midway point, therefore, which commands the thoughts and feelings of the two Sages whom we have represented in contrast, does the Author of that species of composition, the laws of which it is our present purpose to explain, take his stand. Accordingly, recurring to the twofold desire of guarding the remains of the deceased and preserving their memory, it may be said that a sepulchral monument is a tribute to a man as a human being; and that an epitaph (in the ordinary meaning attached to the word) includes this general feeling and something more; and is a record to preserve the memory of the dead, as a tribute due to his individual worth, for a satisfaction to the sorrowing hearts of the survivors, and for the common benefit of the living: which record is to be accomplished, not in a general manner, but, where it can, in *close connection with the bodily remains of the deceased:* and these, it may be added, among the modern nations of Europe, are deposited within, or contiguous to, their places of worship. In ancient times, as is well known, it was the custom to bury the dead beyond the walls of towns and cities; and among the Greeks and Romans they were frequently interred by the way-sides.

I could here pause with pleasure, and invite the Reader to indulge with me in contemplation of the advantages which must have attended such a practice. We might ruminate upon the beauty which the monuments, thus placed, must have borrowed from the surrounding images of nature —from the trees, the wild flowers, from a stream running perhaps within sight or hearing, from the beaten road stretching its weary length hard by. Many tender similitudes must these objects have presented to the mind of the traveller leaning upon one of the tombs, or reposing in the coolness of its shade, whether he had halted from weariness or in compliance with the invitation, 'Pause, Traveller!' so often found upon the monuments. And to its epitaph also must have been supplied strong appeals to visible appearances or immediate impressions, lively and affecting analogies of life as a journey—death as a sleep overcoming the tired wayfarer—of misfortune as a storm that falls suddenly upon him—of beauty as a flower that passeth away, or of innocent pleasure as one that may be gathered—of virtue that standeth firm as a rock against the beating waves;—of hope 'undermined insensibly like the poplar by the side of the river that has fed it,' or blasted in a moment like a pine-tree by the stroke of lightning upon the mountain-top—of admonitions and heart-stirring remembrances, like a refreshing breeze that comes without warning, or the taste of the waters of an unexpected fountain. These, and similar suggestions, must have given, formerly, to the language of the senseless stone a voice enforced and endeared by the benignity of that nature with which it was in unison.—We, in modern times, have lost much of these advantages; and they are

but in a small degree counterbalanced to the inhabitants of large towns and cities, by the custom of depositing the dead within, or contiguous to, their places of worship; however splendid or imposing may be the appearance of those edifices, or however interesting or salutary the recollections associated with them. Even were it not true that tombs lose their monitory virtue when thus obtruded upon the notice of men occupied with the cares of the world, and too often sullied and defiled by those cares, yet still, when death is in our thoughts, nothing can make amends for the want of the soothing influences of nature, and for the absence of those types of renovation and decay, which the fields and woods offer to the notice of the serious and contemplative mind. To feel the force of this sentiment, let a man only compare in imagination the unsightly manner in which our monuments are crowded together in the busy, noisy, unclean, and almost grassless churchyard of a large town, with the still seclusion of a Turkish cemetery, in some remote place; and yet further sanctified by the grove of cypress in which it is embosomed. Thoughts in the same temper as these have already been expressed with true sensibility by an ingenious Poet of the present day. The subject of his poem is 'All Saints' Church, Derby:' he has been deploring the forbidding and unseemly appearance of its burial-ground, and uttering a wish, that in past times the practice had been adopted of interring the inhabitants of large towns in the country:—

'Then in some rural, calm, sequestered spot,
Where healing Nature her benignant look
Ne'er changes, save at that lorn season, when,
With tresses drooping o'er her sable stole,
She yearly mourns the mortal doom of man,
Her noblest work, (so Israel's virgins erst,
With annual moan upon the mountains wept
Their fairest gone,) there in that rural scene,
So placid, so congenial to the wish
The Christian feels, of peaceful rest within
The silent grave, I would have stayed.

 .   .   .   .   .

—wandered forth, where the cold dew of heaven
Lay on the humbler graves around, what time
The pale moon gazed upon the turfy mounds,
Pensive, as though like me, in lonely muse,
'Twere brooding on the dead inhumed beneath.
There while with him, the holy man of Uz,
O'er human destiny I sympathised,
Counting the long, long periods prophecy
Decrees to roll, ere the great day arrives
Of resurrection, oft the blue-eyed Spring
Had met me with her blossoms, as the Dove,
Of old, returned with olive leaf, to cheer
The Patriarch mourning o'er a world destroyed:
And I would bless her visit; for to me
'Tis sweet to trace the consonance that links
As one, the works of Nature and the word
Of God.'—

JOHN EDWARDS.

A village churchyard, lying as it does in the lap of nature, may indeed be most favourably contrasted with that of a town of crowded population; and sepulture therein combines many of the best tendencies which belong to the mode practised by the Ancients, with others peculiar to itself. The sensations of pious cheerfulness, which attend the celebration of the sabbath-day in rural places, are profitably chastised by the sight of the graves of kindred and friends, gathered together in that general home towards which the thoughtful yet happy spectators themselves are journeying. Hence a parish-church, in the stillness of the country, is a visible centre of a community of the living

NOTES

and the dead; a point to which are habitually referred the nearest concerns of both.

As, then, both in cities and in villages, the dead are deposited in close connection with our places of worship, with us the composition of an epitaph naturally turns, still more than among the nations of antiquity, upon the most serious and solemn affections of the human mind; upon departed worth—upon personal or social sorrow and admiration—upon religion, individual and social—upon time, and upon eternity. Accordingly, it suffices in ordinary cases, to secure a composition of this kind from censure, that it contain nothing that shall shock or be inconsistent with this spirit. But, to entitle an epitaph to praise, more than this is necessary. It ought to contain some thought or feeling belonging to the mortal or immortal part of our nature touchingly expressed; and if that be done, however general or even trite the sentiment may be, every man of pure mind will read the words with pleasure and gratitude. A husband bewails a wife; a parent breathes a sigh of disappointed hope over a lost child; a son utters a sentiment of filial reverence for a departed father or mother; a friend perhaps inscribes an encomium recording the companionable qualities, or the solid virtues, of the tenant of the grave, whose departure has left a sadness upon his memory. This and a pious admonition to the living, and a humble expression of Christian confidence in immortality, is the language of a thousand churchyards; and it does not often happen that anything, in a greater degree discriminate or appropriate to the dead or to the living, is to be found in them. This want of discrimination has been ascribed by Dr. Johnson, in his Essay upon the epitaphs of Pope, to two causes; first, the scantiness of the objects of human praise; and, secondly, the want of variety in the characters of men; or, to use his own words, 'to the fact, that the greater part of mankind have no character at all.' Such language may be holden without blame among the generalities of common conversation; but does not become a critic and a moralist speaking seriously upon a serious subject. The objects of admiration in human nature are not scanty, but abundant: and every man has a character of his own, to the eye that has skill to perceive it. The real cause of the acknowledged want of discrimination in sepulchral memorials is this: That to analyse the characters of others, especially of those whom we love, is not a common or natural employment of men at any time. We are not anxious unerringly to understand the constitution of the minds of those who have soothed, whom we have cheered, who have supported us: with whom we have been long and daily pleased or delighted. The affections are their own justification. The light of love in our hearts is a satisfactory evidence that there is a body of worth in the minds of our friends or kindred, whence that light has proceeded. We shrink from the thought of placing their merits and defects to be weighed against each other in the nice balance of pure intellect; nor do we find much temptation to detect the shades by which a good quality or virtue is discriminated in them from an excellence known by the same general name as it exists in the mind of another; and, least of all, do we incline to these refinements when under the pressure of sorrow, admiration, or regret, or when actuated by any of those feelings which incite men to prolong the memory of their friends and kindred, by records placed in the bosom of the all-uniting and equalising receptacle of the dead.

The first requisite, then, in an Epitaph is, that it should speak, in a tone which shall sink into the heart, the general language of humanity as connected with the subject of death—the source from which an epitaph proceeds—of death, and of life. To be born and to die are the two points in which all men feel themselves to be in absolute coincidence. This general language may be uttered so strikingly as to entitle an epitaph to high praise; yet it cannot lay claim to the highest unless other excellencies be superadded. Passing through all intermediate steps, we will attempt to determine at once what these excellencies are, and wherein consists the perfection of this species of composition.—It will be found to lie in a due proportion of the common or universal feeling of humanity to sensations excited by a distinct and clear conception, conveyed to the reader's mind, of the individual, whose death is deplored and whose memory is to be preserved; at least of his character as, after death, it appeared to those who loved him and lament his loss. The general sympathy ought to be quickened, provoked, and diversified, by particular thoughts, actions, images,—circumstances of age, occupation, manner of life, prosperity which the deceased had known, or adversity to which he had been subject; and these ought to be bound together and solemnised into one harmony by the general sympathy. The two powers should temper, restrain, and exalt each other. The reader ought to know who and what the man was whom he is called upon to think of with interest. A distinct conception should be given (implicitly where it can, rather than explicitly) of the individual lamented.—But the writer of an epitaph is not an anatomist, who dissects the internal frame of the mind; he is not even a painter, who executes a portrait at leisure and in entire tranquillity: his delineation, we must remember, is performed by the side of the grave; and, what is more, the grave of one whom he loves and admires. What purity and brightness is that virtue clothed in, the image of which must no longer bless our living eyes! The character of a deceased friend or beloved kinsman is not seen, no—nor ought to be seen, otherwise than as a tree through a tender haze or a luminous mist, that spiritualises and beautifies it; that takes away, indeed, but only to the end that the parts which are not abstracted may appear more dignified and lovely; may impress and affect the more. Shall we say, then, that this is not truth, not a faithful image; and that, accordingly, the purposes of commemoration cannot be answered?—It *is* truth, and of the highest order; for, though doubtless things are not apparent which did exist; yet, the object being looked at through this medium, parts and proportions are brought into distinct view which before had been only imperfectly or unconsciously seen: it is truth hallowed by love—the joint offspring of the worth of the dead and the affections of the living! This may easily be brought to the test. Let one, whose eyes have been sharpened by personal hostility to discover what was amiss in the character of a good man, hear the tidings of his death, and what a change is wrought in a moment! Enmity melts away; and, as it disappears, unsightliness, disproportion, and deformity, vanish; and, through the influence of commiseration, a harmony of love and beauty succeeds. Bring such a man to the tombstone on which shall be inscribed an epitaph on his adversary, composed in the spirit which we have recommended. Would he turn from it as from an idle tale? No;—the thoughtful look, the sigh, and perhaps the involuntary tear, would testify that it had a sane, a generous, and good

731

NOTES

meaning; and that on the writer's mind had remained an impression which was a true abstract of the character of the deceased; that his gifts and graces were remembered in the simplicity in which they ought to be remembered. The composition and quality of the mind of a virtuous man, contemplated by the side of the grave where his body is mouldering, ought to appear, and be felt as something midway between what he was on earth walking about with his living frailties, and what he may be presumed to be as a Spirit in heaven.

It suffices, therefore, that the trunk and the main branches of the worth of the deceased be boldly and unaffectedly represented. Any further detail, minutely and scrupulously pursued, especially if this be done with laborious and antithetic discriminations, must inevitably frustrate its own purpose; forcing the passing Spectator to this conclusion,—either that the dead did not possess the merits ascribed to him, or that they who have raised a monument to his memory, and must therefore be supposed to have been closely connected with him, were incapable of perceiving those merits; or at least during the act of composition had lost sight of them; for, the understanding having been so busy in its petty occupation, how could the heart of the mourner be other than cold? and in either of these cases, whether the fault be on the part of the buried person or the survivors, the memorial is unaffecting and profitless.

Much better is it to fall short in discrimination than to pursue it too far, or to labour it unfeelingly. For in no place are we so much disposed to dwell upon those points, of nature and condition, wherein all men resemble each other, as in the temple where the universal Father is worshipped, or by the side of the grave which gathers all human Beings to itself, and 'equalises the lofty and the low.' We suffer and we weep with the same heart; we love and are anxious for one another in one spirit; our hopes look to the same quarter; and the virtues by which we are all to be furthered and supported, as patience, meekness, good-will, justice, temperance, and temperate desires, are in an equal degree the concern of us all. Let an Epitaph, then, contain at least these acknowledgments to our common nature; nor let the sense of their importance be sacrificed to a balance of opposite qualities or minute distinctions in individual character; which if they do not, (as well for the most part be the case,) when examined, resolve themselves into a trick of words, will, even when they are true and just, for the most part be grievously out of place; for, as it is probable that few only have explored these intricacies of human nature, so can the tracing of them be interesting only to a few. But an epitaph is not a proud writing shut up for the studious: it is exposed to all—to the wise and the most ignorant; it is condescending, perspicuous, and lovingly solicits regard; its story and admonitions are brief, that the thoughtless, the busy, and indolent, may not be deterred, nor the impatient tired: the stooping old man cons the engraven record like a second horn-book;—the child is proud that he can read it;—and the stranger is introduced through its mediation to the company of a friend: it is concerning all, and for all:—in the churchyard it is open to the day; the sun looks down upon the stone, and the rains of heaven beat against it.

Yet, though the writer who would excite sympathy is bound in this case, more than in any other, to give proof that he himself has been moved, it is to be remembered, that to raise a monument is a sober and a reflective act; that the inscription which it bears is intended to be permanent, and for universal perusal; and that, for this reason, the thoughts and feelings expressed should be permanent also—liberated from that weakness and anguish of sorrow which is in nature transitory, and which with instinctive decency retires from notice. The passions should be subdued, the emotions controlled; strong, indeed, but nothing ungovernable or wholly involuntary. Seemliness requires this, and truth requires it also: for how can the narrator otherwise be trusted? Moreover, a grave is a tranquillising object: resignation in course of time springs up from it as naturally as the wild flowers, besprinkling the turf with which it may be covered, or gathering round the monument by which it is defended. The very form and substance of the monument which has received the inscription, and the appearance of the letters, testifying with what a slow and laborious hand they must have been engraven, might seem to reproach the author who had given way on this occasion to transports of mind, or to quick turns of conflicting passion; though the same might constitute the life and beauty of a funeral oration or elegiac poem.

These sensations and judgments, acted upon perhaps unconsciously, have been one of the main causes why epitaphs so often personate the deceased, and represent him as speaking from his own tomb-stone. The departed Mortal is introduced telling you himself that his pains are gone; that a state of rest is come; and he conjures you to weep for him no longer. He admonishes with the voice of one experienced in the vanity of those affections which are confined to earthly objects, and gives a verdict like a superior Being, performing the office of a judge, who has no temptations to mislead him, and whose decision cannot but be dispassionate. Thus is death disarmed of its sting, and affliction unsubstantialised. By this tender fiction, the survivors bind themselves to a sedater sorrow, and employ the intervention of the imagination in order that the reason may speak her own language earlier than she would otherwise have been enabled to do. This shadowy interposition also harmoniously unites the two worlds of the living and the dead by their appropriate affections. And it may be observed, that here we have an additional proof of the propriety with which sepulchral inscriptions were referred to the consciousness of immortality as their primal source.

I do not speak with a wish to recommend that an epitaph should be cast in this mould preferably to the still more common one, in which what is said comes from the survivors directly; but rather to point out how natural those feelings are which have induced men, in all states and ranks of society, so frequently to adopt this mode. And this I have done chiefly in order that the laws, which ought to govern the composition of the other, may be better understood. This latter mode, namely, that in which the survivors speak in their own persons, seems to me upon the whole greatly preferable: as it admits a wider range of notices; and, above all, because, excluding the fiction which is the groundwork of the other, it rests upon a more solid basis.

Enough has been said to convey our notion of a perfect epitaph; but it must be borne in mind that one is meant which will best answer the *general* ends of that species of composition. According to the course pointed out, the worth of private life, through all varieties of situation and character, will be most honourably and profitably preserved in memory. Nor would the model recommended

732

NOTES

less suit public men, in all instances save of those persons who by the greatness of their services in the employments of peace or war, or by the surpassing excellence of their works in art, literature, or science, have made themselves not only universally known, but have filled the heart of their country with everlasting gratitude. Yet I must here pause to correct myself. In describing the general tenour of thought which epitaphs ought to hold, I have omitted to say, that if it be the *actions* of a man, or even some *one* conspicuous or beneficial act of local or general utility, which have distinguished him, and excited a desire that he should be remembered, then, of course, ought the attention to be directed chiefly to those actions or that act: and such sentiments dwelt upon as naturally arise out of them or it. Having made this necessary distinction, I proceed.—The mighty benefactors of mankind, as they are not only known by the immediate survivors, but will continue to be known familiarly to latest posterity, do not stand in need of biographic sketches, in such a place; nor of delineations of character to individualise them. This is already done by their Works, in the memories of men. Their naked names, and a grand comprehensive sentiment of civic gratitude, patriotic love, or human admiration—or the utterance of some elementary principle of true virtue;—or a declaration touching that pious humility and self-abasement, which are ever most profound as minds are most susceptible of genuine exaltation—or an intuition, communicated in adequate words, of the sublimity of intellectual power; —these are the only tribute which can here be paid—the only offering that upon such an altar would not be unworthy.

'What needs my Shakspeare for his honoured bones
The labour of an age in piled stones,
Or that his hallowed reliques should be hid
Under a star-ypointing pyramid?
Dear Son of Memory, great Heir of Fame,
What need'st thou such weak witness of thy name?
Thou in our wonder and astonishment
Hast built thyself a livelong monument,
And so sepulchred, in such pomp dost lie,
That kings for such a tomb would wish to die.'
W.

Page 654.

'And spires whose "silent finger points to heaven".'] An instinctive taste teaches men to build their churches in flat countries with spire-steeples, which as they cannot be referred to any other object, point as with silent finger to the sky and stars, and sometimes, when they reflect the brazen light of a rich though rainy sunset, appear like a pyramid of flame burning heavenward. See 'The Friend,' by S. T. Coleridge, No. 14, p. 223.

Page 675.

'That sycamore, which annually holds
Within its shade, as in a stately tent.']
'This Sycamore oft musical with Bees;
Such Tents the Patriarchs loved.'
S. T. COLERIDGE.

Page 680.

'Perish the roses and the flowers of kings.'] The 'Transit gloria mundi' is finely expressed in the Introduction to the Foundation-charters of some of the ancient Abbeys. Some expressions here used are taken from that of the Abbey of St. Mary's Furness, the translation of which is as follows:—

'Considering every day the uncertainty of life, that the roses and flowers of Kings, Emperors, and Dukes, and the crowns and palms of all the great, wither and decay; and that all things, with an uninterrupted course, tend to dissolution and death: I therefore,' &c.—W.

Page 682.

——————'Earth has lent
Her waters, Air her breezes.']

In treating this subject, it was impossible not to recollect, with gratitude, the pleasing picture, which, in his Poem of the Fleece, the excellent and amiable Dyer has given of the influences of manufacturing industry upon the face of this Island. He wrote at a time when machinery was first beginning to be introduced, and his benevolent heart prompted him to augur from it nothing but good. Truth has compelled me to dwell upon the baneful effects arising out of an ill-regulated and excessive application of powers so admirable in themselves.—W.

Page 692.

'Binding herself by statute.'] The discovery of Dr. Bell affords marvellous facilities for carrying this into effect; and it is impossible to overrate the benefit which might accrue to humanity from the universal application of this simple engine under an enlightened and conscientious government.—W.

PREFACES

ETC., ETC.

MUCH the greatest part of the foregoing Poems has been so long before the Public that no prefatory matter, explanatory of any portion of them, or of the arrangement which has been adopted, appears to be required; and had it not been for the observations contained in those Prefaces upon the principles of Poetry in general they would not have been reprinted even as an Appendix in this Edition. [W. W. ed. 1849–50.]

PREFACE TO THE SECOND EDITION OF SEVERAL OF THE FOREGOING POEMS PUBLISHED, WITH AN ADDITIONAL VOLUME, UNDER THE TITLE OF 'LYRICAL BALLADS.'

[*Note.*—In succeeding Editions, when the Collection was much enlarged and diversified, this Preface was transferred to the end of the Volumes as having little of a special application to their contents.]

THE first Volume of these Poems has already been submitted to general perusal. It was published, as an experiment, which, I hoped, might be of some use to ascertain, how far, by fitting to metrical arrangement a selection of the real language of men in a state of vivid sensation, that sort of pleasure and that quantity of pleasure may be imparted, which a Poet may rationally endeavour to impart.

I had formed no very inaccurate estimate of the probable effect of those Poems: I flattered myself that they who should be pleased with them would read them with more than common pleasure: and, on the other hand, I was well aware, that by those who should dislike them, they would be read with more than common dislike. The result has differed from my expectation in this only, that a greater number have been pleased than I ventured to hope I should please.

. . . .

Several of my Friends are anxious for the success of these Poems, from a belief, that, if the views with which they were composed were indeed realised, a class of Poetry would be produced, well adapted to interest mankind permanently, and not unimportant in the quality, and in the multiplicity of its moral relations: and on this account they have advised me to prefix a systematic defence of the theory upon which the Poems were written. But I was unwilling to undertake the task, knowing that on this occasion the Reader would look coldly upon my arguments, since I might be suspected of having been principally influenced by the selfish and foolish hope of *reasoning* him into an approbation of these particular Poems: and I was still more unwilling to undertake the task, because, adequately to display the opinions, and fully to enforce the arguments, would require a space wholly disproportionate to a preface. For, to treat the subject with the clearness and coherence of which it is susceptible, it would be necessary to give a full account of the present state of the public taste in this country, and to determine how far this taste is healthy or depraved; which, again, could not be determined, without pointing out in what manner language and the human mind act and re-act on each other, and without retracing the revolutions, not of literature alone, but likewise of society itself. I have therefore altogether declined to enter regularly upon this defence; yet I am sensible, that there would be something like impropriety in abruptly obtruding upon the Public, without a few words of introduction, Poems so materially dif-

ferent from those upon which general approbation is at present bestowed.

It is supposed, that by the act of writing in verse an Author makes a formal engagement that he will gratify certain known habits of association; that he not only thus apprises the Reader that certain classes of ideas and expressions will be found in his book, but that others will be carefully excluded. This exponent or symbol held forth by metrical language must in different eras of literature have excited very different expectations: for example, in the age of Catullus, Terence, and Lucretius, and that of Statius or Claudian; and in our own country, in the age of Shakspeare and Beaumont and Fletcher, and that of Donne and Cowley, or Dryden, or Pope. I will not take upon me to determine the exact import of the promise which, by the act of writing in verse, an Author in the present day makes to his reader: but it will undoubtedly appear to many persons that I have not fulfilled the terms of an engagement thus voluntarily contracted. They who have been accustomed to the gaudiness and inane phraseology of many modern writers, if they persist in reading this book to its conclusion, will, no doubt, frequently have to struggle with feelings of strangeness and awkwardness: they will look round for poetry, and will be induced to inquire by what species of courtesy these attempts can be permitted to assume that title. I hope therefore the reader will not censure me for attempting to state what I have proposed to myself to perform; and also (as far as the limits of a preface will permit) to explain some of the chief reasons which have determined me in the choice of my purpose: that at least he may be spared any unpleasant feeling of disappointment, and that I myself may be protected from one of the most dishonourable accusations which can be brought against an Author; namely, that of an indolence which prevents him from endeavouring to ascertain what is his duty, or, when his duty is ascertained, prevents him from performing it.

The principal object, then, proposed in these Poems was to choose incidents and situations from common life, and to relate or describe them, throughout, as far as was possible in a selection of language really used by men, and, at the same time, to throw over them a certain colouring of imagination, whereby ordinary things should be presented to the mind in an unusual aspect; and, further, and above all, to make these incidents and situations interesting by tracing in them, truly though not ostentatiously, the primary laws of our nature: chiefly, as far as regards the manner in which we associate ideas in a state of excitement. Humble and rustic life was generally chosen, because, in that condition, the essential passions of the heart find a better soil in which they can attain their maturity, are less under restraint, and speak a plainer and more emphatic language; because in that condition of life our elementary feelings coexist in a state of greater simplicity, and, consequently, may be more accurately contemplated, and more forcibly communicated; because the manners of rural life germinate from those elementary feelings, and, from the necessary character of rural occupations, are more easily comprehended, and are more durable; and, lastly, because in that condition the passions of men are incorporated with the beautiful and permanent forms of nature. The language, too, of these men has been adopted (purified indeed from what appear to be its real defects, from all lasting and rational causes of dislike or disgust) because such men hourly communicate with the best objects from which the best part of language is originally derived; and because, from their rank in society and the sameness and narrow circle of their intercourse, being less under the influence of social vanity, they convey their feelings and notions in simple and unelaborated expressions. Accordingly, such a language, arising out of repeated experience and regular feelings, is a more permanent, and a far more philosophical language, than that which is frequently substituted for it by Poets, who think that they are conferring honour upon themselves and their art, in proportion as they separate themselves from the sympathies of men, and indulge in arbitrary and capricious habits of expression, in order to furnish food for fickle tastes, and fickle appetites, of their own creation[1].

I cannot, however, be insensible to the present outcry against the triviality and meanness, both of thought and language, which some of my contemporaries have occasionally introduced into their metrical compositions; and I acknowledge that this defect, where it exists, is more dishonourable to the Writer's own character than false refinement or arbitrary innovation, though I should contend at the same time, that it is far less pernicious in the sum of its consequences. From such verses the Poems in these volumes will be found distinguished at least by one mark of difference, that each of them has a worthy *purpose*. Not that I always began to write with a distinct purpose formally conceived; but habits of meditation have, I trust, so prompted and regulated my feelings, that my descriptions of such objects as strongly excite those feelings, will be found to carry along with them a *purpose*. If this opinion be erroneous, I can have little right to the name of a Poet. For all good poetry is the spontaneous overflow of powerful feelings: and though this be true, Poems to which any value can be attached were never produced on any variety of subjects but by a man who, being possessed of more than usual organic sensibility, had also thought long and deeply. For our continued influxes of feeling are modified and directed by our thoughts, which are indeed the representatives of all our past feelings; and, as by contemplating the relation of these general representatives to each other, we discover what is really important to men, so, by the repetition and continuance of this act, our feelings will be connected with important subjects, till at length, if we be originally possessed of much sensibility, such habits of mind will be produced, that, by obeying blindly and mechanically the impulses of those habits, we shall describe objects, and utter

[1] It is worth while here to observe, that the affecting parts of Chaucer are almost always expressed in language pure and universally intelligible even to this day.

sentiments, of such a nature, and in such connection with each other, that the understanding of the Reader must necessarily be in some degree enlightened, and his affections strengthened and purified.

It has been said that each of these poems has a purpose. Another circumstance must be mentioned which distinguishes these Poems from the popular Poetry of the day; it is this, that the feeling therein developed gives importance to the action and situation, and not the action and situation to the feeling.

A sense of false modesty shall not prevent me from asserting, that the Reader's attention is pointed to this mark of distinction, far less for the sake of these particular Poems than from the general importance of the subject. The subject is indeed important! For the human mind is capable of being excited without the application of gross and violent stimulants; and he must have a very faint perception of its beauty and dignity who does not know this, and who does not further know, that one being is elevated above another, in proportion as he possesses this capability. It has therefore appeared to me, that to endeavour to produce or enlarge this capability is one of the best services in which, at any period, a Writer can be engaged; but this service, excellent at all times, is especially so at the present day. For a multitude of causes, unknown to former times, are now acting with a combined force to blunt the discriminating powers of the mind, and, unfitting it for all voluntary exertion, to reduce it to a state of almost savage torpor. The most effective of these causes are the great national events which are daily taking place, and the increasing accumulation of men in cities, where the uniformity of their occupations produces a craving for extraordinary incident, which the rapid communication of intelligence hourly gratifies. To this tendency of life and manners the literature and theatrical exhibitions of the country have conformed themselves. The invaluable works of our elder writers, I had almost said the works of Shakspeare and Milton, are driven into neglect by frantic novels, sickly and stupid German Tragedies, and deluges of idle and extravagant stories in verse.—When I think upon this degrading thirst after outrageous stimulation, I am almost ashamed to have spoken of the feeble endeavour made in these volumes to counteract it; and, reflecting upon the magnitude of the general evil, I should be oppressed with no dishonourable melancholy, had I not a deep impression of certain inherent and indestructible qualities of the human mind, and likewise of certain powers in the great and permanent objects that act upon it, which are equally inherent and indestructible; and were there not added to this impression a belief, that the time is approaching when the evil will be systematically opposed, by men of greater powers, and with far more distinguished success.

Having dwelt thus long on the subjects and aim of these Poems, I shall request the Reader's permission to apprise him of a few circumstances relating to their *style*, in order, among other reasons, that he may not censure me for not having performed what I never attempted. The Reader will find that personifications of abstract ideas rarely occur in these volumes; and are utterly rejected, as an ordinary device to elevate the style, and raise it above prose. My purpose was to imitate, and, as far as possible, to adopt the very language of men; and assuredly such personifications do not make any natural or regular part of that language. They are, indeed, a figure of speech occasionally prompted by passion, and I have made use of them as such; but have endeavoured utterly to reject them as a mechanical device of style, or as a family language which Writers in metre seem to lay claim to by prescription. I have wished to keep the Reader in the company of flesh and blood, persuaded that by so doing I shall interest him. Others who pursue a different track will interest him likewise; I do not interfere with their claim, but wish to prefer a claim of my own. There will also be found in these volumes little of what is usually called poetic diction; as much pains has been taken to avoid it as is ordinarily taken to produce it; this has been done for the reason already alleged, to bring my language near to the language of men; and further, because the pleasure which I have proposed to myself to impart, is of a kind very different from that which is supposed by many persons to be the proper object of poetry. Without being culpably particular, I do not know how to give my Reader a more exact notion of the style in which it was my wish and intention to write, than by informing him that I have at all times endeavoured to look steadily at my subject; consequently, there is I hope in these Poems little falsehood of description, and my ideas are expressed in language fitted to their respective importance. Something must have been gained by this practice, as it is friendly to one property of all good poetry, namely, good sense: but it has necessarily cut me off from a large portion of phrases and figures of speech which from father to son have long been regarded as the common inheritance of Poets. I have also thought it expedient to restrict myself still further, having abstained from the use of many expressions, in themselves proper and beautiful, but which have been foolishly repeated by bad Poets, till such feelings of disgust are connected with them as it is scarcely possible by any art of association to overpower.

If in a poem there should be found a series of lines, or even a single line, in which the language, though naturally arranged, and according to the strict laws of metre, does not differ from that of prose, there is a numerous class of critics, who, when they stumble upon these prosaisms, as they call them, imagine that they have made a notable discovery, and exult over the Poet as over a man ignorant of his own profession. Now these men would establish a canon of criticism which the Reader will conclude he must utterly reject, if he wishes to be pleased with these volumes. And it would be a most easy task to prove to him, that not only the language of a large portion of every good poem, even of the most elevated character, must necessarily, except with reference to the metre, in no respect differ from that of good prose, but likewise that some of the most interesting parts of the best poems will be found to be strictly the language of prose when prose is well written. The truth of this assertion might be demonstrated by innumerable passages from almost all the poetical writings, even of Milton himself. To illustrate the subject in a general manner, I will here adduce a short composition of Gray, who was at the head of those who, by their reasonings, have attempted to widen the space of separation betwixt Prose and Metrical composition, and was more than any other man curiously elaborate in the structure of his own poetic diction.

'In vain to me the smiling mornings shine,
And reddening Phoebus lifts his golden fire:
The birds in vain their amorous descant join,
Or cheerful fields resume their green attire.
These ears, alas! for other notes repine;
A different object do these eyes require;
My lonely anguish melts no heart but mine;
And in my breast the imperfect joys expire;
Yet morning smiles the busy race to cheer,
And new-born pleasure brings to happier men;
The fields to all their wonted tribute bear;
To warm their little loves the birds complain.
I fruitless mourn to him that cannot hear,
And weep the more because I weep in vain.'

It will easily be perceived, that the only part of this Sonnet which is of any value is the lines printed in Italics; it is equally obvious, that, except in the rhyme, and in the use of the single word 'fruitless' for fruitlessly, which is so far a defect, the language of these lines does in no respect differ from that of prose.

By the foregoing quotation it has been shown that the language of Prose may yet be well adapted to Poetry; and it was previously asserted, that a large portion of the language of every good poem can in no respect differ from that of good Prose. We will go further. It may be safely affirmed, that there neither is, nor can be, any *essential* difference between the language of prose and metrical composition. We are fond of tracing the resemblance between Poetry and Painting, and, accordingly, we call them Sisters: but where shall we find bonds of connection sufficiently strict to typify the affinity betwixt metrical and prose composition? They both speak by and to the same organs; the bodies in which both of them are clothed may be said to be of the same substance, their affections are kindred, and almost identical, not necessarily differing even in degree; Poetry[1] sheds no tears 'such as Angels weep,' but natural and human tears; she can boast of no celestial ichor that distinguishes her vital juices from those of prose; the same human blood circulates through the veins of them both.

If it be affirmed that rhyme and metrical arrangement of themselves constitute a distinction which overturns what has just been said on the strict affinity of metrical language with that of prose, and paves the way for other artificial distinctions which the mind voluntarily admits, I answer that the language of such Poetry as is here recommended is, as far as is possible, a selection of the language really spoken by men; that this selection, wherever it is made with true taste and feeling, will of itself form a distinction far greater than would at first be imagined, and will entirely separate the composition from the vulgarity and meanness of ordinary life; and, if metre be superadded thereto, I believe that a dissimilitude will be produced altogether sufficient for the gratification of a rational mind. What other distinction would we have? Whence is it to come? And where is it to exist? Not, surely, where the Poet speaks through the mouths of his characters: it cannot be necessary here, either for elevation of style, or any of its supposed ornaments: for, if the Poet's subject be judiciously chosen, it will naturally, and upon fit occasion, lead him to passions the lan-

[1] I here use the word 'Poetry' (though against my own judgment) as opposed to the word Prose, and synonymous with metrical composition. But much confusion has been introduced into criticism by this contradistinction of Poetry and Prose, instead of the more philosophical one of Poetry and Matter of Fact, or Science. The only strict antithesis to Prose is Metre; nor is this, in truth, a *strict* antithesis, because lines and passages of metre so naturally occur in writing prose, that it would be scarcely possible to avoid them, even were it desirable.

guage of which, if selected truly and judiciously, must necessarily be dignified and variegated, and alive with metaphors and figures. I forbear to speak of an incongruity which would shock the intelligent Reader, should the Poet interweave any foreign splendour of his own with that which the passion naturally suggests: it is sufficient to say that such addition is unnecessary. And, surely, it is more probable that those passages, which with propriety abound with metaphors and figures, will have their due effect, if, upon other occasions where the passions are of a milder character, the style also be subdued and temperate.

But, as the pleasure which I hope to give by the Poems now presented to the Reader must depend entirely on just notions upon this subject, and, as it is in itself of high importance to our taste and moral feelings, I cannot content myself with these detached remarks. And if, in what I am about to say, it shall appear to some that my labour is unnecessary, and that I am like a man fighting a battle without enemies, such persons may be reminded, that, whatever be the language outwardly holden by men, a practical faith in the opinions which I am wishing to establish is almost unknown. If my conclusions are admitted, and carried as far as they must be carried if admitted at all, our judgments concerning the works of the greatest Poets both ancient and modern will be far different from what they are at present, both when we praise, and when we censure: and our moral feelings influencing and influenced by these judgments will, I believe, be corrected and purified.

Taking up the subject, then, upon general grounds, let me ask, what is meant by the word Poet? What is a Poet? To whom does he address himself? And what language is to be expected from him?—He is a man speaking to men: a man, it is true, endowed with more lively sensibility, more enthusiasm and tenderness, who has a greater knowledge of human nature, and a more comprehensive soul, than are supposed to be common among mankind; a man pleased with his own passions and volitions, and who rejoices more than other men in the spirit of life that is in him; delighting to contemplate similar volitions and passions as manifested in the goings-on of the Universe, and habitually impelled to create them where he does not find them. To these qualities he has added a disposition to be affected more than other men by absent things as if they were present; an ability of conjuring up in himself passions, which are indeed far from being the same as those produced by real events, yet (especially in those parts of the general sympathy which are pleasing and delightful) do more nearly resemble the passions produced by real events, than anything which, from the motions of their own minds merely, other men are accustomed to feel in themselves:—whence, and from practice, he has acquired a greater readiness and power in expressing what he thinks and feels, and especially those thoughts and feelings which, by his own choice, or from the structure of his own mind, arise in him without immediate external excitement.

But whatever portion of this faculty we may suppose even the greatest Poet to possess, there cannot be a doubt that the language which it will suggest to him, must often, in liveliness and truth, fall short of that which is uttered by men in real life, under the actual pressure of those passions, certain shadows of which the Poet thus produces, or feels to be produced, in himself.

However exalted a notion we would wish to cherish of the character of a Poet, it is obvious,

that while he describes and imitates passions, his employment is in some degree mechanical, compared with the freedom and power of real and substantial action and suffering. So that it will be the wish of the Poet to bring his feelings near to those of the persons whose feelings he describes, nay, for short spaces of time, perhaps, to let himself slip into an entire delusion, and even confound and identify his own feelings with theirs; modifying only the language which is thus suggested to him by a consideration that he describes for a particular purpose, that of giving pleasure. Here, then, he will apply the principle of selection which has been already insisted upon. He will depend upon this for removing what would otherwise be painful or disgusting in the passion; he will feel that there is no necessity to trick out or to elevate nature: and, the more industriously he applies this principle, the deeper will be his faith that no words, which his fancy or imagination can suggest, will be to be compared with those which are the emanations of reality and truth.

But it may be said by those who do not object to the general spirit of these remarks, that, as it is impossible for the Poet to produce upon all occasions language as exquisitely fitted for the passion as that which the real passion itself suggests, it is proper that he should consider himself as in the situation of a translator, who does not scruple to substitute excellencies of another kind for those which are unattainable by him; and endeavours occasionally to surpass his original, in order to make some amends for the general inferiority to which he feels that he must submit. But this would be to encourage idleness and unmanly despair. Further, it is the language of men who speak of what they do not understand; who talk of Poetry as of a matter of amusement and idle pleasure; who will converse with us as gravely about a taste for Poetry, as they express it, as if it were a thing as indifferent as a taste for rope-dancing, or Frontiniac or Sherry. Aristotle, I have been told, has said, that Poetry is the most philosophic of all writing: it is so: its object is truth, not individual and local, but general, and operative; not standing upon external testimony, but carried alive into the heart by passion; truth which is its own testimony, which gives competence and confidence to the tribunal to which it appeals, and receives them from the same tribunal. Poetry is the image of man and nature. The obstacles which stand in the way of the fidelity of the Biographer and Historian, and of their consequent utility, are incalculably greater than those which are to be encountered by the Poet who comprehends the dignity of his art. The Poet writes under one restriction only, namely, the necessity of giving immediate pleasure to a human Being possessed of that information which may be expected from him, not as a lawyer, a physician, a mariner, an astronomer, or a natural philosopher, but as a Man. Except this one restriction, there is no object standing between the Poet and the image of things; between this, and the Biographer and Historian, there are a thousand.

Nor let this necessity of producing immediate pleasure be considered as a degradation of the Poet's art. It is far otherwise. It is an acknowledgment of the beauty of the universe, an acknowledgment the more sincere, because not formal, but indirect; it is a task light and easy to him who looks at the world in the spirit of love: further, it is a homage paid to the native and naked dignity of man, to the grand elementary principle of pleasure, by which he knows, and feels, and lives, and moves. We have no sympathy but what is propagated by pleasure: I would not be misunderstood; but wherever we sympathise with pain, it will be found that the sympathy is produced and carried on by subtle combinations with pleasure. We have no knowledge, that is, no general principles drawn from the contemplation of particular facts, but what has been built up by pleasure, and exists in us by pleasure alone. The Man of science, the Chemist and Mathematician, whatever difficulties and disgusts they may have had to struggle with, know and feel this. However painful may be the objects with which the Anatomist's knowledge is connected, he feels that his knowledge is pleasure; and where he has no pleasure he has no knowledge. What then does the Poet? He considers man and the objects that surround him as acting and re-acting upon each other, so as to produce an infinite complexity of pain and pleasure; he considers man in his own nature and in his ordinary life as contemplating this with a certain quantity of immediate knowledge, with certain convictions, intuitions, and deductions, which from habit acquire the quality of intuitions; he considers him as looking upon this complex scene of ideas and sensations, and finding everywhere objects that immediately excite in him sympathies which, from the necessities of his nature, are accompanied by an over-balance of enjoyment.

To this knowledge which all men carry about with them, and to these sympathies in which, without any other discipline than that of our daily life, we are fitted to take delight, the Poet principally directs his attention. He considers man and nature as essentially adapted to each other, and the mind of man as naturally the mirror of the fairest and most interesting properties of nature. And thus the Poet, prompted by this feeling of pleasure, which accompanies him through the whole course of his studies, converses with general nature, with affections akin to those, which, through labour and length of time, the Man of science has raised up in himself, by conversing with those particular parts of nature which are the objects of his studies. The knowledge both of the Poet and the Man of science is pleasure; but the knowledge of the one cleaves to us as a necessary part of our existence, our natural and unalienable inheritance; the other is a personal and individual acquisition, slow to come to us, and by no habitual and direct sympathy connecting us with our fellow-beings. The Man of science seeks truth as a remote and unknown benefactor; he cherishes and loves it in his solitude: the Poet, singing a song in which all human beings join with him, rejoices in the presence of truth as our visible friend and hourly companion. Poetry is the breath and finer spirit of all knowledge; it is the impassioned expression which is in the countenance of all Science. Emphatically may it be said of the Poet, as Shakspeare hath said of man, 'that he looks before and after.' He is the rock of defence for human nature; an upholder and preserver, carrying everywhere with him relationship and love. In spite of difference of soil and climate, of language and manners, of laws and customs: in spite of things silently gone out of mind, and things violently destroyed; the Poet binds together by passion and knowledge the vast empire of human society, as it is spread over the whole earth, and over all time. The objects of the Poet's thoughts are everywhere; though the eyes and senses of man are, it is true, his favourite guides, yet he will follow wheresoever he can find an atmosphere of sensation in which to move his wings. Poetry is the first and last of all knowledge

—it is as immortal as the heart of man. If the labours of Men of science should ever create any material revolution, direct or indirect, in our condition, and in the impressions which we habitually receive, the Poet will sleep then no more than at present; he will be ready to follow the steps of the Man of science, not only in those general indirect effects, but he will be at his side, carrying sensation into the midst of the objects of the science itself. The remotest discoveries of the Chemist, the Botanist, or Mineralogist, will be as proper objects of the Poet's art as any upon which it can be employed, if the time should ever come when these things shall be familiar to us, and the relations under which they are contemplated by the followers of these respective sciences shall be manifestly and palpably material to us as enjoying and suffering beings. If the time should ever come when what is now called science, thus familiarised to men, shall be ready to put on, as it were, a form of flesh and blood, the Poet will lend his divine spirit to aid the transfiguration, and will welcome the Being thus produced, as a dear and genuine inmate of the household of man.—It is not, then, to be supposed that any one, who holds that sublime notion of Poetry which I have attempted to convey, will break in upon the sanctity and truth of his pictures by transitory and accidental ornaments, and endeavour to excite admiration of himself by arts, the necessity of which must manifestly depend upon the assumed meanness of his subject.

What has been thus far said applies to Poetry in general; but especially to those parts of composition where the Poet speaks through the mouths of his characters; and upon this point it appears to authorise the conclusion that there are few persons of good sense, who would not allow that the dramatic parts of composition are defective, in proportion as they deviate from the real language of nature, and are coloured by a diction of the Poet's own, either peculiar to him as an individual Poet or belonging simply to Poets in general; to a body of men who, from the circumstance of their compositions being in metre, it is expected will employ a particular language.

It is not, then, in the dramatic parts of composition that we look for this distinction of language; but still it may be proper and necessary where the Poet speaks to us in his own person and character. To this I answer by referring the Reader to the description before given of a Poet. Among the qualities there enumerated as principally conducing to form a Poet, is implied nothing differing in kind from other men, but only in degree. The sum of what was said is, that the Poet is chiefly distinguished from other men by a greater promptness to think and feel without immediate external excitement, and a greater power in expressing such thoughts and feelings as are produced in him in that manner. But these passions and thoughts and feelings are the general passions and thoughts and feelings of men. And with what are they connected? Undoubtedly with our moral sentiments and animal sensations, and with the causes which excite these; with the operations of the elements, and the appearances of the visible universe; with storm and sunshine, with the revolutions of the seasons, with cold and heat, with loss of friends and kindred, with injuries and resentments, gratitude and hope, with fear and sorrow. These, and the like, are the sensations and objects which the Poet describes, as they are the sensations of other men, and the objects which interest them. The Poet thinks and feels in the

PREFACES, ETC.

spirit of human passions. How, then, can his language differ in any material degree from that of all other men who feel vividly and see clearly? It might be *proved* that it is impossible. But supposing that this were not the case, the Poet might then be allowed to use a peculiar language when expressing his feelings for his own gratification, or that of men like himself. But Poets do not write for Poets alone, but for men. Unless therefore we are advocates for that admiration which subsists upon ignorance, and that pleasure which arises from hearing what we do not understand, the Poet must descend from this supposed height; and, in order to excite rational sympathy, he must express himself as other men express themselves. To this it may be added, that while he is only selecting from the real language of men, or, which amounts to the same thing, composing accurately in the spirit of such selection, he is treading upon safe ground, and we know what we are to expect from him. Our feelings are the same with respect to metre; for, as it may be proper to remind the Reader, the distinction of metre is regular and uniform, and not, like that which is produced by what is usually called POETIC DICTION, arbitrary, and subject to infinite caprices upon which no calculation whatever can be made. In the one case, the Reader is utterly at the mercy of the Poet, respecting what imagery or diction he may choose to connect with the passion; whereas, in the other, the metre obeys certain laws, to which the Poet and Reader both willingly submit because they are certain, and because no interference is made by them with the passion, but such as the concurring testimony of ages has shown to heighten and improve the pleasure which co-exists with it.

It will now be proper to answer an obvious question, namely, Why, professing these opinions, have I written in verse? To this, in addition to such answer as is included in what has been already said, I reply, in the first place, Because, however I may have restricted myself, there is still left open to me what confessedly constitutes the most valuable object of all writing, whether in prose or verse; the great and universal passions of men, the most general and interesting of their occupations, and the entire world of nature before me—to supply endless combinations of forms and imagery. Now, supposing for a moment that whatever is interesting in these objects may be as vividly described in prose, why should I be condemned for attempting to superadd to such description the charm which, by the consent of all nations, is acknowledged to exist in metrical language? To this, by such as are yet unconvinced, it may be answered that a very small part of the pleasure given by Poetry depends upon the metre, and that it is injudicious to write in metre, unless it be accompanied with the other artificial distinctions of style with which metre is usually accompanied, and that, by such deviation, more will be lost from the shock which will thereby be given to the Reader's associations than will be counterbalanced by any pleasure which he can derive from the general power of numbers. In answer to those who still contend for the necessity of accompanying metre with certain appropriate colours of style in order to the accomplishment of its appropriate end, and who also, in my opinion, greatly underrate the power of metre in itself, it might, perhaps, as far as relates to these Volumes, have been almost sufficient to observe, that poems are extant, written upon more humble subjects, and in a still more naked and simple style, which have continued to give pleasure from generation to genera-

tion. Now, if nakedness and simplicity be a defect, the fact here mentioned affords a strong presumption that poems somewhat less naked and simple are capable of affording pleasure at the present day; and, what I wished *chiefly* to attempt, at present, was to justify myself for having written under the impression of this belief.

But various causes might be pointed out why, when the style is manly, and the subject of some importance, words metrically arranged will long continue to impart such a pleasure to mankind as he who proves the extent of that pleasure will be desirous to impart. The end of Poetry is to produce excitement in co-existence with an overbalance of pleasure; but, by the supposition, excitement is an unusual and irregular state of the mind; ideas and feelings do not, in that state, succeed each other in accustomed order. If the words, however, by which this excitement is produced be in themselves powerful, or the images and feelings have an undue proportion of pain connected with them, there is some danger that the excitement may be carried beyond its proper bounds. Now the co-presence of something regular, something to which the mind has been accustomed in various moods and in a less excited state, cannot but have great efficacy in tempering and restraining the passion by an intertexture of ordinary feeling, and of feeling not strictly and necessarily connected with the passion. This is unquestionably true; and hence, though the opinion will at first appear paradoxical, from the tendency of metre to divest language, in a certain degree, of its reality, and thus to throw a sort of half-consciousness of unsubstantial existence over the whole composition, there can be little doubt but that more pathetic situations and sentiments, that is, those which have a greater proportion of pain connected with them, may be endured in metrical composition, especially in rhyme, than in prose. The metre of the old ballads is very artless; yet they contain many passages which would illustrate this opinion; and, I hope, if the following Poems be attentively perused, similar instances will be found in them. This opinion may be further illustrated by appealing to the Reader's own experience of the reluctance with which he comes to the re-perusal of the distressful parts of 'Clarissa Harlowe,' or the 'Gamester;' while Shakspeare's writings, in the most pathetic scenes, never act upon us, as pathetic, beyond the bounds of pleasure—an effect which, in a much greater degree than might at first be imagined, is to be ascribed to small, but continual and regular impulses of pleasurable surprise from the metrical arrangement.—On the other hand (what it must be allowed will much more frequently happen) if the Poet's words should be incommensurate with the passion, and inadequate to raise the Reader to a height of desirable excitement, then, (unless the Poet's choice of his metre has been grossly injudicious) in the feelings of pleasure which the Reader has been accustomed to connect with metre in general, and in the feeling, whether cheerful or melancholy, which he has been accustomed to connect with that particular movement of metre, there will be found something which will greatly contribute to impart passion to the words, and to effect the complex end which the Poet proposes to himself.

If I had undertaken a SYSTEMATIC defence of the theory here maintained, it would have been my duty to develope the various causes upon which the pleasure received from metrical language depends. Among the chief of these causes is to be

739

reckoned a principle which must be well known to those who have made any of the Arts the object of accurate reflection; namely, the pleasure which the mind derives from the perception of similitude in dissimilitude. This principle is the great spring of the activity of our minds, and their chief feeder. From this principle the direction of the sexual appetite, and all the passions connected with it, take their origin: it is the life of our ordinary conversation; and upon the accuracy with which similitude in dissimilitude, and dissimilitude in similitude are perceived, depend our taste and our moral feelings. It would not be a useless employment to apply this principle to the consideration of metre, and to show that metre is hence enabled to afford much pleasure, and to point out in what manner that pleasure is produced. But my limits will not permit me to enter upon this subject, and I must content myself with a general summary.

I have said that poetry is the spontaneous overflow of powerful feelings: it takes its origin from emotion recollected in tranquillity: the emotion is contemplated till, by a species of reaction, the tranquillity gradually disappears, and an emotion, kindred to that which was before the subject of contemplation, is gradually produced, and does itself actually exist in the mind. In this mood successful composition generally begins, and in a mood similar to this it is carried on; but the emotion, of whatever kind, and in whatever degree, from various causes, is qualified by various pleasures, so that in describing any passions whatsoever, which are voluntarily described, the mind will, upon the whole, be in a state of enjoyment. If Nature be thus cautious to preserve in a state of enjoyment a being so employed, the Poet ought to profit by the lesson held forth to him, and ought especially to take care, that, whatever passions he communicates to his Reader, those passions, if his Reader's mind be sound and vigorous, should always be accompanied with an overbalance of pleasure. Now the music of harmonious metrical language, the sense of difficulty overcome, and the blind association of pleasure which has been previously received from works of rhyme or metre of the same or similar construction, an indistinct perception perpetually renewed of language closely resembling that of real life, and yet, in the circumstance of metre, differing from it so widely—all these imperceptibly make up a complex feeling of delight, which is of the most important use in tempering the painful feeling always found intermingled with powerful descriptions of the deeper passions. This effect is always produced in pathetic and impassioned poetry; while, in lighter compositions, the ease and gracefulness with which the Poet manages his numbers are themselves confessedly a principal source of the gratification of the Reader. All that it is *necessary* to say, however, upon this subject, may be effected by affirming, what few persons will deny, that, of two descriptions, either of passions, manners, or characters, each of them equally well executed, the one in prose and the other in verse, the verse will be read a hundred times where the prose is read once.

Having thus explained a few of my reasons for writing in verse, and why I have chosen subjects from common life, and endeavoured to bring my language near to the real language of men, if I have been too minute in pleading my own cause, I have at the same time been treating a subject of general interest; and for this reason a few words shall be added with reference solely to these particular poems, and to some defects which will

probably be found in them. I am sensible that my associations must have sometimes been particular instead of general, and that, consequently, giving to things a false importance, I may have sometimes written upon unworthy subjects; but I am less apprehensive on this account, than that my language may frequently have suffered from those arbitrary connections of feelings and ideas with particular words and phrases, from which no man can altogether protect himself. Hence I have no doubt, that, in some instances, feelings, even of the ludicrous, may be given to my Readers by expressions which appeared to me tender and pathetic. Such faulty expressions, were I convinced they were faulty at present, and that they must necessarily continue to be so, I would willingly take all reasonable pains to correct. But it is dangerous to make these alterations on the simple authority of a few individuals, or even of certain classes of men; for where the understanding of an Author is not convinced, or his feelings altered, this cannot be done without great injury to himself: for his own feelings are his stay and support; and, if he set them aside in one instance, he may be induced to repeat this act till his mind shall lose all confidence in itself, and become utterly debilitated. To this it may be added, that the critic ought never to forget that he is himself exposed to the same errors as the Poet, and, perhaps, in a much greater degree: for there can be no presumption in saying of most readers, that it is not probable that they will be so well acquainted with the various stages of meaning through which words have passed, or with the fickleness or stability of the relations of particular ideas to each other; and, above all, since they are so much less interested in the subject, they may decide lightly and carelessly.

Long as the Reader has been detained, I hope he will permit me to caution him against a mode of false criticism which has been applied to Poetry, in which the language closely resembles that of life and nature. Such verses have been triumphed over in parodies, of which Dr. Johnson's stanza is a fair specimen:—

> 'I put my hat upon my head
> And walked into the Strand,
> And there I met another man
> Whose hat was in his hand.'

Immediately under these lines let us place one of the most justly-admired stanzas of the 'Babes in the Wood.'

> 'These pretty Babes with hand in hand
> Went wandering up and down;
> But never more they saw the Man
> Approaching from the Town.'

In both these stanzas the words, and the order of the words, in no respect differ from the most unimpassioned conversation. There are words in both, for example, 'the Strand,' and 'the Town,' connected with none but the most familiar ideas; yet the one stanza we admit as admirable, and the other as a fair example of the superlatively contemptible. Whence arises this difference? Not from the metre, not from the language, not from the order of the words; but the *matter* expressed in Dr. Johnson's stanza is contemptible. The proper method of treating trivial and simple verses, to which Dr. Johnson's stanza would be a fair parallelism, is not to say, this is a bad kind of poetry, or, this is not poetry; but, this wants sense; it is neither interesting in itself, nor can *lead* to anything interesting; the images neither originate in that sane state of feeling which arises out of thought, nor can excite thought or feeling in the

PREFACES, ETC.

Reader. This is the only sensible manner of dealing with such verses. Why trouble yourself about the species till you have previously decided upon the genus? Why take pains to prove that an ape is not a Newton, when it is self-evident that he is not a man?

One request I must make of my reader, which is, that in judging these Poems he would decide by his own feelings genuinely, and not by reflection upon what will probably be the judgment of others. How common is it to hear a person say, I myself do not object to this style of composition, or this or that expression, but, to such and such classes of people it will appear mean or ludicrous! This mode of criticism, so destructive of all sound unadulterated judgment, is almost universal: let the Reader then abide, independently, by his own feelings, and, if he finds himself affected, let him not suffer such conjectures to interfere with his pleasure.

If an Author, by any single composition, has impressed us with respect for his talents, it is useful to consider this as affording a presumption, that on other occasions where we have been displeased, he, nevertheless, may not have written ill or absurdly; and further, to give him so much credit for this one composition as may induce us to review what has displeased us, with more care than we should otherwise have bestowed upon it. This is not only an act of justice, but, in our decisions upon poetry especially, may conduce, in a high degree, to the improvement of our own taste; for an *accurate* taste in poetry, and in all the other arts, as Sir Joshua Reynolds has observed, is an *acquired* talent, which can only be produced by thought and a long-continued intercourse with the best models of composition. This is mentioned, not with so ridiculous a purpose as to prevent the most inexperienced Reader from judging for himself, (I have already said that I wish him to judge for himself;) but merely to temper the rashness of decision, and to suggest, that, if Poetry be a subject on which much time has not been bestowed, the judgment may be erroneous; and that, in many cases, it necessarily will be so.

Nothing would, I know, have so effectually contributed to further the end which I have in view, as to have shown of what kind the pleasure is, and how that pleasure is produced, which is confessedly produced by metrical composition essentially different from that which I have here endeavoured to recommend: for the Reader will say that he has been pleased by such composition; and what more can be done for him? The power of any art is limited; and he will suspect, that, if it be proposed to furnish him with new friends, that can be only upon condition of his abandoning his old friends. Besides, as I have said, the Reader is himself conscious of the pleasure which he has received from such composition, composition to which he has peculiarly attached the endearing name of Poetry; and all men feel an habitual gratitude, and something of an honourable bigotry, for the objects which have long continued to please them: we not only wish to be pleased, but to be pleased in that particular way in which we have been accustomed to be pleased. There is in these feelings enough to resist a host of arguments; and I should be the less able to combat them successfully, as I am willing to allow, that, in order entirely to enjoy the Poetry which I am recommending, it would be necessary to give up much of what is ordinarily enjoyed. But, would my limits have permitted me to point out how this pleasure is produced, many obstacles might have been removed, and the Reader assisted in perceiving that the powers of language are not so limited as he may suppose: and that it is possible for poetry to give other enjoyments, of a purer, more lasting, and more exquisite nature. This part of the subject has not been altogether neglected, but it has not been so much my present aim to prove, that the interest excited by some other kinds of poetry is less vivid, and less worthy of the nobler powers of the mind as to offer reasons for presuming, that if my purpose were fulfilled, a species of poetry would be produced, which is genuine poetry; in its nature well adapted to interest mankind permanently, and likewise important in the multiplicity and quality of its moral relations.

From what has been said, and from a perusal of the Poems, the Reader will be able clearly to perceive the object which I had in view: he will determine how far it has been attained; and, what is a much more important question, whether it be worth attaining: and upon the decision of these two questions will rest my claim to the approbation of the Public.

APPENDIX

See page 739—'by what is usually called POETIC DICTION.'

PERHAPS, as I have no right to expect that attentive perusal, without which, confined, as I have been, to the narrow limits of a preface, my meaning cannot be thoroughly understood, I am anxious to give an exact notion of the sense in which the phrase poetic diction has been used; and for this purpose, a few words shall here be added, concerning the origin and characteristics of the phraseology, which I have condemned under that name.

The earliest poets of all nations generally wrote from passion excited by real events; they wrote naturally, and as men: feeling powerfully as they did, their language was daring, and figurative. In succeeding times, Poets, and Men ambitious of the fame of Poets, perceiving the influence of such language, and desirous of producing the same effect without being animated by the same passion, set themselves to a mechanical adoption of these figures of speech, and made use of them, sometimes with propriety, but much more frequently applied them to feelings and thoughts with which they had no natural connection whatsoever. A language was thus insensibly produced, differing materially from the real language of men in *any situation*. The Reader or Hearer of this distorted language found himself in a perturbed and unusual state of mind: when affected by the genuine language of passion he had been in a perturbed and unusual state of mind also: in both cases he was willing that his common judgment and understanding should be laid asleep, and he had no instinctive and infallible perception of the true to make him reject the false; the one served as a passport for the other. The emotion was in both cases delightful, and no wonder if he confounded the one with the other, and believed them both to be produced by the same, or similar causes.

741

PREFACES, ETC.

Besides, the Poet spake to him in the character of a man to be looked up to, a man of genius and authority. Thus, and from a variety of other causes, this distorted language was received with admiration; and Poets, it is probable, who had before contented themselves for the most part with misapplying only expressions which at first had been dictated by real passion, carried the abuse still further, and introduced phrases composed apparently in the spirit of the original figurative language of passion, yet altogether of their own invention, and characterised by various degrees of wanton deviation from good sense and nature.

It is indeed true, that the language of the earliest Poets was felt to differ materially from ordinary language, because it was the language of extraordinary occasions; but it was really spoken by men, language which the Poet himself had uttered when he had been affected by the events which he described, or which he had heard uttered by those around him. To this language it is probable that metre of some sort or other was early superadded. This separated the genuine language of Poetry still further from common life, so that whoever read or heard the poems of these earliest Poets felt himself moved in a way in which he had not been accustomed to be moved in real life, and by causes manifestly different from those which acted upon him in real life. This was the great temptation to all the corruptions which have followed: under the protection of this feeling succeeding Poets constructed a phraseology which had one thing, it is true, in common with the genuine language of poetry, namely, that it was not heard in ordinary conversation; that it was unusual. But the first Poets, as I have said, spake a language which, though unusual, was still the language of men. This circumstance, however, was disregarded by their successors; they found that they could please by easier means: they became proud of modes of expression which they themselves had invented, and which were uttered only by themselves. In process of time metre became a symbol or promise of this unusual language, and whoever took upon him to write in metre, according as he possessed more or less of true poetic genius, introduced less or more of this adulterated phraseology into his compositions, and the true and the false were inseparably interwoven until, the taste of men becoming gradually perverted, this language was received as a natural language: and at length, by the influence of books upon men, did to a certain degree really become so. Abuses of this kind were imported from one nation to another, and with the progress of refinement this diction became daily more and more corrupt, thrusting out of sight the plain humanities of nature by a motley masquerade of tricks, quaintnesses, hieroglyphics, and enigmas.

It would not be uninteresting to point out the causes of the pleasure given by this extravagant and absurd diction. It depends upon a great variety of causes, but upon none, perhaps, more than its influence in impressing a notion of the peculiarity and exaltation of the Poet's character, and in flattering the Reader's self-love by bringing him nearer to a sympathy with that character; an effect which is accomplished by unsettling ordinary habits of thinking, and thus assisting the Reader to approach to that perturbed and dizzy state of mind in which if he does not find himself, he imagines that he is balked of a peculiar enjoyment which poetry can and ought to bestow.

The sonnet quoted from Gray, in the Preface, except the lines printed in Italics, consists of little

else but this diction, though not of the worst kind; and indeed, if one may be permitted to say so, it is far too common in the best writers both ancient and modern. Perhaps in no way, by positive example, could more easily be given a notion of what I mean by the phrase *poetic diction* than by referring to a comparison between the metrical paraphrase which we have of passages in the Old and New Testament, and those passages as they exist in our common Translation. See Pope's 'Messiah' throughout; Prior's 'Did sweeter sounds adorn my flowing tongue,' &c. &c. 'Though I speak with the tongues of men and of angels,' &c. &c. 1st Corinthians, chap. xiii. By way of immediate example take the following of Dr. Johnson:—

'Turn on the prudent Ant thy heedless eyes,
Observe her labours, Sluggard, and be wise;
No stern command, no monitory voice,
Prescribes her duties, or directs her choice;
Yet, timely provident, she hastes away
To snatch the blessings of a plenteous day;
When fruitful Summer loads the teeming plain,
She crops the harvest, and she stores the grain.
How long shall sloth usurp thy useless hours,
Unnerve thy vigour, and enchain thy powers?
While artful shades thy downy couch enclose,
And soft solicitation courts repose,
Amidst the drowsy charms of dull delight,
Year chases year with unremitted flight,
Till Want now following, fraudulent and slow,
Shall spring to seize thee, like an ambush'd foe.'

From this hubbub of words pass to the original. 'Go to the Ant, thou Sluggard, consider her ways, and be wise: which having no guide, overseer, or ruler, provideth her meat in the summer, and gathereth her food in the harvest. How long wilt thou sleep, O Sluggard? when wilt thou arise out of thy sleep? Yet a little sleep, a little slumber, a little folding of the hands to sleep. So shall thy poverty come as one that travelleth, and thy want as an armed man.' Proverbs, chap. vi.

One more quotation, and I have done. It is from Cowper's Verses supposed to be written by Alexander Selkirk:—

'Religion! what treasure untold
Resides in that heavenly word!
More precious than silver and gold,
Or all that this earth can afford.
But the sound of the church-going bell
These valleys and rocks never heard,
Ne'er sighed at the sound of a knell,
Or smiled when a sabbath appeared.

'Ye winds, that have made me your sport
Convey to this desolate shore
Some cordial endearing report
Of a land I must visit no more.
My Friends, do they now and then send
A wish or a thought after me?
O tell me I yet have a friend,
Though a friend I am never to see.'

This passage is quoted as an instance of three different styles of composition. The first four lines are poorly expressed; some Critics would call the language prosaic; the fact is, it would be bad prose, so bad, that it is scarcely worse in metre. The epithet 'church-going' applied to a bell, and that by so chaste a writer as Cowper, is an instance of the strange abuses which Poets have introduced into their language, till they and their Readers take them as matters of course, if they do not single them out expressly as objects of admiration. The two lines 'Ne'er sighed at the sound,' &c., are, in my opinion, an instance of the language of passion wrested from its proper use, and, from the mere

742

circumstance of the composition being in metre, applied upon an occasion that does not justify such violent expressions; and I should condemn the passage, though perhaps few Readers will agree with me, as vicious poetic diction. The last stanza is throughout admirably expressed: it would be equally good whether in prose or verse, except that the Reader has an exquisite pleasure in seeing such natural language so naturally connected with metre. The beauty of this stanza tempts me to conclude with a principle which ought never to be lost sight of, and which has been my chief guide in all I have said,—namely, that in works of *imagination and sentiment*, for of these only have I been treating, in proportion as ideas and feelings are valuable, whether the composition be in prose or in verse, they require and exact one and the same language. Metre is but adventitious to composition, and the phraseology for which that passport is necessary, even where it may be graceful at all, will be little valued by the judicious.

ESSAY, SUPPLEMENTARY TO THE PREFACE

WITH the young of both sexes, Poetry is, like love, a passion; but, for much the greater part of those who have been proud of its power over their minds, a necessity soon arises of breaking the pleasing bondage; or it relaxes of itself;—the thoughts being occupied in domestic cares, or the time engrossed by business. Poetry then becomes only an occasional recreation; while to those whose existence passes away in a course of fashionable pleasure, it is a species of luxurious amusement. In middle and declining age, a scattered number of serious persons resort to poetry, as to religion, for a protection against the pressure of trivial employments, and as a consolation for the afflictions of life. And, lastly, there are many, who, having been enamoured of this art in their youth, have found leisure, after youth was spent, to cultivate general literature; in which poetry has continued to be comprehended *as a study*.

Into the above classes the Readers of poetry may be divided; Critics abound in them all; but from the last only can opinions be collected of absolute value, and worthy to be depended upon, as prophetic of the destiny of a new work. The young, who in nothing can escape delusion, are especially subject to it in their intercourse with Poetry. The cause, not so obvious as the fact is unquestionable, is the same as that from which erroneous judgments in this art, in the minds of men of all ages, chiefly proceed; but upon Youth it operates with peculiar force. The appropriate business of poetry, (which, nevertheless, if genuine, is as permanent as pure science,) her appropriate employment, her privilege and her *duty*, is to treat of things not as they *are*, but as they *appear;* not as they exist in themselves, but as they *seem* to exist in the *senses*, and to the *passions*. What a world of delusion does this acknowledged obligation prepare for the inexperienced! what temptations to go astray are here held forth for them whose thoughts have been little disciplined by the understanding, and whose feelings revolt from the sway of reason!—When a juvenile Reader is in the height of his rapture with some vicious passage, should experience throw in doubts, or common-sense suggest suspicions, a lurking consciousness that the realities of the Muse are but shows, and that her liveliest excitements are raised by transient shocks of conflicting feeling and successive assemblages of contradictory thoughts—is ever at hand to justify extravagance, and to sanction absurdity. But, it may be asked, as these illusions are unavoidable, and, no doubt, eminently useful to the mind as a process, what good can be gained by making observations, the tendency of which is to diminish the confidence of youth in its feelings, and thus to abridge its innocent and even profitable pleasures? The reproach implied in the question could not be warded off, if Youth were incapable of being delighted with what is truly excellent; or, if these errors always terminated of themselves in due season. But, with the majority, though their force be abated, they continue through life. Moreover, the fire of youth is too vivacious an element to be extinguished or damped by a philosophical remark; and, while there is no danger that what has been said will be injurious or painful to the ardent and the confident, it may prove beneficial to those who, being enthusiastic, are, at the same time, modest and ingenuous. The intimation may unite with their own misgivings to regulate their sensibility, and to bring in, sooner than it would otherwise have arrived, a more discreet and sound judgment.

If it should excite wonder that men of ability, in later life, whose understandings have been rendered acute by practice in affairs, should be so easily and so far imposed upon when they happen to take up a new work in verse, this appears to be the cause;—that, having discontinued their attention to poetry, whatever progress may have been made in other departments of knowledge, they have not, as to this art, advanced in true discernment beyond the age of youth. If, then, a new poem fall in their way, whose attractions are of that kind which would have enraptured them during the heat of youth, the judgment not being improved to a degree that they shall be disgusted, they are dazzled; and prize and cherish the faults for having had power to make the present time vanish before them, and to throw the mind back, as by enchantment, into the happiest season of life. As they read, powers seem to be revived, passions are regenerated, and pleasures restored. The Book was probably taken up after an escape from the burden of business, and with a wish to forget the world, and all its vexations and anxieties. Having obtained this wish, and so much more, it is natural that they should make report as they have felt.

If Men of mature age, through want of practice, be thus easily beguiled into admiration of absurdities, extravagances, and misplaced ornaments, thinking it proper that their understandings should enjoy a holiday, while they are unbending their minds with verse, it may be expected that such Readers will resemble their former selves also in strength of prejudice, and an inaptitude to be moved by the unostentatious beauties of a pure style. In the higher poetry, an enlightened Critic chiefly looks for a reflection of the wisdom of the heart and the grandeur of the imagination. Wherever these appear, simplicity accompanies them; Magnificence herself, when legitimate, depending upon a simplicity of her own, to regulate her ornaments. But it is a well-known property of human nature, that our estimates are ever governed by comparisons, of which we are conscious with

743

various degrees of distinctness. Is it not, then, inevitable (confining these observations to the effects of style merely) that an eye, accustomed to the glaring hues of diction by which such Readers are caught and excited, will for the most part be rather repelled than attracted by an original Work, the colouring of which is disposed according to a pure and refined scheme of harmony? It is in the fine arts as in the affairs of life, no man can *serve* (*i.e.* obey with zeal and fidelity) two Masters.

As Poetry is most just to its own divine origin when it administers the comforts and breathes the spirit of religion, they who have learned to perceive this truth, and who betake themselves to reading verse for sacred purposes, must be preserved from numerous illusions to which the two Classes of Readers, whom we have been considering, are liable. But, as the mind grows serious from the weight of life, the range of its passions is contracted accordingly; and its sympathies become so exclusive, that many species of high excellence wholly escape, or but languidly excite, its notice. Besides, men who read from religious or moral inclinations, even when the subject is of that kind which they approve, are beset with misconceptions and mistakes peculiar to themselves. Attaching so much importance to the truths which interest them, they are prone to overrate the Authors by whom those truths are expressed and enforced. They come prepared to impart so much passion to the Poet's language, that they remain unconscious how little, in fact, they receive from it. And, on the other hand, religious faith is to him who holds it so momentous a thing, and error appears to be attended with such tremendous consequences, that, if opinions touching upon religion occur which the Reader condemns, he not only cannot sympathise with them, however animated the expression, but there is, for the most part, an end put to all satisfaction and enjoyment. Love, if it before existed, is converted into dislike; and the heart of the Reader is set against the Author and his book.—To these excesses, they, who from their professions ought to be the most guarded against them, are perhaps the most liable; I mean those sects whose religion, being from the calculating understanding, is cold and formal. For when Christianity, the religion of humility, is founded upon the proudest faculty of our nature, what can be expected but contradictions? Accordingly, believers of this cast are at one time contemptuous; at another, being troubled, as they are and must be, with inward misgivings, they are jealous and suspicious;—and at all seasons, they are under temptation to supply by the heat with which they defend their tenets, the animation which is wanting to the constitution of the religion itself.

Faith was given to man that his affections, detached from the treasures of time, might be inclined to settle upon those of eternity;—the elevation of his nature, which this habit produces on earth, being to him a presumptive evidence of a future state of existence; and giving him a title to partake of its holiness. The religious man values what he sees chiefly as an 'imperfect shadowing forth' of what he is incapable of seeing. The concerns of religion refer to indefinite objects, and are too weighty for the mind to support them without relieving itself by resting a great part of the burthen upon words and symbols. The commerce between Man and his Maker cannot be carried on but by a process where much is represented in little, and the Infinite Being accommodates himself to a finite capacity. In all this may be perceived the affinity between religion and poetry; between religion—making up the deficiencies of reason by faith; and poetry—passionate for the instruction of reason; between religion—whose element is infinitude, and whose ultimate trust is the supreme of things, submitting herself to circumscription, and reconciled to substitutions; and poetry—ethereal and transcendent, yet incapable to sustain her existence without sensuous incarnation. In this community of nature may be perceived also the lurking incitements of kindred error;—so that we shall find that no poetry has been more subject to distortion, than that species, the argument and scope of which is religious; and no lovers of the art have gone farther astray than the pious and the devout.

Whither then shall we turn for that union of qualifications which must necessarily exist before the decisions of a critic can be of absolute value? For a mind at once poetical and philosophical; for a critic whose affections are as free and kindly as the spirit of society, and whose understanding is severe as that of dispassionate government? Where are we to look for that initiatory composure of mind which no selfishness can disturb? For a natural sensibility that has been tutored into correctness without losing anything of its quickness; and for active faculties, capable of answering the demands which an Author of original imagination shall make upon them, associated with a judgment that cannot be duped into admiration by aught that is unworthy of it?— among those and those only, who, never having suffered their youthful love of poetry to remit much of its force, have applied to the consideration of the laws of this art the best power of their understandings. At the same time it must be observed—that, as this Class comprehends the only judgments which are trust-worthy, so does it include the most erroneous and perverse. For to be mistaught is worse than to be untaught; and no perverseness equals that which is supported by system, no errors are so difficult to root out as those which the understanding has pledged its credit to uphold. In this Class are contained censors, who, if they be pleased with what is good, are pleased with it only by imperfect glimpses, and upon false principles; who, should they generalise rightly, to a certain point, are sure to suffer for it in the end; who, if they stumble upon a sound rule, are fettered by misapplying it, or by straining it too far; being incapable of perceiving when it ought to yield to one of higher order. In it are found critics too petulant to be passive to a genuine poet, and too feeble to grapple with him; men, who take upon them to report of the course which *he* holds whom they are utterly unable to accompany,—confounded if he turn quick upon the wing, dismayed if he soar steadily 'into the region;'— men of palsied imaginations and indurated hearts; in whose minds all healthy action is languid, who therefore feed as the many direct them, or, with the many, are greedy after vicious provocatives;— judges, whose censure is auspicious, and whose praise ominous! In this class meet together the two extremes of best and worst.

The observations presented in the foregoing series are of too ungracious a nature to have been made without reluctance; and, were it only on this account, I would invite the reader to try them by the test of comprehensive experience. If the number of judges who can be confidently relied upon be in reality so small, it ought to follow that partial notice only, or neglect, perhaps long continued, or attention wholly inadequate to their merits— must have been the fate of most works in the higher departments of poetry; and that, on the other hand, numerous productions have blazed into popularity, and have passed away, leaving scarcely a trace behind them: it will be further found, that when Authors shall have at length raised themselves into general admiration and maintained their ground, errors and prejudices have prevailed concerning their genius and their works, which the few who are conscious of those errors and prejudices would deplore; if they were not recompensed by perceiving that there are select Spirits for whom it is ordained that their fame shall be in the world an existence like that of Virtue, which owes its being to the struggles it makes, and its vigour to the enemies whom it provokes;—a vivacious quality, ever doomed to meet with opposition, and still triumphing over it; and, from the nature of its dominion, incapable of being brought to the sad conclusion of Alexander, when he wept that there were no more worlds for him to conquer.

Let us take a hasty retrospect of the poetical literature of this Country for the greater part of the last two centuries, and see if the facts support these inferences.

Who is there that now reads the 'Creation' of Dubartas? Yet all Europe once resounded with his praise; he was caressed by kings; and, when his Poem was translated into our language, the 'Faery Queen' faded before it. The name of Spenser, whose genius is of a higher order than even that of Ariosto, is at this day scarcely known beyond the limits of the British Isles. And if the value of his works is to be estimated from the attention now paid to them by his countrymen, compared with that which they bestow on those of some other writers, it must be pronounced small indeed.

'The laurel, meed of mighty conquerors
And poets *sage*'—

are his own words; but his wisdom has, in this particular, been his worst enemy: while its opposite, whether in the shape of folly or madness, has been *their* best friend. But he was a great power, and hears a high name: the laurel has been awarded to him.

A dramatic Author, if he write for the stage, must adapt himself to the taste of the audience, or they will not endure him; accordingly the mighty genius of Shakspeare was listened to. The people were delighted: but I am not sufficiently versed in stage antiquities to determine whether they did not flock as eagerly to the representation of many pieces of contemporary Authors, wholly undeserving to appear upon the same boards. Had there been a formal contest for superiority among dramatic writers, that Shakspeare, like his predecessors Sophocles and Euripides, would have often been subject to the mortification of seeing the prize adjudged to sorry competitors, becomes too probable, when we reflect that the admirers of Settle and Shadwell were, in a later age, as numerous, and reckoned as respectable in point of talent, as those of Dryden. At all events, that Shakspeare stooped to accommodate himself to the People, is sufficiently apparent; and one of the most striking proofs of his almost omnipotent genius, is, that he could turn to such glorious purpose those materials which the prepossessions of the age compelled him to make use of. Yet even this marvellous skill appears not to have been enough to prevent his rivals from having some advantage over him in public estimation; else how can we account for passages and scenes that exist in his works, unless

upon a supposition that some of the grossest of them, a fact which in my own mind I have no doubt of, were foisted in by the Players, for the gratification of the many?

But that his Works, whatever might be their reception upon the stage, made but little impression upon the ruling Intellects of the time, may be inferred from the fact that Lord Bacon, in his multifarious writings, nowhere either quotes or alludes to him[1]. His dramatic excellence enabled him to resume possession of the stage after the Restoration; but Dryden tells us that in his time two of the plays of Beaumont and Fletcher were acted for one of Shakspeare's. And so faint and limited was the perception of the poetic beauties of his dramas in the time of Pope, that, in his Edition of the Plays, with a view of rendering to the general reader a necessary service, he printed between inverted commas those passages which he thought most worthy of notice.

At this day, the French Critics have abated nothing of their aversion to this darling of our Nation: 'the English, with their bouffon de Shakspeare,' is as familiar an expression among them as in the time of Voltaire. Baron Grimm is the only French writer who seems to have perceived his infinite superiority to the first names of the French Theatre; an advantage which the Parisian Critic owed to his German blood and German education. The most enlightened Italians, though well acquainted with our language, are wholly incompetent to measure the proportions of Shakspeare. The Germans only, of foreign nations, are approaching towards a knowledge and feeling of what he is. In some respects they have acquired a superiority over the fellow-countrymen of the Poet: for among us it is a current, I might say, an established opinion, that Shakspeare is justly praised when he is pronounced to be 'a wild irregular genius, in whom great faults are compensated by great beauties.' How long may it be before this misconception passes away, and it becomes universally acknowledged that the judgment of Shakspeare in the selection of his materials, and in the manner in which he has made them, heterogeneous as they often are, constitute a unity of their own, and contribute all to one great end, is not less admirable than his imagination, his invention, and his intuitive knowledge of human Nature?

There is extant a small Volume of miscellaneous poems, in which Shakspeare expresses his own feelings in his own person. It is not difficult to conceive that the Editor, George Steevens, should have been insensible to the beauties of one portion of that Volume, the Sonnets; though in no part of the writings of this Poet is found, in an equal compass, a greater number of exquisite feelings felicitously expressed. But, from regard to the Critic's own credit, he would not have ventured to talk of an[2] act of parliament not being strong

[1] The learned Hakewill (a third edition of whose book bears date 1635), writing to refute the error 'touching Nature's perpetual and universal decay,' cites triumphantly the names of Ariosto, Tasso, Bartas, and Spenser, as instances that poetic genius had not degenerated; but he makes no mention of Shakspeare.

[2] This flippant insensibility was publicly reprehended by Mr. Coleridge in a course of Lectures upon Poetry given by him at the Royal Institution. For the various merits of thought and language in Shakspeare's Sonnets, see Numbers, 27, 29, 30, 32, 33, 54, 64, 66, 68, 73, 76, 86, 91, 92, 93, 97, 98, 105, 107, 108, 109, 111, 113, 114, 116, 117, 129, and many others.

enough to compel the perusal of those little pieces, if he had not known that the people of England were ignorant of the treasures contained in them: and if he had not, moreover, shared the too common propensity of human nature to exult over a supposed fall into the mire of a genius whom he had been compelled to regard with admiration, as an inmate of the celestial regions—'there sitting where he durst not soar.'

Nine years before the death of Shakspeare, Milton was born; and early in life he published several small poems, which, though on their first appearance they were praised by a few of the judicious, were afterwards neglected to that degree, that Pope in his youth could borrow from them without risk of its being known. Whether these poems are at this day justly appreciated, I will not undertake to decide: nor would it imply a severe reflection upon the mass of readers to suppose the contrary; seeing that a man of the acknowledged genius of Voss, the German poet, could suffer their spirit to evaporate; and could change their character, as is done in the translation made by him of the most popular of those pieces. At all events, it is certain that these Poems of Milton are now much read, and loudly praised; yet were they little heard of till more than 150 years after their publication; and of the Sonnets, Dr. Johnson, as appears from Boswell's Life of him, was in the habit of thinking and speaking as contemptuously as Steevens wrote upon those of Shakspeare.

About the time when the Pindaric odes of Cowley and his imitators, and the productions of that class of curious thinkers whom Dr. Johnson has strangely styled metaphysical Poets, were beginning to lose something of that extravagant admiration which they had excited, the 'Paradise Lost' made its appearance. 'Fit audience find though few,' was the petition addressed by the Poet to his inspiring Muse. I have said elsewhere that he gained more than he asked; this I believe to be true; but Dr. Johnson has fallen into a gross mistake when he attempts to prove, by the sale of the work, that Milton's Countrymen were '*just* to it' upon its first appearance. Thirteen hundred Copies were sold in two years; an uncommon example, he asserts, of the prevalence of genius in opposition to so much recent enmity as Milton's public conduct had excited. But, be it remembered that, if Milton's political and religious opinions, and the manner in which he announced them, had raised him many enemies; who, as all personal danger was passed away at the time of publication, would be eager to procure the master-work of a man whom they revered, and whom they would be proud of praising. Take, from the number of purchasers, persons of this class, and also those who wished to possess the Poem as a religious work, and but few I fear would be left who sought for it on account of its poetical merits. The demand did not immediately increase; 'for,' says Dr. Johnson, 'many more readers' (he means persons in the habit of reading poetry) 'than were supplied at first the Nation did not afford.' How careless must a writer be who can make this assertion in the face of so many existing title-pages to belie it! Turning to my own shelves, I find the folio of Cowley, seventh edition 1681. A book near it is Flatman's Poems, fourth edition, 1686; Waller, fifth edition, same date. The Poems of Norris of Bemerton not long after went, I believe, through nine editions. What further demand there might be for these works I do not know; but I well remember, that,

twenty-five years ago, the booksellers' stalls in London swarmed with the folios of Cowley. This is not mentioned in disparagement of that able writer and amiable man; but merely to show—that, if Milton's work were not more read, it was not because readers did not exist at the time. The early editions of the 'Paradise Lost' were printed in a shape which allowed them to be sold at a low price, yet only three thousand copies of the Work were sold in eleven years; and the Nation, says Dr. Johnson, had been satisfied from 1623 to 1664, that is, forty-one years, with only two editions of the Works of Shakspeare; which probably did not together make one thousand Copies; facts adduced by the critic to prove the 'paucity of Readers.'—There were readers in multitudes; but their money went for other purposes, as their admiration was fixed elsewhere. We are authorised, then, to affirm, that the reception of the 'Paradise Lost,' and the slow progress of its fame, are proofs as striking as can be desired that the positions which I am attempting to establish are not erroneous[1].—How amusing to shape to one's self such a critique as a Wit of Charles's days, or a Lord of the Miscellanies or trading Journalist of King William's time, would have brought forth, if he had set his faculties industriously to work upon this Poem, everywhere impregnated with *original* excellence.

So strange indeed are the obliquities of admiration, that they whose opinions are much influenced by authority will often be tempted to think that there are no fixed principles[2] in human nature for this art to rest upon. I have been honoured by being permitted to peruse in MS. a tract composed between the period of the Revolution and the close of that century. It is the Work of an English Peer of high accomplishments, its object to form the character and direct the studies of his son. Perhaps nowhere does a more beautiful treatise of the kind exist. The good sense and wisdom of the thoughts, the delicacy of the feelings, and the charm of the style, are, throughout, equally conspicuous. Yet the Author, selecting among the Poets of his own country those whom he deems most worthy of his son's perusal, particularises only Lord Rochester, Sir John Denham, and Cowley. Writing about the same time, Shaftesbury, an author at present unjustly depreciated, describes the English Muses as only yet lisping in their cradles.

The arts by which Pope, soon afterwards, contrived to procure to himself a more general and a higher reputation than perhaps any English Poet ever attained during his life-time, are known to the judicious. And as well known is it to them, that the undue exertion of those arts is the cause why Pope has for some time held a rank in literature, to which, if he had not been seduced by an over-love of immediate popularity, and had confided more in his native genius, he never could have descended. He bewitched the nation by his melody, and dazzled it by his polished style, and was himself blinded by his own success. Having wandered from humanity in his Eclogues with

---

[1] Hughes is express upon this subject: in his dedication of Spenser's Works to Lord Somers, he writes thus: 'It was your Lordship's encouraging a beautiful edition of "Paradise Lost" that first brought that incomparable Poem to be generally known and esteemed.'

[2] This opinion seems actually to have been entertained by Adam Smith, the worst critic, David Hume not excepted, that Scotland, a soil to which this sort of weed seems natural, has produced.

boyish inexperience, the praise, which these compositions obtained, tempted him into a belief that Nature was not to be trusted, at least in pastoral Poetry. To prove this by example, he put his friend Gay upon writing those Eclogues which their author intended to be burlesque. The instigator of the work, and his admirers, could perceive in them nothing but what was ridiculous. Nevertheless, though these Poems contain some detestable passages, the effect, as Dr. Johnson well observes, 'of reality and truth became conspicuous even when the intention was to show them grovelling and degraded.' The Pastorals, ludicrous to such as prided themselves upon their refinement, in spite of those disgusting passages, 'became popular, and were read with delight, as just representations of rural manners and occupations.'

Something less than sixty years after the publication of the 'Paradise Lost' appeared Thomson's 'Winter;' which was speedily followed by his other Seasons. It is a work of inspiration; much of it is written from himself, and nobly from himself. How was it received? 'It was no sooner read,' says one of his contemporary biographers, 'than universally admired: those only excepted who had not been used to feel, or to look for anything in poetry, beyond a *point* of satirical or epigrammatic wit, a smart *antithesis* richly trimmed with rhyme, or the softness of an *elegiac* complaint. To such his manly classical spirit could not readily commend itself; till, after a more attentive perusal, they had got the better of their prejudices, and either acquired or affected a truer taste. A few others stood aloof, merely because they had long before fixed the articles of their poetical creed, and resigned themselves to an absolute despair of ever seeing anything new and original. These were somewhat mortified to find their notions disturbed by the appearance of a poet, who seemed to owe nothing but to nature and his own genius. But, in a short time, the applause became unanimous; every one wondering how so many pictures, and pictures so familiar, should have moved them but faintly to what they felt in his descriptions. His digressions too, the overflowings of a tender benevolent heart, charmed the reader no less; leaving him in doubt, whether he should more admire the Poet or love the Man.'

This case appears to bear strongly against us:—but we must distinguish between wonder and legitimate admiration. The subject of the work is the changes produced in the appearances of nature by the revolution of the year: and, by undertaking to write in verse, Thomson pledged himself to treat his subject as became a Poet. Now, it is remarkable that, excepting the nocturnal Reverie of Lady Winchilsea, and a passage or two in the 'Windsor Forest' of Pope, the poetry of the period intervening between the publication of the 'Paradise Lost' and the 'Seasons' does not contain a single new image of external nature; and scarcely presents a familiar one from which it can be inferred that the eye of the Poet had been steadily fixed upon his object, much less that his feelings had urged him to work upon it in the spirit of genuine imagination. To what a low state knowledge of the most obvious and important phenomena had sunk, is evident from the style in which Dryden has executed a description of Night in one of his Tragedies, and Pope his translation of the celebrated moonlight scene in the 'Iliad.' A blind man, in the habit of attending accurately to descriptions casually dropped from the lips of those around him, might easily depict these appearances with more truth. Dryden's lines are vague, bombastic, and senseless[1]; those of Pope, though he had Homer to guide him, are throughout false and contradictory. The verses of Dryden, once highly celebrated, are forgotten; those of Pope still retain their hold upon public estimation,—nay, there is not a passage of descriptive poetry, which at this day finds so many and such ardent admirers. Strange to think of an enthusiast, as may have been the case with thousands, reciting those verses under the cope of a moonlight sky, without having his raptures in the least disturbed by a suspicion of their absurdity!—If these two distinguished writers could habitually think that the visible universe was of so little consequence to a poet, that it was scarcely necessary for him to cast his eyes upon it, we may be assured that those passages of the elder poets which faithfully and poetically describe the phenomena of nature, were not at that time holden in much estimation, and that there was little accurate attention paid to those appearances.

Wonder is the natural product of Ignorance; and as the soil was *in such good condition* at the time of the publication of the 'Seasons,' the crop was doubtless abundant. Neither individuals nor nations become corrupt all at once, nor are they enlightened in a moment. Thomson was an inspired poet, but he could not work miracles; in cases where the art of seeing had in some degree been learned, the teacher would further the proficiency of his pupils, but he could do little *more;* though so far does vanity assist men in acts of self-deception, that many would often fancy they recognized a likeness when they knew nothing of the original. Having shown that much of what his biographer deemed genuine admiration must in fact have been blind wonderment—how is the rest to be accounted for?—Thomson was fortunate in the very title of his poem, which seemed to bring it home to the prepared sympathies of every one: in the next place, notwithstanding his high powers, he writes a vicious style; and his false ornaments are exactly of that kind which would be most likely to strike the undiscerning. He likewise abounds with sentimental common-places, that, from the manner in which they were brought forward, bore an imposing air of novelty. In any well-used copy of the 'Seasons' the book generally opens of itself with the rhapsody on love, or with one of the stories (perhaps 'Damon and Musidora'); these also are prominent in our collections of Extracts, and are the parts of his Work which, after all, were probably most efficient in first recommending the author to general notice. Pope, repaying praises which he had received, and wishing to extol him to the highest, only styles him 'an elegant and philosophical Poet;' nor are we able to collect any unquestionable proofs that the true characteristics of Thomson's genius as an imaginative poet[2] were perceived, till the elder Warton, almost forty years

---

[1]   CORTES *alone in a night-gown.*

'All things are hush'd as Nature's self lay dead;
The mountains seem to nod their drowsy head.
The little Birds in dreams their songs repeat,
And sleeping Flowers beneath the Night-dew
  sweat:
Even Lust and Envy sleep; yet Love denies
Rest to my soul, and slumber to my eyes.'
                    DRYDEN'S *Indian Emperor.*

[2] Since these observations upon Thomson were written, I have perused the second edition of his 'Seasons,' and find that even *that* does not contain the most striking passages which Warton points out for admiration; these, with other improvements, throughout the whole work, must have been added at a later period.

after the publication of the 'Seasons,' pointed them out by a note in his Essay on the 'Life and Writings of Pope.' In the 'Castle of Indolence' (of which Gray speaks so coldly) these characteristics were almost as conspicuously displayed, and in verse more harmonious, and diction more pure. Yet that fine poem was neglected on its appearance, and is at this day the delight only of a few!

When Thomson died, Collins breathed forth his regrets in an Elegiac Poem, in which he pronounces a poetical curse upon *him* who should regard with insensibility the place where the Poet's remains were deposited. The Poems of the mourner himself have now passed through innumerable editions, and are universally known; but if, when Collins died, the same kind of imprecation had been pronounced by a surviving admirer, small is the number whom it would not have comprehended. The notice which his poems attained during his lifetime was so small, and of course the sale so insignificant, that not long before his death he deemed it right to repay to the bookseller the sum which he had advanced for them, and threw the edition into the fire.

Next in importance to the 'Seasons' of Thomson, though at considerable distance from that work in order of time, come the 'Reliques of Ancient English Poetry;' collected, new-modelled, and in many instances (if such a contradiction in terms may be used) composed by the Editor, Dr. Percy. This work did not steal silently into the world, as is evident from the number of legendary tales, that appeared not long after its publication; and had been modelled, as the authors persuaded themselves, after the old Ballad. The Compilation was however ill suited to the then existing taste of city society; and Dr. Johnson, 'mid the little senate to which he gave laws, was not sparing in his exertions to make it an object of contempt. The critic triumphed, the legendary imitators were deservedly disregarded, and, as undeservedly, their ill-imitated models sank, in this country, into temporary neglect; while Bürger, and other able writers of Germany, were translating or imitating these Reliques, and composing, with the aid of inspiration thence derived, poems which are the delight of the German nation. Dr. Percy was so abashed by the ridicule flung upon his labours from the ignorance and insensibility of the persons with whom he lived, that, though while he was writing under a mask he had not wanted resolution to follow his genius into the regions of true simplicity and genuine pathos (as is evinced by the exquisite ballad of 'Sir Cauline' and by many other pieces), yet when he appeared in his own person and character as a poetical writer, he adopted, as in the tale of the 'Hermit of Warkworth,' a diction scarcely in any one of its features distinguishable from the vague, the glossy, and unfeeling language of his day. I mention this remarkable fact[1] with regret, esteeming the genius of Dr. Percy in this kind of writing superior to that of any other man by whom in modern times it has been cultivated. That even Bürger (to whom

[1] Shenstone, in his 'Schoolmistress,' gives a still more remarkable instance of this timidity. On its first appearance (see D'Israeli's 2nd Series of the 'Curiosities of Literature') the Poem was accompanied with an absurd prose commentary, showing, as indeed some incongruous expressions in the text imply, that the whole was intended for burlesque. In subsequent editions, the commentary was dropped, and the People have since continued to read in seriousness, doing for the Author what he had not courage openly to venture upon for himself.

Klopstock gave, in my hearing, a commendation which he denied to Goethe and Schiller, pronouncing him to be a genuine poet, and one of the few among the Germans whose works would last) had not the fine sensibility of Percy, might be shown from many passages, in which he has deserted his original only to go astray. For example,

'Now daye was gone, and night was come,
And all were fast asleepe,
All save the Lady Emeline,
Who sate in her bowre to weepe:

'And soone she heard her true Love's voice
Low whispering at the walle,
Awake, awake, my dear Ladye,
'Tis I thy true-love call.'

Which is thus tricked out and dilated:

'Als nun die Nacht Gebirg' und Thal
Vermummt in Rabenschatten,
Und Hochburgs Lampen überall
Schon ausgeflimmert hatten,
Und alles tief entschlafen war;
Doch nur das Fräulein immerdar,
Voll Fieberangst, noch wachte,
Und seinen Ritter dachte:
Da horch! Ein süsser Liebeston
Kam leis' empor geflogen.
"Ho, Trudchen, ho! Da bin ich schon!
Frisch auf! Dich angezogen!"'

But from humble ballads we must ascend to heroics. All hail, Macpherson! hail to thee, Sire of Ossian! The Phantom was begotten by the snug embrace of an impudent Highlander upon a cloud of tradition—it travelled southward, where it was greeted with acclamation, and the thin Consistence took its course through Europe, upon the breath of popular applause. The Editor of the 'Reliques' had indirectly preferred a claim to the praise of invention, by not concealing that his supplementary labours were considerable! how selfish his conduct, contrasted with that of the disinterested Gael, who, like Lear, gives his kingdom away, and is content to become a pensioner upon his own issue for a beggarly pittance!—Open this far-famed Book!—I have done so at random, and the beginning of the 'Epic Poem Temora,' in eight Books, presents itself. 'The blue waves of Ullin roll in light. The green hills are covered with day. Trees shake their dusky heads in the breeze. Grey torrents pour their noisy streams. Two green hills with aged oaks surround a narrow plain. The blue course of a stream is there. On its banks stood Cairbar of Atha. His spear supports the king; the red eyes of his fear are sad. Cormac rises on his soul with all his ghastly wounds.' Precious memorandums from the pocket-book of the blind Ossian!

If it be unbecoming, as I acknowledge that for the most part it is, to speak disrespectfully of Works that have enjoyed for a length of time a widely-spread reputation, without at the same time producing irrefragable proofs of their unworthiness, let me be forgiven upon this occasion.—Having enabled the good fortune to be born and reared in a mountainous country, from my very childhood I have felt the falsehood that pervades the volumes imposed upon the world under the name of Ossian. From what I saw with my own eyes, I knew that the imagery was spurious. In nature everything is distinct, yet nothing defined into absolute independent singleness. In Macpherson's work, it is exactly the reverse; everything (that is not stolen) is in this manner defined, insulated, dislocated, deadened,—yet nothing distinct. It will always be so when words are substituted for things. To say that the characters never could exist, that the manners are impossible, and that a dream has more substance than the whole state of society, as there depicted, is doing nothing more than pronouncing a censure which Macpherson defied; when, with the steeps of Morven before his eyes, he could talk so familiarly of his Car-borne heroes; —of Morven, which, if one may judge from its appearance at the distance of a few miles, contains scarcely an acre of ground sufficiently accommodating for a sledge to be trailed along its surface.—Mr. Malcolm Laing has ably shown that the diction of this pretended translation is a motley assemblage from all quarters; but he is so fond of making out parallel passages as to call upon Macpherson to account for his 'ands' and his 'buts!' and he has weakened his argument by conducting it as if he thought that every striking resemblance was a *conscious* plagiarism. It is enough that the coincidences are too remarkable for its being probable or possible that they could arise in different minds without communication between them. Now as the Translators of the Bible, and Shakspeare, Milton, and Pope, could not be indebted to Macpherson, it follows that he must have owed his fine feathers to them; unless we are prepared gravely to assert, with Madame de Staël, that many of the characteristic beauties of our most celebrated English Poets are derived from the ancient Fingallian; in which case the modern translator would have been but giving back to Ossian his own.—It is consistent that Lucien Buonaparte, who could censure Milton for having surrounded Satan in the infernal regions with courtly and regal splendour, should pronounce the modern Ossian to be the glory of Scotland;—a country that has produced a Dunbar, a Buchanan, a Thomson, and a Burns! These opinions are of ill omen for the Epic ambition of him who has given them to the world.

Yet, much as those pretended treasures of antiquity have been admired, they have been wholly uninfluential upon the literature of the Country. No succeeding writer appears to have caught from them a ray of inspiration; no author, in the least distinguished, has ventured formally to imitate them—except the boy, Chatterton, on their first appearance. He had perceived, from the successful trials which he himself had made in literary forgery, how few critics were able to distinguish between a real ancient medal and a counterfeit of modern manufacture; and he set himself to the work of filling a magazine with *Saxon Poems,*—counterparts of those of Ossian, as like his as one of his misty stars is to another. This incapability to amalgamate with the literature of the Island, is, in my estimation, a decisive proof that the book is essentially unnatural; nor should I require any other to demonstrate it to be a forgery, audacious as worthless.—Contrast, in this respect, the effect of Macpherson's publication with the 'Reliques' of Percy, so unassuming, so modest in their pretensions!—I have already stated how much Germany is indebted to this latter work; and for our own country, its poetry has been absolutely redeemed by it. I do not think that there is an able writer in verse of the present day who would not be proud to acknowledge his obligations to the 'Reliques;' I know that it is so with my friends; and, for myself, I am happy in this occasion to make a public avowal of my own.

Dr. Johnson, more fortunate in his contempt of the labours of Macpherson than those of his modest friend, was solicited not long after to furnish Prefaces biographical and critical for the works of some of the most eminent English Poets. The booksellers took upon themselves to make the collection; they referred probably to the most popular miscellanies, and, unquestionably, to their books of accounts; and decided upon the claim of authors to be admitted into a body of the most eminent, from the familiarity of their names with the readers of that day, and by the profits, which, from the sale of his works, each had brought and was bringing to the Trade. The Editor was allowed a limited exercise of discretion, and the Authors whom he recommended are scarcely to be mentioned without a smile. We open the volume of Prefatory Lives, and to our astonishment the *first* name we find is that of Cowley!—What is become of the morning-star of English Poetry? Where is the bright Elizabethan constellation? Or, if names be more acceptable than images, where is the ever-to-be-honoured Chaucer? where is Spenser? where Sidney? and, lastly, where he, whose rights as a poet, contra-distinguished from those which he is universally allowed to possess as a dramatist, we have vindicated,—where Shakspeare?—These, and a multitude of others not unworthy to be placed near them, their contemporaries and successors, we have *not*. But in their stead, we have (could better be expected when precedence was to be settled by an abstract of reputation at any given period made, as in this case before us?) Roscommon, and Stepney, and Phillips, and Walsh, and Smith, and Duke, and King, and Spratt—Halifax, Granville, Sheffield, Congreve, Broome, and other reputed Magnates—metrical writers utterly worthless and useless, except for occasions like the present, when their productions are referred to as evidence what a small quantity of brain is necessary to procure a considerable stock of admiration, provided the aspirant will accommodate himself to the likings and fashions of his day.

As I do not mean to bring down this retrospect to our own times, it may with propriety be closed at the era of this distinguished event. From the literature of other ages and countries, proofs equally cogent might have been adduced, that the opinions announced in the former part of this Essay are founded upon truth. It was not an agreeable office, nor a prudent undertaking, to declare them; but their importance seemed to render it a duty. It may still be asked, where lies the particular relation of what has been said to these Volumes?—The question will be easily answered by the discerning Reader who is old enough to remember the taste that prevailed when some of these poems were first published, seventeen years ago; who has also observed to what degree the poetry of this Island has since that period been coloured by them; and who is further aware of the unremitting hostility with which, upon some principle or other, they have each and all been opposed. A sketch of my own notion of the constitution of Fame has been given; and, as far as concerns myself, I have cause to be satisfied. The love, the admiration, the indifference, the slight, the aversion, and even the contempt, with which these Poems have been received, knowing, as I do, the source within my own mind, from which they have proceeded, and the labour and pains, which, when labour and pains appeared needful, have been bestowed upon them, must all, if I think consistently, be received as pledges and tokens, bearing the same general impression, though widely different in value;—they are all proofs that for the present time I have not laboured in vain; and afford assurances, more or less authentic, that the products of my industry will endure.

If there be one conclusion more forcibly pressed upon us than another by the review which has been given of the fortunes and fate of poetical Works, it is this,—that every author, as far as he is great and at the same time *original*, has had the task of *creating* the taste by which he is to be enjoyed: so has it been, so will it continue to be. This remark was long since made to me by the philosophical Friend for the separation of whose poems from my own I have previously expressed my regret. The predecessors of an original Genius of a high order will have smoothed the way for all that he has in common with them;—and much he will have in common; but, for what is peculiarly his own, he will be called upon to clear and often to shape his own road:—he will be in the condition of Hannibal among the Alps.

And where lies the real difficulty of creating that taste by which a truly original poet is to be relished? Is it in breaking the bonds of custom, in overcoming the prejudices of false refinement, and displacing the aversions of inexperience? Or, if he labour for an object which here and elsewhere I have proposed to myself, does it consist in divesting the reader of the pride that induces him to dwell upon those points wherein men differ from each other, to the exclusion of those in which all men are alike, or the same; and in making him ashamed of the vanity that renders him insensible of the appropriate excellence which civil arrangements, less unjust than might appear, and Nature illimitable in her bounty, have conferred on men who may stand below him in the scale of society? Finally, does it lie in establishing that dominion over the spirits of readers by which they are to be humbled and humanised, in order that they may be purified and exalted?

If these ends are to be attained by the mere communication of *knowledge*, it does *not* lie here.—TASTE, I would remind the reader, like IMAGINATION, is a word which has been forced to extend its services far beyond the point to which philosophy would have confined them. It is a metaphor, taken from a *passive* sense of the human body, and transferred to things which are in their essence *not* passive,—to intellectual *acts* and *operations*. The word, Imagination, has been overstrained, from impulses honourable to mankind, to meet the demands of the faculty which is perhaps the noblest of our nature. In the instance of Taste, the process has been reversed; and from the prevalence of dispositions at once injurious and discreditable, being no other than that selfishness which is the child of apathy,—which, as Nations decline in productive and creative power, makes them value themselves upon a presumed refinement of judging. Poverty of language is the primary cause of the use which we make of the word, Imagination; but the word, Taste, has been stretched to the sense which it bears in modern Europe by habits of self-conceit, inducing that inversion in the order of things whereby a passive faculty is made paramount among the faculties conversant with the fine arts. Proportion and congruity, the requisite knowledge being supposed, are subjects upon which taste may be trusted; it is competent to this office;—for in its intercourse with these the mind is *passive*, and is affected painfully or pleasurably as by an instinct. But the profound and the exquisite in feeling, the lofty and universal in thought and imagination; or, in ordinary language, the pathetic and the sublime;—

are neither of them, accurately speaking, objects of a faculty which could ever without a sinking in the spirit of Nations have been designated by the metaphor—*Taste*. And why? Because without the exertion of a co-operating *power* in the mind of the Reader, there can be no adequate sympathy with either of these emotions: without this auxiliary impulse, elevated or profound passion cannot exist.

Passion, it must be observed, is derived from a word which signifies *suffering*; but the connection which suffering has with effort, with exertion, and *action*, is immediate and inseparable. How strikingly is this property of human nature exhibited by the fact, that, in popular language, to be in a passion, is to be angry!—But,

'Anger in hasty *words* or *blows*
Itself discharges on its foes.'

To be moved, then, by a passion, is to be excited, often to external, and always to internal, effort; whether for the continuance and strengthening of the passion, or for its suppression, accordingly as the course which it takes may be painful or pleasurable. If the latter, the soul must contribute to its support, or it never becomes vivid,—and soon languishes, and dies. And this brings us to the point. If every great poet with whose writings men are familiar, in the highest exercise of his genius, before he can be thoroughly enjoyed, has to call forth and to communicate *power*, this service, in a still greater degree, falls upon an original writer, at his first appearance in the world. —Of genius the only proof is, the act of doing well what is worthy to be done, and what was never done before: Of genius, in the fine arts, the only infallible sign is the widening the sphere of human sensibility, for the delight, honour, and benefit of human nature. Genius is the introduction of a new element into the intellectual universe: or, if that be not allowed, it is the application of powers to objects on which they had not before been exercised, or the employment of them in such a manner as to produce effects hitherto unknown. What is all this but an advance, or a conquest, made by the soul of the poet? Is it to be supposed that the reader can make progress of this kind, like an Indian prince or general—stretched on his palanquin, and borne by his slaves? No; he is invigorated and inspirited by his leader, in order that he may exert himself; for he cannot proceed in quiescence, he cannot be carried like a dead weight. Therefore to create taste is to call forth and bestow power, of which knowledge is the effect; and *there* lies the true difficulty.

As the pathetic participates of an *animal* sensation, it might seem—that, if the springs of this emotion were genuine, all men, possessed of competent knowledge of the facts and circumstances, would be instantaneously affected. And, doubtless, in the works of every true poet will be found passages of that species of excellence, which is proved by effects immediate and universal. But there are emotions of the pathetic that are simple and direct, and others—that are complex and revolutionary; some—to which the heart yields with gentleness; others—against which it struggles with pride; these varieties are infinite as the combinations of circumstance and the constitutions of character. Remember, also, that the medium through which, in poetry, the heart is to be affected, is language; a thing subject to endless fluctuations and arbitrary associations. The genius of the poet melts these down for his purpose; but they retain their shape and quality to him who is not capable of exerting, within his own mind, a corresponding energy. There is also a meditative, as well as a human, pathos; an enthusiastic, as well as an ordinary, sorrow; a sadness that has its seat in the depths of reason, to which the mind cannot sink gently of itself—but to which it must descend by treading the steps of thought. And for the sublime,—if we consider what are the cares that occupy the passing day, and how remote is the practice and the course of life from the sources of sublimity, in the soul of Man, can it be wondered that there is little existing preparation for a poet charged with a new mission to extend its kingdom, and to augment and spread its enjoyments?

Away, then, with the senseless iteration of the word, *popular*, applied to new works in poetry, as if there were no test of excellence in this first of the fine arts but that all men should run after its productions, as if urged by an appetite, or constrained by a spell!—The qualities of writing best fitted for eager reception are either such as startle the world into attention by their audacity and extravagance; or they are chiefly of a superficial kind, lying upon the surfaces of manners; or arising out of a selection and arrangement of incidents, by which the mind is kept upon the stretch of curiosity, and the fancy amused without the trouble of thought. But in everything which is to send the soul into herself, to be admonished of her weakness, or to be made conscious of her power;—wherever life and nature are described as operated upon by the creative or abstracting virtue of the imagination; wherever the instinctive wisdom of antiquity and her heroic passions uniting, in the heart of the poet, with the meditative wisdom of later ages, have produced that accord of sublimated humanity, which is at once a history of the remote past and a prophetic enunciation of the remotest future, *there*, the poet must reconcile himself for a season to few and scattered hearers.—Grand thoughts (and Shakspeare must often have sighed over this truth), as they are most naturally and most fitly conceived in solitude, so can they not be brought forth in the midst of plaudits, without some violation of their sanctity. Go to a silent exhibition of the productions of the sister Art, and be convinced that the qualities which dazzle at first sight, and kindle the admiration of the multitude, are essentially different from those by which permanent influence is secured. Let us not shrink from following up these principles as far as they will carry us, and conclude with observing—that there never has been a period, and perhaps never will be, in which vicious poetry, of some kind or other, has not excited more zealous admiration, and been far more generally read, than good; but this advantage attends the good, that the *individual*, as well as the species, survives from age to age; whereas, of the depraved, though the species be

immortal, the individual quickly *perishes;* the object of present admiration vanishes, being supplanted by some other as easily produced; which, though no better, brings with it as least the irritation of novelty,—with adaptation, more or less skilful, to the changing humours of the majority of those who are most at leisure to regard poetical works when they first solicit their attention.

Is it the result of the whole, that, in the opinion of the Writer, the judgment of the People is not to be respected? The thought is most injurious; and, could the charge be brought against him, he would repel it with indignation. The People have already been justified, and their eulogium pronounced by implication, when it was said, above—that, of *good* poetry, the *individual*, as well as the species, *survives*. And how does it survive but through the People? What preserves it but their intellect and their wisdom?

'——Past and future, are the wings
On whose support, harmoniously conjoined,
Moves the great Spirit of human knowledge——.'
                                                        MS.

The voice that issues from this Spirit, is that Vox Populi which the Deity inspires. Foolish must he be who can mistake for this a local acclamation, or a transitory outcry—transitory though it be for years, local though from a Nation. Still more lamentable is his error who can believe that there is anything of divine infallibility in the clamour of that small though loud portion of the community, ever governed by factitious influence, which, under the name of the PUBLIC, passes itself, upon the unthinking, for the PEOPLE. Towards the Public, the Writer hopes that he feels as much deference as it is entitled to: but to the People, philosophically characterised, and to the embodied spirit of their knowledge, so far as it exists and moves, at the present, faithfully supported by its two wings, the past and the future, his devout respect, his reverence, is due. He offers it willingly and readily; and, this done, takes leave of his Readers, by assuring them—that, if he were not persuaded that the contents of these Volumes, and the Work to which they are subsidiary, evince something of the 'Vision and the Faculty divine;' and that, both in words and things, they will operate in their degree, to extend the domain of sensibility for the delight, the honour, and the benefit of human nature, not withstanding the many happy hours which he has employed in their composition, and the manifold comforts and enjoyments they have procured to him, he would not, if a wish could do it, save them from immediate destruction;—from becoming at this moment, to the world, as a thing that had never been.

1815.

DEDICATION

PREFIXED TO THE EDITION OF 1815

TO SIR GEORGE HOWLAND BEAUMONT, BART.

MY DEAR SIR GEORGE,
    Accept my thanks for the permission given me to dedicate these Volumes to you. In addition to a lively pleasure derived from general considerations, I feel a particular satisfaction; for, by inscribing these Poems with your Name, I seem to myself in some degree to repay, by an appropriate

honour, the great obligation which I owe to one part of the Collection—as having been the means of first making us personally known to each other. Upon much of the remainder, also, you have a peculiar claim,—for some of the best pieces were composed under the shade of your own groves, upon the classic ground of Coleorton; where I was animated by the recollection of those illustrious Poets of your name and family, who were born in that neighbourhood; and, we may be assured, did not wander with indifference by the dashing stream of Grace Dieu, and among the rocks that diversify the forest of Charnwood.—Nor is there any one to whom such parts of this Collection as have been inspired or coloured by the beautiful Country from which I now address you, could be presented with more propriety than to yourself—to whom it has suggested so many admirable pictures. Early in life, the sublimity and beauty of this region excited your admiration; and I know that you are bound to it in mind by a still strengthening attachment.

Wishing and hoping that this Work, with the embellishments it has received from your pencil,[1] may survive as a lasting memorial of a friendship, which I reckon among the blessings of my life,

I have the honour to be,
My dear Sir George,
Yours most affectionately and faithfully,
WILLIAM WORDSWORTH.

RYDAL MOUNT, WESTMORELAND,
February 1, 1815.

[1] The state of the plates has, for some time, not allowed them to be repeated.

PREFACE TO THE EDITION OF 1815

THE powers requisite for the production of poetry are: first, those of Observation and Description,—*i.e.* the ability to observe with accuracy things as they are in themselves, and with fidelity to describe them, unmodified by any passion or feeling existing in the mind of the describer; whether the things depicted be actually present to the senses, or have a place only in the memory. This power, though indispensable to a Poet, is one which he employs only in submission to necessity, and never for a continuance of time: as its exercise supposes all the higher qualities of the mind to be passive, and in a state of subjection to external objects, much in the same way as a translator or engraver ought to be to his original. 2ndly, Sensibility,—which, the more exquisite it is, the wider will be the range of a poet's perceptions; and the more will he be incited to observe objects, both as they exist in themselves and as re-acted upon by his own mind. (The distinction between poetic and human sensibility has been marked in the character of the Poet delineated in the original preface.) 3rdly, Reflection,—which makes the Poet acquainted with the value of actions, images, thoughts, and feelings; and assists the sensibility in perceiving their connection with each other. 4thly, Imagination and Fancy,—to modify, to create, and to associate. 5thly, Invention,—by which characters are composed out of materials supplied by observation; whether of the Poet's own heart and mind, or of external life and nature; and such incidents and situations produced as are most impressive to the imagination, and most fitted to do justice to the characters, sentiments, and passions, which the Poet undertakes to illustrate. And, lastly, Judgment,—to decide how and where, and in what degree, each of these faculties ought to be exerted; so that the less shall not be sacrificed to the greater; nor the greater, slighting the less, arrogate, to its own injury, more than its due. By judgment, also, is determined what are the laws and appropriate graces of every species of composition.[1]

The materials of Poetry, by these powers collected and produced, are cast, by means of various moulds, into divers forms. The moulds may be enumerated, and the forms specified, in the following order. 1st, The Narrative,—including the Epopœia, the Historic Poem, the Tale, the Romance, the Mock-heroic, and, if the spirit of Homer will tolerate such neighbourhood, that

[1] As sensibility to harmony of numbers, and the power of producing it, are invariably attendants upon the faculties above specified, nothing has been said upon those requisites.

dear production of our days, the metrical Novel. Of this Class, the distinguishing mark is, that the Narrator, however liberally his speaking agents be introduced, is himself the source from which everything primarily flows. Epic Poets, in order that their mode of composition may accord with the elevation of their subject, represent themselves as *singing* from the inspiration of the Muse, 'Arma virumque *cano;*' but this is a fiction, in modern times, of slight value: the 'Iliad' or the 'Paradise Lost' would gain little in our estimation by being chanted. The other poets who belong to this class are commonly content to *tell* their tale;—so that of the whole it may be affirmed that they neither require nor reject the accompaniment of music.

2ndly, The Dramatic,—consisting of Tragedy, Historic Drama, Comedy, and Masque, in which the Poet does not appear at all in his own person, and where the whole action is carried on by speech and dialogue of the agents; music being admitted only incidentally and rarely. The Opera may be placed here, inasmuch as it proceeds by dialogue; though depending, to the degree that it does, upon music, it has a strong claim to be ranked with the lyrical. The characteristic and impassioned Epistle, of which Ovid and Pope have given examples, considered as a species of monodrama, may, without impropriety, be placed in this class.

3rdly, The Lyrical,—containing the Hymn, the Ode, the Elegy, the Song, and the Ballad; in all which, for the production of their *full* effect, an accompaniment of music is indispensable.

4thly, The Idyllium,—descriptive chiefly either of the processes and appearances of external nature, as the 'Seasons' of Thomson; or of characters, manners, and sentiments, as are Shenstone's 'Schoolmistress,' 'The Cotter's Saturday Night' of Burns, 'The Twa Dogs' of the same Author; or of these in conjunction with the appearances of Nature, as most of the pieces of Theocritus, the 'Allegro' and 'Penseroso' of Milton, Beattie's 'Minstrel,' Goldsmith's 'Deserted Village.' The Epitaph, the Inscription, the Sonnet, most of the epistles of poets writing in their own persons, and all loco-descriptive poetry, belong to this class.

5thly, Didactic,—the principal object of which is direct instruction; as the Poem of Lucretius, the 'Georgics' of Virgil, 'The Fleece' of Dyer, Mason's 'English Garden,' &c.

And, lastly, philosophical Satire, like that of Horace and Juvenal; personal and occasional Satire rarely comprehending sufficient of the general in the individual to be dignified with the name of poetry.

Out of the three last has been constructed a com-

PREFACES, ETC.

posite order, of which Young's 'Night Thoughts,' and Cowper's 'Task,' are excellent examples.

It is deducible from the above, that poems, apparently miscellaneous, may with propriety be arranged either with reference to the powers of mind *predominant* in the production of them; or to the mould in which they are cast; or, lastly, to the subjects to which they relate. From each of these considerations, the following Poems have been divided into classes; which, that the work may more obviously correspond with the course of human life, and for the sake of exhibiting in it the three requisites of a legitimate whole, a beginning, a middle, and an end, have been also arranged, as far as it was possible, according to an order of time, commencing with Childhood, and terminating with Old Age, Death, and Immortality. My guiding wish was, that the small pieces of which these volumes consist, thus discriminated, might be regarded under a two-fold view; as composing an entire work within themselves, and as adjuncts to the philosophical Poem, 'The Recluse.' This arrangement has long presented itself habitually to my own mind. Nevertheless, I should have preferred to scatter the contents of these volumes at random, if I had been persuaded that, by the plan adopted, anything material would be taken from the natural effect of the pieces, individually, on the mind of the unreflecting Reader. I trust there is a sufficient variety in each class to prevent this; while, for him who reads with reflection, the arrangement will serve as a commentary unostentatiously directing his attention to my purposes, both particular and general. But, as I wish to guard against the possibility of misleading by this classification, it is proper first to remind the Reader, that certain poems are placed according to the powers of mind, in the Author's conception, predominant in the production of them; *predominant*, which implies the exertion of other faculties in less degree. Where there is more imagination than fancy in a poem, it is placed under the head of imagination, and *vice versâ*. Both the above classes might without impropriety have been enlarged from that consisting of 'Poems founded on the Affections;' as might this latter from those, and from the class 'proceeding from Sentiment and Reflection.' The most striking characteristics of each piece, mutual illustration, variety, and proportion, have governed me throughout.

None of the other Classes, except those of Fancy and Imagination, require any particular notice. But a remark of general application may be made. All Poets, except the dramatic, have been in the practice of feigning that their works were composed to the music of the harp or lyre: with what degree of affectation this has been done in modern times, I leave to the judicious to determine. For my own part, I have not been disposed to violate probability so far, or to make such a large demand upon the Reader's charity. Some of these pieces are essentially lyrical; and, therefore, cannot have their due force without a supposed musical accompaniment; but, in much the greatest part, as a substitute for the classic lyre or romantic harp, I require nothing more than an animated or impassioned recitation, adapted to the subject. Poems, however humble in their kind, if they be good in that kind, cannot read themselves; the law of long syllable and short must not be so inflexible, —the letter of metre must not be so impassive to the spirit of versification,—as to deprive the Reader of all voluntary power to modulate, in subordination to the sense, the music of the poem;—

in the same manner as his mind is left at liberty, and even summoned, to act upon its thoughts and images. But, though the accompaniment of a musical instrument be frequently dispensed with, the true Poet does not therefore abandon his privilege distinct from that of the mere Proseman;

'He murmurs near the running brooks
A music sweeter than their own.'

Let us come now to the consideration of the words Fancy and Imagination, as employed in the classification of the following Poems. 'A man,' says an intelligent author, 'has imagination in proportion as he can distinctly copy in idea the impressions of sense: it is the faculty which *images* within the mind the phenomena of sensation. A man has fancy in proportion as he can call up, connect, or associate, at pleasure, those internal images (φαντάζειν is to cause to appear) so as to complete ideal representations of absent objects. Imagination is the power of depicting, and fancy of evoking and combining. The imagination is formed by patient observation; the fancy by a voluntary activity in shifting the scenery of the mind. The more accurate the imagination, the more safely may a painter, or a poet, undertake a delineation, or a description, without the presence of the objects to be characterised. The more versatile the fancy, the more original and striking will be the decorations produced.'—*British Synonyms discriminated, by W. Taylor.*

Is not this as if a man should undertake to supply an account of a building, and be so intent upon what he had discovered of the foundation, as to conclude his task without once looking up at the superstructure? Here, as in other instances throughout the volume, the judicious Author's mind is enthralled by Etymology; he takes up the original word as his guide and escort, and too often does not perceive how soon he becomes its prisoner, without liberty to tread in any path but that to which it confines him. It is not easy to find out how imagination, thus explained, differs from distinct remembrance of images; or fancy from quick and vivid recollection of them: each is nothing more than a mode of memory. If the two words bear the above meaning, and no other, what term is left to designate that faculty of which the Poet is 'all compact;' he whose eye glances from earth to heaven, whose spiritual attributes body forth what his pen is prompt in turning to shape; or what is left to characterise Fancy, as insinuating herself into the heart of objects with creative activity?—Imagination, in the sense of the word as giving title to a class of the following Poems, has no reference to images that are merely a faithful copy, existing in the mind, of absent external objects; but is a word of higher import, denoting operations of the mind upon those objects, and processes of creation or of composition, governed by certain fixed laws. I proceed to illustrate my meaning by instances. A parrot *hangs* from the wires of his cage by his beak or by his claws; or a monkey from the bough of a tree by his paws or his tail. Each creature does so literally and actually. In the first Eclogue of Virgil, the shepherd, thinking of the time when he is to take leave of his farm, thus addresses his goats:—

'Non ego vos posthac viridi projectus in antro
Dumosa *pendere* procul de rupe videbo.'

'half way down
Hangs one who gathers samphire,'

is the well-known expression of Shakespeare,

753

delineating an ordinary image upon the cliffs of Dover. In these two instances is a slight exertion of the faculty which I denominate imagination, in the use of one word: neither the goats nor the samphire-gatherer do literally hang, as does the parrot or the monkey; but, presenting to the senses something of such an appearance, the mind in its activity, for its own gratification, contemplates them as hanging.

'As when far off at sea a fleet descried
Hangs in the clouds, by equinoctial winds
Close sailing from Bengala, or the isles
Of Ternate or Tidore, whence merchants bring
Their spicy drugs; they on the trading flood
Through the wide Ethiopian to the Cape
Ply, stemming nightly toward the Pole: so seemed
Far off the flying Fiend.'

Here is the full strength of the imagination involved in the word *hangs*, and exerted upon the whole image: First, the fleet, an aggregate of many ships, is represented as one mighty person, whose track, we know and feel, is upon the waters; but, taking advantage of its appearance to the senses, the Poet dares to represent it as *hanging in the clouds*, both for the gratification of the mind in contemplating the image itself, and in reference to the motion and appearance of the sublime objects to which it is compared.

From impressions of sight we will pass to those of sound; which, as they must necessarily be of a less definite character, shall be selected from these volumes:

'Over his own sweet voice the Stock-dove *broods;*'

of the same bird,

'His voice was *buried* among trees,
Yet to be come at by the breeze;'

'O, Cuckoo! shall I call thee *Bird,*
Or but a wandering *Voice?*'

The stock-dove is said to *coo*, a sound well imitating the note of the bird; but, by the intervention of the metaphor *broods*, the affections are called in by the imagination to assist in marking the manner in which the bird reiterates and prolongs her soft note, as if herself delighting to listen to it, and participating of a still and quiet satisfaction, like that which may be supposed inseparable from the continuous process of incubation. 'His voice was buried among trees,' a metaphor expressing the love of *seclusion* by which this Bird is marked; and characterising its note as not partaking of the shrill and the piercing, and therefore more easily deadened by the intervening shade; yet a note so peculiar and withal so pleasing, that the breeze, gifted with that love of the sound which the Poet feels, penetrates the shades in which it is entombed, and conveys it to the ear of the listener.

'Shall I call thee Bird,
Or but a wandering Voice?'

This concise interrogation characterises the seeming ubiquity of the voice of the cuckoo, and dispossesses the creature almost of a corporeal existence; the Imagination being tempted to this exertion of her power by a consciousness in the memory that the cuckoo is almost perpetually heard throughout the season of spring, but seldom becomes an object of sight.

Thus far of images independent of each other, and immediately endowed by the mind with properties that do not inhere in them, upon an incitement from properties and qualities the existence of which is inherent and obvious. These processes of imagination are carried on either by conferring additional properties upon an object, or abstracting from it some of those which it actually possesses, and thus enabling it to re-act upon the mind which hath performed the process, like a new existence.

I pass from the Imagination acting upon an individual image to a consideration of the same faculty employed upon images in a conjunction by which they modify each other. The Reader has already had a fine instance before him in the passage quoted from Virgil, where the apparently perilous situation of the goat, hanging upon the shaggy precipice, is contrasted with that of the shepherd contemplating it from the seclusion of the cavern in which he lies stretched at ease and in security. Take these images separately, and how unaffecting the picture compared with that produced by their being thus connected with, and opposed to, each other!

'As a huge stone is sometimes seen to lie
Couched on the bald top of an eminence,
Wonder to all who do the same espy
By what means it could thither come, and whence,
So that it seems a thing endued with sense,
Like a sea-beast crawled forth, which on a shelf
Of rock or sand reposeth, there to sun himself.

Such seemed this Man; not all alive nor dead
Nor all asleep, in his extreme old age.

. . . .

Motionless as a cloud the old Man stood,
That heareth not the loud winds when they call,
And moveth altogether if it move at all.'

In these images, the conferring, the abstracting, and the modifying powers of the Imagination, immediately and mediately acting, are all brought into conjunction. The stone is endowed with something of the power of life to approximate it to the sea-beast; and the sea-beast stripped of some of its vital qualities to assimilate it to the stone; which intermediate image is thus treated for the purpose of bringing the original image, that of the stone, to a nearer resemblance to the figure and condition of the aged Man; who is divested of so much of the indications of life and motion as to bring him to the point where the two objects unite and coalesce in just comparison. After what has been said, the image of the cloud need not be commented upon.

Thus far of an endowing or modifying power: but the Imagination also shapes and *creates;* and how? By innumerable processes; and in none does it more delight than in that of consolidating numbers into unity, and dissolving and separating unity into number,—alternations proceeding from, and governed by, a sublime consciousness of the soul in her own mighty and almost divine powers. Recur to the passage already cited from Milton. When the compact Fleet, as one Person, has been introduced 'sailing from Bengala,' 'They,' *i.e.* the 'merchants,' representing the fleet resolved into a multitude of ships, 'ply' their voyage towards the extremities of the earth: 'So,' (referring to the word 'As' in the commencement) 'seemed the flying Fiend;' the image of his Person acting to recombine the multitude of ships into one body,—the point from which the comparison set out. 'So seemed,' and to whom seemed? To the heavenly Muse who dictates the poem, to the eye of the Poet's mind, and to that of the Reader, present at one moment in the wide Ethiopian, and the next in the solitudes, then first broken in upon, of the infernal regions!

'Modo me Thebis, modo ponit Athenis.'

PREFACES, ETC.

Hear again this mighty Poet,—speaking of the Messiah going forth to expel from heaven the rebellious angels,

'Attended by ten thousand thousand Saints
He onward came: far off his coming shone,'—

the retinue of Saints, and the Person of the Messiah himself, lost almost and merged in the splendour of that indefinite abstraction 'His coming!'

As I do not mean here to treat this subject further than to throw some light upon the present Volumes, and especially upon one division of them, I shall spare myself and the Reader the trouble of considering the Imagination as it deals with thoughts and sentiments, as it regulates the composition of characters, and determines the course of actions: I will not consider it (more than I have already done by implication) as that power which, in the language of one of my most esteemed Friends, 'draws all things to one; which makes things animate or inanimate, beings with their attributes, subjects with their accessories, take one colour and serve to one effect[1].' The grand storehouses of enthusiastic and meditative Imagination, of poetical, as contra-distinguished from human and dramatic Imagination, are the prophetic and lyrical parts of the Holy Scriptures, and the works of Milton; to which I cannot forbear to add those of Spenser. I select these writers in preference to those of ancient Greece and Rome, because the anthropomorphitism of the Pagan religion subjected the minds of the greatest poets in those countries too much to the bondage of definite form; from which the Hebrews were preserved by their abhorrence of idolatry. This abhorrence was almost as strong in our great epic Poet, both from circumstances of his life, and from the constitution of his mind. However imbued the surface might be with classical literature, he was a Hebrew in soul; and all things tended in him towards the sublime. Spenser, of a gentler nature, maintained his freedom by aid of his allegorical spirit, at one time inciting him to create persons out of abstractions; and, at another, by a superior effort of genius, to give the universality and permanence of abstractions to his human beings, by means of attributes and emblems that belong to the highest moral truths and the purest sensations,—of which his character of Una is a glorious example. Of the human and dramatic Imagination the works of Shakspeare are an inexhaustible source.

'I tax not you, ye Elements, with unkindness,
I never gave you kingdoms, call'd you Daughters!'

And if, bearing in mind the many Poets distinguished by this prime quality, whose names I omit to mention; yet justified by recollection of the insults which the ignorant, the incapable, and the presumptuous, have heaped upon these and my other writings, I may be permitted to anticipate the judgment of posterity upon myself, I shall declare (censurable, I grant, if the notoriety of the fact above stated does not justify me) that I have given in these unfavourable times, evidence of exertions of this faculty upon its worthiest objects, the external universe, the moral and religious sentiments of Man, his natural affections, and his acquired passions; which have the same ennobling tendency as the productions of men, in this kind, worthy to be holden in undying remembrance.

To the mode in which Fancy has already been characterised as the power of evoking and combining, or, as my friend Mr. Coleridge has styled

[1] Charles Lamb upon the genius of Hogarth.

it, 'the aggregative and associative power,' my objection is only that the definition is too general. To aggregate and to associate, to evoke and to combine, belong as well to the Imagination as to the Fancy; but either the materials evoked and combined are different; or they are brought together under a different law, and for a different purpose. Fancy does not require that the materials which she makes use of should be susceptible of change in their constitution, from her touch; and, where they admit of modification, it is enough for her purpose if it be slight, limited, and evanescent. Directly the reverse of these, are the desires and demands of the Imagination. She recoils from everything but the plastic, the pliant, and the indefinite. She leaves it to Fancy to describe Queen Mab as coming,

'In shape no bigger than an agate-stone
On the fore-finger of an alderman.'

Having to speak of stature, she does not tell you that her gigantic Angel was as tall as Pompey's Pillar; much less that he was twelve cubits, or twelve hundred cubits high; or that his dimensions equalled those of Teneriffe or Atlas;—because these, and if they were a million times as high it would be the same, are bounded: The expression is, 'His stature reached the sky!' the illimitable firmament!—When the Imagination frames a comparison, if it does not strike on the first presentation, a sense of the truth of the likeness, from the moment that it is perceived, grows—and continues to grow—upon the mind; the resemblance depending less upon outline of form and feature, than upon expression and effect; less upon casual and outstanding, than upon inherent and internal, properties: moreover, the images invariably modify each other.—The law under which the processes of Fancy are carried on is as capricious as the accidents of things, and the effects are surprising, playful, ludicrous, amusing, tender, or pathetic, as the objects happen to be appositely produced or fortunately combined. Fancy depends upon the rapidity and profusion with which she scatters her thoughts and images; trusting that their number, and the felicity with which they are linked together, will make amends for the want of individual value: or she prides herself upon the curious subtilty and the successful elaboration with which she can detect their lurking affinities. If she can win you over to her purpose, and impart to you her feelings, she cares not how unstable or transitory may be her influence, knowing that it will not be out of her power to resume it upon an apt occasion. But the Imagination is conscious of an indestructible dominion;—the Soul may fall away from it, not being able to sustain its grandeur; but, if once felt and acknowledged, by no act of any other faculty of the mind can it be relaxed, impaired, or diminished.—Fancy is given to quicken and to beguile the temporal part of our nature, Imagination to incite and to support the eternal.—Yet is it not the less true that Fancy, as she is an active, is also, under her own laws and in her own spirit, a creative faculty. In what manner Fancy ambitiously aims at a rivalship with Imagination, and Imagination stoops to work with the materials of Fancy, might be illustrated from the compositions of all eloquent writers, whether in prose or verse; and chiefly from those of our own Country. Scarcely a page of the impassioned parts of Bishop Taylor's Works can be opened that shall not afford examples.—Referring the Reader to those inestimable volumes, I will content myself with placing a conceit (ascribed to Lord Chesterfield)

755

in contrast with a passage from the 'Paradise Lost':—

'The dews of the evening most carefully shun,
They are the tears of the sky for the loss of the sun.'

After the transgression of Adam, Milton, with other appearances of sympathising Nature, thus marks the immediate consequence,

'Sky lowered, and, muttering thunder, some sad drops
Wept at completion of the mortal sin.'

The associating link is the same in each instance: Dew and rain, not distinguishable from the liquid substance of tears, are employed as indications of sorrow. A flash of surprise is the effect in the former case; a flash of surprise, and nothing more; for the nature of things does not sustain the combination. In the latter, the effects from the act, of which there is this immediate consequence and visible sign, are so momentous, that the mind acknowledges the justice and reasonableness of the sympathy in nature so manifested; and the sky weeps drops of water as if with human eyes, as 'Earth had before trembled from her entrails, and Nature given a second groan.'

Finally, I will refer to Cotton's 'Ode upon Winter,' an admirable composition, though stained with some peculiarities of the age in which he lived, for a general illustration of the characteristics of Fancy. The middle part of this ode contains a most lively description of the entrance of Winter, with his retinue, as 'A palsied king,' and yet a military monarch,—advancing for conquest with his army; the several bodies of which, and their arms and equipments, are described with a rapidity of detail, and a profusion of *fanciful* comparisons, which indicate on the part of the poet extreme activity of intellect, and a correspondent hurry of delightful feeling. Winter retires from the foe into his fortress, where

———'a magazine
Of sovereign juice is cellared in;
Liquor that with the siege maintain
Should Phœbus ne'er return again.'

Though myself a water-drinker, I cannot resist the pleasure of transcribing what follows, as an instance still more happy of Fancy employed in the treatment of feeling than, in its preceding passages, the Poem supplies of her management of forms.

''Tis that, that gives the poet rage,
And thaws the gelid blood of age;
Matures the young, restores the old,
And makes the fainting coward bold.

'It lays the careful head to rest,
Calms palpitations in the breast,
Renders our lives' misfortune sweet;

. . . .

'Then let the chill Sirocco blow,
And gird us round with hills of snow,
Or else go whistle to the shore,
And make the hollow mountains roar,

'Whilst we together jovial sit
Careless, and crowned with mirth and wit,
Where, though bleak winds confine us home
Our fancies round the world shall roam.

'We'll think of all the Friends we know,
And drink to all worth drinking to;
When having drunk all thine and mine,
We rather shall want healths than wine.

'But where Friends fail us, we'll supply
Our friendships with our charity;
Men that remote in sorrows live,
Shall by our lusty brimmers thrive.

'We'll drink the wanting into wealth,
And those that languish into health,
The afflicted into joy; th' opprest
Into security and rest.

'The worthy in disgrace shall find
Favour return again more kind,
And in restraint who stifled lie,
Shall taste the air of liberty.

'The brave shall triumph in success
The lover shall have mistresses,
Poor unregarded Virtue, praise,
And the neglected Poet, bays.

'Thus shall our healths do others good,
Whilst we ourselves do all we would;
For, freed from envy and from care,
What would we be but what we are?'

When I sate down to write this Preface, it was my intention to have made it more comprehensive; but, thinking that I ought rather to apologise for detaining the reader so long, I will here conclude.

POSTSCRIPT

1835

IN the present volume, as in those that have preceded it, the reader will have found occasionally opinions expressed upon the course of public affairs, and feelings given vent to as national interests excited them. Since nothing, I trust, has been uttered but in the spirit of reflective patriotism, those notices are left to produce their own effect; but, among the many objects of general concern, and the changes going forward, which I have glanced at in verse, are some especially affecting the lower orders of society; in reference to these, I wish here to add a few words in plain prose.

Were I conscious of being able to do justice to those important topics, I might avail myself of the periodical press for offering anonymously my thoughts, such as they are, to the world; but I feel that, in procuring attention, they may derive some advantage, however small, from my name, in addition to that of being presented in a less fugitive shape. It is also not impossible that the state of mind which some of the foregoing poems may have produced in the reader, will dispose him to receive more readily the impression which I desire to make, and to admit the conclusions I would establish.

I. The first thing that presses upon my attention is the Poor-Law Amendment Act. I am aware of the magnitude and complexity of the subject, and the unwearied attention which it has received from men of far wider experience than my own; yet I cannot forbear touching upon one point of it, and to this I will confine myself, though not insensible to the objection which may reasonably be brought against treating a portion of this, or any other, great scheme of civil polity separately from the whole. The point to which I wish to

PREFACES, ETC.

draw the reader's attention is, that *all* persons who cannot find employment, or procure wages sufficient to support the body in health and strength, are entitled to a maintenance by law.

This dictate of humanity is acknowledged in the Report of the Commissioners; but is there not room for apprehension that some of the regulations of the new act have a tendency to render the principle nugatory by difficulties thrown in the way of applying it? If this be so, persons will not be wanting to show it, by examining the provisions of the act in detail,—an attempt which would be quite out of place here; but it will not. therefore, be deemed unbecoming in one who fears that the prudence of the head may, in framing some of those provisions, have supplanted the wisdom of the heart, to enforce a principle which cannot be violated without infringing upon one of the most precious rights of the English people, and opposing one of the most sacred claims of civilized humanity.

There can be no greater error, in this department of legislation, than the belief that this principle does by necessity operate for the degradation of those who claim, or are so circumstanced as to make it likely they may claim, through laws founded upon it, relief or assistance. The direct contrary is the truth: it may be unanswerably maintained that its tendency is to raise, not to depress; by stamping a value upon life, which can belong to it only where the laws have placed men who are willing to work, and yet cannot find employment, above the necessity of looking for protection against hunger and other natural evils, either to individual and casual charity, to despair and death, or to the breach of law by theft, or violence.

And here, as in the Report of the Commissioners the fundamental principle has been recognised, I am not at issue with them any farther than I am compelled to believe that their 'remedial measures' obstruct the application of it more than the interests of society require.

And, calling to mind the doctrines of political economy which are now prevalent, I cannot forbear to enforce the justice of the principle, and to insist upon its salutary operation.

And first for its justice: If self-preservation be the first law of our nature, would not every one in a state of nature be morally justified in taking to himself that which is indispensable to such preservation, where, by so doing, he would not rob another of that which might be equally indispensable to *his* preservation? And if the value of life be regarded in a right point of view, may it not be questioned whether this right of preserving life, at any expense short of endangering the life of another, does not survive man's entering into the social state; whether this right can be surrendered or forfeited, except when it opposes the divine law, upon any supposition of a social compact, or of any convention for the protection of mere rights of property?

But, if it be not safe to touch the abstract question of man's right in a social state to help himself even in the last extremity, may we not still contend for the duty of a christian government, standing *in loco parentis* towards all its subjects, to make such effectual provision, that no one shall be in danger of perishing either through the neglect or harshness of its legislation? Or, waiving this, is it not indisputable that the claim of the state to the allegiance, involves the protection, of the subject? And, as all rights in one party impose a correlative duty upon another, it follows that the right of the state to require the services of its

members, even to the jeoparding of their lives in the common defence, establishes a right in the people (not to be gainsaid by utilitarians and economists) to public support when, from any cause, they may be unable to support themselves.

Let us now consider the salutary and benign operation of this principle. Here we must have recourse to elementary feelings of human nature, and to truths which from their very obviousness are apt to be slighted, till they are forced upon our notice by our own sufferings or those of others. In the 'Paradise Lost,' Milton represents Adam, after the Fall, as exclaiming, in the anguish of his soul—

'Did I request Thee, Maker, from my clay
To mould me man; did I solicit Thee
From darkness to promote me?
. . . . My will
Concurred not to my being.'

Under how many various pressures of misery have men been driven thus, in a strain touching upon impiety, to expostulate with the Creator! and under few so afflictive as when the source and origin of earthly existence have been brought back to the mind by its impending close in the pangs of destitution. But as long as, in our legislation, due weight shall be given to this principle, no man will be forced to bewail the gift of life in hopeless want of the necessaries of life.

Englishmen have, therefore, by the progress of civilisation among them, been placed in circumstances more favourable to piety and resignation to the divine will, than the inhabitants of other countries, where a like provision has not been established. And as Providence, in this care of our countrymen, acts through a human medium, the objects of that care must, in like manner, be more inclined towards a grateful love of their fellow-men. Thus, also, do stronger ties attach the people to their country, whether while they tread its soil, or, at a distance, think of their native land as an indulgent parent, to whose arms, even they who have been imprudent and undeserving may, like the prodigal son, betake themselves, without fear of being rejected.

Such is the view of the case that would first present itself to a reflective mind; and it is in vain to show, by appeals to experience, in contrast with this view, that provisions founded upon the principle have promoted profaneness of life, and dispositions the reverse of philanthropic, by spreading idleness, selfishness, and rapacity: for these evils have arisen, not as an inevitable consequence of the principle, but for want of judgment in framing laws based upon it; and, above all, from faults in the mode of administering the law. The mischief that has grown to such a height from granting relief in cases where proper vigilance would have shown that it was not required, or in bestowing it in undue measure, will be urged by no truly enlightened statesman, as a sufficient reason for banishing the principle itself from legislation.

Let us recur to the miserable states of consciousness that it precludes.

There is a story told, by a traveller in Spain, of a female who, by a sudden shock of domestic calamity, was driven out of her senses, and ever after looked up incessantly to the sky, feeling that her fellow-creatures could do nothing for her relief. Can there be Englishmen who, with a good end in view, would, upon system, expose their brother Englishmen to a like necessity of looking upwards only; or downwards to the earth, after it shall contain no spot where the destitute can demand,

757

by civil right, what by right of nature they are entitled to?

Suppose the objects of our sympathy not sunk into this blank despair, but wandering about as strangers in streets and ways, with the hope of succour from casual charity; what have we gained by such a change of scene? Woeful is the condition of the famished Northern Indian, dependent, among winter snows, upon the chance-passage of a herd of deer, from which one, if brought down by his rifle-gun, may be made the means of keeping him and his companions alive. As miserable is that of some savage Islander, who, when the land has ceased to afford him sustenance, watches for food which the waves may cast up, or in vain endeavours to extract it from the inexplorable deep. But neither of these is in a state of wretchedness comparable to that, which is so often endured in civilised society: multitudes, in all ages, have known it, of whom may be said:—

'Homeless, near a thousand homes they stood,
And near a thousand tables pined, and wanted food.'

Justly might I be accused of wasting time in an uncalled-for attempt to excite the feelings of the reader, if systems of political economy, widely spread, did not impugn the principle, and if the safeguards against such extremities were left unimpaired. It is broadly asserted by many, that every man who endeavours to find work, *may* find it: were this assertion capable of being verified, there still would remain a question, what kind of work, and how far may the labourer be fit for it? For if sedentary work is to be exchanged for standing; and some light and nice exercise of the fingers, to which an artisan has been accustomed all his life, for severe labour of the arms; the best efforts would turn to little account, and occasion would be given for the unthinking and the unfeeling unwarrantably to reproach those who are put upon such employment, as idle, froward, and unworthy of relief, either by law or in any other way! Were this statement correct, there would indeed be an end of the argument, the principle here maintained would be superseded. But, alas! it is far otherwise. That principle, applicable to the benefit of all countries, is indispensable for England, upon whose coast families are perpetually deprived of their support by shipwreck, and where large masses of men are so liable to be thrown out of their ordinary means of gaining bread, by changes in commercial intercourse, subject mainly or solely to the will of foreign powers; by new discoveries in arts and manufactures; and by reckless laws, in conformity with theories of political economy, which, whether right or wrong in the abstract, have proved a scourge to tens of thousands, by the abruptness with which they have been carried into practice.

But it is urged,—refuse altogether compulsory relief to the able-bodied, and the number of those who stand in need of relief will steadily diminish through a conviction of an absolute necessity for greater forethought, and more prudent care of a man's earnings. Undoubtedly it would, but so also would it, and in a much greater degree, if the legislative provisions were retained, and parochial relief administered under the care of the upper classes, as it ought to be. For it has been invariably found, that wherever the funds have been raised and applied under the superintendence of gentlemen and substantial proprietors, acting in vestries, and as overseers, pauperism has diminished accordingly. Proper care in that quarter would effectually check what is felt in some districts to

be one of the worst evils in the poor law system, viz. the readiness of small and needy proprietors to join in imposing rates that seemingly subject them to great hardships, while, in fact, this is done with a mutual understanding, that the relief each is ready to bestow upon his still poorer neighbours will be granted to himself, or his relatives, should it hereafter be applied for.

But let us look to inner sentiments of a nobler quality, in order to know what we have to build upon. Affecting proofs occur in every one's experience, who is acquainted with the unfortunate and the indigent, of their unwillingness to derive their subsistence from aught but their own funds or labour, or to be indebted to parochial assistance for the attainment of any object, however dear to them. A case was reported, the other day, from a coroner's inquest, of a pair who, through the space of four years, had carried about their dead infant from house to house, and from lodging to lodging, as their necessities drove them, rather than ask the parish to bear the expense of its interment:—the poor creatures lived in the hope of one day being able to bury their child at their own cost. It must have been heart-rending to see and hear the mother, who had been called upon to account for the state in which the body was found, make this deposition. By some, judging coldly, if not harshly, this conduct might be imputed to an unwarrantable pride, as she and her husband had, it is true, been once in prosperity. But examples, where the spirit of independence works with equal strength, though not with like miserable accompaniments, are frequently to be found even yet among the humblest peasantry and mechanics. There is not, then, sufficient cause for doubting that a like sense of honour may be revived among the people, and their ancient habits of independence restored, without resorting to those severities which the new Poor Law Act has introduced.

But even if the surfaces of things only are to be examined, we have a right to expect that lawgivers should take into account the various tempers and dispositions of mankind: while some are led, by the existence of a legislative provision, into idleness and extravagance, the economical virtues might be cherished in others by the knowledge that, if all their efforts fail, they have in the Poor Laws a 'refuge from the storm and a shadow from the heat.' Despondency and distraction are no friends to prudence: the springs of industry will relax, if cheerfulness be destroyed by anxiety; without hope men become reckless, and have a sullen pride in adding to the heap of their own wretchedness. He who feels that he is abandoned by his fellow-men will be almost irresistibly driven to care little for himself; will lose his self-respect accordingly, and with that loss what remains to him of virtue?

With all due deference to the particular experience, and general intelligence of the individuals who framed the Act, and of those who in and out of parliament have approved of and supported it; it may be said, that it proceeds too much upon the presumption that it is a labouring man's own fault if he be not, as the phrase is, beforehand with the world. But the most prudent are liable to be thrown back by sickness, cutting them off from labour, and causing to them expense: and who but has observed how distress creeps upon multitudes without misconduct of their own; and merely from a gradual fall in the price of labour, without a correspondent one in the price of provisions; so that men who may have ventured upon the marriage state with a fair prospect of maintaining their families in comfort and happiness, see them reduced to a pittance which no effort of theirs can increase? Let it be remembered, also, that there are thousands with whom vicious habits of expense are not the cause why they do not store up their gains; but they are generous and kind-hearted, and ready to help their kindred and friends; moreover, they have a faith in Providence that those who have been prompt to assist others, will not be left destitute, should they themselves come to need. By acting from these blended feelings, numbers have rendered themselves incapable of standing up against a sudden reverse. Nevertheless, these men, in common with all who have the misfortune to be in want, if many theorists had their wish, would be thrown upon one or other of those three sharp points of condition before adverted to, from which the intervention of law has hitherto saved them.

All that has been said tends to show how the principle contended for makes the gift of life more valuable, and has, it may be hoped, led to the conclusion that its legitimate operation is to make men worthier of that gift: in other words, not to degrade but to exalt human nature. But the subject must not be dismissed without adverting to the indirect influence of the same principle upon the moral sentiments of a people among whom it is embodied in law. In our criminal jurisprudence there is a maxim, deservedly eulogised, that it is better that ten guilty persons should escape, than that one innocent man should suffer; so, also, might it be maintained, with regard to the Poor Laws, that it is better for the interests of humanity among the people at large, that ten undeserving should partake of the funds provided, than that one morally good man, through want of relief, should either have his principles corrupted, or his energies destroyed; than that such a one should either be driven to do wrong, or be cast to the earth in utter hopelessness. In France, the English maxim of criminal jurisprudence is reversed; there, it is deemed better that ten innocent men should suffer, than one guilty escape: in France, there is no universal provision for the poor; and we may judge of the small value set upon human life in the metropolis of that country, by merely noticing the disrespect with which, after death, the body is treated, not by the thoughtless vulgar, but in schools of anatomy, presided over by men allowed to be, in their own art and in physical science, among the most enlightened in the world. In the East, where countries are overrun with population as with a weed, infinitely more respect is shown to the remains of the deceased; and what a bitter mockery is it, that this insensibility should be found where civil polity is so busy in minor regulations, and ostentatiously careful to gratify the luxurious propensities, whether social or intellectual, of the multitude! Irreligion is, no doubt, much concerned with this offensive disrespect, shown to the bodies of the dead in France; but it is mainly attributable to the state in which so many of the living are left by the absence of compulsory provision for the indigent so humanely established by the law of England.

Sights of abject misery, perpetually recurring, harden the heart of the community. In the perusal of history, and of works of fiction, we are not, indeed, unwilling to have our commiseration excited by such objects of distress as they present to us; but, in the concerns of real life, men know that such emotions are not given to be indulged for their own sakes: there, the conscience declares

to them that sympathy must be followed by action; and if there exist a previous conviction that the power to relieve is utterly inadequate to the demand, the eye shrinks from communication with wretchedness, and pity and compassion languish, like any other qualities that are deprived of their natural aliment. Let these considerations be duly weighed by those who trust to the hope that an increase of private charity, with all its advantages of superior discrimination, would more than compensate for the abandonment of those principles, the wisdom of which has been here insisted upon. How discouraging, also, would be the sense of injustice, which could not fail to arise in the minds of the well-disposed, if the burden of supporting the poor, a burden of which the selfish have hitherto by compulsion borne a share, should now, or hereafter, be thrown exclusively upon the benevolent.

By having put an end to the Slave Trade and Slavery, the British people are exalted in the scale of humanity; and they cannot but feel so, if they look into themselves, and duly consider their relation to God and their fellow-creatures. That was a noble advance; but a retrograde movement will assuredly be made, if ever the principle, which has been here defended, should be either avowedly abandoned or but ostensibly retained.

But after all, there may be little reason to apprehend permanent injury from any experiment that may be tried. On the one side will be human nature rising up in her own defence, and on the other prudential selfishness acting to the same purpose, from a conviction that, without a compulsory provision for the exigencies of the labouring multitude, that degree of ability to regulate the price of labour, which is indispensable for the reasonable interest of arts and manufactures, cannot, in Great Britain, be upheld.

II. In a poem of the foregoing collection, allusion is made to the state of the workmen congregated in manufactories. In order to relieve many of the evils to which that class of society are subject and to establish a better harmony between them and their employers, it would be well to repeal such laws as prevent the formation of joint-stock companies. There are, no doubt, many and great obstacles to the formation and salutary working of these societies, inherent in the mind of those whom they would obviously benefit. But the combinations of masters to keep down, unjustly, the price of labour would be fairly checked by them, as far as they were practicable; they would encourage economy, inasmuch as they would enable a man to draw profit from his savings, by investing them in buildings or machinery for processes of manufacture with which he was habitually connected. His little capital would then be working for him while he was at rest or asleep; he would more clearly perceive the necessity of capital for carrying on great works; he would better learn to respect the larger portions of it in the hands of others; he would be less tempted to join in unjust combinations; and, for the sake of his own property, if not for higher reasons, he would be slow to promote local disturbance, or endanger public tranquillity; he would, at least, be loth to act in that way *knowingly:* for it is not to be denied that such societies might be nurseries of opinions unfavourable to a mixed constitution of government, like that of Great Britain. The democratic and republican spirit which they might be apt to foster would not, however, be dangerous in itself, but only as it might act without being sufficiently counterbalanced, either by landed proprietorship, or by a Church extending itself so as to embrace an ever-growing and ever-shifting population of mechanics and artisans. But if the tendencies of such societies would be to make the men prosper who might belong to them, rulers and legislators should rejoice in the result, and do their duty to the state by upholding and extending the influence of that Church to which it owes, in so great a measure, its safety, its prosperity, and its glory.

This, in the temper of the present times, may be difficult, but it is become indispensable, since large towns in great numbers have sprung up, and others have increased tenfold, with little or no dependence upon the gentry and the landed proprietors; and apart from those mitigated feudal institutions, which, till of late, have acted so powerfully upon the composition of the House of Commons. Now it may be affirmed that, in quarters where there is not an attachment to the Church, or the landed aristocracy, and a pride in supporting them, *there* the people will dislike both, and be ready, upon such incitements as are perpetually recurring, to join in attempts to overthrow them. There is no neutral ground here: from want of due attention to the state of society in large towns and manufacturing districts, and ignorance or disregard of these obvious truths, innumerable well-meaning persons became zealous supporters of a Reform Bill, the qualities and powers of which, whether destructive or constructive, they would otherwise have been afraid of; and even the framers of that bill, swayed as they might be by party resentments and personal ambition, could not have gone so far, had not they too been lamentably ignorant or neglectful of the same truths both of fact and philosophy.

But let that pass; and let no opponent of the bill be tempted to compliment his own foresight, by exaggerating the mischiefs and dangers that have sprung from it: let not time be wasted in profitless regrets; and let those party distinctions vanish to their very names that have separated men who, whatever course they may have pursued, have ever had a bond of union in the wish to save the limited monarchy, and those other institutions that have, under Providence, rendered for so long a period of time this country the happiest and worthiest of which there is any record since the foundation of civil society.

III. A philosophic mind is best pleased when looking at religion in its spiritual bearing; as a guide of conduct, a solace under affliction, and a support amid the instabilities of mortal life: but the Church having been forcibly brought by political considerations to my notice, while treating of the labouring classes, I cannot forbear saying a few words upon that momentous topic.

There is a loud clamour for extensive change in that department. The clamour would be entitled to more respect if they who are the most eager to swell it with their voices were not generally the most ignorant of the real state of the Church, and the service it renders to the community. *Reform* is the word employed. Let us pause and consider what sense it is apt to carry, and how things are confounded by a lax use of it. The great religious Reformation, in the sixteenth century, did not profess to be a new construction, but a restoration of something fallen into decay, or put out of sight. That familiar and justifiable use of the word seems to have paved the way for fallacies with respect to the term reform, which it is difficult to escape from. Were we to speak of improvement, and the

correction of abuses, we should run less risk of being deceived ourselves, or of misleading others. We should be less likely to fall blindly into the belief, that the change demanded is a renewal of something that has existed before, and that, therefore, we have experience on our side; nor should we be equally tempted to beg the question, that the change for which we are eager must be advantageous. From generation to generation, men are the dupes of words; and it is painful to observe, that so many of our species are most tenacious of those opinions which they have formed with the least consideration. They who are the readiest to meddle with public affairs, whether in church or state, fly to generalities, that they may be eased from the trouble of thinking about particulars; and thus is deputed to mechanical instrumentality the work which vital knowledge only can do well.

'Abolish pluralities,' is a favourite cry; but, without adverting to other obstacles in the way of this specious scheme, it may be asked what benefit would accrue from its *indiscriminate* adoption to counterbalance the harm it would introduce, by nearly extinguishing the order of curates, unless the revenues of the church should grow with the population, and be greatly increased in many thinly peopled districts, especially among the parishes of the North.

The order of curates is so beneficial, that some particular notice of it seems to be required in this place. For a church poor as, relatively to the numbers of people, that of England is, and probably will continue to be, it is no small advantage to have youthful servants, who will work upon the wages of hope and expectation. Still more advantageous is it to have, by means of this order, young men scattered over the country, who being more detached from the temporal concerns of the benefice, have more leisure for improvement and study, and are less subject to be brought into secular collision with those who are under their spiritual guardianship. The curate, if he reside at a distance from the incumbent, undertakes the requisite responsibilities of a temporal kind, in that modified way which prevents him, as a new-comer, from being charged with selfishness: while it prepares him for entering upon a benefice of his own, with something of a suitable experience. If he should act under and in co-operation with a resident incumbent, the gain is mutual. His studies will probably be assisted; and his training, managed by a superior, will not be liable to relapse in matters of prudence, seemliness, or in any of the highest cares of his functions; and by way of return for these benefits to the pupil, it will often happen that the zeal of a middle-aged or declining incumbent will be revived, by being in near communion with the ardour of youth, when his own efforts may have languished through a melancholy consciousness that they have not produced as much good among his flock as, when he first entered upon the charge, he fondly hoped.

Let one remark, and that not the least important, be added. A curate, entering for the first time upon his office, comes from college after a course of expense, and with such inexperience in the use of money, that, in his new situation, he is apt to fall unawares into pecuniary difficulties. If this happens to him, much more likely is it to happen to the youthful incumbent; whose relations, to his parishioners and to society, are more complicated; and, his income being larger and independent of another, a costlier style of living is required of him by public opinion. If embarrass-

760

PREFACES, ETC.

ment should ensue, and with that unavoidably some loss of respectability, his future usefulness will be proportionably impaired: not so with the curate, for he can easily remove and start afresh with a stock of experience and an unblemished reputation; whereas the early indiscretions of an incumbent being rarely forgotten, may be impediments to the efficacy of his ministry for the remainder of his life. The same observations would apply with equal force to doctrine. A young minister is liable to errors, from his notions being either too lax or overstrained. In both cases it would prove injurious that the error should be remembered, after study and reflection, with advancing years, shall have brought him to a clearer discernment of the truth, and better judgment in the application of it.

It must be acknowledged that, among the regulations of ecclesiastical polity, none at first view are more attractive than that which prescribes for every parish a resident incumbent. How agreeable to picture to one's self, as has been done by poets and romance-writers, from Chaucer down to Goldsmith, a man devoted to his ministerial office, with not a wish or a thought ranging beyond the circuit of its cares! Nor is it in poetry and fiction only that such characters are found; they are scattered, it is hoped not sparingly, over real life, especially in sequestered and rural districts, where there is but small influx of new inhabitants, and little change of occupation. The spirit of the Gospel, unaided by acquisitions of profane learning and experience in the world,—that spirit, and the obligations of the sacred office may, in such situations, suffice to effect most of what is needful. But for the complex state of society that prevails in England, much more is required, both in large towns, and in many extensive districts of the country. A minister there should not only be irreproachable in manners and morals, but accomplished in learning, as far as is possible without sacrifice of the least of his pastoral duties. As necessary, perhaps more so, is it that he should be a citizen as well as a scholar; thoroughly acquainted with the structure of society, and the constitution of civil government, and able to reason upon both with the most expert; all ultimately in order to support the truths of Christianity, and to diffuse its blessings.

A young man coming fresh from the place of his education, cannot have brought with him these accomplishments; and if the scheme of equalising church incomes, which many advisers are much bent upon, be realised, so that there should be little or no secular inducement for a clergyman to desire a removal from the spot where he may chance to have been first set down; surely not only opportunities for obtaining the requisite qualifications would be diminished, but the motives for desiring to obtain them would be proportionably weakened. And yet these qualifications are indispensable for the diffusion of that knowledge, by which alone the political philosophy of the New Testament can be rightly expounded, and its precepts adequately enforced. In these times, when the press is daily exercising so great a power over the minds of the people, for wrong or for right as may happen, *that* preacher ranks among the first of benefactors who, without stooping to the direct treatment of current politics and passing events, can furnish infallible guidance through the delusions that surround them; and who, appealing to the sanctions of Scripture, may place the grounds of its injunctions in so clear a light, that disaffection shall cease to be cultivated as a laudable propensity, and loyalty cleansed from the dishonour of a blind and prostrate obedience.

It is not, however, in regard to civic duties alone, that this knowledge in a minister of the Gospel is important; it is still more so for softening and subduing private and personal discontents. In all places, and at all times, men have gratuitously troubled themselves, because their survey of the dispensations of Providence has been partial and narrow; but now that readers are so greatly multiplied, men judge as they are *taught*, and repinings are engendered everywhere, by imputations being cast upon the government; and are prolonged or aggravated by being ascribed to misconduct or injustice in rulers, when the individual himself only is in fault. If a Christian pastor be competent to deal with these humours, as they may be dealt with, and by no members of society so successfully, both from more frequent and more favourable opportunities of intercourse, and by aid of the authority with which he speaks; he will be a teacher of moderation, a dispenser of the wisdom that blunts approaching distress by submission to God's will, and lightens, by patience, grievances which cannot be removed.

We live in times when nothing, of public good at least, is generally acceptable, but what we believe can be traced to preconceived intention, and specific acts and formal contrivances of human understanding. A Christian instructor thoroughly accomplished would be a standing restraint upon such presumptuousness of judgment, by impressing the truth that—

> 'In the unreasoning progress of the world
> A wiser spirit is at work for us,
> A better eye than ours.'—*MS.*

Revelation points to the purity and peace of a future world; but our sphere of duty is upon earth; and the relations of impure and conflicting things to each other must be understood, or we shall be perpetually going wrong, in all but goodness of intention; and goodness of intention will itself relax through frequent disappointment. How desirable, then, is it, that a minister of the Gospel should be versed in the knowledge of existing facts, and be accustomed to a wide range of social experience! Nor is it less desirable for the purpose of counterbalancing and tempering in his own mind that ambition with which spiritual power is as apt to be tainted as any other species of power which men covet or possess.

It must be obvious that the scope of the argument is to discourage an attempt which would introduce into the Church of England an equality of income, and station, upon the model of that of Scotland. The sounder part of the Scottish nation know what good their ancestors derived from their church, and feel how deeply the living generation is indebted to it. They respect and love it, as accommodated in so great a measure to a comparatively poor country, through the far greater portion of which prevails a uniformity of employment; but the acknowledged deficiency of theological learning among the clergy of that church is easily accounted for by this very equality. What else may be wanting there, it would be unpleasant to inquire, and might prove invidious to determine: one thing, however, is clear; that in all countries the temporalities of the Church Establishment should bear an analogy to the state of society, otherwise it cannot diffuse its influence through the whole community. In a country so rich and luxurious as England, the character of its clergy must unavoidably sink, and their influence be everywhere impaired, if individuals from the upper ranks, and men of leading talents, are to have no inducements to enter into that body but such as are purely spiritual. And this 'tinge of secularity' is no reproach to the clergy, nor does it imply a deficiency of spiritual endowments. Parents and guardians, looking forward to sources of honourable maintenance for their children and wards, often direct their thoughts early towards the church, being determined partly by outward circumstances, and partly by indications of seriousness, or intellectual fitness. It is natural that a boy or youth, with such a prospect before him, should turn his attention to those studies, and be led into those habits of reflection, which will in some degree tend to prepare him for the duties he is hereafter to undertake. As he draws nearer to the time when he will be called to these duties, he is both led and compelled to examine the Scriptures. He becomes more and more sensible of their truth. Devotion grows in him; and what might begin in temporal considerations, will end (as in a majority of instances we trust it does) in a spiritual-mindedness not unworthy of that Gospel, the lessons of which he is to teach, and the faith of which he is to inculcate. Not inappositely may be here repeated an observation which, from its obviousness and importance, must have been frequently made, viz. that the impoverishing of the clergy, and bringing their incomes much nearer to a level, would not cause them to become less worldly-minded: the emoluments, howsoever reduced, would be as eagerly sought for, but by men from lower classes in society; men who, by their manners, habits, abilities, and the scanty measure of their attainments, would unavoidably be less fitted for their station, and less competent to discharge its duties.

Visionary notions have in all ages been afloat upon the subject of best providing for the clergy; notions which have been sincerely entertained by good men, with a view to the improvement of that order, and eagerly caught at and dwelt upon, by the designing, for its degradation and disparagement. Some are beguiled by what they call the *voluntary system,* not seeing (what stares one in the face at the very threshold) that they who stand in most need of religious instruction are unconscious of the want, and therefore cannot reasonably be expected to make any sacrifices in order to supply it. Will the licentious, the sensual, and the depraved, take from the means of their gratifications and pursuits, to support a discipline that cannot advance without uprooting the trees that bear the fruit which they devour so greedily? Will *they* pay the price of that seed whose harvest is to be reaped in an invisible world? A voluntary system for the religious exigencies of a people numerous and circumstanced as we are! Not more absurd would it be to expect that a knot of boys should draw upon the pittance of their pocket-money to build schools, or out of the abundance of their discretion be able to select fit masters to teach and keep them in order! Some, who clearly perceive the incompetence and folly of such a scheme for the agricultural part of the people, nevertheless think it feasible in large towns, where the rich might subscribe for the religious instruction of the poor. Alas! they know little of the thick darkness that spreads over the streets and alleys of our large towns. The parish of Lambeth, a few years since, contained not more than one church and three or four small proprietary chapels, while dissenting chapels, of every denomination were still more scantily found there; yet the in-

habitants of the parish amounted at that time to upwards of 50,000. Were the parish church and the chapels of the Establishment existing there, an *impediment* to the spread of the Gospel among that mass of people? Who shall dare to say so? But if any one, in the face of the fact which has just been stated, and in opposition to authentic reports to the same effect from various other quarters, should still contend, that a voluntary system is sufficient for the spread and maintenance of religion, we would ask, what kind of religion? wherein would it differ, among the many, from deplorable fanaticism?

For the preservation of the Church Establishment, all men, whether they belong to it or not, could they perceive their true interest, would be strenuous: but how inadequate are its provisions for the needs of the country! and how much is it to be regretted that, while its zealous friends yield to alarms on account of the hostility of dissent, they should so much over-rate the danger to be apprehended from that quarter, and almost over-look the fact that hundreds of thousands of our fellow-countrymen, though formally and nominally of the Church of England, never enter her places of worship, neither have they communication with her ministers! This deplorable state of things was partly produced by a decay of zeal among the rich and influential, and partly by a want of due expansive power in the constitution of the Establishment as regulated by law. Private benefactors, in their efforts to build and endow churches, have been frustrated, or too much impeded by legal obstacles: these, where they are unreasonable or unfitted for the times, ought to be removed; and, keeping clear of intolerance and injustice, means should be used to render the presence and powers of the church commensurate with the wants of a shifting and still-increasing population.

This cannot be effected, unless the English Government vindicate the truth, that, as her church exists for the benefit of all (though not in equal degree), whether of her communion or not, all should be made to contribute to its support. If this ground be abandoned, cause will be given to fear that a moral wound may be inflicted upon the heart of the English people, for which a remedy cannot be speedily provided by the utmost efforts which the members of the Church will themselves be able to make.

But let the friends of the church be of good courage. Powers are at work, by which, under Divine Providence, she may be strengthened and the sphere of her usefulness extended; not by alterations in her Liturgy, accommodated to this or that demand of finical taste, nor by cutting off this or that from her articles or Canons, to which the scrupulous or the overweening may object. Covert schism, and open nonconformity, would survive after alterations, however promising in the eyes of those whose subtilty had been exercised in making them. Latitudinarianism is the parhelion of liberty of conscience, and will ever successfully lay claim to a divided worship. Among Presbyterians, Socinians, Baptists, and Independents, there will always be found numbers who will tire of their several creeds, and some will come over to the Church. Conventicles may disappear, congregations in each denomination may fall into decay or be broken up, but the conquests which the National Church ought chiefly to aim at, lie among the thousands and tens of thousands of the unhappy outcasts who grow up with no religion at all. The wants of these cannot but be feelingly remembered. Whatever may be the disposition of the new constituencies under the reformed parliament, and the course which the men of their choice may be inclined or compelled to follow, it may be confidently hoped that individuals acting in their private capacities, will endeavour to make up for the deficiencies of the legislature. Is it too much to expect that proprietors of large estates, where the inhabitants are without religious instruction, or where it is sparingly supplied, will deem it their duty to take part in this good work; and that thriving manufacturers and merchants will, in their several neighbourhoods, be sensible of the like obligation, and act upon it with generous rivalry?

Moreover, the force of public opinion is rapidly increasing: and some may bend to it, who are not so happy as to be swayed by a higher motive; especially they who derive large incomes from lay-impropriations, in tracts of country where ministers are few and meagrely provided for. A claim still stronger may be acknowledged by those who, round their superb habitations, or elsewhere, walk over vast estates which were lavished upon their ancestors by royal favouritism or purchased at insignificant prices after church-spoliation; such proprietors, though not conscience-stricken (there is no call for that) may be prompted to make a return for which their tenantry and dependents will learn to bless their names. An impulse has been given; an accession of means from these several sources, co-operating with a *well*-considered change in the distribution of some parts of the property at present possessed by the church, a change scrupulously founded upon due respect to law and justice, will, we trust, bring about so much of what her friends desire, that the rest may be calmly waited for, with thankfulness for what shall have been obtained.

Let it not be thought unbecoming in a layman, to have treated at length a subject with which the clergy are more intimately conversant. All may, without impropriety, speak of what deeply concerns all; nor need an apology be offered for going over ground which has been trod before so ably and so often: without pretending, however, to anything of novelty, either in matter or manner, something may have been offered to view, which will save the writer from the imputation of having little to recommend his labour, but goodness of intention.

It was with reference to thoughts and feelings expressed in verse, that I entered upon the above notices, and with verse I will conclude. The passage is extracted from my MSS. written above thirty years ago: it turns upon the individual dignity which humbleness of social condition does not preclude, but frequently promotes. It has no direct bearing upon clubs for the discussion of public affairs, nor upon political or trade-unions; but if a single workman—who, being a member of one of those clubs, runs the risk of becoming an agitator, or who, being enrolled in a union, must be left without a will of his own, and therefore a slave—should read these lines, and be touched by them, I should indeed rejoice, and little would I care for losing credit as a poet with intemperate critics, who think differently from me upon political philosophy or public measures, if the sober-minded admit that, in general views, my affections have been moved, and my imagination exercised, under and *for* the guidance of reason.

'Here might I pause, and bend in reverence
To Nature, and the power of human minds;
To men as they are men within themselves.
How oft high service is performed within,
When all the external man is rude in show;
Not like a temple rich with pomp and gold,
But a mere mountain chapel that protects
Its simple worshippers from sun and shower!
Of these, said I, shall be my song; of these,
If future years mature me for the task,
Will I record the praises, making verse
Deal boldly with substantial things—in truth
And sanctity of passion, speak of these,
That justice may be done, obeisance paid
Where it is due. Thus haply shall I teach,
Inspire, through unadulterated ears
Pour rapture, tenderness, and hope; my theme
No other than the very heart of man,
As found among the best of those who live,
Not unexalted by religious faith,
Nor uninformed by books, good books, though
        few.
In Nature's presence: thence may I select
Sorrow that is not sorrow, but delight,
And miserable love that is not pain
To hear of, for the glory that redounds
Therefrom to human kind, and what we are
Be mine to follow with no timid step
Where knowledge leads me; it shall be my pride
That I have dared to tread this holy ground,
Speaking no dream, but things oracular,
Matter not lightly to be heard by those
Who to the letter of the outward promise
Do read the invisible soul; by men adroit
In speech, and for communion with the world
Accomplished, minds whose faculties are then
Most active when they are most eloquent,
And elevated most when most admired.
Men may be found of other mould than these;
Who are their own upholders, to themselves
Encouragement and energy, and will;
Expressing liveliest thoughts in lively words
As native passion dictates. Others, too,
There are, among the walks of homely life,
Still higher, men for contemplation framed;
Shy, and unpractised in the strife of phrase;
Meek men, whose very souls perhaps would sink
Beneath them, summoned to such intercourse.
Theirs is the language of the heavens, the power,
The thought, the image, and the silent joy:
Words are but under-agents in their souls;
When they are grasping with their greatest strength
They do not breathe among them; this I speak
In gratitude to God, who feeds our hearts
For his own service, knoweth, loveth us,
When we are unregarded by the world.'

INDEX OF TITLES

INDEX OF TITLES

INDEX OF TITLES

INDEX OF TITLES

INDEX OF TITLES

INDEX OF TITLES

INDEX OF TITLES

INDEX OF OPENING WORDS

INDEX OF OPENING WORDS

INDEX OF OPENING WORDS

INDEX OF OPENING WORDS

INDEX OF OPENING WORDS

INDEX OF OPENING WORDS

INDEX OF OPENING WORDS

INDEX OF OPENING WORDS

OXFORD

MORE OXFORD PAPERBACKS

Details of a selection of other books follow. A complete list
of Oxford Paperbacks, including The World's Classics,
Twentieth-Century Classics, OPUS, Past Masters, Oxford
Authors, Oxford Shakespeare, and Oxford Paperback
Reference, is available in the UK from the General Publicity
Department, Oxford University Press (JN), Walton Street,
Oxford OX2 6DP.

In the USA, complete lists are available from the Paperbacks
Marketing Manager, Oxford University Press, 200 Madison
Avenue, New York, NY 10016.

Oxford Paperbacks are available from all good bookshops. In
case of difficulty, customers in the UK can order direct from
Oxford University Press Bookshop, 116 High Street, Oxford,
Freepost, OX1 4BR, enclosing full payment. Please add 10 per
cent of published price for postage and packing.

THE PRELUDE

William Wordsworth

Edited by Ernest de Selincourt and Stephen Gill

The Prelude, Wordsworth's great autobiographical poem is crucial to our understanding of his life and poetry. It was written between 1798 and 1805, when it was read to Coleridge, but the text, first published in 1850 after the poet's death, had been subjected to intensive revision in his later years. This volume contains the original version of 1805, edited from manuscripts and with an Introduction and notes by Ernest de Selincourt. Text and notes have been revised by Stephen Gill.

LETTERS OF DOROTHY WORDSWORTH

Edited by Alan G. Hill

In the letters of Dorothy Wordsworth we find the most authentic biography of William's 'exquisite sister' that we have, and a unique picture of the circle in which she moved. No other observer was so close to Wordsworth and Coleridge, shared so completely their feelings and aims, and had such an eye for the landscape that inspired them.

Seventy complete letters have been chosen to provide a portrait of the writer and her milieu. They can be read as a continuous narrative, following the course of her life from youth until the onset of her last tragic illness. Through her words we are faced with a remarkable group of people and this is her enduring achievement.